5

The 20
AIM
Guide

Incorporating the

BAKER TILLY

ADVISER DIRECTORY

From the *Growth Company Investor* team

www.growthcompany.co.uk

THE 2004 AIM GUIDE

EDITOR
Christopher Spink

JOURNALISTS
Leslie Copeland, James Crux,
Elliott Davis, Robert Tyerman, Vikki Kunz

RESEARCHERS
Alex Tomlin, Julian Ellis, Oliver Haill

PRODUCTION
Neill Purvis, Richard Cooke

FRONT COVER DESIGN
Solutions

ADVERTISING & SPONSORSHIP
Chris Broadbent – 020-7421 3449
James Cassley – 020-7421 3450

GROWTH COMPANY INVESTOR LTD

95 Aldwych
London WC2B 4JF
Telephone: 020-7430 9777
Fax: 020-7430 9888
E-mail: aimguide@growthcompany.co.uk
www.growthcompany.co.uk
Growth Company Investor Ltd is regulated by the
Financial Services Authority

Foreword

It is a pleasure to provide a foreword for the latest edition of *The AIM Guide*. Since being appointed Head of AIM in February this year I have been impressed by the huge strides that the market has made and the great potential for its future development and growth.

AIM is a vital element of London's capital markets and plays a key role in maintaining the competitiveness of the UK economy. Against a backdrop of continuing challenging equity market conditions, last year was again highly successful for AIM.

A brief glance at 2003's figures shows an 80 per cent increase in market value, a quadruple increase in the value of shares traded and 162 new companies joining AIM, including over half of all Western European IPOs. These IPOs raised £2.1 billion of new money, more than double the total of the previous year.

International marketing efforts paid off as well – there was an increase of 20 per cent in the number of overseas companies on AIM and their total market value rose by an impressive 256 per cent.

The success of AIM has largely been due to the quality of its regulation and its unique, flexible structure. We want to ensure these qualities are preserved. We have worked hard to make AIM more attractive for UK and international companies, and also to protect the market from well-meaning, but potentially harmful, regulation.

We achieved this by committing significant resources to important areas, including lobbying EU policymakers to make changes to the Prospectus Directive. The Treasury has now agreed in principle that we will be able to operate AIM as an 'Exchange-regulated' market once the EU Prospectus Directive takes effect. This classification will allow us to maintain AIM's current regulatory framework, with its focus on appropriate regulation for its target audience of smaller, growing companies.

Secondly, to increase AIM's attractiveness as the market of choice for overseas companies, we have introduced a fast track admissions process that provides companies from approved international markets with more direct access to AIM.

Thirdly, my appointment as Head of AIM is part of a new management structure that will give AIM greater management focus and ensure that it has the resources needed to take it onto the next stage in its development.

As an entry point to public equity markets for smaller companies and pipeline for companies that aspire to join the Main Market, AIM is a vital part of the London Stock Exchange's business. It also serves as a significant contributor to the competitiveness of the UK economy and is a vital asset when promoting the value of London's capital markets.

I am confident that AIM will continue to go from strength to strength in 2004.

Martin Graham
Head of AIM
London Stock Exchange

CONTENTS

Editorial

CONTENTS

Companies Section   1

Baker Tilly Adviser Directory   397

Introduction

Nobody can doubt that AIM has revived in spectacular fashion over the past year. Last year the AIM Index rose nearly 39 per cent and one in six AIM companies saw their share prices double, as detailed in our Spotlight on AIM feature (page vii). No less than 32 companies joined the market in December, emphasising its position as the market of choice for fast-growing enterprises.

However, few would have expected the revival to continue at the same frenetic pace during the first quarter of the current year. Nevertheless the AIM Index has improved a respectable 8.5 per cent, which compares favourably with a 0.5 per cent decline for the FTSE All-Share Index. And, more impressively, March was another bumper month for new issues, with 34 companies joining AIM.

Solid prospects?

The key question now for prospective companies and investors is whether this momentum can be sustained.

There are signs of speculation creeping in. The great resources run, reflecting the rise in the price of gold, looks like turning into a rush. Nearly a third of the companies joining AIM in March were mineral explorers or producers. Five others are plain cash shells. Liquidity has now reached levels last seen at the height of the dotcom boom, with bargains averaging almost 8,000 per day.

However, a significant number of companies floating are profitable concerns, raising money at reasonable valuations for expansion, either organically or by acquisition. Others, such as Centaur Publishing, are using AIM as a legitimate means for founders or private equity backers to sell a business cost effectively to new institutional shareholders. Even FTSE 100 property giant Canary Wharf could shortly join AIM via this method.

The other factor that could underpin AIM's continued good health is Gordon Brown's decision in March's Budget to double the income tax relief that investors in Venture Capital Trusts (VCTs) receive from 20 per cent to 40 per cent. This should see significant sums of money explicitly ear-marked for AIM companies, perhaps as much as £250 million a year.

At this rate, as Peter Webb and Sean O'Flanagan of Unicorn Asset Management point out in their article, AIM will soon have more companies than the Full List of the London Stock Exchange.

Comprehensive

Growth Company Investor has followed AIM's fortunes for over seven years now. During that time the AIM Guide has gained a reputation as the comprehensive and trusted reference work on the market.

Growth Company Investor's team of analysts have commented on all 774 companies listed on AIM, providing an independent assessment of each one's prospects. Baker Tilly's Adviser Directory also gives companies wishing to join AIM, information on the nominated advisers, brokers, lawyers, accountants, public relations firms and other professionals they will need to use when they float.

We hope you find the guide useful, whatever your interest is in the market.

Christopher Spink, *Growth Company Investor*

Spotlight on AIM

AIM is in rude health. No less than 32 companies joined the market in December. This ensured AIM ended the year with a 754 companies listed – valued at £18.4 billion – its highest amount ever.

Whilst this is good news for companies needing fresh capital to expand their businesses, the activity makes it harder for investors to sift through the market in search of decent investment opportunities. However, we have ranked the market by different criteria, throwing up some intriguing investment ideas.

2003's best performing shares

One in six AIM companies saw their share prices double last year. This happened as the AIM Index rose over 58 per cent from its record low at the start of last April.

Four of the top ten best performers (see Table 1) were speculative mining exploration concerns, led by **Caledon Resources**, a venture seeking gold in China that reversed into failed online auctions business **Finelot**.

The other dominant sector was media, which started to pull out of its three-year post-dotcom recession. Web services business **Iomart**, which was valued at less than its net cash in March, has since won large orders enabling it to breakeven on a monthly basis.

2003'S BEST PERFORMING SHARES		1
Company	Share price (p)	% gain
Caledon Resources	15.5	+1020.0
Iomart Group	47.5	+804.8
Oxus Mining	84.25	+802.8
Premier Direct	595.0	+744.0
OverNet	50.5	+741.7
YooMedia	53.5	+716.7
Innovision	100.5	+644.4
7 Group	1.05	+607.6
Petrel Resources	26.75	+585.7
Southern African Resources	17.25	+570.0

Another company to come back from the dead is **YooMedia**, a leading provider of simple interactive services, such as dating and games, for digital television. The shares posted a similar rise after the group won a significant contract with UK digital TV leader BSkyB.

However, a more sizeable operation to prosper in 2003 was shopping-at-work specialist **Premier Direct**. The group returned to profit last year and is expected to double the size of its business this year after buying Kleeneze's operations in this space for a bargain £3.8 million.

2003's worst performing shares

AIM also had its fair share of failures during 2003, with 112 companies leaving the market.

One of the worst performing sectors was speciality finance. This sector has suffered from the ravages of the three-year bear market as well as uncertainty about the Financial Services Authority's reinvigorated regulatory regime. Topping the list of poor performers in Table 2 was independent financial adviser **Inter-Alliance**.

Other struggling businesses were affected by the downturn in the football sector. Football agent **First Artist** saw trading sharply deteriorate, sports IFA Kingsbridge is now a cash shell as is **Leisure Ventures**, which has ceased its football training business.

Overall, nine of the top 20 fallers are still operating their original businesses, the rest being cash shells. The survivors could become interesting recovery plays. All told, the best performers in 2003 tended to be companies restored to health after an extensive period of tricky trading.

2003'S WORST PERFORMING SHARES 2		
Company	Share price (p)	% gain
Inter-Alliance	2.12	-97.93
Parallel Media	3.0	-94.55
Comeleon	3.25	-93.50
XecutiveResearch	0.1	-92.50
Scipher	3.5	-88.33
Kingsbridge	1.12	-87.14
Fortfield Investments	3.0	-86.67
Mezzanine	0.62	-86.54
PNC Telecom	1.375	-85.53
Transware	0.62	-85.29

Fastest growing companies by sales

The driving force of many AIM companies is to expand their business by increasing revenues. A company that starts with a tiny turnover can see this shoot up exponentially as it starts to register significant sales. For this reason, Table 3 excludes companies whose 'previous' turnover starts below £250,000.

Making acquisitions is the way to expand rapidly, as has been shown by **Gaming Corporation** and **ukbetting**, both of which have snapped up cash-strapped online gambling ventures for bargain prices. This has enabled their turnovers to rise quickly as these operations can be easily integrated into their existing systems.

The top-line growth of telecoms group **CybIT** may be slightly flattering since the company has made maximum use of expensive factoring and invoice discounting facilities to bring forward sales to the current year. Nevertheless, this is still impressive progress.

FASTEST GROWING COMPANIES BY SALES			3
Company	2003 turnover (£m)	2002 turnover (£m)	% gain
Mean Fiddler Music	39.03	3.67	963
Gaming Corporation	8.60	0.84	920
CybIT	5.07	0.62	714
ukbetting	39.08	5.16	657
First Property	2.28	0.37	513
Intellexis	1.38	0.26	441
Staffing Ventures	9.43	1.77	433
TripleArc	7.01	1.44	387
Maverick Entertainment	1.48	0.331	347
Galleon	1.21	0.277	337

Similarly, a change of business strategy at **First Property**, enabling the company to extract fees at an earlier stage of its advice process, explains the growth here. Music promoter **Mean Fiddler** moved into managing venues as well. Sales of low margin tickets at these venues explains why turnover jumped here.

Companies exhibiting cleaner, principally organic growth included restaurant operator **Prezzo**, whose revenues rose 245 per cent, housebuilder **Telford Homes**, with sales up 188 per cent, and DNA producer **Cobra Biomanufacturing**, registering a 137 per cent improvement in turnover.

In all, 63 companies managed to double their turnover over the past year.

Fastest growing companies by earnings

If measuring turnover growth is tricky, then accounting for earnings growth is even harder to do, being plagued by exceptional events.

Accountancy services group **Numerica** exemplifies this. Last year's earnings do not include 3.6p of goodwill charges relating to a flurry of recent acquisitions. Add these back and the company would plummet down the table.

FASTEST GROWING COMPANIES BY EARNINGS			4
Company	2003 earnings (p)	2002 earnings (p)	% gain
Cape	8.1	0.2	3950
CA Coutts	9.8	0.7	1300
International Brand Licensing	2.4	0.2	1100
John Swan & Sons	11.8	1.0	1080
Numerica	4.3	0.4	975
Radamec	11.8	1.1	973
Universe	2.5	0.4	525
Genus	8.3	1.7	388
Bizspace	2.8	0.7	300
Stylo	12.2	3.3	270

Many AIM companies run businesses at a reasonably early stage of development. These tend to be loss-making. Only 315, or less than half of AIM companies, make profits. And, of these, about half managed to grow earnings last year, and only 22 managed to double them.

Again, as with sales growth, the principal reason for major rises in earnings include exceptional changes of direction in the business, such as at cattle market operator **John Swan**, which sold off some of its freehold premises, or software producer **Radamec**, which divested one of its businesses.

The top two companies in Table 4, building contractor **Cape** and retail marketing display maker **CA Coutts**, both bounced back from trading setbacks in the previous year. Jewellery designer **Theo Fennell** is starting to produce decent profits.

Other solid businesses that have doubled earnings organically include IT services concern **ComputerLand UK**, travel promoter **Landround** and online training company **Epic**.

Christopher Spink, *Growth Company Investor*

This is extracted from a 16 page report entitled 'Spotlight on AIM' compiled by *Growth Company Investor*. The report is available in PDF format pieced £75 + VAT. To order a copy call 020-7430 9777.

Many thanks to Lawrence Graham, a leading law firm providing legal services to both UK and international companies, financial institutions and private clients, who helped with compiling this report.

Growth Company Awards 2004

First established in April 2001, the Growth Company Awards – sponsored by KBC Peel Hunt – strive to identify and reward those contributing most to enhance the reputation of the growth company sector in the UK.

The research that *Growth Company Investor* undertook to generate the shortlists for each category is, in our opinion, the most unique and objective way of identifying the leading players in each field.

The Institutional Investor of the Year shortlist and Company of the Year shortlists were compiled using very strict and objective performance criteria.

For the adviser awards, we conducted a comprehensive survey of all AIM companies, asking every single chief executive or finance director to rate the performance of their of their nominated adviser, broker, lawyer and accountant. In total, 330 AIM companies responded to this survey. In all but the last of these categories, customer satisfaction reached record levels. Indeed, a staggering 82.8 per cent described the service received from their Nomad as being either 'Good' or 'Very Good', a near 12 percentage point improvement on 2003.

We believe that, given the methodology involved and the input of our distinguished panel of judges, each and every winner, runner-up and shortlisted firm should feel proud of their achievements over the past 12 months.

AIM Company of the Year 2004

Sponsored by Seymour Pierce

Winner:	**Armour Group**
Runner-up:	Cape
Shortlisted:	Stream Group
	Galahad Gold
	John Swan & Sons

The contest for the AIM Company of the Year title is traditionally the most closely fought of all our awards. Electronics and in-car entertainment systems developer Armour Group finally prevailed, capping off a phenomenal year for the Tunbridge Wells-based company. Over the last 12 months it has not only witnessed its share price quadruple but it recently announced a £1 million surge in first half profits to £1.3 million, as sales doubled to £13.9 million.

Runner-up Cape was very close behind. The past year has seen it complete its restructuring, reduce its debts levels substantially and ensure all its remaining operations are growing both profits and turnover.

As in previous years, the shortlist for this category was drawn up from *Growth Company Investor*'s own research, focusing primarily on improvements in earnings per share over the past 12 months. Other issues – such as the trading performance since the last reported full year results, exceptional items and other business developments – were factored in.

A panel of six independent experts ranked the short-listed companies in order of preference.

AIM Adviser of the Year 2004
Sponsored by Lewis Silkin

Winner:	**KBC Peel Hunt**
Runner-up:	Rowan Dartington & Co
Shortlisted:	John East & Partners
	Noble & Co
	Westhouse Securities

AIM Broker of the Year 2004
Sponsored by Rosenblatt

Winner:	**Evolution Beeson Gregory**
Joint runners-up:	KBC Peel Hunt
	Charles Stanley
Shortlisted:	Numis Securities
	Westhouse Securities

AIM Accountant of the Year 2004

Winner:	**Baker Tilly**
Runner-up:	Ernst & Young
Shortlisted:	KPMG
	PKF
	RSM Robson Rhodes

AIM Lawyer of the Year 2004

Winner:	**Memery Crystal**
Joint runners-up:	Faegre Benson Hobson Audley
	Jones Day Gouldens
Shortlisted:	Burges Salmon
	Maclay Murray & Spens

As already mentioned, the shortlists for each of the adviser categories were derived from a survey of AIM companies. The *Growth Company Investor* team sent a questionnaire to each and every AIM chief executive, asking them to rate the performance of their advisers on a five-point scale ranging from 'Very Poor' to 'Very Good'. From these responses the names of the five most highly regarded advisers in each category were then sent to the judges who then ranked them in order of their own preference.

As in previous years no judge was asked to vote on a category in which his own firm was eligible.

Apart from our winners, Numis and Ernst & Young deserve special mention as the only two firms to have been nominated in an individual category (respectively Broker of the Year and Accountant of the Year) in 2001, 2002, 2003 and 2004.

Institutional Investor of the Year 2004

Sponsored by MRI Moores Rowland

Winner:	**Artemis Fund Managers**
Runner-up:	Marlborough Fund Managers
Shortlisted:	Close Brothers
	Discretionary Unit Fund Managers
	ISIS Asset Management

Following an analysis of small cap fund and venture capital trust net asset value performance over the past five years, these five firms were identified as being the leading institutional investment lights in the growth company sector. The judges were, once again, asked to rank the shortlisted firms in order of preference and their individual scores were then aggregated.

OFEX Company of the Year 2004

Sponsored by Gateway Securities

Winner:	**Oakdene Homes**
Runner-up:	Printing.com
Shortlisted:	Britannia Finance
	Litcomp
	Northampton Saints

The five shortlisted firms for this award were identified using a similar methodology to that employed in the AIM Company of the Year category. In what was perhaps the closest of all this year's contests, Oakdene narrowly edged out Printing.com into first place.

OFEX Adviser of the Year 2004

Winner:	**JM Finn & Co**
Runner-up:	Ruegg & Co
Shortlisted:	Acorn Corporate Finance
	Loeb Aron & Co
	St Helen's Capital

This shortlist was constructed by asking each and every OFEX firm to rate the performance of their lead adviser on a similar five-point scale to that used for AIM Advisers. Our panel of judges believed that JM Finn, a stalwart amongst OFEX advisers, was most deserving of the title.

Finally we would like to thank all of the AIM and OFEX company chief executives who took the time to share their opinions with us and all of those kind enough to act as judges – without their support these awards would not have been possible.

The judges were:

Adam Hart, KBC Peel Hunt   **Andrew Buchanan**, Close Brothers   **Chilton Taylor**, Baker Tilly   **Chris Akers**, Sports Resource   **Jeff Harris**, PKF   **Ken Ford**, Teather & Greenwood   **Leslie Copeland**, Vitesse Media   **Michael Cunningham**, Rathbones   **Michael Storar**, Lawrence Graham   **Nick Hasell**, The Times   **Peter Webb**, Unicorn Asset Management   **Richard Feigen**, Seymour Pierce   **Richard Oldworth**, Buchanan   **Simon Brickles**, OFEX   **Stephen Hazell-Smith**, Hoodless Brennan

Steps to a flotation

Suitability for listing

If a company's management team is to market its business to the public successfully, it must have a clear vision of the firm's ultimate direction and business aspirations.

Thus the key document is the company's strategic or business plan. This should include the business' background and history, details of current trading, incorporating financial and other information, information on the management team, and the company's trading prospects.

Prospective AIM advisers will review this document to form an initial view on the company's suitability for listing. They consider the business' sector, competitive position, growth opportunities, financial strength and, not least, the strength of its management team.

It is important that it is a well thought out and carefully written document. Companies preparing a business plan may wish to seek advice from accountants or other financial advisers.

Flotations are also an opportunity to consider introducing one or more share option schemes. Professional advice should be sought on the suitability of the various schemes available.

Appointment of advisers

The next step is to appoint various professional advisers: the nominated adviser, (often referred to as the 'nomad'), broker, reporting accountant, solicitors, and other professionals. Reporting accountants or solicitors who are experienced in this field should be able to help introduce a nomad to prospective AIM companies.

For a smooth and timely transaction, it is fundamental that all the parties appointed are experienced. They must also be able to work well as a team, and with the company's management.

The nomad assesses the company's suitability for the AIM market, manages the flotation process, and helps ensure that AIM's rules are adhered to. The company is also required to retain the nomad to advise the directors after flotation.

The broker is responsible for raising funds from the initial public offering, and subsequently managing the after-market. The broker will frequently be the same company as the nomad.

A list of nomads can be obtained from the AIM team at the London Stock Exchange or www.londonstockexchange.com/aim.

The timetable

The nomad is responsible for drafting the timetable and allocating responsibilities to all respective parties. It is important that all of these parties ensure the timetable is realistic. Once agreed, it is imperative everyone adheres to it. The management team must appreciate the significant amount of time that will be taken up by the flotation process. Consequently, this must be built into the management's plans so that the process is not detrimental to the business. There will usually be numerous drafting and other meetings with all parties.

The due diligence process (including working capital)

At an early stage in the process the reporting accountant starts work on a detailed report known as the 'long form report' – the starting point for which is usually the company's business plan. This report details the firm's history, structure, operations, organisation, and its historical and future trading position. The main distinction between this and the business plan is that it is an independent review of the company. Potential areas of concern are highlighted.

The nomad uses the long form report as the basis for a large proportion of the information to be included with the prospectus. In practice, the timing is such that the first draft of the prospectus is prepared while due diligence work is still in progress.

While the reporting accountants are carrying out financial due diligence, the solicitors focus their attention on legal due diligence and any specialist input sought, such as environmental due diligence or asset valuation.

Legal due diligence covers areas such as the company's memorandum and articles, employment contracts, title to assets, key customer and supplier contracts, and any legal areas specific to the business.

AIM's rules require the prospectus to contain a statement from the directors that there is, in their opinion, sufficient working capital in the company for its current requirements – for at least one year from the date of admission.

The company's fully-integrated forecasts (profit and loss account, balance sheet and cashflow) are then reviewed by the reporting accountant. The accountant's work will include close scrutiny of the stated assumptions and sensitivity testing.

It is often necessary, or desirable, to effect the re-organisation of a group of companies or form a new holding company. This will usually require tax clearances, and it is important that these are considered at an early stage to avoid delays.

Profit forecast, estimate or projection

The nomad will sometimes require the inclusion of a profit forecast, estimate or projection. The directors must prepare this and make a statement that they have done so after due and careful enquiry, supported by the bases and assumptions on which it has been prepared. The nomad is required to confirm to the applicant that it is satisfied the forecast, estimate or projection has been made after due and careful enquiry by the directors, and will normally support this by delegating the review to the reporting accountants. A formal letter from these accountants is sometimes published in the document.

Admission document

AIM rules require an admission document to comply with the Public Offers of Securities Regulations 1995 (POS). The document must contain information about the company, its management and fundraising. It includes the reporting accountant's short form report, which typically includes the company's financial information for the past three years, or a shorter period since the firm was formed. The solicitors are responsible for drafting the admission document's statutory and general information sections.

The nomad has responsibility for coordinating the production of the admission document. As it evolves, the solicitors begin the formal verification process to ensure that all of the statements made in the prospectus are properly supported and not misleading. This process must not be underestimated. It is a criminal offence to make false statements in a prospectus. Alongside the verification process, the AIM broker will be informally sounding out the market to see who might be interested in the new share issue.

A pathfinder prospectus is a marketing tool used by the AIM broker to generate interest from potential investors and determine the share price. It is a replica of the admission document, minus information about the share price and numbers, and is normally made available two to three weeks before flotation. During this period the directors will be heavily involved with their broker and PR company, making presentations to potential investors.

Completion board meeting

At the completion meeting all the documents are signed, including board minutes, directors' service contracts, the short form report, working capital and long form report. The directors approve the final admission document and printing is authorised. If the document comprises a formal prospectus under POS, it is filed at Companies House and subsequently distributed to potential investors. The nomad applies for the company's share capital to be admitted to AIM, with admission occurring three days later.

A company applying for a listing on AIM should expect the whole process to take about three months.

To speak to a Baker Tilly partner about AIM please contact Chilton Taylor or Paul Watts on 020-7413 5100

ShareMark parallel trading: enhancing AIM's liquidity

Trading in less-liquid stocks has always proved a perplexing conundrum for all involved in the investing process.

Market makers need to cover the additional costs and hence bid-offer spreads tend to widen as liquidity falls. Investors on the other hand are deterred by wide spreads, often unwilling to accept the need for what can be a significant rise in share value simply to recoup the overall cost of their original investment. This reticence can lead to reduced liquidity, fuelling still wider spreads.

The typical spread on shares in the FTSE 100 Index is under 0.5 per cent. In the FTSE All-Share Index it's around 2.75 per cent, whereas for AIM stocks the average is typically 12.5 per cent. Indeed, it's not uncommon for less frequently traded stocks to have a spread as wide as 50 per cent.

Wide spreads work against the best interests of the company and its shareholders in three main ways:

- Investors are discouraged from investing because, on occasions, they might need to see a large rise in a share price simply to get back the price they paid;
- There's often no way of establishing what the supply and demand levels are for any individual stock, so investors can find themselves 'shooting in the dark' when trying to gauge the right price at which to buy or sell; and
- Because there are fewer investors buying or selling, companies see less liquidity in their shares. This leads to disillusioned investors and an inefficient market in the shares. Such a situation can adversely affect a company's attempts to raise further equity capital.

ShareMark's solution

ShareMark, the share-trading platform for both AIM-listed and unquoted companies, now provides a fresh alternative for investors and the potential for improved investor-relations for companies.

The market was originally conceived to overcome the shortcomings of existing markets for smaller quoted companies. The wide spreads and inadequate pre-trade visibility of these markets are an inevitable consequence of their market maker-based continuous trading systems. These problems have not been allowed to feature within the ShareMark proposition.

ShareMark operates by scheduled periodic auctions, concentrating available order flow so as to achieve optimum price formation. There is no bid-offer spread, and full price transparency is in place via the Internet at www.sharemark.co.uk on an around the clock continuous basis. Rather than simply replicating a bulletin board system, ShareMark goes further by actually setting the price. This price formation process is based on an algorithm, which assesses the point at which demand equals supply.

Of particular interest to all involved in the AIM market, however is ShareMark's launch of a 'parallel trading service' for AIM companies.

Dual trading attraction

Existing AIM companies can seek a complementary quotation on ShareMark, enabling ShareMark to potentially form a single dealing price for investors within the AIM bid-offer spread. Those investors wishing to deal in size and who require immediacy will naturally favour AIM. However, smaller investors prepared to await the next auction in that stock may benefit from a keener price.

Safeguards have been built into the service for private investors. Orders submitted for inclusion within the parallel trading service carry a limit price and are checked on a real-time basis against the price on AIM. Should the limit price be achieved on AIM at any point prior to the next scheduled auction, the order will automatically be withdrawn from ShareMark and dealt on AIM, thereby ensuring that a client can never be disadvantaged. Orders that cannot be dealt go to form the ShareMark order book. One would anticipate that over time, the effect of such a trading service would be to assist in narrowing the bid-offer spread on AIM.

AIM companies who have already taken advantage of this innovative service include RingProp, Elektron, fountains and Vitesse Media. And whilst there's an ongoing cost to the company of £1,250 a quarter plus VAT, the investor relations benefit could significantly outweigh this charge.

ShareMark also provides a platform on which Open Ended Investment Company (OEIC) or Unit Trust Fund Managers can administer their funds' investments. OEIC shares and Unit Trust units are traded on the basis of their 'net asset value' (NAV), rather than using the demand and supply model that applies to equities. Consequently, the ShareMark price shown is an indicative valuation of shares/units in the Fund, based on the London Stock Exchange's '15-minute delayed' prices.

And, of course, all of these services can be accessed by investors, companies and brokers alike. Indeed, many private client stockbrokers already have Authorised Stockbroker accounts open with ShareMark, allowing them to place orders on ShareMark on behalf of their clients.

Following the appointment of The Share Centre, ShareMark's sister company, to act as Market Operator to the Birmingham Local Business Exchange, ShareMark may soon take on a more regional dimension as well. The purpose of the exchange will be to bridge the equity gap for developing SMEs, which fits neatly with ShareMark's own aspirations.

Iain Wallace
Managing Director
ShareMark

ShareMark®

... a great fit whatever your investment focus

Private Investor, Corporate Adviser, Venture Capital Fund Manager, EIS Fund Manager, Broker ...

Whatever your investment focus, make sure you check out the exciting new developments underway at ShareMark.

For details about how you can benefit from this innovative market, tailored to your specific interests, simply complete and return the coupon below.

**ShareMark, P.O. Box 2000, Aylesbury, Bucks. HP21 8ZB.
Tel: 08000 28 28 12 Email: sharemark@share.co.uk
www.sharemark.co.uk**

ShareMark is administered by The Share Centre, which is a member of the London Stock Exchange and is authorised and regulated by the Financial Services Authority.

Please send me details about how ShareMark is tailored to my interests and then keep me up to date on new developments.

Name:

Company:
(if applicable)

Job Title:
(if applicable)

Address:

Post Code:

Tel. No.:   (STD code)

Email: @

Please tick the box to indicate your investment focus:

Private Investor ☐   Venture Capital / EIS Fund Manager ☐

Corporate Adviser ☐   Broker ☐

Please send your completed coupon to :

ShareMark, FREEPOST NATW536, Aylesbury, Bucks. HP21 9ZS.

SEYMOUR PIERCE

AIM's most popular adviser and broker

Investment Banking
Stockbroking

SEYMOUR
PIERCE

AIM and the EU Financial Services Action Plan

At the time of writing, the European Commission is in the midst of a flurry of activity as it seeks to settle the final elements of the Financial Services Action Plan (FSAP) before its April 2004 deadline.

Whilst the FSAP was established with the laudable aim of creating a single market for financial services, its bid for uniformity and a standardisation of regulation throughout the EU has caused concerns for a number of participants in the European financial markets, not least for AIM.

AIM was established to provide a market for companies seeking a less onerous and more flexible regulatory environment in which to operate. Its success as one of Europe's premier growth markets is now perceived to be under threat, to some extent at least, by some of the measures which make up the FSAP.

Prospectus Directive

One of those measures is the Prospectus Directive, which was adopted at the end of 2003 and must be implemented by member states by 1 July 2005. The Directive is intended to harmonise the requirements for the content and approval of prospectuses required to be published when securities are offered to the public or admitted to trading on a regulated market in the EU. As we shall see, the definition of 'regulated market' is key, for it currently encompasses AIM.

The principal objective of the Prospectus Directive is to create a 'single passport' for issuers, so that once a prospectus has been approved by its 'home member state' competent authority, the issuer may then use that prospectus for offerings and applications for admission in all member states without having to amend the contents for particular markets or seek further approvals from other regulatory authorities.

Impact of Prospectus Directive on AIM

The Prospectus Directive will require all prospectuses to be pre-vetted by the competent authority of the issuer's home member state, which in the case of the UK will be the Financial Services Authority (FSA). Concern has been expressed as to the potentially negative impact of this requirement on AIM's attractiveness to issuers in terms of efficiency and cost-effectiveness. Currently, AIM admission documents are not required to be pre-vetted by either the London Stock Exchange or the FSA. Instead, the issuer appoints a 'nominated adviser' who is obliged to confirm to the London Stock Exchange that the AIM Rules, including their specific content requirements for admission documents, have been complied with.

The London Stock Exchange has expressed concern that this regulatory framework established by the Prospectus Directive is more appropriate for large companies than for AIM's target, smaller company, market. There is, it is true, some flexibility built into the Prospectus Directive in that the FSA, as the UK's competent authority, will be able to delegate the responsibility to vet prospectuses to other bodies, though this power to delegate will be reviewed after five years and cannot last beyond eight years. In this way, the FSA could, at least temporarily, delegate responsibility for the approval of an AIM company's prospectus to its nominated adviser, so maintaining the status quo.

However, the search for a permanent solution to this issue has led the London Stock Exchange to undertake discussions with the Treasury, the outcome of which is expected to be that AIM will continue to operate as an Exchange-regulated market once the Prospectus Directive is implemented. This would involve removing AIM from the list of 'regulated markets' which the UK submits each year to the Commission and which are incorporated by the Commission into an overall list of the 'regulated markets' of the EU. If no longer a 'regulated market', AIM would not fall within the ambit of the Prospectus Directive and would continue to be run and regulated, as it is now, by the London Stock Exchange, with responsibility for ensuring that an AIM admission document complies with the AIM Rules falling, as it does currently, upon the company, its directors and its nominated adviser.

It should be noted though, that once the Prospectus Directive is in force, if an issuer makes an offer of securities to the public in the EU it will be obliged to publish a prospectus pursuant to the Directive (unless an exemption applies), irrespective of whether the securities being offered are also being admitted to a regulated market. It is to be expected, however, that AIM offers will generally fall within one of the applicable exemptions, in particular that which will apply where an offer is made to fewer than 100 persons per member state (other than qualified investors).

Transparency Directive

Maintaining its status as an Exchange-regulated market would also allow AIM to escape from some of the other burdens of the FSAP. This includes the Transparency Directive, which proposes the imposition of certain continuing disclosure obligations (principally in terms of financial reporting and substantial share-holdings) upon issuers with securities admitted to trading on an EU regulated market. Whilst, in broad terms, the AIM Rules impose similar disclosure obligations, there are certain notable differences. For instance, the Directive will require share issuers to publish interim management statements between their annual and half-yearly financial reports, though this would not apply to issuers who already publish quarterly financial reports. As there is no current requirement in the AIM Rules for quarterly reporting, this would create additional disclosure obligations for AIM companies were AIM still to be a 'regulated market' when the Directive comes into force (though it is due for adoption shortly, member states are expected to be given a further two years to implement the Directive into their national laws).

Also, the AIM Rules allow a company's annual audited accounts to be prepared in accordance with any of UK GAAP, US GAAP or International Financial Reporting Standards (also known as International Accounting Standards or IAS). This flexibility is not present, however, in the Transparency Directive, which will require both annual and half-yearly accounts to be prepared in accordance with IAS. The EU Commission will be able to recognise other standards as 'equivalent' to IAS, but has not yet made any official statement in this regard (although US GAAP, at least, is expected to qualify).

IAS Regulation

For UK and other EU companies listed on AIM, this question of having to prepare IAS-compliant accounts will, in any event, have already arisen before the time comes for compliance with the Transparency Directive. In 2002 the EU adopted the IAS Regulation, which will require EU companies whose securities are admitted to trading on a regulated market to prepare their consolidated accounts, for financial years starting on or after I January 2005, in accordance with IAS.

Assuming, however, that AIM is removed from the category of 'regulated markets', neither these additional disclosure requirements of the Transparency Directive nor the IAS Regulation will apply to AIM companies, which will continue to be governed by the AIM Rules in terms of what constitute acceptable disclosure and financial reporting standards.

It may be that, whether required to or not, many AIM companies will move to the adoption of IAS-compliant reporting in any event. However, we expect that there will still be some benefit in AIM maintaining the flexibility it is currently afforded to allow companies to report in one of a number of internationally recognised accounting standards and which may give it a potentially significant competitive edge over other, more prescriptive, markets.

Stephanie Bates
Mayer, Brown, Rowe & Maw LLP

Corporate governance on AIM

Corporate governance has become a critical issue in determining both the strength and value of quoted companies at the current time. Corporate scandals, such as Enron, WorldCom and, more recently, Parmalat, have caused worldwide debate about the way in which companies have been governed and the way in which they should be governed in the future.

In the US this led to the passing of the Sarbanes-Oxley Act. This has had an effect worldwide, not only because of its extra territorial limitations, but also because of the influence that its provisions have in other parts of the world. All this has led to a widespread expectation of improvements in corporate governance. Investors expect this, not only in large companies, but also in small companies.

The combined code

Strictly speaking, the combined code on corporate governance does not apply to AIM companies. However, most AIM companies recognise that to function properly and successfully in the modern environment, it is important that they adhere to, and are seen to adhere to, 'appropriate' standards of corporate governance.

What does 'appropriate' mean? It means that there should be an effective board, which should include a balance of executive and non-executive directors. In fact, these are the first two principles of the combined code, so one can see that whilst the code does not formally apply to AIM companies, its principles are such that any well run and properly governed company will take heed of them. In addition, the company's nominated adviser is likely to insist upon a certain standard of corporate governance as a condition of being prepared to accept this role.

From my own experience, both as a non-executive director and as a lawyer advising AIM companies, the large majority of AIM companies do comply with most of the code of best practice and, in particular, usually have a separate chief executive and chairman, a balanced board including at least two non-executive directors and separate audit and remuneration committees.

The cost of complying with an increasing corporate governance burden is one that most companies are prepared to bear and do not regard as unnecessary or wasted. The days are long gone when non-executive directors were regarded in the way that Tiny Rowland once described them – as being like 'baubles on a Christmas tree'.

Directors' obligations

Directors are expected to perform to increasingly high expectations and the responsibility of being a non-executive director is growing all the time.

The concept of a non-executive director is problematic because there is no legal or statutory definition. The Companies Act only defines a director but draws no distinction between those having executive responsibilities and those that do not. Non-executive directors are therefore, in effect, independent directors who hold no executive responsibility but have all the duties of executive directors.

This places a great responsibility and burden on non-executive directors and anybody taking on this job must not take it on lightly and must be aware that they will be required to perform to the highest standards. Their role is being regarded increasingly as a control and check on the exercise of powers by the executive directors. In fact, they must be prepared to have the necessary experience and knowledge of the business to be able to ask the right questions.

Attracting non-executives

It is this increasing responsibility and burden which may make it more difficult for small companies to attract the appropriate type of non-executive director. The rewards are not great but the risks are high. It is a concern that needs to be recognised in order to create an environment that may be attractive to proposed appointees. In order to encourage the right type of candidate it may be that they should be permitted to participate in a share option or performance related scheme even if this is contrary to the definition of 'independence' in the combined code.

AIM companies are therefore in a unique position in that they are not under a legal or regulatory obligation to comply with any codes or rules on corporate governance and are able to consider with their nominated adviser and other professional advisers what would be appropriate and right for each individual company.

It is a great credit to the majority of such companies that they do accept the need for proper corporate governance. I hope that this position will remain, because, quite clearly, certain provisions of the combined code are not appropriate to small companies. I believe that the current system serves AIM companies well and is one of which this market can be proud.

Clive Garston
Senior Partner
Halliwell Landau
(020-7929 1900 / cgarston@halliwells.co.uk)

New Issues taking off

Since the last edition of the AIM Guide was published at the beginning of October, a staggering 84 companies have joined the market in the six months to the end of March.

Between them these newcomers raised £836 million. This is still lower than at the height of the dotcom boom – for instance, £3 billion was raised in 2000. But this still shows the renewed appetite for backing small cap companies.

December and March stand out as easily the busiest two of these six months. No less than 29 ventures came to AIM in December, which is normally a quiet time for new issues, whilst 24 concerns floated in March.

Within this broad range of companies were traditional growth businesses, such as property services play **Erinaceous**, Full List migrants like tool hire venture **Multi**, and overseas companies seeking an AIM quote, for example Toronto-listed **Brazilian Diamonds**.

Popular brokers and advisers

Mining and exploration concerns continued to prove popular as evidenced by broker Canaccord Capital, the Canadian resource specialist. This outfit acted as broker to nine new issues, making it the most popular broker jointly with Seymour Pierce.

The latter company was behind some excellent floats, raising £15 million for public sector software developer **Civica**, which made a £9.1 million pre-tax profit on £90.3 million revenue in the year to September. **Asfare**, the maker of ladders for the rescue services, has also performed well since receiving £2.4 million from a Seymour Pierce-sponsored placing.

Canaccord brought titanium oxide miner **Aricom**, Toronto-quoted **Yamana Gold** and oil and gas explorer **Oilexco**, another Toronto company, to the market, amongst others. The group was also behind raising £40.6 million for **Oriel Resources**.

Other busy firms included Manchester-based WH Ireland, which acted as broker for eight companies, KBC Peel Hunt, which performed broking services for seven, followed by Terry Smith's Collins Stewart with six and Numis with five.

Amongst companies that act purely as Nomads, Grant Thornton remained prolific, acting for four new AIM ventures: media sites and billboards group **Network**, drug researcher **EiRx Therapeutics** and two miners, **Namibian Resources** and **Gippsland**.

Accelerated IPOs

So-called 'accelerated' IPOs, which involve large fundraising exercises whereby brokers buy flotation candidates outright and then try and find fresh institutional backers for them, skewed these statistics somewhat.

Two companies accounted for £377 million, or 45 per cent, of the £836 million raised during this period.

Holiday village operator **Center Parcs (UK)** was sold by its private equity investors to a purpose-made vehicle controlled by Collins Stewart, which then raised £245 million by floating the company in December. In the year to last April Center Parcs registered a £160.7 million turnover.

And £132 million was raised when business magazine publisher **Centaur** was floated by Numis. The broker, led by Oliver Hemsley, also raked in £47.5 million for **Moneybox**, the ATM outfit that joined AIM this March.

Sector themes

AIM continues to attract a fair proportion of international mining concerns. Notable recent entrants include Australian outfit Gippsland, which has a promising tantalum and feldspar deposit in Egypt. Gippsland raised £700,000 in March through broker Hoodless Brennan.

The same month also saw the debut of Canadian gold explorer **Medoro Resources**. Others included **Eureka Mining** and **Marakand Minerals**, both handled by Williams de Broe, as well as WH Ireland-sponsored gold and silver explorer **Palladex**.

Media and software companies are also coming back into fashion. Teather & Greenwood, steered by Ken Ford, brought mobile phone content provider **Monstermob** to the market. The firm also raised £5 million for in-store radio broadcaster **Immedia**, whose chief executive is DJ Bruno Brookes. Teathers also attracted £4.5 million for profitable internet service provider **Business Serve**, chaired by Lord Baker.

James Crux, *Growth Company Investor*

You're focused on AIM. So are we.

WE'RE LAWYERS WHO SPECIALISE IN THE AIM MARKET. AND WE'VE GOT THE RESOURCES TO HELP YOU GROW.

If you're looking at an AIM flotation, you want lawyers who have been there. We've done dozens of AIM deals and travelled with the London Stock Exchange around the world to promote the AIM market. The head of our London corporate group, Max Audley, serves on the London Stock Exchange's AIM Advisory Group.

With experienced lawyers in corporate, intellectual property, employment, real estate and litigation, we can take your company to the next level. And we're part of a firm that reaches around the world to Europe, Asia, and the U.S. So if you're taking a close look at AIM, you should be looking at us.

AIM IPO
THE ROUTE TO SUCCESS

If you are planning an IPO on the Alternative Investment Market then you can't afford to miss this seminar

KEY SPEAKERS

Ashley Reeback
A partner in the Corporate Finance Department and Head of its AIM team at Finers Stephens Innocent, Ashley specialises in all forms of public company fundraising work with a particular emphasis in advising on AIM flotations and related transactions. During 2003 FSI advised on 14 AIM transactions and now has an established client base of some 12 AIM listed client companies as well as advising numerous nomads and brokers on flotations and AIM related transactions

Peter Jackson
Peter is a Director of Corporate Finance at W.H. Ireland, heading up the firm's London corporate finance activities. A chartered accountant, having qualified with a predecessor firm of PriceWaterhouseCoopers, Peter has been involved in a great variety of public and private transaction work throughout his career, including spending six years at the London Stock Exchange where he was ultimately Head of AIM and Sponsor Regulation. Immediately prior to joining W. H. Ireland Peter also worked in the venture capital industry.

Leesa Peters
Leesa is Director of AIM Companies at Conduit PR, has spoken at many international conferences run by the LSE on listing and advised many companies on the process. Conduit PR has its head office in the UK with affiliated offices including Johannesburg, Perth, Sydney and Toronto. The firm started from the need to provide a dedicated financial public relations and investor relations service for small to mid cap companies in Europe.

Stephen Bourne
Stephen Bourne joined BDO Stoy Hayward in 1997 to head up the Corporate Finance department. Since then the team has trebled in size, with 30 partners and 100 staff nationwide. BDO Stoy Hayward Corporate Finance advises on IPOs, mergers and acquisitions, private equity and debt fund raisings, investigations, public company transactions and private finance initiatives. Stephen specialises in advising on IPOs and grooming companies for flotation.

Paul Dudley
Prior to joining W. H. Ireland as associate director in corporate finance, Paul was previously a director of corporate development for a private equity fund manager making primary investments in early and developing stage companies. He had previously qualified as a chartered accountant with PriceWaterhouseCoopers (PWC), where he worked in the Banking division. Whilst at PWC he spent over a year seconded to the Listing Department of the London Stock Exchange where he was responsible for the approval of a variety of listed company transactions.

> The seminar will be held on Thursday 29 September 2004 at the Grocers Hall, London EC2.
> For more information or to book your place contact Michelle Senyah on 020 7430 9777
> michelle.senyah@growthcompany.co.uk

Improving AIM

From very humble beginnings, AIM has been incredibly successful in raising new money for fledgling businesses. Since inception in 1995, more than £10 billion has been raised and there are now over 750 companies listed on the market.

The success of AIM in attracting new businesses has been quite remarkable when put in context – by comparison, there are just 1,083 companies, excluding investment trusts, listed on the main market, which, after all, has existed for 200 years.

The growth of intermediaries serving this market has been equally remarkable. Today there are a mere 68 nominated advisers, 52 brokers, 30 reporting accountants, 67 solicitors, 46 PR companies and 8 registrars catering for companies' and their investors' every need.

Focus on profits

Whilst there is no doubt that AIM is now recognised as the 'market of choice' for growth companies, it has in recent years struggled somewhat to meet investor expectations. In hindsight, the rapid growth associated with the market has led to quality issues.

In the past, it has often been the case that investments driven by tax considerations have failed to deliver. The abundance of 'pre-revenue' businesses – formerly called blue-sky concepts – has been a major factor in this disappointing performance.

Many entrepreneurs, advisers and investors seem to have forgotten that it is profits, not dreams, which ultimately drive share prices.

Tax assistance?

AIM was established as a market to help bridge the so-called 'equity funding gap' for small and medium sized businesses (SMEs). The Government offers generous tax incentives to the shareholders of qualifying investments through a myriad of offerings including Venture Capital Trusts (VCTs) and Enterprise Investment Schemes.

It was hoped that the injection of capital into SMEs would lead to greater productivity growth and wealth creation. The ultimate goal was of course to increase the number of successful businesses within the UK, create more jobs and increase general levels of taxation.

Unfortunately, the decision to link the tax incentives to capital gains delivered a wall of money for investment at a time when global equity markets were close to their cyclical peak. During the early part of this decade, stock markets have experienced significant declines and in order to receive their tax breaks investors have had to invest when prospects for growth were far from exciting.

The various qualifying criteria for investments initially concentrated investment on a relatively small number of qualifiers. However, it did not take long for the multitude of advisers to flood the market with new companies that were not affected by the economic downturn. Profitless start-ups had not disappointed everyone.

The Government's recent proposals to eliminate VCTs' dependence upon capital gains for the lion's share of their fundraisings may well lead to a much steadier flow of new investment. However, we believe that a complete review of the reasons for, and objectives behind, the tax incentives for the AIM market are long overdue.

For example, we fail to see the logic of the £15 million gross asset test. This prevents many worthy SMEs from attracting monies from willing investors. The Government should also be aware that the equity gap is not exclusive to AIM companies and is in fact shared by many companies within the lower echelons of the main market.

International vision?

Recent attempts by the London Stock Exchange to internationalise AIM leave us somewhat bemused. What can be the point of increasing political, economic and currency risks for investors in this market? At present, the mining exploration sector on AIM is exhibiting all the characteristics of the TMT Sector during the dotcom era. Mouth-watering valuations built on the certainty of failure are perhaps the underlying truth.

However, we should never doubt the powers of persuasion of those with vested interests. The growth of intermediaries serving this market has indeed been remarkable. With so many mouths to feed, it is no surprise that investors are seldom left with little more than crumbs from the table.

The future of AIM is dependent on its success in rejuvenating the entire stock market. To date, winners have been few and far between. Three-quarters of AIM constituents remain unprofitable.

It is quality and value that the market needs and sadly high calibre companies such as support services specialist **Mears**, retailer **Majestic Wine** and pizza chain **Ask Central** are currently rarer than long-term winners in the mining exploration sector.

Peter Webb and Sean O'Flanagan
Unicorn Asset Management

Mayer, Brown, Rowe & Maw's Corporate Group has the specialist knowledge and resources to handle any corporate or corporate finance transaction.

Unlock your potential

Contact:

Stephanie Bates
Corporate Partner on +44 (0)20 7782 8833
Email: sbates@mayerbrownrowe.com

Stephen Bottomley
Corporate Partner on +44 (0)20 7782 8825
Email: sbottomley@mayerbrownrowe.com

www.mayerbrownrowe.com

Great deals

MAYER
BROWN
ROWE
& MAW

Choosing a Registrar for today and tomorrow

The role of the registrar has changed to meet the challenges of the 21st century using a mixture of tradition and technology.

In the past, many saw the role of the registrar as an obligatory service, necessary to maintain a company's Register of Shareholders, process their transfers and produce a list of the shareholders when required.

For companies proposing to float on AIM, the role of the receiving agent has been viewed in a similar way. It must though be remembered that if the initial public offering process does not go smoothly, the reputation of the company and its advisers can be damaged for a long time.

However, in today's business climate the registrar and receiving agent should be able to offer significantly more than just keeping the list of shareholders up to date.

Managing the flotation process

The experienced registrar, acting as receiving agent, will be able to manage the application process smoothly and, from the time a company floats, their expertise can be an invaluable asset. This allows the directors to focus on their business strategy, secure in the knowledge that their shareholders' expectations are being fully met.

As the flotation date approaches, the company's board is required to spend more and more time preparing for the big event. With meetings between these directors and their corporate advisers becoming longer and more frequent, too often the last item to be considered by the finance director and company secretary is the appointment of a registrar.

As a result the decision can be made in haste and is often based upon the precept that the lowest quotation is good enough. However, selecting the registrar should be given more consideration. The relationship between a company and its registrar should be viewed as a long-term one and one in which the registrar can provide a breadth of expertise in all corporate events, at the time of flotation and in the future.

Picking the right registrar

Most service registrars offer the traditional services, however, the company should be looking towards the future and choosing a registrar that offers much more than that.

Initially, the registrar's proven ability to successfully handle large or small IPOs will be the key criteria, as will their technological capabilities and project management skills.

Many registrars can offer the services of a specialist IPO team that deals with all enquiries and will have a London office for the receipt of documents from institutional investors. Other services to consider are the registrars' internet capabilities and possible in-house printing facilities.

A successful, ongoing relationship with your Registrar entails provision of a range of services to meet your changing or growing needs.

One such service may be a full range of employee share plans. Research, both here in the UK and in North America, shows that a major issue facing companies in today's climate of skills shortages and shifting employment patterns is how to retain and motivate their key staff.

No longer is salary alone sufficient to entice or retain the best staff and companies are now offering a variety of incentives to create an attractive salary and benefits package. Owning shares in the company is one of the more popular of such benefits.

Shareholder communication

Once a company takes on the responsibilities of shareholders, their registrar plays a major role in communicating with those shareholders. A share registrar with internet technology can facilitate this communication on the company's behalf, whilst delivering substantial cost savings at the same time.

Online services for shareholders and clients alike can deliver convenient, flexible, user-friendly solutions. A modern registrar has to continually explore the possibilities of using advances in technology to widen the ways in which they can communicate.

Whether a company is considering expansion and raising capital through their shareholders or expanding by acquisition, the right registrar will be flexible enough to manage any corporate action regardless of size or scope.

They should have the experience and expertise to ensure that the technical processes comprising the corporate action comply with all the necessary deadlines, rules and regulatory constraints. Their reputation will deliver peace of mind as they manage the risks on the company's behalf and are conscious of the need for total confidentiality in all aspects of the work.

A relationship for the future

The right registrar can help companies optimise their strategy regarding their shareholders and employees as well as providing support through a productive and long-term relationship.

A registrar that combines all the benefits of a modern, dynamic service registrar, with the proven track record of a long established and respected company, can deliver a level of service that a company requires for itself, and demands for their shareholders, both now and in the future.

Paul Etheridge is Senior Manager Business Development at Capita Registrars. If you would like further information about the services Capita Registrars provide please contact him on 020-7800 4116 or development@capitaregistrars.com.

Tax reliefs

Shares traded on AIM are regarded by the Inland Revenue as unquoted. The various tax-reliefs outlined below are those that relate to investments in all qualifying unquoted companies. Tax reliefs are updated to include those proposed in the March 2004 Budget and it is assumed that such proposals will be enacted.

This is only a brief summary of the tax-reliefs and some of the principal qualifying criteria. It is not the intention to provide the full terms of relevant legislation, which is often complex. Meanwhile the relevance of, and ability to, claim particular reliefs will generally depend on individual circumstance. Professional advice is recommended.

The tax reliefs available include:

For individual investors:

- Capital gains tax (CGT) - business asset taper relief
- Capital gains tax (CGT) - gift relief
- The Enterprise Investment Scheme (EIS)
- Inheritance tax (IHT) - business property relief
- Relief for losses
- Venture capital trusts (VCTs)

For corporate investors:

- The Corporate Venturing Scheme (CVS)

CGT business asset taper relief

Shares in qualifying AIM companies with substantial trading activities are classed as 'business' assets and qualify for business asset taper relief. After a two-year holding period, this can reduce the effective rate of tax for higher rate taxpayers to 10 per cent.

CGT gift relief

If shares or securities in an AIM-trading company are transferred, other than at arm's length, the deemed capital gain can be 'held over'. That is, the CGT liability is postponed until a subsequent arm's length disposal by the transferee, who effectively inherits the transferor's base cost.

Enterprise Investment Scheme

The EIS can benefit individual investors who subscribe for new ordinary shares in AIM companies that are qualifying trading firms. Qualifying investments of up to £200,000 in aggregate in a tax year (a husband and wife may each invest £200,000) may entitle an investor to the following tax reliefs:

- 20 per cent initial income tax relief
- CGT exemption on disposal
- Loss relief on failure/sale at a loss

The first two reliefs apply only where the shares are held for a period of three years and the company qualifies throughout.

CGT deferral under the EIS

In addition, or alternatively, investors may defer assessment to capital gains tax on other gains by reinvesting in subscriptions for new ordinary shares, in companies qualifying under EIS rules.

Reinvestment must be made up to one year before, and three years after, the relevant disposal. Deferral continues until the investment is disposed of or the investee company ceases to qualify. There is basically no limit to the amount of the gain before taper relief that can be deferred. Investors must be UK residents at time of original gain, its reinvestment, and for three years thereafter.

EIS Conditions

These include:

- The shares issued must be subscribed for wholly in cash, fully paid up on issue, with no preferential rights to dividends or assets on a winding up.
- Funds from the same share issue must be employed wholly for the purpose of a qualifying business activity, carried on wholly or mainly in the UK – 80 per cent within 12 months of the date of subscription, the remainder in the following 12 months.
- Aggregate gross assets must not exceed £15 million before investment and £16 million immediately after.
- Throughout a three-year period, generally from the issue of shares, the company must satisfy various conditions, including being unquoted and not controlled by another company. Subsidiary companies must be at least 75 per cent-owned (51 per cent for shares issued on or after 17 March 2004) but 90 per cent if the subsidiary uses EIS funds.

Qualifying business activities under the EIS

Most trades (not investment activities) qualify, but some activities do not, including:

- Property development
- Letting of property
- Dealing in land, commodities, futures, shares or securities
- Dealing in goods other than by normal wholesale or retail

- Banking, insurance, money-lending, debt-factoring, hire-purchase or other financial activities
- Legal or accountancy services
- Farming, market gardening, forestry woodlands or timber
- Operating or managing property-backed establishments such as hotels, guest houses, nursing homes, residential care homes, or managing property used for any of these activities

IHT business property relief

Investments in qualifying AIM-trading companies, as defined by the rules above, can attract 100 per cent relief from IHT provided the investment is held for at least two years before a chargeable transfer for IHT purposes.

Relief for capital losses

It may be possible to relieve capital losses arising from investments in qualifying AIM-trading companies against the capital gains of the year in which the loss arises, or a subsequent year. It may also be possible to relieve the loss against income of the current or previous year. Professional advice should be taken as to the nature and eligibility of the losses available for relief.

Venture capital trusts

A VCT is a fully-listed company, similar to a quoted investment trust and approved by the Inland Revenue. Investors in VCTs can therefore gain indirect access to a professionally-managed portfolio of unquoted investments – which can include shares in qualifying AIM companies.

Investments in VCTs (either purchased in the market or subscribed for) of up to £200,000 in any tax year entitle individual investors to the following tax exemptions:

- From tax on dividends
- From CGT on the disposal of shares in the VCT

In addition, for subscriptions of up to £200,000 per year in new ordinary shares issued by a VCT on or after 6 April 2004, there is 40 per cent initial income tax relief on the amount invested, provided the shares are held for three years.

The qualifying criteria for investee companies is essentially as under the EIS, but restrictions on the employment of funds relate only to those from VCTs.

Corporate Venturing Scheme

The CVS has been described as the equivalent of the EIS for companies because of the similarities in the issuing companies that qualify and reliefs available to investing companies. The CVS entitles investing companies to the following tax reliefs:

- 20 per cent corporation tax relief on investment
- Deferral of tax on CVS gains

• Relief against income for capital losses

It is stressed that available tax reliefs should not be the principal reason for investment, and should never outweigh the commercial criteria of investment proposals. However, they can enhance financial returns, as well as assist in an investor's tax planning.

Chilton Taylor

Partner

Baker Tilly

The London Stock Exchange and Baker Tilly have published a booklet 'A Guide to AIM tax benefits'. It provides additional information on the various reliefs outlined above. It also considers special situations, such as the status of non-UK incorporated or resident companies; firms moving from AIM to the main market, or vice versa; and obtaining clearance from the Revenue. In addition, it contains two pull-out summaries for investors and companies respectively.

You can either request a copy or download the booklet by visiting: www.londonstockexchange.com/aim or http://www.bakertilly.co.uk

The AIM rules

Investors and aspirant AIM companies may wonder how the Alternative Investment Market differs from the Official List of the United Kingdom Listing Authority (the "Official List"). Well, unlike fully-listed companies, prospective AIM companies do not need to be a minimum size, have a three-year trading record or keep 25 per cent of their shares in public hands.

An AIM company must appoint and retain a nominated adviser (a "nomad") from the list of 70 or so suitable firms approved by London Stock Exchange plc (the "Stock Exchange"). The nomad provides guidance to the company to ensure its compliance with the regulatory requirements of the Stock Exchange.

An AIM company must also retain a broker, which may well be the same firm as the nomad, to ensure there is a market for the company's shares.

AIM has its own rules (the 'AIM Rules') – set out by the Stock Exchange which cover both entry into, and the operation of, the market, and the latest version (December 2003) can be accessed on the Stock Exchange website www.londonstockexchange.com/aim/rules.asp. In relation to admissions to AIM, these rules are currently based on the Public Offers of Securities Regulations 1995 (the 'POS Regs'), but differ in certain respects. A new streamlined AIM admission regime for companies already listed on certain major international stock markets (including the Australian Stock Exchange, Deutsche Börse, Johannesburg Stock Exchange, Nasdaq, NYSE and the Toronto Stock Exchange) as specified on the Stock Exchange's website ('Designated Markets') was introduced in May 2003, the benefits of which are set out below.

All AIM companies have certain obligations to fulfil. The main points of these are listed below.

Flotation rules

For admission to AIM, a company must:

- be duly incorporated and validly established under the laws of its country of incorporation.
- be a UK public company or the equivalent in its country of incorporation so that it can offer its securities to the public.
- have published accounts conforming to UK or US generally accepted accounting principles or international financial reporting standards, and prepared in accordance with its national law (unless it is a new company).
- ensure that its securities are freely transferable on AIM subject to limited exceptions and that appropriate settlement arrangements are in place.
- ensure that its directors and applicable employees do not deal in the company's AIM securities, both while in possession of unpublished price sensitive information and in the period prior to the announcement of results.
- retain a nomad and broker at all times.

Additional requirements

Companies seeking a listing on AIM that are not already listed on a Designated Market must prepare an admission document which in addition to containing the information required for a prospectus under the POS Regs must:

- include a confirmation from the company that, having made due and careful enquiries, the available working capital – from the time the securities to which the admission document relates are admitted to AIM – is sufficient to meet the company's present requirements.

- where a profit estimate or forecast is included, a statement by the directors and the nomad that this has been made after due and careful enquiry by the directors; and a clear statement of the principal assumptions for each factor that could have a material effect on the forecast.

- include a risk warning on the front page in prominent lettering confirming that AIM is a market for emerging or smaller companies to which a higher investment risk tends to be attached; that AIM securities are not admitted to the Official List; and that the Stock Exchange has not reviewed the prospectus.

- include a statement about any restrictions on the disposal of securities agreed by directors, applicable employees, substantial shareholders and other related parties.

- in relation to the company's directors, provide full details of the name, age and all the directorships held in the last five years, unspent convictions in relation to indictable offences; all bankruptcies or individual voluntary arrangements; receiverships, liquidations, administrations, company voluntary arrangements or similar arrangements of companies or partnerships of which an individual was a director or partner at the time or within the preceding 12 months of such event; any public criticisms by statutory or regulatory authorities of such individuals; and whether a director has been disqualified by a court from acting as a director or from acting in the management or conduct of the affairs of any company.

- contain the name and full details of the relationship of any person who has either received within 12 months preceding an AIM admission application, or has entered into contractual arrangements to receive on or after admission, fees of £10,000 or securities in the company of £10,000 or more, calculated by reference to the issue or opening price or any other benefit with a value of £10,000 or more at the date of admission.

- include the name of any person who, as far as the company is aware, is interested in 3 per cent or more of the company's capital, and the percentage amount of such interest.

- include any other factual information which the company reasonably considers necessary for investors to form a full understanding of the matters contained in the admission document or prospectus.

- disclose any related financial product dealings, such as fixed odds or spread bets, undertaken by directors in relation to the company's AIM securities, both in the admission document or prospectus and on an ongoing basis.

- If it is an investment company, include details of its investment strategy.

Companies listed on Designated Markets do not have to produce an admission document and need only provide an expanded pre-admission announcement 20 days before admission. This announcement must disclose certain details relating to the company together with any information that the company has not previously disclosed on its Designated Market but would have been required to disclose in an admission document.

More information, including the full AIM rules, is available free of charge from the Stock Exchange's AIM team and is also available on the Exchange's website: http://www.londonstockexchange.com

Jan Mellmann, of international law firm Watson Farley & Williams, prepared this outline of the AIM rules (email: jmellmann@wfw.com, tel: 020 7814 8000, web site: www.wfw.com).

Companies joining and leaving AIM between October 2003 and March 2004

ADMISSIONS

Date joined	Company name	Sector	Mkt cap (£m)	Money raised (£m)
15/10/03	Canisp	Speciality & Other Finance	3.44	2.06
15/10/03	IP2IPO	Speciality & Other Finance	111.76	31.49
17/10/03	Noble Investments	Speciality & Other Finance	1.18	0.84
20/10/03	Deal Group Media	Media & Photography	11.95	1.75
20/10/03	Southampton Leisure	Leisure, Entertainment & Hotels	10.70	n/a
20/10/03	Stepquick	Speciality & Other Finance	14.99	0.17
23/10/03	Conygar Investment	Speciality & Other Finance	4.60	4.00
28/10/03	General Industries	Speciality & Other Finance	1.05	0.57
28/10/03	Melrose	Speciality & Other Finance	13.12	12.10
29/10/03	Quayle Munro	Investment Companies	14.24	n/a
29/10/03	The Telecommunications Group	Telecommunication Services	26.48	n/a
30/10/03	Netbenefit	Media & Photography	6.94	n/a
30/10/03	Ocean Power Technologies	Electronic & Electrical	62.84	25.00
31/10/03	Crown Corporation	Investment Companies	283.14	n/a
03/11/03	Community Broking Group	Speciality & Other Finance	2.83	0.80
06/11/03	Romag	Building & Construction	19.00	8.01
07/11/03	Straight	Chemicals	5.52	1.52
10/11/03	Clapham House Group	Leisure, Entertainment & Hotels	15.05	14.75
11/11/03	RWS	Support Services	42.52	21.08
17/11/03	Multi	Building & Construction	2.50	2.04
24/11/03	Monstermob	General Retailers	32.08	5.30
24/11/03	Network	Media & Photography	12.08	n/a
25/11/03	Trans-Siberian	Mining	42.83	16.00
27/11/03	Scott Tod	Electronic & Electrical	6.75	2.50
27/11/03	Erinaceous Group	Support Services	57.96	14.14
28/11/03	Yamana Gold	Mining	140.80	n/a
01/12/03	Monsoon	General Retailers	254.43	n/a
02/12/03	Access Intelligence	Media & Photography	10.45	0.20
04/12/03	CES Software	Media & Photography	13.30	4.31
04/12/03	Marakand Minerals	Mining	39.37	n/a
08/12/03	Brazilian Diamonds	Mining	37.41	2.04
08/12/03	Pixology	Software & Computer Services	28.00	10.00
11/12/03	Center Parcs	Leisure, Entertainment & Hotels	245.00	245.00
11/12/03	Eureka Mining	Mining	20.45	7.00
11/12/03	Sinclair Pharma	Pharmaceuticals	61.82	10.80
12/12/03	Asfare Group	Engineering & Machinery	4.20	2.40
12/12/03	Cater Barnard (USA)	Investment Companies	1.67	0.19
12/12/03	Flightstore Group	Software & Computer Services	10.04	2.00

ADMISSIONS

Date joined	Company name	Sector	Mkt cap (£m)	Money raised (£m)
12/12/03	Immedia Broadcasting	Media & Photography	12.88	5.05
12/12/03	IndigoVision	Software & Computer Services	2.46	n/a
16/12/03	BKN International	Media & Photography	10.24	n/a
17/12/03	Raven Mount	Property	46.66	n/a
18/12/03	BWA	Speciality & Other Finance	0.36	0.31
18/12/03	City Lofts Group	Real Estate	47.00	7.00
18/12/03	Croma Group	Aerospace & Defence	2.84	1.65
18/12/03	Napier Brown Foods	Food Producers & Processors	25.11	10.00
19/12/03	Strategic Retail	General Retailers	11.91	0.35
19/12/03	Vista Group	Building & Construction	14.61	0.25
19/12/03	Wilshaw	Automobiles & Parts	5.29	n/a
22/12/03	Farley Group	Property	3.11	n/a
23/12/03	Alliance Pharma	Pharmaceuticals	17.73	3.67
23/12/03	Oilexco	Oil & Gas	57.97	12.82
24/12/03	Avesco	Media & Photography	24.56	n/a
31/12/03	Aricom	Chemicals	14.02	4.00
31/12/03	Feedback	Electronic & Electrical	3.61	n/a
06/01/04	INVU	Software & Computer Services	8.60	3.00
13/01/04	EiRx Therapeutics	Pharmaceuticals	6.12	0.78
16/01/04	Amberley Group	Chemicals	1.70	n/a
19/01/04	Enition	Software & Computer Services	10.17	0.30
22/01/04	Planit	Software & Computer Services	27.03	n/a
23/01/04	Tottenham Hotspur	Leisure, Entertainment & Hotels	25.00	15.00
02/02/04	Palladex	Mining	5.44	5.30
03/02/04	Business Serve	Media & Photography	18.04	4.50
03/02/04	Camelot Capital	Speciality & Other Finance	2.96	1.38
04/02/04	Supercart	Support Services	10.25	4.00
13/02/04	ADL	Health	3.73	n/a
16/02/04	Meon Capital	Investment Companies	4.03	n/a
01/03/04	Civica	Software & Computer Services	79.00	15.00
02/03/04	Medoro Resources	Mining	27.20	n/a
05/03/04	Interactive Gaming	Software & Computer Services	1.40	0.25
08/03/04	Reflexion Cosmetics	Investment Companies	1.20	0.37
08/03/04	Felix Group	Media & Photography	27.60	0.50
09/03/04	Gippsland	Mining	5.10	0.70
09/03/04	Skiddaw Capital	Investment Companies	3.75	1.20
10/03/04	Screen FX	Media & Photography	5.00	5.00
10/03/04	Centaur	Media & Photography	148.00	131.90
10/03/04	Compass Finance	Speciality & Other Finance	32.10	0.61
11/03/04	Roshni Investments	Investment Companies	1.80	0.25
11/03/04	Oriel Resources	Mining	123.80	40.60
11/03/04	Offshore Hydrocarbon Mapping	Mining	49.30	10.00
11/03/04	2 ergo	Support Services	36.00	3.00
16/03/04	RAB Capital	Investment Companies	124.90	8.00
17/03/04	ANGLE	Support Services	24.00	9.00

Companies due to float on AIM

Company name	Sector	Due to float
Asia Energy	Mining	tbc
Imperial Energy	Oil & Gas	05 Apr 04
NETeller	Speciality & Other Finance	08 Apr 04
Robinson	Food Producers & Processors	29 Apr 04
Sovereign Reversions	Investment Companies	16 Apr 04
Station Plan	Telecommunication Services	02 Apr 04
Tantalum Australia	Mining	tbc
The 4Less Group	Speciality & Other Finance	15 Apr 04
Titan Europe	Engineering & Machinery	07 Apr 04
Toledo Copper	Mining	05 Apr 04

DELETIONS

Company name	Sector	Reason
Access Plus	Media & Photography	At the company's request
Arcolectric	Electronic & Electrical	Shares cancelled after suspension
Aspinalls Online	Leisure, Entertainment & Hotels	At the company's request
Auiron Energy	Mining	At the company's request
AWG Services	Support Services	Acquired and became Oak Holdings
Blavod Black Vodka	Beverages	Acquired Extreme Beverages and became Blavod Extreme Spirits
Bradstock	Investment Companies	At the company's request
Comeleon	Support Services	Acquired and became Tanfield
Compass Software	Software & Computer Services	At the company's request
Convergent Communications	Telecommunication Services	Shares cancelled after suspension
Darwen Capital	Investment Companies	Acquired and became Scott Tod
Forever Broadcasting	Media & Photography	At the company's request
Fusion & Oil	Oil & Gas	At the company's request
Galahad Capital	Mining	Acquired Shambhala Gold and became Galahad Gold
Galileo Innovation	Media & Photography	Shares cancelled after suspension
Getmapping	Media & Photography	At the company's request
Giardino	Leisure, Entertainment & Hotels	At the company's request
Guiton	Media & Photography	At the company's request
Health Media Group	Support Services	Acquired Bybrook and became RWS Holdings

IBNet	Software & Computer Services	Acquired and became Deal Group Media
IFTE	Support Services	At the company's request
Intelliplus	Telecommunication Services	At the company's request
Mezzanine	Leisure, Entertainment & Hotels	At the company's request
Names.co Internet	Software & Computer Services	Acquired Larchland and became Triple Plate Junction
Peerless Technology	Pharmaceuticals	Acquired and became Alliance Pharma
Po Na Na Group	Leisure, Entertainment & Hotels	At the company's request
Safestore	Support Services	At the company's request
Saltmark	Investment Companies	Acquired and became Noble Investments
Shaw (Arthur)	Media & Photography	Shares cancelled after suspension
Staffing Ventures	Support Services	Acquired Parys Snowdon Payroll and became Supporta
Systems Integrated Research	Media & Photography	Acquired Linetex and became SiRViS IT
Topnotch Health Clubs	Leisure, Entertainment & Hotels	Failure to appoint an adviser
Transware	Software & Computer Services	At the company's request

NB. The following companies have come to AIM since going to press:

Attentiv Systems Group
Award International
Aztec Resources
Central African Gold
Cobra Capital
European Goldfields
European Nickel
Floors 2 Go
Healthcare Holdings
Moneybox
Nadlan
Namibian Resources
Polaron
Quintessentially English
Sky Capital Enterprises

Note: In the main companies section of the Guide asterisks (*) are sometimes placed beside directors and main shareholders. This indicates that the asterisked items are linked. For example, the chairman might hold his shares in the company through a separate investment company

we take

aim

you take stock

The Watson, Farley & Williams team has been involved with AIM since its inception in 1995 and has developed considerable experience of transactions involving new applications for admission to trading on AIM.

We act for Nominated Advisers and Brokers as well as several companies on AIM and those considering applications for admission to AIM. In addition, we have advised on secondary fund raising exercises, acquisitions and disposals and reverse take-over transactions.

We have continued to broaden our experience of AIM related transactions and are in a strong position to deal with such transactions efficiently and professionally and at competitive rates. We are looking forward to continuing our activity on AIM in 2004.

For further information on the services we provide, please contact:

Jan Mellmann, Charles Walford
or Jonathan Martin.

Watson, Farley & Williams
15 Appold Street
London EC2A 2HB

Tel: +44 (0)20 7814 8000
Fax: +44 (0)20 7814 8141
Email: jmellmann@wfw.com

Watson, Farley & Williams
www.wfw.com

Market Makers key

ABN	ABN Amro Equities	HSBC	HSBC Securities
AITK	Aitken Campbell & Co	INV.	Investec Bank (UK)
ALTI	Altium Capital	JEFF	Jefferies
ARBT	Arbuthnot Securities	JPMS	JP Morgan Securities
BARD	Robert W Baird	KBCS	KBC Peel Hunt
BEST	Bear Stearns	KLWT	Dresdner Kleinwort Wasserstein
BGWL	Bridgewell	LEHM	Lehman Brothers
CAZR	Cazenove Securities	MLSB	Merrill Lynch International
CITI	Citigroup	NMRA	Nomura International
CLS.	Credit Lyonnais Securities	NUMS	Numis Securities
CSCS	Collins Stewart	PMUR	Panmure Gordon
DAVY	J & E Davy	SCAP	Shore Capital Stockbrokers
DEUT	Deutsche Bank AG	SGSL	SG Securites (London)
DURM	Durlacher	TEAM	Teather & Greenwood
EVO	Evolution Beeson Gregory	UBS.	UBS Warburg
GOOD	Goodbody Stockbrokers	WDBM	Williams De Broe
HOOD	Hoodless Brennan	WINS	Winterflood Securites

The AllStars awards are designed to reward the achievement of investors who operate in early stage venture capital investing up to £10m.

Last year the awards attracted over 350 attendees and headline sponsorship from Barclays Bank, Olswang, MTI and Nesta.

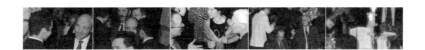

This year's event will be held on Wednesday 13th October 2004 at the Inter-continental Hotel, London,W1

For more details, or to book a table, please call Michelle Senyah on 020 7430 9777

COMPANIES
SECTION

We have included detailed information on 774 AIM companies.

10 Group (TGR)

Holding company

10 Clement Street, Birmingham, B1 2SL Tel: 01862-827787; Fax: 01926-889336; e-mail: info@10group.co.uk

		holding %
Chairman	Neil McGowan	0.0
Chief Executive		
Finance Director		
Director	Jonathan Burrow	0.0

Main Shareholders:

Fiske Nominees	27.2
Pershing Keen Noms	10.2
Scoreloop	4.1

Percentage of free market capital: 58.6%

Nominated Adviser:	City Financial Associates, London
AIM Broker:	Seymour Pierce, London
Solicitors:	Field Fisher Waterhouse, London
Market Makers:	KBCS; MLSB; SCAP; WINS
Auditors:	Moore Stephens, Birmingham
Registrars:	Computershare Investor Services

Entry on AIM:	30/6/1998	Recent price:	2.0p
Interim results:	Sep	Market cap:	£0.49m
Final results:	Jun	Issue price:	n/a
Year end:	Dec	Current no of shares:	
Accounts due:	Apr		24,482,068
Int div paymnt:	n/a	No of shares after	
Fin div paymnt:	n/a	dilution:	n/a
Int net div per share:	nil	P/E ratio:	n/a
Fin net div per share:	nil	Probable CGT?	No

LATEST REPORTED RESULTS:	2002	PREVIOUS REPORTED RESULTS:	2001
Turnover:	£1.02m	Turnover:	£4.49m
PTP:	£(2.69m)	PTP:	£(1.5m)
EPS:	(0.1)p	EPS:	(0.2)p

Comments:

Cash shell 10 has at last found a viable business. £0.4m has been spent on Oakburn Import/Export Ltd, a supplier of flooring products. Oakburn made profits of £56,918 on sales of £1.5m last year. 10 will pay £50,000 in cash and issue 35m shares to cover the cost. A further 10m shares will be issued if Oakburn hits certain profit targets. An open offer is also underway to raise £0.5m via the issue of no less than 49m shares. Every two shares gets a free warrant.

1st Dental Laboratories (FDT)

Dental laboratory services

Chesterton House, 2 Rectory Place, Loughborough, Leicestershire LE11 1UW Tel: 01509-211616; Fax: 01509-211717

		holding %
Chairman	Andrew Garner	21.9
Managing Director	Ian Bryer	1.0
Finance Director	Roy Butterworth	15.0
Technical Director	Bradley Moore	1.0

Main Shareholders:

Rathbone Investment	17.2
Northern AIM VCT	9.7
Close Brothers AIM VCT	9.7
BWD Aim VCT	7.0
Stika Health fund VCT	7.0

Percentage of free market capital: 10.2%

Nominated Adviser:	Corporate Synergy, London
AIM Broker:	Corporate Synergy, London
Solicitors:	Halliwell Landau, Manchester
Market Makers:	HOOD; WINS
Auditors:	Godkin & Co, 105 Derby Road, Loughborough, Leics LE11 5AE
Registrars:	Capita Registrars

Entry on AIM:	2/5/2002	Recent price:	29.25p
Interim results:	Aug	Market cap:	£3.95m
Final results:	Feb	Issue price:	27.0p
Year end:	Nov	Current no of shares:	
Accounts due:	May		13,514,620
Int div paymnt:	n/a	No of shares after	
Fin div paymnt:	n/a	dilution:	n/a
Int net div per share:	nil	P/E ratio:	n/a
Fin net div per share:	nil	Probable CGT?	Yes

LATEST REPORTED RESULTS:	2003	PREVIOUS REPORTED RESULTS:	25 JUL '02 TO 30 NOV '02
Turnover:	£4.36m	Turnover:	£2.80m
PTP:	£(295,000)	PTP:	£(202,000)
EPS:	(2.5)p	EPS:	(2.7)p

Comments:

This group came to AIM in an attempt to consolidate the makers of false teeth, bridges, crowns and other dental devices. Previously this £350m market has been run as an informal 'cottage' industry. Entrepreneurial Andrew Garner made two acquisitions last year, enabling annualised turnover to rise 27% to £4.3m. The seven strong business is now breaking even on a monthly basis. Garner wants to make more purchases and thinks new regulations may force many smaller players to capitulate.

2 ergo
(RGO)
Telecommunications support services company
St Mary's Chambers, Haslingden Road, Rawtenstall, Lancashire BB4 6QX Tel: 01706-221777; Fax: 01706-221888;
e-mail: admin@2ergo.com

		holding %
Chairman	Keith Seeley	2.8
Joint Managing Director	Barry Sharples	26.3
Finance Director	Jillian Collighan	0.03
Joint Managing Director	Neale Graham	26.2

Main Shareholders:

Michael Kilgannon	8.6
Trevor Bladon	7.1
Lammtara Industries	4.7

Percentage of free market capital: 23.5%

Comments:

2 ergo arrived on AIM having raised £2.3m net in a placing at 120p. The company, which turned profitable in 2003, makes its money from a range of telecom-sector focused services. In particular it focuses on providing mobile content (sports results, logos, ring tones, etc) and message and billing services to the likes of Vodafone, Orange, MMO2, T-Mobile and Virgin. In addition 2 ergo recently picked up four 118 Directory Enquiry licences from OFTEL.

Nominated Adviser:	Numis, London
AIM Broker:	Numis, London
Solicitors:	Wacks Caller, Manchester
Market Makers:	WINS
Auditors:	KPMG, St James' Square, Manchester M2 6DS
Registrars:	Computershare Investor Services

ENTRY ON AIM:	11/3/2004	**Recent price:**	125.5p
Interim results:	Jun	**Market cap:**	£36.36m
Final results:	Dec	**Issue price:**	120.0p
Year end:	Aug	**Current no of shares:**	
Accounts due:	Feb		28,970,100
Int div paymnt:	n/a	**No of shares after**	
Fin div paymnt:	n/a	**dilution:**	n/a
Int net div per share:	nil	**P/E ratio:**	54.6
Fin net div per share:	nil	**Probable CGT?**	YES

LATEST REPORTED RESULTS:	2003	PREVIOUS REPORTED RESULTS:	2002
Turnover:	£4.58m	**Turnover:**	£1.55m
PTP:	£453,000	**PTP:**	£(194,000)
EPS:	2.3p	**EPS:**	(0.7)p

2 Travel
(TLG)
Bus & coach operator
Upper Bank, Pentrechwyth, Swansea, SA1 7DB Tel: 01792-48040; Fax: 01792-652422;
web site: www.2travelgroup.co.uk

		holding %
Chairman	Sir Richard Needham	0.3
Chief Executive	Bev Fowles	31.9
Finance Director	Carl Waters	0.0
Operations Director	David Rhys Fowles	0.0

Main Shareholders:

Jupiter Asset management	9.9
Teather & Greenwood	7.0
Downing Classic VCT 3	4.6
Giltspur Nominees	3.8

Percentage of free market capital: 10.7%

Comments:

In a tough year for tourism 2 Travel moved its coach business away from tour work towards more pre-dictable domestic business. In more upbeat news, its bus operations benefited from new commercial and local authority tendered routes gained towards the end of the year. The financials showed rising turnover, but a move into losses. These were caused by exceptional flotation costs, depot and route development costs, as well as rising staff costs and higher insurance premiums.

Nominated Adviser:	City Financial Associates, London
AIM Broker:	CFA Securities, Manchester
Solicitors:	Eversheds, Cardiff
Market Makers:	KBCS; SCAP; WINS
Auditors:	Bevan & Buckland, Swansea
Registrars:	Melton Registrars

Entry on AIM:	20/1/2003	**Recent price:**	7.25p
Interim results:	May	**Market cap:**	£3.56m
Final results:	Feb	**Issue price:**	7.0p
Year end:	Aug	**Current no of shares:**	
Accounts due:	Mar		49,048,123
Int div paymnt:	n/a	**No of shares after**	
Fin div paymnt:	n/a	**dilution:**	n/a
Int net div per share:	nil	**P/E ratio:**	n/a
Fin net div per share:	nil	**Probable CGT?**	YES

LATEST REPORTED RESULTS:	2003	PREVIOUS REPORTED RESULTS:	2002
Turnover:	£4.25m	**Turnover:**	£3.68m
PTP:	£(997,000)	**PTP:**	£212,000
EPS:	n/a	**EPS:**	n/a

3DM Worldwide   (TDM)
Plastics moulding technology
Keble House, Church End, South Leigh, Oxfordshire OX29 6UR Tel: 01993-779468; Fax: 01993-776480;
e-mail: info@3dmworldwide.com; web site: www.3dmworldwide.com

		holding %
Chairman	Kenneth Brooks	1.4
Chief Executive	William Widger	1.7
Finance Director		
Director	William Lopshire	0.0

Main Shareholders:	
Battlebridge	13.6
Universities Superannuation Scheme	5.0

Percentage of free market capital: 78.3%

Nominated Adviser:	Grant Thornton, London
AIM Broker:	JM Finn, London
Solicitors:	Charles Russell, London
Market Makers:	KBCS; WINS
Auditors:	Solomon Hare, Bristol
Registrars:	Capita Registrars

ENTRY ON AIM:	23/10/2002	**Recent price:**		161.0p
Interim results:	Sep	**Market cap:**		£106.68m
Final results:	Aug	**Issue price:**		86.0p
Year end:	Dec	**Current no of shares:**		
Accounts due:	May			66,262,297
Int div paymnt:	n/a	**No of shares after**		
Fin div paymnt:	n/a	**dilution:**		n/a
Int net div per share:	nil	**P/E ratio:**		n/a
Fin net div per share:	nil	**Probable CGT?**		YES

LATEST REPORTED RESULTS: 2002		PREVIOUS REPORTED RESULTS: 2001	
Turnover:	£403,000	Turnover:	£648,000
PTP:	£(8.99m)	PTP:	£(3.22m)
EPS:	(15.5)p	EPS:	(11.4)p

Comments:
The plastics technology intellectual property play acquired two plastics making processes back in 2001. Powder Impression Moulding, or PIM, produces a strong composite with the strength of metal. PIM has huge applications in fields like the construction and car industry. Whilst 3-Dimensional Blow Moulding helps the manufacture of complex components with reduced weight, creating cost savings. In an encouraging half to June, losses were pared back to £700,000 from £4.4m.

---

7 Group (suspended 29 Sep 2003)   (SVG)
Cash shell looking for food and leisure opportunities
52/54 Broadwick Street, London, W1V 1FF Tel: 020-7439 4444; Fax: 020-7439 2222; e-mail: info@7group.co.uk

		holding %
Chairman	Mario Palmonella	0.0
Chief Executive		
Finance Director		
Director	Anita Madhas	0.0

Main Shareholders:	
10 Group	29.8
Anzcorp Trust	20.8
W S Nominees	9.3
Robert Upchurch	7.2
J Pordum	7.0

Percentage of free market capital: 4.5%

Nominated Adviser:	Beaumont Cornish, London
AIM Broker:	WH Ireland, Manchester
Solicitors:	Field Fisher Waterhouse, London
Market Makers:	WINS
Auditors:	Hacker Young, Hove
Registrars:	Capita Registrars

Entry on AIM:	8/7/1996	**Recent price:**		1.05p
Interim results:	Mar	**Market cap:**		£3.03m
Final results:	Nov	**Issue price:**		3.0p
Year end:	May	**Current no of shares:**		
Accounts due:	Dec			288,850,000
Int div paymnt:	n/a	**No of shares after**		
Fin div paymnt:	n/a	**dilution:**		n/a
Int net div per share:	nil	**P/E ratio:**		n/a
Fin net div per share:	nil	**Probable CGT?**		YES

LATEST REPORTED RESULTS: 2002		PREVIOUS REPORTED RESULTS: 2001	
Turnover:	£527,000	Turnover:	n/a
PTP:	£(32,000)	PTP:	£(1.83m)
EPS:	0.0p	EPS:	(1.0)p

Comments:
The erstwhile shell, scouring for a reverse deal since selling Bon Appetite Food & Wine, is now the owner of Azzurra Air. Back in November, the investment group flagged up its taking control of Air Littoral, a private French regional airline that offers more than 120 connections between Southern Europe's largest cities. Apparently the board's strategy now is to drive synergies between the two airlines and become a 'regional airline with a Mediterranean vocation'.

A Cohen & Co (CHEN)

Non-ferrous scrap metal trader

Purland Road, London, SE28 0AT Tel: 020-8320 4210; Fax: 020-8310 1506

		holding %
Executive Chairman	Royce Ritchie	0.0
Managing Director	James Ferguson	0.0
Finance Director		
Non-Exec Director	Russel Sincock	0.0

Main Shareholders:

HSBC	23.2
Fitel Nominees	7.3
Gilspur	6.8
D J Massie	6.3
N J Tod	6.3

Percentage of free market capital: 42.5%

Nominated Adviser:	Beaumont Cornish, London
AIM Broker:	Arbuthnot, London
Solicitors:	Faegre Benson Hobson Audley
Market Makers:	ARBT; WINS
Auditors:	Rees Pollock, 7 Pilgrim Street, London, EC4V 6DR
Registrars:	Computershare Investor Services

ENTRY ON AIM:	30/9/2003	Recent price:	7.9p
Interim results:	Sep	Market cap:	£1.2m
Final results:	Mar	Issue price:	n/a
Year end:	Dec	Current no of shares:	
Accounts due:	May		15,160,482
Int div paymnt:	n/a	No of shares after	
Fin div paymnt:	n/a	dilution:	n/a
Int net div per share:	nil	P/E ratio:	n/a
Fin net div per share:	nil	Probable CGT?	No

LATEST REPORTED RESULTS: 2002		PREVIOUS REPORTED RESULTS: 2001	
Turnover:	£8.50m	Turnover:	£9.07m
PTP:	£(1.57m)	PTP:	£(424,000)
EPS:	(11.4)p	EPS:	(7.8)p

Comments:

A Cohen & Co has closed its international metals trading business and its restructuring is substantially complete. It holds a 24% interest in ROO Media Europe and 33.3% of Money Products International, a developer of smart charge and credit card dispensing equipment. Latest financials were interims to June. These showed wider pre-tax losses of £717,000 (£188,000) on £3.7m (£4.3m) sales. The deficit arose on its exit from the phospor-copper business.

Abingdon Capital (ANC)

Corporate financier and stockbroker

223a Kensington High Street, London, W8 6SG Tel: 020-7937 4445; Fax: 020-7937 4446

		holding %
Chairman	Oliver Vaughan	5.8
Chief Executive	Edward Vandyk	9.3
Finance Director	Christopher Roberts	0.2

Main Shareholders:

Thurloe Holdings	8.5
St Clements Lane Investments	8.4
Symphony Investments	8.3
UBS AG, Hong Kong	3.1

Percentage of free market capital: 46.5%

Nominated Adviser:	KBC Peel Hunt, London
AIM Broker:	KBC Peel Hunt, London
Solicitors:	Stringer Saul, London
Market Makers:	KBCS; MLSB; SCAP; WINS
Auditors:	Moore Stephens, St Paul's House, Warwick Lane, London EC4P 4BN
Registrars:	Capita Registrars

Entry on AIM:	11/1/1996	Recent price:	12.0p
Interim results:	Aug	Market cap:	£6.95m
Final results:	Apr	Issue price:	100.0p
Year end:	Dec	Current no of shares:	
Accounts due:	Apr		57,937,851
Int div paymnt:	n/a	No of shares after	
Fin div paymnt:	n/a	dilution:	n/a
Int net div per share:	nil	P/E ratio:	n/a
Fin net div per share:	nil	Probable CGT?	Yes

LATEST REPORTED RESULTS: 2002		PREVIOUS REPORTED RESULTS: 2001	
Turnover:	£832,000	Turnover:	n/a
PTP:	£(1.1m)	PTP:	£(789,000)
EPS:	(2.5)p	EPS:	(2.2)p

Comments:

Abingdon consists of investment entity Mountcashel and financial boutique Corporate Synergy. The former's biotech investments have been sold or hived-off into AIM-listed Bionex. FSA-regulated Corporate Synergy is leading the formation of an integrated stockbroking and corporate advisory business. Mountcashel hopes to become a regulated hedge fund under Paul Spence's direction. Interim losses halved to £0.23m. Cash stands at £5.3m.

Abraxus Investments (AXU)
Cash shell

Lacon House, Theobald's Road, London, WC1X 8RW Tel: 020-7401 7182; Fax: 020-7643 5301;
web site: 08004homes.com

		holding %
Chairman	Phil Edmonds	0.0
Chief Executive		
Finance Director		
Director	Douglas Blausten	0.0

Main Shareholders:

Grosvenor Land Holdings	29.3
Immoconsult Leasing Gesellschaft	7.0
Hornbuckle Mitchell	5.2
Pershing Keen Nominees	4.0
Capela Overseas	3.6

Percentage of free market capital: 36.7%

Nominated Adviser:	Seymour Pierce, London
AIM Broker:	Seymour Pierce, London
Solicitors:	Nabarro Nathanson, Reading
Market Makers:	KBCS; SCAP; WINS
Auditors:	Deloitte & Touche, 1 Little New St, London EC4A 3TR
Registrars:	Capita Registrars

ENTRY ON AIM: 23/12/1999		**Recent price:**	7.5p
Interim results:	Dec	Market cap:	£1.79m
Final results:	Jul	Issue price:	25.0p
Year end:	Mar	Current no of shares:	
Accounts due:	Aug		23,879,444
Int div paymnt:	n/a	No of shares after	
Fin div paymnt:	n/a	dilution:	n/a
Int net div per share:	nil	P/E ratio:	n/a
Fin net div per share:	nil	Probable CGT?	YES

LATEST REPORTED RESULTS:		PREVIOUS REPORTED RESULTS:	
	2003		2002
Turnover:	n/a	Turnover:	£78,000
PTP:	£(221,000)	PTP:	£(1.81m)
EPS:	(1.1)p	EPS:	(9.6)p

Comments:
Phil Edmonds and the team from his property vehicle Grosvenor Land took over cash shell Property Internet with the aim of using it to invest in commercial property in Russia. The company is now looking to benefit from the expansion of the EU and is looking for investment opportunities in Central and Eastern Europe. In the interim to September pre-tax losses were small at £29,823 and with a healthy cash balance of £2.1m, it's in a good position to invest.

Access Intelligence (formerly Readymarket) (ACC)
Information & services provider

6 Ralli Courts, West Riverside, Manchester, M3 5FT

		holding %
Chairman	Edmund Savage	0.6
Chief Executive	Brendan Austin	14.7
Finance Director	Colin Davies	9.2
Non-Exec Director	Alwin Thompson	6.1

Main Shareholders:

Jeremy Hamer	7.5
Michael Halsall	6.0
Paul Stanton	4.0
Bernard Higgins	4.0

Percentage of free market capital: 46.9%

Nominated Adviser:	WH Ireland, Manchester
AIM Broker:	WH Ireland, Manchester
Solicitors:	DWF, Manchester
Market Makers:	EVO; WINS
Auditors:	Chadwick, Television House, Manchester
Registrars:	Neville Registrars

Entry on AIM:	1/12/2003	**Recent price:**	42.5p
Interim results:	Sep	Market cap:	£12.01m
Final results:	Mar	Issue price:	37.0p
Year end:	Nov	Current no of shares:	
Accounts due:	May		28,253,378
Int div paymnt:	n/a	No of shares after	
Fin div paymnt:	n/a	dilution:	n/a
Int net div per share:	nil	P/E ratio:	n/a
Fin net div per share:	nil	Probable CGT?	YES

LATEST REPORTED RESULTS:		PREVIOUS REPORTED RESULTS:	
	2002		2001
Turnover:	£511,000	Turnover:	£415,000
PTP:	£(200,000)	PTP:	£(375)
EPS:	n/a	EPS:	n/a

Comments:
Like some other new AIM entrants, Access Intelligence consists of three separate but inter-linked operations. The first is The Marketing Guild, a tiny marketing advice business aimed at small-and medium -sized enterprises with 700 subscribers. The second division is The Wired Gov, a supplier of government press releases to SMEs with 5000 'users'. The last operation is Backup & Running, a modest disaster recovery software supplier to SMEs. Following admission, £800,000 sits in the company coffers.

Acquisitor (ACQ)

Investment company

9 Walton Street, London, SW3 2JD Tel: 020-7581 4455; Fax: 0870-134 1720; e-mail: information@acquisitor.com; web site: www.acquisitor.com

		holding %
Chairman	John Radziwill*	0.0
Managing Director	Duncan Soukup*	0.0
Finance Director	Tim Lovell	0.0
Non-Exec Director	Christopher Mills	15.2

Main Shareholders:

Lionheart*	24.8
Scottish Value Trust	21.4
Framlington Invest. Mangement	8.7
Polaris Partners	6.3
Peter Melhado	6.3

Percentage of free market capital: 22.7%

*Lionheart, Inc. and/or its affiliates holds 705,000 Ordinary Shares pursuant to its discretionary fund management arrangements on behalf of clients including Mr Radziwill and Mr Soukup

Nominated Adviser:	KBC Peel Hunt, London
AIM Broker:	KBC Peel Hunt, London
Solicitors:	Pinsents, London
Market Makers:	KBCS; TEAM; WINS
Auditors:	KPMG, London
Registrars:	Capita Registrars

Entry on AIM:	10/1/2000	**Recent price:**	51.0p
Interim results:	May	**Market cap:**	£1.46m
Final results:	Nov	**Issue price:**	31.5p
Year end:	Sep	**Current no of shares:**	
Accounts due:	May		2,857,145
Int div paymnt:	n/a	**No of shares after**	
Fin div paymnt:	n/a	**dilution:**	n/a
Int net div per share:	nil	**P/E ratio:**	28.3
Fin net div per share:	nil	**Probable CGT?**	No

LATEST REPORTED RESULTS: 2003		PREVIOUS REPORTED RESULTS: 2002	
Turnover:	n/a	Turnover:	n/a
PTP:	£(70,000)	PTP:	£1.21m
EPS:	1.8p	EPS:	26.2p

Comments:

This is the UK version of a company that has successfully realised value in a number of US cash-rich companies. At the year end net assets stood at £1.1m, or 39p a share. The group realised its stakes in IndigoVision and marketing concern Protagona. This leaves the group with an 11% stake in fully listed Nettec. The prime focus, however, is on seeking a business that could reverse into the company.

Acquisitor (Bermuda) (AOB)

Holding company

Clarendon House, 2 Church Street, Hamilton HM 11, Bermuda

		holding %
Chairman	John Radziwill*	0.0
Managing Director	Duncan Soukup*	0.0
Finance Director		
Non-Exec Director	Luke Johnson	6.3

Main Shareholders:

Lionheart*	24.7
Scottish Value Trust	21.2
North Atlantic Smaller Companies	15.2
Framlington Investments	8.7
Swiss Life	6.8

Percentage of free market capital: 12.1%

*Mr Soukup & Mr Radziwill have a combined interest in these shares

Nominated Adviser:	KBC Peel Hunt, London
AIM Broker:	KBC Peel Hunt, London
Solicitors:	Pinsents, London; Conyers Dill & Pearlman, Bermuda
Market Makers:	CSCS; TEAM; WINS
Auditors:	KPMG, Crown House, 4 Par-la-Ville Road, Hamilton HM08 Bermuda
Registrars:	Capita Registrars

Entry on AIM:	8/10/2002	**Recent price:**	36.5p
Interim results:	May	**Market cap:**	£10.05m
Final results:	Oct	**Issue price:**	27.5p
Year end:	Jul	**Current no of shares:**	
Accounts due:	Nov		27,532,950
Int div paymnt:	n/a	**No of shares after**	
Fin div paymnt:	n/a	**dilution:**	n/a
Int net div per share:	nil	**P/E ratio:**	n/a
Fin net div per share:	nil	**Probable CGT?**	No

LATEST REPORTED RESULTS: 7 OCT 2002 TO 30 SEPT 2003		PREVIOUS REPORTED RESULTS: N/A	
Turnover:	n/a	Turnover:	n/a
PTP:	$(957,000)	PTP:	n/a
EPS:	(0.0)c	EPS:	n/a

Comments:

This offshore vehicle bought the majority of the assets of fellow AIM company Acquisitor so that shareholders in the parent could avoid tax. At the year end the group had stakes in five public companies, worth $9.8m, and net cash or current assets of $7.1m. Acquisitor aims to invest in undervalued situations and then aggressively realise value. It managed to do this successfully with Colorado MEDtech. The group has recently built an 8.2% stake in internet security group Baltimore.

actif (ACT)
Branded clothing designer, wholesaler & retailer
20 Little Portland Street, London, WIN 5AE Tel: 020-7436 3330; Fax: 020-7436 3303; e-mail: info@actif.com; web site: www.actifgroup.com

		holding %
Chairman	David Brock	1.5
Chief Executive	Mark Evans	0.3
Finance Director	Julian Ghinn	0.0
Non-Exec Director	Lindsay Page	0.1

Main Shareholders:

Ted Baker Investments (Jersey)	13.5
Hatziannou	10.7
Martin Lent*	9.2
Michael Benjamin	4.5
Oakdown	3.5

Percentage of free market capital: 56.8%

*Includes 523,734 Ordinary Shares held by a person connected with Martin Lent

Nominated Adviser:	Seymour Pierce, London
AIM Broker:	Seymour Pierce, London
Solicitors:	Joelson Wilson, London
Market Makers:	SCAP; WINS
Auditors:	BDO Stoy Hayward, Tweedy Road, Bromley, Kent
Registrars:	Capita Registrars

ENTRY ON AIM:	31/1/2000	**Recent price:**	7.5p
Interim results:	Apr	**Market cap:**	£4.9m
Final results:	Oct	**Issue price:**	15.0p
Year end:	Jul	**Current no of shares:**	
Accounts due:	Dec		65,344,571
Int div paymnt:	n/a	**No of shares after**	
Fin div paymnt:	n/a	**dilution:**	n/a
Int net div per share:	nil	**P/E ratio:**	15.0
Fin net div per share:	nil	**Probable CGT?**	YES

LATEST REPORTED RESULTS:	2003	PREVIOUS REPORTED RESULTS:	2002
Turnover:	£25.58m	Turnover:	£24.88m
PTP:	£333,000	PTP:	£315,000
EPS:	0.5p	EPS:	0.7p

Comments:

The clothes retailer and wholesaler, which produces the Elle brand, is back into profits and has experienced 15% improved sales in the first quarter. Having restructured, the company opened four flagship stores in Meadowhall, Reading, Glasgow and Brimingham during 2003 as well as three new concessions in department stores. Last year, debt was cut by 39% and gearing reduced from 47% to 27%. The Spring/Summer 2004 wholesale collections are apparently selling well.

ADL (formerly Matrix Healthcare) (AD.)
Nursing home operator
Corby Steps, Chieveley, Berkshire RG20 8UD Tel: 01635-247400; Fax: 01635-248704

		holding %
Chairman	Peter Dewe-Mathews	1.0
Managing Director	Jenny Davies	47.8
Finance Director	Richard Ellert	16.9
Director	Pearl Jackson	11.3

Main Shareholders:

BEST Investment	3.8

Percentage of free market capital: 19.3%

Nominated Adviser:	Durlacher, London
AIM Broker:	Durlacher, London
Solicitors:	DLA, Leeds
Market Makers:	KBCS; WINS
Auditors:	Deloitte & Touche, 1 City Square, Leeds LS1 2AL
Registrars:	Capita Registrars

Entry on AIM:	19/6/1996	**Recent price:**	41.5p
Interim results:	Dec	**Market cap:**	£3.69m
Final results:	Jun	**Issue price:**	120.0p
Year end:	Mar	**Current no of shares:**	
Accounts due:	Jun		8,885,694
Int div paymnt:	n/a	**No of shares after**	
Fin div paymnt:	n/a	**dilution:**	n/a
Int net div per share:	nil	**P/E ratio:**	n/a
Fin net div per share:	nil	**Probable CGT?**	YES

LATEST REPORTED RESULTS:	2003	PREVIOUS REPORTED RESULTS:	2002
Turnover:	£2.41m	Turnover:	£2.56m
PTP:	£661,000	PTP:	£(518,000)
EPS:	26.7p	EPS:	(22.7)p

Comments:

This used to be nursing home operator Matrix Healthcare, which has long disappointed investors. The shares doubled after shareholders were offered a cash exit of 40p a share. Jeremy Davies and Richard Ellert will reverse two nursing home companies they run into Matrix and in the process pay off the company's debt to Best Investment. Last year Matrix made a pre-tax profit of £661,000, which was more than the value of the company before the offer was made.

AdVal (ADL)

HR and business services

Ringwood House, Walton Street, Aylesbury, Buckinghamshire HP21 7QP Tel: 01296-388100; Fax: 01296-388110;
e-mail: info@adval.co.uk; web site: www.adval.co.uk

		holding %
Chairman	Lars Ahrell	1.2
Chief Executive	Nick Dredge	0.1
Finance Director	Richard Horsley	0.1
Deputy Chairman	Dennis Quilter	10.8

Main Shareholders:

RBSTB Nominees	6.7
Capita Trust	6.7
CM Doyle	6.5
Sinjul Nominees	4.8

Percentage of free market capital: 46.6%

Comments:

Following recent losses and board room upheavals AdVal's immediate goal is to make modest monthly profits by the end of the financial year. Costs have been cut, salaries reduced and a non-core development training arm sold to its senior management. Figures for the first half to September showed a loss before tax of £495,000 (£393,000) on total turnover of £1.7m (£2.5m). However in August, spirits were buoyed with news of a 2-year £2.5m deal with Alvis Vickers.

Nominated Adviser:	Arbuthnot, London
AIM Broker:	Arbuthnot, London
Solicitors:	Speechly Bircham, London
Market Makers:	ARBT; DURM; KBCS; WINS
Auditors:	Grant Thornton, Central Milton Keynes
Registrars:	Capita Registrars

Entry on AIM:	25/6/1998	**Recent price:**	3.9p
Interim results:	Nov	**Market cap:**	£1.34m
Final results:	Aug	**Issue price:**	65.0p
Year end:	Mar	**Current no of shares:**	
Accounts due:	Jul		34,408,069
Int div paymnt:	n/a	**No of shares after**	
Fin div paymnt:	n/a	**dilution:**	n/a
Int net div per share:	nil	**P/E ratio:**	n/a
Fin net div per share:	nil	**Probable CGT?**	Yes

LATEST REPORTED RESULTS:	2003	PREVIOUS REPORTED RESULTS:	2002
Turnover:	£4.47m	**Turnover:**	£5.17m
PTP:	£(4.40m)	**PTP:**	£(3.53m)
EPS:	(14.1)p	**EPS:**	(13.9)p

Advance Capital Invest (ACN)

Investment company

63 Queen Victoria Street, London, EC4N 4ST Tel: 020-7796 4133; Fax: 020-7329 4000

		holding %
Chairman	Nigel Whittaker	2.5
Managing Director	David Laurie	2.5
Finance Director	Charles Fairbairn	1.5
Non-Exec Director	Geoffrey Westmore	1.5

Main Shareholders:

Command Fund	40.0
Marlborough Fund Managers	5.9
Richard Joseph (Non-Exec Director)	2.5

Percentage of free market capital: 43.6%

Comments:

Formed in 2000, the investment vehicle chaired by entrepreneur Nigel Whittaker is yet to do a deal. Preliminary numbers showed losses trimmed thanks to the board's decision to halve its remuneration. Advance Capital Invest still looks an attractive vehicle, sitting as it does, on 16.4p net assets per share, predominantly in cash. Directors believe finding a suitable reversal is easier now than at any time in the past two years, because investor sentiment is more positive.

Nominated Adviser:	Evolution Beeson Gregory, London
AIM Broker:	Evolution Beeson Gregory, London
Solicitors:	KLegal/McGrigor Donald, London
Market Makers:	BGMM; WINS
Auditors:	HW Fisher & Company, London
Registrars:	Computershare Investor Services

Entry on AIM:	1/12/2000	**Recent price:**	12.75p
Interim results:	Aug	**Market cap:**	£1.03m
Final results:	Feb	**Issue price:**	25.0p
Year end:	Oct	**Current no of shares:**	
Accounts due:	Mar		8,100,000
Int div paymnt:	n/a	**No of shares after**	
Fin div paymnt:	n/a	**dilution:**	8,220,000
Int net div per share:	nil	**P/E ratio:**	n/a
Fin net div per share:	nil	**Probable CGT?**	No

LATEST REPORTED RESULTS:	2003	PREVIOUS REPORTED RESULTS:	2002
Turnover:	n/a	**Turnover:**	n/a
PTP:	£(30,000)	**PTP:**	£(68,000)
EPS:	(0.4)p	**EPS:**	(0.8)p

Advance Visual Communications (ACV)

Cash shell

Units 3/4, Colbeck Row Business Park, Birstall, Batley, WF17 9NR Tel: 01274-854900; Fax: 01274-854909;
e-mail: investor@advancevisual.com; web site: www.advancevisual.com

		holding %		
Chairman	Barclay Douglas	1.9		
Managing Director				
Finance Director				
Non-Exec Director	Graham Leask	0.5		

Main Shareholders:	
IHL	36.4
Friends Ivory and Sime	12.0
Friends Provident	9.5
Singer & Friedlander	7.3
Concentric	3.9
Percentage of free market capital:	28.6%

Nominated Adviser:	Shore Capital, London
AIM Broker:	Shore Capital, London
Solicitors:	DLA, Leeds
Market Makers:	KBCS; MLSB; SCAP; WINS
Auditors:	Deloitte & Touche, 10-12 East Parade, Leeds, LS1 2AJ
Registrars:	Capita Registrars

ENTRY ON AIM: 16/11/2000		Recent price:	0.4p
Interim results:	Mar	Market cap:	£0.65m
Final results:	Sep	Issue price:	10.0p
Year end:	Jun	Current no of shares:	
Accounts due:	Oct		161,575,486
Int div paymnt:	n/a	No of shares after	
Fin div paymnt:	n/a	dilution:	180,501,159
Int net div per share:	nil	P/E ratio:	n/a
Fin net div per share:	nil	Probable CGT?	No

LATEST REPORTED RESULTS: 2003		PREVIOUS REPORTED RESULTS: 2002	
Turnover:	n/a	Turnover:	£1.08m
PTP:	£(198,000)	PTP:	£(4.42m)
EPS:	(0.1)p	EPS:	(2.8)p

Comments:
The telecoms services venture threw in the towel in 2002 and put its trading subsidiaries into liquidation. This left the group as a cash shell with £130,000, seeking a 'good quality, profitable business' wishing to reverse into it. The company no longer has any full-time employees and 'minimal' operating costs of around £100,000 a year.

Advanced Medical Solutions (AMS)

Manufacture of a range of advanced wound dressings

Road Three, Winsford Industrial Estate, Winsford, Cheshire CW7 3PD Tel: 01606-863500; Fax: 01606-863600;
e-mail: info@admedsol.com; web site: www.admedsol.com

		holding %
Chairman	Geoffrey Vernon	0.4
Chief Executive	Donald Evans	0.4
Finance Director	Mary Tavener	0.03
Non-Exec Director	Ralph Harris	0.1

Main Shareholders:	
Newton Investment Management	14.8
The Royal Bank of Scotland	14.4
Close Finsbury Asset Management	13.0
Merrill Lynch	6.2
INVESCO English and International Trust	5.5
Percentage of free market capital:	26.4%

Nominated Adviser:	Baird, London
AIM Broker:	Baird, London
Solicitors:	Wragge & Co, Birmingham
Market Makers:	KLWT; GRAB; MLSB; WINS;
Auditors:	Baker Tilly, Number One, Old Hall Street, Liverpool L3 9SX
Registrars:	Capita Registrars

Entry on AIM: 30/4/2002		Recent price:	11.1p
Interim results:	Sep	Market cap:	£15.77m
Final results:	Mar	Issue price:	8.5p
Year end:	Dec	Current no of shares:	
Accounts due:	Jun		142,082,536
Int div paymnt:	n/a	No of shares after	
Fin div paymnt:	n/a	dilution:	145,565,404
Int net div per share:	nil	P/E ratio:	n/a
Fin net div per share:	nil	Probable CGT?	Yes

LATEST REPORTED RESULTS: 2002		PREVIOUS REPORTED RESULTS: 2001	
Turnover:	£8.37m	Turnover:	£7.37m
PTP:	£(1.69m)	PTP:	£(1.60m)
EPS:	(1.1)p	EPS:	(1.6)p

Comments:
The developer of technology that treats plasters and other wound dressings with substances such as seaweed and silver compounds so that the wound heals better, has suffered from the perception that its products are merely plasters. However, it is concentrating on higher-margin sales. Revenue stayed flat at £4.1m in the first-half, making house broker Baird's prediction of a full year profit optimistic. Recent deals with Johnson & Johnson may help efforts though. Cash remains healthy at £4m.

Advanced Power Components (APC)

Electronic component maker and distributor
47 Riverside, Medway City Estate, Rochester, Kent ME2 4DP Tel: 01634-290588; Fax: 01634-290591;
e-mail: sales@apc-plc.co.uk; web site: www.apc-plc.co.uk

		holding %
Chairman	Rex Thorne	0.0
Managing Director	Mark Robinson*	2.0
Finance Director	Hugh Edmonds	0.0
Non-Exec Director	Timothy Ford	0.0

Main Shareholders:

Eaglet Investment	25.2
John Mitchell	18.7

Percentage of free market capital: 54.0%

*In addition to his direct holding, Mark Robinson also has a beneficial interest in 861,500 Ordinary Shares held by the Robinson Family Trust

Nominated Adviser:	Evolution Beeson Gregory, London
AIM Broker:	Evolution Beeson Gregory, London
Solicitors:	Ashursts, London
Market Makers:	EVO; KLWT; MLSB; WINS
Auditors:	PricewaterhouseCoopers, Maidstone
Registrars:	Capita Registrars

Entry on AIM:	12/11/2002	**Recent price:**	16.75p
Interim results:	May	**Market cap:**	£4.37m
Final results:	Jan	**Issue price:**	10.5p
Year end:	Aug	**Current no of shares:**	
Accounts due:	Mar		26,114,513
Int div paymnt:	n/a	**No of shares after**	
Fin div paymnt:	n/a	**dilution:**	n/a
Int net div per share:	nil	**P/E ratio:**	n/a
Fin net div per share:	nil	**Probable CGT?**	No

Comments:
Having sold its mobile communications equipment subsidiary to BelFuse, Advanced has recently acquired Go! technology and Silver Birch Marketing. The debt-free group now distributes electronic components via divisions Hi-rel, SB and Go! It is recruiting personnel and seeking further distribution agreements. At the end of August cash levels stood at £2.1m. Pre-tax losses for the year were slashed by two thirds.

LATEST REPORTED RESULTS: 2003		PREVIOUS REPORTED RESULTS: 2002	
Turnover:	£4.41m	Turnover:	£6.31m
PTP:	£(552,000)	PTP:	£(1.48m)
EPS:	(2.0)p	EPS:	(5.0)p

Advanced Technology (AVT)

Short-range, secure radio communications provider
7 Enterprise Way, Aviation Park, Bournemouth Int'l Airport, Christchurch, Dorset BH23 6HB Tel: 01202-592000;
Fax: 01202-592001; e-mail: admin@atr-group.com; web site: www.atl-systems.com

		holding %
Chairman	Greg Morgan	2.0
Managing Director	John Howell	0.3
Finance Director	David Collinson	0.0
Technical Director	Peter Garrard	3.0

Main Shareholders:

Universities Superannuation Scheme	11.5
Peter Hibbitt	8.2

Percentage of free market capital: 74.8%

Nominated Adviser:	KBC Peel Hunt, London
AIM Broker:	KBC Peel Hunt, London
Solicitors:	TLT, Bristol
Market Makers:	KBCS; MLSB; WINS
Auditors:	KPMG, Dukes Keep, Marsh Lane, Southampton SO14 3EX
Registrars:	Capita Registrars

Entry on AIM:	14/4/2000	**Recent price:**	34.25p
Interim results:	Nov	**Market cap:**	£16.19m
Final results:	Jun	**Issue price:**	250.0p
Year end:	Dec	**Current no of shares:**	
Accounts due:	Apr		47,266,477
Int div paymnt:	n/a	**No of shares after**	
Fin div paymnt:	n/a	**dilution:**	n/a
Int net div per share:	nil	**P/E ratio:**	n/a
Fin net div per share:	nil	**Probable CGT?**	Yes

Comments:
Advanced Technology has developed a number of short-range, low-power communications systems that enable meters to be analysed and controlled remotely via a one- or two-way system. It is currently in advanced negotiations with the Ghanian government to provide two-way fixed network metering and with a utility company in Asia. As the discussions have had delays, it also had to raise £850,000 via convertible loan nores and a placing to meet working capital requirements.

LATEST REPORTED RESULTS: 2002		PREVIOUS REPORTED RESULTS: 2001	
Turnover:	£7.63m	Turnover:	£6.01m
PTP:	£(3.9m)	PTP:	£(4.96m)
EPS:	(14.0)p	EPS:	(17.8)p

ADVFN.com (AFN)
Financial website operator
26 Throgmorton Street, London, EC2N 2AN Tel: 020-7070 0909; Fax: 020-7070 0959; web site: www.advfn.com

		holding %
Chairman	Michael Hodges*	0.3
Managing Director	Clement Chambers*	2.1
Finance Director	David Crump	0.038
Exec Director	Ray Negus	0.0

Main Shareholders:

On-line*	33.3
Fidelity International	10.0
SG Asset Management	6.2
Peter O'Reilly	3.0

Percentage of free market capital: 44.9%

*Michael Hodges and Clement Chambers are deemed to be connected with On-line as they each hold more than 20 per cent of the issued share capital of On-line

Comments:
There's a tremendous sense of optimism from this financial website operator. Interims saw the group increase sales to £1.3m and reduce losses to £147,000. The board claimed that user numbers have improved 48%, from December 02 to March 04, to over 300,000. Subscribers have also apparently improved over this period, although the exact number of paying users was not released. Information on UK, US, Canadian, Russian and German stocks is now available on ADVFN's site.

Nominated Adviser:	Canaccord Capital, London
AIM Broker:	Canaccord Capital, London
Solicitors:	Field Fisher Waterhouse, London
Market Makers:	DURM; MLSB; SCAP; WINS
Auditors:	Grant Thornton, 21 Dyke Road, Brighton BN1 3GD
Registrars:	Capita Registrars

ENTRY ON AIM:	20/3/2000	Recent price:	6.25p
Interim results:	Mar	Market cap:	£25.42m
Final results:	Dec	Issue price:	10.0p
Year end:	Jun	Current no of shares:	
Accounts due:	Nov		406,783,177
Int div paymnt:	n/a	No of shares after	
Fin div paymnt:	n/a	dilution:	n/a
Int net div per share:	nil	P/E ratio:	n/a
Fin net div per share:	nil	Probable CGT?	YES

LATEST REPORTED RESULTS: 2003		PREVIOUS REPORTED RESULTS: 2002	
Turnover:	£2.26m	Turnover:	£1.64m
PTP:	£(1.22m)	PTP:	£(2.48m)
EPS:	(0.3)p	EPS:	(0.8)p

Aero Inventory (AI.)
E-based procurement and inventory management
30 Lancaster Road, New Barnet, Hertfordshire EN4 8AP Tel: 020-8449 9263; Fax: 020-8449 3555; web site: www.aero-inventory.com

		holding %
Chairman	Frank Turner	0.7
Chief Executive	Rupert Lewin	7.4
Finance Director	Hugh Bevan	0.3
Exec Dep. Chair	Laurence Heyworth	5.2

Main Shareholders:

Singer and Friedlander Investment Management	10.0
Rathbone	6.7
Scottish Widows	5.5
Liontrust	3.2

Percentage of free market capital: 57.7%

Comments:
Aero Inventory has reported a dramatic drop in interim profits to December and warned annual profits will be 'well below' expectations. First half profits plummeted from £1.54m to £562,000 despite an 8% sales rise to £7.8m. The numbers were hit by the after-effects of SARS, higher overhead and start-up costs on new deals and there being but a one-month contribution from its major contract with SR Technics. Aero has also announced a contract with Abu Dhabi-based GAMCO.

Nominated Adviser:	Evolution Beeson Gregory, London
AIM Broker:	Evolution Beeson Gregory, London
Solicitors:	Taylor Wessing, London
Market Makers:	BGMM; WINS
Auditors:	Horwath Clark Whitehill London
Registrars:	Capita Registrars

Entry on AIM:	25/5/2000	Recent price:	445.0p
Interim results:	Mar	Market cap:	£69.52m
Final results:	Sep	Issue price:	123.0p
Year end:	Jun	Current no of shares:	
Accounts due:	Oct		15,623,049
Int div paymnt:	May	No of shares after	
Fin div paymnt:	Dec	dilution:	n/a
Int net div per share:	3.0p	P/E ratio:	n/a
Fin net div per share:	2.3p	Probable CGT?	YES

LATEST REPORTED RESULTS: 2003		PREVIOUS REPORTED RESULTS: 2002	
Turnover:	£15.87m	Turnover:	£9.11m
PTP:	£2.82m	PTP:	£1.62m
EPS:	19.6p	EPS:	14.0p

Aerobox (ARX)

Air freight sector materials developer

3rd Floor, 345 Stockport Road, Manchester, M13 0LF Tel: 0161-273 6050; Fax: 0161-276172

		holding %
Chairman	David Sebire	0.0
Chief Executive	Robert Bushman	5.2
Finance Director		
Non-Exec Director	Anthony Leon	0.0

Main Shareholders:

Brookspey	8.5
Innobox	5.7
Highland Capital	5.2
Highland Specialist	4.6
Athabasca Int.	3.3

Percentage of free market capital: 64.1%

Nominated Adviser:	Seymour Pierce, London
AIM Broker:	Seymour Pierce, London
Solicitors:	Kuit Steinart Levy, Manchester
Market Makers:	EVO; JEFF; SCAP; WINS
Auditors:	Horwath Clark Whitehall, Manchester
Registrars:	Capita Registrars

Entry on AIM:	20/3/2003	Recent price:	32.75p
Interim results:	Sep	Market cap:	£30.53m
Final results:	Mar	Issue price:	20.0p
Year end:	Dec	Current no of shares:	
Accounts due:	Apr		93,231,250
Int div paymnt:	n/a	No of shares after	
Fin div paymnt:	n/a	dilution:	n/a
Int net div per share:	nil	P/E ratio:	n/a
Fin net div per share:	nil	Probable CGT?	Yes

LATEST REPORTED RESULTS: PERIOD FROM 2 OCT 02 TO 31 JAN 03		PREVIOUS REPORTED RESULTS: N/A	
Turnover:	n/a	Turnover:	n/a
PTP:	£(31,000)	PTP:	n/a
EPS:	n/a	EPS:	n/a

Comments:

Aerobox has developed a unique air freight and baggage container – lighter, stronger, more durable and easier to repair than traditional aluminium containers. It can reduce repair costs for airlines. Intriguingly, this January the company announced the first commercial sales of the Aerobox product, following a successful three-month trial with Aer Lingus and Virgin Atlantic. Its new-generation air containers are being trialed with other major airlines around the world.

AFA Systems (AFA)

Provider of software solutions for companies in financial markets

Bury House, 31 Bury Street, London, EC3A 5AR Tel: 020-7337 7250; Fax: 020-7337 7251; e-mail: info@afa-systems.com; web site: www.afa-systems.com

		holding %
Chairman	Michael Hart	6.9
Chief Executive	as above	
Finance Director	Henry Sallitt	0.8
Technical Director	Annabel Levin	1.1

Main Shareholders:

Gartmore	10.4
Artemis	9.9
FMR	7.8
Fidelity	7.7
NW Brown Asset management	6.7

Percentage of free market capital: 20.2%

Nominated Adviser:	Bridgewell, London
AIM Broker:	Bridgewell, London
Solicitors:	Gold Mann & Co, London, Eversheds, Birmingham
Market Makers:	ALTI; BGWL; CLS; KBCS; KLWT; MLSB; WINS
Auditors:	KPMG Audit, Birmingham
Registrars:	Neville Registrars

Entry on AIM:	8/1/2003	Recent price:	26.0p
Interim results:	Sep	Market cap:	£12.27m
Final results:	Mar	Issue price:	17.75p
Year end:	Dec	Current no of shares:	
Accounts due:	May		47,182,549
Int div paymnt:	n/a	No of shares after	
Fin div paymnt:	n/a	dilution:	n/a
Int net div per share:	nil	P/E ratio:	n/a
Fin net div per share:	nil	Probable CGT?	Yes

LATEST REPORTED RESULTS: 2003		PREVIOUS REPORTED RESULTS: 2002	
Turnover:	£6.45m	Turnover:	£6.01m
PTP:	£(3.04m)	PTP:	£(10.64m)
EPS:	(4.3)p	EPS:	(42.0)p

Comments:

Unveiling improved results for 2003 AFA chief executive Mike Hart claimed to be in 'cautiously optimistic' mood with regard to the year ahead, suggesting that 'all the indicators are there to suggest that things are picking up'. Like many of its peers AFA does not expect to reap the full benefits until 2005/2006 and yet customer enquiries are rising, the likes of Artemis, Fidelity and ISIS have all upped their stakes in the company and £2.4m sits in the bank.

African Diamonds

(AFD)

Diamond miner

162 Clontarf Road, Dublin 3, Ireland, Tel: 00-353-1 833 2833; Fax: 00-353-1 833 3505;
web site: www.africandiamonds.co.za

		holding %
Chairman	John Teeling	3.3
Chief Executive		
Finance Director		
Exec Director	Mark Scowcroft*	9.4

Main Shareholders:

Ashdale	4.7
City Equities	3.7
Courtfield Industries	3.7
Forest Nominees	3.7
Gartmore	3.7

Percentage of free market capital: 48.2%

*Shares registered in the name of Kimberlite Exploration Services

Comments:

Steered by colourful Irish entrepreneur John Teeling, African Diamonds has already found some gems in drilling its Orapa licence area in Botswana (where its shares are also listed). Elsewhere, the company, whose losses soared from £44,000 to £264,000 last year, has a mining licence for the Kono region of Sierra Leone, containing tailings from 30 years of previous mining by others.

Nominated Adviser:	Rowan Dartington, London		
AIM Broker:	Rowan Dartington, London		
Solicitors:	McEvoy, Dublin		
Market Makers:	SCAP; WINS		
Auditors:	Deloitte & Touche, Earlsfort Terrace Dublin 2 Ireland		
Registrars:	Computershare Investor Services		

ENTRY ON AIM:	14/7/2003	**Recent price:**	51.5p
Interim results:	Jan	**Market cap:**	£28.19m
Final results:	Sep	**Issue price:**	7.0p
Year end:	Jun	**Current no of shares:**	
Accounts due:	Oct		54,741,149
Int div paymnt:	n/a	**No of shares after**	
Fin div paymnt:	n/a	**dilution:**	n/a
Int net div per share:	nil	**P/E ratio:**	n/a
Fin net div per share:	nil	**Probable CGT?**	No

LATEST REPORTED RESULTS: 2003		PREVIOUS REPORTED RESULTS: 13 MONTHS TO 30 JUN 02	
Turnover:	n/a	Turnover:	n/a
PTP:	£(264,000)	PTP:	£(44,000)
EPS:	(0.6)p	EPS:	(0.5)p

African Eagle Resources

(AFE)

Mineral explorer

2nd Floor, 6-7 Queen Street, London EC4N 1SP Tel: 020-7248 6059; Fax: 020-7691 7745;
e-mail: info@africaneagle.co.uk; web site: www.africaneagle.co.uk

		holding %
Chairman	John Park	4.6
Managing Director	Mark Parker	3.0
Finance Director		
Operations Director	Christopher Davies	0.4

Main Shareholders:

RAB Capital	25.9
Orogen	9.1
Carmignac managed funds	7.3
JPMF Natural Resource	5.9
B Rowan	4.0

Percentage of free market capital: 38.7%

Comments:

The Gold Fields mining giant decided not to exercise its option to join African Eagle to develop its Miyabi gold prospect in Tanzania, but kept its 20% AE stake. African Eagle, which lost an interim £143,000, said it would go on exploring there. December's £1.1m funding at 16.5p was followed by 'Promising' drilling results at the company's Eagle Eye copper-gold prospect in Zambia.

Nominated Adviser:	Nabarro Wells, London		
AIM Broker:	Durlacher, London		
Solicitors:	Cobbetts, Manchester		
Market Makers:	DURM; WINS		
Auditors:	Grant Thornton, Barnes Wallis Road, Segensworth, Hampshire PO15 5GT		
Registrars:	Capita Registrars		

Entry on AIM:	25/6/2003	**Recent price:**	19.0p
Interim results:	Sep	**Market cap:**	£14.52m
Final results:	Mar	**Issue price:**	6.0p
Year end:	Dec	**Current no of shares:**	
Accounts due:	Jun		76,439,569
Int div paymnt:	n/a	**No of shares after**	
Fin div paymnt:	n/a	**dilution:**	121,615,979
Int net div per share:	n/a	**P/E ratio:**	n/a
Fin net div per share:	n/a	**Probable CGT?**	No

LATEST REPORTED RESULTS: 2002		PREVIOUS REPORTED RESULTS: 2001	
Turnover:	n/a	Turnover:	n/a
PTP:	£(522,000)	PTP:	£(135,000)
EPS:	(0.7)p	EPS:	(2.0)p

African Gold (AFG)

Gold prospector & producer

162 Clontarf Road, Dublin 3, Ireland Tel: 00-353 1 833 2833; Fax: 00-353 1 833 3505; e-mail: afgold@iol.ie;
web site: www.africangoldplc.com

		holding %
Chairman	John J Teeling	8.1
Managing Director	Dipti Mehta	0.0
Financial Controller	James Finn	1.1
Deputy Chairman	David Horgan	2.8

Main Shareholders:

Yewpole	6.6
Michael Begley	4.4

Percentage of free market capital: 69.2%

Nominated Adviser:	Rowan Dartington, Bristol
AIM Broker:	Rowan Dartington, Bristol
Solicitors:	Taylor Wessing, London
Market Makers:	MLSB; SCAP; WINS
Auditors:	Deloitte & Touche, Earlsfort Terrace, Dublin 2
Registrars:	Computershare Investor Services

ENTRY ON AIM:	29/9/1995	**Recent price:**	10.6p
Interim results:	Jan	**Market cap:**	£24.9m
Final results:	Aug	**Issue price:**	7.25p
Year end:	Mar	**Current no of shares:**	
Accounts due:	Oct		234,867,699
Int div paymnt:	n/a	**No of shares after**	
Fin div paymnt:	n/a	**dilution:**	n/a
Int net div per share:	nil	**P/E ratio:**	n/a
Fin net div per share:	nil	**Probable CGT?**	No

LATEST REPORTED RESULTS: 2003		PREVIOUS REPORTED RESULTS: 2002	
Turnover:	£28,000	Turnover:	£389,000
PTP:	£(121,000)	PTP:	£(34,000)
EPS:	(0.1)p	EPS:	(0.0)p

Comments:
Once Zimbabwe-focused, African Gold, which cut interim losses from £129,000 to £72,000, is pursuing West African prospects, after the merger of the Ashanti and Anglo giants. Wheeler-dealing boss John Teeling induced influential mining figures to buy 29% of Afgold (at a big discount) and the company won an exclusive option to buy Ghana's Avanta gold property, with potential for 'a bulk-minable open-pit deposit'.

Air Music & Media (AMU)

Developer and acquirer of music copyrights

Chiltern House, 184 High Street, Berkhamstead, Hertfordshire HP4 3AP Tel: 01442-877018; Fax: 01442-877015;
e-mail: info@airmusicandmedia.com; web site: www.airmusicandmedia.co.uk

		holding %
Chairman	Frederick French	0.0
Chief Executive	Mark Frey*	55.3
Finance Director	Ruth Salsbury	0.0
Commercial Director	Michael Infante	23.6

Main Shareholders:

Capital International	3.6

Percentage of free market capital: 13.7%

*Mark Frey's shares are held by Galaxy Management Corporation

Nominated Adviser:	Seymour Pierce, London
AIM Broker:	Seymour Pierce, London
Solicitors:	Nicholson Graham Jones, London
Market Makers:	SCAP; WINS
Auditors:	Kingston Smith, Devonshire House, 60 Goswell Road, London EC1M 7AD
Registrars:	Neville Registrars

Entry on AIM:	4/7/2002	**Recent price:**	7.75p
Interim results:	Nov	**Market cap:**	£15.18m
Final results:	Jun	**Issue price:**	5.0p
Year end:	Mar	**Current no of shares:**	
Accounts due:	Aug		195,919,701
Int div paymnt:	n/a	**No of shares after**	
Fin div paymnt:	n/a	**dilution:**	n/a
Int net div per share:	nil	**P/E ratio:**	19.4
Fin net div per share:	nil	**Probable CGT?**	Yes

LATEST REPORTED RESULTS: 2003		PREVIOUS REPORTED RESULTS: 2002	
Turnover:	£8.03m	Turnover:	£4.37m
PTP:	£909,000	PTP:	£804,000
EPS:	0.4p	EPS:	0.4p

Comments:
This cash generative budget CD and DVD supplier is in rude health. Interims showed sales almost doubled to £5.7m and pre-tax profits lifted 70% to £597,872. The strong results were partly due to its Legacy Entertainment and Hollywood DVD acquisitions, which were completed at the end of last year. However, the recent £3m acquisition of The Original Record Company, which trades as low price CD label New Sound 2000, should boost overall group performance again this year.

Airbath
(ATU)
Bathroom products designer & maker
Crossley House, Belle Vue Park, Hopwood Lane, Halifax, HX1 5EB Tel: 01422-349401; Fax: 01422-349396;
e-mail: info@airbath.fsnet.co.uk; web site: www.airbathgroup.co.uk

		holding %
Chairman	John Parkinson	1.1
Chief Executive		
Finance Director	Michael Dunn	0.1
Non-Exec Director	Alan Bottomley	0.2

Main Shareholders:
Tony Gartland* 54.1

Percentage of free market capital: 44.5%

*Tony Gartland has 58.92% shareholding in GWB, which has 54% holding in Airbath

Nominated Adviser:	Westhouse Securities, Manchester
AIM Broker:	Westhouse Securities, London
Solicitors:	Walker Morris, Leeds
Market Makers:	KBCS; SCAP; WINS
Auditors:	KPMG Audit, St James Square, Manchester, M60 2EP
Registrars:	Capita Registrars

ENTRY ON AIM:	17/8/2001	**Recent price:**	2.5p
Interim results:	Dec	Market cap:	£0.64m
Final results:	Jul	Issue price:	10.0p
Year end:	Mar	Current no of shares:	
Accounts due:	Jul		25,408,461
Int div paymnt:	Jan	No of shares after	
Fin div paymnt:	n/a	dilution:	n/a
Int net div per share:	0.1p	P/E ratio:	2.8
Fin net div per share:	n/a	Probable CGT?	Yes

LATEST REPORTED RESULTS:	2003	PREVIOUS REPORTED RESULTS: 41 WEEKS TO 31 MAR '02	
Turnover:	£15.30m	Turnover:	£12.89m
PTP:	£559,000	PTP:	£56,000
EPS:	0.9p	EPS:	(0.7)p

Comments:
Erstwhile executive chairman Clive Gilham parted company with Airbath (and sister company Collins & Hayes), after ending his relationship with main stake holder Gartland Whalley Barker. News of his departure came less than a month after the specialist bath and spa manufacturer unveiled disappointing interim numbers, profits tumbling from £500,000 to £11,000 as sales slumped 16% to £6.7m. Although management remains upbeat, longer term a full year loss seems likely.

Airsprung Furniture
(APG)
Bed & upholstey manufacturer
Canal Road, Trowbridge, Wiltshire BA14 8RQ Tel: 01225-754411; Fax: 01225-777423;
e-mail: group@airsprung-furniture.co.uk; web site: www.airsprung-furniture.co.uk

		holding %
Chairman	Philip Bradshaw	0.1
Chief Executive	Antonio Lisanti	0.0
Finance Director	Tean Dallaway	0.0
Director	Jeremy Yates	9.7

Main Shareholders:

Redbird	23.1
CM Yates	22.6
Schroder Investment Management	7.4
Fidelity	4.0

Percentage of free market capital: 22.6%

Nominated Adviser:	Rowan Dartington, Bristol
AIM Broker:	Rowan Dartington, Bristol
Solicitors:	Burges Salmon, London
Market Makers:	EVO; WINS
Auditors:	PricewaterhouseCoopers, 31 Great George Street, Bristol BS1 5QD
Registrars:	Capita Registrars

Entry on AIM:	1/8/2003	Recent price:	65.5p
Interim results:	Dec	Market cap:	£15.65m
Final results:	May	Issue price:	n/a
Year end:	Mar	Current no of shares:	
Accounts due:	Jun		23,888,698
Int div paymnt:	n/a	No of shares after	
Fin div paymnt:	n/a	dilution:	n/a
Int net div per share:	nil	P/E ratio:	n/a
Fin net div per share:	nil	Probable CGT?	Yes

LATEST REPORTED RESULTS:	2003	PREVIOUS REPORTED RESULTS:	2002
Turnover:	£66.45m	Turnover:	£74.01m
PTP:	£(471,000)	PTP:	£505,000
EPS:	(1.1)p	EPS:	2.3p

Comments:
Beds and upholstery manufacturer and supplier Airsprung continues to disappoint – a February trading statement confirming that, following a poor start to the second half, full year results will fall short of market expectations. Despite the setback, management claims the company's woes reflect a wider dip in sales across the sector and confidently predicts that a series of additional catalogue listings will boost trading. Benefits aren't expected until early 2005, however.

AIT

(AGP)

Provider of customer relationship management software

The Smith Centre, The Fairmile, Henley on Thames, Oxfordshire RG9 6AB Tel: 01491-416600; Fax: 01491-416601;
e-mail: kirsty.shearer@aitgroup.com; web site: www.aitgroup.com

		holding %
Chairman	Richard Hicks	9.4
Chief Executive	Nicholas Randall	6.6
Financial Controller	Matthew White	0.0
Head of Distribution	Geoffrey Probert	0.0

Main Shareholders:

Bessemer Investors	18.4
Close Brothers Group	10.2
Arbib Family Interests	9.5
Quester VCT 4	5.7
The Royal Bank of Scotland	3.8
Percentage of free market capital:	**33.1%**

Nominated Adviser:	Arbuthnot, London
AIM Broker:	Arbuthnot, London
Solicitors:	Taylor Wessing, London
Market Makers:	ARBT; WINS
Auditors:	Deloitte & Touche, Columbia Centre, Market Street, Bracknell, Berkshire RG12 1PA
Registrars:	Capita Registrars

ENTRY ON AIM:	10/9/2002	**Recent price:**	74.5p
Interim results:	Nov	**Market cap:**	£37.47m
Final results:	Jun	**Issue price:**	87.5p
Year end:	Mar	**Current no of shares:**	
Accounts due:	Sep		50,290,820
Int div paymnt:	Jan	**No of shares after**	
Fin div paymnt:	n/a	**dilution:**	n/a
Int net div per share:	1.30p	**P/E ratio:**	n/a
Fin net div per share:	nil	**Probable CGT?**	Yes

LATEST REPORTED RESULTS:	2003	PREVIOUS REPORTED RESULTS:	2002
Turnover:	£17.58m	**Turnover:**	£36.22m
PTP:	£(41.23m)	**PTP:**	£(9.27m)
EPS:	(0.0)p	**EPS:**	(0.0)p

Comments:

Interim figures from AIT revealed an anticipated return to the black. 2002's staggering £37m first half loss was transformed into a £1m profit on sales up £1.5m at £10m as operating expenses were slashed by around £13m. In its new leaner form, AIT has also re-focused and now says it aims to provide clients with 'leading edge' customer relationship management solutions. New alliances have been signed and new clients won as the company revels in its new role as a textbook software turnaround.

Akaei

(AKI)

Shell company

Crown House, Linton Road, Barking, Essex IG11 8HJ Tel: 020-8591 1125; Fax: 020-8591 0110; e-mail: mikeh@akaei.com;
web site: www.akaei.com

		holding %
Chairman	Michael Hodges	0.0
Managing Director		
Finance Director	David Crump	0.0
Director	Clement Chambers	0.0

Main Shareholders:

On-Line	84.3

Percentage of free market capital: 11.9%

Nominated Adviser:	Grant Thornton, London
AIM Broker:	Hoodless Brennan, London
Solicitors:	Field Fisher Waterhouse, London
Market Makers:	HOOD; SCAP; WINS
Auditors:	Grant Thornton, Lees House, 21 Dyke Road, Brighton, East Sussex BN1 3GD
Registrars:	Capita Registrars

Entry on AIM:	25/7/2001	**Recent price:**	23.5p
Interim results:	Jun	**Market cap:**	£0.54m
Final results:	May	**Issue price:**	10.0p
Year end:	Jun	**Current no of shares:**	
Accounts due:	Oct		2,300,362
Int div paymnt:	n/a	**No of shares after**	
Fin div paymnt:	n/a	**dilution:**	n/a
Int net div per share:	nil	**P/E ratio:**	5.6
Fin net div per share:	nil	**Probable CGT?**	Yes

LATEST REPORTED RESULTS:	2003	PREVIOUS REPORTED RESULTS:	2002
Turnover:	£98,000	**Turnover:**	£445,000
PTP:	£26,000	**PTP:**	£(1.66m)
EPS:	4.2p	**EPS:**	(211.7)p

Comments:

Trading in this tiny cash shell was suspended following the board's announcement that it was in early-stage negotiations regarding a possible reverse takeover.

Akers Biosciences

(AKR)

Developer and manufacturer of diagnostic screening and testing products

201 Grove Road, Thorofare, New Jersey 08086, United States of America Tel: 00-1 856 848 8698;
e-mail: info@akersbiosciences.com

		holding %
Chairman	David Wilbraham	0.4
Chief Executive	Raymond Akers Jr	9.0
Finance Director	Paul Freedman	0.4
Research Director	Daniel Seckinger	0.4

Main Shareholders:

Milan Holdings	11.2
Dolores Akers	6.4
DMI Investments	6.3

Percentage of free market capital: 63.9%

Nominated Adviser:	KBC Peel Hunt, London
AIM Broker:	KBC Peel Hunt, London
Solicitors:	Hale and Dorr, Oxford
Market Makers:	KBCS; WINS
Auditors:	McGladrey & Pullen, 1777 Sentry Parkway West, PA 19422-2211, USA
Registrars:	Capita Registrars

ENTRY ON AIM:	22/5/2002	**Recent price:**	94.0p
Interim results:	Sep	**Market cap:**	£44.7m
Final results:	Jun	**Issue price:**	136.0p
Year end:	Dec	**Current no of shares:**	
Accounts due:	Apr		47,551,915
Int div paymnt:	n/a	**No of shares after**	
Fin div paymnt:	n/a	**dilution:**	n/a
Int net div per share:	nil	**P/E ratio:**	n/a
Fin net div per share:	nil	**Probable CGT?**	No

Comments:

US-based Akers designs and makes 'rapid diagnostic screening and testing products' that check for diseases like HIV, hepatitis, syphilis and malaria. These can be used in the field by the military. The company suffered after much-trumpeted orders from Kenya, worth £22.5m, were delayed. Interim revenue fell 13% to $0.46m, producing a loss of $1.5m. A distribution deal has since been signed. Net current liabilities stand at $3.4m but various debt-for-equity arrangements should tide the group over.

LATEST REPORTED RESULTS:	2002	PREVIOUS REPORTED RESULTS:	2001
Turnover:	$812,000	**Turnover:**	$621,000
PTP:	$(6.07m)	**PTP:**	$(5.25m)
EPS:	(0.2)p	**EPS:**	(0.2)p

Albemarle & Bond

(ABM)

Pawnbroker, jewellery retailer & cheque cashing facilitator

12 Station Road, Reading, RG1 1JX Tel: 0118-955 8100; Fax: 0118-956 9072; e-mail: albemarlebond@dial.pippx.com;
web site: www.albemarlebond.com

		holding %
Chairman	Charles Nicolson	1.7
Chief Executive	Greville V Nicholls	1.6
Finance Director	David Pattinson	0.0
Non-Exec Director	Nicholas Taylor	3.1

Main Shareholders:

Ezcorp International	29.5
Heritable Nominees	6.4
SBS Nominees	6.3
BNY (OCS) Nominees	5.8
Schroder Investments Management	5.5

Percentage of free market capital: 33.0%

Nominated Adviser:	Solomon Hare, Bristol
AIM Broker:	Collins Stewart, London
Solicitors:	Burges Salmon, Bristol
Market Makers:	CSCS; WINS
Auditors:	Solomon Hare, Oakfield Grove, Clifton, Bristol BS8 2BN
Registrars:	Capita Registrars

Entry on AIM:	25/9/1995	**Recent price:**	101.5p
Interim results:	Mar	**Market cap:**	£46.63m
Final results:	Sep	**Issue price:**	12.0p
Year end:	Jun	**Current no of shares:**	
Accounts due:	Sep		45,941,556
Int div paymnt:	May	**No of shares after**	
Fin div paymnt:	Jan	**dilution:**	47,045,207
Int net div per share:	1.0p	**P/E ratio:**	15.1
Fin net div per share:	1.75p	**Probable CGT?**	Yes

Comments:

The UK's largest pawnbroker, which lends cash against the security of gold jewellery or diamonds, turned in some impressive interims to December. Pre-tax profits put on 14% to £2.6m as turnover sparked up from £10.7m to £11.9m. Encouragingly, the pawn loan book grew 12.7%, overall retail sales soared 13%, although pay day advances waned 3.3%. The post New Year period, traditionally important for the company, has seen strong growth in the pawn loan book.

LATEST REPORTED RESULTS:	2003	PREVIOUS REPORTED RESULTS:	2002
Turnover:	£20.23m	**Turnover:**	£17.83m
PTP:	£3.70m	**PTP:**	£2.46m
EPS:	6.7p	**EPS:**	5.7p

Alibi Communications   (ALC)

Film and television group

35 Long Acre, London, WC2E 9JT Tel: 020-7845 0400; Fax: 020-7379 7035; e-mail: alc@alibifilms.co.uk;
web site: www.alibifilms.co.uk

		holding %
Chairman	Lord Romsey	8.8
Chief Executive	Roger Holmes	14.5
Finance Director		
Exec Director	Linda James*	14.9

Main Shareholders:

Pershing Keen Nominees	11.3
Jeffrey Curtis	8.6
Herald Investments	8.2
HSBC Global Custody Nominees	6.8
Hillary Davis	4.7

Percentage of free market capital: -5.5%

*Includes shares held by Linda James' husband Stephen Bayley

Comments:

A new lease of life has been breathed into Alibi, the struggling film and TV group. The group has purchased Coolebah Ltd, a business with fledgling brand and entertainment properties, for £102,000. The business owns the rights to Peppars Patrol, a new property from Rob Lee, the man who created Fireman Sam. The business was bought from William Harris, the entrepreneur who built Gullane into a substantial intellectual property rights firm. He has joined the board in a non-executive capacity.

Nominated Adviser:	Grant Thornton, London
AIM Broker:	Seymour Pierce, London
Solicitors:	SJ Berwin, London
Market Makers:	SCAP; WINS
Auditors:	AGN Shipleys, London
Registrars:	Capita Registrars

ENTRY ON AIM:	1/6/1999	Recent price:	9.25p
Interim results:	Mar	Market cap:	£2.0m
Final results:	Nov	Issue price:	75.0p
Year end:	Jun	Current no of shares:	
Accounts due:	Nov		21,662,532
Int div paymnt:	n/a	No of shares after	
Fin div paymnt:	n/a	dilution:	n/a
Int net div per share:	nil	P/E ratio:	n/a
Fin net div per share:	nil	Probable CGT?	No

LATEST REPORTED RESULTS:	2003	PREVIOUS REPORTED RESULTS:	2002
Turnover:	£2.66m	Turnover:	£3.93m
PTP:	£(292,000)	PTP:	£(218,000)
EPS:	(4.8)p	EPS:	(3.6)p

Alkane Energy   (ALK)

Coal miner

Edwinstowe House, High Street, Edwinstowe, Nottinghamshire NG21 9PR Tel: 01623-827927; Fax: 01623-827930;
e-mail: info@alkane.co.uk

		holding %
Chairman	Cameron Davies	4.2
Chief Executive	David Cross	0.9
Finance Director	Stephen Goalby	0.5
Technical Director	David Oldham	1.8

Main Shareholders:

Apax	37.5
Morgan Nominees	10.0
Tipacs	6.7
Chase Nominees	3.6

Percentage of free market capital: 34.8%

Comments:

Bombed-out Alkane claims its £2.8m acquisition of German electricity generation and gas equipment supplier Pro2 is bearing fruit. Pro2 started 2004 with 'its strongest ever order book'. Alkane lost an interim £20m on suspending and writing down loss-making UK coal mine methane recovery operations. Pro2 equipment is used to extract and use methane from sewage, decomposed organic substances and landfill. Speculative.

Nominated Adviser:	Brewin Dolphin, Leeds
AIM Broker:	Brewin Dolphin, Leeds
Solicitors:	Ashursts, London
Market Makers:	EVO; KBCS; SCAP; WINS
Auditors:	Ernst & Young, Nottingham
Registrars:	Computershare Investor Services

Entry on AIM:	19/9/2003	Recent price:	15.25p
Interim results:	Sep	Market cap:	£13.68m
Final results:	Mar	Issue price:	12.25p
Year end:	Dec	Current no of shares:	
Accounts due:	May		89,683,855
Int div paymnt:	n/a	No of shares after	
Fin div paymnt:	n/a	dilution:	n/a
Int net div per share:	nil	P/E ratio:	n/a
Fin net div per share:	nil	Probable CGT?	No

LATEST REPORTED RESULTS:	2002	PREVIOUS REPORTED RESULTS:	2001
Turnover:	£995,000	Turnover:	£1.02m
PTP:	£(567,000)	PTP:	£407,000
EPS:	(0.6)p	EPS:	0.5p

Alliance Pharma (formerly Peerless Technology) (APH)

Holding company for a pharmaceutical distribution business

Nidderdale House, Otley Road, Beckwith Knowle, Harrogate, HG3 1SA Tel: 01423-850 000; Fax: 01423-877581

		holding %
Chairman	Michael Gatenby	0.0
Chief Executive	John Dawson	56.2
Finance Director	Madeleine Scott	0.5
Sales & Mktg Director	Anthony Booley	6.1

Main Shareholders:
n/a

Percentage of free market capital: 37.3%

Nominated Adviser:	Numis, London
AIM Broker:	Numis, London
Solicitors:	Norton Rose, London
Market Makers:	NUMS; WINS
Auditors:	Grant Thornton, London
Registrars:	Capita Registrars

ENTRY ON AIM:	1/9/2001	Recent price:	20.5p
Interim results:	Sep	Market cap:	£22.71m
Final results:	May	Issue price:	16.0p
Year end:	Dec	Current no of shares:	
Accounts due:	Apr		110,793,903
Int div paymnt:	n/a	No of shares after	
Fin div paymnt:	n/a	dilution:	n/a
Int net div per share:	nil	P/E ratio:	n/a
Fin net div per share:	nil	Probable CGT?	YES

LATEST REPORTED RESULTS: 2002		PREVIOUS REPORTED RESULTS: 2001	
Turnover:	n/a	Turnover:	n/a
PTP:	£(70,000)	PTP:	£(37,000)
EPS:	(0.5)p	EPS:	(1.0)p

Comments:
Alliance reversed into cash shell Peerless Technology last November. The group buys rights to drugs at the latter stages of development and then exploits them commercially. Currently it holds the rights to 23 branded products for therapies to combat heart disease, Parkinson's, nasal infections and dermatological conditions. Most are prescription-only drugs sold direct to hospitals. Annual sales should rise 25% to £10.4m.

Alltracel Pharmaceuticals (AP.)

Biopharmaceutical research and development

10 Church Place, Sallynoggin, Co.Dublin Ireland, Tel: 00-353 1 2352162; Fax: 00-353 1 235 2165;
e-mail: Investor.Relations@alltracel.com; web site: www.alltracel.com

		holding %
Chairman	Padraic O'Connor	0.2
Chief Executive	Gerard Brandon	27.0
Chief Financial Officer	Anthony Richardson	1.3
Managing Director	Donal O'Brien	0.0

Main Shareholders:

New Opportunities Investment Trust	12.7
Jubilee Investment Trust	9.3

Percentage of free market capital: 49.5%

Nominated Adviser:	J&E Davy, Dublin
AIM Broker:	Seymour Pierce, London
Solicitors:	O'Donnell Sweeney, Dublin
Market Makers:	SCAP; WINS
Auditors:	Ernst & Young Dublin 2
Registrars:	Computershare Investor Services

Entry on AIM:	19/7/2001	Recent price:	31.25p
Interim results:	Sep	Market cap:	£24.51m
Final results:	May	Issue price:	89.0p
Year end:	Dec	Current no of shares:	
Accounts due:	Apr		78,435,070
Int div paymnt:	n/a	No of shares after	
Fin div paymnt:	n/a	dilution:	n/a
Int net div per share:	nil	P/E ratio:	n/a
Fin net div per share:	nil	Probable CGT?	No

LATEST REPORTED RESULTS: 2002		PREVIOUS REPORTED RESULTS: 2001	
Turnover:	£527,000	Turnover:	n/a
PTP:	£(32,000)	PTP:	£(1.83m)
EPS:	0.0p	EPS:	(1.0)p

Comments:
This Irish/Czech company's main product is m.doc, a chemical derived from cellulose that can stop bleeding in less than two minutes. The development process eats up cash, and money has been raised from various sources recently. However, last year sales rose 61% to £0.67m as a frenzy of distributing deals were signed, including in the US – where the product will be called Seal-On – and across Europe. A dental version and a cholesterol-reducing supplement are also in the pipeline.

Amberley (AMB)

Property investment

Victoria Square House, Victoria Square, Birmingham, B2 4DL

		holding %
Chairman	Roger Fletcher	0.0
Chief Executive		
Finance Director	Alan Sime	0.0
Non-Exec Director	William Jessup	0.0

Main Shareholders:

JO Hambro & Oryx	14.9
Deutsche Asset Management	9.1
ForwardIssue	7.5
Totalassist	7.5
Schroder Investment Management	4.6

Percentage of free market capital: 56.4%

Nominated Adviser:	Arbuthnot, Birmingham
AIM Broker:	Arbuthnot, Birmingham
Solicitors:	DLA, London
Market Makers:	CSCS; EVO; MLSB; SCAP; WINS
Auditors:	KPMG, 2 Cornwall Street, Birmingham B3 2DL
Registrars:	Capita Registrars

ENTRY ON AIM:	16/1/2004	**Recent price:**	10.4p
Interim results:	Dec	Market cap:	£2.44m
Final results:	Aug	Issue price:	n/a
Year end:	Apr	Current no of shares:	
Accounts due:	Oct		23,461,439
Int div paymnt:	n/a	No of shares after	
Fin div paymnt:	n/a	dilution:	n/a
Int net div per share:	nil	P/E ratio:	n/a
Fin net div per share:	nil	Probable CGT?	No

LATEST REPORTED RESULTS: 2003		PREVIOUS REPORTED RESULTS: 13 MONTHS TO 30 APR 2002	
Turnover:	n/a	Turnover:	£49.35m
PTP:	£(74,000)	PTP:	£(28.44m)
EPS:	(0.2)p	EPS:	(43.6)p

Comments:

After selling its four operations in speciality mineral and chemical manufacture, Amberley dropped down from the full list to AIM in January. It has only £690,000 cash in hand and freehold properties in Hull. Recently, an offer was made to the company by directors GA Naggar and PR Klimt through Dawnay Day Corporate Finance at 7.5p per share, valuing the company at £1.76m. So far, Dawnay has 50.18% of the issued share capital of Amberley.

Ambient (ABI)

Communications & marketing services provider

8th Floor, Cardinal Tower, 12 Farringdon Road, London, EC1M 3NN Tel: 020-7452 5200; Fax: 020-7452 5223; e-mail: stimpson@ambientplc.com; web site: www.ambientplc.com

		holding %
Chairman	Vincent Isaacs	26.1
Managing Director	Andrew Stimpson	5.3
Finance Director	Kevin Beerling	0.1
Non-Exec Director	Peter Revell-Smith	0.5

Main Shareholders:

The Appleton Group	14.5
Herald Investment Trust	8.4
European Spirit	5.6
Mark Armitage	4.3
Insight Investment Management	3.1

Percentage of free market capital: 31.3%

Nominated Adviser:	Numis, London
AIM Broker:	Numis, London
Solicitors:	Olswang, London
Market Makers:	ALTI; SCAP; WINS
Auditors:	Deloitte & Touche, 20 Old Bailey, London EC4M 4AR
Registrars:	Capita Registrars

Entry on AIM:	20/5/1998	**Recent price:**	73.5p
Interim results:	Nov	Market cap:	£41.06m
Final results:	Mar	Issue price:	90.0p
Year end:	Jan	Current no of shares:	
Accounts due:	Jun		55,862,444
Int div paymnt:	n/a	No of shares after	
Fin div paymnt:	n/a	dilution:	n/a
Int net div per share:	nil	P/E ratio:	n/a
Fin net div per share:	nil	Probable CGT?	YES

LATEST REPORTED RESULTS: 2003		PREVIOUS REPORTED RESULTS: 2002	
Turnover:	£37.45m	Turnover:	£25.46m
PTP:	£(13.21m)	PTP:	£(16.35m)
EPS:	(21.2)p	EPS:	(25.6)p

Comments:

Having now demerged promising ATM business Moneybox and disposed of business intelligence subsidiary WMA, Ambient is free to focus on guiding its remaining interests through to profitability. Much of its cash will be used to develop Touch, the group's on-line marketing subsidiary, which saw revenues rise 11% on a like-for-like basis to £2.5m last year as losses halved to £800,000. Without Moneybox's contribution, group revenues will be significantly reduced in 2004.

AMCO   (ARP)

Diversified contracting mini-conglomerate

Amco House, 25 Moorgate Road, Rotherham, S Yorkshire S60 2AD Tel: 01709-828218; Fax: 01709-828499;
e-mail: info@amco-corporation.plc.uk; web site: www.amco-corporation.plc.uk

		holding %
Chairman	Stuart N Gordon	8.3
Managing Director		
Finance Director	Ian Swire	0.1
Commercial	D Jackson	0.0
Director		

Main Shareholders:

Amco Investments	50.9
Bedell & Cristin Trustees	9.0
Franklyn Finance	7.5
Leonard Samuel	3.9

Percentage of free market capital: 20.3%

Comments:
AMCO, whose activities range from civil engineering and steelwork contracting to property development and mining consultancy, warned in November of big losses in a contracting subsidiary, whose managers had previously hidden them. Legal proceedings were instituted. An interim deficit of £628,000 was blamed on problem contracts in Scotland, hikes in employer's liability premiums and losses on structural steel supplies.

Nominated Adviser:	Brewin Dolphin, London
AIM Broker:	Brewin Dolphin, London
Solicitors:	Eversheds, Birmingham
Market Makers:	WINS
Auditors:	Grant Thornton, 8 West Walk, Leicester LE1 7NH
Registrars:	Capita Registrars

ENTRY ON AIM:	29/9/1995	**Recent price:**	61.5p
Interim results:	Sep	**Market cap:**	£8.54m
Final results:	Apr	**Issue price:**	94.0p
Year end:	Dec	**Current no of shares:**	
Accounts due:	Mar		13,879,327
Int div paymnt:	n/a	**No of shares after**	
Fin div paymnt:	n/a	**dilution:**	n/a
Int net div per share:	nil	**P/E ratio:**	n/a
Fin net div per share:	nil	**Probable CGT?**	Yes

LATEST REPORTED RESULTS:	2002	PREVIOUS REPORTED RESULTS:	2001
Turnover:	£90.64m	Turnover:	£91.2m
PTP:	£1.58m	PTP:	£3.45m
EPS:	9.8p	EPS:	25.3p

America Mineral Fields   (AMF)

Mineral explorer

St George's House, 15 Hanover Square, London, W1S 1HS

		holding %
Chairman	Bernard Vavala	0.0
Chief Executive	Timothy Read	0.0
Finance Director		
Director	Patrick Walsh	0.0

Main Shareholders:

Gondwana Investments/J Boulle	25.9
Umicore S A	9.8
Exploration Capital Partners	4.4
Roytor & Co	3.9

Percentage of free market capital: 56.0%

Comments:
Strong copper and cobalt prices have supported Toronto-listed America Mineral Fields after last year's £20m AIM launch fund raising. The company, which increased shareholders' equity fourfold to £14.4m last year, hopes to go ahead in 2005 with its ambitious Kolwezi copper and cobalt tailings project in Congo and is looking at zinc and diamond possibilities in Congo and Angola. Speculative but with strong potential.

Nominated Adviser:	Canaccord Capital, London
AIM Broker:	Canaccord Capital, London
Solicitors:	Stikeman Elliott, London
Market Makers:	EVO; JEFF; KBCS; WINS
Auditors:	KPMG, 999-777 Dunsmuir Street, Vancouver, British Columbia, Canada V7Y 1K3
Registrars:	Computershare Investor Services

Entry on AIM:	26/9/2003	**Recent price:**	86.0p
Interim results:	Sep	**Market cap:**	£59.52m
Final results:	Jan	**Issue price:**	50.0p
Year end:	Oct	**Current no of shares:**	
Accounts due:	Apr		69,205,416
Int div paymnt:	n/a	**No of shares after**	
Fin div paymnt:	n/a	**dilution:**	n/a
Int net div per share:	nil	**P/E ratio:**	n/a
Fin net div per share:	nil	**Probable CGT?**	No

LATEST REPORTED RESULTS:	2003	PREVIOUS REPORTED RESULTS:	2002
Turnover:	n/a	Turnover:	n/a
PTP:	£(3.54m)	PTP:	£(3.53m)
EPS:	(0.1)p	EPS:	(0.1)p

Andrews Sykes (ASY)

Support services

Premier House, Darlington Street, Wolverhampton, WV1 4JJ Tel: 01902-328700; Fax: 01902-422466;
e-mail: info@andrews-sykes.com; web site: www.andrews-sykes.com

	holding %
Chairman	Jacques Gaston Murray 83.1
Chief Executive	R J Stevens 0.8
Finance Director	Anthony Bourne 0.0
Non-Exec Director	J-C Pillois 0.9

Main Shareholders:

n/a

Percentage of free market capital: 14.0%

Nominated Adviser:	Ernst & Young, Leeds
AIM Broker:	Brewin Dolphin, Leeds
Solicitors:	n/a
Market Makers:	KLWT; WINS
Auditors:	Deloitte & Touche, 2 Colmore Row, Birmingham B3 2BN
Registrars:	Lloyds Bank Registrars

ENTRY ON AIM: 24/12/2001		Recent price:	197.0p
Interim results:	Sep	Market cap:	£114.24m
Final results:	May	Issue price:	95.5p
Year end:	Dec	Current no of shares:	
Accounts due:	Jul		57,991,003
Int div paymnt:	n/a	No of shares after	
Fin div paymnt:	n/a	dilution:	63,846,648
Int net div per share:	nil	P/E ratio:	17.1
Fin net div per share:	nil	Probable CGT?	YES

LATEST REPORTED RESULTS:	2002	PREVIOUS REPORTED RESULTS:	2001
Turnover:	£70.54m	Turnover:	£84.18m
PTP:	£12.12m	PTP:	£12.25m
EPS:	11.5p	EPS:	10.5p

Comments:

Andrews Sykes is a specialist hire solutions outfit, as well as a cash-generative corporate beast that continues to buy back its own shares. But aside from these developments, there's been little to update shareholders on since much-improved interim figures to 28 June were posted. These numbers showed the benefits of its core UK business reorganisation. Ongoing sales were up 7.7% at £32.4m, and pre-tax profits burgeoned 23.3% to £5.6m.

Angus & Ross (AGU)

Gold & explorer

St Chad's House, Piercy End, Kirkbymoorside, York, YO62 6DQ Tel: 01751-430988; Fax: 01751-430991;
e-mail: angusandross1@btinternet.com; web site: www.angusandross.com

	holding %
Chairman	Robin Andrews 5.8
Managing Director	as above
Finance Director	Axel Steenberg 0.2
Non-Exec Director	Ian Plimer 0.7

Main Shareholders:

Bruce Rowan	19.0
Cabot G B	12.3
RAB Capital	7.9

Percentage of free market capital: 52.3%

Nominated Adviser:	Brewin Dolphin, Edinburgh
AIM Broker:	Brewin Dolphin, Edinburgh
Solicitors:	Hewetsons, Cambridge
Market Makers:	WDBM; WINS
Auditors:	Buzzacott, 12 New Fetter Lane, London EC4A 1AG
Registrars:	Capita Registrars

Entry on AIM: 28/8/2001		Recent price:	13.0p
Interim results:	Sep	Market cap:	£6.62m
Final results:	Jun	Issue price:	2.0p
Year end:	Feb	Current no of shares:	
Accounts due:	Jun		50,949,403
Int div paymnt:	n/a	No of shares after	
Fin div paymnt:	n/a	dilution:	n/a
Int net div per share:	nil	P/E ratio:	n/a
Fin net div per share:	nil	Probable CGT?	No

LATEST REPORTED RESULTS:	2003	PREVIOUS REPORTED RESULTS:	2002
Turnover:	n/a	Turnover:	n/a
PTP:	£(752,000)	PTP:	£(496,000)
EPS:	(2.5)p	EPS:	(2.1)p

Comments:

A&R, which lost £446,000 in the six months to August, has been regaining stockmarket friends with its Rutherford Table gold property in Queensland, where a tailings dam is to be built for an estimated 20,000 oz of gold from an old mine, with more around it. Chairman Robin Andrews argues local mineralisation could suggest a deep epithermal gold source nearby. Initial drilling elsewhere at Top Camp has yielded nothing.

Antonov (ATV)

Automotive transmission technology licenser

100 Barbiroll Square, Manchester, M2 3AB Tel: 0161-831 2706; Fax: 0161-838 2706;
web site: www.antonov-transmission.com

		holding %
Chairman	Roumen Antonov	10.5
Chief Executive	Martin Schinzig	0.0
Finance Director	David Bovell	0.5
Director	Cornelis Minnaar**	6.9

Main Shareholders:

GG Enterprises BVBA**	6.9
Green Investments BVBA*	6.6
Delta Lloyd Verzekeringsgroep NV	4.9
WWP	4.7
Garrick Holdings BVBA	3.3

Percentage of free market capital: 55.0%

*D Bovell is a director of Green Investments, but not a shareholder
**C Minnaar's interest is held by GG

Comments:

After ten years of development, Antonov has signed a much anticipated heads of agreement with an un-named 'tier 1' transmission manufacturer to develop its six-speed automatic gearboxes. Production will begin in 2005, but due to its royalty strategy, revenues will not occur until 2005. Its deal with Honda as a manufactur-ing licensee has also yet to produce any revenue. With no immediate sales, further fundraising is likely. Patience is definitely required.

Nominated Adviser:	Brewin Dolphin, Manchester
AIM Broker:	Brewin Dolphin, Manchester
Solicitors:	Halliwell Landau
Market Makers:	CLS; MLSB; WINS
Auditors:	Ernst & Young, 100 Barbirolli Square, Manchester M2 3AB
Registrars:	Capita Registrars

Entry on AIM:	25/8/1995	**Recent price:**	45.5p
Interim results:	Aug	**Market cap:**	£47.92m
Final results:	Feb	**Issue price:**	24.0p
Year end:	Dec	**Current no of shares:**	
Accounts due:	Jun		105,319,348
Int div paymnt:	n/a	**No of shares after**	
Fin div paymnt:	n/a	**dilution:**	n/a
Int net div per share:	nil	**P/E ratio:**	n/a
Fin net div per share:	nil	**Probable CGT?**	Yes

LATEST REPORTED RESULTS: 2002		PREVIOUS REPORTED RESULTS: 2001	
Turnover:	£139,000	Turnover:	£16,000
PTP:	£(1.98m)	PTP:	£(2.18m)
EPS:	(2.0)p	EPS:	(2.5)p

Antrim Energy (AEY)

Energy company

3100, 324 8th Avenue, SW Calgary, Alberta, Canada T2P 2Z2 Tel: 00-1 403 264 5111; Fax: 00-1 403 264 5113;
web site: www.antrimenergy.com

		holding %
Chairman	Stephen Greer	13.7
Chief Executive	as above	0.0
Finance Director	Anthony Potter	0.0
Director	Vyvyan Martin	0.0

Main Shareholders:

n/a

Percentage of free market capital: 86.3%

Comments:

Toronto-listed Antrim, the second foreign company to list via AIM's 'fast-track' procedure, recently raised £5.5 million at the equivalent of a heavily discounted 5p plus half a warrant at 72p a share, to explore and develop oil and gas properties in the UK (including the North Sea), Tanzania, Argentina and Australia. This year, Antrim, which lost an interim £1m, is to drill its first well, South Galapagos, on Australia's North West Shelf.

Nominated Adviser:	Canaccord Capital, London
AIM Broker:	Canaccord Capital, London
Solicitors:	Burstall Winge, Alberta
Market Makers:	KBCS; WINS
Auditors:	PricewaterhouseCoopers LLP, Calgary, Alberta
Registrars:	Capita Registrars

Entry on AIM:	30/7/2003	**Recent price:**	55.0p
Interim results:	Oct	**Market cap:**	£17.19m
Final results:	Mar	**Issue price:**	n/a
Year end:	Dec	**Current no of shares:**	
Accounts due:	Jun		31,255,983
Int div paymnt:	n/a	**No of shares after**	
Fin div paymnt:	n/a	**dilution:**	n/a
Int net div per share:	nil	**P/E ratio:**	550.0
Fin net div per share:	nil	**Probable CGT?**	No

LATEST REPORTED RESULTS: 2002		PREVIOUS REPORTED RESULTS: 2001	
Turnover:	£5.17m	Turnover:	£3.93m
PTP:	£1.38m	PTP:	£(4.22m)
EPS:	0.1p	EPS:	(0.2)p

AorTech (AOR)

Medical devices developer, maker and distributor

Phoenix Crescent, Strathclyde Business Park, Bellshill, Lanarkshire ML4 3NJ Scotland Tel: 01698-746699;
Fax: 01698-748474; e-mail: info@aortech.com; web site: www.aortech.com

		holding %
Chairman	Laurie Rostron	0.0
Chief Executive	Frank Maguire	0.0
Finance Director	Ian Cameron	0.04
Non-Exec Director	William Strachan	0.1

Main Shareholders:

ISIS Asset Management	20.2
Active Capital Trust	12.4
Caricature Investments	11.7
Melody Investments	11.5
Erudite	9.6

Percentage of free market capital: 23.7%

Nominated Adviser:	Brewin Dolphin, Glasgow
AIM Broker:	Brewin Dolphin, Glasgow
Solicitors:	Biggart Baillie, Glasgow
Market Makers:	ALTI; BGWL; CLS; KBCS; KLWT; MLSB; WINS
Auditors:	PricewaterhouseCoopers, Glasgow
Registrars:	Lloyds TSB Registrars

ENTRY ON AIM: 18/12/2002	Recent price:	160.0p
Interim results:	Nov	Market cap:	£6.1m
Final results:	Jun	Issue price:	7.75p
Year end:	Mar	Current no of shares:	
Accounts due:	Aug		3,810,278
Int div paymnt:	n/a	No of shares after	
Fin div paymnt:	n/a	dilution:	n/a
Int net div per share:	nil	P/E ratio:	n/a
Fin net div per share:	nil	Probable CGT?	YES

Comments:

Last year AorTech returned to AIM after two years on the Full List and took a £20m impairment charge, giving a £39m full year loss. In order to survive, the heart valve businesses have been sold. The company, which had 250 staff at its peak and now has 15, is focusing on the research and development of innovative 'Elast-Eon' biomaterials. Interim losses were cut to £1m and bid rumours surround the stock. Cash stands at £6.2m.

LATEST REPORTED RESULTS: 2003		PREVIOUS REPORTED RESULTS: 2002	
Turnover:	£1.38m	Turnover:	£4.63m
PTP:	£(39.36m)	PTP:	£(12.88m)
EPS:	(103.3)p	EPS:	(34.7)p

ARC Risk Management (ARC)

Security risk management consultant

4th Floor, 73 Watling Street, London, EC4M 9BL Tel: 020-7332 5600; Fax: 020-7236 3918;
e-mail: contactus@arcrisk.com; web site: www.arcrisk.com

		holding %
Chairman	Simon Richards*	0.2
Chief Executive	Robert Whiting	6.0
Finance Director		
Operations Director	Maldwyn Worsley-Tonks	0.6

Main Shareholders:

Sidebell*	19.8
Regent Trust	8.5
Markel International	6.8
Galloway	4.5

Percentage of free market capital: 49.3%

*Simon Richards is a director of and has an interest in the share capital of Sidebell

Nominated Adviser:	Seymour Pierce, London
AIM Broker:	Seymour Pierce Ellis, Crawley
Solicitors:	Wedlake Bell, London
Market Makers:	SCAP; WINS
Auditors:	Baker Tilly, London
Registrars:	Capita Registrars

Entry on AIM: 13/5/1999	Recent price:	1.6p
Interim results:	Nov	Market cap:	£3.51m
Final results:	Jul	Issue price:	1.25p
Year end:	Dec	Current no of shares:	
Accounts due:	Apr		219,210,836
Int div paymnt:	n/a	No of shares after	
Fin div paymnt:	n/a	dilution:	n/a
Int net div per share:	nil	P/E ratio:	n/a
Fin net div per share:	nil	Probable CGT?	YES

Comments:

The global security play came to AIM via a reversal into shell Perthshire Leisure. Its latest success is a deal with World Access for its red24 security information service, which offers telephone or web-based communication with security experts – this follows earlier red24 deals with HSBC and Hiscox. In the half to September, ARC's pre-tax loss widened from £189,000 to £328,000 but this was half the deficit incurred in the six months to March. Turnover was £507,000 (£132,000).

LATEST REPORTED RESULTS: 2003		PREVIOUS REPORTED RESULTS: 15 MONTHS TO 31 MAR 02	
Turnover:	£621,000	Turnover:	£1.17m
PTP:	£(903,000)	PTP:	£(994,000)
EPS:	(1.1)p	EPS:	(2.9)p

Archipelago Resources (AR.)

Investor in gold mining & exploration
190 Strand, London, WC2R 1JN

		holding %
Chairman		
Managing Director	Colin Loosemore	24.6
Finance Director		
Non-Exec Director	Barry Casson	0.0

Main Shareholders:
Ocean Resources Capital 38.5

Percentage of free market capital: 13.4%

Nominated Adviser:	Grant Thornton, London	
AIM Broker:	Durlacher, London	
Solicitors:	Lawrence Graham, London	
Market Makers:	DURM; WINS	
Auditors:	Ernst & Young, One Colemore Row, Birmingham B3 2DB	
Registrars:	Share Registrars	

ENTRY ON AIM:	9/9/2003	**Recent price:**	36.5p
Interim results:	Oct	**Market cap:**	£17.78m
Final results:	Mar	**Issue price:**	23.5p
Year end:	Dec	**Current no of shares:**	
Accounts due:	Jun		48,720,771
Int div paymnt:	n/a	**No of shares after**	
Fin div paymnt:	n/a	**dilution:**	n/a
Int net div per share:	nil	**P/E ratio:**	n/a
Fin net div per share:	nil	**Probable CGT?**	No

LATEST REPORTED RESULTS: PERIOD ENDED 31 DEC '02		PREVIOUS REPORTED RESULTS:	N/A
Turnover:	n/a	Turnover:	n/a
PTP:	£(632,000)	PTP:	n/a
EPS:	(4.1)p	EPS:	n/a

Comments:
Headed by entrepeneur Colin Loosemore, Archipelago is paying development capital group Arlington £5m to provide processing equipment from Chile for Archipelago's Toka Tindung gold and silver project in Indonesia, with 1.75m oz of gold identified. Share swap group Ocean Capital has 38% of Archipelago, which also has rights to copper and gold projects in the Philippines.

Aricom (TIO)

Titanium oxide miner, producer and distributer
10-11 Grosvenor Place, London, SW1X 7HH Tel: 020-7201 8939; Fax: 020-7201 8938; e-mail: info@aricom.plc.uk; web site: www.aricom.com

		holding %
Chairman	Malcolm Field	0.5
Chief Executive	Thomas Swithenbank	0.0
Finance Director	Peter Howes	0.0
Non-Exec Director	Pavel Maslovsky	0.0

Main Shareholders:

Macaria Investments	22.2
Viscaria Investments	15.1
Nutraco	10.5
Clients of Merril Lynch	8.8
Morstan Nominees	8.0

Percentage of free market capital: 8.3%

Nominated Adviser:	Canaccord Capital, London	
AIM Broker:	Canaccord Capital, London	
Solicitors:	Norton Rose, London	
Market Makers:	EVO; KBCS; WINS	
Auditors:	Moore Stephens, London	
Registrars:	Capita Registrars	

Entry on AIM:	31/12/2003	**Recent price:**	48.0p
Interim results:	Sep	**Market cap:**	£45.66m
Final results:	Mar	**Issue price:**	15.0p
Year end:	Dec	**Current no of shares:**	
Accounts due:	May		95,118,684
Int div paymnt:	n/a	**No of shares after**	
Fin div paymnt:	n/a	**dilution:**	n/a
Int net div per share:	n/a	**P/E ratio:**	n/a
Fin net div per share:	n/a	**Probable CGT?**	No

LATEST REPORTED RESULTS: 2002		PREVIOUS REPORTED RESULTS: 2001	
Turnover:	n/a	Turnover:	n/a
PTP:	n/a	PTP:	n/a
EPS:	n/a	EPS:	n/a

Comments:
Peter Hambro is a director of Aricom, which floated after raising £3.5m at 15p, to take Peter Hambro Mining's titanium interests in Russia. The money was earmaked for a feasibility study on a titanium dioxide plant in Russia's Amur region and due diligence on 'Titan', a potential joint venture in the Ukraine. The comany has acquired 74% of a project to develop titanium deposits at Olekma.

Arko (formerly Arko Energy Holdings) (AKO)

Chinese energy conglomerate

12 St. James's Square, London, SW1Y 4RB Tel: 020-8228 1838; Fax: 020-8228 1839; e-mail: admin@arkoenergy.com;
web site: www.arkoholdings.com

		holding %
Chairman	Chin Kam Chiu*	0.0
Chief Executive	Angela Leung	0.04
Finance Director	Shi Yan	0.0
Exec Director	Qin Bing Qiang	0.0

Main Shareholders:
Keen Lloyd Holdings*	93.2

Percentage of free market capital: 6.7%

*These shares are held in the name of Keen Lloyd

Comments:
Vehicle for Hong Kong entrepreneur and 94%-owner KC Chin, Arko, which doubled interim profits to £2m, is building a role as vertically-integrated Chinese energy company by buying quarries, mines, power generation and shipping interests. Arko recently bought a chunk of such companies in exchange for 190m shares to be issued if their combined EBITDA exceeds £3.8m.

Nominated Adviser:	Nabarro Wells, London
AIM Broker:	Keith Bayley Rogers, London
Solicitors:	McFadden, London
Market Makers:	BGMM; KBCS; WINS
Auditors:	Yeung & Co, 14 Grange Drive, Chislehurst, Kent BR1 5ES
Registrars:	Capita Registrars

Entry on AIM:	27/6/2000	Recent price:	4.6p
Interim results:	Jun	Market cap:	£99.67m
Final results:	Dec	Issue price:	0.5p
Year end:	Dec	Current no of shares:	
Accounts due:	Jul		2,166,844,720
Int div paymnt:	n/a	No of shares after	
Fin div paymnt:	n/a	dilution:	n/a
Int net div per share:	nil	P/E ratio:	23.0
Fin net div per share:	nil	Probable CGT?	No

LATEST REPORTED RESULTS: 9 MONTHS ENDED 31 DEC 2002		PREVIOUS REPORTED RESULTS: YEAR ENDED 31 MAR 2002	
Turnover:	£37.81m	Turnover:	£187,000
PTP:	£3.59m	PTP:	£(162,000)
EPS:	0.2p	EPS:	(0.2)p

Arlington (ARL)

Investment Company

18 Pall Mall, London, SW1Y 5LU Tel: 020-7389 5010; Fax: 0845-345 6729; e-mail: CBrookes@ArlingtonGroup.co.uk;
web site: www.arlingtongroup.co.uk

		holding %
Chairman	Nicholas Barham	58.8
Chief Executive	Craig Niven	0.2
Finance Director	Colin Hill	0.5
Investment Director	Geoffrey Nash	0.0

Main Shareholders:
Fidelity	5.1
Ashton Graham	4.8
Ferlim Nominees	3.3
Pershing Keen Nominees	3.3

Percentage of free market capital: 30.9%

Comments:
The investment company benefited from improved UK and US stock markets during the half to September. The company committed almost £7m to new projects in both equity and bridge finance transactions. These included a £3m placing and open offer with Ennstone and a £2.65m MBO transaction in Ster Century Cinemas. Interims showed profits improved to £1.3m (£0.18m). Cash remained robust at £21.8m, with uncommitted balances equating to 25p a share.

Nominated Adviser:	Evolution Beeson Gregory, London
AIM Broker:	Evolution Beeson Gregory, London
Solicitors:	Pinsents, London
Market Makers:	WINS
Auditors:	Solomon Hare, Bristol
Registrars:	Capita Registrars

Entry on AIM:	29/11/2000	Recent price:	36.5p
Interim results:	Sep	Market cap:	£24.05m
Final results:	May	Issue price:	n/a
Year end:	Mar	Current no of shares:	
Accounts due:	Jul		65,894,277
Int div paymnt:	n/a	No of shares after	
Fin div paymnt:	n/a	dilution:	75,663,419
Int net div per share:	nil	P/E ratio:	73.0
Fin net div per share:	nil	Probable CGT?	Yes

LATEST REPORTED RESULTS: 2003		PREVIOUS REPORTED RESULTS: 2002	
Turnover:	£14.36m	Turnover:	£370,000
PTP:	£357,000	PTP:	£(9.79m)
EPS:	0.5p	EPS:	(13.8)p

Armour Group   (AMR)
Electronic equipment designer & maker
Lonsdale House, 7/9 Lonsdale Gardens, Tunbridge Wells, Kent, TN1 1NU Tel: 01892-502700; Fax: 01892-502707

		holding %
Chairman	Bob Morton*	1.0
Chief Executive	George Dexter	0.6
Finance Director	John Harris	0.2
Non-Exec Director	Stephen Bodger	0.3

Main Shareholders:

Southwind*	21.7
Fleming Mercantile Investment	5.17
Montanaro New Millennium Fund	3.85
Anin Investment Holdings	3.4
Universities Superannuation Scheme	3.1

Percentage of free market capital: 60.7%

*Mr Morton has a non-beneficial interest in these shares, Mr Morton's pension scheme holds 400,000 shares (1%) which is beneficial

Comments:

Armour continues to prosper, with its audio electronic division trading ahead of expectations for the current financial year – enhanced by the acquisition of Veda, Qed, Golding and IMI for a consideration of £12m. In February, it also announced it had signed an agreement with Hyundai to supply its Veba in-car entertainment equipment to four of its models. The deal is worth an initial £400,000. Pre-tax profits of £2.7m are expected for the year.

Nominated Adviser:	KBC Peel Hunt, London
AIM Broker:	KBC Peel Hunt, London
Solicitors:	Arnold & Porter, London
Market Makers:	KBCS; WINS
Auditors:	BDO Stoy Hayward, 69 Tweedy Rd, Bromley, Kent BR1 3WA
Registrars:	Capita Registrars

ENTRY ON AIM:	2/7/2002	Recent price:	88.0p
Interim results:	Apr	Market cap:	£46.29m
Final results:	Oct	Issue price:	18.0p
Year end:	Aug	Current no of shares:	
Accounts due:	Dec		52,603,274
Int div paymnt:	n/a	No of shares after	
Fin div paymnt:	Dec	dilution:	n/a
Int net div per share:	nil	P/E ratio:	35.2
Fin net div per share:	0.35p	Probable CGT?	Yes

LATEST REPORTED RESULTS:	2003	PREVIOUS REPORTED RESULTS:	2002
Turnover:	£16.08m	Turnover:	£13.30m
PTP:	£1.40m	PTP:	£246,000
EPS:	2.5p	EPS:	0.3p

Artisan (UK)   (ART)
Housebuilder and property developer
Mace House, Sovereign Court, Spitfire Close, Ermine Business Park, Huntingdon, Cambs PE29 6XU Tel: 01480-436666; Fax: 01480-436231; e-mail: email@artisan-plc.co.uk; web site: www.artisan.plc.co.uk

		holding %
Chairman	Michael Stevens*	10.3
Chief Executive	Martyn Freeman	0.1
Finance Director	Christopher Musselle	0.1
Non-Exec Director	Norman Saunders	0.02

Main Shareholders:

n/a

Percentage of free market capital: 89.5%

*These shares are held by Aspen Finance

Comments:

Returning to concentrate on house-building and commercial development has been a smart move for Artisan. Rippon Homes, its East Midlands home-builder exceeded budgeted targets by selling 55 new homes last year. In order to reduce the mammoth debt incurred during the past few years, the sale of non-core and surplus assets assisted in a 68% reduction of debt to £6m. Non-core assets sold in Mallorca in May for £1.43m enabled gearing to drop 88.5% to 46.8%.

Nominated Adviser:	Seymour Pierce, London
AIM Broker:	Seymour Pierce, London
Solicitors:	Philip Speer, Cambridge
Market Makers:	KBCS; MLSB; SCAP; WINS
Auditors:	BDO Stoy Hayward, 8 Baker Street, London W1M 1DA
Registrars:	Capita Registrars

Entry on AIM:	8/12/1998	Recent price:	2.75p
Interim results:	Dec	Market cap:	£7.93m
Final results:	Jul	Issue price:	4.0p
Year end:	Mar	Current no of shares:	
Accounts due:	Aug		288,529,426
Int div paymnt:	Feb	No of shares after	
Fin div paymnt:	n/a	dilution:	291,992,760
Int net div per share:	0.25p	P/E ratio:	n/a
Fin net div per share:	nil	Probable CGT?	Yes

LATEST REPORTED RESULTS:	2003	PREVIOUS REPORTED RESULTS:	2002
Turnover:	£35.29m	Turnover:	£59.46m
PTP:	£(5.34m)	PTP:	£(12.83m)
EPS:	(2.0)p	EPS:	(4.7)p

Asfare   (ASF)
Fire and safety equipment maker & distributor
25 Upper Brook Street, Mayfair, London, W1K 7QD

		holding %
Chairman	Timothy Wightman	11.9
Chief Executive	David Chisnall	15.4
Finance Director		
Non-Exec Director	Adrian Bradshaw*	40.2

Main Shareholders:
n/a

Percentage of free market capital: 32.5%

These shares are held by Bradmount acting as nominee for Adrian Bradshaw and Peter Mountford

Comments:
The maker of ladders for the rescue services joined AIM in December via a £2.4m placing priced at 100p. The listing gives Asfare greater kudos overseas, will help expand its business in the US and Australia and also provide acquisition currency. Asfare's main customers include fire brigades, airports and the police. Crucially, the company has been in profit since 1989 and turned over about £4m last year. Growth will come from health and safety legislation and concerns.

Nominated Adviser:	Seymour Pierce, London	
AIM Broker:	Seymour Pierce, London	
Solicitors:	Olswang, London	
Market Makers:	SCAP; WINS	
Auditors:	Grant Thornton, Fareham	
Registrars:	Computershare Investor Services	

ENTRY ON AIM: 12/12/2003		**Recent price:**	128.0p
Interim results:	Oct	**Market cap:**	£5.38m
Final results:	Jul	**Issue price:**	100.0p
Year end:	Mar	**Current no of shares:**	
Accounts due:	Sep		4,200,000
Int div paymnt:	n/a	**No of shares after**	
Fin div paymnt:	n/a	**dilution:**	n/a
Int net div per share:	nil	**P/E ratio:**	n/a
Fin net div per share:	nil	**Probable CGT?**	YES

LATEST REPORTED RESULTS:	2003	PREVIOUS REPORTED RESULTS:	2002
Turnover:	£4.19m	Turnover:	£3.50m
PTP:	£775,000	PTP:	£463,000
EPS:	n/a	EPS:	n/a

ASITE   (ASE)
E-procurement services for the construction industry
Leconfield House, Curzon Street, London, W1J 5JA Tel: 020-7647 5151; Fax: 020-7647 5155;
e-mail: marketing@asite.com; web site: www.asite.com

		holding %
Chairman	John Egan	0.0
Chief Executive	Tom Dengenis	0.5
Finance Director		
Deputy Chairman	Walter Goldsmith	0.5

Main Shareholders:

B & C Plaza	25.9
Plane Investments	15.0
Stanhope	11.9
Warrencity Invest Corp	8.7
Aurora Investments	6.6

Percentage of free market capital: 30.6%

Comments:
ASITE is an intriguing e-tendering business with a board headed by construction industry reformer Sir John Egan. Financial results have been less than impressive so far, although losses have continued to drop. Through core business ASITE Solutions it has rolled out four new systems in the past year, Tender, Workspace, Negotiate and Integration, with a number of contractors. One of the number is Laing O'Rourke, using the systems for BAA's Heathrow Terminal 5 project.

Nominated Adviser:	Deloitte & Touche, London	
AIM Broker:	Insinger Townsley, London	
Solicitors:	Eversheds, London	
Market Makers:	MLSB; SCAP; WINS	
Auditors:	Mazars, London	
Registrars:	Capita Registrars	

Entry on AIM:	12/3/1998	**Recent price:**	3.9p
Interim results:	Jul	**Market cap:**	£4.01m
Final results:	Jun	**Issue price:**	30.0p
Year end:	Dec	**Current no of shares:**	
Accounts due:	May		102,910,633
Int div paymnt:	n/a	**No of shares after**	
Fin div paymnt:	n/a	**dilution:**	n/a
Int net div per share:	nil	**P/E ratio:**	n/a
Fin net div per share:	nil	**Probable CGT?**	YES

LATEST REPORTED RESULTS:	2002	PREVIOUS REPORTED RESULTS:	2001
Turnover:	£1.60m	Turnover:	£5.09m
PTP:	£(5.39m)	PTP:	£(8.35m)
EPS:	(4.7)p	EPS:	(12.3)p

ASK Central   (AKC)

Pizza and pasta restaurant operator

20 High Street, St Albans, Hertfordshire AL3 4EL Tel: 01727-735800; Fax: 01727-735899; web site: www.askcentral.co.uk

		holding %
Chairman	George Cracknell	0.2
Managing Director	Adam Kaye	3.6
Finance Director	Martin Eckersley	0.1
Exec Director	Sam Kaye	3.6

Main Shareholders:

FMR, Fidelity Intl + Mr EC Johnson	11.7
ISIS Asset Management	7.9
Phillip Kaye	5.5
Stanlife Nominees	5.5
M & G Investment	3.7
Percentage of free market capital: 53.9%	

Nominated Adviser:	Evolution Beeson Gregory, London
AIM Broker:	Evolution Beeson Gregory, London
Solicitors:	Howard Kennedy, London;
	Glovers, London
Market Makers:	ARBT; BGMM; CSFB; HSBC; KBCS; MLSB; WINS
Auditors:	BDO Stoy Hayward, London
Registrars:	Computershare Investor Services

ENTRY ON AIM:	3/10/1995	**Recent price:**	217.5p
Interim results:	Sep	**Market cap:**	£209.25m
Final results:	Mar	**Issue price:**	35.0p
Year end:	Dec	**Current no of shares:**	
Accounts due:	Apr		96,205,603
Int div paymnt:	Nov	**No of shares after**	
Fin div paymnt:	Jul	**dilution:**	99,560,603
Int net div per share:	0.4p	**P/E ratio:**	17.7
Fin net div per share:	0.5p	**Probable CGT?**	Yes

LATEST REPORTED RESULTS:	2002	PREVIOUS REPORTED RESULTS:	2001
Turnover:	£95.84m	Turnover:	£78.91m
PTP:	£16.67m	PTP:	£13.58m
EPS:	12.3p	EPS:	10.3p

Comments:

Having recently rebuffed The Restaurant Group's offer, ASK is asking its shareholders to accept the all-cash 220p per share offer from Riposte, a company formed by private equity company TDR Capital and Capricorn Ventures International, which also purchased Pizza Express in July last year. The offer values ASK at £212.9m. There are currently two major chains – ASK itself and Zizzi. A grill operation called Jo Shmo's is also being launched.

ASOS (formerly asSeenonScreen)   (ASC)

Media and retail website operator

1 Kingsway, London, WC2B 6XF Tel: 020-7240 7070; Fax: 020-7240 9990; e-mail: nick@asos.com; web site: www.asos.com

		holding %
Chairman	Lord Waheed Alli	0.0
Chief Executive	Nick Robertson	16.1
Finance Director	John Morgan	0.0
Bus Dev Director	Quentin Griffiths	16.2

Main Shareholders:

Brookspey	8.5
Deborah Thorpe	5.6
Credit Suisse First Boston	5.0
Percentage of free market capital: 48.6%	

Nominated Adviser:	Seymour Pierce, London
AIM Broker:	Seymour Pierce Ellis, Crawley
Solicitors:	Kuit Steinart Levy, Manchester
Market Makers:	SCAP; WINS
Auditors:	Horwarth Clark, London
Registrars:	Capita Registrars

Entry on AIM:	3/10/2001	**Recent price:**	11.75p
Interim results:	Sep	**Market cap:**	£7.99m
Final results:	Jun	**Issue price:**	20.0p
Year end:	Mar	**Current no of shares:**	
Accounts due:	Apr		67,969,759
Int div paymnt:	n/a	**No of shares after**	
Fin div paymnt:	n/a	**dilution:**	70,157,330
Int net div per share:	nil	**P/E ratio:**	n/a
Fin net div per share:	nil	**Probable CGT?**	Yes

LATEST REPORTED RESULTS:	2002	PREVIOUS REPORTED RESULTS:	2001
Turnover:	£4.10m	Turnover:	£1.70m
PTP:	£(1.70m)	PTP:	£(1.11m)
EPS:	(2.8)p	EPS:	(2.6)p

Comments:

ASOS, which stands for As Seen On Screen, sells clothes and accessories 'as seen on' celebrities like David Beckham and Cameron Diaz, through the website ASOS.com. Sales have grown strongly in recent times, with the company producing first time pre-tax profits for 2003. It now has 283,000 registered users and had a much healthier £1.3m cash position. It is looking to sell its profitable Entertainment Marketing (UK) division.

ATA (ATP)
Recruitment & training consultant
Kingston House, Oaklands Business Park, Armstrong Way, Yate, South Gloucestershire BS37 5NA, Tel: 01454-310069;
Fax: 01454-333129; e-mail: admin@ata-group.co.uk; web site: www.ata-group.co.uk

		holding %	
Chairman	Bill Douie	17.0	
Chief Executive	Clive Chapman	18.8	
Finance Director			
Non-Exec Director	John Hustler	0.2	

Main Shareholders:

	holding %
Direct Nominees	9.4
Sinjul Nominees	9.0
North Castle Street Nominees	9.0
Graham J Chivers	7.1
Vidacos Nominees	3.4
Percentage of free market capital: 25.6%	

Comments:

Encouragingly ATA has broadened its coverage with London Underground through a 10-year deal with 'Tube Lines' for the training of technical staff. The support services company also clinched a 3-year deal supplying on-track labour to the Thames Valley Area of Network Rail. Back in September, the board pleased investors with interims to June set against a tough market. Pre-tax profits perked up 18% to £450,000 on sales 21% ahead at £7.5m.

Nominated Adviser:	Williams de Broe, London
AIM Broker:	Williams de Broe, London
Solicitors:	Lawrence Graham, London
Market Makers:	TEAM; WINS
Auditors:	PKF, Promenade, Clifton, Bristol BS2 8RZ
Registrars:	Computershare Investor Services

ENTRY ON AIM:	15/6/1998	Recent price:	113.5p
Interim results:	Sep	Market cap:	£9.24m
Final results:	Apr	Issue price:	134.0p
Year end:	Dec	Current no of shares:	
Accounts due:	Apr		8,142,204
Int div paymnt:	Oct	No of shares after	
Fin div paymnt:	Jul	dilution:	n/a
Int net div per share:	2.1p	P/E ratio:	10.0
Fin net div per share:	3.8p	Probable CGT?	Yes

LATEST REPORTED RESULTS: 2002		PREVIOUS REPORTED RESULTS: 2001	
Turnover:	£13.13m	Turnover:	£13.09m
PTP:	£1.42m	PTP:	£1.07m
EPS:	11.4p	EPS:	9.6p

Athelney Trust (ATY)
Investment company
2 Queen Anne's Gate Buildings, Dartmouth Street, London, SW1H 9BP Tel: 020-7222 8989; Fax: 020-7222 8998;
e-mail: chelverton@fastnet.co.uk

		holding %
Chairman	Hugo Deschampsneufs*	7.2
Managing Director	Robin Boyle*	26.9
Finance Director		
Non-Exec Director	David Horner	0.3
Main Shareholders:		
Dartington		26.3
Principal Nominees		14.4
Pershing Keen		11.4
Rock Nominees		4.5

Percentage of free market capital: 9.0%
*These holdings include 58,000 shares held in a pension scheme in which these directors are jointly interested

Comments:

Final figures for this tiny small cap investment trust are awaited. In the six months to June, NAV rose 11% to 92.2p. However, compared with a year ago NAV fell 7%. Since then NAV should have improved markedly in line with the buoyant small cap indices. MD Robin Boyle's style is to pick decent small companies with steady growth plans that are neglected by larger funds. Athelney aims to maintain last year's payout level of 1.7p.

Nominated Adviser:	Noble & Co, Edinburgh
AIM Broker:	Speirs & Jeffrey, Glasgow
Solicitors:	n/a
Market Makers:	KBCS; WINS
Auditors:	Clement Keys, Birmingham
Registrars:	Park Circus

Entry on AIM:	19/6/1995	Recent price:	80.5p
Interim results:	Sep	Market cap:	£1.45m
Final results:	Mar	Issue price:	53.0p
Year end:	Dec	Current no of shares:	
Accounts due:	Mar		1,802,802
Int div paymnt:	n/a	No of shares after	
Fin div paymnt:	May	dilution:	n/a
Int net div per share:	nil	P/E ratio:	n/a
Fin net div per share:	1.7p	Probable CGT?	No

LATEST REPORTED RESULTS: 2002		PREVIOUS REPORTED RESULTS: 2001	
Turnover:	£60,330	Turnover:	£86,420
PTP:	£(270,000)	PTP:	£25,000
EPS:	(11.0)p	EPS:	2.0p

Atlantic Global (ATL)

Provider of business management software applications

Maple House, Woodland Park, Bradford Rd, Chain Bar, Cleckheaton, BD19 6BW Tel: 01274-863300; Fax: 01274-865966;
e-mail: info@atlantic-global.co.uk; web site: www.atlanticglobal.co.uk

		holding %
Chairman	David Cox	0.1
Managing Director	Eugene Blaine	50.8
Finance Director Designate	Rupert Hutton	0.2
Commercial Director	Samuel Howcroft	3.5

Main Shareholders:

AIM Distribution Trust	6.4
Paul Gleghorn	4.3
Leggmason Investors	3.3
Northern AIM VCT	3.3
Ian Needs	3.1
Percentage of free market capital:	23%

Nominated Adviser:	Collins Stewart, London
AIM Broker:	Collins Stewart, London
Solicitors:	Robert Muckle, Newcastle-Upon-Tyne
Market Makers:	CSCS; KBCS; WINS
Auditors:	KPMG, Newcastle-Upon-Tyne
Registrars:	Capita Registrars

Entry on AIM:	4/6/2001	Recent price:	66.5p
Interim results:	Sep	Market cap:	£15.13m
Final results:	Mar	Issue price:	25.0p
Year end:	Dec	Current no of shares:	
Accounts due:	Mar		22,747,026
Int div paymnt:	n/a	No of shares after	
Fin div paymnt:	May	dilution:	25,669,026
Int net div per share:	nil	P/E ratio:	n/a
Fin net div per share:	0.5p	Probable CGT?	Yes

Comments:

Business and resource management software star Atlantic Global has been boosted by details of two new contracts worth a combined £200,000 to the company. The first stems from insurance giant Norwich Union, the second from its rival Friends Provident and between them they concern licences for 2,250 of Atlantic's Adeo software – a near-10% addition to the products user base. First half profits hit £231,000 on sales of £907,000. Analysts expect a full year surplus of £700,000.

	LATEST REPORTED RESULTS: 2002	PREVIOUS REPORTED RESULTS: 2001
Turnover:	£1.55m	Turnover: £1.21m
PTP:	£235,000	PTP: £314,000
EPS:	0.6p	EPS: 1.4p

Auto Indemnity (AUT)

Accident management service provider

Indemnity House, Sir Frank Whittle Way, Blackpool Business Park, Blackpool, FY4 2FB Tel: 0870-889 2200;
Fax: 0870-889 2211; e-mail: info@autoindemnity.co.uk; web site: www.autoindemnity.co.uk

		holding %
Chairman	Charles Good	14.1
Chief Executive	Adrian M Palmer	0.0
Finance Director	Geoffrey Orme	0.03
Non-Exec Director	David Gorton	5.0

Main Shareholders:

Chase Nominees	24.0
RBSTB Nominees	10.7
Close Brothers Group	9.9
Andrew Gorton	4.9
HSBC Global Custody Nominee	3.5
Percentage of free market capital:	21.1%

Nominated Adviser:	Teather & Greenwood, London
AIM Broker:	Teather & Greenwood, London
Solicitors:	Wedlake Bell, London
Market Makers:	SCAP; TEAM; WINS
Auditors:	RSM Robson Rhodes, Manchester
Registrars:	Computershare Investor Services

Entry on AIM:	21/12/1999	Recent price:	34.25p
Interim results:	Feb	Market cap:	£20.96m
Final results:	Sep	Issue price:	42.0p
Year end:	Jun	Current no of shares:	
Accounts due:	Sep		61,198,688
Int div paymnt:	Apr	No of shares after	
Fin div paymnt:	Nov	dilution:	63,353,225
Int net div per share:	0.25	P/E ratio:	n/a
Fin net div per share:	0.25p	Probable CGT?	Yes

Comments:

The car accident management venture's second interims – for the 12 months to December – were excellent and beat forecasts from the house broker. Profits rocketed up 191.1% to £1.9m and turnover was lifted 33.4% to £19.7m. Auto Indemnity is now one of the biggest volume suppliers of replacement cars amongst the accident management groups. For the year to June, analysts suggest profits of £2m, giving earnings of 2.53p.

	LATEST REPORTED RESULTS: 2002	PREVIOUS REPORTED RESULTS: 2001
Turnover:	£14.75m	Turnover: £10.42m
PTP:	£341,000	PTP: £384,000
EPS:	1.3p	EPS: 0.7p

Avanti Capital (AVA)

Cash shell/investments

2 Motcomb Street, Knightsbridge, London, SW1X 8JU Tel: 020-7070 7070; Fax: 020-7070 7077; web site: www.avanticap.com

		holding %
Chairman	Philip Crawford	1.4
Joint Chief Executive	Julian Fellerman	0.6
CEO & CFO	Richard Kleiner	2.1
Non-Exec Director	William Crewdson	0.0

Main Shareholders:

Laxey Partners	11.5

Percentage of free market capital: 84.4%

Nominated Adviser:	Collins Stewart, London
AIM Broker:	KBC Peel Hunt, London
Solicitors:	Stringer Saul, London
Market Makers:	KBCS; MLSB; SCAP; WINS
Auditors:	Ernst & Young, 7 Rolls Buildings, London EC4A 1NH
Registrars:	Melton Registrars

ENTRY ON AIM:	6/10/1997	**Recent price:**	154.0p
Interim results:	Mar	**Market cap:**	£3.65m
Final results:	Sep	**Issue price:**	2.5p
Year end:	Jun	**Current no of shares:**	
Accounts due:	Sep		2,369,358
Int div paymnt:	n/a	**No of shares after**	
Fin div paymnt:	n/a	**dilution:**	n/a
Int net div per share:	nil	**P/E ratio:**	n/a
Fin net div per share:	nil	**Probable CGT?**	No

LATEST REPORTED RESULTS: 2003		PREVIOUS REPORTED RESULTS: 2002	
Turnover:	£201,000	**Turnover:**	£83,000
PTP:	£47,000	**PTP:**	£(3.42m)
EPS:	0.0p	**EPS:**	(0.7)p

Comments:

The former internet investor-cum-corporate financier has done its first private equity deal, providing £7m to the management team rescuing late night bar chain Po Na Na from administration. This deal gave the group net assets of £19.7m, or 190p per share, at the end of December. The 28 Po Na Na bars are trading profitably in line with expectations. The £2m tech portfolio is dominated by text-messaging company mBlox, which accounts for half of the value of this portfolio.

Avesco (AVS)

Service provider to the media sector

Unit E2, Sussex Manor Business Park, Gatwick Road, Crawley, RH10 9NH Tel: 020-8974 1234; Fax: 020-8974 1622

		holding %
Chairman	Ian Martin	0.3
Chief Executive	David Nicholson	0.2
Finance Director	John Christmas	0.0
Non-Exec Director	Richard Murray	19.1

Main Shareholders:

Prudential	15.0
The Fleming Mercantile Trust	9.3
Complete Communications	5.2

Percentage of free market capital: 50.7%

Nominated Adviser:	Durlacher, London
AIM Broker:	Durlacher, London
Solicitors:	Norton Rose, London
Market Makers:	DURM; EVO; KBCS; WINS
Auditors:	KPMG, Crawley
Registrars:	Capita Registrars

Entry on AIM:	24/12/2003	**Recent price:**	148.5p
Interim results:	Jan	**Market cap:**	£24.9m
Final results:	Jul	**Issue price:**	n/a
Year end:	Mar	**Current no of shares:**	
Accounts due:	Sep		16,764,342
Int div paymnt:	n/a	**No of shares after**	
Fin div paymnt:	n/a	**dilution:**	n/a
Int net div per share:	nil	**P/E ratio:**	n/a
Fin net div per share:	nil	**Probable CGT?**	Yes

LATEST REPORTED RESULTS: 2003		PREVIOUS REPORTED RESULTS: 2002	
Turnover:	£60.14m	**Turnover:**	£65.17m
PTP:	£(6.02m)	**PTP:**	£2.97m
EPS:	(35.2)p	**EPS:**	24.7p

Comments:

Avesco came to AIM to de-merge its Core Services arm – a UK and US provider of specialist services to the corporate presentation, entertainment and broadcast markets. The remaining Media Rights division owns 49% of CCCL (a producer of shows such as Who Wants to be a Millionaire) and 23.6% of AIM-listed Medal Entertainment & Media. A £1.8m interim loss was produced. Since then, the board has warned of a deterioration of trade in its soon-to-be demerged Core Services division.

Avingtrans (AVG)

Precision engineering

Precision House, Derby Road, Sandiacre, Nottingham, NG10 5HU Tel: 0115-949 9020; Fax: 0115-949 9024; web site: www.avingtrans.plc.uk

		holding %
Chairman	Kenneth Baker	8.9
Chief Executive	Steve Lawrence	2.9
Finance Director	Stephen King	0.6
Non-Exec Director	Jeremy Hamer	0.8

Main Shareholders:

Nigel Wray	10.7
Bill Stanway	5.4
Intrinsic Value	4.8
Guy Thomas	4.3
David Abell	3.3

Percentage of free market capital: 55.6%

Nominated Adviser:	Bridgewell, London
AIM Broker:	Gilbert Eliott, London
Solicitors:	Nabarro Nathanson, London
Market Makers:	KBCS, WINS
Auditors:	Pricewaterhousecoopers, St Albans
Registrars:	Capita Registrars

ENTRY ON AIM:	19/3/2002	Recent price:	43.5p
Interim results:	Feb	Market cap:	£3.07m
Final results:	Sep	Issue price:	55.0p
Year end:	May	Current no of shares:	
Accounts due:	Sept		7,049,804
Int div paymnt:	n/a	No of shares after	
Fin div paymnt:	n/a	dilution:	n/a
Int net div per share:	nil	P/E ratio:	n/a
Fin net div per share:	nil	Probable CGT?	YES

LATEST REPORTED RESULTS: 2003		PREVIOUS REPORTED RESULTS: 2002	
Turnover:	4.65m	Turnover:	n/a
PTP:	£291,000	PTP:	£(309,000)
EPS:	3.3p	EPS:	(4.9)p

Comments:

Avingtrans, the actuators and spindles play that acquired Jena via reversal, is a supplier of precision equipment and 'critical services' to manufacturing in the UK, Germany and the USA. These days it is a broader beast, having acquired powered spindles supplier B&T last September. Interim figures to November showed sales rising 32.2% to £2.6m, although profits fell 5.2% to £163,000. Markets for its products remain depressed.

Avionic Services (ASR)

Air traffic control system developer

53 Portland Road, Kingston, Surrey KT1 2SH Tel: 020-8974 5225; Fax: 020-8974 5023; e-mail: Marketing@avionicservices.co.uk; web site: www.avionicservices.co.uk

		holding %
Chairman	William Price	1.2
Chief Executive	as above	
Finance Director		
Operations Director	David Bartlett	2.8

Main Shareholders:

Rathbone Brothers	7.0
Grange Nominees	4.7
Trafalgar Catalyst Fund	3.4
GAM London Limited	3.4

Percentage of free market capital: 73.1%

Nominated Adviser:	Noble & Co, Edinburgh
AIM Broker:	Noble & Co, Edinburgh
Solicitors:	Memery Crystal, London
Market Makers:	HOOD; KBCS; WINS
Auditors:	KPMG, Salisbury Court, London EC4Y 8BB
Registrars:	Capita Registrars

Entry on AIM:	31/5/2002	Recent price:	5.25p
Interim results:	Feb	Market cap:	£4.5m
Final results:	Dec	Issue price:	21.0p
Year end:	Jun	Current no of shares:	
Accounts due:	Oct		85,735,342
Int div paymnt:	n/a	No of shares after	
Fin div paymnt:	n/a	dilution:	n/a
Int net div per share:	nil	P/E ratio:	n/a
Fin net div per share:	nil	Probable CGT?	YES

LATEST REPORTED RESULTS: 2003		PREVIOUS REPORTED RESULTS: 2002	
Turnover:	£1.02m	Turnover:	£3.11m
PTP:	£(3.36m)	PTP:	£240,000
EPS:	(15.2)p	EPS:	(5.9)p

Comments:

The air traffic engineering business has suffered in the wake of 9/11 and the Iraqi liberation, but looks to have turned the corner. Interim figures showed losses trimmed by 65% to £452,175 on sales up a staggering 122% to £1.5m. In December, Avionic raised £1.6m to help finance larger contracts. The strategy now is to balance 'lumpy' income from systems integration activities with more regular contracted income by developing its flight inspection and consultancy work.

Avocet Mining (AVM)

Gold miner

7th Floor, 9 Berkeley Street, London, W1J 8DW Tel: 020-7907 9000; Fax: 020-7907 9019;
e-mail: avocetmining@avocet.co.uk; web site: www.avocet.co.uk

		holding %
Chairman	N G McNair Scott	4.9
Chief Executive	John Catchpole	1.0
Finance Director	Jonathan Henry	0.1
Non-Exec Director	R A Pilkington	0.2

Main Shareholders:

Elliott Associates LP	27.8
Artemis	14.3
INVESCO	6.3

Percentage of free market capital: 45.3%

Nominated Adviser:	Evolution Beeson Gregory, London
AIM Broker:	Fiske, London
Solicitors:	Field Fisher Waterhouse, London
Market Makers:	WDBM; WINS
Auditors:	Grant Thornton, Melton St, Euston Sq, London NW1 2EP
Registrars:	Lloyds TSB Registrars

ENTRY ON AIM:	26/7/2002	**Recent price:**	64.5p
Interim results:	Nov	**Market cap:**	£66.88m
Final results:	Jul	**Issue price:**	13.0p
Year end:	Mar	**Current no of shares:**	
Accounts due:	Aug		103,696,530
Int div paymnt:	n/a	**No of shares after**	
Fin div paymnt:	n/a	dilution:	n/a
Int net div per share:	nil	P/E ratio:	n/a
Fin net div per share:	nil	**Probable CGT?**	No

LATEST REPORTED RESULTS:	2003	PREVIOUS REPORTED RESULTS:	2002
Turnover:	£31.38m	Turnover:	£25.47m
PTP:	£2.36m	PTP:	£(10.93m)
EPS:	2.0p	EPS:	(16.6)p

Comments:

Gold producer Avocet, which boosted interim profits threefold to £3.5m pre-tax, increased output from Penjom in Malaysia and Zeravshan in Tajikistan by 53% to 135,124 oz in the nine months to December. Chief executive John Catchpole hopes to start production at North Lanut in Indonesia in the second half of this year. After a good run, the shares have marked time, but could go further.

Azure (formerly Room Service) (AZH)

Cash shell

65 Maygrove Road, Kilburn, London, NW6 2EH Tel: 020-7644 6666; Fax: 020-7644 6644

		holding %
Chairman	Nicolas Greenstone	0.0
Managing Director	Gerald Gold	0.0
Finance Director		
Non-Exec Director	Raymond Harris	0.0

Main Shareholders:

Chiddingfold	19.28
Microcap Equities	8.0
Winterflood Securities	4.2
Laurence Davis	3.8

Percentage of free market capital: 64.7%

Nominated Adviser:	John East, London
AIM Broker:	John East, London
Solicitors:	Penningtons, London
Market Makers:	MLSB; SCAP; WINS
Auditors:	Baker Tilly, 2 Bloomsbury Street, London WC1B 3ST
Registrars:	Capita Registrars

Entry on AIM:	28/2/2000	**Recent price:**	1.4p
Interim results:	Mar	**Market cap:**	£0.47m
Final results:	May	**Issue price:**	17.0p
Year end:	Dec	**Current no of shares:**	
Accounts due:	Apr		33,231,569
Int div paymnt:	n/a	**No of shares after**	
Fin div paymnt:	n/a	dilution:	n/a
Int net div per share:	nil	P/E ratio:	n/a
Fin net div per share:	nil	**Probable CGT?**	Yes

LATEST REPORTED RESULTS:	2002	PREVIOUS REPORTED RESULTS:	2001
Turnover:	£17,000	Turnover:	£991,000
PTP:	£(2.84m)	PTP:	£(5.5m)
EPS:	(2.3)p	EPS:	(13.9)p

Comments:

This company started AIM life as Cube8.com, then acquired food delivery company Room Service. After racking up losses and sinking into creditors' voluntary liquidation, it was left with no trading activities and 'virtually no cash'. Since then the company has been cleaned up, with debts repaid and converted into equity. Azure is now in a position to search for a reverse deal, with money having been raised to fund due diligence and professional fees.

Bakery Services (BKE)

Bakeries in supermarkets and shopping centres

3 Horsted Sq, Bellbrook Bus Park, Uckfield, East Sussex TN22 1QG Tel: 01825-761415; Fax: 01825-761418;
e-mail: info@bakeryservices.co.uk; web site: www.bakeryservices.co.uk

		holding %
Chairman	Richard Worthington	3.9
Managing Director	Keith Bentley	13.9
Finance Director	as chairman	
Comm Director	David Drury	9.0
Main Shareholders:		
Diggle Investments		7.2

Percentage of free market capital: 65.9%

Nominated Adviser:	Smith & Williamson, London
AIM Broker:	Seymour Pierce Ellis, Crawley
Solicitors:	Memery Crystal, London
Market Makers:	SCAP; WINS
Auditors:	Hill Wooldridge, 107 Hindes Road, Harrow, HA1 1RU
Registrars:	Capita Registrars

ENTRY ON AIM:	7/7/1997	Recent price:	0.7p
Interim results:	Nov	Market cap:	£0.99m
Final results:	Sep	Issue price:	3.0p
Year end:	Mar	Current no of shares:	
Accounts due:	Jul		140,833,333
Int div paymnt:	n/a	No of shares after	
Fin div paymnt:	n/a	dilution:	n/a
Int net div per share:	nil	P/E ratio:	n/a
Fin net div per share:	nil	Probable CGT?	YES

LATEST REPORTED RESULTS: 2003		PREVIOUS REPORTED RESULTS: 2002	
Turnover:	£4.09m	Turnover:	£4.55m
PTP:	£(697,000)	PTP:	£(1.75m)
EPS:	(0.5)p	EPS:	(1.3)p

Comments:
Bakery Services managed an interim pre-tax profit of £3,000. The company now has two UK divisions, Inbake (which operates in-store bakeries in Co-Ops) and retail bakery/café franchise Don Millers, which has now reached eight stores plus one managed store. It is also pursuing a legal claim against its former solicitors over the acquisition of Don Miller for £400,000. The sale of an investment that realised £250,000 will be used for further development.

Bank Restaurant (BKR)

Restaurant operator

15 - 19 Kingsway, London, WC2B 6UN Tel: 020-7379 5088; Fax: 020-7379 5070; e-mail: info@bankrestaurants.com;
web site: www.bankrestaurants.com

		holding %
Chairman	Leigh Collins	1.9
Managing Director	Christian Delteil	1.2
Finance Director	Geoffrey Smith	2.1
Operations Director	David Colcombe	0.0
Main Shareholders:		
Coran		24.9
John Moxon		21.6
Evolution Beeson Gregory		12.1
Giltspur Nominees		6.4
Pershing Keen		6.1

Percentage of free market capital: 9.3%

Nominated Adviser:	Evolution Beeson Gregory, London
AIM Broker:	Evolution Beeson Gregory, London
Solicitors:	Pinsents, London
Market Makers:	BGMM; KBCS; SCAP; WINS
Auditors:	Ernst & Young, London
Registrars:	Hartford Registrars

Entry on AIM:	23/11/2000	Recent price:	2.4p
Interim results:	Jul	Market cap:	£1.74m
Final results:	Feb	Issue price:	20.0p
Year end:	Oct	Current no of shares:	
Accounts due:	Mar		72,500,000
Int div paymnt:	n/a	No of shares after	
Fin div paymnt:	n/a	dilution:	n/a
Int net div per share:	nil	P/E ratio:	n/a
Fin net div per share:	nil	Probable CGT?	YES

LATEST REPORTED RESULTS: 2003		PREVIOUS REPORTED RESULTS: 2002	
Turnover:	£8.60m	Turnover:	£9.0m
PTP:	£(346,000)	PTP:	£(2.38m)
EPS:	(0.7)p	EPS:	(5.6)p

Comments:
Restaurant operator Bank is still feeling the effects of a slump in the London tourist trade, but thanks to cost-cutting measures, losses before tax shrank significantly. Conran Holdings made a strategic investment in the company – it now owns 29.9% of Bank but has declined to make an offer for the company. Instead, it is supporting Bank in its sales and marketing efforts. Net debt in October stood at £2.4m but the company has secured a new long-term bank facility.

Base Group
(BS.)

Sports management company

25 City Road, London, EC1Y 1BQ Tel: 020-7448 8959; Fax: 020-7638 9426; e-mail: info@digitalsport.co.uk

		holding %
Chairman	Adrian Bradshaw	0.0
Chief Executive		
Finance Director		
Non-Exec Director	Gary Smith	10.6

Main Shareholders:

Socknersh Investments**	7.2
Richard Ellis	5.3
James Allen	5.3
Eurobet (UK)	4.1
Sky Capital UK Nominees*	3.1

Percentage of free market capital: 54.6%

*These shares are being held for Shawall Limited
** Socknersh Investments is controlled by Crispin Barker

Comments:

These days Base is a shell exploring 'all avenues', including possible acquisitions – at the last count it had £350,000 'free cash'. An erstwhile sports management play, it sold its only trading operations to ex-director Leon Angel's company for £1 apiece. The board had to do this or risk running out of money by the spring. This crisis followed a dire half to August with losses before tax coming in at £905,000 (£1.28m) on lower turnover of £332,000 (£428,000).

Nominated Adviser:	Collins Stewart, London
AIM Broker:	Collins Stewart, London
Solicitors:	Eversheds, London
Market Makers:	BGMM; CLS.; KBCS; SCAP; WINS
Auditors:	KPMG Audit, 2 Cornwall Street, Birmingham B3 2DL
Registrars:	Capita Registrars

Entry on AIM: 29/11/2000		**Recent price:**	0.2p
Interim results:	Sep	**Market cap:**	£1.68m
Final results:	Jun	**Issue price:**	2.0p
Year end:	Feb	**Current no of shares:**	
Accounts due:	Jun		839,944,149
Int div paymnt:	n/a	**No of shares after**	
Fin div paymnt:	n/a	**dilution:**	n/a
Int net div per share:	nil	**P/E ratio:**	n/a
Fin net div per share:	nil	**Probable CGT?**	Yes

LATEST REPORTED RESULTS: 14 MONTHS TO 28 FEB 2003		PREVIOUS REPORTED RESULTS: 2001	
Turnover:	£1.53m	Turnover:	£812,000
PTP:	£(2.24m)	PTP:	£(1.09m)
EPS:	(0.3)p	EPS:	(0.2)p

Basepoint
(BNT)

Managed business, innovation and enterprise centre operator

9 Charlecote Mews, Staple Gardens, Winchester, Hampshire SO23 8SR Tel: 01962-842244; Fax: 01962-867037; e-mail: hq@basepoint.co.uk; web site: www.basepoint.co.uk

		holding %
Chairman	Viscount James Lifford	1.4
Chief Executive	Robert Cleaver	3.4
Finance Director	David Boakes	1.3
Non-Exec Director	Brian Keys	4.5

Main Shareholders:

ACG Developments	30.3
Ronverworth	4.8

Percentage of free market capital: 52.1%

Comments:

Basepoint is the developer and operator of Managed Business, Innovation and Enterprise Centres which accommodate and provide infrastructure support packages to SMEs on short term licence agreements. With so many individual businesses about, this is a huge market. In a splendid first half to 31 August, pre-tax profits improved from £368,000 to £760,000, and earnings rose 43%, on a 64% sales hike to £2.6m. Investors were treated to a maiden interim dividend.

Nominated Adviser:	Smith & Williamson, London
AIM Broker:	Teather & Greenwood, London
Solicitors:	Olswang, London
Market Makers:	SCAP; WINS
Auditors:	Blueprint Audit, Eastleigh
Registrars:	Capita Registrars

Entry on AIM:	14/6/2000	**Recent price:**	171.5p
Interim results:	Oct	**Market cap:**	£19.16m
Final results:	May	**Issue price:**	123.0p
Year end:	Feb	**Current no of shares:**	
Accounts due:	Jun		11,169,588
Int div paymnt:	n/a	**No of shares after**	
Fin div paymnt:	Jul	**dilution:**	n/a
Int net div per share:	nil	**P/E ratio:**	19.9
Fin net div per share:	2.2p	**Probable CGT?**	Yes

LATEST REPORTED RESULTS: 2003		PREVIOUS REPORTED RESULTS: 2002	
Turnover:	£3.69m	Turnover:	£2.43m
PTP:	£876,000	PTP:	£628,000
EPS:	8.6p	EPS:	6.3p

Beauford   (BFRD)

Engineering ceramic products manufacturer

35-37 Cavendish Way, Southfield Industrial Estate, Glenrothes, Fyffe, KY6 2SB Tel: 01592-630505; Fax: 01592-773192; web site: www.vzs-seagoe.com

		holding %
Chairman	Alastair Ritchie	0.0
Chief Executive		
Finance Director		
Director	Laurie Hoskisson	0.8
Main Shareholders:		
Roger Fletcher		10.1
Hermes Investment Management		8.6
Asset Value Realisation		3.7

Percentage of free market capital: 76.5%

Nominated Adviser:	Brewin Dolphin, Edinburgh
AIM Broker:	Brewin Dolphin, Edinburgh
Solicitors:	Burness, Edinburgh
Market Makers:	KBCS; MLSB; WINS
Auditors:	Deloitte & Touche, Edinburgh
Registrars:	Capita Registrars

ENTRY ON AIM:	3/9/2001	Recent price:	0.4p
Interim results:	Feb	Market cap:	£0.32m
Final results:	Jun	Issue price:	1.75p
Year end:	Dec	Current no of shares:	
Accounts due:	May		80,976,280
Int div paymnt:	n/a	No of shares after	
Fin div paymnt:	n/a	dilution:	n/a
Int net div per share:	nil	P/E ratio:	n/a
Fin net div per share:	nil	Probable CGT?	YES

Comments:

Beauford's sole trading business is ceramic products play VZS Technical Ceramics, now that its Craigavon operation has been closed. Yet there's been no word from the taciturn company since its thread-bare half year statement way back in September, when the board flagged up small signs of improvement in its markets. The pre-tax loss was pared from £829,000 to £153,000 on £1.98m (£1.73m) of sales. This result was 'broadly in line with the board's expectation'.

LATEST REPORTED RESULTS:	2002	PREVIOUS REPORTED RESULTS:	2001
Turnover:	£4.74m	Turnover:	£6.39m
PTP:	£(741,000)	PTP:	£(1.87m)
EPS:	(1.0)p	EPS:	(2.4)p

Beaufort (suspended 12 Mar 2004)   (BFG)

Business service provider

152 Buckingham Palace Road, London, SW1W 9TR Tel: 020-7259 8000; Fax: 020-7259 8001; e-mail: info@beaufort-international.com; web site: www.beaufort-international.com

		holding %
Chairman	Kenneth Harvey	1.5
Chief Executive	Harry Cowan	2.9
Finance Director	Alan Chamberlin	0.0
Main Shareholders:		
David Stewart		6.8
Gordon Stewart		4.4

Percentage of free market capital: 84.4%

Nominated Adviser:	City Financial Asociates, London
AIM Broker:	Seymour Pierce Ellis, Crawley
Solicitors:	Ashursts, London & Marriott Harrison, London
Market Makers:	MLSB; SCAP; WINS
Auditors:	Smith & Williamson, 1 Riding Hse St, London W1A 3AS
Registrars:	Capita Registrars

Entry on AIM:	7/11/1996	Recent price:	0.1p
Interim results:	Dec	Market cap:	£1.32m
Final results:	Sep	Issue price:	3.0p
Year end:	Mar	Current no of shares:	
Accounts due:	Aug		1,323,444,090
Int div paymnt:	n/a	No of shares after	
Fin div paymnt:	n/a	dilution:	n/a
Int net div per share:	nil	P/E ratio:	n/a
Fin net div per share:	nil	Probable CGT?	YES

Comments:

These days Beaufort International is a more focused consultancy seeing a pick up in its markets. It cut operating losses to £205,000 (£447,000) in the half to September thanks to continued rationalising of its operations. However the loss before tax burgeoned to £696,000 (£493,000) after £470,000 of exceptional costs. During the year, it has added new 'prestigious' clients like Costain, National Grid Transco and Morley Fund Management.

LATEST REPORTED RESULTS:	2003	PREVIOUS REPORTED RESULTS:	2002
Turnover:	£3.63m	Turnover:	£4.45m
PTP:	£(2.17m)	PTP:	£(990,000)
EPS:	(0.3)p	EPS:	(0.2)p

Belgravium Technologies (BVM)

Engineering & electronic data capture

Belgravium House, 2 Campus Road, Listerhills Science Park, Bradford, West Yorkshire BD7 1HR Tel: 01274-718800; Fax: 01274-718801; e-mail: investor@belgravium.com; web site: www.belgravium.com

		holding %
Chairman	John Kembery	7.3
Chief Executive		
Finance Director		
Non-Exec Director	Roderick McDougall	2.4

Main Shareholders:

Perfecta Asset Management	4.4
Britel Fund Nominees	3.7

Percentage of free market capital: 82.1%

Nominated Adviser:	KPMG, Leeds
AIM Broker:	Teather and Greenwood, London
Solicitors:	DLA, Birmingham
Market Makers:	MLSB; SCAP; TEAM; WINS
Auditors:	PricewaterhouseCoopers, Manchester
Registrars:	Capita Registrars

Entry on AIM:	24/1/2001	Recent price:	15.0p
Interim results:	Aug	Market cap:	£10.17m
Final results:	Feb	Issue price:	n/a
Year end:	Dec	Current no of shares:	
Accounts due:	Mar		67,825,759
Int div paymnt:	Dec	No of shares after	
Fin div paymnt:	May	dilution:	69,621,547
Int net div per share: 0.12p		P/E ratio:	16.7
Fin net div per share: 0.24p		Probable CGT?	Yes

LATEST REPORTED RESULTS: 2003		PREVIOUS REPORTED RESULTS: 2002	
Turnover:	£3.90m	Turnover:	£4.19m
PTP:	£795,000	PTP:	£1.41m
EPS:	0.9p	EPS:	1.5p

Comments:

The designer and maker of real-time electronic data capture systems reported lower sales and profits last year in a cautious logistics industry suffering from a confidence crisis. Nevertheless, Belgravium has invested in products, has a strong balance sheet – cash in the bank rose 52% to £2m – and looks well placed for when the market turns. Encouragingly, there were 'significantly more contracts' in negotiation than a year ago, as the company entered 2004.

Bella Media (formerly MobileFuture) (BLL)

Cinema developer & owner

9 West Halkin Street, London, SW1 8JL Tel: 01920-443600; Fax: 01920-443601

		holding %
Chairman	Emmanuel Olympitis	0.0
Chief Executive	Fred Weinert	0.0
Finance Director	Timothy Le Druillenec	0.0
Joint Deputy Chairman	Clive Ng	0.0

Main Shareholders:

Pacific Media	25.0
S G Investment	9.3
Richard Armstrong	7.3
A J Bennett	3.4

Percentage of free market capital: 55.1%

Nominated Adviser:	Beaumont Cornish, London
AIM Broker:	Fiske, London
Solicitors:	Simmons & Simmons, London
Market Makers:	BGMM; WINS
Auditors:	Baker Tilly, 2 Bloomsbury Street, London WC1B 3ST
Registrars:	Capita Registrars

Entry on AIM:	1/11/2000	Recent price:	0.2p
Interim results:	Jan	Market cap:	£0.14m
Final results:	Nov	Issue price:	72.0p
Year end:	Jun	Current no of shares:	
Accounts due:	Oct		67,825,759
Int div paymnt:	n/a	No of shares after	
Fin div paymnt:	n/a	dilution:	n/a
Int net div per share:	nil	P/E ratio:	0.7
Fin net div per share:	nil	Probable CGT?	Yes

LATEST REPORTED RESULTS: 2003		PREVIOUS REPORTED RESULTS: 2002	
Turnover:	n/a	Turnover:	£479,000
PTP:	£(84,000)	PTP:	£(4.11m)
EPS:	0.3p	EPS:	(9.4p)

Comments:

Following an injection of new management, erstwhile mobile internet business MobileFuture has changed both its name and business focus. The group is now into the development, construction and ownership of Imax and large screen cinemas. Plans are in motion to develop the first cinema in Springfield, USA. This is one of AIM's more risk-intense operations.

Bema Gold (BAU)

Gold and silver miner

Suite 3100, Three Bentall Centre, 595 Burrard Street, PO Box 49143, Vancouver, British Columbia V7X 1J1 Canada;
web site: www.bema.com

		holding %
Chairman	Clive Johnson	0.0
Chief Executive	as above	
Finance Director		
Director	Barry Rayment	0.0

Main Shareholders:

CDS & Co	70.8
CEDE & Co	20.4

Percentage of free market capital: 8.8%

Comments:

A strong rand has increased cash costs at Canadian gold producer Bema's Petrex mine in South Africa to $398 an ounce — more than the recent $393 price — though gains on a rand/gold put option cut this to $358. With operations in Chile and Russia too, Bema, geared to a high gold price, more than doubled output last year to 250,315 oz and targets 300,000 oz for 2004, despite a fire interrupting production in Russia.

Nominated Adviser:	Canaccord Capital, London
AIM Broker:	Canaccord Capital, London
Solicitors:	Charles Russell, Lonodn
Market Makers:	JEFF; KBCS; WINS
Auditors:	PricewaterhouseCoopers LLP, British Columbia, Canada
Registrars:	Computershare Investor Services

ENTRY ON AIM:	30/9/2003	Recent price:	196.0p
Interim results:	Sep	Market cap:	£689.86m
Final results:	Mar	Issue price:	n/a
Year end:	Dec	Current no of shares:	
Accounts due:	May		351,971,523
Int div paymnt:	n/a	No of shares after	
Fin div paymnt:	n/a	dilution:	n/a
Int net div per share:	nil	P/E ratio:	n/a
Fin net div per share:	nil	Probable CGT?	No

LATEST REPORTED RESULTS:	2002	PREVIOUS REPORTED RESULTS:	2001
Turnover:	$36.29m	Turnover:	$21.21m
PTP:	$(2.56m)	PTP:	$(11.34m)
EPS:	(0.02)c	EPS:	(0.07)c

Bertam (BTM)

Plantations operator & real estate developer

3 Clanricarde Gardens, Tunbridge Wells, Kent TN1 1HQ Tel: 01892-516333; Fax: 01892-518639

		holding %
Chairman	Peter Hadsley-Chaplin	0.1
Chief Executive	as above	
Finance Director	Philip Fletcher	0.0
Deputy Chairman	Angus Fraser	0.02

Main Shareholders:

Rowe Evans Investments	48.3
Sungkai	10.4
Kulim	3.5
Alcatel Bell Pensioenfond VZW	3.1

Percentage of free market capital: 34.2%

Comments:

Bertam has been enjoying profits from a firm palm oil market – its main activity in Malaysia. The company also develops property and has enjoyed higher sales on the back of the palm oil boom. Its Straits Beach development has encountered problems with planning permission but work should commence in March with an end of year completion. Its cotton interests in Australia remains dependent on the continent's drought ending.

Nominated Adviser:	Westhouse Securities, London
AIM Broker:	Westhouse Securities, London
Solicitors:	Lovells, London
Market Makers:	WINS
Auditors:	Deloitte & Touche, Crawley
Registrars:	M P Evans

Entry on AIM:	28/10/2002	Recent price:	290.0p
Interim results:	Sep	Market cap:	£77.98m
Final results:	Apr	Issue price:	185.0p
Year end:	Dec	Current no of shares:	
Accounts due:	May		26,888,349
Int div paymnt:	n/a	No of shares after	
Fin div paymnt:	Jun	dilution:	n/a
Int net div per share:	nil	P/E ratio:	36.3
Fin net div per share:	5.5p	Probable CGT?	No

LATEST REPORTED RESULTS:	2002	PREVIOUS REPORTED RESULTS:	2001
Turnover:	£3.53m	Turnover:	£3.05m
PTP:	£3.18m	PTP:	£2.48m
EPS:	8.0p	EPS:	6.5p

betinternet.com (BET)

Tax-free internet bookmaker

4th floor, Viking House, Nelson Street, Douglas, Isle of Man IM1 2AH Tel: 01624-665000; Fax: 01624-629698;
e-mail: info@betinternet.com; web site: www.betinternet.com

		holding %
Chairman	Denham Eke	0.0
Chief Executive	Paul Doona	0.3
Finance Director		
Technical Director	William Mummery	0.0

Main Shareholders:

Burnbrae	22.4
Vincent Caldwell	13.6
Mill Properties	11.4
Merrion Stockbrokers Nominees	9.5
Pershing Keen Nominees	5.9

Percentage of free market capital: 27.8%

Nominated Adviser:	Williams de Broe, London
AIM Broker:	Williams de Broe, London
Solicitors:	Berwin Leighton Paisner, London
Market Makers:	KBCS; WINS
Auditors:	KPMG, Douglas
Registrars:	Capita Registrars

Entry on AIM:	9/5/2000	Recent price:	7.75p
Interim results:	Feb	Market cap:	£9.04m
Final results:	Jul	Issue price:	45.0p
Year end:	May	Current no of shares:	
Accounts due:	Oct		116,687,027
Int div paymnt:	n/a	No of shares after	
Fin div paymnt:	n/a	dilution:	119,761,902
Int net div per share:	nil	P/E ratio:	n/a
Fin net div per share:	nil	Probable CGT?	No

LATEST REPORTED RESULTS: 2003		PREVIOUS REPORTED RESULTS: 2002	
Turnover:	£57.06m	Turnover:	£52.63m
PTP:	£(131,000)	PTP:	£(1.98m)
EPS:	(0.1)p	EPS:	(2.3)p

Comments:

The online gaming play has lapsed back into the red. Interims to November showed a loss before tax of £1.1m. Turnover increased 65% to £40.8m comparatively. Meanwhile, cost cutting measures continued, with staff reductions of 23%. Some consolation is provided by joint venture Euro Off-Track, which saw turnover leap an incredible 4,550% to £14.6m and created a first-time profit of £338,000. Not surprisingly, it is actively looking to enter into more joint ventures.

Bidtimes (BDT)

Investment company

Meriden House, 6 Great Cornbow, Halesowen, West Midlands B63 3AB Tel: 0121-5040965; Fax: 0121-5040981;
e-mail: info@bidtimes.com; web site: www.bidtimes.com

		holding %
Chairman	Brian North	0.3
Managing Director	Russell Stevens	0.5
Finance Director		
Non-Exec Director	Brent Fitzpatrick	0.8

Main Shareholders:

Lanman Asset Management	8.5
Meriden	7.5
Tim Royce	6.3

Percentage of free market capital: 44.4%

Nominated Adviser:	John East, London
AIM Broker:	Seymour Pierce, London
Solicitors:	Eversheds, Birmingham
Market Makers:	SCAP; WINS
Auditors:	Grant Thornton, Birmingham
Registrars:	Neville Registrars

Entry on AIM:	4/7/2000	Recent price:	3.25p
Interim results:	Nov	Market cap:	£0.56m
Final results:	Oct	Issue price:	25.0p
Year end:	Feb	Current no of shares:	
Accounts due:	Jun		17,373,523
Int div paymnt:	n/a	No of shares after	
Fin div paymnt:	n/a	dilution:	17,637,372
Int net div per share:	nil	P/E ratio:	n/a
Fin net div per share:	nil	Probable CGT?	Yes

LATEST REPORTED RESULTS: PERIOD ENDED 28 FEB 2003		PREVIOUS REPORTED RESULTS: 2001	
Turnover:	£13,000	Turnover:	n/a
PTP:	£(1.12m)	PTP:	£(148,000)
EPS:	(10.3)p	EPS:	(2.9)p

Comments:

Bidtimes has changed itself into an investment company investing in fellow AIM companies SRS Technology and Innobox, plus it has a holding in private company Blue Chip Casinos. Of late it has begun to invest solely in residential property and currenty owns five 'show homes' built by Barratt. Russell Stevenson is now chairman and chief executive after Brian North retired. Innobox has performed well but SRS' share price continues to fall.

Billam   (BLLM)

Pan-European investment company

32 Clerkenwell Green, London, EC1R 0DU Tel: 020-7336 1300; Fax: 020-7336 1310; e-mail: Info@billamplc.co.uk;
web site: www.billamplc.co.uk

		holding %
Chairman	Victor Beamish	1.0
Managing Director	Angus Forrest	10.0
Finance Director		
Director	Juliet Hoskins	0.3

Main Shareholders:

Barcleyshare	6.1
TD Waterhouse Nominees	4.5
Teawood Nominees	3.6

Percentage of free market capital: 74.5%

Nominated Adviser:	KBC Peel Hunt, London
AIM Broker:	KBC Peel Hunt, London; Seymour Pierce Ellis, Crawley
Solicitors:	Pinsents, London
Market Makers:	KBCS; MLSB; SCAP; WINS
Auditors:	Grant Thornton, 28 Kenwood Park Road, Sheffield S7 1NG
Registrars:	Computershare Investor Services

ENTRY ON AIM:	3/7/1997	**Recent price:**	27.5p
Interim results:	Nov	**Market cap:**	£4.45m
Final results:	Jun	**Issue price:**	0.1p
Year end:	Dec	**Current no of shares:**	
Accounts due:	Apr		16,172,312
Int div paymnt:	n/a	**No of shares after**	
Fin div paymnt:	n/a	**dilution:**	n/a
Int net div per share:	nil	**P/E ratio:**	3.1
Fin net div per share:	nil	**Probable CGT?**	No

LATEST REPORTED RESULTS: 2003		PREVIOUS REPORTED RESULTS: 2002	
Turnover:	n/a	**Turnover:**	n/a
PTP:	£1.44m	**PTP:**	£(2.41m)
EPS:	8.9p	**EPS:**	(16.0)p

Comments:

Beleaguered engineer Billam has been revived as a venture capital vehicle. During 2003, net assets improved to £10.7 million but on a per share basis dropped marginally to 65.3p. The major portfolio member is AIM-listed telematics company Cybit, in which Billam is the largest shareholder. The group plans to turnaround other early stage technology ventures. A particular focus is healthcare concerns, such as drug developers Eirx, which floated in January, and Physiomics, which might float later this year.

BioFocus   (BIO)

Chemistry service provider and specialist library producer

Sittingbourne Research Centre, Sittingbourne, Kent ME9 8AZ Tel: 01795-412300; Fax: 01795-47123;
e-mail: info@biofocus.com; web site: www.biofocus.com

		holding %
Chairman	David Stone	3.2
Chief Executive	Geoffrey McMillan	0.0
Finance Director	Stephen France	0.9
Non-Exec Director	Brian Adger	0.01

Main Shareholders:

ISIS Asset Management	15.4
Friends Ivory and Sime	13.0
North Castle Street Nominees	7.5
RBSTB Nominees	4.2
John Harris	4.0

Percentage of free market capital: 33.5%

Nominated Adviser:	Nomura, London
AIM Broker:	Teather & Greenwood, London; Nomura, London
Solicitors:	Barlow Lyde & Gilbert, London
Market Makers:	KBCS; MLSB; NMRA; TEAM; WINS
Auditors:	Baker Tilly, 2 Bloomsbury Street, London WC1B 3ST
Registrars:	Capita Registrars

Entry on AIM:	21/8/2000	**Recent price:**	210.0p
Interim results:	Sep	**Market cap:**	£32.29m
Final results:	Feb	**Issue price:**	290.0p
Year end:	Dec	**Current no of shares:**	
Accounts due:	Apr		15,375,037
Int div paymnt:	n/a	**No of shares after**	
Fin div paymnt:	n/a	**dilution:**	n/a
Int net div per share:	nil	**P/E ratio:**	n/a
Fin net div per share:	nil	**Probable CGT?**	Yes

LATEST REPORTED RESULTS: 2003		PREVIOUS REPORTED RESULTS: 2002	
Turnover:	£15.84m	**Turnover:**	£14.45m
PTP:	£(316,000)	**PTP:**	£993,000
EPS:	(1.0)	**EPS:**	2.7p

Comments:

The chemistry services business is rehabilitating after a tough start to last year. Some high-margin service contracts were delayed but revenue from technology and research income more than compensated for this in the final quarter of the year. The group will also save costs by moving to a single site near Cambridge. However, the associated costs pushed the group into the red last year. BioFocus now has interests in 38 of its clients' promising drug candidates.

Bionex Investments

(BNX)

Investment company

223a Kensington High Street, London, W8 6SG Tel: 020-7937 4445; Fax: 020-7937 4446; e-mail: graham@bionex.co.uk

		holding %
Chairman	Christopher Roberts	0.2
Chief Executive		
Finance Director	as above	
Non-Exec Director	Julian Noble	1.4

Main Shareholders:

Newbourne	10.6
Pershing Keen	7.6
Bioprojects International	6.3
Twenty/Twenty L.P	5.1
Thurloe Holdings	3.9

Percentage of free market capital: 49.0%

Nominated Adviser:	W H Ireland, Manchester
AIM Broker:	W H Ireland, Manchester
Solicitors:	Stringer Saul, London
Market Makers:	KBCS; SCAP; WINS
Auditors:	Chantrey Vellacott, London
Registrars:	Melton Registrars

Entry on AIM:	27/1/2003	**Recent price:**	2.3p
Interim results:	Jun	**Market cap:**	£3.63m
Final results:	Dec	**Issue price:**	2.25p
Year end:	Sep	**Current no of shares:**	
Accounts due:	Mar		157,925,634
Int div paymnt:	n/a	**No of shares after**	
Fin div paymnt:	n/a	**dilution:**	n/a
Int net div per share:	n/a	**P/E ratio:**	n/a
Fin net div per share:	n/a	**Probable CGT?**	No

LATEST REPORTED RESULTS: 2003		PREVIOUS REPORTED RESULTS: 2002	
Turnover:	n/a	Turnover:	n/a
PTP:	£(384,000)	PTP:	£(390,000)
EPS:	(0.3)p	EPS:	(0.4)p

Comments:

Bionex has stakes in eight life sciences ventures. Most are unquoted and range from start-ups to pre-IPO enterprises, although some short-term biotech share bets have been made. The group is connected with Abingdon Capital, owner of Nomad Corporate Synergy. Christopher Roberts has recently replaced Graham Wylie as chief executive following the board's decision to use its £1m cash to support existing investments rather than make new ones. Net assets fell £0.3m to £3.4m last year.

BioProgress

(BPRG)

Pharmaceutical equipment developer

14 Hostmoor Avenue, March, Cambridgeshire PE15 0AX Tel: 01354-655674; Fax: 01354-655858;

web site: www.bioprogress.com

		holding %
Chairman	Peter Glynn-Jones	0.0
Chief Executive	Graham Hind	0.5
Finance Director	Elizabeth Edwards	0.0
Technical Director	Malcolm Brown	5.3

Main Shareholders:

Barry Muncaster	12.3
Schweco Nominees	6.3
Ormiston-Gore Securities	4.2
The Jade Partnership	3.3

Percentage of free market capital: 67.8%

Nominated Adviser:	Collins Stewart, London
AIM Broker:	Collins Stewart, London
Solicitors:	Dechert, London
Market Makers:	CSCS; KBCS; SCAP; WINS
Auditors:	Grant Thornton, Cambridge
Registrars:	Capita Registrars

Entry on AIM:	22/5/2003	**Recent price:**	118.0p
Interim results:	Oct	**Market cap:**	£133.38m
Final results:	Mar	**Issue price:**	16.0p
Year end:	Dec	**Current no of shares:**	
Accounts due:	Jun		113,033,937
Int div paymnt:	n/a	**No of shares after**	
Fin div paymnt:	n/a	**dilution:**	n/a
Int net div per share:	nil	**P/E ratio:**	n/a
Fin net div per share:	nil	**Probable CGT?**	No

LATEST REPORTED RESULTS: FROM 22 MAY TO 31 DEC '03		PREVIOUS REPORTED RESULTS: N/A	
Turnover:	£947,000	Turnover:	n/a
PTP:	£(1.67m)	PTP:	£(408,000)
EPS:	(3.4)p	EPS:	n/a

Comments:

The developer of novel ways of delivering drugs, particularly via soluble gelatin-free films, has seen its shares jump more than sixfold since moving from Nasdaq to AIM last May. The group has signed some aggressive licensing deals and has recently taken over a US company that already has revenue from contracts with Boots and Wrigleys for its breath-freshening strips. Placings at 50p and 110p give the group over £17m cash to build up its commercial activities.

BioProjects (BIP)

Provider of funding and advice to early-stage biotechs

Inglisfield, Gifford, East Lothian, EH41 4JH Tel: 01620-810183; Fax: 01620-810167; e-mail: invest@bioprojects.com; web site: www.bioprojects.com

		holding %
Chairman	James Slater	9.1
Managing Director	Terence Bond	3.0
Finance Director		
Chief Operating Officer	John Broome	4.0
Main Shareholders:		
Atlas Capital S A		5.8
European Technology		4.0
Mountcashel		3.3
Northglen Investments		3.3

Percentage of free market capital: 66.3%

Nominated Adviser:	Seymour Pierce, London
AIM Broker:	Seymour Pierce, London
Solicitors:	Faegre Benson Hobson Audley, London
Market Makers:	SCAP; WINS
Auditors:	BDO Stoy Hayward, 8 Baker Street, London W1U 3LL
Registrars:	Capita Registrars

ENTRY ON AIM:	21/5/2002	Recent price:	6.5p
Interim results:	Dec	Market cap:	£17.23m
Final results:	Jun	Issue price:	6.0p
Year end:	Mar	Current no of shares:	
Accounts due:	Jul		265,000,000
Int div paymnt:	n/a	No of shares after	
Fin div paymnt:	n/a	dilution:	n/a
Int net div per share:	nil	P/E ratio:	n/a
Fin net div per share:	nil	Probable CGT?	YES

LATEST REPORTED RESULTS: 2003		PREVIOUS REPORTED RESULTS: 2002	
Turnover:	£25,000	Turnover:	£47,000
PTP:	£(2.40m)	PTP:	£(885,000)
EPS:	(1.0)p	EPS:	(0.5)p

Comments:

This is the vehicle that veteran investors Jim Slater and Terry Bond use to back early stage biotech and medical devices ventures, spun out of universities and government research agencies. The focus is on a handful of more promising projects, such as NASA spin-out ViaLogy, which has developed signal processing software for use in drug discovery, and Acolyte Biomedica, which is developing a technique to screen rapidly for hospital superbugs. Net assets stand at £5.8m, including £0.6m cash.

Birmingham City (BMC)

Professional football club operator

St Andrew's Stadium, Birmingham, B9 4NH Tel: 0121-772 0101; Fax: 0121-766 7866; web site: www.bcfc.com

		holding %
Chairman	David Sullivan*	0.0
Managing Director	Karren Brady	0.02
Finance Director	Roger Bannister	0.02
Non-Exec Director	Paul Richardson	0.5
Main Shareholders:		
Sport Newspapers*		77.5

Percentage of free market capital: 22.0%

*David Sullivan is a director of Sport Newspapers

Nominated Adviser:	Shore Capital, London
AIM Broker:	Shore Capital, London
Solicitors:	Henri Brandman, London; SJ Berwin, London
Market Makers:	MLSB; SCAP; WINS
Auditors:	RSM Robson Rhodes, Birmingham
Registrars:	Capita Registrars

Entry on AIM:	7/3/1997	Recent price:	16.5p
Interim results:	May	Market cap:	£13.2m
Final results:	Dec	Issue price:	50.0p
Year end:	Aug	Current no of shares:	
Accounts due:	Jan		80,000,000
Int div paymnt:	n/a	No of shares after	
Fin div paymnt:	n/a	dilution:	n/a
Int net div per share:	nil	P/E ratio:	3.9
Fin net div per share:	nil	Probable CGT?	YES

LATEST REPORTED RESULTS: 2003		PREVIOUS REPORTED RESULTS: 2002	
Turnover:	£36.48m	Turnover:	£15.18m
PTP:	£3.34m	PTP:	£(6.40m)
EPS:	4.2p	EPS:	(7.9)p

Comments:

The Midlands football club enjoyed an excellent year to August both financially and on the pitch. In its first season in the Premier League, the team finished thirteenth. Over the year, turnover more than doubled and Birmingham City swung into profit. Commercial income rose 27%, merchandising sales were up 19%, and the club now has 22,500 season ticket holders. Though a hefty 54% of turnover is spent on wages, that figure has to rise to improve the squad.

Bits Corp (BIT)

Video game software developer

112 Cricklewood Lane, London, NW2 2DP   Tel: 020-8282 7200; Fax: 020-8450 9966; web site: www.bitscorp.com

		holding %
Chairman	John Corre	0.0
Chief Executive	Foo Katan	2.4
Finance Director	Rob Hakim	0.02
Non-Exec Director	Julian Levy	1.3

Main Shareholders:

I Robot Holdings	30.4
Chase Nominees	18.2
New York Nominees	13.7
Mikto Pension Scheme	5.9
Chargegovern	4.8

Percentage of free market capital: 16.8

Comments:

Business seems to be improving at last for computer games developer Bits, which posted a small profit of £23,000 for the interim period against a loss of £556,000 in 2002. Sales increased 67.8% to £1.06m. Chief exec Foo Katan attributes much of the turnaround to improved risk-management systems. High hopes are reserved for a deal with leading industry figure Capcom to distribute Rogue Ops in Europe. However, interest in the company's last major project, Die Hard: Vendetta, was disappointing.

Nominated Adviser:	Collins Stewart, London
AIM Broker:	Collins Stewart, London
Solicitors:	Jones Day, London
Market Makers:	CSCS; WINS
Auditors:	Averbach Hope, 58-60 Berners Street, London W1T 3JS
Registrars:	Capita Registrars

Entry on AIM:	21/9/2000	**Recent price:**	3.1p
Interim results:	Dec	**Market cap:**	£1.36m
Final results:	Sep	**Issue price:**	60.0p
Year end:	Mar	**Current no of shares:**	
Accounts due:	Sep		43,991,690
Int div paymnt:	n/a	**No of shares after**	
Fin div paymnt:	n/a	**dilution:**	n/a
Int net div per share:	nil	**P/E ratio:**	n/a
Fin net div per share:	nil	**Probable CGT?**	**Yes**

LATEST REPORTED RESULTS: 2003		PREVIOUS REPORTED RESULTS: 2002	
Turnover:	£1.70m	Turnover:	£994,000
PTP:	£(572,000)	PTP:	£(1.73m)
EPS:	(1.3)p	EPS:	(5.5)p

Bizspace (BIZ)

Business accommodation provider

94-96 Great North Road, London, N2 0NL Tel: 020-8815 1616; Fax: 020-8815 1617; e-mail: info@biz-space.co.uk; web site: www.biz-space.co.uk

		holding %
Chairman	Larry Lipman*	0.6
Managing Director	Neil Corderey	0.2
Finance Director	Paul Davis	0.1
Non-Exec Director	Jonathen Radgick	0.0
Main Shareholders:		

Safeland*	17.5
Schroders Nominees	10.2
Safeland Holdings corporation	9.7
RBSTB Nominees	8.1
Chase Nominees	6.7

Percentage of free market capital: 18.6%

*Larry Lipman has a one-third beneficial interest in the issued share capital of Safeland

Comments:

Bizspace is a provider of flexible managed workspace to small- and medium-sized businesses. In November, it acquired seven new sites situated in the Greater Manchester region for £15.8m, which currently have a net income of £1.6m and over 80% occupancy levels. This was follwed in December with two further acquisitions in the Midlands for £2.4m. Its Newport business centre was sold in February for £2.05m. It had cost £1.25m three years ago.

Nominated Adviser:	Teather & Greenwood, London
AIM Broker:	Teather & Greenwood, London
Solicitors:	Dechert, London
Market Makers:	KBCS; MLSB; SCAP; WINS
Auditors:	Deloitte and Touche, London
Registrars:	Capita Registrars

Entry on AIM:	3/7/2000	**Recent price:**	36.0p
Interim results:	Aug	**Market cap:**	£13.69m
Final results:	Jun	**Issue price:**	70.0p
Year end:	Feb	**Current no of shares:**	
Accounts due:	Jun		38,026,351
Int div paymnt:	n/a	**No of shares after**	
Fin div paymnt:	n/a	**dilution:**	n/a
Int net div per share:	nil	**P/E ratio:**	12.9
Fin net div per share:	nil	**Probable CGT?**	**Yes**

LATEST REPORTED RESULTS: 2003		PREVIOUS REPORTED RESULTS: 2002	
Turnover:	£4.69m	Turnover:	£2.99m
PTP:	£1.32m	PTP:	407,000
EPS:	2.8p	EPS:	0.7p

BKN International (BKN)

Animated children's television programme distributor and marketer

Zulpicher Strabe 217, Cologne, 50937 Germany,

		holding %
Chairman	Allen Bohbot	9.4
Chief Executive	as above	
Finance Director	Wayne Mowat	0.4
Director	Jack Kugler	9.4

Main Shareholders:

Gordon Group	11.7
Eric Vik	6.7
Sony Pictures Family Entertainment	5.9
Capital Research	4.4
Star Asset Management	3.2

Percentage of free market capital: 48.9%

Comments:

Global animation venture BKN, which boasts Highlander in its film library, was the first company listed on the Frankfurt Stock Exchange to list on AIM under new 'fast track' rules. BKN distributes and markets animated kids' TV shows and related consumer products.

Nominated Adviser:	Teather & Greenwood, London		
AIM Broker:	Westhouse Securities, London		
Solicitors:	Maclay Murray Spens, London		
Market Makers:	TEAM; WINS		
Auditors:	BTR Beratung und Treuhand Ring GmbHWirtschaft, Düsseldorf, Germany		
Registrars:	Capita Registrars		

ENTRY ON AIM: 16/12/2003		**Recent price:**	192.5p
Interim results:	Sep	**Market cap:**	£26.0m
Final results:	Jan	**Issue price:**	n/a
Year end:	Sep	**Current no of shares:**	
Accounts due:	Apr		13,506,484
Int div paymnt:	n/a	**No of shares after**	
Fin div paymnt:	n/a	**dilution:**	n/a
Int net div per share:	nil	**P/E ratio:**	n/a
Fin net div per share:	nil	**Probable CGT?**	No

LATEST REPORTED RESULTS: 2003		PREVIOUS REPORTED RESULTS: 2002	
Turnover:	£403,000	**Turnover:**	£648,000
PTP:	£(8.99m)	**PTP:**	£(3.22m)
EPS:	(15.5)p	**EPS:**	(11.4)p

Black Arrow (BLKA)

Office furniture distributor, contractor & finance provider

748 London Road, Hounslow, Middlesex TW3 1PD Tel: 020-8572 7474; Fax: 020-8572 9188

		holding %
Chairman	Arnold Edward	16.2
Chief Executive	as above	
Finance Director	Ronald Waxman	0.0
Director	Maurice Edward	15.3

Main Shareholders:

Mrs A Marsden	7.6
S Harris	4.5
Paul Edward	4.4
Peter Edward	3.8

Percentage of free market capital: 40.8%

Comments:

Office furniture manufacturer and distributor Black Arrow dropped from the Full List to AIM in April 2003 in a bid to cut costs. From the look of the company's interims, however, which revealed an alarming slump in profits from £938,000 to just £56,000, much still needs to be done. In addition to its core furniture business, Black Arrow also provides a contracting and fit-out service for offices and offers leasing finance for plant and machinery.

Nominated Adviser:	Ernst & Young, London		
AIM Broker:	WH Ireland, London		
Solicitors:	Kidd Rapinet, London		
Market Makers:	KBCS; MLSB; SCAP; WINS		
Auditors:	Ernst & Young LLP, Rolls House, 7 Rolls Buildings, Fetter Lane, London EC4A 1NH		
Registrars:	Computershare Investor Services		

Entry on AIM: 16/4/2003		**Recent price:**	65.0p
Interim results:	Nov	**Market cap:**	£13.26m
Final results:	Jul	**Issue price:**	n/a
Year end:	Mar	**Current no of shares:**	
Accounts due:	Sep		20,394,819
Int div paymnt:	n/a	**No of shares after**	
Fin div paymnt:	Mar	**dilution:**	n/a
Int net div per share:	nil	**P/E ratio:**	15.9
Fin net div per share:	2.0p	**Probable CGT?**	Yes

LATEST REPORTED RESULTS: 2003		PREVIOUS REPORTED RESULTS: 2002	
Turnover:	£17.30m	**Turnover:**	£18.17m
PTP:	£1.17m	**PTP:**	£613,000
EPS:	4.1p	**EPS:**	2.0p

Black Rock Oil & Gas   (BLR)

Oil & gas explorer
30 Farringdon Street, London, EC4A 4HJ Tel: 0207-544 5677; Fax: 0207-544 5565;
web site: www.blackrockpetroleum.com.au

		holding %
Chairman	David Steinepreis*	10.3
Managing Director	as above	
Finance Director		
Non-Exec Director	Gary Steinepreis	0.0

Main Shareholders:

C Rowan	14.8
N&J Mitchell	8.8
Cezanne Investments	8.0
Agon Investments	7.0
John Scott*	5.6

Percentage of free market capital: 32.9%

*Shares held by these directors are non-beneficial

Comments:
After a bruising period of aborted projects, Black Rock has been sounding optimistic about impending appraisal drilling at the Isle of Wight's Sandhills 2 well, which it says could be part of a potential deposit containing 9.7 million 'probable' barrels of oil and 15.3 million 'potential' barrels. The company, which reduced its losses from £2.8m to £787,000 last year, has a 5% free carried interest in the well and remains a high-risk punt.

Nominated Adviser:	Corporate Synergy, London
AIM Broker:	Corporate Synergy, London
Solicitors:	Watson, Farley & Williams, London
Market Makers:	HOOD; WINS
Auditors:	Hacker Young, London
Registrars:	Computershare Investor Services

ENTRY ON AIM:	25/4/2001	**Recent price:**	2.0p
Interim results:	Mar	Market cap:	£2.31m
Final results:	Dec	Issue price:	5.0p
Year end:	Jun	Current no of shares:	
Accounts due:	Oct		115,265,200
Int div paymnt:	n/a	No of shares after	
Fin div paymnt:	n/a	dilution:	n/a
Int net div per share:	nil	P/E ratio:	n/a
Fin net div per share:	nil	Probable CGT?	No

LATEST REPORTED RESULTS:	2003	PREVIOUS REPORTED RESULTS:	2002
Turnover:	n/a	Turnover:	n/a
PTP:	£(787,000)	PTP:	£(2.77m)
EPS:	(0.8)p	EPS:	(3.3)p

Blavod Extreme Spirits   (BES)

Independent drinks company
202 Fulham Road, London, SW10 9PJ Tel: 020-7352 2096; Fax: 020-7823 3510; e-mail: info@blavod.com;
web site: www.blavod.com

		holding %
Chairman	Allan Shiach	0.6
Chief Executive	Jeffrey Hopmayer	2.7
Finance Director	Fred Read	0.0
Managing Director	Richard Ambler	0.0

Main Shareholders:

Extreme	15.1
Bero SCA	10.7
Artemis	8.5
Herrick Investissements SAS	4.1

Percentage of free market capital: 58.5%

Comments:
The black vodka drinks group is taking a shot at the US with the purchase of American spirits company Extreme Beverage, which produces vodka, rum and gin, via a reverse takeover. Interim losses decreased almost 50% to £247,000. Turnover was down to £557,000 but gross profit margins grew to 36.5%. With UK distribution of Domaines Baron de Rothschild wines and Mickey Finns Schnapps increasing, it expects to be in the black next year.

Nominated Adviser:	Evolution Beeson Gregory, London
AIM Broker:	Evolution Beeson Gregory, London
Solicitors:	Maclay, Murray Spens, London
Market Makers:	MLSB; WINS
Auditors:	Nexia Audit, Loondon
Registrars:	Capita Registrars

Entry on AIM:	26/2/2001	**Recent price:**	37.5p
Interim results:	Dec	Market cap:	£24.54m
Final results:	Jun	Issue price:	24.5p
Year end:	Mar	Current no of shares:	
Accounts due:	Oct		65,443,633
Int div paymnt:	n/a	No of shares after	
Fin div paymnt:	n/a	dilution:	n/a
Int net div per share:	nil	P/E ratio:	n/a
Fin net div per share:	nil	Probable CGT?	YES

LATEST REPORTED RESULTS:	2003	PREVIOUS REPORTED RESULTS:	2002
Turnover:	£1.51m	Turnover:	£1.15m
PTP:	£(581,000)	PTP:	£(1.16m)
EPS:	(3.9)p	EPS:	(7.9)p

Blooms of Bressingham (BBR)

Garden centre operator

Bath Road, Haresfield, Nr. Stonehouse, Gloucester GL10 3DP Tel: 01452-887530; Fax: 01452-722445;
e-mail: rs@blooms-uk.com; web site: www.blooms-online.com

		holding %
Chairman	Charles Good	9.1
Chief Executive	Jon Kitching	5.2
Finance Director	Wendy King	0.0
Deputy Chairman	Christopher Baker	0.04

Main Shareholders:

Ari Zaphiriou-Zarifi	8.7
Bank of New York Nominees	7.9
Direct Nominees	6.0
Singer & Friedlander AIM 3	5.3

Percentage of free market capital: 34.1%

Nominated Adviser:	Teather & Greenwood, London	
AIM Broker:	Teather & Greenwood, London	
Solicitors:	Wedlake Bell, London	
Market Makers:	KBCS; WINS	
Auditors:	Grant Thornton, Southampton	
Registrars:	Capita Registrars	

ENTRY ON AIM: 20/12/1999		**Recent price:**	44.5p
Interim results:	Oct	**Market cap:**	£10.96m
Final results:	Jun	**Issue price:**	125.0p
Year end:	Jan	**Current no of shares:**	
Accounts due:	May		24,628,872
Int div paymnt:	n/a	**No of shares after**	
Fin div paymnt:	n/a	**dilution:**	n/a
Int net div per share:	nil	**P/E ratio:**	n/a
Fin net div per share:	nil	**Probable CGT?**	YES

LATEST REPORTED RESULTS: 2003		PREVIOUS REPORTED RESULTS: 2002	
Turnover:	£18.45m	Turnover:	£16.93m
PTP:	£(596,000)	PTP:	£(3.96m)
EPS:	(2.4)p	EPS:	(22.0)p

Comments:

Blooms, named after the famous gardens at Bressingham in Norfolk, has apparently been undergoing a 'quiet but highly significant revolution' during the past 18 months as it moved to profitability. For the year to mid-January like-for-likes were up 9.2% and group sales increased 1.5%. It has also just completed the sale of five small non-core leasehold centres and will buy the freehold of its Cardiff garden centre for £2.5m.

BNB Resources (BNB)

Human resources solutions provider

30 Farringdon Street, London, EC4A 4EA Tel: 020-7634 1200; Fax: 020-7489 9330; e-mail: clairep@bnb.co.uk;
web site: www.bnb-global.com

		holding %
Chairman	Julian Treger	0.1
Acting Chief Executive	Simon Grinstead	2.5
Finance Director	Paul Turner	0.3
Non-Exec Director	John Redwood	0.1

Main Shareholders:

Montelle Properties	21.9
Xanthus	21.0
Round Enterprises	19.6
Electra Quoted Management	6.1
The & Trust	4.4

Percentage of free market capital: 22.4%

Nominated Adviser:	Shore Capital, London	
AIM Broker:	Shore Capital, London	
Solicitors:	Stephenson Harwood, London	
Market Makers:	CAZR; SCAP; WINS	
Auditors:	RSM Robson Rhodes, 186 City Road, London EC1V 2NU	
Registrars:	Capita Registrars	

Entry on AIM:	10/1/2002	**Recent price:**	15.0p
Interim results:	Sep	**Market cap:**	£11.64m
Final results:	Apr	**Issue price:**	39.5p
Year end:	Dec	**Current no of shares:**	
Accounts due:	Apr		77,631,175
Int div paymnt:	n/a	**No of shares after**	
Fin div paymnt:	n/a	**dilution:**	n/a
Int net div per share:	nil	**P/E ratio:**	n/a
Fin net div per share:	nil	**Probable CGT?**	YES

LATEST REPORTED RESULTS: 2002		PREVIOUS REPORTED RESULTS: 2001	
Turnover:	£116.87m	Turnover:	£139.29m
PTP:	£(4.52m)	PTP:	£(18.92m)
EPS:	(12.7)p	EPS:	(87.0)p

Comments:

Restructured BNB made an overall loss last year, but continuing losses before exceptionals were cut significantly and turnover rose nearly 6% in a tough recruitment market. Management was particularly pleased with the Barkers recruitment arm, which grew market share. And its Norman Broadbent and Garfield Robbins businesses saw improved conditions and demand in the year's second half. BNB is also buying the Apollo Group, aided by an £8m fundraising.

Bond International Software (BDI)

Specialist software provider

Courtlands, Parklands Avenue, Goring-by-Sea, West Sussex BN12 4NG Tel: 01903-707070; Fax: 01903-707080;
e-mail: mclements@bond.co.uk; web site: www.bondadapt.com

		holding %
Chairman	Martin Baldwin	0.2
Chief Executive	Stephen R Russell	53.3
Finance Director	Bruce Morrison	0.0
European CEO	Timothy Richards	6.2

Main Shareholders:

Westpool Investment Trust	11.8
Advent VCT	5.4
Capita Trust	3.2

Percentage of free market capital: 19.5%

Nominated Adviser:	Grant Thornton, Fareham
AIM Broker:	Seymour Pierce, London
Solicitors:	Coole & Haddock, Horsham
Market Makers:	DURM; KBCS; SCAP; WINS
Auditors:	Baker Tilly, London
Registrars:	Melton Registrars

Comments:

As well as the expected return to profits Bond's full year figures also brought news of the $5m acquisition of EZaccess, a rival recruitment-sector software supplier with a particularly strong presence in the US. Having generated $2.5m of revenue last year, EZaccess is expected to be earnings enhancing from the off, and with Bond itself noting an uptick in activity across all its core markets in recent months, 2004 looks likely to be a strong year for the company.

ENTRY ON AIM: 30/12/1997	Recent price:	50.5p
Interim results: Sep	Market cap:	£7.41m
Final results: Mar	Issue price:	65.0p
Year end: Dec	Current no of shares:	
Accounts due: Apr		14,666,232
Int div paymnt: n/a	No of shares after	
Fin div paymnt: n/a	dilution:	n/a
Int net div per share: nil	P/E ratio:	23.0
Fin net div per share: nil	Probable CGT?	Yes

LATEST REPORTED RESULTS: 2003	PREVIOUS REPORTED RESULTS: 2002
Turnover: £7.04m	Turnover: £6.4m
PTP: £451,000	PTP: £(1.97m)
EPS: 2.2p	EPS: (13.8)p

Booth Industries (BTHI)

Engineering and related services

PO Box 50, Nelson Street, Bolton, Lancashire BL3 2AP Tel: 01204-366333; Fax: 01204-380888;
web site: www.booth-industries.co.uk

		holding %
Chairman	Derek Ablett	0.2
Managing Director	William Robson	0.0
Finance Director	Christopher Lewis-Jones	0.0
Non-Exec Director	Roger McDowell	0.0

Main Shareholders:

Willbro Nominees	29.9
Otani	17.3
Intrinsic Value	9.3
Fircroft	7.1
W Robson	3.2

Percentage of free market capital: 29.8%

Nominated Adviser:	Brewin Dolphin, London
AIM Broker:	Brewin Dolphin, London
Solicitors:	Martineau Johnson, Birmingham
Market Makers:	KBCS; WINS
Auditors:	Ernst & Young, 1 Colmore Row, Birmingham B3 2DB
Registrars:	Capita Registrars

Comments:

The Full List refugee saw a drop in continuing turnover, particularly at Jordan Projects, as well as reduced operating losses. But the year was dominated by two projects – the refocusing of Jordan away from certain markets towards its core skills in the nuclear industry. And the sale of Oakland Elevators, which is normally Booth's 'strongest contributor'. Oakland disappointed and was sold for £7.7m in September.

Entry on AIM: 2/7/2003	Recent price:	30.5p
Interim results: Oct	Market cap:	£4.07m
Final results: Jan	Issue price:	12.5p
Year end: Sep	Current no of shares:	
Accounts due: Apr		13,353,606
Int div paymnt: n/a	No of shares after	
Fin div paymnt: n/a	dilution:	n/a
Int net div per share: nil	P/E ratio:	n/a
Fin net div per share: nil	Probable CGT?	Yes

LATEST REPORTED RESULTS: 2002	PREVIOUS REPORTED RESULTS: 2001
Turnover: £54.83m	Turnover: £31.59m
PTP: £(2.39m)	PTP: £339,000
EPS: (17.9)p	EPS: 2.0p

Bradstock (suspended 29 Sep 2003)   (BDK)
Reinsurance broker
Knollys House, 9-13 Byward Streeet, London, EC3R 5AS Tel: 020-7712 7500; Fax: 020-7712 1212;
web site: www.bradstock.co.uk

		holding %
Chairman	N M Bryce-Smith	0.8
Chief Executive	as above	
Finance Director	David Griffiths	0.6
Director	R Jeffreys	0.5

Main Shareholders:

Belgate PTY Ltd	12.7
B Austin	6.8
P W J Cresswell	5.5
Capital Cranfield Trustees Ltd	4.8
Rieg Gibson	4.5

Percentage of free market capital: 62.8%

Nominated Adviser:	Credit Lyonnais, London
AIM Broker:	Credit Lyonnais, London
Solicitors:	Berwin Leighton Paisner, London
Market Makers:	WINS
Auditors:	Deloitte & Touche, 1 Little New St, London EC4A 3TR
Registrars:	Lloyds TSB Registrars

ENTRY ON AIM:	3/3/2003	Recent price:	44.0p
Interim results:	Jun	Market cap:	£1.23m
Final results:	Jan	Issue price:	105.0p
Year end:	Sep	Current no of shares:	
Accounts due:	Mar		2,799,992
Int div paymnt:	n/a	No of shares after	
Fin div paymnt:	n/a	dilution:	n/a
Int net div per share:	nil	P/E ratio:	n/a
Fin net div per share:	nil	Probable CGT?	No

LATEST REPORTED RESULTS:	2002	PREVIOUS REPORTED RESULTS:	2001
Turnover:	£2.22m	Turnover:	£5.22m
PTP:	£4.84m	PTP:	£(8.29m)
EPS:	(3.8)p	EPS:	(0.3)p

Comments:
Shares in reinsurance broker Bradstock have been suspended since September 2003, when the company was unable to obtain professional indemnity cover following pension mis-selling problems and £1.7m net liabilities arising from its own big pension fund deficit. Gareth Hughes and Martin Fishman of accountant Ernst & Young were appointed joint provisional liquidators.

Brainspark   (BSP)
Internet-related business incubator
The Lightwell, 12/16 Laystall Street, Clerkenwell, London, EC1R 4PF Tel: 020-7843 6600; Fax: 020-7843 6601;
e-mail: email@brainspark.com; web site: www.brainspark.com

		holding %
Chairman	Alberta Agosta	0.0
Chief Executive	Francesco Gardin	0.0
Finance Director		
Non-Exec Director	David Meacher	0.0

Main Shareholders:

Cross Atlantic Technology	27.1
HATT III LP	21.2
Uni-invest Special Aktier	5.3

Percentage of free market capital: 46.4%

Nominated Adviser:	Beaumont Cornish, London
AIM Broker:	Evolution Beeson Gregory, London
Solicitors:	Jones Day Gouldens, London
Market Makers:	DURM; KBCS; MLSB; SCAP; SSSB; WINS
Auditors:	PricewaterhouseCoopers, Reading, Berkshire RG1 1JG
Registrars:	Capita Registrars

Entry on AIM:	7/4/2000	Recent price:	1.0p
Interim results:	Sep	Market cap:	£1.87m
Final results:	Jun	Issue price:	125.0p
Year end:	Dec	Current no of shares:	
Accounts due:	Apr		187,404,909
Int div paymnt:	n/a	No of shares after	
Fin div paymnt:	n/a	dilution:	n/a
Int net div per share:	nil	P/E ratio:	n/a
Fin net div per share:	nil	Probable CGT?	No

LATEST REPORTED RESULTS:	2002	PREVIOUS REPORTED RESULTS:	2001
Turnover:	n/a	Turnover:	n/a
PTP:	£(12.93m)	PTP:	£(14.56m)
EPS:	(10.5)p	EPS:	(14.9)p

Comments:
Internet incubator Brainspark now has stakes in a dozen or so web-related businesses, following a merger with Italian consultant AISoftware and its own investment vehicle Infusion. Interim losses doubled to £1.6m, reflecting write-downs which saw net assets fall 24% in the first half to £5.1m. Cashflow remains a problem. Directors are now paid in shares rather than cash and a £500,000 loan note issue was arranged with an Italian bank.

Brazilian Diamonds (BDY)

Diamond exploration & kimberlite developer

Suite 209, 475 Howe Street, Vancouver, British Columbia V6C 2B3 Canada,

		holding %
Chairman	Kenneth Judge	0.0
Chief Executive		
President	Stephen Fabian	0.0
Non-Exec Director	Roger Morton	0.0

Main Shareholders:
n/a

Percentage of free market capital: 100.0%

Comments:
Run by entrepreneur Ken Judge, Toronto-star Brazilian Diamonds is pursuing gem prospects in the Brazilian state of Minas Gerais and secured £330,000 from local joint venture partners COMIG (a royalty holder) and MRN. Judge has claimed 'encouraging' grades of 6.3 to 21.77 grammes a tonne at the company's Cata Preta gold project.

Nominated Adviser:	Westhouse Securities, London
AIM Broker:	Westhouse Securities, London
Solicitors:	Growling Lafleur Henderson, Vancouver
Market Makers:	KBCS; WINS
Auditors:	PricewaterhouseCoopers, British Columbia, Canada
Registrars:	Capita Registrars

ENTRY ON AIM:	8/12/2003	Recent price:	29.5p
Interim results:	n/a	Market cap:	£30.95m
Final results:	n/a	Issue price:	n/a
Year end:	n/a	Current no of shares:	
Accounts due:	n/a		104,899,608
Int div paymnt:	n/a	No of shares after	
Fin div paymnt:	n/a	dilution:	n/a
Int net div per share:	nil	P/E ratio:	n/a
Fin net div per share:	nil	Probable CGT?	No

LATEST REPORTED RESULTS: 2003		PREVIOUS REPORTED RESULTS: 2002	
Turnover:	n/a	Turnover:	n/a
PTP:	$(4.41m)	PTP:	$(12.45m)
EPS:	(0.1)c	EPS:	(0.2)c

Successful investing with Growth Company Investor

Growth Company Investor is widely regarded as the UK's leading magazine on fast-growing companies. Published 10 times a year it offers Growth Company Investor unrivalled insight into high-potential smaller companies.

Each issue is packed full to the brim with share recommendations, informative features, directors' dealings and brokers' tips. Subscribers also benefit from online services at www.growthcompany.co.uk, including daily recommendations, company updates, prices and charts.

To subscribe at the reduced rate of just £59.50 for the first year (normally £119.50), simply call 020 7430 9777 or visit www.growthcompany.co.uk today.

Growth Company Investor is published by Growth Company Investor Ltd, a wholly owned subsidiary of Vitesse Media plc, 95 Aldwych, London WC2B 4JF

Bright Futures (BRF)

Provider of enabling information and mobility products for disabled customers

Unit 21, Planetary Road, Willenhall, West Midlands, WV13 3XA Tel: 0121-609 7238

		holding %
Chairman	Anthony Leon	0.1
Chief Executive	Stephen Harpin	9.1
Finance Director	Lance Hickman	12.8
Non-Exec Director	Emma Edelson	0.2

Main Shareholders:

Fiske Nominees	25.9
Ortho-Kinetics	22.7
Joseph Rajko	9.7
Michael Holoway	6.1
Wick Holdings	3.6

Percentage of free market capital: 16.5%

Nominated Adviser:	Altium Capital, London
AIM Broker:	Fiske, London
Solicitors:	Kuit Steinart Levy, Manchester
Market Makers:	SCAP; WINS
Auditors:	Horwath Clark Whitehill, Manchester
Registrars:	Capita Registrars

ENTRY ON AIM:	5/8/2002	Recent price:	8.25p
Interim results:	Dec	Market cap:	£2.75m
Final results:	Jun	Issue price:	20.0p
Year end:	Dec	Current no of shares:	
Accounts due:	Apr		33,350,020
Int div paymnt:	n/a	No of shares after	
Fin div paymnt:	n/a	dilution:	n/a
Int net div per share:	nil	P/E ratio:	n/a
Fin net div per share:	nil	Probable CGT?	Yes

LATEST REPORTED RESULTS: FROM 19 NOV '01 TO 31 DEC '02		PREVIOUS REPORTED RESULTS:	N/A
Turnover:	£1.96m	Turnover:	n/a
PTP:	£(2.83m)	PTP:	n/a
EPS:	(22.0)p	EPS:	n/a

Comments:

Bright Futures is the holding vehicle for The Mobility Group, Scootermart and Youreable.com, and sells 'age and disability' equipment. Its management is now able to concentrate on the company's retail store opening programme, following the sale of its 49% stake in joint venture route2mobility, a non-core financing business, to the joint venture partner. In the first half of the year to 30 June, Bright Futures made £66,888 before goodwill on £2.63m sales.

Bristol & London (BTL)

Vehicle credit hire company

1st & 2nd Floor Offices, 21 - 23 High Street, Portishead, Bristol, BS20 6AD Tel: 01275-858888; Fax: 01275-851888;
e-mail: info@bristolandlondon.com; web site: www.bristolandlondon.com

		holding %
Chairman	Robert Woods	0.03
Chief Executive	Richard Abel	95.3
Finance Director	Andrew Daw	0.0
Non-Executive Director	Robert Bailey	0.0

Main Shareholders:

n/a

Percentage of free market capital: 4.7%

Nominated Adviser:	Rowan Dartington, Bristol
AIM Broker:	Rowan Dartington, Bristol
Solicitors:	Burges Salmon, Bristol
Market Makers:	SCAP; WINS
Auditors:	KPMG, 100 Temple Street, Bristol BS1 6AG
Registrars:	Neville Registrars

ENTRY ON AIM:	25/9/2003	Recent price:	87.0p
Interim results:	Oct	Market cap:	£21.05m
Final results:	Mar	Issue price:	130.0p
Year end:	Jan	Current no of shares:	
Accounts due:	May		24,197,352
Int div paymnt:	n/a	No of shares after	
Fin div paymnt:	n/a	dilution:	n/a
Int net div per share:	nil	P/E ratio:	11.4
Fin net div per share:	nil	Probable CGT?	No

LATEST REPORTED RESULTS: 2003		PREVIOUS REPORTED RESULTS: 2002	
Turnover:	£7.26m	Turnover:	£3.46m
PTP:	£2.66m	PTP:	£1.04m
EPS:	7.6p	EPS:	3.0p

Comments:

Shares in the provider of vehicle credit hire facilities have drifted since joining AIM last September, after issuing a profit warning, saying that margins had been affected by increasing competition. Founder and chief executive Richard Abel, who still owns 95% of the company, plans to declare a dividend of 1.5 times earnings. The group's business is to hire out prestige cars to blameless road accident victims.

Bristol & West Investments (BWE)

Provider of short-term property finance

12 Eclipse Office Park, High Street, Staple Hill, Bristol, BS16 5EL Tel: 0117-970 2703; Fax: 0117-970 2303;
e-mail: info@bridgingloans.com; web site: www.bridgingloans.com

		holding %
Chairman	Royston Smith	26.2
Managing Director	Martyn Smith	10.6
Finance Director		
Non-Exec Director	Stanley Cohen*	30.2
Main Shareholders:		
Joseph Cummings		4.3

Percentage of free market capital: 28.3%

*Includes the holdings of Glenmore Investments, a company controlled by Stanley Cohen

Comments:
The bridging loans specialist continues to prosper from the buoyant property market. In the first half pre-tax profits perked up 11% to £0.84m as sales surged 22% to £1.66m. Gross mortgage advances – the actual value of the bridging loans – rose 29% to £21.1m. For the full year Rowan Dartington forecasts a £1.75m pre-tax profit, giving EPS of 1.3p, and a 0.24p payout. This superb performance has prompted an unsuccessful bid approach.

Nominated Adviser:	Rowan Dartington, Bristol
AIM Broker:	Rowan Dartington, Bristol
Solicitors:	Osborne Clarke, Bristol; TLT, Bristol
Market Makers:	MLSB; SCAP; WINS
Auditors:	Bentley Jennison, Bristol
Registrars:	Computershare Investor Services

ENTRY ON AIM:	6/3/2000	Recent price:	10.0p
Interim results:	Oct	Market cap:	£9.29m
Final results:	May	Issue price:	7.0p
Year end:	Mar	Current no of shares:	
Accounts due:	Jun		92,857,143
Int div paymnt:	Jan	No of shares after	
Fin div paymnt:	Jul	dilution:	97,562,143
Int net div per share:	0.06p	P/E ratio:	9.1
Fin net div per share:	0.14p	Probable CGT?	YES

LATEST REPORTED RESULTS:	2003	PREVIOUS REPORTED RESULTS:	2002
Turnover:	£3.04m	Turnover:	£2.51m
PTP:	£1.52m	PTP:	£1.25m
EPS:	1.1p	EPS:	1.0p

Buckland (BUC)

Industrial investor

3 Draycott Place, London, SW3 2SE Tel: 01285-831492

		holding %
Chairman	Patrick C R C Rogers*	15.6
Managing Director	as above	
Finance Director		
Non-Exec Director	Lee Sharples*	15.6
Main Shareholders:		
Wharton Holdings Corporation*		15.6
CI Law Trustees		13.7
Groupe Industriel Electronique		13.7
Philip E Palmer		13.7

Percentage of free market capital: 57.0%

*Shares held on behalf of a discretionary trust, in which Mr Rogers' & Dr Sharples' families are beneficiaries

Comments:
Towards the end of 2003, a £200,000 placing priced at 0.5p bolstered the working capital position at Buckland. In the first half to June, the supplier of CRT sockets and SCART connectors to consumer electronics makers achieved pre-exceptional profits of £21,000 on higher sales of £2.35m (£2.29m). Unfortunately, an £81,000 exceptional hit concerning a factory closure and transfer to Bangkok pulled the company to losses of £60,000 (£61,000).

Nominated Adviser:	Seymour Pierce, London
AIM Broker:	Seymour Pierce, London
Solicitors:	McFadden, Pilkington & Ward, London
Market Makers:	MLSB; WINS
Auditors:	BDO Stoy Hayward, 8 Baker Street, London WIM 1DA
Registrars:	Capita Registrars

ENTRY ON AIM:	6/3/1998	Recent price:	0.6p
Interim results:	Sep	Market cap:	£1.14m
Final results:	Jul	Issue price:	15.0p
Year end:	Dec	Current no of shares:	
Accounts due:	Jun		190,779,408
Int div paymnt:	n/a	No of shares after	
Fin div paymnt:	n/a	dilution:	n/a
Int net div per share:	nil	P/E ratio:	6.0
Fin net div per share:	nil	Probable CGT?	YES

LATEST REPORTED RESULTS:	2002	PREVIOUS REPORTED RESULTS:	2001
Turnover:	£4.79m	Turnover:	£5.81m
PTP:	£122,000	PTP:	£(86,000)
EPS:	0.1p	EPS:	(0.6p)

Bullion Resources (BLO)

Holding company for gold mining companies in South Africa

1 The Green, Richmond, Surrey TW9 1PL Tel: 020-7409 0890; Fax: 0207-409 2750; web site: www.bullionresources.net

		holding %
Chairman	J B Meiring*	10.6
Chief Executive		
Finance Director	D M Bank	1.6
Non-Exec Director	A T Ogilvie Thompson	0.0

Main Shareholders:

S F Mellett	22.4
Elcor	17.7
J van den Berg	11.3
Golden Prospect	6.4

Percentage of free market capital: 30.1%

* Shares are held through JBM Gold Holdings

Comments:

Bullion Resources has been looking for a deal since ex-boss Johnny van den Berg and director Fanie Mellett quit over queries about assets claimed in 2002's £5m AIM prospectus. South Africa's Council of Natural Scientific Professions has ruled that Dr Vermaakt, author of the 'competent persons"report in the prospectus, 'transgressed the council's Code of Professional Conduct ' and 'misled the public'.

Nominated Adviser:	Grant Thornton, London
AIM Broker:	Insinger Townsley, London
Solicitors:	Amhurst Brown Colombotti, London
Market Makers:	KBCS; SCAP; WINS
Auditors:	Grant Thornton, Segensworth, Hampshire PO15 5GT
Registrars:	Melton Registrars

ENTRY ON AIM:	10/6/2002	Recent price:	5.0p
Interim results:	Oct	Market cap:	£2.31m
Final results:	May	Issue price:	40.0p
Year end:	Feb	Current no of shares:	
Accounts due:	Jul		46,250,000
Int div paymnt:	n/a	No of shares after	
Fin div paymnt:	n/a	dilution:	n/a
Int net div per share:	nil	P/E ratio:	n/a
Fin net div per share:	nil	Probable CGT?	No

LATEST REPORTED RESULTS: 2002		PREVIOUS REPORTED RESULTS: N/A	
Turnover:	n/a	Turnover:	n/a
PTP:	£(1.66m)	PTP:	n/a
EPS:	(6.2)p	EPS:	n/a

Business Serve (BRV)

Internet service provider

Riversway House, Morecombe Road, Lancaster, Lancashire LA1 2SS Tel: 08707-555565; Fax: 08707-555567

		holding %
Chairman	Lord Baker	2.9
Managing Director	Simon Cleaver	28.3
Finance Director	Christopher Baron	0.0
Operations Director	Tim Longton	0.0

Main Shareholders:

EBT	9.7
Carl Holt	4.3
Canada Life Marketing	3.5

Percentage of free market capital: 51.3%

Comments:

Aside from its famous chairman, Business Serve's other claim to fame is its ability to make profits in an area where many others have tried and failed. The group's ISP service has around 18,000 customers, ranging from SMEs to large blue chips. Teather & Greenwood's placing raised no less than £17.5m. As certain existing shareholders were selling, the amount of new money actually raised for the company was £3.9m after expenses. An interesting play in a fragmented market.

Nominated Adviser:	Teather & Greenwood, London
AIM Broker:	Teather & Greenwood, London
Solicitors:	DWF, Manchester
Market Makers:	WINS
Auditors:	Baker Tilly, Manchester
Registrars:	Capita Registrars

ENTRY ON AIM:	3/2/2004	Recent price:	74.5p
Interim results:	Jan	Market cap:	£16.8m
Final results:	Jul	Issue price:	78.0p
Year end:	Mar	Current no of shares:	
Accounts due:	Sep		22,544,716
Int div paymnt:	n/a	No of shares after	
Fin div paymnt:	n/a	dilution:	n/a
Int net div per share:	nil	P/E ratio:	n/a
Fin net div per share:	nil	Probable CGT?	No

LATEST REPORTED RESULTS: 2003		PREVIOUS REPORTED RESULTS: 2002	
Turnover:	£8.09m	Turnover:	£5.52m
PTP:	£52,000	PTP:	£(513,000)
EPS:	nil	EPS:	nil

BWA (BWP)
Cash Shell
50 Broadway, Westminster, London, SW1H 0BL

		holding %
Chairman	David Steavenson	3.4
Chief Executive		
Finance Director		
Non-Exec Director	Richard Battersby	1.7

Main Shareholders:

Percentage of free market capital: 95.0%

Nominated Adviser:	Beaumont Cornish, London
AIM Broker:	Fiske, London
Solicitors:	Bircham Dyson Bell, London
Market Makers:	SCAP; WINS
Auditors:	Malthouse & Company, Liverpool
Registrars:	Capita Registrars

ENTRY ON AIM: 18/12/2003		Recent price:	2.1p
Interim results:	n/a	Market cap:	£0.38m
Final results:	n/a	Issue price:	n/a
Year end:	n/a	Current no of shares:	
Accounts due:	n/a		17,966,627
Int div paymnt:	n/a	No of shares after	
Fin div paymnt:	n/a	dilution:	n/a
Int net div per share:	nil	P/E ratio:	n/a
Fin net div per share:	nil	Probable CGT?	No

LATEST REPORTED RESULTS: N/A		PREVIOUS REPORTED RESULTS: N/A	
Turnover:	n/a	Turnover:	n/a
PTP:	n/a	PTP:	n/a
EPS:	n/a	EPS:	n/a

Comments:
This cash shell has been resurrected by Peter Redmond and Richard Armstrong from the ashes of fully-listed British World Aviation, which fell into receivership after September 11th 2001. Outstanding liabilities have been tidied up and £310,000 has been raised by Fiske. The aim is to find a suitable business, possibly in the manufacturing or support systems sectors, to reverse into the shell and restore shareholder's fortunes. If nothing has happened after two years, remaining proceeds will be returned to shareholders.

CA Coutts (CAH)
In-store displays & packaging designer & manufacturer
Violet Road, London, E3 3QL Tel: 020-7510 9292; Fax: 020-7510 9293; e-mail: investor@crc-uk.com; web site: www.cacouttsholdings.com

		holding %
Chairman	Robert Essex	8.8
Chief Executive	as above	
Finance Director	Graeme Harris	0.2
Deputy Chairman	Stuart Alexander	2.4

Main Shareholders:

NA Essex	11.0
Close Finsbury Asset Management	8.3
Framlington	7.3
Singer & Friedlander	5.8
ISIS	5.0

Percentage of free market capital: 43.2%

Nominated Adviser:	Williams de Broe, London
AIM Broker:	Williams de Broe, London
Solicitors:	Nabarro Nathanson, London
Market Makers:	BGMM; WINS, WDBM
Auditors:	Ernst & Young, London
Registrars:	Capita Registrars

ENTRY ON AIM:	9/5/1996	Recent price:	119.5p
Interim results:	Sep	Market cap:	£15.32m
Final results:	Mar	Issue price:	105.0p
Year end:	Dec	Current no of shares:	
Accounts due:	Mar		12,823,276
Int div paymnt:	Oct	No of shares after	
Fin div paymnt:	May	dilution:	n/a
Int net div per share:	1.25p	P/E ratio:	12.2
Fin net div per share:	3.25p	Probable CGT?	Yes

LATEST REPORTED RESULTS: 2002		PREVIOUS REPORTED RESULTS: 2001	
Turnover:	£37.71m	Turnover:	£38.26m
PTP:	£1.62m	PTP:	£(19,000)
EPS:	9.8p	EPS:	0.7p

Comments:
Retail communications group CA Coutts continues to perform well, identifiably enhancing the product sales of companies as diverse as Disney and Manor Bakeries (as well as a host of other blue chip, household names). A January trading statement reinforced the company's progress, confirming that it had experienced a strong second half of the year, particularly in the run up to Christmas. Full-year profits are thus likely to be 'materially higher' than the £1.18m previously forecast.

Cabouchon (CBO)

Retailer of costume jewellery

Imperial House, 2-14 High Street, Margate, Kent CT9 1DW   Tel: 01843-221122; Fax: 01843-221000;
e-mail: support@cabouchon.com; web site: www.cabouchon.com

		holding %
Chairman	David Pearl	7.4
Managing Director	Julie Wing	50.0
Finance Director	Kenneth Bone	0.02
Non-Exec Director	Jake Hughes	0.02

Main Shareholders:

Jubilee Investment Trust	29.4

Percentage of free market capital: 13.2%

Nominated Adviser:	Grant Thornton, London
AIM Broker:	Christows, London
Solicitors:	Field Fisher Waterhouse, London
Market Makers:	SCAP; WINS
Auditors:	Grant Thornton, Southampton, SO15 2EW
Registrars:	Melton Registrars

ENTRY ON AIM: 14/12/2001		Recent price:	3.4p
Interim results:	Oct	Market cap:	£1.04m
Final results:	Sep	Issue price:	25.0p
Year end:	Mar	**Current no of shares:**	
Accounts due:	Nov		30,600,000
Int div paymnt:	n/a	**No of shares after**	
Fin div paymnt:	n/a	dilution:	n/a
Int net div per share:	nil	P/E ratio:	n/a
Fin net div per share:	nil	Probable CGT?	Yes

LATEST REPORTED RESULTS: 2003		PREVIOUS REPORTED RESULTS: 8 MONTHS TO 31 MAR 2002	
Turnover:	£148,000	Turnover:	£60,000
PTP:	£(1.44m)	PTP:	£(211,000)
EPS:	(6.0)p	EPS:	(1.0)p

Comments:

Costume jewellery business Cabouchon continues to struggle, having generated just £70,357 of revenue and a £144,322 loss in the first half of 2003/04. In a bid to improve the situation, management recently launched the company's first mail order catalogue and extended its relationship with TV shopping channel Ideal World, a business owned by AIM peer Ideal Shopping Direct. Cabouchon, which sources its products from Spain and the Far East, has traditionally sold its products via a network of sales agents.

Caledon Resources (formerly Finelot) (CDN)

East Asia gold explorer

18 Upper Brook Street, London, W1K 7PU Tel: 0845-108 2835; Fax: 020-7409 3139;
web site: www.caledonresources.com

		holding %
Chairman	Stephen Dattels	15.6
Managing Director	George Salamis	0.0
Finance Director		
Non-Exec Director	Robert Alford	0.4

Main Shareholders:

Standard Mercantile Bancorp	6.0
Framlington Innovative Growth Trust	5.0
NRI	4.8
Lonti Ebers	4.5
Baybak Family Partners	3.0

Percentage of free market capital: 55.4%

Nominated Adviser:	Williams de Broe, London
AIM Broker:	Williams de Broe, London
Solicitors:	Nicholson Graham & Jones, London
Market Makers:	MLSB; WDBM; WINS
Auditors:	PricewaterhouseCoopers, London
Registrars:	Computershare Investor Services

ENTRY ON AIM: 7/12/2000		Recent price:	10.5p
Interim results:	Apr	Market cap:	£22.4m
Final results:	Jan	Issue price:	35.0p
Year end:	Jul	**Current no of shares:**	
Accounts due:	Nov		213,363,999
Int div paymnt:	n/a	**No of shares after**	
Fin div paymnt:	n/a	dilution:	n/a
Int net div per share:	nil	P/E ratio:	n/a
Fin net div per share:	nil	Probable CGT?	Yes

LATEST REPORTED RESULTS: 17 MONTHS TO 31 DEC '03		PREVIOUS REPORTED RESULTS: 2002	
Turnover:	£7,000	Turnover:	£175,000
PTP:	£(1.40m)	PTP:	£(448,000)
EPS:	(1.2)p	EPS:	(1.8)p

Comments:

Created by a reversal into failed online auctioneer Finelot, Caledon is investigating four gold projects in southern China and hopes to define a resource for one, Longtoushan, by the end of 2004. Favoured for its long-term possibilities, the company, which lost £1.9m last year, raised £2.2m in 2003 in several issues, at prices rising from 3.5p to 12p.

Caledonian Trust (CNN)

Property investor

61 North Castle Street, Edinburgh, EH2 3LJ Tel: 0131-220 0416; Fax: 0131-220 0417; e-mail: mail@caledoniantrust.com

		holding %
Chairman	Ian D Lowe	78.8
Chief Executive	as above	
Finance Director	Michael J Baynham	4.5
Non-Exec Director	Bryan J Rankin	0.8

Main Shareholders:

Aberdeen City Council	3.0

Percentage of free market capital: 12.8%

Nominated Adviser:	Noble & Co, London
AIM Broker:	Numis, London
Solicitors:	Dickinson Dees, Newcastle
Market Makers:	KBCS; WINS
Auditors:	KPMG, 20 Castle Terrace, Edinburgh EH1 2EG
Registrars:	Lloyds TSB Registrars

Comments:
Edinburgh-based property investor Caledonian has won favour with a mixed office, development and retail portfolio, mostly in Edinburgh (and some in South London). Fixed assets rose £4m to £18.6m last year and shareholders' funds gained £800,000 to £19.6m. Selling Caledonian's St Magnus House and Stoneywood properties halved rents to £963,000 and pre-tax profits fell from £3.6m to £503,000.

ENTRY ON AIM:	29/9/1995	Recent price:	141.5p
Interim results:	Sep	Market cap:	£16.29m
Final results:	Mar	Issue price:	75.0p
Year end:	Dec	Current no of shares:	
Accounts due:	May		11,510,269
Int div paymnt:	Apr	No of shares after	
Fin div paymnt:	Jan	dilution:	11,940,269
Int net div per share:	1.0p	P/E ratio:	32.2
Fin net div per share:	1.0p	Probable CGT?	No

LATEST REPORTED RESULTS: 2003		PREVIOUS REPORTED RESULTS: 2002	
Turnover:	£1.69m	Turnover:	£3.07m
PTP:	£503,000	PTP:	£3.62m
EPS:	4.4p	EPS:	27.6p

CamAxys (CAX)

Information management software systems supplier

8 The Meadow, Meadow Lane, St Ives, Cambridgeshire PE27 4LG Tel: 01480-497739; Fax: 01480-497759;
web site: www.fieldens.co.uk

		holding %
Chairman	Derek Bonham	14.9
Chief Executive	Andrew Arends	14.9
Finance Director		
Exec Director	Colin West	3.9

Main Shareholders:

RBC Trustees	16.0
Barbara Fielden	10.4
Alan James	8.5
HSBC Global Custody Nominees	5.2

Percentage of free market capital: 21.9%

Nominated Adviser:	Shore Capital, London
AIM Broker:	Shore Capital, London
Solicitors:	Slaughter and May, London
Market Makers:	SCAP; WINS
Auditors:	PKF, Colchester
Registrars:	Capita Registrars

Comments:
Erstwhile tractor-tyre manufacturer Fieldens has reinvented itself as a supplier of environmental and health & safety risk management systems. As the final assets of the Fieldens business were only sold off in November, however, there has been little for the company to report on its new activities thus far. Efforts are currently being focused on bulking up the company's sales and marketing capabilities. With cash fairly tight, a raft of fundraising options are also being considered.

ENTRY ON AIM:	10/6/1996	Recent price:	22.0p
Interim results:	Mar	Market cap:	£1.57m
Final results:	Oct	Issue price:	48.5p
Year end:	Jun	Current no of shares:	
Accounts due:	Oct		7,136,944
Int div paymnt:	n/a	No of shares after	
Fin div paymnt:	n/a	dilution:	n/a
Int net div per share:	nil	P/E ratio:	n/a
Fin net div per share:	nil	Probable CGT?	Yes

LATEST REPORTED RESULTS: 2003		PREVIOUS REPORTED RESULTS: 2002	
Turnover:	£1.23m	Turnover:	£3.31m
PTP:	£(915,000)	PTP:	£(202,000)
EPS:	(14.5)p	EPS:	(4.0)p

Cambrian Mining (CBM)

Mining investment company

4th Floor, 55 St James's Street, London, SW1A 1LA Tel: 020-7409 0890; Fax: 020-7409 2750;
e-mail: info@cambrianmining.com; web site: www.cambrianmining.com

		holding %
Chairman	Charles de Chezelles	0.2
Chief Executive	John Byrne	20.3
Finance Director		
Exec Director	Jonathan Malins	0.1

Main Shareholders:

Resources Investment Trust	20.5
Tiger Resources	7.0
Investika	4.7

Percentage of free market capital: 47.3%

Nominated Adviser:	Grant Thornton, London
AIM Broker:	Christows, London
Solicitors:	Trowers & Hamlins, London
Market Makers:	EVO; SCAP; WINS
Auditors:	Chapman Davis & Co, London
Registrars:	Capita Registrars

ENTRY ON AIM:	5/8/2003	Recent price:	63.5p
Interim results:	Oct	Market cap:	£16.51m
Final results:	Jun	Issue price:	30.0p
Year end:	Jun	Current no of shares:	
Accounts due:	Jan		26,005,601
Int div paymnt:	n/a	No of shares after	
Fin div paymnt:	n/a	dilution:	n/a
Int net div per share:	nil	P/E ratio:	n/a
Fin net div per share:	nil	Probable CGT?	No

LATEST REPORTED RESULTS: 2003		PREVIOUS REPORTED RESULTS: N/A	
Turnover:	£111,000	Turnover:	n/a
PTP:	£163,000	PTP:	n/a
EPS:	1.6p	EPS:	n/a

Comments:

Fixed asset sales outweighed operating losses (swollen by directors' pay and other fees) to enable Cambrian to make £187,000 pre-tax last year. Headed by entrepreneurial Aussie John Byrne, Cambrian has a key stake in Ghana's promising Subranum gold project . Other interests include Deepgreen Energy, set to float Bangladeshi coal hopeful Asia Energy this year. Backers include RAB Capital.

Cambridge Mineral Resources (CMR)

Mineral explorer & developer

Simmonds House, Simmonds Buildings, Bristol Road, Hambrook, Bristol, BS16 1RY Tel: 0117-573666;
Fax: 0117-56666; e-mail: office@cambmin.co.uk; web site: www.cambmin.co.uk

		holding %
Executive Chairman	Michael Thomsen	0.1
Chief Executive		
Finance Director	Michael Burton	0.1
Managing Director	David Bramhill	2.5

Main Shareholders:

Ashdale Investment Trust	7.7

Percentage of free market capital: 81.9%

Nominated Adviser:	Westhouse Securities, London
AIM Broker:	Westhouse Securities, London
Solicitors:	Osborne Clarke, Bristol
Market Makers:	HOOD; KBCS; MLSB; SCAP; WINS
Auditors:	Grant Thornton, 31 Carlton Crescent, Soton SO15 2EW
Registrars:	Capita Registrars

ENTRY ON AIM:	7/3/1997	Recent price:	14.5p
Interim results:	Sep	Market cap:	£19.57m
Final results:	Jun	Issue price:	16.0p
Year end:	Dec	Current no of shares:	
Accounts due:	Aug		134,946,824
Int div paymnt:	n/a	No of shares after	
Fin div paymnt:	n/a	dilution:	n/a
Int net div per share:	nil	P/E ratio:	n/a
Fin net div per share:	nil	Probable CGT?	No

LATEST REPORTED RESULTS: 2002		PREVIOUS REPORTED RESULTS: 2001	
Turnover:	n/a	Turnover:	n/a
PTP:	£(731,000)	PTP:	£(464,000)
EPS:	(1.2)p	EPS:	(0.9)p

Comments:

Cambridge, steered by David Bramhill, is persisting with its Lomero Poyatos polymetallic project in Spain and has 11.5% of a new company, Falkland Minerals, controlled by Cambridge backer RAB Capital, that is looking to probe onshore mineral prospects in the Falkland Islands. Cambridge, which lost an interim £503,000, expects an eventual Falkland Minerals float. The appeal is speculative.

Camelot Capital (CMT)

Investment company
The Hawthornes, Wareside, Hertfordshire SG12 7RL

		holding %
Chairman	Jeremy Peace	3.6
Chief Executive		
Finance Director	Paul Brigden	1.8
Non-Exec Director	Guy Sangster	1.8

Main Shareholders:
Salic   43.6

Percentage of free market capital: 49.2%

Nominated Adviser:	Seymour Pierce, London
AIM Broker:	Seymour Pierce Ellis, Crawley
Solicitors:	Memery Crystal, London
Market Makers:	WINS
Auditors:	Rees Pollock, 7 Pilgrim Street, London EC4V 6DR
Registrars:	Neville Registrars

ENTRY ON AIM:	3/2/2004	Recent price:	5.9p
Interim results:	n/a	Market cap:	£3.25m
Final results:	n/a	Issue price:	5.0p
Year end:	n/a	Current no of shares:	
Accounts due:	n/a		55,000,000
Int div paymnt:	n/a	No of shares after	
Fin div paymnt:	n/a	dilution:	n/a
Int net div per share:	nil	P/E ratio:	n/a
Fin net div per share:	nil	Probable CGT?	No

LATEST REPORTED RESULTS:	N/A	PREVIOUS REPORTED RESULTS:	N/A
Turnover:	n/a	Turnover:	n/a
PTP:	n/a	PTP:	n/a
EPS:	n/a	EPS:	n/a

Comments:
This ready-made shell raised £1.26m net on admission. The directors hope to find one or more businesses with 'the potential for generating significant, sustainable growth and profitability'. These are likely to be in the leisure, healthcare, services and TMT sectors. The search is being led by West Bromwich Albion chairman Jeremy Peace and associates who most recently sat on the board of fellow AIM speculation Galahad Gold.

Campus Media (CPM)

Youth radio broadcaster
109a Regent's Park Rd, London, NW1 8UR Tel: 020-7691 4777; Fax: 020-7691 4666

		holding %
Chairman	Jonathan Durden	0.0
Chief Executive	Tony Harbron	0.0
Finance Director		0.0
Deputy Chairman	Adam Driscoll	0.0

Main Shareholders:

Channelfly	29.3
Simon Lynds	12.3
Liontrust Investment Funds	13.0
Herald Investments	12.69

Percentage of free market capital: 32.8%

Nominated Adviser:	Seymour Pierce, London
AIM Broker:	Seymour Pierce, London
Solicitors:	Wragge & Co, Birmingham
Market Makers:	WDBM; WINS
Auditors:	Ernst & Young LLP, Cambridge
Registrars:	Computershare Investor Services

ENTRY ON AIM:	26/2/2002	Recent price:	14.5p
Interim results:	Apr	Market cap:	£2.4m
Final results:	Nov	Issue price:	65.0p
Year end:	Jul	Current no of shares:	
Accounts due:	Nov		16,546,145
Int div paymnt:	n/a	No of shares after	
Fin div paymnt:	n/a	dilution:	n/a
Int net div per share:	nil	P/E ratio:	n/a
Fin net div per share:	nil	Probable CGT?	Yes

LATEST REPORTED RESULTS:	2003	PREVIOUS REPORTED RESULTS:	2002
Turnover:	£346,000	Turnover:	£64,000
PTP:	£(3.95m)	PTP:	£(549,000)
EPS:	(41.7)p	EPS:	(16.4)p

Comments:
2003 results were very disappointing from Campus, the student marketing and broadcast services venture. A chunk of the hefty pre-tax loss (£2.5m) was related to a goodwill impairment charge at its Student Broadcast Network, although operating losses prior to this were already north of £1m. Since the year end the group has raised £665,000 via a placing and acquired The Campus Marketing Company for a maximum of £282,800, satisfied by the issue of shares. Given its level of turnover, much remains to be done here.

Canisp (CN.)

Telecommunications investor
Kitwell House, The Warren, Radlett, Herts WD7 7DU

		holding %
Chairman	John Leat	1.0
Chief Executive		
Finance Director		
Exec Director	John Maundrell	2.0

Main Shareholders:
Everdene	29.0
Tigerhawk	7.8
Maycot Investments	5.0

Percentage of free market capital: 52.1%

Comments:
Canisp acquired telecommunications service provider Airtime Group (TAG) in December for £980,500. Loss-making TAG sells telephone minutes through global calling cards and prepaid calling cards. It also resells telephone capacity through fixed lines. Recently it completed the establishment of service provider status with BT Wholesale. This will enable savings for customers on line and call charges and severs the tie between the customer and BT.

Nominated Adviser:	Canaccord Capital, London	
AIM Broker:	Canaccord Capital, London	
Solicitors:	Fladgate Fielder, London	
Market Makers:	EVO; KBCS; SCAP; WINS	
Auditors:	Grant Thornton, Birmingham	
Registrars:	Capita Registrars	

ENTRY ON AIM: 15/10/2003		**Recent price:**	55.0p
Interim results:	n/a	**Market cap:**	£6.88m
Final results:	n/a	**Issue price:**	27.5p
Year end:	n/a	**Current no of shares:**	
Accounts due:	n/a		12,500,000
Int div paymnt:	n/a	**No of shares after**	
Fin div paymnt:	n/a	**dilution:**	n/a
Int net div per share:	nil	**P/E ratio:**	n/a
Fin net div per share:	nil	**Probable CGT?**	YES

LATEST REPORTED RESULTS:		PREVIOUS REPORTED RESULTS:	
	N/A		N/A
Turnover:	n/a	**Turnover:**	n/a
PTP:	n/a	**PTP:**	n/a
EPS:	n/a	**EPS:**	n/a

Canterbury Foods (formerly Global) (CBY)

Food manufacturer
Cranbrook House, Redlands, Surrey CR5 2HT Tel: 020-8668 9344; Fax: 020-8660 4640

		holding %
Chairman	Christian Williams	0.0
Chief Executive	Paul Ainsworth	0.0
Finance Director	Alison Everatt	0.0
Non-Exec Director	Andrew Baker	0.0

Main Shareholders:
Alphagen Volantis Fund	5.3

Percentage of free market capital: 94.7%

Comments:
The meat and pastry products manufacturer is charging ahead with its restructuring and anticipates returning to profit in 2004. It sold its meat trading division in September for £11.3m in order to focus on its food manufacturing operations. Results for the year to December are anticipated to show a substantial loss, reflecting the goodwill write-off of the businesses disposed of and reorganisation costs associated with restructuring.

Nominated Adviser:	Teather & Greenwood, London	
AIM Broker:	Teather & Greenwood, London	
Solicitors:	Eversheds, London	
Market Makers:	KBCS; SCAP; TEAM; WINS	
Auditors:	PKF, New Garden House, London	
Registrars:	Capita Registrars	

ENTRY ON AIM:	9/9/2003	**Recent price:**	43.0p
Interim results:	Sep	**Market cap:**	£7.05m
Final results:	Apr	**Issue price:**	32.5p
Year end:	Dec	**Current no of shares:**	
Accounts due:	Jun		16,398,821
Int div paymnt:	n/a	**No of shares after**	
Fin div paymnt:	n/a	**dilution:**	n/a
Int net div per share:	nil	**P/E ratio:**	n/a
Fin net div per share:	nil	**Probable CGT?**	YES

LATEST REPORTED RESULTS:		PREVIOUS REPORTED RESULTS:	
	2002		2001
Turnover:	£143.03m	**Turnover:**	£165.37m
PTP:	£(2.27m)	**PTP:**	£(6.17m)
EPS:	(1.2)p	**EPS:**	(3.7)p

Capcon (CPC)

Provider of audit, stocktaking and commercial investigation services

Rembrandt House, Whippendell Road, Watford, WD18 7PP Tel: 01923-242202; Fax: 01923-240518;
e-mail: enquiries@capconuk.com; web site: www.capcon.plc.com

		holding %
Chairman	Ken Dulieu	15.4
Managing Director	Clifford Cavender	3.0
Finance Director		
Non-Exec Director	Paul Jackson	14.9

Main Shareholders:

Singer & Friedlander Trust	13.0
P K Ashton	3.5

Percentage of free market capital: 49.1%

Comments:

The only UK-listed investigations and risk management company scored terrific annual numbers with profits up 89% and sales rising 43%, including a £1.24m contribution from acquisition Argen. Capcon is seeing rising sales and margins at VSA, an insurance fraud investigator bought in 2002. And the board is on the lookout for further acquisitions. This company should benefit from compliance issues in financial services and a crackdown on corporate fraud.

Nominated Adviser:	Williams de Broe, London
AIM Broker:	Williams de Broe, London
Solicitors:	Duane Morris, London
Market Makers:	SCAP; WINS
Auditors:	BDO Stoy Hayward, 8 Baker Street, London
Registrars:	Capita Registrars

ENTRY ON AIM:	31/5/2001	Recent price:	50.5p
Interim results:	Jun	Market cap:	£4.66m
Final results:	Jan	Issue price:	80.0p
Year end:	Sep	Current no of shares:	
Accounts due:	Feb		9,233,776
Int div paymnt:	Jul	No of shares after	
Fin div paymnt:	Dec	dilution:	n/a
Int net div per share:	0.73p	P/E ratio:	50.5
Fin net div per share:	1.46p	Probable CGT?	Yes

LATEST REPORTED RESULTS:	2003	PREVIOUS REPORTED RESULTS:	2002
Turnover:	£7.10m	Turnover:	£4.96m
PTP:	£133,000	PTP:	£105,000
EPS:	1.0p	EPS:	0.7p

Cape (CIU)

Industrial scaffolding and insulation supplier

Iver Lane, Uxbridge, Middlesex UB8 2JQ Tel: 01895-463463; Fax: 01895-232962; web site: www.capeplc.com

		holding %
Chairman	Martin May	0.1
Chief Executive	Ian Maclellan	0.0
Finance Director	Michael Reynolds	0.0
Managing Director	Paul Ainley	0.0

Main Shareholders:

M & G Investment Management Limited	14.9
Royal Bank of Scotland	14.1
Unibank A/S	9.3
BNY (OCS) Nominees	8.9
Active Capital Trust	5.5

Percentage of free market capital: 42.9%

Comments:

The industrial services concern is reaping the benefits of restructuring, and its core business Cape Industrial Services (CIS) is outperforming. 2003 numbers beat forecasts, showing rising sales and profits at CIS, with turnover up 19.1% and operating profits lifted by 8.7% to £10m. Also encouraging was lower year-end net debt, cut back from £19.3m to £5.4m. Analysts have since upgraded 2004 pre-tax profit forecasts from £8.1m to £9.4m, giving earnings of 14.2p.

Nominated Adviser:	Evolution Beeson Gregory, London
AIM Broker:	Evolution Beeson Gregory, London
Solicitors:	Herbert Smith, London; Davies Arnold Cooper, London
Market Makers:	KLWT; WINS
Auditors:	PricewaterhouseCoopers, London
Registrars:	Capita Registrars

ENTRY ON AIM:	27/1/2003	Recent price:	74.5p
Interim results:	Aug	Market cap:	£40.47m
Final results:	Mar	Issue price:	13.0p
Year end:	Dec	Current no of shares:	
Accounts due:	May		54,326,021
Int div paymnt:	n/a	No of shares after	
Fin div paymnt:	n/a	dilution:	n/a
Int net div per share:	nil	P/E ratio:	9.2
Fin net div per share:	nil	Probable CGT?	Yes

LATEST REPORTED RESULTS:	2002	PREVIOUS REPORTED RESULTS:	2001
Turnover:	£189.3m	Turnover:	£215.1m
PTP:	£14.6m	PTP:	£(32.4m)
EPS:	8.1p	EPS:	0.2p

Capital Management and Investment (CMIP)

Investment company

4th Floor, 54 Baker Street, London W1U 1FB Tel: 020-7725 0800; Fax: 020-7725 0808

		holding %
Chairman	Alan McIntosh	6.4
Managing Director		
Finance Director	Hugh Osmond	6.6
Non-Exec Director	Daniel Taylor	1.4

Main Shareholders:

J P Morgan Fleming	10.2
Bipolar Holdings	6.8
e-xentric Employee Share Trust	6.4
Zurich Financial Services	5.2
Riverbay Properties Limited*	4.7

Percentage of free market capital: 19.1%

*The registered holders of these shares are Fitel Nominees Limited

Comments:

There's been little to report from Capital Management and Investment, the buy-out vehicle of pubs entrepreneur Hugh Osmond, since it announced interims for the six months to July. These revealed a swing from a £545,000 profit to losses of £7.3m due to one-off expenses after it failed with its bold swoop for Six Continents. At that time, the company's balance sheet showed cash reserves of £34.8m. It continues to search for lucrative investment opportunities.

Nominated Adviser:	Brewin Dolphin, London
AIM Broker:	Brewin Dolphin, London; Credit Suisse First Boston, London; Collins Stewart, London; Lehman Brothers, London
Solicitors:	Pinsents, London
Market Makers:	CSCS; KBCS; WINS
Auditors:	BDO Stoy Hayward, 8 Baker Street, London W1M 1DA
Registrars:	Capita Registrars

ENTRY ON AIM:	8/8/1997	**Recent price:**	11.5p
Interim results:	Sep	**Market cap:**	£26.78m
Final results:	Feb	**Issue price:**	72.5p
Year end:	Jan	**Current no of shares:**	
Accounts due:	May		232,834,988
Int div paymnt:	n/a	**No of shares after**	
Fin div paymnt:	n/a	**dilution:**	n/a
Int net div per share:	nil	**P/E ratio:**	38.3
Fin net div per share:	nil	**Probable CGT?**	Yes

LATEST REPORTED RESULTS: 2003		PREVIOUS REPORTED RESULTS: 2002	
Turnover:	n/a	**Turnover:**	n/a
PTP:	£1.01m	**PTP:**	£1.68m
EPS:	0.3p	**EPS:**	0.6p

Capricorn Resources (CIR)

Acquirer of African mining projects

15, Gloucester Place Mews, London, W1U 8BE Tel: 020-7224 2522; Fax: 020-7224 3348

		holding %
Chairman	Phil Edmonds	14.8
Chief Executive	as above	
Finance Director		
Non-Exec Director	Bruce Rowan	45.7

Main Shareholders:

n/a

Percentage of free market capital: 25.7%

Comments:

Capricorn Resources, floated last year by entrepreneurial ex-cricketer Phil Edmonds, has won favour with a declared stategy of pursuing resource and mining opportunities in Angola, Congo, Mozambique, Zambia and other African countries, helped by locally well-connected director Moreti Motau. The company, which lost an interim £34,000, raised £150,000 at 1.5p in September and has motored since then.

Nominated Adviser:	Grant Thornton, London
AIM Broker:	Hichens Harrison, London
Solicitors:	Salans, London
Market Makers:	SCAP; WINS
Auditors:	Baker Tilly, 2 Bloomsbury Street, London WC1B 3ST
Registrars:	Capita Registrars

ENTRY ON AIM:	18/2/2003	**Recent price:**	12.25p
Interim results:	n/a	**Market cap:**	£7.83m
Final results:	n/a	**Issue price:**	1.0p
Year end:	n/a	**Current no of shares:**	
Accounts due:	n/a		63,950,000
Int div paymnt:	n/a	**No of shares after**	
Fin div paymnt:	n/a	**dilution:**	n/a
Int net div per share:	nil	**P/E ratio:**	n/a
Fin net div per share:	nil	**Probable CGT?**	No

LATEST REPORTED RESULTS: N/A		PREVIOUS REPORTED RESULTS: N/A	
Turnover:	n/a	**Turnover:**	n/a
PTP:	n/a	**PTP:**	n/a
EPS:	n/a	**EPS:**	n/a

Carbo (CAB)

Industrial abrasives producer

Lakeside, Trafford Park Road, Trafford Park, Manchester, M17 1HP Tel: 0161-872 2381; Fax: 0161-953 2982; web site: www.carbogb.co.uk

		holding %
Chairman	Lord Hodgson	0.1
Chief Executive	Lars Nyqvist	0.0
Finance Director	Stuart Dootson	0.0
Non-Exec Director	Sven Olsson	0.0

Main Shareholders:

Prudential Portfolio Managers	14.3
Silverslaggan AB	8.24
Perpetual Unit Trust Managers	8.0
Schroder Investment Management	5.8
Henry Cooke	4.5
Percentage of free market capital: 43.7%	

Nominated Adviser: Deloitte & Touche, London
AIM Broker: Collins Stewart, London
Solicitors: DLA, Leeds
Market Makers: CSCS; MLSB; SCAP; WINS
Auditors: PricewaterhouseCoopers, Manchester
Registrars: Capita Registrars

ENTRY ON AIM:	6/11/2000	**Recent price:**	15.0p
Interim results:	Oct	**Market cap:**	£3.44m
Final results:	Jul	**Issue price:**	n/a
Year end:	Jan	**Current no of shares:**	
Accounts due:	Jun		22,902,218
Int div paymnt:	n/a	**No of shares after**	
Fin div paymnt:	n/a	**dilution:**	n/a
Int net div per share:	nil	**P/E ratio:**	n/a
Fin net div per share:	nil	**Probable CGT?**	YES

LATEST REPORTED RESULTS:	2003	PREVIOUS REPORTED RESULTS:	2002
Turnover:	£56.09m	Turnover:	£64.2m
PTP:	£(4.49m)	PTP:	£(10.0m)
EPS:	(54.9)p	EPS:	(106.0)p

Comments:

Products from the industrial abrasives maker and distributor are supplied under brand names including BMA and Carborundum. In a spot of welcome good news, Carbo recently completed its refinancing programme. Now the company plans to concentrate on coated abrasives as its core business, where it is one of the world leaders. Carbo was still making losses when it reported for the half to 31 July – almost £2m was lost on sales of £29.4m (£27.1m).

Cardpoint (CASH)

Owner & operator of cash machines

The Old Fire Station, 55 Hove Road, Lytham St Annes, Lancashire FY8 1XH Tel: 01253-785800; Fax: 01253-789214; e-mail: mark.mills@Cardpointplc.com; web site: www.cardpointplc.com

		holding %
Chairman	Peter Smyth	0.2
Chief Executive	Mark Mills	9.4
Finance Director	Chris Hanson	0.9
Sales & Mktg Director	Nigel Mills	5.5

Main Shareholders:

ProVen VCT	7.1
David Jones	5.3
Singer & Friedlander AIM 3 Venture Capital	3.8
John Barker	3.7
Universities Superannuation Scheme	3.5
Percentage of free market capital: 60.5%	

Nominated Adviser: Evolution Beeson Gregory, London
AIM Broker: Evolution Beeson Gregory, London
Solicitors: Halliwell Landau, Manchester
Market Makers: BGMM; WINS
Auditors: Grant Thornton, Manchester
Registrars: Capita Registrars

ENTRY ON AIM:	10/6/2002	**Recent price:**	141.0p
Interim results:	May	**Market cap:**	£46.09m
Final results:	Nov	**Issue price:**	43.0p
Year end:	Sept	**Current no of shares:**	
Accounts due:	Dec		32,686,334
Int div paymnt:	n/a	**No of shares after**	
Fin div paymnt:	n/a	**dilution:**	n/a
Int net div per share:	nil	**P/E ratio:**	n/a
Fin net div per share:	nil	**Probable CGT?**	YES

LATEST REPORTED RESULTS:	2003	PREVIOUS REPORTED RESULTS:	2002
Turnover:	£12.17m	Turnover:	£3.10m
PTP:	£(608,000)	PTP:	£(757,000)
EPS:	0.2p	EPS:	(5.4)p

Comments:

Cardpoint is the rapidly growing independent ATM deployer and mobile phone top-up terminal operator. In recent bullish news, it renewed its ATM deal with largest corporate customer Welcome Break. This followed an excellent set of full year numbers, with Cardpoint scoring a near-fourfold rise in sales and a move into pre-goodwill pre-tax profits. For the current year, analysts at the house broker predict a £2.4m profit and earnings of 6.7p, on sales of £31.7m.

Carlisle   (CLH)

Support services provider

60 Market Square, Belize City, Belize; e-mail: info@carlisleholdings.com; web site: www.carlisleholdings.com

		holding %
Chairman	Michael A Ashcroft	32.0
Managing Director		
Finance Director	Peter Gaze	0.0
Exec Dep. Chair	David B Hammond	0.0

Main Shareholders:

Strand Partners	29.9
Nigel W Wray	12.3
Schroder Asset Management	8.8
Fleming Mercantile Inv Trust	5.0
Friends Provident	3.2

Percentage of free market capital: 8.9%

Comments:

Best known for the involvement of tycoon Lord Ashcroft as its chairman, Carlisle provides janitorial, landscaping and repair and maintenance services through its OneSource brand in the US, and also business services in the UK and Ireland. In the nine months to December the company improved net income to $30.2m ($26.3m) on revenues of $835.3m ($861m). Carlisle recently sold its 52.46% stake in Belize Telecommunications to the Government of Belize to cut debts.

Nominated Adviser:	Panmure Gordon, London		
AIM Broker:	Fyshe Horton Finney, Birmingham		
Solicitors:	Ozannes, St. Peter Port; Allen & Overy, London		
Market Makers:	KBCS; MLSB; WINS		
Auditors:	PricewaterhouseCoopers, London		
Registrars:	Capita Registrars		

ENTRY ON AIM:	2/6/1999	**Recent price:**	312.5p
Interim results:	Sep	**Market cap:**	£193.02m
Final results:	May	**Issue price:**	10.57p
Year end:	Mar	**Current no of shares:**	
Accounts due:	Jun		61,765,830
Int div paymnt:	n/a	**No of shares after**	
Fin div paymnt:	n/a	**dilution:**	79,431,246
Int net div per share:	nil	**P/E ratio:**	n/a
Fin net div per share:	nil	**Probable CGT?**	YES

LATEST REPORTED RESULTS:		PREVIOUS REPORTED RESULTS:	
	2003		2002
Turnover:	$291.4m	Turnover:	$295.4m
PTP:	$52.1m	PTP:	$47.8m
EPS:	0.6c	EPS:	0.5c

Carrwood (formerly Downtex)   (CAW)

Cash shell

George House, 48 George Street, Manchester, M1 4HF Tel: 0161-236 6555; Fax: 0161-236 5777; e-mail: dmond@downtex.co.uk; web site: www.downtex.co.uk

		holding %
Chairman	Gerald Carey	0.2
Managing Director	Jonathan Mond*	40.0
Finance Director	David Mond*	40.0

Main Shareholders:

Oliver Mond	5.3
Raymond Donn	3.2

Percentage of free market capital: 11.3%

*These shares are held by a Life Settlement Trust and a Maintenance and Accumulation Trust in which these directors are interested

Comments:

On the back of an 125% rise in interim losses to £420,645, perennially beleaguered Downtex transformed itself into cash shell Carrwood in December. The company's loss-making textiles operations were offloaded to directors Jonathan and David Mond for just £50,000. As part of the deal the Monds assumed Downtex's liabilities in full. Carrwood's revised strategy of 'acquiring interests in businesses... which the directors believe will provide a return to investors' seems vague, though.

Nominated Adviser:	Grant Thornton, London		
AIM Broker:	WH Ireland, Manchester		
Solicitors:	Halliwell Landau, Manchester		
Market Makers:	SCAP; WINS		
Auditors:	Baker Tilly, Manchester		
Registrars:	Neville Registrars		

ENTRY ON AIM:	4/8/1998	**Recent price:**	3.75p
Interim results:	Aug	**Market cap:**	£0.47m
Final results:	Feb	**Issue price:**	25.0p
Year end:	Dec	**Current no of shares:**	
Accounts due:	Mar		12,490,641
Int div paymnt:	n/a	**No of shares after**	
Fin div paymnt:	n/a	**dilution:**	12,890,641
Int net div per share:	nil	**P/E ratio:**	n/a
Fin net div per share:	nil	**Probable CGT?**	YES

LATEST REPORTED RESULTS:		PREVIOUS REPORTED RESULTS:	
	2002		2001
Turnover:	£6.12m	Turnover:	£6.14m
PTP:	£(559,000)	PTP:	£10,000
EPS:	(3.6)p	EPS:	0.0p

Cassidy Brothers (CDY)

Toy & nursery goods manufacturer

Mitcham Rd, Blackpool, FY4 4QW Tel: 01253-766411; Fax: 01253-691486; e-mail: toys@casdon.co.uk;
web site: www.casdon.co.uk

		holding %
Chairman	Paul Cassidy	48.1
Managing Director	as above	
Finance Director	S Wilkinson	0.5
Joint MD	K Hopkinson	0.6
Main Shareholders:		
I G Cassidy		10.6
E G Cassidy		4.4

Percentage of free market capital: 27.2%

Nominated Adviser:	Charles Stanley, London	
AIM Broker:	Charles Stanley, London	
Solicitors:	Addie Jones, Fleetwood	
Market Makers:	KBCS; WINS	
Auditors:	BDO Stoy Hayward, Blackpool	
Registrars:	Stanley Wilkinson	

ENTRY ON AIM:	2/10/1995	**Recent price:**	42.5p
Interim results:	Jan	**Market cap:**	£2.35m
Final results:	Jun	**Issue price:**	45.0p
Year end:	Apr	**Current no of shares:**	
Accounts due:	Jul		5,524,350
Int div paymnt:	Apr	**No of shares after**	
Fin div paymnt:	Sep	**dilution:**	n/a
Int net div per share:	1.0p	**P/E ratio:**	12.5
Fin net div per share:	2.0p	**Probable CGT?**	YES

LATEST REPORTED RESULTS:	2003	PREVIOUS REPORTED RESULTS:	2002
Turnover:	£5.34m	Turnover:	£6.3m
PTP:	£194,000	PTP:	£662,000
EPS:	3.4p	EPS:	10.5p

Comments:
The delay of toy maker Cassidy's deal with confectioner Cadbury's to market a range of licensed items hit interim numbers to October. The results were also affected by consumer purchasing moving ever closer to Christmas. Pre-tax profits waned by two thirds from £340,000 to £114,000 on a 29% wane in revenues to £2.3m. However, the company's three KFC-licensed products proved a success, as have recent launches of Pick & Mix and Cadbury Heroes.

Cater Barnard (CRB)

Financial services

Lloyds Avenue House, 6 Lloyds Avenue, London, EC3N 3AX Tel: 0870-066 0830; Fax: 0870-066 0831

		holding %
Chairman	David Williams	0.0
Chief Executive		
Finance Director		
Non-Exec Director	Aidan Mills-Thomas	0.0
Main Shareholders:		
Hetmoor		14.3
Winston		12.3
Ethel Austin		9.0
Pershing Keen Nominees		7.2
Meynard Freres		6.7
S Edwards		4.9

Percentage of free market capital: 35.5%

Nominated Adviser:	Beaumont Cornish, London	
AIM Broker:	Seymour Pierce Ellis, London	
Solicitors:	Philip Speer & Co, London	
Market Makers:	KBCS; MLSB; SCAP; WINS	
Auditors:	Spokes & Co, Hildenborough, Kent	
Registrars:	Capita Registrars	

ENTRY ON AIM:	24/8/1999	**Recent price:**	0.5p
Interim results:	Jun	**Market cap:**	£5.18m
Final results:	Dec	**Issue price:**	5.0p
Year end:	Sep	**Current no of shares:**	
Accounts due:	Dec		1,035,331,981
Int div paymnt:	n/a	**No of shares after**	
Fin div paymnt:	n/a	**dilution:**	n/a
Int net div per share:	nil	**P/E ratio:**	n/a
Fin net div per share:	nil	**Probable CGT?**	No

LATEST REPORTED RESULTS:	2003	PREVIOUS REPORTED RESULTS:	2002
Turnover:	£944,000	Turnover:	783,000
PTP:	£(6.87m)	PTP:	£(13.29m)
EPS:	(0.9)p	EPS:	(2.5)p

Comments:
Colourful financier Stephen Dean has resigned as director and sold his majority stake in the company following the acquisition of property services concern Navitas Hemway. This business's chief executive David Williams has replaced Dean as chairman. Cater Barnard owns 40% of Navitas with an option to acquire the remaining 60% by October. Williams plans to make several acquisitions in this space. The group has wound down its venture capital activities, recently selling its stake in US enterprise Dialog.

Cavanagh   (CVH)

Financial advisers

The Courtyard, Staplefield Road, Cuckfield, West Sussex, RH17 5JT Tel: 01444-475400; Fax: 01444-475405;
web site: www.cavanagh.co.uk

		holding %
Chairman	John Campbell	0.7
Chief Executive	Andrew Fay	23.3
Finance Director	Robert Smyth	0.0
Managing Director	Simon Redgrove	23.3

Main Shareholders:

Neill Millard (Director)	23.3
Vidacos Nominees	4.0
Simon Taylor	3.7

Percentage of free market capital: 12.7%

Nominated Adviser:	Brewin Dolphin, Leeds
AIM Broker:	Brewin Dolphin, Leeds
Solicitors:	Dundas Wilson, Edinburgh
Market Makers:	KBCS; WINS
Auditors:	Baker Tilly, Brazennose House, Manchester
Registrars:	Capita Registrars

ENTRY ON AIM: 23/12/2003		**Recent price:**	219.0p
Interim results:	Jan	**Market cap:**	£21.9m
Final results:	Sep	**Issue price:**	n/a
Year end:	Jun	**Current no of shares:**	
Accounts due:	Nov		10,000,000
Int div paymnt:	n/a	**No of shares after**	
Fin div paymnt:	n/a	**dilution:**	n/a
Int net div per share:	nil	**P/E ratio:**	n/a
Fin net div per share:	nil	**Probable CGT?**	Yes

LATEST REPORTED RESULTS: 2003	PREVIOUS REPORTED RESULTS: 13 MONTHS TO 31 OCT '02
Turnover: £4.69m	Turnover: £3.79m
PTP: £(250,000)	PTP: £(45,000)
EPS: (2.0)p	EPS: (0.6)p

Comments:

The fast-growing independent financial adviser has completed a £3m takeover of the financial advice arm of 'big four' accountant Ernst & Young. The group, based in the south-east, was set up in 1996 by 3 IFAs from Royal Insurance but, following the E&Y deal now boasts 200 advisers in 11 locations. Cavanagh's clients are principally barristers and City lawyers. Most growth up until now has been organic but this deal should transform the business.

Celltalk   (CLT)

Mobile phone direct retailer

24th Floor Sunley Tower, Piccadilly Plaza, Manchester, M1 4BT Tel: 0161-609 5370; Fax: 0161-609 5105;
e-mail: ann@celltalk.co.uk; web site: www.clubmobile.co.uk

		holding %
Chairman	Derek Joseph	0.4
Chief Executive	Ian Pegler	0.0
Finance Director		
Joint Managing Director	Richard Marsden	39.1

Main Shareholders:

Jesse Meredith–Watts (Joint MD)	39.1

Percentage of free market capital: 16.1%

Nominated Adviser:	Charles Stanley, London
AIM Broker:	Charles Stanley, London
Solicitors:	Halliwell Landau, Manchester
Market Makers:	SCAP; WINS
Auditors:	KPMG Audit, Cardiff
Registrars:	Capita Registrars

ENTRY ON AIM: 21/6/2000		**Recent price:**	12.0p
Interim results:	Nov	**Market cap:**	£2.92m
Final results:	Jul	**Issue price:**	115.0p
Year end:	Mar	**Current no of shares:**	
Accounts due:	Aug		24,310,000
Int div paymnt:	n/a	**No of shares after**	
Fin div paymnt:	n/a	**dilution:**	n/a
Int net div per share:	nil	**P/E ratio:**	120.0
Fin net div per share:	nil	**Probable CGT?**	Yes

LATEST REPORTED RESULTS: 2003	PREVIOUS REPORTED RESULTS: 15 MONTHS TO 31 MAR 02
Turnover: £8.33m	Turnover: £24.47m
PTP: £38,000	PTP: £(4.22m)
EPS: 0.1p	EPS: (17.4)p

Comments:

Celltalk has continued to comply with the conditions of its Company Voluntary Arrangement (CVA) to return to the market. Half of this year's profits will go straight to the CVA supervisor, while competition is hotting up in the market. In the interim to September, profits before tax were small at £24,000 and debts were still high at £1.6m. However, trading since is apparently significantly ahead of last year, with commission levels more realistic.

Celtic Resources

(CER)

Owner & operator of gold mines

Enterprise House, 59-65 Upper Ground, Blackfriars Rd, London, SE1 9PQ Tel: 0207-593 0001; Fax: 020-7593 0002;
e-mail: londonoffice@celticresources.com; web site: www.celticresources.com

		holding %
Chairman	Peter Hannen*	1.3
Chief Executive	Kevin Foo**	8.0
Finance Director	Michael Palmer	0.7
Exec Director	Euan Worthington	0.3

Main Shareholders:

Deutsche Bank AG	14.3
Resources Investment Trust	4.9
Family Investments	4.7
Mr L G M and Mrs B Hannen	4.6
GNI	4.1

Percentage of free market capital: 47.4%

*Shares are registered in the name of Hannen & company
**Shares are registered in the name of H J Resources

Comments:

Headed by Kevin Foo, Celtic Resources has become a rare AIM mining company to propose a dividend, in the form of half its remaining 44% stake in Eureka Mining, its Kazakhstan gold and molybdenum arm that was recently floated on AIM for £7m. Celtic is focusing on gold at Susdal and Zherek in Kazakhstan and Nezhdaninskoye in Russia. Among backers is aggressive RAB Capital. More corporate moves are on the cards.

Nominated Adviser:	Williams de Broe, London
AIM Broker:	Williams de Broe, London
Solicitors:	Kerman & CO, London; O'Donnell Sweeney, Dublin
Market Makers:	GBMM; HOOD; KBCS;WDBM; WINS
Auditors:	Deloitte & Touche, Earlsfort Terrace, Dublin 2, Ireland
Registrars:	Computershare Investor Services

ENTRY ON AIM: 14/10/2002		**Recent price:**	496.5p
Interim results:	Aug	**Market cap:**	£175.18m
Final results:	Mar	**Issue price:**	135.0p
Year end:	Dec	**Current no of shares:**	
Accounts due:	May		35,283,343
Int div paymnt:	n/a	**No of shares after**	
Fin div paymnt:	n/a	**dilution:**	n/a
Int net div per share:	nil	**P/E ratio:**	n/a
Fin net div per share:	nil	**Probable CGT?**	No

LATEST REPORTED RESULTS:	2002	**PREVIOUS REPORTED RESULTS:**	2001
Turnover:	9.27m	Turnover:	n/a
PTP:	$2.32m	PTP:	$334,000
EPS:	(0.0)c	EPS:	(0.0)c

CeNeS

(CEN)

Drug developer

Company House, Vision Park, Chivers Way, Histon, Cambridge, CB2 9ZR Tel: 01223-266 466; Fax: 01223-266 467;
web site: www.cenes.com

		holding %
Chairman	Alan Goodman	6.8
Chief Executive		
Finance Director	Neil Clark	0.0
Non-Exec Director	Thomas Irwin	0.01

Main Shareholders:

Avlar Bioventures Fund II	9.1
Barclayshare	7.2
NY Nominees	6.5
M&G Investment Management	5.8
GlaxoSmithKline	5.0

Percentage of free market capital: 48.6%

Comments:

The developer of pain-reducing drugs is moving forwards after a financial restructuring, culminating in a £65m write-off. Now the group has two painkillers in late-stage clinical trials and enough cash for two years. Recently TheraSci was bought for £3.7m. The concern owns the rights to a GlaxoSmithKline programme developing 'short-acting sedatives for the use in day case procedures'.

Nominated Adviser:	Piper Jaffray, London
AIM Broker:	Piper Jaffray, London
Solicitors:	Weil, Gotshal & Manges, London; Eversheds, London
Market Makers:	EVO; KBCS; KLWT; MLSB; WINS
Auditors:	PricewaterhouseCoopers, London
Registrars:	Lloyds TSB

ENTRY ON AIM: 8/8/2003		**Recent price:**	11.6p
Interim results:	Sep	**Market cap:**	£29.64m
Final results:	Apr	**Issue price:**	n/a
Year end:	Dec	**Current no of shares:**	
Accounts due:	Aug		255,482,342
Int div paymnt:	n/a	**No of shares after**	
Fin div paymnt:	n/a	**dilution:**	n/a
Int net div per share:	nil	**P/E ratio:**	n/a
Fin net div per share:	nil	**Probable CGT?**	Yes

LATEST REPORTED RESULTS:	2002	**PREVIOUS REPORTED RESULTS:**	2001
Turnover:	£5.23m	Turnover:	£5.30m
PTP:	£(6.55m)	PTP:	£(66.21m)
EPS:	(3.7)p	EPS:	(40.7)p

Centamin Egypt (CEY)

Gold explorer and project developer

57 Kishorn Road, Mount Pleasant, Perth, Western Australia 6153 Tel: 00-61 8 9316 2640; Fax: 00-61 8 9316 2650;
e-mail: centamin@iinet.net.au ; web site: www.centamin.com.au

		holding %
Chairman	Sami El-Raghy	20.0
Managing Director	Josef El-Raghy	0.4
Financial Controller	Cecilia Tyndall	0.0
Non-Exec Director	Colin Cowden	0.1

Main Shareholders:

NEFCo Nominees	13.9
National Nominees	7.1
Willbro Nominees	6.4
Nordana	6.3
Goldman Sachs Securities	3.3

Percentage of free market capital: 45.33%

Comments:

Progress at Centamin's Sukari project in the Egyptian desert, where the company claims an estimated 3m oz of gold, remains stalled by delays in renewing staff security passes. Centamin, which lost an interim £540,000 (after directors' fees trebled to £355,000) on £290,000 revenues, has been continuing talks with the Egyptian Geological Survey and Mining Authority to break the impasse.

Nominated Adviser:	Williams de Broe, London
AIM Broker:	Williams de Broe, London
Solicitors:	Wojtowicz Kelly, Perth, Australia
Market Makers:	SGSL; WDBM; WINS
Auditors:	Deloitte Touche Tohmatsu, Perth WA
Registrars:	Computershare Investor Services

ENTRY ON AIM: 21/12/2001	Recent price:	12.0p
Interim results:	Mar	Market cap:	£46.88m
Final results:	Sep	Issue price:	6.0p
Year end:	Jun	Current no of shares:	
Accounts due:	Oct		390,665,923
Int div paymnt:	n/a	No of shares after	
Fin div paymnt:	n/a	dilution:	529,329,986
Int net div per share:	nil	P/E ratio:	n/a
Fin net div per share:	nil	Probable CGT?	No

LATEST REPORTED RESULTS: 2002		PREVIOUS REPORTED RESULTS: 2001	
Turnover:	A$141,000	Turnover:	A$231,000
PTP:	A$(1.16m)	PTP:	A$(117,000)
EPS:	Ac(0.3)	EPS:	Ac(0.0)

Centaur (CAU)

Publishing company

St Giles House, 50 Poland Street, London, W1F 7AX Tel: 020-7970 4000

		holding %
Chairman	Graham Sherren	4.6
Chief Executive	as above	
Finance Director	Geoffrey Wilmot	0.0
Non-Exec Director	Patrick Taylor	0.1

Main Shareholders:

Griffin Land & Nurseries	4.4

Percentage of free market capital: 90.7%

Comments:

Centuar's AIM float caused a stir. Fully listed Incisive Media had hoped to buy the company. However, broking firm Numis, which was also adviser to Incisive at the time, ended up effectively buying the company itself and selling its entire stake in the IPO to various institutional investors. Centaur publishes a range of well known business, legal and finance titles including Marketing Week, New Media Age and Mortgage Strategy. It is pinning growth hopes on the belief that the media recession is well and truly over.

Nominated Adviser:	Numis, London
AIM Broker:	Numis, London
Solicitors:	Travers Smith Braithwaite, London
Market Makers:	WINS
Auditors:	PricewaterhouseCoopers, 1 Embankment Place, London WC2N 6RH
Registrars:	Share Registrars

ENTRY ON AIM: 10/3/2004	Recent price:	98.0p
Interim results:	Sep	Market cap:	£145.03m
Final results:	Mar	Issue price:	100.0p
Year end:	Dec	Current no of shares:	
Accounts due:	Apr		147,994,118
Int div paymnt:	n/a	No of shares after	
Fin div paymnt:	n/a	dilution:	n/a
Int net div per share:	nil	P/E ratio:	6.0
Fin net div per share:	nil	Probable CGT?	No

LATEST REPORTED RESULTS: 2003		PREVIOUS REPORTED RESULTS: 2002	
Turnover:	£62.6m	Turnover:	£68.7m
PTP:	£16.2m	PTP:	£(8.23m)
EPS:	16.3p	EPS:	7.7p

Center Parcs (UK) (CPK)
Short break holiday village operator
c/o Simmons & Simmons, CityPoint, One Ropemaker Street, London, EC2Y 9SS

		holding %
Chairman	Martin Robinson	0.0
Chief Executive	Martin Dalby	0.0
Finance Director	Simon Lane	0.0
Non-Exec Director	John Matthews	0.0

Main Shareholders:

ISIS Asset Management	11.4
Treadneedle Investment	7.6
UBS Asset Manaement	7.2
Tudor Capital	5.8
Henderson Investors	5.3

Percentage of free market capital: 31.3%

Nominated Adviser:	Collins Stewart, London
AIM Broker:	Collins Stewart, London
Solicitors:	Simmons & Simmons, London
Market Makers:	BARD; CSCS; WINS
Auditors:	PricewaterhouseCoopers, East Midlands DE74 2UZ
Registrars:	Capita Registrars

ENTRY ON AIM: 11/12/2003	Recent price:	95.0p
Interim results: Jan	Market cap:	£242.45m
Final results: Jul	Issue price:	100.0p
Year end: Apr	Current no of shares:	
Accounts due: Aug		255,208,332
Int div paymnt: n/a	No of shares after	
Fin div paymnt: n/a	dilution:	n/a
Int net div per share: nil	P/E ratio:	29.7
Fin net div per share: nil	Probable CGT?	Yes

LATEST REPORTED RESULTS: 2003	PREVIOUS REPORTED RESULTS: 2002
Turnover: £160.72m	Turnover: £166.29m
PTP: £72.15m	PTP: £(48.82m)
EPS: 3.2p	EPS: (8.4)p

Comments:
The short-break holiday operator has listed on AIM as a stop-gap before moving to the Full List next year. With four 'villages' focusing on a 'subtropical swimming paradise', the leisure operator has healthy sales and profits. Last year its Elveden site in Suffolk was closed due to a fire. In the six months to September, net sales at its three other sites have increased 11.7% and bookings at the reopened Elveden are ahead of budget.

Central African Mining & Exploration (CFM)
Mining & exploration for tantalum and associated minerals
15 Gloucester Place Mews, London, W1U 8BE Tel: 020-7224 2522; Fax: 020-7224 3348;
e-mail: philedmonds@camec-plc.com; web site: www.camec-plc.com

		holding %
Chairman	Philippe Edmonds	11.6
Chief Executive	as above	
Finance Director		
Dvlpmt Director	Andrew Groves	8.2

Main Shareholders:

Bruce Rowan	29.9
Namibian Resources	16.0
Southern Africa Growth Area Investments	9.8
Africa Growth Area Investments	6.9

Percentage of free market capital: 13.3%

Nominated Adviser:	Seymour Pierce, London
AIM Broker:	Seymour Pierce Ellis, Crawley
Solicitors:	Salans, Hertzfeld & Heilbronn, London
Market Makers:	EVO; SCAP; WINS
Auditors:	Baker Tilly, 2 Bloomsbury Street, London WC1B 3ST
Registrars:	Capita Registrars

ENTRY ON AIM: 9/10/2002	Recent price:	11.0p
Interim results: Nov	Market cap:	£48.67m
Final results: Sep	Issue price:	3.0p
Year end: Mar	Current no of shares:	
Accounts due: Sep		442,439,802
Int div paymnt: n/a	No of shares after	
Fin div paymnt: n/a	dilution:	n/a
Int net div per share: nil	P/E ratio:	55.0
Fin net div per share: nil	Probable CGT?	No

LATEST REPORTED RESULTS: 2003	PREVIOUS REPORTED RESULTS: 9 MONTHS TO 31(MONTH) 2002
Turnover: £199,000	Turnover: £35,000
PTP: £606,000	PTP: £(186,000)
EPS: 0.2p	EPS: (0.1)p

Comments:
Sister company to Phil Edmonds' Southern African Resources, Central African Mining & Exploration (CAMEC) has pleased punters with its copper and cobalt projects in Congo, from which shipments began last year. CAMEC, which lost £151,000 last year on turnover up from £48,000 to £1.3m, recently raised £2.5m at 4p. The company claimed assets of £5.2m, including a stake in Southern African valued at cost.

Centurion Electronics (CUC)

Conception, design, marketing & distribution of automotive audio-visual products

Satellite House, City Park, Welwyn Garden City, Hertfordshire AL7 1LY Tel: 01707-330550; Fax: 01707-330866;
e-mail: info@ceplc.net; web site: www.ceplc.net

		holding %
Chairman	Brian Hendon	0.1
Chief Executive		
Finance Director	Amanda Thorneycroft	0.1
Technical Director	Alistair Powell	1.4

Main Shareholders:

Steven Cunningham (Deceased)	37.6
Unicorn AIM VCT	8.3
Electra Quoted Management	6.4

Percentage of free market capital: 46.0%

Comments:
Strong UK sales of Centurion's second-generation 'plug & play' in-car entertainment systems have buoyed the company as orders for its other retail products quietened. After the tragic death of chief executive Steve Cunningham, Brian Hendon has stepped in as interim chairman. Meanwhile, Centurion's original equipment manufacturer business model continues to expand – Centurion now supplies its screens to Toyota and is also in talks with Kia.

Nominated Adviser:	Charles Stanley, London	
AIM Broker:	Charles Stanley, London	
Solicitors:	Finers Stephens Innocent, London	
Market Makers:	SCAP; WINS	
Auditors:	BDO Stoy Hayward, Hatfield,	
Registrars:	Capita Registrars	

ENTRY ON AIM:	2/12/2002	Recent price:	123.5p
Interim results:	May	Market cap:	£29.91m
Final results:	Dec	Issue price:	30.0p
Year end:	Sep	Current no of shares:	
Accounts due:	Feb		24,214,761
Int div paymnt:	n/a	No of shares after	
Fin div paymnt:	n/a	dilution:	n/a
Int net div per share:	nil	P/E ratio:	27.4
Fin net div per share:	0.8p	Probable CGT?	Yes

LATEST REPORTED RESULTS: 2003		PREVIOUS REPORTED RESULTS: 2002	
Turnover:	£6.25m	Turnover:	£4.14m
PTP:	£1.18m	PTP:	£435,000
EPS:	4.5p	EPS:	2.8p

Centurion Energy (CUX)

Oil & gas explorer & producer

Suite 800, 205 – 5th Avenue S W, Calgary, Alberta, Canada T2P 2Y7; Fax: (403) 263-5998;
web site: www.centurionenergy.com

		holding %
Chairman	Michael Miller	1.8
Chief Executive	Said Arrata	2.2
Finance Director	Barry Swan	0.5
Non-Exec Director	Derrick Armstrong	0.3

Main Shareholders:

Delta Oil	24.5
ARC Canadian energy venture	7.3

Percentage of free market capital: 63.3%

Comments:
Centurion, which produces and explores for oil and gas in Tunisia and Egypt, is seeking new assets — and companies owning them — in order to double daily output to 20,000 barrels. The intention is to drill 23 new wells this year and next, with an £18m exploration budget largely funded from producing wells. Claiming reserves of £20m and a breakeven oil price of $10 a barrel, Centurion has high hopes for its Mellita project in Tunisia.

Nominated Adviser:	Williams de Broe, London	
AIM Broker:	Williams de Broe, London	
Solicitors:	Memery Crystal, London	
Market Makers:	WDBM; WINS	
Auditors:	PricewaterhouseCoopers, Canada	
Registrars:	Capita Registrars	

ENTRY ON AIM:	12/6/2003	Recent price:	148.0p
Interim results:	Sep	Market cap:	£107.52m
Final results:	Mar	Issue price:	57.5p
Year end:	Dec	Current no of shares:	
Accounts due:	May		72,651,581
Int div paymnt:	n/a	No of shares after	
Fin div paymnt:	n/a	dilution:	n/a
Int net div per share:	nil	P/E ratio:	1480.0
Fin net div per share:	nil	Probable CGT?	No

LATEST REPORTED RESULTS: 2002		PREVIOUS REPORTED RESULTS: 2001	
Turnover:	£34.37m	Turnover:	£14.89m
PTP:	£10.88m	PTP:	£5.90m
EPS:	0.1p	EPS:	0.1p

CES Software
(CES)

Technology company
267 Richmond Street West, Toronto, Ontario M5V 3M6 Canada, ; web site: www.columbiaexchange.com

		holding %
Executive Chairman	Andrew Rivkin*	24.5
Chief Executive	Lorne Abony	18.1
Finance Director		
Chief Operating Officer	Anatoly Plotkin	0.0
Main Shareholders:		
Scott Paterson Family Trust		4.6

Percentage of free market capital: 52.8%

*These shares are held by Stampee Technologies

Comments:
CES develops and supplies a range of gaming software solutions for sports bookmaking firms operating in the UK, mainland Europe and Asia. At its helm is Andrew Rivkin – founder of the similarly focused Cryptologic, which floated on the Full List with a market cap of £85m in September. Like TradingSports Exchange, another recently floated rival, CES makes its money by taking a small commission against each processed transaction. CES raised £3.7m net on arrival.

Nominated Adviser:	Canaccord Capital, London
AIM Broker:	Canaccord Capital, London
Solicitors:	Osborne Clarke, London
Market Makers:	EVO; KBCS; WINS
Auditors:	KPMG, Toronto, Ontario, M2P 2H3, Canada
Registrars:	Capita Registrars

ENTRY ON AIM:	4/12/2003	Recent price:	107.0p
Interim results:	Sep	Market cap:	£20.92m
Final results:	Mar	Issue price:	68.0p
Year end:	Dec	Current no of shares:	
Accounts due:	Jun		19,554,000
Int div paymnt:	n/a	No of shares after	
Fin div paymnt:	n/a	dilution:	n/a
Int net div per share:	nil	P/E ratio:	n/a
Fin net div per share:	nil	Probable CGT?	No

LATEST REPORTED RESULTS: 6 MONTHS TO 30 JUNE '03		PREVIOUS REPORTED RESULTS: FROM 9 MAY TO 31 DEC '02	
Turnover:	n/a	Turnover:	n/a
PTP:	£(226,000)	PTP:	£(428,000)
EPS:	n/a	EPS:	n/a

CFA Capital
(CFP)

Financial services group
Pountney Hill House, 6 Laurence Pountney Hill, London, EC4R 0BL Tel: 020-7090 7800; Fax: 020-7283 6300;
e-mail: enquiry@cityfin.co.uk

		holding %
Chairman	Stephen Barclay	11.7
Dep Chief Executive	John Shaw	5.3
Finance Director	Ian Buckley	0.6
Main Shareholders:		
Pershing Keen		19.3
A P Rawlinson		3.1

Percentage of free market capital: 59.9%

Comments:
Small-cap specialist Stephen Barclay, also behind Seymour Pierce's flotation, reversed nomad City Financial Associates and Galleon Assets Management into his Abinger cash shell in 2002. In the first half the finance house notched up an overall loss of £0.5m on lower turnover of £0.6m. This prompted a placing at 0.25p to raise £0.3m and the sale of its execution-only brokerage. However, the market anticiptes that the second half was busier and should prove profitable.

Nominated Adviser:	Shore Capital, London
AIM Broker:	Seymour Pierce Ellis, Crawley
Solicitors:	Field Fisher Waterhouse, London
Market Makers:	KBCS; SCAP; WINS
Auditors:	CLB, Aldwych House, 81 Aldwych, London WC2B 4HP
Registrars:	Capita Registrars

ENTRY ON AIM:	12/6/2001	Recent price:	0.7p
Interim results:	Sep	Market cap:	£3.88m
Final results:	Mar	Issue price:	1.0p
Year end:	Dec	Current no of shares:	
Accounts due:	Mar		554,000,000
Int div paymnt:	n/a	No of shares after	
Fin div paymnt:	n/a	dilution:	n/a
Int net div per share:	nil	P/E ratio:	n/a
Fin net div per share:	nil	Probable CGT?	YES

LATEST REPORTED RESULTS: 2002		PREVIOUS REPORTED RESULTS: 2001	
Turnover:	£1.63m	Turnover:	£134,000
PTP:	£(2.39m)	PTP:	£(290,000)
EPS:	(0.6)p	EPS:	(0.3)p

Charlton Athletic (CLO)

Professional football club operator

The Valley, Floyd Road, London, SE7 8BL Tel: 020-8333 4000; Fax: 020-8333 4001; e-mail: info@cafc.co.uk; web site: www.cafc.co.uk

		holding %
Chairman	Richard Murray	25.1
Chief Executive	Peter Varney	0.0
Finance Director	Nigel Capelin	0.0
Deputy Chairman	Robert Whitehand	11.7

Main Shareholders:

Vidacos Nominees	5.3
J Steven Ward	3.8
David White	3.8
David Hughes	3.7

Percentage of free market capital: 21.9%

Comments:

The South London club has secured Premiership status for next season. Interims to December revealed a swing from a £64,000 profit to losses of £690,000 after a charge against the value of a single purchased player. Sales rose an encouraging 20% to £21.3m thanks to broadcasting contracts with the Premier League, rising matchday activity and sponsorship revenues. Full year figures will enjoy a one off gain on the £10m sale of Scott Parker to Chelsea.

Nominated Adviser:	Teather & Greenwood, London
AIM Broker:	Teather & Greenwood, London
Solicitors:	Brachers, Maidstone & London
Market Makers:	KBCS; MLSB; TEAM; WINS
Auditors:	Nunn Hayward, New Malden
Registrars:	Capita Registrars

ENTRY ON AIM:	21/3/1997	**Recent price:**	21.5p
Interim results:	Mar	**Market cap:**	£11.82m
Final results:	Oct	**Issue price:**	80.0p
Year end:	Jun	**Current no of shares:**	
Accounts due:	Oct		54,969,293
Int div paymnt:	n/a	**No of shares after**	
Fin div paymnt:	n/a	**dilution:**	55,256,793
Int net div per share:	nil	**P/E ratio:**	n/a
Fin net div per share:	nil	**Probable CGT?**	YES

LATEST REPORTED RESULTS: 2003		PREVIOUS REPORTED RESULTS: 2002	
Turnover:	£35.14m	**Turnover:**	£30.64m
PTP:	£(464,000)	**PTP:**	£(10.73m)
EPS:	(0.8)p	**EPS:**	(19.5)p

Charterhouse Communications (CHO)

Financial media company

Arnold House, 36-41 Holywell Lane, London, EC2A 3SF Tel: 020-7827 5454; Fax: 020-7827 0567; web site: www.charterhouse-communications.co.uk

		holding %
Chairman	Brian Rowbotham	0.9
Deputy Chairman	Ivan Elliott	9.3
Finance Director	Michael Shipman	1.1
Managing Director	Geoffrey Gamble	9.2

Main Shareholders:

Friends Ivory & Sime	14.0
The Aim Trust	9.0
Cooperation Retirement Benefits Fund	8.1
Nigel Wray	6.9
ISIS Asset Management*	4.5

Percentage of free market capital: 33.8%

*These shares are held in addition to the shares it holds through The Aim Trust

Comments:

The financial media house reduced interim pre-tax losses by 21% to £197,000. Stripping out amortisation of goodwill, an improved profit of £243,000 was recorded. The group said its mortgage magazines continued to trade strongly but its personal finance operations were still struggling. Like many similar publishers, Charterhouse is hoping for a sustained economic recovery, particularly in the financial sphere. Its wishes may come true if economic portents remain good for UK PLC.

Nominated Adviser:	Teather & Greenwood, London
AIM Broker:	Teather & Greenwood, London
Solicitors:	Maxwell Batley, London
Market Makers:	MLSB; SCAP; TEAM; WINS
Auditors:	Grant Thornton, London
Registrars:	Capita Registrars

ENTRY ON AIM:	27/11/1996	**Recent price:**	4.75p
Interim results:	Feb	**Market cap:**	£5.81m
Final results:	Sep	**Issue price:**	5.0p
Year end:	May	**Current no of shares:**	
Accounts due:	Sep		122,344,631
Int div paymnt:	n/a	**No of shares after**	
Fin div paymnt:	Nov	**dilution:**	125,184,631
Int net div per share:	nil	**P/E ratio:**	n/a
Fin net div per share:	0.23p	**Probable CGT?**	YES

LATEST REPORTED RESULTS: 2003		PREVIOUS REPORTED RESULTS: 2002	
Turnover:	£10.24m	**Turnover:**	£12.86m
PTP:	£(266,000)	**PTP:**	£(9.34m)
EPS:	(0.3)p	**EPS:**	(7.6)p

Charteris (CAE)

Business and IT management consultancy

Charteris House, 39/40 Barthollemew Close, London EC1A 7JN Tel: 020-7600 9199; Fax: 020-7600 9212;
e-mail: info@charteris.com; web site: www.charteris.com

		holding %
Chairman	David Mann	22.3
Chief Executive	David Pickering	8.1
Finance Director	Marsali Harwood	0.03
Deputy Chairman	Clifford Preddy	21.6

Main Shareholders:

Chris Rees	10.5
Charteris General Employee Benefit Trust	5.7
Victory Capital	3.9

Percentage of free market capital: 14.1%

Nominated Adviser:	KBC Peel Hunt, London
AIM Broker:	KBC Peel Hunt, London
Solicitors:	Masons, London
Market Makers:	TEAM; WINS
Auditors:	Baker Tilly, 2 Bloomsbury Street, London, WC1B 3ST
Registrars:	Capita Registrars

ENTRY ON AIM:	1/11/2000	**Recent price:**	25.0p
Interim results:	Mar	**Market cap:**	£10.47m
Final results:	Oct	**Issue price:**	90.0p
Year end:	Jul	**Current no of shares:**	
Accounts due:	Nov		41,873,514
Int div paymnt:	n/a	**No of shares after**	
Fin div paymnt:	Dec	**dilution:**	n/a
Int net div per share:	nil	**P/E ratio:**	n/a
Fin net div per share:	0.4p	**Probable CGT?**	YES

LATEST REPORTED RESULTS: 2003		PREVIOUS REPORTED RESULTS: 2002	
Turnover:	£12.17m	Turnover:	£19.09m
PTP:	£(625,000)	PTP:	£1.59m
EPS:	(1.3)p	EPS:	2.9p

Comments:

At its December AGM the business and IT management consultant said trading was meeting expectations and its deal with Microsoft would be worth £1m in revenues this financial year. After some tough times, Charteris may well be turning the corner, having cut costs and boasting a healthier sales pipeline. Last year it moved into a loss before tax on lower turnover, suffering from slow sales and order delays within the important financial services sector.

Cheerful Scout (CLS)

Corporate communication videos and video/DVD editing

25-27 Riding House Street, London, W1W 7DU Tel: 020-7291 0444; Fax: 020-7291 0445;
web site: www.cheerfulscout.com

		holding %
Chairman	Stuart Appleton	1.6
Chief Executive		
Finance Director		
Non-Exec Director	Richard Owen	0.0

Main Shareholders:

RTI	11.5

Percentage of free market capital: 19.6%

Nominated Adviser:	Seymour Pierce, London
AIM Broker:	Seymour Pierce Ellis, Crawley
Solicitors:	Finers Stephens Innocent, London
Market Makers:	SCAP; WINS
Auditors:	A V Audit Limited, 66 Wigmore Street, London W1H 0HQ
Registrars:	Capita Registrars

ENTRY ON AIM:	1/5/2002	**Recent price:**	1.5p
Interim results:	May	**Market cap:**	£2.93m
Final results:	Nov	**Issue price:**	2.5p
Year end:	Jun	**Current no of shares:**	
Accounts due:	Oct		195,000,000
Int div paymnt:	n/a	**No of shares after**	
Fin div paymnt:	n/a	**dilution:**	n/a
Int net div per share:	nil	**P/E ratio:**	n/a
Fin net div per share:	nil	**Probable CGT?**	YES

LATEST REPORTED RESULTS: 2003		PREVIOUS REPORTED RESULTS: 2002	
Turnover:	£733,000	Turnover:	£195,000
PTP:	£(206,000)	PTP:	£62,000
EPS:	(0.1)p	EPS:	0.1p

Comments:

Interim results from the corporate communicatons, DVD and post production services group were very disappointing. Sales dropped to just £252,142 and losses rose to £229,270. A lot of progress needs to be made this year if this group is to justify its public company listing.

Chelford (CHR)

Supply chain and collaborative commerce business

SSI House, Hampshire International Business Park, Crockford Lane, Basingstoke, Hampshire RG24 8WH
Tel: 01256-685400; Fax: 01256-685201; web site: www.chelfordgroup.com

		holding %
Chairman	William Birkett	8.6
Chief Executive	Trevor Lewis	12.8
Finance Director	Martin Anderson	0.0
Non-Exec Director	Stephen Lord	11.6

Main Shareholders:

Adrian de Ferranti	24.9
Dale Stephen Barrington	3.8

Percentage of free market capital: 38.4%

Nominated Adviser:	Arbuthnot, London		
AIM Broker:	Arbuthnot, London		
Solicitors:	Nabarro Nathanson, Reading		
Market Makers:	KBCS; SCAP; WINS		
Auditors:	KPMG, Norfolk House, Silbury Boulevard, Central Milton Keynes, MK9 2HA		
Registrars:	Capita Registrars		

ENTRY ON AIM:	23/3/2000	**Recent price:**	2.9p
Interim results:	Sep	**Market cap:**	£19.2m
Final results:	Apr	**Issue price:**	2.0p
Year end:	Dec	**Current no of shares:**	
Accounts due:	Mar		662,166,667
Int div paymnt:	n/a	**No of shares after**	
Fin div paymnt:	n/a	**dilution:**	n/a
Int net div per share:	nil	**P/E ratio:**	n/a
Fin net div per share:	nil	**Probable CGT?**	YES

LATEST REPORTED RESULTS:	2002	**PREVIOUS REPORTED RESULTS:**	2001
Turnover:	£7.3m	**Turnover:**	£7.81m
PTP:	£(1.03m)	**PTP:**	£(1.05m)
EPS:	(0.2)p	**EPS:**	(0.2)p

Comments:

Software and IT services business Chelford has consolidated upon an improved first-half performance, a period during which sales rose 31% to £4.3m. In a January trading statement, management confirmed that 'Chelford will have achieved a profit before tax and goodwill amortisation for 2003 as a whole'. Cash reserves, meanwhile, are said to have increased by £30,000 to £1.35m. With contracted revenues already covering 70% of costs, a strong 2004 is now expected.

Chepstow Racecourse (CRC)

Racecourse operator

Chepstow, Monmouthshire NP16 6BE Tel: 01291-622260; Fax: 01291-627061; e-mail: info@chepstow-racecourse.co.uk;
web site: www.chepstow-racecourse.co.uk

		holding %
Chairman	Stanley Clarke	57.1
Chief Executive		
Finance Director		
Non-Exec Director	Peter Grodzinski	5.7

Main Shareholders:

St Modwen	27.2

Percentage of free market capital: 3.2%

Nominated Adviser:	Brewin Dolphin, Cardiff		
AIM Broker:	Williams de Broe, London		
Solicitors:	Palser Grossman, Cardiff		
Market Makers:	TEAM; WINS		
Auditors:	KPMG, Cardiff		
Registrars:	Computershare Investor Services		

ENTRY ON AIM:	4/1/2002	**Recent price:**	219.0p
Interim results:	Sep	**Market cap:**	£77.17m
Final results:	Mar	**Issue price:**	162.5p
Year end:	Dec	**Current no of shares:**	
Accounts due:	May		35,236,480
Int div paymnt:	n/a	**No of shares after**	
Fin div paymnt:	Jun	**dilution:**	n/a
Int net div per share:	nil	**P/E ratio:**	27.4
Fin net div per share:	1.1p	**Probable CGT?**	YES

LATEST REPORTED RESULTS:	2002	**PREVIOUS REPORTED RESULTS:**	2001
Turnover:	£3.35m	**Turnover:**	£2.5m
PTP:	£655,000	**PTP:**	£371,000
EPS:	8.0p	**EPS:**	4.1p

Comments:

2003 was a most successful year for Chepstow, which is now one of the UK's three leading racecourse operators. The group has nine racecourses following the acquisition of Northern Racing, an important deal which has enhanced its commercial opportunities and left it better placed to capitalise on opportunities in the evolving horseracing industry. 2003 turnover rocketed up 131%, operating profits powered up 115% and profits at the pre-tax line were lifted 101%.

Chicago Environmental (CEV)

Investment company
c/o Barings Limited, St James's Chambers, Athol Street, Douglas, Isle of Man

		holding %
Chairman	Richard Sandor	2.1
Chief Executive		
Finance Director		
Non-Exec Director	Neil Eckert	2.1

Main Shareholders:
Goldman Sachs	10.0

Percentage of free market capital: 85.8%

Nominated Adviser:	Collins Stewart, London
AIM Broker:	Collins Stewart, London
Solicitors:	Taylor Wessing, London
Market Makers:	CSCS; WINS
Auditors:	KPMG, Heritage Court, Isle of Man IM99 1HN
Registrars:	Computershare Investor Services

Entry on AIM:	18/9/2003	**Recent price:**	102.0p
Interim results:	n/a	**Market cap:**	£15.3m
Final results:	n/a	**Issue price:**	100.0p
Year end:	n/a	**Current no of shares:**	
Accounts due:	n/a		15,000,000
Int div paymnt:	n/a	**No of shares after**	
Fin div paymnt:	n/a	**dilution:**	n/a
Int net div per share:	nil	**P/E ratio:**	n/a
Fin net div per share:	nil	**Probable CGT?**	No

LATEST REPORTED RESULTS:	N/A	PREVIOUS REPORTED RESULTS:	
Turnover:	n/a	Turnover:	n/a
PTP:	n/a	PTP:	n/a
EPS:	n/a	EPS:	n/a

Comments:
CE is an environmental investment company, formed to invest $15m (£9m) in CCX – operator of a US trading exchange focused on the reduction of greenhouse gas (GHG) emissions. The exchange works by allowing firms to offset their emissions against each other, the theory being that this will lead to a reduction in overall US GHGs pollution. Having raised a total of £15m on launch, CE will also look to invest in other promising environmentally friendly businesses. No update has yet been given.

Chorion (COR)

Brand management and creation business
4th floor, Aldwych House, 81 Aldwych, London, WC2B 4HN Tel: 020-7061 3800; Fax: 020-7061 3801;
web site: www.chorion.co.uk

		holding %
Chairman	William Astor	0.0
Managing Director	Nicholas Williams	0.0
Finance Director	Jeremy Banks	0.0
Deputy Chairman	The Lord Alli	0.8

Main Shareholders:
Schoder Investment Management	7.6
Canada Life Marketing Group	6.0
UBS Asset Management	5.9
Merrill Lynch Investment Managers	4.2
M & G Investement Management	4.0

Percentage of free market capital: 63.2%

Nominated Adviser:	Evolution Beeson Gregory, London
AIM Broker:	Evolution Beeson Gregory, London
Solicitors:	Norton Rose & Berwin Leighton Paisner, London
Market Makers:	ARBT; CSFB; KBCS; MLSB; SCAP; WEST; WINS
Auditors:	KPMG Audit, London
Registrars:	Capita Registrars

Entry on AIM:	17/5/2002	**Recent price:**	212.5p
Interim results:	Sep	**Market cap:**	£36.66m
Final results:	Apr	**Issue price:**	11.25p
Year end:	Dec	**Current no of shares:**	
Accounts due:	Apr		17,250,764
Int div paymnt:	n/a	**No of shares after**	
Fin div paymnt:	n/a	**dilution:**	n/a
Int net div per share:	nil	**P/E ratio:**	31.3
Fin net div per share:	nil	**Probable CGT?**	Yes

LATEST REPORTED RESULTS:	2003	PREVIOUS REPORTED RESULTS:	2002
Turnover:	£18.57m	Turnover:	£9.27m
PTP:	£3.15m	PTP:	£433,000
EPS:	6.8p	EPS:	(0.2)p

Comments:
Entertainment brands business Chorion produced vastly improved full year results, spurred on by the success of children's character Noddy both in the UK and overseas. Having signed a new deal with ITV to produce a minimum of four new Miss Marple or Poirot dramas each year the future is looking increasingly bright too. And recent news that the company is also negotiating the purchase of the already established Mr Men licensing business is set to add further momentum.

Churchill China (CHH)

Ceramic tableware maker

Marlborough Pottery, High Street, Tunstall, Stoke on Trent, Staffordshire ST6 5NZ Tel: 01782-577566;
Fax: 01782-837239; e-mail: churchill@churchillchina.plc.uk; web site: www.churchillchina.com

		holding %
Chairman	Stephen Roper	11.2
Chief Executive	Andrew Roper	7.2
Finance Director	David Taylor	0.1
Operations Director	David O'Connor	0.04

Main Shareholders:

Steelite International	17.2
M Roper	10.9
LandFinance	5.2
Miss S Roper	3.7

Percentage of free market capital: 44.3%

Nominated Adviser:	Williams de Broe, Birmingham
AIM Broker:	Williams de Broe, Birmingham
Solicitors:	Addleshaw Goddard, Manchester
Market Makers:	KLWT; WDBM; WINS
Auditors:	PricewaterhouseCoopers, Birmingham
Registrars:	Lloyds TSB Registrars

ENTRY ON AIM:	22/4/2003	**Recent price:**	216.5p
Interim results:	Aug	Market cap:	£23.17m
Final results:	Mar	Issue price:	n/a
Year end:	Dec	**Current no of shares:**	
Accounts due:	May		10,704,376
Int div paymnt:	Dec	**No of shares after**	
Fin div paymnt:	Jun	dilution:	n/a
Int net div per share:	3.3p	P/E ratio:	16.2
Fin net div per share:	6.0p	Probable CGT?	YES

LATEST REPORTED RESULTS: 2003		PREVIOUS REPORTED RESULTS: 2002	
Turnover:	£49.47m	Turnover:	£50.9m
PTP:	£1.16m	PTP:	£1.78m
EPS:	5.7p	EPS:	13.4p

Comments:

Interims from ceramics business Churchill China were something of a disappointment, profits flat at £500,000 on sales reduced £600,000 to £23.7m – although they did include £1.3m of exceptional restructuring costs. With this hit now taken, however, a brighter 2004 is forecast and dividend payments remain strong. When 2003 figures are published, they are expected to show a profit of £2.7m before tax and exceptionals, rising to £3.7m in 2004.

CI Traders (CI.)

Holding company for businesses in the retail, brewing, hotel and leisure sectors

1-3 L'Avenue, le Bas, Longueville, St Saviour, Jersey JE4 8NB Tel: 01534-508400

		holding %
Chairman	Thomas Hays Scott	13.7
Chief Executive	David Bralsford	3.3
Finance Director	Donal Duff	0.0
Deputy Chairman	Michael Wilkes	0.02

Main Shareholders:

Cadic	13.9
HSBC	4.5
Forest Nominees	4.5
Calvet	3.7

Percentage of free market capital: 55.8%

Nominated Adviser:	Collins Stewart, London
AIM Broker:	Collins Stewart, London
Solicitors:	Clifford Chance, London
Market Makers:	CSCS; WINS
Auditors:	Deloitte & Touche, Jersey & KPMG, London
Registrars:	Computershare Investor Services

ENTRY ON AIM:	15/8/2002	**Recent price:**	69.0p
Interim results:	Dec	Market cap:	£161.53m
Final results:	Apr	Issue price:	83.0p
Year end:	Jan	**Current no of shares:**	
Accounts due:	May		234,104,054
Int div paymnt:	Dec	**No of shares after**	
Fin div paymnt:	Jun	dilution:	n/a
Int net div per share:	1.25p	P/E ratio:	12.3
Fin net div per share:	2.0p	Probable CGT?	No

LATEST REPORTED RESULTS: 2003 (53 WEEKS)		PREVIOUS REPORTED RESULTS: 2002	
Turnover:	£275.8m	Turnover:	£258.2m
PTP:	£17.1m	PTP:	£16.3m
EPS:	5.6p	EPS:	5.2p

Comments:

The consumer and leisure conglomerate has suffered from difficult trading conditions in the Channel Islands and is set only to reach interim profits in line with last year. The Guernsey hotels' sales fell 2.7% but since receiving a casino licence for its St. Pierre Park Hotel last September, the company will spend £15m on the first two phases of a total redevelopment. The big news on the horizon is a full property revaluation at the end of January. A lot of unrealised gains are expected.

City Lofts
(CTF)

Property company

Town Centre House, Cheltenham Cresent, Harrogate, Yorkshire HG1 1DQ Tel: 0142-356 9556; Fax: 0142-353 6777

		holding %
Chairman	Nigel Denby	0.0
Chief Executive	Stuart Wright	22.2
Finance Director	Mark Hadcock	3.9
Commercial Director	Ross Mansori-Dara	22.0

Main Shareholders:

Melvin Morris	7.8
Nicholas Moody	3.9

Percentage of free market capital: 14.8%

Nominated Adviser:	Collins Stewart, London
AIM Broker:	Collins Stewart, London
Solicitors:	Lawrence Graham, London
Market Makers:	CSCS; WINS
Auditors:	Baker Tilly, 2 Whitehall Quay, Leeds LS1 4HG
Registrars:	Capita Registrars

ENTRY ON AIM:	18/12/2004	**Recent price:**	99.5p
Interim results:	Jan	**Market cap:**	£46.77m
Final results:	Jul	**Issue price:**	100.0p
Year end:	Mar	**Current no of shares:**	
Accounts due:	Sep		47,000,032
Int div paymnt:	n/a	**No of shares after**	
Fin div paymnt:	n/a	**dilution:**	n/a
Int net div per share:	nil	**P/E ratio:**	n/a
Fin net div per share:	nil	**Probable CGT?**	No

LATEST REPORTED RESULTS: 18 MONTHS TO 31 MAR '03		PREVIOUS REPORTED RESULTS: 2001	
Turnover:	£1.99m	**Turnover:**	£663,000
PTP:	£(373,000)	**PTP:**	£(179,000)
EPS:	n/a	**EPS:**	n/a

Comments:
City Lofts raised £7m on admission. As a developer of urban mixed-use property schemes, the company prides itself on maintaining high quality. In fact, City Lofts use Conran for architectural and interior design. Interim pre-tax profit to September reached £839,000 compared to losses of £373,000 for the previous 18 months. Of the nine developments completed, eight are expected to generate £193m in revenue in the next two years.

Cityblock (formerly Easyroad)
(CLK)

Student accommodation provider

Fleet House, New Road, Lancaster, LA1 1EZ Tel: 01524-541200; Fax: 01524-541201; web site: www.cityblock.co.uk

		holding %
Chairman	Martin Higginson	26.1
Managing Director	Trevor Bargh	26.0
Finance Director		
Non-Exec Director	Richard Hughes	17.6

Main Shareholders:

n/a

Percentage of free market capital: 30.4%

Nominated Adviser:	WH Ireland, Manchester
AIM Broker:	WH Ireland, Manchester
Solicitors:	Wacks Caller, Manchester
Market Makers:	WINS
Auditors:	PKF, Sovereign House, Queen Street, Manchester M2 6WH
Registrars:	Capita Registrars

ENTRY ON AIM:	29/7/2003	**Recent price:**	80.0p
Interim results:	n/a	**Market cap:**	£17.47m
Final results:	n/a	**Issue price:**	48.0p
Year end:	n/a	**Current no of shares:**	
Accounts due:	n/a		21,842,097
Int div paymnt:	n/a	**No of shares after**	
Fin div paymnt:	n/a	**dilution:**	n/a
Int net div per share:	nil	**P/E ratio:**	n/a
Fin net div per share:	nil	**Probable CGT?**	No

LATEST REPORTED RESULTS: N/A		PREVIOUS REPORTED RESULTS: N/A	
Turnover:	n/a	**Turnover:**	n/a
PTP:	n/a	**PTP:**	n/a
EPS:	n/a	**EPS:**	n/a

Comments:
Cityblock is looking to be to student accommodation what Harvey Nichols is to London shopping in offering secure upmarket off-campus accommodation. Its first site in Lancaster with 30 rooms was sold as soon as the sites became available and it is currently building a second larger site comprising 77 rooms. Losses for the interim to September were £10,300. Executive chairman Higginson was voted North West Entrepreneur for 2002. Cash stands at £697,000.

Civica (CIV)

Software company
2 Burston Road, Putney, London, Tel: 020-7760 2800

		holding %
Chairman	Laurence Vaughan	0.03
Chief Executive	Simon Downing	0.5
Finance Director	Michael Stoddard	0.6
Non-Exec Director	Mark Pearman	0.01

Main Shareholders:

Alchemy Partners	38.9

Percentage of free market capital: 60.0%

Nominated Adviser:	Seymour Pierce, London
AIM Broker:	Seymour Pierce, London
Solicitors:	DLA, London
Market Makers:	WINS
Auditors:	KPMG, 1 TheEmbankment, Neville Street, Leeds LS1 4DW
Registrars:	Capita Registrars

ENTRY ON AIM:	1/3/2004	Recent price:	191.5p
Interim results:	Jun	Market cap:	£86.66m
Final results:	Dec	Issue price:	175.0p
Year end:	Sep	Current no of shares:	
Accounts due:	Mar		45,255,690
Int div paymnt:	n/a	No of shares after	
Fin div paymnt:	n/a	dilution:	n/a
Int net div per share:	nil	P/E ratio:	14.5
Fin net div per share:	nil	Probable CGT?	Yes

LATEST REPORTED RESULTS: 2003		PREVIOUS REPORTED RESULTS: 2002	
Turnover:	£90.30m	Turnover:	£91.39m
PTP:	£9.32m	PTP:	£6.75m
EPS:	13.2p	EPS:	10.5p

Comments:
Public sector-focused IT business Civica arrived on AIM having raised £15m of new cash and a further £30m for existing investors to provide them with an exit. The money raised by the company directly will be used to pay bank debts down to £18m. Already strongly profitable, Civica derives most of its revenue from software sales at present. However, management also has high hopes for its consulting and managed services arms. Further improvements in sales and pre-exceptional pre-tax profits are expected this year.

Civilian Content (CCN)

Film and television financier and producer
4th Floor, Portland House, 4 Great Portland Street, London, W1W 8QJ Tel: 020-7612 0030; Fax: 020-7612 0031; e-mail: reception@civiliancontent.com; web site: www.civiliancontent.com

		holding %
Chairman	Crispin Barker	27.0
Managing Director	Chris Auty	0.7
Finance Director	Norman Humphrey	0.1
Director	Aline Perry	0.0

Main Shareholders:

Fandango	29.0
Richard Thompson*	24.3
Vidacos Nominees	18.3
Chase Nominees	9.2
Rizona (Hong Kong)	8.6

Percentage of free market capital: n/a

*These shares are registered in the name of Burj Properties

Nominated Adviser:	KBC Peel Hunt, London
AIM Broker:	KBC Peel Hunt, London
Solicitors:	The Simkins Partnership, London
Market Makers:	KBCS; MLSB; SCAP; WINS
Auditors:	AGN Shipleys, London
Registrars:	Capita Registrars

ENTRY ON AIM:	1/7/1999	Recent price:	7.75p
Interim results:	Sep	Market cap:	£3.51m
Final results:	Mar	Issue price:	n/a
Year end:	Dec	Current no of shares:	
Accounts due:	Apr		45,254,817
Int div paymnt:	n/a	No of shares after	
Fin div paymnt:	n/a	dilution:	n/a
Int net div per share:	nil	P/E ratio:	n/a
Fin net div per share:	nil	Probable CGT?	Yes

LATEST REPORTED RESULTS: 2002		PREVIOUS REPORTED RESULTS: 2001	
Turnover:	£6.66m	Turnover:	£14.44m
PTP:	£103,000	PTP:	£(5.47m)
EPS:	0.3p	EPS:	(13.7)p

Comments:
Most of Civilian's activity comes from its film distribution arm The Works. Three films were selected for the Berlin Film Festival and the rights of film Country of my Skull has been sold to Sony Classics/Columbia Tri-Star with expected revenues of US$700,000. Unfortunately, the income will fall in the first half of 2004, negatively impacting 2003 results. Italian Independent film production and distribution company Fandango has taken a 29% stake in the company.

Clan Homes (CNH)

Residential property manager

1a Greenhill Avenue, Giffnock, Glasgow, G46 6QX Tel: 0141-621 2165; Fax: 0141-638 0781

		holding %
Chairman	Alan Thomson	12.8
Chief Executive		
Finance Director		
Director	David Hickey	9.3

Main Shareholders:

West Caledonian Assests	81.3

Percentage of free market capital: -3.3%

Nominated Adviser:	Brewin Dolphin, Edinburgh
AIM Broker:	Brewin Dolphin, Edinburgh
Solicitors:	McClure Naismith, Glasgow
Market Makers:	WINS
Auditors:	Ernst & Young, 50 Huntly Street, Aberdeen, AB10 1ZN
Registrars:	Park Circus

ENTRY ON AIM: 25/10/1995		**Recent price:**	98.5p
Interim results:	Dec	**Market cap:**	£1.06m
Final results:	Sep	**Issue price:**	100.0p
Year end:	Mar	**Current no of shares:**	
Accounts due:	Oct		1,080,654
Int div paymnt:	n/a	**No of shares after**	
Fin div paymnt:	n/a	**dilution:**	n/a
Int net div per share:	nil	**P/E ratio:**	n/a
Fin net div per share:	nil	**Probable CGT?**	No

LATEST REPORTED RESULTS: 2003		PREVIOUS REPORTED RESULTS: 2002	
Turnover:	£80,000	Turnover:	£108,000
PTP:	£(51,000)	PTP:	£(49,000)
EPS:	(5.3)p	EPS:	(5.0)p

Comments:

Scottish property manager Clan has been disposing of its entire property portfolio since last year. Benefiting from rising property prices, Clan intends to use the proceeds to become a cash shell with no debt with the intention of achieving shareholder value by procuring a reverse takeover. Major shareholder Western Caledonian Assets recently agreed to sell 200,000 shares to David Hickey, who has previous experience of reverse takeovers, and other 'investors'.

Clarity Commerce Solutions (CCS)

Software solutions provider

One Netherhampton Business Centre, Netherhampton, Salisbury, Wiltshire SP2 8PU Tel: 01722-746200; Fax: 01722-746224; e-mail: investor@clarity.plc.uk; web site: www.claritycommerce.com

		holding %
Chairman	Bob Morton*	7.1
Managing Director	Graham York	25.1
Finance Director		
Technical Director	David Shearmon	1.2

Main Shareholders:

Southwind*	9.6
Close Investments	9.6
RBSTB Nominees	9.2
Gartmore Investment	7.6

Percentage of free market capital: 30.7%

*Southwind is an investment company wholly owned by a trust established by Bob Morton for his children

Nominated Adviser:	Williams de Broe, Birmingham
AIM Broker:	Williams de Broe, Birmingham
Solicitors:	Hammonds, Birmingham
Market Makers:	KBCS; WDBM; WINS
Auditors:	Solomon Hare, Bristol
Registrars:	Capita Registrars

ENTRY ON AIM: 26/7/2000		**Recent price:**	60.0p
Interim results:	Dec	**Market cap:**	£9.26m
Final results:	Jul	**Issue price:**	125.0p
Year end:	Mar	**Current no of shares:**	
Accounts due:	May		15,427,402
Int div paymnt:	n/a	**No of shares after**	
Fin div paymnt:	n/a	**dilution:**	n/a
Int net div per share:	nil	**P/E ratio:**	31.6
Fin net div per share:	nil	**Probable CGT?**	YES

LATEST REPORTED RESULTS: 2003		PREVIOUS REPORTED RESULTS: 2002	
Turnover:	£7.26m	Turnover:	£7.62m
PTP:	£315,000	PTP:	£(221,000)
EPS:	1.9p	EPS:	(2.5)p

Comments:

IT business Clarity Commerce has admitted that full year profits will fail to match analyst expectations, yet there remain many positives for the company. An earlier expected need to invest in product upgrades at recently acquired cinema ticketing software supplier Pacer/Cats appears to have triggered the warning. Longer term, however, this is likely to work in Clarity's favour. Annual profits 'significantly above' the £315,000 achieved last year are still forecast.

Clean Diesel Technologies (CDT)

Developer of cleaner and more efficient diesel engines

300 Atlantic St, Suite 702, Stamford, CT 6901 USA, Tel: 00-1 203 327 7050; Fax: 00-1 203.323.0461;
e-mail: information@cdti.com; web site: www.cdti.com

		holding %
Chairman	Derek Gray	0.4
Chief Executive	Jeremy Peter-Hoblyn	0.0
Finance Officer	David Whitwell	0.1
Non-Exec Director	Derek Gray	2.4

Main Shareholders:

Fuel-Tech	16.3
Positive Securities	9.8
Waltham Forest Friendly Society	9.5
Cadogan Settled Estates	9.4
J A Kanis	3.2

Percentage of free market capital: 48.5%

Comments:

This intriguing speciality chemical company has patented products slashing emissions from diesel engines. Last year, CDT scored higher revenues thanks to rising sales of the Platinum Plus fuel-borne catalyst, though these were partially offset by lower ARIS license and royalty income. Annual losses widened on higher development costs. The year's fourth quarter was a milestone one, marked by Platinum Plus verification by the Environmental Protection Agency (EPA).

Nominated Adviser:	Nabarro Wells, London
AIM Broker:	Durlacher, London
Solicitors:	Faegre Benson Hobson Audley, London
Market Makers:	KBCS; WINS
Auditors:	Ernst & Young, USA
Registrars:	Capita Registrars

ENTRY ON AIM: 28/12/2001		**Recent price:**	165.0p
Interim results:	Aug	**Market cap:**	£14.25m
Final results:	Mar	**Issue price:**	140.0p
Year end:	Dec	**Current no of shares:**	
Accounts due:	Apr		8,633,616
Int div paymnt:	n/a	**No of shares after**	
Fin div paymnt:	n/a	**dilution:**	12,782,669
Int net div per share:	nil	**P/E ratio:**	n/a
Fin net div per share:	nil	**Probable CGT?**	No

LATEST REPORTED RESULTS:	2002	PREVIOUS REPORTED RESULTS:	2001
Turnover:	$441,000	Turnover:	$1.60m
PTP:	$(2.67m)	PTP:	$(936,000)
EPS:	$(0.2)	EPS:	$(1.1)

Clipper Ventures (CLV)

Round-the-world yacht race organiser

Shamrock Quay, William Street, Northam, Southampton, SO14 5QL Tel: 023-8023 7088; Fax: 023-80237 081;
e-mail: HQ@clipper-ventures.com; web site: www.clipper-ventures.com

		holding %
Chairman	Robin Knox-Johnston	10.9
Chief Executive	William Ward	29.2
Finance Director	Jeremy Knight	0.0
Non-Exec Director	Robert Dench	0.0

Main Shareholders:

Stasson Investment Group	10.1
Close Bros VCT	6.8
Chelverton Growth Trust	6.2
Close Bros Protected VCT	4.8

Percentage of free market capital: 32.0%

Comments:

Although interim results were weak with turnover at £1.5m and the small £13,000 pre-tax profit last year turning into a huge loss of £545,000, things are beginning to look up. For the Clipper 2005/6 around the world race, it has gained three hosts, with Liverpool providing £1.8m in sponsorship and Durban, South Africa, entering into a £427,000 deal. Perth in Western Australia has also signed up for the 12-stage race. The monies received should be reflected in the next results.

Nominated Adviser:	ARM Corporate Finance, London
AIM Broker:	Hoodless Brennan, London
Solicitors:	Memery Crystal, London
Market Makers:	HOOD; SCAP; WINS
Auditors:	MacIntyre Hudson, Northampton
Registrars:	Capita Registrars

ENTRY ON AIM: 26/8/1999		**Recent price:**	17.25p
Interim results:	Mar	**Market cap:**	£4.33m
Final results:	Oct	**Issue price:**	40.0p
Year end:	Apr	**Current no of shares:**	
Accounts due:	Nov		25,104,724
Int div paymnt:	n/a	**No of shares after**	
Fin div paymnt:	n/a	**dilution:**	n/a
Int net div per share:	nil	**P/E ratio:**	n/a
Fin net div per share:	nil	**Probable CGT?**	Yes

LATEST REPORTED RESULTS:	2003	PREVIOUS REPORTED RESULTS:	2002
Turnover:	£2.80m	Turnover:	£2.25m
PTP:	£(468,000)	PTP:	£(314,000)
EPS:	(3.4)p	EPS:	(2.4)p

Clover (CLR)

Manufacturer & supplier of edible oils for healthcare & nutritional sectors

7 Sefton Road, Thornleigh NSW 2120, Australia, Tel: 00-61 2 9956 8200; Fax: 00-61 2 9484 1166;
e-mail: andrewf@clovercorp.com.au; web site: www.clovercorp.com.au

		holding %
Chairman	Peter Robinson	0.03
Managing Director		
Finance Director		
Non-Exec Director	Hamish Drummond	18.5

Main Shareholders:

Washington H Soul Pattinson & Co	28.6

Percentage of free market capital: 52.8%

Nominated Adviser:	KBC Peel Hunt, London
AIM Broker:	KBC Peel Hunt, London
Solicitors:	Sparke Helmore, Sydney
Market Makers:	KBCS; WINS
Auditors:	Lawler Partners, Sydney
Registrars:	Computershare Investor Services

ENTRY ON AIM:	16/5/2001	Recent price:	17.5p
Interim results:	Jan	Market cap:	£26.44m
Final results:	Aug	Issue price:	8.5p
Year end:	Jun	Current no of shares:	
Accounts due:	Oct		151,110,933
Int div paymnt:	n/a	No of shares after	
Fin div paymnt:	n/a	dilution:	165,350,000
Int net div per share:	nil	P/E ratio:	n/a
Fin net div per share:	nil	Probable CGT?	No

LATEST REPORTED RESULTS: 2003		PREVIOUS REPORTED RESULTS: 2002	
Turnover:	A$12.01m	Turnover:	A$10.55m
PTP:	A$809,000	PTP:	A$(5.57m)
EPS:	0.3Ac	EPS:	(3.7)Ac

Comments:

Clover, which owns the intellectual property over a nutritional supplement called Omega3, derived from tuna fish oil, saw profits before tax to December increase 135% to A$871,000 on 73% improved revenues of A$9m. It has also recently entered into a joint venture for soy processing and applications with Moree Seed Grades where a soy flour milling facility will be constructed. It has a strong balance sheet with A$14.7m in cash.

Clubhaus (CHA)

Country club operator

Bath Road, Knowl Hill, Reading, RG10 9AL Tel: 0870-240 8924; Fax: 0870-240 8925; e-mail: info@clubhaus.com; web site: www.clubhaus.com

		holding %
Chairman	Paul Sellars	0.1
Managing Director	Charlie Parker	0.4
Finance Director	Paul Stephens	0.1
Non-Exec Director	John Hume	0.0

Main Shareholders:

Morley Fund Management	9.3
MWB	8.7
Deutsche Bank AG	8.6
M & G	7.3
Fidelity International	7.2

Percentage of free market capital: 27.2%

Nominated Adviser:	KBC Peel Hunt, London
AIM Broker:	KBC Peel Hunt, London
Solicitors:	Ashursts, London
Market Makers:	GRAB; KBCS; MLSB; SCAP; WINS
Auditors:	Baker Tilly, 2 Bloomsbury Street, London WC1B 3ST
Registrars:	Capita Registrars

ENTRY ON AIM:	29/10/2001	Recent price:	0.3p
Interim results:	May	Market cap:	£2.74m
Final results:	Dec	Issue price:	3.75p
Year end:	Sep	Current no of shares:	
Accounts due:	Dec		914,614,165
Int div paymnt:	n/a	No of shares after	
Fin div paymnt:	n/a	dilution:	n/a
Int net div per share:	nil	P/E ratio:	n/a
Fin net div per share:	nil	Probable CGT?	No

LATEST REPORTED RESULTS: 2003		PREVIOUS REPORTED RESULTS: 2002	
Turnover:	£27.15m	Turnover:	£34.1m
PTP:	£(704,000)	PTP:	£(14.29m)
EPS:	(0.1)p	EPS:	(3.2)p

Comments:

Debts still dominate at Clubhaus. In 2002, high yield bond holders converted £45m of their bonds into shares representing around 80% of the group. However, as at last September it sill had net debts of £55.9m, which included £15.9m of high yield bonds. The group paid the interest on this for 2003 by issuing, wait for it, £1.6m of high yield bonds. The interest per year on these bonds is 12%. In amongst all of this is a business operating country clubs. These are likely to be sold.

Cluff Mining

(CLU)

Mineral deposits identifier, acquirer and developer

29 St James's Place, London, SW1A 1NR Tel: 020-7495 2030; Fax: 020-7495 2245; e-mail: admin@cluff-mining.com;
web site: www.cluff-mining.com

		holding %
Chairman	John Cluff	4.2
Chief Executive	Terence Wilkinson	0.3
Finance Director	Donald McAlister	0.0
Non-Exec Director	Mzi Khumalo**	13.7

Main Shareholders:

Russell Investment Corporation	23.4
J Cluff*	17.9
The Africa Emerging Markets Fund	5.4
Odey Asset Management	4.8
Hitchcock/Rushbury/Tang/Murray	4.8

Percentage of free market capital: 33.6%

*Includes Ordinary Shares held by St. Cross Trustee & J Cluff
**Through his interest in Rosario International Investments Limited and Gibbs International Holdings Limited, Mr Khumalo is interested in 13.49%

Comments:
Algy Cluff has resigned as chief executive of Cluff Mining to work on floating its gold assets in a new company, Cluff Gold. Terry Wilkinson, ex-platinum boss at Lonmin, now runs Cluff Mining, which lost an interim £1.25m and is focused on platinum group metals in South Africa's Bushveld. Still out of favour with investors, Cluff Mining has a £3.2m facility from Standard Bank, which has a million Cluff Mining three-year options at 120p.

Nominated Adviser:	Investec, London		
AIM Broker:	Canaccord, London		
Solicitors:	Slaughter and May, London		
Market Makers:	IHCS; KBCS; WINS		
Auditors:	KPMG Audit, 8 Salisbury Square, London EC4Y 8BB		
Registrars:	Capita Registrars		

ENTRY ON AIM:	5/5/2000	**Recent price:**	83.5p
Interim results:	Sep	**Market cap:**	£21.75m
Final results:	Apr	**Issue price:**	220.0p
Year end:	Dec	**Current no of shares:**	
Accounts due:	Apr		26,044,345
Int div paymnt:	n/a	**No of shares after**	
Fin div paymnt:	n/a	**dilution:**	n/a
Int net div per share:	nil	**P/E ratio:**	n/a
Fin net div per share:	nil	**Probable CGT?**	No

LATEST REPORTED RESULTS: 2002		PREVIOUS REPORTED RESULTS: 2001	
Turnover:	$414,000	**Turnover:**	$3.83m
PTP:	$(9.62m)	**PTP:**	$(8.18m)
EPS:	(46.0)c	**EPS:**	(59.0)c

CMS Webview

(CWV)

Collector and distributor of real-time financial data

2nd Floor, Hermitage Court, 8-10 Sampson Street, London, E1W 1NA Tel: 020-7265 0772; Fax: 020-7265 0875;
e-mail: sales@cms.co.uk; web site: www.cms.co.uk

		holding %
Chairman	Keppel Simpson	0.5
Chief Executive	Robert Antell	25.9
Finance Director	Stephen Hill	1.5
Vice Chairman	Keith Young	19.6

Main Shareholders:

Singer & Friedlander	5.0

Percentage of free market capital: 47.6%

Comments:
Interim results from CMS showed further progress in the company's long trek back to profitability. Sales surged 55% to £905,000 as demand for the firm's transactional data interface products rose and this, in turn, enabled CMS to slash losses from £345,000 to £116,000. The company's recently signed distribution deal with US software producer Data Transmission Network also appears to have played a key role in the figures with nine new sales having been made in the first half.

Nominated Adviser:	Smith & Williamson, London		
AIM Broker:	Corporate Synergy, Crawley		
Solicitors:	DLA, London		
Market Makers:	SCAP; WINS		
Auditors:	Grant Thornton, London		
Registrars:	Capita Registrars		

ENTRY ON AIM:	4/8/2000	**Recent price:**	13.0p
Interim results:	Jun	**Market cap:**	£10.4m
Final results:	May	**Issue price:**	10.0p
Year end:	Dec	**Current no of shares:**	
Accounts due:	Apr		80,000,000
Int div paymnt:	n/a	**No of shares after**	
Fin div paymnt:	n/a	**dilution:**	n/a
Int net div per share:	nil	**P/E ratio:**	n/a
Fin net div per share:	nil	**Probable CGT?**	Yes

LATEST REPORTED RESULTS: 2002		PREVIOUS REPORTED RESULTS: 2001	
Turnover:	£1.21m	**Turnover:**	£1.12m
PTP:	£(683,000)	**PTP:**	£(880,000)
EPS:	(1.1)p	**EPS:**	(1.6)p

Cobra Bio-Manufacturing (CBF)

Manufacturer of DNA and protein based pharmaceuticals for clinical trials

Stephenson Building, Keele University Science Park, Keele, Staffordshire, ST5 5SP Tel: 01782-382205; Fax: 01782-714168; e-mail: info@cobrabio.com; web site: www.cobrabio.com

		holding %
Chairman	Peter Fothergill	0.1
Chief Executive	David Thatcher	0.1
Finance Director	Peter Coleman	0.02
Non-Exec Director	David Bloxham	0.04

Main Shareholders:

ML Laboratories	5.1
Britannic Investment Managers*	6.3
INVESCO English and International Trust	6.0
Fidelity Investments	5.8
Standard Life	5.1

Percentage of free market capital: 67.5%

*These shares are registered in the name of Vidacos Nominees

Nominated Adviser:	Collins Stewart, London
AIM Broker:	Collins Stewart, London
Solicitors:	Gateley Wareing, Birmingham
Market Makers:	CSCS; WINS
Auditors:	Ernst & Young, 100 Barbirolli Square, Manchester M2 3EY
Registrars:	Capita Registrars

ENTRY ON AIM:	13/6/2002	**Recent price:**	80.0p
Interim results:	May	**Market cap:**	£15.6m
Final results:	Dec	**Issue price:**	100.0p
Year end:	Sept	**Current no of shares:**	
Accounts due:	Jan		19,500,000
Int div paymnt:	n/a	**No of shares after**	
Fin div paymnt:	n/a	**dilution:**	n/a
Int net div per share:	nil	**P/E ratio:**	11.6
Fin net div per share:	nil	**Probable CGT?**	YES

LATEST REPORTED RESULTS: 2003		PREVIOUS REPORTED RESULTS: 2002	
Turnover:	£6.02m	Turnover:	£2.57m
PTP:	£817,000	PTP:	£(937,000)
EPS:	6.9p	EPS:	1.0p

Comments:

The producer of DNA that is resistant to antibiotics, used by biotech companies wishing to develop novel genetic therapies, has disappointed investors with an unexpected profit warning. This came shortly after Cobra reported a maiden annual profit. The group, which has recently expanded capacity, was predicted to make a profit this year, but now only reckons it will break even. Sales will rise by 30 per cent rather than 80 per cent due to delayed orders.

Coburg (CGG)

Importer and distributor of coffee & tea

3 Harrington Way, Warspite Road, Woolwich, London, SE18 5NU Tel: 020-8317 0103; Fax: 020-8855 5664

		holding %
Chairman	Konrad Legg*	19.4
Chief Executive	Alistair Summers	14.0
Finance Director		
Non-Exec Director	Anne Higgins	0.7

Main Shareholders:

Tudeley Holdings*	11.9
Michael Cronk	8.9
Westcombe Investments	6.0

Percentage of free market capital: 38.5%

*Konrad Legg is interested in these shares

Nominated Adviser:	Grant Thornton, London
AIM Broker:	Fiske, London
Solicitors:	James Stallard, London
Market Makers:	MLSB, WINS
Auditors:	Lees, 1 Purley Road, Purley, Surrey CR8 2HA
Registrars:	Capita Registrars

ENTRY ON AIM:	25/9/2002	**Recent price:**	10.75p
Interim results:	Jan	**Market cap:**	£1.78m
Final results:	Jul	**Issue price:**	n/a
Year end:	Apr	**Current no of shares:**	
Accounts due:	Oct		16,590,914
Int div paymnt:	n/a	**No of shares after**	
Fin div paymnt:	n/a	**dilution:**	n/a
Int net div per share:	nil	**P/E ratio:**	n/a
Fin net div per share:	nil	**Probable CGT?**	No

LATEST REPORTED RESULTS: 2003		PREVIOUS REPORTED RESULTS: 2002	
Turnover:	£1.91m	Turnover:	£1.84m
PTP:	£(33,000)	PTP:	£(236,000)
EPS:	(0.3)p	EPS:	(2.3)p

Comments:

The tea and coffee importer saw turnover increase 30% to £1.25m in the interim to October and profits before tax came in at £5,000. This compares with a loss of £24,000 last time. It is planning to develop Colchester-based Ashby's as a coffee franchise brand as well as raising the profile of last year's acquisition Rizzi as a genuine Italian brand. Coburg has warned it is aware that conditions in the high street remain challenging for many of its clients.

CODASciSys (CSY)

Computer software provider

Methuen Park, Chippenham, Wiltshire SN14 0GB Tel: 01249-466466; Fax: 01249-466666;
e-mail: marketing@scisys.co.uk; web site: www.codascisys.co.uk

		holding %
Chairman	Mike Love	10.8
Chief Executive	Graham Steinsberg	3.3
Finance Director	Ruth McRitchie	0.02
Dir & MD (Space)	John Haynes	3.7

Main Shareholders:

Science Systems Employee Share Trust	7.4

Percentage of free market capital: 69.9%

Nominated Adviser:	Rowan Dartington, Bristol
AIM Broker:	Rowan Dartington, Bristol
Solicitors:	Burges Salmon, Bristol
Market Makers:	KBCS; WINS
Auditors:	KPMG, 100 Temple Street, Bristol BS1 6AG
Registrars:	Computershare Investor Services

ENTRY ON AIM:	25/9/1997	**Recent price:**	377.5p
Interim results:	Sep	**Market cap:**	£95.88m
Final results:	Mar	**Issue price:**	129.0p
Year end:	Dec	**Current no of shares:**	
Accounts due:	Apr		25,399,571
Int div paymnt:	Jan	**No of shares after**	
Fin div paymnt:	Jul	**dilution:**	n/a
Int net div per share:	1.0p	**P/E ratio:**	21.8
Fin net div per share:	2.4p	**Probable CGT?**	YES

LATEST REPORTED RESULTS: 2002		PREVIOUS REPORTED RESULTS: 2001	
Turnover:	£66.38m	Turnover:	£64.82m
PTP:	£5.73m	PTP:	£5.05m
EPS:	17.3p	EPS:	12.7p

Comments:

IT services and financial solutions provider CODA bounced back from a May profit warning as it revealed that full year results are likely 'to slightly exceed [revised] market expectations'. A string of deferred contracts from the Government and utilities sectors had hindered first half progress but, with these orders flowing at last, hopes for the future are once again high. Despite spending £10.8m on acquisitions during the year, more than £6m remains in the bank.

COE (COE)

Video network technology provider

Photon House, Percey Street, Leeds, LS12 1EG Tel: 0113-230 8800; Fax: 0113-279 9229; e-mail: sales@coe.co.uk;
web site: www.coe.co.uk

		holding %
Chairman	Dick Eykel	0.2
Chief Executive		
Finance Officer	Michael Sandpearl	0.0
Technical Director	Mark Marriage	3.3

Main Shareholders:

Vivendi Universal S A	24.8
Banque de Gestion Financiere	7.9
Laxey Investors	7.4
R Zimet	5.2
Gall & Eke	4.8

Percentage of free market capital: 39.0%

Nominated Adviser:	Deloitte & Touche, London
AIM Broker:	Durlacher, London
Solicitors:	DLA, Leeds
Market Makers:	DURM; MLSB; WINS
Auditors:	BDO Stoy Hayward, Epsom
Registrars:	Computershare Investor Services

ENTRY ON AIM:	5/6/2003	**Recent price:**	15.75p
Interim results:	Mar	**Market cap:**	£1.95m
Final results:	Aug	**Issue price:**	20.5p
Year end:	Jun	**Current no of shares:**	
Accounts due:	Oct		12,399,474
Int div paymnt:	n/a	**No of shares after**	
Fin div paymnt:	n/a	**dilution:**	n/a
Int net div per share:	nil	**P/E ratio:**	n/a
Fin net div per share:	nil	**Probable CGT?**	YES

LATEST REPORTED RESULTS: 2002		PREVIOUS REPORTED RESULTS: 2001	
Turnover:	£9.36m	Turnover:	£4.28m
PTP:	£511,000	PTP:	£(429,000)
EPS:	n/a	EPS:	n/a

Comments:

COE, which provides networked analogue and digital video solutions for commercial surveillance – working on the London congestion charging scheme amongst other projects, reversed into shell Timeload in May. With client-led delays affecting sales revenue, it effected a overhead reduction by culling 35 employees. Finance director Michael Sandpearl is currently acting as interim chief executive after Brian Wadsworth left in November.

Coffee Republic

Coffee bar operator

(CFE)

Ground Floor, 109-123 Clifton Rd, London, EC2A 4LD Tel: 020-7940 1750; Fax: 020-7407 6360

		holding %
Chairman	Bobby Hashemi	2.0
Chief Executive		
Finance Director	Simon Drysdale	0.1
Non-Exec Director	Nitin Shah	0.6

Main Shareholders:

Julian Richer and The Richer Partnership	16.6
Prudential & its subsidiaries*	11.9
Cafe Nero	5.6

Percentage of free market capital: 62.9%

*Subsidiaries include M & G

Comments:

Interim figures showed some improvement but the coffee bar chain is far from profitable. Sales fell 26% to £11.4m but losses before tax dropped substantially from £4m to £1m. A £2m placing in November has 'ensured financial stability' and an opportunity to roll out its Republic Deli concept this Spring. Currently two bars are being trialled with positive results. It also hopes to dispose of 17 bars to reach a target of maintaining 50 bars.

Nominated Adviser:	Teather & Greenwood, London
AIM Broker:	Teather & Greenwood, London
Solicitors:	Lawrence Graham, London
Market Makers:	KBCS; MLSB; SCAP; TEAM; WINS
Auditors:	BDO Stoy Hayward, 8 Baker Street, London W1M 1DA
Registrars:	Capita Registrars

Entry on AIM: 14/11/2002		**Recent price:**	1.13p
Interim results:	Dec	**Market cap:**	£4.83m
Final results:	Sep	**Issue price:**	2.25p
Year end:	Mar	**Current no of shares:**	
Accounts due:	Aug		427,765,304
Int div paymnt:	n/a	**No of shares after**	
Fin div paymnt:	n/a	**dilution:**	n/a
Int net div per share:	nil	**P/E ratio:**	n/a
Fin net div per share:	nil	**Probable CGT?**	Yes

LATEST REPORTED RESULTS:	2003	PREVIOUS REPORTED RESULTS:	2002
Turnover:	£30.30m	Turnover:	£27.82m
PTP:	£(9.82m)	PTP:	£(7.49m)
EPS:	(1.8)p	EPS:	(0.8)p

coffeeheaven (COH)

Polish coffee and sandwich bar group

3 Horsted Square, Bellbrook Business Park, Uckfield, East Sussex TN22 1QG Tel: 01825-761415; Fax: 01825-766712;
web site: www.coffeeheaven.eu.com

		holding %
Chairman	Richard Worthington*	3.5
Chief Executive		
Finance Director		
Non-Exec Director	Jonathan Cooper	0.4

Main Shareholders:

Keith Bentley	10.5
Diggle Investments*	10.5
David Drury	6.9
Michael Ovadenko	3.3

Percentage of free market capital: 64.6%

*Richard Worthington is a director of Diggle Investments

Comments:

Coffeeheaven has been busy building up its coffee bar business, opening its 19th site in Poland and its first site in Czechoslovakia. It also acquired an airside site at Warsaw's international airport. For the interim, turnover improved 70% to £1m but pre-tax losses more than doubled to £215,000. Trading for the third quarter to December has seen like-for-like sales improve 15%, but the company has fundraised twice in the last three months for working capital purposes.

Nominated Adviser:	Seymour Pierce, London
AIM Broker:	Seymour Pierce Ellis, Crawley
Solicitors:	Eversheds, London
Market Makers:	SCAP; WINS
Auditors:	Grant Thornton, London
Registrars:	Capita Registrars

ENTRY ON AIM:	3/12/2001	Recent price:	1.4p
Interim results:	Dec	Market cap:	£4.08m
Final results:	Aug	Issue price:	1.0p
Year end:	Mar	Current no of shares:	
Accounts due:	Apr		291,459,460
Int div paymnt:	n/a	No of shares after	
Fin div paymnt:	n/a	dilution:	n/a
Int net div per share:	nil	P/E ratio:	n/a
Fin net div per share:	nil	Probable CGT?	No

LATEST REPORTED RESULTS:	2003	PREVIOUS REPORTED RESULTS:	2002
Turnover:	£1.49m	Turnover:	£729,000
PTP:	£(184,000)	PTP:	£(66,000)
EPS:	(0.1)p	EPS:	(0.0)p

Coliseum (CSM)

Sports bars operator

9th Floor, Winchester House, 259 Old Marylebone Road, London, NW1 5RA Tel: 020-7643 5360; Fax: 020-7643 5301;
web site: www.coliseumgroup.com

		holding %
Chairman	Ian Lenagan	0.9
Chief Executive	William Balkou	20.8
Finance Director	Rodger Sargeant	4.8
Non-Exec Director	Christopher Akers	4.9

Main Shareholders:

Grant Thornton	20.7

Percentage of free market capital: 28.0%

Comments:

Coliseum, owner of the well-known Sports Café brand has arranged a £5.8m facility to enable it to roll out its next five proposed units to add to its current three in London, Manchester and Birmingham. The Glasgow site was meant to have opened in March but is still not completed. In order to cut losses it has lowered head office costs by relocating. Its sponsorship deal with Betdeal is underway in London with screens avaiable providing sports information.

Nominated Adviser:	Panmure Gordon, London
AIM Broker:	Panmure Gordon, London
Solicitors:	Norton Rose, London
Market Makers:	WEST; WINS
Auditors:	Grant Thornton, London
Registrars:	Capita Registrars

ENTRY ON AIM:	3/7/2001	Recent price:	27.5p
Interim results:	Sep	Market cap:	£10.61m
Final results:	Apr	Issue price:	25.0p
Year end:	Dec	Current no of shares:	
Accounts due:	Jul		38,566,613
Int div paymnt:	n/a	No of shares after	
Fin div paymnt:	n/a	dilution:	n/a
Int net div per share:	nil	P/E ratio:	n/a
Fin net div per share:	nil	Probable CGT?	Yes

LATEST REPORTED RESULTS:	2002	PREVIOUS REPORTED RESULTS:	FROM 3 JULY 01 TO 31 DEC 01
Turnover:	£6.44m	Turnover:	£477,000
PTP:	£(1.11m)	PTP:	£189,000
EPS:	(2.7)p	EPS:	2.2p

Collins & Hayes (CIY)

Upholstered furniture manufacturer

Crossley House, Belle Vue Park, Hopwood Lane, Halifax, HX1 5EB Tel: 01424-720027; Fax: 01424-720270;
web site: www.collinsandhayesgroup.co.uk

		holding %
Chairman	Phillip Bennett	0.0
Chief Executive		
Finance Director	Brian Heather	0.1
Managing Director	Nicholas Hayes	0.0

Main Shareholders:

GWB	49.8
Peter Hayes	6.2
BFS Small Companies Trust	5.6
Trustees of the GWB Employee Benefit Trust	5.1
Stargas Nominees	3.4

Percentage of free market capital: 26.2%

Nominated Adviser:	Westhouse Securities, Manchester
AIM Broker:	Westhouse Securities, London
Solicitors:	Walker Morris, Leeds
Market Makers:	KBCS; WINS
Auditors:	PricewaterhouseCoopers, Leeds
Registrars:	Capita Registrars

ENTRY ON AIM:	30/7/2001	**Recent price:**	24.0p
Interim results:	Oct	**Market cap:**	£6.18m
Final results:	Apr	**Issue price:**	60.0p
Year end:	Jan	**Current no of shares:**	
Accounts due:	Apr		25,760,777
Int div paymnt:	Oct	**No of shares after**	
Fin div paymnt:	Jul	dilution:	26,670,160
Int net div per share:	1.0p	**P/E ratio:**	3.3
Fin net div per share:	2.1p	**Probable CGT?**	Yes

LATEST REPORTED RESULTS: 2003		PREVIOUS REPORTED RESULTS: 2002 (PRO FORMA)	
Turnover:	£23.2m	**Turnover:**	£16.07m
PTP:	£2.7m	**PTP:**	£1.76m
EPS:	7.3p	**EPS:**	4.5p

Comments:

Collins & Hayes has endured a difficult time of late. First came October's news of a £400,000 fall in interim profits to £1.1m and just three months later the company was rocked by news of the departure of chief executive Clive Gilham and managing director Bill Soutar. Hitherto non-executive chairman Phillip Bennett is now at the helm. With first half debts reduced but still nudging £6.9m, meanwhile, a £1.4m sale and leaseback of the company's Hastings headquarters has been completed.

Comland Commercial (COM)

Property investor & developer

Lunar House, Mercury Park, Wooburn Green, Bucks HP10 0HH Tel: 01628-535777; Fax: 01628-535700;
e-mail: info@comland.co.uk; web site: www.comland.co.uk

		holding %
Chairman	S J Crossley	48.2
Managing Director	as above	
Finance Director	C Martin	47.8
Director	J Collinson	0.0

Main Shareholders:

n/a

Percentage of free market capital: 4.0%

Nominated Adviser:	Deloitte & Touche. London
AIM Broker:	Teather & Greenwood, London
Solicitors:	Manches, London
Market Makers:	TEAM; WINS
Auditors:	Smith & Williamson, London
Registrars:	Capita Registrars

ENTRY ON AIM:	9/12/1997	**Recent price:**	275.0p
Interim results:	Dec	**Market cap:**	£13.22m
Final results:	Aug	**Issue price:**	n/a
Year end:	Mar	**Current no of shares:**	
Accounts due:	n/a		4,808,896
Int div paymnt:	n/a	**No of shares after**	
Fin div paymnt:	n/a	dilution:	n/a
Int net div per share:	nil	**P/E ratio:**	458.3
Fin net div per share:	nil	**Probable CGT?**	No

LATEST REPORTED RESULTS: 2003		PREVIOUS REPORTED RESULTS: 2002	
Turnover:	n/a	**Turnover:**	£940,000
PTP:	£82,000	**PTP:**	£1.62m
EPS:	0.6p	**EPS:**	39.5p

Comments:

The Buckinghamshire-based company is suffering due to the downturn in commercial property. At its Mercury Park development in Beaconsfield rents are 20% lower since its peak in 2002. Despite this pre-tax profits for the interim to September were up 275% to £1.24m. It also acquired Parade Court in Bourne End for £600,000 and The Red Lion at High Wycombe for £8.3m. But its DOCTORnow private general practice is haemorrhaging £20-30,000 per month.

Community Broking

(CB.)

Insurance broker

Barton Hall, Hardy Street, Eccles, Manchester, M30 7NB Tel: 0161-920 0200; Fax: 0161-920 0169

		holding %
Chairman	David Worsley	4.6
Managing Director	Martin Lewis	2.6
Finance Director		
Sales Director	Michael Askew	2.6

Main Shareholders:

Texas Holdings	19.9
Michael McDonald	6.4
Laurence Turnball	4.5
David Goddard	4.2
Guardrange	3.3

Percentage of free market capital: 51.9%

Nominated Adviser:	Insinger de Beaufort, London
AIM Broker:	Insinger Townsley, London
Solicitors:	Pannone & Partners, Manchester
Market Makers:	KBCS; SCAP; WINS
Auditors:	Chadwick, Manchester
Registrars:	Capita Registrars

ENTRY ON AIM:	3/11/2003	**Recent price:**	38.0p
Interim results:	Sep	Market cap:	£2.98m
Final results:	Mar	Issue price:	36.0p
Year end:	Dec	Current no of shares:	
Accounts due:	Jun		7,848,950
Int div paymnt:	n/a	**No of shares after**	
Fin div paymnt:	n/a	dilution:	n/a
Int net div per share:	nil	P/E ratio:	14.1
Fin net div per share:	nil	Probable CGT?	No

LATEST REPORTED RESULTS: 2003		PREVIOUS REPORTED RESULTS: 2002	
Turnover:	£1.51m	Turnover:	£1.15m
PTP:	£306,000	PTP:	£143,000
EPS:	2.7p	EPS:	n/a

Comments:

This Manchester-based insurance broker has built up business over the past three years both organically and by making five acquisitions. Clients are predominantly small and medium sized businesses. The £0.6m net raised on admission will continue this acquisition policy in this fragmented area – most recently snapping up Cloughley for £0.44m. The group also provides personal insurance needs for directors and executives of client companies.

Compact Power

(CPO)

Waste treatment business

Hydro House, St Andrew's Road, Avonmouth, Bristol, BS11 9HZ Tel: 0117-980 2900; Fax: 0117-980 2901;
e-mail: info@compactpower.co.uk; web site: www.compactpower.co.uk

		holding %
Chairman	Nicholas Cooper	1.0
Chief Executive	John Acton	2.2
Finance Director	Gonzalo Trujillo	0.4
Commercial	David Bulman	1.6
Director		

Main Shareholders:

Cooper Holdings	23.3
HSBC Global Custody Nominees	10.0
Channel House Trustees	6.9
BHP Mineral Resources	6.3

Percentage of free market capital: 48.4%

Nominated Adviser:	Rowan Dartington, Bristol
AIM Broker:	Rowan Dartington, Bristol
Solicitors:	Burgess Salmon, Bristol
Market Makers:	WINS
Auditors:	Solomon Hare, Bristol
Registrars:	Computershare Investor Services

ENTRY ON AIM:	24/4/2002	**Recent price:**	15.0p
Interim results:	Nov	Market cap:	£4.37m
Final results:	Jun	Issue price:	90.0p
Year end:	Mar	Current no of shares:	
Accounts due:	Jul		29,150,986
Int div paymnt:	n/a	**No of shares after**	
Fin div paymnt:	n/a	dilution:	n/a
Int net div per share:	nil	P/E ratio:	n/a
Fin net div per share:	nil	Probable CGT?	Yes

LATEST REPORTED RESULTS: 2003		PREVIOUS REPORTED RESULTS: 2002	
Turnover:	£411,000	Turnover:	£98,000
PTP:	£(4.13m)	PTP:	£(4.28m)
EPS:	(13.3)p	EPS:	(41.6)p

Comments:

The owner and developer of a waste-to-energy technology hopes to benefit from falling landfill availability and the tighter processing requirements for certain types of waste. In the first half to September, losses were trimmed from £2.4m to £1.4m. This was achieved on a 43% revenue rise to £244,000, wrought from processing waste at its plant in Avonmouth. Reported half-time cash balances were £1.3m, and the company has said it will try to raise more money.

Compass Finance (CAF)

Consumer finance company

Compass House, New Hall Hey Road, Rawtenstall, Rossendale, BB4 6HH Tel: 01706-833100; Fax: 01706-833101;
web site: wwwcompassfinance.co.uk

		holding %
Chairman	Grenville Folwell	0.0
Chief Executive	Christopher Smith	0.0
Finance Director		
Chief Operating Officer	Mark Butterwick	0.0

Main Shareholders:
n/a

Percentage of free market capital: 100.0%

Comments:

Compass acts as a broker of loans, both secured and unsecured, to individuals, introducing them to suitable lenders. Last year this thriving market saw the company produce an 140% increase in turnover to £8.26m as operating profits soared 231%. The growth has continued since the year-end, with turnover up 67% in the four months to January. The board estimates it will organise lending worth £165m this year and thinks rising interest rates will increase business.

Nominated Adviser:	WH Ireland, London
AIM Broker:	WH Ireland, London
Solicitors:	Wacks Caller, London
Market Makers:	WINS
Auditors:	n/a
Registrars:	Neville Registrars

ENTRY ON AIM:	10/3/2004	**Recent price:**	55.0p
Interim results:	Sep	Market cap:	£36.82m
Final results:	Mar	Issue price:	n/a
Year end:	Dec	Current no of shares:	
Accounts due:	Apr		66,949,792
Int div paymnt:	n/a	No of shares after	
Fin div paymnt:	n/a	dilution:	n/a
Int net div per share:	nil	P/E ratio:	28.9
Fin net div per share:	nil	Probable CGT?	No

LATEST REPORTED RESULTS: 2003		PREVIOUS REPORTED RESULTS: 2002	
Turnover:	£8.26m	Turnover:	£3.45m
PTP:	£1.79m	PTP:	£120,000
EPS:	1.9p	EPS:	0.1p

ComProp (CPP)

Channel Islands property developer

La Rue Fondon, Jersey JE3 7BF Channel Islands, Tel: 01534-835500; Fax: 01534-835501;
e-mail: group-ho@comprop.co.je; web site: www.compropinc.com

		holding %
Chairman	Tom Scott*	0.7
Chief Executive	Nigel Jones	0.6
Finance Director	Stephen Down	0.0
Non-Exec Director	John Henwood	0.6

Main Shareholders:

Lapwing Investments*	29.7
Forest Nominees	7.9
C I Traders	7.7

Percentage of free market capital: 52.6%

*Interested in the shares of Lapwing Investments

Comments:

Having sold its media interests in 2002, the company is focusing on property development. It has now completed a retail warehouse for DIY giants B&Q and will revalue the site in March. Its two Flagship office buildings on Guernsey's seafront are under construction but have already been pre-let. For the half-year to September pre-tax profits improved slightly to £260,000 while turnover rose 12% to £2.2m Net debt rose 40% to £40m.

Nominated Adviser:	Collins Stewart, London
AIM Broker:	Collins Stewart, Channel Islands
Solicitors:	Bedell Cristin, Jersey
Market Makers:	CSCS; MLSB; SCAP; WINS
Auditors:	HLB AV Audit, Southampton
Registrars:	Capita Registrars

ENTRY ON AIM:	29/9/1995	**Recent price:**	111.5p
Interim results:	Nov	Market cap:	£39.75m
Final results:	Jun	Issue price:	80.0p
Year end:	Mar	Current no of shares:	
Accounts due:	Jul		35,649,858
Int div paymnt:	n/a	No of shares after	
Fin div paymnt:	n/a	dilution:	n/a
Int net div per share:	nil	P/E ratio:	79.6
Fin net div per share:	nil	Probable CGT?	No

LATEST REPORTED RESULTS: 2003		PREVIOUS REPORTED RESULTS: 2002	
Turnover:	£4.06m	Turnover:	£4.31m
PTP:	£506,000	PTP:	£486,000
EPS:	1.4p	EPS:	1.6p

Computer Software Group (formerly Software For Sport) (CSW)
Software supplier for the sports industry

Integra House, 138-140 Alexandra Road, Wimbledon, London, SW19 7JY Tel: 020-8879 3939; Fax: 020-8879 7880;
e-mail: glenn.jackson@software4sport.com; web site: www.software4sport.com

		holding %
Chairman	Michael Jackson	3.0
Chief Executive		
Finance Director		
Exec Director	Glenn Jackson	1.4

Main Shareholders:

Elderstreet Capital Partners*	23.7
Natwest IT Fund	18.3
Northern Venture Managers	12.0
Elderstreet Downing VCT	10.3
The Royal Bank of Scotland	8.4

Percentage of free market capital: 7.2%

*Elderstreet Capital Partners Limited Partnership is benficially interested in 19.66% of the Company's issued share capital

Comments:

The company formerly known as Software for Sport posted positive half-year results, showing an operating profit of £161,000 before goodwill amortisation. Thanks mainly to its purchase of Chorus Application Software in May, turnover was up almost 40%, at £2.5m. Overall, the loss before taxation was down 9.1% to £632,000 and broker Seymour Pierce is now quietly confident for the company's future progress. Further acquisitions are expected in the not-too-distant future.

Nominated Adviser:	Seymour Pierce, London
AIM Broker:	Seymour Pierce, London
Solicitors:	CMS Cameron McKenna, London
Market Makers:	KBCS; SCAP; WINS
Auditors:	PKF, Pannell House, Guildford
Registrars:	Capita Registrars

ENTRY ON AIM:	17/8/2000	Recent price:	42.5p
Interim results:	Nov	Market cap:	£13.6m
Final results:	Aug	Issue price:	10.0p
Year end:	Feb	Current no of shares:	
Accounts due:	Jun		32,007,019
Int div paymnt:	n/a	No of shares after	
Fin div paymnt:	n/a	dilution:	n/a
Int net div per share:	nil	P/E ratio:	n/a
Fin net div per share:	nil	Probable CGT?	Yes

LATEST REPORTED RESULTS:	2003	PREVIOUS REPORTED RESULTS:	2002
Turnover:	£3.58m	Turnover:	£3.03m
PTP:	£(1.40m)	PTP:	£(1.63m)
EPS:	(1.0)p	EPS:	(1.2)p

ComputerLand UK (CPU)
Computer services & products provider

Discovery House, Mere Way, Ruddington Fields, Ruddington, Nottingham, NG11 6JW Tel: 0115-931 8000;
Fax: 0115-931 8222; web site: www.computerland.co.uk

		holding %
Chairman	Graham Gilbert	46.6
Managing Director	as above	
Finance Director	Michael Kent	0.0
Sales Director	Simon Lawless	1.2

Main Shareholders:

Eaglet Investment Trust	6.1
John Spiers	6.1
Best Investment	5.6
North Castle Street Nominees	4.8
Unicorn Free Spirit Fund	4.0

Percentage of free market capital: 38.0%

Comments:

IT service provider ComputerLand continues to impress. Latest interims were the best yet as pre-tax profits surged 21% to £900,000 and, since then, the hardware maintenance business of rival IT Solutions has been purchased for £1.7m, a deal expected to be earnings enhancing from the off. Prior to this acquisition, net cash topped £6m and, perhaps most encouragingly of all, contracted revenues continue to rise steadily.

Nominated Adviser:	Charles Stanley, London
AIM Broker:	Charles Stanley, London
Solicitors:	Eversheds, Nottingham
Market Makers:	BGMM; KBCS; MLSB; WINS
Auditors:	BDO Stoy Hayward, Gregory Blvd, Notts NG7 6LH
Registrars:	Capita Registrars

ENTRY ON AIM:	19/9/1997	Recent price:	196.5p
Interim results:	Dec	Market cap:	£20.59m
Final results:	Jun	Issue price:	100.0p
Year end:	Apr	Current no of shares:	
Accounts due:	n/a		10,479,248
Int div paymnt:	Mar	No of shares after	
Fin div paymnt:	Sep	dilution:	n/a
Int net div per share:	1.1p	P/E ratio:	18.7
Fin net div per share:	2.2p	Probable CGT?	Yes

LATEST REPORTED RESULTS:	2003	PREVIOUS REPORTED RESULTS:	2002
Turnover:	£54.84m	Turnover:	£37.62m
PTP:	£1.51m	PTP:	£611,000
EPS:	10.5p	EPS:	4.7p

Concurrent Technologies (CNC)

Single-board computer designer & producer

4 Gilberd Court, Newcomen Way, Colchester, Essex CO4 9WN Tel: 01206-752626; Fax: 01206-751116;
e-mail: info@cct.co.uk; web site: www.cct.co.uk

		holding %
Chairman	Michael Collins	1.2
Managing Director	Glen Fawcett	2.3
Finance Director		
Non-Exec Director	Anthony Hurley	3.3

Main Shareholders:

Eaglet Trust	13.0
Ivor Keeler	11.5
KF Burnett	7.8
Active Capital Trust*	7.1
Direct Nominees	6.6

Percentage of free market capital: 36.9%

*The shares are registered in the name of Chase Nominees

Nominated Adviser:	Brewin Dolphin, Glasgow
AIM Broker:	Brewin Dolphin, Glasgow
Solicitors:	DLA, London
Market Makers:	MLSB; WDBM; WINS
Auditors:	Baker Tilly, 2 Bloomsbury Street, London WC1B 3ST
Registrars:	MSP Secretaries

ENTRY ON AIM:	4/7/1996	**Recent price:**	20.5p
Interim results:	Sep	**Market cap:**	£14.86m
Final results:	Feb	**Issue price:**	15.0p
Year end:	Dec	**Current no of shares:**	
Accounts due:	Apr		72,505,012
Int div paymnt:	Nov	**No of shares after**	
Fin div paymnt:	May	**dilution:**	n/a
Int net div per share: 0.25p		**P/E ratio:**	34.2
Fin net div per share: 0.35p		**Probable CGT?**	**YES**

LATEST REPORTED RESULTS:	2003	PREVIOUS REPORTED RESULTS:	2002
Turnover:	£7.30m	Turnover:	£7.54m
PTP:	£280,000	PTP:	£553,000
EPS:	0.5p	EPS:	0.6p

Comments:

Concurrent failed to match profit expectations for 2003, its results being dragged down by Intel's unexpected decision to cease production of one of its long-life processors. The one upside is that Concurrent has since been accepted into the Intel Communications Alliance and should therefore receive a heads-up on any similar issues in future. Despite these problems Concurrent remained profitable last year. A strong 2004 recovery is now expected thanks to increased defence and security spending in the US.

Conder Environmental (CDE)

Environmental equipment

21/22 Britannia Chambers, Town Quay, Southampton, SO14 2AQ Tel: 023-8082 8903; Fax: 023-8021 1344;
e-mail: info@conderenvironmental.co.uk; web site: www.conderenvironmental.co.uk

		holding %
Chairman	Michael Killingley	1.3
Managing Director	Glyn Humphries	0.3
Finance Director	Jon Varney	0.1
Director	Robert Turner	0.03

Main Shareholders:

Chase Nominees	20.5
G V R Batchelor	12.5
Royal & Sun Alliance Trust	11.3
Sinjul Nominees	8.5
S G Linn	6.2

Percentage of free market capital: 29.7%

Nominated Adviser:	Teather & Greenwood, London
AIM Broker:	Teather & Greenwood, London
Solicitors:	DLA, London
Market Makers:	KBCS; TEAM; WINS
Auditors:	KPMG, Dukes Keep, Marsh Lane, Southampton, SO14 3EX
Registrars:	Capita Registrars

ENTRY ON AIM:	18/12/2000	**Recent price:**	12.75p
Interim results:	Oct	**Market cap:**	£4.75m
Final results:	Jun	**Issue price:**	20.0p
Year end:	Apr	**Current no of shares:**	
Accounts due:	Aug		37,254,309
Int div paymnt:	n/a	**No of shares after**	
Fin div paymnt:	Aug	**dilution:**	39,054,309
Int net div per share:	nil	**P/E ratio:**	11.6
Fin net div per share:	0.5p	**Probable CGT?**	**YES**

LATEST REPORTED RESULTS:	2003	PREVIOUS REPORTED RESULTS:	2002
Turnover:	£21.82m	Turnover:	£14.65m
PTP:	£560,000	PTP:	£(1.28m)
EPS:	1.1p	EPS:	(3.2)p

Comments:

Environmental equipment play Conder retreated from 2003 highs on warning results for the year to April would 'significantly' disappoint. Conder, which made £560,000 pre-tax in 2002-03 but later lost an interim £520,000, feared late orders, a weak dollar and the receivership of a distributor of sewage treatment 'membranes' would knock £350,000 off the bottom line. But the company would show an 'improved' order book.

Conister Trust (CTU)

Isle Of Man retail bank, specialising in asset finance

Conister Ho, 16/18 Finch Rd, Douglas, Isle Of Man IM1 2 PT Tel: 01624-694694; Fax: 01624-624278;
e-mail: info@conistertrust.com; web site: www.conistertrust.com

		holding %
Chairman	Peter Hammonds	1.6
Managing Director		
Finance Director		
Non-Exec Director	Michael Marshall	1.3

Main Shareholders:

Croftdene	24.1
Island Farms	14.9
Chase Nominees	7.6

Percentage of free market capital: 49.5%

Nominated Adviser:	KBC Peel Hunt, London
AIM Broker:	KBC Peel Hunt, London
Solicitors:	Cains, Isle of Man
Market Makers:	KBCS; WINS
Auditors:	KPMG, 41 Athol St, Douglas, Isle of Man IM99 1HN
Registrars:	Conister Trust

ENTRY ON AIM:	22/9/1995	**Recent price:**	30.0p
Interim results:	Sep	**Market cap:**	£9.3m
Final results:	Mar	**Issue price:**	25.0p
Year end:	Dec	**Current no of shares:**	
Accounts due:	Mar		31,009,935
Int div paymnt:	Oct	**No of shares after**	
Fin div paymnt:	May	**dilution:**	n/a
Int net div per share:	0.3p	**P/E ratio:**	30.0
Fin net div per share:	0.6p	**Probable CGT?**	No

LATEST REPORTED RESULTS: 2003		PREVIOUS REPORTED RESULTS: 2002	
Turnover:	n/a	Turnover:	n/a
PTP:	£506,000	PTP:	£220,000
EPS:	2.0p	EPS:	1.0p

Comments:
Peter Hammonds, who succeeded Ernie Thorn after 15 years, wants to make this asset finance specialist more efficient. The business, split between the Isle of Man and the north of England, recently raised £0.8m to expand its lending activities, particularly in the litigation funding market, supporting clients who pursue legal action. A first half recovery was seen in the motor area but the commercial business is still very competitive. Deposits stand at £40m.

Connaught (CNT)

Facilities management & building services provider

Connaught House, Pynes Hill, Rydon Lane, Exeter, EX2 5TZ Tel: 01392-444546; Fax: 01392-444543;
e-mail: timothy.ross@connaught.plc.uk; web site: www.connaughtplc.com

		holding %
Chairman	Timothy Ross	0.03
Managing Director	Mark Tincknell	7.2
Finance Director	David Pike	0.03
Non-Exec Director	Tony Williams	0.0

Main Shareholders:

Chase Nominees	20.0

Percentage of free market capital: 70.4%

Nominated Adviser:	Altium Capital, London
AIM Broker:	KBC Peel Hunt, London
Solicitors:	Burges Salmon, Bristol
Market Makers:	KBCS, WINS
Auditors:	KPMG, 100 Temple Street, Bristol BS1 6AG
Registrars:	Capita Registrars

ENTRY ON AIM:	30/11/1998	**Recent price:**	410.0p
Interim results:	May	**Market cap:**	£77.61m
Final results:	Nov	**Issue price:**	125.0p
Year end:	Aug	**Current no of shares:**	
Accounts due:	Nov		18,928,777
Int div paymnt:	Jun	**No of shares after**	
Fin div paymnt:	Jan	**dilution:**	n/a
Int net div per share:	2.6p	**P/E ratio:**	24.3
Fin net div per share:	5.1p	**Probable CGT?**	Yes

LATEST REPORTED RESULTS: 2003		PREVIOUS REPORTED RESULTS: 2002	
Turnover:	£159.42m	Turnover:	£108.34m
PTP:	£5.06m	PTP:	£3.33m
EPS:	16.9p	EPS:	21.7p

Comments:
Fund managers' favourite Connaught is active in both the public and private sectors, owns the country's biggest commercial gas servicing business, and recently clinched a ten-year regeneration partnership with South Somerset Homes (SSH) worth a combined £100m. At the January AGM, Connaught boasted about a £740m forward order book. The company wowed the market with its last annual numbers, which showed profits up a staggering 76% on a 47.1% sales hike.

Conroy Diamonds & Gold   (CDG)
Precious metals developer

10 Upper Pembroke Street, Dublin 2, Ireland, Tel: 00-353 1 661 8958; Fax: 00-353 1 662 1213;
e-mail: conroydg@indigo.ie; web site: www.conroydiamondsandgold.com

		holding %
Chairman	Richard Conroy	11.6
Managing Director	Maureen Jones	2.3
Finance Director	James Jones	1.1
Non-Exec Director	Louis Maguire	1.0

Main Shareholders:	
Gartmore	7.2
Hoodless Brennan	6.4

Percentage of free market capital: 67.8%

Nominated Adviser:	Seymour Pierce, London
AIM Broker:	Seymour Pierce Ellis, Crawley
Solicitors:	William Fry, Dublin
Market Makers:	KBCS; SCAP; WINS
Auditors:	KPMG, 1 Harbourmaster Place, IFSC, Dublin 1
Registrars:	Capita Registrars

ENTRY ON AIM:	30/5/2000	**Recent price:**	4.5p
Interim results:	Mar	**Market cap:**	£2.6m
Final results:	Nov	**Issue price:**	25.0p
Year end:	May	**Current no of shares:**	
Accounts due:	Nov		57,691,070
Int div paymnt:	n/a	**No of shares after**	
Fin div paymnt:	n/a	**dilution:**	n/a
Int net div per share:	nil	**P/E ratio:**	4.1
Fin net div per share:	nil	**Probable CGT?**	YES

LATEST REPORTED RESULTS: 2003		**PREVIOUS REPORTED RESULTS:** 2002	
Turnover:	n/a	Turnover:	n/a
PTP:	£(342,000)	PTP:	£(348,000)
EPS:	(0.0)p	EPS:	(0.0)p

Comments:
Investors have been waiting for the first mineral resource estimate of Conroy's gold properties near the Irish border. Chairman Richard Conroy said the company, which lost an interim £1m, made five gold finds within a 6.5km section and SRK Consulting has been preparing the resource estimate. Conroy raised £1.25m in September at 5p, but re-rating chances hang on a resource figure.

94

Consolidated Minerals (CNM)

Exploration, mining & processing of manganese and chromite ores

62 Colin Street, West Perth, Western Australia 6005 Australia, Tel: 00-61 8 9321 3633; Fax: 00-61 8 9321 3644;
web site: www.consminerals.com.au

		holding %
Chairman	Colin Smith	1.2
Chief Executive	Michael Kiernan	4.3
Finance Director	David Macoboy	1.7
Operations Director	Allan Quadrio	1.0

Main Shareholders:

Noble Resources	15.9
Portfolio Partners	13.1
Jenkins Investment Management	5.1
Fortescue Metal	5.17
Invesco Australia	4.8
AMP Life	3.6

Percentage of free market capital: 25.1%

Comments:

'Down Under'-based Consolidated Minerals, which lifted interim profits 40% to £3.5m, is studying how to raise manganese output from Woodie Woodie in Western Australia from 600,000 tonnes a year in order to meet booming Chinese demand. The company, which has also increased its chromite output, has been high-flying since its AIM launch and claims a hedging programme protects it from adverse currency moves.

Nominated Adviser:	RFC Corporate Finance, Perth
AIM Broker:	Numis, London
Solicitors:	Watson Farley & Williams, London
Market Makers:	NUMS; WINS
Auditors:	Ernst & Young, Perth, Western Australia
Registrars:	Computershare Investor Services

Entry on AIM:	14/4/2003	Recent price:	53.5p
Interim results:	Feb	Market cap:	£82.39m
Final results:	Oct	Issue price:	6.0p
Year end:	Jun	Current no of shares:	
Accounts due:	Dec		153,991,884
Int div paymnt:	Mar	No of shares after	
Fin div paymnt:	Jun	dilution:	n/a
Int net div per share:	2.25c	P/E ratio:	n/a
Fin net div per share:	5.0c	Probable CGT?	No

LATEST REPORTED RESULTS: 2002		PREVIOUS REPORTED RESULTS: 2001	
Turnover:	A$91.29m	Turnover:	A$80.73m
PTP:	A$15.60m	PTP:	A$17.81m
EPS:	7.4c	EPS:	11.0c

Constellation (CST)

Human resources

6 Derby Street, London, W1J 7AD Tel: 020-7629 8822; Fax: 020-7629 8833; e-mail: info@constellationcorporation.com;
web site: www.constellationcorporation.com

		holding %
Chairman	John Bartle	0.7
Chief Executive	Andrew Garner	33.2
Finance Director		
Non-Exec Director	Roger Hingley	0.2

Main Shareholders:

P Cunningham	5.7
D Keith	5.7

Percentage of free market capital: 50.5%

Comments:

Constellation Corporation is a taciturn corporate beast – there's been no news since it posted improved first-half figures to June way back in August! Those numbers revealed an encouraging £56,000 profit, versus earlier pre-tax losses of £586,000. And revenues reached an encouraging £690,000 (£578,000). These days, the company is chasing longer-term 'retainer' agreements with certain clients, because these offer a secure income stream.

Nominated Adviser:	John East, London
AIM Broker:	Insinger Townsley, London
Solicitors:	Stephenson Harwood, London
Market Makers:	KBCS; MLSB; SCAP; WINS
Auditors:	Deloitte & Touche, 2 Colmore Row, Birmingham B3 2BN
Registrars:	Capita Registrars

Entry on AIM:	6/11/2000	Recent price:	0.4p
Interim results:	Aug	Market cap:	£3.63m
Final results:	Jun	Issue price:	n/a
Year end:	Jul	Current no of shares:	
Accounts due:	Nov		907,118,358
Int div paymnt:	n/a	No of shares after	
Fin div paymnt:	n/a	dilution:	n/a
Int net div per share:	nil	P/E ratio:	n/a
Fin net div per share:	nil	Probable CGT?	Yes

LATEST REPORTED RESULTS: 2002		PREVIOUS REPORTED RESULTS: 2001	
Turnover:	£1.34m	Turnover:	£1.88m
PTP:	£(858,000)	PTP:	£(5.59m)
EPS:	(0.1)p	EPS:	(0.6)p

Contemporary Enterprises (CPY)

Software development

Broadmarsh Innovation Centre, Harts Farm Way, Havant, PO9 1HS Tel: 0870-350 1051; Fax: 0870-350 1052;
e-mail: Admin@ceplc.com; web site: www.ausped.co.uk

		holding %
Chairman	Henry Edwards	16.8
Managing Director	Martin Gladding	11.5
Finance Director	Anthony Edwards*	5.5
Director	Kenneth Tinkler	0.5

Main Shareholders:

Milestone Group**	21.2
Adint Charitable Trust*	14.5

Percentage of free market capital: 24.5%

*Anthony Edwards has a non-beneficial interest in the shares held by Adint Charirable Trust
**Milestone Group is 95%-owned by Non-Exec Director Andrew Craig

Comments:

This cash shell originally wanted to build a business in the hotel and catering service market using its £1m float proceeds. But the directors, experienced hotel managers, instead acquired AuSPeD, a developer of mobile software technologies, in a £1m reverse takeover funded by the issue of 1.6m shares at 60p. AuSPeD's products can be used in hospitals, at railway stations and airports to monitor time-sensitive operations manually using short-wave radio. Contract delays meant a full year loss was made.

Nominated Adviser:	KBC Peel Hunt, London
AIM Broker:	KBC Peel Hunt, London
Solicitors:	Howard Kennedy, London
Market Makers:	KBCS; WINS
Auditors:	Grant Thornton, Fareham, Hampshire
Registrars:	Capita Registrars

ENTRY ON AIM:	28/3/2001	**Recent price:**	47.5p
Interim results:	May	**Market cap:**	£1.81m
Final results:	Dec	**Issue price:**	50.0p
Year end:	Sep	**Current no of shares:**	
Accounts due:	Dec		3,800,000
Int div paymnt:	n/a	**No of shares after**	
Fin div paymnt:	n/a	**dilution:**	n/a
Int net div per share:	nil	**P/E ratio:**	n/a
Fin net div per share:	nil	**Probable CGT?**	YES

LATEST REPORTED RESULTS: 17 MONTHS TO 30 SEPT 2003		PREVIOUS REPORTED RESULTS: 18 MONTHS TO 30 APR 2003	
Turnover:	286,000	Turnover:	n/a
PTP:	£(208,000)	PTP:	£(100,000)
EPS:	(2.9)p	EPS:	(6.2)p

Conygar Investment (CIC)

Real estate related investment company

7th Floor, 39 St James's Street, London, SW1A 1JD

		holding %
Chairman	Robert Ware	27.2
Chief Executive		
Finance Director	Peter Batchelor	0.9
Property Director	Gavin Davidson	1.8

Main Shareholders:

Blydenstein Nominees	5.4
Stephen East	4.4
Pershing Keen	4.4
Rulegale Nominees	4.2
State Street Nominees	3.3

Percentage of free market capital: 43.1%

Comments:

Headed by Robert Ware, former deputy chief executive of the MEPC property giant, Conygar was well received by the market with its strategy of hands-on investment in assets and companies in the property arena. The company raised £465,000 in February at 90p, nearly twice last October's 50p float price.

Nominated Adviser:	Deloitte & Touche, London
AIM Broker:	Bridgewell, London
Solicitors:	Macfarlanes, London
Market Makers:	BGWL; SCAP; WINS
Auditors:	Rees Pollock, 7 Pilgrim Street, London EC4V 6DR
Registrars:	Share Registrars

ENTRY ON AIM:	23/10/2003	**Recent price:**	106.5p
Interim results:	n/a	**Market cap:**	£10.35m
Final results:	n/a	**Issue price:**	50.0p
Year end:	n/a	**Current no of shares:**	
Accounts due:	n/a		9,722,001
Int div paymnt:	n/a	**No of shares after**	
Fin div paymnt:	n/a	**dilution:**	n/a
Int net div per share:	nil	**P/E ratio:**	n/a
Fin net div per share:	nil	**Probable CGT?**	No

LATEST REPORTED RESULTS:		PREVIOUS REPORTED RESULTS:	
	N/A		
Turnover:	n/a	Turnover:	n/a
PTP:	n/a	PTP:	n/a
EPS:	n/a	EPS:	n/a

Corac (CRA)

Producer of compressed air technology

Brunel Science Park, Kingston Lane, Uxbridge, Middlesex UB8 3PQ Tel: 01895-813463; Fax: 01895-813505;
e-mail: info@corac.co.uk; web site: www.corac.co.uk

		holding %
Chairman	Gerald Musgrave	0.1
Chief Executive		
Finance Director	Roberta Miles	0.01
Non-Exec Director	John Grant	0.5
Main Shareholders:		
Morstan Nominees		17.7
S P Angel Nominees		5.0

Percentage of free market capital: 74.8%

Nominated Adviser:	Numis, London
AIM Broker:	Numis, London
Solicitors:	Charles Russell, London
Market Makers:	NUMS; WEST; WINS
Auditors:	Grant Thornton, 1 Westminster Way, Oxford OX2 0PZ
Registrars:	Capita Registrars

ENTRY ON AIM:	4/7/2001	Recent price:	28.0p
Interim results:	Sep	Market cap:	£19.22m
Final results:	Mar	Issue price:	105.0p
Year end:	Dec	Current no of shares:	
Accounts due:	Apr		68,628,808
Int div paymnt:	n/a	No of shares after	
Fin div paymnt:	n/a	dilution:	77,095,420
Int net div per share:	nil	P/E ratio:	n/a
Fin net div per share:	nil	Probable CGT?	Yes

LATEST REPORTED RESULTS:	2002	PREVIOUS REPORTED RESULTS:	2001
Turnover:	£61,000	Turnover:	£82,000
PTP:	£(1.64m)	PTP:	£(2.03m)
EPS:	(2.2)p	EPS:	(2.9)p

Comments:

Losses at the compressed air technology developer increased last year, but the company is close to clinching several deals with major companies, yielding up-front payments, continuing royalties and development contracts. Corac has also recruited German industrial air expert Gerd Comm to help it tap into a £24bn global market. The group has £8m in tax losses to carry forward and funding for two years. Investors await the imminent signing of a licensing deal.

Corpora (CP.)

Software development & sales

1 Farnham Road, Guildford, Surrey GU2 4RG

		holding %
Chairman	Robert Lowe	0.7
Chief Executive	Mark Thompson	15.1
Finance Director		
Sales & Mktg	James Wye	1.4
Director		
Main Shareholders:		
Sinjul Nominees		10.7
Chase Nominees		10.0
Investment Ventures		8.6
Prudential Assurance		5.7
Framlington		3.7

Percentage of free market capital: 24.6%

Nominated Adviser:	Nabarro Wells, London
AIM Broker:	Bridgewell, London
Solicitors:	Hill Dickinson, London
Market Makers:	BGWL; WINS
Auditors:	CLB, Aldwych House, 81 Aldwych, London WC2B 4HP
Registrars:	Neville Registrars

ENTRY ON AIM:	28/8/2003	Recent price:	44.0p
Interim results:	Jan	Market cap:	£6.15m
Final results:	May	Issue price:	25.0p
Year end:	Mar	Current no of shares:	
Accounts due:	Jul		13,987,200
Int div paymnt:	n/a	No of shares after	
Fin div paymnt:	n/a	dilution:	n/a
Int net div per share:	nil	P/E ratio:	n/a
Fin net div per share:	nil	Probable CGT?	Yes

LATEST REPORTED RESULTS:	2003	PREVIOUS REPORTED RESULTS:	2002
Turnover:	£289,000	Turnover:	£194,000
PTP:	£(433,000)	PTP:	£(1.26m)
EPS:	n/a	EPS:	n/a

Comments:

Corpora's main product is Jump!, a clever piece of document navigation software that enables users to jump 'around, within and between documents' to find information that is important to them. Although commercialisation remains at an early stage, the plan is to target the software initially towards the pharmaceutical, legal and financial services markets. First half losses hit £678,091 from flat revenues of £150,713.

Corvus Capital (suspended 9 Feb 2004)   (CVS)

Investment Company

PO Box 605, La Marchant House, La Marchant Street, St Peter Port, Guernsey GY1 4NP Tel: 020-7070 7283; Fax: 020-7070 7288

		holding %
Chairman	Ian Tickler	0.0
Chief Executive		
Finance Director		
Non-Exec Director	Richard Griffiths	0.0

Main Shareholders:

The Strawberry Fund	22.7
Matthew Tawse	8.4
Brookspey	8.4

Percentage of free market capital: 60.5%

Nominated Adviser:	Canaccord Capital, London
AIM Broker:	Canaccord Capital, London
Solicitors:	Berwin Leighton Paisner, London
Market Makers:	SCAP; WINS
Auditors:	BDO Stoy Hayward, 8 Baker Street, London, W1M 1DA
Registrars:	Elan Corporate Services

ENTRY ON AIM:	4/7/2000	**Recent price:**	7.5p
Interim results:	Nov	**Market cap:**	£1.12m
Final results:	Aug	**Issue price:**	25.0p
Year end:	Mar	**Current no of shares:**	
Accounts due:	Jun		14,980,000
Int div paymnt:	n/a	**No of shares after**	
Fin div paymnt:	n/a	**dilution:**	22,380,000
Int net div per share:	nil	**P/E ratio:**	n/a
Fin net div per share:	nil	**Probable CGT?**	No

LATEST REPORTED RESULTS:	2003	PREVIOUS REPORTED RESULTS:	2002
Turnover:	n/a	**Turnover:**	n/a
PTP:	£(787,000)	**PTP:**	£(1.3m)
EPS:	(5.5)p	**EPS:**	(9.1)p

Comments:
Founding chief executive Haresh Kanabar has left the investment company, which raised £3.1m in July 2000. Under his direction the group backed ten fledgling technology companies, several at flotation, including Silentpoint, another Kanabar company. The shares are suspended whilst new director Ian Tickler completes the reversal of his offshore fund management business Regent into Corvus. This will cost £0.25m. Cash remains tight after a £0.16m interim loss was made.

County Contact Centres   (CUY)

Contact centres and related software

2 Melford Court, The Havens, Ransomes Bureau Park, Ipswich, Suffolk IP3 9FJ Tel: 024-7643 0410; Fax: 01473-321801; web site: www.countyweb.com

		holding %
Chairman	Peter Brown	4.1
Managing Director	William Catchpole*	4.6
Finance Director	Stuart Gordon	1.0
Technical Director	GeoffreyForsyth	0.9

Main Shareholders:

Suffolk Life Annuities	13.7
Peter Wildey	9.3
GWR	3.7

Percentage of free market capital: 62.8%

*54,220 of such Ordinary Shares are held by or on behalf of Mr Catchpole's wife and/or son

Nominated Adviser:	Brewin Dolphin, London
AIM Broker:	Brewin Dolphin, London
Solicitors:	Stringer Saul, London
Market Makers:	KBCS; WINS
Auditors:	Grant Thornton, London
Registrars:	Lloyds TSB Registrars

ENTRY ON AIM:	29/9/2000	**Recent price:**	8.0p
Interim results:	Feb	**Market cap:**	£2.38m
Final results:	Aug	**Issue price:**	100.0p
Year end:	Jun	**Current no of shares:**	
Accounts due:	Sep		29,700,743
Int div paymnt:	n/a	**No of shares after**	
Fin div paymnt:	n/a	**dilution:**	n/a
Int net div per share:	nil	**P/E ratio:**	n/a
Fin net div per share:	nil	**Probable CGT?**	Yes

LATEST REPORTED RESULTS:	2003	PREVIOUS REPORTED RESULTS:	2002
Turnover:	£1.28m	**Turnover:**	£1.3m
PTP:	£(840,000)	**PTP:**	£(535,000)
EPS:	(2.8)p	**EPS:**	(1.6)p

Comments:
CCC has yet to reach its goal of monthly break-even, however pre-tax losses in the interim dropped 59% to £206,658. Contributing to the improving figures was a 26% reduction in administrative expenses. Ansaback, its call centre services operation, performed well with sales growing 24%. The CallScripter software division was less impressive as sales remained flat but, since reorganising mid-year, a number of orders from overseas have been placed.

CPL Resources (CPS)

IT recruitment

83 Merrion Square, Dublin 2, Ireland Tel: 00-353 1 614 6000; Fax: 00-353 1 614 6011; e-mail: info@cpl.ie;
web site: www.cplresources.ie

		holding %
Chairman	John Hennessy	1.7
Managing Director	Anne Heraty*	54.5
Finance Director	Josephine Tierney	0.0
Bus. Dvlpmt Director	Paul Carroll*	17.0

Main Shareholders:

n/a

Percentage of free market capital: 26.5%

*Anne Heraty and Paul Carroll are husband and wife

Comments:
Diversification is paying off for the Irish staffer, which operates in sectors such as finance, engineering, healthcare, and light industrial. This has helped CPL mitigate the tech sector downturn. In a tricky half to December, profits powered ahead 35% to 941,000 on a 48% turnover hike to 34.7m. Encouragingly, the company also boasted considerable balance sheet strength. Net cash balances at half time were 4.3m, a 2.1m improvement from a year before.

Nominated Adviser:	J&E Davy, Dublin		
AIM Broker:	J&E Davy, Dublin		
Solicitors:	William Fry, Dublin		
Market Makers:	GBMM; KBCS; SCAP; WINS		
Auditors:	Deloitte & Touche, Dublin		
Registrars:	Computershare Investor Services		

ENTRY ON AIM:	29/6/1999	**Recent price:**	60.0p
Interim results:	Sep	**Market cap:**	£22.01m
Final results:	Mar	**Issue price:**	50.0p
Year end:	Jun	**Current no of shares:**	
Accounts due:	Oct		36,677,825
Int div paymnt:	Apr	**No of shares after**	
Fin div paymnt:	Nov	**dilution:**	n/a
Int net div per share:	0.3c	**P/E ratio:**	n/a
Fin net div per share:	0.4c	**Probable CGT?**	No

LATEST REPORTED RESULTS:	2003	PREVIOUS REPORTED RESULTS:	2002
Turnover:	n/a	Turnover:	n/a
PTP:	£(1.66m)	PTP:	n/a
EPS:	(6.2)p	EPS:	n/a

Cradley (CDLY)

Maker of lithographic printing equipment

Chester Road, Cradley Heath, Warley, West Midlands B64 6AB Tel: 01384-414100; Fax: 01384-414102;
e-mail: info@cradleygp.co.uk; web site: www.cradleygp.co.uk

		holding %
Chairman	John Wheatley	0.1
Managing Director	Christopher Jordan	26.4
Finance Director	as chairman	
Sales Director	Nicholas Jordan	26.5

Main Shareholders:

n/a

Percentage of free market capital: 20.5%

Comments:
Cradley has turned its attention from prinitng consumer magazines to commercial work and claims that in the first quarter a number of new contracts have been won. In the two months to December the company apparently operated profitably. However, Cradley saw its pre-tax losses for the year jump 53% and net debt is still high at £5.8m. To redress the situation it has cut staffing levels and changed the management structure.

Nominated Adviser:	Arbuthnot, Birmingham		
AIM Broker:	Arbuthnot, Birmingham		
Solicitors:	DLA, Birmingham		
Market Makers:	ARBT; WINS		
Auditors:	Clement Keys, 4/5 Calthorpe Rd, Birmingham B15 1RL		
Registrars:	Capita Registrars		

ENTRY ON AIM:	17/5/2002	**Recent price:**	16.5p
Interim results:	Feb	**Market cap:**	£5.34m
Final results:	Oct	**Issue price:**	5.5p
Year end:	Jun	**Current no of shares:**	
Accounts due:	Oct		32,358,604
Int div paymnt:	n/a	**No of shares after**	
Fin div paymnt:	n/a	**dilution:**	n/a
Int net div per share:	nil	**P/E ratio:**	n/a
Fin net div per share:	nil	**Probable CGT?**	Yes

LATEST REPORTED RESULTS:	2003	PREVIOUS REPORTED RESULTS:	2002
Turnover:	£24.28m	Turnover:	£28.68m
PTP:	£(2.64m)	PTP:	£(1.68m)
EPS:	(6.4)p	EPS:	(3.7)p

CRC   (CCG)

Service and repair specialist in IT, telecoms and media communications

Unit 20 Thames Park Business Centre, Wenman Road, Thame, Oxfordshire OX9 3XA Tel: 01844-261900;
Fax: 01844-219411; e-mail: enquiries@crc-group.com; web site: www.crc-group.com

		holding %
Chairman	David Ryan	0.0
Chief Executive	Alan McLaughlin	0.1
Finance Director	Christopher Matthews	0.1
Non-Exec Director	Colin Holland	4.6

Main Shareholders:

AID Directors Pension Scheme	4.9
D Dale	3.4
Patrick J Conafray	3.1
PM Watson	3.1

Percentage of free market capital: 71.7%

Nominated Adviser:	Williams de Broe, London
AIM Broker:	Williams de Broe, London
Solicitors:	Hale and Dorr, Oxford
Market Makers:	KBCS; MLSB; WDBM; WINS
Auditors:	Grant Thornton, 1 Westminster Way, Oxford OX2 0PZ
Registrars:	Capita Registrars

Entry on AIM:	5/11/1997	Recent price:	158.5p
Interim results:	Aug	Market cap:	£38.67m
Final results:	Feb	Issue price:	90.0p
Year end:	Dec	Current no of shares:	
Accounts due:	Feb		24,399,677
Int div paymnt:	Sep	No of shares after	
Fin div paymnt:	May	dilution:	24,470,978
Int net div per share:	2.5p	P/E ratio:	14.4
Fin net div per share:	4.5p	Probable CGT?	Yes

LATEST REPORTED RESULTS:	2003	PREVIOUS REPORTED RESULTS:	2002
Turnover:	£71.24m	Turnover:	£109.6m
PTP:	£3.65m	PTP:	£7.56m
EPS:	11.0p	EPS:	21.1p

Comments:

Fears for the future of electronic equipment repairer CRC emerged last year as mobile phone giant (and major revenue source) Nokia, renegotiated its contract with the company. But while 2003 figures showing sales down 35% were disappointing, they did demonstrate an ability to turn a profit without having to rely on a single dominant customer. A string of additional contracts with the likes of Siemens, Telewest and NTL have been signed and analysts are forecasting profits in excess of £7m in 2004.

Creative Recruitment Solutions (formerly jobs.co.uk)   (CRT)

Internet portal providing recruitment information

Queen Anne House, 131 High Street, Coleshill, Birmingham, B46 3BP Tel: 01675-469613; e-mail: info@jobs.co.uk

		holding %
Chairman	Tim Watts	0.0
Chief Executive	Craig Holborn	0.0
Finance Director		
Chief Technical Officer	Christopher Traynor	0.0

Main Shareholders:

Pretemps	35.0
Peter Gold	10.0
Warm Welcome Management	9.0
Gary Raime	4.3
Heather Kenny	4.1

Percentage of free market capital: 4.7%

Nominated Adviser:	Rowan Dartington, London
AIM Broker:	Rowan Dartington, London
Solicitors:	Shakespeares, Birmingham
Market Makers:	WINS
Auditors:	Hazlewoods, Windsor House, Brunswick Road, Gloucester GL1 1JR
Registrars:	Computershare Investor Services

Entry on AIM:	11/11/1999	Recent price:	1.25p
Interim results:	Sep	Market cap:	£1.57m
Final results:	Mar	Issue price:	n/a
Year end:	Dec	Current no of shares:	
Accounts due:	Apr		125,627,625
Int div paymnt:	n/a	No of shares after	
Fin div paymnt:	n/a	dilution:	103,905,124
Int net div per share:	nil	P/E ratio:	n/a
Fin net div per share:	nil	Probable CGT?	Yes

LATEST REPORTED RESULTS:	2002	PREVIOUS REPORTED RESULTS:	2001
Turnover:	£779,000	Turnover:	£98,000
PTP:	£(2.32m)	PTP:	£(517,000)
EPS:	(3.2)p	EPS:	(1.0)p

Comments:

CRS provides a range of recruitment-focused software solutions to both corporate and specialist agency clients. Despite the company's troubled past (as perennially loss-making Jobs.co.uk) its prospects now seem to be gradually improving. First half numbers showed a swing from loss (of £506,000) to profit (£182,000) before tax and goodwill, while an association with enterprise solutions giant Peoplesoft has recently been signed.

Croma (CMG)

Surveillance & security products supplier

215a Holme Lacy Road, Rotherwas, Hereford, HR2 6BQ Tel: 01432-373030; Fax: 01432-373031;
e-mail: info@cromadefence.com

		holding %
Chairman	John French	1.2
Chief Executive	as above	
Finance Director	David Bretel	0.01
Technical Director	Robert Layton	0.0

Main Shareholders:

HSBC	7.3
Chase Nominees	7.0
Goldman Sachs	5.9
London & Boston Investments	4.7
Nortrust Nominees	4.4
Percentage of free market capital: 66.2%	

Comments:

Croma develops surveillance equipment and security-related products for the military, the police as well as customs and immigration authorities. Products include Cobalt, a covert monochrome camera, and the Zeus Tactical Light, which illuminates space remotely allowing the user to hide. Croma also has an acoustic information system that can locate gunshots, and a 'Passive Infra-Red Suit'. Last financial year, operating losses were £529,000 on sales of £142,100.

Nominated Adviser:	Seymour Pierce, London
AIM Broker:	Seymour Pierce, London
Solicitors:	Irwin Mitchell, London
Market Makers:	EVO; HOOD; SCAP; WINS
Auditors:	Saffery Champness, London
Registrars:	Neville Registrars

ENTRY ON AIM: 18/12/2003		**Recent price:**	6.5p
Interim results:	Mar	**Market cap:**	£3.38m
Final results:	Sep	**Issue price:**	5.5p
Year end:	Jun	**Current no of shares:**	
Accounts due:	Oct		51,961,742
Int div paymnt:	n/a	**No of shares after**	
Fin div paymnt:	n/a	**dilution:**	n/a
Int net div per share:	nil	**P/E ratio:**	n/a
Fin net div per share:	nil	**Probable CGT?**	**YES**

LATEST REPORTED RESULTS: 2003		PREVIOUS REPORTED RESULTS: 2002	
Turnover:	£142,000	**Turnover:**	£95,000
PTP:	£(770,000)	**PTP:**	£(590,000)
EPS:	(5.1)p	**EPS:**	(4.1)p

Crown Corporation (CCO)

Investment company

Canon's Court, 22 Victoria Street, Hamilton HM 12 Bermuda

		holding %
Chairman	Mariusz Rybak	10.9
Chief Executive	as above	
Finance Director	Jean-Pierre Regli	0.0
Non-Exec Director	Friedrich Kramer	0.0

Main Shareholders:

Lambert Financial	59.1
Wolfgang Menzel	10.9
Ursula Gruman Demagistri	4.9
Pierre Demagistri	4.8
Pierre Michelutti	4.7
Percentage of free market capital: 1.2%	

Comments:

Investment company Crown raised 200m when it launched onto AIM in October 2003. The group intends to take significant stakes (a minimum of 51%) in under-performing companies with a view to turning them around. The group is registered in Bermuda (for tax purposes), its shares are held almost exclusively by European investors and it intends to invest in Canadian and US ventures.

Nominated Adviser:	Nabarro Wells, London
AIM Broker:	Insinger Townsley, London
Solicitors:	Lawrence Graham, London
Market Makers:	KBCS; WINS
Auditors:	Baker Tilly, 2 Bloomsbury Street, London WC1B 3ST
Registrars:	Capita Registrars

ENTRY ON AIM: 31/10/2003		**Recent price:**	675.0p
Interim results:	n/a	**Market cap:**	£472.5m
Final results:	n/a	**Issue price:**	405.0p
Year end:	n/a	**Current no of shares:**	
Accounts due:	n/a		70,000,000
Int div paymnt:	n/a	**No of shares after**	
Fin div paymnt:	n/a	**dilution:**	n/a
Int net div per share:	n/a	**P/E ratio:**	n/a
Fin net div per share:	n/a	**Probable CGT?**	**No**

LATEST REPORTED RESULTS: N/A		PREVIOUS REPORTED RESULTS: N/A	
Turnover:	n/a	**Turnover:**	n/a
PTP:	n/a	**PTP:**	n/a
EPS:	n/a	**EPS:**	n/a

CSS Stellar
(CSS)

Sports and entertainment management services

Drury House, 34-43 Russell Street, London, WC2B 5HA Tel: 020-7978 1400; Fax: 020-7078 1401;
e-mail: enquiries@css-stellar.com; web site: www.css-stellar.com

		holding %
Chairman	John Webber	7.2
Joint Chief Executive	Julian Jakobi	16.4
Finance Director	Kevin Rose	0.0
Joint Chief Executive	Sean Kelly	0.7

Main Shareholders:

Fidelity International	8.76
Banque de Luxembourg	6.1
Julian Hill	4.1
Barrie Gill	3.9

Percentage of free market capital: 49.4%

Nominated Adviser:	Bridgewell, London
AIM Broker:	Bridgewell, London
Solicitors:	Berwin Leighton Paisner, London
Market Makers:	GRAB, KLWT; WINS
Auditors:	Grant Thornton, London
Registrars:	Capita Registrars

ENTRY ON AIM: 12/12/2000		**Recent price:**	44.5p
Interim results:	Sep	Market cap:	£11.81m
Final results:	May	Issue price:	180.0p
Year end:	Dec	**Current no of shares:**	
Accounts due:	Mar		26,531,142
Int div paymnt:	n/a	**No of shares after**	
Fin div paymnt:	Apr	dilution:	n/a
Int net div per share:	nil	P/E ratio:	n/a
Fin net div per share:	1.0p	**Probable CGT?**	YES

LATEST REPORTED RESULTS: 2003		PREVIOUS REPORTED RESULTS: 2002	
Turnover:	£72.92m	Turnover:	£48.46m
PTP:	£(4.21m)	PTP:	£6,000
EPS:	(17.2)p	EPS:	(1.8)p

Comments:

The entertainment and sports marketing play disappointed investors by recording a significant loss for 2003. However, the bulk of this related to its ARB business, which has since been sold. This now leaves the group with four divisions that are all operating profitably. Moreover, an improvement in its market place and its lower cost base – not to mention a considerable improvement in working capital – are buoying management spirits for 2004. The market is expecting a profit of £2.55m.

CustomVis
(CUS)

Laser eye treatment specialist equipment developer

c/o 7 Devonshire Square, Cutlers Gardens, London, EC2M 4YH Tel: 0870-839 0000; Fax: 0870-839 1001

		holding %
Chairman	William Colvin	0.0
Chief Executive	Dr Paul Saarloos	38.3
Finance Director	Hugh Grant	0.0
Managing Director	Simon Gordon	0.6

Main Shareholders:

Asian Lasers	6.2
Custom Lasers	6.2
Poynton & Partners	4.0

Percentage of free market capital: 32.2%

Nominated Adviser:	Collins Stewart, London
AIM Broker:	Collins Stewart, London
Solicitors:	Hammonds, London
Market Makers:	CSCS; WINS
Auditors:	PKF, New Garden House, London
Registrars:	Capita Registrars

ENTRY ON AIM: 8/7/2003		**Recent price:**	42.5p
Interim results:	Jan	Market cap:	£14.76m
Final results:	Aug	Issue price:	91.0p
Year end:	Jun	**Current no of shares:**	
Accounts due:	Nov		34,719,148
Int div paymnt:	n/a	**No of shares after**	
Fin div paymnt:	n/a	dilution:	n/a
Int net div per share:	nil	P/E ratio:	n/a
Fin net div per share:	nil	**Probable CGT?**	YES

LATEST REPORTED RESULTS: 2003		PREVIOUS REPORTED RESULTS: 2002	
Turnover:	£23,000	Turnover:	£(84,000)
PTP:	£(658,000)	PTP:	£42,000
EPS:	(7.6)p	EPS:	n/a

Comments:

The developer of the next generation of laser eye surgery equipment saw its shares plunge after admitting production delays would mean only five instead of 12 machines would be made this year – its first on AIM since raising £10m net last summer. The first machine is currently being tested. The aim is to overcome many of the faults of existing laser machines used to correct mild short-sight. These shave off sections of the cornea to improve vision. CustomVis will measure each eye before surgery.

CW Residential (CWE)

Residential property owner & developer

1 Riding House Street, London, W1A 3AS Tel: 020-7637 5377; Fax: 020-7631 0741

		holding %
Chairman	Robert Dory**	20.4
Managing Director	as above	
Finance Director		
Non-Exec Director	Gareth Pearce	10.6

Main Shareholders:

Smith & Williamson Nominees*	21.7
Dory Estates	13.8
Clients of Smith & Williamson Nominees	6.2

Percentage of free market capital: 64.6%

*Includes Gareth Pearce's holding of 10.58%
**Includes Dory Estates holding of 13.83%

Comments:

Interim pre-tax profits at residential property group CW halved to £162,144 and fixed assets were £140,000 lighter at £3.2m, though cash was seven times higher at £1.5m. The company sold two investment properties for £180,050. CW had found it hard to buy at 'sensible' prices, but expected house price inflation assumptions to fall, offering opportunities for the future.

Nominated Adviser:	Teather & Greenwood, London		
AIM Broker:	Teather & Greenwood, London		
Solicitors:	Bircham Dyson Bell, London		
Market Makers:	TEAM; WINS		
Auditors:	BDO Stoy Hayward, Harrow		
Registrars:	Capita Registrars		

Entry on AIM:	2/10/1995	**Recent price:**	149.0p
Interim results:	Aug	**Market cap:**	£5.76m
Final results:	Mar	**Issue price:**	40.0p
Year end:	Dec	**Current no of shares:**	
Accounts due:	Mar		3,865,000
Int div paymnt:	Sep	**No of shares after**	
Fin div paymnt:	Apr	**dilution:**	n/a
Int net div per share:	1.5p	**P/E ratio:**	10.2
Fin net div per share:	1.35p	**Probable CGT?**	No

LATEST REPORTED RESULTS:	2003	PREVIOUS REPORTED RESULTS:	2002
Turnover:	£714,000	**Turnover:**	£3.61m
PTP:	£205,000	**PTP:**	£807,000
EPS:	4.4p	**EPS:**	14.6p

Cyberes (CYB)

Booking systems and software provider

Mitre House, North Park Road, Harrogate, HG1 5RX Tel: 01423-857400; Fax: 01423-857405;
e-mail: enquiries@cyberes.co.uk; web site: www.cyberes.co.uk

		holding %
Chairman	Ian McNeill	9.7
Managing Director	Tariq Malik	16.0
Finance Director	Mark Cant	1.4
Commercial Director	David Collick	4.5

Main Shareholders:

Active Capital Trust	13.0
Herald Investment Trust	9.8
Liontrust	6.3
Capital for Companies	4.5
Anthony Rowe	3.4

Percentage of free market capital: 28.0%

Comments:

The supplier of travel booking and fares systems to travel agents slashed pre-tax losses for the year-end. Holding flight agreements with 55 airlines, it is branching out to ferry bookings and low cost hotel reservations. In December, it acquired Corporate Travel for £2m and will see its scale increase three times. It expects to be cashflow positive this year and has reshuffled its management team with former finance director Mark Cant as the new chief executive.

Nominated Adviser:	Nabarro Wells, London		
AIM Broker:	Durlacher, London		
Solicitors:	Hammonds, Leeds		
Market Makers:	WDBM; WINS		
Auditors:	KPMG, 1 The Embankment, Neville Street, Leeds, LS1 4DW		
Registrars:	Capita Registrars		

Entry on AIM:	21/12/2000	**Recent price:**	12.25p
Interim results:	Jun	**Market cap:**	£4.52m
Final results:	Dec	**Issue price:**	55.0p
Year end:	Sep	**Current no of shares:**	
Accounts due:	Jan		36,866,376
Int div paymnt:	n/a	**No of shares after**	
Fin div paymnt:	n/a	**dilution:**	n/a
Int net div per share:	nil	**P/E ratio:**	n/a
Fin net div per share:	nil	**Probable CGT?**	Yes

LATEST REPORTED RESULTS:	2003	PREVIOUS REPORTED RESULTS:	2002
Turnover:	£14.60m	**Turnover:**	£12.03m
PTP:	£(1.16m)	**PTP:**	£(1.96m)
EPS:	(4.1)p	**EPS:**	(9.4)p

CybIT (CYH)

Provider of telematics and online services

IT House, Chord Business Park, London Road, Godmanchester, Cambridgeshire PE29 2NU Tel: 01480-389100;
Fax: 01480-389101; e-mail: enquiries@cybit.co.uk; web site: www.cybit.co.uk

		holding %
Chairman	Neil Johnson	2.6
Managing Director	Richard Horsman	2.4
Finance Director	Kevin Lawrence	0.2
Sales & Mktg Director	John Wisdom	0.5

Main Shareholders:

Billam	21.2
Brian Robins	10.6
P R Bligh	3.0

Percentage of free market capital: 59.4%

Nominated Adviser:	KBC Peel Hunt, London
AIM Broker:	KBC Peel Hunt, London
Solicitors:	Pinsents, London
Market Makers:	KBCS; MLSB; SCAP; WINS
Auditors:	Grant Thornton, Cambridge
Registrars:	Capita Registrars

ENTRY ON AIM:	16/3/2001	Recent price:	2.7p
Interim results:	Nov	Market cap:	£26.74m
Final results:	Jun	Issue price:	3.5p
Year end:	Mar	Current no of shares:	
Accounts due:	Jun		990,211,017
Int div paymnt:	n/a	No of shares after	
Fin div paymnt:	n/a	dilution:	n/a
Int net div per share:	nil	P/E ratio:	n/a
Fin net div per share:	nil	Probable CGT?	YES

Comments:

CybIT, the telematic service provider, announced maiden pre-tax profits of £38,000 in the interim to September. Turnover also increased 79% to £4m. In the past year, its volume of business has more than doubled. New contracts have been prolific of late with three deals in the past two months generating an initial value of £475,000. But its factoring and invoice discounting policy, where it outsources its debtor book to a financing company, cost it £517,322, 41% more than last year.

LATEST REPORTED RESULTS:		PREVIOUS REPORTED RESULTS:	
	2003	15 MONTHS TO 31 MAR 02	
Turnover:	£5.07m	Turnover:	£623,000
PTP:	£(787,000)	PTP:	£(1.65m)
EPS:	(0.1)p	EPS:	(0.3)p

CYC (formerly CyberChina) (CYC)

Financial support for Chinese companies

Hillyfields House, Woodhill Lane, Shamley Green, Guildford, Surrey GU5 0SP Tel: 01483-894627; Fax: 01483-894818;
e-mail: management@cyberchinaholdings.com; web site: www.cyberchinaholdings.com

		holding %
Chairman	Viscount Torrington	1.6
CEO & Dep Chairman	Michael McAlister	3.3
Finance Director	Michael Lindsay	0.0
Non-Exec Director	Paul Harris	0.4

Main Shareholders:

Fiske Nominees	13.8
Leo Wang	9.7
Cabinet Trust	6.5
Dartington Portfolio Nominees	3.4
Pinegrove Enterprise	3.3

Percentage of free market capital: 54.9%

Nominated Adviser:	Rowan Dartington, Bristol
AIM Broker:	Rowan Dartington, Bristol
Solicitors:	Kuit Stewart Lev, Manchester
Market Makers:	KBCS; MLSB; SCAP; WINS
Auditors:	Horwath Clarke Whitehill, London
Registrars:	Capita Registrars

ENTRY ON AIM:	13/10/2000	Recent price:	2.7p
Interim results:	Jun	Market cap:	£8.32m
Final results:	Jan	Issue price:	2.0p
Year end:	Oct	Current no of shares:	
Accounts due:	Feb		308,000,000
Int div paymnt:	n/a	No of shares after	
Fin div paymnt:	n/a	dilution:	n/a
Int net div per share:	nil	P/E ratio:	n/a
Fin net div per share:	nil	Probable CGT?	No

Comments:

China play CYC, formerly CyberChina, recently raised £250,000 at 10p for Sinovation, a Chinese company with 'pioneering' electronic data input technology that has reversed into an ex-OFEX shell, ahead of an OFEX float. CYC, which lost £230,000 last year, has pleased punters with prospects for two AIM floats, one a packaging machinery maker and the other boasting a 'new generation' of oil-refining catalysts.

LATEST REPORTED RESULTS:		PREVIOUS REPORTED RESULTS:	
	2003		2002
Turnover:	n/a	Turnover:	£7,000
PTP:	£(232,000)	PTP:	£(259,000)
EPS:	(0.1)p	EPS:	(0.1)p

Cyprotex (CRX)

Drug discovery software

15 Beech Lane, Macclesfield, Cheshire SK10 2DR Tel: 01625-505100; Fax: 01625-505199; e-mail: info@cyprotex.com; web site: www.cyprotex.com

		holding %
Chairman	Robert Atwater	0.0
Chief Executive	as above	
Finance Director		
Chief Scientific Officer	David Leahy	0.02

Main Shareholders:

Nordan	29.9
Dresdner Kleinwort Wasserstein Securities	19.7
Stephen Toon	3.5

Percentage of free market capital: 39.2%

Comments:

Cyprotex, which tests compounds to see how they will react in the human body, is moving on from the controversy surrounding its float. This was marred by a £5m spread-bet that major backer Paul 'the Plumber' Davidson made – forcing Dresdner effectively to underwrite the offer. The share price plunged below 1p and Davidson, who was fined by the FSA, sold some of his stake to new chairman Robert Atwater. A further £3m has been raised at 10p a share and promising deals signed with AstraZeneca and Roche amongst others.

Nominated Adviser:	Durlacher, London
AIM Broker:	Durlacher, London
Solicitors:	Addleshaw Goddard, Manchester
Market Makers:	ALTI; KBCS; WINS
Auditors:	Ernst & Young, 100 Barbirolli Square, Manchester, M2 3EY
Registrars:	Capita Registrars

Entry on AIM:	15/2/2002	**Recent price:**	17.75p
Interim results:	Sep	**Market cap:**	£22.5m
Final results:	Apr	**Issue price:**	29.0p
Year end:	Dec	**Current no of shares:**	
Accounts due:	Mar		126,737,131
Int div paymnt:	n/a	**No of shares after**	
Fin div paymnt:	n/a	**dilution:**	149,008,497
Int net div per share:	nil	**P/E ratio:**	n/a
Fin net div per share:	nil	**Probable CGT?**	Yes

LATEST REPORTED RESULTS: 14 MONTHS TO 31 DEC 02		PREVIOUS REPORTED RESULTS: 7 MONTHS TO 31 OCT 01	
Turnover:	£648,000	Turnover:	£99,000
PTP:	£(3.51m)	PTP:	£(387,000)
EPS:	(4.0)p	EPS:	(0.8)p

Cytomyx (CYX)

Genomic research services provider

6/7 Technopark, Newmarket Road, Cambridge, CB5 8PB Tel: 01223-508191; Fax: 01223-508198; e-mail: services@cytomyx.com; web site: www.cytomyx.com

		holding %
Chairman	William Mason	1.0
Chief Executive	Michael Kerins	3.7
Finance Director	Max Dyer Bartlett	0.0
Non-Exec Director	Alan Seeley	14.6

Main Shareholders:

Vidacos Nominees	7.2
Rathbone Nominees	6.5
Pennine Downing AIM VCT II	5.7
Michael Kerins	3.7

Percentage of free market capital: 44.4%

Comments:

The protein reagent specialist is turning itself from a biotech services provider to a supplier of products to pharmaceutical groups for research and development. To this end, Cytomyx has bought Cambridge BioScience, a distributor of new reagent products, for £1m and US drug discoverer Clinomics Bioscience, owner of 750,000 human tissue samples, for up to $1m in shares. A recent institutional placing also raised £1.9m. Profits could be made in the current year.

Nominated Adviser:	Corporate Synergy, London
AIM Broker:	Teather & Greenwood, London
Solicitors:	Memery Crystal, London
Market Makers:	HOOD; TEAM; WINS
Auditors:	Deloitte & Touche, Cambridge
Registrars:	Capita Registrars

Entry on AIM:	29/5/2001	**Recent price:**	21.5p
Interim results:	Jun	**Market cap:**	£8.99m
Final results:	Dec	**Issue price:**	0.5p
Year end:	Sep	**Current no of shares:**	
Accounts due:	Jan		41,792,358
Int div paymnt:	n/a	**No of shares after**	
Fin div paymnt:	n/a	**dilution:**	n/a
Int net div per share:	nil	**P/E ratio:**	n/a
Fin net div per share:	nil	**Probable CGT?**	Yes

LATEST REPORTED RESULTS: 2003		PREVIOUS REPORTED RESULTS: 2002	
Turnover:	£5.10m	Turnover:	£930,000
PTP:	£(477,000)	PTP:	£(893,000)
EPS:	n/a	EPS:	n/a

DA (formerly Digital Animations) (DAG)

Interactive computer games, digital animation effects developer

70 Mitchell Street, Glasgow, G1 3LX Tel: 0141-582 0600; Fax: 0141-582 0699; e-mail: info@digital-animations.com; web site: www.digital-animations.com

		holding %
Chairman	Rob Walker	0.0
Chief Executive	Michael Antliff	18.5
Finance Director	Paul McCaffrey	0.0
Deputy Chairman	Adrian Shinwell	0.1

Main Shareholders:

Colin McNab	10.1
Catriona A S Paton	7.6
Northern & Midland Nominees	7.1
T D Waterhouse Nominees	6.8
Sharelink Nominees	4.0

Percentage of free market capital: 42.8%

Nominated Adviser:	Deloitte & Touche, London
AIM Broker:	Durlacher, London
Solicitors:	Dundas & Wilson, Edinburgh
Market Makers:	DURM; KBCS; MLSB; SCAP; WINS
Auditors:	Ernst & Young, 50 George Sq, Glasgow G2 1RR
Registrars:	Capita Registrars

Entry on AIM:	24/7/1996	**Recent price:**	42.0p
Interim results:	Dec	**Market cap:**	£12.53m
Final results:	Jun	**Issue price:**	71.0p
Year end:	Mar	**Current no of shares:**	
Accounts due:	Aug		29,841,608
Int div paymnt:	n/a	**No of shares after**	
Fin div paymnt:	n/a	**dilution:**	n/a
Int net div per share:	nil	**P/E ratio:**	n/a
Fin net div per share:	nil	**Probable CGT?**	Yes

Comments:

DA's core business is now the development and deployment of 'avatars', animated characters which it anticipates will increasingly become a liaison between the 'digital world and the human one'. Applications have already been found in the e-learning market place, as well as in local government and the marketing sector. Yet for all of its technological wizardry and ample cash reserves, DA continues to run up losses, reporting a deficit of £1.3m at the interim stage.

LATEST REPORTED RESULTS: 2003		PREVIOUS REPORTED RESULTS: 2002	
Turnover:	£1.54m	Turnover:	£1.42m
PTP:	£(2.61m)	PTP:	£(743,000)
EPS:	(8.5)p	EPS:	(2.6)p

DataCash (formerly auxinet) (DATA)

E-commerce payment solutions provider

Floor 2, Descartes House, 8 Gate House, London, WC2A 3HP Tel: 0870-727 4760; Fax: 0870-7274 781; e-mail: info@datacash.com

		holding %
Chairman	David Bailey	1.5
Chief Executive	as above	
Finance Director		
Director	Gavin Breeze	26.1

Main Shareholders:

Fidelity International	10.0
AMVESCAP	10.0
INVESCO English & International Trust	4.0
Close Brothers Investment Management	3.8
Universities Superannuation Scheme	3.4

Percentage of free market capital: 32.5%

Nominated Adviser:	Collins Stewart, London
AIM Broker:	Collins Stewart, London
Solicitors:	Teacher, Stern, Selby, London
Market Makers:	CSCS; MLSB; SCAP; WINS
Auditors:	Baker Tilly, London
Registrars:	Capita Registrars

Entry on AIM:	1/11/1996	**Recent price:**	71.5p
Interim results:	Aug	**Market cap:**	£31.99m
Final results:	Apr	**Issue price:**	3.0p
Year end:	Dec	**Current no of shares:**	
Accounts due:	Mar		44,738,912
Int div paymnt:	n/a	**No of shares after**	
Fin div paymnt:	n/a	**dilution:**	45,951,004
Int net div per share:	nil	**P/E ratio:**	n/a
Fin net div per share:	nil	**Probable CGT?**	Yes

Comments:

Payments processor DataCash – formerly known as Auxinet – pleased its followers with a bullish pre-close update. Apparently 2003 was a good year – pre-goodwill pre-tax profits came in at more than £700,000, a resounding result given the loss recorded in 2002. And year-end cash balances 'more than doubled' from the £666,000 figure a year earlier. There was some impressive transaction growth, particularly in the fourth quarter, buoyed by new deals with high street retailers.

LATEST REPORTED RESULTS: 2002		PREVIOUS REPORTED RESULTS: 2001	
Turnover:	£2.70m	Turnover:	£3.04m
PTP:	£(2.37m)	PTP:	£(6.85m)
EPS:	(5.4)p	EPS:	(17.0)p

DawMed Systems (DSY)
Medical devices business
Eden Close, Hellaby, Rotherham, South Yorkshire S66 8RW Tel: 01709-730730; Fax: 01709-730000

		holding %
Chairman	Kevin Gilmore*	39.2
Chief Executive	John Crispin	10.8
Finance Director	Barry Dale	0.0
Non-Exec Director	Gordon Arbib	9.8

Main Shareholders:

The SVM OFEX Fund	5.4
Viatrade	5.0

Percentage of free market capital: 25.5%

*Kevin Gilmore's interests include the shareholding of his wife

Nominated Adviser:	Beaumont Cornish, London
AIM Broker:	Hichens Harrison, London & Hoodless Brennan, London
Solicitors:	BPE Solicitors, Cheltenham
Market Makers:	SCAP; WINS
Auditors:	Baker Tilly, City Plaza, Temple Row, Birmingham B2 5AF
Registrars:	Neville Registrars

Entry on AIM: 14/10/2002		**Recent price:**	22.0p
Interim results:	Jun	**Market cap:**	£4.06m
Final results:	Dec	**Issue price:**	27.5p
Year end:	Sep	**Current no of shares:**	
Accounts due:	Jan		18,463,292
Int div paymnt:	n/a	**No of shares after**	
Fin div paymnt:	n/a	**dilution:**	n/a
Int net div per share:	nil	**P/E ratio:**	n/a
Fin net div per share:	nil	**Probable CGT?**	**Yes**

LATEST REPORTED RESULTS: 2003		PREVIOUS REPORTED RESULTS: 2002	
Turnover:	£4.53m	Turnover:	£3.70m
PTP:	£(293,000)	PTP:	£9,000
EPS:	(1.9)p	EPS:	0.1p

Comments:
DawMed makes special washers for use in hospitals. These help disinfect and decontaminate surgical instruments and other items used medically. The group joined OFEX before moving to AIM, raising £150,000 to develop a new product. The NHS has earmarked £200m to upgrade decontamination equipment. The group has developed a bench-top version for use in dental surgeries, which is soon to be launched. Delays pushed the group into the red.

DCS (DCS)
IT solutions & services provider
1 Sun Street, London, EC2A 2EP Tel: 020-7920 0200; Fax: 020-7920 6290; e-mail: marketing@dcsgroup.co.uk; web site: www.dcsgroup.co.uk

		holding %
Chairman	Colin Amies	0.2
Chief Executive	Stephen Yapp	0.04
Finance Director		
Chief Technical Officer	Andrew Forsyth	1.3

Main Shareholders:

Morley Fund management	14.8
AVIVA	10.9
HSBC	10.5
Wilbro Nominees	6.8
Southwind	6.8

Percentage of free market capital: 48.6%

Nominated Adviser:	Close Brothers, London
AIM Broker:	KBC Peel Hunt, London
Solicitors:	CMS Cameron McKenna, London
Market Makers:	KBCS; KLWT; MLSB; WINS
Auditors:	KPMG, 8 Salisbury Square, London EC4Y 8BB
Registrars:	Capita Registrars

Entry on AIM: 30/5/2003		**Recent price:**	17.5p
Interim results:	Sep	**Market cap:**	£4.38m
Final results:	Apr	**Issue price:**	11.5p
Year end:	Dec	**Current no of shares:**	
Accounts due:	Jun		25,040,363
Int div paymnt:	n/a	**No of shares after**	
Fin div paymnt:	n/a	**dilution:**	n/a
Int net div per share:	nil	**P/E ratio:**	n/a
Fin net div per share:	nil	**Probable CGT?**	**Yes**

LATEST REPORTED RESULTS: 2002		PREVIOUS REPORTED RESULTS: 2001	
Turnover:	£69.8m	Turnover:	£104.9m
PTP:	£(14.2m)	PTP:	£(4.6m)
EPS:	(57.1)p	EPS:	(22.6)p

Comments:
Beleaguered IT services business DCS continues to struggle. First half figures were depressing, losses hitting £4m as sales slumped from £37.8m to £30.2m, while company debts now stand in excess of £20m. Following a series of cost-cutting disposals erstwhile finance director Colin Campbell has also been axed. His departure reflects the company's decision to pass his responsibilities on to its divisional finance teams.

DDD (DDD)

Developer of 3-D technology

The Little House, Quenington, Cirencester, Gloucestershire GL7 5BW Tel: 00-1 310 566 3340; Fax: 00-1 310 566 3380; web site: www.ddd.com

		holding %
Chairman	Paul Kristensen	0.9
Chief Executive	Christopher Yewdall	0.8
Finance Director	Mark McGowan	0.0
Technology Officer	Philip Harman	1.0

Main Shareholders:

Elliott Associates	26.7
Schroder Investment Management	15.9
Sofaer	8.1
Motorola	5.3
Red Reef*	4.0

Percentage of free market capital: 36.1%
*includes 160,000 shares held on behalf of directors Yewdall, Schwartz and Harman

Comments:

DDD continues to announce new corporate agreements at a prodigious rate, most recently declaring a three-year publishing agreement with 3D-movie producer nWave pictures. The deal will see the company encode films in order to prepare them for viewing on a new generation of 3D display systems – the Sharp Actius laptop, with which DDD is also strongly affiliated, included. Despite the strong deal flow, however, it remains to be seen when and if DDD can turn a profit.

Nominated Adviser:	Arbuthnot, London
AIM Broker:	Arbuthnot, London
Solicitors:	Norton Rose, London
Market Makers:	ARBT; WINS
Auditors:	Grant Thornton, London
Registrars:	Computershare Investor Services

Entry on AIM:	3/1/2002	**Recent price:**	37.0p
Interim results:	Sep	**Market cap:**	£13.07m
Final results:	Mar	**Issue price:**	65.0p
Year end:	Dec	**Current no of shares:**	
Accounts due:	Apr		35,337,349
Int div paymnt:	n/a	**No of shares after**	
Fin div paymnt:	n/a	dilution:	38,086,822
Int net div per share:	nil	**P/E ratio:**	n/a
Fin net div per share:	nil	**Probable CGT?**	Yes

LATEST REPORTED RESULTS: 2002		PREVIOUS REPORTED RESULTS: 2001	
Turnover:	£182,000	Turnover:	£172,000
PTP:	£(2.63m)	PTP:	£(3.42m)
EPS:	(7.5)p	EPS:	(14.6)p

Deal Group Media (formerly IBNet) (DGM)

Internet surveillance and intelligence gathering system developer

19 Cavendish Square, London, W1A 2AW Tel: 020-7691 1880; Fax: 020-7691 1881; e-mail: sales@dealgroupmedia.com; web site: www.dealgroupmedia.com

		holding %
Chairman	David Lees	1.5
Chief Executive	Adrian Moss	11.3
Finance Director		
Non-Exec Director	Keith Lassman	0.4

Main Shareholders:

I-Spire	21.4
JO Hamro	5.7
Eureka Fund	5.6
Capita Trust	5.2
Toby Smallpeice	4.4

Percentage of free market capital: 44.5%

Comments:

Online advertising specialist Deal Group Media reversed into AIM-listed search-engine marketing concern IBNet in September in a £7m deal. The company focuses on solutions such as affiliate marketing, where revenues are shared between online advertisers, and the rates they are paid by companies are based on performance measures such as sales, click-throughs and registrations. Deal Group generated a £583,000 pre-tax profit from £7.4m of turnover last year.

Nominated Adviser:	KBC Peel Hunt, London
AIM Broker:	KBC Peel Hunt, London
Solicitors:	Howard Kennedy, London; Memery Crystal, London
Market Makers:	EVO; HOOD; KBCS; SCAP
Auditors:	Grant Thornton, Slough
Registrars:	Capita Registrars

Entry on AIM:	9/3/2000	**Recent price:**	6.9p
Interim results:	Sep	**Market cap:**	£24.65m
Final results:	Apr	**Issue price:**	3.41p
Year end:	Dec	**Current no of shares:**	
Accounts due:	Jul		357,254,636
Int div paymnt:	n/a	**No of shares after**	
Fin div paymnt:	n/a	dilution:	364,304,636
Int net div per share:	nil	**P/E ratio:**	n/a
Fin net div per share:	nil	**Probable CGT?**	Yes

LATEST REPORTED RESULTS: 2003		PREVIOUS REPORTED RESULTS: 9 MONTHS TO 31 MAR 02	
Turnover:	£1.88m	Turnover:	£1.19m
PTP:	£(1.58m)	PTP:	£(1.84m)
EPS:	(1.8)p	EPS:	(3.1)p

Debt Free Direct (DFD)

Provider of advice on debt issues

55 St Thomas's Road, Chorley, Lancashire PR7 1JH Tel: 01257-240500; Fax: 01257-240501;
e-mail: tjones@debtfreedirect.co.uk

		holding %
Chairman	Grenville Folwell	0.0
Chief Executive	Andrew Redmond	17.7
Finance Director	John Reynard	22.3
Director	Paul Latham	22.3

Main Shareholders:

Keith Seeley	12.7
Derek Oakley	5.9
Peter Byrne	3.8

Percentage of free market capital: 14.7%

Nominated Adviser:	WH Ireland, Manchester
AIM Broker:	WH Ireland, Manchester
Solicitors:	Eversheds, London
Market Makers:	KBCS; SCAP; WINS
Auditors:	Horwath Clark Whitehill, Manchester
Registrars:	Capita Registrars

ENTRY ON AIM: 16/12/2002	**Recent price:**	68.5p
Interim results:	Oct	**Market cap:**	£21.2m
Final results:	Jul	**Issue price:**	40.0p
Year end:	Apr	**Current no of shares:**	
Accounts due:	Sep		30,949,187
Int div paymnt:	n/a	**No of shares after**	
Fin div paymnt:	n/a	dilution:	n/a
Int net div per share:	nil	**P/E ratio:**	n/a
Fin net div per share:	nil	**Probable CGT?**	**YES**

LATEST REPORTED RESULTS: PERIOD FROM 26 APR 02 TO 30 APR 03	PREVIOUS REPORTED RESULTS: N/A
Turnover: £1.06m	**Turnover:** n/a
PTP: £(175,000)	**PTP:** n/a
EPS: (1.3)p	**EPS:** n/a

Comments:

The company, set up by insolvency practitioners from accountants Lathams, aims to help 'unfortunates' who have fallen into debt through an unlucky event such as divorce or redundancy, but are willing to pay it off in an Individual Voluntary Arrangement (IVA) with their creditors. Nearly all Debt Fee's revenues come from fees it receives for setting up IVAs. Maiden interims produced a £111,000 pre-tax profit on £1.86m turnover. Revenue per month has increased 50% to £300,000. Political changes may increase business.

Deep-Sea Leisure (DSL)

Aquarium visitor attractions owner

Forthside Terrace, North Queensferry, Fife KY11 1JR Tel: 01383-411880; Fax: 01383-410514;
e-mail: info@deepseaworld.co.uk; web site: www.deepsealeisure.com

		holding %
Chairman	Angel Barrachina	0.0
Managing Director	Stuart Earley	0.0
Financial Controller	Sue Howarth	0.0
Non-Exec Director	Norman Yarrow	0.4

Main Shareholders:

Net Ein	29.9
Philip Crane	23.4

Percentage of free market capital: 45.4%

Nominated Adviser:	Hawkpoint Partners, Edinburgh
AIM Broker:	Brewin Dolphin, Edinburgh
Solicitors:	Shepherd & Wedderburn, Edinburgh
Market Makers:	WINS
Auditors:	KPMG Audit, 20 Castle Terrace, Edinburgh EH1 2EG
Registrars:	Royal Bank of Scotland

ENTRY ON AIM: 31/10/1996	**Recent price:**	32.5p
Interim results:	Jul	**Market cap:**	£6.24m
Final results:	Mar	**Issue price:**	160.0p
Year end:	Oct	**Current no of shares:**	
Accounts due:	Apr		19,199,783
Int div paymnt:	n/a	**No of shares after**	
Fin div paymnt:	n/a	dilution:	n/a
Int net div per share:	nil	**P/E ratio:**	8.8
Fin net div per share:	nil	**Probable CGT?**	**YES**

LATEST REPORTED RESULTS: 2003	PREVIOUS REPORTED RESULTS: 8 MONTHS TO 31 OCT '02
Turnover: £6.14m	**Turnover:** £5.06m
PTP: £1.04m	**PTP:** £886,000
EPS: 3.7p	**EPS:** 2.8p

Comments:

The operator of two UK marine life aquariums improved its margins and spend per head in a tough year for tourism. This seasonal business sees 88% of customers between February and October – so with last summer being one of the hottest in recent years and its aquariums wholly indoor attractions, a rising per capita spend was a decent achievement. The chairman said the business held up admirably last year and the current year has started in line with budget.

Delcam (DLC)

Computer software developer & marketer

Talbot Way, Small Heath Business Park, Birmingham, B10 0HJ Tel: 0121-766 5544; Fax: 0121-766 5511;
e-mail: marketing@delcam.com; web site: www.delcam.com

		holding %
Chairman	Thomas Kinsey	0.6
Managing Director	Hugh Humphreys	16.1
Finance Director	Kulwant Singh	0.5
Technical Director	Edward Lambourne	15.2

Main Shareholders:

Steve Hobbs	4.8
Delcam Trustees Limited	3.6
Nigel Whalley	3.5

Percentage of free market capital: 51.2%

Nominated Adviser:	Williams de Broe, Birmingham
AIM Broker:	Williams de Broe, Birmingham
Solicitors:	Wragge & Co, Birmingham
Market Makers:	KBCS; WDBM; WINS
Auditors:	Deloitte & Touche, 2 Colmore Row, Birmingham B3 2BN
Registrars:	Neville Registrars

ENTRY ON AIM:	15/7/1997	**Recent price:**	219.0p
Interim results:	Aug	**Market cap:**	£13.24m
Final results:	Mar	**Issue price:**	260.0p
Year end:	Dec	**Current no of shares:**	
Accounts due:	Apr		6,044,478
Int div paymnt:	Sep	**No of shares after**	
Fin div paymnt:	May	**dilution:**	6,097,059
Int net div per share:	0.95p	**P/E ratio:**	15.6
Fin net div per share:	2.55p	**Probable CGT?**	YES

LATEST REPORTED RESULTS: 2002		PREVIOUS REPORTED RESULTS: 2001	
Turnover:	£18.91m	Turnover:	£18.25m
PTP:	£1.07m	PTP:	£854,000
EPS:	14.0p	EPS:	9.9p

Comments:

Design and manufacture software developer Delcam continues to perform well. Indeed in January management revealed that the group had 'achieved record sales in December' and that full year numbers would, as a result, surpass analyst expectations of a £1.1m profit before tax for 2003. The one cloud on the horizon concerns an expected pension fund deficit, which is likely to be addressed in the near future.

Deltex Medical (DEMG)

Heart monitoring equipment maker and marketer

Terminus Road, Chichester, West Sussex PO19 8TX Tel: 01243-774837; Fax: 01243-532534;
e-mail: info@deltexmedical.com; web site: www.deltexmedical.com

		holding %
Chairman	Nigel Keen	5.8
Chief Executive	Andy Hill	0.1
Finance Director	Ewan Phillips	0.8
Vice Chairman	Edwin Snape	4.7

Main Shareholders:

Close Finsbury Asset Management	14.9
Close Brothers	14.6
Framlington Investment Management	9.6
LeggMason Investors Asset Managers	6.7
Euroclear & Clearstream	6.7

Percentage of free market capital: 25.3%

Nominated Adviser:	Charles Stanley, London
AIM Broker:	Charles Stanley, London
Solicitors:	Eversheds, London
Market Makers:	BGMM; WINS
Auditors:	PricewaterhouseCoopers, Southampton
Registrars:	Capita Registrars

ENTRY ON AIM:	8/11/2001	**Recent price:**	25.25p
Interim results:	Aug	**Market cap:**	£15.58m
Final results:	Apr	**Issue price:**	25.0p
Year end:	Dec	**Current no of shares:**	
Accounts due:	Apr		61,701,957
Int div paymnt:	n/a	**No of shares after**	
Fin div paymnt:	n/a	**dilution:**	n/a
Int net div per share:	nil	**P/E ratio:**	n/a
Fin net div per share:	nil	**Probable CGT?**	YES

LATEST REPORTED RESULTS: 2002		PREVIOUS REPORTED RESULTS: 2001	
Turnover:	£1.8m	Turnover:	£1.3m
PTP:	£(3.1m)	PTP:	£(3.3m)
EPS:	(7.8)p	EPS:	(17.4)p

Comments:

Shares in the maker of the CardioQ heart monitor have shot up over the past year. Placings at 7p and 15p, raising £2m, have helped the group improve annual sales 70% to £3.1m with 35,000 probes sold. These are used in operating theatres and intensive care units, by forcing a probe down the patient's throat. The unit reduces the length of a patient's post-operative stay in hospital by about 30%. The technology can also be used to constantly monitor patients in less critical conditions.

Densitron Technologies (DSN)

Display technologies developer

Unit 4, Airport Trading Estate, Biggin Hill, Westerham, Kent TN16 3BW Tel: 01959-542000; Fax: 01959-542001;
e-mail: sales@densitron.co.uk; web site: www.densitron.com

		holding %
Chairman	Philip Lawler	0.0
Chief Executive	David McQuiggan	0.2
Finance Director	Robert Smith	0.2
Technical Director	Nicholas Jarmany	0.7

Main Shareholders:

Peter Gyllenhammar	14.6
Goldman Sachs	13.1
Clifford Hardcastle	10.6
Shigemi Degawa	6.8
Michael Hardcastle	3.6

Percentage of free market capital: 50.3%

Nominated Adviser:	Rowan Dartington, London	
AIM Broker:	Rowan Dartington, London	
Solicitors:	Addleshaw Goddard, London	
Market Makers:	EVO; KBCS; KLWT; MLSB; WINS	
Auditors:	Deloitte and Touche, London,	
Registrars:	Capita Registrars	

ENTRY ON AIM:	24/7/2003	**Recent price:**	16.25p
Interim results:	Nov	**Market cap:**	£10.51m
Final results:	Mar	**Issue price:**	n/a
Year end:	Dec	**Current no of shares:**	
Accounts due:	Jun		64,669,106
Int div paymnt:	n/a	**No of shares after**	
Fin div paymnt:	n/a	**dilution:**	n/a
Int net div per share:	nil	**P/E ratio:**	n/a
Fin net div per share:	nil	**Probable CGT?**	YES

LATEST REPORTED RESULTS:	2002	PREVIOUS REPORTED RESULTS:	2001
Turnover:	£25.49m	**Turnover:**	£28.43m
PTP:	£(5.29m)	**PTP:**	£(551,000)
EPS:	(20.0)p	**EPS:**	(2.5)p

Comments:

Densitron has emerged from an offer period after two potential buyers walked away. Now talks are over, management time has been freed up at the display technologies concern, which moved down to AIM last summer. Encouragingly for investors, the company returned to profitability in the first half, but flagged up challenging US and European markets. Profits hit £6,000, after stripping out a £6m charge, versus losses of £2.8m. And sales hiked up 22% to £14.7m.

Designer Vision (DVS)

Car audio-visual entertainment systems supplier

Designer House, 75 Capitol Way, London, NW9 0EW Tel: 020-8200 1515; Fax: 020-8200 0022;
e-mail: info@designervision.co.uk; web site: www.designervision.co.uk

		holding %
Chairman	Godfrey Bilton	10.0
Managing Director	Mark Peach	2.9
Finance Director	Martin Peters	0.0
Non-Exec Director	Anthony Fabrizi	1.6

Main Shareholders:

A Panayiotou	65.3
M Coleman	4.2

Percentage of free market capital: 16.0%

Nominated Adviser:	City Financial Associates, London	
AIM Broker:	City Financial Associates, London	
Solicitors:	Field Fisher Waterhouse, London	
Market Makers:	EVO; KBCS; SCAP; WINS	
Auditors:	CLB, Aldwych House, 81 Aldwych, London WC2B 4HP	
Registrars:	Capita Registrars	

ENTRY ON AIM:	12/8/2003	**Recent price:**	13.5p
Interim results:	Sep	**Market cap:**	£7.1m
Final results:	Mar	**Issue price:**	10.0p
Year end:	Dec	**Current no of shares:**	
Accounts due:	Jul		52,600,000
Int div paymnt:	n/a	**No of shares after**	
Fin div paymnt:	n/a	**dilution:**	n/a
Int net div per share:	nil	**P/E ratio:**	n/a
Fin net div per share:	nil	**Probable CGT?**	YES

LATEST REPORTED RESULTS:	14 MONTHS TO DEC 2002	PREVIOUS REPORTED RESULTS:	N/A
Turnover:	£897,000	**Turnover:**	n/a
PTP:	£(11,000)	**PTP:**	n/a
EPS:	n/a	**EPS:**	n/a

Comments:

Loss-making Designer Vision has been active lately, gaining an OEM order from Volvo to supply in-car audio visual equipment for its UK market worth £1.3m, and winning a contract to supply Ford with an in-car DVD system. Blaupunkt has chosen the group for a strategic partnership for in-car cinema and integrated satellite navigation system development. Non-board member Angelo Panayiotou has a checkered history having seen numerous business interests go into liquidation.

Desire Petroleum (DES)

Oil & gas explorer

Mathon Court, Mathon, Malvern, Worcestershire WR13 5NZ Tel: 01684-892242; Fax: 01684-575226;
e-mail: dpl@desireplc.co.uk; web site: www.desireplc.co.uk

		holding %
Chairman	Colin Phipps	0.0
Managing Director		
Finance Director		
Non-Exec Director	Stephen Phipps*	0.0

Main Shareholders:

Phipps & Co*	24.7
Westmount Energy	5.4
Greenwich Resources	5.1

Percentage of free market capital: 61.4%

*these shares are held by Phipps & Company Ltd

Comments:

Trading at less than 10% of its 1998 float price, Desire, a high-risk recovery speculation that cut interim losses by a third to £213,000, managed to raise £7 million at 10p in January. The money was to fund a seismic survey of its offshore Falkland Islands oil prospects and to repay a loan from, and pay fees to, chairman and key shareholder Colin Phipps.

Nominated Adviser:		Seymour Pierce, London	
AIM Broker:		Seymour Pierce, London	
Solicitors:		Osborne Clarke, Bristol	
Market Makers:		KBCS; MLSB; SCAP; SGSL; WINS	
Auditors:		Hacker Young, 79 Oxford St, Manchester M1 6HT	
Registrars:		Capita Registrars	

Entry on AIM:	17/6/1998	**Recent price:**	10.75p
Interim results:	Jul	**Market cap:**	£17.75m
Final results:	Apr	**Issue price:**	125.0p
Year end:	Dec	**Current no of shares:**	
Accounts due:	Apr		165,105,799
Int div paymnt:	n/a	**No of shares after**	
Fin div paymnt:	n/a	**dilution:**	n/a
Int net div per share:	nil	**P/E ratio:**	n/a
Fin net div per share:	nil	**Probable CGT?**	No

LATEST REPORTED RESULTS: 2002		PREVIOUS REPORTED RESULTS: 2001	
Turnover:	n/a	Turnover:	n/a
PTP:	£(377,000)	PTP:	£(7.11m)
EPS:	(0.4)p	EPS:	(6.8)p

Dickinson Legg (DKL)

Manufacturer of parts for tobacco processing equipment

Moorside Road, Winnal Trading Estate, Winchester, Hampshire SO23 7SS Tel: 01962-842227; Fax: 01962-840567;
e-mail: sales@dickinsonlegg.com; web site: www.dickinsonlegg.com

		holding %
Chairman	Barry Stevenson	0.0
Chief Exec & MD	Thomas Mackie	0.3
Finance Director	David Heath	0.0
Non-Exec Director	Trevor Swete	0.0

Main Shareholders:

Schroder Institutional Recovery Fund	19.1
Aberdeen Asset Management	12.4
Clients of Veer Plathe Voute NV	12.3
Invesco Asset Management	4.6
Universities Superannuation Scheme	4.1

Percentage of free market capital: 43.7%

Comments:

The tobacco processing and air drying equipment maker declared its first interim dividend despite the decline of sales and profits in the half to December. Operating profit waned to £116,000 (£647,000) on lower turnover of £18.5m (£21.8m). Its core tobacco machine business started the year with a lower order book, though it remained in profit. And margins were also tight at Spooner Industries, the air drying equipment maker. There's little evidence of imminent improvement in the group's markets.

Nominated Adviser:		Rowan Dartington, London	
AIM Broker:		Rowan Dartington, London	
Solicitors:		Osborne Clarke, Bristol	
Market Makers:		GRAB; KLWT; WINS	
Auditors:		PricewaterhouseCoopers, Southampton	
Registrars:		Computershare Investor Services	

Entry on AIM:	16/12/2002	**Recent price:**	28.5p
Interim results:	Feb	**Market cap:**	£10.36m
Final results:	Sep	**Issue price:**	42.5p
Year end:	Jun	**Current no of shares:**	
Accounts due:	Oct		36,354,913
Int div paymnt:	n/a	**No of shares after**	
Fin div paymnt:	Jul	**dilution:**	n/a
Int net div per share:	nil	**P/E ratio:**	5.5
Fin net div per share:	1.5p	**Probable CGT?**	Yes

LATEST REPORTED RESULTS: 2002		PREVIOUS REPORTED RESULTS: 2001	
Turnover:	£49.19m	Turnover:	£54.16m
PTP:	£2.22m	PTP:	£5.8m
EPS:	5.2p	EPS:	14.6p

Digital Classics (DTC)

Broadcaster of audio transmissions over the internet

Fraser House, 29 Albemarle Street, London, W1S 4JB Tel: 020-7636 1400; Fax: 020-7637 1355;
e-mail: team@onlineclassics.com; web site: www.onlineclassics.com

		holding %
Chairman	Richard Price	1.8
CEO	Christopher Hunt	23.6
Finance Director	Michael Barton	0.9
Artistic Director	Alan Sievewright	6.6

Main Shareholders:

Prudential 13.8

Percentage of free market capital: 9.4%

Nominated Adviser:	Grant Thornton, London
AIM Broker:	Durlacher, London
Solicitors:	Field Fisher Waterhouse, London
Market Makers:	HSBC; WINS
Auditors:	Grant Thornton, Southampton
Registrars:	Melton Registrars

Comments:

Digital managed to shrink pre-tax losses 87% to £385,646 in the interim although turnover fell 40% to £722,806. Iambic was affected by the non-transmission of its programme on Michael Jackson – due to be televised on the day the star was arrested for child molestation – but it will receive over £500,000 for its programme celebrating Swedish supergroup Abba. It has also launched a subscription website and recently placed 158m shares to acquire R M Associates Distribution.

ENTRY ON AIM: 13/12/1999	**Recent price:**	1.6p
Interim results:	Mar	**Market cap:**	£4.93m
Final results:	Sep	**Issue price:**	1.0p
Year end:	Jun	**Current no of shares:**	
Accounts due:	Nov		308,124,263
Int div paymnt:	n/a	**No of shares after**	
Fin div paymnt:	n/a	**dilution:**	n/a
Int net div per share:	nil	**P/E ratio:**	n/a
Fin net div per share:	nil	**Probable CGT?**	**Yes**

LATEST REPORTED RESULTS: 2003		PREVIOUS REPORTED RESULTS: 2002	
Turnover:	£1.20m	Turnover:	£1.37m
PTP:	£(2.89m)	PTP:	£(12.28m)
EPS:	(2.2)p	EPS:	(34.1)p

Dimension Resources (DMR)

Dimension stone extractor & processor

2 Church Street, Hamilton, Bermuda HM11 Tel: 00-27 21-852 8349; Fax: 00-27 21-851 7560

		holding %
Chairman	Brian Moritz	7.2
Managing Director	Steve Taylor	2.4
Finance Director		
Non-Exec Director	Geoffrey Hoodless	12.2

Main Shareholders:

Halewood International Futures Limited 21.9

Percentage of free market capital: 54.3%

Nominated Adviser:	Grant Thornton, London
AIM Broker:	Hoodless Brennan, London
Solicitors:	Field Fisher Waterhouse, London
Market Makers:	KBCS; WINS
Auditors:	Kessel Feinstein, 14 Long St, Cape Town 8001, South Africa
Registrars:	Melton Registrars

Comments:

Chairman Brian Moritz blamed the rand's strength against the dollar for continuing interim losses of £66,4000 at South African decorative stone quarrier Dimension. The company, which has been working on a Rustenburg black granite quarry, raised £300,000 last year at 0.5p in a placing that brought stockbroker Geoffrey Hoodless a 12.2% stake and a seat on the board.

ENTRY ON AIM: 18/5/1998	**Recent price:**	0.7p
Interim results:	Sep	**Market cap:**	£1.38m
Final results:	Jun	**Issue price:**	30.0p
Year end:	Dec	**Current no of shares:**	
Accounts due:	Apr		197,042,498
Int div paymnt:	n/a	**No of shares after**	
Fin div paymnt:	n/a	**dilution:**	208,951,996
Int net div per share:	nil	**P/E ratio:**	n/a
Fin net div per share:	nil	**Probable CGT?**	**No**

LATEST REPORTED RESULTS: 2002		PREVIOUS REPORTED RESULTS: 2001	
Turnover:	£234,000	Turnover:	£184,000
PTP:	£(294,000)	PTP:	£(430,000)
EPS:	(0.3)p	EPS:	(0.5)p

Dinkie Heel (DINK)
Footwear manufacturer
St Ivel Way, Warmley, Bristol BS30 8TY Tel: 0117-961 3163; Fax: 0117-935 2162; e-mail: info@dinkie.co.uk; web site: www.dinkie.com

		holding %
Chairman	Richard Organ	1.9
Managing Director	C R Ball	4.5
Finance Director	Geoff Martin	0.0
General Manager	M J Stowey	8.7

Main Shareholders:

HSBC	8.4
Dartington Portfolio Nominees	4.9
J Abell	4.5
The Bank of New York	3.4
Gilt Fund Securities	3.2

Percentage of free market capital: 51.6%

Nominated Adviser:	City Financial Associates, London
AIM Broker:	Rowan Dartington, Bristol
Solicitors:	Burges Salmon, Bristol
Market Makers:	WINS
Auditors:	PricewaterhouseCoopers, Bristol BS1 5QD
Registrars:	Capita Registrars

ENTRY ON AIM:	29/7/1998	**Recent price:**	4.5p
Interim results:	Sep	**Market cap:**	£0.71m
Final results:	May	**Issue price:**	n/a
Year end:	Dec	**Current no of shares:**	
Accounts due:	Apr		15,706,056
Int div paymnt:	n/a	**No of shares after**	
Fin div paymnt:	n/a	**dilution:**	n/a
Int net div per share:	nil	**P/E ratio:**	n/a
Fin net div per share:	nil	**Probable CGT?**	YES

LATEST REPORTED RESULTS: 2001		PREVIOUS REPORTED RESULTS: 2000	
Turnover:	£9.34m	Turnover:	£10.15m
PTP:	£(1.56m)	PTP:	£(475,000)
EPS:	(10.6)p	EPS:	(3.2)p

Comments:
Dinkie Heel's paramount objective is to reorganise and return to profit. Interims to June showed lower sales of £2.7m (£3.5m) and wider losses of £462,000 (£163,000). However all premises surplus to requirements have been sold, with toe cap manufacturing transferred to Botswana. And, although toe cap sales were down 47% in the first half, the move to Botswana should help. Davies Odell should benefit from seasonal upturn in its matting and footwear markets.

Dipford (DIP)
Corporate finance and business transfer agency
Pynes, Upton Pyne, Exeter, EX5 5EF Tel: 01392-256800; Fax: 01392-256801; e-mail: info@dipford.com; web site: www.dipford.com

		holding %
Chairman	J. Custance Baker	19.8
Managing Director	Rupert Cattell	10.6
Finance Director	Miles MacEacharn	2.9
Non-Exec Director	Christopher Pople	0.0

Main Shareholders:

Rathbones	11.6
Aberdeen Asset Management	8.0

Percentage of free market capital: 47.1%

Nominated Adviser:	Rowan Dartington, Bristol
AIM Broker:	Rowan Dartington, Bristol
Solicitors:	Burges Salmon, Bristol
Market Makers:	WINS
Auditors:	Francis Clark, Exeter
Registrars:	Computershare Investor Services

ENTRY ON AIM:	12/2/2002	**Recent price:**	50.0p
Interim results:	Dec	**Market cap:**	£3.06m
Final results:	Aug	**Issue price:**	49.0p
Year end:	Apr	**Current no of shares:**	
Accounts due:	Oct		6,113,343
Int div paymnt:	n/a	**No of shares after**	
Fin div paymnt:	n/a	**dilution:**	n/a
Int net div per share:	nil	**P/E ratio:**	n/a
Fin net div per share:	nil	**Probable CGT?**	YES

LATEST REPORTED RESULTS: 2003		PREVIOUS REPORTED RESULTS: 12 FEB 02 TO 30 APR 02	
Turnover:	£1.04m	Turnover:	£6,000
PTP:	£(476,000)	PTP:	£(107,000)
EPS:	(19.4)p	EPS:	(4.6)p

Comments:
Ex-Exeter Investment chief executive Custance Baker wants to consolidate the corporate finance market for private companies worth less than £10m. So far it has bought business valuer and transfer agency Redwoods for £1.4m and profitable Dowling Kerr for £2.1m, using cash and shares. Dipford sees retaining independence from accountants as a virtue. A £35,000 interim loss was made on £1m turnover, with delays in its Prism corporate finance arm still evident.

Dobbies Garden Centres   (DGC)

Garden centre operator

Melville Nursery, Lasswade, Midlothian EH18 1AZ Tel: 0131-663 6778; Fax: 0131-654 2548;
e-mail: postmaster@dobbies.com; web site: www.dobbies.com

		holding %
Chairman	A. Hammond-Chambers	1.3
Chief Executive	James Barnes	1.1
Finance Director	Sharon Brown	0.03
Operations Director	John Trotter	2.4

Main Shareholders:

Chase Nominees	9.9
Brewin Nominees	7.3
Nortrust Nominees	6.8
BNY/DGS Nominees	4.4
Ashleybank Investments	4.2
Percentage of free market capital:	51.0%

Nominated Adviser:	Brewin Dolphin, Edinburgh
AIM Broker:	Brewin Dolphin, Glasgow
Solicitors:	Tods Murray, Edinburgh
Market Makers:	ALTI; KBCS; NUMS; WINS
Auditors:	Deloitte & Touche, Edinburgh EH2 2HZ
Registrars:	Lloyds TSB Registrars

ENTRY ON AIM:	10/3/1997	Recent price:	470.0p
Interim results:	Jun	Market cap:	£45.97m
Final results:	Feb	Issue price:	200.0p
Year end:	Oct	Current no of shares:	
Accounts due:	n/a		9,780,810
Int div paymnt:	Oct	No of shares after	
Fin div paymnt:	Apr	dilution:	10,006,610
Int net div per share:	2.65p	P/E ratio:	15.9
Fin net div per share:	4.9p	Probable CGT?	YES

LATEST REPORTED RESULTS: 2003		PREVIOUS REPORTED RESULTS: 2002	
Turnover:	£46.12m	Turnover:	£38.36m
PTP:	£4.15m	PTP:	£6.01m
EPS:	29.6p	EPS:	50.6p

Comments:

Scottish group Dobbies continues to bloom, thanks largely to an unseasonably warm spring and summer. Founded back in 1865, it has completed the Atherstone site, which is one of the largest garden centres in the UK, at a cost of £4.9m. A store in Ayr is due to open in March, bringing the total chain to 18. Moreover, Dobbies has submitted planning permission for two further stores. Seymour Pierce is forecasting profits to increase to £5.1m in 2004.

Documedia Solutions   (DOC)

Digital print services group

Trustcott House, 32-42 East Road, London, N1 6AD Tel: 020-7553 6600; Fax: 020-7833 5252;
e-mail: bertie@ctrlp.com; web site: www.documedia.co.uk

		holding %
Chairman	Warren Tayler*	13.8
Managing Director	Mark O'Connor	0.0
Finance Director	Herbert Maxwell	0.6
Technical Director	Antony Hodgson	0.0

Main Shareholders:

Exebridge Investment*	18.2
Mercator Trust	12.2
Peter O'Reilly	4.8

Percentage of free market capital: 42.3%

*Warren Tayler has a beneficial interest in the shares held by Exebridge Investment

Nominated Adviser:	City Financial Associates, London
AIM Broker:	Collins Stewart, London
Solicitors:	Taylor Wessing, London
Market Makers:	CSCS; WINS
Auditors:	Hazlewoods, Barnett Way, Gloucester GL4 3RT
Registrars:	Capita Registrars

ENTRY ON AIM:	10/5/2000	Recent price:	2.6p
Interim results:	Oct	Market cap:	£1.04m
Final results:	Jul	Issue price:	60.0p
Year end:	Feb	Current no of shares:	
Accounts due:	Aug		40,113,340
Int div paymnt:	n/a	No of shares after	
Fin div paymnt:	n/a	dilution:	n/a
Int net div per share:	nil	P/E ratio:	n/a
Fin net div per share:	nil	Probable CGT?	YES

LATEST REPORTED RESULTS: 2003		PREVIOUS REPORTED RESULTS: 2002	
Turnover:	£9.08m	Turnover:	£2.54m
PTP:	£(2.53m)	PTP:	£(1.7m)
EPS:	(7.3)p	EPS:	(5.0)p

Comments:

Documedia is the restructured print management venture providing 'high impact' marketing support materials to clients across sectors such as property, leisure and retail. Effectively, this company creates, publishes and controls its clients' marketing campaigns for them. Some 60% of its revenues are now generated through an e-commerce system. Figures for the half year to August were encouraging, with narrower losses of £365,386 (£1.05m) on turnover of £4.1m (£4.75m).

Domino's Pizza UK & Ireland (DOM)

Pizza delivery service provider

Domino's House, Lasborough Road, Kingston, Milton Keynes MK10 0AB Tel: 01908-580000; Fax: 01908-588000; e-mail: investor.relations@dominos.co.uk; web site: www.dominos.co.uk

		holding %
Chairman	Colin Halpern	24.4
CEO	Stephen Hemsley	4.7
Finance Director		
Sales & Mktg	Christopher Moore	0.0
Director		
Main Shareholders:		
Nigel Wray (Non-Exec Director)		27.6
FMR Corp and FIL		7.2
Moonpal Grewal		3.5

Percentage of free market capital: 32.1%

Nominated Adviser:	Numis, London
AIM Broker:	Numis, London
Solicitors:	McDermott, Will and Emery, London
Market Makers:	KBCS; MLSB; SCAP; WINS
Auditors:	Ernst & Young, 400 Capability Green, Luton LU1 3LU
Registrars:	Capita Registrars

ENTRY ON AIM: 24/11/1999		Recent price:	217.5p
Interim results:	Jul	Market cap:	£115.64m
Final results:	Feb	Issue price:	50.0p
Year end:	Dec	Current no of shares:	
Accounts due:	Apr		53,168,711
Int div paymnt:	Sep	No of shares after	
Fin div paymnt:	Apr	dilution:	56,400,000
Int net div per share: 1.32p		P/E ratio:	24.2
Fin net div per share: 3.5p		Probable CGT?	YES

LATEST REPORTED RESULTS: 2003		PREVIOUS REPORTED RESULTS: 2002	
Turnover:	£61.56m	Turnover:	£53.11m
PTP:	£6.54m	PTP:	£4.24m
EPS:	9.0p	EPS:	5.6p

Comments:

The pizza delivery group continues to go from strength to strength. It opened a record 50 new stores in 2003 and with a current tally of 318 units the group is on track to reach its target of 500 stores by the end of 2006. The company has also extended its sponsorship of the Simpsons on Sky TV until 2006 as part of its branding strategy. In 2003, it managed to repay its £8.2m bank debt and has healthy cash resources of £3.7m to fund further growth.

Dream Direct (DDG)

Mail order retailer of family-oriented software

Granville Way, Bicester, Oxfordshire OX26 4JT Tel: 01869-328200; web site: www.edream.co.uk

		holding %
Chairman	Robert Silver	0.1
Chief Executive	Robert Colquhoun	8.1
Finance Director	Patrick Huggins	0.0
Exec Director	Oliver Vintcent	7.3
Main Shareholders:		
Gerald Dennis' family		18.4
Russell Duckworth		5.8
Artemis AIM VCT		4.0
Carol Galley		3.5
Axa Equity and Law Life Assurance		3.4

Percentage of free market capital: 40.3%

Nominated Adviser:	KBC Peel Hunt, London
AIM Broker:	KBC Peel Hunt, London
Solicitors:	Hammonds, London
Market Makers:	KBCS; WINS
Auditors:	Grant Thornton, London NW1 2EP
Registrars:	Capita Registrars

ENTRY ON AIM: 2/5/2002		Recent price:	81.0p
Interim results:	Dec	Market cap:	£6.98m
Final results:	Jul	Issue price:	88.0p
Year end:	Mar	Current no of shares:	
Accounts due:	Aug		8,612,979
Int div paymnt:	n/a	No of shares after	
Fin div paymnt:	n/a	dilution:	n/a
Int net div per share:	nil	P/E ratio:	n/a
Fin net div per share:	nil	Probable CGT?	YES

LATEST REPORTED RESULTS: 2003		PREVIOUS REPORTED RESULTS: 2002	
Turnover:	£7.39m	Turnover:	£3.75m
PTP:	£(782,000)	PTP:	£(991,000)
EPS:	n/a	EPS:	n/a

Comments:

Despite announcing greatly improved interim figures – losses reduced 30% to £366,000 on sales up 52% to £3.8m – family software retailer DD has conceded that its full year results will fall short of expectations. Like many direct retailers the company claims to have been badly affected by November's postal strikes, management suggesting that the resulting profit shortfall could equal anything up to £200,000. More positive was news that DD generated one-week sales in excess of £1m for the first time in early December.

Dwyka Diamonds (DWY)

Diamond miner

Level 4, HPPL House, 28-42 Ventnor Avenue, West Perth, WA 6005 Australia, Tel: 00-61 8 9324 2955;
Fax: 00-61 8 9324 2977; e-mail: info@dwykadiamonds.com; web site: www.dwykadiamonds.com

		holding %
Chairman	Edward Nealon	1.6
Chief Executive	Melissa Sturgess	1.6
Finance Director		
Technical Director	Evan Kirby	0.4

Main Shareholders:

Daltonvale	11.6
National Nominees	9.6
Chase Nominnes	4.7
Poductive Walk Nominees	4.0
Grosspoint	3.3

Percentage of free market capital: 57.2%

Nominated Adviser:	Williams de Broe, London
AIM Broker:	Williams de Broe, London
Solicitors:	Nabarro Nathanson, London
Market Makers:	BGMM; SGSL; WINS
Auditors:	PricewaterhouseCoopers, Perth WA6000, Australia
Registrars:	Computershare Investor Services

ENTRY ON AIM:	7/12/2001	Recent price:	23.75p
Interim results:	Mar	Market cap:	£14.55m
Final results:	Sep	Issue price:	40.0p
Year end:	Jun	Current no of shares:	
Accounts due:	Oct		61,281,611
Int div paymnt:	n/a	No of shares after	
Fin div paymnt:	n/a	dilution:	61,713,977
Int net div per share:	nil	P/E ratio:	n/a
Fin net div per share:	nil	Probable CGT?	No

LATEST REPORTED RESULTS: 2002		PREVIOUS REPORTED RESULTS: 2001	
Turnover:	A$5.26m	Turnover:	n/a
PTP:	A$(4.49m)	PTP:	A$(709,000)
EPS:	(10.9)Ac	EPS:	(4.6)Ac

Comments:
After major restructuring, Australian-based Dwyka turned a £6m interim loss into a £450,000 first-half profit, having refocused its Nooitgedacht operation in South Africa onto low-cost alluvial mining. With an average grade of 1.07 carats, the company sold one 55.5 carat stone for £268,000. Dwyka professes high hopes for its Indian gem prospecting alliance with mining giant BHP Billiton and exploration in Andrha Pradesh.

Dynamic Commercial Finance (DCF)

Provider of sales finance for small companies

38-42 South Road, Haywards Heath, West Sussex RH16 4LA Tel: 01444-884646; Fax: 01444-884647;
e-mail: info@dcfplc.com; web site: www.dcfplc.com

		holding %
Chairman	Tony Caplin	0.6
Chief Executive	Paul Hird*	4.7
Finance Director	Paul Billett	0.0
Risk & Ops Director	Phil Woodward	3.0

Main Shareholders:

Eaglet Investment Trust	28.9
Close Brothers	16.1
Liontrust Investment Services	12.6

Percentage of free market capital: 31.1%

* includes shares held by spouse

Nominated Adviser:	Williams de Broe, London
AIM Broker:	Williams de Broe, London
Solicitors:	Hammonds, London
Market Makers:	WDBM; WINS
Auditors:	KPMG, Crawley
Registrars:	Capita Registrars

ENTRY ON AIM:	20/12/2000	Recent price:	88.5p
Interim results:	Sep	Market cap:	£3.47m
Final results:	Mar	Issue price:	153.0p
Year end:	Dec	Current no of shares:	
Accounts due:	Apr		3,918,465
Int div paymnt:	n/a	No of shares after	
Fin div paymnt:	n/a	dilution:	4,571,428
Int net div per share:	nil	P/E ratio:	n/a
Fin net div per share:	nil	Probable CGT?	Yes

LATEST REPORTED RESULTS: 2002		PREVIOUS REPORTED RESULTS: 2001	
Turnover:	£2.88m	Turnover:	£884,000
PTP:	£(96,000)	PTP:	£(663,000)
EPS:	2.6p	EPS:	(16.9)p

Comments:
Fast-growing DCF hopes to become a leading invoice discounter for SMEs. Discount invoicing is similar to factoring, but the responsibility for collecting the original debt remains with the customer. Against a background of increased competition the group made a small interim profit as turnover rose 73% to £1.9m, culled from £15.9m of funds factored out to 171 clients. Capital is provided by a £25m facility with Lloyds TSB, agreed last spring. Less than half has been used so far, giving enough scope for two years of growth.

e-primefinancial (EPF)

Investor in growth companies

4th Floor, Landseer House, 19 Charing Cross Road, London WC2H 0ES Tel: 020-7839 4132; Fax: 020-7839 5164;
e-mail: investor.relations@eprimefinancial.com; web site: www.epf.com

		holding %
Chairman	Lance O'Neill	6.7
Chief Executive		
Finance Director	Nigel Duxbury	5.4
Non-Exec Director	Jeremy Peace	1.6

Main Shareholders:

Hamilton Trustees	17.0
Shallotte Investments	14.0
Gene Grant	14.4

Percentage of free market capital: 38.6%

Nominated Adviser:	Seymour Pierce, London
AIM Broker:	Seymour Pierce, London
Solicitors:	Memery Crystal, London
Market Makers:	MLSB; SCAP; WINS
Auditors:	Rees Pollock, 7 Pilgrim Street, London EC4V 6DR
Registrars:	Capita Registrars

ENTRY ON AIM: 16/12/1999	Recent price:	25,000.00p
Interim results: Aug	Market cap:	£7.5m
Final results: Jun	Issue price:	2.0p
Year end: Dec	Current no of shares:	
Accounts due: Apr		29,981
Int div paymnt: n/a	No of shares after	
Fin div paymnt: n/a	dilution:	n/a
Int net div per share: nil	P/E ratio:	n/a
Fin net div per share: nil	Probable CGT?	No

Comments:

This group, which wanted to form a US bank, failed to raise sufficient capital to obtain a banking licence. It now wants to use its £10.4m cash pile for acquisitions. Former chief executive Gene Grant got the board to run a tender offer last year to return some of the cash to shareholders. The company bought back 40% of the shares, spending £5.36m in all. A share consolidation has since taken place. A £0.64m interim loss was made but cost cuts should make the company profitable soon.

LATEST REPORTED RESULTS: 2002	PREVIOUS REPORTED RESULTS: 2001
Turnover: n/a	Turnover: n/a
PTP: £(1.57m)	PTP: £(2.24m)
EPS: (0.5)p	EPS: (0.6)p

Eagle Eye Telematics (EIT)

Developer of vehicle communication technologies

Apollo House, 41 Halton Station Road, Sutton Weaver, Runcorn, Cheshire WA7 3DN Tel: 01928-795400;
Fax: 01928-795401; web site: www.eagle-eye.co.uk

		holding %
Chairman	Nigel Whittaker	1.0
Chief Executive	Neil Arnott	0.0
Finance Director	Chris Stubbs	0.04
Non-Exec Director	Ralph Stross	25.5

Main Shareholders:

Terry Krell (Non-exec Director)	25.0
Command Fund	5.3

Percentage of free market capital: 40.6%

Nominated Adviser:	WH Ireland, London
AIM Broker:	WH Ireland, London
Solicitors:	Halliwell Landau, Manchester
Market Makers:	ALTI; BGMM; SCAP; WINS
Auditors:	PricewaterhouseCoopers, Manchester
Registrars:	Capita Registrars

ENTRY ON AIM: 3/2/2000	Recent price:	7.0p
Interim results: Aug	Market cap:	£1.82m
Final results: Mar	Issue price:	25.0p
Year end: Nov	Current no of shares:	
Accounts due: Mar		26,027,579
Int div paymnt: n/a	No of shares after	
Fin div paymnt: n/a	dilution:	26,904,246
Int net div per share: nil	P/E ratio:	n/a
Fin net div per share: nil	Probable CGT?	YES

Comments:

Last year was one of overhaul for the vehicle telematics technology supplier, which adversely affected turnover short term. Disappointingly, Eagle Eye's losses widened after an exceptional stock write off and the charging of goodwill – no dividend was proposed. Now the company has a leaner overhead base and a more focussed sales strategy. The board is convinced the long-mooted 'explosion' in the take-up of telematics is about to happen.

LATEST REPORTED RESULTS: 2002	PREVIOUS REPORTED RESULTS: 2001
Turnover: £2.24m	Turnover: £2.28m
PTP: £(4.34m)	PTP: £(4.12m)
EPS: (16.7)p	EPS: (15.8)p

Earthport (EPO)

E-commerce secure payment systems provider

7-10 Chandos Street, London, W1G 9DQ   Tel: 020-7907 1100; Fax: 020-7907 1101; e-mail: info@earthport.com; web site: www.earthport.com

		holding %
Chairman	Andy Ripley	0.0
Chief Executive	Robert Cunningham	2.3
Finance Director	Christopher Hall	0.0
Non-Exec Director	Robert Rakison	4.2

Main Shareholders:

Metropole Europe Corporation	13.5
Tallulah Properties	7.2
Gelande Holdings	6.1
Savoy Investment Management	4.7
Java Services	4.0
Percentage of free market capital: 60.0%	

Nominated Adviser:	Beaumont Cornish, London
AIM Broker:	Seymour Pierce, London
Solicitors:	GMR, London
Market Makers:	CHMM; KBCS; MLSB; NMRA; WINS
Auditors:	Ernst & Young, Fetter Lane, London
Registrars:	Capita Registrars

Entry on AIM:	30/1/2001	**Recent price:**	3.0p
Interim results:	Mar	Market cap:	£16.12m
Final results:	Sep	Issue price:	125.0p
Year end:	Jun	Current no of shares:	
Accounts due:	Oct		537,489,387
Int div paymnt:	n/a	No of shares after	
Fin div paymnt:	n/a	dilution:	n/a
Int net div per share:	nil	P/E ratio:	n/a
Fin net div per share:	nil	Probable CGT?	Yes

LATEST REPORTED RESULTS: 2003		PREVIOUS REPORTED RESULTS: 2002	
Turnover:	£513,000	Turnover:	£248,000
PTP:	£(12.93m)	PTP:	£(12.48m)
EPS:	(6.4)p	EPS:	(11.4)p

Comments:

Beleaguered OFEX-graduate Earthport specialises in the provision of secure electronic payment solutions to corporate clients in a range of industries from banking through to on-line gaming. On a trading level the past few years have, without doubt, been appalling and yet management now states that the company's 'salvage and reconstruction period' is over. A recent £3.6m fundraising affords a degree of financial stability.

---

easier (EZR)

Cash shell

Somerset House, 30 Wynnstay Road, Colwyn Bay, LL29 8NB   Tel: 01492-536642; Fax: 01492-535863; web site: www.easier.co.uk

		holding %
Chairman	David Gough	0.0
Chief Executive		
Finance Director		
Non-Exec Director	Richard Guy Thomas	6.5

Main Shareholders:

Sterling Trust	25.2
Simon Eagle	12.2
AMVESCAP	10.6
Fuji Investment Management	9.9
Neville Buch	8.5
Percentage of free market capital: 12.8%	

Nominated Adviser:	Beaumont Cornish, London
AIM Broker:	n/a
Solicitors:	Jones Day Gouldens, London
Market Makers:	KBCS; WINS
Auditors:	Deloitte & Touche, Cardiff
Registrars:	Capita Registrars

Entry on AIM:	4/2/2000	**Recent price:**	20.0p
Interim results:	Sep	Market cap:	£4.93m
Final results:	Jun	Issue price:	150.0p
Year end:	Dec	Current no of shares:	
Accounts due:	Apr		24,666,800
Int div paymnt:	n/a	No of shares after	
Fin div paymnt:	n/a	dilution:	n/a
Int net div per share:	nil	P/E ratio:	n/a
Fin net div per share:	nil	Probable CGT?	Yes

LATEST REPORTED RESULTS: 2002		PREVIOUS REPORTED RESULTS: 2001	
Turnover:	n/a	Turnover:	n/a
PTP:	£63,000	PTP:	£(329,000)
EPS:	0.3p	EPS:	(1.3)p

Comments:

Now a shell with around £5.4m of cash, easier originally raised £11.2m net to operate a residential property website, but failed to make much money from it. After perusing a number of opportunities and mulling over reverse takeover ideas, the company is now moving away from structured finance investments and is looking at investment opportunities in property and real estate investment trusts. Recent board changes have been made.

Eckoh Technologies (ECK)

Designer and manager of speech solutions

Telford House, Corner Hall, Hemel Hempstead, Hertfordshire HP3 9HN Tel: 0870-110 0200; Fax: 0870-110 7107;
web site: www.365corp.com

		holding %
Chairman	D Best	0.04
Chief Executive	M Turner	0.0
Finance Director	B McArthur Muscroft	0.0
Chief Operating Officer	N Philpot	0.9

Main Shareholders:

Gartmore	10.5
Herald Investment	7.2
UBS Global Asset Management	4.7
Bank of Bermuda	4.1
Invesco English & International	4.0
Percentage of free market capital:	**65.6%**

Nominated Adviser:	Evolution Beeson Gregory, London
AIM Broker:	Evolution Beeson Gregory, London
Solicitors:	Freshfields Bruckhaus Deringer, London
Market Makers:	DURM; EVO; JEFF; KBCS; KLWT; MLSB; SCAP; WINS
Auditors:	PricewaterhouseCoopers, London
Registrars:	Capita Registrars

Entry on AIM:	27/6/2003	**Recent price:**	13.75p
Interim results:	Sep	**Market cap:**	£36.63m
Final results:	Apr	**Issue price:**	n/a
Year end:	Mar	**Current no of shares:**	
Accounts due:	Jul		266,408,961
Int div paymnt:	n/a	**No of shares after**	
Fin div paymnt:	n/a	**dilution:**	n/a
Int net div per share:	nil	**P/E ratio:**	n/a
Fin net div per share:	nil	**Probable CGT?**	Yes

LATEST REPORTED RESULTS: 2003		PREVIOUS REPORTED RESULTS: 2002	
Turnover:	£55.09m	Turnover:	£54.92m
PTP:	£(9.08m)	PTP:	£(33.46m)
EPS:	(4.4)p	EPS:	(16.5)p

Comments:

The speech application services play moved down to AIM last summer, then gobbled up rival Intelliplus in an all-share deal. It has since become the interactive telephony partner for ITV, which followed welcome news that its alliance with BT had been extended until December 2006. Half-year results to September revealed a 4% rise in continuing sales to £21.8m, whilst the net loss was slashed from £9.4m to £1.3m. The market for speech solutions is picking up 'real momentum'.

Education Development International (EDD)

Learning assessment system developers

The Old School, Holly Walk, Leamington Spa, Warwickshire CV32 4GL Tel: 01926-458600; Fax: 01926-887676;
e-mail: info@goalplc.co.uk; web site: www.goalplc.co.uk

		holding %
Chairman	Bryan Nicholson	0.0
Chief Executive	Nigel Snook	0.1
Finance Director	Kumaresan Padmanathan	0.1
Non-Exec Director	Wynford Dore	20.6

Main Shareholders:

LCCI Commercial Education Trust	48.5
Gareth Newman	28.6
Percentage of free market capital:	**1.9%**

Nominated Adviser:	Williams de Broe, Birmingham
AIM Broker:	Williams de Broe, Birmingham
Solicitors:	Pinsents, Birmingham
Market Makers:	WDBM; WINS
Auditors:	RSM Robson Rhodes, 7 Hill Street, Birmingham B5 4UU
Registrars:	Capita Registrars

Entry on AIM:	28/4/2000	**Recent price:**	8.75p
Interim results:	Mar	**Market cap:**	£4.25m
Final results:	Nov	**Issue price:**	225.0p
Year end:	Mar	**Current no of shares:**	
Accounts due:	Jul		48,514,851
Int div paymnt:	n/a	**No of shares after**	
Fin div paymnt:	n/a	**dilution:**	n/a
Int net div per share:	nil	**P/E ratio:**	n/a
Fin net div per share:	nil	**Probable CGT?**	Yes

LATEST REPORTED RESULTS: 18 MONTHS TO 30 SEP '03		PREVIOUS REPORTED RESULTS: 2002	
Turnover:	£8.57m	Turnover:	£589,000
PTP:	£(4.73m)	PTP:	(2.07m)p
EPS:	(12.2)p	EPS:	(8.5)p

Comments:

The group was formed when online assessment business GOAL acquired the London Chamber of Commerce and Industry Examinations Board (LCCIEB) in a reverse deal. Restructuring of the bigger corporate entity has taken out £1.2m of annualised overheads. Though the venture has had a challenging time in tough markets, its reported net cash as of 30 September was £1.3m. Apparently this is enough to support the business given sales growth and cost reductions.

Einstein

(EIC)

Digital TV channel operator

4 Lower Park Row, Bristol, BS1 5BJ Tel: 0117-927 7473; Fax: 0117-923 0862; e-mail: generalenquiries@tenmedia.co.uk; web site: www.einstein-group.tv

		holding %
Chairman	John Sanderson	0.4
Chief Executive	Stephen Timmins	8.3
Finance Director	Paul Fowler	0.0

Main Shareholders:

n/a

Percentage of free market capital: 91.3%

Comments:

Einstein, one of AIM's least successful ventures, went into administration last year and just recently had its creditors voluntary arrangement approved. The group is currently mulling over various board appointments and a possible fundraising.

Nominated Adviser:	Grant Thornton, London
AIM Broker:	Daniel Stewart, London
Solicitors:	Stringer Saul, London
Market Makers:	SCAP; WDBM; WINS
Auditors:	Moores Rowland, London
Registrars:	Capita Registrars

ENTRY ON AIM:	2/3/2000	**Recent price:**	1.1p
Interim results:	Sep	**Market cap:**	£1.41m
Final results:	Mar	**Issue price:**	40.0p
Year end:	Dec	**Current no of shares:**	
Accounts due:	Apr		128,150,326
Int div paymnt:	n/a	**No of shares after**	
Fin div paymnt:	n/a	**dilution:**	162,550,326
Int net div per share:	nil	**P/E ratio:**	n/a
Fin net div per share:	nil	**Probable CGT?**	YES

LATEST REPORTED RESULTS: 2002		PREVIOUS REPORTED RESULTS: 2001	
Turnover:	£1.42m	**Turnover:**	£3.11m
PTP:	£(6.82m)	**PTP:**	£(4.49m)
EPS:	(5.9)p	**EPS:**	(13.9)p

EiRx Therapeutics

(ERX)

Drug researcher

2800 Cork Airport Business Park, Kinsale Road, Cork, EC1R 0DU Ireland, Tel: 353 (0)21 4320847; Fax: 353 (0)21 4320848

		holding %
Chairman	John Pool	0.5
Chief Executive	Ian Hayes	0.0
Finance Director	Nicholas Strong	0.0
Chief Scientific Officer	Thomas Cotter	0.0

Main Shareholders:

EiRx Pharma	81.7
Peter Hoskins	4.5
Billam	3.7

Percentage of free market capital: 9.5%

Comments:

Irish drug discoverer EiRx raised £0.58m net on admission after being spun out of AIM-listed Billam. The thrust of the company's research is genes involved in apoptosis. This is the process through which most cell death takes place. The idea being that new therapies might be discovered, by replicating this process artificially, to kill unwanted cancerous cells or arresting the cell destruction wrought by degenerative diseases such as Alzheimers. Revenue will eventually come through licence fees.

Nominated Adviser:	Grant Thornton, London
AIM Broker:	Hoodless Brennan, London
Solicitors:	Bircham Dyson Bell, London
Market Makers:	HOOD; WINS
Auditors:	Grant Thornton, 95 Bothwell Street, Glasgow G2 7JZ
Registrars:	Capita Registrars

ENTRY ON AIM:	13/1/2004	**Recent price:**	8.5p
Interim results:	Mar	**Market cap:**	£10.4m
Final results:	Sep	**Issue price:**	5.0p
Year end:	Jun	**Current no of shares:**	
Accounts due:	Nov		122,349,997
Int div paymnt:	n/a	**No of shares after**	
Fin div paymnt:	n/a	**dilution:**	n/a
Int net div per share:	n/a	**P/E ratio:**	n/a
Fin net div per share:	n/a	**Probable CGT?**	No

LATEST REPORTED RESULTS: 2003		PREVIOUS REPORTED RESULTS: 2002	
Turnover:	n/a	**Turnover:**	n/a
PTP:	£(477,000)	**PTP:**	£(893,000)
EPS:	n/a	**EPS:**	n/a

Electric Word (ELE)

Provider of mixed-media for consumer and professional markets

67-71 Goswell Road, London, EC1V 7EP Tel: 020-7251 9035; Fax: 020-7251 9045; web site: www.electricwordplc.com

		holding %
Chairman	Nigel Wray	14.4
Chief Executive	Julian Turner	1.7
Finance Director		
Exec Director	Sylvester Stein	12.1

Main Shareholders:

Pinkberry Consultants	7.0
Owen Anderson	6.7
Robert Troop	5.9
Alasdair Buchan	4.0
Rosalind Buchan	4.0

Percentage of free market capital: 37.7%

Comments:

The publisher of professional development information for managers, as well as practitioners in health, education and local government, moved into profit – before product development and exceptionals – last year. Turnover rose by a decent 22%. Electric Word is growing both organically and by acquisition. The year concluded with its fourth and largest acquisition to date, PFP Publishing. The board claims breakeven is a realistic target for 2004.

Nominated Adviser:	Seymour Pierce, London
AIM Broker:	Seymour Pierce, London
Solicitors:	Memery Crystal, London
Market Makers:	SCAP; WINS
Auditors:	Baker Tilly, 2 Bloomsbury Street, London WC1B 3ST
Registrars:	Computershare Investor Services

Entry on AIM:	29/3/2000	**Recent price:**	7.9p
Interim results:	Jul	**Market cap:**	£7.7m
Final results:	Feb	**Issue price:**	5.0p
Year end:	Nov	**Current no of shares:**	
Accounts due:	Mar		97,513,854
Int div paymnt:	n/a	**No of shares after**	
Fin div paymnt:	n/a	**dilution:**	n/a
Int net div per share:	nil	**P/E ratio:**	n/a
Fin net div per share:	nil	**Probable CGT?**	Yes

LATEST REPORTED RESULTS: 2003		PREVIOUS REPORTED RESULTS: 2002	
Turnover:	£3.05m	**Turnover:**	£2.49m
PTP:	£(557,000)	**PTP:**	£(480,000)
EPS:	(0.5)p	**EPS:**	(0.6)p

Elektron (EKT)

Electronic component designer and manufacturer

131-133 New London Road, Chelmsford, Essex CM2 0QN Tel: 020-8477 9300; Fax: 01245-211939;
e-mail: mail@bulgin.plc.uk; web site: www.elektronplc.com

		holding %
Executive Chairman	Adrian Girling	0.0
Chief Executive	as above	
Finance Director	C M Leigh	0.1
Non-Exec Director	Keith Daley	0.0

Main Shareholders:

John Kinder	13.9
Trustees of A F Bulgin Sttlmnts*	12.1
Rathbone Nominees	9.6
Ronald Bulgin	5.0
James Capel Nominees	4.6

Percentage of free market capital: 42.5%

*J A D Skailes is a trustee of A F Bulgin Settlements

Comments:

Elektron has been busy of late acquiring three dormant companies with cash resources to provide working capital in return for shares. It also acquired AIM-suspended Arcoelectric Switches from administrative receivership for a consideration of £352,000 plus the assumption of £1.5m lease finance debt repayable after five years. In February, it sold its loss-making Milmega division to Framefair for £1m. The proceeds will be used to reduce borrowings.

Nominated Adviser:	Beaumont Cornish, London
AIM Broker:	The Share Centre, London
Solicitors:	Wollastons, London
Market Makers:	MLSB; TEAM; WINS
Auditors:	Bright Grahame Murray, London W1H 6AA
Registrars:	Capita Registrars

Entry on AIM:	19/4/1999	**Recent price:**	7.5p
Interim results:	Sep	**Market cap:**	£7.37m
Final results:	May	**Issue price:**	n/a
Year end:	Jan	**Current no of shares:**	
Accounts due:	Jun		98,332,036
Int div paymnt:	n/a	**No of shares after**	
Fin div paymnt:	n/a	**dilution:**	n/a
Int net div per share:	nil	**P/E ratio:**	n/a
Fin net div per share:	nil	**Probable CGT?**	Yes

LATEST REPORTED RESULTS: 2003		PREVIOUS REPORTED RESULTS: 2002	
Turnover:	£14.64m	**Turnover:**	£16.91m
PTP:	£(3.37m)	**PTP:**	£(2.65m)
EPS:	(6.2)p	**EPS:**	(4.5)p

Elite Strategies   (ETS)
Independent financial adviser
Greenhill House, Thorpe Wood, Peterborough, PE3 6RU Tel: 01733-264265; Fax: 01733-265855

		holding %
Chairman	Christopher Roberts	0.0
Chief Executive	Jonathan Fry	0.0
Finance Director	Peter Holmes	0.0
Non-Exec Director	Terence O'Neill	3.6

Main Shareholders:

Aroon Kumar Maharajh	4.7
IceMobile	4.4
Concept	3.4
Paul Kingston	3.2

Percentage of free market capital: 51.7%

Comments:
IFA Elite struggled in a tough financial services industry – the half to December revealed a swing to losses of £968,519 after month to month trading remained loss-making. Subsequently, Elite is selling its operating businesses to Croesus Holdings, a company with which its chief executive Fry is connected. Directors feel Elite is too small to sustain the costs of a public listing – the shell will have around £100,000 in cash reserves and remains on AIM with an eye on a reverse deal.

Nominated Adviser:	Corporate Synergy, London
AIM Broker:	Seymour Pierce, London
Solicitors:	Eversheds, Cambridge
Market Makers:	KBCS; SCAP; WINS
Auditors:	Rees Pollock, 7 Pilgrim Street, London, EC4V 6DR
Registrars:	Capita Registrars

ENTRY ON AIM:	5/10/2000	Recent price:	0.4p
Interim results:	Mar	Market cap:	£1.65m
Final results:	Oct	Issue price:	9.0p
Year end:	Jun	Current no of shares:	
Accounts due:	Oct		413,320,605
Int div paymnt:	n/a	No of shares after	
Fin div paymnt:	n/a	dilution:	n/a
Int net div per share:	nil	P/E ratio:	n/a
Fin net div per share:	nil	Probable CGT?	Yes

LATEST REPORTED RESULTS: 2003		PREVIOUS REPORTED RESULTS: 2002	
Turnover:	£1.13m	Turnover:	£1.03m
PTP:	£(225,000)	PTP:	£370,000
EPS:	(0.1)p	EPS:	0.1p

EmdexTrade   (EMD)
Operator of bespoke web-based trading platform
1 The Green, Richmond, Surrey TW9 1PL Tel: 020-8334 9953; Fax: 020-8940 0649; e-mail: info@pumphrey.co.uk

		holding %
Chairman	Ian Salter	0.5
Chief Executive	Eren Nil	84.2
Finance Director	Patrick Kennedy	0.3
Director	Layla Hollender	1.8

Main Shareholders:

n/a

Percentage of free market capital: 12.2%

Comments:
The trading platform operator has offloaded loss-making US division EmdexTrade Delaware (ETD) to Watamu Trading, a Bahrainian-registered company controlled by Emdex CEO and main shareholder Erin Nil. This division generated a £606,935 loss last year and £475,866 of debt owed to Emdex has been assumed elsewhere in the group. But while the transfer improves Emdex's balance sheet, it remains to be seen when and if Emdex will generate any form of profit.

Nominated Adviser:	Nabarro Wells, London
AIM Broker:	Keith Bayley Rogers, London
Solicitors:	Field Fisher Waterhouse, London
Market Makers:	SCAP; WINS
Auditors:	RSM Robson Rhodes, 186 City Road, London EC1V 2NU
Registrars:	Capita Registrars

ENTRY ON AIM:	14/6/2001	Recent price:	6.75p
Interim results:	Jul	Market cap:	£3.0m
Final results:	Apr	Issue price:	10.0p
Year end:	Oct	Current no of shares:	
Accounts due:	Mar		44,444,444
Int div paymnt:	n/a	No of shares after	
Fin div paymnt:	n/a	dilution:	n/a
Int net div per share:	nil	P/E ratio:	n/a
Fin net div per share:	nil	Probable CGT?	Yes

LATEST REPORTED RESULTS: 2002		PREVIOUS REPORTED RESULTS: 15 MONTHS TO OCT 01	
Turnover:	£780,000	Turnover:	£313,000
PTP:	£(654,000)	PTP:	£(69,000)
EPS:	(1.6)p	EPS:	n/a

Empire Interactive
(EMP)

Computer games developer and publisher

The Spires, 677 High Road, North Finchley, London, N12 0DA Tel: 020-8343 7337; Fax: 020-8343 7447; web site: www.empireinteractive.com

		holding %
Chairman	Sir Rodney Walker	1.8
Chief Executive	Ian Higgins	31.1
Finance Director		
Managing Director	Simon Jeffrey	31.1

Main Shareholders:

Mercury Asset Management	5.4
Herald Investment Trust	4.7

Percentage of free market capital: 25.9%

Nominated Adviser:	Altium Capital, London
AIM Broker:	Altium Capital, London
Solicitors:	DLA, Leeds
Market Makers:	ALTI; WINS
Auditors:	Grant Thornton, Melton St, Euston Sq, London NW1 2EP
Registrars:	Capita Registrars

ENTRY ON AIM:	25/7/2000	**Recent price:**	10.5p
Interim results:	Sep	**Market cap:**	£7.13m
Final results:	Mar	**Issue price:**	60.0p
Year end:	Dec	**Current no of shares:**	
Accounts due:	Apr		67,861,002
Int div paymnt:	n/a	**No of shares after**	
Fin div paymnt:	n/a	**dilution:**	n/a
Int net div per share:	nil	**P/E ratio:**	6.6
Fin net div per share:	nil	**Probable CGT?**	YES

LATEST REPORTED RESULTS:	2003	PREVIOUS REPORTED RESULTS:	2002
Turnover:	£30.44m	**Turnover:**	£22.57m
PTP:	£611,000	**PTP:**	£(2.9m)
EPS:	1.6p	**EPS:**	(4.3)p

Comments:

Computer games publisher Empire Interactive boosts a strong portfolio of film-related licences ranging all the way through from Bad Boys 2 and Starsky & Hutch to the slightly less high profile BulletProof Monk. With offices in the UK, US, France, Germany, Italy and Spain – and experience of publishing titles for a variety of next-generation platforms – Empire has the infrastructure in place to succeed. Significantly the company moved from loss to profit in the first half.

Enition
(ENT)

Software company

Third Floor, 345 Stockport Road, Manchester, M13 0LF

		holding %
Chairman	Anthony Leon	0.0
Chief Executive	Raymond Dutton	11.3
Finance Director		
Non-Exec Director	Michael Scott	1.5

Main Shareholders:

Terra Energy	12.5
R Ryndziewicz	4.1
E Bartlett	3.9

Percentage of free market capital: 66.0%

Nominated Adviser:	Seymour Pierce, London
AIM Broker:	Seymour Pierce, London
Solicitors:	Kuit Steinart Levy, Manchester
Market Makers:	EVO; SCAP; WINS
Auditors:	Horwath Clark Whitehall, Manchester
Registrars:	Capita Registrars

ENTRY ON AIM:	19/1/2004	**Recent price:**	15.5p
Interim results:	Sep	**Market cap:**	£31.51m
Final results:	Mar	**Issue price:**	5.0p
Year end:	Dec	**Current no of shares:**	
Accounts due:	Jun		203,305,780
Int div paymnt:	n/a	**No of shares after**	
Fin div paymnt:	n/a	**dilution:**	n/a
Int net div per share:	nil	**P/E ratio:**	n/a
Fin net div per share:	nil	**Probable CGT?**	YES

LATEST REPORTED RESULTS:	15 MONTHS TO 31 DEC '02	PREVIOUS REPORTED RESULTS:	15 MONTHS TO 30 SEP '01
Turnover:	£10,000	**Turnover:**	n/a
PTP:	£(1.97m)	**PTP:**	£(504,000)
EPS:	n/a	**EPS:**	n/a

Comments:

Database-management software developer Enition came to AIM with £300,000 to its name following a Seymour Pierce-arranged private placing. On arrival the firm acquired CDE Solutions and will now combine this business's suite of products with IBM's information integration platform, creating a clever piece of software that will enable users to update a multitude of separate databases as one. OEM and partnership agreements with IBM have already been signed.

Enneurope (ENU)

Acquisition vehicle for aggregates businesses in Central Europe

Breedon Hall, Breedon-on-the-Hill, Derby, DE73 1AN Tel: 01332-694444; Fax: 01332-694445;
e-mail: mail@ennstone.co.uk; web site: www.ennstone.co.uk

		holding %
Chairman	Vaughan McLeod	0.0
Chief Executive		
Finance Director	John Barlow	0.0
Non-Exec Director	Timothy Ross	0.0

Main Shareholders:
Arlington 71.2

Percentage of free market capital: 28.8%

Nominated Adviser:	Altium Capital, London
AIM Broker:	KBC Peel Hunt, London
Solicitors:	Jones Day Gouldens, London
Market Makers:	SCAP; WINS
Auditors:	KPMG Audit, 2 Cornwall Street, Birmingham B3 2DL
Registrars:	Capita Registrars

Entry on AIM: 21/12/2001		Recent price:	11.0p
Interim results:	Jun	Market cap:	£3.08m
Final results:	Mar	Issue price:	50.0p
Year end:	Sep	Current no of shares:	
Accounts due:	Apr		27,980,000
Int div paymnt:	n/a	No of shares after	
Fin div paymnt:	n/a	dilution:	n/a
Int net div per share:	nil	P/E ratio:	n/a
Fin net div per share:	nil	Probable CGT?	No

Comments:
Enneurope, which lost a trebled £1.6m last year, has added to its Polish aggregates business by paying £75,000 for ready mixed concrete outfit Betonex and additional land. Having raised £3m at 15p from the Arlington investment group, chairman Vaughan Macleod said Enneurope was poised to exploit Poland's scheduled EU entry this May. Hope has been long deferred, though it might conceivably bear fruit one day.

LATEST REPORTED RESULTS: 2003		PREVIOUS REPORTED RESULTS: PRELIMS FOR 9 MONTHS TO 30 SEP 2002	
Turnover:	£482,000	Turnover:	£229,000
PTP:	£(1.62m)	PTP:	£(583,000)
EPS:	(20.4)p	EPS:	(11.9)p

Ensor (ESR)

Manufacture, supply and distribution of building materials

Ellard House, Dallimore Road, Manchester, M23 9NX Tel: 0161-945 5953; Fax: 0161-945 5851; e-mail: mail@ensor.co.uk;
web site: www.ensor.co.uk

		holding %
Chairman	Kenneth Harrison	54.4
Chief Executive	Anthony Coyne	0.1
Finance Director	Marcus Chadwick	0.1
Non-Exec Director	Brian Morgan	3.6

Main Shareholders:

n/a

Percentage of free market capital: 41.8%

Nominated Adviser:	Westhouse Securities, Manchester
AIM Broker:	Westhouse Securities, London
Solicitors:	n/a
Market Makers:	WINS
Auditors:	Grant Thornton, Manchester
Registrars:	Capita Registrars

Entry on AIM:	2/5/2002	Recent price:	17.5p
Interim results:	Dec	Market cap:	£5.14m
Final results:	Jun	Issue price:	10.0p
Year end:	Mar	Current no of shares:	
Accounts due:	Jul		29,395,659
Int div paymnt:	Dec	No of shares after	
Fin div paymnt:	Jun	dilution:	n/a
Int net div per share:	0.3p	P/E ratio:	9.7
Fin net div per share:	0.45p	Probable CGT?	Yes

Comments:
Mini-conglomerate Ensor continues to improve as interim results to September saw sales increase 12% to £11.5m and profits before tax improve 30% to £539,000. Despite strong competition in the construction materials sector, all divisions contributed towards profitability and it was helped by enhanced purchasing from its office in China. It does admit though that its weak cash position must be improved during 2004.

LATEST REPORTED RESULTS: 2003		PREVIOUS REPORTED RESULTS: 2002	
Turnover:	£20.43m	Turnover:	£17.05m
PTP:	£746,000	PTP:	£(124,000)
EPS:	1.8p	EPS:	(0.5)p

Enterprise (ETR)

Support services

Lancaster House, Centurion Way, Leyland, Preston, PR26 6TX Tel: 01772-819000; Fax: 01772-819001;
e-mail: headoffice@enterprise.plc.uk; web site: www.enterprise.plc.uk

		holding %
Chairman	Owen McLaughlin	9.5
Chief Executive	Jack McGrory	0.0
Finance Director	Neil Kirkby	0.0
Commercial Director	John Gavan	0.6
Main Shareholders:		
Deutsche Bank		13.5
Guild Ventures		4.1
Prudential		3.8
Framlington		3.5
Scottish Widows		3.4
Percentage of free market capital: 54.8%		

Nominated Adviser:	KBC Peel Hunt, London; Close Brothers, London
AIM Broker:	KBC Peel Hunt, London
Solicitors:	DLA, Manchester
Market Makers:	KBCS; WINS
Auditors:	Deloitte & Touche, Manchester
Registrars:	Capita Registrars

ENTRY ON AIM:	6/10/1995	Recent price:	321.5p
Interim results:	Sep	Market cap:	£238.96m
Final results:	Mar	Issue price:	n/a
Year end:	Dec	Current no of shares:	
Accounts due:	Apr		74,328,103
Int div paymnt:	Sep	No of shares after	
Fin div paymnt:	May	dilution:	n/a
Int net div per share:	2.6p	P/E ratio:	25.3
Fin net div per share:	3.2p	Probable CGT?	YES

LATEST REPORTED RESULTS: 2003		PREVIOUS REPORTED RESULTS: 2002	
Turnover:	£303.5m	Turnover:	£272.5m
PTP:	£15.9m	PTP:	£12.9m
EPS:	14.0p	EPS:	12.7p

Comments:

Profits powered up 23% in 2003 at this AIM giant. Enterprise has increased its work in the utility and public sector markets, buoyed by the acquisition of Subterra from Thames Water, which strengthened its position as a supplier to the water industry, and by increased work with BT. Other highlights included the award to Enterprise-Liverpool, the venture formed with Liverpool City Council, of a £70m street cleansing contract and a £60m deal maintaining Liverpool's social housing.

---

enterpriseAsia (EPA)

Education & training services provider

Parkland Business Centre, Greengates, Bradford, West Yorkshire BD10 9TQ Tel: 01274-623478; Fax: 01274-622032;
e-mail: contact-us@enterpriseasia.com.hk; web site: www.enterpriseasia.com.hk

		holding %
Chairman	Davie Auyeung	0.0
Chief Executive	Ka Hang Lai	0.0
Finance Director		
Non-Exec Director	Phillip Brown	4.2
Main Shareholders:		
Try On		24.9
Europasia Education		4.2
Clarest		4.2
Percentage of free market capital: 62.5%		

Nominated Adviser:	Insinger de Beaufort, London
AIM Broker:	Fiske, London
Solicitors:	Taylor Wessing, London
Market Makers:	MLSB; SCAP; WINS
Auditors:	Pridie Brewster, 23-31 Greville Street, London EC1N 8RB
Registrars:	Capita Registrars

ENTRY ON AIM:	22/2/2000	Recent price:	0.5p
Interim results:	Sep	Market cap:	£1.2m
Final results:	Jun	Issue price:	5.0p
Year end:	Dec	Current no of shares:	
Accounts due:	Jun		239,598,496
Int div paymnt:	n/a	No of shares after	
Fin div paymnt:	n/a	dilution:	242,200,000
Int net div per share:	nil	P/E ratio:	n/a
Fin net div per share:	nil	Probable CGT?	NO

LATEST REPORTED RESULTS: 2002		PREVIOUS REPORTED RESULTS: 2001	
Turnover:	£23,000	Turnover:	£24,000
PTP:	£(8.09m)	PTP:	£(1.18m)
EPS:	(3.4)p	EPS:	(0.5)p

Comments:

EnterpriseAsia is changing course. The plan is no longer to seek out IT-related investments in the Far East. Instead management will now look to develop a portfolio of firms that provide education and training services to those in the 'Greater China' region – the first is a summer camp operator. The holdings in inter-active games developer Net Fun and securities trading system developer Value Convergence, have been completely written-off.

Envesta Telecom
Specialist telecoms operator
Lloyd's Avenue House, 6 Lloyd's Avenue, London, EC3N 3AX Tel: 0870-767 7778; Fax: 0870-767 7779;
e-mail: enquiries@envestaplc.com; web site: www.envestaplc.com

		holding %
Chairman	Lyndon Chapman	0.2
Chief Executive	as above	
Finance Director	Kevin McGovern	0.2
Non-Exec Director	David Hunter	0.0

Main Shareholders:

New Opportunities Investment Trust	14.5

Percentage of free market capital: 33.6%

Nominated Adviser:	Corporate Synergy, L
AIM Broker:	Seymour Pierce Ellis, Cɪ
Solicitors:	P. Speer, Cambridge
Market Makers:	KBCS; SCAP; WINS
Auditors:	Deloitte & Touche, I Little New St, London EC4A 3TR
Registrars:	Capita Registrars

ENTRY ON AIM:	4/4/1997	**Recent price:**	2.0p
Interim results:	Mar	**Market cap:**	£4.59m
Final results:	Sep	**Issue price:**	40.0p
Year end:	Jun	**Current no of shares:**	
Accounts due:	Dec		229,589,759
Int div paymnt:	n/a	**No of shares after**	
Fin div paymnt:	n/a	**dilution:**	n/a
Int net div per share:	nil	**P/E ratio:**	n/a
Fin net div per share:	nil	**Probable CGT?**	**YES**

LATEST REPORTED RESULTS: 2003		PREVIOUS REPORTED RESULTS: 2002	
Turnover:	£10.82m	**Turnover:**	£4.91m
PTP:	£(907,000)	**PTP:**	£(1.13m)
EPS:	(0.8)p	**EPS:**	(1.1)p

Comments:
The self-styled alternative telecoms operator, claims it is suffering from ferocious price competition. This significantly reduced margins, leading to a likely operating loss for the first half. Despite its trading woes, Envesta bought a 27% interest in Formjet, a company established by chairman Lyndon Chapman to undertake a management buyout of Software Dialogue Group, a UK software distribution business of which Chapman was chairman, for £100,000.

Epic   (EPI)
Online learning and solutions provider
52 Old Steine, Brighton, East Sussex BN1 1NH Tel: 01273-728686; Fax: 01273-821567; e-mail: marketing@epic.co.uk;
web site: www.epic.co.uk

		holding %
Chairman	Michael Inwards	1.3
Chief Executive	Donald Clark	7.9
Finance Director	Stephen Oliver	0.0
Non-Exec Director	Ian Ritchie	0.1

Main Shareholders:

Framlington	13.3
ABN AMRO Asset Management	10.8
Scottish Widows Investment Partnership	7.8
Morley Fund Management	6.2
Eaglet Investment Trust	4.2

Percentage of free market capital: 44.3%

Nominated Adviser:	Altium Capital, London
AIM Broker:	Altium Capital, London
Solicitors:	DMH, Brighton
Market Makers:	ALTI; ARBT; MLSB; SCAP; WINS
Auditors:	Baker Tilly, Brighton
Registrars:	Lloyds TSB Registrars

ENTRY ON AIM:	23/5/1996	**Recent price:**	86.5p
Interim results:	Feb	**Market cap:**	£22.56m
Final results:	Jul	**Issue price:**	105.0p
Year end:	May	**Current no of shares:**	
Accounts due:	Aug		26,083,076
Int div paymnt:	Apr	**No of shares after**	
Fin div paymnt:	n/a	**dilution:**	27,559,576
Int net div per share:	0.4p	**P/E ratio:**	12.7
Fin net div per share:	1.0p	**Probable CGT?**	**YES**

LATEST REPORTED RESULTS: 2003		PREVIOUS REPORTED RESULTS: 2002	
Turnover:	£8.75m	**Turnover:**	£7.23m
PTP:	£1.80m	**PTP:**	£835,000
EPS:	6.8p	**EPS:**	3.2p

Comments:
Epic's annual profits will beat market expectations – this follows earlier warnings that poor orders would depress the second half. In February, Epic reported a weaker half to November, yet remained profitable and cash generative. Both sales and profits were pegged back by 20%. But Epic's cash balances increased by £300,000 to stand at a bumper £12m. And future acquisitions will widen Epic's ability to offer integrated learning solutions.

...estments (EPB)

...ouglas, Isle of Man IM99 1PP

	holding %
...nia	0.0
...rnon	0.0
...vesco	20.0
Threadneedle Investments	9.9
Insight Investment	9.0
Artemis Investment	8.0
Jupiter Asset Management	7.0

Percentage of free market capital: 16.4%

Nominated Adviser:	Collins Stewart, London
AIM Broker:	Collins Stewart, London
Solicitors:	Latham & Watkins, London
Market Makers:	CSCS; WINS
Auditors:	KPMG, Audit, Douglas, Isle of Man
Registrars:	Computershare Investor Services

ENTRY ON AIM:	2/1/2003	Recent price:	82.5p
Interim results:	n/a	Market cap:	£41.27m
Final results:	n/a	Issue price:	102.0p
Year end:	n/a	Current no of shares:	
Accounts due:	n/a		50,023,000
Int div paymnt:	n/a	No of shares after	
Fin div paymnt:	n/a	dilution:	n/a
Int net div per share:	nil	P/E ratio:	n/a
Fin net div per share:	nil	Probable CGT?	No

LATEST REPORTED RESULTS:		PREVIOUS REPORTED RESULTS:	
	N/A		N/A
Turnover:	n/a	Turnover:	n/a
PTP:	n/a	PTP:	n/a
EPS:	n/a	EPS:	n/a

Comments:

Epic, which raised £50m at IPO, is a joint venture with Lornamead Group, the Jatania family's personal care products company, which has £25m available to invest with Epic. Together they will put £5-50m in a range of household and personal care brands sold by re-focusing multinationals, such as Unilever. So far, five acquisitions have been made, including a DIY tooth-whitening product, a beauty products maker as well as some of Lornamead's brands such as Lipsyl lip-balm, Harmony hairspray and Amplex deodorant.

Epic Reconstruction (ERN)

Financial company
St James's Chambers, Athol Street, Douglas, Isle of Man, IM99 1PP

		holding %
Chairman	Donald Adamson	0.0
Chief Executive		
Finance Director		
Non-Exec Director	Robert Quayle	0.0

Main Shareholders:

Lehman Brothers	36.7
Brit Insurance	16.7
Jupiter Asset Management	10.0
Deutsche Asset Management	10.0
Henderson Global	9.2

Percentage of free market capital: 2.3%

Nominated Adviser:	Numis, London
AIM Broker:	Numis, London
Solicitors:	Latham & Watkins, London
Market Makers:	KBCS; NUMS; WINS
Auditors:	KPMG, Douglas, Isle of Man
Registrars:	Barings

ENTRY ON AIM:	16/9/2003	Recent price:	105.0p
Interim results:	n/a	Market cap:	£31.5m
Final results:	n/a	Issue price:	100.0p
Year end:	n/a	Current no of shares:	
Accounts due:	n/a		30,000,000
Int div paymnt:	n/a	No of shares after	
Fin div paymnt:	n/a	dilution:	n/a
Int net div per share:	nil	P/E ratio:	n/a
Fin net div per share:	nil	Probable CGT?	No

LATEST REPORTED RESULTS:		PREVIOUS REPORTED RESULTS:	
	N/A		
Turnover:	n/a	Turnover:	n/a
PTP:	n/a	PTP:	n/a
EPS:	n/a	EPS:	n/a

Comments:

Epic, which raised £30m on admission to help re-finance 'businesses emerging from distressed situations', has done its first deal backing the MBO of Abingdon Flooring from the receivers. The main mover behind the investment process is Andrew Castle, an established adviser on financing insolvent concerns. Castle aims to choose cash-generative enterprises hampered by debt. This is a tried and tested private equity investment method. Epic will principally provide asset-based lending.

eq (EQI)

Marketing Services

Crossley House, Hopwood Lane, Halifax, West Yorkshire HX1 5EB Tel: 01422-301917; Fax: 01422-349399;
web site: www.eqgroup.co.uk

		holding %
Chairman	Phillip Bennett	0.3
Chief Executive	Robert Bond	0.2
Finance Director	Brian Heather	0.1
Non-Exec Director	Michael Waterhouse	0.0

Main Shareholders:

GWB	68.4
M Drye	13.0
R Eckert	7.0

Percentage of free market capital: 10.4%

Nominated Adviser:	KBC Peel Hunt, London
AIM Broker:	KBC Peel Hunt, London
Solicitors:	DLA, Manchester
Market Makers:	KBCS; WINS
Auditors:	PricewaterhouseCoopers, Leeds
Registrars:	Capita Registrars

Entry on AIM:	19/5/2000	**Recent price:**	195.0p
Interim results:	Sep	**Market cap:**	£13.61m
Final results:	Jun	**Issue price:**	100.0p
Year end:	Dec	**Current no of shares:**	
Accounts due:	Apr		6,980,196
Int div paymnt:	n/a	**No of shares after**	
Fin div paymnt:	n/a	**dilution:**	n/a
Int net div per share:	nil	**P/E ratio:**	39.8
Fin net div per share:	nil	**Probable CGT?**	Yes

LATEST REPORTED RESULTS: 2003		PREVIOUS REPORTED RESULTS: 2002	
Turnover:	£8.91m	**Turnover:**	£5.15m
PTP:	£634,000	**PTP:**	£132,000
EPS:	4.9p	**EPS:**	1.0p

Comments:
Marketing and advertising services business eq enjoyed a strong 2003 as life returned to the hitherto depressed media market. The building up of an impressive client roster – Hilton, Sony and Tesco to name just three – enabled the company to report significant improvements in both sales and profits. Debts, meanwhile, fell 18% to £5.4m. Hopes for further strong progress in 2004 are high, though investors should note that 50% of all revenues are generated from just 20 clients.

Equator (EQG)

Film producer & distributor

6 Heddon Street, London, W1B 4BT Tel: 020-7025 7400; Fax: 020-7025 7401

		holding %
Chairman	Ian Robinson	1.0
Managing Director	as above	
Finance Director		
Operations Director	Peter Parkinson	0.0

Main Shareholders:

Cartier	28.8
Winchester Group	27.2
Southbrook Group	10.7
Clipperton	7.2
3M Trustees	6.7

Percentage of free market capital: 9.6%

Nominated Adviser:	John East, London
AIM Broker:	Insinger Townsley, London
Solicitors:	Field Fisher Waterhouse, London
Market Makers:	KBCS; WINS
Auditors:	BDO Stoy Hayward, 8 Baker Street, London W1M 1DA
Registrars:	Capita Registrars

Entry on AIM:	11/4/1997	**Recent price:**	9.5p
Interim results:	Oct	**Market cap:**	£2.95m
Final results:	Jul	**Issue price:**	25.0p
Year end:	Dec	**Current no of shares:**	
Accounts due:	May		31,099,832
Int div paymnt:	n/a	**No of shares after**	
Fin div paymnt:	n/a	**dilution:**	n/a
Int net div per share:	nil	**P/E ratio:**	n/a
Fin net div per share:	nil	**Probable CGT?**	Yes

LATEST REPORTED RESULTS: 2002		PREVIOUS REPORTED RESULTS: 2001	
Turnover:	£369,000	**Turnover:**	£1.36m
PTP:	£(1.17m)	**PTP:**	£475,000
EPS:	(3.9)p	**EPS:**	1.4p

Comments:
Very little has come out of this company since its failed bid to buy Handmade Films from Cartier Investments, a group which owns 28% of Equator. It did manage to acquire two minor films, one called 'Charlie' and one called 'The Pursuit of Happiness'. Most attention however was focused on another poor set of results. Its film library assets were valued in the books at £9.7m last year.

Erinaceous (ERG)
Property services
Phoenix House, 11 Wellesley Road, Croydon, London, CR0 2NW Tel: 0870-703 9898; Fax: 0870-703 9899;
e-mail: info@erinaceous.com; web site: www.erinaceous.com

		holding %
Chairman	Nigel Turnball	0.2
Chief Executive	Neil Bellis	19.9
Finance Director	Michael Pearson	0.1
Commercial Director	Lucy Cummings	17.7

Main Shareholders:
n/a

Percentage of free market capital: 37.9%

Nominated Adviser:	Collins Stewart, London
AIM Broker:	Collins Stewart, London
Solicitors:	Memery Crystal, London
Market Makers:	CSCS, WINS
Auditors:	Grant Thornton, Slough
Registrars:	Capita Registrars

ENTRY ON AIM: 27/11/2003	**Recent price:**	130.0p
Interim results: Jan	**Market cap:**	£57.96m
Final results: Jul	**Issue price:**	130.0p
Year end: Mar	**Current no of shares:**	
Accounts due: Jul		44,582,764
Int div paymnt: n/a	**No of shares after**	
Fin div paymnt: n/a	**dilution:**	n/a
Int net div per share: nil	**P/E ratio:**	15.5
Fin net div per share: nil	**Probable CGT?**	YES

LATEST REPORTED RESULTS:	2003	**PREVIOUS REPORTED RESULTS:**	2002
Turnover:	£33.74m	**Turnover:**	£21.49m
PTP:	£2.19m	**PTP:**	£2.01m
EPS:	8.4p	**EPS:**	8.8p

Comments:
Erinaceous is the fast growing 'one-stop shop property services group' operating in both the public and private sectors. It debuted on AIM last November, raising £10m in a private institutional placing. Recently its Haywards subsidiary flagged up two major contracts with a total income value of £6.5m. One, with Brighton & Hove District Council, is worth more than £5m over 5 years, whilst the deal with Hounslow Homes has a total fee of £1.5m.

ESV (ESV)
Port investor, developer & operator
77 South Audley Street, London, W1K 1JG

		holding %
Chairman	Masoud Alikhani	0.0
Managing Director	Ronny Maas	0.0
Finance Director	Ronald Wunsh	0.0
Exec Director	Guillaume Guldentops	0.0

Main Shareholders:

Labeto NV	66.5
Meunerie Liegois SA	33.4

Percentage of free market capital: 0.1%

Nominated Adviser:	Beaumont Cornish, London
AIM Broker:	Hichens Harrison, London
Solicitors:	Beachcroft Wansbroughs, London
Market Makers:	WINS
Auditors:	Deloitte & Touche, Hellerup, Denmark
Registrars:	Vaerdipapircentralen

ENTRY ON AIM: 28/7/2003	**Recent price:**	1.25p
Interim results: n/a	**Market cap:**	£0.64m
Final results: n/a	**Issue price:**	0.75p
Year end: n/a	**Current no of shares:**	
Accounts due: n/a		51,426,540
Int div paymnt: n/a	**No of shares after**	
Fin div paymnt: n/a	**dilution:**	n/a
Int net div per share: nil	**P/E ratio:**	n/a
Fin net div per share: nil	**Probable CGT?**	No

LATEST REPORTED RESULTS: PERIOD FROM 1 OCT 02 TO 31 MAY 03		**PREVIOUS REPORTED RESULTS:**	N/A
Turnover:	n/a	**Turnover:**	n/a
PTP:	£(90,000)	**PTP:**	n/a
EPS:	n/a	**EPS:**	n/a

Comments:
This Danish concern has Belgian shareholders and plans to develop port facilities on the Black Sea shore of the Ukraine and other sites in Eastern Europe. The group wants to invest in the improvement of these businesses and related activities, such as transport, warehousing and other infrastructure. The Ukraine is a major exporter of grains, vegetable oils and fertilisers. The directors and shareholders have experience in this area of trade. £240,000 cash remains after an initial £246,000 interim loss was made.

Eurasia Mining

Russian precious metals miner

14-16 Regent Street, London, SW1Y 4PH Tel: 020-7976 1222; Fax: 020-7976 1422; e-mail: info@eurasia–mining.p
web site: www.eurasia–mining.plc.uk

		holding %
Chairman	John Mitchell	0.4
Managing Director	Christian Schaffalitzky	2.0
Finance Director	Robert Jenkins	0.7
Deputy Chairman	Michael Martineau	1.1

Main Shareholders:

Bruce Rowan	13.7
Gartmore Asset Management	6.8
Golden Prospect	5.7
INVESCO English and International Trust	4.7
NatWest Smaller Companies Investment Trust	4.0

Percentage of free market capital: 51.4%

Nominated Adviser:	Grant Thornton, London
AIM Broker:	WH Ireland, London
Solicitors:	Eversheds, London
Market Makers:	KBCS; MLSB; SCAP; WINS
Auditors:	KPMG Audit, 8 Salisbury Square, London EC4Y 0NH
Registrars:	Capita Registrars

ENTRY ON AIM: 2/10/1996	Recent price:	7.0p
Interim results:	Sep	Market cap:	£5.39m
Final results:	Apr	Issue price:	310.0p
Year end:	Dec	Current no of shares:	
Accounts due:	May		77,000,875
Int div paymnt:	n/a	No of shares after	
Fin div paymnt:	n/a	dilution:	n/a
Int net div per share:	nil	P/E ratio:	n/a
Fin net div per share:	nil	Probable CGT?	No

LATEST REPORTED RESULTS: 2002		PREVIOUS REPORTED RESULTS: 2001	
Turnover:	n/a	Turnover:	n/a
PTP:	£(1.53m)	PTP:	£(502,000)
EPS:	(3.8)p	EPS:	(1.6)p

Comments:

Eurasia shares have lost 98% of their value since listing in 1996, as a Urals gold prospector. Now pursuing platinum group metals prospects under managing director Christian Schaffalitzky, the company raised £1 million at 7p in November to probe Russia's Kola Peninsula and has a prospecting licence at Kliprivier in South Africa's Bushveld, near Anglo Plat's Drr Brochen project and Aquarius's Evest South property.

Eureka Mining (EKA)

Mining company

Level 1, Enterprise House, 59-65 Upper Ground, Blackfriars Road, London, SE1 9PQ

		holding %
Chairman	Kevin Foo	0.4
Chief Executive	David Bartley	0.0
Finance Director	Malcolm James	0.0
Exec Director	Andrzej Sliwa	0.0

Main Shareholders:

Celtic Resources	44.4
RAB Capital	10.7
RCM	4.5
Gartmore Investment Management	3.2

Percentage of free market capital: 36.8%

Nominated Adviser:	Williams de Broe, London
AIM Broker:	Williams de Broe, London
Solicitors:	Kerman & Co, London
Market Makers:	JEFF; WDBM; WINS
Auditors:	Deloitte & Touche, Earlsfort Terrace, Dublin 2, Ireland
Registrars:	Computershare Investor Services

ENTRY ON AIM: 11/12/2003	Recent price:	128.5p
Interim results:	n/a	Market cap:	£21.9m
Final results:	n/a	Issue price:	120.0p
Year end:	n/a	Current no of shares:	
Accounts due:	n/a		17,044,166
Int div paymnt:	n/a	No of shares after	
Fin div paymnt:	n/a	dilution:	n/a
Int net div per share:	nil	P/E ratio:	n/a
Fin net div per share:	nil	Probable CGT?	No

LATEST REPORTED RESULTS: N/A		PREVIOUS REPORTED RESULTS: N/A	
Turnover:	n/a	Turnover:	n/a
PTP:	n/a	PTP:	n/a
EPS:	n/a	EPS:	n/a

Comments:

Spun-off from Celtic Resources, Eureka raised £7m at 120p to develop gold and, in particular, molybdenum projects in Kazakhstan, to tap nearby China's thirst for steelmaking ingredients. Boss David Bartley claims Eureka's Shorskoye deposit could produce 10,000 tonnes of molybdenum and 3,000 of copper a year. Celtic moved to halve its stake to 23% by giving 3.5m Eureka shares to its own investors.

...naged Services (EKM)

...Queen Square, Brighton, East Sussex BN1 3FD Tel: 01273-200100; Fax: 01273-205005;
...n; web site: www.emsplc.com

		holding %
	George Kynoch	0.0
	David Wood	0.1
Fi... ...r		
Non-E... ...ctor	Jim Carr	0.4

Main Shareholders:

Chrysalis Trustees	95.2

Percentage of free market capital: 4.4%

Nominated Adviser:	John East, London
AIM Broker:	Durlacher, London
Solicitors:	Hammonds, London
Market Makers:	DURM; WINS
Auditors:	BDO Stoy Hayward, Brighton
Registrars:	Capita Registrars

ENTRY ON AIM:	11/8/1999	Recent price:	40.0p
Interim results:	Dec	Market cap:	£4.16m
Final results:	Aug	Issue price:	100.0p
Year end:	Mar	Current no of shares:	
Accounts due:	Aug		10,400,000
Int div paymnt:	n/a	No of shares after	
Fin div paymnt:	n/a	dilution:	10,936,795
Int net div per share:	nil	P/E ratio:	33.3
Fin net div per share:	nil	Probable CGT?	YES

LATEST REPORTED RESULTS: 2003		PREVIOUS REPORTED RESULTS: 2002	
Turnover:	£9.15m	Turnover:	£9.23m
PTP:	£204,000	PTP:	£155,000
EPS:	1.2p	EPS:	0.5p

Comments:

IT consultancy Eurolink has failed to consolidate upon last year's strong results, swinging from a profit (of £17,000) to a £96,000 loss in the first half of 2003/04. The reversal came as revenues plunged from £4.5m to £3.8m. On a more positive note, however, early March saw the company announce that it has picked up a new three-year IT service contract worth more than £5m from Northern Rock. The full impact of this deal is unlikely to be felt until 2004/05.

Europasia Education (formerly StartIT.com) (EPE)
Educational promoter

Parkland Business Centre, Greengates, Bradford, West Yorkshire BD10 9TQ Tel: 01274-623478; Fax: 01274-622032;
e-mail: pbrown@start-it.co.uk; web site: www.start-it.co.uk

		holding %
Chairman	James Holmes	16.1
Chief Executive	as above	
Finance Director	Simon Littlewood	0.0
Non-Exec Director	George Allnutt	0.0

Main Shareholders:

Phill A Brown*	11.9
Rich Projects International	8.2
Vintage Investments*	8.2
Pershing Keen	4.8
Temima Investement	3.1

Percentage of free market capital: 44.7%

*Phill Brown is a director of Vintage Investments

Nominated Adviser:	Insinger de Beaufort, London
AIM Broker:	Hoodless Brennan, London
Solicitors:	Taylor Wessing, London
Market Makers:	SCAP; WINS
Auditors:	Pridie Brewster, London
Registrars:	Capita Registrars

ENTRY ON AIM:	3/8/1999	Recent price:	1.5p
Interim results:	Sep	Market cap:	£1.41m
Final results:	Jun	Issue price:	5.0p
Year end:	Dec	Current no of shares:	
Accounts due:	Jul		93,781,250
Int div paymnt:	n/a	No of shares after	
Fin div paymnt:	n/a	dilution:	n/a
Int net div per share:	nil	P/E ratio:	n/a
Fin net div per share:	nil	Probable CGT?	YES

LATEST REPORTED RESULTS: 2002		PREVIOUS REPORTED RESULTS: 2001	
Turnover:	£11,000	Turnover:	26,000
PTP:	£(2.27m)	PTP:	£(473,000)
EPS:	(4.8)p	EPS:	(1.0)p

Comments:

Sharing directors with London Asia Capital, speculative Europasia offers fee-paying Chinese and other overseas students English and Australian academic and commercial qualifications, with MBAs from Sunderland, Northumbria and South Queensland universities. The company, which cut interim losses from £2m to £143,000 and runs a language school in Canterbury, paid consultant Study World £180,000 in shares.

European Diamonds   (EPD)
Diamond explorer
22 Grosvenor Square, London, W1K 6LF Tel: 020-7529 7502; Fax: 020-7491 2244;
e-mail: enquiries@europeandiamondsplc.com; web site: www.europeandiamondsplc.com

		holding %
Chairman	Tony Williams	9.7
Chief Executive	Roy Spencer	11.8
Finance Director		
Non-Exec Director	George Beaton	2.3

Main Shareholders:

Beaucourt Mining	14.5
William M Parente	5.2
Active Capital Trust	4.5
Framlington Innovative Growth Trust	3.8
Zo Media	3.5
Percentage of free market capital: 34.9	

Nominated Adviser:	Numis, London
AIM Broker:	Numis, London
Solicitors:	Ashursts, London
Market Makers:	BGMM; KBCS; MLSB; SCAP; WDBM; WINS
Auditors:	PKF, London
Registrars:	Computershare Investor Services

Entry on AIM: 11/12/2000		**Recent price:**	61.0p
Interim results:	Mar	**Market cap:**	£15.74m
Final results:	Oct	**Issue price:**	70.0p
Year end:	Jun	**Current no of shares:**	
Accounts due:	Oct		25,802,911
Int div paymnt:	n/a	**No of shares after**	
Fin div paymnt:	n/a	**dilution:**	n/a
Int net div per share:	nil	**P/E ratio:**	n/a
Fin net div per share:	nil	**Probable CGT?**	No

LATEST REPORTED RESULTS: 2003		**PREVIOUS REPORTED RESULTS:** 2002	
Turnover:	n/a	**Turnover:**	n/a
PTP:	£(623,000)	**PTP:**	£(609,000)
EPS:	(3.5)p	**EPS:**	(3.7)p

Comments:
European Diamonds, which lost £623,000 last year, recently bought MineGem of Canada, with both 'near-term potential' to produce 200,000 carats a year and Lesotho's Satellite pipe, for which veteran wheeler-dealer David Rowland supplied a £6m debt facility to European. Rowland's son Jonathan's Resurge outfit had bought into a £1.5m fundraising at 75p to fund drilling at the company's Lentira prospect in Finland.

Eurovestech   (EVT)
Investment fund
29 Curzon Street, London, W1Y 7AE Tel: 020-7491 0770; Fax: 020-7491 9595; e-mail: enquiries@eurovestech.com;
web site: www.eurovestech.com

		holding %
Chairman	Richard Grogan	1.1
Chief Executive	Richard Bernstein	23.3
Finance Director		
Non-Exec Director	Quentin Solt	0.8

Main Shareholders:

Scottish Value Trust	19.0
CG Asset Management	4.7
Insinger NetC@pital	4.4
Percentage of free market capital: 46.7%	

Nominated Adviser:	John East, London
AIM Broker:	Insinger Townsley, London
Solicitors:	SJ Berwin, London
Market Makers:	KBCS; MLSB; SCAP; WINS
Auditors:	Grant Thornton, Euston Square, London WC1X 8HB
Registrars:	Capita Registrars

Entry on AIM: 13/3/2000		**Recent price:**	10.75p
Interim results:	Dec	**Market cap:**	£27.97m
Final results:	Sep	**Issue price:**	5.0p
Year end:	Mar	**Current no of shares:**	
Accounts due:	Jul		260,171,055
Int div paymnt:	n/a	**No of shares after**	
Fin div paymnt:	n/a	**dilution:**	292,096,608
Int net div per share:	nil	**P/E ratio:**	n/a
Fin net div per share:	nil	**Probable CGT?**	Yes

LATEST REPORTED RESULTS: 2003		**PREVIOUS REPORTED RESULTS:** 2002	
Turnover:	£93,000	**Turnover:**	£230,000
PTP:	£(551,000)	**PTP:**	£(572,000)
EPS:	(2.1)p	**EPS:**	(0.1)p

Comments:
The internet investment vehicle saw net assets revive 49% to £7.1m in the six months to September. The portfolio performed even better after removing the £0.87m loss, helped by revaluing retail and petrol consultant KSS, which is growing strongly. Other promising investments include teenage girls e-magazine Mykindaplace, which has reached profitability and has a two-year deal with BSkyB, and Paris-based software concern Cjudge, which is also profitable. A placing pulled in £1.7m in October.

Excel Airways (EXA)

Charter passenger airline & aviation seat broking company

Mitre Court, Fleming Way, Crawley, West Sussex RH10 9NJ Tel: 0870-1677 737; Fax: 0870-1677 767

		holding %
Chairman	Eamonn Mullaney	2.3
Chief Executive	Philip Wyatt	10.0
Finance Director	Paul Roberts	0.3
Deputy Chairman	Andreas Drakou	0.0

Main Shareholders:

Air Atlanta	40.5
Libra Holidays	39.5

Percentage of free market capital: 5.3%

Comments:

Air Atlanta is now a 40.5% shareholder in Excel Airways, one of the UK's major charter passenger airlines, having bought 38.9m shares from Libra. The transaction provides Excel with a long term source of flexible seasonal capacity – one of its key strategies is flexing aircraft capacity to seasonal demand. Excel's preliminary numbers beat expectations, with profits up 296%. Analysts predict improved profits of £15.3m this year, rising to £16.7m for 2005.

Nominated Adviser:	Brewin Dolphin, Glasgow	
AIM Broker:	Brewin Dolphin, Glasgow	
Solicitors:	DLA, London	
Market Makers:	WINS	
Auditors:	BDO Stoy Hayward, Epsom	
Registrars:	Capita Registrars	

ENTRY ON AIM: 20/11/2002		**Recent price:**	162.5p
Interim results:	Jun	**Market cap:**	£156.0m
Final results:	Dec	**Issue price:**	123.0p
Year end:	Oct	**Current no of shares:**	
Accounts due:	Mar		96,000,000
Int div paymnt:	n/a	**No of shares after**	
Fin div paymnt:	n/a	**dilution:**	n/a
Int net div per share:	nil	**P/E ratio:**	16.8
Fin net div per share:	nil	**Probable CGT?**	YES

LATEST REPORTED RESULTS: 2003		PREVIOUS REPORTED RESULTS: 2002	
Turnover:	£247.31m	Turnover:	£182.34m
PTP:	£13.37m	PTP:	£3.38m
EPS:	9.7p	EPS:	2.7p

Expomedia (EXP)

Organiser and manager of exhibitions

Unit 1& 2 Verney House, 1B Hollywood Road, Fulham, London, SW10 9HS Tel: 020-7376 3300; Fax: 020-7795 1424;
e-mail: info@expocentres.com; web site: www.expocentres.com

		holding %
Chairman	Roger Shashoua**	36.9
Chief Executive	Mark Shashoua	20.2
Finance Director	Darra Comyn*	0.01
Director	Barbara Hanlon*	0.01

Main Shareholders:

ABN AMRO Danube Ventures	19.9
Stancroft Trust	17.7

Percentage of free market capital: 5.3%

*These directors are potential beneficiaries of an option over 3,511,841 shares held by the Perseus Trust. **Shares held under Rodemadan Holdings

Comments:

Earnings are still proving elusive at this international operator of exhibitions and events, although sales are being driven forward and the cash outflow is being curtailed. In 2003 Expomedia organised 62 events and, following expansion into Russia, Hungary, Poland and India, it expects to organise 130 events this year. Advance booking for 2004 is up 60% on last year. But profits would be preferred. €6m was raised last year, net debt stands at €1.8m and net assets at €23.7m.

Nominated Adviser:	Durlacher, London	
AIM Broker:	Charles Stanley, London	
Solicitors:	Nicholson, Graham & Jones, London	
Market Makers:	SCAP; WINS	
Auditors:	KPMG Audit, 8 Salisbury Square, London EC4Y 6AX	
Registrars:	Capita Registrars	

ENTRY ON AIM: 14/12/2001		**Recent price:**	171.5p
Interim results:	Sep	**Market cap:**	£70.61m
Final results:	Mar	**Issue price:**	75.0p
Year end:	Dec	**Current no of shares:**	
Accounts due:	Apr		41,169,178
Int div paymnt:	n/a	**No of shares after**	
Fin div paymnt:	n/a	**dilution:**	41,328,853
Int net div per share:	nil	**P/E ratio:**	n/a
Fin net div per share:	nil	**Probable CGT?**	YES

LATEST REPORTED RESULTS: 2003		PREVIOUS REPORTED RESULTS: 2002	
Turnover:	Eur11.0m	Turnover:	Eur7.03m
PTP:	Eur(3.71m)	PTP:	Eur(2.57m)
EPS:	Eur(0.1)	EPS:	Eur(0.1)

Fairplace Consulting (FCO)

Corporate career services provider

36-38 Cornhill, London, EC3V 3PQ Tel: 020-7816 0707; Fax: 020-7816 0708; e-mail: fairplace@fairplace.com;
web site: www.fairplace.com

		holding %
Chairman	Mark Allsup	9.0
Chief Executive	Michael Moran	0.0
Finance Director	Clare Hanson	0.3
Director	Jim Horsted	3.6

Main Shareholders:

Select Appointments	26.0
Blomfield	14.5
Beacon Investment Fund	7.9

Percentage of free market capital: 32.2%

Comments:
First-half figures to 31 December from the outplacement consultant were disappointing, with a swing to pre-tax losses of £365,476 from a £104,492 profit. Sales waned by 11.3% to £2.35m as City outplacement demand fell over the key autumn period – there were lower levels of restructuring carried out by financial institutions. On the plus side, the UK and distance-based businesses made excellent progress and sales at Fairplace Italy have started to pick up.

Nominated Adviser:	Williams de Broe, London
AIM Broker:	Williams de Broe, London
Solicitors:	Pinsents, London; Beaumont, London
Market Makers:	SCAP; WDBM; WINS
Auditors:	Rees Pollock, 7 Pilgrim Street, London EC4V 6DR
Registrars:	Melton Registrars

ENTRY ON AIM:	28/7/1997	**Recent price:**	86.5p
Interim results:	Feb	**Market cap:**	£4.76m
Final results:	Sep	**Issue price:**	3.0p
Year end:	Jun	**Current no of shares:**	
Accounts due:	Oct		5,500,174
Int div paymnt:	Apr	**No of shares after**	
Fin div paymnt:	Oct	dilution:	5,516,351
Int net div per share:	2.1p	**P/E ratio:**	n/a
Fin net div per share:	3.0p	**Probable CGT?**	Yes

LATEST REPORTED RESULTS: 2003		PREVIOUS REPORTED RESULTS: 2002	
Turnover:	£5.34m	Turnover:	£5.27m
PTP:	£149,000	**PTP:**	£501,000
EPS:	(0.1)p	**EPS:**	6.2p

Falkland Islands Holdings (FKL)

Holding company for companies trading in the Falklands

Charringtons House, The Causeway, Bishop's Stortford, Hertfordshire CM23 2ER Tel: 01279-461630; Fax: 01279-461631;
e-mail: ficuk@aol.com

		holding %
Chairman	David Hudd	0.0
Chief Executive	Bryan McGreal	0.0
Finance Director	Anthony Knightley	0.0
Non-Exec Director	Leonard Licht	19.4

Main Shareholders:

Amvescap	8.1
Channel Hotels	8.1
Jupiter Asset Management	6.9
Alfred Bader	5.2

Percentage of free market capital: 42.1%

Comments:
Falkland Islands, which made an interim £300,000 pre-tax profit, is extending its interests with a 22.5% stake in Falklands Minerals, set up with Cambridge Mineral Resources and Global Petroleum to research mineral deposits on the islands. RAB Capital will have 51% of the new company and fund most of a £710,000 exploration programme. An eventual float for Falkland Minerals is on the cards.

Nominated Adviser:	Dawnay Day, London
AIM Broker:	Collins Stewart, London
Solicitors:	Addleshaw Goddard, London
Market Makers:	CSCS; WINS
Auditors:	KPMG Audit, 8 Salisbury Square, London, EC4Y 8BB
Registrars:	Capita Registrars

ENTRY ON AIM:	13/1/2003	**Recent price:**	229.0p
Interim results:	Dec	**Market cap:**	£14.13m
Final results:	Jul	**Issue price:**	197.5p
Year end:	Mar	**Current no of shares:**	
Accounts due:	Aug		6,170,037
Int div paymnt:	n/a	**No of shares after**	
Fin div paymnt:	Nov	dilution:	n/a
Int net div per share:	nil	**P/E ratio:**	19.4
Fin net div per share:	5.5p	**Probable CGT?**	No

LATEST REPORTED RESULTS: 2003		PREVIOUS REPORTED RESULTS: 2002	
Turnover:	£11.45m	Turnover:	£11.81m
PTP:	£1.03m	**PTP:**	£1.0m
EPS:	11.8p	**EPS:**	10.9p

Farley Group (FGR)

Estate agents

Channel House, Forest Lane, St Peters Port, Guernsey, GY1 4HL

		holding %
Chairman	Timothy James	18.9
Managing Director	Patricia Farley	31.4
Finance Director		
Non-Exec Director	Simon Wharmby	7.5

Main Shareholders:
n/a

Percentage of free market capital: 42.2%

Nominated Adviser:	Corporate Synergy, London
AIM Broker:	Corporate Synergy, London
Solicitors:	Stringer Saul, London
Market Makers:	HOOD; KBCS; SCAP; WINS
Auditors:	Chantrey Vellacott DFK, London
Registrars:	Capita Registrars

ENTRY ON AIM: 22/12/2003		**Recent price:**	33.0p
Interim results:	Sep	**Market cap:**	£3.76m
Final results:	Dec	**Issue price:**	25.0p
Year end:	Sep	**Current no of shares:**	
Accounts due:	Mar		11,405,000
Int div paymnt:	n/a	**No of shares after**	
Fin div paymnt:	n/a	**dilution:**	n/a
Int net div per share:	nil	**P/E ratio:**	n/a
Fin net div per share:	nil	**Probable CGT?**	**No**

LATEST REPORTED RESULTS: 2003		PREVIOUS REPORTED RESULTS: 2002	
Turnover:	£2.55m	Turnover:	£2.51m
PTP:	£155,000	PTP:	£(225,000)
EPS:	n/a	EPS:	n/a

Comments:
The estate agent floated in December after being acquired by cash shell Dealstore II for £2.15m. Focusing on the letting, selling and management of properties in Kensington and Chelsea, it will acquire and consolidate smaller estate agents and property management companies witihn London. Farley was loss making until 2003 due to directors' salaries. History may repeat itself as the directors plan to award themselves £200,000 per annum excluding benefits.

Faroe Petroleum (FPM)

Oil & gas explorer

51 Eastcheap, London, EC3M 1JP Tel: 01224-652810; Fax: 01224-643243

		holding %
Chairman	Joseph Darby	0.02
Chief Executive	Graham Stewart	0.2
Finance Director		
Non-Exec Director	Meinhard Jacobsen	0.01

Main Shareholders:

Faroe Petroleum Investments	17.7
MHR	15.7
Dana	13.8
3i	10.2
Colette Lynch	3.5

Percentage of free market capital: 38.9%

Nominated Adviser:	Williams de Broe, London
AIM Broker:	Williams de Broe, London
Solicitors:	Clyde & Co, London
Market Makers:	WDBM; WINS
Auditors:	KPMG, PO Box 695, London
Registrars:	Capita Registrars

ENTRY ON AIM: 27/6/2003		**Recent price:**	60.5p
Interim results:	Sep	**Market cap:**	£26.0m
Final results:	Mar	**Issue price:**	103.5p
Year end:	Dec	**Current no of shares:**	
Accounts due:	Jul		42,970,945
Int div paymnt:	n/a	**No of shares after**	
Fin div paymnt:	n/a	**dilution:**	n/a
Int net div per share:	nil	**P/E ratio:**	n/a
Fin net div per share:	nil	**Probable CGT?**	**No**

LATEST REPORTED RESULTS: 2002		PREVIOUS REPORTED RESULTS: 2001	
Turnover:	n/a	Turnover:	n/a
PTP:	£(628,000)	PTP:	£(601,000)
EPS:	(0.0)p	EPS:	(0.0)p

Comments:
Faroe is the holding company for Foroya Kolveni, which has 25% of two oil and gas exploration licences offshore the Faroe Islands, west of Norway. With £14m from its flotation fundraising, the company abandoned one unpromising well, 002 Marimas, and failed to agree terms to buy properties off the Shetland Islands from Italy's Eni group. Faroe, which lost an interim £447,000, is looking for new opportunities.

Farsight (FAR)

IT & security support services

The Observatory, Leofric Square, Vicarage Farm Road, Peterborough, PE1 5TP Tel: 01733-317614

		holding %
Chairman	Alan Wix	4.7
Chief Executive	Christopher Thomas	0.0
Finance Director		
Commercial Director	Carol Booth	0.03
Main Shareholders:		
Robert Davies		10.0
John Dalton		10.0
Michael James		10.0

Percentage of free market capital: 65.4%

Nominated Adviser:	Rowan Dartington, Bristol
AIM Broker:	Rowan Dartington, Bristol
Solicitors:	M & A, Cardiff
Market Makers:	MLSB; SCAP; WINS
Auditors:	AGN Shipley, London
Registrars:	Capita Registrars

ENTRY ON AIM: 24/10/2000		**Recent price:**	1.6p
Interim results:	Feb	**Market cap:**	£4.89m
Final results:	Nov	**Issue price:**	n/a
Year end:	May	**Current no of shares:**	
Accounts due:	Dec		305,927,072
Int div paymnt:	n/a	**No of shares after**	
Fin div paymnt:	n/a	**dilution:**	n/a
Int net div per share:	nil	**P/E ratio:**	n/a
Fin net div per share:	nil	**Probable CGT?**	YES

LATEST REPORTED RESULTS: 2003		PREVIOUS REPORTED RESULTS: 2002	
Turnover:	£1.03m	Turnover:	£3.15m
PTP:	£(2.46m)	PTP:	£(3.35m)
EPS:	(1.0)p	EPS:	(2.9)p

Comments:

The security services and remote video surveillance venture reported a half to November of ongoing reorganisation – losses were £501,000 (£978,000) on £431,000 (£597,000) turnover. But Farsight also enjoyed growing month-by-month 'remote video monitoring' revenues. Encouragingly, it has secured a major deal using e-surveillance software with Johnson Workplace Management that should be worth at least £250,000 over the next two years.

Faupel Trading (FAT)

Designer, importer and distributor of household textiles

Faupel House, Giggs Hill Road, Thames Ditton, Surrey KT7 0TR Tel: 020-8339 3100; Fax: 020-8398 5810;
e-mail: jamesmcclean@faupel.co.uk

		holding %
Chairman	David Newbigging	4.3
Chief Executive	Laurence Mead*	0.0
Finance Director	James McClean	0.0
Non-Exec Director	Stephen Redfarn	17.0
Main Shareholders:		
Max Money Resources*		20.1
Stephen Redfarn (Supervisory Board Spokesman)		17.0
T S Anderson		7.2

Percentage of free market capital: 12.1%

*Director Laurence Mead has a 40% holding in Max Money Resources

Nominated Adviser:	Evolution Beeson Gregory, London
AIM Broker:	Evolution Beeson Gregory, London
Solicitors:	Taylor Joynson Garrett, London
Market Makers:	MLSB; WINS
Auditors:	KPMG, 1 Forest Gate, Brighton Rd, Crawley, Sussex RH11 9PT
Registrars:	Computershare Investor Services

ENTRY ON AIM: 14/12/2001		**Recent price:**	24.0p
Interim results:	Nov	**Market cap:**	£3.77m
Final results:	Jun	**Issue price:**	14.5p
Year end:	Mar	**Current no of shares:**	
Accounts due:	Jul		15,709,447
Int div paymnt:	n/a	**No of shares after**	
Fin div paymnt:	n/a	**dilution:**	15,739,447
Int net div per share:	nil	**P/E ratio:**	n/a
Fin net div per share:	nil	**Probable CGT?**	YES

LATEST REPORTED RESULTS: 2003		PREVIOUS REPORTED RESULTS: 2002	
Turnover:	£26.94m	Turnover:	£35.38m
PTP:	£(875,000)	PTP:	£(2.2m)
EPS:	(5.6)p	EPS:	(17.1)p

Comments:

Faupel, the UK-based company that designs and then imports and distributes home furnishings, clothes and safety equipment from China and the Far East, continues to improve steadily. Latest interims from the company showed losses down 87% at £40,000 on reduced sales of £12.7m as margins edged up and unprofitable areas of business were closed. Debts, meanwhile, were written down 15% to £4.1m.

Fayrewood (FWY)

Pan-European computer software & hardware distributor

2nd Floor, 19/21 Clarendon Rd, Watford, WD17 1JR Tel: 01923-252996; Fax: 01923-252978;
e-mail: info@fayrewood.co.uk; web site: www.fayrewood.co.uk

		holding %
Chairman	Pierce A Casey	9.1
Managing Director	Paul Griffiths	0.9
Finance Director	Dick Lynch	0.0
Deputy Chairman	David Kleeman*	4.1

Main Shareholders:

Mario Legorburu	10.1
Herald Investment Management	6.9
BMPS Nominees (CI)*	4.3
Singer and Friedlander	3.2

Percentage of free market capital: 56.6%

*David Kleeman has a beneficial interest in these shares

Comments:

The Pan-European computer hardware and software distributor enjoyed a record 2003, with profits up 68% on a 14% sales hike. It expects better times in the European IT sector this year. Fayrewood has two operating arms, a niche distribution division as well as its 51% stake in ComputerLinks, a business quoted on the German NEMAX 50. Overall, this was a great year for Fayrewood. For 2004, City analysts expect profits of £13.2m on £465m of sales.

Nominated Adviser:	Arbuthnot, London
AIM Broker:	Arbuthnot, London
Solicitors:	Matheson Ormsby Prentice, London
Market Makers:	ALTI; ARBT; MLSB; SCAP; WINS
Auditors:	Ernst & Young, 7 Rolls Bldg, London EC4A 1NH
Registrars:	Capita Registrars

ENTRY ON AIM:	15/7/1996	Recent price:	116.5p
Interim results:	Aug	Market cap:	£56.89m
Final results:	Feb	Issue price:	36.0p
Year end:	Dec	Current no of shares:	
Accounts due:	Apr		48,830,760
Int div paymnt:	Apr	No of shares after	
Fin div paymnt:	Oct	dilution:	n/a
Int net div per share: 0.22p		P/E ratio:	n/a
Fin net div per share: 0.25p		Probable CGT?	Yes

LATEST REPORTED RESULTS:	2003	PREVIOUS REPORTED RESULTS:	2002
Turnover:	£434.13m	Turnover:	£380.14m
PTP:	£12.76m	PTP:	£7.57m
EPS:	11.8p	EPS:	6.8p

Feedback (FDBK)

Maker of electronic & computer equipment for education and industry

Park Road, Crowborough, East Sussex TN6 2QR Tel: 01892-653322; Fax: 01892-669077;
e-mail: enquiries@feedback.plc.uk

		holding %
Chairman	David Harding	13.4
Managing Director	David Sawyer	0.0
Finance Director		
Director	Andrew Whiteley	0.0

Main Shareholders:

Executors of PF Blackman	20.7
TWG Charlton	9.9
Hargreave Hale	4.4

Percentage of free market capital: 51.6%

Comments:

The Full List refugee makes electrical, electronic and microprocessor-based equipment for educational and industrial training. In a frustrating half to September losses came in at £496,000 on a 17% sales slump to £4.22m. Feedback Instruments was hit by delays in big contracts, notably in the Middle East. Feedback Data operated profitably and Feedback Incorporated broke even. In January, struggling e-learning subsidiary Teknical was sold to a division of Serco.

Nominated Adviser:	Charles Stanley, London
AIM Broker:	Charles Stanley, London
Solicitors:	Cripps Harries Hall, Kent
Market Makers:	SCAP; WINS
Auditors:	BDO Stoy Hayward, 69 Tweedy Road, Kent BR1 3WA
Registrars:	Capita Registrars

ENTRY ON AIM:	31/12/2003	Recent price:	22.5p
Interim results:	Jan	Market cap:	£2.71m
Final results:	Jun	Issue price:	n/a
Year end:	Mar	Current no of shares:	
Accounts due:	Aug		12,045,846
Int div paymnt:	n/a	No of shares after	
Fin div paymnt:	n/a	dilution:	n/a
Int net div per share:	nil	P/E ratio:	75.0
Fin net div per share:	nil	Probable CGT?	Yes

LATEST REPORTED RESULTS:	2003	PREVIOUS REPORTED RESULTS:	2002
Turnover:	£10.56m	Turnover:	£8.76m
PTP:	£179,000	PTP:	£(593,000)
EPS:	0.3p	EPS:	(5.7)p

Felix (FLX)

Interactive media company
Third Floor, 345 Stockport, Manchester, M13 0LF

		holding %
Chairman	Michael Neville	0.0
Chief Executive	Alasdair Waddell	0.0
Finance Director		
Non-Exec Director	Hugh Stewart	19.4

Main Shareholders:

Urgel	13.8
Mark Horrocks	5.9
Highland Capital	3.7
Dewscope	3.4
Atlas Telecoms	3.0
Percentage of free market capital: 31.2%	

Comments:

Felix's main offering is Everyone's A Winner, an interactive sales promotion 'game', where 'the participant is asked to stop a clock in a given time frame' in order to win a prize. The prize is always guaranteed to be worth more than twice the cost of participating and players can take part either by calling a premium phone line or using a touch screen 'cabinet version', which are set to be sold to a range of retail and leisure outlets.

Nominated Adviser:	Seymour Pierce, London
AIM Broker:	Seymour Pierce, London
Solicitors:	Hammonds, London
Market Makers:	WINS
Auditors:	Horwath Clark Whirehall, Manchester
Registrars:	Capita Registrars

ENTRY ON AIM:	8/3/2004	**Recent price:**	35.25p
Interim results:	Jun	**Market cap:**	£33.5m
Final results:	Dec	**Issue price:**	20.0p
Year end:	Aug	**Current no of shares:**	
Accounts due:	Jan		95,027,905
Int div paymnt:	n/a	**No of shares after**	
Fin div paymnt:	n/a	**dilution:**	n/a
Int net div per share:	nil	**P/E ratio:**	n/a
Fin net div per share:	nil	**Probable CGT?**	YES

LATEST REPORTED RESULTS: 2003		PREVIOUS REPORTED RESULTS: PERIOD ENDED 31 AUG 2002	
Turnover:	£521,000	**Turnover:**	n/a
PTP:	£(1.20m)	**PTP:**	£(158,000)
EPS:	n/a	**EPS:**	n/a

FFastFill (FFA)

Financial markets software developer
10 Arthur Street, London, EC4R 9AY Tel: 020-7665 8900; Fax: 020-7665 8905; e-mail: sales@ffastfill.com; web site: www.ffastfill.com

		holding %
Chairman	Keith Todd	5.8
Chief Executive		
Finance Director		
Deputy Chairman	Nigel McCorkell	0.2

Main Shareholders:

Ian Kergel	9.4
Robert White	5.3
Gartmore	4.6
Intrinsic Value	4.5
David Shaw	4.5
Percentage of free market capital: 44.8%	

Comments:

Financial markets trading software developer FFastFill is slowly moving in the right direction. Interims showed sales surging 317% to £1.6m, while losses more than halved to £1.2m. A new managed service of the company's software has been launched – DRW Capital Markets becoming the first customer to opt for this model – while a £1m placing was recently completed to strengthen the balance sheet. Nonetheless, profits remain some way off.

Nominated Adviser:	KBC Peel Hunt, London
AIM Broker:	KBC Peel Hunt, London
Solicitors:	Field Fisher Waterhouse, London
Market Makers:	KBCS; WINS
Auditors:	Baker Tilly, 2 Bloomsbury Street, London WC1B 3ST
Registrars:	Capita Registrars

ENTRY ON AIM:	14/11/2000	**Recent price:**	7.75p
Interim results:	Dec	**Market cap:**	£7.91m
Final results:	Sep	**Issue price:**	175.0p
Year end:	Mar	**Current no of shares:**	
Accounts due:	Jul		102,008,190
Int div paymnt:	n/a	**No of shares after**	
Fin div paymnt:	n/a	**dilution:**	n/a
Int net div per share:	nil	**P/E ratio:**	n/a
Fin net div per share:	nil	**Probable CGT?**	YES

LATEST REPORTED RESULTS: 2003		PREVIOUS REPORTED RESULTS: 2002	
Turnover:	£1.37m	**Turnover:**	£896,000
PTP:	£(4.93m)	**PTP:**	£(8.02m)
EPS:	(10.1)p	**EPS:**	(16.7)p

Finsbury Food
(FIF)

Speciality cakes and bread maker

25 City Road, London, EC1Y 1BQ Tel: 020-7448 8950; Fax: 020-7638 9426; e-mail: finsbury@city-group.com

		holding %
Chairman	Lord Saatchi	0.0
Chief Executive	David Brooks	0.5
Finance Director	John Lomer	0.0
Non-Exec Director	Edward Beale	0.4

Main Shareholders:

Landau Enterprises*	28.2
London Finance & Investment	25.1
JP Morgan Fleming Asset Management	15.7
Richard Ashness	11.3

Percentage of free market capital: 18.6%

* Lord Saatchi is interested in 4,798,774 shares via this company.

Comments:

The cake and bread manufacturer has been hit by a double whammy. It is likely only to break-even for the year as increased sales of Christmas lines exhausted the local supply of suitable labour. This led to significant inefficiencies in the manufacturing processes, which was compounded by pressure from rising raw material costs. On a brighter note, Finsbury rolled off its first products for Nestlé in January and has gained new distribution channels such as convenience and impulse outlets.

Nominated Adviser:	Durlacher, London
AIM Broker:	Durlacher, London
Solicitors:	SJ Berwin, London
Market Makers:	SCAP; WINS
Auditors:	Horwarth Clark Whitehall, London
Registrars:	CI Registrars

ENTRY ON AIM:	23/8/1996	Recent price:	36.5p
Interim results:	Mar	Market cap:	£7.65m
Final results:	Sep	Issue price:	12.5p
Year end:	Jun	Current no of shares:	
Accounts due:	Oct		20,963,562
Int div paymnt:	n/a	No of shares after	
Fin div paymnt:	Dec	dilution:	n/a
Int net div per share:	nil	P/E ratio:	28.1
Fin net div per share:	1.0p	Probable CGT?	YES

LATEST REPORTED RESULTS: 2003		PREVIOUS REPORTED RESULTS: 2002	
Turnover:	£35.25m	Turnover:	£284,000
PTP:	£392,000	PTP:	£(355,000)
EPS:	1.3p	EPS:	(0.9)p

Firestone Diamonds
(FDI)

Diamond miner & explorer

PO Box 23727, London, SW5 9FU Tel: 020-7370 6452; Fax: 020-7460 2457; e-mail: info@firestonediamonds.com; web site: www.firestonediamonds.com

		holding %
Chairman	James F Kenny	1.7
Managing Director	Philip Kenny*	1.8
Finance Director		
Deputy Chairman	Hugh C D Jenner-Clarke	1.9

Main Shareholders:

Elfin Trust	47.4

Percentage of free market capital: 46.4%

*Potential beneficiaries of a discretionary trust holding 7,200,000 ordinary shares

Comments:

Volatile diamond producer and explorer Firestone, whose pre-tax profits slid £31,000 to £163,000, has several operations in South Africa and Botswana. It has been making much of Bonte Koe in Namaqualand, a joint venture with black-empowerment group African Star, funded with a £2m placing at 33p. Boss Philip Kenny says this could produce 158,000 carats over four years and generate £17m revenues.

Nominated Adviser:	Brewin Dolphin, Glasgow
AIM Broker:	Brewin Dolphin, Edinburgh
Solicitors:	Reynolds Porter Chamberlain, London
Market Makers:	KBCS; MLSB; SCAP; WINS
Auditors:	PKF, 78 Hatton Garden, London EC1N 8JA
Registrars:	Capita Registrars

ENTRY ON AIM:	14/8/1998	Recent price:	40.0p
Interim results:	Mar	Market cap:	£16.11m
Final results:	Dec	Issue price:	114.0p
Year end:	Jun	Current no of shares:	
Accounts due:	Dec		40,265,469
Int div paymnt:	n/a	No of shares after	
Fin div paymnt:	n/a	dilution:	47,111,469
Int net div per share:	nil	P/E ratio:	200.0
Fin net div per share:	nil	Probable CGT?	YES

LATEST REPORTED RESULTS: 2003		PREVIOUS REPORTED RESULTS: 2002	
Turnover:	£1.16m	Turnover:	£842,000
PTP:	£163,000	PTP:	£193,000
EPS:	0.2p	EPS:	0.4p

First Artist (FAN)

Sports management

87 Wembley Hill Road, Wembley, Middlesex HA9 8BU Tel: 020-8900 1818; Fax: 020-8903 2964;
e-mail: admin@firstartist.com ; web site: www.firstartist.com

		holding %
Chairman	Brian Baldock	0.4
Chief Executive	Jonathan Smith*	21.1
Finance Director	Jonathan Lees	0.0
Chief Operating Officer	Philip Smith*	14.1

Main Shareholders:

Vinicio Fioranelli	15.9
Vincenzio Morabito (Director)	15.7
Smith Family Trust*	5.2
Singer & Friedlander	4.1

Percentage of free market capital: 23.5%

*These directors have a beneficial interest in the Smith Family Trust

Comments:

This leading sports management and representation business is focussed heavily on the football sector. The cash crisis at many clubs, FIFA's imposition of the 'transfer window', the reduction in TV income and other factors (notably a goodwill impairment charge of £14.8m) contributed to a loss of £15m for the 16 months to October 2003. Apparently the recent deal between BSKyB and the Premier League, its own reorganisation and a pick up in other areas, should ensure this year is much improved. Time will tell.

Nominated Adviser:	Seymour Pierce, London
AIM Broker:	Seymour Pierce, London
Solicitors:	SJ Berwin, London
Market Makers:	SCAP; WINS
Auditors:	Baker Tilly, 2 Bloomsbury Street, London WC1B 3ST
Registrars:	Capita Registrars

Entry on AIM: 21/12/2001		Recent price:	2.75p
Interim results:	Mar	Market cap:	£1.48m
Final results:	Oct	Issue price:	50.0p
Year end:	Jun	Current no of shares:	
Accounts due:	Oct		53,903,537
Int div paymnt:	n/a	No of shares after	
Fin div paymnt:	n/a	dilution:	54,703,537
Int net div per share:	nil	P/E ratio:	n/a
Fin net div per share:	nil	Probable CGT?	Yes

LATEST REPORTED RESULTS:		PREVIOUS REPORTED RESULTS:	
	2003		2002
Turnover:	£2.46m	Turnover:	£6.7m
PTP:	£(14.54m)	PTP:	£642,000
EPS:	(25.9)p	EPS:	0.7p

First Calgary Petroleums (FPL)

Oil & gas exploration and development

Suite 900, 520 - 5th Avenue S W, Calgary T2P 3R7, Alberta, Canada Tel: 00-1 403 264 6697; Fax: 00-1 403 264 3955;
web site: www.fcpl.ca

		holding %
Chairman	Richard Anderson	1.3
Chief Executive	as above	
Vice-Pres Finance	Kenneth Rutherford	0.1
Non-Exec Director	Darryl Raymaker	0.2

Main Shareholders:

CDS & Co	69.3
Everest Assets Management	9.5
Lynminister	9.5
Weighbridge Trust	4.8

Percentage of free market capital: 5.3%

Comments:

Shares in First Calgary have risen sixfold since its 2002 AIM launch on a flow of cheering drilling news from its MLE oil and gas prospect in Algeria. The Canadian company, which raised £60m last year at 170p a share to fund its programme, says independent experts reckon the MLE pool could contain the equivalent of 5.7 trillion cubic feet of gas. Recent flow rates from wells drilled have been encouraging.

Nominated Adviser:	Nabarro Wells, London
AIM Broker:	Canaccord Capital, London
Solicitors:	SJ Berwin, London
Market Makers:	KBCS; SCAP; WINS
Auditors:	KPMG, Calgary T2P 4B9, Alberta, Canada
Registrars:	Computershare Investor Services

Entry on AIM: 30/7/2002		Recent price:	322.0p
Interim results:	Sep	Market cap:	£510.11m
Final results:	Mar	Issue price:	52.0p
Year end:	Dec	Current no of shares:	
Accounts due:	May		158,420,046
Int div paymnt:	n/a	No of shares after	
Fin div paymnt:	n/a	dilution:	n/a
Int net div per share:	nil	P/E ratio:	n/a
Fin net div per share:	nil	Probable CGT?	No

LATEST REPORTED RESULTS:		PREVIOUS REPORTED RESULTS:	
	2002		2001
Turnover:	$266,000	Turnover:	$298,000
PTP:	$(3.64m)	PTP:	$(1.33m)
EPS:	(0.0)c	EPS:	(0.0)c

First Derivatives (FDP)

Software solutions provider

First Derivatives House, Kilmorey Business Park, Kilmorey Street, Newry, Co.Down, BT34 2DH N. Ireland

Tel: 028-3025 2242 ; Fax: 028-3025 2060 ; e-mail: enquiries@firstderivatives.com; web site: www.firstderivatives.com

		holding %		
Chairman	David Anderson	0.0	Nominated Adviser:	Corporate Synergy, London
Managing Director	Brian Conlon	73.7	AIM Broker:	Corporate Synergy, London
Finance Director				
Operations Director	Michael O'Neill	8.4	Solicitors:	Mills Selig, Belfast
			Market Makers:	WINS
Main Shareholders:				
n/a			Auditors:	KPMG, Stokes House, Belfast
			Registrars:	Melton Registrars

Percentage of free market capital: 17.9%		ENTRY ON AIM: 28/3/2002	Recent price:	82.5p
		Interim results: Nov	Market cap:	£9.93m
		Final results: May	Issue price:	50.0p
		Year end: Feb	Current no of shares:	

Comments:

Derivatives trading system developer FD bounced back from a slightly disappointing 2002/03 to practically double both profits and sales in the first half of the current year (to £251,000 and £1.2m respectively). Growth across all of the company's core business areas – systems support, software and consulting – was reported as new long-term contracts were picked up from two large investment banks. A broadband joint venture with BT is currently under development.

Accounts due:	Jul	Current no of shares:	12,041,667
Int div paymnt:	n/a	No of shares after	
Fin div paymnt:	n/a	dilution:	12,060,000
Int net div per share:	nil	P/E ratio:	34.4
Fin net div per share:	nil	Probable CGT?	YES

LATEST REPORTED RESULTS: 2003		PREVIOUS REPORTED RESULTS: 2002	
Turnover:	£1.65m	Turnover:	£1.78m
PTP:	£406,000	PTP:	£612,000
EPS:	2.4p	EPS:	4.3p

First Property (FPO)

Property services

17 Quayside Lodge, William Morris Way, London, SW6 2UZ Tel: 020-7731 2844; Fax: 020-7731 8644;

e-mail: george.digby@fprop.com; web site: www.fprop.com

		holding %		
Chairman	Alasdair Locke	8.6	Nominated Adviser:	Baird, London
Chief Executive	Benyamin Habib	14.7	AIM Broker:	Baird, London
Finance Director	George Digby	0.0	Solicitors:	Harbottle & Lewis, London; Pinsents, London
			Market Makers:	MLSB; SCAP; WINS
Main Shareholders:			Auditors:	Haines Watts, Sterling House, Kidlington, Oxford OX5 2DH
John Kottler		14.1		
FPD Savills Commercial		6.9	Registrars:	Capita Registrars
Russell Duckworth		3.2		

Percentage of free market capital: 52.6%	ENTRY ON AIM: 29/9/1995	Recent price:	18.25p
	Interim results: Nov	Market cap:	£16.99m
	Final results: Jun	Issue price:	60.0p
	Year end: Mar	Current no of shares:	

Comments:

'Fprop' is now trading in the black after achieving pre-tax profits of £175,000 in the six months to September. Turnover soared 314% to £1.6m. Under its Asset Management arm it now has two fully invested funds with £7m under management and has launched a third fund at almost twice the size of previous funds. Interest in a fourth fund has been expressed. In order to retain the quality of its Commercial Property Database at a lower cost, the company has expanded its team in Pakistan.

Accounts due:	Aug	Current no of shares:	93,085,698
Int div paymnt:	n/a	No of shares after	
Fin div paymnt:	Sep	dilution:	n/a
Int net div per share:	nil	P/E ratio:	n/a
Fin net div per share:	0.05p	Probable CGT?	YES

LATEST REPORTED RESULTS: 2003		PREVIOUS REPORTED RESULTS: 2002	
Turnover:	£2.28m	Turnover:	372,000
PTP:	£(2.81m)	PTP:	£(3.92m)
EPS:	(2.7)p	EPS:	(4.4)p

First Quantum Minerals (FQM)
Copper mining

1st Floor, Mill House, Mill Bay Lane, Horsham, West Sussex RH12 1SS Tel: 01403-273484; Fax: 01403-273494;
e-mail: clive.newall@first-quantum.com; web site: www.first-quantum.com

		holding %
Chairman	Philip Pascall	2.2
Chief Executive	as above	
Finacial Director	Martin Rowley	0.6
President	Clive Newall	1.6

Main Shareholders:

CDS & Co	44.1
Cede & Co	16.3
Good Luck	10.2
Roytor & Co	6.0
Pridewood Management Bahamas	4.2

Percentage of free market capital: 9.9%

Comments:

Toronto and AIM-quoted First Quantum has been cash hungry, but the markets have been happy to oblige on the strength of its copper and cobalt prospects in Zambia and Congo. The loss-making company recently fixed a £124.5m debt package to develop its Kansanshi project in northern Zambia and issued £50m of shares at 690p. January brought a promising cobalt find at Lufua in Congo's mineral-rich Katanga province.

Nominated Adviser:	Canaccord Capital, London
AIM Broker:	Canaccord Capital, London
Solicitors:	SJ Berwin, London
Market Makers:	KBCS; WINS
Auditors:	PricewaterhouseCoopers, Vancouver, Canada
Registrars:	Computershare Investor Services

ENTRY ON AIM:	9/4/2001	**Recent price:**	625.0p
Interim results:	May	**Market cap:**	£364.1m
Final results:	Mar	**Issue price:**	145.5p
Year end:	Dec	**Current no of shares:**	
Accounts due:	Feb		58,256,624
Int div paymnt:	n/a	**No of shares after**	
Fin div paymnt:	n/a	**dilution:**	n/a
Int net div per share:	nil	**P/E ratio:**	n/a
Fin net div per share:	nil	**Probable CGT?**	No

LATEST REPORTED RESULTS: 13 MONTHS TO 31 DEC 2002		PREVIOUS REPORTED RESULTS: 2001	
Turnover:	$51.34m	**Turnover:**	$138.1m
PTP:	$(5.48m)	**PTP:**	$(17.91m)
EPS:	$(0.1)	**EPS:**	$(0.6)

Fiske (FKE)
Broker-dealer services

Salisbury House, London Wall, London, EC2M 5QS Tel: 020-7448 4700; Fax: 020-7256 5365; e-mail: info@fiskeplc.com

		holding %
Chairman	Geoffrey Maitland Smith	0.1
Chief Executive	Clive Fiske Harrison	28.8
Finance Director		
Deputy Chairman	Steven Cockburn	9.9

Main Shareholders:

Jove Investment Trust	15.0
Gartmore	5.7
Constance Short	4.5
Alexander Fiske Harrison*	3.9
Byron Fiske Harrison*	3.6

Percentage of free market capital: 20.9%

*Alexander Harrison and Byron Harrison are the adult sons of Clive Harrison

Comments:

Stockbroker Fiske currently represents a dozen AIM companies. And though it is seemingly yet to benefit directly from the recent resurgence in London's IPO market the general upswing in market activity has boosted prospects somewhat. First half numbers showed a welcome return to profits – last year's £403,000 deficit becoming a £262,000 surplus. A £900,000 surge in revenues to £2m triggered the improvement.

Nominated Adviser:	Grant Thornton, London
AIM Broker:	Fiske, London
Solicitors:	Dechert, London
Market Makers:	KBCS; MLSB; WINS
Auditors:	Deloitte & Touche, London
Registrars:	Capita Registrars

ENTRY ON AIM:	30/3/2000	**Recent price:**	85.0p
Interim results:	Jan	**Market cap:**	£7.03m
Final results:	Aug	**Issue price:**	135.0p
Year end:	May	**Current no of shares:**	
Accounts due:	Aug		8,273,092
Int div paymnt:	Feb	**No of shares after**	
Fin div paymnt:	Sep	**dilution:**	n/a
Int net div per share:	2.0p	**P/E ratio:**	n/a
Fin net div per share:	1.75p	**Probable CGT?**	No

LATEST REPORTED RESULTS: 2003		PREVIOUS REPORTED RESULTS: 2002	
Turnover:	£1.83m	**Turnover:**	£1.72m
PTP:	£(793,000)	**PTP:**	£457,000
EPS:	(8.3)p	**EPS:**	4.5p

Fitzhardinge (FHG)

Property and hotels consultancy

9 Marylebone Lane, London, W1U 1HL Tel: 020-7935 4499; Fax: 020-7409 3124; e-mail: info@fitzhardingeplc.com; web site: www.fitzhardingeplc.com

		holding %
Chairman	John Ritblat	1.4
Managing Director	David Izzet	0.1
Finance Director	Thomas Tidy	0.1
Deputy Chairman	John Manser	0.0

Main Shareholders:

Delancey	37.0
The Trustee*	15.7
ISIS	6.9
Northern Venture Managers	4.3

Percentage of free market capital: 32.1%

*Barclays Private Bank & Trust (IoM) as a trustee of the Consultancies Group employee share ownership plan

Nominated Adviser:	Shore Capital, London
AIM Broker:	Shore Capital, London
Solicitors:	S J Berwin, London
Market Makers:	SCAP; WINS
Auditors:	Baker Tilly, 2 Bloomsbury Street, London WC1B 3ST
Registrars:	Capita Registrars

Entry on AIM:	2/8/2001	**Recent price:**	132.5p
Interim results:	Sep	**Market cap:**	£40.52m
Final results:	Apr	**Issue price:**	115.0p
Year end:	Dec	**Current no of shares:**	
Accounts due:	Sep		30,579,400
Int div paymnt:	n/a	**No of shares after**	
Fin div paymnt:	May	**dilution:**	n/a
Int net div per share: 1.05p		**P/E ratio:**	11.9
Fin net div per share: 2.10p		**Probable CGT?**	Yes

LATEST REPORTED RESULTS: YEAR TO 31 DEC 02		PREVIOUS REPORTED RESULTS: 5 MONTHS TO 31 DEC 01	
Turnover:	£38.21m	Turnover:	£15.26m
PTP:	£3.19m	PTP:	£2.01m
EPS:	11.1p	EPS:	7.2p

Comments:

Fitzhardinge is a property consultancy with an additional fund management team. After integrating acquisitions Gooch Webster and Fisher Wilson, the company has been busy advising in the shopping centre market and M&A deals. Its new division Colliers Capital, a bespoke property advice service to private clients and those creating new funds is apparently performing well. The company is almost at break-even.

Flightstore (FLG)

Producer of inflight software

Castlegate House, 14 London Road, Reigate, Surrey RH2 9HY Tel: 01737-228960; Fax: 0845-280 1909

		holding %
Chairman	David Sebire	4.9
Managing Director	Derek Jewson	0.0
Finance Director		
Technical Director	Ian Walberg	9.5

Main Shareholders:

Watermark Group	7.7
Strathclyde Pension Fund	3.3
Matrix Venture Fund	3.2

Percentage of free market capital: 62.4%

Nominated Adviser:	Seymour Pierce, London
AIM Broker:	Seymour Pierce, London
Solicitors:	Davies Lavery, London
Market Makers:	EVO; SCAP; WINS
Auditors:	KPMG LLP, 8 Salisbury Square, London EC4Y 8BB
Registrars:	Neville Registrars

Entry on AIM:	12/12/2003	**Recent price:**	13.75p
Interim results:	Sep	**Market cap:**	£13.8m
Final results:	Mar	**Issue price:**	10.0p
Year end:	Dec	**Current no of shares:**	
Accounts due:	Jun		100,376,460
Int div paymnt:	n/a	**No of shares after**	
Fin div paymnt:	n/a	**dilution:**	n/a
Int net div per share:	nil	**P/E ratio:**	n/a
Fin net div per share:	nil	**Probable CGT?**	Yes

LATEST REPORTED RESULTS: 2002		PREVIOUS REPORTED RESULTS: 2001	
Turnover:	£44,000	Turnover:	£5,000
PTP:	£(858,000)	PTP:	£(881,000)
EPS:	n/a	EPS:	n/a

Comments:

In-flight advertising business FlightStore arrived on AIM with £2m in the bank following an oversubscribed placing. Chaired by AeroBox chief David Sebire, the company has developed a system enabling airline passengers to access information and purchase goods and services through seat-back TVs. Thus far demand has been encouraging. The likes of Continental, Delta Song and KLM have already signed up and this affords the group an annual audience of 10m.

Flintstone Technologies (FLT)

Technology developer & investor

52 Mount Pleasant, Liverpool, L3 5UN Tel: 0151-706 0626; Fax: 0151-706 0627; e-mail: information@flintstoneplc.com;
web site: www.flintstoneplc.com

		holding %
Chairman	Glyn Hirsch	1.1
Chief Executive	David Chestnutt	2.1
Finance Director		
Non-Exec Director	Pavel Shashkov	2.1

Main Shareholders:

Ian Woodcock	12.0
HSBC	11.6
AXA Investment Managers	8.2
Schroder Investment Management	6.8
The Throgmorton Trust	5.7
Percentage of free market capital: 43.4%	

Nominated Adviser:	Collins Stewart, London
AIM Broker:	Collins Stewart, London
Solicitors:	Kingsley Napley, London
Market Makers:	CSCS; WINS
Auditors:	PKF, 52 Mount Pleasant, Liverpool L3 5UN
Registrars:	Capita Registrars

Entry on AIM:	28/6/2002	**Recent price:**	12.75p
Interim results:	Dec	**Market cap:**	£6.06m
Final results:	Jun	**Issue price:**	33.0p
Year end:	Mar	**Current no of shares:**	
Accounts due:	Jul		47,554,000
Int div paymnt:	n/a	**No of shares after**	
Fin div paymnt:	n/a	**dilution:**	n/a
Int net div per share:	nil	**P/E ratio:**	n/a
Fin net div per share:	nil	**Probable CGT?**	No

Comments:

This business accelerator has stakes in six fledgling enterprises, originally developed in the former Soviet Union. UK-based Biocote, which makes anti-bacterial coating, plans to float on AIM. Hardide, which produces super-resistant metal powders, has raised £2m recently. Other ventures are at an earlier stage, including one to develop a new ultra-efficient electric motor. Annual portfolio costs are a steep £0.7m but there is enough cash for two years. NAV has fallen slghtly to £5.7m.

LATEST REPORTED RESULTS: 2003		PREVIOUS REPORTED RESULTS: 2002	
Turnover:	£127,000	**Turnover:**	£324,000
PTP:	£(1.40m)	**PTP:**	£(535,000)
EPS:	(3.1)p	**EPS:**	(2.3)p

Flomerics (FLO)

Virtual prototyping software developer & supplier

81 Bridge Road, Hampton Court, Surrey, KT8 9HH Tel: 020-8941 8810; Fax: 020-8941 8730;
e-mail: info@flomerics.co.uk; web site: www.flomerics.com

		holding %
Chairman	David W Mann	1.3
Chief Executive	David G Tatchell	9.1
Finance Director	Chris Ogle	0.1
Deputy Chairman	T R Rowbotham	1.2

Main Shareholders:

ISIS Asset Management	17.0
Fidelity Investments	9.9
E Rosten	8.0
The Bank of New York (Nominees)	5.5
Sharelink Nominees	3.4
Percentage of free market capital: 44.3%	

Nominated Adviser:	Teather & Greenwood, London
AIM Broker:	Teather & Greenwood, London
Solicitors:	Hammonds, London
Market Makers:	KBCS; SCAP; TEAM; WINS
Auditors:	BDO Stoy Hayward, 8 Baker Street, London W1M 1DA
Registrars:	Capita Registrars

Entry on AIM:	6/12/1995	**Recent price:**	81.0p
Interim results:	Jul	**Market cap:**	£11.86m
Final results:	Feb	**Issue price:**	26.0p
Year end:	Dec	**Current no of shares:**	
Accounts due:	Mar		14,646,580
Int div paymnt:	n/a	**No of shares after**	
Fin div paymnt:	May	**dilution:**	14,737,000
Int net div per share:	nil	**P/E ratio:**	28.9
Fin net div per share:	1.0p	**Probable CGT?**	Yes

Comments:

Electronics analysis software supplier Flomerics announced disappointing 2003 results, as a weak US dollar and a dearth of new customer signings reversed previous revenue growth. Nonetheless chief executive David Tatchell claims the future is now looking a little brighter as existing customers continue to renew their annual licences and signs are starting to emerge that IT budgets are once again expanding. Around £2.5m remains in the coffers.

LATEST REPORTED RESULTS: 2003		PREVIOUS REPORTED RESULTS: 2002	
Turnover:	£10.22m	**Turnover:**	£11.71m
PTP:	£455,000	**PTP:**	£635,000
EPS:	2.8p	**EPS:**	3.3p

Focus Solutions (FSG)

Software and e-commerce developer for financial services industry

Cranford House, Kenilworth Road, Leamington Spa, Warwickshire CV32 6RQ Tel: 01926-468300; Fax: 01926-468400;
e-mail: info@focus-solutions.co.uk; web site: www.focus-solutions.co.uk

		holding %
Chairman	Alastair Taylor	0.1
Chief Executive	John Streets	29.4
Finance Director	Martin Clements	0.4
Operations Director	Mark Thelwell	2.1

Main Shareholders:

Hatt III LP	22.3
Liontrust Investment Funds	11.0
Active Capital Trust*	7.1
Unibank	5.6
Close Brothers	5.6

Percentage of free market capital: 14.0%

*These shares are registered in the name of Chase Nominees

Comments:

Trading conditions remain tough for this financial-sector-focused software business. Yet, a raft of cost cuts (lead by a reduction in headcount) did enable the company to shrug aside a near £300,000 slip in first-half sales to report a significantly reduced loss of £663,000 (£1.9m). Cutbacks aside, there have been several other positives – principally a £400,000 three-year deal with Credit Suisse subsidiary Winterthur Life. £568,000 of cash remains.

Nominated Adviser:	Evolution Beeson Gregory, London
AIM Broker:	Evolution Beeson Gregory, London
Solicitors:	Hammond Suddards Edge, Birmingham
Market Makers:	BGMM; WINS
Auditors:	Deloitte & Touche, Birmingham
Registrars:	Capita Registrars

ENTRY ON AIM:	16/3/2000	**Recent price:**	56.0p
Interim results:	Dec	**Market cap:**	£15.92m
Final results:	Jun	**Issue price:**	195.0p
Year end:	Mar	**Current no of shares:**	
Accounts due:	Jun		28,429,358
Int div paymnt:	n/a	**No of shares after**	
Fin div paymnt:	n/a	**dilution:**	n/a
Int net div per share:	nil	**P/E ratio:**	n/a
Fin net div per share:	nil	**Probable CGT?**	YES

LATEST REPORTED RESULTS:	2003	PREVIOUS REPORTED RESULTS:	2002
Turnover:	£6.58m	Turnover:	£5.07m
PTP:	£(3.83m)	PTP:	£(2.59m)
EPS:	(13.4)p	EPS:	(10.3)p

Forbidden Technologies (FBT)

Video technology developer

3rd Floor, 2-4 St. George's Road, Wimbledon, London, SW19 4DP Tel: 020-8879 7245; Fax: 020-8946 4871;
e-mail: info@forbidden.co.uk; web site: www.forbidden.co.uk

		holding %
Chairman	Victor Steel	0.3
Chief Executive	Stephen Streater	84.1
Finance Director	Douglas Blaikie	0.1
Non-Exec Director	Peter Main	0.0

Main Shareholders:

n/a

Percentage of free market capital: 15.5%

Comments:

The story scarcely seems to change at video compression specialist Forbidden. The technology is exciting but the revenues remain minimal and all the while much larger rivals continue to develop similar systems. The only significant development of late concerns a new agreement signed with Mediaconcept Srl, a company established in order to develop and promote Forbidden's products in the Italian market. It remains to be seen what impact this deal will have on revenues.

Nominated Adviser:	Brewin Dolphin, Glasgow
AIM Broker:	Brewin Dolphin, Glasgow
Solicitors:	Tarlo Lyons, London
Market Makers:	KBCS; MLSB; SCAP; WINS
Auditors:	KPMG, 1 Puddle Dock, Blackfriars, London EC4V 3PD
Registrars:	Capita Registrars

ENTRY ON AIM:	2/3/2000	**Recent price:**	41.0p
Interim results:	Sep	**Market cap:**	£30.94m
Final results:	Mar	**Issue price:**	20.0p
Year end:	Dec	**Current no of shares:**	
Accounts due:	Apr		75,475,000
Int div paymnt:	n/a	**No of shares after**	
Fin div paymnt:	n/a	**dilution:**	77,182,500
Int net div per share:	nil	**P/E ratio:**	n/a
Fin net div per share:	nil	**Probable CGT?**	YES

LATEST REPORTED RESULTS:	2002	PREVIOUS REPORTED RESULTS:	2001
Turnover:	£9,000	Turnover:	£3,000
PTP:	£(431,000)	PTP:	£(251,000)
EPS:	(0.6)p	EPS:	(0.3)p

Forever Broadcasting (FOB)

Radio broadcaster

4 Osborne Road, Newcastle upon Tyne, NE2 2AA Tel: 0191-281 1222; Fax: 0191-281 4111;
e-mail: mail@foreverbroadcasting.com; web site: www.foreverbroadcasting.com

		holding %
Chairman	John Josephs	7.9
Managing Director	as above	
Finance Director		
Programme Director	Steve King	0.01

Main Shareholders:

The Wireless Group	16.1
Peter Coates	9.3
Maurice Dobson	7.9
Sound Advice	3.7
Wayne Chadwick	3.4

Percentage of free market capital: 44.5%

Nominated Adviser:	Baird, London
AIM Broker:	Baird, London
Solicitors:	Mincoffs, Newcastle upon Tyne
Market Makers:	GRAB; WINS
Auditors:	PricewaterhouseCoopers, Newcastle upon Tyne
Registrars:	Capita Registrars

ENTRY ON AIM:	2/8/2000	**Recent price:**	43.25p
Interim results:	May	**Market cap:**	£9.31m
Final results:	Nov	**Issue price:**	155.0p
Year end:	Sep	**Current no of shares:**	
Accounts due:	Dec		21,519,225
Int div paymnt:	n/a	**No of shares after**	
Fin div paymnt:	n/a	**dilution:**	21,869,225
Int net div per share:	nil	**P/E ratio:**	n/a
Fin net div per share:	nil	**Probable CGT?**	YES

Comments:

Following the acceptance of an offer from Wireless, the radio company run by ex-Sun editor Kelvin Mackenzie, Forever's shares have been delisted. The offer at 37.6p a share valued Forever at £8.1 million.

	LATEST REPORTED RESULTS: 2003		PREVIOUS REPORTED RESULTS: 2002
Turnover:	£5.38m	**Turnover:**	£3.80m
PTP:	£(4.77m)	**PTP:**	£(8.38m)
EPS:	(22.2)p	**EPS:**	(8.38)p

Formscan (FSA)

Total document solutions supplier

Apex House, West End, Frome, Somerset BA11 3AS Tel: 01373-452555; Fax: 01373-461269;
e-mail: info@formscan.com; web site: www.formscan.com

		holding %
Chairman	Allan M Harle	42.4
Managing Director	John F Harvey	16.8
Finance Director	Joanne DiGiacomo	0.8
Non-Exec Director	Peter J Harris	0.1

Main Shareholders:

Sharelink Nominees	7.3
Trevor Brown	6.3

Percentage of free market capital: 26.4%

Nominated Adviser:	Shore Capital, London
AIM Broker:	Shore Capital, London
Solicitors:	Nabarro Nathanson, London; Harris & Harris, Somerset
Market Makers:	SCAP; WINS
Auditors:	Moore Stephens, Bath
Registrars:	Neville Registrars

ENTRY ON AIM:	19/6/1995	**Recent price:**	12.5p
Interim results:	Apr	**Market cap:**	£1.49m
Final results:	Nov	**Issue price:**	51.0p
Year end:	Jul	**Current no of shares:**	
Accounts due:	Nov		11,890,904
Int div paymnt:	n/a	**No of shares after**	
Fin div paymnt:	n/a	**dilution:**	n/a
Int net div per share:	nil	**P/E ratio:**	n/a
Fin net div per share:	nil	**Probable CGT?**	YES

Comments:

Formscan develops and delivers document management solutions ranging all the way through from data capture to document storage and preservation. Yet despite recently completing a 'prestige' order for 48 camera systems in Japan – a deal which helped boost full year revenues by around £1m – the company continues to run up losses. With the push for profits Formscan's priority, management is increasingly turning its attention to the US market.

	LATEST REPORTED RESULTS: 2003		PREVIOUS REPORTED RESULTS: N/A
Turnover:	£4.70m	**Turnover:**	£4.23m
PTP:	£(453,000)	**PTP:**	£(308,000)
EPS:	(1.1)p	**EPS:**	(2.8)p

Fortfield Investments (formerly SMF Technologies) (FIV)

Cash shell

Plassey, Limerick, Ireland Tel: 00-353 1 61 201030 ; Fax: 00-353 1 61 330812; e-mail: info@smftechnologies.com; web site: www.smftechnologies.com

		holding %
Chairman		
Managing Director	John McDonnell	0.0
Finance Director		
Non-Exec Director	James M O'Donovan	3.5

Main Shareholders:

Martin O'Donoghue	32.4
Savoy Investment Management	17.2
HSBC	10.3
Bank of New York Nominees	7.5
Nontrust Nominees	7.1
Percentage of free market capital:	17.1%

Nominated Adviser:	Insinger de Beaufort, London
AIM Broker:	Insinger Townsley, London
Solicitors:	O'Donnell Sweeney, Dublin
Market Makers:	GBMM; WINS
Auditors:	Deloitte & Touche, ICC House, Charlotte Quay, Limerick
Registrars:	Computershare Investor Services

ENTRY ON AIM:	23/7/1998	**Recent price:**	3.5p
Interim results:	Oct	**Market cap:**	£0.96m
Final results:	Jul	**Issue price:**	97.5p
Year end:	Mar	**Current no of shares:**	
Accounts due:	Jun		27,321,171
Int div paymnt:	n/a	**No of shares after**	
Fin div paymnt:	n/a	**dilution:**	n/a
Int net div per share:	nil	**P/E ratio:**	n/a
Fin net div per share:	nil	**Probable CGT?**	YES

LATEST REPORTED RESULTS:	2003	PREVIOUS REPORTED RESULTS:	2002
Turnover:	£5.07m	**Turnover:**	£623,000
PTP:	£(787,000)	**PTP:**	(1.65m)
EPS:	(3.8)p	**EPS:**	(4.1)p

Comments:

Having sold its operating businesses last June, the company is currently a cash shell after 205,000 euros was ploughed into it. For the interim, pre-tax losses were 114,256 euros, which reflected the costs of disposing of its business. It is now looking to secure a reverse takeover. A further fundraising is contemplated for 2004. The directors have been behind such AIM disasters as Zoa Corporation, Future Internet Technologies and World Sport. Tread warily.

Fountains (FNT)

Environmental support services provider

PO Box 307, Malthouse Walk, Banbury, Oxon OX16 5PU Tel: 01295-750000; Fax: 01295-753253; e-mail: info@fountainsplc.com; web site: www.fountainsplc.com

		holding %
Chairman	Barry Gamble	17.0
Chief Executive	as above	
Finance Director	Doug Eadie	0.04
Exec Director	Peter Neighbour	0.02

Main Shareholders:

George McRobbie	9.9
Robert White	6.7
M Pattison	6.6
Asplundh Tree Expert	5.7
Percentage of free market capital:	52.9%

Nominated Adviser:	Collins Stewart, London
AIM Broker:	Collins Stewart, London
Solicitors:	Pinsents, Birmingham
Market Makers:	CSCS; KBCS; WINS
Auditors:	PricewaterhouseCoopers, 35 Bull St, Birmingham B4 6JT
Registrars:	Capita Registrars

ENTRY ON AIM:	19/12/1996	**Recent price:**	149.25p
Interim results:	May	**Market cap:**	£15.8m
Final results:	Nov	**Issue price:**	75.0p
Year end:	Sep	**Current no of shares:**	
Accounts due:	Dec		10,583,344
Int div paymnt:	Jul	**No of shares after**	
Fin div paymnt:	Feb	**dilution:**	10,985,024
Int net div per share:	0.85p	**P/E ratio:**	18.2
Fin net div per share:	1.92p	**Probable CGT?**	YES

LATEST REPORTED RESULTS:	2003	PREVIOUS REPORTED RESULTS:	2002
Turnover:	£35.61m	**Turnover:**	£34.49m
PTP:	£1.20m	**PTP:**	£1.03m
EPS:	8.2p	**EPS:**	9.4p

Comments:

2003 was another year of good profits and cash generation for the environmental support services outfit. Fountains also reported a £70m order book stretching to 2007 and raised the dividend 12%. At the more recent AGM, announced business wins included £2m worth of contracts for local authorities and utilities, a 1-year vegetation management deal with Yorkshire Electricity, and the renewal of a 5-year contract managing woodland owned by Southern Water.

FTV   (FTG)
Advertising space provider
22 Grosvenor Square, London, London W1K 6LF Tel: 020-7569 9065; Fax: 020-7569 9075;
e-mail: info@ftvgroup.com; web site: www.ftvgroup.com

		holding %
Chairman	Anthony Vickers	9.2
Chief Executive	Martin Johnston	0.02
Finance Director	as above	
Non-Exec Director	Alastair Gunning	0.0

Main Shareholders:

Strategic Finance (UK)	30.0
New Star Asset Management	8.1
Alasdair Locke	7.1
Michael Luckwell	4.4
Petercam Moneta Country & Sector Assets Discount	4.4

Percentage of free market capital: 29.2%

Comments:
This failed petrol station TV channel operator is now a cash shell with under £0.5m in the bank.

Nominated Adviser:	Numis, London
AIM Broker:	Numis, London
Solicitors:	Shepherd & Wedderburn, London
Market Makers:	KBCS; MLSB; NUMS; WINS
Auditors:	BDO Stoy Hayward, 69 Tweedy Rd, Bromley, Kent BR1 3WA
Registrars:	Capita Registrars

ENTRY ON AIM:	27/9/2000	**Recent price:**	1.2p
Interim results:	Mar	**Market cap:**	£0.66m
Final results:	Dec	**Issue price:**	73.0p
Year end:	Jun	**Current no of shares:**	
Accounts due:	Oct		55,056,390
Int div paymnt:	n/a	**No of shares after**	
Fin div paymnt:	n/a	**dilution:**	n/a
Int net div per share:	nil	**P/E ratio:**	n/a
Fin net div per share:	nil	**Probable CGT?**	Yes

LATEST REPORTED RESULTS: 2003		PREVIOUS REPORTED RESULTS: 2002	
Turnover:	n/a	Turnover:	n/a
PTP:	£(420,000)	PTP:	£(6.86m)
EPS:	(0.8)p	EPS:	(12.5)p

Fulcrum Pharma   (FUL)
Drug development services provider
5th Floor, Kodak House, Station Road, Hemel Hempstead, Hertfordshire HP1 1JY Tel: 01442-283600;
Fax: 01442-283613; e-mail: infomation@fulcrumpharma.com; web site: www.fulcrumpharma.com

		holding %
Chairman	Charles George	0.3
CEO	Jonathan Court	6.1
Finance Director	Geoffrey Smith	0.3
Chief Op Officer	Alastair Devlin	5.7

Main Shareholders:

Chase Nominees	10.0
Robert Miller	5.7
Gareth Walters	5.7

Percentage of free market capital: 60.3%

Comments:
A strong second half failed to prevent a full year loss for the provider of outsourcing services, such as carrying out early clinical trials, to biotechs and major drug companies. However, revenues rose 36%. Several 'step-changes', which saw staff numbers double and costs increase as offices were opened in Europe, the US and Japan, pushed the group into the red though. The group retains £3.5m cash and looks likely to exceed forecasts for the current year of £1.1m pre-tax profit and 0.6p earnings per share.

Nominated Adviser:	Seymour Pierce, London
AIM Broker:	Seymour Pierce, London
Solicitors:	Pinsents, London
Market Makers:	KBCS; MLSB; SCAP; WINS
Auditors:	PricewaterhouseCoopers, Cambridge
Registrars:	Capita Registrars

ENTRY ON AIM:	15/3/2000	**Recent price:**	8.0p
Interim results:	May	**Market cap:**	£9.75m
Final results:	Nov	**Issue price:**	33.0p
Year end:	Aug	**Current no of shares:**	
Accounts due:	Oct		121,862,320
Int div paymnt:	Jun	**No of shares after**	
Fin div paymnt:	n/a	**dilution:**	127,228,478
Int net div per share:	0.2p	**P/E ratio:**	n/a
Fin net div per share:	nil	**Probable CGT?**	Yes

LATEST REPORTED RESULTS: 2003		PREVIOUS REPORTED RESULTS: 2002	
Turnover:	£7.81m	Turnover:	£5.74m
PTP:	£(947,000)	PTP:	£1.67m
EPS:	(0.6)p	EPS:	1.4p

Fundamental-e Investments (FEI)

Computer components distributor

c/o Computer Components Marketing, Units L & M, Lyon Ind Est, Atlantic St, Altrincham, Cheshire WA14 5DH

Tel: 0161-929 9124; Fax: 0161-929 9125

		holding %
Chairman	Simon Eagle	10.0
Chief Executive		
Finance Director	Ian Ashworth	0.0
Director	Jonathan Nelson	0.0

Main Shareholders:

Winterway Investment Corporation	10.0
TW Hosier	3.0

Percentage of free market capital: 77.0%

*The beneficial owner of these shares is Nirland Limited

Comments:

Fundamental has been busy of late, moving away from distributing computer components to snapping up Purely Plasma, which intends to sell flat screens via the internet. Following the appointment of Simon Eagle as chairman the company has also made two new investments – one in Proactive Games, which acquires and distributes computer games, and the other in Europass Telecoms, a supplier of premium and discount rate telephone calls in the UK and Spain.

Nominated Adviser:	City Financial Associates, London		
AIM Broker:	City Financial Associates, London		
Solicitors:	Wacks Caller, Manchester;		
	Memery Crystal, London		
Market Makers:	SCAP; WINS		
Auditors:	BKR Haines Watts, Hale, Altrincham WA14 2UT		
Registrars:	Capita Registrars		

ENTRY ON AIM:	1/7/1998	**Recent price:**	7.0p
Interim results:	Jun	**Market cap:**	£11.55m
Final results:	Jan	**Issue price:**	10.0p
Year end:	Sep	**Current no of shares:**	
Accounts due:	Dec		165,000,000
Int div paymnt:	Jun	**No of shares after**	
Fin div paymnt:	n/a	**dilution:**	170,000,000
Int net div per share:	0.3p	**P/E ratio:**	70.0
Fin net div per share:	nil	**Probable CGT?**	YES

LATEST REPORTED RESULTS: 2003		PREVIOUS REPORTED RESULTS: 2002	
Turnover:	£9.56m	Turnover:	£13.48m
PTP:	£201,000	PTP:	£611,000
EPS:	0.1p	EPS:	0.3p

Futura Medical (FUM)

Pharmaceutical products developer specialising in sexual dysfunction

Surrey Technology Centre, 40 Occam, Surrey Research Park, Guildford, Surrey GU2 7YG Tel: 01483-685670

		holding %
Chairman	Dr William Potter	0.0
Chief Executive	James Barder	1.5
Finance Director	Anothony Claydon	0.0
Dvlpmt Director	David Davies	0.03

Main Shareholders:

Morstan Nominees	12.1
Medinvest	9.7
Christopher Crabtree	9.2
Robin Lamb	6.1

Percentage of free market capital: 61.4%

Comments:

The developer of products to combat sexual dysfunction in both men and women has completed phase II trials for its topical cream that can be rubbed onto the affected part to arouse it into action. At an earlier stage of development is a condom on which a special gel can be smeared so that the member retains maximum rigidity during intercourse. The group has an agreement with leading condom maker SSL. Cash levels remain healthy at over £4m following a series of placings.

Nominated Adviser:	Williams de Broe, London		
AIM Broker:	Williams de Broe, London		
Solicitors:	Memery Crystal, London		
Market Makers:	KBCS; WDBM; WINS		
Auditors:	BDO Stoy Hayward, Reading		
Registrars:	Capita Registrars		

ENTRY ON AIM:	22/7/2003	**Recent price:**	80.0p
Interim results:	Sep	**Market cap:**	£38.87m
Final results:	Mar	**Issue price:**	71.5p
Year end:	Dec	**Current no of shares:**	
Accounts due:	Jun		48,583,601
Int div paymnt:	n/a	**No of shares after**	
Fin div paymnt:	n/a	**dilution:**	n/a
Int net div per share:	nil	**P/E ratio:**	n/a
Fin net div per share:	nil	**Probable CGT?**	YES

LATEST REPORTED RESULTS: 2003		PREVIOUS REPORTED RESULTS: 2002	
Turnover:	n/a	Turnover:	n/a
PTP:	£(1.46m)	PTP:	£(1.24m)
EPS:	(3.2)p	EPS:	(2.7)p

Future Internet Technologies

(FTI)

Shell

Unit 3B, Farm Lane Trading Estate, 101 Farm Lane, London, SW6 1QJ Tel: 020-7381 7800; Fax: 020-7381 7801

		holding %
Chairman	Richard Armstrong	5.6
Managing Director		
Finance Director		
Non-Exec Director	Peter Redmond	2.5

Main Shareholders:

Savoy Investment Management	20.9
R.A.J. de Mendonca	5.6
Merchant House	5.3
antfactory	5.1
Exhibit SRL	5.1

Percentage of free market capital: 21.3%

Comments:

Having offloaded its software and internet services business back in August 2001 FIT remains on AIM as a shell on the look out for suitable acquisition targets. Recently a placing at 5p raised £480,000 giving the group £614,000 in all, thus enhancing its charms as an attractive cash shell. Fellow AIM concern Savoy Asset Management has picked up a 22% stake in the group, suggesting a deal may not be far away.

Nominated Adviser:	Insinger English Trust, London
AIM Broker:	Fiske, London
Solicitors:	Field Fisher Waterhouse, London
Market Makers:	KBCS; MLSB; SCAP; WINS
Auditors:	Grant Thornton, Southampton
Registrars:	Capita Registrars

ENTRY ON AIM:	28/2/2000	**Recent price:**	9.75p
Interim results:	Mar	**Market cap:**	£1.56m
Final results:	Dec	**Issue price:**	1.0p
Year end:	Jun	**Current no of shares:**	
Accounts due:	Jan		15,979,954
Int div paymnt:	n/a	**No of shares after**	
Fin div paymnt:	n/a	**dilution:**	n/a
Int net div per share:	nil	**P/E ratio:**	2.0
Fin net div per share:	nil	**Probable CGT?**	No

LATEST REPORTED RESULTS:		**PREVIOUS REPORTED RESULTS:**	
	2003		2002
Turnover:	n/a	**Turnover:**	£10,000
PTP:	£(151,000)	**PTP:**	£(2.14m)
EPS:	(5.0)p	**EPS:**	(198.9)p

Galahad Gold (formerly Galahad Capital)

(GLA)

Gold miner

39 Cornhill, London, EC3V 3RR Tel: 020-7626 4193; Fax: 020-7626 4194; e-mail: info@galahadcapital.com; web site: www.galahadcapital.com

		holding %
Chairman	Ian Watson	39.5
Managing Director	Alastair King	0.5
Finance Director	James Slater	13.8
Operations Director	Brian Mountford	6.5

Main Shareholders:

Salic Investments	17.0
Jeremy Peace's entities	3.2
Peter O'Reilly	3.0

Percentage of free market capital: 3.7%

Comments:

Galahad Gold, backed by veteran wheeler-dealer Jim Slater and his son Mark, raised pre-tax profits from £174,000 to £2.5 million last year. The company is focused on the Skaergaard gold, platinum and palladium project in Greenland and has 33.25% of Canada's Northern Dynasty Minerals, with the right to acquire Alaska's potentially massive low-grade Pebble copper and gold deposit. Highly geared to metal prices.

Nominated Adviser:	Seymour Pierce, London
AIM Broker:	Seymour Pierce, London
Solicitors:	Nicholson Graham Jones, London
Market Makers:	CSCS; SCAP; WINS
Auditors:	Rees Pollock, 7 Pilgrim Street, London EC4V 6DR
Registrars:	Neville Registrars

ENTRY ON AIM:	22/1/2001	**Recent price:**	14.75p
Interim results:	Sep	**Market cap:**	£73.52m
Final results:	Apr	**Issue price:**	10.0p
Year end:	Dec	**Current no of shares:**	
Accounts due:	Mar		498,429,167
Int div paymnt:	n/a	**No of shares after**	
Fin div paymnt:	n/a	**dilution:**	n/a
Int net div per share:	nil	**P/E ratio:**	n/a
Fin net div per share:	nil	**Probable CGT?**	No

LATEST REPORTED RESULTS:		**PREVIOUS REPORTED RESULTS:**	
	2003		2002
Turnover:	£5.02m	**Turnover:**	£990,000
PTP:	£2.53m	**PTP:**	£173,000
EPS:	2.3p	**EPS:**	0.2p

Galleon   (GON)

Content provider in multimedia broadcast and interactive software

Galleon House, 35 Hagley Road, Stourbridge, West Midlands DY8 1QR Tel: 01384-358328; Fax: 01384-358367;
e-mail: info@galleonplc.com; web site: www.galleonplc.com

		holding %
Chairman	James Driscoll	23.5
Chief Executive	Simon Driscoll	0.02
Finance Director	Keith Palmer	0.02
Non-Exec Director	Andrew Flatt	0.4

Main Shareholders:

Richard Thompson	17.2
Catherine Copestake	13.8
Kevin Bulmer	13.8
Pershing Keen	9.7
Halb Nominees	8.8
Percentage of free market capital:	12.7%

Nominated Adviser:	Nabarro Wells, London
AIM Broker:	S.P. Angel, London
Solicitors:	DLA, Birmingham
Market Makers:	WINS
Auditors:	Grant Thornton, 32-34 Queens Road, Coventry, CV1 3FJ
Registrars:	Computershare Investor Services

Entry on AIM:	29/1/2001	**Recent price:**	1.0p
Interim results:	Dec	**Market cap:**	£7.92m
Final results:	Sep	**Issue price:**	1.0p
Year end:	Mar	**Current no of shares:**	
Accounts due:	Oct		792,471,719
Int div paymnt:	n/a	**No of shares after**	
Fin div paymnt:	n/a	dilution:	n/a
Int net div per share:	nil	P/E ratio:	n/a
Fin net div per share:	nil	Probable CGT?	Yes

Comments:

This intellectual property group owns the rights to a range of children's characters, including shortly-to-be-premiered Astro Knights and Pepper's Patrol, developed in association with Coolebah, a company chaired by ex-Gullane CEO William Harris. Another asset is the 'Oggies'. The group recently issued 'innovative' television production bonds of at least £0.5m to fund the first 13 episodes of this series. The half time numbers showed losses of £609,000 on sales of £329,000.

LATEST REPORTED RESULTS:	2003	PREVIOUS REPORTED RESULTS:	2002
Turnover:	£1.21m	Turnover:	£277,000
PTP:	£(8.83m)	PTP:	£(812,000)
EPS:	(1.1)p	EPS:	(0.3)p

Looking for the right advisers to help you grow your business?

Choosing the right advisers is important for any business leader. With the right advisers, you are more likely to raise capital when required and successfully negotiate the various steps of your growth plan.

www.growthbusiness.co.uk is a new website from Vitesse Media, publishers of Business XL. It specifically helps you appoint the best advisers and target the most appropriate venture capitalists for you and your business.

The site is free to access and enables you to:

- View comprehensive directories of all AIM and OFEX advisers and venture capitalists
- Study all the Aim, Ofex and VC deals as they happen
- Search all deals by type, sector and amount raised
- Find contact details for all key individuals that have worked on each deal
- Use our unique Deals Barometer to view the current climate for raising money
- Sign up for our fortnightly bulletin, Deal Alert

152

Gaming Corporation   (GMC)

Online gaming company

2nd Floor, The Plaza, 535 King's Road, Chelsea, London, SW10 0SZ Tel: 020-7349 4300; Fax: 020-7349 4310;
e-mail: justindrummond@gamingcorp.net; web site: www.gamingcorp.net

		holding %
Chairman	Justin Drummond	15.5
Chief Executive	as above	
Finance Director	Peter Williams	3.2
Director	Charles Black	3.9

Main Shareholders:

Barnard Nominees	16.3
Pershing Keen Nominees	11.2
Clydesdale Bank Custodian Nominees	9.4
Boss Media AB	5.1

Percentage of free market capital: 30.4%

Comments:

Originally set up to acquire defunct internet incubators, the group is now building up an online casino in collaboration with leading gaming software group Boss, using its profitable casino.co.uk website. Another successful venture is TV listings software package onthebox. When issuing finals, which saw turnover rise tenfold, the group also raised £520,000 from directors possibly to fund future acquisitions. If this organic growth continues a profit may be made this year.

Nominated Adviser:	Evolution Beeson Gregory, London		
AIM Broker:	Evolution Beeson Gregory, London		
Solicitors:	Hardwick Stallards, London		
Market Makers:	KBCS; SCAP; WINS		
Auditors:	Gerald Edelman, 25 Harley way, London W1G 9BR		
Registrars:	Capita Registrars		

ENTRY ON AIM: 23/10/2000		**Recent price:**	2.5p
Interim results:	May	**Market cap:**	£3.37m
Final results:	Nov	**Issue price:**	10.0p
Year end:	Sep	**Current no of shares:**	
Accounts due:	Dec		134,802,054
Int div paymnt:	n/a	**No of shares after**	
Fin div paymnt:	n/a	**dilution:**	n/a
Int net div per share:	nil	**P/E ratio:**	n/a
Fin net div per share:	nil	**Probable CGT?**	YES

LATEST REPORTED RESULTS: 2003		PREVIOUS REPORTED RESULTS: 2002	
Turnover:	£8.60m	Turnover:	£843,000
PTP:	£(734,000)	PTP:	£(2.51m)
EPS:	1.0p	EPS:	(5.3)p

Gaming Insight   (GIN)

Internet-based games operator

22 Soho Square, London, W1D 4NS Tel: 020-7070 7280; Fax: 020-7070 7240;
e-mail: l.alabaster@ginplc.com; web site: www.gaminginsight.com

		holding %
Chairman	Nigel Robertson	13.2
Chief Executive		
Finance Director	Haresh Kanabar	0.0
Non-Exec Director	David Warren	
		0.0

Main Shareholders:

Richard Kay	30.5
The Strawberry Fund	26.2
Highland Capital	10.5
Lansdowne Partners	9.7
Sporting Resorts	3.1

Percentage of free market capital: 6.8%

Comments:

Gaming Insight has had a dire recent history, culminating in the wind up of interactive greyhound racing subsidiary Gobarkingmad last summer. Now it is scouring for new businesses in the same sector – its future depends on finding a new strategy and finding funding to follow it through. The company fiinally published its 2002 accounts and its interims June 2003. The interims showed pre-tax losses of £2.1m (£6.2m loss), and a lower turnover of £2.1m (£7.8m).

Nominated Adviser:	Seymour Pierce, London		
AIM Broker:	Seymour Pierce, London		
Solicitors:	Berwin Leighton Paisner, London		
Market Makers:	ARBT; MLSB; SCAP; WINS		
Auditors:	Grant Thornton, London		
Registrars:	Capita Registrars		

Entry on AIM:	10/1/2000	**Recent price:**	0.4p
Interim results:	Sep	**Market cap:**	£3.31m
Final results:	Jun	**Issue price:**	6.0p
Year end:	Dec	**Current no of shares:**	
Accounts due:	Apr		827,029,839
Int div paymnt:	n/a	**No of shares after**	
Fin div paymnt:	n/a	**dilution:**	n/a
Int net div per share:	nil	**P/E ratio:**	n/a
Fin net div per share:	nil	**Probable CGT?**	YES

LATEST REPORTED RESULTS: 2002		PREVIOUS REPORTED RESULTS: 2001	
Turnover:	£12.34m	Turnover:	£12.99m
PTP:	£(13.82m)	PTP:	£(19.68m)
EPS:	(4.1)p	EPS:	(9.1)p

Gamingking (GGK)

Lottery and gaming company

Cedar House, Hainault Business Park, 56-57 Peregrine Rd, Hainault, Essex IG6 3SZ Tel: 020-8501 5511;
Fax: 020-8509 8114; e-mail: admin@thebiz.co.uk; web site: www.thebiz.co.uk

		holding %
Chairman	Leslie R Hurst	14.7
Chief Executive	Nick Watkins	1.0
Finance Director	Guy van Zwanenberg	0.8
Managing Director	Brian A Nichols	6.5

Main Shareholders:

Alan Stack	17.5
Barry Stack	10.9

Percentage of free market capital: 48.1%

Nominated Adviser:	Smith & Williamson, London
AIM Broker:	Evolution Beeson Gregory, London
Solicitors:	Mayer, Brown, Rowe & Maw, London
Market Makers:	MLSB; SCAP; WINS
Auditors:	Grant Thornton, London
Registrars:	Capita Registrars

ENTRY ON AIM:	11/7/1996	Recent price:	2.0p
Interim results:	Dec	Market cap:	£5.06m
Final results:	Jul	Issue price:	3.0p
Year end:	Apr	Current no of shares:	
Accounts due:	Aug		253,017,391
Int div paymnt:	n/a	No of shares after	
Fin div paymnt:	n/a	dilution:	n/a
Int net div per share:	nil	P/E ratio:	n/a
Fin net div per share:	nil	Probable CGT?	YES

Comments:

This leisure group, formerly known as TheBiz.com, specialises in lotteries for private members, clubs. It has a total of 3000 machines installed at its customers' sites and has ambitions of launching a complementary website offering. The interim results showed turnover increasing 49% to £1.36m and losses before tax of £60,000. Management continue to search for 'business development opportunities'.

LATEST REPORTED RESULTS:	2003	PREVIOUS REPORTED RESULTS:	2002
Turnover:	£2.16m	Turnover:	£1.69m
PTP:	£(162,000)	PTP:	£(138,000)
EPS:	(0.0)p	EPS:	(0.1)p

General Industries (GNI)

Investment company

56 Station Road, Egham, Surrey TW20 9LF Tel: 017-8443 7444

		holding %
Chairman	Richard Wollenberg	16.7
Chief Executive		
Finance Director	Anthony Shakesby	1.4
Non-Exec Director	Ian Reynolds	14.3

Main Shareholders:

The Cardiff Property Company	9.5

Percentage of free market capital: 55.2%

Nominated Adviser:	KBC Peel Hunt, London
AIM Broker:	KBC Peel Hunt, London
Solicitors:	Morgan Cole, London
Market Makers:	KBCS; WINS
Auditors:	KPMG, Cardiff
Registrars:	Computershare Investor Services

ENTRY ON AIM:	28/10/2003	Recent price:	36.25p
Interim results:	n/a	Market cap:	£1.52m
Final results:	n/a	Issue price:	25.0p
Year end:	n/a	Current no of shares:	
Accounts due:	n/a		4,200,000
Int div paymnt:	n/a	No of shares after	
Fin div paymnt:	n/a	dilution:	n/a
Int net div per share:	nil	P/E ratio:	n/a
Fin net div per share:	nil	Probable CGT?	No

Comments:

This is the latest shell company of Cardiff property entrepreneur Richard Wollenberg, who reversed social housing consultancy Hacas into a previous shell. The company is seeking an unquoted business that wants to make the most of a public quote to grow rapidly by paper-based acquisition. However, the current set of directors plan to take an active role in any investment made. Wollenberg hopes to complete a deal within three years. The float raised £510,000 net.

LATEST REPORTED RESULTS:	N/A	PREVIOUS REPORTED RESULTS:	N/A
Turnover:	n/a	Turnover:	n/a
PTP:	n/a	PTP:	n/a
EPS:	n/a	EPS:	n/a

Genus (GNS)

Agricultural technology and service provider

Alpha Buildings, London Road, Nantwich, Cheshire CW5 7JW Tel: 01270-616616; Fax: 01270-616702;
e-mail: investor.relations@genus-plc.co.uk; web site: www.genusplc.com

		holding %
Chairman	John Beckett	0.2
Chief Executive	Richard Wood	0.2
Finance Director	Michael Roller	0.0
Non-Exec Director	Edwin White	0.1

Main Shareholders:

NFU Mutual	18.9

Percentage of free market capital: 80.6%

Nominated Adviser:	Bridgewell, Manchester
AIM Broker:	Panmure Gordon, London
Solicitors:	DLA, London
Market Makers:	KBCS; TEAM; WINS
Auditors:	Ernst & Young, 100 Barbirolli Square, Manchester, M2 3EY
Registrars:	Lloyds TSB Registrars

ENTRY ON AIM:	6/7/2000	**Recent price:**	188.5p
Interim results:	Nov	**Market cap:**	£66.3m
Final results:	May	**Issue price:**	180.0p
Year end:	Mar	**Current no of shares:**	
Accounts due:	Jul		35,173,374
Int div paymnt:	n/a	**No of shares after**	
Fin div paymnt:	Aug	**dilution:**	n/a
Int net div per share:	nil	**P/E ratio:**	22.7
Fin net div per share:	5.50p	**Probable CGT?**	YES

LATEST REPORTED RESULTS:		PREVIOUS REPORTED RESULTS:	
	2003		2002
Turnover:	£172.79m	Turnover:	£160.42m
PTP:	£5.14m	PTP:	£2.95m
EPS:	8.3p	EPS:	1.7p

Comments:
The well-regarded international bovine genetics play reported a 12% profits fall to £4.5m in the first half to September. This was caused by some depressed agricultural markets – the USA and Australia came in for particular mention – and a late selling season for Bovine Genetics this year. Turnover improved 14% to £93.5m. Because of the late selling season, net debt burgeoned by £4.7m to £16.9m, giving gearing of 35%. The board expects trading to improve in the second half.

Georgica (GGA)

Sports bars, leisure site and fast food restaurant operator and tenpin operator

8 Clarendon Drive, Wymbush, Milton Keynes, MK8 8ED Tel: 01908-208020; Fax: 01908-208021

		holding %
Chairman	Don Hanson	0.6
Chief Executive	Nicholas Oppenheim	0.5
Finance Director	Peter Haspel	0.0
Director	Clive Preston	0.6

Main Shareholders:

Schroder Investment Management	19.9
M&G Investment Management	11.2
Fidelity Investment	10.0
UBS Global	7.2
Insight Investment	4.6

Percentage of free market capital: 45.3%

Nominated Adviser:	Panmure Gordon, London
AIM Broker:	Panmure Gordon, London & Investec, London
Solicitors:	Herbert Smith, London
Market Makers:	CHMM; IHCS; MLSB; WEST; WINS
Auditors:	Deloitte & Touche, London
Registrars:	Capita Registrars

ENTRY ON AIM:	9/10/2000	**Recent price:**	89.5p
Interim results:	Sep	**Market cap:**	£88.74m
Final results:	Mar	**Issue price:**	n/a
Year end:	Dec	**Current no of shares:**	
Accounts due:	Apr		99,150,000
Int div paymnt:	n/a	**No of shares after**	
Fin div paymnt:	n/a	**dilution:**	n/a
Int net div per share:	nil	**P/E ratio:**	n/a
Fin net div per share:	nil	**Probable CGT?**	YES

LATEST REPORTED RESULTS:		PREVIOUS REPORTED RESULTS:	
	2003		2002
Turnover:	£96.25m	Turnover:	£83.86m
PTP:	£(7.49m)	PTP:	£(11.25m)
EPS:	(9.7)p	EPS:	(14.8)p

Comments:
Georgica is making gradual progress as its Rileys pool and snooker bars and Cue Sports businesses are trading well. It has also ended its 'unfortunate joint venture' with Duke Street Capital by buying the half of troubled Megabow, Duke owned for £1 plus £22.7m in debts. Megabowl still has £52.4m debts overall but the company expects to turn the venture around and make a profit this year. Gloucester's Megabowl suffered a fire over Christmas, but will reopen by the end of 2004.

Gippsland (GIP)

Natural resources developer

Suite 34, Level 2, 18 Stirling Highway, Nedlands, WA 6009 Australia; web site: www.gippslandltd.com.au

		holding %
Chairman	Robert Telford	0.0
Chief Executive		
Finance Director		
Exec Director	John Kenny	0.0

Main Shareholders:

Situate	8.1
Eco International	8.0
King Town Holdings	4.7
Sandstone Securities	4.4
Taveroam	4.2

Percentage of free market capital: 66.9%

Comments:

The first Aussie company joining AIM via its 'fast track' route, Gippsland, run by entrepreneur Jack Telford, has two tantalum and feldspar projects in Egypt, with possibly 138m tonnes of ore, at Abu Dabbab and Muweibi. Telford says Gippsland, which lost an interim £727,000, needs £28m, mostly debt, to take Abu Dabbab to production and sees payback in three years.

Nominated Adviser:	Grant Thornton, London
AIM Broker:	Hoodless Brennan, London
Solicitors:	Blakiston & Crabb, Australia
Market Makers:	WINS
Auditors:	Grant Thornton, Perth WA
Registrars:	Computershare Investor Services

ENTRY ON AIM:	9/3/2004	Recent price:	3.75p
Interim results:	Mar	Market cap:	£5.23m
Final results:	Sep	Issue price:	n/a
Year end:	Jun	**Current no of shares:**	
Accounts due:	Oct		139,528,359
Int div paymnt:	n/a	**No of shares after**	
Fin div paymnt:	n/a	dilution:	n/a
Int net div per share:	nil	P/E ratio:	n/a
Fin net div per share:	nil	Probable CGT?	No

LATEST REPORTED RESULTS: 2003		PREVIOUS REPORTED RESULTS: 2002	
Turnover:	£9.58m	Turnover:	£5.17m
PTP:	£(755,000)	PTP:	£(606,000)
EPS:	(0.8)p	EPS:	(0.8)p

Gladstone (GLD)

Supplier of software to the health & fitness industry

Hithercroft Road, Wallingford, Oxfordshire OX10 9BT Tel: 01491-201010; Fax: 01491-201020;
e-mail: info@gladstonemrm.com; web site: www.gladstoneplc.com

		holding %
Chairman	Simon Preston	2.1
Chief Executive	Ben Merrett	1.1
Finance Director		
Non-Exec Director	Jeremy Stokes	16.7

Main Shareholders:

Mr Guiver	5.7
Nutraco Nominees	5.5
BNY (OCS) Nominees	3.3
Pershing Keen Nominees	3.2

Percentage of free market capital: 56.8%

Comments:

Gladstone continues to impress, having moved from loss to profit last year. Unusually, this maiden profit was achieved in spite of an 8% revenue reduction, attributed by chief executive Ben Merrett to reduced sales of low-margin hardware. The company's plan to switch clients away from outright software purchasing and towards a leasing model (reducing up-front turnover but increasing stability) also appears to have paid off with rental revenues now accounting for 37% of all sales.

Nominated Adviser:	Brewin Dolphin, London
AIM Broker:	Brewin Dolphin, London
Solicitors:	Addleshaw Goddard, London
Market Makers:	BGMM; KBCS; MLSB; SCAP; WINS
Auditors:	Hacker Young, London
Registrars:	Capita Registrars

ENTRY ON AIM:	28/5/2002	Recent price:	14.25p
Interim results:	Feb	Market cap:	£6.22m
Final results:	Dec	Issue price:	7.75p
Year end:	Jun	**Current no of shares:**	
Accounts due:	Sept		43,616,996
Int div paymnt:	n/a	**No of shares after**	
Fin div paymnt:	n/a	dilution:	n/a
Int net div per share:	nil	P/E ratio:	28.5
Fin net div per share:	nil	Probable CGT?	Yes

LATEST REPORTED RESULTS: 2003		PREVIOUS REPORTED RESULTS: 2002	
Turnover:	£7.94m	Turnover:	£8.6m
PTP:	£184,000	PTP:	£(1.75m)
EPS:	0.5p	EPS:	(4.5)p

Glisten (GLI)

Confectionery manufacturer

Hill Street, Blackburn, Lancashire BB1 3HG Tel: 01254-266300; Fax: 01254-266330;
e-mail: enquiries@glisten.uk.com; web site: www.glisten.uk.com

		holding %
Chairman	Jeremy Hamer	4.6
Chief Executive	Paul Simmonds	8.0
Finance Director	Robert Davies	0.2

Main Shareholders:

Artemis AIM VCT	9.8
Unicorn Asset Management	8.9
BWD AIM VCT	6.6
Menton Investments	6.4
New Star Asset Management	5.5

Percentage of free market capital: 29.3%

Comments:

The acquisitive food manufacturer served up tasty interims to 31 December, with profits sweetening up 11.5% to £950,000 on an 11% turnover hike to £9.4m. Recent acquisitions include Sunya, a maker of foiled wrapped chocolate balls and eggs, wine gum and fruit pastilles business Fravigar, and boiled sweets business Penguin. Sales in the first nine weeks of the second half were up 18% on last year. The house broker predicts full year profits of £1.82m on £21m sales.

Nominated Adviser:	Charles Stanley, London
AIM Broker:	Charles Stanley, London
Solicitors:	Eversheds, Leeds
Market Makers:	MLSB; WINS
Auditors:	PKF, Pannell House, 6 Queen Street, Leeds LS1 2TW
Registrars:	Capita Registrars

ENTRY ON AIM:	28/6/2002	**Recent price:**	286.0p
Interim results:	Mar	**Market cap:**	£26.0m
Final results:	Sep	**Issue price:**	80.0p
Year end:	Jun	**Current no of shares:**	
Accounts due:	Oct		9,090,018
Int div paymnt:	n/a	**No of shares after**	
Fin div paymnt:	n/a	**dilution:**	n/a
Int net div per share:	nil	**P/E ratio:**	34.5
Fin net div per share:	nil	**Probable CGT?**	YES

LATEST REPORTED RESULTS: 2003		PREVIOUS REPORTED RESULTS: 2002 PRO FORMA	
Turnover:	£15.59m	Turnover:	£14.26m
PTP:	£1.06m	PTP:	£1.17m
EPS:	8.3p	EPS:	n/a

Global Energy Development (GED)

Oil & gas producer and explorer

580 WestLake Park Boulevard, Suite 750, Houston, Texas, 77079 Tel: 00-1 281 504-6400; Fax: 00-1 281 504-6450;
e-mail: webmaster@globalenergyplc.com; web site: www.globalenergyplc.com

		holding %
Chairman	Mikel Faulkner	0.3
Managing Director	Stephen Voss	0.035
Finance Director		
Non-Exec Director	David Quint	0.1

Main Shareholders:

Delaware	93.9

Percentage of free market capital: 5.7%

Comments:

A subsidiary of controversial US oil group Harken Energy, Global, which scored an interim turnaround from a £244,000 loss to £199,000 profits, has production and exploration interests in Colombia, Costa Rica and Peru. The company, whose past performance has been mixed, has previously swapped shares with New Opportunities Investment Trust and claimed net assets of nearly £20m. The tightly-held shares are an illiquid market.

Nominated Adviser:	RP & C International, London
AIM Broker:	Canaccord Capital, London
Solicitors:	Norton Rose, London
Market Makers:	KBCS; SCAP; WINS
Auditors:	Ernst & Young, London
Registrars:	Capita Registrars

ENTRY ON AIM:	25/3/2002	**Recent price:**	45.5p
Interim results:	Sep	**Market cap:**	£12.73m
Final results:	Apr	**Issue price:**	50.0p
Year end:	Dec	**Current no of shares:**	
Accounts due:	Apr		27,971,831
Int div paymnt:	n/a	**No of shares after**	
Fin div paymnt:	n/a	**dilution:**	31,642,746
Int net div per share:	nil	**P/E ratio:**	n/a
Fin net div per share:	nil	**Probable CGT?**	No

LATEST REPORTED RESULTS: 2002		PREVIOUS REPORTED RESULTS: 2001	
Turnover:	$7.62m	Turnover:	$8.29m
PTP:	$(1.91m)	PTP:	$(15.75m)
EPS:	(0.1)c	EPS:	n/a

Glow Communications (GLW)

Telecoms reseller via affinity partners

20A The Coda Centre, 189 Munster Road, London, SW6 6AW Tel: 020-7385 2340; Fax: 020-7385 2579;
e-mail: glowtelecom.com

		holding %
Chairman	Duncan Hickman	0.0
Chief Executive	as above	
Finance Director	Graeme Cummings	0.0
Director of Business Development	Derek Griffiths	0.9

Main Shareholders:

Curran Holdings	13.6
Belgravia	12.7
J M Finn	11.2
The Bank of New York	7.2
R C Greig Nominees	4.2

Percentage of free market capital: 42.9%

Comments:

Loss-making Glow, the telecoms marketing affinity company, recently sold non-core Primary storage to ex-director Terry Boland for £1. Indeed, the company has been financially restructuring itself and issued 74m shares, which equares to 12.7% of its issued share capita,l to telecoms investment group Belgravia. Combined with a 2.5m share option exercise and issuing 7.1m shares to Gem Global Yield Fund, in four months it diluted shareholders by 16.6%.

Nominated Adviser:	Grant Thornton, London		
AIM Broker:	Durlacher, London		
Solicitors:	Clarke Willmott & Clarke, Southampton		
Market Makers:	ARBT; MLSB; SCAP; WINS		
Auditors:	PricewaterhouseCoopers, Birmingham		
Registrars:	Capita Registrars		

ENTRY ON AIM: 19/10/2000		**Recent price:**	1.25p
Interim results:	Aug	**Market cap:**	£7.38m
Final results:	Apr	**Issue price:**	3.0p
Year end:	Nov	**Current no of shares:**	
Accounts due:	Mar		590,594,489
Int div paymnt:	n/a	**No of shares after**	
Fin div paymnt:	n/a	**dilution:**	612,219,572
Int net div per share:	nil	**P/E ratio:**	n/a
Fin net div per share:	nil	**Probable CGT?**	YES

LATEST REPORTED RESULTS: 2002		PREVIOUS REPORTED RESULTS: 2001	
Turnover:	£8.35m	Turnover:	£5.08m
PTP:	£(4.13m)	PTP:	£(3.53m)
EPS:	(0.8)p	EPS:	(0.7)p

GMA Resources (GMA)

Gold miner & explorer

Fraser House, 29 Albermarle Street, London, W1S 4JB

		holding %
Chairman	Richard Linnell	4.2
Chief Executive	Colin Ikin	40.1
Finance Director	Simon Farrell	0.0
Technical Director	Simon Bunn	4.5

Main Shareholders:

Behan	17.0
MOBFI SA	9.0
Sahara Investment	9.0
Golden Valley Mines	7.2
Carmignac Gestion	4.4

Percentage of free market capital: 4.6%

Comments:

Hoping to develop partly-privatised Saharan gold assets in Algeria, GMA, which lost £408,300 from February to June last year, won initial favour with its Amesmessa and Tirek projects. The company, which launched a £3.35m placing at 25p in October, says it could take £10m to develop them with its partner Sonatrach. GMA puts potential resources at four million oz. Preliminary drilling results showed grades from 0.57 to 53 grammes a tonne.

Nominated Adviser:	Canaccord Capital, London		
AIM Broker:	Canaccord Capital, London		
Solicitors:	Field Fisher Waterhouse, London		
Market Makers:	EVO; SCAP; WINS		
Auditors:	Grant Thornton, Crawley		
Registrars:	Capita Registrars		

ENTRY ON AIM: 14/5/2003		**Recent price:**	27.0p
Interim results:	Oct	**Market cap:**	£30.72m
Final results:	Mar	**Issue price:**	1.0p
Year end:	Dec	**Current no of shares:**	
Accounts due:	Apr		113,788,522
Int div paymnt:	n/a	**No of shares after**	
Fin div paymnt:	n/a	**dilution:**	n/a
Int net div per share:	nil	**P/E ratio:**	n/a
Fin net div per share:	nil	**Probable CGT?**	NO

LATEST REPORTED RESULTS: 9 MONTHS TO 30 SEP 2002		PREVIOUS REPORTED RESULTS: 2001	
Turnover:	£2.44m	Turnover:	£773,000
PTP:	£(1.18m)	PTP:	£(859,000)
EPS:	n/a	EPS:	n/a

Gold Mines of Sardinia (GMN)

Gold explorer and developer in Sardinia

The Little House, Quenington, Cirencester, Gloucestershire GL7 5BW Tel: 01285-750001; Fax: 01285-750002;
e-mail: enquiries@gmslimited.co.uk; web site: www.gmslimited.co.uk

		holding %
Chairman	Jon Pither	0.2
Chief Executive	John C Morris	3.6
Finance Director		
Non-Exec Director	John Chappell	0.4

Main Shareholders:

Arrow Resources	20.2
Lehman Brothers International	3.6

Percentage of free market capital: 71.2%

Nominated Adviser:	Williams de Broe, London
AIM Broker:	Williams de Broe, London
Solicitors:	Fox Brooks Marshall, Manchester
Market Makers:	KBCS; MLSB; SGSL; WINS
Auditors:	Ernst & Young, 152-158 St George's Terrace, Perth, Aus
Registrars:	Capita Registrars

ENTRY ON AIM:	20/6/1996	Recent price:	1.5p
Interim results:	Sep	Market cap:	£4.12m
Final results:	Mar	Issue price:	0.3p
Year end:	Dec	Current no of shares:	
Accounts due:	Apr		274,350,555
Int div paymnt:	n/a	No of shares after	
Fin div paymnt:	n/a	dilution:	n/a
Int net div per share:	nil	P/E ratio:	n/a
Fin net div per share:	nil	Probable CGT?	No

Comments:
Gold Mines of Sardinia has only a vestigial AIM presence after combining its operating assets with Canada's Full Riches Investment to form Medoro Resources. GMS holders took one Medoro share for each GMS one. The hope is that Full Riches director Serafino Iacono will be better able than the GFMS team to overcome political obstacles clogging progess at its Furtei mine in Sardinia.

LATEST REPORTED RESULTS: 2002		PREVIOUS REPORTED RESULTS: 2001	
Turnover:	£4.38m	Turnover:	£5.79m
PTP:	£(5.77m)	PTP:	£(2.69m)
EPS:	(2.2)p	EPS:	(1.0)p

Golden Prospect (GOL)

Mining investor

138 Park Lane, London, W1K 7AS Tel: 020-7409 3500; Fax: 020-7409 3507

		holding %
Chairman	Malcolm Burne	0.5
Chief Executive		
Finance Director	Nathan Steinberg	0.0
Non-Exec Director	Richard Lockwood	1.4

Main Shareholders:

AMVESCAP	16.8
Scottish Widows Investment	10.8
Clontary Investments	6.2
Perilya	4.6
S Cawkwell & family	4.2

Percentage of free market capital: 54.7%

Nominated Adviser:	Grant Thornton, London
AIM Broker:	Fiske, London
Solicitors:	Stringer Saul, London
Market Makers:	SCAP; WINS
Auditors:	Grant Thornton, Southampton
Registrars:	Melton Registrars

ENTRY ON AIM:	19/2/1999	Recent price:	34.5p
Interim results:	Sep	Market cap:	£30.84m
Final results:	Jun	Issue price:	29.5p
Year end:	Dec	Current no of shares:	
Accounts due:	Jul		89,384,958
Int div paymnt:	n/a	No of shares after	
Fin div paymnt:	n/a	dilution:	90,284,958
Int net div per share:	nil	P/E ratio:	172.5
Fin net div per share:	nil	Probable CGT?	No

Comments:
The company holds quoted and – jointly with Mano River and Jubilee Platinum – unquoted junior mining shares, with Australians prominent. These have fared well for the company, which made a reduced £329,500 interim profit. Only Bullion Resources has been a problem for Golden Prospect, which recently bought into fellow AIM counter Eurasia Mining. The shares have been trading at 20% below claimed assets of 43p.

LATEST REPORTED RESULTS: 2002		PREVIOUS REPORTED RESULTS: 2001	
Turnover:	£4.52m	Turnover:	£1.91m
PTP:	£240,000	PTP:	£274,000
EPS:	0.2p	EPS:	0.3p

Gooch & Housego (GHH)

Precision optical component manufacturer

The Old Magistrates Court, Ilminster, Somerset TA19 0AB Tel: 01460-52271; Fax: 01460-54972;
e-mail: avirgin@goochandhousego.com; web site: www.goochandhousego.com

		holding %
Chairman	Archie Gooch	6.4
Chief Executive	Gareth Jones	0.04
Finance Director	Ian Bayer	0.1
Non-Exec Director	JA Melles	0.1

Main Shareholders:

Gooch/Virgin Discretionary Trust	16.7
Heather Virgin	15.2
Active Capital Trust	8.6
David Irish	5.6

Percentage of free market capital: 47.4%

Nominated Adviser:	Rowan Dartington, London
AIM Broker:	Rowan Dartington, London
Solicitors:	Burges Salmon, Bristol
Market Makers:	SCAP; WINS
Auditors:	PricewaterhouseCoopers, Bristol BS1 5QD
Registrars:	Capita Registrars

ENTRY ON AIM: 12/12/1997	Recent price:	103.25p
Interim results:	Jun	Market cap:	£18.58m
Final results:	Dec	Issue price:	105.0p
Year end:	Sep	Current no of shares:	
Accounts due:	Jan		17,999,162
Int div paymnt:	Jul	No of shares after	
Fin div paymnt:	Feb	dilution:	n/a
Int net div per share:	1.1p	P/E ratio:	14.1
Fin net div per share:	2.0p	Probable CGT?	Yes

Comments:

The acousto-optic and electro-optic device maker grew profits 8.4% last year despite tough markets and a falling dollar – two thirds of sales are won in the US. Each of its four companies made positive contributions, with Optronic Laboratories, an optical instrumentation business, returning to profit. Gooch & Housego's single most important product is the Q-switch, which turns a laser into an industrial tool, holding up power and then unleashing it at a far greater force.

LATEST REPORTED RESULTS: 2003		PREVIOUS REPORTED RESULTS: 2002	
Turnover:	£15.91m	Turnover:	£15.59m
PTP:	£2.19m	PTP:	£2.02m
EPS:	7.3p	EPS:	7.0p

GR (GRH)

Leisure, hotel, land & property investor

6 Sloane Square, London, SW1W 8EE Tel: 020-7730 8799; Fax: 020-7730 7273

		holding %
Chairman	AD Stalbow	0.0
Chief Executive		
Finance Director		
Director	JA Stalbow	0.0

Main Shareholders:

A Stanford & Co	75.1
Mrs Z Pomson	8.2
M Cohen	7.7

Percentage of free market capital: 9.0%

Nominated Adviser:	Evolution Beeson Gregory, London
AIM Broker:	Evolution Beeson Gregory, London
Solicitors:	Eversheds, London
Market Makers:	WINS
Auditors:	Gerald Kreditor, Llanvanor Rd, London NW2 2AQ
Registrars:	Lloyds TSB Registrars

ENTRY ON AIM: 5/8/1997	Recent price:	50.0p
Interim results:	Mar	Market cap:	£6.58m
Final results:	Nov	Issue price:	n/a
Year end:	Jun	Current no of shares:	
Accounts due:	Oct		13,168,100
Int div paymnt:	n/a	No of shares after	
Fin div paymnt:	n/a	dilution:	n/a
Int net div per share:	nil	P/E ratio:	n/a
Fin net div per share:	nil	Probable CGT?	No

Comments:

GR is the quiet, loss-making conglomerate that never gives investors any more than the bare bones of its news. The company operates Grayshott Hall Health Fitness Retreat and sells Morlands footwear and sheepskin car rugs. In its last financial year, pre-tax losses widened despite a rise in turnover driven by better occupancy at Grayshott. Net cash improved. Turnover at Morlands fell by 15%. Since the end of the year, trading has deteriorated.

LATEST REPORTED RESULTS: 2003		PREVIOUS REPORTED RESULTS: 2002	
Turnover:	£4.66m	Turnover:	£4.41m
PTP:	£(164,000)	PTP:	£(118,000)
EPS:	(2.5)p	EPS:	(2.0)p

Greenchip Investments (GRE)

Holding company for an early-stage technology venture

138 Park Lane, London, W1K 7AS Tel: 020-7409 3500; Fax: 020-7409 3507; web site: www.greenchip.co.uk

		holding %
Chairman	Colin Hill	0.0
Chief Executive	Robert Downie	0.0
Non-Exec Director	Malcolm Burne	1.8

Main Shareholders:

Arlington	30.0
New Opportunities Investment Trust	15.6
Capita Trust	12.1
Robert Downie	7.7
EBC Security Services	4.6

Percentage of free market capital: 20.3%

Comments:

Greenchip finally gave up the investment company ghost in 2003 – offloading its only interest, in loss-making degradable plastics business Programmable Life, in November after failing to secure a sufficient level of development funding. All of the company's other subsidiaries have since been sold (for a nominal figure), as have the company's warrants in the New Opportunities Investment Trust. Possible reverse takeover targets are now being sought.

Nominated Adviser:	Grant Thornton, London
AIM Broker:	Fiske, London
Solicitors:	Faegre Benson Hobson Audley, London
Market Makers:	KBCS; WINS
Auditors:	FW Smith Riches & Co, London
Registrars:	Melton Registrars

Entry on AIM: 30/10/2000	**Recent price:**	1.5p
Interim results: Sep	**Market cap:**	£2.4m
Final results: May	**Issue price:**	n/a
Year end: Dec	**Current no of shares:**	
Accounts due: Jun		160,281,597
Int div paymnt: n/a	**No of shares after**	
Fin div paymnt: n/a	**dilution:**	163,781,597
Int net div per share: nil	**P/E ratio:**	n/a
Fin net div per share: nil	**Probable CGT?**	Yes

LATEST REPORTED RESULTS: 2003		PREVIOUS REPORTED RESULTS: 2002	
Turnover:	£58.17m	Turnover:	£80.86m
PTP:	£(40,000)	PTP:	£(5.14m)
EPS:	(0.0)p	EPS:	(3.7)p

Griffin (formerly Cater Barnard (USA)) (GFF)

Financial company

17 State Street, New York, 10004 US

		holding %
Chairman	Stephen Dean	19.4
Chief Executive	Adrian Stecyk	24.0
Finance Director	Vince Nicholls	0.0
Director	Chrystyna Bedrij	0.9

Main Shareholders:

Michal Garvin	6.7

Percentage of free market capital: 25.4%

Comments:

The coporate financial adviser has interests on both sides of the Atlantic and wants to build up its research capabilities in order to win new business under the Griffin banner. Most recently the group has focused on biotech companies, where it aims to organise fund raisings of up to $10m, charging 10% commission in cash plus 10% in warrants. Stephen Dean was in charge at building group Artisan before he was ousted. A placing raised £140,000 to pay for the cost of the company graduating from Ofex.

Nominated Adviser:	Beaumont Cornish, London
AIM Broker:	Seymour Pierce Ellis, London
Solicitors:	Bechcroft Wansbroughs, London
Market Makers:	KBCS; SCAP; WINS
Auditors:	Spokes & Company, Kent
Registrars:	Capita Registrars

Entry on AIM: 12/12/2003	**Recent price:**	5.5p
Interim results: Jun	**Market cap:**	£1.84m
Final results: Dec	**Issue price:**	n/a
Year end: Sep	**Current no of shares:**	
Accounts due: Mar		33,483,629
Int div paymnt: n/a	**No of shares after**	
Fin div paymnt: n/a	**dilution:**	n/a
Int net div per share: nil	**P/E ratio:**	27.5
Fin net div per share: nil	**Probable CGT?**	No

LATEST REPORTED RESULTS: 2003		PREVIOUS REPORTED RESULTS: 2002	
Turnover:	£657,000	Turnover:	£384,000
PTP:	£42,000	PTP:	£(1.62m)
EPS:	0.2p	EPS:	(8.3)p

Griffin Mining (GFM)

Mineral explorer & developer

6th Floor, 60 St James's Street, London, SW1A 1LE Tel: 020-7629 7772; Fax: 020-7629 7773;
e-mail: roger@griffinmining.demon.co.uk; web site: www.griffinmining.com

		holding %
Chairman	Mladen Ninkov	0.03
Chief Executive	Adrian Stecyk	28.2
Finance Director	Roger Goodwin	0.2
Director	Dal Brynelsen	0.0

Main Shareholders:

Global Investments	23.6
Trellas Partners	16.3
RAB Capital	13.4
Gartmore	12.0

Percentage of free market capital: 6.2%

Comments:

Griffin shares recently paused after soaring on hopes for its Chinese zinc project at Caijiaying, which the company claims could hold 1.2m tonnes and start with annual output of 22,000 tonnes. With £3.6m earmarked for nearby gold targets, Griffin recently raised £8.75m at 25p and gave 9.5m three-year options at 27p to chairman Mladen Ninkov and several millions to other directors.

Nominated Adviser:	Charles Stanley, London
AIM Broker:	Charles Stanley, London
Solicitors:	Denton Wilde, London
Market Makers:	MLSB; SCAP; WINS
Auditors:	Grant Thornton, Manor Court, Segesworth, Fareham, Hampshire PO15 5ST
Registrars:	Capita Registrars

ENTRY ON AIM:	30/6/1997	Recent price:	26.25p
Interim results:	Sep	Market cap:	£44.68m
Final results:	Apr	Issue price:	25.0p
Year end:	Dec	Current no of shares:	
Accounts due:	Apr		170,227,731
Int div paymnt:	n/a	No of shares after	
Fin div paymnt:	n/a	dilution:	n/a
Int net div per share:	nil	P/E ratio:	n/a
Fin net div per share:	nil	Probable CGT?	No

LATEST REPORTED RESULTS:	2002	PREVIOUS REPORTED RESULTS:	2001
Turnover:	$8,000	Turnover:	n/a
PTP:	$(230,000)	PTP:	$(543,000)
EPS:	(0.2)c	EPS:	(0.6)c

Grosvenor Land (GVR)

Property manager

22 Gilbert Street, Grosvenor Square, London, W1K 5EJ Tel: 020-7408 2222; Fax: 020-7493 2482

		holding %
Chairman	Philippe Edmonds	1.4
Chief Executive	Douglas Blausten*	4.2
Finance Director		
Non-Exec Director	Robert Dyson	6.3

Main Shareholders:

Maland Pension Fund	25.3
Andrew Perloff	24.9
Oakburn Properties (incl. *)	10.9
Mark Futter	5.8

Percentage of free market capital: 46.7%
* Douglas Blausten and Simon Blausten each own 10% of the share capital of Oakburn Properties

Comments:

Property group Grosvenor was the target of a hostile takeover bid by Panther Securities, a vehicle owned by serial investor Andrew Perloff, who attempted first to throw the directors off the board and then made an offer for Oakburn Properties, which owns 29.34% of the company. This was resolved when director Douglas Blausten teamed up with fellow AIM-listed property group Terrace Hill and made a successful bid for Oakburn. Grosvenor is expected to delist on April 6.

Nominated Adviser:	Seymour Pierce, London
AIM Broker:	Seymour Pierce Ellis, Crawley
Solicitors:	n/a
Market Makers:	KBCS; SCAP; WINS
Auditors:	BDO Stoy Hayward, 8 Baker Street, London W1M 1DA
Registrars:	Capita Registrars

ENTRY ON AIM:	11/9/1996	Recent price:	17.75p
Interim results:	Dec	Market cap:	£6.13m
Final results:	Sep	Issue price:	12.5p
Year end:	Mar	Current no of shares:	
Accounts due:	Aug		34,559,964
Int div paymnt:	n/a	No of shares after	
Fin div paymnt:	Nov	dilution:	n/a
Int net div per share:	nil	P/E ratio:	16.1
Fin net div per share:	0.2p	Probable CGT?	No

LATEST REPORTED RESULTS:	2003	PREVIOUS REPORTED RESULTS:	2002
Turnover:	£1.17m	Turnover:	£1.26m
PTP:	£440,000	PTP:	£123,000
EPS:	1.1p	EPS:	0.3p

GTL Resources

(GTL)

Conversion of natural gas into methanol

60 St James's Street, London, SW1A 1LE Tel: 020-7493 3393; Fax: 020-7493 3394;
e-mail: enquiries@gtlresources.com; web site: www.gtlresources.com

		holding %
Chairman	Peter Middleton	0.0
Chief Executive	as above	
Finance Director		
Deputy Chairman	Michael Fox	13.0

Main Shareholders:

RAB Capital	15.8
Resources Investment Trust	7.2
Kevin Alexander	5.8
Bank of New York Nominees	5.7
Cantor Fitzgerald (Europe)	3.7

Percentage of free market capital: 24.6%

Comments:

GTL recently told increasingly impatient shareholders only one material contract remained to be completed before it could arrange finance for its ambitious £270m project to convert non-commercial gas to liquid methanol at Dampier in Western Australia. A distinctly high-risk investment, the company, which lost an interim £1.1m, raised £2.75m at 8p in October and expects to have a 70% stake in this 'Liquigas' project.

Nominated Adviser:	Durlacher, London
AIM Broker:	Durlacher, London
Solicitors:	Norton Rose, London
Market Makers:	KBCS; MLSB; SCAP; SGSL; WINS
Auditors:	KPMG Audit, Newcastle
Registrars:	Computershare Investor Services

ENTRY ON AIM:	29/9/1998	**Recent price:**	6.5p
Interim results:	Dec	**Market cap:**	£17.28m
Final results:	Jun	**Issue price:**	30.0p
Year end:	Mar	**Current no of shares:**	
Accounts due:	Sep		265,910,465
Int div paymnt:	n/a	**No of shares after**	
Fin div paymnt:	n/a	**dilution:**	n/a
Int net div per share:	nil	**P/E ratio:**	n/a
Fin net div per share:	nil	**Probable CGT?**	No

LATEST REPORTED RESULTS: 2003		PREVIOUS REPORTED RESULTS: 2002	
Turnover:	n/a	**Turnover:**	n/a
PTP:	$(5.13m)	**PTP:**	$(3.04m)
EPS:	(0.0)c	**EPS:**	(0.0)c

GW Pharmaceuticals

(GWP)

Cannabis-derived medicine developer

Porton Down Science Park, Salisbury, Wiltshire SP4 0JQ Tel: 01980-557000; Fax: 01980-557111;
e-mail: info@gwpharm.com; web site: www.gwpharm.com

		holding %
Chairman	Geoffrey Guy	21.2
Chief Executive	Justin Gover	3.3
Finance Director	David Kirk	0.006
Scientific Director	Brian Whittle	9.6

Main Shareholders:

Preston Parish	8.5
Troy Asset Management	4.1
Michael Lester	3.2

Percentage of free market capital: 49.7%

Comments:

GW, which has a licence from the Government to use cannabis to develop pain-relief prescription medicines, expects to launch its first product, after gaining regulatory approval, this summer. This will help patients with multiple sclerosis. Trials to test the herb's effectiveness against other ailments are also being carried out. Cash stands at a healthy £32m following a £20m placing at 200p. Directors sold some shares at the same time. The group has a £28m tie-up with Germany's Bayer.

Nominated Adviser:	Hoare Govett, London
AIM Broker:	Hoare Govett, London
Solicitors:	Mayer Brown Rowe & Maw, London
Market Makers:	CSCS; KBCS; MLSBL SCAP; WINS
Auditors:	Deloitte & Touche, Reading,
Registrars:	Capita Registrars

ENTRY ON AIM:	28/6/2001	**Recent price:**	200.5p
Interim results:	Jun	**Market cap:**	£221.42m
Final results:	Jan	**Issue price:**	182.0p
Year end:	Sep	**Current no of shares:**	
Accounts due:	Jan		110,434,679
Int div paymnt:	n/a	**No of shares after**	
Fin div paymnt:	n/a	**dilution:**	n/a
Int net div per share:	nil	**P/E ratio:**	n/a
Fin net div per share:	nil	**Probable CGT?**	YES

LATEST REPORTED RESULTS: 2003		PREVIOUS REPORTED RESULTS: 2002	
Turnover:	£5.0m	**Turnover:**	n/a
PTP:	£(9.63m)	**PTP:**	£(12.17m)
EPS:	(7.8)p	**EPS:**	(11.6)p

Gympie Gold (suspended 29 Dec 2003)   (GGD)

Gold and coal miner

Level 9 Goldfields House, I Alfred Street, Sydney, NSW Australia 2000, Tel: 00-61 2 9251 2777; Fax: 00-61 2 9251 2666;
e-mail: info@gympiegold.com.au; web site: www.gympiegold.com.au

		holding %
Chairman	Michael Darling*	31.6
Chief Executive	Harry Adams	1.4
Financial Director	Arthur Gillen	0.0
Director	Peter Cadwallader	0.3

Main Shareholders:

Pilatus Capital*	27.9
Citicorps Nominees	8.4
Mafed Investments*	3.2

Percentage of free market capital: 27.1%

*These companies are associated with Michael Darling

Nominated Adviser:	Nabarro Wells, London
AIM Broker:	Numis, London
Solicitors:	Faegre Benson Hobson Audley, London
Market Makers:	SGSL; WINS
Auditors:	Ernst & Young, Australia
Registrars:	Computershare Investor Services

ENTRY ON AIM: 28/11/2001	Recent price:	19.5p
Interim results: Mar	Market cap:	£45.8m
Final results: Aug	Issue price:	30.0p
Year end: Jun	Current no of shares:	
Accounts due: Oct		234,858,575
Int div paymnt: n/a	No of shares after	
Fin div paymnt: n/a	dilution:	n/a
Int net div per share: nil	P/E ratio:	n/a
Fin net div per share: nil	Probable CGT?	No

Comments:

A 'devastating' fire over the Christmas holiday put paid to loss-making Aussie counter Gympie's stated hopes of a £20m EBITDA contribution from its Southland colliery Down Under. Chairman Michael Darling, who made the forecast, had to abort a £10m funding and, with the shares down at 19.5p, call in adminstrators. HSBC, as agent for Gympie's corporate loan facility, appointed receivers on December 30.

LATEST REPORTED RESULTS: 2003	PREVIOUS REPORTED RESULTS: 2002
Turnover: A$96.9m	Turnover: A$85.73m
PTP: A$(24.8m)	PTP: A$(3.3m)
EPS: (1.7)Ac	EPS: 5.0Ac

Halladale   (HDG)

Property trader and developer

93 West George Street, Glasgow, G2 IPB Tel: 0141-204 4633; Fax: 0141-204 4655;
e-mail: all@halladale.co.uk; web site: www.halladale.co.uk

		holding %
Chairman	Alfred Shedden	0.1
Chief Executive	David Lockhart	26.1
Finance Director	Mark Harkin	0.1
Property Director	Kenneth Lindsay	0.1

Main Shareholders:

3i	24.0
Finsbury Trust	11.1
DASL Liferent Trust	8.3
Solus UK Special Situations Fund	6.9
Frank Nominees	4.4

Percentage of free market capital: 18.9%

Nominated Adviser:	Collins Stewart, London
AIM Broker:	Collins Stewart, London
Solicitors:	Eversheds, London
Market Makers:	TEAM; WINS
Auditors:	Deloitte & Touche, Glasgow G2
Registrars:	Capita Registrars

ENTRY ON AIM: 27/4/2001	Recent price:	78.5p
Interim results: Dec	Market cap:	£15.0m
Final results: Jul	Issue price:	50.0p
Year end: Apr	Current no of shares:	
Accounts due: Sep		19,107,500
Int div paymnt: Feb	No of shares after	
Fin div paymnt: Sep	dilution:	n/a
Int net div per share: 0.7p	P/E ratio:	10.9
Fin net div per share: 1.04p	Probable CGT?	No

Comments:

Adopting an 'active' policy of continually buying, redeveloping, selling and moving on, Halladale increased interim profits before tax 7% to £1m. 85% of its portolio is invested in retail property. Sites in Glasgow and Brentwood are being developed. The company is also investing in recovery buys such as the South East office market. The aggregate value of acquisitions and disposals fell 56% to £28m but many transactions are expected to fall into the second half.

LATEST REPORTED RESULTS: 2003	PREVIOUS REPORTED RESULTS: 2002
Turnover: £30.36m	Turnover: £22.24m
PTP: £1.69m	PTP: £1.15m
EPS: 7.2p	EPS: 5.3p

Hansard (HSD)

Public relations company

14 Kinnerton Place South, London, SW1X 8EH Tel: 020-7245 1100; Fax: 020-7245 0909;
e-mail: mail@hansardcommunications.com; web site: www.hansardcommunications.com

		holding %
Chairman	Anthony Caplin	1.5
Chief Executive	Adam Reynolds*	33.2
Finance Director	Paul Foulger	1.7
Non-Exec Director	Sir Richard Needham	0.0

Main Shareholders:

David Newton	10.0
Glyn Hirsh	9.3
Nomihold Securities	9.3
NCL Investments	5.0
Teawood	4.2

Percentage of free market capital: 22.2%
*5,000 shares are held by Adam Reynolds wife & 40,000 are held on behalf of his children

Comments:
After a tough 12 months, financial PR consultancy Hansard will be hoping that the recent upturn in flotations and corporate transactions proves to be sustainable. First half numbers were fairly flat. Revenues rose just £10,000 to £319,000 and profits before tax climbed from £16,000 to £19,000. A recent placing raised £175,710, bringing David Newton and NCL Investments onto the shareholder register.

Nominated Adviser:	Seymour Pierce, London		
AIM Broker:	Seymour Pierce, London		
Solicitors:	Halliwell Landau, London		
Market Makers:	KBCS; SCAP; WINS		
Auditors:	Gerald Edelman, 25 Harley Street, London, W1N 2BR		
Registrars:	Computershare Investor Services		

ENTRY ON AIM: 16/11/2000		**Recent price:**	18.25p
Interim results:	Sep	**Market cap:**	£2.47m
Final results:	Jul	**Issue price:**	25.0p
Year end:	Feb	**Current no of shares:**	
Accounts due:	Oct		13,549,754
Int div paymnt:	n/a	**No of shares after**	
Fin div paymnt:	n/a	**dilution:**	n/a
Int net div per share:	nil	**P/E ratio:**	n/a
Fin net div per share:	nil	**Probable CGT?**	Yes

LATEST REPORTED RESULTS:	2003	PREVIOUS REPORTED RESULTS:	2002
Turnover:	£617,000	Turnover:	£454,000
PTP:	£(106,000)	PTP:	£128,000
EPS:	(0.7)p	EPS:	(1.1)p

Hardman Resources (HNR)

Oil and gas exploration and production

Ground Floor, 5 Ord Street, West Perth 6005, West Australia, Australia Tel: 00-61 8 9321 6881; Fax: 00-61 8 9321 2375;
e-mail: office@hdr.com.au; web site: www.hdr.com.au

		holding %
Chairman	Alan Burns	0.0
Chief Executive	Edward Ellyard	0.7
Finance Director		
Exec Director	Scott Spencer	0.8

Main Shareholders:

Woodside Mauritania Investments	9.9

Percentage of free market capital: 88.6%

Comments:
Hardman began the year well, declaring its Chinguetti oil prospect in Mauritania to be commercial and suggesting its Tiof prospect there could be bigger. The company lost an interim $11m (£6.1m), after $7m of asset write-downs and currency losses, and sold assets in Australia's Perth Basin for $7.6m. With interests in Uganda, Gabon and New Zealand, potential assets in the ground could be between $300m and $500m.

Nominated Adviser:	Nabarro Wells, London		
AIM Broker:	Oriel, London; Collins Stewart, London		
Solicitors:	Watson, Farley & Williams, London		
Market Makers:	KBCS; SGSL		
Auditors:	Grant Thornton, Australia		
Registrars:	Computershare Investor Services		

ENTRY ON AIM: 19/3/2002		**Recent price:**	51.25p
Interim results:	Mar	**Market cap:**	£247.03m
Final results:	Sep	**Issue price:**	23.75p
Year end:	Jun	**Current no of shares:**	
Accounts due:	Oct		482,010,028
Int div paymnt:	n/a	**No of shares after**	
Fin div paymnt:	n/a	**dilution:**	n/a
Int net div per share:	nil	**P/E ratio:**	n/a
Fin net div per share:	nil	**Probable CGT?**	No

LATEST REPORTED RESULTS:	2003	PREVIOUS REPORTED RESULTS:	2002
Turnover:	A$11.43m	Turnover:	A$11.49m
PTP:	A$(1.75m)	PTP:	A$(4.08m)
EPS:	0.4Ac	EPS:	1.0Ac

165

Harrier (HRR)

Internet and network security and networked data storage integrater

2nd Floor, Cromwell House, Bartley Wood Business Park, Hook, Hampshire RG27 9XA Tel: 01256-760081;
Fax: 01256-760 091; e-mail: info@harrier.com; web site: www.harrier.com

		holding %
Chairman	Bob Morton*	29.9
Chief Executive	Jim Stoddart	0.0
Finance Director	Mark Rowlinson	0.5
Commercial	Trevor Meredith**	6.0
Director		

Main Shareholders:

Southwind*	30.0
Wayne Bugden	6.1
Framlington	4.3
David Cheesman	4.0
Julia Nicholl	3.8

Percentage of free market capital: 33.47%
*The beneficial holder of these shares is Southwind
**100,000 shares held by Sandra Ann Meredith

Nominated Adviser:	KBC Peel Hunt, London
AIM Broker:	KBC Peel Hunt, London
Solicitors:	Addleshaw Goddard, London
Market Makers:	KBCS; MLSB; SCAP; WINS
Auditors:	Saffery Champness, London
Registrars:	Capita Registrars

ENTRY ON AIM:	4/11/1999	Recent price:	30.25p
Interim results:	Sep	Market cap:	£8.85m
Final results:	Mar	Issue price:	110.0p
Year end:	Dec	Current no of shares:	
Accounts due:	Apr		29,241,930
Int div paymnt:	n/a	No of shares after	
Fin div paymnt:	n/a	dilution:	29,564,569
Int net div per share:	nil	P/E ratio:	43.2
Fin net div per share:	nil	Probable CGT?	YES

LATEST REPORTED RESULTS: 2003		PREVIOUS REPORTED RESULTS: 2002	
Turnover:	£9.03m	Turnover:	£9.54m
PTP:	£200,000	PTP:	£(19.01m)
EPS:	0.7p	EPS:	(66.2p)

Comments:

Following a return to profitability last year Harrier is now actively scouting for acquisitions – chairman Bob Morton says management has been poring over possibilities recently. As for the existing businesses, last year's improvements, says chief executive Jim Stoddart, 'were the result of chasing quality business with sensible profit margins, rather than just revenues'. House broker Peel Hunt expects profits of £750,000 in 2004 on sales of £11.0m.

Harrogate (HGP)

Investment companies

Empress Buildings, 380 Chester Road, Manchester, M16 9EA Tel: 0161-877 2199 ; Fax: 0161-877 3751;
e-mail: contact@harrogategroup.com; web site: www.harrogategroup.com

		holding %
Chairman	Keith Chadwick	0.0
Chief Executive	Mark Housley	21.8
Finance Director		
Director	Peter Scott	4.9

Main Shareholders:

n/a

Percentage of free market capital: 73.3%

Nominated Adviser:	Nabarro Wells, London
AIM Broker:	Fiske, London
Solicitors:	Bowmans, Manchester
Market Makers:	MLSB; SCAP; WINS
Auditors:	BDO Stoy Hayward, Preston
Registrars:	Capita Registrars

ENTRY ON AIM:	15/6/2000	Recent price:	0.5p
Interim results:	Dec	Market cap:	£2.38m
Final results:	Sep	Issue price:	2.5p
Year end:	Mar	Current no of shares:	
Accounts due:	Sep		476,000,000
Int div paymnt:	n/a	No of shares after	
Fin div paymnt:	n/a	dilution:	n/a
Int net div per share:	nil	P/E ratio:	n/a
Fin net div per share:	nil	Probable CGT?	YES

LATEST REPORTED RESULTS: 2003		PREVIOUS REPORTED RESULTS: 2002	
Turnover:	£737,000	Turnover:	£551,000
PTP:	£(568,000)	PTP:	£(8.34m)
EPS:	(0.1)p	EPS:	(1.8)p

Comments:

Harrogate owns Axiom Internet, a behavioural profiling software business. Axiom makes software for the medical, legal and scientific research market and has organised distribution deals in various international territories. Harrogate has abandoned plans to spin off Axiom onto Ofex. The group also owns half of a document management software venture. Cost cuts saw interim losses reduced from £466,000 to £93,000 as sales doubled to £369,000. Cash stands at £330,000.

Hartest (HTH)

Supplier of laboratory equipment and furniture

275 King Henry's Drive, New Addington, Croydon, Suffolk CR0 0AE Tel: 01689-800799; Fax: 01689-800405;
e-mail: Hartest@labspace.co.uk

		holding %
Chairman	David Leeming	11.1
Chief Executive	as above	
Finance Director	Max Dyer-Barlett	1.9
Non-Exec Director	John Whitfield	6.5

Main Shareholders:

C S Inglefield	3.8
BWD AIM	3.3
Micro Quoted Growth Trust	3.2

Percentage of free market capital: 67.3%

Comments:

Hartest has a tender to supply its Swissray digital imaging system to North Tees and Hartlepool NHS Trust. Having ditched its underperforming laboratory furnishings division, the company is looking to grow revenues in its medical division. Hartest recently raised £700,000 via a placing at 4p with directors and institutions – the bulk for working capital and to reduce debts. In the half to August, the company made £259,000 pre-tax on £9.6m of continuing sales.

Nominated Adviser:	Corporate Synergy, London
AIM Broker:	Corporate Synergy, London
Solicitors:	Wedlake Bell, London
Market Makers:	HOOD; SCAP; WINS
Auditors:	Bright Grahame Murray, London
Registrars:	Capita Registrars

ENTRY ON AIM:	16/7/2001	Recent price:	5.5p
Interim results:	Oct	Market cap:	£7.55m
Final results:	Jun	Issue price:	n/a
Year end:	Feb	Current no of shares:	
Accounts due:	Jul		137,359,542
Int div paymnt:	Apr	No of shares after	
Fin div paymnt:	Oct	dilution:	n/a
Int net div per share:	0.13p	P/E ratio:	n/a
Fin net div per share:	0.13p	Probable CGT?	Yes

LATEST REPORTED RESULTS:	2003	PREVIOUS REPORTED RESULTS:	2002
Turnover:	£25.65m	Turnover:	£17.96m
PTP:	£(435,000)	PTP:	£227,000
EPS:	(0.1)p	EPS:	0.1p

Hartford (HAR)

Restaurant and bar group

Africa House, 64-78 Kingsway, London, WC2B 6BG Tel: 020-7269 6370; Fax: 020-7405 7180;
web site: www.hartfordgroup.co.uk

		holding %
Chairman	Stephen Thomas	7.5
Chief Executive	James Kowszun	0.7
Finance Director	Urvashi Parekh	0.0
Operations Director	Jeremy Spencer	0.0

Main Shareholders:

Prestbury Investments	27.2
Aberdeen Asset Management	6.9
Marlborough fund Managers	4.6
UBS Asset Management	4.0

Percentage of free market capital: 49.2%

Comments:

Hartford might be turning the corner. On the up side, in the year to September 2003 it delivered its first positive EBITDA. That said, losses on ordinary activities before tax more than doubled. This was mainly due to the closing of The Wells, a bar in Ascot, and two cash-draining restaurants: The Dakota and Pharmacy in Notting Hill. The group has one remaining restaurant left, Canyon, which is trading strongly. Other costs materialised from refurbishment of the 17-strong Jamies Bar chain.

Nominated Adviser:	Investec, London
AIM Broker:	Investec, London
Solicitors:	CMS Cameron McKenna, London
Market Makers:	IHCS; KBCS; SCAP; WINS
Auditors:	BDO Stoy Hayward, 8 Baker Street, London W1M 1DA
Registrars:	Capita Registrars

ENTRY ON AIM:	17/6/1998	Recent price:	1.5p
Interim results:	Jun	Market cap:	£8.02m
Final results:	Mar	Issue price:	2.0p
Year end:	Dec	Current no of shares:	
Accounts due:	Apr		534,978,960
Int div paymnt:	n/a	No of shares after	
Fin div paymnt:	n/a	dilution:	n/a
Int net div per share:	nil	P/E ratio:	n/a
Fin net div per share:	nil	Probable CGT?	Yes

LATEST REPORTED RESULTS:	2003	PREVIOUS REPORTED RESULTS:	9 MONTHS TO 28 SEP '02
Turnover:	£14.29m	Turnover:	£4.88m
PTP:	£(1.84m)	PTP:	£(728,000)
EPS:	(0.3)p	EPS:	(0.3)p

Hartstone (HST)

Distributor of leather goods in the US under the Etienne Aigner brand

17 Chiltern Business Centre, 63/65 Woodside Road, Amersham, Bucks HP6 6AA Tel: 01494-787700; Fax: 01494-787707

		holding %
Chairman	Shaun Dowling	7.3
Chief Executive		
Finance Director		
Non-Exec Director	William McBride	0.0

Main Shareholders:

J O Hambro	13.9
HENK HEYST	8.5
Schroders	6.7
Veers Palthe Voute	4.2
Barclayshare	3.1

Percentage of free market capital: 56.3%

Comments:
Hartstone has entered a footwear licensing agreement with Bennett Footwear, a footwear sourcing and distribution business. Hartstone will now receive 5% royalty fees for all Etienne Aigner shoes sold through Bennett's 63 retail outlets. Hartstone has managed to reduce its bank borrowings to £9.5m but interim results remained poor with losses of £1.8m. The small accessory business, which Harstone will retain, increased sales by 46%. Total sales fell 12% overall to £33.1m though.

Nominated Adviser:	Collins Stewart, London
AIM Broker:	Collins Stewart, London
Solicitors:	Travers Smith Braithwaite, London
Market Makers:	EVO; SCAP; MLSB; SCAP; UBS; WINS
Auditors:	RSM Robson Rhodes, 186 City Road, London EC1V 2NU
Registrars:	Capita Registrars

ENTRY ON AIM:	10/9/2003	**Recent price:**	1.5p
Interim results:	Dec	**Market cap:**	£2.38m
Final results:	Jul	**Issue price:**	0.68p
Year end:	Mar	**Current no of shares:**	
Accounts due:	Aug		158,487,044
Int div paymnt:	n/a	**No of shares after**	
Fin div paymnt:	n/a	**dilution:**	n/a
Int net div per share:	nil	**P/E ratio:**	n/a
Fin net div per share:	nil	**Probable CGT?**	**No**

LATEST REPORTED RESULTS:	2003	PREVIOUS REPORTED RESULTS:	2002
Turnover:	£75.08m	Turnover:	£99.59m
PTP:	£(7.04m)	PTP:	£1.12m
EPS:	(4.9)p	EPS:	0.6p

Hat Pin (HTP)

Advertising industry recruitment consultant

50-60 Hallam Street, London, W1W 6JL Tel: 020-7907 4433; Fax: 020-7907 4459;
e-mail: gay@ktlondon.co.uk; web site: www.hatpin.co.uk

		holding %
Chairman	Gay Haines	22.4
Chief Executive	as above	
Finance Director	Michael Marks	4.3
Non-Exec Director	Stephen Raven	4.7

Main Shareholders:

Mr & Mrs A Morton	18.2
HSBC Private Bank (Jersey)	8.8
Michael Jackson	6.0
Ms S Ching	5.1
Camilla Sparkes	4.1

Percentage of free market capital: 19.4%

Comments:
Improved trading in the communications industry, particularly in the UK and US, helped the recruiter led by Gay Haines move into the black for 2003. Hat Pin also reported a positive performance in Hong Kong. Last year's turnover sparked up by 14% and the group's net margin continued to show improvement. Directors are convinced the industry is poised for upturn, and Hat Pin wants to grow aggressively, both organically and through acquisition.

Nominated Adviser:	Evolution Beeson Gregory, London
AIM Broker:	Evolution Beeson Gregory, London
Solicitors:	Lewis Silkin, London
Market Makers:	SCAP; TEAM; WINS
Auditors:	BDO Stoy Hayward, 8 Baker Street, London W1M 1DA
Registrars:	Capita Registrars

ENTRY ON AIM:	17/7/1996	**Recent price:**	57.5p
Interim results:	Sep	**Market cap:**	£6.3m
Final results:	Apr	**Issue price:**	68.0p
Year end:	Dec	**Current no of shares:**	
Accounts due:	Apr		10,948,270
Int div paymnt:	Dec	**No of shares after**	
Fin div paymnt:	Apr	**dilution:**	n/a
Int net div per share:	nil	**P/E ratio:**	n/a
Fin net div per share:	nil	**Probable CGT?**	**Yes**

LATEST REPORTED RESULTS:	2002	PREVIOUS REPORTED RESULTS:	2001
Turnover:	£3.12m	Turnover:	£9.17m
PTP:	£(202,000)	PTP:	£(1.08m)
EPS:	(2.2)p	EPS:	(13.1)p

Hawthorn (formerly Poptones) (suspended 4 November 2003) (HAW)

Independent record label & retailer

Pop Art Mansions, Berkeley Grove, London, NW1 8XY Tel: 020-7483 2541; Fax: 020-7586 5556;
web site: www.poptones.co.uk

		holding %
Chairman	Michael Blackburn	2.5
Chief Executive		
Finance Director	Ian Aspinall	0.0
Non-Exec Director	Julian Richer	14.0

Main Shareholders:

Alan McGee	38.6
Joseph Foster	7.2
Robert Devereux	4.3
Katherine Holmes	3.4
Oxygen Investors	3.0

Percentage of free market capital: 23.6%

Comments:

This venture became cash shell Hawthorn after selling off record label Poptones to Alan McGee last June following some tough trading in the music industry. It then started to look to entice suitable companies with its cash and AIM listing. The latest news is Hawthorn has signed heads of terms on a forthcoming reverse takeover and is carrying out the due diligence – its shareholders are waiting with bated breath. At the last count, cash at the bank was £140,000.

Nominated Adviser:	Altium Capital, Manchester
AIM Broker:	Rowan Dartington, Bristol
Solicitors:	Kuit Steinart Levy, Manchester
Market Makers:	KBCS; MLSB; SCAP; WINS
Auditors:	Horwath Clark Whitehill, Manchester
Registrars:	Capita Registrars

ENTRY ON AIM:	8/8/2000	**Recent price:**	3.75p
Interim results:	Mar	**Market cap:**	£0.21m
Final results:	Sep	**Issue price:**	2.0p
Year end:	Jun	**Current no of shares:**	
Accounts due:	Oct		5,720,870
Int div paymnt:	n/a	**No of shares after**	
Fin div paymnt:	n/a	**dilution:**	n/a
Int net div per share:	nil	**P/E ratio:**	n/a
Fin net div per share:	nil	**Probable CGT?**	**YES**

LATEST REPORTED RESULTS: 2003		PREVIOUS REPORTED RESULTS: 2002	
Turnover:	£69,000	**Turnover:**	£1.72m
PTP:	£(488,000)	**PTP:**	¢(350,000)
EPS:	(8.5)p	**EPS:**	(6.1)p

Headway (HDW)

Management of property workspace

Calderdale Business Park, Club Lane, Ovenden, Halifax, HX2 8DB Tel: 01422-330433; Fax: 01422-351400;
e-mail: headwayplc@btinternet.com; web site: www.headwayplc.co.uk

		holding %
Chairman	William Cran	1.2
Chief Executive	Andrew Staniland	0.9
Finance Director	Stephen Thornton	0.0
Non-Exec Director	John Lees	27.2

Main Shareholders:

Country & Metropolitan	26.72
Fleet Property	11.4
Jupiter Asset Management	7.1

Percentage of free market capital: 25.4%

Comments:

The managed workspace provider announced healthy interim results with profits before tax up 9.2% to £501,000. NAV rose 1.3% to 111p. It has recently signed a ten-year lease to a local housing trust in Bradford. Fully listed housebuilder C&M has increased its stake in the company to 26.7%. The company has also confirmed it is in discussions which may lead to an offer near the current share price.

Nominated Adviser:	KPMG Corporate Finance, Leeds
AIM Broker:	Numis, London
Solicitors:	DLA, Leeds
Market Makers:	BGMM; KBCS; WINS
Auditors:	KPMG, 1 The Embankment, Neville Street, Leeds LS1 4DW
Registrars:	Capita Registrars

ENTRY ON AIM:	21/6/2001	**Recent price:**	104.0p
Interim results:	Jan	**Market cap:**	£16.89m
Final results:	Sep	**Issue price:**	n/a
Year end:	Jun	**Current no of shares:**	
Accounts due:	Oct		16,240,503
Int div paymnt:	Apr	**No of shares after**	
Fin div paymnt:	Dec	**dilution:**	16,400,503
Int net div per share:	0.77p	**P/E ratio:**	28.1
Fin net div per share:	1.61p	**Probable CGT?**	**No**

LATEST REPORTED RESULTS: 2003		PREVIOUS REPORTED RESULTS: 2002	
Turnover:	£2.12m	**Turnover:**	£2.03m
PTP:	£875,000	**PTP:**	£967,000
EPS:	3.7p	**EPS:**	4.6p

Healthcare Enterprise (formerly Interactivity) (HCEG)
Health investment vehicle
15 Stratton Street, London, W1J 8LQ Tel: 020-7659 6158

		holding %
Chairman	Stuart Bruck	37.7
Chief Executive	Gordon Wood	0.0
Finance Director	Lyndon Gaborit	0.0
Director	Michael Low	0.0

Main Shareholders:

LPMCC, LLC	37.7
Medical Investment group	23.9
European Life Sciences	9.1

Percentage of free market capital: 8.4%

Nominated Adviser:	Numis, London
AIM Broker:	Numis, London
Solicitors:	Norton Rose, London
Market Makers:	MLSB; SCAP; WINS
Auditors:	HLB AV AUDIT, 66 Wigmore Street, London W1H 0HQ
Registrars:	Capita Registrars

ENTRY ON AIM:	3/5/2000	Recent price:	2.25p
Interim results:	Jun	Market cap:	£63.17m
Final results:	Feb	Issue price:	n/a
Year end:	Sep	Current no of shares:	
Accounts due:	Apr		2,807,586,702
Int div paymnt:	n/a	No of shares after	
Fin div paymnt:	n/a	dilution:	n/a
Int net div per share:	n/a	P/E ratio:	n/a
Fin net div per share:	n/a	Probable CGT?	YES

Comments:

Healthcare Enterprise, led by sector specialist Stuart Bruck, has made a 'foundation acquisition' of occupational health concern SAFA Group, a profitable provider of first-aid kits and other medical goods. SAFA, set up by entrepreneurial Gordon Wood, also owns SafaTec, which has nine investments in Israeli healthcare development ventures. SafaTec products likely to reach market first include Ebiox molecular decontamination tools.

LATEST REPORTED RESULTS: 2002		PREVIOUS REPORTED RESULTS: 2001	
Turnover:	n/a	Turnover:	£189,000
PTP:	£(49,000)	PTP:	£(739,000)
EPS:	(0.0)p	EPS:	(0.0)p

Heavitree Brewery (The) (HVT)
Devon pub chain operator
Trood Lane, Matford, Exeter EX2 8YP Tel: 01392-217733; Fax: 01392-229939

		holding %
Chairman	WP Tucker	19.2
Managing Director	NHP Tucker	37.6
Finance Director	GJ Crocker	4.8
Director	Rodney Glanville	0.2

Main Shareholders:

PA Bennett	6.0
EMA Pease-Watkin	5.8
JHF Pease-Watkin	5.8
RH Duncan	5.3
SM Duncan	3.3

Percentage of free market capital: 13.5%

Nominated Adviser:	Credit Lyonnais, London
AIM Broker:	Credit Lyonnais, London
Solicitors:	Ford Simey, Exeter; SJ Berwin, London
Market Makers:	WINS
Auditors:	Ernst & Young, Southern Hay West, Exeter EX1 1LF
Registrars:	Computershare Investor Services

ENTRY ON AIM:	1/7/1996	Recent price:	350.0p
Interim results:	Jun	Market cap:	£13.62m
Final results:	Feb	Issue price:	275.0p
Year end:	Oct	Current no of shares:	
Accounts due:	Mar		3,892,365
Int div paymnt:	Jul	No of shares after	
Fin div paymnt:	Apr	dilution:	n/a
Int net div per share:	3.5p	P/E ratio:	18.8
Fin net div per share:	5.25p	Probable CGT?	YES

Comments:

Devon-based pub operator Heavitree is rather elusive as it only ever releases the barest amount of information and acts more like a private concern than a listed company. Latest results for 2003 provided an increase in pre-tax profits, despite chairman WP Tucker admitting that conditions were difficult during the year. Dividends were also 9.75% up.

LATEST REPORTED RESULTS: 2003		PREVIOUS REPORTED RESULTS: 2002	
Turnover:	£12.31m	Turnover:	£11.91m
PTP:	£1.25m	PTP:	£973,000
EPS:	18.6p	EPS:	12.8p

Hemisphere Properties (HPE)
Property trader and developer
2 Bloomsbury Street, London, WC1B 3ST

		holding %
Chairman	Donald McCrickard	3.0
Chief Executive	Desmond Bloom	26.7
Finance Director	Ivan Minter	2.6
Director		

Main Shareholders:

INFH Inc	14.9
Margaret Mountfalcon	13.6

Percentage of free market capital: 39.2%

Nominated Adviser:	Nabarro Wells, London
AIM Broker:	Christows, London
Solicitors:	Field Fisher Waterhouse, London
Market Makers:	EVO; SCAP; WINS
Auditors:	Baker Tilly, 2 Bloomsbury Street, London EC2V 3ND
Registrars:	Share Registrars

ENTRY ON AIM:	5/8/2003	Recent price:	5.25p
Interim results:	Apr	Market cap:	£1.65m
Final results:	Sep	Issue price:	5.0p
Year end:	Mar	Current no of shares:	
Accounts due:	Nov		31,406,666
Int div paymnt:	n/a	No of shares after	
Fin div paymnt:	n/a	dilution:	n/a
Int net div per share:	nil	P/E ratio:	n/a
Fin net div per share:	nil	Probable CGT?	No

LATEST REPORTED RESULTS: 2003		PREVIOUS REPORTED RESULTS: FROM 10 AUG '01 TO 31 MAR '02	
Turnover:	£50,000	Turnover:	n/a
PTP:	£(6,000)	PTP:	£(63,000)
EPS:	n/a	EPS:	n/a

Comments:

Hemisphere was established by property entrepreneur Desmond Bloom and raised £500,000 of a planned £2m. Its aim is to build up a portfolio of property, whether in the form of offices, industrial or retail premises, either in the UK or overseas. It has acquired Downside, which holds one retail property in London and recently also bought two properties in Scotland that are fully let for £2.7m. Bloom's last AIM venture Eurocity performed woefully, attracting investor wrath.

hemscott (HEM)
Business & financial information solutions
2nd Floor, Finsbury Tower, 103-105 Bunhill Row, London, EC1Y 8TY Tel: 020-7496 0055; Fax: 020-7847 1719;
e-mail: Corpcomms@Hemscott.co.uk; web site: www.hemscott.com

		holding %
Chairman	Michael Grade	0.1
Chief Executive	Rosalyn Wilton	0.4
Financial Director	Angus Watson	0.0
Chief Technology Officer	Stephen Roche	0.02

Main Shareholders:

Finmedia	55.0
INVESCO English and International Trust	5.7
Intrinsic Value	5.6
Co-operation Ret Ben Fund	4.4
SG Asset Management	4.2

Percentage of free market capital: 24.3%

Nominated Adviser:	KBC Peel Hunt, London
AIM Broker:	KBC Peel Hunt, London
Solicitors:	Richards Butler, London
Market Makers:	KBCS; WINS
Auditors:	Deloitte & Touche, 180 The Strand, London WC2R 1BL
Registrars:	Capita Registrars

ENTRY ON AIM:	15/8/2000	Recent price:	40.5p
Interim results:	Jul	Market cap:	£13.02m
Final results:	Feb	Issue price:	2.25p
Year end:	Dec	Current no of shares:	
Accounts due:	Mar		32,136,419
Int div paymnt:	n/a	No of shares after	
Fin div paymnt:	n/a	dilution:	37,193,587
Int net div per share:	nil	P/E ratio:	n/a
Fin net div per share:	nil	Probable CGT?	YES

LATEST REPORTED RESULTS: 2003		PREVIOUS REPORTED RESULTS: 2002	
Turnover:	£6.42m	Turnover:	£5.16m
PTP:	£(1.14m)	PTP:	£(2.4m)
EPS:	(3.5)p	EPS:	(7.5)p

Comments:

Hemscott reduced losses last year as the company's business information products chipped in £5.1m revenues, a 27.5% improvement on 2002. More than 90 customers, mostly financial institutions, now take 'Company Guru', while around 350 firms have signed up for the investor relations service. By comparison, progress at Hemscott's media division has been more measured. £6m of cash remains in the bank although house broker KBC Peel Hunt doesn't reckon the group will break even until 2005.

Henderson Morley (HML)

Developer of therapies to combat herpes and other DNA viruses

Metropolitan House, 2 Salisbury Road, Mosely, Birmingham, B13 8JS Tel: 0121-442 4600; Fax: 0121-442 4611;
e-mail: info@henderson-morley.com; web site: www.henderson-morley.com

		holding %
Chairman	Andrew Knight	39.0
Chief Executive	Ian Pardoe	19.8
Finance Director	Christopher Pate	0.0015
Non-Exec Director	Michael Fowler	0.0

Main Shareholders:

Iken Communications	5.0

Percentage of free market capital: 35.1%

Nominated Adviser:	Brewin Dolphin, Leeds
AIM Broker:	Hoodless Brennan, London
Solicitors:	Wragge & Co, Birmingham
Market Makers:	KBCS; SCAP; WINS
Auditors:	Moore Stephens, Birmingham
Registrars:	Neville Registrars

ENTRY ON AIM:	11/9/2001	Recent price:	1.75p
Interim results:	Jan	Market cap:	£3.66m
Final results:	Jul	Issue price:	4.0p
Year end:	Apr	Current no of shares:	
Accounts due:	Aug		209,200,349
Int div paymnt:	n/a	No of shares after	
Fin div paymnt:	n/a	dilution:	n/a
Int net div per share:	nil	P/E ratio:	n/a
Fin net div per share:	nil	Probable CGT?	YES

LATEST REPORTED RESULTS:	2003	PREVIOUS REPORTED RESULTS:	2002
Turnover:	£11,000	Turnover:	£22,000
PTP:	£(685,000)	PTP:	£(587,000)
EPS:	(0.4)p	EPS:	(0.4)p

Comments:

This ex-Ofex stock is looking for a cure for herpes, especially the genital variety. It has developed ICVT, a proprietary anti-viral technology, and has licensed this out to German drugs group Croma Pharma, who will fund Phase II trials on ICVT's use on treating certain eye conditions. In return, Croma has invested £0.35m in ReGen. An ear application is also being tested. At the end of October cash stood at £354,000 following a £377,000 interim loss. Funding remains a concern.

Hereward Ventures (HEV)

Investor in natural resource exploration

Simmonds House, Simmonds Buildings, Bristol Road, Bristol, BS16 1RY Tel: 0117-957 3666; Fax: 0117-956 2666;
e-mail: enquiry@hereward.com; web site: www.hereward.com

		holding %
Chairman	Michael Thomsen	0.0
Managing Director	David Bramhill	0.8
Finance Director		
Operations Director	Colin Andrew	1.3

Main Shareholders:

Orogen	6.1
Cambridge Mineral Resources	4.7
Douglas Wright	4.6
Ashdale Investment Trust Services	3.3
Crosslane	3.1

Percentage of free market capital: 63.4%

Nominated Adviser:	Westhouse Securities, London
AIM Broker:	Westhouse Securities, London
Solicitors:	Osborne Clarke, Bristol
Market Makers:	MLSB; SCAP; WINS
Auditors:	Grant Thornton, Southampton
Registrars:	Capita Registrars

ENTRY ON AIM:	12/2/2001	Recent price:	7.0p
Interim results:	Dec	Market cap:	£8.09m
Final results:	Sep	Issue price:	5.0p
Year end:	Mar	Current no of shares:	
Accounts due:	Jul		115,589,996
Int div paymnt:	n/a	No of shares after	
Fin div paymnt:	n/a	dilution:	n/a
Int net div per share:	nil	P/E ratio:	n/a
Fin net div per share:	nil	Probable CGT?	No

LATEST REPORTED RESULTS:	2003	PREVIOUS REPORTED RESULTS:	2002
Turnover:	n/a	Turnover:	n/a
PTP:	£(313,000)	PTP:	£(265,000)
EPS:	(0.3)p	EPS:	(0.4)p

Comments:

Hereward has diversified from Balkan gold prospecting to UK oil and gas, farming in to Isle of Wight and southern England prospects with Black Rock Resources. But Hereward, which lost an interim £215,000 and recently raised £720,000 at 4p, is still looking for gold at Chaira in Bulgaria, which it claims could hold much more than the 450,000 oz suggested by local state geologists 20 years ago. Speculative.

Hidefield (HIF)

Mineral explorer and developer

29 Albermarle Street, London, W1S 4JB Tel: 020-7544 5555; Fax: 020-7499 6099; e-mail: kennethbone@hidefield.com

		holding %
Chairman	John Prochnau	14.1
Chief Executive		
Finance Director	Kenneth Bone	0.1
Non-Exec Director	Harry Pearl	0.4

Main Shareholders:

Web Shareshop	16.5
Resources Investment Trust	9.7
Anglo Pacific	6.0
Ashton Agricultural and General	5.5
RAB Special Situations	4.5

Percentage of free market capital: 38.8%

Comments:

Speculative mineral play Hidefield has pleased investors, including Bruce Rowan's Web Shareshop, by buying into gold assets held by Black Swan Resources (now Arko) in exchange for shares. Drilling at one of these, Cata Preta in Brazil, where Hidefeld has 20%, showed 'encouraging' gold grades ranging from 6.3 to 21.77 grammes a tonne.

Nominated Adviser:	Westhouse Securities, London
AIM Broker:	Westhouse Securities, London
Solicitors:	Field Fisher Waterhouse, London
Market Makers:	SCAP; WINS
Auditors:	Kingston Smith, 60 Goswell Road, London, EC1M 7AD
Registrars:	Melton Registrars

Entry on AIM:	7/12/2000	**Recent price:**	7.75p
Interim results:	Jun	**Market cap:**	£9.46m
Final results:	Aug	**Issue price:**	10.0p
Year end:	May	**Current no of shares:**	
Accounts due:	Sep		122,000,000
Int div paymnt:	n/a	**No of shares after**	
Fin div paymnt:	n/a	**dilution:**	n/a
Int net div per share:	nil	**P/E ratio:**	n/a
Fin net div per share:	nil	**Probable CGT?**	No

LATEST REPORTED RESULTS: 2002		PREVIOUS REPORTED RESULTS: 2001	
Turnover:	£1.71m	Turnover:	£8.21m
PTP:	£(454,000)	PTP:	£(1.02m)
EPS:	(1.0)p	EPS:	(3.3)p

Highams Systems Services (HSS)

IT products & business services supplier

Quadrant House, 33/45 Croydon Road, Caterham, Surrey CR3 6PB Tel: 01883-341144; Fax: 01883-346699; e-mail: group@highams.co.uk; web site: www.highams.co.uk

		holding %
Chairman	Nigel Graham Maw	0.5
Chief Executive	Ted Andrews	17.4
Finance Director	Tony Eve	0.3
Deputy Chairman	John Higham*	36.3

Main Shareholders:

Denis Drinan	11.2
John Higham Family Trust*	6.3
New Town Nominees	3.5
Chase Nominees	3.5

Percentage of free market capital: 41.9%

*JE Higham's interests includes 1,230,000 shares held by the John Higham Family Trust

Comments:

Having sold its business solutions arm, Highams Systems Services is now focusing its financial resources – buoyed by sale proceeds – on developing and expanding its recruitment activities, where it provides permanent and contract IT personnel to the insurance and finance sector. Interims to September showed narrower losses of £102,000 (£212,000) on turnover of £4.8m (£5.6m), with £4m related to recruiting. Cash remained strong at £904,000.

Nominated Adviser:	Charles Stanley, London
AIM Broker:	Charles Stanley, London
Solicitors:	Withers, London
Market Makers:	TEAM; WINS
Auditors:	BDO Stoy Hayward, 69 Tweedy Rd, Bromley, Kent BR1 3WA
Registrars:	Capita Registrars

Entry on AIM:	16/12/1996	**Recent price:**	13.25p
Interim results:	Dec	**Market cap:**	£2.59m
Final results:	Aug	**Issue price:**	36.0p
Year end:	Mar	**Current no of shares:**	
Accounts due:	Jun		19,574,298
Int div paymnt:	n/a	**No of shares after**	
Fin div paymnt:	n/a	**dilution:**	20,434,177
Int net div per share:	nil	**P/E ratio:**	n/a
Fin net div per share:	nil	**Probable CGT?**	Yes

LATEST REPORTED RESULTS: 2003		PREVIOUS REPORTED RESULTS: 2002	
Turnover:	£11.10m	Turnover:	£16.78m
PTP:	£(195,000)	PTP:	£(298,000)
EPS:	(1.0)p	EPS:	(1.2)p

Highland Gold Mining   (HGM)
Russian gold mining projects developer
Le Gallais Chambers, 54 Bath Street, St Helier, Jersey JE4 8YD

		holding %
Chairman	Lord Daresbury	1.6
Chief Executive	Ivan Koulakov	20.4
Finance Director	Denis Alexandrov	0.0
Non-Exec Director	Christopher Palmer-Tomkinson	0.5

Main Shareholders:

Barrick Gold	17.0
Hightops Gold	6.8
Posaune	4.0
London & Lochside Investments	3.2

Percentage of free market capital: 31.3%

Nominated Adviser:	W H Ireland, Manchester
AIM Broker:	W H Ireland, Manchester
Solicitors:	Fox Brooks Marshall, Manchester
Market Makers:	KBCS; NUMS; SCAP; WINS
Auditors:	Ernst & Young, Becket House, 1 Lambeth Palace Road, SE1 7EU
Registrars:	Capita Registrars

ENTRY ON AIM: 17/12/2002		**Recent price:**	267.5p
Interim results:	Oct	**Market cap:**	£320.57m
Final results:	Apr	**Issue price:**	190.0p
Year end:	Dec	**Current no of shares:**	
Accounts due:	Apr		119,838,260
Int div paymnt:	n/a	**No of shares after**	
Fin div paymnt:	n/a	**dilution:**	n/a
Int net div per share:	nil	**P/E ratio:**	n/a
Fin net div per share:	nil	**Probable CGT?**	No

LATEST REPORTED RESULTS: 184 DAY PERIOD TO DEC 02		PREVIOUS REPORTED RESULTS:	N/A
Turnover:	$27.42m	Turnover:	n/a
PTP:	$9.43m	PTP:	n/a
EPS:	6.9c	EPS:	n/a

Comments:
Canada's Barrick Gold has nearly 17% of Russia-focused Highland, after the placing of South African group Harmony's 32% stake at 235p. Barrick and Highland have agreed a four-year co-operation deal in Russia and discussed a joint venture at the Mayskoye project. Highland, which raised interim profits 62% to £7.3m, lifted output at its Mnogovershinnoye mine 9% to 194,000 oz last year.

Highland Timber   (HTB)
Forestry investor & timber harvester
23 Cathedral Yard, Exeter, EX1 1HB Tel: 01392-412122; Fax: 01392-253282;
e-mail: fim@fimltd.co.uk; web site: www.fimltd.co.uk

		holding %
Chairman	Ian Henderson	15.0
Chief Executive		
Finance Director		
Non-Exec Director	Timothy Congdon	2.2

Main Shareholders:

Rathbone Brothers	11.7
Lord Weinstock	4.7

Percentage of free market capital: 66.2%

Nominated Adviser:	Arbuthnot, London
AIM Broker:	Arbuthnot, London
Solicitors:	Brodies, Edinburgh
Market Makers:	WINS
Auditors:	Grant Thornton, 1 Westminster Way, Oxford OX2 0PZ
Registrars:	Computershare Investor Services

ENTRY ON AIM: 17/6/1997		**Recent price:**	71.5p
Interim results:	Aug	**Market cap:**	£6.32m
Final results:	Feb	**Issue price:**	124.0p
Year end:	Dec	**Current no of shares:**	
Accounts due:	Mar		8,832,266
Int div paymnt:	n/a	**No of shares after**	
Fin div paymnt:	n/a	**dilution:**	n/a
Int net div per share:	nil	**P/E ratio:**	n/a
Fin net div per share:	nil	**Probable CGT?**	YES

LATEST REPORTED RESULTS: 2003		PREVIOUS REPORTED RESULTS: 2002	
Turnover:	£1.63m	Turnover:	£1.6m
PTP:	£(516,000)	PTP:	£(910,000)
EPS:	(5.8)p	EPS:	(10.3)p

Comments:
Highland continued to cut losses in 2003, however it still remains hampered by weak world timber prices that have yet to show any improvement. Owning nine forests in New Zealand and six in the UK, a significant proportion of its trees are reaching maturity so the company could increase its felling programme should a recovery emerge. The company's net debt was £3.6m in January but worryingly cash at bank and in hand was negative £1.5m.

Holders Technology (HDT)

Provider of products and services to the electronics industry

Northway House, 1379 High Road, Whetstone, London, N20 9LP Tel: 020-8343 7095; Fax: 020-8446 9566;
e-mail: info@holders.co.uk; web site: www.holders.co.uk

		holding %
Chairman	Rudi Weinreich	50.0
Chief Executive	as above	
Finance Director	Jim Shawyer	0.4
Sales & Mktg	Michael Batsch	0.0
Director		

Main Shareholders:

Rath Dhu	9.9
Armstrong Investments	7.8
Hugh Gregory	3.0

Percentage of free market capital: 28.3%

Nominated Adviser:	Rowan Dartington, Bristol
AIM Broker:	Rowan Dartington, Bristol
Solicitors:	Osborne Clarke, Bristol
Market Makers:	WINS
Auditors:	RSM Robson Rhodes, Cambridge
Registrars:	Capita Registrars

ENTRY ON AIM:	8/10/2001	Recent price:	79.0p
Interim results:	Jul	Market cap:	£3.27m
Final results:	Mar	Issue price:	50.0p
Year end:	Nov	Current no of shares:	
Accounts due:	Mar		4,144,551
Int div paymnt:	Sep	No of shares after	
Fin div paymnt:	May	dilution:	4,199,551
Int net div per share:	2.0p	P/E ratio:	29.3
Fin net div per share:	2.5p	Probable CGT?	YES

LATEST REPORTED RESULTS:	2003	PREVIOUS REPORTED RESULTS:	2002
Turnover:	£14.20m	Turnover:	£9.01m
PTP:	£328,000	PTP:	£(133,000)
EPS:	2.7p	EPS:	(2.3)p

Comments:

Holders is a small European distributor of materials and other products to manufacturers of printed circuit boards. In 2003, the group went back into profit thanks to robust UK operations and its enlarged German activities. It still faces challenging conditions in Holland and was adversely impacted in Scandinavia. It has disposed of its holding in loss-making Justfone. The company also has a strong balance sheet with virtually no long-term debt.

Home Entertainment (HET)

Video and DVD rental business

19-24 Manasty Road, Orton Southgate, Peterborough, PE2 6UP Tel: 01733-233464; Fax: 01733-238966;
web site: www.hecplc.com

		holding %
Chairman	Iain Muspratt	29.6
Chief Executive	as above	
Finance Director	John Sealey	0.9
Deputy Chairman	Geoffrey Hopkins	13.0

Main Shareholders:

Diane Gardner	15.1
ABN AMRO Asset Management	14.9
Schroder Investment Management	13.1
British Steel Pension Fund	4.5

Percentage of free market capital: 8.4%

Nominated Adviser:	Teather & Greenwood, London
AIM Broker:	Teather & Greenwood, London
Solicitors:	Nicholson Graham & Jones, London
Market Makers:	TEAM; WINS
Auditors:	Ernst & Young, Cambridge
Registrars:	Lloyds TSB Registrars

ENTRY ON AIM:	25/10/2001	Recent price:	195.0p
Interim results:	Jan	Market cap:	£35.18m
Final results:	Aug	Issue price:	170.0p
Year end:	May	Current no of shares:	
Accounts due:	Oct		18,043,475
Int div paymnt:	Apr	No of shares after	
Fin div paymnt:	Nov	dilution:	18,699,015
Int net div per share:	2.2p	P/E ratio:	9.3
Fin net div per share:	3.8p	Probable CGT?	YES

LATEST REPORTED RESULTS:	2003	PREVIOUS REPORTED RESULTS:	2002
Turnover:	£120.66m	Turnover:	£103.04m
PTP:	£5.95m	PTP:	£4.73m
EPS:	20.9p	EPS:	14.4p

Comments:

HET operates a 213-strong DVD rental chain under the Choices Video brand. Interims saw sales rise 6.3% to £70.4m but pre-tax profits drop 15.3% to £3.3m. Management put this down to the exceptionally good weather at the end of last summer and heavy investment in a new EPOS system. On the internet side, business remained brisk. The second half has started satisfactorily with Xmas and New Year sales holding up. Net assets improved 11.1% to 94.8p per share.

Honeycombe Leisure (HCL)
Pub owner & operator

Marian House, Beech Grove, Ashton, Preston PR2 1DU Tel: 01772-723764; Fax: 01772-722470;
e-mail: info@honeycombe.co.uk; web site: www.honeycombe.co.uk

		holding %
Chairman	Sandy Anderson	40.0
Joint Chief Executive	Bryan Wardman	2.4
Finance Director	Paul Snape	0.02
Joint Chief Executive	James Baer	2.2

Main Shareholders:

Unicorn Asset management	14.5
Rights and Issues Investment	5.7
V Wardman	4.9
Close Finsbury Asset managment	4.9
Electra Quoted Management	4.4

Percentage of free market capital: 21.0%

Comments:

Honeycombe's strategy to manage pubs on behalf of pub owners is beginning to pay off as it received £94,000 in fees in the first half from Nectar Taverns. When the portfolio is fully grown, fees receivable could hit £500,000. Other management deals include six Ma Hubbard sites and 13 Punch pubs. The group has negotiated a new £32m loan to increase working capital facilities. Gearing has dropped but it still has a way to go on this front.

Nominated Adviser:	Charles Stanley, London		
AIM Broker:	Charles Stanley, London		
Solicitors:	Pinsents, London		
Market Makers:	KBCS; WDBM; WINS		
Auditors:	KPMG, Preston		
Registrars:	Capita Registrars		

ENTRY ON AIM:	4/11/1998	**Recent price:**	69.0p
Interim results:	Jan	**Market cap:**	£21.66m
Final results:	Jul	**Issue price:**	55.0p
Year end:	Apr	**Current no of shares:**	
Accounts due:	Aug		31,394,369
Int div paymnt:	Apr	**No of shares after**	
Fin div paymnt:	Oct	**dilution:**	n/a
Int net div per share:	0.9p	**P/E ratio:**	10.5
Fin net div per share:	2.2p	**Probable CGT?**	YES

LATEST REPORTED RESULTS: 2003		**PREVIOUS REPORTED RESULTS:** 2002	
Turnover:	£33.0m	Turnover:	£32.45m
PTP:	£2.58m	PTP:	£0.4m
EPS:	6.6p	EPS:	(0.1)p

Honeygrove (formerly Propan Homes) (HYG)
Residential property developer

Chapel House, 31 London Road, Sevenoaks, Kent TN13 1AR Tel: 01732-743393; Fax: 01732-746282;
e-mail: info@honeygrove.co.uk; web site: www.honeygrove.co.uk

		holding %
Chairman	James Dubois	2.2
Chief Executive	Christopher Johnson	0.4
Finance Director	Terence Negus	2.0
Deputy Chairman	Jeremy Streeten	12.4

Main Shareholders:

Alexander Johnson	15.9
Louise Johnson	15.9
House & Property Venture Capital*	13.7
Nigel Wray	6.5
Pershing Keen Nominees	5.6

Percentage of free market capital: 13.6%
*Alex and Louise Johnson are interested in these shares

Comments:

Honeygrove was formed through the merger of private group Honeygrove Holdings with AIM-listed Propan Homes. Developing luxury accomodation and mid-market starter homes, it currently has over 210 plots with planning consent. The jewel in its crown is its Swaylands site in Penshurst, Kent, where gross development profits have been valued at £15-20m. Chief executive Chris Johnson is predicting pre-tax profits of £5.8m for the year to September.

Nominated Adviser:	Seymour Pierce, London		
AIM Broker:	Seymour Pierce Ellis, Crawley		
Solicitors:	Memery Crystal, London		
Market Makers:	SCAP; WINS		
Auditors:	Baker Tilly, Tunbridge Wells, Kent		
Registrars:	SLC Registrars		

ENTRY ON AIM:	6/3/2001	**Recent price:**	11.5p
Interim results:	Jun	**Market cap:**	£14.12m
Final results:	Jan	**Issue price:**	14.0p
Year end:	Sep	**Current no of shares:**	
Accounts due:	Jan		122,777,096
Int div paymnt:	n/a	**No of shares after**	
Fin div paymnt:	n/a	**dilution:**	n/a
Int net div per share:	nil	**P/E ratio:**	n/a
Fin net div per share:	nil	**Probable CGT?**	No

LATEST REPORTED RESULTS: 2003		**PREVIOUS REPORTED RESULTS:** 2002	
Turnover:	£14.85m	Turnover:	£12.93m
PTP:	£(1.74m)	PTP:	£2.48m
EPS:	n/a	EPS:	3.2p

Honeysuckle (suspended 19 Nov 2003) (HYS)

Shell

25 Upper brook Street, London, W1K 7QD Tel: 020-8228 1642; Fax: 020-8228 1643; e-mail: colin.ingram@honey.co.uk

		holding %
Chairman	Sandy Anderson	50.0
Chief Executive		
Finance Director	Colin Ingram	1.0
Non-Exec Director	hammer	7.0
Main Shareholders:		
Peter Mountford		7.0

Percentage of free market capital: 35.0%

Nominated Adviser:	Collins Stewart, London
AIM Broker:	Collins Stewart, London
Solicitors:	Addleshaw Goddard, London
Market Makers:	CSCS; KBCS; MLSB; SCAP; WINS
Auditors:	Ernst & Young, 14 King Street, Leeds LS1 2JN
Registrars:	Capita Registrars

ENTRY ON AIM:	16/12/1999	Recent price:	0.3p
Interim results:	Mar	Market cap:	£1.44m
Final results:	Nov	Issue price:	2.0p
Year end:	May	Current no of shares:	
Accounts due:	Nov		480,622,500
Int div paymnt:	n/a	No of shares after	
Fin div paymnt:	n/a	dilution:	n/a
Int net div per share:	nil	P/E ratio:	n/a
Fin net div per share:	nil	Probable CGT?	YES

LATEST REPORTED RESULTS: 2002		PREVIOUS REPORTED RESULTS: 2001	
Turnover:	n/a	Turnover:	£1.76m
PTP:	£(576,000)	PTP:	£(804,000)
EPS:	(0.1)p	EPS:	(0.2)p

Comments:
Back in November, Honeysuckle's shares were suspended pending the result of discussions. Directors revealed the company was in talks with a private company that might make an offer, but there's been nothing to report since. Honeysuckle itself had been on the lookout for an acquisition to rejuvenate its fortunes for some time. Latest figures from the company were for the half to November 2002. These revealed pre-tax losses of £154,000 (£240,000) and a loss per share of 0.03p.

Host Europe (HER)

Internet hosting solutions and internet services company

Host Europe House, Kendal Avenue, London, W3 0XA Tel: 020-8896 7500; Fax: 020-8752 1883;
e-mail: invest@hosteurope.com; web site: www.hosteurope.com

		holding %
Chairman	Garry Southern	0.0
Chief Executive	Abby Hardoon	16.6
Finance Director	Stephen Sadler	0.0
Technology Director	Victor Gareh	15.9
Main Shareholders:		
Marcus Lauder		6.3
SG Asset Management		5.8

Percentage of free market capital: 55.4%

Nominated Adviser:	Durlacher, London
AIM Broker:	Durlacher, London
Solicitors:	Hammonds, Manchester
Market Makers:	ALTI; BGMM; MLSB; SCAP; WINS
Auditors:	BDO Stoy Hayward, 8 Baker Street, London W1M 1DA
Registrars:	Capita Registrars

ENTRY ON AIM:	13/9/1999	Recent price:	2.25p
Interim results:	Sep	Market cap:	£26.48m
Final results:	Mar	Issue price:	2.5p
Year end:	Dec	Current no of shares:	
Accounts due:	Apr		1,176,725,619
Int div paymnt:	n/a	No of shares after	
Fin div paymnt:	n/a	dilution:	n/a
Int net div per share:	nil	P/E ratio:	n/a
Fin net div per share:	nil	Probable CGT?	YES

LATEST REPORTED RESULTS: 2002		PREVIOUS REPORTED RESULTS: 2001	
Turnover:	£13.7m	Turnover:	£9.53m
PTP:	£(505,000)	PTP:	£(34.42m)
EPS:	(0.1)p	EPS:	(3.4)p

Comments:
In spite of last summer's much-publicised board upheaval, web services business Host Europe continues to deliver. First-half sales lifted 26% to £8.2m and though losses increased from £269,000 to £657,000 they did include £777,000 of exceptional costs relating to the departure of the entire executive board except for CEO Abby Hardoon. The second half, by all accounts, has been just as successful and cash generation is said to have been strong.

Hot (HOT)

Internet recruitment service and recruitment fair operator

3 Shortlands, London, W6 8JH Tel: 0845-1304422; Fax: 0845-1304433; web site: www.thehotgroup.com

		holding %
Chairman	Anthony Reeves	3.2
Chief Executive		
Finance Director	Stephen Wright	0.3
Managing Director	Harvey Sinclair	1.8

Main Shareholders:

Morley Fund Management	11.3
HSBC	10.2
Chase Nominees	9.3
Vidacos Nominees	9.1
New Star Asset Management	6.6

Percentage of free market capital: 10.5%

Nominated Adviser:	Strand Partners, London
AIM Broker:	Numis, London
Solicitors:	Denton Wilde, London
Market Makers:	SCAP; WINS
Auditors:	Baker Tilly, 2 Bloomsbury Street, London WC1B 3ST
Registrars:	Capita Registrars

Entry on AIM:	1/6/1999	Recent price:	21.25p
Interim results:	May	Market cap:	£32.9m
Final results:	Nov	Issue price:	50.0p
Year end:	Sep	Current no of shares:	
Accounts due:	Jan		154,845,109
Int div paymnt:	n/a	No of shares after	
Fin div paymnt:	n/a	dilution:	n/a
Int net div per share:	nil	P/E ratio:	n/a
Fin net div per share:	nil	Probable CGT?	Yes

LATEST REPORTED RESULTS: 2003		PREVIOUS REPORTED RESULTS: 16 MONTHS TO 31 AUG 02	
Turnover:	£2.63m	Turnover:	£2.83m
PTP:	£(6.06m)	PTP:	£(4.71m)
EPS:	(12.0)p	EPS:	(31.2)p

Comments:

Numis has upgraded forecasts for the recruiter that reversed into RexOnline in 2002. Investors can now expect a £1.7m profit this year, rising to £2.6m in 2005. hot has diversified through acquisitions from online operations into traditional recruiting, and other new areas with good growth prospects. The latest purchase was The Graduate, a recruiter with blue chip clients like Citigroup and Dresdner Kleinwort Wasserstein. Analysts predict healthy year-end net cash of £1.7m.

Hurlingham (HRL)

Residential property investor & hotel developer

Pear Tree Ho, Hopperton, Knaresborough, N Yorks HG5 8NX Tel: 01423-331356; Fax: 01423-331356

		holding %
Chairman	Charles Llewellyn	5.9
Chief Executive	Charles Pettingell	6.0
Finance Director	as above	
Director	Maurice Taylor	5.9

Main Shareholders:

Aberdeen Development Capital	19.3
Acremanor	10.6

Percentage of free market capital: 52.3%

*W Nixon is a director of Aberdeen Development Capital

Nominated Adviser:	Teather & Greenwood, London
AIM Broker:	Teather & Greenwood, London
Solicitors:	Howard Kennedy, London
Market Makers:	KBCS; TEAM; WINS
Auditors:	F W Stephens & Co, London
Registrars:	Capita Registrars

Entry on AIM:	3/4/1996	Recent price:	71.0p
Interim results:	Jun	Market cap:	£1.43m
Final results:	Jan	Issue price:	80.0p
Year end:	Sep	Current no of shares:	
Accounts due:	Mar		2,015,488
Int div paymnt:	Jan	No of shares after	
Fin div paymnt:	Apr	dilution:	n/a
Int net div per share:	0.5p	P/E ratio:	n/a
Fin net div per share:	1.0p	Probable CGT?	No

LATEST REPORTED RESULTS: 2003		PREVIOUS REPORTED RESULTS: 2002	
Turnover:	£1.45m	Turnover:	£1.66m
PTP:	£(206,000)	PTP:	£(69,000)
EPS:	(10.2)p	EPS:	(3.7)p

Comments:

With a continued decline in the tourist industry following 9/11, Hurlingham had a mixed 2003. Its hotel in Perth enjoyed higher occupancy and has benefited from a £111,440 increase in value, but the travel agency subsidiary suffered. Losses to September rose substantially but the company is looking to capture the growing online business with a new division Custom Flights, which will be purely online and focused on the European holiday market. NAV at September was £2.5m.

Huveaux   (HVX)

Acquisition vehicle in the media sector

4 Grosvenor Place, London, SW1X 7DL Tel: 020-7245 0270; Fax: 020-7245 0271

		holding %
Chairman	John van Kuffeler	4.7
Chief Executive		
Finance Director	David Horne	0.0
Non-Exec Director	Timothy Benn	2.9

Main Shareholders:

ISIS Asset management	14.6
Jupiter Asset Management	11.9
Schroders Investment Management	11.4
Singer & Friedlander Investment	10.7
Rathbone Investment management	9.1

Percentage of free market capital: 8.1%

Comments:

Specialist publishing and media business Huveaux is making significant strides with its buy-and-build expansion strategy. Three acquisitions were completed in 2003, in the training, education and political biographical market. Earlier this year it completed its fourth, snapping up the Public Affairs Newsletter for £750,000. Significant earnings and sales growth was recorded last year and much the same is expected this year. An exciting venture.

Nominated Adviser:	Brewin Dolphin, Edinburgh		
AIM Broker:	Brewin Dolphin, Glasgow		
Solicitors:	Eversheds, London		
Market Makers:	KBCS; WINS		
Auditors:	KPMG Audit Plc, London		
Registrars:	Lloyds TSB Registrars		

ENTRY ON AIM: 17/12/2001		Recent price:	61.0p
Interim results:	Aug	Market cap:	£43.59m
Final results:	Feb	Issue price:	25.0p
Year end:	Dec	Current no of shares:	
Accounts due:	May		71,464,730
Int div paymnt:	n/a	No of shares after	
Fin div paymnt:	Dec	dilution:	n/a
Int net div per share:	nil	P/E ratio:	30.5
Fin net div per share:	0.75p	Probable CGT?	YES

LATEST REPORTED RESULTS: 2003		PREVIOUS REPORTED RESULTS: 2002	
Turnover:	£4.58m	Turnover:	£1.05m
PTP:	£1.21m	PTP:	£368,000
EPS:	2.0p	EPS:	2.1p

---

i-documentsystems   (IDOX)

Information management solution provider

10th Floor, 21 New Fetter Lane, London, EC4A 1AJ Tel: 020-7427 0660; Fax: 020-7427 0661;
e-mail: investors@i-documentsystems.com; web site: www.i-documentsystems.com

		holding %
Chairman	John Wisbey	14.2
Chief Executive	Andrew Fraser	10.4
Finance Director	Timothy Bowen	1.3
Non-Exec Director	Peter Lilley	0.0

Main Shareholders:

Lombard Risk Management	10.6
Herald Investment Trust	8.9
ISIS	5.9
Invesco	5.4
Dresdner Kleinwort Wasserstein	4.8

Percentage of free market capital: 18.3%

Comments:

Full year results from local authority-focused IT services business IDOX surpassed analyst expectations as the company moved into profit during the final quarter. There were other positives too. For one, recurring revenues – generated from long-term managed service contracts – almost doubled to £2.3m during the period. For another cash reserves rose slightly to £2.7m even after September's £1.7m acquisition of e-commerce consultancy Mandoforms.

Nominated Adviser:	Noble & Co, London		
AIM Broker:	Noble & Co, London		
Solicitors:	Memery Crystal, London		
Market Makers:	SCAP; WINS		
Auditors:	Grant Thornton, London		
Registrars:	Park Circus		

ENTRY ON AIM: 19/12/2000		Recent price:	10.25p
Interim results:	Jun	Market cap:	£15.7m
Final results:	Dec	Issue price:	12.0p
Year end:	Oct	Current no of shares:	
Accounts due:	Jan		153,178,902
Int div paymnt:	n/a	No of shares after	
Fin div paymnt:	n/a	dilution:	153,830,904
Int net div per share:	nil	P/E ratio:	n/a
Fin net div per share:	nil	Probable CGT?	YES

LATEST REPORTED RESULTS: 2003		PREVIOUS REPORTED RESULTS: 2002	
Turnover:	£4.47m	Turnover:	£3.02m
PTP:	£(595,000)	PTP:	£(1.48m)
EPS:	(0.4)p	EPS:	(1.1)p

I2S (ITS)

Investment company

3rd Floor, Commonwealth House, 2 Chalk Hill Road, London, W6 8DW Tel: 020-8846 2703; Fax: 0870-458 2601;
e-mail: enquiries@i2s.co.uk; web site: www.i2s.co.uk

		holding %
Chairman	Neville Buch*	22.4
Chief Executive		
Finance Director		
Non-Exec Director	Richard Blackburn	11.6

Main Shareholders:

P M Blackburn & J A Wild	5.7
J Denye	4.7

Percentage of free market capital: 49.1%

*Neville Buch's interests are in the shares of N D Buch Life Interest Settlement, Royal Bank of Scotland Trust and Owlcastle

Nominated Adviser:	KBC Peel Hunt, London
AIM Broker:	KBC Peel Hunt, London
Solicitors:	Macfarlanes, London
Market Makers:	KBCS; WINS
Auditors:	PKF, Sovereign House, Queen Street, Manchester, M2 5HR
Registrars:	Computershare Investor Services

ENTRY ON AIM:	29/2/2000	Recent price:	94.5p
Interim results:	Dec	Market cap:	£6.9m
Final results:	May	Issue price:	100.0p
Year end:	Mar	Current no of shares:	
Accounts due:	Jul		7,299,000
Int div paymnt:	n/a	No of shares after	
Fin div paymnt:	n/a	dilution:	9,400,000
Int net div per share:	nil	P/E ratio:	n/a
Fin net div per share:	nil	Probable CGT?	No

LATEST REPORTED RESULTS: 2003		PREVIOUS REPORTED RESULTS: 2002	
Turnover:	n/a	Turnover:	n/a
PTP:	£(307,000)	PTP:	£(972,000)
EPS:	(4.2)p	EPS:	(13.1)p

Comments:

I2S is recommending an offer from hedge fund manager RAB Capital. I2S's NAV waned from 61p to 59.5p over the half to September, with the company again failing to find suitable investment opportunities. Its only investment remains unquoted venture Sit-up, which makes up 11% of the portfolio, with 89% held in cash, amounting to £3.9m at the last count. Turnover was £71,000 (£72,000), principally wrought from cash on deposit, and net losses widened to £108,000 (£68,000).

ID Data (IDD)

Smart card manufacturer

Wansell Road, Weldon North, Corby, Northamptonshire NN17 5LX Tel: 0845-310 0099 (UK) 01536-207000
(International); Fax: 01536-203534; e-mail: enquiry@id-data.co.uk; web site: www.id-data.co.uk

		holding %
Chairman	Mike Blackburn	0.1
Chief Executive	Peter Cox	17.6
Finance Director	Martin Coles	0.5
Director	Michael Stewart	0.1

Main Shareholders:

Even Flow Holdings	24.3
Framlington Investment Management	9.3
Singer & Friedlander Investment Management	6.5
Artemis	3.6

Percentage of free market capital: 12.7%

Nominated Adviser:	KBC Peel Hunt, London
AIM Broker:	KBC Peel Hunt, London
Solicitors:	Simmons & Simmons, London
Market Makers:	CSCS; WINS
Auditors:	PKF, New Garden House, 78 Hatton Garden, EC1N 8JA
Registrars:	Capita Registrars

ENTRY ON AIM:	10/10/2000	Recent price:	7.0p
Interim results:	Nov	Market cap:	£19.18m
Final results:	Jul	Issue price:	63.0p
Year end:	Mar	Current no of shares:	
Accounts due:	Jul		274,017,727
Int div paymnt:	n/a	No of shares after	
Fin div paymnt:	n/a	dilution:	n/a
Int net div per share:	nil	P/E ratio:	n/a
Fin net div per share:	nil	Probable CGT?	YES

LATEST REPORTED RESULTS: 2003		PREVIOUS REPORTED RESULTS: 2002	
Turnover:	£19.65m	Turnover:	£17.86m
PTP:	£(3.38m)	PTP:	£(6.43m)
EPS:	(2.2)p	EPS:	(9.4)p

Comments:

The smart card maker is in transition, moving from making low margin plastic cards to licensing out its technology as the industry introduces chip-based credit cards. Interim revenues fell 48% to £5.4m pushing losses up 31% to £1.7m. Last time the results included the launch of the Nectar Loyalty card. Investors are supporting these strategic moves – over £9m has been raised over the past year via various initiatives. £4m paid for the acquisition of rival Mids & Horsey.

Ideal Shopping Direct (IDS)

TV shopping channel and mail order catalogue operator
Ideal Home House, Newark Road, Peterborough, PE1 5WG Tel: 08700-777002; Fax: 08700-777003;
web site: www.idealworldtv.co.uk

		holding %
Chairman	Paul Wright	34.1
Chief Executive	as above	
Finance Director	Michael Creedon	
Commercial Director	Valerie Kaye	17.9

Main Shareholders:
n/a

Percentage of free market capital: 47.9%

Nominated Adviser:	KBC Peel Hunt, London
AIM Broker:	KBC Peel Hunt, London
Solicitors:	Norton Rose, London
Market Makers:	KBCS; WINS
Auditors:	Grant Thornton, Kettering
Registrars:	Capita Registrars

ENTRY ON AIM:	17/2/2000	Recent price:	47.5p
Interim results:	Sep	Market cap:	£13.79m
Final results:	Mar	Issue price:	157.0p
Year end:	Dec	Current no of shares:	
Accounts due:	Mar		29,025,570
Int div paymnt:	n/a	No of shares after	
Fin div paymnt:	n/a	dilution:	29,502,917
Int net div per share:	nil	P/E ratio:	n/a
Fin net div per share:	nil	Probable CGT?	Yes

Comments:
Ideal Shopping has turned recovery into disaster as it expects to make substantial trading losses for the year – contrary to the small profits forecasted by broker KBC Peel Hunt. To address its issues, it will focus on TV shopping on its two channels. It will sell or close its mail order division and has outsourced its call centre operations to India. It is currently restructuring its buying and product sourcing departments and to put more cash in the bank, it has 'dramatically' reduced its stock levels.

LATEST REPORTED RESULTS:	2002	PREVIOUS REPORTED RESULTS:	2001
Turnover:	£32.63m	Turnover:	£17.65m
PTP:	£3.24m	PTP:	£(3.58m)
EPS:	15.5p	EPS:	(15.3)p

IDN Telecom (IDN)

Telecommunication consultancy
Vienna House, International Square, Birmingham International Park, Bickenhill Lane, Solihull, B37 7GN Tel: 0870-777 1775;
Fax: 0870-777 1776; e-mail: investors@idn.co.uk; web site: www.idn.co.uk

		holding %
Chairman	Barry Roberts	17.5
Chief Executive	Mike Morrison	4.6
Finance Director	Steve Cox	0.0
Sales Director	Alan Hanna	2.8

Main Shareholders:

Michael Wilmott	18.6
Simon Dronfield	6.9

Percentage of free market capital: 41.0%

Nominated Adviser:	Seymour Pierce, London
AIM Broker:	Seymour Pierce, London
Solicitors:	Wragge & Co, Birmingham
Market Makers:	SCAP; WINS
Auditors:	Smith, Hodge and Baxter, Corby
Registrars:	Capita Registrars

ENTRY ON AIM:	21/8/2000	Recent price:	3.0p
Interim results:	Jul	Market cap:	£11.64m
Final results:	Mar	Issue price:	5.0p
Year end:	Oct	Current no of shares:	
Accounts due:	Jan		387,916,660
Int div paymnt:	n/a	No of shares after	
Fin div paymnt:	n/a	dilution:	n/a
Int net div per share:	nil	P/E ratio:	30.0
Fin net div per share:	nil	Probable CGT?	Yes

Comments:
IDN is in rude health after posting a decent profit compared to a loss last year. Overheads fell 32%, due largely to the company ditching its branch office network and consolidating its operation into two offices. Thanks to its billing system, where even if more than one telecoms operator is used clients are all charged on one bill, its has gained many converts particularly in the local government and healthcare sectors. For 2004, Seymour Pierce is forecasting £550,000 pre-tax profits.

LATEST REPORTED RESULTS:	2003	PREVIOUS REPORTED RESULTS:	FROM 1 JUL 01 TO 31 OCT 02
Turnover:	£9.21m	Turnover:	£10.17m
PTP:	£258,000	PTP:	£(2.18m)
EPS:	0.1p	EPS:	(0.7)p

Illuminator (ILM)

Funding and development of European e-commerce business

Brettenham House, 1-19 Lancaster Place, London, WC2E 7EN Tel: 020-7520 6900; Fax: 020-7240 6969;
e-mail: info@illuminator.co.uk; web site: www.illuminator.co.uk

		holding %
Joint Chairman	Brian Myerson	2.7
Chief Executive		
Finance Director		
Joint Chairman	Julian Treger	2.7

Main Shareholders:

Shore Capital	19.7
e.investors	15.7
Marylebone Warwick Balfour Group	3.4

Percentage of free market capital: 23.2%

Comments:

South African entrepreneurs Brian Myerson and Julian Treger are actively seeking a reverse takeover candidate for the former technology investor but are being held up by a dispute with the Inland Revenue about a £275,000 tax bill. Last year the group, which boasts £3.9m of tax losses, returned a cumulative £12.8m to shareholders via a dividend and tender offer. Cash stood at £0.62m at the end of June. Annual overheads stand at £99,000.

Nominated Adviser:	Shore Capital, London		
AIM Broker:	Shore Capital, London		
Solicitors:	Sinclair Roche and Temperley, London		
Market Makers:	KLWT; MLSB; SCAP; WINS		
Auditors:	BDO Stoy Hayward, 8 Baker Street, London W1M 1DA		
Registrars:	Capita Registrars		

ENTRY ON AIM:	9/12/1999	**Recent price:**	7.25p
Interim results:	Sep	**Market cap:**	£10.03m
Final results:	Jun	**Issue price:**	45.0p
Year end:	Dec	**Current no of shares:**	
Accounts due:	Jun		138,295,206
Int div paymnt:	n/a	**No of shares after**	
Fin div paymnt:	n/a	**dilution:**	n/a
Int net div per share:	nil	**P/E ratio:**	n/a
Fin net div per share:	nil	**Probable CGT?**	Yes

LATEST REPORTED RESULTS: 2002		PREVIOUS REPORTED RESULTS: 2001	
Turnover:	£28,000	Turnover:	£657,000
PTP:	£(4.01m)	PTP:	£(1.88m)
EPS:	(3.8)p	EPS:	(1.3)p

Image Scan (IGE)

Imaging product developer

Pera Innovation Park, Nottingham Road, Melton Mowbray, Leicestershire, LE13 0PB Tel: 01664-503600;
Fax: 01664-503601; e-mail: info@ish.co.uk; web site: www.ish.co.uk

		holding %
Chairman		
Managing Director	Nicholas Fox	11.7
Finance Director	Ray Gibbs	1.8
Technical Director	Simon Godber	0.0

Main Shareholders:

ISIS Asset Management	17.4
3PC Investment	8.3
AiM VCT2	8.3
Welsh Industrial Investment	6.1
A P Stirling	4.5

Percentage of free market capital: 19.5%

Comments:

Image Scan is yet to reap the rewards from its 3D, multi-view and x-ray imaging technologies. The company has a manufacturing and marketing agreement with Rapiscan in the baggage scanning machine sector for its AXIS-3D system. Focusing on turning its current product range into sales Image Scan has just signed a contract with nuclear medicine supplier Amersham for its 3D system. Brokers Durlacher are predicting sales increasing to £2.5m in 2004.

Nominated Adviser:	Durlacher, London		
AIM Broker:	Durlacher, London		
Solicitors:	Stallards, London		
Market Makers:	SCAP; WINS		
Auditors:	Deloitte & Touche, Nottingham		
Registrars:	Capita Registrars		

ENTRY ON AIM:	25/4/2002	**Recent price:**	39.5p
Interim results:	Jun	**Market cap:**	£7.65m
Final results:	Dec	**Issue price:**	65.0p
Year end:	Sep	**Current no of shares:**	
Accounts due:	Feb		19,373,630
Int div paymnt:	n/a	**No of shares after**	
Fin div paymnt:	n/a	**dilution:**	n/a
Int net div per share:	nil	**P/E ratio:**	n/a
Fin net div per share:	nil	**Probable CGT?**	Yes

LATEST REPORTED RESULTS: 2003		PREVIOUS REPORTED RESULTS: 2002	
Turnover:	£510,000	Turnover:	£503,000
PTP:	£(839,000)	PTP:	£(665,000)
EPS:	(4.9)p	EPS:	(4.0)p

ImageState (IMA)

Image library
Ramillies House, 1-2 Ramillies Street, London, W1F 7LN Tel: 020-7734 7344; Fax: 020-7287 3933;
e-mail: info@imagestate.co.uk; web site: www.imagestate.co.uk

		holding %
Chairman	Chris Adamson	0.8
Chief Executive	Leslie Hughes	0.0
Finance Director	John McIntosh	0.0
Non-Exec Director	Michael Luckwell	27.9

Main Shareholders:

Pacific Investments	29.0
Alton Investments	16.9

Percentage of free market capital: 21.0%

Comments:

New York and London-based photographic stock agency continues to struggle. Indeed chairman Chris Adamson's recent pronouncement that 'trading since year-end shows an improvement...but is still below expectations' just about sums the company's fortunes up. With cash running out and net debts increased by £3.2m to £8.6m during the period, ImageState's prospects do not look good.

Nominated Adviser:	Evolution Beeson Gregory, London
AIM Broker:	Evolution Beeson Gregory, London
Solicitors:	Taylor Wessing, London
Market Makers:	DMG; WINS
Auditors:	BDO Stoy Hayward, 8 Baker Street, London W1U 3LL
Registrars:	Capita Registrars

Entry on AIM:	21/2/2000	**Recent price:**	0.75p
Interim results:	Mar	**Market cap:**	£1.89m
Final results:	Dec	**Issue price:**	10.0p
Year end:	Jun	**Current no of shares:**	
Accounts due:	Nov		251,485,178
Int div paymnt:	n/a	**No of shares after**	
Fin div paymnt:	n/a	dilution:	264,362,150
Int net div per share:	nil	**P/E ratio:**	n/a
Fin net div per share:	nil	**Probable CGT?**	**Yes**

LATEST REPORTED RESULTS: 2003		**PREVIOUS REPORTED RESULTS:** 2002	
Turnover:	£5.48m	Turnover:	£7.03m
PTP:	£(3.54m)	PTP:	£(22.11m)
EPS:	(1.4)p	EPS:	(9.6)p

Immedia Broadcasting (IME)

Design and operation of in store radio stations
7-9 The Broadway, Newbury, Berkshire RG14 1RS Tel: 01635-572800; Fax: 01635-572801

		holding %
Chairman	Geoff Howard-Spink	0.0
Chief Executive	Trevor Brookes	3.0
Finance Director	Robert Parker	0.3
Non-Exec Director	Peter Teague	0.0

Main Shareholders:

Mark Horricks	11.9
BBME	9.8
Equity Partnership	6.5
Ian Watson	5.0
Allan Cockell	4.6

Percentage of free market capital: 47.0%

Comments:

Run by 80s Radio 1 disc jockey Bruno Brookes, this venture delivers 'in-store radio stations' to shops in the UK. At present, interests include Newagents Radio, picked up by 2,300 shops; and Lloydspharmacy Live, which gets broadcast to no less than 1260 of this chain. £3.77m was raising on admission, to be used as it seeks to expand its Newsagent Radio arm and broker deals with other major retail operators. Given the experience of other similar ventures in the past, investors will need nerves of steel.

Nominated Adviser:	Teather & Greenwood, London
AIM Broker:	Teather & Greenwood, London
Solicitors:	Charles Russell, London
Market Makers:	KBCS; TEAM; WINS
Auditors:	KPMG Audit, Reading
Registrars:	Computershare Investor Services

Entry on AIM:	12/12/2003	**Recent price:**	118.0p
Interim results:	Sep	**Market cap:**	£13.82m
Final results:	Mar	**Issue price:**	110.0p
Year end:	Dec	**Current no of shares:**	
Accounts due:	Jun		11,707,910
Int div paymnt:	n/a	**No of shares after**	
Fin div paymnt:	n/a	dilution:	n/a
Int net div per share:	nil	**P/E ratio:**	n/a
Fin net div per share:	nil	**Probable CGT?**	**Yes**

LATEST REPORTED RESULTS: 2002		**PREVIOUS REPORTED RESULTS:** 2001	
Turnover:	£983,000	Turnover:	£144,000
PTP:	£(651,000)	PTP:	£(1.09m)
EPS:	n/a	EPS:	n/a

Impax (IPX)

Financial consultancy for green businesses

Broughton House, 6-8 Sackville Street, London, W1S 3DG Tel: 020-7434 1122; Fax: 020-7434 1123;
e-mail: info@impax.co.uk; web site: www.impax.co.uk

		holding %
Chairman	Keith Falconer	0.0
Joint Managing	Nigel Taunt	0.6
Director	Deborah Fowler	0.0
Finance Director	Stuart Bickerstaff	7.3
Non-Exec Director		

Main Shareholders:

Swan	22.0
AXA Investment Managers	14.8
Clients of Friends Ivory & Sime	11.2
Active Capital Trust	11.2
Aberdeen Asset Managers	8.4

Percentage of free market capital: 14.1%

Comments:

The environmental corporate finance and asset management concern may have announced improved results for the year but losses are still high. The Starks oil field was finally sold netting £767,313. Corporate finance apparently has also achieved significant revenue growth, with increased activity in advising governmental agencies such as the Department of Enterprise, Trade and Investment for Northern Ireland.

Nominated Adviser:	Marshall Securities, London
AIM Broker:	Marshall Securities, London
Solicitors:	Faegre Benson Hobson Audley, London
Market Makers:	KBCS; UBSW; WINS
Auditors:	MRI Moores Rowland, London
Registrars:	Capita Registrars

Entry on AIM: 29/11/1996		**Recent price:**	7.0p
Interim results:	Jun	**Market cap:**	£2.58m
Final results:	Mar	**Issue price:**	50.0p
Year end:	Sep	**Current no of shares:**	
Accounts due:	Mar		36,865,846
Int div paymnt:	n/a	**No of shares after**	
Fin div paymnt:	n/a	**dilution:**	37,198,582
Int net div per share:	nil	**P/E ratio:**	n/a
Fin net div per share:	nil	**Probable CGT?**	Yes

LATEST REPORTED RESULTS: 2003		**PREVIOUS REPORTED RESULTS:** 2002	
Turnover:	£1.18m	Turnover:	£1.42m
PTP:	£(2.63m)	PTP:	£(3.93m)
EPS:	(7.5)p	EPS:	(11.1)p

Imprint Search & Selection (IMP)

Provider of recruitment and training services

2 Sheraton Street, London, W1F 8BH Tel: 020-7287 8585; Fax: 020-7287 7676; web site: www.imprintplc.com

		holding %
Chairman	Pierce Casey	12.8
Chief Executive	Brian Hamill	23.8
Finance Director	John Hunter	0.0
Non-Exec Director	John Gordon	0.1

Main Shareholders:

Eaglet Investment Trust	5.1
FPAM Institutional UK Smaller Co's	4.9
Reyker Nominees	4.0
Singer & Friedlander AIM 3 Venture Capital Trust	3.5

Percentage of free market capital: 45.8%

Comments:

The search and selection outfit turned in its first annual profit in 2003 – only its second full year of trading – on higher turnover. Imprint is winning new clients, broadening its sector offering and taking on more fee earners. Healthy cash generation left the business with £1.46m (£1.05m) cash at the year-end, and with no borrowings. Its UK operations moved into profit and the restructuring of the Asian business is now complete. Investors can expect a much improved 2004.

Nominated Adviser:	Altium Capital, London
AIM Broker:	Altium Capital, London
Solicitors:	Blake Lapthorn, Fareham
Market Makers:	ALTI; WINS
Auditors:	Ernst & Young, London
Registrars:	Capita Registrars

Entry on AIM: 23/5/2001		**Recent price:**	145.0p
Interim results:	Sep	**Market cap:**	£25.15m
Final results:	Mar	**Issue price:**	80.0p
Year end:	Dec	**Current no of shares:**	
Accounts due:	Apr		17,346,730
Int div paymnt:	n/a	**No of shares after**	
Fin div paymnt:	n/a	**dilution:**	20,546,730
Int net div per share:	nil	**P/E ratio:**	50.0
Fin net div per share:	nil	**Probable CGT?**	Yes

LATEST REPORTED RESULTS: 2003		**PREVIOUS REPORTED RESULTS:** 2002	
Turnover:	£4.64m	Turnover:	£3.48m
PTP:	£383,000	PTP:	£(1.20m)
EPS:	2.9p	EPS:	(7.0)p

IMS Maxims   (IMX)

Software supplier
Sandymount, Station Road, Woburn Sands, MK17 8RR Tel: 01908-588800; Fax: 01908-588819;
e-mail: info@imsmaxims.com; web site: www.imsmaxims.com

		holding %
Chairman	David MacDonald	1.5
Chief Executive	B Ennis	19.4
Financial Controller	Stephen Casey	0.0
Technical Director	T Fossey	2.4

Main Shareholders:
Hal Nominees	6.1
RBSTB Nominees	3.0

Percentage of free market capital: 54.7%

Nominated Adviser:	Durlacher, London
AIM Broker:	Durlacher, London
Solicitors:	Taylor Wessing, London
Market Makers:	MLSB; SCAP; WINS
Auditors:	Ernst & Young, 400 Capability Green, Luton LU1 3LU
Registrars:	Capita Registrars

Entry on AIM: 26/10/1999	**Recent price:**	10.0p
Interim results:	Dec	**Market cap:**	£14.52m
Final results:	Sep	**Issue price:**	5.0p
Year end:	Mar	**Current no of shares:**	
Accounts due:	Jul		145,163,332
Int div paymnt:	n/a	**No of shares after**	
Fin div paymnt:	n/a	dilution:	n/a
Int net div per share:	nil	**P/E ratio:**	n/a
Fin net div per share:	nil	**Probable CGT?**	Yes

LATEST REPORTED RESULTS: 2003		PREVIOUS REPORTED RESULTS: 2002	
Turnover:	£3.36m	Turnover:	£5.68m
PTP:	£(4.39m)	PTP:	£296,000
EPS:	(3.2)p	EPS:	0.2p

Comments:
IMS supplies software and IT services to the public sector: its primary focus being the NHS. But while a significant increase in Government health spending has been anticipated for some time now, the company has yet to reap any tangible benefits. Interim sales were up slightly, by 12% to £1.9m, however, losses increased 30% to £1.3m. Debts now top £6m and though management predicts the NHS-focus will ensure long-term success, an improvement is required far sooner.

Incite (suspended 2 Feb 2004)   (INC)

Telecommunications company
102 Fulham Palace Road, London, W6 9PL

		holding %
Chairman		
Chief Executive	Simon Hellier	22.7
Finance Director	Anthony Davies	21.5
Media Rights Director	Martin Boulton	5.4

Main Shareholders:
Barnard Nominees Limited (a/c Richard Griffiths)	18.3
Elenora International Investments	7.1
Bruce Pleckinger	5.6
Kinsale Management	5.5
Chase Nominees	4.4

Percentage of free market capital: 2.1%

Nominated Adviser:	Beaumont Cornish, London
AIM Broker:	Christows, London
Solicitors:	Atlantic Law, London
Market Makers:	EVO; KLWT; SCAP; WINS
Auditors:	BDO Stoy Hayward, 8 Baker Street, London W1U 3LL
Registrars:	Capita Registrars

Entry on AIM: 12/9/2003	**Recent price:**	43.5p
Interim results:	Sep	**Market cap:**	£12.76m
Final results:	Jan	**Issue price:**	25.0p
Year end:	Oct	**Current no of shares:**	
Accounts due:	Mar		29,339,030
Int div paymnt:	n/a	**No of shares after**	
Fin div paymnt:	n/a	dilution:	n/a
Int net div per share:	nil	**P/E ratio:**	n/a
Fin net div per share:	nil	**Probable CGT?**	Yes

LATEST REPORTED RESULTS: 13 MONTHS TO 31 OCT '02		PREVIOUS REPORTED RESULTS: N/A	
Turnover:	n/a	Turnover:	n/a
PTP:	£(66,000)	PTP:	n/a
EPS:	(114.2)p	EPS:	n/a

Comments:
The mobile media specialists allows organisations to become 'virtual network operators', to get information, sound, images and video footage out to their customers in return for annual or monthly fees. Clients include Tottenham Hotspur, West Ham United and Leeds United. It also has Orange distributing its ((on!)) product range. Shares have been suspended as it is in discussions to acquire 'substantial mobile assets' in conjunction with a placing.

IndigoVision (IND)
Video technology
The Edinburgh Technopole, Bush Loan, Edinburgh, EH26 0PJ Tel: 0131-475 7200; Fax: 0131-475 7201;
e-mail: IR@indigovision.com; web site: www.indigovision.com

		holding %
Chairman	Hamish Grossart	1.6
Chief Executive	Oliver Vellacott	19.8
Finance Director	Marcus Kneen	0.4
Chief Technology Officer	Barry Keenpeace	0.2

Main Shareholders:

UBS-IB	18.99
Patrick Porteous	4.34

Percentage of free market capital: 76.6%

Nominated Adviser:	Brewin Dolphin, Glasgow
AIM Broker:	Brewin Dolphin, Glasgow
Solicitors:	Shepherd & Wedderburn, Edinburgh
Market Makers:	CAZR; KBCS; MLSB; WINS
Auditors:	KPMG, Saltire Court, 20 Castle Terrace, Edinburgh EH1 2ET
Registrars:	Computerhare

Comments:

Once valued at more than £500m, this beleagured video technology business dropped from the Full List to AIM with management claiming the junior market 'is more appropriate to the [company's] scale and stage'. As you would expect – given the company's tumbling valuation – trading remains tough, although a recent move away from licensing and towards product manufacture has reduced losses. A half-year cash pile of £6.2m offers scope for a turnaround.

Entry on AIM: 15/12/2003		**Recent price:**	65.0p
Interim results:	Mar	**Market cap:**	£4.5m
Final results:	Nov	**Issue price:**	n/a
Year end:	Jul	**Current no of shares:**	
Accounts due:	Nov		6,919,976
Int div paymnt	n/a	**No of shares after**	
Fin div paymnt:	n/a	**dilution:**	n/a
Int net div per share:	nil	**P/E ratio:**	n/a
Fin net div per share:	nil	**Probable CGT?**	Yes

LATEST REPORTED RESULTS: 2003		PREVIOUS REPORTED RESULTS: 2002	
Turnover:	£1.79m	Turnover:	£2.25m
PTP:	£(3.64m)	PTP:	£(10.28m)
EPS:	(6.4)p	EPS:	(15.0)p

Inditherm (IDM)
Developer of electrical heating technology
Inditherm House, Houndhill Park, Bolton Road, Wath-upon-Dearne, Rotherham, S63 7JY Tel: 01709-761000;
Fax: 01709-761066; e-mail: sales@pjoinditherm.co.uk; web site: www.pjoinditherm.co.uk

		holding %
Chairman	Mark Abrahams	0.3
Chief Executive	Colin Tarry	2.7
Finance Director	Ian Smith	0.0
Director	Patrick O'Grady	33.2

Main Shareholders:

AXA Investment Managers UK	13.5
Cazenove	13.0
Brymarc	11.9
RBS Custody Bank	5.0
Allianz	4.6

Percentage of free market capital: 5.0%

Nominated Adviser:	Collins Stewart, London
AIM Broker:	Collins Stewart, London
Solicitors:	Freeth Cartwright, Nottingham
Market Makers:	CSCS; WINS
Auditors:	Blueprint Audit, Nottingham
Registrars:	Capita Registrars

Comments:

Inditherm produces a flexible polymer that heats uniformly by an energy efficient low voltage charge. Its products include frost protection solutions for pipelines and pizza delivery bags. Although the company asserted it expects to reach break-even in the second half, it recently raised £4.8m through a placing in order to expand its UK direct sales, to increase its international presence and to open distribution channels to the medical business.

Entry on AIM: 14/12/2001		**Recent price:**	54.0p
Interim results:	Sep	**Market cap:**	£11.38m
Final results:	Mar	**Issue price:**	97.0p
Year end:	Dec	**Current no of shares:**	
Accounts due:	Apr		21,069,980
Int div paymnt:	n/a	**No of shares after**	
Fin div paymnt:	n/a	**dilution:**	n/a
Int net div per share:	nil	**P/E ratio:**	n/a
Fin net div per share:	nil	**Probable CGT?**	Yes

LATEST REPORTED RESULTS: 2002		PREVIOUS REPORTED RESULTS: 2001	
Turnover:	£683,000	Turnover:	£477,000
PTP:	£(739,000)	PTP:	£(256,000)
EPS:	(6.8)p	EPS:	(3.0)p

Inflexion (IFX)

Private equity investor

40 George Street, London, W1U 7DW Tel: 020-7487 9888; Fax: 020-7487 2774;
e-mail: info@inflexion.com; web site: www.inflexion.com

		holding %
Chairman	Andrew Shaw	0.0
Joint Chief Executive	John Hartz	12.5
Finance Director		
Joint Chief Executive	Simon Turner	12.2

Main Shareholders:

Newton Investment Management	9.6
Scudder Threadneedle	8.9
Shore Capital	8.8
Luke Johnson	7.9
Employee Benefit Trust	6.8

Percentage of free market capital: 6.7%

Nominated Adviser:	Grant Thornton, London
AIM Broker:	Schroders, London
Solicitors:	Ashursts, London
Market Makers:	KBCS; MLSB; SCAP; SSSB; WINS
Auditors:	PricewaterhouseCoopers, London
Registrars:	Lloyds TSB Registrars

Entry on AIM:	10/4/2000	**Recent price:**	16.75p
Interim results:	Nov	**Market cap:**	£36.48m
Final results:	Aug	**Issue price:**	100.0p
Year end:	Mar	**Current no of shares:**	
Accounts due:	Jul		217,782,761
Int div paymnt:	n/a	**No of shares after**	
Fin div paymnt:	n/a	**dilution:**	n/a
Int net div per share:	nil	**P/E ratio:**	n/a
Fin net div per share:	nil	**Probable CGT?**	No

LATEST REPORTED RESULTS: 2003		PREVIOUS REPORTED RESULTS: 2002	
Turnover:	n/a	Turnover:	n/a
PTP:	£(4.37m)	PTP:	£(12.18m)
EPS:	(7.2)p	EPS:	(20.0)p

Comments:

By last September Inflexion's original £36m portfolio had fallen to £13.4m, following a series of write-offs. £9.5m cash remained. Since then the group has acquired a £12m portfolio from FTSE 250 member London Merchant Securities, who have also subscribed for £15m of shares, giving it a 59% stake in Inflexion. The group wants to focus on managing institutional funds, raising £26m for a buy-out fund. This has backed the buy-out of cinema multiplex group Ster Century. A £2.1m interim loss was made.

Ingenta (IGA)

Online professional and academic research provider

23-38 Hythe Bridge Street, Oxford, OX1 2ET Tel: 01865-799000; Fax: 01865-799111;
e-mail: info@ingenta.co.uk; web site: www.ingenta.co.uk

		holding %
Chairman	Martyn Rose	4.5
Chief Executive	Mark Rowse	11.0
Finance Director		
Chief Operating Officer	Simon Dessain	0.4

Main Shareholders:

Macguire Childrens Trust	8.1
Dominic Collins	5.6
Invesco English and International Trust	5.5
Chatham Holdings	4.6
Stanlife Nominees	3.9

Percentage of free market capital: 46.4%

Nominated Adviser:	Collins Stewart, London
AIM Broker:	Collins Stewart, London
Solicitors:	n/a
Market Makers:	ARBT; CHMM; MLSB; SCAP; WINS
Auditors:	Grant Thornton, Westminster way, Oxford OX2 0PZ
Registrars:	Capita Registrars

Entry on AIM:	3/6/1997	**Recent price:**	13.75p
Interim results:	Jun	**Market cap:**	£15.06m
Final results:	Dec	**Issue price:**	n/a
Year end:	Sep	**Current no of shares:**	
Accounts due:	Jan		109,542,201
Int div paymnt:	n/a	**No of shares after**	
Fin div paymnt:	n/a	**dilution:**	n/a
Int net div per share:	nil	**P/E ratio:**	n/a
Fin net div per share:	nil	**Probable CGT?**	Yes

LATEST REPORTED RESULTS: 2003		PREVIOUS REPORTED RESULTS: 2002	
Turnover:	£8.5m	Turnover:	£9.3m
PTP:	£(2.9m)	PTP:	£(26.4m)
EPS:	(2.0)p	EPS:	(45.0)p

Comments:

After focusing on cost cutting in the year to September, the specialist academic publication website creator is now aiming for growth and looking forward to the new year with 'confidence'. Losses were reduced by 59%. Operations in Oxford, Bath and in the US were consolidated and streamlined and the workforce was cut 23% to 127. New business totalling £2m has been generated since September but it may suffer from the fall in the US dollar.

Innobox (INO)

Hotelier

Meriden House, 6 Great Cornbow, Halesowen, West Midlands B63 3AB Tel: 0121-585 6655; Fax: 0121-585 6228;
e-mail: info@innobox.co.uk; web site: www.innobox.co.uk

		holding %
Chairman	Arthur Baker	3.2
Chief Executive	Russell Stevens	9.7
Finance Director		
Non-Exec Director	Mark Jones	3.3

Main Shareholders:

Bidtimes	15.0
Corvus Capital	12.4
Personal Pension Management	4.4
Maxima	4.0
No Boundary	4.0

Percentage of free market capital: 29.9%

Nominated Adviser:	Brown Shipley, London
AIM Broker:	Brown Shipley, London
Solicitors:	Berwin Leighton Paisner, London
Market Makers:	SCAP; WINS
Auditors:	PKF, Birmingham
Registrars:	Neville Registrars

ENTRY ON AIM:	22/1/2001	Recent price:	10.0p
Interim results:	Jan	Market cap:	£1.25m
Final results:	May	Issue price:	10.0p
Year end:	Apr	Current no of shares:	
Accounts due:	Nov		12,500,000
Int div paymnt:	n/a	No of shares after	
Fin div paymnt:	n/a	dilution:	13,500,000
Int net div per share:	nil	P/E ratio:	n/a
Fin net div per share:	nil	Probable CGT?	Yes

LATEST REPORTED RESULTS: 2003		PREVIOUS REPORTED RESULTS: 2002	
Turnover:	n/a	Turnover:	n/a
PTP:	£596,000	PTP:	£(62,000)
EPS:	4.8p	EPS:	(0.5)p

Comments:

After acquiring the Moss Cottage Hotel in Derbyshire, Innobox made a small interim turnover of £74,823 and notched up pre-tax losses of £130,690. It has completed renovations, which give the hotel 16 letting rooms. The company has also just purchased the Three Tuns Coaching Inn in Ipswich, Suffolk for £625,000 and intends to add an extra 17 rooms to the existing 11. Selling 1m shares in spin-out Aerobox gave a decent £142,5000 profit.

Innovision Research & Technology (INN)

Electronics technology solutions provider

Ash Court, 23 Rose Street, Wokingham, Berkshire RG40 1XS Tel: 0118-979 2000; Fax: 0118-979 1500;
e-mail: enquiries@innovision-group.com; web site: www.innovision-group.com

		holding %
Chairman	Barton Clarke	0.3
Chief Executive	Marc Borrett	22.3
Finance Director	Michael Wroe	0.01
Technical Director	Peter Symons	0.0

Main Shareholders:

Vidacos Nominees	8.0
Herald Investment Trust	6.2
C Low	5.7
P D Roy	5.7
Chase Nominees	4.0

Percentage of free market capital: 23.9%

Nominated Adviser:	KBC Peel Hunt, London
AIM Broker:	KBC Peel Hunt, London
Solicitors:	Ashursts, London
Market Makers:	KBCS; WINS
Auditors:	Baker Tilly, 2 Bloomsbury Street, London WC1B 3ST
Registrars:	Computershare Investor Services

ENTRY ON AIM:	6/4/2001	Recent price:	125.0p
Interim results:	Dec	Market cap:	£49.96m
Final results:	Jun	Issue price:	101.0p
Year end:	Mar	Current no of shares:	
Accounts due:	Jul		39,970,390
Int div paymnt:	n/a	No of shares after	
Fin div paymnt:	n/a	dilution:	42,094,390
Int net div per share:	nil	P/E ratio:	n/a
Fin net div per share:	nil	Probable CGT?	Yes

LATEST REPORTED RESULTS: 2003		PREVIOUS REPORTED RESULTS: 2002	
Turnover:	£802,000	Turnover:	£1.11m
PTP:	£(3.57m)	PTP:	£(2.26m)
EPS:	(8.7)p	EPS:	(5.4)p

Comments:

The radio frequency identification solutions company recently signed further licenses for its 'Jewel' contactless transport ticketing chip. In an encouraging half year to 30 September, its losses were pared from £1.77m to £735,000. And tight control of cash left the business with £3.9m (£4.5m) cash at the half-year. Turnover sparked up from £214,000 to £1.02m, thanks to management's focus on work with market leading customers on high-quality funded development work.

InTechnology (ITO)

IT services

1 Threadneedle Street, London EC2R 8BE Tel: 020-7786 3443; Fax: 020-7786 3444; web site: www.intechnology.co.uk

		holding %
Chairman	Peter Wilkinson	56.8
Chief Executive	Charles Cameron	0.0
Finance Director	Andrew Kaberry	7.2
Non-Executive President	Lord Parkinson	0.0

Main Shareholders:

Artemis Investment Management	9.3
Jon Wood	7.7

Percentage of free market capital: 14.7%

Comments:

IT services specialist InTechnology reduced its loss in the six months to September from £4.7m to £3.6m. The company's performance was aided by a strong contribution from IT security products distributor Allasso – acquired for £17.6m in July. The deal did, however, see the company's strong net cash position reverse into £13.3m of debt. More encouragingly, the third quarter to December is said to have been 'particularly strong' and further progress is expected in 2004.

Nominated Adviser:	Dresdner Kleinwort Wasserstein, London
AIM Broker:	Dresdner Kleinwort Wasserstein, London
Solicitors:	Norton Rose, London
Market Makers:	GRAB; MLSB; NUMS; SCAP; UBSW; WEST; WINS
Auditors:	PricewaterhouseCoopers, Leeds
Registrars:	Capita Registrars

Entry on AIM:	2/3/2000	**Recent price:**	88.5p
Interim results:	Nov	**Market cap:**	£122.5m
Final results:	Jun	**Issue price:**	25.0p
Year end:	Mar	**Current no of shares:**	
Accounts due:	Jul		138,414,996
Int div paymnt:	n/a	**No of shares after**	
Fin div paymnt:	n/a	dilution:	n/a
Int net div per share:	n/a	P/E ratio:	n/a
Fin net div per share:	n/a	Probable CGT?	Yes

LATEST REPORTED RESULTS: 2003		PREVIOUS REPORTED RESULTS: 2002	
Turnover:	£156.9m	Turnover:	£158.11m
PTP:	£(6.68m)	PTP:	£(82.49m)
EPS:	(5.1)p	EPS:	(60.2)p

Integrated Asset Management (IAM)

Private client & institutional investment manager

4 Hill Street, London, W1J 5NE Tel: 020-7514 0550; Fax: 020-7481 8523;
e-mail: contact@integratedam.com; web site: www.integratedam.com

		holding %
Chairman	John Booth	6.3
Chief Executive	Emanuel M Arbib	3.4
Finance Director	Keith Williams	0.0
Non-Exec Director	Mark Segall	0.0

Main Shareholders:

Asset Management Investment Co	19.4
Nicholas Levene	5.5
Norman Epstein	4.7
SIS SEGA	4.7
Capital Management	4.0

Percentage of free market capital: 48.6%

Comments:

Integrated has ambitious plans to build a financial services group. First half turnover was slightly down at £2.43m but pre-tax losses were reduced by a third to £0.6m as a result of cost cuts. The group now has $450m under management, over a third of which is hedge funds. The money has been bolstered by a flurry of small acquisitions, including Appleton International, a South African set-up, and the broking business of Investory. Profits still look some way off though.

Nominated Adviser:	Insinger de Beaufort, London
AIM Broker:	Seymour Pierce, London
Solicitors:	Bircham Dyson Bell, London
Market Makers:	DURM; KBCS; WINS
Auditors:	Moore Stephens, Warwick Lane, London EC4P 4BN
Registrars:	Capita Registrars

Entry on AIM:	19/5/1997	**Recent price:**	51.5p
Interim results:	Oct	**Market cap:**	£6.44m
Final results:	Jun	**Issue price:**	100.0p
Year end:	Dec	**Current no of shares:**	
Accounts due:	May		12,500,871
Int div paymnt:	n/a	**No of shares after**	
Fin div paymnt:	n/a	dilution:	n/a
Int net div per share:	nil	P/E ratio:	n/a
Fin net div per share:	nil	Probable CGT?	Yes

LATEST REPORTED RESULTS: 2002		PREVIOUS REPORTED RESULTS: 8 MONTHS TO 31 DEC 01	
Turnover:	£4.98m	Turnover:	£2.3m
PTP:	£(1.63m)	PTP:	£(1.46m)
EPS:	(17.9)p	EPS:	(25.1)p

Intellexis (ILX)

Financial training provider

Lyric House, 149 Hammersmith Road, London, W14 0QL Tel: 020-7371 4444; Fax: 020-7371 6556;
e-mail: info@intellexis.com; web site: www.intellexis.com

		holding %
Chairman	Paul Lever	0.0
Chief Executive	Kenneth Scott	1.1
Financial Director	Jon Pickles	1.2
President	Paul Palmarozza	14.0

Main Shareholders:

Park Row	27.4
Singer & Friedlander AIM 3	8.95

Percentage of free market capital: 53%

Nominated Adviser:	Teather & Greenwood, London
AIM Broker:	Teather & Greenwood, London
Solicitors:	City Law, London
Market Makers:	MLSB; SCAP; WINS
Auditors:	Saffery Champness, London
Registrars:	Capita Registrars

ENTRY ON AIM: 12/12/2000		**Recent price:**	92.5p
Interim results:	Oct	**Market cap:**	£8.51m
Final results:	Jun	**Issue price:**	1.0p
Year end:	Mar	**Current no of shares:**	
Accounts due:	Jul		9,200,881
Int div paymnt:	n/a	**No of shares after**	
Fin div paymnt:	n/a	**dilution:**	n/a
Int net div per share:	nil	**P/E ratio:**	n/a
Fin net div per share:	nil	**Probable CGT?**	Yes

LATEST REPORTED RESULTS:	2003	PREVIOUS REPORTED RESULTS:	2002
Turnover:	£1.38m	**Turnover:**	£255,000
PTP:	£(2.04m)	**PTP:**	£(1.82m)
EPS:	(0.1)p	**EPS:**	(0.1)p

Comments:

Despite a quiet summer and tough markets, the financial training firm returned to trading profitability at operational level in a decent half to September. Encouragingly, pre-tax losses were pared back from £1.5m to only £79,000. Gross margins were a healthy 82%, with most of Intellexis' business, a bumper 88%, coming from its existing clients. Intellexis recently acquired Key Skills, a provider of computer-based multimedia training courses, in a deal worth £2.4m.

Intelligent Environments (IEN)

Internet & intranet software tools developer

Riverview House, 20 Old Bridge Street, Kingston-on-Thames, Surrey KT1 4BU Tel: 020-8614 9800;
Fax: 020-8614 9801; e-mail: info@ie.com; web site: www.ie.com

		holding %
Chairman	Clive Richards	11.9
Chief Executive	Phillip Blundell	0.7
Finance Director	as above	
Non-Exec Director	Laurence T Shafe	1.2

Main Shareholders:

Close Brothers Group	24.1
Singer & Friedlander	17.0
Friends Ivory & Sime	13.4
Aberdeen Asset Management	6.3
Herald Investment Trust	6.1

Percentage of free market capital: 16.2%

Nominated Adviser:	Bridgewell, London
AIM Broker:	Bridgewell, London
Solicitors:	Taylor Wessing, Carmelite, London
Market Makers:	HSBC; MLSB; SCAP; WINS
Auditors:	Baker Tilly, 2 Bloomsbury Street, London WC1B 3ST
Registrars:	Computershare Investor Services

ENTRY ON AIM: 28/6/1996		**Recent price:**	12.0p
Interim results:	Sep	**Market cap:**	£17.95m
Final results:	May	**Issue price:**	94.0p
Year end:	Dec	**Current no of shares:**	
Accounts due:	Jun		149,577,181
Int div paymnt:	n/a	**No of shares after**	
Fin div paymnt:	n/a	**dilution:**	n/a
Int net div per share:	nil	**P/E ratio:**	n/a
Fin net div per share:	nil	**Probable CGT?**	Yes

LATEST REPORTED RESULTS:	2002	PREVIOUS REPORTED RESULTS:	2001
Turnover:	£2.67m	**Turnover:**	£3.11m
PTP:	£(2.87m)	**PTP:**	£(6.98m)
EPS:	(2.1)p	**EPS:**	(13.5)p

Comments:

The faith many have shown in IE's recovery prospects finally appears to be paying off. In a pre-results trading update management confirmed that the company is 'expected to breakeven' for the full year thanks, in part, to an anticipated 30% rise in revenue to around £3.5m. Moreover, the outlook for 2004 is said to be optimistic thanks to 'a healthy backlog of orders, strong pipeline activity, a wider portfolio of products to sell and encouraging signs in the market'.

Inter Link Foods (ITF)

Cake & pastry manufacturer & supplier

Shadsworth Road, Sett End Road West, Blackburn, Lancashire BB1 2PT Tel: 01254-55495; Fax: 01254-663602;
e-mail: int@interlinkfoods.co.uk; web site: www.interlinkfoods.co.uk

		holding %
Chairman	Jeremy J Hamer	0.2
Chief Executive	Alwin Thompson	3.1
Finance Director	Christopher Neilson	0.2
Non-Exec Director	Colin E Davies	2.8

Main Shareholders:

Friends Ivory & Sime*	12.9
Pension Servies	4.7
Gartmore	4.5
Canada Life Marketing	4.4

Percentage of free market capital: 44.4%

*4.63% held by Baronsmead VCT 2, 5.66% held by Baronsmead VCT

Comments:

Inter Link served up interim profits before tax improved 42% to £2.3m. It will also be able to cover most of the cake market now it has acquired Hoppers Farmhouse Bakery, a Christmas products specialist. Even more intriguing though is a new licensing agreement with Disney. The agreement allows Inter Link exclusively to produce all 'small cake' products based on major Disney characters including Winnie the Pooh, Cinderella and the Lion King.

Nominated Adviser:	Brewin Dolphin, Manchester
AIM Broker:	Brewin Dolphin, Manchester & Numis, London
Solicitors:	DWF, Manchester
Market Makers:	KBCS; MLSB; WINS
Auditors:	Grant Thornton, Manchester,
Registrars:	Capita Registrars

ENTRY ON AIM:	21/8/1998	**Recent price:**	450.0p
Interim results:	Jan	**Market cap:**	£43.8m
Final results:	Jul	**Issue price:**	110.0p
Year end:	Apr	**Current no of shares:**	
Accounts due:	Aug		9,732,916
Int div paymnt:	Mar	**No of shares after**	
Fin div paymnt:	Sep	**dilution:**	n/a
Int net div per share:	1.67p	**P/E ratio:**	17.1
Fin net div per share:	3.3p	**Probable CGT?**	Yes

LATEST REPORTED RESULTS: 2003		PREVIOUS REPORTED RESULTS: 2002	
Turnover:	£51.38m	Turnover:	£45.99m
PTP:	£2.96m	PTP:	£2.69m
EPS:	26.3p	EPS:	25.2p

Inter-Alliance (IAL)

National independent financial adviser

27-37 St Georges Road, Wimbledon, London, SW19 4DS Tel: 020-8971 4400; Fax: 020-8947 2210;
web site: www.inter-alliance.com

		holding %
Chairman	Keith Carby	0.7
Chief Executive	as above	
Finance Director	Steven Hartley	0.3
Non-Exec Director	Tom Morton	0.0

Main Shareholders:

Henderson Global Investors	14.4
Friends Provident	10.0
Gartmore Investment Management	9.1
Lansdowne Partners Limited Partnership	4.2
HBOS	4.2

Percentage of free market capital: 36.8%

Comments:

The perennially struggling IFA network with 1,350 members is in merger talks with fellow IFA Berkeley Berry Birch. This would spell the end of Inter-Alliance's independence. Evolution Beeson Gregory arranged two rescue fundraisings last year, raising over £30m. July's was priced at just 2p after a profit warning. Interim losses rose 9.5% to £19.4m as turnover fell 12.7% to £21.2m. However the group hopes to be 'cashflow positive during the first half of 2004 without recourse to further funds'.

Nominated Adviser:	Credit Lyonnais, London
AIM Broker:	Credit Lyonnais, London
Solicitors:	Lawrence Graham, London
Market Makers:	MLSB; WINS
Auditors:	Deloitte & Touche, 20 Old Bailey, London EC4M 7AN
Registrars:	Capita Registrars

ENTRY ON AIM:	26/5/1998	**Recent price:**	2.0p
Interim results:	Sep	**Market cap:**	£18.21m
Final results:	Apr	**Issue price:**	325/425p
Year end:	Dec	**Current no of shares:**	
Accounts due:	May		91,043,7113
Int div paymnt:	n/a	**No of shares after**	
Fin div paymnt:	n/a	**dilution:**	n/a
Int net div per share:	nil	**P/E ratio:**	n/a
Fin net div per share:	nil	**Probable CGT?**	Yes

LATEST REPORTED RESULTS: 2002 (AFTER EXCEPTIONAL ITEMS)		PREVIOUS REPORTED RESULTS: 2001 (AFTER EXCEPTIONAL ITEMS)	
Turnover:	£45.72m	Turnover:	£45.54m
PTP:	£(17.77m)	PTP:	£(25.2m)
EPS:	(21.3)p	EPS:	(52.9)p

Interactive Digital Solutions (IGL)

Entertainment and business software developer

Suite 3 Quayside Offices, Basin Road South, Portslade, East Sussex BN41 1WF Tel: 01273-426005;
Fax: 01273-426004; web site: www.ids-plc.com

		holding %
Chairman	Dorian Marks	0.0
Chief Executive	Gareth Pearce-Thomas	26.7
Finance Director	Kevin Hamilton	0.0
Chief Operating Officer	Keith Lawrence	14.4
Main Shareholders:		
Ian Stephen		10.0
BNY (OLS) Nominees		9.4
John Burren		7.2
Talsiman House VCT		6.7
Fiske Nominees		6.6

Percentage of free market capital: 19.0%

Comments:

Delays continue to afflict progress at IDS. Last summer interest mounted after the group won a £3m deal with Spanish media firm Intrasat, to install 25,000 home communication and entertainment systems (offering phone, TV and internet services) over the next two years. However, technical problems have held up the implementation of this contract. Thus turnover slipped 21% and another hefty loss was incurred. Cash remains a more immediate problem and a further fundraising looks likely.

Nominated Adviser:	City Financial Associates, London
AIM Broker:	City Financial Associates, London
Solicitors:	Stone Odell & Frankston, Surrey
Market Makers:	KBCS; WINS
Auditors:	Grant Thornton, Brighton
Registrars:	Capita Registrars

ENTRY ON AIM:	20/8/2001	Recent price:	3.6p
Interim results:	Jun	Market cap:	£6.19m
Final results:	Feb	Issue price:	2.5p
Year end:	Sep	Current no of shares:	
Accounts due:	Jan		172,033,000
Int div paymnt:	n/a	No of shares after	
Fin div paymnt:	n/a	dilution:	n/a
Int net div per share:	nil	P/E ratio:	n/a
Fin net div per share:	nil	Probable CGT?	YES

LATEST REPORTED RESULTS:	2002	PREVIOUS REPORTED RESULTS:	2001
Turnover:	£243,000	Turnover:	n/a
PTP:	£(1.22m)	PTP:	£(152,000)
EPS:	(0.7)p	EPS:	(0.5)p

Interactive Gaming (IGH)

Cash shell

32 Rathbone Place, London, W1T 1JQ Tel: 0207-290 0290; Fax: 0207-290 0299;
e-mail: investor@igamingholdings.com

		holding %
Chairman	Thomas Taule	0.0
Chief Executive	as above	
Exec Director	Mitchell Petchenik	0.0
Non-Exec Director	Michael Wesley	0.0
Main Shareholders:		
Pegasus		70.9

Percentage of free market capital: 29.1%

Comments:

IGH is a new company established to acquire content portals and related sites within the online gaming sector. The plan is to seek out 'proven and cash-generative' sites and to then enhance their profitability by improving their 'look and feel'. By acquiring multiple e-gaming businesses, management hopes to benefit from significant economies of scale. £250,000 was raised on admission. This will be used to provide working capital, with further cash to be raised as and when it is needed.

Nominated Adviser:	Insinger de Beaufort, London
AIM Broker:	Insinger Townsley, London
Solicitors:	Salans, London
Market Makers:	WINS
Auditors:	BDO Stoy Hayward, 8 Baker Street, London W1U 3LL
Registrars:	Capita Registrars

ENTRY ON AIM:	5/3/2004	Recent price:	7.5p
Interim results:	n/a	Market cap:	£1.31m
Final results:	n/a	Issue price:	5.0p
Year end:	n/a	Current no of shares:	
Accounts due:	n/a		17,500,000
Int div paymnt:	n/a	No of shares after	
Fin div paymnt:	n/a	dilution:	n/a
Int net div per share:	nil	P/E ratio:	n/a
Fin net div per share:	nil	Probable CGT?	No

LATEST REPORTED RESULTS:	N/A	PREVIOUS REPORTED RESULTS:	N/A
Turnover:	n/a	Turnover:	n/a
PTP:	n/a	PTP:	n/a
EPS:	n/a	EPS:	n/a

Intercede (IGP)

Software developer and supplier

Lutterworth Hall, St Mary's Road, Lutterworth, Leicestershire LE17 4PS Tel: 01455-558111;
Fax: 01455-558222; web site: www.intercedegroup.com

		holding %
Chairman	Richard Parris	27.8
Chief Executive	as above	
Finance Director	Andrew Walker	1.0
Operations Director	Jayne Murphy	6.6

Main Shareholders:

Cogefin	5.3
Trailford	4.6
Plastic Technologies	3.6
React Invest	3.3
E Gutzwiller & Cie Banquiers	3.2

Percentage of free market capital: 44.4%

Comments:

Smart card technology specialist Intercede is yet another of AIM's band of small software companies gradually scrambling to profitability. With revenues increasing by only £2,000 to £878,000, however, a 62% reduction in first half losses to £269,000 owed much to an increase in higher margin own-software sales. As such Intercede's flagship product 'edifice' now accounts for 62% of all group revenue – demand for third party products having fallen. At September £1.3m sat in the bank.

Nominated Adviser:	KBC Peel Hunt, London
AIM Broker:	KBC Peel Hunt, London
Solicitors:	Berwin Leighton Paisner, London
Market Makers:	NUMS; WINS
Auditors:	Deloitte & Touche, Birmingham
Registrars:	Computershare Investor Services

Entry on AIM:	8/1/2001	Recent price:	24.75p
Interim results:	Dec	Market cap:	£8.41m
Final results:	May	Issue price:	60.0p
Year end:	Mar	Current no of shares:	
Accounts due:	Jun		33,963,438
Int div paymnt:	n/a	No of shares after	
Fin div paymnt:	n/a	dilution:	n/a
Int net div per share:	nil	P/E ratio:	n/a
Fin net div per share:	nil	Probable CGT?	Yes

LATEST REPORTED RESULTS: 2003		PREVIOUS REPORTED RESULTS: 2002	
Turnover:	£1.82m	Turnover:	£1.19m
PTP:	£(1.12m)	PTP:	£(2.19m)
EPS:	(5.6)p	EPS:	(11.7)p

Interior Services (ISG)

Occupancy services specialist

15 Appold Street, London, EC2A 2NH Tel: 020-7247 1717; Fax: 020-7247 8656;
e-mail: email@interiorplc.com; web site: www.theoccupancybusiness.com

		holding %
Executive Chairman	David King	5.9
Managing Director	Robert Horvath	1.1
Finance Director	David Lawther	0.2
Non-Exec Director	Peter David	0.5

Main Shareholders:

Zurich Scudder Investments	13.6
Schroder Investment Management	9.0
Fidelity Investment	7.0
Threadneedle Investment Mngrs	6.9
UBS Global Asset Managment	6.2

Percentage of free market capital: 36.1%

Comments:

With the current year expected to be as challenging as any so far for the occupancy services specialist, half-time numbers to December proved pretty resilient. Profits before tax and goodwill eased off to £3.8m (£4.2m) on a higher turnover of £205m (£198m). Growth in owner-led new build work, property and facilities management work offset yet more decline in occupier-led fit-out work. Prospects are brightening – the interim dividend was hiked up 10% to 2.75p.

Nominated Adviser:	Bridgewell, London
AIM Broker:	Panmure Gordon, London
Solicitors:	CMS Cameron McKenna, London
Market Makers:	CSCS; KBCS; WINS
Auditors:	Deloitte & Touche, 1 Little New St, London EC4A 3TR
Registrars:	Capita Registrars

Entry on AIM:	30/6/1998	Recent price:	182.5p
Interim results:	Mar	Market cap:	£47.31m
Final results:	Sep	Issue price:	126.0p
Year end:	Jun	Current no of shares:	
Accounts due:	Nov		25,921,696
Int div paymnt:	Apr	No of shares after	
Fin div paymnt:	Nov	dilution:	n/a
Int net div per share:	2.5p	P/E ratio:	n/a
Fin net div per share:	5.0p	Probable CGT?	Yes

LATEST REPORTED RESULTS: 2003		PREVIOUS REPORTED RESULTS: 2002	
Turnover:	£402.02m	Turnover:	£406.44m
PTP:	£(2.91m)	PTP:	£7.10m
EPS:	(21.0)p	EPS:	18.4p

International Brand Licensing (IBL)

Sports and lifestyle brands owner and developer

Chariot House, 42 Alie Street, Aldgate, London, E1 8DA Tel: 020-7691 2200; Fax: 020-7387 0489

		holding %
Chairman	Lance Yates	9.1
Chief Executive	Anthony Hutchinson	0.0
Finance Director	Mark Kirkland	0.0
Non-Exec Director	Glyn Hirsch	1.1

Main Shareholders:

Kylemore	23.6
Mark Levinson	21.5
Fleming Mercantile	9.0
Chase Nominees	8.9
Fidelity	6.4

Percentage of free market capital: 12.6%

Comments:

IBL does what its name suggests. It is a brand owner and developer and joined AIM via a demerger from Hay & Robertson. IBL's most recent news was its new agreement with Asda as Admiral licensee for the UK mass market. Nevertheless, the first half of the year was pretty poor. A £173,000 profit gave way to losses of £105,000 as sales waned to £593,000 (£820,000). The figures reflected the continuing impact of previous Admiral licensee Big Hit which went into administration.

Nominated Adviser:	Collins Stewart, London
AIM Broker:	Collins Stewart, London
Solicitors:	Memery Crystal, London
Market Makers:	CSCS; WINS
Auditors:	Ernst & Young, Becket House, 1 Lambeth Palace Road, London SE1 7EU
Registrars:	Capita Registrars

ENTRY ON AIM:	5/6/2002	Recent price:	27.75p
Interim results:	Sep	Market cap:	£8.41m
Final results:	Mar	Issue price:	40.0p
Year end:	Dec	Current no of shares:	
Accounts due:	May		30,313,553
Int div paymnt:	n/a	No of shares after	
Fin div paymnt:	n/a	dilution:	32,518,442
Int net div per share:	nil	P/E ratio:	11.6
Fin net div per share:	nil	Probable CGT?	Yes

LATEST REPORTED RESULTS: 2002		PREVIOUS REPORTED RESULTS: 2001	
Turnover:	£1.62m	Turnover:	£1.10m
PTP:	£335,000	PTP:	£303,000
EPS:	2.4p	EPS:	0.2p

International Greetings (IGR)

Greetings products designer & manufacturer

Belgrave House, Hatfield Business Park, Frobisher Way, Hatfield, Hertfordshire AL10 9TQ Tel: 01707-630630; Fax: 01707-630666; e-mail: lcooke@intg.co.uk; web site: www.internationalgreetings.co.uk

		holding %
Chairman	John Elfed Jones	0.0
Joint Chief Executive	Anders Hedlund	57.1
Finance Director	Mark Collini	0.5
Joint Chief Executive	Nick Fisher	6.4

Main Shareholders:

Artemis Investment Management	7.2
Liberty Wanger Asset	3.1

Percentage of free market capital: 19.5%

Comments:

The greetings card and gift-wrap manufacturer plans to expand into Europe via the 2.5m acquisition of Dutch gift-wrap producer Hoomark. 'We have been aware of the growth potential in Europe for a number of years and have now found the perfect acquisition,' explained joint chief executive Nick Fisher. Meanwhile, the company's UK and US businesses continue to perform solidly, latest interims showing a £4.6m profit and £53.5m of revenue.

Nominated Adviser:	Arbuthnot, London
AIM Broker:	Arbuthnot, London
Solicitors:	Dechert, London
Market Makers:	KBCS; OMSL, WINS
Auditors:	KPMG, Marlborough Hse, Fitzalan Rd, Cardiff CF2 1TE
Registrars:	Capita Registrars

ENTRY ON AIM:	31/10/1995	Recent price:	280.0p
Interim results:	Dec	Market cap:	£118.29m
Final results:	Jul	Issue price:	50.0p
Year end:	Mar	Current no of shares:	
Accounts due:	Jul		42,245,591
Int div paymnt:	Jan	No of shares after	
Fin div paymnt:	Sep	dilution:	n/a
Int net div per share:	1.3p	P/E ratio:	15.1
Fin net div per share:	4.45p	Probable CGT?	Yes

LATEST REPORTED RESULTS: 2003		PREVIOUS REPORTED RESULTS: 2002	
Turnover:	£113.73m	Turnover:	£110.65m
PTP:	£10.93m	PTP:	£8.49m
EPS:	18.5p	EPS:	14.6p

Internet Business Group (IBG)

Internet professional services business

40-42 Osnaburgh Street, London, NW1 3ND Tel: 020-7380 8530; Fax: 020-7380 8545;
e-mail: info@ibg.co.uk; web site: www.ibg.co.uk

		holding %
Chairman	Maziar Darvish	29.5
Chief Executive	as above	
Finance Director	Pierre-Jean De Villiers	0.0
Non-Exec Director	Ricki Bothamley	0.5

Main Shareholders:

Chase Nominees	7.9
Jonkheer Quintus	6.3
Osborne Inc	5.7
Kamal Darvish	5.4
RBSTB Nominees	3.9

Percentage of free market capital: 40.7%

Nominated Adviser:	Altium Capital, London
AIM Broker:	Altium Capital, London
Solicitors:	Jones Day Gouldens, London
Market Makers:	ALTI; KBCS; WINS
Auditors:	KPMG, 1 The Embankment, Neville Street, Leeds LS1 4DW
Registrars:	Capita Registrars

ENTRY ON AIM:	2/5/2000	**Recent price:**	2.9p
Interim results:	Jul	**Market cap:**	£1.84m
Final results:	Apr	**Issue price:**	40.0p
Year end:	Oct	**Current no of shares:**	
Accounts due:	Mar		63,524,445
Int div paymnt:	n/a	**No of shares after**	
Fin div paymnt:	n/a	**dilution:**	67,622,377
Int net div per share:	nil	**P/E ratio:**	n/a
Fin net div per share:	nil	**Probable CGT?**	YES

LATEST REPORTED RESULTS: 2002		PREVIOUS REPORTED RESULTS: 2001	
Turnover:	£1.39m	Turnover:	£1.08m
PTP:	£(537,000)	PTP:	£(2.92m)
EPS:	(0.9)p	EPS:	(5.5)p

Comments:

This 'leading advertising, e-commerce and professional services group' with a emphasis on the application of internet technologies means that the company operates a number of websites ranging from sports equipment e-tailer Sweatband all the way through to 'pay-for-performance' web-advertising business AffiliateFuture. Interim revenues surged 90% to £1.2m as losses were cut from £321,000 to £188,000.

Internet Music & Media (suspended 18 Sep 2003) (IMM)

Music, entertainment and media group

Unit 10, Latimer Road Industrial Estate, Latimer Road, London, W10 6RQ Tel: 020-8962 3350;
Fax: 020-8962 3355; web site: www.groovetech.com

		holding %
Chairman	Nicholas Cowan	36.7
Chief Executive	Jonathon Cunningham	0.0
Finance Director		
Non-Exec Director	Barney Cordell	6.0

Main Shareholders:

Highland Equity	14.8
Ronnie Wood	7.6
Corvus Capital	7.4
Highland Capital	6.8
Highland Specialist Fund	5.0

Percentage of free market capital: 69.9%

Nominated Adviser:	John East, London
AIM Broker:	Insinger Townsley, London
Solicitors:	Berwin Leighton Paisner, London
Market Makers:	SCAP; WINS
Auditors:	Gerald Edelman, 25 Harley Street, London WC1 2BR
Registrars:	Capita Registrars

ENTRY ON AIM:	14/10/1999	**Recent price:**	3.0p
Interim results:	Sep	**Market cap:**	£1.06m
Final results:	Jun	**Issue price:**	25.0p
Year end:	Dec	**Current no of shares:**	
Accounts due:	Aug		35,464,725
Int div paymnt:	n/a	**No of shares after**	
Fin div paymnt:	n/a	**dilution:**	36,085,225
Int net div per share:	nil	**P/E ratio:**	n/a
Fin net div per share:	nil	**Probable CGT?**	YES

LATEST REPORTED RESULTS: 2002		PREVIOUS REPORTED RESULTS: 2001	
Turnover:	£2.07m	Turnover:	£1.26m
PTP:	£(1.76m)	PTP:	£(12.16m)
EPS:	(5.0)p	EPS:	(46.9)p

Comments:

Internet Music & Media, which through its perpetually loss-making internet site Groovetech sold music on vinyl to DJs and broadcast live and achived music from its studios, has continued to have its shares suspended after announcing it was to close the Groovetech arm. The company is best known for the involvement of 7.6% shareholder Ronnie Wood. Shares in the business were suspended at 3p in September pending financial clarification.

Interregnum (ITR)

Internet business management consultancy

22/23 Old Burlington Street, London, W1S 2JJ Tel: 020-7494 3080; Fax: 020-7494 3090; web site: www.interregnum.com

		holding %
Chairman	Ken Olisa	55.0
Chief Executive	as above	
Finance Director	Martin Cooper	0.1
Non-Exec Director	Graham Ransom	3.9

Main Shareholders:

Liontrust	8.9
Browallia Discount	8.6
CIBC	5.9

Percentage of free market capital: 16.7%

Nominated Adviser:	Seymour Pierce, London
AIM Broker:	Seymour Pierce, London
Solicitors:	Osborne Clarke, Reading
Market Makers:	TEAM; WINS
Auditors:	Ernst & Young, London
Registrars:	Capita Registrars

ENTRY ON AIM:	13/3/2000	Recent price:	8.0p
Interim results:	Mar	Market cap:	£5.65m
Final results:	Sep	Issue price:	140.0p
Year end:	Jun	Current no of shares:	
Accounts due:	Oct		70,575,964
Int div paymnt:	n/a	No of shares after	
Fin div paymnt:	n/a	dilution:	90,581,564
Int net div per share:	nil	P/E ratio:	n/a
Fin net div per share:	nil	Probable CGT?	YES

LATEST REPORTED RESULTS:	2003	PREVIOUS REPORTED RESULTS:	2002
Turnover:	£2.06m	Turnover:	£1.33m
PTP:	£(960,000)	PTP:	£(18.4m)
EPS:	(1.4)p	EPS:	(28.1)p

Comments:

The IT investor and adviser is recovering after a tricky few years, as technology spending starts to pick up again. Interim losses were reduced by 61% to £191,000 after the group raked in a tasty fee as client uDate was sold to USA Interactive. Going forward the group plans to buy principal stakes in promising companies rather than small holdings in businesses it can't control. For instance it spent £1.5m on acquiring wireless network player Cellular Design Services.

Inventive Leisure (IVL)

Bar and nightclub operator

21 Old Street, Ashton Under Lyne, Lancashire OL6 6LA Tel: 0161-330 3876; Fax: 0161-343 7144;
web site: www.revolution-bars.co.uk

		holding %
Chairman	John Green	0.3
Chief Executive	Roy Ellis	14.8
Finance Director	Sean Curran	0.0
Dvlptmt Director	Neil McLeod	18.4

Main Shareholders:

John McDonald	12.4
Ian McLeod	9.4
Friends Ivory and Sime	6.2
Lillian McLeod	4.5
Aegon UK	4.1

Percentage of free market capital: 4.7%

Nominated Adviser:	Altium Capital, London
AIM Broker:	Panmure Gordon, London
Solicitors:	DWF Manchester
Market Makers:	ALTI; BGMM; WEST; WINS
Auditors:	PricewaterhouseCoopers, 101 Barbirolli Squre, Manchester M2 3PW
Registrars:	Capita Registrars

ENTRY ON AIM:	22/5/2000	Recent price:	69.0p
Interim results:	Mar	Market cap:	£16.41m
Final results:	Oct	Issue price:	95.0p
Year end:	Jun	Current no of shares:	
Accounts due:	Oct		23,788,270
Int div paymnt:	Apr	No of shares after	
Fin div paymnt:	Nov	dilution:	24,780,505
Int net div per share:	0.65p	P/E ratio:	7.1
Fin net div per share:	1.3p	Probable CGT?	YES

LATEST REPORTED RESULTS:	2003	PREVIOUS REPORTED RESULTS:	2002
Turnover:	£37.65m	Turnover:	£27.85m
PTP:	£3.64m	PTP:	£3.01m
EPS:	9.7p	EPS:	9.7p

Comments:

The vodka bar chain has gone from record profits last year to poor trading. Interim results were relatively upbeat with turnover up 17% to £20.4m and pre-tax profits virtually flat at £1.5m (£1.4m) – considering the high street bar malaise, this was a quite respectable feat. But for the three weeks ending mid-March like-for-like sales have decreased 14.6%, making the average decline for the second half 10.4%. Talks of potential corporate activity still abound.

Inveresk (IVS)

Production & sale of speciality paper products

Carrongrove Paper Mill, Denny, Stirlingshire FK6 5HJ Scotland, Tel: 01324-827200; Fax: 01324-824270;
e-mail: cgv-sls@inveresk.co.uk

		holding %
Chairman	Jan Bernander	8.1
Chief Executive	Alan Walker	1.9
Finance Director	Gordon Thomson	0.4
Director	Kieron Green	0.2

Main Shareholders:

Klippan AB	8.4
UBS Global Asset Management	7.2
Hensjo International	4.8
The Inveresk ESOP	3.7
Isis Asset Management	3.5

Percentage of free market capital: 55.3%

Comments:

Paper maker Inveresk operates from two speciality mills, one at Carrongrove in Scotland and the other at St Cuthberts in Somerset. Encouragingly, the group's first annual results since completing its restructuring and its refinancing in April showed restored underlying profitability. Some £8.2m was raised back in April via a placing underwritten by 17 institutional and other investors. Trading in most of Inveresk's European markets remains tough nonetheless.

Nominated Adviser:	KBC Peel Hunt, London
AIM Broker:	KBC Peel Hunt, London
Solicitors:	Dundas Wilson, Glasgow
Market Makers:	KBCS; KLWT; SCAP; WINS
Auditors:	KPMG Audit, 20 Castle Terrace, Edinburgh EH1 2EG
Registrars:	Computershare Investor Services

ENTRY ON AIM:	23/1/2003	**Recent price:**	19.25p
Interim results:	Aug	**Market cap:**	£27.68m
Final results:	May	**Issue price:**	11.75p
Year end:	Dec	**Current no of shares:**	
Accounts due:	Mar		143,804,750
Int div paymnt:	n/a	**No of shares after**	
Fin div paymnt:	Jul	**dilution:**	n/a
Int net div per share:	nil	**P/E ratio:**	7.1
Fin net div per share:	0.25p	**Probable CGT?**	Yes

LATEST REPORTED RESULTS:	2003	PREVIOUS REPORTED RESULTS: 13 MONTHS TO 31 DEC 2002	
Turnover:	£39.74m	**Turnover:**	£81.94m
PTP:	£3.03m	**PTP:**	£(34.31m)
EPS:	2.7p	**EPS:**	(56.3)p

Investment Management (formerly Seymour Pierce) (IMH)

Stockbroker and adviser

13th Floor, Bucklersbury House, 3 Queen Victoria Street, London EC4N 8FL,
Tel: 202-7107 8000; Fax: 020-7107 8114; e-mail: info@imhplc.com; web site: www.imhplc.com

		holding %
Chairman	Keith Harris	3.4
Chief Executive		
Finance Director	Patrick Ingram	0.0
Non-Exec Director	Nigel Wray*	3.3

Main Shareholders:

J H Whitney IV L.P	14.9
AF Investments	4.6
Pershing Keen Nominees	4.1

Percentage of free market capital: 69.7%

*These shares are held by Syncbeam, a company wholly owned by Nigel Wray

Comments:

This is the rump of Seymour Pierce, the small-cap stockbroker and corporate financier, whose principal operations have been bought by chairman Keith Harris and venture capitalist John Moulton for £7.35m. The board plans to pay out surplus cash of up to £21m, or 2.8p a share, to shareholders. This is far less than the £46.4m capital raised over the years, and understandably some small shareholders are aggrieved. Through Rowan, the group still looks after £400m of clients' funds.

Nominated Adviser:	ING Barings, London
AIM Broker:	ING Barings, London
Solicitors:	Memery Crystal, London
Market Makers:	KBCS; MLSB; SCAP; WINS
Auditors:	Deloitte & Touche, 1 Stonecutter St, London EC4A 4TR
Registrars:	Capita Registrars

ENTRY ON AIM:	12/8/1998	**Recent price:**	2.75p
Interim results:	May	**Market cap:**	£20.64m
Final results:	Dec	**Issue price:**	6.0p
Year end:	Sep	**Current no of shares:**	
Accounts due:	Dec		750,416,700
Int div paymnt:	n/a	**No of shares after**	
Fin div paymnt:	n/a	**dilution:**	n/a
Int net div per share:	nil	**P/E ratio:**	n/a
Fin net div per share:	nil	**Probable CGT?**	Yes

LATEST REPORTED RESULTS:	2003	PREVIOUS REPORTED RESULTS:	2002
Turnover:	£17.44m	**Turnover:**	£20.44m
PTP:	£(7.17m)	**PTP:**	£(31.74m)
EPS:	(1.0)p	**EPS:**	(5.4)p

Invox (INX)

Marketing and consumer services via SMS and e-mail

Galbraith House, 141 Great Charles Street, Birmingham, B3 3LG Tel: 0121-214 9900; Fax: 0121-214 9901

		holding %
Chairman	Stephen Hargrave	12.0
Joint Chief Executive	Carl Tatton	20.9
Finance Director	Jerry Reidy	7.7
Joint Chief Executive	Paul Hargrave	19.7

Main Shareholders:

Peter Henry	7.3
AEGON UK	4.1
Charles Bradshaw-Smith	3.3

Percentage of free market capital: 21.2%

Comments:

Invox is looking to expand by trialing home gaming products, fixed-odds betting and paid-for internet games in order to exploit the 300,000 names proprietary database it has gained through its SMS ringtones and direct marketing services. Pre-tax profits improved slightly to £3.2m despite the disruption by the postal workers' strike last year, which it believes cost an extra £300,000 in profits. Turnover fell 20% to £7.6m. Dividends remain generous.

Nominated Adviser:	Numis, London
AIM Broker:	Numis, London
Solicitors:	Memery Crystal, London
Market Makers:	SCAP; WINS
Auditors:	KPMG Audit, 2 Cornwall Street, Birmingham B3 2DL
Registrars:	Neville Registrars

ENTRY ON AIM:	21/2/2000	**Recent price:**	360.0p
Interim results:	Feb	**Market cap:**	£57.8m
Final results:	Sep	**Issue price:**	3.0p
Year end:	Mar	**Current no of shares:**	
Accounts due:	Jul		16,056,667
Int div paymnt:	Feb	**No of shares after**	
Fin div paymnt:	Nov	**dilution:**	n/a
Int net div per share:	4.0p	**P/E ratio:**	17.7
Fin net div per share:	16.0p	**Probable CGT?**	YES

LATEST REPORTED RESULTS: 2003		PREVIOUS REPORTED RESULTS: 15 MONTHS TO 30 JUN 03	
Turnover:	£18.19m	**Turnover:**	£13.29m
PTP:	£5.01m	**PTP:**	£2.59m
EPS:	20.3p	**EPS:**	14.7p

INVU (NVU)

Document management software supplier

The Beren, Blisworth Hill Farm, Stoke Road, Blisworth, Northamptonshire NN7 3BD

		holding %
Chairman	Daniel Goldman	0.01
Chief Executive	David Morgan	0.0
Finance Director	John Agostini	0.0
Sales & Mktg Director	Jonathon Halestrap	0.1

Main Shareholders:

Tyne and Wear Holdings	25.7
Montague	21.0
Cynthia Goldman	11.0
Cede & Co	4.1

Percentage of free market capital: 36.4%

Comments:

INVU's arrival on AIM was somewhat unusual, as it effectively saw the company switch its listing from the US over-the-counter market to the UK. Explaining the move management commented that 'the group's products are predominantly focused on the UK market', that as a business it 'does not currently operate in, or generate significant revenue from, the US' and that 'the majority of the Company's equity is owned by UK investors'. £2.5m net was raised on arrival.

Nominated Adviser:	Arbuthnot, London
AIM Broker:	Arbuthnot, London
Solicitors:	DLA, Birmingham
Market Makers:	ARBT; WINS
Auditors:	Grant Thornton, Elgin House, Billing Road, Northampton, NN1 5AU
Registrars:	Capita Registrars

ENTRY ON AIM:	6/1/2004	**Recent price:**	14.5p
Interim results:	Sep	**Market cap:**	£9.22m
Final results:	Mar	**Issue price:**	8.5p
Year end:	Jan	**Current no of shares:**	
Accounts due:	May		63,608,056
Int div paymnt:	n/a	**No of shares after**	
Fin div paymnt:	n/a	**dilution:**	n/a
Int net div per share:	nil	**P/E ratio:**	n/a
Fin net div per share:	nil	**Probable CGT?**	YES

LATEST REPORTED RESULTS: 2003		PREVIOUS REPORTED RESULTS: 2002	
Turnover:	£1.68m	**Turnover:**	£1.09m
PTP:	£(439,000)	**PTP:**	£(947,000)
EPS:	n/a	**EPS:**	n/a

iomart (IOM)
Network security software and web services
Fleming Pavilion, Todd Campus, West of Scotland Science Park, Glasgow, G20 0XA Tel: 0141-931 7000;
Fax: 0141-931 7001; web site: www.iomart.com

		holding %
Chairman	Nick Kuensberg	1.6
Chief Executive	Angus MacSween	37.9
Finance Director		
Bus. Dvlpmt Director	Bill Dobbie	16.0
Main Shareholders:		
Pensions Services		3.0

Percentage of free market capital: 40.2%

Comments:
Resurgent content management software developer-cum-web services business Iomart has agreed to shell out £250,000 in cash for domain name registrar Internetters. It's one of only 12 accredited registrars in the UK and offers hosting services. The deal, when coupled with the purchase of rival NicNames in July 2003, affords a roster of some 35,000 clients. Interim results showed a 253% surge in revenue to £2.9m and losses practically halved to £779,000.

Nominated Adviser:	KBC Peel Hunt, London
AIM Broker:	KBC Peel Hunt, London
Solicitors:	KLegal/McGrigor Donald, London
Market Makers:	KBCS; WINS
Auditors:	Deloitte & Touche, 39 St Vincent Place, Glasgow, G1 2QQ
Registrars:	Capita Registrars

ENTRY ON AIM:	19/4/2000	**Recent price:**	66.75p
Interim results:	Nov	**Market cap:**	£35.91m
Final results:	May	**Issue price:**	127.0p
Year end:	Mar	**Current no of shares:**	
Accounts due:	Apr		53,801,169
Int div paymnt:	n/a	**No of shares after**	
Fin div paymnt:	n/a	**dilution:**	n/a
Int net div per share:	nil	**P/E ratio:**	n/a
Fin net div per share:	nil	**Probable CGT?**	Yes

LATEST REPORTED RESULTS: 2003		PREVIOUS REPORTED RESULTS: 15 MONTHS TO 31 MAR 02	
Turnover:	£2.19m	Turnover:	£5.40m
PTP:	£(2.22m)	PTP:	£(7.90m)
EPS:	(3.5)p	EPS:	(14.7)p

IP2IPO (IPO)
Commercialisation of university research
59 St Aldates, Oxford, OX1 1ST Tel: 01865-799150; Fax: 01865-724414

		holding %
Chairman	Bruce Smith	0.1
Chief Executive	David Norwood	0.9
Financial Director	John Davies	0.01
Non-Exec Director	Andrew Beeson	0.1
Main Shareholders:		
The Evolution Group		40.6
Lansdowne Partners		9.4
Barclays		7.2
Artemis		7.0

Percentage of free market capital: 34.7%

Comments:
Chess grandmaster David Norwood raised £30m net for his grand tech-transfer endeavour. Major supporters are Evolution Beeson Gregory, where Norwood used to work. The group has long-term agreements with Oxford University's chemistry department, King's College London as well as Southampton and York Universities. These allow the company to take stakes in ventures spun out of these bodies. The current portfolio of early stage ventures is theoretically worth around £135m.

Nominated Adviser:	KBC Peel Hunt, London
AIM Broker:	KBC Peel Hunt, London
Solicitors:	Masons, London
Market Makers:	KBCS; KLWT; WINS
Auditors:	PricewaterhouseCoopers LLP, 1 Embankment Place, London WC2N 6RH
Registrars:	Capita Registrars

ENTRY ON AIM:	15/10/2003	**Recent price:**	457.5p
Interim results:	Oct	**Market cap:**	£185.92m
Final results:	Mar	**Issue price:**	275.0p
Year end:	Dec	**Current no of shares:**	
Accounts due:	Jun		40,638,910
Int div paymnt:	n/a	**No of shares after**	
Fin div paymnt:	n/a	**dilution:**	n/a
Int net div per share:	nil	**P/E ratio:**	n/a
Fin net div per share:	nil	**Probable CGT?**	No

LATEST REPORTED RESULTS: 2002		PREVIOUS REPORTED RESULTS: 2001	
Turnover:	n/a	Turnover:	n/a
PTP:	£(1.56m)	PTP:	£(326,000)
EPS:	(6.3)p	EPS:	(1.7)p

IQ-Ludorum

(IQL)

Gaming software developer

28 Eccleston Squre, Victoria, London, SW1V 1NS Tel: 020-7932 2451; Fax: 020-7932 2439;
e-mail: invest@iq-l.com; web site: www.iq-l.com

		holding %
Chairman	Nicholas Wills	0.6
Chief Executive	Roger Stone	0.3
Finance Director	Antony Norris	0.0
Director	Gurcharan Singh*	25.7

Main Shareholders:

Norbellis Foundation*	11.3
Kempson Holdings	7.1
Repasi Consulting	6.3
BNY Nominees	5.4
ISI Executive Trust*	5.3

Percentage of free market capital: 32.0%
*In addition G Singh is also interested in the shares owned by the Norbellis Foundation and ISI Executive Holdings

Comments:

IQ-Ludorum supplies a range of 'wagering software solutions' to the burgeoning e-gaming industry. Its products help the operators of on-line casinos and betting shops to run all of their games off a sole account for each customer. With offices in the UK, US, Costa Rica and India the company also possesses an international presence, yet for all that it continues to run-up significant losses. Interim numbers showed a deficit of $1.7m from sales down 30% at $2.1m.

Nominated Adviser:	KBC Peel Hunt, London
AIM Broker:	KBC Peel Hunt, London
Solicitors:	CMS Cameron McKenna, London
Market Makers:	KBCS; WINS
Auditors:	BDO Stoy Hayward, 8 Baker Street, London, W1M 1DA
Registrars:	Capita Registrars

Entry on AIM:	9/8/2000	**Recent price:**	2.4p
Interim results:	Sep	Market cap:	£1.92m
Final results:	Jun	Issue price:	75.0p
Year end:	Dec	Current no of shares:	
Accounts due:	Mar		79,959,036
Int div paymnt:	n/a	No of shares after	
Fin div paymnt:	n/a	dilution:	83,326,702
Int net div per share:	nil	P/E ratio:	n/a
Fin net div per share:	nil	Probable CGT?	Yes

LATEST REPORTED RESULTS: 2002		PREVIOUS REPORTED RESULTS: 2001	
Turnover:	$5.88m	Turnover:	£6.04m
PTP:	$(7.45m)	PTP:	£(7.64m)
EPS:	(9.3)c	EPS:	(9.6)c

IQE

(IQE)

Manufacturer of advanced semi-conductor materials

Cyress Drive, St Mellons, Cardiff, CF3 0EG Tel: 02920-839400; Fax: 02920-839401; e-mail: investors@iqep.com

		holding %
Chairman	Godfrey Ainsworth	0.5
Chief Executive	Andrew Nelson	8.5
Finance Director		
Director	Martin Lamb	1.2

Main Shareholders:

Michael Scott	8.3
T L Hierl	8.7
Morley Fund Management	3.7

Percentage of free market capital: 69.1%

Comments:

IQE transferred from the Full List in September, identifying the junior market as a more suitable home for a company of this size. A former darling of the IT sector the manufacturer of epitaxial wafers for the semiconductor industry has seen its share price plummet in recent years, though a recent revival accompanied first signs of a trading improvement. Latest interims showed a £6.8m loss from £10.1m of sales with around £10.7m in the bank. Full year results will be affected by the weakness of the dollar.

Nominated Adviser:	Evolution Beeson Gregory, London
AIM Broker:	Evolution Beeson Gregory, London
Solicitors:	M and A Solicitors, London
Market Makers:	EVO; JEFF; KBCS; KLWT; MLSB; WINS
Auditors:	Deloitte & Touche, Cardiff
Registrars:	Capita Registrars

Entry on AIM:	30/9/2003	**Recent price:**	15.75p
Interim results:	Sep	Market cap:	£49.68m
Final results:	Mar	Issue price:	n/a
Year end:	Dec	Current no of shares:	
Accounts due:	May		315,434,016
Int div paymnt:	n/a	No of shares after	
Fin div paymnt:	n/a	dilution:	n/a
Int net div per share:	nil	P/E ratio:	n/a
Fin net div per share:	nil	Probable CGT?	Yes

LATEST REPORTED RESULTS: 2002		PREVIOUS REPORTED RESULTS: 2001	
Turnover:	£22.96m	Turnover:	£42.05m
PTP:	£(118,000)	PTP:	£(5.85m)
EPS:	(63.1)p	EPS:	(3.4)p

ITIS (ITH)

Supplier of local information to motorists

Fifth Floor, Station House, Stamford New Road, Altrincham, Cheshire WA14 1EP Tel: 0161-929 5788;
Fax: 0161-929 5074; e-mail: info@itisholdings.com; web site: www.itisholdings.com

		holding %
Chairman	Trevor Chinn	0.5
Chief Executive	Stuart Marks	31.7
Finance Director	Andrew Forrest	0.03
Joint Managing Director	Giles Harridge	0.4

Main Shareholders:

Peter Smedvig Capital	10.2
Deutsche Asset Management	9.2
ITIS Employee Benefit Trust	6.7
Wireless Internet Portfolio	4.4
Minorplanet Systems	3.7

Percentage of free market capital: 32.5%

Nominated Adviser:	Altium Capital, London
AIM Broker:	Altium Capital, London
Solicitors:	Berwin Leighton Paisner, London; Squires Sanders & Dempsey, London
Market Makers:	ALTI; KBCS; WINS
Auditors:	Deloitte & Touche, Manchester,
Registrars:	Capita Registrars

ENTRY ON AIM: 16/10/2000		Recent price:	33.75p
Interim results:	Nov	Market cap:	£33.22m
Final results:	May	Issue price:	186.0p
Year end:	Mar	Current no of shares:	
Accounts due:	Jul		98,420,884
Int div paymnt:	n/a	No of shares after	
Fin div paymnt:	n/a	dilution:	106,810,347
Int net div per share:	nil	P/E ratio:	n/a
Fin net div per share:	nil	Probable CGT?	YES

LATEST REPORTED RESULTS: 2003		PREVIOUS REPORTED RESULTS: 2002	
Turnover:	£3.82m	Turnover:	£1.48m
PTP:	£(7.67m)	PTP:	£(8.74m)
EPS:	(7.5)p	EPS:	(8.6)p

Comments:

ITIS's stolen vehicle tracking system is the only system installed 'as standard' on Maserati's new Quattroporte range. As well as car security, ITIS provides journey time forecasts and updates through traffic content deals with the likes of Vodafone, Orange and the Highways Agency. Interims to September showed losses pared 14% to £2.97m on a 186% sales hike to £3.2m. Half time cash was £7.5m, which the chief executive claims is enough to see it to profit.

---

iTrain (IRN)

Multimedia training products supplier

1 North Pallant, Chichester, West Sussex PO19 1TJ Tel: 01243-785562; Fax: 01243-785604

		holding %
Chairman	Derek Moore	26.7
Chief Executive	Rainer Illing	35.0
Finance Director	Andrew Henshaw	0.0
Production Director	Michael Griffiths	14.6

Main Shareholders:

David House	13.0

Percentage of free market capital: 10.8%

Nominated Adviser:	Grant Thornton, London
AIM Broker:	Corporate Synergy, London
Solicitors:	Thomas Eggar, West Sussex
Market Makers:	WINS
Auditors:	Grant Thornton, Hampshire
Registrars:	Melton Registrars

ENTRY ON AIM: 26/9/2002		Recent price:	11.75p
Interim results:	Sep	Market cap:	£8.09m
Final results:	Jun	Issue price:	n/a
Year end:	Dec	Current no of shares:	
Accounts due:	May		68,819,750
Int div paymnt:	n/a	No of shares after	
Fin div paymnt:	n/a	dilution:	n/a
Int net div per share:	nil	P/E ratio:	n/a
Fin net div per share:	nil	Probable CGT?	No

LATEST REPORTED RESULTS: 2002		PREVIOUS REPORTED RESULTS: 2001	
Turnover:	£856,000	Turnover:	£1.30m
PTP:	£(319,000)	PTP:	£269,000
EPS:	(5.5)p	EPS:	2.7p

Comments:

iTrain, the supplier of training software to the corporate and local authority markets, needed to raise £650,000 in February to 'strengthen its balance sheet'. The company has apparently extended its library of IT training courses and has over 100 customers. 50% of revenue is derived from repeat business. But it was only slightly profitable in 2004 and its £8m market cap looks very generous.

JAB

(JBH)

Cash shell

Suites 13 & 15, Sarnia House, Le Truchot, St Peter Port, Guernsey GY1 4NA Tel: 01481-727927; Fax: 01481-710348; web site: www.pkfguernsey.com

		holding %
Chairman	Simon Thornton**	1.9
Chief Executive		
Finance Director		
Director	Michael Pappas	0.0

Main Shareholders:

E.Investors*	30.0
Leventis	20.0
John Collins	12.5
Roots Financial	5.3
Sybil Robson	5.0

Percentage of free market capital: 17.9%

*Brian Myerson is a possible beneficiary in a family trust that owns 50% of E.Investors
**These share are now held by The Gold Top Retirement Annuity Trust Scheme

Nominated Adviser:	Altium Capital, London
AIM Broker:	Altium Capital, London
Solicitors:	Tenon Statham Gill Davies, London
Market Makers:	SCAP; WINS
Auditors:	Moore Stephens, Guernsey
Registrars:	Capita Registrars

ENTRY ON AIM:	19/5/2000	**Recent price:**	0.5p
Interim results:	Mar	**Market cap:**	£2.15m
Final results:	Sep	**Issue price:**	5.0p
Year end:	Jun	**Current no of shares:**	
Accounts due:	Oct		429,501,964
Int div paymnt:	n/a	**No of shares after**	
Fin div paymnt:	n/a	**dilution:**	n/a
Int net div per share:	nil	**P/E ratio:**	n/a
Fin net div per share:	nil	**Probable CGT?**	**No**

LATEST REPORTED RESULTS: 2003		PREVIOUS REPORTED RESULTS: 2002	
Turnover:	n/a	**Turnover:**	n/a
PTP:	£(127,000)	**PTP:**	£(191,000)
EPS:	(0.0)p	**EPS:**	(0.0)p

Comments:

This investment minnow has just one holding, a 21% stake in US-based classic car auction business RM. Trading has been encouraging here lately and in the six months to December, JAB received a £95,000 dividend from RM. This more than compensated for JAB's running costs of £63,000 to produce a profit of £36,000. The group has around £330,000 net cash.

Jacques Vert (JQV)

Designer and retailer of women's fashion wear
22 Plumbers Row, London, E1 1EZ Tel: 020-7377 1900; Fax: 020-7247 6487;
e-mail: company.secretary@jacques-vert.co.uk; web site: www.jacques-vert.co.uk

		holding %
Chairman	Derek Lovelock	0.0
Chief Executive	Paul Allen	0.2
Finance Director	Ian Johnson	0.0
Deputy Chairman	Christopher Baker	0.02

Main Shareholders:

Waillim	26.8
Schroders Investment Management	25.2
Littlewoods Home Shopping	16.2
LeggMason Investors Asset Managers	7.7
Cavendish Asset Management	7.2

Percentage of free market capital: 16.8%

Comments:

Jacques Vert has suffered of late as the group's turnover for the six months to October declined 10.5% to £83.6m on a pro-forma basis with the pre-tax line showing a considerable loss of £5.6m. Having purchased competitor Baird in December 2002, it recently netted £3.4m from selling a subsidiary Microtherm International. The proceeds were used to reduce net debt, which now stands at £2.1m. The group now operates 948 outlets but trading continues to be tough.

Nominated Adviser:	Seymour Pierce, London
AIM Broker:	Seymour Pierce, London
Solicitors:	Field Fisher Waterhouse, London
Market Makers:	KLWT; MLSB; WINS
Auditors:	PricewaterhouseCoopers, London
Registrars:	Computershare Investor Services

ENTRY ON AIM:	28/8/2001	Recent price:	19.5p
Interim results:	Nov	Market cap:	£36.75m
Final results:	Jul	Issue price:	10.0p
Year end:	Apr	Current no of shares:	
Accounts due:	Aug		188,444,048
Int div paymnt:	n/a	No of shares after	
Fin div paymnt:	n/a	dilution:	n/a
Int net div per share:	nil	P/E ratio:	n/a
Fin net div per share:	nil	Probable CGT?	YES

LATEST REPORTED RESULTS: 2003		PREVIOUS REPORTED RESULTS: 2002	
Turnover:	£33.54m	Turnover:	£29.58m
PTP:	£(1.49m)	PTP:	£879,000
EPS:	(1.8)p	EPS:	1.8p

James Halstead (JHD)

Vinyl floor coverings maker
Beechfield, Hollinhurst Road, Radcliffe, Manchester, M26 1JN Tel: 0161-767 2500; Fax: 0161-766 7499

		holding %
Chairman	Geoffrey Halstead	3.6
Chief Executive	Mark Halstead	6.1
Finance Director	Gordon Oliver	0.1
Non-Exec Director	Anthony Wild	0.1

Main Shareholders:

J Halstead & H Livesey	15.7
Prudential Client HSBC GIS Nominees	5.1
Chase Nominess	5.1
J Halstead & A Halstead	4.8
Forest Nominees	3.3

Percentage of free market capital: 56.2%

Comments:

James Halstead has businesses under the Polyflor brand name in the UK, Hong Kong and Scandinavia; Halstead in New Zealand and Australia; and Objectflor in central Europe. It also has a motorcycle accessories business called Phoenix Distribution. Recently chairman Geoffrey Halstead announced he was optimistic for the current year as profits and trading are ahead of last year. The company appears reticent to implement an employee pension scheme.

Nominated Adviser:	Westhouse Securities, London
AIM Broker:	Westhouse Securities, London
Solicitors:	n/a
Market Makers:	CAZR; WINS
Auditors:	PricewaterhouseCoopers, Manchester
Registrars:	Computershare Investor Services

ENTRY ON AIM:	11/3/2002	Recent price:	413.0p
Interim results:	Mar	Market cap:	£101.98m
Final results:	Sep	Issue price:	256.5p
Year end:	Jun	Current no of shares:	
Accounts due:	Oct		24,692,790
Int div paymnt:	May	No of shares after	
Fin div paymnt:	Dec	dilution:	n/a
Int net div per share:	5.10p	P/E ratio:	12.5
Fin net div per share:	10.0p	Probable CGT?	YES

LATEST REPORTED RESULTS: 2003		PREVIOUS REPORTED RESULTS: 2002	
Turnover:	£99.78m	Turnover:	£93.03m
PTP:	£12.21m	PTP:	£11.28m
EPS:	33.0p	EPS:	28.3p

James R Knowles (JRK)

Construction industry consultant

Vistorm House, 3200 Daresbury Park, Daresbury, Warrington, Cheshire WA4 4BU Tel: 08707-530600;
Fax: 08707-530605; e-mail: info@jrknowles.com; web site: www.jrknowles.com

		holding %
Chairman	Roger Knowles	62.6
Joint Chief Executive	Mike Charlton	7.3
Finance Director	Charlotte Parsons	0.0
Joint Chief Executive	Brian Quinn	0.1

Main Shareholders:
Chase Nominees	10.2

Percentage of free market capital: 19.6%

Nominated Adviser:	Brewin Dolphin, Manchester
AIM Broker:	Brewin Dolphin, Manchester
Solicitors:	Eversheds, Manchester
Market Makers:	MLSB; WINS
Auditors:	KPMG Audit, St James Square, Manchester, M60 2EP
Registrars:	Capita Registrars

Entry on AIM:	2/6/1998	Recent price:	54.5p
Interim results:	Apr	Market cap:	£10.86m
Final results:	Oct	Issue price:	85.0p
Year end:	Jul	Current no of shares:	
Accounts due:	Nov		19,920,967
Int div paymnt:	May	No of shares after	
Fin div paymnt:	Dec	dilution:	20,931,433
Int net div per share:	0.8p	P/E ratio:	30.3
Fin net div per share:	2.1p	Probable CGT?	Yes

LATEST REPORTED RESULTS:	2003	PREVIOUS REPORTED RESULTS:	2002
Turnover:	£32.89m	Turnover:	£31.05m
PTP:	£724,000	PTP:	£101,000
EPS:	1.8p	EPS:	(0.7)p

Comments:

The legal services play has flagged up a strong start to the year with first quarter sales and profit ahead of the prior year. Annual 2003 numbers were buoyed by service expansion overseas allied with cost cutting at home. Knowles Loss Adjusters and Knowles Law both churned out excellent profits. Overseas growth opportunities are immense – the company has an established office and management structure in Asia, the Middle East, North America, Europe and Australia.

Jarvis Porter (JVP)

Glass manufacturer and investment vehicle

PO Box 58, Midland Mills, Valley Road, Bradford, West Yorkshire BD1 4RL Tel: 01274-721910; Fax: 01274-722683;
web site: www.jarvisporter.co.uk

		holding %
Chairman	Christopher Mills	0.0
Chief Executive		
Finance Director	Stephen Bannister	0.0
Non-Exec Director	Michael Maher	0.1

Main Shareholders:
Montpellier*	26.6
North Atlantic Smaller Companies	18.2
Jo Hambro Capital Management/North Atlantic Smaller Companies Investment Trust	17.3
Mistol Associate SA	13.7
Donohoe Trusts	3.9

Percentage of free market capital: 13.3%

  * Peter Gyllenhammar is deputy chairman of Montpellier

Nominated Adviser:	Strand Partners, London
AIM Broker:	Charles Stanley, London
Solicitors:	DLA, London
Market Makers:	CAZR; KBCS; KLWT; WINS
Auditors:	Deloitte & Touche, London
Registrars:	Capita Registrars

Entry on AIM:	14/5/2001	Recent price:	24.0p
Interim results:	Oct	Market cap:	£11.51m
Final results:	May	Issue price:	n/a
Year end:	Feb	Current no of shares:	
Accounts due:	Sep		47,961,560
Int div paymnt:	n/a	No of shares after	
Fin div paymnt:	n/a	dilution:	n/a
Int net div per share:	nil	P/E ratio:	n/a
Fin net div per share:	nil	Probable CGT?	Yes

LATEST REPORTED RESULTS:	2003	PREVIOUS REPORTED RESULTS:	2002
Turnover:	n/a	Turnover:	£31.76m
PTP:	£(1.61m)	PTP:	£(14.37m)
EPS:	(3.4)p	EPS:	(30.7)p

Comments:

Jarvis Porter has changed greatly since disposing of its printing businesses and property, and then buying glass manufacturer Darby. The company has sold its 29.7% interest in European Colour, netting a £1.1m profit. For the interims turnover reached £8.4m with pre-tax profits at £1.8m. The Pro Glass division is suffering but to cut costs it will share the Scunthorpe plant with the glazing division. JP is investing in soft glass coating capabilities for Darby, which is operating profitably.

Jennings Brothers (JBC)

Brewer, pub operator & drinks wholesaler

Castle Brewery, Cockermouth, Cumbria CA13 9NE Tel: 01900-823214; Fax: 01900-827462;
e-mail: jhoughton@jenningsbrewery.co.uk; web site: www.jenningsbrewery.co.uk

		holding %
Chairman	John Rudgard	0.2
Managing Director	Mike Clayton	0.1
Finance Director	David Stevenson	0.0
Non-Exec Director	Ralph Catto	0.1

Main Shareholders:

Frederic Robinson	24.0
Brown Shipley	18.2

Percentage of free market capital: 53.7%

Nominated Adviser:	Arbuthnot, London
AIM Broker:	Arbuthnot, London
Solicitors:	Eversheds, Newcastle
Market Makers:	ARBT; KBCS; WINS
Auditors:	Grant Thornton, Newcastle upon Tyne NE1 6EF
Registrars:	Computershare Investor Services

ENTRY ON AIM:	1/8/1995	Recent price:	255.5p
Interim results:	Oct	Market cap:	£27.22m
Final results:	May	Issue price:	280.0p
Year end:	Feb	Current no of shares:	
Accounts due:	May		10,654,447
Int div paymnt:	Dec	No of shares after	
Fin div paymnt:	Jul	dilution:	n/a
Int net div per share:	2.3p	P/E ratio:	14.5
Fin net div per share:	4.1p	Probable CGT?	YES

LATEST REPORTED RESULTS: 2003		PREVIOUS REPORTED RESULTS: 2002	
Turnover:	£16.36m	Turnover:	£30.25m
PTP:	£2.55m	PTP:	£(6.1m)
EPS:	17.6p	EPS:	(56.5)p

Comments:

The North West traditional brewer and pub owner is still trading well, with like-for-like beer sales to its InnVentures pub business increasing 4.4% and turnover improving 8.5% in the five months to January. Its own beer brands are also selling well with its Cumberland Ale up 27% and it is now brewing and distributing the established South Yorkshire beer, Ward's Best Bitter. It currently has 126 pubs but is likely to acquire another three in the coming months.

John Lewis of Hungerford (JLH)

Kitchen & furniture designer & retailer

Unit 1 Grove Technology Park, Downsview Rd, Wantage, Oxfordshire OX12 9FA Tel: 01235-774300; Fax: 01235-769031;
e-mail: marketing@john-lewis.co.uk; web site: www.john-lewis.co.uk

		holding %
Chairman	John Lewis	64.6
Chief Executive	as above	
Finance Director	Richard Worthington	2.2
Sales & Admin Dir	Linda Lewis	0.0

Main Shareholders:

Warm Welcome	6.1

Percentage of free market capital: 26.9%

Nominated Adviser:	Smith & Williamson, London
AIM Broker:	Seymour Pierce Ellis, Crawley
Solicitors:	Hammonds, London
Market Makers:	MLSB; WINS
Auditors:	Hill Wooldridge, 107 Hindes Road, Harrow, HA1 1RU
Registrars:	Capita Registrars

ENTRY ON AIM:	27/1/1997	Recent price:	2.1p
Interim results:	May	Market cap:	£3.12m
Final results:	Dec	Issue price:	3.0p
Year end:	Aug	Current no of shares:	
Accounts due:	Jan		148,745,519
Int div paymnt:	n/a	No of shares after	
Fin div paymnt:	Apr	dilution:	159,157,705
Int net div per share:	nil	P/E ratio:	10.5
Fin net div per share:	0.041p	Probable CGT?	YES

LATEST REPORTED RESULTS: 2003		PREVIOUS REPORTED RESULTS: 2002	
Turnover:	£4.12m	Turnover:	£3.44m
PTP:	£383,000	PTP:	£(82,000)
EPS:	0.2p	EPS:	(0.1)p

Comments:

The designer, manufacturer and retailer of kitchen and home office furniture swung from losses to profits in the 12 months to August, by reporting its most successful year to date. A 20% sales surge laid the foundations for the record performance – demand for the company's kitchen furniture being particularly strong. Further progress in 2004 is by no means guaranteed, however. Chairman John Lewis admits that first quarter orders 'have been slow'.

John Swan & Sons (SWJ)

Auctioneer, valuer & estate agent

Auction Mart, Newtown St.Boswells, Melrose, TD6 0PP Tel: 0131-443 2301; Fax: 0131-455 7323;
e-mail: stboswells@johnswan.demon.co.uk; web site: www.johnswan.co.uk

		holding %
Chairman	Alastair Ritchie	0.2
Managing Director	Jack Clark	1.3
Finance Director		
Non-Exec Director	James Allen	0.3

Main Shareholders:

David Barry*	9.6
Peregrine Moncreiffe	7.3

Percentage of free market capital: 81.1%

*These shares are registered in the name of Value Investments Limited

Nominated Adviser:	Brewin Dolphin, Edinburgh
AIM Broker:	Brewin Dolphin, Edinburgh
Solicitors:	Shepherd & Wedderburn, Edinburgh
Market Makers:	n/a
Auditors:	Scott-Moncrieff, 17 Melville Street, Edinburgh EH3 7PH
Registrars:	Georghegan & Co

ENTRY ON AIM:	24/9/2001	Recent price:	782.5p
Interim results:	Dec	Market cap:	£4.79m
Final results:	Jun	Issue price:	355.0p
Year end:	Apr	Current no of shares:	
Accounts due:	Aug		612,000
Int div paymnt:	n/a	No of shares after	
Fin div paymnt:	Sep	dilution:	732,000
Int net div per share:	nil	P/E ratio:	66.3
Fin net div per share:	10.0p	Probable CGT?	YES

LATEST REPORTED RESULTS:	2003	PREVIOUS REPORTED RESULTS:	2002
Turnover:	£1.36m	Turnover:	£1.25m
PTP:	£55,434	PTP:	£8,473
EPS:	11.8p	EPS:	1.0p

Comments:

Founded in 1856 by John Swan and his two sons, the company reported an interim turnover of £1.6m and pre-tax profits of £709,207, thanks largely to the sale of Powflats Farm near Edinburgh for £747,000 above book value. The company has reorganised with major board changes and is now concentrating on its auction mart business, which is operating profitably. Its 'Braveheart' venture is suffering due to the importation of beef at discount prices. Net debt at the end of October was £1.4m.

Jourdan (JDR)

Industrial holding company

North Way, Walworth Estate, Andover, Hampshire SP10 5LX Tel: 01264-361710; Fax: 01264-363947

		holding %
Chairman	John Abell	29.9
Chief Executive		
Finance Director		
Deputy Chairman	Jon Pither	1.9

Main Shareholders:

Strand Associates	21.2
Goosegog	10.9
Jupiter Asset Management	3.6
Amodeo Investments	3.2

Percentage of free market capital: 27.4%

Nominated Adviser:	Charles Stanley, London
AIM Broker:	Charles Stanley, London
Solicitors:	Jones Day Gouldens, London
Market Makers:	KBCS; SCAP; WINS
Auditors:	Grant Thornton, 8 West Walk, Leicester LE1 7NH
Registrars:	Lloyds TSB Registrars

ENTRY ON AIM:	25/10/2002	Recent price:	37.5p
Interim results:	Mar	Market cap:	£12.35m
Final results:	Sep	Issue price:	11.0p
Year end:	Jun	Current no of shares:	
Accounts due:	Oct		32,945,258
Int div paymnt:	n/a	No of shares after	
Fin div paymnt:	n/a	dilution:	n/a
Int net div per share:	nil	P/E ratio:	n/a
Fin net div per share:	nil	Probable CGT?	YES

LATEST REPORTED RESULTS:	2003	PREVIOUS REPORTED RESULTS:	2002
Turnover:	£24.63m	Turnover:	£26.73m
PTP:	£(390,000)	PTP:	£(3.35m)
EPS:	(1.5)p	EPS:	(9.9)p

Comments:

The mini-conglomerate scored a recovery in interim profits to December, thanks to better results from electric fires maker Suncrest, trouser press maker John Corby and sterilisation packages business Westfield Medical. In flat or declining markets, Jourdan's pre-tax profits rose from £21,000 to £676,000 on sales of £14.2m (£12.6m). Debts were cut from £5.4m a year earlier to £4m as Jourdan's operations continued to generate cash.

Jubilee Platinum (JLP)

International explorer for platinum group metals
22 Melton Street, London, NW1 2BW Tel: 020-7590 8806; Fax: 020-7589 7806; web site: www.jubileeplatinum.com

		holding %
Chairman	Stephen Kearney	0.0
Chief Executive	Colin Bird	17.0
Finance Director		
Non-Exec Director	John Parker	0.0

Main Shareholders:

Golden Prospect	27.9
Resource Capital	19.8
The Prudent Bear Fund	8.1
Framlington Investment Management	3.5
Gartmore	3.5
Percentage of free market capital: 17.1%	

Comments:

Cash-hungry Jubilee, which lost £550,000 last year, raised £2.6m at 20p and 28p on the strength of platinum group metals projects with claimed potential of one million-plus oz, in South Africa's Bushveld and Madagascar. Jubilee has clinched a South African black-empowerment deal, leading to new potential projects, and has found favour with its 'highly prospective' York project in Sierra Leone.

Nominated Adviser:	Numis, London
AIM Broker:	Numis, London
Solicitors:	Stringer Saul, London
Market Makers:	KBCS; SCAP; WINS
Auditors:	Grant Thornton, Segensworth
Registrars:	Melton Registrars

ENTRY ON AIM:	31/7/2002	**Recent price:**	30.0p
Interim results:	Mar	**Market cap:**	£14.75m
Final results:	Jun	**Issue price:**	16.0p
Year end:	Jun	**Current no of shares:**	
Accounts due:	Aug		49,160,000
Int div paymnt:	n/a	**No of shares after**	
Fin div paymnt:	n/a	dilution:	n/a
Int net div per share:	nil	P/E ratio:	n/a
Fin net div per share:	nil	Probable CGT?	No

LATEST REPORTED RESULTS:	2003	PREVIOUS REPORTED RESULTS:	N/A
Turnover:	n/a	**Turnover:**	n/a
PTP:	£(555,000)	**PTP:**	n/a
EPS:	(1.43)p	**EPS:**	n/a

Judges Capital (JDG)

Investment company
1 Bickenhall Mansions, Bickenhall Estate, London, W1H 3LF Tel: 020-7437 4037; Fax: 020-7437 2607

		holding %
Chairman	Alexander Hambro	0.0
Chief Executive	David Cicurel	25.0
Finance Director	Ralph Elman	0.0
Non-Exec Director	Glynn Reece	0.0

Main Shareholders:

Artemis	10.0
Guy Naggar	9.6
Forward Issue	6.3
Totalassist	6.3
Lloyds TSB Bank	5.0
Percentage of free market capital: 14.7%	

Comments:

Judges targets well managed mature but undervalued companies worth up to £100m in slower growing sectors, which might go private and leave the stock market backed by private equity firms. Chief executive David Cicurel has a reputation for pulling off such deals. He invested £500,000 in the initial £1.8m net placing. Half has so far been invested in candidates, such as Pilkington's Tiles, Lionheart, which has since gone into liquidation, and an unnamed support services company.

Nominated Adviser:	Shore Capital, London
AIM Broker:	Shore Capital, London
Solicitors:	Faegre Benson Hobson Audley, London
Market Makers:	EVO; WINS
Auditors:	Grant Thornton, 8 West Walk, Leicester LE1 7NH
Registrars:	Capita Registrars

ENTRY ON AIM:	7/1/2003	**Recent price:**	112.0p
Interim results:	n/a	**Market cap:**	£2.36m
Final results:	n/a	**Issue price:**	95.0p
Year end:	n/a	**Current no of shares:**	
Accounts due:	n/a		2,106,316
Int div paymnt:	n/a	**No of shares after**	
Fin div paymnt:	n/a	dilution:	n/a
Int net div per share:	nil	P/E ratio:	n/a
Fin net div per share:	nil	Probable CGT?	Yes

LATEST REPORTED RESULTS:	N/A	PREVIOUS REPORTED RESULTS:	N/A
Turnover:	n/a	**Turnover:**	n/a
PTP:	n/a	**PTP:**	n/a
EPS:	n/a	**EPS:**	n/a

Just Car Clinics (formerly BikeNet) (JCR)

Motor vehicle accident repair

York Trading Park, Kettlestring Lane, Clifton, Moorgate, York, LS2 8DD Tel: 01904-476793; Fax: 01904-476772;
web site: www.bikenet.com

		holding %
Chairman	David Hickey	21.2
Chief Executive	Barry Whittles	9.3
Finance Director	Chris Elton	6.3
Non-Exec Director	Ian Davis	0.4

Main Shareholders:
Simon Lunt 19.1

Percentage of free market capital: 43.7%

Nominated Adviser:	Brewin Dolphin, London
AIM Broker:	Brewin Dolphin, London
Solicitors:	Gossehachs, Hull
Market Makers:	KBCS; WINS
Auditors:	Ernst & Young, PO Box 3, Lowgate House, Hull HU1 1JJ
Registrars:	Capita Registrars

ENTRY ON AIM:	25/8/2000	Recent price:	21.0p
Interim results:	Sep	Market cap:	£2.7m
Final results:	Mar	Issue price:	133.0p
Year end:	Dec	Current no of shares:	
Accounts due:	Mar		12,863,892
Int dlv paymnt:	n/a	No of shares after	
Fin div paymnt:	n/a	dilution:	n/a
Int net div per share:	nil	P/E ratio:	n/a
Fin net div per share:	nil	Probable CGT?	YES

LATEST REPORTED RESULTS: 2002		PREVIOUS REPORTED RESULTS: 2001	
Turnover:	£140,000	Turnover:	£1.77m
PTP:	£(121,000)	PTP:	£(784,000)
EPS:	(1.1)p	EPS:	(7.3)p

Comments:
The independent collision repair chain stunned the market with news of a scandalous £370,000 overstatement ahead of maiden preliminary results. In a pre-audit review, the group uncovered false bookkeeping by one of its four accountants, since dismissed. Theft for personal gain has not yet been ruled out. Nevertheless during 2004 Just Car has been profitable and continues to be cash positive. Interim figures to June revealed a pro forma pre-tax profit of £215,000 on £11.2m sales.

K3 Business Technology (KBT)

e-commerce group

RAP House, Harrison Street, Briercliffe, Burnley, Lancashire BB10 2HP Tel: 01282-410685; Fax: 01282-451170;
e-mail: enquiries@k3btg.com; web site: www.k3btg.com

		holding %
Chairman	George Matthews	1.0
Chief Executive	Andrew Makeham	1.9
Finance Director	David Bolton	1.6
Non-Exec Director	Johan Claesson	19.1

Main Shareholders:

Silverslaggan AB*	43.8
P J Claesson	19.2
P Gyllenhammar	4.7

Percentage of free market capital: 42.2%
 * Silverslaggan AB is owned and controlled by Mr P Gyllenhammar

Nominated Adviser:	Rowan Dartington, Bristol
AIM Broker:	Rowan Dartington, Bristol
Solicitors:	Addlestone Keane, Leeds
Market Makers:	WDBM; WINS
Auditors:	Deloitte & Touche, 9 Charlotte St, Manchester M1 4EU
Registrars:	Capita Registrars

ENTRY ON AIM:	14/11/2000	Recent price:	18.25p
Interim results:	Sep	Market cap:	£9.3m
Final results:	Mar	Issue price:	n/a
Year end:	Dec	Current no of shares:	
Accounts due:	Mar		50,962,144
Int div paymnt:	n/a	No of shares after	
Fin div paymnt:	n/a	dilution:	53,767,310
Int net div per share:	nil	P/E ratio:	n/a
Fin net div per share:	nil	Probable CGT?	YES

LATEST REPORTED RESULTS: 2003		PREVIOUS REPORTED RESULTS: 2002	
Turnover:	£7.92m	Turnover:	£8.09m
PTP:	£(199,000)	PTP:	£266,000
EPS:	(0.6)p	EPS:	(3.6)p

Comments:
Customer relationship management and enterprise planning software developer K3 swung from profit to loss in 2003, as management was forced to write off £610,000 of debt relating to its legacy garden hardware business RAP, since disposed. As such, and although the tough market conditions led to a near £1m drop in revenues, cash reserves actually increased by £1.1m to £1.23m over the year. 2004 is likely to be another tough year, though management is confident further progress will be made.

Keryx Biopharmaceuticals (KRX)

Drug discoverer

7 Hartom St, Har Hotzvim, PO Box 23706, Jerusalem, 91236 Israel, Tel: 00-1972 2 541 3500 ; Fax: 00-1972 2 541 3501; e-mail: info@keryx.com; web site: www.keryxbiopharm.com

		holding %
Chairman	Michael Weiss	0.0
Chief Executive	as above	
Finance Director		
Secretary	Bob Trachenberg	1.4

Main Shareholders:

Lindsay Rosenwald	26.8
Children's Medical Centre	4.3
Nomura Bank	3.5

Percentage of free market capital: 51.0%

Nominated Adviser:	Panmure Gordon, London
AIM Broker:	Panmure Gordon, London
Solicitors:	Morgan, Lewis & Bockius, London
Market Makers:	ALTI; WEST; WINS
Auditors:	Somekh Chaikin, Jerusalem, Israel
Registrars:	American Stock Transfer and Trust Company

ENTRY ON AIM:	2/8/2000	**Recent price:**	670.0p
Interim results:	Jun	**Market cap:**	£153.66m
Final results:	Mar	**Issue price:**	687.21p
Year end:	Dec	**Current no of shares:**	
Accounts due:	Apr		22,934,081
Int div paymnt:	n/a	**No of shares after**	
Fin div paymnt:	n/a	**dilution:**	n/a
Int net div per share:	nil	**P/E ratio:**	n/a
Fin net div per share:	nil	**Probable CGT?**	No

LATEST REPORTED RESULTS: 2002		PREVIOUS REPORTED RESULTS: 2001	
Turnover:	n/a	Turnover:	n/a
PTP:	$(11.78m)	PTP:	$(9.81m)
EPS:	(0.6)c	EPS:	(0.5)c

Comments:

New York-headquartered drug developer Keryx is working on products to treat diseases such as diabetes and cancer. Its lead drug is KRX-101, an oral compound to treat diabetic nephropathy – this is a life threatening kidney disease and Keryx is planning its phase 2/3 clinical programs. The company listed on AIM and Nasdaq at the same time in August 2000, raising £30m. The shares have jumped tenfold over the past year, enabling the group to raise £26m, giving it £33m in all.

KeyWorld Investments (KWI)

Single premium life assurance policy operator

46 Crawford Street, London, W1H 1JU Tel: 020-7724 2423; Fax: 020-7724 3433; web site: www.keyworldinvest.com

		holding %
Chairman	Todd Knobel	0.0
Chief Executive		
Finance Director	George Raynor*	0.5
Director	Grant Peires*	46.3

Main Shareholders:

Jubilee Investment Trust	16.0
Duncan Gee*	8.5
Kevin Barker*	8.5
Jaspar Investments	5.1
Fieldfare Investments	5.1

Percentage of free market capital: 4.6

*Lifestyle 2000 is the legal owner of the Ordinary Shares in which the directors are interested

Nominated Adviser:	Grant Thornton, London		
AIM Broker:	Hoodless Brennan, London		
Solicitors:	Denton Wilde, London		
Market Makers:	HOOD; WINS		
Auditors:	Grant Thornton, Portsmouth		
Registrars:	Capita Registrars		

ENTRY ON AIM:	2/3/2001	**Recent price:**	0.75p
Interim results:	Jan	**Market cap:**	£20.22m
Final results:	Oct	**Issue price:**	2.0p
Year end:	Apr	**Current no of shares:**	
Accounts due:	Nov		2,695,759,067
Int div paymnt:	n/a	**No of shares after**	
Fin div paymnt:	n/a	**dilution:**	n/a
Int net div per share:	nil	**P/E ratio:**	n/a
Fin net div per share:	nil	**Probable CGT?**	Yes

LATEST REPORTED RESULTS: 2003		PREVIOUS REPORTED RESULTS: 2002	
Turnover:	n/a	Turnover:	n/a
PTP:	£(508,000)	PTP:	£(1.61m)
EPS:	(0.0)p	EPS:	(0.2)p

Comments:

Keyworld, via its bonds, offers investors 30 years of free holiday accommodation for a single investment of £10,000. It recently signed an agreement with Berkeley Wealth Management to distribute its Keyworld Bonds. Although the concept sounds feasible, in the interim period to October the company failed to generate any income – indeed, nothing in the way of revenues has been generated since its listing in 2001.

Knowledge Technology Solutions (KTS)
Software solutions developer
Wembley Point, I Harrow Road, Wembley, Middlesex HA9 6DE Tel: 020-8795 2700; Fax: 020-8795 2711;
e-mail: enquiries@ktsplc.com; web site: www.ktsplc.com

		holding %
Chairman	Gavin Casey	0.2
CEO	Marc Pinter-Krainer	16.9
Finance Director	Michael Levy	0.3
Commercial Director	Paul McGroary	9.1
Main Shareholders:		
ISIS Asset Management		9.8
Smit Berry (Non-Exec-Director)		8.4
Singer & Friedlander		8.3
The Global Value Investment Portfolio		5.2
Ennis International		4.0
Percentage of free market capital: 34.8%		

Nominated Adviser:	KBC Peel Hunt, London
AIM Broker:	KBC Peel Hunt, London
Solicitors:	Nicholson, Graham & Jones, London
Market Makers:	SCAP; WINS
Auditors:	Solomon Hare, Oakfield Grove, Clifton, Bristol BS8 2BN
Registrars:	Capita Registrars

Entry on AIM:	4/12/2000	Recent price:	9.5p
Interim results:	Mar	Market cap:	£11.35m
Final results:	Sep	Issue price:	4.5p
Year end:	Jun	Current no of shares:	
Accounts due:	Oct		119,443,302
Int div paymnt	n/a	No of shares after	
Fin div paymnt:	n/a	dilution:	n/a
Int net div per share:	nil	P/E ratio:	n/a
Fin net div per share:	nil	Probable CGT?	Yes

LATEST REPORTED RESULTS: 2003		PREVIOUS REPORTED RESULTS: 2002	
Turnover:	£161,000	Turnover:	£77,000
PTP:	£(706,000)	PTP:	£(451,000)
EPS:	(0.7)p	EPS:	(0.6)p

Comments:
KTS' bluster and bravado is finally reaping rewards. Latest interims from the company, which seemed to announce a new contract a fortnight last summer, at last showed a degree of revenue generation – sales hitting £298,232, up 570% on H1 2002. Losses also increased, by £110,000 to £432,656, yet £1.1m sits in the bank and annual revenues are said to top £850,000. Brokers Charles Stanley and Sky Capital are among the latest to sign up for KTS' low-cost stock market terminal.

Kuju (KUJ)
Interactive games software developer
Unit 10, Woodside Park, Catteshall Lane, Godalming, Surrey, GU7 ILG Tel: 01483-414344; Fax: 01483-414287;
web site: www.kuju.com

		holding %
Chairman	Dominic Wheatley	1.7
Managing Director	Jonathan Newth	33.2
Finance Director	David Stanley	0.0
Bus Development Director	Ian Baverstock	33.2
Main Shareholders:		
Command Fund		4.5
Percentage of free market capital: 27.1%		

Nominated Adviser:	Noble & Co, London
AIM Broker:	Noble & Co, London
Solicitors:	Osborne Clarke, London
Market Makers:	CSCS; WINS
Auditors:	Grant Thornton, Farnham, Surrey
Registrars:	Capita Registrars

Entry on AIM:	22/5/2002	Recent price:	17.5p
Interim results:	Nov	Market cap:	£1.47m
Final results:	Jun	Issue price:	96.0p
Year end:	Mar	Current no of shares:	
Accounts due:	Jul		8,385,417
Int div paymnt:	n/a	No of shares after	
Fin div paymnt:	n/a	dilution:	8,411,417
Int net div per share:	nil	P/E ratio:	n/a
Fin net div per share:	nil	Probable CGT?	Yes

LATEST REPORTED RESULTS: 2003		PREVIOUS REPORTED RESULTS: 2002	
Turnover:	£6.12m	Turnover:	£4.72m
PTP:	£(598,000)	PTP:	£345,000
EPS:	(6.1)p	EPS:	4.2p

Comments:
Kuju's interims were pretty terrible, losses hitting £1.5m compared with a £66,480 profit 12 months earlier. Sales dipped 40% to just under £1.9m. Explanations included a poor performance from the company's 'simulation' division, delays in signing new projects, currency fluctuations and restructuring costs. On a brighter note several new contracts have been signed in the second half, but a revival in Kuju's fortunes depend on it successfully completing projects already under development.

Landround   (LDR)

Travel promotions operator

The Quadrant, Sealand Road, Chester, Cheshire CH1 4QR Tel: 01244-370033; Fax: 01244-370911;
e-mail: mail@landround.com; web site: www.landround.com

		holding %
Chairman	Michael Crompton	11.6
Chief Executive	David Lyne	0.3
Finance Director	Clare Dyer	0.1
Non-Exec Director	Peter Carter	0.0

Main Shareholders:

Framlington*	12.7
ISIS	9.3
Employee Share Ownership Plan	3.2

Percentage of free market capital: 62.4%

*The Ordinary Shares are registered in the name of HSBC Global Custody Nominee

Comments:

This travel promotions business posted a spectacular set of results for 2003 largely due to the continued strong performance of its voucher-based travel promotions arm. However, management remain excited by the prospects of 'Buy and Fly!', an 'air miles' type offering that is going great guns. At present, this division accounts for only 17% of sales, yet with an electronic version set to replace the current paper-based option, many more clients are expected to come on board. A profit of at least £2.4m is expected this year.

Nominated Adviser:	Evolution Beeson Gregory, London		
AIM Broker:	Evolution Beeson Gregory, London		
Solicitors:	Eversheds, Manchester		
Market Makers:	BGMM; MLSB; WINS		
Auditors:	Baker Tilly, Steam Mill, Chester CH3 5AN		
Registrars:	Capita Registrars		

Entry on AIM:	13/8/1997	**Recent price:**	389.0p
Interim results:	Jun	**Market cap:**	£23.03m
Final results:	Dec	**Issue price:**	80.0p
Year end:	Sep	**Current no of shares:**	
Accounts due:	Jan		5,919,382
Int div paymnt:	Jul	**No of shares after**	
Fin div paymnt:	Feb	**dilution:**	6,112,404
Int net div per share:	3.5p	**P/E ratio:**	15.3
Fin net div per share:	7.0p	**Probable CGT?**	Yes

LATEST REPORTED RESULTS: 2003		PREVIOUS REPORTED RESULTS: 2002	
Turnover:	£9.89m	Turnover:	£7.07m
PTP:	£1.96m	PTP:	£754,000
EPS:	25.4p	EPS:	8.9p

Lawrence   (LAC)

Agricultural & animal health products supplier

78 Coombe Road, New Malden, Surrey KT3 4QS Tel: 020-8336 2900; Fax: 020-8336 0909;
web site: www.lawrenceplc.com

		holding %
Chairman	Peter Lawrence*	36.4
Chief Executive	Michael Brent	0.2
Finance Director		
Non-Exec Director	Gavin Casey	0.2

Main Shareholders:

Fidelity International	9.9
Schroder Investment Management	6.4
Artemis	5.7
Juliette Levy	3.1
Andrew Levy	3.1

Percentage of free market capital: 28.9%

* and family

Comments:

The maker and distributor of chemical and pharmaceutical products for the farming, animal health and pet markets reported a decent half to September. Pre-tax profits rose to £2.12m (£1.96m) on sales up 5% to £18.2m. Shareholders enjoyed 11% growth in the interim payout. The chairman was particularly pleased that Lawrence maintained sound first half cashflow, even after spending on drug registrations for its fast growing ECO business.

Nominated Adviser:	Charles Stanley, London	
AIM Broker:	Charles Stanley, London; Durlacher, London	
Solicitors:	Haarmann Hemmelrath, London	
Market Makers:	KBCS; WINS	
Auditors:	FW Stephens, Charterhouse Square, London EC1	
Registrars:	Capita Registrars	

Entry on AIM:	26/9/1995	**Recent price:**	402.5p
Interim results:	Dec	**Market cap:**	£107.66m
Final results:	Jul	**Issue price:**	170.0p
Year end:	Mar	**Current no of shares:**	
Accounts due:	Sep		26,747,352
Int div paymnt:	Apr	**No of shares after**	
Fin div paymnt:	Nov	**dilution:**	35.6
Int net div per share:	1.15p	**P/E ratio:**	n/a
Fin net div per share:	8.95p	**Probable CGT?**	Yes

LATEST REPORTED RESULTS: 2003		PREVIOUS REPORTED RESULTS: 2002	
Turnover:	£36.26m	Turnover:	£34.04m
PTP:	£4.55m	PTP:	£761,000
EPS:	11.3p	EPS:	(0.9)p

Leeds (LDSG)

Equipment leasing

Schofield House, Gateway Drive, Yeadon, Leeds, LS19 7XY Tel: 0113-391 9000; Fax: 0113-202 9612;
e-mail: enquiries@leedsgroup.plc.uk; web site: www.leedsgroup.plc.uk

		holding %
Chairman	Bill Cran	0.9
Managing Director	Malcolm Wilson	0.2
Finance Director	Dawn Bowler	0.0
Non-Exec Director	Vin Murria	0.3

Main Shareholders:

Mr J Claesson & Associates	20.4
P Gyllenhammar & Associates	18.4

Percentage of free market capital: 60.0%

Nominated Adviser:	KPMG Corporate Finance, Leeds
AIM Broker:	Numis, London
Solicitors:	Walker Morris, Leeds
Market Makers:	KBCS; WINS
Auditors:	KPMG Audit, Leeds
Registrars:	Capita Registrars

ENTRY ON AIM:	13/3/2002	Recent price:	17.0p
Interim results:	May	Market cap:	£6.22m
Final results:	Dec	Issue price:	31.50p
Year end:	Sept	Current no of shares:	
Accounts due:	Jan		36,598,603
Int div paymnt:	n/a	No of shares after	
Fin div paymnt:	n/a	dilution:	n/a
Int net div per share:	nil	P/E ratio:	n/a
Fin net div per share:	nil	Probable CGT?	No

LATEST REPORTED RESULTS:	2003	PREVIOUS REPORTED RESULTS:	2002
Turnover:	£25.10m	Turnover:	£33.47m
PTP:	£(12.11m)	PTP:	£(6.61m)
EPS:	(33.3)p	EPS:	(16.2)p

Comments:

Dismal full year figures from Leeds reflected the company's decision to pull out of the textiles manufacturing business, indeed £12.8m was written off in relation to one disposal alone. With its textile ties now severed, management is free to concentrate on its ongoing equipment leasing business, which generated a £555,000 profit before tax last year. As you would expect from a leasing firm net debts are high. Borrowings topped £14m at year-end.

Legendary Investments (LEG)

Internet investor

4th Floor, Wembley Point, 1 Harrow Road, London, HA9 6DE Tel: 020-8903 9037;
web site: www.legendaryinvestmentsplc.com

		holding %
Chairman		
Chief Executive	Shami Ahmed	42.3
Finance Director		
Non-Exec Director	Zafarullah Karim	0.0

Main Shareholders:

Swiss Digital Technologies	11.3
The Accessory People	3.9

Percentage of free market capital: 30.7%

Nominated Adviser:	Seymour Pierce, London
AIM Broker:	Seymour Pierce, London
Solicitors:	KLegal, London
Market Makers:	MLSB; SCAP; WINS
Auditors:	Baker Tilly, 2 Bloomsbury Street, London WC1B 3ST
Registrars:	Capita Registrars

ENTRY ON AIM:	2/3/2000	Recent price:	0.7p
Interim results:	Dec	Market cap:	£3.72m
Final results:	Aug	Issue price:	2.0p
Year end:	Mar	Current no of shares:	
Accounts due:	Sep		532,067,198
Int div paymnt:	n/a	No of shares after	
Fin div paymnt:	n/a	dilution:	705,087,729
Int net div per share:	nil	P/E ratio:	n/a
Fin net div per share:	nil	Probable CGT?	Yes

LATEST REPORTED RESULTS:	2003	PREVIOUS REPORTED RESULTS:	2002
Turnover:	n/a	Turnover:	n/a
PTP:	£(2.20m)	PTP:	£(1.91m)
EPS:	(0.4)p	EPS:	(0.4)p

Comments:

Despite not making any major investments over the period Legendary still managed to produce a net profit of £32,000 in the six months to September, due to prudent management of its resources. At the end of the period net assets stood at £2.16m, following last year's £1.3m write off charge. Chief executive Shami Ahmed will continue to look for situations where his hands-on approach will bring benefits. It's debatable whether the shares deserve their premium to NAV though.

Leisure Ventures (LSV)

Cash shell

St James's Court, Brown Street, Manchester, M2 2JF Tel: 0161-831 2691

		holding %
Chairman	Harry Coe	1.2
Chief Executive	Iorwerth Williams	41.4
Finance Director		
Director	Ian Craig	0.6

Main Shareholders:
n/a

Percentage of free market capital: 56.3%

Nominated Adviser:	WH Ireland, Manchester
AIM Broker:	WH Ireland, Manchester
Solicitors:	Halliwell Landau, Manchester
Market Makers:	KBCS; SCAP; WINS
Auditors:	Ernst & Young LLP, Manchester,
Registrars:	Capita Registrars

ENTRY ON AIM:	4/4/2002	**Recent price:**	1.9p
Interim results:	Jan	**Market cap:**	£2.48m
Final results:	Jul	**Issue price:**	7.5p
Year end:	Apr	**Current no of shares:**	
Accounts due:	Sep		130,477,520
Int div paymnt:	n/a	**No of shares after**	
Fin div paymnt:	n/a	**dilution:**	n/a
Int net div per share:	nil	**P/E ratio:**	n/a
Fin net div per share:	nil	**Probable CGT?**	YES

LATEST REPORTED RESULTS: 2003		PREVIOUS REPORTED RESULTS: 4 APR 02 TO 30 APR 02	
Turnover:	£3.52m	Turnover:	n/a
PTP:	£(8.56m)	PTP:	£(9,000)
EPS:	(9.2)p	EPS:	(0.1)p

Comments:
The cash shell brought to market by former MyTravel managing director Harry Coe is an empty vessel on the hunt for deals once more. In the interim to October, turnover was £549,000 and losses before tax were £349,000. Net liabilities are £69,000. It has sold its only business, The International Academy (TIA), to Thomson Travel for an initial consideration of £200,000 with a further potential £1.8m based on TIA's performance during the next four years.

Lendu (LNU)

Farming irrigated-cotton, beef cattle and cereals

3 Clanricarde Gardens, Tunbridge Wells, Kent, TN1 1HQ Tel: 01892-516333; Fax: 01892-518639;
web site: www.mpevans.co.uk

		holding %
Chairman	Peter Hadsley-Chaplin	0.04
Chief Executive	as above	
Finance Director	Philip Fletcher	0.02
Deputy Chairman	Derek Shaw	5.7

Main Shareholders:

Rowe Evans Investments	35.1
Kulim	10.3
Leong Watt Hin Estates	8.0
Aberdeen UK Emerging Companies Fund	7.7
El Oro Mining and Exploration	5.6

Percentage of free market capital: 24.0%

Nominated Adviser:	Westhouse Securities, London
AIM Broker:	Westhouse Securities, London
Solicitors:	Lovells, London; Abbot Tout, Australia
Market Makers:	KBCS; WINS
Auditors:	Deloitte & Touche, Crawley
Registrars:	MP Evans (UK)

ENTRY ON AIM:	27/8/2002	**Recent price:**	52.5p
Interim results:	Mar	**Market cap:**	£7.17m
Final results:	Sep	**Issue price:**	47.0p
Year end:	Jun	**Current no of shares:**	
Accounts due:	Oct		13,662,867
Int div paymnt:	n/a	**No of shares after**	
Fin div paymnt:	Nov	**dilution:**	n/a
Int net div per share:	nil	**P/E ratio:**	12.5
Fin net div per share:	0.25p	**Probable CGT?**	No

LATEST REPORTED RESULTS: 2003		PREVIOUS REPORTED RESULTS: 2002	
Turnover:	£2.51m	Turnover:	£4.11m
PTP:	£378,000	PTP:	£915,000
EPS:	4.2p	EPS:	4.9p

Comments:
Australian irrigated-cotton, beef and cereals producer Lendu reported interim pre-tax losses of £728,000. The company has now decided to sell its three irrigated-cotton properties, valued at A$37m in 2002, with the cotton harvest being adversely affected by the drought. Instead, it will expand into the Aussie beef-cattle sector, as it believes it has a geographical advantage in providing beef to the growing Asian market. It does not anticipate being in profits for the full year.

LiDCO (LID)

Manufacturer of cardio-vascular monitoring devices

16 Orsman Road, London, N1 5QJ Tel: 020-7749 1500; Fax: 020-7749 1501; e-mail: info@lidco.com; web site: www.lidco.com

		holding %
Chairman	Theresa Wallis	0.0
Chief Executive	Terry O'Brien	13.6
Finance Director	Richard Mills	0.7
Sales & Mktg Director	John Barry	0.4

Main Shareholders:

Robert Greenshield	7.0
Merlin Biosciences Fund	4.4
Paul Brewer	4.3
Jiri Kratochvil	4.3
Joe Leitch	3.2

Percentage of free market capital: 48.9%

Nominated Adviser:	Nomura, London
AIM Broker:	Nomura, London
Solicitors:	Herbert Smith, London
Market Makers:	BGMM; TEAM; WINS
Auditors:	Deloitte & Touche, London
Registrars:	Capita Registrars

ENTRY ON AIM:	5/7/2001	**Recent price:**	29.0p
Interim results:	Sep	Market cap:	£22.4m
Final results:	Mar	Issue price:	140p
Year end:	Dec	Current no of shares:	
Accounts due:	Apr		77,235,798
Int div paymnt:	n/a	No of shares after	
Fin div paymnt:	n/a	dilution:	n/a
Int net div per share:	nil	P/E ratio:	n/a
Fin net div per share:	nil	Probable CGT?	YES

LATEST REPORTED RESULTS:	2002	PREVIOUS REPORTED RESULTS:	2001
Turnover:	£2.04m	Turnover:	£1.13m
PTP:	£(5.5m)	PTP:	£(2.80m)
EPS:	(7.7)p	EPS:	(5.7)p

Comments:

The maker of heart monitoring devices is recovering. First-half revenue rose 70% to £1.7m, which helped losses reduce by 31% to £1.8m. A recent £1m placing at 19.5p has bolstered the group's tight cash position. The technology, which injects lithium chloride into the bloodstream to measure electrical conductivity, seems to be attractive and has now gained US and Japanese regulatory approval. The products are seen as safer and less intrusive for patients. A US partner is being sought to accelerate sales.

Lighthouse (LGT)

Financial adviser network

Rydon House, Pynes Hill, Exeter, Devon EX2 5AZ Tel: 020-7776 8890; Fax: 0870-197 7499; web site: www.lighthouseifa.com

		holding %
Chairman	David Hickey*	0.0
Chief Executive	Malcolm Streatfield	3.6
Finance Director	Paivi Grigg	3.5
Deputy Chairman	Matthew Goldsmith	0.03

Main Shareholders:

Atlas Trust Advisors Scheme	23.8
RBSTB Nominees	5.1
Ferlim Nominees	4.1
HSBC	4.1

Percentage of free market capital: 27.4%

*David Hickey is interested in the Atlas Trust Employee Scheme

Nominated Adviser:	Durlacher, London
AIM Broker:	Durlacher, London
Solicitors:	Faegre Benson Hobson Audley, London
Market Makers:	KBCS; WINS
Auditors:	PricewaterhouseCoopers, Bristol
Registrars:	Capita Registrars

ENTRY ON AIM:	27/10/2000	**Recent price:**	25.5p
Interim results:	Sep	Market cap:	£9.13m
Final results:	Mar	Issue price:	160.0p
Year end:	Dec	Current no of shares:	
Accounts due:	Apr		35,808,029
Int div paymnt:	n/a	No of shares after	
Fin div paymnt:	n/a	dilution:	n/a
Int net div per share:	nil	P/E ratio:	n/a
Fin net div per share:	nil	Probable CGT?	YES

LATEST REPORTED RESULTS:	2002	PREVIOUS REPORTED RESULTS:	2001
Turnover:	£14.89m	Turnover:	£5.17m
PTP:	£(2.25m)	PTP:	£(2.82m)
EPS:	(20.4)p	EPS:	(63.5)p

Comments:

The IFA sector remains troubled but Lighthouse, which boasts 600 advisers, looks better prepared to cope than many, with net cash of £4m. The recent major acquisitions of Berkeley Woodhouse Associates and RJ Temple helped interim turnover rise 30% to £9.5m. Pre-tax losses only increased 11% to £1m, which shows progress is being achieved. A better market may help matters in the coming year. Annualised turnover is estimated at £22m and costs will be 30% of turnover.

Linton Park   (LPK)

Agriculture, horticulture & chemical producer & trader

Linton Park, Linton, Nr Maidstone, Kent ME17 4AB Tel: 01622-746655; Fax: 01622-747422

		holding %
Chairman	M C Perkins	0.1
Managing Director	as above	
Finance Director	Anil Mathur	0.0
Deputy Chairman	D Bowley	0.0

Main Shareholders:

Camellia Plc	79.4
Alcatel Bell Pensioenfonds	4.2

Percentage of free market capital: 16.3%

Nominated Adviser:	Credit Lyonnais, London
AIM Broker:	Credit Lyonnais, London
Solicitors:	Penningtons, London
Market Makers:	CLS.; MLSB; WINS
Auditors:	PricewaterhouseCoopers, I Embankment Place, London WC2N 6RN
Registrars:	Capita Registrars

ENTRY ON AIM: 18/11/1998		**Recent price:**	432.5p
Interim results:	Sep	**Market cap:**	£85.96m
Final results:	Apr	**Issue price:**	n/a
Year end:	Dec	**Current no of shares:**	
Accounts due:	May		19,876,002
Int div paymnt:	Nov	**No of shares after**	
Fin div paymnt:	Jul	**dilution:**	n/a
Int net div per share: 3.00p		**P/E ratio:**	8.8
Fin net div per share: 13.0p		**Probable CGT?**	No

LATEST REPORTED RESULTS: 2002		PREVIOUS REPORTED RESULTS: 2001	
Turnover:	£132.23m	Turnover:	£154.03m
PTP:	£14.61m	PTP:	£12.79m
EPS:	49.3p	EPS:	47.4p

Comments:

Linton Park is a diversified conglomerate, which operates in various sectors throughout the globe. It produces tea and coffee, farms macadamia, pistachio nuts and citrus fruits and makes table and wine grapes. In addition it has a food storage and distribution business, an engineering division and pharmaceutical subsidiary Siegfried. Drought in South Africa and Australia has caused problems on the agricultural side and the profitable Siegfried expects lower sales too.

Lloyds British Testing   (LBT)

Lifting equipment services

319 Shady Lane, Great Barr, Birmingham, B44 9XA Tel: 0121-325 2700; Fax: 0121-3252799;
e-mail: sales@lloydsgroup.co.uk; web site: www.lloydsgroup.co.uk

		holding %
Chairman	Brian Ralley	1.9
Chief Executive	Ian White	19.9
Finance Director	Hayden Davis	0.4
Non-Exec Director	Aubrey Brocklebank	0.2

Main Shareholders:

Bank of New York	15.4
Rathbone Nominees	10.6
Sinjul Nominees	7.8
Teawood Nominees	7.5
Graham Osmond	6.9

Percentage of free market capital: 5.5%

Nominated Adviser:	Nabarro Wells, London
AIM Broker:	Teather & Greenwood, Liverpool
Solicitors:	Gateley Wareing, Birmingham
Market Makers:	TEAM; WINS
Auditors:	Grant Thornton, Enterprise House, 115 Edmund Street, Birmingham B3 2HJ
Registrars:	Capita Registrars

ENTRY ON AIM: 31/7/2002		**Recent price:**	11.25p
Interim results:	Sep	**Market cap:**	£3.57m
Final results:	May	**Issue price:**	20.5p
Year end:	Dec	**Current no of shares:**	
Accounts due:	Apr		31,769,620
Int div paymnt:	n/a	**No of shares after**	
Fin div paymnt:	Aug	**dilution:**	n/a
Int net div per share:	nil	**P/E ratio:**	28.1
Fin net div per share: 0.25p		**Probable CGT?**	Yes

LATEST REPORTED RESULTS: 2002		PREVIOUS REPORTED RESULTS: 2001	
Turnover:	£7.27m	Turnover:	£15.27m
PTP:	£202,000	PTP:	£413,000
EPS:	0.4p	EPS:	n/a

Comments:

Lifting equipment services company Lloyds, which was founded in 1812, admitted profits to December 2003 will be lower than expected. With its short-term support services and tool hire business highly operationally geared, a small drop in turnover results in a large reduction in operating profit. Adding to its woes, the company was unable to sell its Power Access division, and will now have to decide whether to keep it within the business and, if so, how to properly structure it.

Lo-Q (LOQ)

Installer & developer of electronic queuing systems

New Close, Greenlands, Henley on Thames, Oxfordshire RG9 3AL Tel: 01491-577210; Fax: 01491-577270;
e-mail: info@lo-q.com; web site: www.lo-q.com

		holding %
Chairman	Jeff McManus	0.0
Managing Director	Leonard Sim	31.1
Finance Director		0.0
Non-Exec Director	Anthony Bone	1.3

Main Shareholders:

Singer and Friedlander	5.3
Adam & Co International Nominees	3.8
Henrieheta Sim	3.7
Manulife International Investment Management	3.5
LeggMason Investors Asset Managers	3.4

Percentage of free market capital: 44.8%

Comments:
Continued poor attendance levels at US theme parks have dogged the fortunes of beleaguered virtual queuing system developer Lo-Q. The company has completed the development of 'e-line', a low cost functionality version of the Q-Bot system but with a precarious cash position, it cannot depend on its deal with US theme park operator Six Flags alone and is in talks with other theme parks in the US and Europe. Firm orders have yet to be secured.

Nominated Adviser:	Corporate Synergy, London		
AIM Broker:	Daniel Stewart, London		
Solicitors:	Garretts, Reading		
Market Makers:	SCAP; WINS		
Auditors:	BDO Stoy Hayward, Basingstoke		
Registrars:	Capita Registrars		

Entry on AIM:	24/4/2002	**Recent price:**	6.4p
Interim results:	Jun	**Market cap:**	£0.92m
Final results:	Feb	**Issue price:**	100.0p
Year end:	Sep	**Current no of shares:**	
Accounts due:	Jan		14,347,837
Int div paymnt:	n/a	**No of shares after**	
Fin div paymnt:	n/a	**dilution:**	16,209,667
Int net div per share:	nil	**P/E ratio:**	n/a
Fin net div per share:	nil	**Probable CGT?**	Yes

LATEST REPORTED RESULTS: 2003		PREVIOUS REPORTED RESULTS: 2002	
Turnover:	£2.32m	Turnover:	£886,000
PTP:	£(1.41m)	PTP:	£(1.70m)
EPS:	(0.1)p	EPS:	(0.1)p

Loades (LOD)

Engineer & designer

Bayton Rd, Exhall, Coventry, CV7 9EJ Tel: 02476-644999; Fax: 02476-644888; e-mail: info@loadesplc.co.uk;
web site: www.loades.com

		holding %
Chairman	Tony Loades	17.7
Managing Director	Rob Loades	17.7
Finance Director		
President	Edward Loades	44.1

Main Shareholders:

n/a

Percentage of free market capital: 20.5%

Comments:
The family-owned business has turned into a commercial property developer. Loades Dynamics, a precision engineer to the automotive and aerospace sectors, is the only remnant of its engineering empire. Currently, a significant amount of its commercial property space is available but it hopes to benefit from its proximity to the M6 toll toad. Pre-tax losses fell 83% but it is all a far cry from the swinging '60s when Loades was a principal contractor to Jaguar.

Nominated Adviser:	Arbuthnot, Birmingham		
AIM Broker:	Arbuthnot, Birmingham		
Solicitors:	Martineau Johnson, Birmingham		
Market Makers:	ARBT; WINS		
Auditors:	Baker Tilly, 2 Bloomsbury Street, London WC1B 3ST		
Registrars:	Neville Registrars		

Entry on AIM:	12/2/1997	**Recent price:**	290.0p
Interim results:	Jul	**Market cap:**	£5.34m
Final results:	Mar	**Issue price:**	25.0p
Year end:	Sep	**Current no of shares:**	
Accounts due:	Dec		1,842,000
Int div paymnt:	n/a	**No of shares after**	
Fin div paymnt:	n/a	**dilution:**	n/a
Int net div per share:	nil	**P/E ratio:**	n/a
Fin net div per share:	nil	**Probable CGT?**	Yes

LATEST REPORTED RESULTS: 2003		PREVIOUS REPORTED RESULTS: 2002	
Turnover:	£4.21m	Turnover:	£9.80m
PTP:	£(935,000)	PTP:	£(5.40m)
EPS:	(37.4)p	EPS:	(269.5)p

Lok 'n Store (LOK)

Storage unit provider

12 Skerne Road, Kingston upon Thames, Surrey KT2 5AD Tel: 020-8547 2288; Fax: 020-8549 2777;
e-mail: info@loknstore.co.uk; web site: www.loknstore.co.uk

		holding %
Chairman	Andrew Jacobs	19.1
Chief Executive	Simon Thomas	8.8
Finance Director	Raymond Davies	0.0
Non-Exec Director	Richard Holmes	0.3

Main Shareholders:

Universities Superannuation Scheme	8.0
Rock	5.9
Canada Life	4.2
Lok'n Store Employee Benefit Trust	3.9
Aegon	3.1

Percentage of free market capital: 46.7%

Nominated Adviser:	Investec, London
AIM Broker:	Investec, London
Solicitors:	The City Law Partnership, London
Market Makers:	WEST; WINS
Auditors:	Baker Tilly, 2 Bloomsbury Street, London, EC1A 2AL
Registrars:	Capita Registrars

Entry on AIM:	28/6/2000	**Recent price:**	112.0p
Interim results:	Apr	Market cap:	£39.74m
Final results:	Sep	Issue price:	175.0p
Year end:	Jul	Current no of shares:	
Accounts due:	Nov		35,481,083
Int div paymnt:	n/a	No of shares after	
Fin div paymnt:	n/a	dilution:	n/a
Int net div per share:	nil	P/E ratio:	n/a
Fin net div per share:	nil	Probable CGT?	Yes

LATEST REPORTED RESULTS:	2003	PREVIOUS REPORTED RESULTS:	2002
Turnover:	£5.61m	Turnover:	£5.0m
PTP:	£(430,000)	PTP:	£(399,000)
EPS:	(1.5)p	EPS:	(1.8)p

Comments:

Half time figures to 31 January from the self-storage operator revealed a swing to the red of £41,830 from a £24,179 profit. Before exceptionals, Lok 'n Store made an operating profit though. Interim turnover rose 11.4% to £3.13m. The board insists the group's best opportunities lie in the South and South East of England. At the end of 2003, an approach at 115p was rejected since it undervalued the business and its prospects.

London Asia Capital (LDC)

Investor in internet-related ventures

Gerry Desler, 11 Central House, High Street, Ongar, Essex CM5 9AA Tel: 01277-366558; Fax: 01277-366580

		holding %
Chairman	Jack Wigglesworth	0.4
Chief Executive	Simon Littlewood*	18.6
Finance Director		
Director	George Allnutt	15.5

Main Shareholders:

RAB Capital	21.6
The Throgmorton Trust	12.8
Guoping	9.9
Xiang Qu	6.7
Raven Nominees	6.4

Percentage of free market capital: 3.6%

*Simon Littlewood's shares are held by Temima Investments

Nominated Adviser:	Grant Thornton, London
AIM Broker:	Insinger Townsley, London
Solicitors:	Paisner & Co, London
Market Makers:	KBCS; MLSB; SCAP; WINS
Auditors:	Gerald Edelman, 25 Harley Street, London W1N 2BR
Registrars:	Capita Registrars

Entry on AIM:	6/8/1999	**Recent price:**	17.25p
Interim results:	Feb	Market cap:	£11.78m
Final results:	Nov	Issue price:	25.0p
Year end:	May	Current no of shares:	
Accounts due:	Dec		68,317,734
Int div paymnt:	n/a	No of shares after	
Fin div paymnt:	n/a	dilution:	n/a
Int net div per share:	nil	P/E ratio:	n/a
Fin net div per share:	nil	Probable CGT?	Yes

LATEST REPORTED RESULTS:	2003	PREVIOUS REPORTED RESULTS:	2002
Turnover:	n/a	Turnover:	n/a
PTP:	£(215,000)	PTP:	£(3.58m)
EPS:	(1.45)p	EPS:	(32.4)p

Comments:

London Asia excited punters last year with its Chinese investments, notably financial analysis play Beijing Success Technology. Aiming to nurse companies to flotation and steered by Simon Littlewood and Victor Ng, the company, which lost an interim £113,000, is tapping Wuhan Eastlake New Technology Development Zone to find candidates for listing outside China. RAB Capital bought in last year at half the market price.

London & Boston Investments (LBN)

Investment company

133 Ebury Street, London, SW1W 9QU Tel: 020-7881 0800; Fax: 020-7881 0707;
e-mail: enquiries@london-boston@.com; web site: www.london-boston.com

		holding %
Chairman	Stephen Komlosy	5.6
Chief Executive		
Finance Director	John May	0.0
Non-Exec Director	Edward Adams	0.5

Main Shareholders:

Willbro Nominees	15.8
Nat West Bank Nominees WN1196	7.8
Frank Nominees	6.5
Energy Technique	6.0
Alma	3.3

Percentage of free market capital: 34.7%

Nominated Adviser:	Matrix Securities, London
AIM Broker:	Keith Bayley Rogers, London
Solicitors:	Wallace & Partners, London
Market Makers:	SCAP; WINS
Auditors:	Milsted Langdon, Winchester House, Deane Gate Avenue, Somerset TA1 2UH
Registrars:	Capita Registrars

Entry on AIM:	16/4/2002	Recent price:	8.25p
Interim results:	Dec	Market cap:	£6.91m
Final results:	Jul	Issue price:	6.0p
Year end:	Mar	Current no of shares:	
Accounts due:	Aug		83,801,934
Int div paymnt:	n/a	No of shares after	
Fin div paymnt:	n/a	dilution:	n/a
Int net div per share:	nil	P/E ratio:	n/a
Fin net div per share:	nil	Probable CGT?	No

LATEST REPORTED RESULTS: 2003		PREVIOUS REPORTED RESULTS: 2002	
Turnover:	£1.71m	Turnover:	£146,000
PTP:	£(1.10m)	PTP:	£(920,000)
EPS:	(1.4)p	EPS:	(1.5)p

Comments:

Stephen Komlosy has managed to persuade canny investor Bob Morton to up his stake in this investment vehicle. This sent the shares shooting up above latest NAV of £3.8m. The present portfolio includes fellow AIM concerns Croma, Merchant House and Netcentric Systems. A £0.74m interim loss was made, mainly composed of investment write-downs. The group wants to become a trading company, following the purchase of Audiotel and is in discussions about buying another profitable business.

London Security (formerly London Securities) (LSC)

Fire extinguisher maker, seller and servicer

Wistons Lane, Elland, West Yorkshire HX5 9DS Tel: 01422-372852; Fax: 01422-379569;
web site: www.londonsecurities.co.uk

		holding %
Chairman	Jacques Gaston Murray	98.2
Managing Director		
Finance Director	Jean-Christophe Pillois	0.0
Director	Jean-Jacques Murray	0.0

Main Shareholders:

n/a

Percentage of free market capital: 2.0%

Nominated Adviser:	Ernst & Young, London
AIM Broker:	Teather & Greenwood, London
Solicitors:	Walker Morris, Leeds
Market Makers:	KBCS; WINS
Auditors:	PricewaterhouseCoopers, Leeds
Registrars:	Capita Registrars

Entry on AIM:	30/12/1999	Recent price:	1400.5p
Interim results:	Sep	Market cap:	£202.72m
Final results:	Apr	Issue price:	92.0p
Year end:	Dec	Current no of shares:	
Accounts due:	Apr		14,474,816
Int div paymnt:	Nov	No of shares after	
Fin div paymnt:	Jun	dilution:	n/a
Int net div per share:	2.0p	P/E ratio:	44.0
Fin net div per share:	5.0p	Probable CGT?	Yes

LATEST REPORTED RESULTS: 2002		PREVIOUS REPORTED RESULTS: 2001	
Turnover:	£48.08m	Turnover:	£45.01m
PTP:	£8.44m	PTP:	£7.73m
EPS:	31.8p	EPS:	31.2p

Comments:

When it unveiled its interims to June, London Security said its main aim was to find acquisitions in the fire and security sector. There's been little news for investors on that front since. The fire security play raised the interim payout by 50%, after profits steamed up to £5.1m (£4.8m). Sales growth was a decent 9% at £26.7m. The first half results felt the benefits of 2002 acquisitions Asco, CFP Cavelle and HUG, as well as favourable exchange rate movements.

London Town (LTW)

Residential development manager and adviser

Aria House, 23 Craven Street, London, WC2N 5NT Tel: 020-7839 5588; Fax: 020-7839 4488;
e-mail: info@londontownplc.co.uk; web site: www.londontownplc.co.uk

		holding %
Chairman	Andrew Wilson	0.0
Chief Executive		
Finance Director	John Dodwell	0.1
Director	Jo Welman	0.0

Main Shareholders:

The Horizon Charitable Trust	54.2
Jonathan Buchanan	13.6
Don McCrickard	6.7
Aberdeen Trust Managers	5.3

Percentage of free market capital: 20.0%

Comments:
Property development manager London Town fell from earlier highs, after being beset by debts (one involving its majority holder Horizon Charitable Trust) and delays in obtaining planning permission for a project near London's Tate Modern art gallery. The company has disposed of contracts in Brighton and London's Westbourne Grove to Capital City Developments, to which it agreed to pay £145,000.

Nominated Adviser:	Strand Partners, London
AIM Broker:	City Financial Associates, London
Solicitors:	Goodman Derrick, London
Market Makers:	KBCS; TEAM; WINS
Auditors:	BDO Stoy Hayward, Emerald House, East Street, Epsom, Surrey KT17 1HS
Registrars:	SLC Registrars

Entry on AIM: 24/11/1995	**Recent price:**	15.5p
Interim results:	Sep	**Market cap:**	£8.23m
Final results:	Apr	**Issue price:**	70.0p
Year end:	Dec	**Current no of shares:**	
Accounts due:	Apr		53,087,656
Int div paymnt:	Nov	**No of shares after**	
Fin div paymnt:	n/a	**dilution:**	n/a
Int net div per share:	1.8p	**P/E ratio:**	n/a
Fin net div per share:	nil	**Probable CGT?**	No

LATEST REPORTED RESULTS: 2002		PREVIOUS REPORTED RESULTS: 2001	
Turnover:	£3.0m	Turnover:	£6.9m
PTP:	£(3.04m)	PTP:	£2.25m
EPS:	(36.7)p	EPS:	28.0p

Longbridge (LGI)

Recruitment & HR consultant

85 Gracechurch Street, London, EC3V 0AA Tel: 020-7208 5858; Fax: 020-7208 5859; web site: www.longbridge.com

		holding %
Chairman	Frank Javier Varela	55.8
Managing Director	as above	
Finance Director	Bruce Page	2.1
Non-Exec Director	Keith Lassman	0.1

Main Shareholders:

Liontrust Investment Services	11.8
Amer Deen	8.3
T James	6.3
Friends Ivory & Sime	4.6

Percentage of free market capital: 11.0%

Comments:
A well-supported placing at 80p a share boosted the balance sheet at recruiter Longbridge International, and will help it manage borrowings and take advantage of market recovery. In September, interims to June revealed weaker sales caused by restructuring and the strains of a tricky market. Sales fell from £4.5m to £2.7m, though profits improved to £337,617 (£98,861). The legal business performed well and banking and financial services were improving.

Nominated Adviser:	Noble & Co, London
AIM Broker:	Noble & Co, London
Solicitors:	Howard Kennedy, London
Market Makers:	BGMM; WINS
Auditors:	BDO Stoy Hayward, 8 Baker Street, London W1M 1DA
Registrars:	Capita Registrars

Entry on AIM: 6/5/1997	**Recent price:**	84.5p
Interim results:	Sep	**Market cap:**	£6.5m
Final results:	Jun	**Issue price:**	100.0p
Year end:	Dec	**Current no of shares:**	
Accounts due:	Apr		7,690,503
Int div paymnt:	n/a	**No of shares after**	
Fin div paymnt:	n/a	**dilution:**	n/a
Int net div per share:	nil	**P/E ratio:**	n/a
Fin net div per share:	nil	**Probable CGT?**	Yes

LATEST REPORTED RESULTS: 2002		PREVIOUS REPORTED RESULTS: 2001	
Turnover:	£7.50m	Turnover:	£10.12m
PTP:	£(419,000)	PTP:	£(4.66m)
EPS:	(7.6)p	EPS:	(104.3)p

Longmead (LGM)

Ceramic bathroom accessories manufacturer

Millwey Industrial Estate, Axminster, Devon EX13 5HU Tel: 01297-32578; Fax: 01297-32710;
e-mail: info@longmead-group.co.uk; web site: www.longmead-group.co.uk

		holding %
Chairman	Raymond Newman	28.1
Managing Director	Nigel Newman	5.7
Finance Director		
Sales & Mktg	Mark Toolan	0.0
Director		

Main Shareholders:

Rensburg Client Nominees A/c CLT	12.8
Oliver Marriott	12.5
Christopher Newman	6.8
BNY Gil Client a/c (Nominees)	6.2
PH Nominees	4.0
Percentage of free market capital: 15.3%	

Nominated Adviser:	Smith & Williamson, London
AIM Broker:	Teather & Greenwood, London
Solicitors:	Clyde & Co, London
Market Makers:	TEAM; WINS
Auditors:	Deloitte & Touche, 69-71 Queen Sq, Bristol BS1 4JP
Registrars:	Capita Registrars

ENTRY ON AIM: 31/12/1997		Recent price:	21.0p
Interim results:	Mar	Market cap:	£1.17m
Final results:	Jan	Issue price:	135.0p
Year end:	Oct	Current no of shares:	
Accounts due:	Feb		5,584,391
Int div paymnt:	n/a	No of shares after	
Fin div paymnt:	n/a	dilution:	5,602,390
Int net div per share:	nil	P/E ratio:	n/a
Fin net div per share:	nil	Probable CGT?	YES

LATEST REPORTED RESULTS:		PREVIOUS REPORTED RESULTS:	
	2003	15 MONTHS TO 2 NOV 2002	
Turnover:	£2.60m	Turnover:	£3.92m
PTP:	£(734,000)	PTP:	£(554,000)
EPS:	(13.2)p	EPS:	(11.8)p

Comments:

Last year, Longmead's losses widened after exceptionals although trading results for the second half were considerably better than the first. The group has been totally reorganised, lowering its cost base and revamping its product range. It has now stopped making door furniture – all now imported – though it still makes ceramic bathroom accessories in the UK when it can't get quality from the Far East. The key items sold now are metal products, where demand is rising.

Lonrho Africa (LAF)

Motor vehicle supplier, agriculture, distribution and hotels

Lancaster House, Mercury Court, Tithebarn Street, Liverpool, L2 2RG Tel: 0151-443 5300; Fax: 0151-236 2190;
e-mail: jhughes@lonaf.co.uk

		holding %
Chairman	Bernard Asher	0.01
Chief Executive		
Finance Director		
Non-Exec Director	Michael Wilson	0.3

Main Shareholders:

Blakeney Management	11.9
Peter Cundill & Associates	9.7
Peter Gyllenhammar	9.3
Greenbelt/Greensea	7.6
Percentage of free market capital: 30.7%	

Nominated Adviser:	Strand Partners, London
AIM Broker:	Numis, London
Solicitors:	DLA, London
Market Makers:	HSBC; MLSB; UBSW; WINS
Auditors:	KPMG, London
Registrars:	Lloyds TSB Registrars

ENTRY ON AIM: 26/2/2001		Recent price:	11.25p
Interim results:	Jun	Market cap:	£17.73m
Final results:	Mar	Issue price:	20.0p
Year end:	Sep	Current no of shares:	
Accounts due:	Mar		157,572,088
Int div paymnt:	n/a	No of shares after	
Fin div paymnt:	n/a	dilution:	n/a
Int net div per share:	nil	P/E ratio:	10.2
Fin net div per share:	nil	Probable CGT?	No

LATEST REPORTED RESULTS:		PREVIOUS REPORTED RESULTS:	
	2003		2002
Turnover:	£10.8m	Turnover:	£21.1m
PTP:	£1.4m	PTP:	£(1.2m)
EPS:	1.1p	EPS:	(1.0)p

Comments:

Lonrho Africa continues to ditch businesses and assets in Africa and remains on the lookout for opportunities in the UK. At the year-end operations consisted of hotels and Ol Pejeta ranching. Annual turnover fell 15% on depressed trading, with the hotels in particular hit by the Iraq war, forcing them from profit to loss – Kenyan hotels were hit by specific problems in that country. Lonrho has already exited from motor operations and sold wattle extract stocks in Kenya.

LPA (LPA)

Electronic components designer, maker and distributor

Tudor Works, Debden Road, Saffron Walden, Essex, CB11 4AN Tel: 01799-512800; Fax: 01799-526793; web site: www.lpa-group.com

		holding %
Chairman	Michael Rusch	7.4
Chief Executive	Peter Pollock	2.3
Finance Director	Stephen Brett	0.1
Non-Exec Director	Michael Edmonds	6.4

Main Shareholders:

Ellen Rusch	7.4
Michael Winston	5.8
Marilyn Porter	4.9
Ernest Joseph Lott Settlement No 2	4.1
Harriett Nailon	4.0
Percentage of free market capital: 49.0%	

Nominated Adviser:	Teather & Greenwood, London
AIM Broker:	Teather & Greenwood, London
Solicitors:	Eversheds, Birmingham
Market Makers:	MLSB; TEAM; WINS
Auditors:	RSM Robson Rhodes, Daedalus House, Station Road, Cambridge CB1 2RE
Registrars:	Capita Registrars

ENTRY ON AIM:	9/5/2002	Recent price:	21.5p
Interim results:	Jun	Market cap:	£2.34m
Final results:	Jan	Issue price:	10.0p
Year end:	Sep	Current no of shares:	
Accounts due:	Jan		10,903,229
Int div paymnt:	Sep	No of shares after	
Fin div paymnt:	n/a	dilution:	n/a
Int net div per share: 0.25p		P/E ratio:	n/a
Fin net div per share:	nil	Probable CGT?	YES

LATEST REPORTED RESULTS: 2003		PREVIOUS REPORTED RESULTS: 2002	
Turnover:	£12.57m	Turnover:	£13.81m
PTP:	£(208,000)	PTP:	£(318,000)
EPS:	(1.1)p	EPS:	(3.2)p

Comments:

LPA slashed losses by 35% for the year to September but suffered due to Britain's 'chaotic' railway industry. Things weren't helped by its largest customer going into administration. Two of its divisions LPA Niphon and LPA Channel Electric are performing well as demand in international rail vehicle refurbishment and upgrades have picked up. LPA's two other divisions fared less well – the company depends upon its markets reviving.

LTG Technologies (LTG)

Manufacturer of sheet metal decorating machinery

42 Portman Road, Reading, Berks RG30 1EA; web site: www.ltg-technologies.com

		holding %
Chairman	David Smith	5.6
Chief Executive	Albert Klein	0.0
Finance Director	Michael Williamson	0.0
Sales Director	Peter Heizmann	0.0

Main Shareholders:

LTG Metal Decorating GMBH	27.4
LTG Holding GMBH	15.2
LBBW Trust GMBH	7.9
Smallcap World Fund	7.7
Artemis	4.5
Percentage of free market capital: 27.2%	

Nominated Adviser:	Seymour Pierce, London
AIM Broker:	Seymour Pierce, London
Solicitors:	Maclay Murray & Spens, London
Market Makers:	KBCS; MLSB; WDBM; WINS
Auditors:	Ernst & Young, 7 Rolls Buildings, London EC4A 1NH
Registrars:	Capita Registrars

ENTRY ON AIM:	26/9/2003	Recent price:	13.75p
Interim results:	Sep	Market cap:	£33.32m
Final results:	Mar	Issue price:	9.75p
Year end:	Dec	Current no of shares:	
Accounts due:	May		242,338,635
Int div paymnt:	n/a	No of shares after	
Fin div paymnt:	n/a	dilution:	n/a
Int net div per share:	nil	P/E ratio:	n/a
Fin net div per share:	nil	Probable CGT?	No

LATEST REPORTED RESULTS: 2003		PREVIOUS REPORTED RESULTS: 2002	
Turnover:	£58.84m	Turnover:	£57.88m
PTP:	£(10.64m)	PTP:	£(18.63m)
EPS:	(4.7)p	EPS:	(11.6)p

Comments:

Impressively, this metal decorating and packaging services play pared its losses on a 19% hike in ongoing sales last year. The improvement reflected sales growth in both the LTG Mailaender and Imagelinx divisions. LTG Mailaender grew sales 19% to £49m in tough markets and returned to profitability. At Imagelinx, where revenues rose 10%, costs have been brought more in line with sales after a recent bout of expansion, and new clients include Uniq and Boots Retail.

MacLellan (MLG)

Specialist cleaner and facilities manager

Enterprise House, Castle Street, Worcester, WR1 3AD Tel: 01905-744400; Fax: 01905-611686;
e-mail: enquiries@maclellangroup-plc.com; web site: www.maclellan-group.plc.uk

		holding %
Chairman	Bob Morton	0.3
Chief Executive	John R Foley	0.8
Finance Director	Stephen R Shipley	0.1
Non-Exec Director	Graham WS Lockyer	0.1

Main Shareholders:

M&G Investment Management	8.8
Seraffina Holdings	6.1
Fidelity	6.1
Universities Superannuation Scheme	4.0
Invesco	3.4
Percentage of free market capital: 70.4%	

Nominated Adviser:	Investec, London
AIM Broker:	Williams de Broe, Birmingham
Solicitors:	n/a
Market Makers:	KBCS; MLSB; WDBM; WINS
Auditors:	PricewaterhouseCoopers, Castle Donnington
Registrars:	Capita Registrars

ENTRY ON AIM:	6/10/1995	**Recent price:**	71.0p
Interim results:	Sep	**Market cap:**	£56.35m
Final results:	Mar	**Issue price:**	57.0p
Year end:	Dec	**Current no of shares:**	
Accounts due:	May		79,361,165
Int div paymnt:	n/a	**No of shares after**	
Fin div paymnt:	Jul	**dilution:**	n/a
Int net div per share:	nil	**P/E ratio:**	26.3
Fin net div per share:	0.5p	**Probable CGT?**	Yes

LATEST REPORTED RESULTS: 2003		PREVIOUS REPORTED RESULTS: 2002	
Turnover:	£153.27m	**Turnover:**	£141.54m
PTP:	£3.28m	**PTP:**	£2.65m
EPS:	2.6p	**EPS:**	2.7p

Comments:

The award winning facilities manager chaired by serial AIM player Morton reported another record result for 2003, with turnover lifted 19% and profits boosted by 27%. Acquisitions included Tasker, which created a national commercial window cleaning business and Attlaw, a business with security industry expertise in the retail, leisure and transport markets. MacLellan reported a forward order book of £485m, and 2004 has started well with sizeable contract wins in key sectors.

Madisons Coffee (MCF)

Coffee bar and restaurant operator

3rd Floor Eternity House, 56-58 Putney High Street, Putney, London SW15 1SF Tel: 020-8394 5555;
Fax: 020-8788 5544; web site: www.madisonscoffee.co.uk

		holding %
Chairman	Nigel Whittaker	1.4
Chief Executive	Gareth Lloyd-Jones	7.3
Financial Controller	Susan Ludley	0.0
Non-Exec Director	Mark Horrocks	17.9

Main Shareholders:

The Richer Partnership	27.2
Christopher Akers *	18.3

Percentage of free market capital: 18.6%

* This holding is registered in the name of Strand Nominees Limited

Nominated Adviser:	Teather & Greenwood, London
AIM Broker:	Teather & Greenwood, London
Solicitors:	Dechert, London
Market Makers:	MLSB; TEAM; WINS
Auditors:	KPMG Audit, 8 Salisbury Square, London EC4Y 8BB
Registrars:	Capita Registrars

ENTRY ON AIM:	16/6/1998	**Recent price:**	7.0p
Interim results:	Mar	**Market cap:**	£3.83m
Final results:	Sep	**Issue price:**	100.0p
Year end:	Jun	**Current no of shares:**	
Accounts due:	Oct		54,772,808
Int div paymnt:	n/a	**No of shares after**	
Fin div paymnt:	n/a	**dilution:**	55,944,361
Int net div per share:	nil	**P/E ratio:**	n/a
Fin net div per share:	nil	**Probable CGT?**	Yes

LATEST REPORTED RESULTS: 2003		PREVIOUS REPORTED RESULTS: 2002	
Turnover:	£11.43m	**Turnover:**	£13.32m
PTP:	£(748,000)	**PTP:**	£(1.15m)
EPS:	(1.4)p	**EPS:**	(2.1)p

Comments:

Madisons has posted its first pre-tax profits since listing in 1998 following the disposal of its coffee bar operations. It sold its City Gourmets and Carwardine coffee companies to the Out of Town Group for £2.2m. This affected turnover for the six months to January, which fell 20.4% to £5.3m. Profits before tax reached £1.1m. The sale of its coffee operations has provided the company with a healthy cash position of £2m and it now intends to expand the Richoux brand.

Maelor   (MLR)
Pharmaceuticals & medical devices developer
Riversdale, Cae Gwilym Road, Newbridge, Wrexham, LL14 3JG Tel: 01978-810153; Fax: 01978-810169;
e-mail: enquiries@maelor.plc.uk; web site: www.maelor.plc.uk

		holding %
Chairman	Alastair Macpherson	0.4
Chief Executive	Stephen Applebee	0.3
Finance Director	Paul Williams	0.1
Non-Exec Director	John Gregory	0.1

Main Shareholders:

HSBC Global	10.4
BNY Nominees	5.9
Barclayshare	3.5

Percentage of free market capital: 79.3%

Nominated Adviser:	Insinger de Beaufort, London
AIM Broker:	Numis, London
Solicitors:	Brabner Chaffe Street, Liverpool
Market Makers:	NUMS; SCAP; WINS
Auditors:	Baker Tilly, 1 Old Hall Street, Liverpool L3 9SX
Registrars:	Capita Registrars

ENTRY ON AIM: 21/11/1997		Recent price:	30.5p
Interim results:	Oct	Market cap:	£10.4m
Final results:	May	Issue price:	88.0p
Year end:	Mar	Current no of shares:	
Accounts due:	Jul		34,104,583
Int div paymnt:	n/a	No of shares after	
Fin div paymnt:	n/a	dilution:	n/a
Int net div per share:	nil	P/E ratio:	n/a
Fin net div per share:	nil	Probable CGT?	YES

LATEST REPORTED RESULTS: 2003		PREVIOUS REPORTED RESULTS: 2002	
Turnover:	£1.17m	Turnover:	£582,000
PTP:	£(2.32m)	PTP:	£(1.99m)
EPS:	(9.4)p	EPS:	(8.5)p

Comments:
Maelor develops niche medical devices that are commonly used, such as Optiflo, which cleans catheter equipment, and Volplex, a substitute for blood plasma made from colloid. Anaesthetic lubricant gel TendaGel and another anaesthetic Micelle Propofol are close to commercialisation too. The group raised £2.9m net at 25p a year ago. Interim losses were reduced by 43% to £0.75m on sales up 5% to £0.32m. The group has since signed a distribution deal for Volplex in China and is itself in takeover talks.

Magnum Power (suspended 27 Aug 2003)   (MGP)
Shell company
4 Michaelson Square, Kirkton Campus, Livingston, EH54 7DP Tel: 01506-463330; Fax: 01506-463320;
e-mail: sales@mpsl.demon.co.uk; web site: www.magnumpower.com

		holding %
Chairman	Brian McGhee	0.3
Chief Executive	Sandy Morrison	0.1
Finance Director		
Director	Edward Adams	20.0

Main Shareholders:

n/a

Percentage of free market capital: 19.6%

Nominated Adviser:	Beaumont Cornish, Edinburgh
AIM Broker:	Williams de Broe, Edinburgh
Solicitors:	Shepherd & Wedderburn, Edinburgh
Market Makers:	MLSB; SCAP; WDBM; WINS
Auditors:	PricewaterhouseCoopers, Glasgow
Registrars:	Capita Registrars

ENTRY ON AIM: 25/10/1996		Recent price:	1.25p
Interim results:	Mar	Market cap:	£0.06m
Final results:	Nov	Issue price:	35.0p
Year end:	May	Current no of shares:	
Accounts due:	Mar		4,999,344
Int div paymnt:	n/a	No of shares after	
Fin div paymnt:	n/a	dilution:	n/a
Int net div per share:	nil	P/E ratio:	n/a
Fin net div per share:	nil	Probable CGT?	No

LATEST REPORTED RESULTS: 2003		PREVIOUS REPORTED RESULTS: 2002	
Turnover:	n/a	Turnover:	n/a
PTP:	£(20.26m)	PTP:	£(230,000)
EPS:	(20.3)p	EPS:	(0.2)p

Comments:
Magnum was finally forced to sell its built-in power supplies business in January 2003, after running out of cash. The company is now a shell but has agreed to buy the Stack Leisure Park in Dundee for £7.1m, conditional on it raising the finance to complete the deal. The site is composed of seven units, five of which are vacant. The other two are occupied by a Gala bingo hall and a Megabowl ten-pin bowling venue, which between them bring in £0.6m in rent per year, with leases expiring in 2016.

Maisha (suspended 15 Jan 2004)   (MSA)
Computer consultancy
6th Floor, 52 Haymarket, London, SW1Y 4RP Tel: 020-7976 2299; Fax: 020-7839 2296

		holding %
Chairman	Mumtaz Khan*	0.0
Chief Executive		
Finance Director	Guy Neely	0.0
Non-Exec Director	Horatius Rose**	0.0

Main Shareholders:

The Antonion Trust**	19.6
Gamma Ventures	15.0
Salman Mahmood	15.0
Croxley	13.6
Jackal Investments*	3.8

Percentage of free market capital: 32.9%

*Mr Khan is interested in these shares
**These shares are owned by Mr Da Gama Rose and family

Comments:

Full List refugee Maisha has returned to the drawing board following its disastrous acquisition of computer consultancy Pearl Micro. The plan was to use Pearl as a means of switching from the healthcare to the IT sector. However, less than six months after completion, management conceded that the net asset value of Pearl had failed to meet expectations and that there were doubts over its ability to continue to trade. Pearl boss Salman Mahmood, who had been appointed group CEO following the deal, has resigned.

Nominated Adviser:	ARM Corporate Finance, London
AIM Broker:	Keith Bayley Rogers, London
Solicitors:	Stallard, London
Market Makers:	MLSB; WINS
Auditors:	Wilkins Kennedy, London
Registrars:	Capita Registrars

ENTRY ON AIM:	26/8/2003	**Recent price:**	2.75p
Interim results:	Feb	**Market cap:**	£0.94m
Final results:	Sep	**Issue price:**	n/a
Year end:	Aug	**Current no of shares:**	
Accounts due:	Nov		34,061,783
Int div paymnt:	n/a	**No of shares after**	
Fin div paymnt:	n/a	dilution:	n/a
Int net div per share:	nil	P/E ratio:	n/a
Fin net div per share:	nil	**Probable CGT?**	**YES**

LATEST REPORTED RESULTS: 2003		PREVIOUS REPORTED RESULTS: 2002	
Turnover:	n/a	Turnover:	n/a
PTP:	£(395,000)	PTP:	£(170,000)
EPS:	(1.6)p	EPS:	(0.7)p

Majestic Wine   (MJW)
Wine merchant
Majestic House, Otterspool Way, Watford, Herts WD25 8WW Tel: 01923-298200; Fax: 01923-819105;
e-mail: info@majestic.co.uk; web site: www.majestic.co.uk

		holding %
Chairman	John Apthorp*	0.0
Managing Director	Timothy How	1.0
Finance Director	Nigel Alldritt	0.0
Trading Director	Anthony Mason	0.1

Main Shareholders:

P & L Trust, JP Labesse & LM Williams*	31.2
ABN Amro	6.1
Gartmore	5.3
Jupiter	3.1
Standard Life Investments	3.1

Percentage of free market capital: 36.0%

*John Apthorp holds his shares via P&L Trust, J.P.Labesse, L.M.Williams & Mrs J Apthorp

Comments:

Majestic has 113 wine warehouses in the UK and consistently beats expectations despite heavy discounting by large supermarket chains. Like-for-like sales in the UK in the eight weeks to December were 7.4% higher. It has also seen rising numbers of customers on its database that have made purchases over the past 12 months – database customer numbers are up 10.1% to 320,000. Analysts predict pre-tax profits of £10.3m for the current year.

Nominated Adviser:	Teather & Greenwood, London
AIM Broker:	Teather & Greenwood, London
Solicitors:	Osborne Clarke, London
Market Makers:	TEAM; WDBM; WINS
Auditors:	Ernst & Young, 400 Capability Green, Luton LU1 3LU
Registrars:	Capita Registrars

ENTRY ON AIM:	11/11/1996	**Recent price:**	825.0p
Interim results:	Nov	**Market cap:**	£129.36m
Final results:	Jun	**Issue price:**	160.0p
Year end:	Apr	**Current no of shares:**	
Accounts due:	Jun		15,680,115
Int div paymnt:	Jan	**No of shares after**	
Fin div paymnt:	Aug	dilution:	16,009,558
Int net div per share:	3.0p	P/E ratio:	23
Fin net div per share:	8.0p	**Probable CGT?**	**YES**

LATEST REPORTED RESULTS: 2003		PREVIOUS REPORTED RESULTS: 2002	
Turnover:	£125.68m	Turnover:	£104.6m
PTP:	£7.97m	PTP:	£5.88m
EPS:	35.8p	EPS:	26.4p

Mano River Resources   (MANA)

Mineral prospector & miner

Suite 600, 890 West Pender Street, Vancouver BC, Canada V6C 1K4   Tel: 00-1 604 689-1700;   Fax: 00-1 604 687-1327;
e-mail: mano@manoriver.com;   web site: www.manoriver.com

		holding %
Co-Chairman	P Anthony Rhatigan	2.8
President & CEO	Tom Elder	0.0
Finance Director		
Co-Chairman	Guy Pas	0.5

Main Shareholders:

Eastbound Resources	19.0
Mining Capital Partners	16.5
Golden Prospect	6.4
Beacon Sutton Gold Fund	4.3
Beacon Pioneer Investment Fund	3.8
Percentage of free market capital:	43.9%

Comments:

Miner and prospector Mano River has rallied to within hail of its 1998 float price on hopes for its Sonfon and Kono diamond prospects in Sierra Leone, now extended with a 9,700 sq km exploration licence. Mano, with interests in Liberia and elsewhere, lost a nine-month £388,000, and has farmed American group Golden Star into its Sierra Leone gold licences. Splitting Mano into a diamond and a gold play is on the cards.

Nominated Adviser:	Grant Thornton, London
AIM Broker:	Seymour Pierce Ellis, Crawley
Solicitors:	Stringer Saul, London
Market Makers:	SCAP; WINS
Auditors:	Deloitte & Touche, Vancouver, Can. V7X 1P4
Registrars:	Melton Registrars

ENTRY ON AIM:	18/9/1998	**Recent price:**	14.25p
Interim results:	Oct	**Market cap:**	£28.76m
Final results:	Jun	**Issue price:**	18.0p
Year end:	Jan	**Current no of shares:**	
Accounts due:	Jun		201,816,826
Int div paymnt:	n/a	**No of shares after**	
Fin div paymnt:	n/a	**dilution:**	n/a
Int net div per share:	nil	**P/E ratio:**	n/a
Fin net div per share:	nil	**Probable CGT?**	No

LATEST REPORTED RESULTS: 2003		PREVIOUS REPORTED RESULTS: 2002	
Turnover:	$8.18m	Turnover:	$17,000
PTP:	$(352,000)	PTP:	$(2.28m)
EPS:	(0.0)c	EPS:	(0.0)c

Manpower Software   (MNS)

Producer of planning and scheduling software

The Communications Building, 48 Leicester Square, London, WC2H 7DB   Tel: 020-7389 9500;   Fax: 020-7389 9588;
e-mail: enquiries@manpowersoftware.com ;   web site: www.manpowersoftware.com

		holding %
Chairman	Robert Drummond	8.7
Managing Director	Paul Scandrett	0.2
Finance Director	Simon Thorne	1.7
Non-Exec Director	Ian Lang	1.4

Main Shareholders:

Herald GP Limited	26.5
SOCGEN Nominees	12.7
Bank of New York Nominees	11.9
Singer and Friedlander	8.1
Herald Investment Trust	4.6
Percentage of free market capital:	8.3%

Comments:

Manpower Software continues its recovery as interim revenues rose 184% to £2.5m and pre-tax profits reached £260,000 compared to losses of £1.3m. Since last June, the company has gained four substantial contracts including the sale of its MAPS Forge Force software to the UK Defence Medical Services worth £1.2m over the next four and a half years. Manpower has continued to secure significant orders and £3.1m of revenue has already been contracted for the next 12 months.

Nominated Adviser:	Strand Partners, London
AIM Broker:	Shore Capital, London
Solicitors:	Maclay Murray & Spens, London
Market Makers:	KLWT; MLSB; WINS
Auditors:	Grant Thornton, London
Registrars:	Capita Registrars

ENTRY ON AIM:	16/5/2002	**Recent price:**	40.75p
Interim results:	Feb	**Market cap:**	£18.03m
Final results:	Sep	**Issue price:**	13.0p
Year end:	May	**Current no of shares:**	
Accounts due:	Sep		44,245,086
Int div paymnt:	n/a	**No of shares after**	
Fin div paymnt:	n/a	**dilution:**	46,555,687
Int net div per share:	nil	**P/E ratio:**	n/a
Fin net div per share:	nil	**Probable CGT?**	Yes

LATEST REPORTED RESULTS: 2003		PREVIOUS REPORTED RESULTS: 2002	
Turnover:	£3.56m	Turnover:	£3.15m
PTP:	£(802,000)	PTP:	£(1.25m)
EPS:	(1.8)p	EPS:	(5.1)p

Marakand Minerals   (MKD)
Mineral mining
105 Picadilly, London, W1J 7NJ Tel: 020-7907 2000; Fax: 020-7907 2001

		holding %
Chairman	William Trew	0.3
Chief Executive	Alasdair Stuart	0.3
Finance Director		
Non-Exec Director	Richard Shead	0.3

Main Shareholders:

Oxus Gold	78.2
RAB Special Situations	6.8

Percentage of free market capital: 14.2%

Comments:
Spun out from Oxus Gold in a £4m placing at 20p, Marakand, which incurred a pro forma interim loss of £941,258, is focused on the Khandiza zinc deposit in Uzbekistan. After drastic cost cuts, RBC Capital Markets said this could need £45m capital to earn an eventual £765m. The shares are geared to the zinc price (swayed by Chinese demand) and any political risk.

Nominated Adviser:	Williams de Broe, London
AIM Broker:	Williams de Broe, London
Solicitors:	Stringer Saul, London
Market Makers:	WINS
Auditors:	BDO Isle of Man, Douglas
Registrars:	Capita Registrars

Entry on AIM:	4/12/2003	**Recent price:**	47.75p
Interim results:	Jun	**Market cap:**	£48.23m
Final results:	Jan	**Issue price:**	n/a
Year end:	Oct	**Current no of shares:**	
Accounts due:	Nov		101,000,000
Int div paymnt:	n/a	**No of shares after**	
Fin div paymnt:	n/a	**dilution:**	n/a
Int net div per share:	nil	**P/E ratio:**	n/a
Fin net div per share:	nil	**Probable CGT?**	No

LATEST REPORTED RESULTS: 2003		PREVIOUS REPORTED RESULTS: 2002	
Turnover:	n/a	Turnover:	n/a
PTP:	£(200,000)	PTP:	£(4.55m)
EPS:	(1.8)p	EPS:	(46.0)p

Mark Kingsley   (MKP)
Cash shell
65 New Cavendish Street, London, W1M 7RD Tel: 01372-845600; Fax: 01372-845656

		holding %
Chairman	Rodney Wells	60.7
Chief Executive	as above	
Finance Director	Stephen Garbutta	0.9
Technical Director	John Stadius	0.4

Main Shareholders:

Southwind	10.4
Eaglet Investment Trust	9.9

Percentage of free market capital: 17.8%

Comments:
Mark Kingsley is the shell remaining after digital sound console maker Soundtracs sold its business to a consortium of US investors, called DiGiCo UK, for £1.1m (more than double its book value). The company has a net asset value of £2.7m. During 2003, it was apparently close to making two deals as well as considering setting up a 'leisure sector concept' but none came to fruition. It now states it is looking to focus on a single transaction.

Nominated Adviser:	Teather & Greenwood, London
AIM Broker:	Teather & Greenwood, London
Solicitors:	Shoosmiths, Northampton
Market Makers:	TEAM; WINS
Auditors:	BDO Stoy Hayward, 69 Tweedy Rd, Bromley, Kent BR1 3WA
Registrars:	Capita Registrars

Entry on AIM:	20/12/1996	**Recent price:**	20.75p
Interim results:	Jun	**Market cap:**	£2.1m
Final results:	Jan	**Issue price:**	40.0p
Year end:	Oct	**Current no of shares:**	
Accounts due:	Feb		10,106,000
Int div paymnt:	n/a	**No of shares after**	
Fin div paymnt:	n/a	**dilution:**	10,494,500
Int net div per share:	nil	**P/E ratio:**	n/a
Fin net div per share:	nil	**Probable CGT?**	No

LATEST REPORTED RESULTS: 2003		PREVIOUS REPORTED RESULTS: 2002	
Turnover:	n/a	Turnover:	£1.06m
PTP:	£(94,000)	PTP:	£129,000
EPS:	(1.0)p	EPS:	1.9p

Marshall Edwards (MSH)
Drug developer

c/o The Corporation Trust Company, The Corporation Trust Centre, 1209 Orange Street, Wilmington, Delaware, USA 19801 Tel: 00-1 302 658 7581; web site: www.marshalledwardsinc.com

		holding %
Chairman	Graham Kelly	9.2
Chief Executive	Christopher Naughton	0.3
Finance Director		
Non-Exec Director	Philip Johnson	0.1

Main Shareholders:

National Nominees	20.5
ANZ Nominees	11.2
Oppenheimer Funds	6.4
Westpac Custodian Nominees	6.3
Bende Holdings	4.8

Percentage of free market capital: 32.3%

Nominated Adviser:	KBC Peel Hunt, London
AIM Broker:	KBC Peel Hunt, London
Solicitors:	Morgan, Lewis & Bockius, London
Market Makers:	KBCS; WINS
Auditors:	Ernst & Young, Rolls House, Fetter Lane, London EC4A 1HN
Registrars:	Capita Registrars

ENTRY ON AIM:	22/5/2002	**Recent price:**	535.0p
Interim results:	Mar	**Market cap:**	£304.62m
Final results:	Sep	**Issue price:**	$4.0
Year end:	Jun	**Current no of shares:**	
Accounts due:	Oct		56,938,000
Int div paymnt:	n/a	**No of shares after**	
Fin div paymnt:	n/a	**dilution:**	n/a
Int net div per share:	nil	**P/E ratio:**	n/a
Fin net div per share:	nil	**Probable CGT?**	No

LATEST REPORTED RESULTS: 2003		PREVIOUS REPORTED RESULTS: 2002	
Turnover:	$145,000	Turnover:	$7,000
PTP:	$(3.03m)	PTP:	$(122,000)
EPS:	(0.0)c	EPS:	(0.0)c

Comments:

Drug developer Marshall Edwards is now carrying out phase II and phase III trials of anti-cancer therapy phenoxodiol, after raising $26m when gaining a dual listing on Nasdaq's small-cap market. Phenoxodiol is being tested on patients with both early and late stage cancers of the cervix and vagina. The group, whose major shareholder remains Novogen from whom it was spun out in 2002, now has $32.3m cash, after burning $5.8m in the first half.

Martin Shelton (SHM)
Advertising gifts manufacturer

37 Burley Road, Leeds, LS3 1JT Tel: 0113-244 8454; Fax: 0113-246 7463

		holding %
Chairman	Nicholas Richardson	0.0
Chief Executive	Paul Martin	12.8
Finance Director	Nicholas Reynolds	2.5
Non-Exec Director	Amer Deen	0.0

Main Shareholders:

James Capel Nominees	7.3
Paul Lawrence	4.2
Sinjul Nominees	3.6
Trevor Brown	3.5
Marcus Yeoman	3.3

Percentage of free market capital: 30.6%

Nominated Adviser:	KBC Peel Hunt, London
AIM Broker:	KBC Peel Hunt, London
Solicitors:	Wedlake Bell, London
Market Makers:	KBCS; MLSB; WINS
Auditors:	PricewaterhouseCoopers, 33 Wellington St, Leeds LS1 4JP
Registrars:	Capita Registrars

ENTRY ON AIM:	12/3/1997	**Recent price:**	27.5p
Interim results:	Dec	**Market cap:**	£1.47m
Final results:	Sep	**Issue price:**	76.5p
Year end:	Sep	**Current no of shares:**	
Accounts due:	Jun		5,345,000
Int div paymnt:	Jan	**No of shares after**	
Fin div paymnt:	Jul	**dilution:**	5,360,000
Int net div per share:	0.5p	**P/E ratio:**	7.2
Fin net div per share:	1.25p	**Probable CGT?**	Yes

LATEST REPORTED RESULTS: 2003		PREVIOUS REPORTED RESULTS: 2002	
Turnover:	£7.02m	Turnover:	£7.29m
PTP:	£227,000	PTP:	£(482,000)
EPS:	3.8p	EPS:	(6.3)p

Comments:

Having exited leather goods, Martin Shelton is focused on business gifts. However trading in the second half of the year has disappointed and annual sales – excluding the leather goods arm – won't even beat the previous year's. Management consultancy Mosaique holds 11.2% of the company these days. In a boardroom shake-up, chairman and chief executive Richardson and Deen were appointed to Martin Shelton's board to bring in fresh thinking.

Matisse (formerly Prestige Publishing)   (MAT)

Investor in printing, publishing and interactive entertainment

8 Hinde Street, Manchester Square, London, W1M 5RG   Tel: 020-7486 2240; Fax: 020-7637 9116

		holding %
Chairman	Raymond Harris	1.06
Chief Executive		
Finance Director		
Director	Nicholas Greenstone	1.06

Main Shareholders:

Peter Catto	16.6
netvest.com	16.2
Arc Securities BVI	12.4
Garnham & Co	8.2
Mark Bushnell	4.5

Percentage of free market capital: 5.2%

Comments:

This failed publishing venture is now a shell company awaiting a suitable acquisition. Trading in the oft-suspended shares was once again curtailed in February pending the announcement of a possible reverse takeover deal. Not for the faint hearted.

Nominated Adviser:	John East, London		
AIM Broker:	John East, London		
Solicitors:	Fladgate Fielder, London		
Market Makers:	WINS		
Auditors:	HW Fisher, Acre House, London		
Registrars:	Capita Registrars		

ENTRY ON AIM: 28/11/2001		**Recent price:**	5.75p
Interim results:	Aug	**Market cap:**	£2.64m
Final results:	Feb	**Issue price:**	4.0p
Year end:	Nov	**Current no of shares:**	
Accounts due:	Mar		45,991,700
Int div paymnt:	n/a	**No of shares after**	
Fin div paymnt:	n/a	**dilution:**	n/a
Int net div per share:	nil	**P/E ratio:**	n/a
Fin net div per share:	nil	**Probable CGT?**	Yes

LATEST REPORTED RESULTS: 2002		**PREVIOUS REPORTED RESULTS:** 2001	
Turnover:	£14,000	Turnover:	£5,000
PTP:	£(293,000)	PTP:	£(143,000)
EPS:	(0.2)p	EPS:	(0.1)p

Matrix Communications (formerly Offshore Telecom)   (MXC)

Telecommunications and internet services supplier

Hamble Point Marina, Hamble, Southampton, Hampshire SO31 4NB Tel: 01342-871850; Fax: 023-8045 3711; e-mail: info@offshoretele.com; web site: www.offshoretele.com

		holding %
Chairman	Michael Frank	1.3
Chief Executive		
Finance Director		
Non-Exec Director	Keith Mills	5.9

Main Shareholders:

Michael Yarrow*	8.0
Patrick Roberts	5.9
New Opportunities Investment Trust	5.6
David Bland	4.3

Percentage of free market capital: 31%

*These shares are held by Yarrow Bros Small Self Administered Pension Fund

Comments:

Offshore was originally set up to provide satellite-based communications for the yachting fraternity but has now disposed of its satcom assets. It focuses on providing IT network solutions and has acquired a 50% interest in Norwood Adams Technical Services as well as Intrinsic Networks. Despite being loss-making in 2003, it reported strong first quarter trading and has recently won contracts with a numerous companies including the London Internet Exhange.

Nominated Adviser:	Daniel Stewart, London		
AIM Broker:	Daniel Stewart, London		
Solicitors:	Pinsents, Leeds		
Market Makers:	HOOD; WINS		
Auditors:	Macintyre Hudson, Northampton		
Registrars:	Capita Registrars		

ENTRY ON AIM: 12/1/2001		**Recent price:**	3.1p
Interim results:	Jul	**Market cap:**	£29.95m
Final results:	Apr	**Issue price:**	2.5p
Year end:	Oct	**Current no of shares:**	
Accounts due:	Feb		966,209,696
Int div paymnt:	n/a	**No of shares after**	
Fin div paymnt:	n/a	**dilution:**	n/a
Int net div per share:	nil	**P/E ratio:**	n/a
Fin net div per share:	nil	**Probable CGT?**	Yes

LATEST REPORTED RESULTS: 2003		**PREVIOUS REPORTED RESULTS:** 2002	
Turnover:	£1.66m	Turnover:	£260,000
PTP:	£(428,000)	PTP:	£(665,000)
EPS:	(0.1)p	EPS:	(0.3)p

Maverick Entertainment (MVK)

Provider and merchandiser of children's entertainment products

Belmont House, 13 Upper High Street, Thame, Oxfordshire OX9 3ER Tel: 01844-260858; Fax: 01844-215055;
e-mail: maverickltd@aol.com

		holding %
Chairman	Derek Morris	14.5
Managing Director	Michael Diprose	12.7
Finance Director	Sooka Raveendran	0.0

Main Shareholders:

John Howson	12.7
n/a	

Percentage of free market capital: 60.1%

Nominated Adviser:	Seymour Pierce, London
AIM Broker:	Seymour Pierce Ellis, Crawley
Solicitors:	Gold Mann & Co, London
Market Makers:	SCAP; WINS
Auditors:	Morgan Brown & Spofforth, 82 St John Street, London EC1M 4JN
Registrars:	Neville Registrars

ENTRY ON AIM:	14/5/2001	**Recent price:**	2.0p
Interim results:	Sep	**Market cap:**	£6.11m
Final results:	Apr	**Issue price:**	3.0p
Year end:	Dec	**Current no of shares:**	
Accounts due:	May		305,688,886
Int div paymnt:	n/a	**No of shares after**	
Fin div paymnt:	n/a	**dilution:**	n/a
Int net div per share:	nil	**P/E ratio:**	20
Fin net div per share:	nil	**Probable CGT?**	**YES**

LATEST REPORTED RESULTS: 2002		PREVIOUS REPORTED RESULTS: 2001	
Turnover:	£1.48m	**Turnover:**	£331,000
PTP:	£262,000	**PTP:**	£(226,000)
EPS:	0.1p	**EPS:**	(0.2)p

Comments:

Maverick raised £2.0m in a placing at the end of October 2003 to help develop its Muffin the Mule show and launch its new DVD/Video catalogue. The funds were much needed. The group lost £320,000 at the half way stage and is expected to make a further loss when full year results are announced soon. John Howson recently stepped down as CEO.

Mayborn (MBY)

Babycare, fabric dye and other household products designer & manufacturer

Dylon House, Worsley Bridge Road, Lower Sydenham, London, SE26 5HD Tel: 020-663 4801; Fax: 020-8650 9876;
e-mail: info@mayborngroup.com; web site: www.mayborngroup.com

		holding %
Chairman	Peter Sechiari	0.4
Chief Executive	Michael Samuel	41.0
Finance Director	Ian Hartley	0.1
Non-Exec Director	Viscount Bearsted	12.1

Main Shareholders:

Henderson Smaller Companies	4.5
Discretionary Unit Trust	3.1

Percentage of free market capital: 34.6%

Nominated Adviser:	Collins Stewart, London
AIM Broker:	Collins Stewart, London
Solicitors:	Pinsents, London
Market Makers:	CSCS; WINS
Auditors:	Haysmacintyre, Southampton House, 317 High Holborn, London WC1V 7NL
Registrars:	Capita Registrars

ENTRY ON AIM:	29/5/2003	**Recent price:**	274.5p
Interim results:	Sep	**Market cap:**	£60.68m
Final results:	Mar	**Issue price:**	104.0p
Year end:	Dec	**Current no of shares:**	
Accounts due:	May		22,105,528
Int div paymnt:	Nov	**No of shares after**	
Fin div paymnt:	May	**dilution:**	n/a
Int net div per share:	1.7p	**P/E ratio:**	42.9
Fin net div per share:	1.9p	**Probable CGT?**	**YES**

LATEST REPORTED RESULTS: 2002		PREVIOUS REPORTED RESULTS: 2001	
Turnover:	£56.59m	**Turnover:**	£56.84m
PTP:	£2.32m	**PTP:**	£3.06m
EPS:	6.4p	**EPS:**	10.3p

Comments:

2003 pre-tax profits from the babycare and household products group beat market forecasts, on a 10% sales improvement. This was achieved on the back of a strong performance from the baby products division, where further production was switched to China. Household product profits fell slightly on a higher turnover. Mayborn also doubled the total dividend, and pared net debt from £7.2m to £2.8m despite buying back shares, thanks to excellent cash generation.

Mean Fiddler Music (MEF)

Music festival and venue promoter

16 High Street, Harlesden, London, NW10 4LX Tel: 020-8961 5490; Fax: 020-8838 1748;
web site: www.meanfiddler.com

		holding %
Chairman	Vince Power	34.9
Chief Executive	Melvin Benn	5.3
Finance Director	Jon Hale	0.0
Chief Operating Officer	Dean James	0.0

Main Shareholders:

MCD Production	24.3
Ashwell	7.4
Scanfrost	7.2

Percentage of free market capital: 20.9%

Nominated Adviser:	Grant Thornton, London
AIM Broker:	Daniel Stewart, London
Solicitors:	Olswang, London
Market Makers:	HOOD; MLSB; SCAP; WINS
Auditors:	Gerald Edelman, 25 Harley Street, London, W1N 2BR
Registrars:	Melton Registrars

Entry on AIM:	24/5/2000	**Recent price:**	48.0p
Interim results:	Sep	**Market cap:**	£29.6m
Final results:	Jun	**Issue price:**	7.0p
Year end:	Dec	**Current no of shares:**	
Accounts due:	Apr		61,661,698
Int div paymnt.	n/a	**No of shares after**	
Fin div paymnt:	n/a	**dilution:**	63,997,015
Int net div per share:	nil	**P/E ratio:**	n/a
Fin net div per share:	nil	**Probable CGT?**	Yes

LATEST REPORTED RESULTS: 2002		PREVIOUS REPORTED RESULTS: 2001	
Turnover:	£39.03m	Turnover:	£3.67m
PTP:	£(8.31m)	PTP:	£(1.56m)
EPS:	(12.8)p	EPS:	(13.6)p

Comments:

The music events and promotion business lost a total of £3.7m on sales of £13.4m at the half way stage, but there was much to cheer investors. There was a substantial inflow of cash, the restructuring process has proved successful and all divisions are now profitable. Since these figures, chairman Power has increased the capacity of the Leeds Festival and secured the 2004 European tour of R&B superstar Usher. On a separate note, Power sold 10m of his shares to Denis Desmond, a leading music entrepreneur in Ireland.

Mears (MER)

Support services provider

The Leaze, 40 Salter Street, Berkeley, Gloucestershire GL13 9DB Tel: 01453-511911; Fax: 01453-511914;
e-mail: info@mearsgroup.co.uk; web site: www.mearsgroup.co.uk

		holding %
Chairman	Robert Holt	9.1
Managing Director		
Finance Director	David Robertson	0.4
Director	Phillip Molloy	7.0

Main Shareholders:

Unicorn Asset Management funds	12.5
Newton Managed Funds	7.2
Fidelity Investments	4.2
Gartmore	4.1
Close	4.1

Percentage of free market capital: 42.5%

Nominated Adviser:	Arbuthnot, Birmingham
AIM Broker:	Arbuthnot, Birmingham
Solicitors:	Bretherton Price Elgoods Cheltenham
Market Makers:	ALTI; ARBT; MLSB; SCAP; WINS
Auditors:	Grant Thornton, Imperial Sq, Cheltenham GL50 1PZ
Registrars:	Neville Registrars

Entry on AIM:	4/10/1996	**Recent price:**	145.0p
Interim results:	Aug	**Market cap:**	£83.17m
Final results:	Mar	**Issue price:**	10.0p
Year end:	Dec	**Current no of shares:**	
Accounts due:	May		57,356,434
Int div paymnt:	Nov	**No of shares after**	
Fin div paymnt:	Jul	**dilution:**	58,040,567
Int net div per share:	0.35p	**P/E ratio:**	32.2
Fin net div per share:	0.6p	**Probable CGT?**	Yes

LATEST REPORTED RESULTS: 2002		PREVIOUS REPORTED RESULTS: 2001	
Turnover:	£78.83m	Turnover:	£68.58m
PTP:	£3.61m	PTP:	£2.51m
EPS:	4.5p	EPS:	4.0p

Comments:

The essential support services play scored record 2003 results — profits surged 39.2% higher on a 42.4% turnover hike. Mears' order book increased to a record £550m (£300m), and stretches as far ahead as 2019. The core business, providing maintenance services to the social housing and central government sectors, makes up 65% of sales and is unaffected by discretionary spending trends. Mears' profits have shown an annual compound growth rate of 43% since listing in 1996.

Medal Entertainment & Media   (MME)

Intellectual property rights developer

11 Churchill Court, 58 Station Road, North Harrow, HA2 7SA Middlesex, Tel: 020-8427 2277; Fax: 020-8427 4277

		holding %
Chairman	Brook Land	0.8
Chief Executive	Stephen Ayres	2.9
Finance Director	Mariana Spater	0.1
Non-Exec Director	Christopher Stainforth	0.8

Main Shareholders:

Fountain	23.4
Artemis Investment Management	9.4
Rank Organisation	9.4
Singer & Friedlander AIM 3 VCT	9.4
Baronsmead VCT2	5.6

Percentage of free market capital: 21.6%

Nominated Adviser:	Durlacher, London
AIM Broker:	Durlacher, London; Teather & Greenwood, London
Solicitors:	Nabarro Nathanson, London
Market Makers:	DURM; TEAM
Auditors:	Deloitte & Touche, Hill House, 1 Little New Street, London EC4A 3TR
Registrars:	Capita Registrars

Entry on AIM:	9/11/2001	**Recent price:**	81.5p
Interim results:	Dec	**Market cap:**	£12.2m
Final results:	Jun	**Issue price:**	70.0p
Year end:	Mar	**Current no of shares:**	
Accounts due:	Aug		14,964,033
Int div paymnt:	n/a	**No of shares after**	
Fin div paymnt:	n/a	**dilution:**	n/a
Int net div per share:	nil	**P/E ratio:**	15.1
Fin net div per share:	nil	**Probable CGT?**	No

LATEST REPORTED RESULTS: 2003		PREVIOUS REPORTED RESULTS: 7 Mar 01 to 31 Mar 02	
Turnover:	£6.56m	**Turnover:**	n/a
PTP:	£605,000	**PTP:**	£(121,000)
EPS:	5.4p	**EPS:**	(14.5)p

Comments:

IP rights developer Medal saw first half revenues rise 87.5% to £4.8m, yet losses also increased, from £170,000 to £340,000, during the period. The company currently owns two core businesses. Fountain Television, an independent TV studio, and Leisureview, a DVD and video publisher. A 30% stake in DVD publishing business Maximum Entertainment has also been secured. And, despite debts in the region of £4m, a recent £3.2m placing has secured cash for further expansion.

Media Square   (MSQ)

Provider of marketing and media solutions over the internet

99 Cato Street, Nechells, Birmingham, B7 4TS Tel: 0121-333 6094; Fax: 0121-333 4780;
e-mail: info@mediasquare.co.uk; web site: www.mediasquare.co.uk

		holding %
Chairman	Kevin Steeds	1.3
Chief Executive		
Finance Director	Graeme Burns	1.9
Operations Director	Jeremy Middleton	13.7

Main Shareholders:

Pertemps	13.0
Artemis	6.5
Electra Kingsway VCT	6.5
First State Investments	4.9
Hargreave Hale Stockbrokers	4.5

Percentage of free market capital: 43.5%

Nominated Adviser:	Collins Stewart, London
AIM Broker:	Westhouse Securities, London
Solicitors:	Browne Jacobson, Nottingham
Market Makers:	SCAP; WINS
Auditors:	Grant Thornton, Enterprise House, 115 Edmund Street, Birmingham, B3 2HJ
Registrars:	Neville Registrars

Entry on AIM:	14/9/2000	**Recent price:**	22.0p
Interim results:	Jun	**Market cap:**	£16.81m
Final results:	Jan	**Issue price:**	25.0p
Year end:	Oct	**Current no of shares:**	
Accounts due:	Jan		76,397,164
Int div paymnt:	n/a	**No of shares after**	
Fin div paymnt:	n/a	**dilution:**	n/a
Int net div per share:	nil	**P/E ratio:**	31.4
Fin net div per share:	nil	**Probable CGT?**	Yes

LATEST REPORTED RESULTS: 2003		PREVIOUS REPORTED RESULTS: 2002	
Turnover:	£8.33m	**Turnover:**	£4.89m
PTP:	£256,000	**PTP:**	£(923,000)
EPS:	0.7p	**EPS:**	(4.5)p

Comments:

The successful transformation wrought by chief executive Kevin Steeds at this marketing solutions business was writ large all over the results for the year to October. Revenues soared (after no less than six acquisitions), profits were posted and, by the end of the year, the reorganisation was complete. £3m was raised from the market in October and a further £0.75m in November. Revenues in the first quarter of this year were twice those posted last time. Another acquisition was completed in February.

Medical Marketing International (MMG)

Manager of medical and bioscience technologies

The Bioscience Innovation Centre, Cowley Road, Cambridge CB4 0DS Tel: 01223-477677; Fax: 01223-477678;
e-mail: email@mmigroup.co.uk; web site: www.mmigroup.co.uk

		holding %
Executive Chairman	David Best	38.8
Chief Executive		
Finance Director	John Hustler	0.1
IT Director	Margaret Mitchell	20.1

Main Shareholders:

n/a

Percentage of free market capital: 41.0%

Nominated Adviser:	Brewin Dolphin, Leeds
AIM Broker:	Brewin Dolphin, Leeds
Solicitors:	Eversheds, London
Market Makers:	KBCS; MLSB; WINS
Auditors:	Deloitte & Touche, Cambridge
Registrars:	Capita Registrars

ENTRY ON AIM: 14/11/2000		Recent price:	60.5p
Interim results:	Nov	Market cap:	£28.37m
Final results:	Jul	Issue price:	100.0p
Year end:	Mar	Current no of shares:	
Accounts due:	Jul		46,885,763
Int dlv paymnt:	n/a	No of shares after	
Fin div paymnt:	n/a	dilution:	n/a
Int net div per share:	nil	P/E ratio:	n/a
Fin net div per share:	nil	Probable CGT?	Yes

LATEST REPORTED RESULTS: 2003		PREVIOUS REPORTED RESULTS: 2002	
Turnover:	£461,000	Turnover:	£284,000
PTP:	£(1.39m)	PTP:	£(1.55m)
EPS:	(3.3)p	EPS:	(4.0)p

Comments:

The biotech incubator's shares have recovered strongly over the past year. The group's interests include a large stake in CellFactors and an advisory role to Bioscience VCT. MMI is also behind the Cambridge Bioscience Innovation Centre and a similar plant in Edinburgh. Most interest currently comes from the group's HIV research joint venture and a cancer therapy project. Interim losses remained high at £0.69m as revenues fell 29% to £0.17m but a recent £1.9m institutional placing will tide MMI over for the next year.

Mediwatch (MDW)

Project funding for the diagnosis and treatment of prostate disease

Swift House, Cosford Lane, Swift Valley Industrial Estate, Rugby, Warwickshire CV21 1QN Tel: 01788-547888;
Fax: 01788-536434; e-mail: info@mediwatch.com; web site: www.mediwatch.com

		holding %
Chairman	Frank Davies	0.0
Chief Executive	Philip Stimpson	18.4
Finance Director	Kevin Middis	0.0
Technical Director	Mark Emberton	5.6

Main Shareholders:

Singer & Friedlander AIM 3 VCT	10.0

Percentage of free market capital: 49.4p

Nominated Adviser:	Canaccord Capital, London
AIM Broker:	Canaccord Capital, London
Solicitors:	Field Fisher Waterhouse, London
Market Makers:	HOOD; MLSB; SCAP; WINS
Auditors:	Grant Thornton, Southampton
Registrars:	Melton Registrars

ENTRY ON AIM:	5/6/2000	Recent price:	11.25p
Interim results:	Jan	Market cap:	£9.23m
Final results:	Sep	Issue price:	60.0p
Year end:	Apr	Current no of shares:	
Accounts due:	Sep		82,035,296
Int div paymnt:	n/a	No of shares after	
Fin div paymnt:	n/a	dilution:	n/a
Int net div per share:	nil	P/E ratio:	n/a
Fin net div per share:	nil	Probable CGT?	Yes

LATEST REPORTED RESULTS: 2003		PREVIOUS REPORTED RESULTS: 2002	
Turnover:	£1.54m	Turnover:	£564,000
PTP:	£(5.46m)	PTP:	£(2.0m)
EPS:	(17.6)p	EPS:	(9.3)p

Comments:

The developer of a bladder scanner to test for prostate diseases has gained FDA approval for its device and is close to signing a significant US distribution deal. Mediwatch already has a five year distribution deal with Bard to sell its bladder scanner in the UK, Europe and Canada, which could bring in up to £5m. Deals have been done in Japan and Australia as well. Interim revenue fell 50% to £0.39m but losses were reduced by 7% to £0.64m. Cash stands at a meagre £0.42m though.

Medoro Resources (MRL)

Gold exploration & development company
110 Yonge Street, Suite 1502, Toronto, Ontario M5C 1TA Canada

		holding %
Chairman	Giuseppe Pozzo	1.8
Chief Executive		
Non-Exec Director	Gordon Keep	0.6
Non-Exec Director	Jose Arata	1.8

Main Shareholders:

Willbro Nominees	10.6
Orogen	6.1
Chase Nominees	5.6
Endeavour Mining	3.9

Percentage of free market capital: 67.9%

Nominated Adviser:	Williams de Broe, London
AIM Broker:	Williams de Broe, London
Solicitors:	Charles Russell, London
Market Makers:	WINS
Auditors:	Deloitte & Touche, Canada
Registrars:	Capita Registrars

ENTRY ON AIM:	2/3/2004	**Recent price:**	31.0p
Interim results:	Sep	**Market cap:**	£25.38m
Final results:	Apr	**Issue price:**	n/a
Year end:	Dec	**Current no of shares:**	
Accounts due:	May		81,882,043
Int div paymnt:	n/a	**No of shares after**	
Fin div paymnt:	n/a	**dilution:**	n/a
Int net div per share:	nil	**P/E ratio:**	n/a
Fin net div per share:	nil	**Probable CGT?**	No

LATEST REPORTED RESULTS:	2002	**PREVIOUS REPORTED RESULTS:**	2001
Turnover:	£4.38m	Turnover:	£5.79m
PTP:	£(5.51m)	PTP:	£(2.69m)
EPS:	n/a	EPS:	n/a

Comments:

Medoro was created by merging the operating subsidiary of Gold Mines of Sardinia with Canadian-quoted Full Riches Investment. Headed by Italian politician Guiseppe Pozzo, Medoro has links with Bolivar, a partner in GMS's Monte Ollasteddu project, and is seen as able to circumvent political obstacles at GMS's existing Furtei mine. Decidedly speculative.

Melrose (MRO)

Acquisition company
90 Long Acre, London, WC2E 9RZ

		holding %
Chairman	Christopher Miller	17.4
Chief Executive	David Roper	2.9
Finance Director		
Chief Operating Officer	Simon Peckham	2.0

Main Shareholders:

Schroders	11.4
JP Morgan Chase & Co	10.7
FMR	8.8
Fleming Mercantile	7.6
Threadneedle Investments	3.2

Percentage of free market capital: 44.5%

Nominated Adviser:	Investec, London
AIM Broker:	Investec, London
Solicitors:	Clifford Chance, London
Market Makers:	INV; WINS
Auditors:	Deloitte & Touche, 180 Strand, London WC2V 7QP
Registrars:	Computershare Investor Services

ENTRY ON AIM:	28/10/2003	**Recent price:**	128.0p
Interim results:	n/a	**Market cap:**	£16.79m
Final results:	n/a	**Issue price:**	100.0p
Year end:	n/a	**Current no of shares:**	
Accounts due:	n/a		13,120,000
Int div paymnt:	n/a	**No of shares after**	
Fin div paymnt:	n/a	**dilution:**	n/a
Int net div per share:	nil	**P/E ratio:**	n/a
Fin net div per share:	nil	**Probable CGT?**	No

LATEST REPORTED RESULTS:	PERIOD ENDED 31 DEC '03	**PREVIOUS REPORTED RESULTS:**	N/A
Turnover:	n/a	Turnover:	n/a
PTP:	£(133,000)	PTP:	n/a
EPS:	(1.0)p	EPS:	n/a

Comments:

The executive directors of this shell worked together at fully listed industrial concern Wassall. This group produced an annual compound return of 18% to shareholders over 12 years from 1988 to 2000. The team want to repeat their success with Melrose by turning around businesses that have the potential for operational improvement. Notable acquisitions at Wassall included Thorn Lighting for £363m in 1998. The flotation raised £11.8m net. Monthly costs are roughly £100,000.

Meon Capital

(MC.)

Investment company

Centurion House, 37 Jewry Street, London, EC3N 2ER Tel: 020-7423 1000; Fax: 020-7481 3002

		holding %
Chairman	David Massie	24.6
Chief Executive		
Finance Director	Edmund Barber	4.3
Non-Exec Director	Graham Ashley	8.9

Main Shareholders:
Gresham House — 9.7

Percentage of free market capital: 45.3%

Nominated Adviser:	KBC Peel Hunt, London
AIM Broker:	KBC Peel Hunt, London
Solicitors:	Stallard, London
Market Makers:	WINS
Auditors:	AGN Shipleys, London
Registrars:	Neville Registrars

ENTRY ON AIM:	16/2/2004	Recent price:	24.0p
Interim results:	n/a	Market cap:	£4.2m
Final results:	n/a	Issue price:	23.5p
Year end:	n/a	Current no of shares:	
Accounts due:	n/a		17,500,000
Int div paymnt:	n/a	No of shares after	
Fin div paymnt:	n/a	dilution:	n/a
Int net div per share:	nil	P/E ratio:	n/a
Fin net div per share:	nil	Probable CGT?	No

LATEST REPORTED RESULTS:		PREVIOUS REPORTED RESULTS:	
	N/A		N/A
Turnover:	n/a	Turnover:	n/a
PTP:	n/a	PTP:	n/a
EPS:	n/a	EPS:	n/a

Comments:
This is the second ready made shell that entrepreneur David Massie has floated on AIM. The previous venture Darwen Capital morphed into Scott Tod, a maker of cash machines. KBC Peel Hunt has raised £1.15m for the shell following a £156,000 private placing with directors at 10p a share. Massie plans to find a quoted or unquoted concern that is 'undervalued' and where his proactive approach can prove useful.

Merchant House

(MHG)

Merchant bank and financial services

7th Floor, Aldermary House, 10-15 Queens Street, London, EC4N 1TX Tel: 020-7332 2200; Fax: 020-7332 2201

		holding %
Chairman	Peter Cotgrove	0.2
Chief Executive		
Finance Director	as chairman	
Non-Exec Director	James Fleming	0.0

Main Shareholders:

Delphic Global Opportunities Fund	50.9
London & Boston Investments	25.0

Percentage of free market capital: 21.6%

Nominated Adviser:	Shore Capital, London
AIM Broker:	Shore Capital, London
Solicitors:	Berwin Leighton Paisner, London
Market Makers:	KBCS; WINS
Auditors:	PKF Birmingham
Registrars:	Capita Registrars

ENTRY ON AIM:	10/10/2000	Recent price:	11.25p
Interim results:	Sep	Market cap:	£1.5m
Final results:	Jun	Issue price:	25.0p
Year end:	Dec	Current no of shares:	
Accounts due:	Apr		13,300,000
Int div paymnt:	n/a	No of shares after	
Fin div paymnt:	n/a	dilution:	13,600,000
Int net div per share:	nil	P/E ratio:	n/a
Fin net div per share:	nil	Probable CGT?	YES

LATEST REPORTED RESULTS:		PREVIOUS REPORTED RESULTS:	
	2002	17 JULY 00 - 31 DECEMBER 01	
Turnover:	£100,000	Turnover:	n/a
PTP:	£(272,000)	PTP:	£(52,000)
EPS:	(4.0)p	EPS:	(0.8)p

Comments:
Merchant House's gradual transformation from cash shell to merchant bank is picking up pace. FSA approval to carry out corporate finance and investment advisory business has been received. £650,000 was recently raised at 10p to aid expansion, possibly by acquisition. In addition the group retains a stake in several AIM shells, including MobileFuture and Future Internet Technologies, the former of which is in the process of acquiring a US-based IMAX cinema project.

Mercury Recycling (MRG)

Recycler of products containing mercury

Unit G, Canalside North, John Gilbert Way, Trafford Park, Manchester, M17 1DP Tel: 0161-877 0977; Fax: 0161-877 0390;
e-mail: info@mercuryrecycling.co.uk; web site: www.mercuryrecycling.co.uk

		holding %
Chairman	Rt Hon The Lord Barnett	9.5
Chief Executive	Simon Lebor	15.5
Finance Director	as above	
Non-Exec Director	Anthony Leon	0.6

Main Shareholders:

Caledonian Heritable Investments*	13.8
City Equities Limited	3.5
Fiske Nominees	3.4

Percentage of free market capital: 44.1%

*The interests of of K Doyle are held by Caledonian Heritable Investments

Comments:

Mercury Recycling pleased investors with a move to pre-goodwill operating profits of £73,000 against losses of £38,000 in the year's first half to June. Turnover grew over 30% to £484,000 and cash improved to £333,000 (£266,000) thanks to frugal financial controls. Since then 'Mercury' has acquired Simister. This business, a collector of fluorescent tubes and street lighting, complements Mercury's existing operations with a site in the South of England.

Nominated Adviser:	Rowan Dartington, Bristol
AIM Broker:	Rowan Dartington, Bristol
Solicitors:	Kuit Steinart Levy, Manchester
Market Makers:	ALTI; SCAP; WINS
Auditors:	Hacker Young, St James' Building, 79 Oxford Street, Manchester M2 2JA
Registrars:	Capita Registrars

ENTRY ON AIM:	4/5/2001	**Recent price:**	12.25p
Interim results:	Sep	**Market cap:**	£4.09m
Final results:	May	**Issue price:**	20.0p
Year end:	Dec	**Current no of shares:**	
Accounts due:	Jun		33,359,490
Int div paymnt:	n/a	**No of shares after**	
Fin div paymnt:	n/a	**dilution:**	n/a
Int net div per share:	nil	**P/E ratio:**	n/a
Fin net div per share:	nil	**Probable CGT?**	Yes

LATEST REPORTED RESULTS: 2002		PREVIOUS REPORTED RESULTS: 2001	
Turnover:	£770,000	**Turnover:**	£405,000
PTP:	£(195,000)	**PTP:**	£(247,000)
EPS:	(0.8)p	**EPS:**	(1.7)p

Meriden (MRD)

Business services group

Meriden House, 6 Great Cornbow, Halesowen, West Midlands B63 3AB Tel: 0121-585 6655; Fax: 0121-585 6228;
e-mail: info@meriden-group.co.uk; web site: www.meriden-group.co.uk

		holding %
Chairman	Derek Hall	0.1
Chief Executive	Russell Stevens	74.8
Finance Director		

Main Shareholders:

n/a

Percentage of free market capital: 25.1%

Comments:

Annual numbers to July from the business services play were pregnant with promise, showing both improved sales and profits. During the year the company branched out from its West Midlands base, opening a second 'centre of e-xcellence' in London. A third centre in Wales was 'under evaluation'. Meriden's client base continues to grow, with bigger corporations and government agencies joining SMEs as clients. Post year-end Meriden made its first acquisition, Eltora Digital.

Nominated Adviser:	Seymour Pierce, London
AIM Broker:	Hoodless Brennan, London
Solicitors:	Eversheds, Birmingham
Market Makers:	HOOD; SCAP; WINS
Auditors:	PKF, Birmingham
Registrars:	Neville Registrars

ENTRY ON AIM:	14/8/2001	**Recent price:**	2.4p
Interim results:	Feb	**Market cap:**	£6.96m
Final results:	Sep	**Issue price:**	25.0p
Year end:	Jul	**Current no of shares:**	
Accounts due:	Oct		290,000,000
Int div paymnt:	n/a	**No of shares after**	
Fin div paymnt:	Oct	**dilution:**	n/a
Int net div per share:	nil	**P/E ratio:**	12.0
Fin net div per share:	0.2p	**Probable CGT?**	Yes

LATEST REPORTED RESULTS: 2003		PREVIOUS REPORTED RESULTS: INTERIM RESULTS TO 31 JAN 02	
Turnover:	£5.79m	**Turnover:**	£5.51m
PTP:	£705,000	**PTP:**	£609,000
EPS:	0.2p	**EPS:**	0.2p

Metnor (MTG)

Anti-corrosion steel galvaniser, mechanical and electrical contractor

Metnor Ho, Mylord Cresc, Killingworth, Newcastle upon Tyne, NE12 5YD Tel: 0191-268 4000; Fax: 0191-268 5491;
e-mail: enquiries@metnor.co.uk; web site: www.metnor.co.uk

		holding %
Chairman	Jon Pither	2.1
Managing Director	S Rankin	26.5
Finance Director	Keith Atkinson	0.0
Deputy Chairman	A Rankin	26.4

Main Shareholders:

J R Rankin	21.7
Direct Nominees	4.2
Active Capital Trust	4.2

Percentage of free market capital: 14.8%

Comments:

The diversified group operating in hot dip galvanising, powder coating, and mechanical and electrical contracting, says 2003 continuing profits will meet forecasts despite a slow start to the year in mechanical and electrical contracting and the closure of Norstead South East in London. Chaired by serial entrepreneur Pither, Metnor has already reported glowing figures for the half to June – sales burgeoned 39% higher to £26.9m and profits rose 10% to £2.4m.

Nominated Adviser:	Brewin Dolphin, Newcastle
AIM Broker:	Brewin Dolphin, Newcastle
Solicitors:	Mincoffs, Newcastle upon Tyne
Market Makers:	KBCS; WINS
Auditors:	KPMG, Newcastle upon Tyne
Registrars:	Capita Registrars

ENTRY ON AIM:	8/6/1999	**Recent price:**	250.0p
Interim results:	Sep	**Market cap:**	£38.22m
Final results:	Apr	**Issue price:**	100.0p
Year end:	Dec	**Current no of shares:**	
Accounts due:	Apr		15,286,110
Int dlv paymnt:	Oct	**No of shares after**	
Fin div paymnt:	Jun	**dilution:**	n/a
Int net div per share:	2.0p	**P/E ratio:**	12.4
Fin net div per share:	3.7p	**Probable CGT?**	YES

LATEST REPORTED RESULTS:	2002	**PREVIOUS REPORTED RESULTS:**	2001
Turnover:	£57.43m	Turnover:	£48.98m
PTP:	£4.63m	PTP:	£5.78m
EPS:	20.1p	EPS:	25.8p

Metrodome (MRM)

Film distributor, video marketing distributor & record company

33 Charlotte St, London, W1T 1RR Tel: 020-7153 4421; Fax: 020-71534401; e-mail: tina@metrodomegroup.com;
web site: www.metrodomegroup.com

		holding %
Chairman	Bruce Fireman	0.8
Chief Executive	Andrew Keyte	0.1
Finance Director	Elaine Edwards	0.0
Non-Exec Director	Markus Schafer	0.0

Main Shareholders:

Vidacos Nominees	9.2
The Micro Quoted Growth Trust	6.7
John Hall	6.4
LM Investments	6.3
Westcombe Investments and Associates	4.4

Percentage of free market capital: 59.3%

Comments:

Interims from film and television programme distributor Metrodome showed a first pre-tax profit (of £63,000) in three and half years, thanks to the phenomenal success of cult movie Donnie Darko. Sales increased 11% during the period to £2.2m largely on account of demand for the film. More of the same is likely to have been seen in the second half, the film's profile having been dramatically increased by end-credit song Mad World's topping of the UK's music chart over Christmas.

Nominated Adviser:	KBC Peel Hunt, London
AIM Broker:	KBC Peel Hunt, London; Seymour Pierce, London
Solicitors:	Bircham Dyson Bell, London
Market Makers:	DURM; KBCS; SCAP; WINS
Auditors:	Smith & Williamson, London
Registrars:	Capita Registrars

ENTRY ON AIM:	28/9/1995	**Recent price:**	10.25p
Interim results:	Dec	**Market cap:**	£7.31m
Final results:	Jul	**Issue price:**	200.0p
Year end:	Mar	**Current no of shares:**	
Accounts due:	Jul		71,309,543
Int div paymnt:	n/a	**No of shares after**	
Fin div paymnt:	n/a	**dilution:**	n/a
Int net div per share:	nil	**P/E ratio:**	n/a
Fin net div per share:	nil	**Probable CGT?**	YES

LATEST REPORTED RESULTS:	2003	**PREVIOUS REPORTED RESULTS:**	2002
Turnover:	£4.94m	Turnover:	£19.23m
PTP:	£(1.11m)	PTP:	£(3.30m)
EPS:	(4.2)p	EPS:	(29.5)p

MG Capital   (MAP)
Operation of investment funds
Ocean House, 10/12 Little Trinity Lane, London, EC4V 2DH Tel: 020-7332 2040; Fax: 020-7332 2060;
e-mail: marketing@moneyguru.co.uk; web site: www.moneyguru.co.uk

		holding %
Chairman	Charles Fowler	20.4
Managing Director		
Finance Director		
Non-Exec Director	Michael Baines	1.8

Main Shareholders:

Newland	28.3
Toucan	9.9
John Mather	7.8
Jupiter Split Trust	7.0
Kidz.net	6.6

Percentage of free market capital: 18.1%

Comments:
Wealth manager MG Capital emerged from the ashes of stock research outfit Money Guru. The adviser's products include a global 'macro' investment fund, a UK equity unit trust geared towards 'income with growth', a SIPP, and the Resources and New Opportunities investment trusts, which swap shares with companies in need of collateral. Although losses were reduced by 78% last year, continuing turnover declined. More worryingly the group has negative NAV and needs funds to continue.

Nominated Adviser:	Nabarro Wells, London
AIM Broker:	Keith Bayley Rogers, London
Solicitors:	Richards Butler, London
Market Makers:	SCAP; WINS
Auditors:	Cooper Lancaster Brewers, Aldwych House, 81 Aldwych, London WC2B 4HP
Registrars:	Capita Registrars

ENTRY ON AIM:	8/5/2001	**Recent price:**	0.6p
Interim results:	Mar	**Market cap:**	£2.14m
Final results:	Dec	**Issue price:**	3.5p
Year end:	Jun	**Current no of shares:**	
Accounts due:	Aug		356,231,421
Int div paymnt:	n/a	**No of shares after**	
Fin div paymnt:	n/a	**dilution:**	n/a
Int net div per share:	nil	**P/E ratio:**	n/a
Fin net div per share:	nil	**Probable CGT?**	Yes

LATEST REPORTED RESULTS: 2003		PREVIOUS REPORTED RESULTS: 2002	
Turnover:	£710,000	**Turnover:**	£796,000
PTP:	£(408,000)	**PTP:**	£(1.85m)
EPS:	(0.2)p	**EPS:**	(0.8)p

Micap   (MIC)
Micro-encapsulation technology developer
Ashton House, No 1 The Parks, Lodge Lane, Newton-le-Willows, WA12 0JQ Tel: 01925-664200;
e-mail: info@micap.co.uk; web site: www.micap.com

		holding %
Chairman	Ian Gowrie-Smith*	0.0
Chief Executive	Michael Brennand	3.5
Finance Director	Michael Norris	0.2
Technical Director	Gordon Nelson	0.4

Main Shareholders:

SkyePharma*	18.2
Framlington	13.1
Sigma Technology Investments	7.3
Sigma Technology Venture Fund**	5.3
Nortrust Nominees	3.2

Percentage of free market capital: 45.5%

*Ian Gowrie-Smith is executive chairman of SkyePharma

Comments:
Micap raised £4.7m net to continue the development of its microscopic technology. The group's process focuses on yeast cells which can be used as capsules to protect and deliver flavours, drugs and fertilisers more efficiently. A licensing deal has been signed with global flavour concern Firmenich and the group has a partnership with Skyepharma in the drugs area. Some of the float proceeds enabled the group to buy patents from Unilever. The market is potentially immense. A £0.57m interim loss was made.

Nominated Adviser:	Brewin Dolphin, Glasgow
AIM Broker:	Brewin Dolphin, Glasgow
Solicitors:	Shepherd & Wedderburn, London
Market Makers:	KBCS; SCAP; TEAM; WINS
Auditors:	Bowmans, 88-96 Market St West, Preston PR1 2EU
Registrars:	Computershare Investor Services

ENTRY ON AIM:	7/8/2003	**Recent price:**	70.5p
Interim results:	Mar	**Market cap:**	£20.32m
Final results:	Aug	**Issue price:**	55.0p
Year end:	Mar	**Current no of shares:**	
Accounts due:	Sep		28,825,229
Int div paymnt:	n/a	**No of shares after**	
Fin div paymnt:	n/a	**dilution:**	n/a
Int net div per share:	nil	**P/E ratio:**	n/a
Fin net div per share:	nil	**Probable CGT?**	Yes

LATEST REPORTED RESULTS: 2003		PREVIOUS REPORTED RESULTS: 2002	
Turnover:	£290,000	**Turnover:**	£736,000
PTP:	£(4.22m)	**PTP:**	£(6.82m)
EPS:	n/a	**EPS:**	n/a

Microcap Equities (formerly Underwriting and Subscription) (MEQ)

Provides funds for early stage companies
1 Great Cumberland Place, London, W1H 7AL Tel: 020-7262 6445; Fax: 020-7637 9116

		holding %
Chairman	Raymond Harris	0.8
Managing Director		
Finance Director		
Director	Barry Gold	1.1

Main Shareholders:

Evolution Beeson Gregory	23.8
Libra Investments	19.7

Percentage of free market capital: 53.7%

Nominated Adviser:	n/a
AIM Broker:	n/a
Solicitors:	Paisner & Co, London
Market Makers:	HOOD; WINS
Auditors:	Gerald Edelman, 25 Harley Street, London W1N 2BR
Registrars:	Capita Registrars

ENTRY ON AIM: 17/12/1999		**Recent price:**	9.5p
Interim results:	Sep	Market cap:	£2.91m
Final results:	Jun	Issue price:	23.5p
Year end:	Dec	Current no of shares:	
Accounts due:	Aug		30,649,727
Int div paymnt:	n/a	**No of shares after**	
Fin div paymnt:	n/a	dilution:	n/a
Int net div per share:	nil	P/E ratio:	n/a
Fin net div per share:	nil	**Probable CGT?**	**YES**

LATEST REPORTED RESULTS: 2001		PREVIOUS REPORTED RESULTS: 2000	
Turnover:	n/a	Turnover:	n/a
PTP:	£(1.25m)	PTP:	£(918,000)
EPS:	(9.4)p	EPS:	(0.1)p

Comments:
This tiny shell has had a crazy time lately. At the end of June net liabilities stood at £286,000 and the shares hovered below 1p. Since then they have leapt to 15p. This follows the departure of chairman Peter Catto, who arranged a debt-for-equity deal with Hanover Capital. The new directors have taken stakes at 1p a share, alongside friendly investors. The group's Nomad and broker also resigned. Despite this, the company picked up a 2.5% stake in Interactive Sports Store, the online football kit retailer. A fundraising is imminent.

Milestone (MSG)

Media company
Manor Lane Studios, Oare, Hermitage, Berkshire RG18 9SE Tel: 01635-202700; Fax: 01635-202800

		holding %
Chairman	Julian Blackwell	6.9
Chief Executive	Andrew Craig	11.4
Finance Director	Brain Chester	0.1
Non-Exec Director	Mark Levine	0.0

Main Shareholders:

Elliott International	19.1
Banco Nominees	6.9
Elliott Associates	6.8
INVESCO	5.2
Landfinance	4.5

Percentage of free market capital: 36.1%

Nominated Adviser:	Collins Stewart, London
AIM Broker:	Collins Stewart, London
Solicitors:	Lawrence Graham, London
Market Makers:	CSCS; WINS
Auditors:	BDO Stoy Hayward, 8 Baker Street, London W1U 3LL
Registrars:	Capita Registrars

ENTRY ON AIM:	1/7/2003	**Recent price:**	66.0p
Interim results:	May	Market cap:	£14.26m
Final results:	Jan	Issue price:	100.0p
Year end:	Sep	Current no of shares:	
Accounts due:	Mar		21,599,976
Int div paymnt:	n/a	**No of shares after**	
Fin div paymnt:	n/a	dilution:	n/a
Int net div per share:	nil	P/E ratio:	n/a
Fin net div per share:	nil	**Probable CGT?**	**YES**

LATEST REPORTED RESULTS: 2002		PREVIOUS REPORTED RESULTS: 2001	
Turnover:	£3.35m	Turnover:	£3.48m
PTP:	£(89,000)	PTP:	£297,000
EPS:	(0.0)p	EPS:	n/a

Comments:
Milestone raised £8m net on admission via a Collins Stewart-led fundraising. These funds have proved very useful indeed as the group lost no less than £3.6m last year on sales of £5.8m. Apparently all of this was in line with management expectations, although the market has been spooked enough to mark the shares down significantly. The group's business comprises radio stations, newspapers and local TV stations in Oxford, Berkshire and Staffordshire.

Millfield (MIL)

Independent financial adviser

Knollys House, 17 Addiscombe Road, Croydon, Surrey CR0 6SR Tel: 020-8680 5200; Fax: 020-8680 5900;
e-mail: dbadmin@millfield-partnership.co.uk; web site: www.millfield-partnership.co.uk

		holding %
Chairman	Richard Mansell-Jones	0.2
Chief Executive	Paul Tebbutt	2.3
Finance Director	Harry Roome	0.01
Sales Director	Bryan Beeston	2.4

Main Shareholders:

AMVESCAP	17.1
Insight Investment	10.6
HBOS	9.8
Lansdowne Partners	6.0
Artemis	4.1

Percentage of free market capital: 40.3%

Comments:

IFA Millfield has raised £25m in all to make acquisitions in this consolidating area. Several have since been made, giving the group 640 advisers. Its agents generate annual income of £100,000 each, a figure it wants to increase. Norwich Union has backed Millfield's Lifetime portfolio services venture. Despite seeing interim turnover improve 66% to £23.5m, pre-tax losses stuck at £5.7m. The group still has £12.5m net cash to weather the next year.

Nominated Adviser:	Collins Stewart, London
AIM Broker:	Collins Stewart, London
Solicitors:	Lawrence Graham, London
Market Makers:	CSCS; KBCS; WINS
Auditors:	Deloitte & Touche, Stonecutter Court, 1 Stonecutter Street, London EC4A 4TR
Registrars:	Capita Registrars

ENTRY ON AIM:	1/3/2001	**Recent price:**	85.5p
Interim results:	Nov	**Market cap:**	£78.03m
Final results:	Jun	**Issue price:**	118.0p
Year end:	Mar	**Current no of shares:**	
Accounts due:	Jul		91,263,278
Int div paymnt:	n/a	**No of shares after**	
Fin div paymnt:	n/a	**dilution:**	n/a
Int net div per share:	nil	**P/E ratio:**	n/a
Fin net div per share:	nil	**Probable CGT?**	YES

LATEST REPORTED RESULTS: 2003		PREVIOUS REPORTED RESULTS: 2002	
Turnover:	£31.34m	**Turnover:**	£20.51m
PTP:	£(12.34m)	**PTP:**	£(7.41m)
EPS:	(18.3)p	**EPS:**	(14.2)p

Millwall (MWH)

Football club operator

The Den, Zampa Road, London, SE16 3LN Tel: 020-7232 1222; Fax: 020-7231 3663; web site: www.millwallfc.co.uk

		holding %
Chairman	Theo Paphitis	1.9
Chief Executive	as above	
Finance Director		
Vice Chairman	Peter Mead	0.7

Main Shareholders:

n/a

Percentage of free market capital: 97.1%

Comments:

South London football club Millwall is seeing quite low average home attendances, so it continues to balance ambition on the field of play with the need to run a tight ship. Interim figures to 30 November from 'The Lions' revealed narrower losses of just under £1.2m (£2.5m) on turnover of £3.05m (£2.82m). Excluding player trading, however, the deficit reached £3m. Encouragingly, in a tricky transfer market, Millwall managed to sell midfielder Steven Reid for £1.8m.

Nominated Adviser:	Seymour Pierce, London
AIM Broker:	Seymour Pierce Ellis, Crawley
Solicitors:	Richards Butler, London
Market Makers:	KBCS; MLSB; SCAP; WINS
Auditors:	BDO Stoy Hayward, London
Registrars:	Computershare Investor Services

ENTRY ON AIM:	13/8/2001	**Recent price:**	0.25p
Interim results:	Feb	**Market cap:**	£12.73m
Final results:	Sep	**Issue price:**	0.7p
Year end:	May	**Current no of shares:**	
Accounts due:	Sep		5,092,087,167
Int div paymnt:	n/a	**No of shares after**	
Fin div paymnt:	n/a	**dilution:**	n/a
Int net div per share:	nil	**P/E ratio:**	n/a
Fin net div per share:	nil	**Probable CGT?**	YES

LATEST REPORTED RESULTS: 2003		PREVIOUS REPORTED RESULTS: 2002	
Turnover:	£6.50m	**Turnover:**	£10.58m
PTP:	£(4.68m)	**PTP:**	£60,000
EPS:	(0.2)p	**EPS:**	0.0p

Minco (MIO)

Minerals exploration

162 Clontarf Road, Dublin 3, Ireland, Tel: 00-353 1 833 2833; Fax: 00-353 1 833 3505; e-mail: minco@iol.ie; web site: www.minco.ie

		holding %
Chairman	John Teeling	3.0
Managing Director		
Finance Director	James Finn	1.5
Deputy Chairman	Roger Turner	5.8

Main Shareholders:

Juno	22.0
Vladimer Karpovics	4.3
Strategic Lines Asset Management	4.3
City Equities	1.2

Percentage of free market capital: 37.2%

Comments:

After two years of poor performance, Irish entrepreneur John Teeling's speculative Minco mining hopeful has recovered to well above its float price with an option on a possible 300,000-oz Siberian gold deposit. Jitendera Patel's Sassan Holdings has put £400,000 into Minco, which has mused on splitting this business from its silver tailings operation in Mexico.

Nominated Adviser:	Rowan Dartington, Bristol
AIM Broker:	Rowan Dartington, Bristol
Solicitors:	Ivor Fitzpatrick & Co, Dublin
Market Makers:	WINS
Auditors:	Deloitte & Touche, Dublin
Registrars:	Computershare Investor Services

ENTRY ON AIM:	29/1/2001	Recent price:	17.75p
Interim results:	Feb	Market cap:	£16.86m
Final results:	Oct	Issue price:	IRp12.5
Year end:	Apr	Current no of shares:	
Accounts due:	Nov		94,975,287
Int div paymnt:	n/a	No of shares after	
Fin div paymnt:	n/a	dilution:	n/a
Int net div per share:	nil	P/E ratio:	n/a
Fin net div per share:	nil	Probable CGT?	No

LATEST REPORTED RESULTS: 2003		PREVIOUS REPORTED RESULTS: 2002	
Turnover:	n/a	Turnover:	n/a
PTP:	£724,000	PTP:	£101,000
EPS:	(0.3)p	EPS:	(0.3)p

Mondas (MDS)

Business management software developer

3rd Floor, 17-29 Sun Street, London, EC2M 2PT Tel: 01923-897333; Fax: 01923-897323; e-mail: info@mondas.com; web site: www.mondas.com

		holding %
Chairman	Tim Simon*	22.5
Managing Director	as above	
Finance Director	Ian Selby	0.2
Sales Director	Jarlath McGee	0.0

Main Shareholders:

n/a

Percentage of free market capital: 69.2%

* 458,250 (7.6%) of these shares are registered in the name of his wife Mrs G Simon

Comments:

Banking- and education-sector software provider Mondas continues to make slow progress. December's interims revealed a 28% reduction in losses to £1.1m, on sales up £400,000 at £1.8m. Further positive signs emerged early in H2 as the company secured significant contracts from HSBC (worth £750,000) and Credit Suisse First Boston, while a £1.4m fundraising conducted in July 2003 has provided a degree of financial security. Prior to goodwill the company is expected to break-even for the year.

Nominated Adviser:	John East, London
AIM Broker:	Teather & Greenwood, London
Solicitors:	Richards Butler, London
Market Makers:	KBCS; MLSB; TEAM; WINS
Auditors:	RSM Robson Rhodes, 186 City Road, London EC1V 4DD
Registrars:	Capita Registrars

ENTRY ON AIM:	18/11/1998	Recent price:	40.5p
Interim results:	Dec	Market cap:	£10.59m
Final results:	Jun	Issue price:	75.0p
Year end:	Apr	Current no of shares:	
Accounts due:	Sep		26,141,634
Int div paymnt:	n/a	No of shares after	
Fin div paymnt:	n/a	dilution:	n/a
Int net div per share:	nil	P/E ratio:	n/a
Fin net div per share:	nil	Probable CGT?	Yes

LATEST REPORTED RESULTS: 2003		PREVIOUS REPORTED RESULTS: 2002	
Turnover:	£3.71m	Turnover:	£3.74m
PTP:	£(2.22m)	PTP:	£(2.18m)
EPS:	(10.1)p	EPS:	(10.1)p

Monsoon (MSN)

Sale of women's & children's clothes & accessories, homeware & gifts

Monsoon Building, 179 Harrow Road, London, W2 6NB   Tel: 020-7313 3000;   Fax: 020-7313 3040

		holding %
Chairman	Peter Simon*	63.0
Chief Executive	Rose Foster	0.0
Finance Director	John Clark	0.0
Dvlpmt Director	John Spooner	0.0

Main Shareholders:

Credit Suisse Trust	12.5
Deutsche Bank AktianGesellschaft London	8.9
Goldman Sachs Intenational	3.3

Percentage of free market capital: 12.3%

*Includes the interests of the Beauchamp Trust and a personal holding

Comments:

Monsoon, which relocated from the Full List to AIM, notched up record interim pre-tax profits of £21m and turnover rose 22% to £131.1m. Under the Monsoon and Accessorize brands, 16 new stores were opened in the UK and Ireland, including flagship stores at Marble Arch in London and the Bullring in Birmingham. 30 new stores were also opened internationally bringing its total to 429 stores. With net funds of £38.1m, it is looking to make further acquisitions internationally.

Nominated Adviser:	Numis, London
AIM Broker:	Numis, London
Solicitors:	Berwin Leighton Paisner, London; Allen & Overy, London; Ashursts, London
Market Makers:	KBCS; MLSB; NUMS; WINS
Auditors:	PricewaterhouseCoopers, London
Registrars:	Capita Registrars

ENTRY ON AIM:	1/12/2003	**Recent price:**	153.0p
Interim results:	Jan	**Market cap:**	£273.18m
Final results:	Jul	**Issue price:**	n/a
Year end:	May	**Current no of shares:**	
Accounts due:	Aug		178,549,992
Int div paymnt:	Mar	**No of shares after**	
Fin div paymnt:	Oct	**dilution:**	n/a
Int net div per share:	1.5p	**P/E ratio:**	10.2
Fin net div per share:	3.5p	**Probable CGT?**	YES

LATEST REPORTED RESULTS: 53 WEEKS TO 31 MAY '03		PREVIOUS REPORTED RESULTS: 2002	
Turnover:	£231.2m	**Turnover:**	£203.6m
PTP:	£38.2m	**PTP:**	£32.1m
EPS:	15.0p	**EPS:**	12.7p

Monstermob (MOB)

Mobile telephone entertainment content and services provider

76 Church Street, Lancaster, LA1 1ET   Tel: 01524-841155;   Fax: 01524-841166;
e-mail: info@monstermob.com;   web site: www.monstermob.com

		holding %
Chairman	Lord Baker	3.7
Chief Executive	Matin Higginson	49.8
Finance Director	Lee Dudack	3.8
Operations Director	Gavin Whyte	3.8

Main Shareholders:

Northern Edge	10.5

Percentage of free market capital: 24.0%

Comments:

Monstermob raised just shy of £5m (plus £2.76m for existing shareholders) prior to listing. The group specialises in mobile phone content for the 14-30 year age group and saw operating profits rise substantially in the first half – to £0.9m – on revenues of £6.6m. The group believes this growth rate is sustainable as the global market in messaging is expected to increase from 65.7m in 2003 to 427m in 2006. The float proceeds have been earmarked for European expansion.

Nominated Adviser:	Teather & Greenwood, London
AIM Broker:	Teather & Greenwood, London
Solicitors:	DWF, Manchester
Market Makers:	WINS
Auditors:	Ernst & Young, 100 Barbirolli Street, Manchester M2 3EY
Registrars:	Computershare Investor Services

ENTRY ON AIM:	24/11/2003	**Recent price:**	174.5p
Interim results:	Sep	**Market cap:**	£41.67m
Final results:	Mar	**Issue price:**	135.0p
Year end:	Dec	**Current no of shares:**	
Accounts due:	Jun		23,881,638
Int div paymnt:	n/a	**No of shares after**	
Fin div paymnt:	n/a	**dilution:**	n/a
Int net div per share:	nil	**P/E ratio:**	30.1
Fin net div per share:	nil	**Probable CGT?**	YES

LATEST REPORTED RESULTS: 2003		PREVIOUS REPORTED RESULTS: 2002	
Turnover:	£13.91m	**Turnover:**	£7.91m
PTP:	£1.50m	**PTP:**	£313,000
EPS:	5.8p	**EPS:**	2.1p

Monterrico Metals   (MNA)
Developer of base and precious metals
No 2, London Wall Buildings, London, EC2M 5UU Tel: 020-7448 5088; Fax: 020-7448 5089;
e-mail: info@monterrico.co.uk; web site: www.monterrico.co.uk

		holding %
Chairman	James Mancuso	4.0
Chief Executive	Christopher Eager	11.7
Finance Director		
Chief Operating Officer	Raymond Angus	11.8

Main Shareholders:

Framlington Investment Management	14.6
Throgmorton	7.9
INVESCO English and International Trust	7.4
RAB Capital	3.7

Percentage of free market capital: 36.2%

Nominated Adviser:	Collins Stewart, London
AIM Broker:	Collins Stewart, London
Solicitors:	Cannings Connolly, London
Market Makers:	CSCS: WINS
Auditors:	Grant Thornton, London
Registrars:	Capita Registrars

ENTRY ON AIM:	21/6/2002	Recent price:	235.5p
Interim results:	Sep	Market cap:	£47.55m
Final results:	Mar	Issue price:	54.0p
Year end:	Dec	Current no of shares:	
Accounts due:	May		20,191,068
Int div paymnt:	n/a	No of shares after	
Fin div paymnt:	n/a	dilution:	n/a
Int net div per share:	nil	P/E ratio:	n/a
Fin net div per share:	nil	Probable CGT?	No

LATEST REPORTED RESULTS: 9 MONTHS TO 31 DEC 2002		PREVIOUS REPORTED RESULTS: N/A	
Turnover:	n/a	Turnover:	n/a
PTP:	£(368,000)	PTP:	n/a
EPS:	(4.2)p	EPS:	n/a

Comments:
One of the market's brighter performers, Monterrico, headed by ex-Rothschild banker Chris Eager, raised £10.9m at 135p in October for a feasibility study on its Rio Blanco copper project in Peru, where Eager sees a potential 200m-tonne resource at 1% copper. The study made a 'successful' start in March. Monterrico, which lost an interim £324,119, is to develop Peru's Pico Machay gold deposit with local group Calipuy.

Montpellier   (MPL)
Construction services and property development
39 Cornhill, London, EC3V 3NU Tel: 020-7522 3200; Fax: 020-7522 3213; e-mail: info@yjl.plc.co.uk

		holding %
Chairman	Cedric Scroggs	0.01
Managing Director	Paul Sellars*	0.02
Finance Director	Peter Hall	0.0
Non-Exec Dep Chair	Peter Gyllenhammar**	0.0

Main Shareholders:

Browallia International**	33.7
Carlton Telecom	13.6
Glyn Merrett and family	3.1

Percentage of free market capital: 49.6%
*900 shares held by P Sellars' daughter Bryony Sellars **Peter Gyllenhammar is an executive director of Browallia International

Nominated Adviser:	Rowan Dartington, Bristol
AIM Broker:	Rowan Dartington, Bristol
Solicitors:	Charles Russell, Cheltenham
Market Makers:	KLWT; MLSB; WINS
Auditors:	PricewaterhouseCoopers, London
Registrars:	Capita Registrars

ENTRY ON AIM:	29/10/2001	Recent price:	36.5p
Interim results:	May	Market cap:	£28.65m
Final results:	Dec	Issue price:	25.0p
Year end:	Sep	Current no of shares:	
Accounts due:	Jan		78,494,513
Int div paymnt:	Jul	No of shares after	
Fin div paymnt:	Mar	dilution:	81,795,251
Int net div per share:	0.5p	P/E ratio:	5.0
Fin net div per share:	1.1p	Probable CGT?	YES

LATEST REPORTED RESULTS: 2003		PREVIOUS REPORTED RESULTS: 2002	
Turnover:	£434.06m	Turnover:	£445.24m
PTP:	£4.68m	PTP:	£4.85m
EPS:	7.3p	EPS:	7.3p

Comments:
The construction and property group reported disappointing numbers in a year of restructuring, with both profits and sales dropping off slightly as its construction division under performed. Still, the business is now wholly focused on its core construction activities, and since September, the investment division has been sold to Peter Gyllenhammar's Browallia. Year-end cash looked strong at over £20m, buoyed by further property disposals.

MOS International (MOI)

Producer and supplier of specialist products primarily to the oil industry

Units D & E, Upper Floor, Shipley Wharf, Wharf Street, Shipley, West Yorkshire BD17 7DW Tel: 01274-531862; Fax: 01274-531716; e-mail: sales@mosltd.bdx.co.uk; web site: www.mosltd.co.uk

		holding %
Chairman	Philip Wood	0.0
Chief Executive	Stewart Wild	0.0
Finance Director	Terence Shuttleworth	1.6
Director	Keith Osborne	8.1

Main Shareholders:

Jubilee Investment	20.2
Wendy Larkin	12.2
Brendan Larkin	11.6

Percentage of free market capital: 46.3%

Nominated Adviser:	Seymour Pierce, London
AIM Broker:	Seymour Pierce, London
Solicitors:	Irwin Mitchell, Leeds
Market Makers:	HOOD; WINS
Auditors:	Baker Tilly, 2 Whitehall Quay, Leeds, LS1 4HG
Registrars:	Capita Registrars

Entry on AIM:	23/8/2001	Recent price:	1.5p
Interim results:	Dec	Market cap:	£7.44m
Final results:	Sep	Issue price:	4.0p
Year end:	Mar	Current no of shares:	
Accounts due:	Sep		496,012,500
Int div paymnt:	n/a	No of shares after	
Fin div paymnt:	n/a	dilution:	n/a
Int net div per share:	nil	P/E ratio:	n/a
Fin net div per share:	nil	Probable CGT?	Yes

Comments:

MOS recently purchased bespoke marine and industrial winch manufacturer NIM Engineering for £675,000. At the interims, turnover surged 45% to £1.84m and losses were reduced to £10,793. A restructuring has seen ex-Sheffield United boss Philip Wood assume the executive chairman position. In another change, broker Hoodless Brennan was replaced by Seymour Pierce. The group is now focusing on its core mechanical handling business.

LATEST REPORTED RESULTS:	2003	PREVIOUS REPORTED RESULTS:	2002
Turnover:	£3.33m	Turnover:	£3.49m
PTP:	£(1.74m)	PTP:	£(1.06m)
EPS:	(0.7)p	EPS:	(0.5)p

Mosaique (MQE)

Financial services group

6 Imperial Court, Empire Way, Wembley, London, Middlesex HA9 0RS Tel: 020-8782 2220; Fax: 020-8903 3717; e-mail: info@mosaiqueplc.com; web site: www.mosaiqueplc.com

		holding %
Chairman	Nicholas Richardson	2.9
Chief Executive	Amer Deen	24.0
Finance Director	Stephen Pearce	0.0
Operations Director	Leon Blumenthal	0.0

Main Shareholders:

Zurich International Life	9.8
Jupiter Asset Management	9.0
Iain Batty	6.8
M. Walker	6.7

Percentage of free market capital: 40.8%

Nominated Adviser:	City Financial Associates, London
AIM Broker:	City Financial Associates, London
Solicitors:	Field Fisher Waterhouse, London
Market Makers:	EVO, WINS
Auditors:	CLB, London
Registrars:	Capita Registrars

Entry on AIM:	6/6/1996	Recent price:	47.0p
Interim results:	Feb	Market cap:	£3.71m
Final results:	Sep	Issue price:	100.0p
Year end:	Mar	Current no of shares:	
Accounts due:	Oct		7,900,814
Int div paymnt:	n/a	No of shares after	
Fin div paymnt:	n/a	dilution:	8,064,820
Int net div per share:	nil	P/E ratio:	n/a
Fin net div per share:	nil	Probable CGT?	Yes

Comments:

Mosaique is a financial services business that specialises in selling offshore products to high net worth individuals, mortgage and finance broking, management consultancy services and several other activities not currently covered by the Financial Services Authority's regulatory requirements. The company intends to seek the appropriate regulatory approval and then morph into a more traditional IFA-type business.

LATEST REPORTED RESULTS:	FROM 1 JUN '02 TO 31 MAR '03	PREVIOUS REPORTED RESULTS:	2002
Turnover:	n/a	Turnover:	£4.18m
PTP:	£(93,000)	PTP:	£(6.07m)
EPS:	(1.4)p	EPS:	(92.2)p

Motion Media   (MMD)

Designer, developer & supplier of video technology and products

Motion Media Technology Centre, Severn Bridge, Aust, Bristol, BS35 4BL Tel: 01454-635400; Fax: 01454-635401;
web site: www.motion-media.com

		holding %
Chairman	Rex Thorne	0.6
Chief Executive	Graham Brown	1.0
Finance Director	Iain Silvester	0.3
Non-Exec Director	Alan MacKenzie	1.5

Main Shareholders:

C Blackbourn	9.3

Percentage of free market capital: 87.5%

Nominated Adviser:	ARM Corporate Finance, London
AIM Broker:	Charles Stanley, London
Solicitors:	Burges Salmon, Bristol
Market Makers:	KLWT; SCAP; TEAM; WINS
Auditors:	Deloitte & Touche, Bristol
Registrars:	Capita Registrars

ENTRY ON AIM:	2/1/2003	Recent price:	12.5p
Interim results:	Sep	Market cap:	£27.95m
Final results:	Mar	Issue price:	3.5p
Year end:	Dec	Current no of shares:	
Accounts due:	Apr		223,573,935
Int div paymnt:	n/a	No of shares after	
Fin div paymnt:	n/a	dilution:	n/a
Int net div per share:	nil	P/E ratio:	n/a
Fin net div per share:	nil	Probable CGT?	YES

LATEST REPORTED RESULTS: 2002		PREVIOUS REPORTED RESULTS: 2001	
Turnover:	£2.15m	Turnover:	£2.72m
PTP:	£(6.85m)	PTP:	£(6.89m)
EPS:	(6.4)p	EPS:	(6.6)p

Comments:

Motion Media designs and develops a range of sophisticated internet protocol video phone products for the corporate, IT, health and other markets. Unfortunately the group has only been able to post routine losses. To turn things around, the management has been revamped and costs pared back even further. The last set of interims saw losses hit £2m on reduced sales of just £0.9m. Since then a few deals have been signed, although none of any significance.

Mulberry   (MUL)

International brand designer & retailer

Kilver Court, Shepton Mallet, Somerset BA4 5NF Tel: 01749-340500; Fax: 01749-346976;
e-mail: enquiries@mulberry.com; web site: www.mulberry.com

		holding %
Chairman	Godfrey P Davis	4.3
Chief Executive	as above	
Finance Director	Guy Rutherford	0.0
Non-Exec Director	Bernard Heng	0.0

Main Shareholders:

Challice	52.7
Artemis	10.0
Fidelity	10.0
Dresdner RCM Global	7.2
Roger J Saul	3.6

Percentage of free market capital: 20.5%

Nominated Adviser:	Teather & Greenwood, London
AIM Broker:	Teather & Greenwood, London
Solicitors:	Osborne Clarke, Bristol
Market Makers:	MLSB; TEAM; WINS
Auditors:	Deloitte & Touche, 69-71 Queen Square, Bristol BS1 4JP
Registrars:	Computershare Investor Services

ENTRY ON AIM:	23/5/1996	Recent price:	53.0p
Interim results:	Dec	Market cap:	£25.84m
Final results:	Aug	Issue price:	153.0p
Year end:	Mar	Current no of shares:	
Accounts due:	Aug		48,760,586
Int div paymnt:	n/a	No of shares after	
Fin div paymnt:	n/a	dilution:	n/a
Int net div per share:	nil	P/E ratio:	n/a
Fin net div per share:	nil	Probable CGT?	YES

LATEST REPORTED RESULTS: 2003		PREVIOUS REPORTED RESULTS: 2002	
Turnover:	£28.18m	Turnover:	£27.82m
PTP:	£(2.11m)	PTP:	£(1.75m)
EPS:	(6.6)p	EPS:	(5.4)p

Comments:

Mulberry designs, manufactures, distributes and retails a range of accessories, clothing and home furnishings for the luxury market. But whereas the likes of fully listed Burberry have flourished in recent years Mulberry continues to flounder. Latest interims revealed a £1.2m shortfall in sales to £12.1m, with losses falling to £615,000, although on a brighter note like-for-likes sales at the start of the second half were running around 3% ahead of the comparable period last year.

Multi (MLT)

Small tool hire services provider

Chrisopher Wren Yard, 117 High Street, Croydon, Surrey CR0 1QG Tel: 08701-602901; Fax: 08701-602993

		holding %
Chairman	Oliver Cooke	0.0
Chief Executive		
Finance Director	Andrew Brundle	2.6

Main Shareholders:

Southwind	53.9
F R Bracegirdle	7.6
Eaglet Investment Trust	6.3
Michael EW Jackson	4.0
Rights & Issues Investment Trust	4.0

Percentage of free market capital: 21.6%

Comments:

2003 was the most difficult that tool-hire services firm Multi has ever faced, with underperforming acquisitions and large sums spent on a foray into a new software programme straining its cash resources. But Multi has now been refinanced, ditching loss making businesses and the prospects for the remaining tool hire operations are much improved. The November fundraising introduced two new investors, Michael Jackson and Bob Morton's Southwind, both well-known to the City.

Nominated Adviser:	Corporate Synergy, London
AIM Broker:	Corporate Synergy, London
Solicitors:	Memery Crystal, London
Market Makers:	KBCS; SCAP; WDBM; WINS
Auditors:	BDO, Stoy Hayward, Emerald House, East Street, Ewell, Epsom, Surrey KT17 1HS
Registrars:	Capita Registrars

ENTRY ON AIM: 17/11/2003		**Recent price:**	6.4p
Interim results:	Sep	Market cap:	£16.03m
Final results:	Mar	Issue price:	1.0p
Year end:	Dec	Current no of shares:	
Accounts due:	Jun		250,394,923
Int div paymnt:	n/a	No of shares after	
Fin div paymnt:	n/a	dilution:	n/a
Int net div per share:	nil	P/E ratio:	n/a
Fin net div per share:	nil	Probable CGT?	YES

LATEST REPORTED RESULTS: 2003		PREVIOUS REPORTED RESULTS: 2002	
Turnover:	£13.99m	Turnover:	£15.85m
PTP:	£(3.62m)	PTP:	£(3.06m)
EPS:	(4.2)p	EPS:	(6.6)p

Murchison United NL (MUU)

Mineral deposits developer

Level 2, 1 Havelock Street, West Perth, WA 6005 Western Australia, Tel: 00-61 8 9321 7448; Fax: 00-61 8 9321 7747; e-mail: murchison@munl.com.au; web site: www.murchisonunited.com.au

		holding %
Chairman	Bruno Camarri	1.8
Managing Director	Paul Atherley	6.7
Finance Director	Stacey Apostolou	0.0
Non-Exec Director	David Hutchins	0.0

Main Shareholders:

FMR Corp & Fidelity International	10.2
BNY Nominees	8.4
J P Morgan Nominees	6.4
National Nominees	4.5
NEFCO Nominees	3.3

Percentage of free market capital: 58.7%

Comments:

Murchison languishes on the floor. The Lisbon government's veto of its stake in, and management of, Portugal's Neves Corvo copper and zinc project fades into memory, but its Renison Bell mining arm in Tasmania remains in administration. The company has slashed its £25m original debts, but retains a £1m liability on guaranteeing insurance of Renison Bell's treatment facility.

Nominated Adviser:	Evolution Beeson Gregory, London
AIM Broker:	Evolution Beeson Gregory, London
Solicitors:	Wright Legal, West Perth WA
Market Makers:	BGMM; CSFB; MLSB; WDBM; WINS
Auditors:	KPMG, Perth
Registrars:	Computershare Investor Services

ENTRY ON AIM: 3/7/2000		**Recent price:**	1.0p
Interim results:	Mar	Market cap:	£1.66m
Final results:	Sep	Issue price:	30.0p
Year end:	Jun	Current no of shares:	
Accounts due:	Oct		165,778,150
Int div paymnt:	n/a	No of shares after	
Fin div paymnt:	n/a	dilution:	179,603,150
Int net div per share:	nil	P/E ratio:	n/a
Fin net div per share:	nil	Probable CGT?	No

LATEST REPORTED RESULTS: 2002		PREVIOUS REPORTED RESULTS: 2001	
Turnover:	A$37.07m	Turnover:	A$91.14m
PTP:	A$(26.28m)	PTP:	A$(29.66m)
EPS:	(25.9)Ac	EPS:	(36.6)Ac

Murgitroyd (MUR)

Patent and trademark attorney group

Scotland House, 165-169 Scotland Street, Glasgow, G5 8PL Tel: 0141-307 8400; Fax: 0141-307 8401;
e-mail: mail@murgitroyd.com; web site: www.murgitroyd.com

		holding %
Chairman	Ian Murgitroyd	40.8
Chief Executive	Keith Young	0.0
Finance Director		
Director	Roisin McNally	0.0

Main Shareholders:

Chase Nominees	10.0
Schroder Investment Management	8.5
BNY (OCS) Nominees	5.0
Elizabeth-Anne Thomson	4.7
Morgan Nominees	3.9

Percentage of free market capital: 22.4%

Nominated Adviser:	Noble & Co, Edinburgh
AIM Broker:	Noble & Co, London
Solicitors:	McClure Naismith, Glasgow
Market Makers:	KBCS; WINS
Auditors:	KPMG, 24 Blythswood Square, Glasgow G2 4QS
Registrars:	Capita Registrars

Comments:

The patent and trade mark attorney's push on Europe, aided by last year's Cabinet Bonneau acquisition in France, is progressing well. Interims to November were greatly improved, with pre-tax profits jumping from £7,000 to £243,000 as costs were taken out. Turnover edged up a decent 14% to £5.8m. Looking ahead, Murgitroyd looks well placed to benefit from the burgeoning European patent application growth being fuelled by research spending from key industries.

Entry on AIM: 30/11/2001		**Recent price:**	150.0p
Interim results:	Jan	**Market cap:**	£12.42m
Final results:	Aug	**Issue price:**	121.0p
Year end:	May	**Current no of shares:**	
Accounts due:	Aug		8,277,887
Int div paymnt:	n/a	**No of shares after**	
Fin div paymnt:	Sep	dilution:	8,463,051
Int net div per share:	nil	**P/E ratio:**	75
Fin net div per share: 1.57p		**Probable CGT?**	**Yes**

LATEST REPORTED RESULTS: 2003		PREVIOUS REPORTED RESULTS: 2002	
Turnover:	£10.56m	**Turnover:**	£9.05m
PTP:	£704,000	**PTP:**	£634,000
EPS:	2.0p	**EPS:**	2.0p

Murray Financial (now called Leisureplay, LPY) (MFC)

Cash shell

Greenside House, 25 Greenside Place, Edinburgh, EH1 3AA Tel: 0131-466 6666; Fax: 0131-466 6667;
e-mail: info@murray-financial.com

		holding %
Chairman	Philip Reid	0.0
Chief Executive		
Finance Director		
Non-Exec Director	Jonathan Hall	0.0

Main Shareholders:

Resurge	29.9
Peter Gyllenhammar	11.3
Faisal Mohamed Al-Youssef	10.0

Percentage of free market capital: 48.7%

Nominated Adviser:	ARM Corporate Finance, London
AIM Broker:	KBC Peel Hunt, London
Solicitors:	Lovell White Durrant, London
Market Makers:	KBCS; WINS
Auditors:	PricewaterhouseCoopers, Edinburgh
Registrars:	Lloyds TSB Registrars

Comments:

Controversy stalks loss-making Murray, which was set up to carpet-bag building societies and then backed an insurance dot com. A new board, installed by AIM-listed Resurge, is now in dispute with former boss Ken Murray, who is claiming £0.75m on the termination of his contract. Resurge says £0.85m is missing from the company. The group, now called Leisureplay, has since bought ChartCity, which owns seven pubs trading as 'the Front Room'.

Entry on AIM: 29/6/1998		**Recent price:**	2.75p
Interim results:	Feb	**Market cap:**	£2.75m
Final results:	Nov	**Issue price:**	10.0p
Year end:	May	**Current no of shares:**	
Accounts due:	Dec		100,000,002
Int div paymnt:	n/a	**No of shares after**	
Fin div paymnt:	n/a	dilution:	110,020,002
Int net div per share:	nil	**P/E ratio:**	n/a
Fin net div per share:	nil	**Probable CGT?**	**Yes**

LATEST REPORTED RESULTS: 2003		PREVIOUS REPORTED RESULTS: 2002	
Turnover:	£212,000	**Turnover:**	£407,000
PTP:	£(1.19m)	**PTP:**	£(1.48m)
EPS:	(1.2)p	**EPS:**	(1.5)p

Myratech.net (suspended 25 Mar 2004)　　　　(MYA)

Software and services provider

Vittoria House, 1-7 Vittoria Street, Birmingham, B1 3ND Tel: 0121-628 6000; Fax: 0121-212 1573;
e-mail: info@myratech.net; web site: www.myratech.net

		holding %
Chairman	Nicholas Hamilton	0.03
Chief Executive	Duncan Sperry	6.0
Finance Director	Tony Mobley	6.0
Non-Exec Director	Peter Reynolds	4.8

Main Shareholders:

Lawrie Elwell	4.7
James Walker	3.5

Percentage of free market capital: 19.3%

Nominated Adviser:	Teather & Greenwood, London
AIM Broker:	Teather & Greenwood, London
Solicitors:	Lee Crowder, Birmingham
Market Makers:	TEAM; WINS
Auditors:	Baker Tilly, 154 St Botolph Street, London EC3A 7QR
Registrars:	Capita Registrars

ENTRY ON AIM:	3/4/2000	Recent price:	2.5p
Interim results:	Sep	Market cap:	£0.74m
Final results:	Jun	Issue price:	130.0p
Year end:	Dec	Current no of shares:	
Accounts due:	Jun		29,595,000
Int div paymnt:	n/a	No of shares after	
Fin div paymnt:	n/a	dilution:	29,900,100
Int net div per share:	nil	P/E ratio:	n/a
Fin net div per share:	nil	Probable CGT?	YES

Comments:
Following its first half loss of £257,000, this Sage software reseller disposed of its business for a mere £160,000 (consisting of £40,000 of cash and the buyers taking on £120,000 debt). It is now a cash shell awaiting a business to reverse into it. Interestingly, Elderstreet Investment is proposing to lend the group at least £50,000 which may be converted into shares representing 29.9% of the issued share capital. The shares were suspended on 25 March.

LATEST REPORTED RESULTS:	2002	PREVIOUS REPORTED RESULTS:	2001
Turnover:	£1.89m	Turnover:	£2.0m
PTP:	£(608,000)	PTP:	£(2.76m)
EPS:	(2.1)p	EPS:	(10.0)p

Napier Brown Foods　　　　(NBF)

Sugar, nut and dairy powder supplier

International House, 1 St Katherine's Way, London, E1W 1XB Tel: 020-7335 2500; Fax: 020-7335 2504

		holding %
Chairman	Patrick Ridgwell	60.2
Chief Executive	Christopher Thomas	0.4
Finance Director	Simon Barrell	0.4
Non-Exec Director	Jeremy Hamer	0.0

Main Shareholders:

Merchant Securities	9.9
JM Finn Nominees	9.3
Rathbones Investment Management	8.8

Percentage of free market capital: 11.0%

Nominated Adviser:	John East, London
AIM Broker:	JM Finn, London
Solicitors:	Joelson Wilson, London
Market Makers:	EVO; KBCS; WINS
Auditors:	Horwath Clark Whitehill, 10 Palace Avenue, Maidstone, Kent ME15 6NF
Registrars:	Capita Registrars

ENTRY ON AIM:	18/12/2003	Recent price:	129.5p
Interim results:	Jan	Market cap:	£29.56m
Final results:	Jul	Issue price:	110.0p
Year end:	Mar	Current no of shares:	
Accounts due:	Aug		22,827,272
Int div paymnt:	n/a	No of shares after	
Fin div paymnt:	n/a	dilution:	n/a
Int net div per share:	nil	P/E ratio:	n/a
Fin net div per share:	nil	Probable CGT?	YES

Comments:
Napier Brown Foods, comprising three food companies, listed on AIM after a £9m placing. The three companies – Napier Brown, Garrett Ingredients and Sefcol Ingredients – were acquired for £35 million and between them supply and distribute sugar, value-added sugar, nut, and dairy powder products to customers such as Thorntons, Cadbury Schweppes and Kelloggs. All three companies are 'cash generative'.

LATEST REPORTED RESULTS:	2003	PREVIOUS REPORTED RESULTS:	2002
Turnover:	£185.4m	Turnover:	£197.42m
PTP:	£4.92m	PTP:	£2.91m
EPS:	n/a	EPS:	n/a

Nature Technology Solutions (NSO)

Operator of marine waste water treatment plants

Kingsgate House, 55 Esplanade, St Helier, Jersey JE2 3QB Tel: 01534-706000; Fax: 01534-706099;
e-mail: enquiry@oesglobal.com; web site: www.oesglobal.com

		holding %
Chairman	Richard Eldridge	5.1
Chief Executive	John McKeown	1.8
Finance Director		
Exec Director	Stig Keller	9.5

Main Shareholders:

Gitle Dysjaland	6.5
Torleiv Bilstad	6.4
Jon Pettersen	4.8

Percentage of free market capital: 64.5%

Nominated Adviser:	Seymour Pierce, London
AIM Broker:	Seymour Pierce Ellis, Crawley
Solicitors:	Masons, London
Market Makers:	SCAP; WINS
Auditors:	Drummonds, Gibraltar
Registrars:	Computershare Investor Services

ENTRY ON AIM:	4/9/2001	**Recent price:**	0.75p
Interim results:	Dec	Market cap:	£2.25m
Final results:	Jun	Issue price:	2.5p
Year end:	Jul	Current no of shares:	
Accounts due:	Apr		299,593,384
Int div paymnt:	n/a	No of shares after	
Fin div paymnt:	n/a	dilution:	n/a
Int net div per share:	nil	P/E ratio:	n/a
Fin net div per share:	nil	Probable CGT?	Yes

LATEST REPORTED RESULTS: FROM 1 AUG 2001 TO 31 DEC 2002		PREVIOUS REPORTED RESULTS: 2001	
Turnover:	£336,000	Turnover:	£92,000
PTP:	£(1.30m)	PTP:	£(193,000)
EPS:	(0.0)p	EPS:	(0.0)p

Comments:

Following a merger and £1.1m fundraising, Nature aims to become a major provider of waste water treatment services for ships and the oil industry. Revenues have been minimal so far, but its joint venture SORT was awarded the overall port waste management contract for the Port of Gibraltar. It has also reduced its interest in its Norwegian waste water treatment plant joint venture by 20% to 60%. Trials in Denmark for its CF200 patented absorbent for a industrial group is continuing.

NBA Quantum (NAQ)

Construction industry consultant

14 Half Moon Street, London W1J 7BD Tel: 020-7318 9780; Fax: 020-7318 9784

		holding %
Executive Chairman	David Ridley	7.8
Managing Director	Peter Elliott-Hughes	32.3
Finance Director	Peter Brasier	0.0
Director	David Fishwick	1.0

Main Shareholders:

Robert G Jervis	26.9
Discovery Trust	7.5
Luthra Investments	5.2

Percentage of free market capital: 19.3%

Nominated Adviser:	Brewin Dolphin, London
AIM Broker:	Brewin Dolphin, London
Solicitors:	Field Fisher Waterhouse, London
Market Makers:	TEAM; WINS
Auditors:	Nunn Hayward, 20 Station Rd, Gerrards Cross, Bucks SL9 8EL
Registrars:	Capita Registrars

ENTRY ON AIM:	17/2/1999	**Recent price:**	53.0p
Interim results:	Mar	Market cap:	£3.2m
Final results:	Nov	Issue price:	105.0p
Year end:	Jun	Current no of shares:	
Accounts due:	Oct		6,035,796
Int div paymnt:	n/a	No of shares after	
Fin div paymnt:	Jan	dilution:	n/a
Int net div per share:	nil	P/E ratio:	n/a
Fin net div per share:	3.5p	Probable CGT?	Yes

LATEST REPORTED RESULTS: 2003		PREVIOUS REPORTED RESULTS: 2002	
Turnover:	£2.34m	Turnover:	£2.87m
PTP:	£(121,000)	PTP:	£278,000
EPS:	(3.0)p	EPS:	2.1p

Comments:

The construction claims consultant has taken an additional 15% of joint venture Bionic Productions and now owns 65%. BPL is a developer and producer of industrial multimedia formed to use high quality visuals in support of NBA's dispute cases. In a mixed past financial year to June, NBA reported falling sales and profits and moved into losses after amortisation. But the current year opened with a 'sound' order book and NBA's prospects are much improved.

Netb2b2 (NEB)

Online business-to-business services

20/26 Brunswick Place, London, N1 6DZ e-mail: IR@netb2b2.com; web site: www.netb2b2.com

		holding %
Chairman	Keith Young	17.9
Managing Director	Andrew Gannon	0.4
Finance Director	Geoffrey Griggs	0.6
Non-Exec Director	Timothy Childs	2.4

Main Shareholders:

Puma Nominees	7.6
Shore Capital	7.6
Andrew de Candole	4.4
Brian Newman	3.1

Percentage of free market capital: 48.6%

Nominated Adviser:	Smith & Williamson, London
AIM Broker:	Seymour Pierce Ellis, London
Solicitors:	Eversheds, London
Market Makers:	SCAP; WINS
Auditors:	Monsoon Blueprint, Salisbury House, 31 Finsbury House, London EC2M 5SQ
Registrars:	Capita Registrars

ENTRY ON AIM:	2/9/1998	Recent price:	1.0p
Interim results:	Mar	Market cap:	£4.64m
Final results:	Nov	Issue price:	32.0p
Year end:	Jun	Current no of shares:	
Accounts due:	Sep		463,913,932
Int div paymnt:	n/a	No of shares after	
Fin div paymnt:	n/a	dilution:	n/a
Int net div per share:	nil	P/E ratio:	n/a
Fin net div per share:	nil	Probable CGT?	YES

LATEST REPORTED RESULTS: 2003		PREVIOUS REPORTED RESULTS: 2002	
Turnover:	£5.36m	Turnover:	£6.03m
PTP:	£(800,000)	PTP:	£(2.38m)
EPS:	(0.3)p	EPS:	(0.9)p

Comments:

Digital services group Netb2b2 operates three main businesses. CScape is a profitable internet consultancy boasting strong links with Microsoft and is targeting the e-government and health sectors at present. ITM provides publishing services. Blue Sky, meanwhile, focuses on providing technical and infrastructure offerings to a range of businesses. Despite its diversity the group continues to run up losses, though further progress towards profitability is expected this year.

Netbenefit (NBT)

Provider of domain name management services, web-hosting and related services

11 Clerkenwell Green, London, EC1R 0DP Tel: 020-7336 6777; Fax: 020-7336 0567;
e-mail: sales@netbenefit.com; web site: www.netbenefit.com

		holding %
Chairman	John Parcell	6.6
Chief Executive	Geoffrey Wicks	0.3
Finance Director	Paul Owens	0.0
Non-Exec Director	Keith Young	16.7

Main Shareholders:

Herald Investment Trust	10.1
Herald G.P Limited	6.1

Percentage of free market capital: 33.1%

Nominated Adviser:	Brewin Dolphin, Edinburgh
AIM Broker:	Brewin Dolphin, Edinburgh
Solicitors:	Nabarro Nathanson, London
Market Makers:	KBCS; WINS
Auditors:	BDO Stoy Hayward, 8 Baker Street, London W1U 3LL
Registrars:	Capita Registrars

ENTRY ON AIM:	30/10/2003	Recent price:	54.5p
Interim results:	Mar	Market cap:	£8.89m
Final results:	Sep	Issue price:	n/a
Year end:	Jun	Current no of shares:	
Accounts due:	Oct		16,317,216
Int div paymnt:	n/a	No of shares after	
Fin div paymnt:	n/a	dilution:	n/a
Int net div per share:	nil	P/E ratio:	545.0
Fin net div per share:	nil	Probable CGT?	YES

LATEST REPORTED RESULTS: 2003		PREVIOUS REPORTED RESULTS: 2002	
Turnover:	£6.25m	Turnover:	£6.08m
PTP:	£(166,000)	PTP:	£(1.19m)
EPS:	0.1p	EPS:	(6.9)p

Comments:

Domain name portfolio management group NetBenefit produced good numbers, showing losses of £303,000 transformed into a £105,000 profit on revenues up 26% to £3.5m. The company is focusing on two market segments, providing both a service for large corporate clients with a portfolio of domain names and one for smaller companies, where the group will host their site. NetBenefit currently has around 275 contracts, including 25% of all FTSE-listed companies.

Netcall (NET)

Computer telephone developer

10 Harding Way, St. Ives, Cambridgeshire DE27 3WR Tel: 01480-495300; Fax: 01480-496717;
web site: www.netcall.com

		holding %
Chairman	Ron Elder	0.1
Chief Executive	Henrik Bang	0.0
Finance Director		
Non-Exec Director	Jeffrey Rubins	12.9

Main Shareholders:

ISIS	15.2
Gartmore	12.3
Edenfield Investments	4.4
Committed Capital	3.1

Percentage of free market capital: 50.3%

Comments:

Netcall has developed a telephone queuing system for the call centre trade. Last year it signed a £1.5m deal with BT and, following the appointment of Ron Elder to spearhead its international development, a Far East distribution deal was signed in Japan. Losses though continue to pile up - increasing 48% to £0.73m at the interim stage on reduced sales of £0.67m (£0.83m). Profits seem far off.

Nominated Adviser:	Evolution Beeson Gregory, London
AIM Broker:	Evolution Beeson Gregory, London
Solicitors:	Halliwell Landau, Manchester
Market Makers:	DURM; MLSB; WINS
Auditors:	Deloitte & Touche, Station Road, Cambridge
Registrars:	Neville Registrars

Entry on AIM:	18/12/1996	**Recent price:**	25.5p
Interim results:	Feb	**Market cap:**	£21.97m
Final results:	Sep	**Issue price:**	5.0p
Year end:	Jun	**Current no of shares:**	
Accounts due:	Nov		86,168,440
Int div paymnt	n/a	**No of shares after**	
Fin div paymnt:	n/a	**dilution:**	n/a
Int net div per share:	nil	**P/E ratio:**	n/a
Fin net div per share:	nil	**Probable CGT?**	Yes

LATEST REPORTED RESULTS: 2003		PREVIOUS REPORTED RESULTS: 2002	
Turnover:	£2.39m	**Turnover:**	£861,000
PTP:	£(332,000)	**PTP:**	£(2.34m)
EPS:	(0.6)p	**EPS:**	(6.4)p

Netcentric Systems (NCS)

Shell company

Pascall House, 51 Gatwick Road, Crawley, West Sussex, RH10 9RD Tel: 01293-456280; Fax: 01293-455432;
e-mail: info@netcentriceurope.com; web site: www.netcentriceurope.com

		holding %
Chairman	Stephen Komlosy*	0.0
Chief Executive		
Finance Director	John May*	0.0
Chief Op Officer	Gerard Thompson	1.8

Main Shareholders:

London and Boston Investments*	40.5
New Opportunities Investment Trust	16.5
Herald IT	7.9
RSTD Nominees	7.9
Foundation	5.5

Percentage of free market capital: 10.4%

Komlosy and May are also directors of London Boston Investments

Comments:

Empty shell company Netcentric continues to scout around for a suitable reverse takeover target, although little progress seems to have been achieved thus far. £331,000 sits in the bank to research and finance possible deals, however, as the company managed to lose more than £200,000 last year without operating a trading business this may not last long.

Nominated Adviser:	Teather & Greenwood, London
AIM Broker:	Teather & Greenwood, London
Solicitors:	Tarlo, London; Simcocks, Isle of Man
Market Makers:	MLSB; SCAP; TEAM; WINS
Auditors:	Milsted Langdon, London
Registrars:	Computershare Investor Services

Entry on AIM:	11/7/2000	**Recent price:**	0.5p
Interim results:	Jun	**Market cap:**	£0.7m
Final results:	Mar	**Issue price:**	25.0p
Year end:	Sep	**Current no of shares:**	
Accounts due:	Feb		139,734,883
Int div paymnt:	n/a	**No of shares after**	
Fin div paymnt:	n/a	**dilution:**	n/a
Int net div per share:	nil	**P/E ratio:**	n/a
Fin net div per share:	nil	**Probable CGT?**	Yes

LATEST REPORTED RESULTS: 2003		PREVIOUS REPORTED RESULTS: 2002	
Turnover:	£11,000	**Turnover:**	£28,000
PTP:	£(289,000)	**PTP:**	£(246,000)
EPS:	(0.2)p	**EPS:**	(0.4)p

Network

Outdoor media production & advertsing
Unit B3, 2-4 Central Avenue, Thornleigh, Sydney, NSW 2120; e-mail: info@networklimited.com;
web site: www.networklimited.com

(NWK)

		holding %
Chairman	Graham Jones	0.1
Chief Executive	Brendon Cook	12.1
Finance Director		
Managing Director	Christopher Bregenhoj	2.5

Main Shareholders:

Consortium Capital	33.4
Debra Cook	11.6
Energy Programmes Int	7.1
HTL	5.8

Percentage of free market capital: 27.0%

Comments:

Loss-making Network, which also sports a listing in Australia, is a broker of outdoor media sites, or billboards, to 40 owners of such sites down-under. Following the purchase of three small companies, it also owns some outdoor sites. Interim revenues to June were £4.6m. Of this, around £300,000 came from certain biotech interests it owns. Prior to moving into the ad game, Network was a biotech operation specialising in patenting proteins. An unusual combination.

Nominated Adviser:	Grant Thornton, London
AIM Broker:	JM Finn, London
Solicitors:	Charles Russell, London
Market Makers:	WINS
Auditors:	PricewaterhouseCoopers, Sydney, NSW
Registrars:	Computershare Investor Services

Entry on AIM: 24/11/2003	**Recent price:**	11.5p
Interim results: Sep	**Market cap:**	£7.94m
Final results: Mar	**Issue price:**	n/a
Year end: Dec	**Current no of shares:**	
Accounts due: Jun		69,020,015
Int div paymnt: n/a	**No of shares after**	
Fin div paymnt: n/a	**dilution:**	n/a
Int net div per share: nil	**P/E ratio:**	6.4
Fin net div per share: nil	**Probable CGT?**	No

LATEST REPORTED RESULTS: 2002		PREVIOUS REPORTED RESULTS: 2001	
Turnover:	$3.33m	Turnover:	$460,000
PTP:	$(1.01m)	PTP:	$(2.81m)
EPS:	1.8c	EPS:	2.5c

NeuTec Pharma

Development of antibodies for hospital-acquired infections
2nd Floor, Clinical Sciences Building, Manchester Royal Infirmiry, Oxford Road, Manchester, M13 9WL
Tel: 0161-276 8827; Fax: 0161-276 8826; e-mail: neutecpharma@hotmail.com; web site: www.neutecpharma.com

(NTP)

		holding %
Chairman	Anthony Martin	1.2
Chief Executive	James Burnie	2.1
Finance Director	Andrew King	0.0
R&D Director	Ruth Matthews	2.1

Main Shareholders:

Victory Capital	7.1
Manchester Technology Developments*	5.6
Employee Benefit Trust	4.9
Hoare Govett	4.3
ABN AMRO Ventures	3.7

Percentage of free market capital: 68.9%
* Nominee for the University of Manchester

Comments:

This spin-out company from Manchester University is developing antibodies to combat infections acquired in hospital, which are major killers. Its two main products, tackling a common yeast infection and the MRSA superbug are currently in Phase II and Phase III trials respectively. A £1.2m interim loss was made. The group plans to lodge a FDA application for the yeast drug so clinical trials can start in the US. Costs will mount but the group currently has £8.2m net cash.

Nominated Adviser:	Hoare Govett, London
AIM Broker:	Hoare Govett, London
Solicitors:	Ashursts, London
Market Makers:	WINS
Auditors:	KPMG Audit, St James' Square, Manchester M2 6DS
Registrars:	Lloyds TSB Registrars

Entry on AIM: 20/2/2002	**Recent price:**	282.5p
Interim results: Mar	**Market cap:**	£66.79m
Final results: Sep	**Issue price:**	150.0p
Year end: Jun	**Current no of shares:**	
Accounts due: Oct		23,642,956
Int div paymnt: n/a	**No of shares after**	
Fin div paymnt: n/a	**dilution:**	25,123,744
Int net div per share: nil	**P/E ratio:**	n/a
Fin net div per share: nil	**Probable CGT?**	Yes

LATEST REPORTED RESULTS: 2003		PREVIOUS REPORTED RESULTS: 2002	
Turnover:	n/a	Turnover:	n/a
PTP:	£(2.95m)	PTP:	£(2.06m)
EPS:	(11.8)p	EPS:	(10.7)p

251

New Media Industries (NMI)

Provider of digital marketing and creative services

Middlesex House, 34-42 Cleveland Street, London, W1T 4JE Tel: 020-7436 5000; Fax: 020-7323 9738;
e-mail: reception@nmigroup.com; web site: www.nmigroup.com

		holding %
Chairman	Martin Boase	0.0
Chief Executive	Jon Summerhill	7.4
Finance Director	Toni Denby	0.0
Managing Director	Paul Nathan	1.9

Main Shareholders:

Willbro Nominees	9.1
Chase Nominess	8.9
Alan Page	8.8
HSBC Global Custody Nominees	4.6
Gerard Cok	4.5

Percentage of free market capital: 41.7%

Nominated Adviser:	Collins Stewart, London		
AIM Broker:	Collins Stewart, London		
Solicitors:	Maclay Murray & Spens, London		
Market Makers:	BGMM; WDBM; WINS		
Auditors:	BDO Stoy Hayward, Epsom		
Registrars:	Capita Registrars		

ENTRY ON AIM:	11/4/2001	**Recent price:**	5.75p
Interim results:	Jan	**Market cap:**	£8.03m
Final results:	Sep	**Issue price:**	10.5p
Year end:	Apr	**Current no of shares:**	
Accounts due:	Aug		139,636,596
Int div paymnt:	n/a	**No of shares after**	
Fin div paymnt:	n/a	**dilution:**	n/a
Int net div per share:	nil	**P/E ratio:**	n/a
Fin net div per share:	nil	**Probable CGT?**	**YES**

LATEST REPORTED RESULTS: 2003		PREVIOUS REPORTED RESULTS: 2002	
Turnover:	£23.71m	Turnover:	£31.46m
PTP:	£(3.38m)	PTP:	£(857,000)
EPS:	(4.6)p	EPS:	(1.6)p

Comments:

New Media Industries is one of many AIM media companies undergoing a resurgence in trading. The six months to last October saw turnover improve significantly to £15m and pre-tax losses reduce to a mere £162,000. At the time NMI's management hinted that growth was returning to the sector, following this in late January with news that the company had secured three significant contracts with Emap, Adidas and Sega Europe. The full year results should prove interesting reading.

252

New Millennium Resources (NML)

Niobium and tantalum miner and explorer
Suite 5, 22 Hardy Street, South Perth, WA 6151 Australia, Tel: 00-61 8 9368 0388; Fax: 00-61 8 9368 0588

		holding %		
Chairman	David Johnston	1.2	AIM Broker:	Seymour Pierce, London
Chief Executive	Nik Zuks	0.0		Seymour Pierce Ellis, Crawley
Finance Director	Dato Azizi Yom Ahmad	5.0	Solicitors:	Memery Crystal, London
Non-Exec Director	Michael Yang	3.6	Market Makers:	WDBM; WINS

Main Shareholders:

Chong-Kiat Lim	7.8	
Sik-Choon Tan	3.9	
Keng-Gin Lee	3.1	

Percentage of free market capital: 65.3%

Auditors: KPMG, Central Park, Perth, WA 6000, Australia
Registrars: Computershare Investor Services

ENTRY ON AIM: 26/11/2001		5.75p
		£6.19m
	Nov	28.5p
	Oct	107,679,495
	n/a	
	n/a	
	nil	n/a
	nil	**Probable CGT?** No

Comments:

Aussie-based New Millennium, a speculative exploration play which halved interim losses to £128,000, lost favour over previous delays at its Safartog tantalum and niobium project in Western Greenland. The company, which raised £600,000 at 2.7p, is now pressing ahead there and starting to drill a diamond prospect at Lapi River in Angola, where micro diamonds have been found.

LATEST REPORTED RESULTS: 2003		PREVIOUS REPORTED RESULTS: 2002	
Turnover:	A$35,000	Turnover:	A$428,000
PTP:	A$(1.02m)	PTP:	A$(1.72m)
EPS:	A$0.0	EPS:	A$(0.0)

Newmark Security (NWT)

Electronic security systems developer
Suite 3, 23 Bruton Street, London, W1J 6QF Tel: 020-7355 0070; Fax: 020-7629 0222;
e-mail: info@newmarkworld.com; web site: www.newmarkworld.com

		holding %		
Executive Chairman	Maurice Dwek	7.8	AIM Broker:	Seymour Pierce, London
Chief Executive				Seymour Pierce Ellis, Crawley
Finance Director	Brian Beecraft	0.0	Solicitors:	Travers Smith Braithwaite, London
Non-Exec Director	Alexander Reid	15.5	Market Makers:	KBCS; MLSB; SCAP; WINS

Main Shareholders:

M V Beheer	6.4
P H Nominees Peclt Account	4.5
Credit Suisse First Boston	3.8
HSBC Global	3.2
Pershing Keen	3.1

Percentage of free market capital: 50.7%

Auditors: BDO Stoy Hayward, Northside House, Kent
Registrars: Capita Registrars

Entry on AIM: 21/11/1997		1.5p
	Jan	£3.14m
	Aug	10.0p
	Apr	
	Oct	209,390,016
	n/a	
	n/a	
	nil	n/a
	nil	**Probable CGT?** Yes

Comments:

The supplier of electronic locking systems has removed a huge drain with the disposal of Drion, part of its asset protection division. In the half to October, Newmark made operating profits of £132,000 on continuing business, versus a £175,000 loss. Safetell, its asset protection division, scored 44% sales growth and new products are broadening into new client areas like the police. However, orders at the secure locking division have been slower than expected.

LATEST REPORTED RESULTS: 2003		PREVIOUS REPORTED RESULTS: 2002	
Turnover:	£8.39m	Turnover:	£12.03m
PTP:	£(2.80m)	PTP:	£2.26m
EPS:	(1.6)p	EPS:	(0.8)p

Newmarket Investments (formerly British Bloodstock Agency) (NWN)

Leisure business investor

Queensberry House, High Street, Newmarket, Suffolk CB8 9WP Tel: 01638-665021; Fax: 01638-660283;

		holding %
Chairman	Piers Pottinger	0.0
Chief Executive	Simon Hayes	5.8
Finance Director		
Exec Director	Paul Foster	5.1

Main Shareholders:

Robert Ogden	8.7
P Bickmore	5.4
Henry Moszkowicz	5.0
BD Cordy	4.5
WJ Turnbull	4.3

Percentage of free market capital: 26.8%

Comments:

Newmarket provided a small interim profit of £22,000 and is now focusing the majority of its attention on GoalStriker – an interactive game billed as 'the ultimate penalty shoot-out experience' that is to be installed in 12 theme parks globally. It also has interests in BBA Shipping & Transport and Sales Breeders' Services businesses as well as GWIN, a US betting advisory company. Its sale of the Queensberry House property in Newmarket gave a £450,000 premium to its book value.

Nominated Adviser:	Williams de Broe, London
AIM Broker:	Williams de Broe, London
Solicitors:	Withers, London
Market Makers:	CAZR, CSCS; KBCS, WINS
Auditors:	Ernst & Young, 80 Newmarket Rd, Cambridge CB5 8DZ
Registrars:	Capita Registrars

Entry on AIM:	19/8/1996	**Recent price:**	47.0p
Interim results:	Dec	**Market cap:**	£2.42m
Final results:	Jun	**Issue price:**	100.0p
Year end:	Mar	**Current no of shares:**	
Accounts due:	Jul		5,150,863
Int div paymnt:	n/a	**No of shares after**	
Fin div paymnt:	Jul	dilution:	n/a
Int net div per share:	nil	**P/E ratio:**	n/a
Fin net div per share:	3.5p	**Probable CGT?**	Yes

LATEST REPORTED RESULTS: 2003		PREVIOUS REPORTED RESULTS: 2002	
Turnover:	£2.28m	**Turnover:**	£1.74m
PTP:	£(1.24m)	**PTP:**	£(2.17m)
EPS:	(31.5)p	**EPS:**	(59.7)p

NewMedia SPARK (NMS)

Venture capital

4th Floor, 33 Glasshouse Street, London, W1B 5DG Tel: 020-7851 7777; Fax: 020-7851 7770;
e-mail: enquiries@newmediaspark.com; web site: www.newmediaspark.com

		holding %
Chairman	Thomas Teichman	4.9
Chief Executive	Michael Whitaker	3.8
Finance Director	Bruno Delacave	0.01
Chief Op Officer	Andrew Carruthers	0.6

Main Shareholders:

Prudential*	13.2
Guinness Peat	5.5
Globalnet	5.3
Deutsche Bank AG	4.8
New Star Asset Management	4.2

Percentage of free market capital: 50.7%

*Held through M&G Investment Management and its subsidiaries

Comments:

The internet investor's NAV stood at 11.6p per share at the end of September, down 13% over the year. Cash amounts to £46.4m with the investment portfolio valued at £24.8m. The group may float some of its holdings during the current year. Property costs, at £1m annually, have proved a drain but two thirds of the office is now sublet. The sale of German subsidiary Spuetz is close to being completed and will give NewMedia a one-off dividend of around £11m.

Nominated Adviser:	Collins Stewart, London
AIM Broker:	Collins Stewart, London
Solicitors:	Nabarro Nathanson, London
Market Makers:	CSCS; KBCS; MLSB; SCAB; WINS
Auditors:	Deloitte & Touche, 1 Little New St, London EC4A 3TR
Registrars:	Capita Registrars

Entry on AIM:	28/10/1999	**Recent price:**	12.25p
Interim results:	Feb	**Market cap:**	£59.9m
Final results:	Aug	**Issue price:**	10.0p
Year end:	Mar	**Current no of shares:**	
Accounts due:	Jul		489,017,528
Int div paymnt:	n/a	**No of shares after**	
Fin div paymnt:	n/a	dilution:	n/a
Int net div per share:	nil	**P/E ratio:**	n/a
Fin net div per share:	nil	**Probable CGT?**	Yes

LATEST REPORTED RESULTS: 2003		PREVIOUS REPORTED RESULTS: 2002	
Turnover:	£1.30m	**Turnover:**	3.01m
PTP:	£(9.09m)	**PTP:**	£(105,000)
EPS:	(2.0)p	**EPS:**	(22.3)p

Newsplayer (NPG)
New media

Portland House, 4 Great Portland Street, London, W1W 8QJ Tel: 020-7927 6699; Fax: 020-7927 6698;
e-mail: info@newsplayer.com; web site: www.newsplayer.com

		holding %
Chairman	David Holdgate	1.4
Chief Executive	Paul Duffen	6.7
Finance Director	David Wiseman	0.0
Marketing Director	Barry Llewellyn	6.7

Main Shareholders:

Goldman Sachs Securities	10.6
Fidelity	6.6
Reef Securities	6.1
HTNM	4.1
Universities Superannuation Scheme	3.2

Percentage of free market capital: 33%

Comments:

Newsplayer's recent figures masked the progress made last year. The group has restructured – acquiring business interests in New York, winning content supply deals with NTL, KPN and EMI amongst others, and raising £1.4m. It has since acquired another business, raised a further £2.75m and wrapped up another significant deal. The board is in negotiations to buy the Satellite Information Services business interests of United News & Media. This could seriously transform the group.

Nominated Adviser:	Durlacher, London		
AIM Broker:	Durlacher, London		
Solicitors:	Lewis Silkin, London		
Market Makers:	IHCS; KBCS; NUMS; WDBM; WINS		
Auditors:	Deloitte & Touche, London		
Registrars:	Capita Registrars		
Entry on AIM:	30/5/2000	**Recent price:**	28.75p
Interim results:	Jul	**Market cap:**	£38.72m
Final results:	Apr	**Issue price:**	84.0p
Year end:	Oct	**Current no of shares:**	
Accounts due:	Feb		134,683,634
Int div paymnt:	n/a	**No of shares after**	
Fin div paymnt:	n/a	dilution:	n/a
Int net div per share:	nil	**P/E ratio:**	n/a
Fin net div per share:	nil	**Probable CGT?**	Yes

LATEST REPORTED RESULTS:	2003	PREVIOUS REPORTED RESULTS:	2002
Turnover:	£265,000	Turnover:	£954,000
PTP:	£(6.53m)	PTP:	£(3.46m)
EPS:	(7.9)p	EPS:	(5.0)p

NMT (NMT)
Medical device manufacturer and developer

New Medical Ho, Oakbank Pk, Livingston, West Lothian EH53 0TH Tel: 01506-445000; Fax: 01506-430444;
web site: www.newmedicaltechnology.com

		holding %
Chairman	Tony Fletcher	0.0
Chief Executive	Roy Smith	0.0
Finance Director	Gerard Cassels	0.0
Non-Exec Director	Laurie Rostron	0.0

Main Shareholders:

Morley Fund Management	10.9
UBS Global	6.4
London Merchants	6.3
Inflexion	6.2
Active Capital Trust	5.7

Percentage of free market capital: 56.9%

Comments:

Results continue to improve at the novel syringe maker which has a history of production problems and litigation issues. Following a placing at 4p the group has £12.8m net cash and sales soared last year to £12.3m thanks to an agreement to supply drug giant Roche with syringes for use with its HIV treatment. Operating losses were reduced to £2m. But 2003's figures contained a £14.5m exceptional charge as the Livingston manufacturing plant was shut down. NMT is working on developing a second generation product.

Nominated Adviser:	Panmure, London		
AIM Broker:	Panmure, London		
Solicitors:	Shepherd & Wedderburn, Edinburgh		
Market Makers:	ALTI; GRAB; MLSB; NUMS; SCAP; WEST; WINS		
Auditors:	PricewaterhouseCoopers, Glasgow, G2 2LW		
Registrars:	Computershare Investor Services		
Entry on AIM:	17/4/1997	**Recent price:**	0.75p
Interim results:	Aug	**Market cap:**	£6.53m
Final results:	Mar	**Issue price:**	50.0p
Year end:	Dec	**Current no of shares:**	
Accounts due:	Apr		871,131,794
Int div paymnt:	n/a	**No of shares after**	
Fin div paymnt:	n/a	dilution:	n/a
Int net div per share:	nil	**P/E ratio:**	n/a
Fin net div per share:	nil	**Probable CGT?**	Yes

LATEST REPORTED RESULTS:	2003	PREVIOUS REPORTED RESULTS:	2002
Turnover:	£12.29m	Turnover:	£2.76m
PTP:	£(16.55m)	PTP:	£(14.25m)
EPS:	(0.2)p	EPS:	(1.3)p

Noble Investments (formerly Saltmark) (NBL)

Rare coin trader and investor

Barton Hall, Hardy Street, Eccles, Manchester, M30 7WJ Tel: 0161-707 9911; Fax: 0161-707 9900

		holding %
Chairman	Roger Newton	1.8
Chairman		
Chief Executive		
Finance Director		

Main Shareholders:
n/a

Percentage of free market capital: 70.9%

Nominated Adviser:	Insinger de Beaufort, London
AIM Broker:	Insinger Townsley, London
Solicitors:	Osborne Clarke, London
Market Makers:	MLSB; SCAP; WINS
Auditors:	PricewaterhouseCoopers, Leeds
Registrars:	Capita Registrars

ENTRY ON AIM:	6/2/2001	Recent price:	47.5p
Interim results:	May	Market cap:	£2.44m
Final results:	Feb	Issue price:	23.0p
Year end:	Aug	Current no of shares:	
Accounts due:	Dec		5,137,177
Int div paymnt:	n/a	No of shares after	
Fin div paymnt:	n/a	dilution:	n/a
Int net div per share:	nil	P/E ratio:	n/a
Fin net div per share:	nil	Probable CGT?	YES

LATEST REPORTED RESULTS:	2003	PREVIOUS REPORTED RESULTS:	2002
Turnover:	£9.07m	Turnover:	£20.06m
PTP:	£10.47m	PTP:	£(23.82m)
EPS:	(1.9)p	EPS:	(3.6)p

Comments:
Following the sale of all its trading assets failed advertising venture Saltmark morphed into Noble Investments at the back end of last year after Ian Goldbart injected his £200,000 coin collection into the group. The plan now is to grow the business into a much more substantial coin dealer and advisory concern. £1m sits in the company coffers for this purpose. Speculative stuff.

Norman Hay (HNN)

Metal processing and industrial equipment supplier

Godiva Place, Coventry, CV1 5PN Tel: 024-7622 9373; Fax: 024-7622 4420; e-mail: nhayplc@aol.com;
web site: www.normanhayplc.com

		holding %
Chairman	Peter Hay	13.3
Managing Director	Victor Bellanti	0.04
Finance Director	as above	
Chief Operating Officer	David Miller	0.3

Main Shareholders:

G Luker	9.4
J Bewsher	9.1
Westcombe Investments	4.0

Percentage of free market capital: 56.2%

Nominated Adviser:	Brewin Dolphin, Manchester
AIM Broker:	Brewin Dolphin, Manchester
Solicitors:	DLA, Sheffield
Market Makers:	KBCS; WINS
Auditors:	BDO Stoy Hayward, Manchester
Registrars:	Lloyds TSB Registrars

Entry on AIM:	10/11/2000	Recent price:	39.5p
Interim results:	Sep	Market cap:	£5.79m
Final results:	Apr	Issue price:	n/a
Year end:	Dec	Current no of shares:	
Accounts due:	May		14,650,000
Int div paymnt:	Nov	No of shares after	
Fin div paymnt:	Jul	dilution:	n/a
Int net div per share:	1.0p	P/E ratio:	n/a
Fin net div per share:	1.2p	Probable CGT?	YES

LATEST REPORTED RESULTS:	2003	PREVIOUS REPORTED RESULTS:	2002
Turnover:	£16.38m	Turnover:	£18.8m
PTP:	£866,000	PTP:	£(86,000)
EPS:	5.8p	EPS:	(0.3)p

Comments:
Nothing to report from this taciturn engineering concern since last September, when the company unfurled first half figures to June. Pre-tax profits fell slightly, from £351,000 to £330,000, on lower turnover of £8.4m (£9.8m). Norman Hay's cash flow remained positive at just over £1m and the interim dividend was maintained at 1p. At the time, the company said it was holding market share in North Sea oil and gas related products and the second half outlook was encouraging.

Northacre (NTA)

Residential property investor

48 Old Church Street, Chelsea, London, SW3 5BY Tel: 020-7349 8000; Fax: 020-7349 8001;
e-mail: moneypenny@northacre.co.uk; web site: www.northacre.co.uk

		holding %
Chairman	Klas Nilsson	26.1
Chief Executive	John Hunter	26.1
Finance Director	Simon Elgar	0.0
Non-Exec Director	Shemeel Khan	0.0

Main Shareholders:

Pershing Keen Nominees	11.4
David Gladman	10.7
Raven Nominees	5.0

Percentage of free market capital: 20.7%

Nominated Adviser:	KBC Peel Hunt, London
AIM Broker:	KBC Peel Hunt, London
Solicitors:	Campbell Hooper, London
Market Makers:	KBCS; WINS
Auditors:	Hacker Young, 2 Fore Street, London EC2Y 5DH
Registrars:	Melton Registrars

Entry on AIM:	25/5/1999	Recent price:	10.0p
Interim results:	Dec	Market cap:	£2.27m
Final results:	Aug	Issue price:	n/a
Year end:	Feb	Current no of shares:	
Accounts due:	Aug		22,713,644
Int div paymnt:	n/a	No of shares after	
Fin div paymnt:	n/a	dilution:	n/a
Int net div per share:	nil	P/E ratio:	n/a
Fin net div per share:	nil	Probable CGT?	No

LATEST REPORTED RESULTS: 2003		PREVIOUS REPORTED RESULTS: 2002	
Turnover:	£3.59m	Turnover:	£6.40m
PTP:	£(3.19m)	PTP:	£(2.55m)
EPS:	(14.3)p	EPS:	(10.7)p

Comments:

The London-based luxury property developer has yet to make a profit. it has completed the purchase of the Vicarage Gate House in Kensington – its joint venture with the Islamic Investment Bank – and has applied for planning consent. Its Kings Chelsea development has sold well. Chairman Klas Nilsson and chief executive John Hunt had made a preliminary approach to takeover the company but were unable to secure the necessary funds.

Northern Petroleum (NOP)

Oil producer & developer

No. 1 Cornhill, London, EC3V 3ND Tel: 020-7743 6080; Fax: 020-7743 6081; e-mail: info@northpet.com;
web site: www.northpet.com

		holding %
Chairman	Richard Latham*	1.6
Managing Director	Derek Musgrove	2.2
Finance Director	Jeremy White	0.2
Non-Exec Director	David Roberts	0.2

Main Shareholders:

Active Capital Trust	5.1
Canada Life Marketing	4.1

Percentage of free market capital: 86.6%
*Mr Latham's holding includes shares held by The Cayzer Trust Company.

Nominated Adviser:	John East, London
AIM Broker:	Evolution Beeson Gregory, London
Solicitors:	Gordons, London
Market Makers:	KBCS; MLSB; SCAP; WINS
Auditors:	Ernst & Young, 1 Lambeth Palace Road, London, SE1 7EU
Registrars:	Neville Registrars

Entry on AIM:	22/12/1995	Recent price:	8.0p
Interim results:	Sep	Market cap:	£17.12m
Final results:	May	Issue price:	75.0p
Year end:	Dec	Current no of shares:	
Accounts due:	May		213,970,900
Int div paymnt:	n/a	No of shares after	
Fin div paymnt:	n/a	dilution:	n/a
Int net div per share:	nil	P/E ratio:	n/a
Fin net div per share:	nil	Probable CGT?	No

LATEST REPORTED RESULTS: 2002		PREVIOUS REPORTED RESULTS: 2001	
Turnover:	£29,000	Turnover:	£266,000
PTP:	£395,000	PTP:	£(6.44m)
EPS:	0.2p	EPS:	(5.1)p

Comments:

Northern has rallied strongly (though still a fraction of its 1995 float price) as it has turned its focus from thwarted Siberian oil projects to the British Isles and Spain. Still speculative, the company, which lost an interim £212,000, has 57% of a group of licences in the Isle of Wight area and an option on 80% of an area covering the New Forest coast and Isle of Wight. Northern's partners include Hereward Ventures and Black Rock Resources.

Numerica (NUG)

Provider of business services

66 Wigmore Street, London, W1U 2HQ Tel: 020-7467 4000; Fax: 020-7467 4040; e-mail: info@numericagroup.com;
web site: www.numericagroup.com

		holding %
Chairman	Christopher McCann	0.9
Chief Executive	Peter Jenkins	1.4
Finance Director		
Director	Derrick Woolf	1.0

Main Shareholders:

Amvescap	19.8
Clerical Medical	8.5
Moore Macro Fund	6.8
Artemis UK Smaller Companies Fund	5.8
Credit Suisse	4.0

Percentage of free market capital: 51.8%

Nominated Adviser:	Numis, London
AIM Broker:	Numis, London
Solicitors:	Berwin Leighton Paisner, London
Market Makers:	CSCS; WINS
Auditors:	Ernst & Young, London
Registrars:	Capita Registrars

ENTRY ON AIM: 30/10/2001		**Recent price:**	36.5p
Interim results:	Dec	Market cap:	£19.03m
Final results:	Jun	Issue price:	100.0p
Year end:	Mar	Current no of shares:	
Accounts due:	Aug		52,123,408
Int div paymnt:	n/a	No of shares after	
Fin div paymnt:	n/a	dilution:	68,549,509
Int net div per share:	nil	P/E ratio:	8.5
Fin net div per share:	nil	Probable CGT?	YES

LATEST REPORTED RESULTS:	2003	PREVIOUS REPORTED RESULTS:	2003
Turnover:	£38.23m	Turnover:	£15.16m
PTP:	£3.16m	PTP:	£384,000
EPS:	4.3p	EPS:	0.4p

Comments:

Numerica joined AIM to buy up medium-sized accountancy practices, starting with London-based Levy Gee. Eight others have since been bought. However, the shares plunged after entrepreneur Tony Sarin, who sold Softtechnet to NewMedia SPARK, resigned as chief executive following a profit warning and failed attempt to sell the business. At the interim, turnover rose 6% to £23m but last time's £1.2m pre-tax profit became a £0.3m loss. A full year £0.6m loss is envisaged.

Numis (NUM)

Financial services provider

Cheapside House, 138 Cheapside, London, EC2V 6LH Tel: 020 7776 1500; Fax: 020-7776 1550;
e-mail: mail@numiscorp.com; web site: www.numiscorp.com

		holding %
Chairman	Michael Spencer	0.0
Chief Executive	Oliver Hemsley	15.9
Finance Director	Duncan Sweetland	0.4
Non-Exec Director	Geoffrey Vero	0.02

Main Shareholders:

Intercapital	10.0
David Poutney	8.6
Mr M Stone & Mrs L Stone	8.6
Fleming Mercantile	3.4
Jupiter	3.2

Percentage of free market capital: 48.4%

Nominated Adviser:	PricewaterhouseCoopers, London
AIM Broker:	Numis, London
Solicitors:	Kendall Freeman, London
Market Makers:	KBCS; WINS
Auditors:	PKF, London
Registrars:	Computershare Investor Services

Entry on AIM:	27/3/1996	Recent price:	717.5p
Interim results:	Apr	Market cap:	£136.45m
Final results:	Dec	Issue price:	25.0p
Year end:	Sep	Current no of shares:	
Accounts due:	Jan		19,017,751
Int div paymnt:	n/a	No of shares after	
Fin div paymnt:	Jan	dilution:	n/a
Int net div per share:	nil	P/E ratio:	20.8
Fin net div per share:	7.5p	Probable CGT?	YES

LATEST REPORTED RESULTS:	2003	PREVIOUS REPORTED RESULTS:	2002
Turnover:	£23.99m	Turnover:	£17.41m
PTP:	£9.40m	PTP:	£7.18m
EPS:	34.5p	EPS:	28.9p

Comments:

Investment bank Numis, which initially made its mark as an insurance specialist, is now a dominant player in the small and mid cap markets. Last year the group enjoyed a golden period, with pre-tax profits up 54% on turnover ahead 38%. The group doubled its client list to 53, for whom it raised £340m. The one question mark surrounded the flotation of Centaur Communications. Earlier in the year a £5.7m placing with Intercapital at 315p brought Michael Spencer on board as chairman.

NWD   (NWD)
Marketing services group
14 Kinnerton Place South, London, SW1X 8EH

		holding %
Chairman	Nigel Gourlay	1.0
Chief Executive	Alan Page	3.3
Finance Director	Stephen Stroud	0.0
Director of Business Development	David Gray	3.0

Main Shareholders:

Sinjul Nominees	13.9
Chase Nominees	11.6
Seymour Pierce Ellis	5.8
Barnett Fletcher	5.6
Evolution Nominees	4.6

Percentage of free market capital: 44.7%

Comments:

Shell concern NWD has finally succeeded in completing a significant deal. The group has issued 34m shares at 6.5p to raise £2.2m at the same time as buying three marketing businesses: 21st Century Communications, &SUMM and Joined Up Marketing Partnership (Jump). 21st is a corporate communications agency, with clients such as Vodafone. &SUMM provides brand strategy advice to retailers and associated businesses whilst Jump is a more adventurous marketing agency.

Nominated Adviser:	Smith & Williamson, London	
AIM Broker:	Seymour Pierce, London	
Solicitors:	Berwin Leighton Paisner, London	
Market Makers:	KBCS; MLSB; SCAP; WINS	
Auditors:	Rees Pollock, 7 Pilgrim Street, London EC4V 6DR	
Registrars:	Capita Registrars	

ENTRY ON AIM:	4/9/2000	**Recent price:**	6.1p
Interim results:	Oct	**Market cap:**	£4.06m
Final results:	Jun	**Issue price:**	2.0p
Year end:	Dec	**Current no of shares:**	
Accounts due:	Jun		66,550,643
Int div paymnt:	n/a	**No of shares after**	
Fin div paymnt:	n/a	**dilution:**	n/a
Int net div per share:	nil	**P/E ratio:**	n/a
Fin net div per share:	nil	**Probable CGT?**	Yes

LATEST REPORTED RESULTS:	2002	**PREVIOUS REPORTED RESULTS:**	2001
Turnover:	£13.7m	Turnover:	£839,000
PTP:	£(578,000)	PTP:	£(4.39m)
EPS:	(0.1)p	EPS:	(0.6)p

NWF   (NWF)
Animal feed manufacturer, grocery & fuel distributor, retailer
Wardle, Nantwich, Cheshire CW5 6BP Tel: 01829-260260; Fax: 01829-261042; e-mail: nwf@nwf.co.uk; web site: www.nwf.co.uk

		holding %
Chairman	J Roy Willis	2.2
Chief Executive	Graham R Scott	0.2
Finance Director	Alan E Fulker	1.0
Non-Exec Director	Mark H Hudson	1.5

Main Shareholders:

n/a

Percentage of free market capital: 94.5%

Comments:

Rising insurance and pension costs dragged on first half profits at NWF, the growing diversified sales and distribution play. Interims to 30 November showed flat profits of £1.5m. Turnover rose 17% to £89.3m on higher fuel volumes and prices. NWF's standout performances came from its distribution and fuels businesses. However, analysts at the house broker have pared back the full year profit forecast to £5.05m due to expected lower profits from feeds.

Nominated Adviser:	Charles Stanley, London	
AIM Broker:	Charles Stanley, London	
Solicitors:	Brabners Chaffe Street, Liverpool	
Market Makers:	ARBT; WINS	
Auditors:	KPMG, Preston	
Registrars:	Capita Registrars	

Entry on AIM:	25/9/1995	**Recent price:**	485.0p
Interim results:	Jan	**Market cap:**	£38.61m
Final results:	Aug	**Issue price:**	285.0p
Year end:	May	**Current no of shares:**	
Accounts due:	Sep		7,961,123
Int div paymnt:	May	**No of shares after**	
Fin div paymnt:	Nov	**dilution:**	8,166,335
Int net div per share:	4.0p	**P/E ratio:**	11.6
Fin net div per share:	10.8p	**Probable CGT?**	Yes

LATEST REPORTED RESULTS:	2003	**PREVIOUS REPORTED RESULTS:**	2002
Turnover:	£168.55m	Turnover:	£154.74m
PTP:	£5.05m	PTP:	£4.21m
EPS:	41.9p	EPS:	36.7p

OAK (formerly AWG Services) (OAH)

Property developers, consultants and managers

15 Half Moon Street, W1J 7AT Tel: 020-7493 5522; Fax: 020-7493 5022; e-mail: michael.will@oakholdings.co.uk

		holding %
Executive Chairman	Malcolm Savage	11.1
Chief Executive	Stephen Lewis	7.1
Finance Director	Michael Hill	0.4
Deputy Chairman	Stephen Thomson	0.8

Main Shareholders:

Productive Nominees	22.1
David Medloch	4.7

Percentage of free market capital: 33.9%

Comments:
Formerly known as AWG Services, this company is now a revitalised beast with encouraging prospects having sold its narrowboat operations and reversed property development company Oak into the shell. Oak's plan is to develop mixed-use leisure based schemes and create a revenue generating property consultancy business. Its key project is to develop a 327-acre Rotherham industrial site into a state-of-the-art leisure centre.

Nominated Adviser:	City Financial Associates, London
AIM Broker:	Fiske, London
Solicitors:	Jones Day Gouldens, London
Market Makers:	KBCS; SCAP; WINS
Auditors:	Hazlewoods, Gloucester
Registrars:	Computershare Investor Services

ENTRY ON AIM:	26/2/1997	**Recent price:**	2.0p
Interim results:	Jul	**Market cap:**	£13.08m
Final results:	Apr	**Issue price:**	100.0p
Year end:	Oct	**Current no of shares:**	
Accounts due:	Jun		653,948,279
Int div paymnt.	n/a	**No of shares after**	
Fin div paymnt:	n/a	**dilution:**	n/a
Int net div per share:	nil	**P/E ratio:**	n/a
Fin net div per share:	nil	**Probable CGT?**	Yes

LATEST REPORTED RESULTS: 2003		PREVIOUS REPORTED RESULTS: 2002	
Turnover:	£86,000	**Turnover:**	£76,000
PTP:	£119,000	**PTP:**	£(781,000)
EPS:	(0.1)p	**EPS:**	(0.5)p

Oakgate (formerly PrimeEnt) (OKG)

Media company

Hampton House, 20 Albert Embankment, London, SE1 7TJ Tel: 020-7468 3443; Fax: 020-7468 3455

		holding %
Chairman		
Chief Operating Officer	Rudolf Irminger	0.0
Finance Director	Richard Prickett	0.5
Non-Exec Director		

Main Shareholders:

Xerius	29.9
Maurice Gould	29.9
Philip Reid	4.1

Percentage of free market capital: 35.6%

Comments:
Much speculation has surrounded this cash shell in 2004. The last press comment surrounded the possibility that the group was due to complete the acquisition of various nickel interests in the Philippines. This prompted the directors to report that they were indeed in negotiations although none of the deals they were looking at were at an advanced stage. A clear case of 'watch this space'.

Nominated Adviser:	Beaumont Cornish, London
AIM Broker:	Hichens Harrison, London
Solicitors:	Stringer Saul, London
Market Makers:	HOOD; MLSB; SCAP; WINS
Auditors:	Ernst & Young, 1 Lambeth Palace Road, London, SE1 7EU
Registrars:	Melton Registrars

Entry on AIM:	19/11/1999	**Recent price:**	28.0p
Interim results:	Dec	**Market cap:**	£2.41m
Final results:	Sep	**Issue price:**	6.0p
Year end:	Jun	**Current no of shares:**	
Accounts due:	Oct		8,596,679
Int div paymnt:	n/a	**No of shares after**	
Fin div paymnt:	n/a	**dilution:**	n/a
Int net div per share:	nil	**P/E ratio:**	n/a
Fin net div per share:	nil	**Probable CGT?**	No

LATEST REPORTED RESULTS: 18 MONTHS TO 31 DEC 01		PREVIOUS REPORTED RESULTS: 2000	
Turnover:	£7.86m	**Turnover:**	£2.44m
PTP:	£(16.43m)	**PTP:**	£(1.46m)
EPS:	(2.2)p	**EPS:**	(0.3)p

Oasis Healthcare (OSH)

Dental care service provider

59 St Benedict's Street, Norwich, NR2 4PQ Tel: 01603-625335; Fax: 01603-629512; e-mail: info@oasis-healthcare.com;
web site: www.oasis-healthcare.co.uk

		holding %
Chairman	Ronald Trenter	1.9
Chief Executive	Malcolm Hughes	0.8
Finance Director	Jeremy Clark	0.01
Deputy Chairman	Joseph King*	5.7

Main Shareholders:

Singer & Friedlander Investment Management	11.3
Advent VCT	9.2
Proven Private Equity	8.2
BWD Aim VCT	4.3
Guinness Flight Venture Capital Trust	4.1

Percentage of free market capital: 50.1%

*These share are held in the J & A King retirement benefit scheme

Comments:

After buying rival Dencare's 36 practices for £19.6m, Oasis wants to consolidate its acquisitions and create an efficient high-margin dental care group. The 127 dental practices generate £73m in annual turnover. However, gearing stands at more than 250% and the group has warned that turnover will be 3% below expectations, thus restricting pre-tax profit before amortisation to £1.2m this year. Interim turnover doubled to £36.7m.

Nominated Adviser:	Oriel Securities, London
AIM Broker:	Oriel Securities, London
Solicitors:	Eversheds, Norwich
Market Makers:	KBCS; SCAP; WINS
Auditors:	PricewaterhouseCoopers, Norwich
Registrars:	Capita Registrars

Entry on AIM:	27/7/2000	**Recent price:**	18.75p
Interim results:	Dec	Market cap:	£15.31m
Final results:	Jun	Issue price:	25.0p
Year end:	Mar	Current no of shares:	
Accounts due:	Jul		81,646,122
Int div paymnt:	n/a	No of shares after	
Fin div paymnt:	n/a	dilution:	n/a
Int net div per share:	nil	P/E ratio:	n/a
Fin net div per share:	nil	Probable CGT?	Yes

LATEST REPORTED RESULTS:	2003	PREVIOUS REPORTED RESULTS:	2002
Turnover:	£46.87m	Turnover:	£22.8m
PTP:	£(2.27m)	PTP:	£(13,000)
EPS:	(2.5)p	EPS:	(0.4)p

Ocean Power Technologies (OPT)

Developer of renewable offshore wave-powered electricity generators

1590 Reed Road, Pennington, New Jersey, 08534 United States

		holding %
Chairman	Eric Ash	0.2
Chief Executive	George Taylor	25.0
Financial Director	Charles Dunleavy	5.5
Non-Exec Director	Seymour Preston III	0.2

Main Shareholders:

JoAnne Burns	12.8
Boston Equities Corp	6.4

Percentage of free market capital: 49.9%

Comments:

OPT is developing an off-shore wave-powered electrical generation system called 'PowerBuoy'. October's float raised £22.4m. These systems allow the efficient production of non-polluting electricity generated by waves in the sea. Maiden figures for the six months to October showed net losses of $3.6m (£2.1m) on revenues up 121% to $2.44m (£1.4m). Sales primarily came from its deal installing PowerBuoys at a US Marine Corps base off the island of Oahu in Hawaii.

Nominated Adviser:	Evolution Beeson Gregory, London
AIM Broker:	Evolution Beeson Gregory, London
Solicitors:	Hale & Dorr, London
Market Makers:	WINS
Auditors:	Deloitte & Touche, New Jersey, USA
Registrars:	Computershare Investor Services

Entry on AIM:	31/10/2003	**Recent price:**	95.5p
Interim results:	Sep	Market cap:	£19.95m
Final results:	Jul	Issue price:	125.0p
Year end:	Apr	Current no of shares:	
Accounts due:	Oct		20,891,554
Int div paymnt:	n/a	No of shares after	
Fin div paymnt:	n/a	dilution:	n/a
Int net div per share:	nil	P/E ratio:	n/a
Fin net div per share:	nil	Probable CGT?	Yes

LATEST REPORTED RESULTS:	2003	PREVIOUS REPORTED RESULTS:	2002
Turnover:	£2.55m	Turnover:	£1.38m
PTP:	£(820,000)	PTP:	£(3.92m)
EPS:	(0.0)p	EPS:	(0.1)p

Ocean Resources Capital

(OCE)

Investment company
Ocean House, 10-12 Little Trinity Lane, London, EC4V 2DH

		holding %
Chairman	Peter Seabrook	0.0
Chief Executive	David Hutchins	0.0
Finance Director		
Exec Director	Merfyn Roberts	0.0

Main Shareholders:

Deutsche Bank AG	12.5
Laxey Partners	11.7
GNI LIMITED	11.7
RAB Capital	11.7
Credit Lyonnias Securities	10.6
Percentage of free market capital: 25.1%	

Nominated Adviser:	Insinger English Trust, London
AIM Broker:	Keith Bayley Rogers, London
Solicitors:	Stallard, London
Market Makers:	WINS
Auditors:	Chantrey Vellacott, London
Registrars:	Capita Registrars

ENTRY ON AIM:	28/2/2003	**Recent price:**	30.0p
Interim results:	Sep	**Market cap:**	£25.57m
Final results:	Mar	**Issue price:**	50.0p
Year end:	Dec	**Current no of shares:**	
Accounts due:	Jun		85,240,978
Int div paymnt:	n/a	**No of shares after**	
Fin div paymnt:	n/a	**dilution:**	n/a
Int net div per share:	nil	**P/E ratio:**	n/a
Fin net div per share:	nil	**Probable CGT?**	No

LATEST REPORTED RESULTS: INTERIM RESULTS TO 30 JUN '03		PREVIOUS REPORTED RESULTS:	N/A
Turnover:	£629,000	Turnover:	n/a
PTP:	£(9.88m)	PTP:	n/a
EPS:	(11.7)p	EPS:	n/a

Comments:

Resource-oriented share swap group Ocean recently claimed its portfolio, including Archipelago Resources, was worth 41p, putting its shares on a 27% discount. Pausing from swaps, Ocean, a volatile performer now seeking to help investee companies raise funds elsewhere, has links with financier Willie West's MoneyGuru. Chief executive David Hutchins has spoken of tapping German interest with a Frankfurt quote.

OFEX

(OFX)

Operator of a market for trading securities
1 Goodman's Yard, London, E1 8AT Tel: 020-7423 0800; Fax: 020-7423 0841; e-mail: enquiries@ofex.com; web site: www.ofex.com

		holding %
Chairman	John Jenkins	29.9
Joint Managing Director	Emma Jenkins	16.8
Finance Director		
Joint Managing Director	Jonathan Jenkins	15.5

Main Shareholders:

Luke Johnson	6.3
Percentage of free market capital: 30.8%	

Nominated Adviser:	Seymour Pierce, London
AIM Broker:	Seymour Pierce, London
Solicitors:	Field Fisher Waterhouse, London
Market Makers:	KBCS; SCAP; WINS
Auditors:	Deloitte & Touche, London
Registrars:	Capita Registrars

Entry on AIM:	30/4/2003	**Recent price:**	27.25p
Interim results:	Oct	**Market cap:**	£5.87m
Final results:	Mar	**Issue price:**	25.0p
Year end:	Dec	**Current no of shares:**	
Accounts due:	May		21,532,701
Int div paymnt:	n/a	**No of shares after**	
Fin div paymnt:	n/a	**dilution:**	n/a
Int net div per share:	nil	**P/E ratio:**	n/a
Fin net div per share:	nil	**Probable CGT?**	No

LATEST REPORTED RESULTS:	2003	PREVIOUS REPORTED RESULTS:	2002
Turnover:	£1.10m	Turnover:	£909,000
PTP:	£(535,000)	PTP:	£(720,000)
EPS:	(3.3)p	EPS:	(14.0)p

Comments:

The tertiary trading facility has introduced an 'expedited route to market' facility to encourage internationally listed companies to join OFEX as well. This will offer 'truly cost-effective access to trading in London... without any superfluous bureaucracy'. This development follows a £1m fundraising to introduce a competing market maker system. Winterfloods, Teather & Greenwood and Hoodless Brennan now make markets alongside JP Jenkins Ltd. Former AIM head Simon Brickles works part time for OFEX.

Offshore Hydrocarbon Mapping   (OHM)

Oil & gas exploration company

The Technology Centre, Offshore Technology Park, Bridge of Don, Aberdeen, AB23 Tel: 0870-429 6581;
Fax: 0870-429 6582

		holding %
Chairman	Pierre Jungels	0.6
Chief Executive	David Pratt	0.1
Finance Director	Garry Allan	0.0
Chief Scientific Officer	Lucy MacGregor	5.4

Main Shareholders:

East Hill	24.7
Southampton Asset Management	24.5
IP2IPO Management	15.9
BNY	6.5
Sulis Seedcorn Fund	4.7

Percentage of free market capital: 5.4%

Nominated Adviser:	KBC Peel Hunt, London
AIM Broker:	KBC Peel Hunt, London
Solicitors:	Masons, London
Market Makers:	WINS
Auditors:	BDO Stoy Hayward, Southampton
Registrars:	Capita Registrars

ENTRY ON AIM:	11/3/2004	**Recent price:**	211.0p
Interim results:	Jun	**Market cap:**	£61.19m
Final results:	Dec	**Issue price:**	170.0p
Year end:	Aug	**Current no of shares:**	
Accounts due:	Jan		28,997,939
Int div paymnt:	n/a	**No of shares after**	
Fin div paymnt:	n/a	**dilution:**	n/a
Int net div per share:	nil	**P/E ratio:**	n/a
Fin net div per share:	nil	**Probable CGT?**	No

LATEST REPORTED RESULTS: 2003		PREVIOUS REPORTED RESULTS: PERIOD ENDED 31 AUG '02	
Turnover:	£1.61m	**Turnover:**	£116,000
PTP:	£(362,000)	**PTP:**	£(83,000)
EPS:	(0.0)p	**EPS:**	(0.0)p

Comments:
AIM newcomer Offshore Hydrocarbon Mapping provides remote electromagnetic sensing services to detect offshore oil and gas. Set up to commercialise research carried out at Southampton University's Oceanography Centre, the company undertook its first commercial survey for a 'major' US oil group, with which it now has a contract to provide deep water exploration services.

Oilexco   (OIL)

Oil & gas explorer

Suite 3200, 715-5th Avenue, SW Calgary, Alberta, T2P 2X6 Canada,

		holding %
Chairman	Don Copeland	0.0
Chief Executive	Arthur Millholland	0.0
Finance Director	Brian Ward	0.0
Director	John Cowan	0.0

Main Shareholders:

n/a

Percentage of free market capital: 100%

Nominated Adviser:	Canaccord Capital, London
AIM Broker:	Canaccord Capital, London
Solicitors:	McCarthy Tetrault, London
Market Makers:	SCAP; WINS
Auditors:	Deloitte & Touche, Calagary, Alberta, Canada T2P 0S7
Registrars:	Computershare Investor Services

Entry on AIM:	23/1/2004	**Recent price:**	91.5p
Interim results:	Sep	**Market cap:**	£54.44m
Final results:	Mar	**Issue price:**	n/a
Year end:	Dec	**Current no of shares:**	
Accounts due:	May		59,500,688
Int div paymnt:	n/a	**No of shares after**	
Fin div paymnt:	n/a	**dilution:**	n/a
Int net div per share:	nil	**P/E ratio:**	n/a
Fin net div per share:	nil	**Probable CGT?**	No

LATEST REPORTED RESULTS: 2002		PREVIOUS REPORTED RESULTS: 2001	
Turnover:	$1.27m	**Turnover:**	$1.48m
PTP:	$(1.65m)	**PTP:**	£(1.48m)
EPS:	(0.1)c	**EPS:**	(0.1)c

Comments:
Toronto-quoted oil and gas explorer Oilexco has performed strongly since December's AIM introduction. The Calgary-based company has a three-well drilling programme in licence P1042 in the UK North Sea. This includes the 'Brenda' oil find in the Moray Firth, where production testing is scheduled after finding 'excellent reservoir characteristics'.

OMG   (OMG)

Supplier of electronics and software products

14 Minns Business Park, West Way, Oxford, OX2 0JB Tel: 01865-261800; Fax: 01865-240527; e-mail: omg@omg3d.com;
web site: www.omg3d.com

		holding %
Chairman	Anthony Simonds-Gooding	0.1
Chief Executive	Julian Morris	28.6
Finance Director	Peter Wharton	1.6
Director	Catherine Robertson	1.3

Main Shareholders:

Herald Investment Trust	8.8
Peter Walton	6.9
Graham Klyne	4.4
Thomas Shannon	3.9
Martin Wood	3.9

Percentage of free market capital: 34.4%

Nominated Adviser:	Smith & Williamson, London
AIM Broker:	Evolution Beeson Gregory, London
Solicitors:	Taylor Joynson Garrett, London
Market Makers:	TEAM; WINS
Auditors:	Grant Thornton, 1 Westminster Way, Oxford OX2 0PZ
Registrars:	Capita Registrars

ENTRY ON AIM:	10/4/2001	**Recent price:**	24.0p
Interim results:	Jun	**Market cap:**	£12.62m
Final results:	Dec	**Issue price:**	75p
Year end:	Sep	**Current no of shares:**	
Accounts due:	Jan		52,582,875
Int div paymnt:	n/a	**No of shares after**	
Fin div paymnt:	n/a	**dilution:**	59,423,080
Int net div per share:	nil	**P/E ratio:**	n/a
Fin net div per share:	nil	**Probable CGT?**	YES

LATEST REPORTED RESULTS: 2003		PREVIOUS REPORTED RESULTS: 2002	
Turnover:	£9.76m	Turnover:	£8.04m
PTP:	£891,000	PTP:	£(1.80m)
EPS:	1.7p	EPS:	(3.2)p

Comments:

OMG is a visual effects and motion capture specialist, supplying its wares to the film, medical, scientific and engineering trade. Its results for the year to September 2003 showed a dramatic turnaround, with sales to the Japanese entertainment market soaring and US sales improving 54%. The focus this year will be to capitalise on this revival and to exploit the potential of its products in the engineering and consumer markets.

On-Line   (ONL)

Internet games developer and internet services

Crown House, Linton Road, Barking, Essex IG11 8HJ Tel: 020-8591 1125; Fax: 020-8591 0110;
e-mail: davidc@on-line.co.uk; web site: www.on-line.co.uk

		holding %
Chairman	Michael Hodges	19.4
Managing Director	as above	
Finance Director	David Crump	1.4
Non-Exec Director	Clement Chambers	23.7

Main Shareholders:

Peter Reilly	3.4

Percentage of free market capital: 49.5%

Nominated Adviser:	Grant Thornton, London
AIM Broker:	Hoodless Brennan, London
Solicitors:	Field Fisher Waterhouse, London
Market Makers:	DURM; HOOD; MLSB; SCAP; WINS
Auditors:	Grant Thornton, 21 Dyke Rd, Brighton, Sussex BN1 3GD
Registrars:	Capita Registrars

Entry on AIM:	18/12/1996	**Recent price:**	57.5p
Interim results:	Mar	**Market cap:**	£4.39m
Final results:	Dec	**Issue price:**	100.0p
Year end:	Jun	**Current no of shares:**	
Accounts due:	Oct		7,642,348
Int div paymnt:	n/a	**No of shares after**	
Fin div paymnt:	n/a	**dilution:**	n/a
Int net div per share:	nil	**P/E ratio:**	n/a
Fin net div per share:	nil	**Probable CGT?**	YES

LATEST REPORTED RESULTS: 2003		PREVIOUS REPORTED RESULTS: 2002	
Turnover:	£205,000	Turnover:	£2.32m
PTP:	£(1.51m)	PTP:	£(2.37m)
EPS:	(19.4)p	EPS:	(42.5)p

Comments:

The main interest in this venture is its 28% stake in financial website operator ADVFN, which is apprently cashflow profitable now. It also owns 78% of AKAEI, a cash shell that could be on the verge of completing an interesting deal. All its other operations have been closed down.

OneClickHR (OCR)

Designer and developer of human resource and personnel software

2 Bromley Road, Beckenham, Kent BR3 5JE Tel: 020-8663 4586; Fax: 020-8663 4550; e-mail: info@oneclickhR.com; web site: www.oneclickHR.com

		holding %
Chairman	Lord Sheppard	5.9
Managing Director	Frank Beechinor	14.0
Finance Director	Angus Dent	0.3
Technical Director	Peter Sedman	15.5

Main Shareholders:

Jeremy White	13.7
Herald Investment Management	9.0
Close Brothers Investment	5.4
Legal & General	3.6
3i Asset Management	3.6

Percentage of free market capital: 23.3%

Comments:

Though human resources software developer OneClick generated a small first half profit of £64,000, management admits that full year figures will disappoint. Analysts had expected a £100,000 profit from £5.5m of sales for the 12-month period, but with many prospective clients still deferring their buying decisions the company says a £500,000 loss is more realistic. Meanwhile, negotiations with a swathe of international distributors are said to be underway.

Nominated Adviser:	Hawkpoint Partners, London
AIM Broker:	Collins Stewart, London
Solicitors:	Nellen, London
Market Makers:	CHMM; CSCS; WINS
Auditors:	PricewaterhouseCoopers, Maidstone
Registrars:	Capita Registrars

Entry on AIM:	16/5/2000	**Recent price:**	6.75p
Interim results:	Aug	**Market cap:**	£3.93m
Final results:	May	**Issue price:**	40.0p
Year end:	Dec	**Current no of shares:**	
Accounts due:	Mar		58,233,673
Int div paymnt:	n/a	**No of shares after**	
Fin div paymnt:	n/a	**dilution:**	n/a
Int net div per share:	nil	**P/E ratio:**	n/a
Fin net div per share:	nil	**Probable CGT?**	Yes

LATEST REPORTED RESULTS:	2002	**PREVIOUS REPORTED RESULTS:**	2001
Turnover:	£4.69m	**Turnover:**	£5.65m
PTP:	£(3.47m)	**PTP:**	£(2.28m)
EPS:	(6.4)p	**EPS:**	(4.5)

Online Travel (ONT)

Internet-based travel agent

Fraser House, 15 London Road, Twickenham, Middlesex TW1 3ST Tel: 0870–887 0100; Fax: 020-8288 0006; e-mail: robertf@otctravel.co.uk; web site: www.onlinetravelcorporation.com

		holding %
Chairman	Tommaso Zanzotto	0.1
Managing Director	Mark Jones	1.9
Finance Director	Mark Simpkins	0.0
Exec Director	Andreas Ekkeshis	0.4

Main Shareholders:

FMR Corp. & Fidelity	6.1
Artemis	8.46
Gartmore	6.6
UBS	3.8
Pension Services	3.8
Herald Investment	3.8
GNI Limited	3.4

Percentage of free market capital: 43.6%

Comments:

The web-based travel agent OTC is recommending lastminute.com's offer priced at 31p a share. This values OTC at £54.9m. Last year was tough for the travel sector, yet OTC managed to expand its business and strengthen its foundations. The company enjoyed 23% growth in gross sales at £104.9m, whilst sales in the leisure division rose 40% to £71.4m. Before exceptional items and web development costs, the company made an EBITDA of £1m.

Nominated Adviser:	Altium Capital, London
AIM Broker:	Altium Capital, London
Solicitors:	Marriott Harrison, London
Market Makers:	DURM; WINS
Auditors:	Baker Tilly, 2 Bloomsbury Street, London WC1B 3ST
Registrars:	LLoyds TSB Registrars

Entry on AIM:	20/6/2000	**Recent price:**	26.25p
Interim results:	Jul	**Market cap:**	£46.56m
Final results:	Jan	**Issue price:**	60.0p
Year end:	Oct	**Current no of shares:**	
Accounts due:	Feb		177,382,128
Int div paymnt:	n/a	**No of shares after**	
Fin div paymnt:	n/a	**dilution:**	n/a
Int net div per share:	nil	**P/E ratio:**	n/a
Fin net div per share:	nil	**Probable CGT?**	Yes

LATEST REPORTED RESULTS:	2003	**PREVIOUS REPORTED RESULTS:**	2002
Turnover:	£86.50m	**Turnover:**	£70.24m
PTP:	£(5.94m)	**PTP:**	£(3.03m)
EPS:	(4.4)p	**EPS:**	(2.7)p

Optimisa (formerly bizzbuild.com)

(OPS)

Cash shell

1st Floor, Roxburghe House, Regent Street, London, W1B 2HA

		holding %
Chairman	Ronald Littleboy	14.6
Chief Executive	as above	
Finance Director	Peter Holmes	4.6

Main Shareholders:

Schweco Nominees	16.1
Paddy International	14.1
D Homes	7.2
Darcina corp	4.8
Alessandro Pio Falcone	4.2

Percentage of free market capital: 19.9%

Comments:

Optimisa has retained a low profile since changing its name from bizzbuild in June 2003. The future continues to look fairly bleak, however, with the plan going forward apparently being (rather familiarly) to invest in under-valued companies. Aside from that, and the fact that the company has a £14m tax write-off available to it, there is currently little more to say.

Nominated Adviser:	Noble, London
AIM Broker:	Noble, London
Solicitors:	Simmons & Simmons, London
Market Makers:	DURM; KBCS; WINS
Auditors:	Baker Tilly, 2 Bloomsbury Street, London WC1B 3ST
Registrars:	Capita Registrars

ENTRY ON AIM:	21/3/2000	Recent price:	222.5p
Interim results:	Sep	Market cap:	£0.79m
Final results:	Apr	Issue price:	250.0p
Year end:	Dec	Current no of shares:	
Accounts due:	Aug		356,066
Int div paymnt:	n/a	No of shares after	
Fin div paymnt:	n/a	dilution:	n/a
Int net div per share:	nil	P/E ratio:	n/a
Fin net div per share:	nil	Probable CGT?	YES

LATEST REPORTED RESULTS:	2002	PREVIOUS REPORTED RESULTS:	2001
Turnover:	n/a	Turnover:	£10,000
PTP:	£(123,000)	PTP:	£(4.74m)
EPS:	(59.5)p	EPS:	(23.6)p

Orad Hi-Tec Systems

(OHT)

TV production technology developer and distributor

PO Box 2177, Kfar Saba 44425, Israel

		holding %
Chairman	Lucien Bronicki*	0.0
Chief Executive	Avi Sharir	11.4
Financial Director	Sarit Sagiv	0.0
Executive Vice Pres	Dr Michael Tamir	11.4

Main Shareholders:

ISMM Participation B V	22.9
Ormat Industries	16.0

Percentage of free market capital: 38.3%

*Lucien Bronicki is chairman of Ormat and is interested in those shares

Comments:

Orad is a developer and distributor of 3D graphic solutions for the broadcasting and advertising markets. Its third quarter results were encouraging, with revenues improving 20% to $12.3m and margins lifting from 55% to 63%. The net loss was reduced from $7.2m to $3.8m. The improvement has been due to an array of contract wins – the most recent with the French Lottery for two of its CyberGraphics systems.

Nominated Adviser:	Shore Capital, London
AIM Broker:	Shore Capital, London
Solicitors:	Berwin Leighton Paisner, London
Market Makers:	LEHM; SCAP; WINS
Auditors:	Kost, Forer & Gabbay, Tel Aviv
Registrars:	n/a

Entry on AIM:	16/7/2003	Recent price:	96.5p
Interim results:	Aug	Market cap:	£10.28m
Final results:	Mar	Issue price:	88.0p
Year end:	Dec	Current no of shares:	
Accounts due:	May		10,650,726
Int div paymnt:	n/a	No of shares after	
Fin div paymnt:	n/a	dilution:	n/a
Int net div per share:	nil	P/E ratio:	n/a
Fin net div per share:	nil	Probable CGT?	No

LATEST REPORTED RESULTS:	2002	PREVIOUS REPORTED RESULTS:	2001
Turnover:	$14.51m	Turnover:	$16.18m
PTP:	$(9.72m)	PTP:	$(20.91m)
EPS:	(0.8)c	EPS:	n/a

Orbis   (OBS)

Property management & services provider
106 Oxford Road, Uxbridge, UB8 1NA Tel: 01895-465500; Fax: 01895-465499; e-mail: info@uk.orbis-opp.com

		holding %
Chairman	John Leach	0.0
Chief Executive	Michael Holmes	0.0
Finance Director	John Jukes	0.0
Exec Director	Michael Warriner	0.0

Main Shareholders:

A Riches	5.2
BBC Pension Trust	4.6
H Capital Trust	4.3
S Bowie	3.3

Percentage of free market capital: 61.3%

Nominated Adviser:	Close Brothers, London
AIM Broker:	Collins Stewart, London
Solicitors:	Ashursts, London
Market Makers:	CSCS; EVO; KBCS; MLSB; SCAP; WINS
Auditors:	KPMG Audit, London
Registrars:	Capita Registrars

ENTRY ON AIM:	26/9/2003	Recent price:	16.25p
Interim results:	Nov	Market cap:	£2.27m
Final results:	Jul	Issue price:	20.25p
Year end:	Mar	Current no of shares:	
Accounts due:	Aug		13,984,640
Int div paymnt:	n/a	No of shares after	
Fin div paymnt:	n/a	dilution:	n/a
Int net div per share:	nil	P/E ratio:	n/a
Fin net div per share:	nil	Probable CGT?	Yes

LATEST REPORTED RESULTS:	2003	PREVIOUS REPORTED RESULTS:	2002
Turnover:	£43.08m	Turnover:	£43.94m
PTP:	£(7.33m)	PTP:	£(8.43m)
EPS:	(4.3)p	EPS:	(5.5)p

Comments:
Orbis, yet another main board migrant, clears and cleans empty properties and tidies up estates. It has restructured and new long-term banking arrangements have been agreed. In the first half to September underlying profits came in at £200,000 (£600,000) on continuing turnover of £20m (£21.3m), though Orbis lost £1.95m after exceptionals and amortisation. Encouragingly, strong cash management generated £4m of cash inflow.

Oriel Resoures   (ORI)

Mining company
18 Upper Brook Street, London, W1K 7QF Tel: 020-7514 0590

		holding %
Chairman	Sergey Kurzin	5.3
Chief Executive	as above	
Finance Director		
Exploration Director	Edward Baker	1.3

Main Shareholders:

Pinnacle Trustees	9.6
Aran Asset Management	5.6
Barham Investment	4.4
Morstan Nominees	3.1

Percentage of free market capital: 68.8%

Nominated Adviser:	Canaccord Capital, London
AIM Broker:	Canaccord Capital, London
Solicitors:	Stringer Saul, London
Market Makers:	WINS
Auditors:	BDO Stoy Hayward, 8 Baker Sreet, London W1U 3LL
Registrars:	Computershre Investor Services

Entry on AIM:	11/3/2004	Recent price:	76.0p
Interim results:	Sep	Market cap:	£122.16m
Final results:	Mar	Issue price:	65.0p
Year end:	Dec	Current no of shares:	
Accounts due:	Apr		160,733,336
Int div paymnt:	n/a	No of shares after	
Fin div paymnt:	n/a	dilution:	n/a
Int net div per share:	nil	P/E ratio:	n/a
Fin net div per share:	nil	Probable CGT?	No

LATEST REPORTED RESULTS:	2003	PREVIOUS REPORTED RESULTS:	2002
Turnover:	n/a	Turnover:	n/a
PTP:	£(10,000)	PTP:	£(9,000)
EPS:	n/a	EPS:	n/a

Comments:
Canaccord raised £40.6m at 65p for Oriel, founded by entrepreneurs Sergey Kurzin and Stephen Dattels, a veteran of Barrick Gold, Caledon Resources and others, to acquire mineral deposits in Russia and other ex-Soviet states. It now has one nickel project at Sevchenko in Kazakhstan and three gold plays, at Arup in the Kurile Islands, Togoluk in Kyrgystan (an option) and 14% of Varinskoye in Kazakhstan.

Osmetech

(OMH)

Medical devices developer and supplier

12 St James's Square, London, SW1 6WZ Tel: 020-7849 6027; Fax: 0270-216030; e-mail: info@osmetech.plc.uk

		holding %
Chairman	Gordon Hall	0.1
Chief Executive	James White	0.2
Financial Director	David Sandilands	0.1
Non-Exec Director	Gordon Kuenster	0.1

Main Shareholders:

Chase Nominees	4.6
T D Waterhouse Nominees	4.5
Sharelink Nominees	4.2
The AGUK Small Cap Fund	4.1
Barclayshare Nominees	3.5

Percentage of free market capital: 75.4%

Nominated Adviser:	Evolution Beeson Gregory, London
AIM Broker:	Evolution Beeson Gregory, London
Solicitors:	Ashursts, London
Market Makers:	BGMM; KBCS; KLWT; MLSB; SCAP; TEAM; WINS
Auditors:	BDO Stoy Hayward, Manchester
Registrars:	Capita Registrars

ENTRY ON AIM:	3/10/2002	Recent price:	4.0p
Interim results:	Jan	Market cap:	£23.23m
Final results:	Jul	Issue price:	2.0p
Year end:	Apr	Current no of shares:	
Accounts due:	Sep		580,669,488
Int div paymnt:	n/a	No of shares after	
Fin div paymnt:	n/a	dilution:	n/a
Int net div per share:	nil	P/E ratio:	n/a
Fin net div per share:	nil	Probable CGT?	YES

LATEST REPORTED RESULTS: 2003		PREVIOUS REPORTED RESULTS: 2002	
Turnover:	£686,000	Turnover:	£41,000
PTP:	£(3.83m)	PTP:	£(4.71m)
EPS:	(0.9)p	EPS:	(1.6)p

Comments:

The developer of 'e-nose' technology has transformed its business by buying the OPTI range of blood gas analysers from Roche. The pharma giant also took a stake in Osmetech. The OPTIs have been selling well, helped by demand from SARS-ridden China. Interim losses were reduced by 75% to £0.55m as sales hit £3.5m. A deal is being sought for the e-noses, which effectively 'sniff' the gases given off by bacteria as they metabolise. Other acquisitons are also being considered.

OverNet Data (suspended 20 Oct 2003)

(OND)

Cash shell

Middlesex House, 34-42 Cleveland Street, London, W1T 4JE Tel: 08453-308 706; Fax: 020-7291 3701;
e-mail: info@overnetdata.com; web site: www.overnetdata.com

		holding %
Chairman	Leo Knifton	0.0
Chief Executive		
Finance Director	David Tilston	1.1
Director	Nigel Weller	0.0

Main Shareholders:

Monument	43.9
Peter Bullen	25.2
Artemis AIM VCT	4.6
James Laurence	4.2

Percentage of free market capital: 14.3%

Nominated Adviser:	City Financial, London
AIM Broker:	Arbuthnot, London
Solicitors:	Speechly Bircham, London
Market Makers:	KBCS; MLSB; SCAP; WINS
Auditors:	KPMG, 8 Salisbury Square, London, EC4Y 8BB
Registrars:	Capita Registrars

Entry on AIM:	27/7/2000	Recent price:	11.0p
Interim results:	Sep	Market cap:	£1.01m
Final results:	Jun	Issue price:	115.0p
Year end:	Dec	Current no of shares:	
Accounts due:	Apr		9,155,648
Int div paymnt:	n/a	No of shares after	
Fin div paymnt:	n/a	dilution:	15,022,886
Int net div per share:	nil	P/E ratio:	n/a
Fin net div per share:	nil	Probable CGT?	YES

LATEST REPORTED RESULTS: 2002		PREVIOUS REPORTED RESULTS: 2001	
Turnover:	£80,000	Turnover:	164,000
PTP:	£(1.41m)	PTP:	£(2.2m)
EPS:	(56.0)p	EPS:	(92.3)p

Comments:

Trading in OverNet's shares was suspended in early October when management announced that the company was on the verge of completing a reverse takeover. Back in October they revealed that negotiations with a third party had begun and though these talks were eventually aborted a rival offer emerged with respect to which heads of terms have been agreed. At the time of writing further details had yet to emerge.

Oxus Gold (formerly Oxus Mining) (OXS)

Gold miner

105 Piccadilly, London, W1J 7NJ Tel: 020-7907 2000; Fax: 020-7907 2001; e-mail: oxus@oxusgold.co.uk;
web site: www.oxusgold.co.uk

		holding %
Chairman	Michael Beckett	0.03
Chief Executive	William Trew	2.9
Finance Director	Jonathan Kipps	1.4
Exec Director	Richard Shead	0.8

Main Shareholders:

MAED	17.9
Capital Group	6.0
MLIIF World Gold Fund	5.7
Carmignac Gestion	3.6

Percentage of free market capital: 58.4%

Nominated Adviser:	Williams de Broe, London
AIM Broker:	Williams de Broe, London
Solicitors:	CMS Cameron McKenna, London
Market Makers:	ARBT; KBCS; SCAP; WINS
Auditors:	BDO Stoy Hayward, Isle of Man
Registrars:	Capita Registrars

ENTRY ON AIM:	4/7/2001	Recent price:	57.75p
Interim results:	Mar	Market cap:	£130.18m
Final results:	Sep	Issue price:	30.0p
Year end:	Jun	Current no of shares:	
Accounts due:	Sep		225,411,704
Int div paymnt:	n/a	No of shares after	
Fin div paymnt:	n/a	dilution:	n/a
Int net div per share:	nil	P/E ratio:	n/a
Fin net div per share:	nil	Probable CGT?	No

LATEST REPORTED RESULTS: 18 MONTHS TO 30 JUN '03		PREVIOUS REPORTED RESULTS: 2001	
Turnover:	$762,000	Turnover:	$177,000
PTP:	$(2.82m)	PTP:	$(1.57m)
EPS:	(1.7)c	EPS:	(2.4)c

Comments:

Oxus came off the boil after peaking on the £4m float of its Marakand zinc arm. Headed by South African Bill Trew, whose MAED construction group has a big stake, Oxus has trebled estimated Uzbekistan gold reserves to 61m oz, where production has started at the Amantaytau oxide mine. July's feasibility report permitting, building a more significant sulphide mine could start in October.

Oystertec (OYS)

Designer and developer of pipe connectors

Ground Floor, Kemutec House, Springwood Way, Tytherington, Macclesfield, SK10 2AD Tel: 01625-430351;
Fax: 01625-430552; e-mail: sales@oystertec.com; web site: www.oystertec.com

		holding %
Chairman	Angus Monro	1.5
Chief Executive	Andrew Evans	0.04
Finance Director	Adrian Binney	1.1
Non-Exec Director	Roger McDowell	0.1

Main Shareholders:

Fidelity International	13.0
Stanlife Nominees	8.1
Stanley Fraser	4.8
Ennismore Fund Management	4.8
Threadneedle Investments	4.1

Percentage of free market capital: 58.2%

Nominated Adviser:	Collins Stewart, London
AIM Broker:	Collins Stewart, London
Solicitors:	Berg & Co, Manchester
Market Makers:	CSCS; SCAP; WINS
Auditors:	Ernst & Young, 100 Barbirolli Square, Manchester M2 3EY
Registrars:	Lloyds TSB Registrars

Entry on AIM:	21/2/2001	Recent price:	19.5p
Interim results:	Sep	Market cap:	£48.9m
Final results:	Mar	Issue price:	23.0p
Year end:	Dec	Current no of shares:	
Accounts due:	Mar		250,782,606
Int div paymnt:	n/a	No of shares after	
Fin div paymnt:	n/a	dilution:	274,744,783
Int net div per share:	nil	P/E ratio:	n/a
Fin net div per share:	nil	Probable CGT?	Yes

LATEST REPORTED RESULTS: 2002		PREVIOUS REPORTED RESULTS: 2001	
Turnover:	£112.43m	Turnover:	£6.62m
PTP:	£465,000	PTP:	£(11.27m)
EPS:	0.0p	EPS:	(8.2)p

Comments:

The fluid connections developer beat forecasts with 2003 numbers in bleak markets. Trading profits were £5.8m, a turnaround from losses of £1.6m. IBP has enjoyed a fantastic profit turnaround in two years, from losses of £6.1m to a £6.7m profit, as has Europower, from losses of £1.1m to a £400,000 profit in under two years. And both are cash generative. Oystertec continues to invest in its licensing division where it has a number of products in advanced testing stages.

Palladex (PLX)

Gold & silver explorer

30 Farringdon Street, London, EC4A 4HJ Tel: 020-7544 5677; Fax: 020-7544 5565; e-mail: johnb@sghlaw.com;
web site: www.palladex.co.uk

		holding %
Chairman	Simon Village	1.5
Chief Executive	Merlin Marr-Johnson	6.8
Finance Director	John Bottomley	0.2
Technical Director	Dasha Longley-Sinitsyna	6.6

Main Shareholders:

Morstan Nominees	14.3
Willbro Nominees	3.2

Percentage of free market capital: 61.1%

Comments:
Merlin Marr-Johnson, 32, former Rio Tinto geologist and HSBC commodities trader, heads Palladex, a speculative venture which aims to develop two deposits in Kyrgystan, reckoned to contain between three and 5.6 million oz of gold. He argues both deposits, Karakala and Aksur, might show larger resources than presently estimated.

Nominated Adviser:	WH Ireland, London
AIM Broker:	WH Ireland, London
Solicitors:	Atlantic Law, London
Market Makers:	WINS
Auditors:	BDO Stoy Hayward, London
Registrars:	Capita Registrars

ENTRY ON AIM:	2/2/2004	**Recent price:**	24.5p
Interim results:	Jun	**Market cap:**	£15.13m
Final results:	Dec	**Issue price:**	20.0p
Year end:	Sep	**Current no of shares:**	
Accounts due:	Mar		61,742,960
Int div paymnt:	n/a	**No of shares after**	
Fin div paymnt:	n/a	**dilution:**	n/a
Int net div per share:	nil	**P/E ratio:**	n/a
Fin net div per share:	nil	**Probable CGT?**	No

LATEST REPORTED RESULTS:	2003	PREVIOUS REPORTED RESULTS:	N/A
Turnover:	n/a	Turnover:	n/a
PTP:	$(356,000)	PTP:	n/a
EPS:	(0.3)c	EPS:	n/a

Palmaris Capital (PMS)

Gold and coal mining investor

Patterson Building, Gartsherrie Road, Coatbridge, ML5 2EU Tel: 01236-440410; Fax: 01236-421467;
e-mail: pattersons.quarries@btinternet.com

		holding %
Chairman	Timothy Noble	1.2
Managing Director	Greg Melgaard*	18.2
Finance Director	Jim Richardson**	24.3

Main Shareholders:

Waverton	33.2
Patersons Quarries	30.8
PDFM	16.9
UBS Asset Management	10.8
Anthony Doulton	5.4

Percentage of free market capital: 31.4%

*Greg Melgaard's holding represents that of Waverton
**Jim Richardson's holding includes that of Patersons Quarries

Comments:
Palmaris, which cut its annual loss from £842,500 to £248,100 and boosted net assets 40% to 11.7p, has caught favour with 23% of Mining Scotland, despite falling recent output, on hopes that world demand will boost coal prices. A 26% stake in Australian gold prospector Perseverance looks promising on prospects at Fosterville in Victoria. In Palmaris's previous incarnation as Waverley Mining, the shares briefly topped £1.

Nominated Adviser:	Noble & Co, London
AIM Broker:	Noble & Co, London
Solicitors:	Shepherd & Wedderburn, Edinburgh
Market Makers:	MLSB; WINS
Auditors:	Scott-Moncrieff, 17 Melville Street, Edinburgh EH3 7PH
Registrars:	Capita Registrars

Entry on AIM:	15/1/2000	**Recent price:**	11.75p
Interim results:	Mar	**Market cap:**	£15.32m
Final results:	Nov	**Issue price:**	n/a
Year end:	Jun	**Current no of shares:**	
Accounts due:	Dec		130,344,504
Int div paymnt:	n/a	**No of shares after**	
Fin div paymnt:	n/a	**dilution:**	n/a
Int net div per share:	nil	**P/E ratio:**	n/a
Fin net div per share:	nil	**Probable CGT?**	No

LATEST REPORTED RESULTS:	2003	PREVIOUS REPORTED RESULTS:	2002
Turnover:	£4.87m	Turnover:	£4.28m
PTP:	£(248,000)	PTP:	£(843,000)
EPS:	(0.2)p	EPS:	(0.7)p

Pan Andean Resources (PRE)

Oil and gas producer and explorer

162 Clontarf Road, Clontarf, Dublin 3, Ireland Tel: 00-353 1 833 2833; Fax: 00-353 1 833 3505; e-mail: panand@iol.ie;
web site: www.panandeanresources.com

		holding %
Chairman	John Teeling	0.5
Managing Director	David Horgan	0.8
Finance Director	Jim Finn	0.1

Main Shareholders:

Scoti	4.6
RBSTB Nominees	3.9
BNY Gil Client Account Nominees	3.5

Percentage of free market capital: 86.6%

Nominated Adviser:	Rowan Dartington, Bristol
AIM Broker:	Rowan Dartington, Bristol
Solicitors:	McEvoy & Partners, Dublin
Market Makers:	KBCS; MLSB; SCAP; WINS
Auditors:	Deloitte & Touche, Earlsfort Terrace, Dublin 2
Registrars:	Computershare Investor Services

Comments:

Ever-volatile, Pan Andean, yet another company from the stable of Irish wheeler-dealer John Teeling, has been pleasing recovery punters with drilling reports from its Danbury Dome leases in Texas. The company, which made an interim £301,000 pre-tax, has 21% of the Vrazel offshore Texas well, where Teeling claims recent drilling has 'enhanced prospectivity'.

Entry on AIM:	28/9/1995	Recent price:	17.25p
Interim results:	Dec	Market cap:	£17.1m
Final results:	Sep	Issue price:	18.0p
Year end:	Mar	Current no of shares:	
Accounts due:	Oct		99,121,979
Int div paymnt:	n/a	No of shares after	
Fin div paymnt:	n/a	dilution:	106,691,979
Int net div per share:	nil	P/E ratio:	n/a
Fin net div per share:	nil	Probable CGT?	No

LATEST REPORTED RESULTS: 2003		PREVIOUS REPORTED RESULTS: 2002	
Turnover:	£4.02m	Turnover:	£3.85m
PTP:	£360,000	PTP:	£(365,000)
EPS:	0.3p	EPS:	(0.4)p

Parallel Media (PAA)

International golf and executive sports rights and marketing business

56 Ennismore Gardens, Knightsbridge, London, SW7 1AJ Tel: 020-7225 2000; Fax: 020-7761 6933;
web site: www.worldsportgroup.com

		holding %
Chairman	David Ciclitira	21.1
Managing Director	Graham Axford	1.3
Finance Director		
Non-Exec Director	Jonathon Crisp	0.017

Main Shareholders:

Ronald Littleboy	14.6
Walbrook	10.1
Seymour Pierce	5.3
Merrill Lynch & Co	4.7
Bizzbuild	3.9

Percentage of free market capital: 33.3%

Nominated Adviser:	City Financial Associates, London
AIM Broker:	City Financial Associates, London
Solicitors:	Denton Wilde Sapte, London
Market Makers:	IHCS; KBCS; MLSB; SCAP; WINS
Auditors:	BDO Stoy Hayward, 8 Baker Street, London W1M 1DA
Registrars:	Capita Registrars

Comments:

The executive sports rights and marketing business is in talks to acquire World Sport Group's interests in 50/50 joint venture Asian PGA Tour. Incidentally, the interim statement to June 2003 was the first formal report from the group since disposing of the World Sport Group businesses. These revealed narrower losses of £2.1m (£7.9m) on a turnover of £2.1m (£12.8m). In other developments, PMG has restructured its board, promoting key internal people.

Entry on AIM:	6/1/1999	Recent price:	4.0p
Interim results:	Mar	Market cap:	£0.89m
Final results:	Dec	Issue price:	n/a
Year end:	Jan	Current no of shares:	
Accounts due:	Dec		22,205,444
Int div paymnt:	n/a	No of shares after	
Fin div paymnt:	n/a	dilution:	n/a
Int net div per share:	nil	P/E ratio:	n/a
Fin net div per share:	nil	Probable CGT?	Yes

LATEST REPORTED RESULTS: PERIOD TO 22 JAN '03		PREVIOUS REPORTED RESULTS: 6 MONTHS TO 30 DEC '01	
Turnover:	£30.28m	Turnover:	£18.46m
PTP:	£(11.63m)	PTP:	£(77.23m)
EPS:	(136.5)p	EPS:	(845.5)p

Paramount (PMN)

Restaurant chain operator

15 Grosvenor Gardens, London SW1W 0BD Tel: 020-7828 3983; Fax: 020-7828 1992; web site: www.dawnayday.com

		holding %
Chairman	Guy Naggar	10.0
Chief Executive	Nick Basing	0.2
Finance Director	R Elman	0.2
Non-Exec Director	D Hudd	0.1

Main Shareholders:

JO Hambro	70.7
P Klimt	9.9

Percentage of free market capital: 8.6%

Nominated Adviser:	Evolution Beeson Gregory, London
AIM Broker:	Evolution Beeson Gregory, London
Solicitors:	Bircham Dyson Bell, London
Market Makers:	DURM; EVO; KBCS; MLSB; WINS
Auditors:	BDO Stoy Hayward, 8 Baker Street, London W1M 1DA
Registrars:	Capita Registrars

ENTRY ON AIM:	15/5/2003	**Recent price:**	26.0p
Interim results:	Nov	**Market cap:**	£20.75m
Final results:	May	**Issue price:**	18.0p
Year end:	Sep	**Current no of shares:**	
Accounts due:	Jun		79,823,266
Int div paymnt:	n/a	**No of shares after**	
Fin div paymnt:	n/a	**dilution:**	n/a
Int net div per share:	nil	**P/E ratio:**	n/a
Fin net div per share:	nil	**Probable CGT?**	**YES**

LATEST REPORTED RESULTS: PERIOD ENDED 29 JUNE '03		PREVIOUS REPORTED RESULTS: 2002	
Turnover:	£6.67m	Turnover:	n/a
PTP:	£(760,000)	PTP:	£26,000
EPS:	(2.0)p	EPS:	0.4p

Comments:

Paramount looks set to return to profitability. Over the six-week period to January like-for-like sales increased 5.7% compared to a negative trend for the previous year. Last year Paramount, a cash shell, bought the Chez Gerard business, which included the Chez Gerard, Livebait, Cafe Fish and Bertorelli brands. After selling five of its restaurants (and closing one unprofitable establishment) during the year, the remaining 20 restaurants are now all cash positive.

Parkdean Holidays (PDH)

Holiday park operator in the UK

One Gosforth ParkWay, Gosforth Busines Park, Newcastle upon Tyne, NE12 8ET Tel: 0191-256 0700; Fax: 0191-268 6004; e-mail: ashleydickinson@parkdeanholidays.com; web site: www.parkdean.com

		holding %
Chairman	Graham Wilson	1.5
Chief Executive	John Waterworth	1.5
Finance Director	Michael Norden	0.2
Non-Exec Director	David Stonehouse	0.1

Main Shareholders:

Deutsche Asset Management	12.0
Artemis	10.5
ISIS	9.3
Merrill Lynch	9.3
Framlington	8.7

Percentage of free market capital: 32.7%

Nominated Adviser:	Charles Stanley, London
AIM Broker:	Charles Stanley, London
Solicitors:	Dickinson Dees, Newcastle upon Tyne
Market Makers:	MLSB; WINS
Auditors:	Ernst & Young, Newcastle upon Tyne
Registrars:	Capita Registrars

Entry on AIM:	30/5/2002	**Recent price:**	226.5p
Interim results:	Jun	**Market cap:**	£89.32m
Final results:	Jan	**Issue price:**	100.0p
Year end:	Oct	**Current no of shares:**	
Accounts due:	Jan		39,433,260
Int div paymnt:	Sep	**No of shares after**	
Fin div paymnt:	Mar	**dilution:**	n/a
Int net div per share:	2.0p	**P/E ratio:**	13.6
Fin net div per share:	3.0p	**Probable CGT?**	**YES**

LATEST REPORTED RESULTS: 2003		PREVIOUS REPORTED RESULTS: 2002	
Turnover:	£53.58m	Turnover:	£43.66m
PTP:	£8.98m	PTP:	£3.43m
EPS:	16.7p	EPS:	12.9p

Comments:

Parkdean continues to impress as advanced bookings on a like-for-like basis remain 10% ahead of last year. Short breaks at its 14 sites start from £75 per week, while a six-berth caravan commands up to £875 per week. The company is investing £9m in a capital expenditure programme this year including the creation of 125 new pitches – the equivalent of a new park – and it will refurbish its retail and leisure facilities. Pre-tax profits for 2004 are expected to improve £100,000 to £9.1m.

Patagonia Gold (formerly HPD Exploration)   (PGD)
Gold explorer
15 Upper Grosvenor Street, London, W1K 7PJ Tel: 020-7409 7444

		holding %
Chairman	Richard Prickett	3.8
Chief Executive	William Humphries	3.8
Finance Director	Gonzalo Tanoira	1.7
Deputy Chairman	Carlos Miguens	15.3

Main Shareholders:

Maria Miguens	7.1
Diego Miguens	6.3
Christina Miguens	6.3

Percentage of free market capital: 55.7%

Nominated Adviser:	Seymour Pierce, London
AIM Broker:	Seymour Pierce, London
Solicitors:	Lawrence Graham, London
Market Makers:	SCAP; WBM; WINS
Auditors:	KPMG Audit, 8 Salisbury Square, London EC4Y 8BB
Registrars:	Melton Registrars

Entry on AIM:	5/3/2003	Recent price:	14.5p
Interim results:	Jun	Market cap:	£32.52m
Final results:	Dec	Issue price:	14.0p
Year end:	Sep	Current no of shares:	
Accounts due:	May		224,281,435
Int div paymnt:	n/a	No of shares after	
Fin div paymnt:	n/a	dilution:	n/a
Int net div per share:	nil	P/E ratio:	n/a
Fin net div per share:	nil	Probable CGT?	No

Comments:
Patagonia is the re-named HPD Exploration, spun out of the successful Brancote mining group, which bought out its 50% Argentine partners, the Miguens-Bemberg family, for shares. Patagonia, which lost £1.7m last year, claims drilling at Cerro Crespo in Agentina indicates 'a significant new epithermal gold discovery' and has drilled 'encouraging' gold and silver intercepts at Cohaique in Chile. Risky but potentially rewarding.

LATEST REPORTED RESULTS: 2002		PREVIOUS REPORTED RESULTS: 2001	
Turnover:	n/a	Turnover:	n/a
PTP:	£(213,000)	PTP:	£(60,000)
EPS:	(0.2)p	EPS:	(0.1)p

Pathfinder Properties   (PFP)
Property refurbisher & developer
Capital House, Michael Road, London, SW6 2YH Tel: 020-7736 9669; Fax: 020-7736 1771;
e-mail: office@pathfinderplc.com; web site: www.pathfinderplc.co.uk

		holding %
Chairman	John Parry	0.03
Chief Executive		
Finance Director	Malcolm Bacchus	0.3
Non-Exec Director	George A Heggie	0.4

Main Shareholders:

Pathfinder Recovery Ventures	13.2
Sunnyview	12.5
Value Investments	3.0

Percentage of free market capital: 70.5%

Nominated Adviser:	Nabarro Wells, London
AIM Broker:	Teather & Greenwood, London
Solicitors:	Masons, London
Market Makers:	SCAP; TEAM; WINS
Auditors:	Baker Tilly, 2 Bloomsbury Street, London WC1B 3ST
Registrars:	Capita Registrars

Entry on AIM:	25/3/1997	Recent price:	14.25p
Interim results:	Sep	Market cap:	£11.4m
Final results:	Jun	Issue price:	17.0p
Year end:	Dec	Current no of shares:	
Accounts due:	Mar		79,971,939
Int div paymnt:	Oct	No of shares after	
Fin div paymnt:	n/a	dilution:	n/a
Int net div per share:	0.25p	P/E ratio:	n/a
Fin net div per share:	nil	Probable CGT?	No

Comments:
Pathfinder has had a rollercoaster time culminating in the dismissal of the board following the successful attempt by the Azouz brothers and Guy Davies to replace them. The company also had a number of parties interested in acquiring it but all discussions have now terminated. It recently sold 2.7 acres of its Newark site for £2.45m and it will start development of its £37m end-value scheme in River Quarter, Manchester in Spring following an acceptable offer of finance.

LATEST REPORTED RESULTS: 2002		PREVIOUS REPORTED RESULTS: 2001	
Turnover:	£15.39m	Turnover:	£527,000
PTP:	£(112,000)	PTP:	£(1.27m)
EPS:	(0.1)p	EPS:	(1.3)p

Patsystems (PTS)

Financial software developer

22 Shand Street, London, SE1 2ES Tel: 020-7940 0490; Fax: 020-7940 0499; e-mail: investorrelations@patsystems.com;
web site: www.patsystems.com

		holding %
Chairman	Stewart Millman	0.2
Chief Executive	Kevin Ashby	1.3
Finance Director	Richard Cooper	0.2
Non-Exec Director	Stewart Douglas-Mann	0.3

Main Shareholders:

Lindy Theys Oostman	13.8
Societe Europeene D'acquisitions Financiere SA	11.7
HSBC	9.4
Artemis	8.3
Hargreave Hale	5.9

Percentage of free market capital: 45.7%

Nominated Adviser:	Seymour Pierce, London
AIM Broker:	Seymour Pierce, London
Solicitors:	Jones Day Gouldens, London
Market Makers:	INV; KBCS; KLWT; WINS
Auditors:	PricewaterhouseCoopers, 1 Embankment Place, London WC2N 6RH
Registrars:	Computershare Investor Services

Entry on AIM:	17/2/2003	Recent price:	24.75p
Interim results:	Jun	Market cap:	£36.18m
Final results:	Mar	Issue price:	4.5p
Year end:	Dec	Current no of shares:	
Accounts due:	May		146,179,597
Int div paymnt:	n/a	No of shares after	
Fin div paymnt:	n/a	dilution:	n/a
Int net div per share:	nil	P/E ratio:	n/a
Fin net div per share:	nil	Probable CGT?	Yes

LATEST REPORTED RESULTS:	2003	PREVIOUS REPORTED RESULTS:	2002
Turnover:	£10.67m	Turnover:	£7.79m
PTP:	£(2.37m)	PTP:	£(9.06m)
EPS:	(1.7)p	EPS:	(7.0)p

Comments:

Patsystems' software is a risk management tool that offers three different levels of sophistication for the derivatives trade. Recent results for last year were vastly improved on 2002 – the company traded profitably in the second half. During the year the group also witnessed a 29 per cent leap in the number of trading system users and a 37 per cent improvement in the number of lots traded through its systems. Broker Seymour Pierce expects profits for 2004 to reach £1.27m.

PC Medics (PMG)

PC support provider

Celtic House, 33 St John's Mews, London, WC1N 2QL Tel: 0870 870 0696; Fax: 020-7242 9111;
e-mail: mail@pc-medics.co.uk; web site: www.pc-medics.co.uk

		holding %
Chairman	Boris Adlam	3.4
Chief Executive	Roger Richardson	15.8
Finance Director	Peter Weller	0.2
Exec Director	Joan Tryzelaar	0.0

Main Shareholders:

Robin Parker	12.5
Ian Shafras	10.2
Richard Marengo	9.7

Percentage of free market capital: 47.8%

Nominated Adviser:	Beaumont Cornish, London
AIM Broker:	WH Ireland, London
Solicitors:	Fladgate Fielder, London
Market Makers:	MLSB; SCAP; WINS
Auditors:	Saffrey Champness, London
Registrars:	Neville Registrars

Entry on AIM:	8/5/2001	Recent price:	0.75p
Interim results:	Dec	Market cap:	£1.89m
Final results:	Jul	Issue price:	2.0p
Year end:	Mar	Current no of shares:	47.8
Accounts due:	Oct		251,851,903
Int div paymnt:	n/a	No of shares after	
Fin div paymnt:	n/a	dilution:	n/a
Int net div per share:	nil	P/E ratio:	n/a
Fin net div per share:	nil	Probable CGT?	Yes

LATEST REPORTED RESULTS:	2002	PREVIOUS REPORTED RESULTS:	2001
Turnover:	£968,000	Turnover:	£712,000
PTP:	£(762,000)	PTP:	£(1.01m)
EPS:	(0.6)p	EPS:	(1.6)p

Comments:

The first half was a dire one for PC Medics' UK business, prompting its attempted sale. When finding a buyer proved unsuccessful, it was put into liquidation. Its new UK subsidiary is Nexus Management, which will mirror the US business model. At the recent AGM, the chairman said losses were cut by 65% in the quarter to December and the company is seeing revenue growth. The company should soon trade profitably month on month.

Peel Holdings   (PEEL)

Property, transport and retail conglomerate

Peel Dome, The Trafford Centre, Manchester, M17 8PL Tel: 0161-629 8200; Fax: 0161-629 8333;
e-mail: nlees@peelholdings.co.uk; web site: www.peelholdings.co.uk

		holding %
Chairman	John Whittaker*	0.2
Managing Director	Peter Scott	0.1
Finance Director	Paul Wainscott	0.0
Non-Exec Director	J Duncan	0.0

Main Shareholders:

Tokenhouse Holdings	63
HSBC Global Nominees	17
Velida Investments	4

Percentage of free market capital: 15.7%

*Mr J Whittaker also has an interest in 41,717,514 ordinary shares as a beneficiary of the JH Whittaker discretionary settlement trust

Comments:

Peel announced healthy interim profits from increased rental income from its Trafford Centre retail centre and a half-year contribution from Clydeport, the £190m Scottish ports concern acquired last year. The group, one of the biggest on AIM by market capitalisation, saw operating profits rise £9m to £54m and turnover increase 24% to £101m. Its 75%-owned Teeside International Airport will see low-cost carrier bmibaby base its aircraft there from March 2004.

Nominated Adviser:	Credit Lyonnais, London		
AIM Broker:	Credit Lyonnais, London		
Solicitors:	Travers Smith Braithwaite, London		
Market Makers:	CLS.; KBCS; WINS		
Auditors:	Binder Hamlyn, Manchester		
Registrars:	Capita Registrars		

ENTRY ON AIM:	27/1/2000	**Recent price:**	875.0p
Interim results:	Dec	**Market cap:**	£1034.22m
Final results:	Jun	**Issue price:**	n/a
Year end:	Mar	**Current no of shares:**	
Accounts due:	Jun		118,196,769
Int div paymnt:	Apr	**No of shares after**	
Fin div paymnt:	Oct	**dilution:**	n/a
Int net div per share:	4.8p	**P/E ratio:**	32.8
Fin net div per share:	10.2p	**Probable CGT?**	No

LATEST REPORTED RESULTS: 2003		PREVIOUS REPORTED RESULTS: 2002	
Turnover:	£161.18m	**Turnover:**	£146.81m
PTP:	£30.15m	**PTP:**	£33.42m
EPS:	26.7p	**EPS:**	34.7p

Peel Hotels   (PHO)

Hotelier

19 Warwick Avenue, London, W9 2PS Tel: 020-7266 1100; Fax: 020-7289 5746; web site: www.peelhotel.com

		holding %
Chairman	Robert Peel	35.2
Managing Director	Norbert Petersen	2.2
Finance Director	John Perkins	0.1
Non-Exec Director	John Govett	2.5

Main Shareholders:

C E W Peel	20.4
JP Morgan Chase	10.5
Merrill Lynch	5.4
Framlington	5.2
David Urquhart	3.7
Galloway	3.3
Schroder	3.1

Percentage of free market capital: 5.5%

Comments:

Peel Hotels owns six hotels in England, the most recent acquisitions being the Avon Gorge Hotel in Bristol and the George Hotel in Wallingford in 2002. It now only manages five hotels on behalf of Grace Hotels. In expectation of the gradual extinction of this revenue, it is looking to lift the profit line in its existing hotels and to that end has moved its administrative office to allow for a conference room to be built at the Golden Lion in Leeds.

Nominated Adviser:	KBC Peel Hunt, London		
AIM Broker:	KBC Peel Hunt, London		
Solicitors:	Nicholson Graham & Jones, London		
Market Makers:	KBCS; WINS		
Auditors:	Deloitte & Touche, 1 Little New St, London EC4A 3TR		
Registrars:	Computershare Investor Services		

Entry on AIM:	23/12/1998	**Recent price:**	91.5p
Interim results:	Sep	**Market cap:**	£11.79m
Final results:	Apr	**Issue price:**	25p
Year end:	Feb	**Current no of shares:**	
Accounts due:	May		12,889,688
Int div paymnt:	n/a	**No of shares after**	
Fin div paymnt:	Jun	**dilution:**	13,318,957
Int net div per share:	nil	**P/E ratio:**	8.4
Fin net div per share:	4.0p	**Probable CGT?**	Yes

LATEST REPORTED RESULTS: 2003		PREVIOUS REPORTED RESULTS: 2002	
Turnover:	£11.0m	**Turnover:**	£8.88m
PTP:	£1.76m	**PTP:**	£1.52m
EPS:	10.9p	**EPS:**	12.1p

Penmc (formerly Kingsbridge) (PNC)

Financial services provider

Kingsbridge House, 15 Castlegate, Nottingham NG1 7AQ Tel: 0115-852 3620; Fax: 0115-947 3042;
e-mail: administrator@kingsbridge.co.uk; web site: www.kingsbridge.co.uk

		holding %
Chairman	Eric Cater	0.1
Chief Executive	Laurie Turnbull	0.0
Finance Director		0.0
Director	Peter McGarvey	2.6

Main Shareholders:

David McKee	11.3
Peter Greswold	4.0
Paul Nash	4.0
Julia Boyes	4.0
David Goddard	3.8

Percentage of free market capital: 56.8%

Nominated Adviser:	Insinger de Beaufort, London
AIM Broker:	Insinger Townsley, London
Solicitors:	Hammonds, Leeds
Market Makers:	TEAM; WINS
Auditors:	Andersen, Manchester
Registrars:	Lloyds TSB Registrars

ENTRY ON AIM:	19/7/2000	Recent price:	0.9p
Interim results:	May	Market cap:	£0.88m
Final results:	Jan	Issue price:	25.0p
Year end:	Aug	Current no of shares:	
Accounts due:	Dec		98,147,196
Int div paymnt:	n/a	No of shares after	
Fin div paymnt:	n/a	dilution:	101502428
Int net div per share:	nil	P/E ratio:	n/a
Fin net div per share:	nil	Probable CGT?	YES

LATEST REPORTED RESULTS:	2003	PREVIOUS REPORTED RESULTS:	2002
Turnover:	£5.33m	Turnover:	£(25.68m)
PTP:	£(7.80m)	PTP:	(25.69m)
EPS:	(7.9)p	EPS:	(26.8)

Comments:

After two horrendous years of trading, the financial adviser that specialises in looking after sports and entertainment stars has sold off its businesses, many of which had been written down severely. This means the group, formerly known as Kingsbridge, is a virtual shell, managed by financier Laurie Turnbull of Texas Holdings. He and his fellow directors are not taking fees at present. The company had net liabilities at the end of September.

Pennant (PEN)

Integrated logistic support solutions

Pennant Ct, Staverton Tech Pk, Cheltenham, GL51 6TL Tel: 01452-714881; Fax: 01452-714882;
e-mail: group@pennantplc.co.uk; web site: www.pennantplc.co.uk

		holding %
Chairman	Christopher Powell	32.2
Chief Executive	Joe Thompson	2.1
Finance Director	John Waller	2.1
Non-Exec Director	Max Pearce	0.2

Main Shareholders:

Rathbone Brothers	14.5
Dartington Nominees	9.1
RBSTB Nominees	6.9
Talbot Nominees	6.6
HSBC Global Nominees	5.8

Percentage of free market capital: 12.2%

Nominated Adviser:	Rowan Dartington, Bristol
AIM Broker:	Rowan Dartington, Bristol
Solicitors:	Charles Russell, Cheltenham
Market Makers:	KBCS; WINS
Auditors:	Hayles Farrar & Partners, Leicester
Registrars:	Capita Registrars

Entry on AIM:	12/3/1998	Recent price:	29.0p
Interim results:	Aug	Market cap:	£9.28m
Final results:	Mar	Issue price:	125.0p
Year end:	Dec	Current no of shares:	
Accounts due:	Mar		32,000,000
Int div paymnt:	n/a	No of shares after	
Fin div paymnt:	n/a	dilution:	n/a
Int net div per share:	nil	P/E ratio:	n/a
Fin net div per share:	nil	Probable CGT?	YES

LATEST REPORTED RESULTS:	2003	PREVIOUS REPORTED RESULTS:	2002
Turnover:	£11.88m	Turnover:	£9.03m
PTP:	£711,000	PTP:	£(1.48m)
EPS:	2.1p	EPS:	(5.3)p

Comments:

Defence training-software developer Pennant has received a further boost through the award of a brace of new contracts. The first, worth up to £4m over three years, is to provide consulting services to the Canadian Department of National Defence. In addition Pennant has been awarded a £2m order to develop a Hawk jet training system for the South African Air Force. The deals add further momentum after Pennant returned to profit in the first half.

Pentagon Protection (PPR)

Developer & supplier of glass-related products to the automotive & other industries

Pentagon House, 44 Action Park Estate, The Vale, Acton, W3 7QE

		holding %
Chairman	David Thomas	32.2
Chief Executive	Graham Bannerman	7.8
Finance Director		
Technical Director	Geoffrey Russell	2.9

Main Shareholders:

Employee Share Benefit Trust	3.6

Percentage of free market capital: 51.3%

Nominated Adviser:	Seymour Pierce, London
AIM Broker:	Seymour Pierce Ellis, London
Solicitors:	Mundays, Surrey
Market Makers:	SCAP; WINS
Auditors:	BDO Stoy Hayward, Epsom
Registrars:	Capita Registrars

ENTRY ON AIM:	2/4/2003	Recent price:	5.9p
Interim results:	May	Market cap:	£7.43m
Final results:	Jan	Issue price:	3.0p
Year end:	Sep	Current no of shares:	
Accounts due:	Mar		125,956,334
Int div paymnt:	n/a	No of shares after	
Fin div paymnt:	n/a	dilution:	n/a
Int net div per share:	nil	P/E ratio:	14.8
Fin net div per share:	nil	Probable CGT?	Yes

LATEST REPORTED RESULTS:		PREVIOUS REPORTED RESULTS:	
	2002		2002
Turnover:	£1.50m	Turnover:	£1.01m
PTP:	£(141,000)	PTP:	£136,000
EPS:	0.4p	EPS:	(0.3)p

Comments:

The maker of protective glazing products to the car, commercial and residential sectors has products that can resist a car thief or protect against bomb blasts. It went public in April 2003 with a £500,000 placing. Its maiden year was one of development and repositioning for future growth, and saw Pentagon swing to a pre-tax loss. In December, the company completed its first acquisition since flotation. Filmtek is an installer of safety, security and solar window film on buildings.

Personal Group (PGH)

Marketer & provider of voluntary employee benefits

John Ormond House, 899 Silbury Boulevard, Central Milton Keynes, MK9 3XL Tel: 01908-605000; Fax: 01908-201711; web site: www.personal-assurance.co.uk

		holding %
Chairman	Christopher Johnson	50.6
Managing Director	as above	0.0
Finance Director	John Barber	0.9
Exec Director	Robert Pease	0.2

Main Shareholders:

Vereinigate Haftpflicht Versicherung VAG	9.4
Refuge Assurance	7.3

Percentage of free market capital: 23.6

Nominated Adviser:	Durlacher, London
AIM Broker:	Durlacher, London
Solicitors:	Howes Percival, Milton Keynes
Market Makers:	KBCS; WINS
Auditors:	Grant Thornton, Central Milton Keynes
Registrars:	Capita Registrars

Entry on AIM:	27/11/2000	Recent price:	181.5p
Interim results:	Sep	Market cap:	£55.44m
Final results:	Mar	Issue price:	n/a
Year end:	Dec	Current no of shares:	
Accounts due:	Apr		30,547,940
Int div paymnt:	Mar	No of shares after	
Fin div paymnt:	Apr	dilution:	n/a
Int net div per share:	1.8p	P/E ratio:	13.8
Fin net div per share:	2.35p	Probable CGT?	Yes

LATEST REPORTED RESULTS:		PREVIOUS REPORTED RESULTS:	
	2002		2001
Turnover:	n/a	Turnover:	n/a
PTP:	£5.61m	PTP:	£4.65m
EPS:	13.2p	EPS:	10.6p

Comments:

Personal, which arranges voluntary employee benefit plans, gives shareholders a curious perk, by paying them three dividends each year. Profitable since 1986, the well-capitalised group lifted its second payout 30% to 5p. Trading is ahead of market expectations. Interim pre-tax profit rose 10% to £2.9m. Personal has over 250,000 policies in force and premiums rarely rise because of the low rate of claims. Clients include employees of the Post Office, Tetley, Northern Foods and more recently Starbucks.

Peter Hambro Mining (POG)

Gold miner and explorer

7 Eccleston Street, Belgravia, London, SW1W 9LX Tel: 020-7393 0102; Fax: 020-7393 0103;
web site: www.peterhambro.com

		holding %
Chairman	Peter Hambro	11.8
Deputy Chairman	Pavel Maslovsky	35.7
Finance Director	Philip Leatham	0.0
Non-Exec Director	Rudolph Agnew	0.01

Main Shareholders:

Nutraco Nominees	8.5
Lansdowne Partners	7.2
G Robert Durham	4.0
State Street Nominees	3.7
Merrill Lynch World Mining Trust	3.4
Percentage of free market capital:	15.8%

Nominated Adviser:	Canaccord Capital, London
AIM Broker:	Canaccord Capital, London
Solicitors:	Norton Rose, London
Market Makers:	KBCS; SCAP; WINS
Auditors:	Moore Stephens, London
Registrars:	Capita Registrars

Entry on AIM:	29/4/2002	**Recent price:**	507.5p
Interim results:	Sept	**Market cap:**	£324.79m
Final results:	Mar	**Issue price:**	130.0p
Year end:	Dec	**Current no of shares:**	
Accounts due:	May		63,998,594
Int div paymnt:	n/a	**No of shares after**	
Fin div paymnt:	n/a	dilution:	n/a
Int net div per share:	nil	P/E ratio:	n/a
Fin net div per share:	nil	**Probable CGT?**	No

LATEST REPORTED RESULTS: 2002		PREVIOUS REPORTED RESULTS: 2001	
Turnover:	$22.77m	Turnover:	$23.72m
PTP:	$9.44m	PTP:	$8.69m
EPS:	n/a	EPS:	n/a

Comments:

A star performer so far, PHM, which made an interim £1.6m pre-tax, has pleased punters by doubling attributable gold production last year to 141,000 oz, most from Pokrovskiy in Russia's Amur region, which consultants say could hold 7.7m oz. Chairman Peter Hambro claims Pioneer in Siberia could be bigger, with a 9.4m oz potential. PHM has sold its titanium interests to AIM newcomer Aricom, where Hambro is a director.

Petra Diamonds (PDL)

Diamond explorer

Building 4, Stratford Office Park, Stratford Road, Lanseria 1748, South Africa, Tel: 00-27 11 467 6710;
Fax: 00- 27 11 467 6725; web site: www.petradiamonds.co.za

		holding %
Chairman	Adonis Pouroulis	0.1
Managing Director	as above	
Finance Director	David Abery	0.02
Chief Operating Officer	David Gadd-Claxton	0.2

Main Shareholders:

n/a

Percentage of free market capital: 93.4%

Nominated Adviser:	Williams de Broe, London
AIM Broker:	Williams de Broe, London
Solicitors:	Addleshaw Goddard, London
Market Makers:	MLSB; WINS
Auditors:	Grant Thornton, 31 Carlton Crescent, Soton SO15 2EW
Registrars:	Capita Registrars

Entry on AIM:	30/4/1997	**Recent price:**	54.0p
Interim results:	Mar	**Market cap:**	£28.08m
Final results:	Oct	**Issue price:**	30.0p
Year end:	Jun	**Current no of shares:**	
Accounts due:	Oct		51,999,976
Int div paymnt:	n/a	**No of shares after**	
Fin div paymnt:	n/a	dilution:	n/a
Int net div per share:	nil	P/E ratio:	n/a
Fin net div per share:	nil	**Probable CGT?**	Yes

LATEST REPORTED RESULTS: 2003		PREVIOUS REPORTED RESULTS: 2002	
Turnover:	n/a	Turnover:	£5,000
PTP:	£(875,000)	PTP:	£(2.28m)
EPS:	(1.8)p	EPS:	(5.2)p

Comments:

Petra announced a 'strategic alliance' with the BHP Billiton mining giant to explore the potential of its Alto Cuilo diamond prospect in Angola and then raised £8m at 50p. BHP is lending £782,000 to Petra, which lost a reduced £875,370 last year, and will convert it to equity if prospects at Alto Cuilo – already partly funded by share and option holder Photon – please. Petra's bid for 51% of South Africa's Alexkorp gem operation is stalled.

Petrel Resources   (PET)
Oil & gas explorer
162 Clontarf Rd, Dublin 3, Ireland, Tel: 00-353 1 833 2833; Fax: 00-353 1 833 3505; e-mail: petrel@iol.ie;
web site: www.petrelresources.com

		holding %
Chairman	John Teeling	6.2
Chief Executive	David Horgan	4.7
Finance Director	Jim Finn	1.7
Director	Guy Delbes	0.3

Main Shareholders:
Gartmore Investment Management   7.5

Percentage of free market capital: 79.6%

Nominated Adviser:	Rowan Dartington, Bristol
AIM Broker:	Rowan Dartington, Bristol;
	Keith, Bayley Rogers, London
Solicitors:	McEvoy & Partners, Dublin
Market Makers:	MLSB; WINS
Auditors:	Deloitte & Touche, Dublin
Registrars:	Computershare Investor Services

Entry on AIM:	18/8/2000	**Recent price:**	30.0p
Interim results:	Sep	**Market cap:**	£16.77m
Final results:	Mar	**Issue price:**	n/a
Year end:	Dec	**Current no of shares:**	
Accounts due:	Apr		55,915,150
Int div paymnt:	n/a	**No of shares after**	
Fin div paymnt:	n/a	**dilution:**	59,160,150
Int net div per share:	nil	**P/E ratio:**	n/a
Fin net div per share:	nil	**Probable CGT?**	No

LATEST REPORTED RESULTS: 2002		PREVIOUS REPORTED RESULTS: 2001	
Turnover:	n/a	**Turnover:**	n/a
PTP:	£(6.53m)	**PTP:**	£(3.46m)
EPS:	(0.5)c	**EPS:**	(0.7)c

Comments:
Another speculative John Teeling resource play, Petrel is a gamble on proposed tenders to develop three oil fields in Iraq, Kirkuk, Hamrin and Subba/Luchais, each with claimed potential of 120,000 barrels a day. Run by Teeling associate David Horgan, Petrel raised £959,000 at 13p to explore 10,000 sq km of Block 6 in Iraq's estern desert. After boycotting the pre-war UN oil-for-food plan, Petrel argues unblushingly it can now go for the big prize.

Petroceltic (formerly Ennex International)   (PCI)
Oil and gas investment
11 Mespil Road, Dublin 4, Tel: + 353 1 667 7310; Fax: + 353 1 667 7311

		holding %
Chairman	Brian Cusack	1.6
Managing Director	John Craven	5.4
Finance Director	Con Casey	0.0
Non-Exec Director	Christian Schaffalitzky	1.3

Main Shareholders:

Graham Wrafter   5.4

Percentage of free market capital: 86.2%

Nominated Adviser:	J&E Davy, Dublin
AIM Broker:	J&E Davy, Dublin
Solicitors:	Whitney Moore & Keller, Dublin
Market Makers:	GBMM; KBCS; MLSB; SCAP; WINS
Auditors:	Ernst & Young, Dublin 2
Registrars:	Computershare Investor Services

Entry on AIM:	26/9/2001	**Recent price:**	8.25p
Interim results:	Sep	**Market cap:**	£36.72m
Final results:	Jun	**Issue price:**	1.5p
Year end:	Dec	**Current no of shares:**	
Accounts due:	Jul		445,082,797
Int div paymnt:	n/a	**No of shares after**	
Fin div paymnt:	n/a	**dilution:**	n/a
Int net div per share:	nil	**P/E ratio:**	n/a
Fin net div per share:	nil	**Probable CGT?**	No

LATEST REPORTED RESULTS: 2002		PREVIOUS REPORTED RESULTS: 2001	
Turnover:	$407,000	**Turnover:**	$11,000
PTP:	$(662,000)	**PTP:**	$(23.12m)
EPS:	(0.3)c	**EPS:**	(10.8)c

Comments:
In true sector style, Petroceltic said it was 'cashed up' after selling its zinc interests for £2.2m and then tapped the market for £4.3m at 5p to fund oil and gas exploration in North Africa. Institutions went for it and Petroceltic, whose founder John Craven sold it in 1996 for £3.3m and later bought it back for £850,000, says Sidi Toui in Tunisia could hold 400m barrels of oil and 160 billion cubic feet of gas. Ksar Hadada in the same region, could be similar.

Photo-Scan (PTO)

Electronic security surveillance systems designer, installer & maintainer
Dolphin Estate, Windmill Road, Sunbury on Thames, Middlesex TW16 7HG Tel: 01932-898500; Fax: 01932-787067;
e-mail: info@photo-scan.com; web site: www.photo-scan.com

		holding %
Chairman	Andrew Nash	0.3
Chief Executive	Peter Hawksworth	0.4
Finance Director	Paul Dinan	0.1
Sales & Mktg Director	David Barrington	0.04

Main Shareholders:

Fortress Finance	16.4
Framlington Investment Management	14.2
Schroder Investment Management	11.8
ISIS Asset Management	11.0
Friends Ivory and Sime	10.7
Percentage of free market capital: 20%	

Nominated Adviser:	Rowan Dartington, Bristol
AIM Broker:	Rowan Dartington, Bristol
Solicitors:	CMS Cameron McKenna, Bristol
Market Makers:	KBCS; WINS
Auditors:	KPMG, Arlington Business Park, Theale, Reading RG7 4SD
Registrars:	Lloyds TSB Registrars

ENTRY ON AIM: 13/10/2000	Recent price:	103.5p
Interim results: Sep	Market cap:	£23.27m
Final results: Mar	Issue price:	n/a
Year end: Dec	Current no of shares:	
Accounts due: Apr		22,481,435
Int div paymnt: Oct	No of shares after	
Fin div paymnt: May	dilution:	22,841,435
Int net div per share: 1.66p	P/E ratio:	8.9
Fin net div per share: 3.85p	Probable CGT?	YES

LATEST REPORTED RESULTS: 2002		PREVIOUS REPORTED RESULTS: 2001	
Turnover:	£24.77m	Turnover:	£18.27m
PTP:	£3.77m	PTP:	£3.65m
EPS:	11.6p	EPS:	10.8p

Comments:

2003 was a transitional year for the security solutions play as it switched strategy. Photo-Scan's sales and profits were temporarily affected by the switch, with both falling last year. Rather than compete for lower margin, low technology sales, Photo-Scan is going for larger scale projects built on client partnerships. The new model seems to be working, evidenced by its 7-year purchase and lease-back deal with NCP and a partnership deal with CrystalEyes.

Pilat Media Global (PGB)

Integrated broadcast management systems
19th Floor, Wembley Point, 1 Harrow Road, Middlesex HA9 6DE Tel: 020-8782 0700; Fax: 020-8782 0701;
e-mail: info@pilatmedia.com; web site: www.pilatmedia.com

		holding %
Chairman	Michael Rosenberg	0.4
Chief Executive	Avi Engel	5.1
Finance Director	Martin Blair	0.3
Non-Exec Director	Samuel Sattath	7.8

Main Shareholders:

Close Brothers	19.2
Michael Zuckerman	7.8
Avigdor Rimmer	5.0
Ronnie Erlichman	4.4
eTechnology VCT	3.5
Percentage of free market capital: 36.5%	

Nominated Adviser:	Shore Capital, London
AIM Broker:	Shore Capital, London
Solicitors:	Olswang, London
Market Makers:	SCAP; WINS
Auditors:	Baker Tilly, 2 Bloomsbury Street, London WC1B 3ST
Registrars:	Capita Registrars

Entry on AIM: 26/2/2002	Recent price:	59.0p
Interim results: Sep	Market cap:	£25.94m
Final results: Mar	Issue price:	20.0p
Year end: Dec	Current no of shares:	
Accounts due: Apr		43,959,344
Int div paymnt: n/a	No of shares after	
Fin div paymnt: n/a	dilution:	47,838,253
Int net div per share: nil	P/E ratio:	n/a
Fin net div per share: nil	Probable CGT?	No

LATEST REPORTED RESULTS: 2002		PREVIOUS REPORTED RESULTS: 2001	
Turnover:	£7.35m	Turnover:	£6.14m
PTP:	£(236,000)	PTP:	£(2.23m)
EPS:	0.1p	EPS:	(7.5)p

Comments:

Since demerging from Pilat Technologies 22 months ago, the integrated broadcast management provider has moved into profit. It now has 28 clients and in the past few months won a contract with Malaysian broadcaster MEASAT worth £1m as well as its largest contract to date with Canadian broadcaster CTV, worth £10m over the next three years. The comany no longer has to pay royalty fees (orginally 11% of its revenue) to BSkyB, for whom it designed the technology.

Pilat Technologies (PIA)

Computer software provider

29 Hendon Lane, London, N3 1PZ Tel: 020-8343 3433; Fax: 020-8343 4656; e-mail: info@pilat.com; web site: www.pilat.com

		holding %
Chairman	Igal Ayal	0.0
Chief Executive	David Sapiro	0.0
Finance Director	Chaim Helfgott	0.049
Director	Avigdon Rimmer	9.6

Main Shareholders:

Michael Zukerman	14.1
Samuel Sattath	13.8
Ronnie Erlichman	10.8
RBSTB Nominees	3.7

Percentage of free market capital: 33.8%

Nominated Adviser:	Westhouse Securities, London
AIM Broker:	Westhouse Securities, London
Solicitors:	Kendall Freeman, London
Market Makers:	IHCS; SCAP; WINS
Auditors:	Zinger, Nir, 120 Igal Alon Street, Tel Aviv 67443, Israel
Registrars:	Capita Registrars

ENTRY ON AIM: 16/12/1996		Recent price:	6.0p
Interim results:	Sep	Market cap:	£1.58m
Final results:	Apr	Issue price:	68.5p
Year end:	Dec	Current no of shares:	
Accounts due:	May		26,279,108
Int div paymnt:	n/a	No of shares after	
Fin div paymnt:	n/a	dilution:	n/a
Int net div per share:	nil	P/E ratio:	n/a
Fin net div per share:	nil	Probable CGT?	YES

LATEST REPORTED RESULTS: 2002		PREVIOUS REPORTED RESULTS: 2001	
Turnover:	£11.48m	Turnover:	£13.84m
PTP:	£(1.48m)	PTP:	£(2.14m)
EPS:	(5.6)p	EPS:	(8.7)p

Comments:

The human resources management consultancy and software group had another challenging year. But it cut costs and made progress towards a return to profitability. In tough markets, PTI scaled back its losses in spite of an 8% drop in sales reflecting the discontinuation of loss-making business. Thankfully revenues were wrought from a large number of customers across the UK, US and Israel – encouragingly there was no dependency on any one single client.

Pilkington's Tiles (PIT)

Ceramic floors and tiles maker

PO Box 4, Rake Lane, Clifton Junction, Manchester, M27 8LP Tel: 0161-727 1000; Fax: 0161-727 1122; e-mail: enquiries@pilkingtons.com; web site: www.tfortiles.co.uk

		holding %
Chairman	Horace Anthony Palmer	0.1
Chief Executive	Mary-Lorraine Hughes	0.2
Finance Director	Mark Hesketh	0.1
Non-Exec Director	David Booth	1.9

Main Shareholders:

David Cicurel*	11.7
Schroder Investments	9.9
Ennismore Fund Management	4.5
Apline Pension Fund	4.4

Percentage of free market capital: 67.3%

*Starlight Investment holds 6.89% of these shares. David Cicurel is a director of this company

Nominated Adviser:	Zeus Capital, Manchester
AIM Broker:	WH Ireland, Manchester
Solicitors:	DLA, Manchester
Market Makers:	ARBT; MLSB; WINS
Auditors:	Ernst & Young, 100 Barbirolli Square, Manchester M2 3EY
Registrars:	Computershare Investor Services

Entry on AIM: 25/4/2002		Recent price:	3.25p
Interim results:	Nov	Market cap:	£6.01m
Final results:	May	Issue price:	5.0p
Year end:	Mar	Current no of shares:	
Accounts due:	Jul		184,948,954
Int div paymnt:	n/a	No of shares after	
Fin div paymnt:	n/a	dilution:	n/a
Int net div per share:	nil	P/E ratio:	n/a
Fin net div per share:	nil	Probable CGT?	YES

LATEST REPORTED RESULTS: 2003		PREVIOUS REPORTED RESULTS: 2002	
Turnover:	£27.37m	Turnover:	£33.48m
PTP:	£(2.70m)	PTP:	£840,000
EPS:	(1.0)p	EPS:	0.4p

Comments:

The tile maker and distributor has made operational improvements but still warned that its profitability for the year will still fall below expectations. Its ceramics businesses, Terrazzo and Access Floor, have improved sales and it closed its Supply & Fix business. Net debt at September was £4.8m. The group recently appointed Zeus Capital as Nomad and WH Ireland as broker. Land held in Poole, Dorset has recently been revalued at between £7m and £14.3m.

PipeHawk (PIP)

Developer of radar products for the construction industry and land mine detection

Systems House, Mill Lane, Alton, Hampshire GU34 2QG Tel: 01420-590990; Fax: 01420-590920;
e-mail: enquiries@pipehawk.com; web site: www.pipehawk.com

		holding %
Chairman	Gordon Watt	14.1
Managing Director	Anthony Norton	0.0
Finance Director		
Technical Director	Richard Chignell	15.2

Main Shareholders:

J Moulton	6.2
David Mahony	5.1
Robert MacDonnell	4.5

Percentage of free market capital: 55%

Comments:

PipeHawk is moving closer to breakeven. For the interim, turnover improved slightly to £571,000, but losses before tax almost halved to £291,000. Having closed its R&D premises in Church Crookham and liquidated Emrad last year, it is now solely focused on four GPR-based businesses. The company's need for working capital is proving very dilutive to its original shareholders. Of the total shares now in issue, 30% has been issued over the last 13 months.

Nominated Adviser:	Grant Thornton, London
AIM Broker:	JM Finn, London
Solicitors:	Lawrence Graham, London
Market Makers:	MLSB; SCAP; WINS
Auditors:	RSM Robson Rhodes, 186 City Road, London EC1V 2NU
Registrars:	Capita Registrars

ENTRY ON AIM:	5/12/2000	**Recent price:**	28.5p
Interim results:	Mar	**Market cap:**	£6.61m
Final results:	Oct	**Issue price:**	52.0p
Year end:	Jun	**Current no of shares:**	
Accounts due:	Oct		23,203,808
Int div paymnt:	n/a	**No of shares after**	
Fin div paymnt:	n/a	**dilution:**	n/a
Int net div per share:	nil	**P/E ratio:**	n/a
Fin net div per share:	nil	**Probable CGT?**	YES

LATEST REPORTED RESULTS: 2003		PREVIOUS REPORTED RESULTS: 2002	
Turnover:	£1.06m	Turnover:	£1.13m
PTP:	£(1.17m)	PTP:	£(1.01m)
EPS:	(6.5)p	EPS:	(7.0)p

PIPEX Communications (formerly GX Networks) (PXC)

Telecommunication service provider

PIPEX House, 4 Falcon Gate, Shire Park, Welwyn Garden City, Hertfordshire AL7 1TW Tel: 0845-077 2455;
Fax: 01707-299502; web site: www.pipex.net

		holding %
Chief Executive	Mike Read	0.0
Finance Director	Stewart Porter	0.02
Vice Chairman	Peter Dubens	19.6
Non-Exec Director	Laurence Blackall	0.0

Main Shareholders:

UBS	17.6
Gartmore	6.6
Jupiter Asset Management	6.0
Close Brothers	5.6

Percentage of free market capital: 33%

Comments:

PIPEX Communications was created after PIPEX Internet reversed into GX Networks, which had been busy consolidating within the fixed line telecoms arena, in a £55m deal. It claims to the fifth largest broadband operator in the UK. The integration of the five acquired businesses are now largely completed and are delivering greater than expected cost savings. For the year to December it states it will be operationally cash generative and EBITDA positive.

Nominated Adviser:	Collins Stewart, London
AIM Broker:	Collins Stewart, London
Solicitors:	Hammonds, London
Market Makers:	CSCS; WINS
Auditors:	KPMG Audit, 1 Puddle Dock, London EC4V 3PD
Registrars:	Capita Registrars

Entry on AIM:	4/7/2000	**Recent price:**	10.5p
Interim results:	Sep	**Market cap:**	£190.06m
Final results:	Jun	**Issue price:**	2.0p
Year end:	Dec	**Current no of shares:**	
Accounts due:	Apr		1,810,072,558
Int div paymnt:	n/a	**No of shares after**	
Fin div paymnt:	n/a	**dilution:**	n/a
Int net div per share:	nil	**P/E ratio:**	3.3
Fin net div per share:	nil	**Probable CGT?**	YES

LATEST REPORTED RESULTS: 2002		PREVIOUS REPORTED RESULTS: 2001	
Turnover:	£8.06m	Turnover:	£3.32m
PTP:	£(11.76m)	PTP:	£(7.48m)
EPS:	3.2p	EPS:	(4.7)p

Pixology (PIX)

Provider of imaging software for the digital photography market

Chancellor Court, 20 Priestley Road, Surrey Research Park, Guildford, Surrey GU2 7YS Tel: 01483-301970;
Fax: 01483-304961; e-mail: info@pixology.com; web site: www.pixology.com

		holding %
Chairman	Lord Young of Graffham	15.6
Chief Executive	Yuval Yashiv	0.8
Finance Director	Edward Issac	0.0
Research Director	Robert Biggs	3.1

Main Shareholders:

3i Group	21.3
Investec	9.7
CDIB Young Associates Capital Partners*	8.0
Threadneedle Investments	7.2
Schroders	3.6
Percentage of free market capital: 21.1%	

Lord Young of Graffham is interested in these shares

Comments:

3i-backed Pixology, which raised £8m on admission, has two main products. One focuses on connectivity – offering consumers the chance to 'print, organise and share' their digital pictures – the other is designed to detect and correct red eye in photographs. A deal with leading photographic retailer Jessops was recently announced and the company hopes to develop a presence both in the Japanese and US markets this year.

Nominated Adviser:	Canaccord Capital, London
AIM Broker:	Canaccord Capital, London
Solicitors:	DLA, London
Market Makers:	EVO; KBCS; WINS
Auditors:	Deloitte & Touche, Reading
Registrars:	Capita Registrars

Entry on AIM:	8/12/2003	**Recent price:**	141.0p
Interim results:	Sep	**Market cap:**	£28.2m
Final results:	Mar	**Issue price:**	140.0p
Year end:	Dec	**Current no of shares:**	
Accounts due:	May		20,000,000
Int div paymnt:	n/a	**No of shares after**	
Fin div paymnt:	n/a	**dilution:**	n/a
Int net div per share:	nil	**P/E ratio:**	n/a
Fin net div per share:	nil	**Probable CGT?**	Yes

LATEST REPORTED RESULTS:		PREVIOUS REPORTED RESULTS:	
	2003		2002
Turnover:	£2.53m	**Turnover:**	£1.55m
PTP:	£(1.92m)	**PTP:**	£(1.93m)
EPS:	(12.7)p	**EPS:**	(17.0)p

Planit (PLN)

Software provider to the woodworking and engineering industries

Inca House, Eureka Science & Business Park, Ashford, Kent TN25 4AB Tel: 01233-635 566; Fax: 01233-645 990;
e-mail: info@planit.com

		holding %
Chairman	Michael Jackson	4.8
Chief Executive	Trevor Semadeni	30.4
Finance Director	Jonathon Lee	0.0
Chief Operating Officer	Bryan Pryce	0.0

Main Shareholders:

Artemis UK Smaller Co Fund	7.8
Southwind	5.3
R A Billett	4.2
Prudential	4.1
Edinburgh Smaller Co Trust	3.4
Percentage of free market capital: 40.1%	

Comments:

Industrial software developer Planit dropped from the Full List to AIM after swinging from profit to loss in 2003. Encouragingly, however, signs of a turnaround are already appearing, December's interims showing a £100,000 increase in pre-tax profits to £742,000 on sales up 24% to £13m. Planit's £6.7m debt pile is a cause for concern to some, yet the presence of Sage chairman Michael Jackson at the helm and forecasts of an intermediate return to full year profit provides reassurance.

Nominated Adviser:	Evolution Beeson Gregory, London
AIM Broker:	Evolution Beeson Gregory, London
Solicitors:	Davies Lavery, Kent
Market Makers:	EVO; KLWT; MLSB; SCAP; WINS
Auditors:	PricewaterhouseCoopers, Gatwick
Registrars:	Capita Registrars

Entry on AIM:	22/1/2004	**Recent price:**	28.5p
Interim results:	Dec	**Market cap:**	£26.16m
Final results:	Jul	**Issue price:**	10.0p
Year end:	Apr	**Current no of shares:**	
Accounts due:	Sep		91,802,429
Int div paymnt:	n/a	**No of shares after**	
Fin div paymnt:	n/a	**dilution:**	92,509,073
Int net div per share:	nil	**P/E ratio:**	n/a
Fin net div per share:	nil	**Probable CGT?**	Yes

LATEST REPORTED RESULTS:		PREVIOUS REPORTED RESULTS:	
	2003		2002
Turnover:	£20.42m	**Turnover:**	£22.35m
PTP:	£(571,000)	**PTP:**	£3.55m
EPS:	(0.6)p	**EPS:**	2.7p

PM (PGP)

On-board vehicle weighing systems maker and servicer

Airedale House, Canal Road, Bradford, BD2 1AG Tel: 01274-771177; Fax: 01274-781178; e-mail: info@pmgroup.plc.uk; web site: www.pmonboard.com

		holding %
Chairman	Kenneth Jackson	0.04
Chief Executive	Geoffrey Mountain	56.9
Finance Director	David Hartley	0.2
Non-Exec Director	Thomas Nairn	0.2

Main Shareholders:

Singer & Friedlander AIM 3 VCT	5.0
BWD Aim VCT	4.0
Close Brothers AIM VCT	3.0

Percentage of free market capital: 30.6%

Nominated Adviser:	Williams de Broe, Leeds
AIM Broker:	Williams de Broe, Leeds
Solicitors:	Hammonds, Leeds
Market Makers:	WDBM; WINS
Auditors:	KPMG, 1 The Embankment, Neville Street, Leeds LS1 4DW
Registrars:	Capita Registrars

ENTRY ON AIM:	2/5/2002	Recent price:	244.0p
Interim results:	Mar	Market cap:	£31.66m
Final results:	Sep	Issue price:	100.0p
Year end:	Jun	Current no of shares:	
Accounts due:	Oct		12,976,051
Int div paymnt:	n/a	No of shares after	
Fin div paymnt:	Nov	dilution:	n/a
Int net div per share:	nil	P/E ratio:	40.7
Fin net div per share:	1.6p	Probable CGT?	YES

LATEST REPORTED RESULTS: 2003		PREVIOUS REPORTED RESULTS: 2002	
Turnover:	£10.05m	Turnover:	£5.78m
PTP:	£1.18m	PTP:	£1.03m
EPS:	6.0p	EPS:	5.3p

Comments:

Interim profits to December rocketed up 31% to £425,000 at this designer and maker of on-board vehicle weighing systems for bulk haulage and waste management. Sales enjoyed a 103% hike to £7.2m. Although the bulk haulage market has remained relatively flat, the waste market has grown in the UK, France, and in Ireland, where PM has won big contracts in Cork and Dublin. The company now has four subsidiaries in Benelux which it is in the midst of rationalising.

PNC Telecom (PTC)

Mobile phone retailer and personal numbering specialist

Cavalino House, Corsley Heath, Warminster, Wiltshre BA12 7PL Tel: 08700-707070; Fax: 08700-707071; e-mail: www.pnctele.com; web site: www.pnctele.com

		holding %
Chairman		
Chief Executive		0.0
Finance Director		
Director	Geremy Thomas	7.6

Main Shareholders:

Strand Nominees	8.9
Darren Ridge	6.5
HSDL Nominees	6.5
Bank of New York Nominees	5.8
Rock Nominees	5.8

Percentage of free market capital: 45.3%

Nominated Adviser:	Seymour Pierce, London
AIM Broker:	Seymour Pierce, London
Solicitors:	Berwin Leighton Paisner, London
Market Makers:	KBCS; SCAP; WINS
Auditors:	RSM Robson Rhodes, 186 City Road, London EC1V 4NU
Registrars:	Capita Registrars

Entry on AIM:	18/12/2002	Recent price:	5.0p
Interim results:	Nov	Market cap:	£2.4m
Final results:	Dec	Issue price:	19.0p
Year end:	Mar	Current no of shares:	
Accounts due:	Apr		48,084,232
Int div paymnt:	n/a	No of shares after	
Fin div paymnt:	n/a	dilution:	n/a
Int net div per share:	nil	P/E ratio:	n/a
Fin net div per share:	nil	Probable CGT?	YES

LATEST REPORTED RESULTS: 2003		PREVIOUS REPORTED RESULTS: 2002	
Turnover:	£52.10m	Turnover:	£58.84m
PTP:	£(10.53m)	PTP:	£(29.83m)
EPS:	(22.3)p	EPS:	(6.3)p

Comments:

PNC began trading on AIM again on 20 January, after the discharge of its administration order. It sold its two trading subsidiaries to Harthall for £2.5m with an additional £1.2m in liabilities. All board members other than non-executive deputy chairman Geremy Thomas have been replaced and the company has £1.4m in cash. Having no ongoing business, it is looking to resolve remaining issues from the disposal and to restore a trading business in a similar field.

Portman (POR)

Iron ore producer

Level 11, The Quadrant, 1 William Street, Perth 6000, Western Australia, Tel: 00-61 8-9426 3333; Fax: 00-61 8-9426 3344; web site: www.portman.com.au

		holding %
Chairman	George Jones	3.6
Managing Director	Barry Eldridge	0.0
Financial Director	Norm Marshall	0.0
Director	Michael Perrott	0.1

Main Shareholders:

Thiess Contractors	13.5
AMP Life	8.1
National Nominees	7.7
ANZ Nominees	5.6
Colonial First State	5.4

Percentage of free market capital: 56%

Comments:

Despite delays in obtaining federal approval for expanding its Koolyanobbing iron ore project in Western Australia, against environmental and Aboriginal opposition, Portman has pleased with near-doubled 2003 profits of £10m and an 18.6% iron ore price hike from this April. The company, which recently launched a share buy-back programme, has upped its Koolyanobbing reserve base to 63.8m tonnes.

Nominated Adviser:	Nabarro Wells, London
AIM Broker:	Canaccord Capital, London
Solicitors:	Blake Dawson Waldron, Perth
Market Makers:	SGSL; WINS
Auditors:	Ernst & Young, 152 St Georges Terrace, Perth WA 6000
Registrars:	Computershare Investor Services

ENTRY ON AIM:	29/1/2001	**Recent price:**	60.5p
Interim results:	Aug	**Market cap:**	£108.82m
Final results:	Feb	**Issue price:**	n/a
Year end:	Dec	**Current no of shares:**	
Accounts due:	Apr		179,862,159
Int div paymnt:	Sep	**No of shares after**	
Fin div paymnt:	Apr	dilution:	n/a
Int net div per share:	Ac4.0	**P/E ratio:**	n/a
Fin net div per share:	Ac6.0	**Probable CGT?**	No

LATEST REPORTED RESULTS: 2003		PREVIOUS REPORTED RESULTS: 2002	
Turnover:	A$145,000	Turnover:	A$129,000
PTP:	A$24.10m	PTP:	A$5.82m
EPS:	9.8c	EPS:	1.9c

Potential Finance (POT)

Finance company for small- & medium-sized businesses

Potential House, 149-157 Kings Road, Brentwood, Essex CM14 4EG Tel: 01277-237177; Fax: 01277-237167; e-mail: info@potentialfinance.com; web site: www.potentialfinance.com

		holding %
Chairman	Frank Lafford	15.9
Chief Executive	Laurence Rutter	6.5
Finance Director	Vivien Ware	0.4
Managing Director	Hugh Craen	6.6

Main Shareholders:

Anthony Jacobs (Non-Exec Director)	14.2
Eaglet Investment Trust	12.3
Erudite	8.2

Percentage of free market capital: 36.1%

Comments:

The SME debtor-financing business blamed bad debts of £1.5m for last year's £1.2m loss. However, the group hopes its new vehicle finance arm will help move it back towards profitability. Potential has now restructured its activities, stripping out bad debts and making several redundancies. Net assets fell 13.5% to £4.5m. The sector is consolidating and Potential hopes to benefit from being an independent player in the market.

Nominated Adviser:	Charles Stanley, London
AIM Broker:	Charles Stanley, London
Solicitors:	Norton Rose, London
Market Makers:	KBCS; MLSB; WINS
Auditors:	Baker Tilly, 2 Bloomsbury Street, London, WC1B 3ST
Registrars:	Capita Registrars

Entry on AIM:	4/8/2000	**Recent price:**	26.5p
Interim results:	Jun	**Market cap:**	£2.78m
Final results:	Dec	**Issue price:**	125p
Year end:	Sep	**Current no of shares:**	
Accounts due:	Jan		10,473,600
Int div paymnt:	n/a	**No of shares after**	
Fin div paymnt:	n/a	dilution:	11,232,748
Int net div per share:	nil	**P/E ratio:**	n/a
Fin net div per share:	nil	**Probable CGT?**	Yes

LATEST REPORTED RESULTS: 2003		PREVIOUS REPORTED RESULTS: 2002	
Turnover:	£3.36m	Turnover:	£3.24m
PTP:	£(1.25m)	PTP:	£173,000
EPS:	(9.8)p	EPS:	3.0p

Premier Direct (PDR)

Direct display marketing

Simonside East Industrial Park, Newcastle Road, Southshields, Tyne & Wear NE34 9AA Tel: 0191-497 4100;
Fax: 0191-497 4101; e-mail: add@pdg.inty.net; web site: www.premierdirectgroup.co.uk

		holding %
Chairman	Jon Pither	8.5
Chief Executive	Barry Moat	25.0
Finance Director	Andrew Dean	0.6
Marketing Director	Eric McClenaghan	10.4

Main Shareholders:

ISIS	6.8
Cantor Fitzgerald	5.0
Kleeneze	4.8
Aberdeen Emerging Companies Unit Trust	4.4
Alan Rankin*	3.3

Percentage of free market capital: 29.5%

*These shares are held by Rock Nominees

Comments:

Premier Direct's formula is a simple one. The company has a team of salespeople who visit offices, hospitals, schools and other workplaces peddling a range of goods from books and toys through to cosmetics. Example products and order forms are left with the organisation for several weeks, with the rep then returning to collect payment and fulfil orders. It is a model that appears to be increasingly successful, with analysts forecasting a £3.9m surplus before tax this year.

Nominated Adviser:		Bridgewell, London	
AIM Broker:		Bridgewell, London	
Solicitors:		Watson Burton, Newcastle	
Market Makers:		SCAP; WINS	
Auditors:		KPMG, Newcastle-upon-Tyne	
Registrars:		Capita Registrars	

Entry on AIM:	5/8/1998	**Recent price:**	684.5p
Interim results:	Apr	**Market cap:**	£27.55m
Final results:	Oct	**Issue price:**	180p
Year end:	Jul	**Current no of shares:**	
Accounts due:	Nov		4,024,851
Int div paymnt:	n/a	**No of shares after**	
Fin div paymnt:	n/a	dilution:	4,025,088
Int net div per share:	nil	**P/E ratio:**	45.9
Fin net div per share:	nil	**Probable CGT?**	Yes

LATEST REPORTED RESULTS:	2003	PREVIOUS REPORTED RESULTS:	2002
Turnover:	£19.37m	**Turnover:**	£14.97m
PTP:	£721,000	**PTP:**	£(690,000)
EPS:	14.9p	**EPS:**	(15.9)p

Premier Management (PMA)

Advisory services

11 Central House, High Street, Ongar, Essex CM5 9AA Tel: 01277-366992; Fax: 01277-369506;
e-mail: pmh@premiermgt.co.uk

		holding %
Chairman	Barry Gold	17.8
Joint Managing	William Jennings	17.9
Director	Gerald Desler	0.4
Finance Director	Stuart Lucas	6.2
Shareholder		

Main Shareholders:

Mark Curtis	17.7
Socgen	7.1
BNY (OCS)Nominees	4.1

Percentage of free market capital: 28.9%

Comments:

The football agent has suffered amid transfer market troubles. But its recent trading statement was bullish. The January transfer window closed strongly after a slow start, with fees up more than 50% compared to the previous year's trading. And though the new financial year kicked off quietly there are good prospects waiting in the wings. Premier Management revealed a drop in interim losses to October from £735,000 to £92,000 on lower turnover of £932,000 (£1.6m).

Nominated Adviser:		Brewin Dolphin, Manchester	
AIM Broker:		Brewin Dolphin, Manchester	
Solicitors:		Nabarro Nathanson, Reading	
Market Makers:		ALTI; WINS	
Auditors:		Gerald Edelman, 25 Harley Street, London W1N 2BR	
Registrars:		Capita Registrars	

Entry on AIM:	20/3/2000	**Recent price:**	5.25p
Interim results:	Dec	**Market cap:**	£1.55m
Final results:	Sep	**Issue price:**	25.0p
Year end:	Apr	**Current no of shares:**	
Accounts due:	Jun		29,440,333
Int div paymnt:	n/a	**No of shares after**	
Fin div paymnt:	n/a	dilution:	n/a
Int net div per share:	nil	**P/E ratio:**	n/a
Fin net div per share:	nil	**Probable CGT?**	Yes

LATEST REPORTED RESULTS:	2003	PREVIOUS REPORTED RESULTS:	2002
Turnover:	£2.14m	**Turnover:**	£1.68m
PTP:	£(4.11m)	**PTP:**	£18,000
EPS:	(15.5)p	**EPS:**	(0.0)p

Prestbury (PBH)

Financial services

Barrington House, Heyes Lane, Alderly Edge, Cheshire SK9 7LA Tel: 01625-591444; Fax: 01625-591567;
web site: www.prestbury.com

		holding %
Chairman	Francis Maude	0.7
Chief Executive	Lee Birkett	48.7
Finance Director	Lynne Birkett	0.0
Chief Operating Officer	Stephen Keenan	16.2

Main Shareholders:

Brit	6.5
New Opportunities Trust	5.5
Principal Corporate Investor	4.3
ISIS	3.9
Laing & Cruickshank	3.8

Percentage of free market capital: 10.3%

Nominated Adviser:	Durlacher, London
AIM Broker:	Durlacher, London
Solicitors:	Dawsons, London
Market Makers:	BGMM; SCAP; WINS
Auditors:	Ford Campbell, Stockport
Registrars:	Melton Registrars

Entry on AIM: 14/10/2002		**Recent price:**	80.5p
Interim results:	May	**Market cap:**	£13.3m
Final results:	Jul	**Issue price:**	80.0p
Year end:	Apr	**Current no of shares:**	
Accounts due:	Aug		16,527,778
Int div paymnt:	n/a	**No of shares after**	
Fin div paymnt:	n/a	**dilution:**	n/a
Int net div per share:	nil	**P/E ratio:**	n/a
Fin net div per share:	nil	**Probable CGT?**	Yes

LATEST REPORTED RESULTS: 2003		PREVIOUS REPORTED RESULTS: 2002	
Turnover:	£4.63m	Turnover:	£2.34m
PTP:	£(2.23m)	PTP:	£(4.76m)
EPS:	(12.8)p	EPS:	£(14.4)

Comments:

Despite doubling turnover Prestbury's losses surged to £2.2m as a result of conservative accounting and delays in processing life insurance applications. The group's deals for its Moneybrain product with the Express and Telegraph newspapers has helped business grow. However, Prestbury has had to set up office infrastructure before the revenue comes in. The group hopes to benefit when the FSA starts to regulate mortgages and life assurance. Last September's placing raised £2.5m at 90p.

Preston North End (PNE)

Professional football club operator

Deepdale Stadium, Sir Tom Finney Way, Preston, Lancashire PR1 6RU Tel: 0870-442 1964; Fax: 01772-693366;
e-mail: enquiries@pnefc.net; web site: www.pnefc.net

		holding %
Chairman	Derek Shaw	29.0
Chief Executive		
Finance Director	Simon Beard	0.0
Deputy Chairman	David W Taylor	0.03

Main Shareholders:

Friends of Preston North End	26.1
Active Capital Trust	20.4
Guild Ventures	12.1

Percentage of free market capital: 12.4%

Nominated Adviser:	WH Ireland, Preston
AIM Broker:	WH Ireland, Preston
Solicitors:	KLegal/McGrigor Donald, London
Market Makers:	KBCS; WINS
Auditors:	KPMG Audit, Edward VII Quay, Preston, Lancs PR2 2YF
Registrars:	Lloyds TSB Registrars

Entry on AIM: 14/9/1995		**Recent price:**	125.0p
Interim results:	Mar	**Market cap:**	£4.12m
Final results:	Sep	**Issue price:**	400.0p
Year end:	Jun	**Current no of shares:**	
Accounts due:	Sep		3,295,692
Int div paymnt:	n/a	**No of shares after**	
Fin div paymnt:	n/a	**dilution:**	n/a
Int net div per share:	nil	**P/E ratio:**	n/a
Fin net div per share:	nil	**Probable CGT?**	Yes

LATEST REPORTED RESULTS: 2003		PREVIOUS REPORTED RESULTS: 2002	
Turnover:	£5.73m	Turnover:	£9.89m
PTP:	£(1.99m)	PTP:	£4.41m
EPS:	(54.3)p	EPS:	132.4p

Comments:

Last season was a period of consolidation at Deepdale, both on and off the pitch. The club known as the Lilywhites moved into the red last year thanks to the ongoing negative implications of the collapse of ITV Digital. The company's turnover was eroded by 42%, and worryingly, the wages as a percentage of turnover increased from 42% to 74%. Nevertheless, there was heart to be taken from the club's strong balance sheet. Year-end net assets were £9m and net debt just £600,000.

Prezzo (PRZ)

Restaurant operator

Bridge House Suite 107, 181 Queen Victoria Street, London, EC4V 4DZ Tel: 020-7436 0007

		holding %
Chairman	Michael Carlton	0.4
Chief Executive	Jonathan Kaye	15.4
Finance Director		
Non-Exec Director	John Lederer	0.1

Main Shareholders:

Phillip Kaye	51.3

Percentage of free market capital: 32.8%

Nominated Adviser:	Evolution Beeson Gregory, London
AIM Broker:	Evolution Beeson Gregory, London
Solicitors:	Howard Kennedy, London
Market Makers:	BGMM; WINS
Auditors:	BDO Stoy Hayward, 8 Baker Street, London, W1U 3LL
Registrars:	Computershare Investor Services

Entry on AIM:	21/3/2002	Recent price:	92.5p
Interim results:	Aug	Market cap:	£41.74m
Final results:	Apr	Issue price:	50.0p
Year end:	Dec	Current no of shares:	
Accounts due:	Apr		45,123,125
Int div paymnt:	n/a	No of shares after	
Fin div paymnt:	n/a	dilution:	n/a
Int net div per share:	nil	P/E ratio:	n/a
Fin net div per share:	nil	Probable CGT?	Yes

LATEST REPORTED RESULTS: 2002		PREVIOUS REPORTED RESULTS: 2001	
Turnover:	£3.79m	Turnover:	£1.10m
PTP:	£(86,000)	PTP:	£94,000
EPS:	(0.5)p	EPS:	0.6p

Comments:

Prezzo has already built up an estate of 22 pizza/pasta restaurants, compared to only four when it listed. Although three sites primarily in leisure complexes have not performed well and will be sold, in November it raised £2.7m by a placing for the expansion of its estate and the fit-out of two freehold sites in Brentwood and Norwich. All in all, it owns 34 sites. 12 are unoccupied but four further restaurants should be opened in the first half. ASK's Kaye family is significantly involved.

Private & Commercial Finance (PCF)

Equipment leasing and finance provider

15 Great College Street, Westminster, London, SW1P 3RX Tel: 020-7222 2426; Fax: 020-7222 2985;
e-mail: enquiries@pcfg.co.uk; web site: www.pcfg.co.uk

		holding %
Chairman	Michael Cumming	0.0
Chief Executive	Anthony Nelson	9.1
Finance Director	Scott Maybury	8.9
Director	Robert Murray	8.9

Main Shareholders:

Pershing Keen	11.8
HSBC Global Custody Nominees	9.1
Nigel Wray	6.5
Forrest Nominees	3.8
Chase Nominees	3.4

Percentage of free market capital: 38.3%

Nominated Adviser:	Westhouse Securities, London
AIM Broker:	Seymour Pierce, London
Solicitors:	Maclay Murray & Spens, London
Market Makers:	DURM; SCAP; WINS
Auditors:	Ernst & Young, 7 Rolls Buildings, London EC4A 1NH
Registrars:	Computershare Investor Services

Entry on AIM:	2/9/1998	Recent price:	43.5p
Interim results:	Sep	Market cap:	£6.55m
Final results:	Mar	Issue price:	65.0p
Year end:	Dec	Current no of shares:	
Accounts due:	Mar		15,064,143
Int div paymnt:	Nov	No of shares after	
Fin div paymnt:	May	dilution:	n/a
Int net div per share:	1.1p	P/E ratio:	6.8
Fin net div per share:	1.1p	Probable CGT?	Yes

LATEST REPORTED RESULTS: 2002		PREVIOUS REPORTED RESULTS: 2001	
Turnover:	£33.16m	Turnover:	£30.99m
PTP:	£1.37m	PTP:	£1.13m
EPS:	6.4p	EPS:	6.0p

Comments:

PCF principally provides finance to consumers wanting to purchase cars as well as companies wishing to lease equipment. The group, whose loan book value stands at £55.1m, raised £3.1m via a loan note issue to launch a chain of car supermarkets. However, development in this competitive area has been delayed. Litigation against a division of Direct Line is also affecting the shares. First-half pre-tax profits fell 20% to £0.6m on flat turnover of £16.1m.

Proactive Sports (PAS)

Football and sports marketing agent

9 -13 Manchester Road, Wilmslow, Cheshire SK9 1BQ Tel: 01625-536411; Fax: 01625-536402;
e-mail: mail@proactivesports.co.uk; web site: www.proactivesports.co.uk

		holding %
Chairman	John Lawrence	0.7
Chief Executive	Neil Rodford	0.9
Finance Director	Mark Page	0.2
Sales Director	Paul Stretford	8.7

Main Shareholders:

Lynette Yates	13.4
Kevin Moran	9.1
Jesper Olsen	8.7
Texas Holdings	5.1
Manro Haydan Trading	3.7

Percentage of free market capital: 40.1%

Nominated Adviser:	Charles Stanley, London
AIM Broker:	Charles Stanley, London
Solicitors:	Hammonds, Leeds
Market Makers:	MLSC; SCAP; TEAM; WINS
Auditors:	Deloitte & Touche, Manchester
Registrars:	Lloyds TSB Registrars

ENTRY ON AIM:	17/5/2001	Recent price:	6.6p
Interim results:	Apr	Market cap:	£7.58m
Final results:	Oct	Issue price:	25.0p
Year end:	Aug	Current no of shares:	
Accounts due:	Nov		114,873,815
Int div paymnt:	n/a	No of shares after	
Fin div paymnt:	n/a	dilution:	n/a
Int net div per share:	nil	P/E ratio:	n/a
Fin net div per share:	nil	Probable CGT?	YES

LATEST REPORTED RESULTS: 2003		PREVIOUS REPORTED RESULTS: 2002	
Turnover:	£10.07m	Turnover:	£8.07m
PTP:	£(12.39m)	PTP:	£1.42m
EPS:	(12.3)p	EPS:	0.6p

Comments:

Proactive Sports is becoming a holistic sports management business. It recently established a new wealth management division with post year-end acquisition Kingsbridge Asset Management. Last financial year the group enjoyed a near 25% turnover hike. Its sports marketing operations performed strongly with sales surging 153%, and the representation arm stayed very profitable in tough markets. The year-end cash position was £2.7m (£3.5m).

Probus Estates (PBE)

Commercial property and leisure investor

4 Vigo Street, London, W1S 3HA Tel: 020-7479 7020; Fax: 020-7479 7030; web site: www.probusplc.com

		holding %
Chairman	Hans Junge	0.0
Chief Executive	as above	
Finance Director	Patrick Browning	0.03

Main Shareholders:

Lars-Erik Magnusson*	28.9
Rocurin Corporation	13.0
Inter IKEA	11.4
Fortress Beheer VI	10.5
Temoc Investment	4.7

Percentage of free market capital: 16.2%

*Mr Magnusson's shareholding is held through Magnusson Investments and Larmag Development, companies he controls.

Nominated Adviser:	Westhouse Securities, London
AIM Broker:	Westhouse Securities, London
Solicitors:	Stringer Saul, London
Market Makers:	MLSB; SCAP; WINS
Auditors:	KPMG, 8 Salisbury Square, London, EC4Y 8BB
Registrars:	Capita Registrars

Entry on AIM:	23/11/1999	Recent price:	0.9p
Interim results:	Sep	Market cap:	£4.91m
Final results:	Jun	Issue price:	n/a
Year end:	Dec	Current no of shares:	
Accounts due:	Apr		545,037,562
Int div paymnt:	n/a	No of shares after	
Fin div paymnt:	n/a	dilution:	n/a
Int net div per share:	nil	P/E ratio:	n/a
Fin net div per share:	nil	Probable CGT?	No

LATEST REPORTED RESULTS: 2002		PREVIOUS REPORTED RESULTS: 2001	
Turnover:	£12.29m	Turnover:	£2.76m
PTP:	£(16.55m)	PTP:	£(14.25m)
EPS:	(2.1)c	EPS:	(0.4)c

Comments:

Probus had to sell its largest remaining asset, the Casino de Mallorca, for £18m to cover gaming tax bills and debts to Duch creditor Uni-invest. It also has the Dutch taxmen on its back for a contingent tax liability. To cap it off, Probus is also in breach of its capital-to-assets covenant terms of its loan from Munchener Hypothekenbank. No action has been taken yet but the double whammy, combined with the company's precarious financial position, suggests crunch time is near.

Profile Media   (PMD)

Sporting & special events guides publisher

5th floor, Mermaid House, 2 Puddle Dock, London, EC2V 3DF Tel: 020-7332 2000; Fax: 020-7332 2001;
e-mail: info@profilemediagroup.co.uk; web site: www.profilemediagroup.co.uk

		holding %
Chairman	John Webber	3.2
Chief Executive	David Ellingham	1.6
Finance Director	Martin Thorneycroft	0.1
Director	Jack Mizel	2.4

Main Shareholders:

Power Consultancy	24.9
Octagon Nominees	8.1
P Stamp	7.2
Abacus Nominees	6.6
Royal Bank of Canada Trust	6.5
Percentage of free market capital: 13.8%	

Comments:

Huge debts – at one point they reached £29m – forced this group to radically restructure its operations. It sold two of its largest subsidiaries for £15.4m, swapped a further chunk of its debt for equity, rejigged its management team, closed various other businesses and raised a much needed £2.3m via a placing. The last depressing set of interims showed sales (from continuing operations) of just £3.0m. Losses came in at £2.55m. The fortunes of what remains of this venture now rest in the hands of an advertising upturn.

Nominated Adviser:	Nabarro Wells, London		
AIM Broker:	Charles Stanley, London; HSBC Investment Bank, London		
Solicitors:	Norton Rose, London		
Market Makers:	ARBT; HSBC; MLSC; SCAP; WINS		
Auditors:	Baker Tilly, 2 Bloomsbury Street, London WC1B 3ST		
Registrars:	Capita Registrars		

Entry on AIM:	24/7/1996	**Recent price:**	2.75p
Interim results:	Mar	**Market cap:**	£7.77m
Final results:	Nov	**Issue price:**	10.0p
Year end:	Jun	**Current no of shares:**	
Accounts due:	Oct		282,622,372
Int div paymnt:	n/a	**No of shares after**	
Fin div paymnt:	n/a	**dilution:**	n/a
Int net div per share:	nil	**P/E ratio:**	n/a
Fin net div per share:	nil	**Probable CGT?**	Yes

LATEST REPORTED RESULTS: 2003		PREVIOUS REPORTED RESULTS: 2002	
Turnover:	£24.03m	**Turnover:**	£26.40m
PTP:	£(14.72m)	**PTP:**	£(19.72m)
EPS:	(14.3)p	**EPS:**	(19.6)p

Protec   (PRC)

Security systems and services provider

Axis 7, Rhodes Way, Watford, Hertfordshire WD24 4TP Tel: 01923-211550; Fax: 01923-211590;
e-mail: investors@sda-protec.co.uk; web site: www.protec-plc.com

		holding %
Chairman	Philip Parker	0.7
Chief Executive	Bruce Hiscock	0.1
Finance Director	Paul Geraghty	0.1
Deputy Chairman	Robert Westcott	19.4

Main Shareholders:

Midia Investments SA	19.7
ISIS Asset Management	12.7
Protec plc AESOP	4.5
Neill Harvey	3.9
Percentage of free market capital: 38.4%	

Comments:

The surveillance systems and facilities management play reported an improved first half with narrower losses of £145,000 (£398,000) on turnover of £20.4m (£18.8m). Core systems business SDA Protec, which has clinched a deal as CCTV supplier to ExxonMobil's European service stations, moved into profit after restructuring. And both its surveillance and services operations are performing well. Protec's directors are confident about a profitable second half.

Nominated Adviser:	Teather & Greenwood, London		
AIM Broker:	Teather & Greenwood, London		
Solicitors:	Lawrence Graham, London		
Market Makers:	SCAP; TEAM; WINS		
Auditors:	PKF, Farringdon Place, 20 Farringdon Road EC1M 3AP		
Registrars:	Computershare Investor Services		

Entry on AIM:	20/6/1996	**Recent price:**	11.5p
Interim results:	Mar	**Market cap:**	£16.65m
Final results:	Nov	**Issue price:**	285p
Year end:	Jun	**Current no of shares:**	
Accounts due:	Nov		144,798,561
Int div paymnt:	n/a	**No of shares after**	
Fin div paymnt:	n/a	**dilution:**	n/a
Int net div per share:	nil	**P/E ratio:**	n/a
Fin net div per share:	nil	**Probable CGT?**	Yes

LATEST REPORTED RESULTS: 2003		PREVIOUS REPORTED RESULTS: 2002	
Turnover:	£40.42m	**Turnover:**	£18.98m
PTP:	£12,000	**PTP:**	£(1.07m)
EPS:	0.0p	**EPS:**	(0.9)p

Proteome Sciences (PRM)
Medical diagnostics researcher & developer

Coveham House, Downside Bridge Road, Cobham, Surrey KT11 3EP Tel: 01932-865065; Fax: 01932-868696;
e-mail: helpdesk@proteome.co.uk; web site: www.proteome.co.uk

		holding %
Chairman	Steve Harris	0.1
Managing Director	Christopher Pearce	4.1
Finance Director	James L Malthouse	0.2
Director	William Dawson	0.01

Main Shareholders:

Aventis R&T	15.8
GNI Limited	7.1
Credit Lyonnais Securities	5.1
Fidelity Investments	4.0
Lansdowne Partners	3.0
Percentage of free market capital: 60.5%	

Nominated Adviser:	Evolution Beeson Gregory, London
AIM Broker:	Evolution Beeson Gregory, London
Solicitors:	Lovells, London; Fulbright & Jaworski LLP, Texas
Market Makers:	ALTI; MLSB; SCAP; WEST; WINS
Auditors:	Deloitte & Touche, Reading
Registrars:	Capita Registrars

ENTRY ON AIM:	3/10/1995	Recent price:	196.0p
Interim results:	Sep	Market cap:	£236.28m
Final results:	Jun	Issue price:	142.0p
Year end:	Dec	Current no of shares:	
Accounts due:	Jul		120,552,197
Int div paymnt:	n/a	No of shares after	
Fin div paymnt:	n/a	dilution:	121,461,721
Int net div per share:	nil	P/E ratio:	n/a
Fin net div per share:	nil	Probable CGT?	YES

LATEST REPORTED RESULTS: 2002		PREVIOUS REPORTED RESULTS: 2001	
Turnover:	£171,000	Turnover:	n/a
PTP:	£(4.45m)	PTP:	£(2.07m)
EPS:	(4.0)p	EPS:	(2.2)p

Comments:
Proteome's shares have surged over the past year as revenue starts to appear. The group's unique applied proteomics uses nanotechnology to identify sub-molecular proteins that indicate the presence of a disease. Two licensing deals, to develop early stage tests for BSE in cattle and human strokes, are in place and talks about others are ongoing. Annual cash burn is £4m but a £5.8m placing in June left the group with £8m cash. The prospects are immense and reflected in the valuation.

Pubs 'n' Bars (PNB)
Public house owner and manager

Standwood House, 10/12 Weir Road, London, SW12 0NA Tel: 020-8228 4800; Fax: 020-8675 1950;
e-mail: enquiries@pubsnbars.co.uk; web site: www.pubsnbars.co.uk

		holding %
Chairman	M C Mealey	0.2
Managing Director	C Belligero	0.2
Finance Director	K Chapman	0.6
Deputy Chairman	S Murphy	19.1

Main Shareholders:

Sinjul Nominees	8.7
Dartington Portfolio Nominees	7.8
The Acorn Trust	6.3
Peetee	3.4
Rathbone Nominees	3.2
Percentage of free market capital: 40.5%	

Nominated Adviser:	Rowan Dartington, Bristol
AIM Broker:	Rowan Dartington, Bristol
Solicitors:	Addleshaw Goddard, London
Market Makers:	MLSB; WINS
Auditors:	Kingston Smith, 60 Goswell Road, London EC1M 7AD
Registrars:	Capita Registrars

Entry on AIM:	13/9/1999	Recent price:	40.5p
Interim results:	Sep	Market cap:	£8.68m
Final results:	Apr	Issue price:	45.0p
Year end:	Dec	Current no of shares:	
Accounts due:	Jun		21,437,207
Int div paymnt:	Dec	No of shares after	
Fin div paymnt:	Jul	dilution:	n/a
Int net div per share:	0.5p	P/E ratio:	9.0
Fin net div per share:	1.0p	Probable CGT?	YES

LATEST REPORTED RESULTS: 2002		PREVIOUS REPORTED RESULTS: 2001	
Turnover:	£14.52m	Turnover:	£14.84m
PTP:	£1.25m	PTP:	£1.22m
EPS:	4.5p	EPS:	4.4p

Comments:
To December, P'n'B was 1.47% ahead in like-for-like sales in its managed estate and 6.7% up in its tenanted estate. It has also acquired 15% in Community Taverns, which in turn has agreed terms to acquire 32 pubs formerly owned and run by Balaclava pubs. It will also manage the acquired pubs and expects to generate an additional £450,000 each year from its fixed fee per pub charge. P'n'B will invest £750,000 in the venture during the next 18 months via loan capital.

Pursuit Dynamics (PDX)

Provider of innovative marine propulsion system

Unit 1, Anglian Business Park, Orchard Road, Royston, Hertfordshire SG8 5TW Tel: 01763-250592; Fax: 01763-250596; web site: wwwpursuitdynamics.com

		holding %
Chairman	Ronald Trenter	0.5
Chief Executive	John Heathcote	32.3
Finance Director	Gary Pyle	0.1
Non-Exec Director	John Clarke	8.3

Main Shareholders:
n/a

Percentage of free market capital: 55.7%

Nominated Adviser:	Durlacher, London
AIM Broker:	Durlacher, London
Solicitors:	n/a
Market Makers:	DURM
Auditors:	PricewaterhouseCoopers, Cambridge
Registrars:	Computershare Investor Services

ENTRY ON AIM:	23/5/2001	Recent price:	124.0p
Interim results:	May	Market cap:	£50.93m
Final results:	Feb	Issue price:	50.0p
Year end:	Sep	Current no of shares:	
Accounts due:	Mar		41,070,063
Int div paymnt:	n/a	No of shares after	
Fin div paymnt:	n/a	dilution:	n/a
Int net div per share:	nil	P/E ratio:	n/a
Fin net div per share:	nil	Probable CGT?	YES

LATEST REPORTED RESULTS:	2003	PREVIOUS REPORTED RESULTS:	2002
Turnover:	n/a	Turnover:	n/a
PTP:	£(1.62m)	PTP:	(1.75m)
EPS:	(3.9)p	EPS:	(4.2)p

Comments:
Pursuit Dynamics is the developer of the intriguing PDX technology, which uses steam as the sole motive power in an innovative process system. Encouragingly the company has announced the first sale of a PDX unit into the prepared food market to 'Welcome Foods'. This should be the first of many units sold or leased to the food processing industry. The technology also has a swathe of applications across industries such as nuclear, oil, healthcare and wastewater.

Quadnetics (QDG)

Provider of advanced CCTV systems and related products

North Court House, Morton Bagot, Studley, Warwickshire B80 7EL Tel: 01527-850 080

		holding %
Chairman	Peter Rae	7.2
Chief Executive	Russell Singleton	8.6
Finance Director	Nigel Poultney	1.67
Non-Exec Director	David Coghlan	17.96

Main Shareholders:

Union and Silverslaggen	14.7
Graphite Enterprise Trust	7.8
Fleming Mercantile	6.2
Carlton Communications	5.0

Percentage of free market capital: 17.4%

Nominated Adviser:	Brewin Dolphin, London
AIM Broker:	Brewin Dolphin, London
Solicitors:	MacFarlanes, London
Market Makers:	KBCS; WINS
Auditors:	PKF, London
Registrars:	Capita Registrars

Entry on AIM:	15/1/2002	Recent price:	312.5p
Interim results:	Feb	Market cap:	£36.18m
Final results:	Sep	Issue price:	107.5p
Year end:	May	Current no of shares:	
Accounts due:	Oct		11,576,691
Int div paymnt:	n/a	No of shares after	
Fin div paymnt:	Dec	dilution:	n/a
Int net div per share:	nil	P/E ratio:	n/a
Fin net div per share:	2.0p	Probable CGT?	YES

LATEST REPORTED RESULTS:	2003	PREVIOUS REPORTED RESULTS:	2002
Turnover:	£20.30m	Turnover:	£17.74m
PTP:	£1.41m	PTP:	£(752,000)
EPS:	17.4p	EPS:	(11.6)p

Comments:
The CCTV and network video group saw first half profits improve to £616,000 on reduced sales of £7.0m. The reduction in revenues occurred because the group has exited from much low-margin subcontract civil work. In January the company bought Look CCTV, a venture supplying CCTV systems to the bus sector for £6.8m, raising £8m via a placing to fund the deal. In February it acquired a specialist manufacturer and supplier of CCTV systems for the marine and oil industry for £1.36m.

Quayle Munro (QYM)

Investment company

8 Charlotte Square, Edinburgh, EH2 4DR Tel: 0131-226 4421; Fax: 0131-225 3391

		holding %
Chairman	Ian Jones	14.2
Chief Executive	John Elliot	10.0
Finance Director	Anthony Ostrowski	2.0
Non-Exec Director	Donald Sutherland	0.3

Main Shareholders:

Uberior Investments	29.0
The Waterloo Corporation	10.4
DM Munro	5.8

Percentage of free market capital: 28%

Nominated Adviser:	KBC Peel Hunt, London
AIM Broker:	KBC Peel Hunt, London
Solicitors:	Dickson Minto, London
Market Makers:	KBCS; MLSB; WINS
Auditors:	Ernst & Young, 10 George Street, Edinburgh
Registrars:	Capita Registrars

Comments:

This Full List refugee specialises in backing companies undertaking work under the Private Finance Initiative (PFI). The group also holds a number of listed and unquoted equity investments, the largest of which is housebuilder the Morris Group. In addition a subsidiary advises on PFI projects as well. Interim pre-tax profits doubled to £0.68m as income rose 50% to £0.99m, prompting a 50p special dividend. Net assets stand at £18.1m, or 513.5p per share, after rising 22% over the year.

ENTRY ON AIM: 29/10/2003		**Recent price:**	485.0p
Interim results:	Mar	**Market cap:**	£17.48m
Final results:	Sep	**Issue price:**	n/a
Year end:	Jun	**Current no of shares:**	
Accounts due:	Oct		3,605,025
Int div paymnt:	Apr	**No of shares after**	
Fin div paymnt:	Nov	**dilution:**	n/a
Int net div per share:	5.5p	**P/E ratio:**	16.7
Fin net div per share:	11.0p	**Probable CGT?**	No

LATEST REPORTED RESULTS: 2003		PREVIOUS REPORTED RESULTS: 2002	
Turnover:	£1.47m	Turnover:	£2.07m
PTP:	£1.09m	PTP:	£1.17m
EPS:	29.0p	EPS:	26.9p

Quiktrak Networks (QTR)

Security product manufacturer

2nd Floor, 9-11 The Quadrant, Richmond, London, TW9 1BP Tel: 0870-010 6044; Fax: 0870-010 6043

		holding %
Chairman	Chrisilios Kyriakou	17.0
Chief Executive	as above	
Finance Director		
Non-Exec Director	Charles de Chezelles	0.6

Main Shareholders:

Investika	18.0
Damelian Automobile	13.2
Westpac Custodian	6.4
SST Partners	4.2

Percentage of free market capital: 40%

Nominated Adviser:	Nabarro Wells, London
AIM Broker:	Phillip Securities, London
Solicitors:	Tenon Statham Gill Davies, London
Market Makers:	EVO; KBCS; SCAP; WINS
Auditors:	Sawin & Edwards, London
Registrars:	Capita Registrars

Comments:

Quiktrak provides a low cost telecom-based tracking system to a variety of customers including courier and mini-cab firms. As the system uses the company's own radio network, rather than existing communications infrastructure, for its base, it is reckoned to be far more reliable than rival products. Though it remains early days a raft of orders – from motorbike security firm Get Bike and London-based courier business Addison Lee among others – have recently been secured.

Entry on AIM:	14/8/2003	Recent price:	22.0p
Interim results:	Sep	Market cap:	£13.12m
Final results:	Mar	Issue price:	37.5p
Year end:	Dec	Current no of shares:	
Accounts due:	Jun		59,629,727
Int div paymnt:	n/a	No of shares after	
Fin div paymnt:	n/a	dilution:	n/a
Int net div per share:	n/a	P/E ratio:	n/a
Fin net div per share:	n/a	Probable CGT?	Yes

LATEST REPORTED RESULTS: 2003		PREVIOUS REPORTED RESULTS: 2002	
Turnover:	n/a	Turnover:	n/a
PTP:	n/a	PTP:	n/a
EPS:	n/a	EPS:	n/a

RAB Capital

(RAB)

Fund management company

I Adam Street, London, WC2N 6LE Tel: 020-7389 7000; Fax: 020-7389 7050

		holding %
Chairman	Michael Buckley	43.8
Chief Executive	Phillip Richards	43.8
Finance Director	Christopher de Mattos	1.1
Director	Schehrezade Sadeque	1.1

Main Shareholders:

n/a

Percentage of free market capital: 10.1%

Nominated Adviser:	KBC Peel Hunt, London
AIM Broker:	KBC Peel Hunt, London
Solicitors:	McGrigors, London
Market Makers:	WINS
Auditors:	Ernst & Young, I More London Place, London SE1 2AF
Registrars:	Computershare Investor Services

ENTRY ON AIM:	18/3/2004	Recent price:	41.0p
Interim results:	Sep	Market cap:	£140.3m
Final results:	Mar	Issue price:	25.0p
Year end:	Dec	Current no of shares:	
Accounts due:	Apr		342,200,000
Int div paymnt:	n/a	No of shares after	
Fin div paymnt:	n/a	dilution:	n/a
Int net div per share:	nil	P/E ratio:	16.4
Fin net div per share:	nil	Probable CGT?	No

LATEST REPORTED RESULTS: 13 MONTHS TO 31 DEC '03		PREVIOUS REPORTED RESULTS: 2002	
Turnover:	£22.24m	Turnover:	£11.20m
PTP:	£10.56m	PTP:	£2.79m
EPS:	2.5p	EPS:	0.6p

Comments:
Lord Lamont, the Chancellor humbled by hedge funds, is a director of popularly floated hedge fund manager RAB Capital, which lifted profits from £2.8m to £10.5m last year, backing junior resource groups, often buying at big discounts. Run by ex-brokers Philip Richards and Michael Alen-Buckley, RAB has open-ended funds, which are a way to ride the mining boom, but a downturn could bring redemptions.

Radamec

(RDM)

Cash shell

Bridge Road, Chertsey, Surrey KT16 8LJ Tel: 01932-561181; Fax: 01932-568775; e-mail: moore@radamec.co.uk

		holding %
Chairman	Leonard Whittaker	49.9
Chief Executive	as above	
Finance Director	Lionel Moore	0.2
Non-Exec Director	Alan Whittaker	16.1

Main Shareholders:

Phaseone Investments	3.7
ABN Amro	3.2

Percentage of free market capital: 26.8%

Nominated Adviser:	Cazenove, London
AIM Broker:	Cazenove, London
Solicitors:	Lovells, London
Market Makers:	CAZR; KLWT; WINS
Auditors:	RSM Robson Rhodes, 186 City Road, London EC3 7PP
Registrars:	Computershare Investor Services

Entry on AIM:	1/7/2002	Recent price:	40.5p
Interim results:	Sep	Market cap:	£7.57m
Final results:	Mar	Issue price:	31.0p
Year end:	Dec	Current no of shares:	
Accounts due:	Apr		18,689,714
Int div paymnt:	Apr	No of shares after	
Fin div paymnt:	Jul	dilution:	n/a
Int net div per share:	1.0p	P/E ratio:	3.4
Fin net div per share:	1.0p	Probable CGT?	YES

LATEST REPORTED RESULTS: 2002		PREVIOUS REPORTED RESULTS: 2001	
Turnover:	£9.32m	Turnover:	£12.34m
PTP:	£2.46m	PTP:	£230,000
EPS:	11.8p	EPS:	1.1p

Comments:
After coming down from the Full List, Radamec immediately began to sell off its assets, ending in the disposal of Radamec Broadcast Systems to Vitec for £4.7m and Radamec Defence Systems to Ultra Electronics for £6m. This left a shell with £8.8m in cash and a sub-lease on the old head office that expires at the end of 2003. After dealing with any liabilities arising from the disposals, the aim is to return the remaining cash to shareholders, though it may remain as a shell.

Raft (RFT)

Software provider for financial institutions

Piercy House, 7 Copthall Avenue, London, EC2R 7NJ Tel: 020-7847 0400; Fax: 020-7847 0401; e-mail: info@raftinternational.com; web site: www.raftinternational.com

		holding %
Chairman	David Priestley*	19.2
Chief Executive	as above	
Finance Director	Sandra Kelly	0.04
Technical Director	Asim Shah	29.8

Main Shareholders:

Frank Mobjerg (Director)	9.4
Ian Tobin	6.3

Percentage of free market capital: 35.2%

*Shares held by the Priestley Trust of which David Priestley is the sole beneficiary

Comments:

Despite a brace of recent contract wins in the operational risk management field, Raft's revival appears to have stalled. Speaking at the company's February AGM chairman David Priestley admitted that the current weakness of the dollar coupled with lingering contract delays will impact first-half figures. With times remaining tough, management continues to slash the company's cost base – hence a recent decision to transfer software development work to India.

Nominated Adviser:	Seymour Pierce, London		
AIM Broker:	Seymour Pierce, London		
Solicitors:	Salans, London		
Market Makers:	SCAP; WINS		
Auditors:	Baker Tilly, 2 Bloomsbury Street, London WC1B 3ST		
Registrars:	Capita Registrars		

ENTRY ON AIM: 11/10/2000		**Recent price:**	14.0p
Interim results:	Jun	**Market cap:**	£9.23m
Final results:	Dec	**Issue price:**	64p
Year end:	Oct	**Current no of shares:**	
Accounts due:	Jan		65,955,974
Int div paymnt:	n/a	**No of shares after**	
Fin div paymnt:	n/a	**dilution:**	72,712,106
Int net div per share:	nil	**P/E ratio:**	n/a
Fin net div per share:	nil	**Probable CGT?**	Yes

LATEST REPORTED RESULTS: 2003		PREVIOUS REPORTED RESULTS: 2002	
Turnover:	£8.56m	Turnover:	£6.67m
PTP:	£(999,000)	PTP:	£(2.11m)
EPS:	(1.5)p	EPS:	(3.1)p

Ramco Energy (ROS)

Oil & gas explorer

62 Queens Road, Aberdeen, AB15 4YE Tel: 01224-352200; Fax: 01224-352211; e-mail: lisa.newman@ramco-plc.com; web site: www.ramco-plc.com

		holding %
Chairman	Steve E Remp	11.1
Chief Executive	as above	
Finance Director	Steven R Bertram	0.5
Chief Operating Officer	Daniel Stover	0.0

Main Shareholders:

Artemis	6.0
M&G Investment	5.9
Gartmore	4.3
The Capital Group Companies Inc	3.8

Percentage of free market capital: 67.2%

Comments:

Ramco has been hit by falling well head pressure caused by water at its 87%-owned Seven Heads field offshore Ireland. This cut output, threatening its delivery obligations. The company decided a 'blow down' and reopening could show how much could be delivered. A £3.5m US court ruling against Ramco in favour of a Houston oil family cannot be enforced until the appeal process is over.

Nominated Adviser:	Canaccord Capital, London		
AIM Broker:	Canaccord Capital, London		
Solicitors:	Ledingham Chalmers, Aberdeen; Burness, Edinburgh		
Market Makers:	ARBT; IHCS; JPMS; KBCS; SSSB; WINS		
Auditors:	PricewaterhouseCoopers, Aberdeen		
Registrars:	Capita Registrars		

Entry on AIM: 14/11/1996		**Recent price:**	82.5p
Interim results:	Sep	**Market cap:**	£25.79m
Final results:	Apr	**Issue price:**	70.0p
Year end:	Dec	**Current no of shares:**	
Accounts due:	May		31,264,713
Int div paymnt:	n/a	**No of shares after**	
Fin div paymnt:	n/a	**dilution:**	n/a
Int net div per share:	nil	**P/E ratio:**	n/a
Fin net div per share:	nil	**Probable CGT?**	No

LATEST REPORTED RESULTS: 2002		PREVIOUS REPORTED RESULTS: 2001	
Turnover:	£16.81m	Turnover:	£14.74m
PTP:	£(9.2m)	PTP:	£(10.81m)
EPS:	(35.9)p	EPS:	(46.2)p

Raven Mount (RAV)

Property company

Adelaide House, London Bridge, London, EC4R 9HA ; e-mail: groupplc@swanhill.co.uk

		holding %
Chairman	James Hyslop	0.1
Chief Executive		
Finance Director		
Exec Director	Anton Bilton	3.4

Main Shareholders:

Schroders	20.2
Silchester	12.3
UBS Global Asset Management	7.8
Jupiter Asset Management	4.3

Percentage of free market capital: 48%

Comments:

Raven Mount came to tne market last year with the all-share acquisition of 'high-value, premium-quality' home builder Swan Hill. The combined group, which made £4.5m in 2002, is run by Anton Bilton, Glyn Hirsch and Bimaljit Sandhu, and has attracted interest from investment groups seeking a potential break-up candidate.

Nominated Adviser:	Panmure, London
AIM Broker:	Shore Capital, London
Solicitors:	Berwin Leighton Paisner, London
Market Makers:	KBCS; MLSB; SCAP; WINS
Auditors:	KPMG Audit, 100 Temple Street, Bristol BS1 6AG
Registrars:	Capita Registrars

Entry on AIM: 17/12/2003		**Recent price:**	100.5p
Interim results:	Sep	**Market cap:**	£62.67m
Final results:	Mar	**Issue price:**	n/a
Year end:	Dec	**Current no of shares:**	
Accounts due:	Jun		62,355,333
Int div paymnt:	n/a	**No of shares after**	
Fin div paymnt:	n/a	**dilution:**	n/a
Int net div per share:	nil	**P/E ratio:**	13.2
Fin net div per share:	nil	**Probable CGT?**	No

LATEST REPORTED RESULTS: 2002		PREVIOUS REPORTED RESULTS: 2001	
Turnover:	£76.5m	Turnover:	£71.99m
PTP:	£5.92m	PTP:	£4.92m
EPS:	7.6p	EPS:	6.1p

Razorback Vehicles (RVC)

Commercial vehicle lifting technology

Suite 15, 201 New South Head Road, Edgecliff, New South Wales NSW 2027 Australia, Tel: 01564-711051; Fax: 01564-711 451; e-mail: steve.wright@razorback-vehicles.com; web site: www.razorback-vehicles.com.au

		holding %
Chairman	Edward Gilly*	1.3
Managing Director	Ronald Manser*	1.0
Finance Director	Allen Robinson**	0.1

Main Shareholders:

SME Investments*	77.9
National Australia Bank	11.7
Bridgestar Pty**	3.8

Percentage of free market capital: 4.2%

*E Gilly, A Robinson, R Manser, all dir.s of SME Investments
**AR Robinson is a director of Bridgestar Pty

Comments:

Razorback technology enables the entire load bed of a commercial vehicle or trailer to lower fully to the ground, eliminating the need for manual lifting. It is still loss-making but is in discussions with Fiat to distribute the Razorback as part of the Fiat Ducato commercial vehicle range. It is also looking to apply its technology to other industries and to realise this has tried to raise funding, with little success. Shareholders are helping but a further A$1.3m of bank guarantees are required.

Nominated Adviser:	KBC Peel Hunt, London
AIM Broker:	KBC Peel Hunt, London
Solicitors:	KPMG Solicitors, London
Market Makers:	KBCS; WINS
Auditors:	KPMG, 45 Clarence Street, Sydney, NSW 2000 Australia
Registrars:	Capita Registrars

Entry on AIM: 10/12/1997		**Recent price:**	24.5p
Interim results:	Feb	**Market cap:**	£6.46m
Final results:	Oct	**Issue price:**	102.0p
Year end:	Jun	**Current no of shares:**	
Accounts due:	Oct		26,377,330
Int div paymnt:	n/a	**No of shares after**	
Fin div paymnt:	n/a	**dilution:**	n/a
Int net div per share:	nil	**P/E ratio:**	n/a
Fin net div per share:	nil	**Probable CGT?**	No

LATEST REPORTED RESULTS: 2003		PREVIOUS REPORTED RESULTS: 2002	
Turnover:	£1.60m	Turnover:	£977,000
PTP:	£800,000	PTP:	£(1.55m)
EPS:	0.0p	EPS:	0.1p

Readybuy   (RBUY)

Holding company for a Chinese ready meal business
6 Ralli Courts, West Riverside, Manchester, M3 5FT

		holding %
Chairman	Colin Davies	3.5
Chief Executive	Brian Bennett	3.0
Finance Director	as chairman	
Non-Exec Director	Kui Yeung	10.0

Main Shareholders:

Kui Shum Yeung	10.0
Ian Currie	9.0
Richard Hughes	9.0
John Armstrong	5.7
Paul Stanton	4.8

Percentage of free market capital: 37%

Nominated Adviser:	WH Ireland, Manchester
AIM Broker:	WH Ireland, Manchester
Solicitors:	DWF, Manchester
Market Makers:	SCAP; WINS
Auditors:	Chadwick, Manchester
Registrars:	Capita Registrars

ENTRY ON AIM:	8/9/2003	**Recent price:**	42.5p
Interim results:	Nov	**Market cap:**	£7.65m
Final results:	Jul	**Issue price:**	48.0p
Year end:	Apr	**Current no of shares:**	
Accounts due:	Sep		17,994,010
Int div paymnt:	n/a	**No of shares after**	
Fin div paymnt:	n/a	**dilution:**	n/a
Int net div per share:	nil	**P/E ratio:**	n/a
Fin net div per share:	nil	**Probable CGT?**	**YES**

LATEST REPORTED RESULTS: 2003		PREVIOUS REPORTED RESULTS: 2002	
Turnover:	n/a	Turnover:	£10.86m
PTP:	£(111,000)	PTP:	£(166,000)
EPS:	n/a	EPS:	n/a

Comments:

Readybuy was set up as a cash shell, joining AIM after acquiring the business of McDonald Yang for £435,000 of shares. It has developed a range of premium chilled ready-made Chinese meals for sale through supermarkets under the Yang Sing brand. It currently has attracted one supermarket, which began selling the product in January. Yang Sing is a renowned Cantonese restaurant in Manchester. Losses in the interim were £114,000 with no turnover.

Real Affinity   (RAF)

Direct marketing designer and supplier
Media House, No. 5 Staithgate Lane, Bradford, BD6 1YA Tel: 01274-421700; Fax: 01274-421605;
e-mail: info@realaffinity.co.uk; web site: www.realaffinity.co.uk

		holding %
Chairman	Anthony Douglas	1.1
Chief Executive	Mark Richardson	10.2
Finance Director	N Muffitt	0.1
Non-Exec Director	Nigel Fitzpatrick	0.3

Main Shareholders:

Rathbones Nominees	14.8
Jean Fallows	8.8
Brendan Larkin	8.2
Wendy Larkin	8.2
Keith Osborne	5.4

Percentage of free market capital: 16.5%

Nominated Adviser:	Seymour Pierce, London
AIM Broker:	Seymour Pierce, London
Solicitors:	Lupton Fawcett, Leeds
Market Makers:	SCAP; WINS
Auditors:	Baker Tilly, Bradford
Registrars:	Capita Registrars

Entry on AIM:	26/3/2001	**Recent price:**	1.25p
Interim results:	Dec	**Market cap:**	£3.06m
Final results:	Sep	**Issue price:**	8.0p
Year end:	Mar	**Current no of shares:**	
Accounts due:	Jul		244,483,839
Int div paymnt:	n/a	**No of shares after**	
Fin div paymnt:	n/a	**dilution:**	n/a
Int net div per share:	nil	**P/E ratio:**	n/a
Fin net div per share:	nil	**Probable CGT?**	**YES**

LATEST REPORTED RESULTS: 2003		PREVIOUS REPORTED RESULTS: 2002	
Turnover:	£5.96m	Turnover:	£8.40m
PTP:	£(804,000)	PTP:	£(333,000)
EPS:	(1.8)p	EPS:	(0.9)p

Comments:

This direct marketing and communication specialist is rapidly recovering. The group's interims showed turnover falling to £2.47m but saw pre-tax losses slashed to £22,461. Since then it has announced the acquisition of sports marketing group Navigator, raised £350,00 via a placing at 1p, and signed a deal with the European Athletics Association. At the end of March it announced that it was in talks regarding the takeover of Onyx Media. If it completes this it will be radically transformed.

Redbus Interhouse (RBI)

Communications company

Masters House, 107 Hammersmith Road, London, W14 0QH Tel: 020-7603 1515; Fax: 020-7603 8448;
e-mail: info@interhouse.redbus.com; web site: www.interhouse.redbus.com

		holding %
Chairman	Oliver Grace	25.7
Chief Executive	Michael Tobin	0.0
Finance Director		
Non-Exec Director	Bo Bendtsen	15.4

Main Shareholders:

Sputnik	25.9
Telos Environmental Services	8.5
Garboldi Investment	4.1

Percentage of free market capital: 20.5%

Nominated Adviser:	Teather & Greenwood, London
AIM Broker:	Teather & Greenwood, London
Solicitors:	Ashursts, London
Market Makers:	CSCS, EVO, KLWT, MLSB, SCAP, WINS
Auditors:	Deloitte & Touche, London
Registrars:	Capita Registrars

ENTRY ON AIM:	21/7/2003	**Recent price:**	8.0p
Interim results:	Sep	**Market cap:**	£18.56m
Final results:	Apr	**Issue price:**	5.5p
Year end:	Dec	**Current no of shares:**	
Accounts due:	Jun		232,060,553
Int div paymnt:	n/a	**No of shares after**	
Fin div paymnt:	n/a	**dilution:**	n/a
Int net div per share:	nil	**P/E ratio:**	n/a
Fin net div per share:	nil	**Probable CGT?**	YES

LATEST REPORTED RESULTS:	2002	PREVIOUS REPORTED RESULTS:	2001
Turnover:	£11.55m	**Turnover:**	£9.31m
PTP:	£(19.12m)	**PTP:**	£(65.19m)
EPS:	(12.7)p	**EPS:**	(43.2)p

Comments:

A £4.3m fundraising at the turn of the year replenished the coffers of this IT services company. At the time, the group assured investors that its cost-cutting strategy was showing signs of working. However, it is still bedeviled with a legal dispute in Luxembourg associated with its former facility there. The landlord of this facility launched a petition against Redbus for the payment of circa 8.8m. This was dismissed by the courts, but he was given leave to pursue a new claim, which he has promptly done, for the same amount.

Reefton Mining (RTM)

Diamond explorer and miner

Level 1, 47 Ord Street, West Perth, W A 6005, Australia Tel: 00-61 8-9322 7822; Fax: 00-61 8-9322 7823

		holding %
Chairman	Bradley Moore	0.4
Chief Executive	Mal Randall	0.0
Finance Director		
Managing Director	Vladimir Nikolaenko	5.5

Main Shareholders:

n/a

Percentage of free market capital: 94%

Nominated Adviser:	Grant Thornton, London
AIM Broker:	Hoodless Brennan, London
Solicitors:	Hammonds, London
Market Makers:	SCAP; WINS
Auditors:	K Westaway & Associates, West Perth W A 6005, Australia
Registrars:	Computershare Investor Services

Entry on AIM:	20/5/2002	**Recent price:**	2.6p
Interim results:	Mar	**Market cap:**	£4.33m
Final results:	Sep	**Issue price:**	3.5p
Year end:	Jun	**Current no of shares:**	
Accounts due:	Oct		166,663,462
Int div paymnt:	n/a	**No of shares after**	
Fin div paymnt:	n/a	**dilution:**	n/a
Int net div per share:	nil	**P/E ratio:**	n/a
Fin net div per share:	nil	**Probable CGT?**	No

LATEST REPORTED RESULTS:	2003	PREVIOUS REPORTED RESULTS:	2002
Turnover:	$58,000	**Turnover:**	$121,000
PTP:	$(1.46m)	**PTP:**	$(1.29m)
EPS:	(1.0)c	**EPS:**	(1.0)c

Comments:

Speculative diamond hopeful Reefton, backed by Aussie entrepreneur Vladimir Nikolaev, raised £220,400 last year for gem exploration on Namibia's Skeleton Coast and recently launched another £205,000 funding. Reefton, whose board includes mining tycoon's son Anthony Ogilvie Thompson, lost an interim £295,000. The company found 'a new diamondiferous beach' and recovered 150 diamonds, the largest being 2.34 carats.

Reflec

Reflective printing inks manufacturer

Road One, Winsford Industrial Estate, Cheshire, CW7 3QQ Tel: 01606-593911; Fax: 01606-559535;
e-mail: info@reflec.com; web site: www.reflec.com

		holding %
Chairman	Peter Smith	0.0
Chief Executive	as above	
Finance Director	David Chiverton	0.0
Non-Exec Director	Brian F Sagar	0.1

Main Shareholders:

JD Waterhouse Nominees	4.2
Sharelink Nominees	4.1

Percentage of free market capital: 91.5%

Nominated Adviser:	Seymour Pierce, London
AIM Broker:	Seymour Pierce, London
Solicitors:	DWF, Liverpool
Market Makers:	KBCS; MLSB; SCAP; WINS
Auditors:	BDO Stoy Hayward, Manchester
Registrars:	Computershare Investor Services

ENTRY ON AIM:	5/8/1997	Recent price:	1.0p
Interim results:	Nov	Market cap:	£5.58m
Final results:	Jul	Issue price:	40.0p
Year end:	Feb	Current no of shares:	
Accounts due:	May		558,033,110
Int div paymnt:	n/a	No of shares after	
Fin div paymnt:	n/a	dilution:	n/a
Int net div per share:	nil	P/E ratio:	n/a
Fin net div per share:	nil	Probable CGT?	YES

LATEST REPORTED RESULTS: 2003		PREVIOUS REPORTED RESULTS: 2002	
Turnover:	£3.21m	Turnover:	£3.41m
PTP:	£(2.09m)	PTP:	£(6.82m)
EPS:	(0.5)p	EPS:	(1.6)p

Comments:

Financial turnaround Reflec produces reflective systems, and its blue screen materials are used by BBC TV and Disney. It is enjoying the benefits of a new strategy and stricter financial controls, with ReflecMedia, ReflecEvolution and ReflecReflectives all accountable for their own results. £1m was recently raised at 0.75p to help speed the growth of ReflecMedia. Earlier, interims to August were much improved with losses culled to £175,000 (£2.1m) on £1.47m (£1.5m) sales.

Reflex   (RFI)

Fitness and leisure facilities operator

19 Elgin Road, Ballsbridge, Dublin 4, Ireland, Tel: 00-353 1 660 0213; Fax: 00-353 1 660 0366

		holding %
Chairman	Tony Kilduff	11.7
Chief Executive	Paul May	6.5
Finance Director	as above	
Non-Exec Director	Luke Johnson	9.7

Main Shareholders:

Howard Landon	14.5
Philip Daw	5.5
Gordon McClure	5.2
Ian Salkeld	5.2
Douglas Johnson	5.0

Percentage of free market capital: 23.3%

Nominated Adviser:	J&E Davy, Dublin
AIM Broker:	J&E Davy, Dublin
Solicitors:	MacFarlanes, London
Market Makers:	GBMM; WINS
Auditors:	Deloitte & Touche, Dublin 1
Registrars:	Computershare Investor Services

Entry on AIM:	10/9/2001	Recent price:	2.0p
Interim results:	Sep	Market cap:	£2.61m
Final results:	Apr	Issue price:	9.0p
Year end:	Dec	Current no of shares:	
Accounts due:	Jul		130,261,771
Int div paymnt:	n/a	No of shares after	
Fin div paymnt:	n/a	dilution:	n/a
Int net div per share:	nil	P/E ratio:	n/a
Fin net div per share:	nil	Probable CGT?	YES

LATEST REPORTED RESULTS: 2002		PREVIOUS REPORTED RESULTS: 2001	
Turnover:	£4.07m	Turnover:	£2.48m
PTP:	£(284,000)	PTP:	£(5.67m)
EPS:	(0.2)p	EPS:	(8.3)p

Comments:

Reflex operates the Motorcise Healthy Living Centres. In February, its board said it was unaware of a specific reason for a significant share price rise. The company has yet to report for the full year, but Reflex experienced a tricky first half with sales culled by half a million to £1.6m and pre-tax losses burgeoning to £359,000 (£119,000) reflecting the struggling health and fitness sector. Reflex has taken out costs and, for now, put a stop on the roll-out of new centres.

osmetics (RFX)

ıny

.nover Square, London, W1S 1HP Tel: 020-7667 5000; Fax: 020-7667 5100

		holding %
Chi. .ve	Nigel Robertson	14.0
Finance ctor	Ratan Daryani	32.0
Non-Exec Director	John Vergopoulos	14.0

Main Shareholders:

Mike Leeke	8.7
Highland Specialist	7.8

Percentage of free market capital: 13.5%

Comments:
Reflexion has raised £375,000 net to fund its hunt for businesses to buy in the toiletries and cosmetics sector. Chief executive Ratan Daryani wants to buy under-performing beauty product brands. Daryani was previously on the board of Victory, the AIM-listed operator of Virgin Cosmetics, which has proved successful. Chairman Nigel Robertson founded scoot.com and now sits on several AIM boards. Seeing this pedigree, the shares have nearly quadrupled.

Nominated Adviser:	WH Ireland, London
AIM Broker:	WH Ireland, London
Solicitors:	Harbottle & Lewis, London
Market Makers:	WINS
Auditors:	Grant Thornton, London
Registrars:	Neville Registrars

Entry on AIM:	8/3/2004	Recent price:	49.5p
Interim results:	n/a	Market cap:	£4.38m
Final results:	n/a	Issue price:	13.0p
Year end:	n/a	Current no of shares:	
Accounts due:	n/a		8,846,154
Int div paymnt:	n/a	No of shares after	
Fin div paymnt:	n/a	dilution:	n/a
Int net div per share:	nil	P/E ratio:	n/a
Fin net div per share:	nil	Probable CGT?	No

LATEST REPORTED RESULTS:	PREVIOUS REPORTED RESULTS:
N/A	N/A
Turnover: n/a	Turnover: n/a
PTP: n/a	PTP: n/a
EPS: n/a	EPS: n/a

Regal Petroleum (RPT)

Oil & gas explorer & producer
7th Floor, Hillgate House, 26 Old Bailey, London, EC4M 7HW

		holding %
Chairman	Vasile Timis	7.9
Chief Executive	Guenter Nolte	0.0
Finance Director	Glenn Featherby	3.6
Non-Exec Director	Lord Bletso	0.0

Main Shareholders:

Ballure Trading	15.8
Commerzbank AG	7.5
Alker Investments	3.8
Voldemort	3.5
Lansdowne Partners	3.0

Percentage of free market capital: 54.9%

Comments:
Headed by colourful Romanian emigre Frank Timmis, eastern Europe-focused oil and gas hopeful Regal has impressed with its Kallirachi oil find in Greece, with a claimed potential of 300m barrels, and its move towards profitability. After raising £24m last autumn at 75p, partly to buy access to Aegean Sea oil prospects, Regal raised £37.5m at £3 in February. Timmis has been musing a separate Sierra Leone diamonds float.

Nominated Adviser:	Evolution Beeson Gregory, London
AIM Broker:	Evolution Beeson Gregory, London
Solicitors:	Osborne Clarke, Reading
Market Makers:	EVO; KBCS; WINS
Auditors:	BDO Stoy Hayward, 8 Baker Street, London W1U 3LL
Registrars:	Computershare Investor Services

Entry on AIM:	27/9/2002	Recent price:	320.0p
Interim results:	Sep	Market cap:	£212.85m
Final results:	Jun	Issue price:	60.0p
Year end:	Dec	Current no of shares:	
Accounts due:	May		66,515,867
Int div paymnt:	n/a	No of shares after	
Fin div paymnt:	n/a	dilution:	n/a
Int net div per share:	nil	P/E ratio:	n/a
Fin net div per share:	nil	Probable CGT?	No

LATEST REPORTED RESULTS:	PREVIOUS REPORTED RESULTS:
2002	2001
Turnover: $583,000	Turnover: n/a
PTP: $(4.49m)	PTP: $(1.01m)
EPS: (10.1)c	EPS: (2.5)c

ReGen Therapeutics (RGT)

Alzheimer's disease therapeutic research

Suite 406, Langham House, 29-30 Margaret Street, London W1W 8SA Tel: 020-7907 0910; Fax: 020-7907 0911;
e-mail: head.office@regentherapeutics.com

		holding %
Chairman	Percy Lomax	2.0
Chief Executive	as above	
Finance Director	Norman Lott	0.04
Deputy Chairman	Malcolm Beveridge	3.6

Main Shareholders:

Friedrich Rentschler (Non-Exec Director)	12.5
P. Garrod	10.7
NY Nominees	8.8
Charles Stanley	8.4
New Opportunities Investment Trust	6.6

Percentage of free market capital: 20.7%

Nominated Adviser:	Nabarro Wells, London
AIM Broker:	Hoodless Brennan, London
Solicitors:	Hale and Dorr, London
Market Makers:	HOOD; KBCS; LMSB; WINS
Auditors:	BDO Stoy Hayward, 8 Baker Street, London W1M 1DA
Registrars:	Capita Registrars

ENTRY ON AIM:	24/3/2000	**Recent price:**	3.25p
Interim results:	Sep	**Market cap:**	£9.1m
Final results:	Mar	**Issue price:**	28.0p
Year end:	Dec	**Current no of shares:**	
Accounts due:	Apr		279,966,542
Int div paymnt:	n/a	**No of shares after**	
Fin div paymnt:	n/a	**dilution:**	n/a
Int net div per share:	nil	**P/E ratio:**	n/a
Fin net div per share:	nil	**Probable CGT?**	**YES**

LATEST REPORTED RESULTS: 2003		PREVIOUS REPORTED RESULTS: 2002	
Turnover:	n/a	Turnover:	n/a
PTP:	£(1.99m)	PTP:	£(2.37m)
EPS:	(1.0)p	EPS:	(3.1)p

Comments:

Cash remains a concern for the developer of Colostrinin, a potential treatment for Alzheimer's Disease from cows' milk. However, following a series of placings and investment trust share sales, £1m cash sits on the balance sheet, making funding problems less critical. Nevertheless losses still hit £2m last year, so more cash will be required shortly. Research is being done on other therapeutic uses for the naturally occurring substance, possibly against cancers, multiple sclerosis and Parkinson's.

Resurge (RUE)

Provider of financing to troubled companies

7 The Sanctuary, London, SW1P 3JS Tel: 020-7233 1006; Fax: 020-7222 4200; e-mail: info@resurgeplc.com;
web site: www.resurgeplc.com

		holding %
Chairman	Anthony Brierley	0.8
Joint Managing Director	Jamie Constable	2.8
Finance Director		
Joint Managing Director	Jonathan Rowland*	0.0

Main Shareholders:

Schweco Nominees	20.2
Lavonia	18.2
Wood Hall Securities	16.8
Graham Hellier	15.8
Porlock Trading	8.3

Percentage of free market capital: 4.2%
*Mr Rowland is interested in the shares held by Lavonia

Nominated Adviser:	Collins Stewart, London
AIM Broker:	Collins Stewart, London
Solicitors:	Halliwell Landau, London
Market Makers:	DURM; SCAP; WINS
Auditors:	Baker Tilly, 2 Bloomsbury Street, London WC1B 3ST
Registrars:	Capita Registrars

Entry on AIM:	24/9/2001	**Recent price:**	7.75p
Interim results:	Jun	**Market cap:**	£5.58m
Final results:	Mar	**Issue price:**	5.0p
Year end:	Dec	**Current no of shares:**	
Accounts due:	Apr		72,025,963
Int div paymnt:	n/a	**No of shares after**	
Fin div paymnt:	Feb	**dilution:**	n/a
Int net div per share:	nil	**P/E ratio:**	9.7
Fin net div per share:	0.11p	**Probable CGT?**	**No**

LATEST REPORTED RESULTS: 2003		PREVIOUS REPORTED RESULTS: 2002	
Turnover:	£1.65m	Turnover:	£536,000
PTP:	£805,000	PTP:	£668,000
EPS:	0.8p	EPS:	0.9p

Comments:

This financier, headed by the son of property man David Rowland, backs distressed companies hoping to turn around their fortunes quickly, using high-interest loans or equity. So far, £4m has been raised to fund activities and over a dozen deals completed. The group supported the bid for estate agent Chesterton; won control of AIM shell Murray Financial but failed to take over London Forfaiting. Since the year-end Chartcity, a 7-strong bar chain, has been reversed into Murray Financial.

Retail Stores   (RER)
Department store operator
I West Garden Place, Kendall Street, London, W2 2AQ Tel: 020-7706 2121; Fax: 020-7706 8181

		holding %
Chairman	Richard Balfour-Lynn*	0.0
Chief Executive	Iain Renwick	0.0
Finance Director	Nick Mather	0.0
Director	John Harrison	0.0

Main Shareholders:

MWB*	57.4
Concerto Capital & Second Concerto	12.6
Cartesian Partners	5.5

Percentage of free market capital: 24.5%

*Richard Balfour-Lynn is a director of MWB

Nominated Adviser:	Deutsche Bank, London
AIM Broker:	Deutsche Bank, London
Solicitors:	Dechert, London
Market Makers:	DMG
Auditors:	KPMG, London
Registrars:	Capita Registrars

ENTRY ON AIM:	14/7/2000	Recent price:	215.0p
Interim results:	Mar	**Market cap:**	£47.24m
Final results:	Sep	**Issue price:**	350.0p
Year end:	Jun	**Current no of shares:**	
Accounts due:	Oct		21,970,547
Int div paymnt:	n/a	**No of shares after**	
Fin div paymnt:	n/a	dilution:	23,642,921
Int net div per share:	nil	**P/E ratio:**	n/a
Fin net div per share:	nil	**Probable CGT?**	YES

LATEST REPORTED RESULTS:	2003	PREVIOUS REPORTED RESULTS:	2002
Turnover:	£46.55m	Turnover:	£46.80m
PTP:	£(4.65m)	PTP:	(15.54m)
EPS:	(24.3)p	EPS:	(73.0)p

Comments:
Retail Stores, the owner of London's renowned Liberty department store, is working hard to return to profitability after continued losses. It has implemented cost-cutting measures, appointed new management in key departments and increased its own-brand offering to improve brand recognition. Having relocated its head office, a further 10,000 sq ft of retailing space has been freed up at Tudor House.

Reversus (formerly TransEDA)   (REV)
Cash shell

4th Floor, Black Horse House, Leigh Road, Eastleigh, Hants SO50 9FH Tel: 02380-683500; Fax: 02380-650805;
e-mail: ir@transeda.com; web site: www.transeda.com

		holding %
Chairman	Bob Quinn	3.3
Chief Executive	Udo Muerle	0.0
Finance Director		
Non-Exec Director	Neil Crabb	0.0

Main Shareholders:

Jupiter Asset Management	6.8
Graham Jenney*	6.3
J D Douglas	5.7
Credit Suisse Smaller Companies	4.6
Solus Investment Company	4.3

Percentage of free market capital: 61.3%

*The registered owner of this holding is Pershing Keen Nominees Limited

Comments:

Having sold the operational assets of TransEDA Technologies in September to rival Valiosys for £800,000, the company changed its name and joined the plethora of cash shells mooching on Aim. With its warrants connected to the sale expiring in March, it is currently reviewing potential reverse takeover targets. However, in the interim the company had no turnover and made a £147,000 pre-tax loss. The cash position in March was £608,000.

Nominated Adviser:	Evolution Beeson Gregory, London
AIM Broker:	Evolution Beeson Gregory, London
Solicitors:	Eversheds, Leeds
Market Makers:	BGMM; KBCS; SCAP; WINS
Auditors:	PKF, Pannell House, Park St, Guildford, Surrey, GU1 4HN
Registrars:	Capita Registrars

ENTRY ON AIM:	28/9/2000	Recent price:	1.0p
Interim results:	Mar	Market cap:	£0.72m
Final results:	Sep	Issue price:	50.0p
Year end:	Jun	Current no of shares:	
Accounts due:	Oct		72,160,707
Int div paymnt:	n/a	No of shares after	
Fin div paymnt:	n/a	dilution:	n/a
Int net div per share:	nil	P/E ratio:	n/a
Fin net div per share:	nil	Probable CGT?	YES

LATEST REPORTED RESULTS: 2002		PREVIOUS REPORTED RESULTS: 26 JUN 00 TO 30 JUN 01	
Turnover:	£5.75m	Turnover:	£6.51m
PTP:	£(7.35m)	PTP:	£592,000
EPS:	(10.6)p	EPS:	0.7p

RII (formerly Riceman Insurance Investments)   (RIN)
Emerging markets insurer & reinsurer

43 Queen Anne Street, London, W1M 9FA Tel: 020-7481 1600; Fax: 020-7587 3789; e-mail: post@riceman.com

		holding %
Chairman		
Managing Director	Robert Stubbs	0.0
Finance Director		
Non-Exec Director	Roland Maguire	0.0

Main Shareholders:

Langham Investment	15.7
Shuman Brothers	7.4
Trustees of the Caspian Settlement	7.1
Balli	6.1
Farhad Moshiri	6.1

Percentage of free market capital: 32.7%

Comments:

Formerly Riceman Insurance Investments and one of AIM's worst performers, RII has rallied as a shell with £172,000 cash after losing an interim £5,600. Russian insurance ambitions have been dropped and chairman Kamran Amin replaced by executive director Robert Stubbs. He hopes to be able to put 'suitable proposals' to develop RII to shareholders in 'the near future'.

Nominated Adviser:	Beaumont Cornish, London
AIM Broker:	Hichens Harrison, London
Solicitors:	Watson, Farley & Williams, London
Market Makers:	NUMS; WINS
Auditors:	Larkings, 31 St George's Pl, Canterbury, Kent CT1 1XD
Registrars:	Capita Registrars

Entry on AIM:	29/9/1995	Recent price:	4.5p
Interim results:	Dec	Market cap:	£2.97m
Final results:	Sep	Issue price:	12.0p
Year end:	Mar	Current no of shares:	
Accounts due:	Oct		65,938,530
Int div paymnt:	n/a	No of shares after	
Fin div paymnt:	n/a	dilution:	66,313,530
Int net div per share:	nil	P/E ratio:	n/a
Fin net div per share:	nil	Probable CGT?	No

LATEST REPORTED RESULTS: 2003		PREVIOUS REPORTED RESULTS: 2002	
Turnover:	n/a	Turnover:	n/a
PTP:	£(73,000)	PTP:	£(48,000)
EPS:	(0.1)p	EPS:	(0.1)p

RingProp   (RPP)

Marine technology developer

Haslar Marine Technology Park, Haslar Road Gosport, Hampshire PO12 2AG Tel: 02392-335780; Fax: 02392-335787;
e-mail: gsweet@ringprop.com; web site: www.ringprop.com

		holding %
Chairman	Denis Mulhall	0.8
Chief Executive	Donovan Hoult*	33.9
Finance Director	Giselle Sweet-Escott	0.2
Operations Director	Mark Chapple	1.3

Main Shareholders:

SPI	8.6
Jonathan Townsend	7.6
Martek	6.4

Percentage of free market capital: 40.4%

*RPPL, a company controlled by Don Hoult's wife, is the registered holder of these shares

Nominated Adviser:	Durlacher, London
AIM Broker:	Durlacher, London
Solicitors:	Thomas Eggar, Chichester
Market Makers:	WINS
Auditors:	BDO Stoy Hayward, Southampton
Registrars:	Lloyds TSB Registrars

Entry on AIM: 22/11/2002	**Recent price:**	337.5p
Interim results:	Jun	**Market cap:**	£20.14m
Final results:	Nov	**Issue price:**	130.0p
Year end:	Sep	**Current no of shares:**	
Accounts due:	Dec		5,968,250
Int div paymnt:	n/a	**No of shares after**	
Fin div paymnt:	n/a	dilution:	n/a
Int net div per share:	nil	P/E ratio:	n/a
Fin net div per share:	nil	**Probable CGT?**	**Yes**

LATEST REPORTED RESULTS: 14 MONTHS TO 30 SEPT 2003		PREVIOUS REPORTED RESULTS: N/A	
Turnover:	n/a	Turnover:	n/a
PTP:	£(907,000)	PTP:	n/a
EPS:	(21.0)p	EPS:	n/a

Comments:

RingProp was formed to exploit the potential of its eponymous and ground-breaking marine propeller technology – the company raised around £3.3m on flotation in late 2002. Having decided to make its range in aluminium (where it can sell at a higher price than with composite materials), initial sales have been delayed. The board now expects commercial production to start this summer. Last financial year, there were no revenues, and reported cash balances were almost £1.9m.

Romag   (ROM)

Glass & plastic composites manufacturer

Lope Hill Road, Leadgate Industrial Estate, Lope Hill, Consett, County Durham DH8 7RS Tel: 01207-500000;
Fax: 01207-591979; e-mail: info@romag.co.uk

		holding %
Chairman	John Kennair	38.6
Chief Executive	Lyn Miles	0.5
Finance Director	David Banks	0.2
Non-Exec Director	Peter Allan	0.1

Main Shareholders:

Schroder Trust	9.7

Percentage of free market capital: 51%

Nominated Adviser:	Brewin Dolphin, Glasgow
AIM Broker:	Brewin Dolphin, Glasgow
Solicitors:	Ward Hadaway, Newcastle
Market Makers:	KBCS; WINS
Auditors:	Ernst & Young, Newcastle
Registrars:	Computershare Investor Services

Entry on AIM:	6/11/2003	**Recent price:**	65.5p
Interim results:	Jun	**Market cap:**	£27.66m
Final results:	Jan	**Issue price:**	45.0p
Year end:	Sep	**Current no of shares:**	
Accounts due:	Mar		42,224,662
Int div paymnt:	Jul	**No of shares after**	
Fin div paymnt:	Feb	dilution:	n/a
Int net div per share:	1.0p	P/E ratio:	24.3
Fin net div per share:	1.0p	**Probable CGT?**	**Yes**

LATEST REPORTED RESULTS: 2003		PREVIOUS REPORTED RESULTS: 2002	
Turnover:	£16.64m	Turnover:	£14.93m
PTP:	£967,000	PTP:	£659,000
EPS:	2.7p	EPS:	1.4p

Comments:

The blast and bullet-resistant glass composites maker floated on AIM in November, raising £7.2m. Last year's figures were much improved, with profits up 46% on sales ahead 11%. Romag is moving towards higher margin products and the development of new photovoltaic products will continue this trend. Photovoltaic glass can be incorporated into the fabric of a building as a window or a tile, allowing the passage of light whilst generating electricity.

Roshni Investments

Telecoms investor

8 Baker Street, London, W1U 3LL

		holding %		
Chairman	Nigel Robertson*	62.5	**Nominated Adviser:**	WH Ireland
Chief Executive			**AIM Broker:**	WH Ireland
Finance Director				
Director of Business	Haresh Kanabar	6.3	**Solicitors:**	Lawrence Graham, London
Development			**Market Makers:**	WINS
Main Shareholders:			**Auditors:**	BDO Stoy Hayward, 8 Baker
n/a				Street, London W1U 3LL
			Registrars:	Neville Registrars

Percentage of free market capital: 31.2%

*These shares are held by Brooksrey

ENTRY ON AIM: 11/3/2004	**Recent price:** 25.5p
Interim results: n/a	**Market cap:** £2.04m
Final results: n/a	**Issue price:** 10.0p
Year end: n/a	**Current no of shares:**
Accounts due: n/a	8,000,000
Int div paymnt: n/a	**No of shares after**
Fin div paymnt: n/a	**dilution:** n/a
Int net div per share: nil	**P/E ratio:** n/a
Fin net div per share: nil	**Probable CGT?** No

Comments:

Roshni has raised £185,000 net to acquire telecom services business. The search is being led by Nigel Robertson, founder of troubled directory business scoot.com, and serial shell director Haresh Kanabar. More money will be sought once an acquisition has been found.

LATEST REPORTED RESULTS:		PREVIOUS REPORTED RESULTS:	
	N/A		N/A
Turnover:	n/a	**Turnover:**	n/a
PTP:	n/a	**PTP:**	n/a
EPS:	n/a	**EPS:**	n/a

Rowe Evans Investments (RWEV)

Oil palm, rubber, cotton & beef-cattle plantations owner & operator

3 Clanricarde Gardens, Tunbridge Wells, Kent TN1 1HQ Tel: 01892-516333; Fax: 01892-518639;
e-mail: philipf@mpevans.co.uk

		holding %		
Chairman	Philip Fletcher	0.9	**Nominated Adviser:**	Westhouse Securities, London
Chief Executive	as above		**AIM Broker:**	Westhouse Securities, London
Finance Director			**Solicitors:**	Ashursts, London
Deputy Chairman	Konrad Legg	0.4	**Market Makers:**	MLSB; WINS
			Auditors:	Deloitte & Touche, London
Main Shareholders:				
Sungkai		24.3	**Registrars:**	M P Evans
Bertam		18.9		
Alcatel Bell				
Pensioenfonds VZW		7.1		
E Hadsley-Chaplin		4.7		
Aberdeen Asian Smaller Companies		3.5		

Percentage of free market capital: 39.2%

Entry on AIM: 28/10/2002	**Recent price:** 160.0p
Interim results: Sep	**Market cap:** £77.42m
Final results: Apr	**Issue price:** 94.0p
Year end: Dec	**Current no of shares:**
Accounts due: May	48,385,073
Int div paymnt: n/a	**No of shares after**
Fin div paymnt: Mar	**dilution:** n/a
Int net div per share: nil	**P/E ratio:** 18.2
Fin net div per share: 4.75p	**Probable CGT?** No

Comments:

Tunbridge Wells-based Rowe Evans has interests in cotton and property in Australia and rubber and palm oil in Indonesia and Malaysia. With firm palm oil and rubber prices, the company remains profitable, although the drought in Australia caused low cotton production. This was offset by selling some of its investments there. Presumably, the weak US dollar – the currency in which palm oil is traded in – will have a negative impact on what was expected to be another good year.

LATEST REPORTED RESULTS:		PREVIOUS REPORTED RESULTS:	
	2002		2001
Turnover:	£6.4m	**Turnover:**	£3.78m
PTP:	£6.7m	**PTP:**	£3.19m
EPS:	8.8p	**EPS:**	4.4p

(RWS)

...ctual property support services

...pa House, Marsham Way, Gerrards Cross, Bucks SL9 8BQ Tel: 01753-480200; Fax: 01753-480280;
...mail: rwstrans@rws.com; web site: www.rws.com

		holding %
Chairman	Andrew Brode	49.2
Chief Executive		
Finance Director	Michael McCarthy	0.0
Exec Director	Elisabeth Lucas	0.0

Main Shareholders:
Canada Life Marketing Group 4.2

Percentage of free market capital: 46.5%

Nominated Adviser:	Collins Stewart, London
AIM Broker:	Collins Stewart, London
Solicitors:	Salans, London
Market Makers:	WINS
Auditors:	BDO Stoy Hayward, 8 Baker Street, London W1U 3LL
Registrars:	Capita Registrars

ENTRY ON AIM: 11/11/2003		Recent price:	156.0p
Interim results:	Sep	Market cap:	£58.94m
Final results:	Mar	Issue price:	112.5p
Year end:	Feb	Current no of shares:	
Accounts due:	Jun		37,782,111
Int div paymnt:	n/a	No of shares after	
Fin div paymnt:	n/a	dilution:	n/a
Int net div per share:	nil	P/E ratio:	n/a
Fin net div per share:	nil	**Probable CGT?**	**YES**

LATEST REPORTED RESULTS: 2003		PREVIOUS REPORTED RESULTS: 2002	
Turnover:	£535,000	Turnover:	£2.0m
PTP:	£(118,000)	PTP:	£(5.35m)
EPS:	(0.5)p	EPS:	(27.0)p

Comments:
Loss-making Health Media reinvented itself as an intellectual property business through the £42m takeover of RWS. Driving the deal through was Andrew Brode, the veteran media company supporter, who was previously the boss of both businesses. In its new guise RWS will focus on translating patents and other IP-related documents. It is expected to make profits of £5.4m this year on sales of around £30m.

Samedaybooks.co.uk   (SDK)

Bookshop operator
3 Tunsgate, Guildford, Surrey GU1 3QT Tel: 01483-300255; Fax: 01483-302147; web site: www.samedaybooks.co.uk

		holding %
Chairman	David Mahony	3.1
Managing Director	Alan Clifford	2.0
Finance Director	Andrew Wells	9.3
IT Director	M Hearn	0.1

Main Shareholders:

Andrew Swanston 7.1

Percentage of free market capital: 78.5%

Nominated Adviser:	Charles Stanley, London
AIM Broker:	Charles Stanley, London
Solicitors:	Charles Russell, Guildford
Market Makers:	MLSB; WINS
Auditors:	Sayers Butterworth, 18 Bentinck St, London W1M 5RL
Registrars:	Capita Registrars

Entry on AIM:	15/4/1997	Recent price:	1.1p
Interim results:	Jun	Market cap:	£1.87m
Final results:	Feb	Issue price:	44.0p
Year end:	Sep	Current no of shares:	
Accounts due:	Feb		170,000,000
Int div paymnt:	n/a	No of shares after	
Fin div paymnt:	n/a	dilution:	n/a
Int net div per share:	nil	P/E ratio:	n/a
Fin net div per share:	nil	Probable CGT?	**YES**

LATEST REPORTED RESULTS: 2003		PREVIOUS REPORTED RESULTS: 2002	
Turnover:	£8.06m	Turnover:	£7.65m
PTP:	£(138,000)	PTP:	£(961,000)
EPS:	(0.1)p	EPS:	(0.5)p

Comments:
Samedaybooks showed a small pre-tax loss for 2003 but also enjoyed 2.5% improved like-for-like sales. After disposing of two loss-making stores, all the other outlets are now making a profit, except for the Canterbury one, which nevertheless is cash generative. Up to Christmas like-for-like sales increased 3.2%. The group is not optimistic for 2004 results but, with improved systems, expects to make further progress during the year.

Samuel Heath & Sons (HSM)

Bathroom accessories manufacturer

Cobden Works, Leopold Street, Birmingham, B12 0UJ Tel: 0121-766 4200; Fax: 0121-772 3334;
e-mail: info@samuel-heath.com; web site: www.samuel-heath.com

		holding %
Chairman	Samuel Heath	18.0
Managing Director	David Pick	0.2
Finance Director	David Richardson	0.1
Non-Exec Director	David Coplestone	3.9

Main Shareholders:

C Heath	14.2
G Heath	14.2
S Perkins	10.5
Svenska Handelsbanken AB	3.5

Percentage of free market capital: 35.1%

Comments:

The family-owned bathroom accessories and hardware maker still faces difficult business conditions. Chairman Sam Heath's updates remain frank. Interim profits before tax fell 15% to £340,000 compared to the second half to March, where profits were attributed to exceptionally early spring sales. The company is making no guarantee that this will occur again in the next half. Turnover decreased to £5.9m. Nevertheless, the group remains profitable, which is reassuring.

Nominated Adviser:	Williams de Broe, Birmingham
AIM Broker:	Williams de Broe, Birmingham
Solicitors:	Shakespeares, Birmingham
Market Makers:	WDBM; WINS
Auditors:	Moore Stephens, Warwick Lane, London EC4P 4BN
Registrars:	Capita Registrars

ENTRY ON AIM:	2/10/2000	**Recent price:**	397.5p
Interim results:	Dec	**Market cap:**	£10.31m
Final results:	Jul	**Issue price:**	n/a
Year end:	Mar	**Current no of shares:**	
Accounts due:	Aug		2,594,968
Int div paymnt:	Mar	**No of shares after**	
Fin div paymnt:	Aug	**dilution:**	n/a
Int net div per share:	5.0p	**P/E ratio:**	12.6
Fin net div per share:	8.5p	**Probable CGT?**	YES

LATEST REPORTED RESULTS: 2003		PREVIOUS REPORTED RESULTS: 2002	
Turnover:	£12.74m	Turnover:	£12.83m
PTP:	£1.06m	PTP:	£1.25m
EPS:	31.5p	EPS:	37.6p

Savoy Asset Management (SMN)

Investment manager

Lilly House, 13 Hanover Square, London, W1S 1HN Tel: 020-7659 8000; Fax: 020-7659 8001;
e-mail: savoy@savoyassetmgt.com; web site: www.savoyassetmgt.com

		holding %
Chairman	Kenneth Clarke	0.1
Chief Executive	Christopher Saunders	7.9
Finance Director	Paul Tarran	0.2
Director	David Kennard	3.6

Main Shareholders:

Global Investment House	29.6
Tom Tutton	7.9
Estates of Brian Banks (deceased)	6.8

Percentage of free market capital: 43.5%

Comments:

The fund manager, chaired by former Chancellor Ken Clarke, continues to expand organically under Howard Hughes, a former SocGen stockbroker. He has brought on ten more employees of his former company who, between them, managed £425m at SocGen. A Bournemouth IFA with £50m under management was also bought. The recovering markets helped Savoy return to modest profit at the interim stage.

Nominated Adviser:	Nabarro Wells, London
AIM Broker:	Charles Stanley, London
Solicitors:	Dechert, London
Market Makers:	KBCS; TEAM; WINS
Auditors:	Saffery Champness, London
Registrars:	Capita Registrars

Entry on AIM:	20/11/1997	**Recent price:**	140.0p
Interim results:	Dec	**Market cap:**	£12.55m
Final results:	Aug	**Issue price:**	95.0p
Year end:	Mar	**Current no of shares:**	
Accounts due:	Aug		8,967,525
Int div paymnt:	Jan	**No of shares after**	
Fin div paymnt:	n/a	**dilution:**	n/a
Int net div per share:	1.0p	**P/E ratio:**	n/a
Fin net div per share:	nil	**Probable CGT?**	YES

LATEST REPORTED RESULTS: 2003		PREVIOUS REPORTED RESULTS: 2002	
Turnover:	£3.59m	Turnover:	£3.67m
PTP:	£(342,000)	PTP:	£(580,000)
EPS:	(3.7)p	EPS:	(3.1)p

SBS (SBG)

IT recruitment consultant

19th Flr, Centre Point, 103 New Oxford St, London, WC1A 1DY Tel: 020-7420 6700; Fax: 020-7420 6767;
e-mail: london@sbsplc.com; web site: www.sbsplc.com

		holding %
Chairman	Leo Knifton	0.0
Chief Executive	Philip Holt	0.03
Finance Director		
Director	Nigel Weller	0.0

Main Shareholders:

Alan Waksman	43.5
David Holroyd	6.4
Neil Wotherspoon	3.2

Percentage of free market capital: 46.9%

Comments:

The former IT recruitment and services business is a re-capitalised shell on the lookout for a reverse deal. This follows the sale of its UK IT staffing operations, receivership and the eventual sale of other operations by the receiver to recruiter Harvey Nash. Since then, the company's creditors and shareholders have approved a creditors voluntary agreement and annual accounts to 31 August have been published. Trading in the shares has been restored.

Nominated Adviser:	City Financial Associates, London
AIM Broker:	City Financial Associates, London
Solicitors:	Addleshaw Goddard, London
Market Makers:	KBCS; WINS
Auditors:	PKF, 78 Hatton Garden, London EC1N 8JA
Registrars:	Capita Registrars

Entry on AIM:	5/6/1997	Recent price:	34.0p
Interim results:	May	Market cap:	£2.57m
Final results:	Feb	Issue price:	100.0p
Year end:	Aug	Current no of shares:	
Accounts due:	Dec		7,569,778
Int div paymnt:	n/a	No of shares after	
Fin div paymnt:	n/a	dilution:	n/a
Int net div per share:	nil	P/E ratio:	n/a
Fin net div per share:	nil	Probable CGT?	Yes

LATEST REPORTED RESULTS: 2003		PREVIOUS REPORTED RESULTS: 2002	
Turnover:	n/a	Turnover:	32.09m
PTP:	£(9.63m)	PTP:	£(2.05m)
EPS:	(66.8)p	EPS:	(19.4)p

Scipher (SIP)

Technology developer & licensor

CRL Dawley Road, Hayes, Middlesex UB3 1HH Tel: 020-8848 6555; Fax: 020-8848 6677;
e-mail: info@scipher.com; web site: www.scipher.com

		holding %
Chairman	Dr Kenneth Gray	4.8
Chief Executive	Rudolph Burger	0.04
Finance Director	Christopher Mutter	0.0
Exec Director	Dr Ashok Vaidya	4.9

Main Shareholders:

Schroder Investment Mangement	7.4
Newton ICVC Managed Fund	4.4
Dr John C White	3.7
Henderson Global Investors	3.6
UBS Global Asset Management	3.2

Percentage of free market capital: 67.9%

Comments:

Pity the poor investors here. The group, which develops and licenses a range of technology, is currently in the midst of a strategic review which will see it reduce its workforce, sell off non-core cash-consumptive divisions and hopefully stem its incredible run of losses. When slimmed down, it will focus on three technologies – secure identification, micro-displays and wireless communications. If it can retain key employees, the support of its bank and keep cashflow in order all should be fine. But that's a big if.

Nominated Adviser:	Evolution Beeson Gregory, London
AIM Broker:	Evolution Beeson Gregory, London
Solicitors:	Ashursts, London
Market Makers:	BARD; EVO; KBCS; KLWT; MLSB; UBS; WINS
Auditors:	PricewaterhouseCoopers, London
Registrars:	Capita Registrars

entry on AIM:	11/7/2003	Recent price:	3.1p
Interim results:	Nov	Market cap:	£8.03m
Final results:	Jul	Issue price:	5.0p
Year end:	Mar	Current no of shares:	
Accounts due:	Sep		259,060,797
Int div paymnt:	n/a	No of shares after	
Fin div paymnt:	n/a	dilution:	n/a
Int net div per share:	nil	P/E ratio:	n/a
Fin net div per share:	nil	Probable CGT?	Yes

LATEST REPORTED RESULTS: 2003		PREVIOUS REPORTED RESULTS: 2002	
Turnover:	£20.26m	Turnover:	£20.78m
PTP:	£(10.5m)	PTP:	£(12.67m)
EPS:	(10.4)p	EPS:	(13.2)p

Scott Tod (formerly Darwen Capital)   (SCD)

Automated teller machine distributor and maintainer

Fitzroy House, 18-20 Grafton Street, London, W1S 4DZ

		holding %
Chairman	David Massie	14.9
Chief Executive	Nicholas Tod	31.5
Finance Director		
Operations Director	Lawrence Watts	5.6

Main Shareholders:

Chase Nominees	8.9
JM Finn Nominees	7.1
Singer & Friedlander	5.9

Percentage of free market capital: 22.4%

Nominated Adviser:	ARM Corporate Finance, London
AIM Broker:	Keith Bayley Rogers & Co, London
Solicitors:	Stallard, London
Market Makers:	EVO; SCAP; WINS
Auditors:	PricewaterhouseCoopers, London
Registrars:	Neville Registrars

ENTRY ON AIM:	27/11/2003	**Recent price:**	58.5p
Interim results:	Mar	**Market cap:**	£15.8m
Final results:	Sep	**Issue price:**	25.0p
Year end:	Jun	**Current no of shares:**	
Accounts due:	Oct		27,000,000
Int div paymnt:	n/a	**No of shares after**	
Fin div paymnt:	n/a	**dilution:**	n/a
Int net div per share:	nil	**P/E ratio:**	n/a
Fin net div per share:	nil	**Probable CGT?**	YES

LATEST REPORTED RESULTS: 15 MONTHS TO 30 JUN 2003		PREVIOUS REPORTED RESULTS: 9 MONTHS TO 31 MAR 2002	
Turnover:	£8.02m	**Turnover:**	£2.44m
PTP:	£197,000	**PTP:**	£42,000
EPS:	n/a	**EPS:**	n/a

Comments:

Growing Scott Tod reversed into Darwen Capital last November. It distributes ATMs and also makes card vending and change machines. Interims to December only reflected five weeks trading from the Scott Tod business, and showed a £7,000 profit on £875,000 sales – cash on the balance sheet was £1.2m. Having reached agreement to supply pub owner Mitchells and Butlers, the company hopes to become the pre-eminent ATM supplier to the leisure sector.

Screen   (SEN)

High-tech security and communications products developer

Stubbings Barn, Burchetts Green Lane, Burchetts Green, Maidenhead, Berkshire SL6 3QP Tel: 01628-820011; Fax: 01628-820015; e-mail: info@screenplc.com; web site: www.screenplc.com

		holding %
Chairman	Timothy Wightman	2.1
Chief Executive		
Finance Director	Christopher Langridge	0.0
Deputy Chairman	Ian Taylor	0.5

Main Shareholders:

Manulife International Investment Management	4.5
MFC Global Investment	3.8

Percentage of free market capital: 88.6%

Nominated Adviser:	Collins Stewart, London
AIM Broker:	Collins Stewart, London; Seymour Pierce Ellis, Crawley
Solicitors:	Hale and Dorr, Oxford
Market Makers:	KBCS; MLSB; SCAP; SGSL; WINS
Auditors:	Deloitte & Touche, 1 Little New St, London EC4A 3TR
Registrars:	Capita Registrars

Entry on AIM:	3/3/1997	**Recent price:**	7.0p
Interim results:	Dec	**Market cap:**	£4.62m
Final results:	Apr	**Issue price:**	20.0p
Year end:	Dec	**Current no of shares:**	
Accounts due:	Jun		66,039,403
Int div paymnt:	n/a	**No of shares after**	
Fin div paymnt:	n/a	**dilution:**	n/a
Int net div per share:	nil	**P/E ratio:**	n/a
Fin net div per share:	nil	**Probable CGT?**	YES

LATEST REPORTED RESULTS: 2002		PREVIOUS REPORTED RESULTS: 2001	
Turnover:	£18.69m	**Turnover:**	£14.25m
PTP:	£(15.15m)	**PTP:**	£(851,000)
EPS:	(27.8)p	**EPS:**	(2.0)p

Comments:

Screen, the provider of security and communication systems, has a very chequered recent history to say the least. It has warned the market that the second-half loss will match the first due to snags at Joyce-Loebl – affected by problems in the rail transport industry – and at Petards Vision. This news disappointed after an encouraging half to June in which losses were pared from £11.9m to £583,000. Revenue growth was strong, with turnover rising to £11.2m (£9.7m).

Screen FX (SFX)
Advertising & communication services provider
Mill House, Mill Lane, Cheadle, Cheshire SK8 2NT Tel: 0161-428 5544; Fax: 0161-428 5599

		holding %
Chairman	Richard Nichols	0.2
Chief Executive	David Clark	14.6
Finance Director		
Chief Operating Officer	Stefan Schultz	14.6
Main Shareholders:		
David Makin		14.6
Simon Hawthorne		14.6

Percentage of free market capital: 41.2%

Comments:
Screen FX raised a useful £5m before expenses in a
Seymour Pierce-led fundraising in early March. The
money will be used to develop the group's digital
screen advertising business. Apparently SFX's digital
screens are 'the logical step in the out of home advertising market'. The screens will be placed in 'high
footfall' shopping areas. All in all, an interesting concept,
but much remains to be done.

Nominated Adviser:	Seymour Pierce, London	
AIM Broker:	Seymour Pierce, London	
Solicitors:	Halliwell Landau, London	
Market Makers:	WINS	
Auditors:	Baker Tilly, Manchester	
Registrars:	Park Circus Registrars	

ENTRY ON AIM:	10/3/2004	**Recent price:**	11.0p
Interim results:	Jan	**Market cap:**	£13.2m
Final results:	Sep	**Issue price:**	10.0p
Year end:	Mar	**Current no of shares:**	
Accounts due:	Oct		120,000,000
Int div paymnt:	n/a	**No of shares after**	
Fin div paymnt:	n/a	**dilution:**	n/a
Int net div per share:	nil	**P/E ratio:**	n/a
Fin net div per share:	nil	**Probable CGT?**	YES

LATEST REPORTED RESULTS:		PREVIOUS REPORTED RESULTS:	
	2003		2002
Turnover:	£602,000	**Turnover:**	£378,000
PTP:	£86,000	**PTP:**	£62,000
EPS:	n/a	**EPS:**	n/a

SectorGuard (SGD)
Security solutions provider
Gainsborough House, Sheering Lower Rd, Sawbridgeworth, Herts CM21 9RG Tel: 01279-724777; Fax: 01279-722899;
e-mail: Adam.Crawford@SectorGuard.plc.uk; web site: www.sectorguard.plc.uk

		holding %
Chairman	Peter Gorty	0.1
Chief Executive	David Marks	18.3
Finance Director		
Non-Exec Director	Gideon Lyons	0.2
Main Shareholders:		
ISIS Asset Management		6.2
Artemis AIM VCT		6.2
Northern AIM VCT		6.2
B Myers		4.7
D Sullivan		4.7

Percentage of free market capital: 53.3%

Comments:
The expanding manned security outfit enjoyed a strong
year with healthy sales and profits growth and year-end
cash growing a staggering 247% to £836,000. Much of
SectorGuard's growth has come via acquisitions that
have bolstered its position in London, the Home
Counties and the Midlands. The company is also making
inroads into the education sector, supplying guards to
colleges. Increased regulation of the industry should
squeeze out weaker operators.

Nominated Adviser:	Seymour Pierce, London	
AIM Broker:	Seymour Pierce Ellis, Crawley	
Solicitors:	Nabarro Nathanson, Reading	
Market Makers:	SCAP; WINS	
Auditors:	Nexia Audit, No1 Riding House Street, London WA1 3AS	
Registrars:	Capita Registrars	

Entry on AIM:	13/3/2002	**Recent price:**	4.25p
Interim results:	Jun	**Market cap:**	£8.74m
Final results:	Jan	**Issue price:**	3.0p
Year end:	Sep	**Current no of shares:**	
Accounts due:	Jan		205,755,476
Int div paymnt:	n/a	**No of shares after**	
Fin div paymnt:	n/a	**dilution:**	n/a
Int net div per share:	nil	**P/E ratio:**	n/a
Fin net div per share:	nil	**Probable CGT?**	YES

LATEST REPORTED RESULTS:		PREVIOUS REPORTED RESULTS:	
	2003		2002
Turnover:	£12.75m	**Turnover:**	£7.37m
PTP:	£742,000	**PTP:**	£502,000
EPS:	0.3p	**EPS:**	0.1p

Sefton Resources (SER)

Oil & gas explorer; property owner and developer

2050 S. Oneida Street, Suite 102, Denver, Colorado 80224 USA, Tel: 00-1 303 759 2700; Fax: 00-1 303 759 2701;
e-mail: seftonresources@aol.com; web site: www.seftonresources.com

		holding %
Chairman	John Ellerton	9.4
Chief Executive	as above	
Finance Director		
Director	Karl Arleth	4.9

Main Shareholders:

Canpet	5.0
Dennis Haugh	4.3
Mendes and Associates	4.0

Percentage of free market capital: 67.8%

Nominated Adviser:	Seymour Pierce, London
AIM Broker:	Seymour Pierce Ellis, Crawley
Solicitors:	Masons, London
Market Makers:	SCAP; WINS
Auditors:	Gordon, Hughes & Brown, Denver, Colorado, USA
Registrars:	Computershare Investor Services

Entry on AIM:	8/12/2000	**Recent price:**	0.5p
Interim results:	Sep	Market cap:	£4.69m
Final results:	Jun	Issue price:	5.0p
Year end:	Dec	Current no of shares:	
Accounts due:	Sep		938,369,500
Int div paymnt:	n/a	No of shares after	
Fin div paymnt:	n/a	dilution:	n/a
Int net div per share:	nil	P/E ratio:	n/a
Fin net div per share:	nil	Probable CGT?	No

Comments:
When big-talking Jim Ellerton floated Sefton, he claimed new technology to unlock 'massive' oil and gas reserves in Southern California. They have yet to appear, though output at one well rose recently. Lately beset by lawsuits with a contractor at its Yule 6 well, Sefton has raised £250,000 at a lowly 0.25p, lost a nine-month £175,000 and says its Tapia Canyon field has shallow gas reserves, so far 'overlooked'.

LATEST REPORTED RESULTS: 2002		PREVIOUS REPORTED RESULTS: 2001	
Turnover:	$454,000	Turnover:	$183,000
PTP:	$(1.01m)	PTP:	$(757,000)
EPS:	(0.0)c	EPS:	(0.0)c

Selector (SLC)

Marketing business

27 Almal Street, Kiriat Aryeh, PO Box 3406, Petach Tikva Israel Tel: 00-972 3 924 5559; Fax: 00-972 3 924 5499

		holding %
Chairman	John Corre	3.0
Managing Director	Ronen Levy	34.6
Finance Director	as above	
Shareholder	Joseph Feldman	12.1

Main Shareholders:

Schlomo Ashur	25.2
Bank Hapoalim	10.3
The Aim Trust	9.6
WS Nominees	5.2
State Street Nominees	3.9

Percentage of free market capital: n/a

Nominated Adviser:	Brewin Dolphin, Glasgow
AIM Broker:	Brewin Dolphin, Glasgow
Solicitors:	Olswang, London
Market Makers:	KBCS; WINS
Auditors:	Goffer, Guilman, Gross, Tel Aviv 63324, Israel
Registrars:	Capita Registrars

Entry on AIM:	23/7/1996	**Recent price:**	2.1p
Interim results:	Sep	Market cap:	£0.94m
Final results:	Jun	Issue price:	66.0p
Year end:	Dec	Current no of shares:	
Accounts due:	Jun		44,775,149
Int div paymnt:	n/a	No of shares after	
Fin div paymnt:	n/a	dilution:	n/a
Int net div per share:	nil	P/E ratio:	n/a
Fin net div per share:	nil	Probable CGT?	No

Comments:
Marketing business Selector continues to struggle. Its very brief interim statement showed sales falling to £634,000 and losses increasing to £152,000. Apparently it has invested in research and development and continues to pursue its Select 100 and European interests. £139,000 was raised in a placing in January. In all likelihood, Selector will continue to limp along for as long as the political situation in Israel remains volatile.

LATEST REPORTED RESULTS: 2002		PREVIOUS REPORTED RESULTS: 2001	
Turnover:	$1.33m	Turnover:	$1.20m
PTP:	$(313,000)	PTP:	$(28,000)
EPS:	0.3c	EPS:	(0.0)c

Setstone (formerly threeW.net) (STN)

Cash shell

Verulam Gardens, 70 Gray's Inn Road, London ,WC1X 8NF Tel: 01727 869 300; Fax: 01727 869 400;
e-mail: enquiries@threew.net; web site: www.threew.net

		holding %
Chairman	Peter Burton	5.4
Chief Executive	Anthony Hoskinson	0.0
Finance Director		
Non-Exec Director	David Hyde	0.0

Main Shareholders:

Ivan Smith	18.4
Jason Smith	17.3
Angola Investments	10.5
Bowmaker Management	10.5
London & Globe Securities	9.0
Percentage of free market capital:	10.6%

Nominated Adviser:	City Financial Associates, London
AIM Broker:	Brewin Dolphin, London
Solicitors:	Edward Lewis, London
Market Makers:	MLSB; SCAP; WINS
Auditors:	Gerald Edelman, 25 Harley Street, London W1N 2BR
Registrars:	Capita Registrars

ENTRY ON AIM:	10/1/2000	**Recent price:**	1.0p
Interim results:	Jul	**Market cap:**	£0.57m
Final results:	Apr	**Issue price:**	25.0p
Year end:	Oct	**Current no of shares:**	
Accounts due:	Mar		57,150,736
Int div paymnt:	n/a	**No of shares after**	
Fin div paymnt:	n/a	**dilution:**	n/a
Int net div per share:	nil	**P/E ratio:**	n/a
Fin net div per share:	nil	**Probable CGT?**	YES

Comments:

This used to be called threeW.net until a new set of investors subscribed for new shares to settle outstanding debts and changed the group's name to Setstone. But the strategy, of finding a company to reverse into the shell, remains the same. Latest interims showed a £12,000 loss. Cash levels have improved following the recent £400,000 of share and loan issues. Serial AIM speculator Jo Malins, via his Bowmaker vehicle, was behind the latest action.

LATEST REPORTED RESULTS:	2002	PREVIOUS REPORTED RESULTS:	2001
Turnover:	£91,000	Turnover:	£447,000
PTP:	£(233,000)	PTP:	£(11.16m)
EPS:	(0.8)p	EPS:	(61.3)p

Sheffield United (SUT)

Professional football club operator

Bramall Lane, Sheffield, S2 4SU Tel: 0870-787 1960; Fax: 0870-787 3345; e-mail: info@sufc.co.uk;
web site: www.sufc.co.uk

		holding %
Chairman	Kevin McCabe	20.7
Chief Executive		
Finance Director	Mark Fenoughty	0.0
Non-Exec Director	Andrew Laver	3.5

Main Shareholders:

Texas Holdings	14.7
Scarborough Property Investment	7.4
B Procter	6.6
C Talbot	5.7
A McDonald	3.9
Percentage of free market capital:	20.5%

Nominated Adviser:	KBC Peel Hunt, London
AIM Broker:	KBC Peel Hunt, London
Solicitors:	DLA, London
Market Makers:	HSBC; KBCS; WINS
Auditors:	Grant Thornton, Melton St, Euston Sq, London NW1 2EP
Registrars:	Capita Registrars

Entry on AIM:	3/6/2003	**Recent price:**	9.0p
Interim results:	Mar	**Market cap:**	£8.07m
Final results:	Oct	**Issue price:**	60.0p
Year end:	Jun	**Current no of shares:**	
Accounts due:	Jan		89,638,480
Int div paymnt:	n/a	**No of shares after**	
Fin div paymnt:	n/a	**dilution:**	n/a
Int net div per share:	nil	**P/E ratio:**	n/a
Fin net div per share:	nil	**Probable CGT?**	YES

Comments:

The Nationwide League club is making progress on and off the field of play, and is in with a shout of promotion this season. Nevertheless, interims to December revealed a net loss, reflecting higher player wages and a lack of first-half player sales. But turnover skipped higher, average crowds were 24% up and season ticket sales improved by 34%. The 'Blades' have also signed an agreement with Las Vegas Sands Inc to develop an 'integrated' entertainment complex at Bramall Lane.

LATEST REPORTED RESULTS:	2003	PREVIOUS REPORTED RESULTS:	2002
Turnover:	£13.0m	Turnover:	£10.04m
PTP:	£(411,000)	PTP:	£(1.84m)
EPS:	(0.0)p	EPS:	(3.7)p

Sibir Energy   (SBE)
Oil & gas explorer & producer
11 Grosvenor Crescent, London, SW1X 7EE Tel: 020-7235 3166; Fax: 020-7235 3616;
e-mail: information@sibirenergy.com; web site: www.sibirenergy.com

		holding %
Chairman	William Guinness	0.8
Chief Executive	Henry Cameron	0.8
Finance Director	Alexander Betsky	0.0
Non-Exec Director	Urs Josef Haener	0.6

Main Shareholders:

Bennfield	40.3
Stancroft Trust	6.1
Angelica Trading	5.2
Charlemagne Capital	3.8

Percentage of free market capital: 38.97

Comments:
Sibir has been a strong performer after raising £24m at 16p in October to develop Rusian oil and gas prospects. These include Salym, a £600m project being developed by Shell and local groups. After many snags and delays, Sibir, which lost an interim £8.3m, has a big chunk of one participant, state-owned Moscow Oil & Gas. Bulls have said this could bring Sibir £150m turnover this year.

Nominated Adviser:	Strand Partners, London
AIM Broker:	Canaccord Capital, London
Solicitors:	Jones Day Gouldens, London
Market Makers:	KBCS; MLSB; SCAP; TEAM; WINS
Auditors:	Ernst & Young, Becket House, 1 Lambeth Palace Road, SE1 7EU
Registrars:	Capita Registrars

Entry on AIM:	8/4/1997	**Recent price:**	28.0p
Interim results:	Sep	**Market cap:**	£467.13m
Final results:	Jun	**Issue price:**	10.0p
Year end:	Dec	**Current no of shares:**	
Accounts due:	Jul		1,668,310,092
Int div paymnt:	n/a	**No of shares after**	
Fin div paymnt:	n/a	**dilution:**	n/a
Int net div per share:	nil	**P/E ratio:**	n/a
Fin net div per share:	nil	**Probable CGT?**	**No**

LATEST REPORTED RESULTS:		PREVIOUS REPORTED RESULTS:	
	2002		2001
Turnover:	£22.52m	**Turnover:**	£47.06m
PTP:	£(10.53m)	**PTP:**	£(29.53m)
EPS:	(0.8)p	**EPS:**	(2.3)p

Sigma Technology   (SGM)
Technology investor and consultant
6th Floor, Bucklersbury House, 83 Cannon Street, London, EC4N 8ST Tel: 020-7653 3200; Fax: 020-7653 3201;
web site: www.sigmatech.co.uk

		holding %
Chairman	Simon Miller	0.2
Joint MD	Graham Barnet	20.2
Finance Director	Marilyn Cole	0.8
Joint MD	Neil Crabb	23.3

Main Shareholders:

Barkley	8.0
Jupiter Primadona Growth Trust	6.6
Cantebury	5.6
Bank of Scotland	4.8
Artemis Investment Management	3.0

Percentage of free market capital: 27.6%

Comments:
Sigma has changed its focus. Rather than make investments directly, the group prefers to manage third-party funds. These stand at £23m at present after raising £6m for the Sigma Innovation Fund. Net assets were £4.8m at the end of 2003, of which £1.8m is cash and £1.2m quoted investments – principally microscopic technology developer Micap. Six investments were made in the second half, when the group managed to break even. 2002's loss relates to portfolio write-offs.

Nominated Adviser:	Oriel Securities, London
AIM Broker:	Oriel Securities, London
Solicitors:	Shepherd & Wedderburn, Edinburgh
Market Makers:	DMG; NUMS; WINS
Auditors:	BDO Stoy Hayward, 8 Baker Street, London W1U 3LL
Registrars:	Capita Registrars

Entry on AIM:	27/4/2000	**Recent price:**	19.5p
Interim results:	Sep	**Market cap:**	£7.04m
Final results:	Feb	**Issue price:**	128p
Year end:	Dec	**Current no of shares:**	
Accounts due:	Mar		36,093,540
Int div paymnt:	n/a	**No of shares after**	
Fin div paymnt:	n/a	**dilution:**	n/a
Int net div per share:	nil	**P/E ratio:**	n/a
Fin net div per share:	nil	**Probable CGT?**	**Yes**

LATEST REPORTED RESULTS:		PREVIOUS REPORTED RESULTS:	
	2003		2002
Turnover:	£1.15m	**Turnover:**	£1.01m
PTP:	£(700,000)	**PTP:**	£(3.63m)
EPS:	(1.9)p	**EPS:**	(10.1)p

Silentpoint (SLP)

Investment company
22 Soho Square, London, W1D 4NS Tel: 020-7070 7283; Fax: 020-7070 7288

		holding %
Chairman	Haresh Kanabar	0.6
Chief Executive	Smit Berry	12.0
Finance Director		
Exec Director	David Rogers	0.6

Main Shareholders:

Eyeconomy Holdings	10.5
Goldman Sachs	6.6
Keith Stanley	6.3
Paul McGroary & Tipakorn Anuvatnujotikul	4.5
Suffolk Life Annuities	4.0

Percentage of free market capital: 48.4%

Comments:
This investment group boasts smaller companies expert Smit Berry as chief executive. Its plan is to keep overheads under control, make small quoted investments, and longer term find a reverse acquisition to increase its cashflow generation. Last year the group managed to make a profit after making a £87,000 gain on successful investments. Recently the group has sold part of its stake in Gaming Corporation. Year-end net assets stood at £1.25m.

Nominated Adviser:	John East, London		
AIM Broker:	Seymour Pierce, London		
Solicitors:	Berwin Leighton Paisner, London		
Market Makers:	SCAP; WINS		
Auditors:	BDO Stoy Hayward, 8 Baker Street, London, W1U 3LL		
Registrars:	Capita Registrars		

ENTRY ON AIM: 20/11/2000		Recent price:	10.0p
Interim results:	Sep	Market cap:	£1.75m
Final results:	Apr	Issue price:	10.0p
Year end:	Oct	Current no of shares:	
Accounts due:	Jan		17,500,000
Int div paymnt:	n/a	No of shares after	
Fin div paymnt:	n/a	dilution:	18,200,000
Int net div per share:	nil	P/E ratio:	n/a
Fin net div per share:	nil	Probable CGT?	Yes

LATEST REPORTED RESULTS: 2003		PREVIOUS REPORTED RESULTS: 2002	
Turnover:	n/a	Turnover:	n/a
PTP:	£55,000	PTP:	£(116,000)
EPS:	0.3p	EPS:	(0.7)p

Sinclair Pharma (SPH)

Pharmaceutical company
Borough Road, Godalming, Surrey GU7 2AB Tel: 01483-426 644; Fax: 01483-427 633

		holding %
Chairman	Steven Harris	0.1
Chief Executive	Michael Flynn	20.8
Finance Director	Jeremy Randall	2.2

Main Shareholders:

ESOT	13.9
Marco Mastrodonato	4.2

Percentage of free market capital: 47.9%

Comments:
Drug company Sinclair raised £8.9m net on admission to develop its nine patented treatments for a variety of conditions affecting the skin, mouth and side-effects connected with cancer therapies. The group focuses on bringing treatments in niche areas at a late stage of development to market. Most products are distributed via appointed licensees. Sinclair will consider moving into other niches as well and also look at making acquisitions. A £1.4m interim loss was made on £0.9m sales.

Nominated Adviser:	Baird, London		
AIM Broker:	Baird, London		
Solicitors:	Eversheds, Nottingham		
Market Makers:	BARD; KBCS; WINS		
Auditors:	Ernst & Young, Southampton		
Registrars:	Capita Registrars		

Entry on AIM: 11/12/2003		Recent price:	142.5p
Interim results:	Mar	Market cap:	£76.84m
Final results:	Oct	Issue price:	115.0p
Year end:	Jun	Current no of shares:	
Accounts due:	Oct		53,919,500
Int div paymnt:	n/a	No of shares after	
Fin div paymnt:	n/a	dilution:	n/a
Int net div per share:	nil	P/E ratio:	109.6
Fin net div per share:	nil	Probable CGT?	Yes

LATEST REPORTED RESULTS: 2003		PREVIOUS REPORTED RESULTS: 2002	
Turnover:	£9.08m	Turnover:	£3.40m
PTP:	£583,000	PTP:	£(1.23m)
EPS:	1.3p	EPS:	(3.9)p

SIRA Business Services

(SIB)

Contract cleaning provider

Chester House, 1-3 Brixton Road, London, SW9 6DE Tel: 020-7793 0093; Fax: 020-7793 1300

		holding %
Acting Chairman	Christopher Gilbey	0.03
Chief Executive		
Finance Director	Paul Hart	0.03

Main Shareholders:

Estate of Peter Fox	28.3
Nicholas Earley	14.9
Raymond Empson	14.9
Ariton Business	12.0

Percentage of free market capital: 30%

Nominated Adviser:	Grant Thornton, London
AIM Broker:	Seymour Pierce Ellis, Crawley
Solicitors:	Nabarro Nathanson, London
Market Makers:	SCAP; WINS
Auditors:	Hacker Young, 2 Fore St, London EC2Y 5DH
Registrars:	Capita Registrars

ENTRY ON AIM:	29/4/1996	**Recent price:**	6.5p
Interim results:	Feb	**Market cap:**	£2.51m
Final results:	Sep	**Issue price:**	3.0p
Year end:	Jun	**Current no of shares:**	
Accounts due:	Oct		38,688,504
Int div paymnt:	n/a	**No of shares after**	
Fin div paymnt:	n/a	**dilution:**	41,448,226
Int net div per share:	nil	**P/E ratio:**	n/a
Fin net div per share:	nil	**Probable CGT?**	YES

LATEST REPORTED RESULTS:		PREVIOUS REPORTED RESULTS:	
	2003		2002
Turnover:	£14.61m	**Turnover:**	£16.94m
PTP:	£441,000	**PTP:**	£(392,000)
EPS:	0.8p	**EPS:**	(0.9)p

Comments:

Contract cleaner SIRA reported slightly improved interim figures to December with profits up 23% to £258,000 on a tiny 2% rise in sales to £7.75m. The company also saw net debt fall from £891,000 to £147,000. However gross margins waned from 25.7% to 25.1% on rising costs, due to increases in the minimum wage and national insurance. And the business is facing high levels of competition with work invariably secured at a tight margin.

Sirius Financial Solutions

(SIR)

Software solutions developer

Sirius House, Reddicroft, Sutton Coldfield, West Midlands B73 6BN Tel: 0121-355 3567; Fax: 0121-354 4259; e-mail: info@siriusfs.com; web site: www.siriusfs.com

		holding %
Chairman	Stephen Verrall	32.6
Chief Executive		
Finance Director	Richard Bowser	8.5
Exec Director	Michael Dodd	0.1

Main Shareholders:

Insight Investments	9.7
Richard Glaves	4.6
F&C Smaller Companies	3.7

Percentage of free market capital: 40.8%

Nominated Adviser:	Collins Stewart, London
AIM Broker:	Collins Stewart, London
Solicitors:	DLA, London
Market Makers:	CSCS; WINS
Auditors:	Deloitte & Touche, Birmingham
Registrars:	Capita Registrars

Entry on AIM:	10/6/2003	**Recent price:**	84.5p
Interim results:	Sep	**Market cap:**	£14.37m
Final results:	Apr	**Issue price:**	96.5p
Year end:	Dec	**Current no of shares:**	
Accounts due:	Jun		17,002,789
Int div paymnt:	Jan	**No of shares after**	
Fin div paymnt:	Nov	**dilution:**	n/a
Int net div per share:	1.0p	**P/E ratio:**	14.1
Fin net div per share:	1.7p	**Probable CGT?**	YES

LATEST REPORTED RESULTS:		PREVIOUS REPORTED RESULTS:	
	2002		2001
Turnover:	£22.68m	**Turnover:**	£17.37m
PTP:	£1.89m	**PTP:**	£(281,000)
EPS:	6.0p	**EPS:**	(4.0)p

Comments:

Sirius may switch its sales model away from a hefty up-front fee and instead opt for a 'more contemporary' licensing strategy, on the back of a full year profit-warning. Explaining the decision, management noted that 'due to some unexpected delays and the increasingly lengthy period of time taken completing contract paperwork' a more 'predictable and sustainable' revenue model is now required. First-half figures were disappointing as sales slipped £300,000 to £10.4m with profits down 97% at £38,000.

Sirvis IT (formerly Systems Integrated Research)   (SRV)

Educational software producer and IT services consultancy

Blackbrook House, Ashbourne Road, Belper, Derbyshire DE56 2DB Tel: 01773-820011; Fax: 01773-820206;
e-mail: Corporate@sirplc.co.uk; web site: www.sirplc.co.uk

		holding %
Chairman	Peter Addison	0.1
Managing Director	Mark Lewis	1.1
Finance Director	Ian Bailey	0.2
Operations Director	Colin Sales	6.7

Main Shareholders:
Berg & Berg   20.9

Percentage of free market capital: 66.3%

Nominated Adviser:	ARM Corporate Finance, London
AIM Broker:	JM Finn, London
Solicitors:	Taylor Wessing, London
Market Makers:	SCAP; WINS
Auditors:	PricewaterhouseCoopers, East Midlands
Registrars:	Capita Registrars

Entry on AIM:	2/4/1996	Recent price:	8.25p
Interim results:	Jan	Market cap:	£9.0m
Final results:	Aug	Issue price:	6.0p
Year end:	May	Current no of shares:	
Accounts due:	Aug		109,066,246
Int div paymnt:	n/a	No of shares after	
Fin div paymnt:	n/a	dilution:	n/a
Int net div per share:	nil	P/E ratio:	n/a
Fin net div per share:	nil	Probable CGT?	Yes

LATEST REPORTED RESULTS: 2003		PREVIOUS REPORTED RESULTS: 2002	
Turnover:	£853,000	Turnover:	£1.22m
PTP:	£(288,000)	PTP:	£(79,000)
EPS:	(2.5)p	EPS:	(0.9)p

Comments:
Having reported increased full year losses and reduced sales back in August, Systems Integrated Research has diversified away from its core educational materials business and into the IT services sector. Precipitating the change was the £5.3m acquisition of profitable IT consultant Linetex, CEO Mark Lewis explaining that 'for a long time now we have been looking for an acquisition to bulk the business and this meets all of our criteria'. Lewis hopes the deal will allow SiRViS to sell IT support into the education sector.

Skiddaw Capital (suspended 24 Mar 2004)   (SKW)

Investment company

Walkers SPV Limited, Walker House, Mary Strret, PO Box 908 George Town, Grand Cayman, Cayman Islands,

		holding %
Chairman	John Leat	0.1
Chief Executive		
Finance Director		
Director	Shahed Mahmood	0.1

Main Shareholders:

Everdene   16.0
Kitwell Holdings   3.0

Percentage of free market capital: 80.8%

Nominated Adviser:	Canaccord Capital, London
AIM Broker:	Canaccord Capital, London
Solicitors:	Fladgate Fielder, London
Market Makers:	WINS
Auditors:	Grant Thornton, Birmingham
Registrars:	Capita Registrars

Entry on AIM:	9/3/2004	Recent price:	14.75p
Interim results:	n/a	Market cap:	£3.69m
Final results:	n/a	Issue price:	6.0p
Year end:	n/a	Current no of shares:	
Accounts due:	n/a		25,000,000
Int div paymnt:	n/a	No of shares after	
Fin div paymnt:	n/a	dilution:	n/a
Int net div per share:	nil	P/E ratio:	n/a
Fin net div per share:	nil	Probable CGT?	No

LATEST REPORTED RESULTS: N/A		PREVIOUS REPORTED RESULTS: N/A	
Turnover:	n/a	Turnover:	n/a
PTP:	n/a	PTP:	n/a
EPS:	n/a	EPS:	n/a

Comments:
Skiddaw's shares were suspended a fortnight after joining AIM, following discussions about a £24m reverse takeover with Crosby Capital Partners. The latter concern is a Hong Kong-based investment bank and a subsidiary of Techpacific. If it goes ahead Techpacific will own 89% of the company. The group also wants to raise up to £1.2m at 12p a share. Prior to this Skiddaw raised £1.07m net at 6p a share. Chairman John Leat managed the Dubai Royal family's affairs for 26 years.

Sky Capital   (SKY)
Financial services
8h Floor, 110 Wall Street, New York, New York 10005 USA, Tel: 00-1 212 709 1900; Fax: 00-1-212 709 1951;
web site: www.skycapitalholdings.com

		holding %
Chairman	Thomas McMillen	0.0
Chief Executive	Ross Mandell	47.0
Finance Director		
Chief Executive - US	Michael Recca	0.0
Main Shareholders:		
Sky Capital Ventures		5.1
Empire Castiglioni		3.6

Percentage of free market capital: 44.3%

Comments:
Transatlantic investment broker Sky is expanding quickly. The group's main directors are US-based but Sky also has a UK presence after buying penny share broker Everett Financial in a £1.6m cash and shares deal to give it a foothold in London. Since then it has acquired Miami-based Cardinal Capital Management for £2.56m. Interim revenue rose to $14.5m but losses jumped to $4.2m. The group raised £20m via an offer of preference shares convertible at a discount to the ordinary share price.

Nominated Adviser:	Grant Thornton, London
AIM Broker:	Sky Capital, London
Solicitors:	Nicholson Graham & Jones, London
Market Makers:	WINS
Auditors:	Baker Tilly, 2 Bloomsbury Street, London WC1B 3ST
Registrars:	Melton Registrars

ENTRY ON AIM:	15/7/2002	**Recent price:**	264.5p
Interim results:	Dec	**Market cap:**	£54.02m
Final results:	Sep	**Issue price:**	185.0p
Year end:	Mar	**Current no of shares:**	
Accounts due:	Aug		20,424,658
Int div paymnt:	n/a	**No of shares after**	
Fin div paymnt:	n/a	**dilution:**	n/a
Int net div per share:	nil	**P/E ratio:**	n/a
Fin net div per share:	nil	**Probable CGT?**	No

LATEST REPORTED RESULTS:	2003	PREVIOUS REPORTED RESULTS:	2002
Turnover:	$5.46m	Turnover:	n/a
PTP:	£(7.98m)	PTP:	n/a
EPS:	(0.5)c	EPS:	n/a

Smart Approach (formerly Robert H Lowe)   (SAG)
Developer of computer-based training systems for the aviation sector
Unit 3, Acorn Business Park, Moss Rd, Grimsbury, North East Lincolnshire DN32 0LT Tel: 01472-250300;
Fax: 01472-251508; e-mail: rh_lowe@wsmith.co.uk

		holding %
Chairman	Rodney Potts	0.0
Chief Executive	John Ormesher	0.0
Finance Director		
Non-Exec Director	Martin Canty	4.5
Main Shareholders:		
Ayston		29.9
Strand Associates		16.2
Herald Investment Trust		5.4
J B Abell		3.8

Percentage of free market capital: 31.1%

Comments:
Smart Approach designs, develops and sells training software to the aviation and security markets and has thus seen a great deal of interest from the US, Middle East and India in recent times. A long-standing agreement with defence giant Lockheed Martin (to train individuals' X-ray screening techniques) is in place and currently contributes around a third of all revenues. Smart Approach lost £2.1m from £731,000 of sales in the first half.

Nominated Adviser:	Strand Partners, London
AIM Broker:	Teather & Greenwood, London
Solicitors:	Walker Morris, Leeds
Market Makers:	INGL; KBCS; MLSB; TEAM; WINS
Auditors:	Ernst & Young, Leeds
Registrars:	Capita Registrars

Entry on AIM:	22/10/2002	**Recent price:**	1.5p
Interim results:	Dec	**Market cap:**	£7.07m
Final results:	Jun	**Issue price:**	2.5p
Year end:	Mar	**Current no of shares:**	
Accounts due:	Apr		471,579,013
Int div paymnt:	n/a	**No of shares after**	
Fin div paymnt:	n/a	**dilution:**	n/a
Int net div per share:	nil	**P/E ratio:**	n/a
Fin net div per share:	nil	**Probable CGT?**	Yes

LATEST REPORTED RESULTS:	2002	PREVIOUS REPORTED RESULTS:	2001
Turnover:	n/a	Turnover:	£11.8m
PTP:	£90,000	PTP:	£368,000
EPS:	(0.1)p	EPS:	0.3p

Solid State Supplies (SSP)

Electronic components distributor

Unit 2, Eastlands Lane, Paddock Wood , Kent TN12 6BU Tel: 01892-836836; Fax: 01892-837837;
e-mail: sales@sssplc.com; web site: www.sssplc.com

		holding %
Chairman	Peter Haining	0.2
Managing Director	Gary Marsh	1.2
Finance Director		
Non-Exec Director	Gordon Comben	44.0

Main Shareholders:
n/a

Percentage of free market capital: 27.2%

Comments:
Solid State has continued to be profitable in difficult conditions although pre-tax profits fell almost three quarters to £57,000 in the interim to September. During the period the company relocated to Redditch, Worcestershire. It also managed to recover £240,000 out of £428,000 owed under a sub-contract. Increased demand from the Far East has brought hope of an upturn and a hardening of prices in the semi-conductor business.

Nominated Adviser:	Charles Stanley, London
AIM Broker:	Charles Stanley, London
Solicitors:	Thomson Snell & Passmore, Tunbridge Wells, Kent
Market Makers:	KBCS; WINS
Auditors:	BDO Stoy Hayward, 8 Baker Street, London W1M 1DA
Registrars:	Capita Registrars

ENTRY ON AIM:	26/6/1996	Recent price:	50.5p
Interim results:	Dec	Market cap:	£3.15m
Final results:	Jun	Issue price:	80.5p
Year end:	Mar	Current no of shares:	
Accounts due:	Jul		6,240,000
Int div paymnt:	Dec	No of shares after	
Fin div paymnt:	Jul	dilution:	n/a
Int net div per share:	1.5p	P/E ratio:	13.3
Fin net div per share:	2.0p	Probable CGT?	YES

LATEST REPORTED RESULTS: 2003		PREVIOUS REPORTED RESULTS: 2002	
Turnover:	£9.01m	Turnover:	£5.99m
PTP:	£240,000	PTP:	£116,000
EPS:	3.8p	EPS:	1.4p

Solitaire (STG)

Residential property manager

Lynwood House, 10 Victors Way, Barnet, Hertfordshire EN5 5TZ Tel: 020-8449 6125; Fax: 020-8364 8506;
web site: www.solitairegroup.com

		holding %
Chairman	George Brutton	0.04
Joint MD	Graham Shapiro	27.5
Finance Director	C J Burton	0.0
Joint MD	H Shulman	27.5

Main Shareholders:

Eaglet Investment Trust	26.0
Aberdeen Asset Management	6.0
Rathbone Fund Management	4.7
Perpetual Investment Management	3.0
Mercury Asset Management	3.0

Percentage of free market capital: 29.64%

Comments:
Many prominent fund managers are holders of property management services stock Solitaire – with good reason. The core property management business is growing, and there is a substantial pipeline of developments coming on stream from housebuilder clients. In September it acquired Freehold Managers for £6m, which made £600,000 pre-tax in the year to June, on £1.5m sales. For the year to December 2003, Williams de Broe forecasts £1.83m pre-tax, rising to £2.35m in 2004.

Nominated Adviser:	Williams de Broe, London
AIM Broker:	Williams de Broe, London
Solicitors:	Osborne Clarke, London
Market Makers:	WDBM; WINS
Auditors:	MacIntyre Hudson, London
Registrars:	Capita Registrars

Entry on AIM:	15/10/1997	Recent price:	510.0p
Interim results:	Sep	Market cap:	£24.96m
Final results:	Apr	Issue price:	148.0p
Year end:	Dec	Current no of shares:	
Accounts due:	Jun		4,894,681
Int div paymnt:	Nov	No of shares after	
Fin div paymnt:	Jun	dilution:	n/a
Int net div per share:	3.0p	P/E ratio:	23.6
Fin net div per share:	7.3p	Probable CGT?	No

LATEST REPORTED RESULTS: 2002		PREVIOUS REPORTED RESULTS: 2001	
Turnover:	£5.91m	Turnover:	£5.06m
PTP:	£1.45m	PTP:	£1.16m
EPS:	21.6p	EPS:	17.6p

Sopheon (SPE)

Knowledge management software and services for R & D

Stirling House, Stirling Road, Surrey Research Park, Guildford, Surrey GU2 7RF Tel: 01483-883000; Fax: 01483-883050;
e-mail: info@sopheon.com; web site: www.sopheon.com

		holding %
Chairman	Barry Mence	10.6
Chief Executive	Andy Michuda	0.1
Finance Director	Arif Karimjee	0.0
Non-Exec Director	Stuart Silcock	0.3

Main Shareholders:

Friends Ivory & Sime	5.5
Aventis Research & Technologies GMBH	4.1
3i	3.8
Discovery Trust	3.4

Percentage of free market capital: 71.7%

Comments:

Though business process software developer Sopheon continues to rack up losses (reporting a £5.6m first half deficit) there have been a few positive signs since the turn of the year. New contracts have been picked up from Austrian cellulose fibre manufacturer Lenzing and US-based textiles business Unifi, while a 10m credit facility has also been secured. Despite these positives, however, profits may yet be some way off.

Nominated Adviser:	Seymour Pierce, London
AIM Broker:	Seymour Pierce, London
Solicitors:	Hammonds, London; Nauta Dutilh, Amsterdam
Market Makers:	DURM; HSBC; KBCS; MLSB; SCAP; WINS
Auditors:	Ernst & Young, Apex Plaza, Reading, Berkshire RG1 1YE
Registrars:	Capita Registrars

ENTRY ON AIM:	10/9/1996	Recent price:	30.75p
Interim results:	Sep	Market cap:	£29.92m
Final results:	Jun	Issue price:	65.0p
Year end:	Dec	Current no of shares:	
Accounts due:	May		97,302,481
Int div paymnt:	n/a	No of shares after	
Fin div paymnt:	n/a	dilution:	n/a
Int net div per share:	nil	P/E ratio:	n/a
Fin net div per share:	nil	Probable CGT?	YES

LATEST REPORTED RESULTS:		PREVIOUS REPORTED RESULTS:	
	2002		2001
Turnover:	£12.35m	Turnover:	£13.96m
PTP:	£(16.18m)	PTP:	£(34.63m)
EPS:	(19.4)p	EPS:	(76.2)p

Southampton Leisure (SOO)

Football club operator

The Friends Provident St Mary's Stadium, Britannia Road, Southampton, Hampshire SO14 5FP Tel: 0870-220 0000;
web site: www.saintsfc.co.uk

		holding %
Chairman	Rupert Lowe	6.2
Managing Director	Andrew Cowen	1.2
Finance Director	David Jones	0.02
Vice Chairman	Francis Askham	3.9

Main Shareholders:

Waterhead	5.4
RM Withers	3.9

Percentage of free market capital: 68.7%

Comments:

The south coast Premier League club and Full List refugee unveiled improved interims to November swelled by the £7m sale of Wayne Bridge to Chelsea. Losses of £3.8m turned round to a £1.9m profit on turnover lifted from £16.4m to £18.7m. Although matchday revenues were marginally down, the top line was boosted by rising commercial and broadcasting income. Admittedly players' and coaches' wages put on 16%, but remained at 56% of turnover.

Nominated Adviser:	Collins Stewart, London
AIM Broker:	Collins Stewart, London
Solicitors:	Pritchard Englefield, London
Market Makers:	CSCS; KBCS; MLSB; WINS
Auditors:	Deloitte & Touche, Southampton
Registrars:	Lloyds TSB Registrars

Entry on AIM:	20/10/2003	Recent price:	42.0p
Interim results:	Feb	Market cap:	£11.99m
Final results:	Sep	Issue price:	n/a
Year end:	May	Current no of shares:	
Accounts due:	Oct		28,540,896
Int div paymnt:	n/a	No of shares after	
Fin div paymnt:	n/a	dilution:	n/a
Int net div per share:	nil	P/E ratio:	n/a
Fin net div per share:	nil	Probable CGT?	YES

LATEST REPORTED RESULTS:		PREVIOUS REPORTED RESULTS:	
	2003		2002
Turnover:	£48.88m	Turnover:	£38.54m
PTP:	£(484,000)	PTP:	£3.29m
EPS:	(1.8)p	EPS:	5.6p

319

Southern African Resources (SFU)

Natural resources investor

4th Floor, Clements House, 14-18 Gresham Street, London, EC2V 7NN Tel: 020-7224 2522

		holding %
Chairman	Phil Edmonds	21.5
Chief Executive	as above	
Finance Director		
Non-Exec Director	Bruce Rowan	16.3

Main Shareholders:

Birkwood	29.6
RAB Capital	23.8
General Metallurgical and Services	9.1
Camec	5.5
Web Shareshop	4.4

Percentage of free market capital: n/a

Comments:

Phil Edmonds' Southern African has repaid backers Bruce Rowan (via Web Shareshop) and Thomas Kaplan of Apex Silver with a stellar share rise. Focused on platinum group metals at Leeuwkop in South Africa (with claimed potential of 56m oz), Southern has pleased by recruiting Roy Pitchford, doughty ex-boss of 300m-oz Zimbabwe Platinum, as chief executive.

Nominated Adviser:	Grant Thornton, London
AIM Broker:	Seymour Pierce Ellis, Crawley
Solicitors:	Salans, London
Market Makers:	SCAP; WINS
Auditors:	Baker Tilly, 2 Bloomsbury Street, London WC1B 3ST
Registrars:	Capita Registrars

Entry on AIM:	31/5/2002	**Recent price:**	33.5p
Interim results:	Dec	**Market cap:**	£78.99m
Final results:	Aug	**Issue price:**	1.0p
Year end:	Mar	**Current no of shares:**	
Accounts due:	Oct		235,787,500
Int div paymnt:	n/a	**No of shares after**	
Fin div paymnt:	n/a	**dilution:**	n/a
Int net div per share:	nil	**P/E ratio:**	n/a
Fin net div per share:	nil	**Probable CGT?**	No

LATEST REPORTED RESULTS: PERIOD ENDED 31 MAR '03		PREVIOUS REPORTED RESULTS: N/A	
Turnover:	n/a	**Turnover:**	n/a
PTP:	£(193,000)	**PTP:**	n/a
EPS:	(0.3)p	**EPS:**	n/a

Southern Vectis (SNV)

Bus operator

Nelson Road, Newport, Isle of Wight PO30 1RD Tel: 01983-827000; Fax: 01983-524961;
e-mail: info@southernvectis.plc.uk; web site: www.southernvectis.com

		holding %
Chairman	Mike Killingly	0.7
Managing Director	Stuart Linn	12.0
Finance Director	Ian Palmer	5.2
Director	Kate Boyes	0.1

Main Shareholders:

G V R Batchelor	23.5
Bank of New York Nominees	7.4
AR Peeling	5.2
J B Peeling	5.0

Percentage of free market capital: 40.9%

Comments:

The bus operator scored a 5% rise in pre-tax profits to £758,000 in the half to 31 October on a meagre 1.5% sales hike to £8.53m. Although operating profits were static, the group's pre-tax line benefited from a lower interest charge. Its Isle of Wight operations enjoyed fine weather and more visitors during the summer season, although traffic congestion remains a problem on the mainland. The chairman expects full year profit to show modest improvement over last year.

Nominated Adviser:	Smith & Williamson, London
AIM Broker:	Teather & Greenwood, London
Solicitors:	Roach Pittis, London
Market Makers:	KBCS; TEAM; WINS
Auditors:	KPMG Audit, Southampton
Registrars:	Capita Registrars

Entry on AIM:	2/10/1995	**Recent price:**	38.0p
Interim results:	Dec	**Market cap:**	£7.51m
Final results:	Jul	**Issue price:**	43.0p
Year end:	Apr	**Current no of shares:**	
Accounts due:	Aug		19,754,309
Int div paymnt:	n/a	**No of shares after**	
Fin div paymnt:	Sep	**dilution:**	n/a
Int net div per share:	nil	**P/E ratio:**	15.2
Fin net div per share:	1.55p	**Probable CGT?**	Yes

LATEST REPORTED RESULTS: 2003		PREVIOUS REPORTED RESULTS: 2002	
Turnover:	£16.02m	**Turnover:**	£15.77m
PTP:	£677,000	**PTP:**	£1.01m
EPS:	2.5p	**EPS:**	3.5p

SouthernEra Resources (SRE)
Platinum producer & diamond miner

111 Richmond Street West, Siute 1002, Toronto, Ontario M5H 2GA, Canada Tel: 00-1 416 359 9282;
Fax: 00-1 416 359 9141; e-mail: inbox@southernera.com; web site: www.southernera.com

		holding %
Chairman	Christopher Jennings	1.6
Chief Executive	Patrick Evans	0.1
Finance Director	Mark Rosslee	0.0
Non-Exec Director	Thomas Dawson	0.1

Main Shareholders:

Fidelity Investments	14.7
Kennecott Canada	13.3

Percentage of free market capital: 69.6%

Nominated Adviser:	Williams de Broe, London
AIM Broker:	Williams de Broe, London
Solicitors:	Faegre Benson Hobson Audley, London
Market Makers:	KBCS; WINS
Auditors:	PricewaterhouseCoopers, Ontario, Canada
Registrars:	Computershare Investor Services

ENTRY ON AIM:	13/8/2002	**Recent price:**	190.0p
Interim results:	Nov	**Market cap:**	£138.63m
Final results:	Mar	**Issue price:**	210.0p
Year end:	Dec	**Current no of shares:**	
Accounts due:	May		72,960,800
Int div paymnt:	n/a	**No of shares after**	
Fin div paymnt:	n/a	**dilution:**	n/a
Int net div per share:	nil	**P/E ratio:**	n/a
Fin net div per share:	nil	**Probable CGT?**	No

LATEST REPORTED RESULTS:	2002	PREVIOUS REPORTED RESULTS:	2001
Turnover:	$3.2m	**Turnover:**	$3.79m
PTP:	$(9.0m)	**PTP:**	$(8.4m)
EPS:	(0.2)c	**EPS:**	(0.3)c

Comments:
The rand's strength has forced Toronto-based SouthernEra to suspend diamond mining at Klipspringer in South Africa. SouthernEra, which lost a third quarter £2.5m, reported strong production gains of platinum group metals, nickel, copper and gold at 72%-owned Messina, also in South Africa, and encouraging returns at Koumba in Gabon. Rio Tinto sold its 9.2% SouthernEra stake in March.

SP Holdings (formerly World Sports Solutions) (SPD)
Sports marketing and financial services business

9th Floor, Oakland House, Talbot Road, Old Trafford, Manchester, M16 0PQ Tel: 0161-868 1710; Fax: 0161-876 0224;
e-mail: jp@worldsportssolutions.com; web site: www.worldsportssolutions.com

		holding %
Chairman	Simon Eagle	5.8
Chief Executive	as above	
Finance Director	Darren Edmonston	0.6
Joint Chief Executive	Anthony Simpson	0.0

Main Shareholders:

Marc Roger	27.2
Michael Farnan	17.0
Marguerite Roger	3.4
Patrick Vieira	3.4
Peter Mead	3.4

Percentage of free market capital: 35.2%

Nominated Adviser:	Altium Capital, Manchester
AIM Broker:	Rowan Dartington, Bristol
Solicitors:	Hammonds, Manchester
Market Makers:	SCAP; WINS
Auditors:	Horwath Clark Whitehill, Manchester
Registrars:	Capita Registrars

Entry on AIM:	28/11/2000	**Recent price:**	21.0p
Interim results:	Jul	**Market cap:**	£4.63m
Final results:	Jul	**Issue price:**	2.0p
Year end:	Oct	**Current no of shares:**	
Accounts due:	May		22,070,138
Int div paymnt:	n/a	**No of shares after**	
Fin div paymnt:	n/a	**dilution:**	n/a
Int net div per share:	nil	**P/E ratio:**	2.5
Fin net div per share:	nil	**Probable CGT?**	YES

LATEST REPORTED RESULTS:	2003	PREVIOUS REPORTED RESULTS:	2002
Turnover:	£776,000	**Turnover:**	n/a
PTP:	£(1.29m)	**PTP:**	£(9.76m)
EPS:	8.4p	**EPS:**	235.0p

Comments:
Over the past year marketing outfit World Sport has undergone sweeping changes. New chairman Simon Eagle has made eight acquisitions, bringing on board experienced marketing specialists, including joint CEO Tony Simpson and Chris Reed of News International. This side of the business remains sports-based but now organises many promotional deals rather than merely representing sports players. On the financial services side, the group offers broad advice to individuals and companies.

Sportingbet (SBT)
Online betting service
7th Floor, Transworld House, 82-100 City Road, London, EC1Y 2BJ Tel: 020-7251 7260; Fax: 020-7251 7270;
e-mail: admin@sportingbet.com; web site: www.sportingbet.com

		holding %
Chairman	Peter Dicks	0.1
Chief Executive	Nigel Payne	0.04
Finance Director	Andrew McIver	0.02
Vice Chairman	Mark Blandford	16.5

Main Shareholders:

Geoffrey Wilkinson	16.8
FMR Corp/Fidelity International	13.2
Trophy Atkiengesellschaft	11.5
GJW International	8.0
Nortrust	3.7

Percentage of free market capital: 25.5%

Comments:
The online bookie moved back into profits in the three months to December. Turnover increased 20% to £360m with profits before tax up 60% to £9m. Operations in Europe contributed an operating profit of £1m compared to a loss of £300,000 last year. Acquisitions to further growth have been ruled out as it believes many smaller companies are struggling and will get squeezed out by bigger players. Gaming regulatory developments will shape its future.

Nominated Adviser:	Dresdner Kleinwort Wasserstein, London
AIM Broker:	Dresdner Kleinwort Wasserstein, London
Solicitors:	Linklaters, London
Market Makers:	KBCS; KLWT; MLSB; SCAP; WINS
Auditors:	BDO Stoy Hayward, 8 Baker Street, London W1M 1DA
Registrars:	Capita Registrars

ENTRY ON AIM:	30/1/2001	Recent price:	73.75p
Interim results:	Oct	Market cap:	£140.47m
Final results:	Jul	Issue price:	120.0p
Year end:	Mar	Current no of shares:	
Accounts due:	Aug		190,464,789
Int div paymnt:	n/a	No of shares after	
Fin div paymnt:	n/a	dilution:	n/a
Int net div per share:	nil	P/E ratio:	92.2
Fin net div per share:	nil	Probable CGT?	No

LATEST REPORTED RESULTS: 2003		PREVIOUS REPORTED RESULTS: 2002	
Turnover:	£1150.3m	Turnover:	£991.5m
PTP:	£1.4m	PTP:	£5.04m
EPS:	0.8p	EPS:	3.4p

Sports & Leisure (suspended 12 Feb 2004) (SOP)
Sports events promoter
75 King William Street, London EC4N 7BN Tel: 020-8558 0538

		holding %
Chairman	Clive Garston	0.9
Chief Executive	Edward Simons	4.1
Finance Director	Simon Metcalf	0.0
Exec Director	Gavin Simons	0.9

Main Shareholders:

HSBC Global Custody Nominee	17.7
Jupiter Asset Management	9.7
Nutraco Nominees	8.4
Forest Nominees	5.9
Nomihold Securities	3.3

Percentage of free market capital: 19%

Comments:
Sports & Leisure is the only quoted company focused on the boxing game through its stake in Frank Warren's Sports Network. In February, its shares were suspended after the company agreed, in principle, to acquire the remaining 74% of Sports Network in a reverse takeover deal. Back in September, interim figures to June revealed a disappointing loss caused by the postponement of various bouts. Pre-tax losses came in at £223,000 on a £1.1m turnover.

Nominated Adviser:	Corporate Synergy, London
AIM Broker:	Collins Stewart, London
Solicitors:	Halliwell Landau, London
Market Makers:	CSCS; HOOD; WINS
Auditors:	Gerald Edelman, 25 Harley Street, London, W1N 2BR
Registrars:	Melton Registrars

Entry on AIM:	26/5/2000	Recent price:	7.0p
Interim results:	Sep	Market cap:	£2.37m
Final results:	Feb	Issue price:	25.0p
Year end:	Dec	Current no of shares:	
Accounts due:	Jul		33,886,201
Int div paymnt:	n/a	No of shares after	
Fin div paymnt:	n/a	dilution:	34,386,201
Int net div per share:	nil	P/E ratio:	14
Fin net div per share:	nil	Probable CGT?	Yes

LATEST REPORTED RESULTS: 2002		PREVIOUS REPORTED RESULTS: 2001	
Turnover:	£2.37m	Turnover:	£90,000
PTP:	£163,000	PTP:	£(360,000)
EPS:	0.5p	EPS:	(3.6p)

Spring Grove Property Maintenance (SGV)

Provider of property maintenance to the social housing sector

Spring Grove House, Ivy Road, Hounslow, Middlesex TW3 2NF Tel: 020-8577 8040; Fax: 020-8814 2885

		holding %
Chairman	Christopher Phillips	0.2
Joint MD	Kevin Childs	20.8
Finance Director	Clark Ray	0.0
Joint MD	Andrew Milne	20.8

Main Shareholders:

Puma II Fund	8.8
Northern Aim VCT	7.3
Pennine Downing Aim VCT II	5.9
Aim VCT2	5.3
Unicorn Aim VCT	5.2

Percentage of free market capital: 13.4%

Nominated Adviser:	Shore Capital, London
AIM Broker:	Shore Capital, London
Solicitors:	Fladgate Fielder, London
Market Makers:	SCAP; WINS
Auditors:	BSG Valentine, London
Registrars:	Capita Registrars

ENTRY ON AIM: 13/12/2001		Recent price:	34.5p
Interim results:	Oct	Market cap:	£4.29m
Final results:	Jun	Issue price:	40.0p
Year end:	Jan	Current no of shares:	
Accounts due:	May		12,428,430
Int div paymnt:	n/a	No of shares after	
Fin div paymnt:	n/a	dilution:	12,538,430
Int net div per share:	nil	P/E ratio:	16.4
Fin net div per share:	nil	Probable CGT?	Yes

LATEST REPORTED RESULTS: 2003		PREVIOUS REPORTED RESULTS: 2002	
Turnover:	£10.79m	Turnover:	£7.4m
PTP:	£395,000	PTP:	£394,000
EPS:	2.1p	EPS:	4.0p

Comments:

The repair and maintenance concern recorded a disappointing move from profits to losses last year on a higher turnover, after it lost a couple of big contracts. Spring Grove lost £113,000 in the first half on account of the slow build-up of work from big deals. And it also lost a significant contract at Robert Hawkins, the late 2002 acquisition that helped it expand into the private sector. Encouragingly however, the business was turned round in a promising second half.

Springboard (SPG)

Provider of investment and support to new ventures

7 Duke of York Street, London, SW1Y 6LA Tel: 0845-600 8001; Fax: 020-7004 2600; e-mail: info@springboardplc.com; web site: www.springboardplc.com

		holding %
Chairman	Stephen Ross	10.8
Chief Executive	Simon Smith	0.7
Finance Director	Gerard Downes	1.6
Non-Exec Director	Mike Hauk	0.1

Main Shareholders:

Commerzbank	13.6
The McDowell Family	10.9
Old Mutual	9.8
JO Hambro Capital Management	9.5
HSBC Global Custody Nominee	9.0

Percentage of free market capital: 4.6%

Nominated Adviser:	Durlacher, London
AIM Broker:	Durlacher, London
Solicitors:	DLA, Manchester
Market Makers:	WDBM; WINS
Auditors:	Deloitte & Touche, 9 Charlotte St, Manchester M1 4EU
Registrars:	Capita Registrars

Entry on AIM: 22/7/1998		Recent price:	120.5p
Interim results:	Mar	Market cap:	£15.85m
Final results:	Sep	Issue price:	125.0p
Year end:	Jun	Current no of shares:	
Accounts due:	Sep		13,156,000
Int div paymnt:	n/a	No of shares after	
Fin div paymnt:	n/a	dilution:	n/a
Int net div per share:	nil	P/E ratio:	n/a
Fin net div per share:	nil	Probable CGT?	Yes

LATEST REPORTED RESULTS: 2003		PREVIOUS REPORTED RESULTS: 2002	
Turnover:	£672,000	Turnover:	£873,000
PTP:	£(4.78m)	PTP:	£(3.44m)
EPS:	(36.3)p	EPS:	(26.2)p

Comments:

The early-stage investment consultancy tries to back proven management teams before venture capital teams invest. In the first half NAV rose 4% to £19.1m, or 145p a share. Roughly a third remains as cash. The group's 19-strong portfolio made cumulative sales of £4.3m and registered a £0.2m loss during the period. The group now has the ability to buyback shares to correct any discount to NAV. Prominent investments include Businesshealth and Directorbank.

323

SpringHealth Leisure

(SGL)

Health club operator

42-46 High Street, Esher, KT10 9QY Tel: 01372-465330; Fax: 01372-463620; web site: www.springhealthl.net

		holding %
Chairman	Sandy Anderson	29.8
Chief Executive	Eric Lowry	0.1
Finance Director	Russell Hudson	0.1
Non-Exec Director	Stanley Henry	29.9

Main Shareholders:

Chase Nominees	7.9
Sinjul Nominees	4.3
Speirs & Jeffery	4.0
Lingfield Properties	3.5

Percentage of free market capital: 20.3%

Nominated Adviser:	Arbuthnot, London
AIM Broker:	Arbuthnot, London
Solicitors:	Morgan Cole, Swansea
Market Makers:	KBCS; SCAP; WDBM; WINS
Auditors:	BDO Stoy Hayward, 8 Baker Street, London W1M 1DA
Registrars:	Capita Registrars

Entry on AIM:	23/4/1999	Recent price:	23.0p
Interim results:	May	Market cap:	£2.01m
Final results:	Feb	Issue price:	n/a
Year end:	Aug	Current no of shares:	
Accounts due:	Feb		8,719,373
Int div paymnt:	n/a	No of shares after	
Fin div paymnt:	n/a	dilution:	n/a
Int net div per share:	nil	P/E ratio:	n/a
Fin net div per share:	nil	Probable CGT?	Yes

LATEST REPORTED RESULTS:	2003	PREVIOUS REPORTED RESULTS:	2002
Turnover:	£11.67m	Turnover:	£12.51m
PTP:	£(13.30m)	PTP:	£(1.61m)
EPS:	(89.4)p	EPS:	(10.9)p

Comments:

Losses widened in the last financial year at the mid-market health and fitness club operator, which has struggled in a very competitive market. SpringHealth has suffered from pressure on membership pricing and joining fees. However, the company managed to sell 9 clubs in 2003 to reduce debts. These included the post year-end sale of its 'Northern clubs' for £4m. And finally there are signs the pace and number of new club openings from rivals is abating.

Springwood (suspended 10 Feb 2004)

(SWO)

Nightclub, bar, pub & restaurant operator

Chancery House, Rosbery Rd, Anstey, Leicestershire LE7 7EL Tel: 0116-237 5055; Fax: 0116-230 2983;
web site: www.springwoodleisure.co.uk

		holding %
Executive Chairman Chief Executive	William Gore	0.0
Finance Director	Steven Mugglestone	0.0
Chief Operating Officer	Jez King	0.0

Main Shareholders:

Adam Page	38.1

Percentage of free market capital: 59.8%

Nominated Adviser:	Grant Thornton, London
AIM Broker:	KBC Peel Hunt, London
Solicitors:	Taylor Wessing, London
Market Makers:	EVO; KBCS; MLSB; TEAM; WINS
Auditors:	Grant Thornton, Melton St, Euston Sq, London NW1 2EP
Registrars:	Capita Registrars

Entry on AIM:	6/6/2003	Recent price:	16.5p
Interim results:	Sep	Market cap:	£3.53m
Final results:	Apr	Issue price:	18.5p
Year end:	Dec	Current no of shares:	
Accounts due:	May		21,401,816
Int div paymnt:	n/a	No of shares after	
Fin div paymnt:	n/a	dilution:	n/a
Int net div per share:	nil	P/E ratio:	n/a
Fin net div per share:	nil	Probable CGT?	Yes

LATEST REPORTED RESULTS:	2002	PREVIOUS REPORTED RESULTS:	2001
Turnover:	£32.37m	Turnover:	£26.62m
PTP:	£2.15m	PTP:	£(772,000)
EPS:	n/a	EPS:	14.9p

Comments:

The crestfallen nightclub operator behind the Zanzibar concept was put into receivership at the behest of directors – receivers are looking to sell the business and assets as a going concern. The crisis arose following woeful trading and then the retirement of chairman Adam Page to keep Springwood's bankers sweet. The first half to June was very disappointing with sales dipping 5.5% lower to £14.1m, although the Zanzibar concept performed well.

SRS Technology   (SGY)
Electronic assistive technology for domestic environmental control

105 Brickyard Road, Aldridge, West Midlands WS9 8SX Tel: 01922-456882; Fax: 01922-456883;
e-mail: enquiries@srstechnology.co.uk; web site: www.srstechnology.co.uk

		holding %
Chairman	David Gration	3.0
Chief Executive	as above	
Finance Director	Mary Young	0.4
Sales Director	Jurek Sikorski	0.5

Main Shareholders:

Firefly Securities	11.4
Jupiter	10.2
Ludgate 181	9.9
David Poutney	6.4
Vivienne Pountney	6.4

Percentage of free market capital: 21.9%

Comments:

SRS substantially shrank interim pre-tax losses to
£492,000 (£819,000) and increased turnover 44% to
£342,000. Losses were blamed on slower growth in the
overseas market and a delay in the launch of a new range
of environmental controllers. SRS recently won an
advance order from Christian charity The Shaftesbury
Group worth a potential £170,000 and has signed up
Huntleigh Technology to distribute its products. In the US
it has had repeat orders from Pride Mobility.

Nominated Adviser:	Grant Thornton, London
AIM Broker:	Hoodless Brennan, Birmingham
Solicitors:	Wragge & Co, Birmingham
Market Makers:	NUMS; WINS
Auditors:	Mazars Neville Russell, Street, Birmingham
Registrars:	Computershare Investor Services

Entry on AIM:	20/8/2001	**Recent price:**	5.5p
Interim results:	Mar	**Market cap:**	£1.89m
Final results:	Sep	**Issue price:**	125.0p
Year end:	Jun	**Current no of shares:**	
Accounts due:	Oct		34,383,586
Int div paymnt:	n/a	**No of shares after**	
Fin div paymnt:	n/a	dilution:	n/a
Int net div per share:	nil	P/E ratio:	n/a
Fin net div per share:	nil	**Probable CGT?**	**Yes**

LATEST REPORTED RESULTS:	2003	PREVIOUS REPORTED RESULTS:	2002
Turnover:	£609,000	Turnover:	£274,000
PTP:	£(1.59m)	PTP:	£(1.59m)
EPS:	(10.5)p	EPS:	(11.3)

St Barbara Mines   (SBM)
Gold miner & explorer

Level 2, 16 Ord Street, West Perth, Western Australia 6005 Tel: 00-61 8 9476 5555; Fax: 00-61 8 9476 5500

		holding %
Chairman	Stephen Miller	0.0
Chief Executive		
Finance Director		
Non-Exec Director	Kevin Dundo	0.03

Main Shareholders:

Resource Capital Fund	24.0
National Nominees	12.0
Strata Mining*	9.4
ANZ Nominees	5.9
Citicorp Nominees	4.4

Percentage of free market capital: 41.2%

*Stephen Miller is a director of Strata Mining

Comments:

A notably dismal performer, Western Australian-based
St Barbara has been selling equipment, as well as
disposing of its 30% stake in the Burnakura gold
project for £410,000, after losing an interim £1.1m. The
company did manage to cut interest-bearing liabilities
60% to £3.9m and hopes to expand its Paddy's Flat
gold resource Down Under. Untempting.

Nominated Adviser:	Evolution Beeson Gregory, London
AIM Broker:	Evolution Beeson Gregory, London
Solicitors:	Fox Brooks Marshall, Manchester
Market Makers:	BGMM; WINS
Auditors:	PricewaterhouseCoopers, Australia 6000
Registrars:	Computershare Investor Services

Entry on AIM:	8/7/2002	**Recent price:**	2.75p
Interim results:	Feb	**Market cap:**	£15.63m
Final results:	Sep	**Issue price:**	8.0p
Year end:	Jun	**Current no of shares:**	
Accounts due:	Nov		568,269,087
Int div paymnt:	n/a	**No of shares after**	
Fin div paymnt:	n/a	dilution:	n/a
Int net div per share:	nil	P/E ratio:	n/a
Fin net div per share:	nil	**Probable CGT?**	**No**

LATEST REPORTED RESULTS:	2003	PREVIOUS REPORTED RESULTS:	2002
Turnover:	A$57.60m	Turnover:	A$86.49m
PTP:	A$(30.02m)	PTP:	A$(18.05m)
EPS:	(8.0)c	EPS:	(7.8)c

Stadium   (SDM)

Engineer

Stephen House, Brenda Rd, Hartlepool, TS25 2BQ Tel: 01429-852 500; Fax: 01429-852 798;
web site: www.stadium.co.uk

		holding %
Chairman	Struan Wiley	0.1
Chief Executive	Nigel Rogers	0.4
MD – Asia	Ken Leung	0.1
MD – Electronics	Kamal Verma	1.1

Main Shareholders:
Halifax	6.2
Barings (Guernsey)	5.9
Framlington	5.6
D Dale	5.5
A E Fry	5.1

Percentage of free market capital: 47.2%

Nominated Adviser:	Brewin Dolphin, Newcastle
AIM Broker:	Brewin Dolphin, Newcastle
Solicitors:	n/a
Market Makers:	MLSB; WINS
Auditors:	PricewaterhouseCoopers, Newcastle upon Tyne
Registrars:	Capita Registrars

ENTRY ON AIM:	23/7/2001	**Recent price:**	79.5p
Interim results:	Sep	**Market cap:**	£22.44m
Final results:	Feb	**Issue price:**	n/a
Year end:	Dec	**Current no of shares:**	
Accounts due:	Mar		28,224,698
Int div paymnt:	Oct	**No of shares after**	
Fin div paymnt:	May	**dilution:**	28,547,198
Int net div per share:	0.95p	**P/E ratio:**	15.3
Fin net div per share:	2.9p	**Probable CGT?**	YES

LATEST REPORTED RESULTS:	2003	PREVIOUS REPORTED RESULTS:	2002
Turnover:	£34.88m	**Turnover:**	£43.86m
PTP:	£1.86m	**PTP:**	£(1.39m)
EPS:	5.2p	**EPS:**	(3.0)p

Comments:

Annual 2003 numbers from the provider of electronic manufacturing services beat expectations despite the negative effects of the weak dollar. Stadium returned to bottom line profit, important customer relationships were brought to fruition and investment was carried out in China, where Stadium Asia enjoyed a 15% sales rise. With its Chinese operations, Stadium is in the right place at the right time as more and more firms look to outsource manufacturing to the Far East.

Stadium Group plc, is a leading provider of turnkey electronic manufacturing services for OEM companies in the consumer, industrial, automotive and telecoms sectors.
Stadium has bulk manufacturing operations in China as well as niche production facilities in the UK offering superior and distinctive electronic manufacturing services at a globally competitive cost.

**Stadium Group plc Stadium House Brenda Road
Hartlepool TS25 2BQ
Tel: +44 (0)1429 852 500 Fax: +44 (0) 1429 852 798
www.stadium.co.uk**

Stagecoach Theatre Arts (STA)

Operator of performing arts schools for children

The Courthouse, Elm Grove, Walton-on-Thames, Surrey KT12 1LZ Tel: 01932-254333; Fax: 01932-222894; web site: www.stagecoach.co.uk

		holding %
Chairman	Graham Cole	0.0
Joint CEO	Stephanie Manuel	31.0
Finance Director	Richard Dawson	0.0
Joint CEO	David Sprigg	25.8

Main Shareholders:

Close Brothers Managed Funds	10.6
Capital for Companies	5.0
Baronsmead VCT2	4.6
Baronsmead VCT3	4.6
Marlborough Fund Managers	4.1
Percentage of free market capital:	14.1%

Nominated Adviser:	Evolution Beeson Gregory, London
AIM Broker:	Evolution Beeson Gregory, London
Solicitors:	Berwin Leighton Paisner, London
Market Makers:	BGMM; WINS
Auditors:	PKF, New Garden House, 78 Hatton Garden, EC1N 8JA
Registrars:	Capita Registrars

ENTRY ON AIM:	14/12/2001	**Recent price:**	112.5p
Interim results:	Feb	**Market cap:**	£10.9m
Final results:	Aug	**Issue price:**	93.0p
Year end:	May	**Current no of shares:**	
Accounts due:	Aug		9,690,172
Int div paymnt:	n/a	**No of shares after**	
Fin div paymnt:	Nov	**dilution:**	n/a
Int net div per share:	nil	**P/E ratio:**	20.5
Fin net div per share:	2.0p	**Probable CGT?**	YES

LATEST REPORTED RESULTS:	2003	**PREVIOUS REPORTED RESULTS:**	2002
Turnover:	£4.96m	**Turnover:**	£3.46m
PTP:	£805,000	**PTP:**	£713,000
EPS:	5.5p	**EPS:**	6.0p

Comments:

Stagecoach is the largest franchise network of part-time performing arts schools for young people aged between four and 16. It currently has 28,300 students with 477 schools and 465 Early Stage classes. Pre-tax losses in the interim were almost halved to £154,000, due to the launch of Mini Stages, aimed at babies and toddlers. The company purchased 90% of Stagecoach Germany and opened its first US franchise. Increased initial franchise fees are expected in the second half.

Stanley Gibbons (SGI)

Online collectors' site

7 Parkside, Christchurch Road, Ringwood, Hampshire BH24 3BR Tel: 01425-472363; Fax: 01425-470247; e-mail: info@stanleygibbons.co.uk; web site: www.stanleygibbons.com

		holding %
Chairman	Paul Fraser	22.3
Chief Executive	Mike Hall	0.0
Finance Director	as above	
Non-Exec Director	Tim Dunningham	9.0

Main Shareholders:

Leonard Licht	3.2
Merseyside Pension Fund	3.0
Percentage of free market capital:	62.5%

Nominated Adviser:	Seymour Pierce, London
AIM Broker:	Seymour Pierce, London
Solicitors:	Nabarro Nathanson, London
Market Makers:	BGMM; CSCS; WINS
Auditors:	Solomon Hare, Bristol
Registrars:	Capita Registrars

Entry on AIM:	19/9/2000	**Recent price:**	77.0p
Interim results:	Jul	**Market cap:**	£19.47m
Final results:	Mar	**Issue price:**	27.0p
Year end:	Dec	**Current no of shares:**	
Accounts due:	Mar		25,282,276
Int div paymnt:	n/a	**No of shares after**	
Fin div paymnt:	n/a	**dilution:**	28,345,351
Int net div per share:	nil	**P/E ratio:**	21.4
Fin net div per share:	nil	**Probable CGT?**	YES

LATEST REPORTED RESULTS:	2003	**PREVIOUS REPORTED RESULTS:**	2002
Turnover:	£8.62m	**Turnover:**	£8.12m
PTP:	£1.23m	**PTP:**	£537,000
EPS:	3.6p	**EPS:**	2.0p

Comments:

The stamp trader produced record profits before tax for 2003. Gibbons' websites now receive 9m hits a month, 50% up from last year. Shareholders will be pleased that it intends to adopt a progressive dividend policy and will also benefit from its holding in Provide Commerce, an e-commerce market place for perishable goods, having a market value of £2.5m after it floated in December. Book value was only £223,000 and its shares can be sold after June.

StatPro (SOG)

Asset management performance software provider

StatPro House, 81-87 Hartfield Road, Wimbledon, London, SW19 3TJ Tel: 020-8410 9876; Fax: 020-8410 9877;
e-mail: investorrelations@statpro.co.uk; web site: www.statpro.com

		holding %
Chairman	Carl Bacon	0.7
Chief Executive	Justin Wheatley	19.0
Finance Director	Andrew Fabian	0.03
Non-Exec Director	Michael Fairbairn	0.5

Main Shareholders:

P T Borel	8.0
HSBC Global Custody Nominee (UK)	6.0
Herald Investment	4.9

Percentage of free market capital: 51.2%

Nominated Adviser:	Credit Lyonnais, London
AIM Broker:	Credit Lyonnais, London
Solicitors:	Faegre Benson Hobson Audley, London
Market Makers:	CLS; HOOD; KBCS; SCAP; WINS
Auditors:	PricewaterhouseCoopers, London
Registrars:	Capita Registrars

ENTRY ON AIM:	16/6/2003	Recent price:	40.0p
Interim results:	Aug	Market cap:	£13.24m
Final results:	Mar	Issue price:	27.5p
Year end:	Dec	Current no of shares:	
Accounts due:	May		33,089,244
Int div paymnt:	n/a	No of shares after	
Fin div paymnt:	n/a	dilution:	n/a
Int net div per share:	nil	P/E ratio:	66.7
Fin net div per share:	nil	Probable CGT?	Yes

LATEST REPORTED RESULTS:	2003	PREVIOUS REPORTED RESULTS:	2002
Turnover:	£8.34m	Turnover:	£7.23m
PTP:	£146,000	PTP:	£(2.37m)
EPS:	0.6p	EPS:	(7.3)p

Comments:
Despite chief executive Justin Wheatley's insistence that times remain tough, asset-management software supplier Statpro eased past analyst expectations for the full year to report a first listed profit. Servicing 25 separate markets around the world (from Canada to South Africa) and boasting a large range of software products Statpro's diversity enabled it to reverse losses into profits. Analyst Howard Brookes of house broker Credit Lyonnais forecasts a £800,000 profit for 2005.

Stepquick (SQK)

Accountancy & consultancy provider

6 Ralli Courts, West Riverside, Manchester, M3 5FT Tel: 0161-703 2500

		holding %
Executive Chairman	Gerard Cosgrove	21.7
Chief Executive		
Finance Director		
Exec Director	Geoffrey Dalimore	21.7

Main Shareholders:

Gerard Mason	5.0
Ronald Robinson	3.3

Percentage of free market capital: 13%

Nominated Adviser:	WH Ireland, Manchester
AIM Broker:	WH Ireland, Manchester
Solicitors:	Wacks Caller, Manchester
Market Makers:	SCAP; WINS
Auditors:	PKF, Sovereign House, Queen Street, Manchester M2 5HR
Registrars:	Capita Registrars

Entry on AIM:	20/10/2003	Recent price:	51.0p
Interim results:	Mar	Market cap:	£15.93m
Final results:	Sep	Issue price:	48.0p
Year end:	Mar	Current no of shares:	
Accounts due:	Oct		31,237,375
Int div paymnt:	n/a	No of shares after	
Fin div paymnt:	n/a	dilution:	n/a
Int net div per share:	nil	P/E ratio:	n/a
Fin net div per share:	nil	Probable CGT?	Yes

LATEST REPORTED RESULTS:	15 MONTHS TO 30 JUNE '03	PREVIOUS REPORTED RESULTS:	2002
Turnover:	£703,000	Turnover:	£483,000
PTP:	£(24,000)	PTP:	£21,000
EPS:	(11.0)p	EPS:	(17.0)p

Comments:
Stepquick paid £2.5m to acquire Champion, a provider of audit, accounting and taxation advice to owner-managed Manchester businesses for 30 years. The group has also expanded into other business service areas, such as offering payroll and book-keeping as well as seminars and corporate finance. For the three months to December a £72,000 profit was made on £0.8m turnover. Gerard Cosgrave plans to acquire other similar businesses in the North West.

Sterling Energy (SEY)
Oil producer & explorer
Mardall House, 7-9 Vaughan Road, Harpenden, Herts AL5 4HU Tel: 01582-463141; Fax: 01582-461221

		holding %
Chairman	Richard O'Toole	2.8
Chief Executive	Henry Wilson	3.4
Finance Director	Graeme Thomson	1.9
Operations Director	Nigel Quinton	2.2

Main Shareholders:

Sterling Management	18.0
Westmount Energy	17.1
HBOS	4.0
Edinburgh Smaller Companies	3.2

Percentage of free market capital: 46.5%

Nominated Adviser:	Evolution Beeson Gregory, London
AIM Broker:	Evolution Beeson Gregory, London
Solicitors:	Ashursts, London
Market Makers:	BGMM; WINS
Auditors:	Deloitte & Touche, 180 Strand, London WC2R 1BL
Registrars:	Capita Registrars

ENTRY ON AIM:	11/8/1997	Recent price:	12.75p
Interim results:	Oct	Market cap:	£101.6m
Final results:	Jun	Issue price:	4.0p
Year end:	Dec	Current no of shares:	
Accounts due:	May		796,849,354
Int div paymnt:	n/a	No of shares after	
Fin div paymnt:	n/a	dilution:	n/a
Int net div per share:	nil	P/E ratio:	n/a
Fin net div per share:	nil	Probable CGT?	No

LATEST REPORTED RESULTS: 2002		PREVIOUS REPORTED RESULTS: 2001	
Turnover:	£588,000	Turnover:	£49,000
PTP:	£(98,000)	PTP:	£(1.49m)
EPS:	(0.1)p	EPS:	(6.7)p

Comments:
Sterling, reversed by Harry Wilson and allies into oil minnow LEPCO, has been expanding recently. The company followed a contested but successful £38m bid for Fusion Oil & Gas with the £22m purchase from Osprey Petroleum of five producing gas fields in the Gulf of Mexico offshore of Texas. Sterling, which made interim profits of £1.1m, said this deal would boost its gas production to 12m cubic feet a day.

Stilo (STL)
Software developer
2nd Floor, North Quay, Temple Back, Bristol, BS1 6FL Tel: 0117-311 6500; Fax: 0117-311 6599;
e-mail: info@stilo.com; web site: www.stilo.com

		holding %
Chairman	Barry Welck	3.2
Chief Executive	Leslie Burnham	9.2
Finance Director		
Non-Exec Director	Roy Pike	9.4

Main Shareholders:

3i	7.7
David Ashman	4.6
113509 Ontario	4.5
Mossland	3.2

Percentage of free market capital: 29.3%

Nominated Adviser:	Charles Stanley, London
AIM Broker:	Charles Stanley, London
Solicitors:	Howard Kennedy, London
Market Makers:	TEAM; WINS
Auditors:	Baker Tilly, 2 Bloomsbury Street, London WC1B 3ST
Registrars:	Capita Registrars

Entry on AIM:	30/8/2000	Recent price:	3.5p
Interim results:	Oct	Market cap:	£1.76m
Final results:	Mar	Issue price:	50.0p
Year end:	Dec	Current no of shares:	
Accounts due:	Apr		50,228,470
Int div paymnt:	n/a	No of shares after	
Fin div paymnt:	n/a	dilution:	n/a
Int net div per share:	nil	P/E ratio:	n/a
Fin net div per share:	nil	Probable CGT?	Yes

LATEST REPORTED RESULTS: 2003		PREVIOUS REPORTED RESULTS: 2002	
Turnover:	£2.28m	Turnover:	£2.35m
PTP:	£(1.45m)	PTP:	£(1.85m)
EPS:	(2.6)p	EPS:	(3.6)p

Comments:
After a year of static sales the XML content engineering software developer wants to raise £1m, through a placing at 2.5p, to fund sales and marketing activities. To make the task easier the company's content engineering and knowledge management businesses have been cleaved into separate divisions: the former being based in the US and mainland Europe and the latter in the UK. A series of new product launches are planned for 2004.

Stockcube (SKC)

Producer of research and analysis for investors

Unit 1.23 Plaza 535, Kings Road, London, SW10 0SZ Tel: 020-7352 4001; Fax: 020-7352 3185;
web site: www.stockcube.com

		holding %
Chairman	Edward Forbes	0.5
Chief Executive	Julian Burney	7.8
Finance Director	Shirley Yeoh	0.1
Non-Exec Director	Dan Veru	0.2

Main Shareholders:

Nigel Wray	13.4
Dominic Hawker	9.8
DSF & VGF	5.9
Timothy Parker	4.7

Percentage of free market capital: 53.3%

Nominated Adviser:	Numis, London
AIM Broker:	Numis, London
Solicitors:	Reynolds Porter Chamberlain, London
Market Makers:	NUMS; WINS
Auditors:	Ernst & Young, London
Registrars:	Capita Registrars

ENTRY ON AIM:	4/5/2000	**Recent price:**	8.25p
Interim results:	Sep	**Market cap:**	£7.93m
Final results:	Mar	**Issue price:**	25.0p
Year end:	Dec	**Current no of shares:**	
Accounts due:	Apr		96,106,300
Int div paymnt:	n/a	**No of shares after**	
Fin div paymnt:	n/a	**dilution:**	104,816,300
Int net div per share:	nil	**P/E ratio:**	n/a
Fin net div per share:	nil	**Probable CGT?**	Yes

LATEST REPORTED RESULTS: 2002		PREVIOUS REPORTED RESULTS: 2001	
Turnover:	£2.05m	Turnover:	£2.14m
PTP:	£(2.01m)	PTP:	£91,000
EPS:	(2.1)p	EPS:	0.0p

Comments:

Financial data analysis firm Stockcube returned to the black during the six months to June, though this had much to do with the £1.6m of exceptional costs, which torpedoed 2002 first-half numbers. Interim figures showed a £34,000 profit before tax (compared with last year's £1.7m), while just under £4m of cash remains sitting in the bank. Since then the group has bought a 34.4% stake in Sportcal, a provider of sports statistics and information, for £0.4m.

Stonemartin (SOA)

Serviced office provider

100 Pall Mall, London, SW1Y 5HP Tel: 020-7321 5666; Fax: 020-321 5665;
e-mail: info@stonemartin.co.uk; web site: www.stonemartin.co.uk

		holding %
Chairman	Richard Mead	0.1
Chief Executive	Colin Peacock	4.0
Finance Director	Graham Ede	0.0
Director	Jonathan Gandy	2.5

Main Shareholders:

Hammerson	15.1
Interior Services	12.4
Cardiff & Provincial Properties	10.6
MEPC	10.0
Frederick Tughan	7.1

Percentage of free market capital: 36.7%

Nominated Adviser:	Bridgewell, London
AIM Broker:	Teather & Greenwood, London
Solicitors:	Nabarro Nathanson, London; Travers Smith Braithwaite, London
Market Makers:	KBCS; TEAM; WINS
Auditors:	Deloitte & Touche, 19 Bedford Street, Belfast BT2 7EJ
Registrars:	Capita Registrars

Entry on AIM:	4/5/2001	Recent price:	9.5p
Interim results:	Dec	Market cap:	£10.6m
Final results:	Jun	Issue price:	25.0p
Year end:	Mar	Current no of shares:	
Accounts due:	Jul		111,571,421
Int div paymnt:	n/a	No of shares after	
Fin div paymnt:	n/a	dilution:	114,401,421
Int net div per share:	nil	P/E ratio:	n/a
Fin net div per share:	nil	Probable CGT?	No

LATEST REPORTED RESULTS: 2003		PREVIOUS REPORTED RESULTS: 2002	
Turnover:	£5.10m	Turnover:	£1.58m
PTP:	£(2.98m)	PTP:	£(4.44m)
EPS:	(2.7)p	EPS:	(4.4)p

Comments:

The serviced and managed office provider has opened three of its planned 12 'IoD Hubs'. Despite recent shuffles with two new non-exec directors and chairman Richard Mead now in place, occupancy at the state-of-the-art offices is low due to a cyclical quiet period in property lettings. A partnership involving Morley and Hermes is funding the purchase of the buildings plus basic fit-out in return for 50% of revenues, but profits aren't anticipated for a long while.

Straight (STT)

Recycling container supplier

31 Eastgate, Leeds, LS2 7LY Tel: 0113-245 2244; Fax: 0113-245 2255;
e-mail: info@straight.co.uk

		holding %
Chairman	James Newman	0.5
Chief Executive	Jonathon Straight	70.6
Finance Director	Colin Glass	0.7
Non-Exec Director	Roger Green	0.3

Main Shareholders:

ISIS	10.9
MacDonald Glencross Approved EIS Fund 4C	4.1
Brewin Dolphin	3.4

Percentage of free market capital: 9.7%

Nominated Adviser:	Durlacher, London
AIM Broker:	Durlacher, London
Solicitors:	Walker Morris, Leeds
Market Makers:	DURM; KBCS; WINS
Auditors:	Grant Thornton, Leeds
Registrars:	Capita Registrars

Comments:

Straight is the supplier of container solutions for waste to local authorities and waste management companies, as well as environmentally friendly home and garden products like compost bins and water butts. It should profit from EU initiatives, rising demand from the private sector and the continuing 'environmental agenda'. Straight raised £1.5m via a placing priced at 80p to fund the acquisition of new tooling and improve marketing and production efficiencies.

Entry on AIM:	7/11/2003	Recent price:	100.5p
Interim results:	Sep	Market cap:	£6.94m
Final results:	Mar	Issue price:	80.0p
Year end:	Dec	Current no of shares:	
Accounts due:	Jun		6,903,750
Int div paymnt:	n/a	No of shares after	
Fin div paymnt:	n/a	dilution:	n/a
Int net div per share:	nil	P/E ratio:	n/a
Fin net div per share:	nil	Probable CGT?	Yes

LATEST REPORTED RESULTS: 2002		PREVIOUS REPORTED RESULTS: 2001	
Turnover:	£5.19m	Turnover:	£3.77m
PTP:	£307,000	PTP:	£304,000
EPS:	n/a	EPS:	n/a

Strategic Retail (SRR)

Holding company for retail outfit

6 Ralli Courts, West Riverside, Manchester, M3 5FT Tel: 0161-831 1512; Fax: 0161-831 1513

		holding %
Chairman	Ian Currie	4.0
Chief Executive		
Finance Director		
Exec Director	Roy Gabbie	8.7

Main Shareholders:

Hugh Robertson	8.7
Raymond Donn	4.9
Richard Hughes	4.0

Percentage of free market capital: 57.1%

Nominated Adviser:	WH Ireland, Manchester
AIM Broker:	WH Ireland, Manchester
Solicitors:	Wacks Caller, Manchester
Market Makers:	EVO; SCAP; WINS
Auditors:	PKF, Sovereign House, Queen Street, Manchester M2 5HR
Registrars:	Neville Registrars

Comments:

Strategic Retail was a cash shell that bought loss-making home decor and furnishings retailer Fads out of administration. It raised £348,450 when listing on AIM. Fads operates 53 outlets in high street locations in the UK. A programme of improvements to the profile and variety of products will be undertaken and new sites are to be sourced. The company also intends to acquire other suitable businesses though no negotiations are currently taking place.

Entry on AIM:	19/12/2003	Recent price:	71.5p
Interim results:	Feb	Market cap:	£9.36m
Final results:	Jul	Issue price:	91.0p
Year end:	Mar	Current no of shares:	
Accounts due:	Aug		13,084,472
Int div paymnt:	n/a	No of shares after	
Fin div paymnt:	n/a	dilution:	n/a
Int net div per share:	nil	P/E ratio:	n/a
Fin net div per share:	nil	Probable CGT?	Yes

LATEST REPORTED RESULTS: 53 WEEKS TO 1 MAR '03		PREVIOUS REPORTED RESULTS: 257 DAYS TO 23 FEB '02	
Turnover:	£21.97m	Turnover:	£18.11m
PTP:	£(2.50m)	PTP:	£202,000
EPS:	n/a	EPS:	n/a

Stream (SEA)

Premium rate telephony and digital content provider

The Mansion House, Benham Valance Speen, Newbury, Berkshire RG20 8LU Tel: 01635-516100; Fax: 01635-516111;
e-mail: info@streamgroup.co.uk; web site: www.streamgroup.co.uk

		holding %
Chairman	Gordon Robson	32.9
Managing Director	Michael Spencer	6.7
Finance Director	Joseph Greene	0.0
Non-Exec Director	Graham Stevens	0.4

Main Shareholders:

Jane Scott	7.4
Schroder Nominees	5.0
Chase Nominees	4.9
Hambros (Guernesey Nominees)	4.7
Pershing Keen Nominees	4.7

Percentage of free market capital: 26.2%

Comments:

Business at this venture is roaring. The group supplies live media services to fixed line and mobile phones and produces all manner of niche products from ring-tones and sports results to psychic and astrological phone updates. Last year profits jumped with mobile revenues alone leaping 117% to £3.9m. Even more significantly in terms of how 2004 pans out, the board said that the German, Spanish and Australian divisions were approaching profitability. Worth watching.

Nominated Adviser:	KBC Peel Hunt, London		
AIM Broker:	KBC Peel Hunt, London		
Solicitors:	Lawrence Graham, London		
Market Makers:	KBCS; TEAM; WINS		
Auditors:	KPMG Audit, Reading,		
Registrars:	Capita Registrars		

ENTRY ON AIM:	30/4/2001	**Recent price:**	45.25p
Interim results:	Sep	**Market cap:**	£26.78m
Final results:	Apr	**Issue price:**	28.0p
Year end:	Dec	**Current no of shares:**	
Accounts due:	Jan		59,185,442
Int div paymnt:	n/a	**No of shares after**	
Fin div paymnt:	n/a	**dilution:**	n/a
Int net div per share:	nil	**P/E ratio:**	22.6
Fin net div per share:	nil	**Probable CGT?**	Yes

LATEST REPORTED RESULTS: 2003		PREVIOUS REPORTED RESULTS: 2002	
Turnover:	£10.83m	**Turnover:**	£8.52m
PTP:	£1.11m	**PTP:**	£152,000
EPS:	2.0p	**EPS:**	0.3p

Streetnames (STM)

Cash shell

3 Manchester Square, London, W1M 5RF Tel: 020-7224 4343; Fax: 020-7724 7055

		holding %
Chairman	The Viscount Astor	13.7
Chief Executive		
Finance Director		
Director	Nicholas Leslau	7.7

Main Shareholders:

Prestbury Investment Holdings	38.4
Nigel Wray	14.8
Keelwalk Properties	5.0

Percentage of free market capital: 20.5%

Comments:

There is still little to report at cash shell Streetnames, aside from the fact that management remains on the lookout for decent investment opportunities. Unlike many other AIM shells, however, the company does at least have a couple of things in favour – namely a near £1.5m cash pile and the backing of well-known invest-ment duo Nick Leslau and Nigel Wray.

Nominated Adviser:	Seymour Pierce, London		
AIM Broker:	Seymour Pierce, London		
Solicitors:	Paisner, London		
Market Makers:	SCAP; WINS		
Auditors:	BDO Stoy Hayward, 8 Baker Street, London W1M 1DA		
Registrars:	Capita Registrars		

Entry on AIM:	19/5/2000	**Recent price:**	1.9p
Interim results:	Dec	**Market cap:**	£2.85m
Final results:	Sep	**Issue price:**	10.0p
Year end:	Mar	**Current no of shares:**	
Accounts due:	Nov		150,000,000
Int div paymnt:	n/a	**No of shares after**	
Fin div paymnt:	n/a	**dilution:**	163,750,000
Int net div per share:	n/a	**P/E ratio:**	n/a
Fin net div per share:	n/a	**Probable CGT?**	Yes

LATEST REPORTED RESULTS: 2003		PREVIOUS REPORTED RESULTS: 2002	
Turnover:	n/a	**Turnover:**	£2,000
PTP:	£(108,000)	**PTP:**	£(347,000)
EPS:	(0.1)p	**EPS:**	(0.2)p

Stylo (STYL)

Holding company for footwear retail & UK property activities

Stylo House, Harrogate Road, Apperley Bridge, Bradford, West Yorkshire BD10 0NW Tel: 01274-617761; Fax: 01274-616111

		holding %
Chairman	Michael Ziff	13.2
Chief Executive	as above	
Finance Director		
Operations Director	John Weaving	0.6

Main Shareholders:

Guinness Peat	9.8
A S Perloff	9.2
Edward Ziff	7.1
Employee Benefit Trust	5.4
A L Manning	4.9

Percentage of free market capital: 30.9%

Nominated Adviser:	Dawnay Day, London
AIM Broker:	Brewin Dolphin, Leeds
Solicitors:	DLA, Leeds & Walker Morris, Leeds
Market Makers:	KBCS; WINS
Auditors:	PricewaterhouseCoopers, 33 Wellington St, Leeds LS1 4JP
Registrars:	Lloyds TSB Registrars

ENTRY ON AIM:	5/8/2002	Recent price:	50.5p
Interim results:	Oct	Market cap:	£21.22m
Final results:	Apr	Issue price:	24.0p
Year end:	Jan	Current no of shares:	
Accounts due:	May		42,010,210
Int div paymnt:	n/a	No of shares after	
Fin div paymnt:	Sep	dilution:	n/a
Int net div per share:	nil	P/E ratio:	4.1
Fin net div per share:	1.25p	Probable CGT?	Yes

LATEST REPORTED RESULTS: 2003		PREVIOUS REPORTED RESULTS: 2002	
Turnover:	£208.85m	Turnover:	£197.23m
PTP:	£6.87m	PTP:	£1.9m
EPS:	12.2p	EPS:	3.3p

Comments:

Stylo has gone from profit to loss in the space of a year. Poor trading at Barratts plus the costs of disposing of Shellys clearance stock has affected turnover and even the better performing Priceless has been hampered by distribution problems. David Patrick, an ex-chief executive of JD Sports and Allsports, has been appointed managing director of the Barratts division. However, it may be a while before the company's fortunes are revived.

Sunbeach Communications (SBH)

Internet service provider

San Remo, Belmont Road, St Michael, Barbados Tel: 00-1 246 430 1569; Fax: 00-1 246 228 6330; web site: www.sunbeach.net

		holding %
Chairman		
Managing Director	Michael Wakley*	0.0
Finance Director	John Moir	3.0
Technical Director	Damian Dunphy	14.1

Main Shareholders:

Tele International*	23.5
TP Clarke	16.4
Christopher Alleyne	13.7
IKC Worrell	5.5
Kensington Finance	3.6

Percentage of free market capital: 16.6%

*Managing director Michael Wakley has an interest in these shares

Nominated Adviser:	KBC Peel Hunt, London
AIM Broker:	KBC Peel Hunt, London
Solicitors:	Irwin Mitchell, London; Chancery Chambers, Barbados
Market Makers:	KBCS; WINS
Auditors:	Toppin, Walker & Co, Barbados
Registrars:	Capita Registrars

Entry on AIM:	13/8/2002	Recent price:	19.0p
Interim results:	May	Market cap:	£9.15m
Final results:	Sep	Issue price:	$0.54
Year end:	Nov	Current no of shares:	
Accounts due:	Apr		48,177,934
Int div paymnt:	n/a	No of shares after	
Fin div paymnt:	n/a	dilution:	n/a
Int net div per share:	nil	P/E ratio:	n/a
Fin net div per share:	nil	Probable CGT?	Yes

LATEST REPORTED RESULTS: 2003		PREVIOUS REPORTED RESULTS: 2002	
Turnover:	$6.01m	Turnover:	n/a
PTP:	$(2.29m)	PTP:	n/a
EPS:	(0.1)c	EPS:	n/a

Comments:

Sunbeach is a Barbados-based internet service provider that has a dual listing on the Barbados Stock Exchange and on AIM. The group's internet division continues to trade profitably and during the past year it has secured a licence from the Barbadian Government to operate a cellular telephone network. The interim stage saw the company achieve sales of B$3.1m and a loss before tax of B$2,085.

Supercart (SC.)

Plastic supermarket trolley distributor

Whitebeams, 11 The Glebefield, Shoreham Lane, Sevenoaks, Kent TN13 1DR Tel: 01732-459898; Fax: 01732-464530

		holding %
Chairman	Victor Segal	0.1
Chief Executive	M. Castledine-Wolfe	19.5
Finance Director	Brian Rowbotham	0.0
Managing Director	Martin Deale	19.6

Main Shareholders:

Venture Global Engineering	21.9
Charles Stanley	5.6
Libertas Capital	4.4

Percentage of free market capital: 24.3%

Nominated Adviser:	Charles Stanley, London
AIM Broker:	Charles Stanley, London
Solicitors:	Berwin Leighton Paisner, London
Market Makers:	WINS
Auditors:	Audit Assure, 82 St. John Street, London EC1M 4JN
Registrars:	Lloyds TSB Registrars

ENTRY ON AIM:	4/2/2004	Recent price:	44.0p
Interim results:	Nov	Market cap:	£9.02m
Final results:	Jun	Issue price:	50.0p
Year end:	Feb	Current no of shares:	
Accounts due:	Aug		20,500,000
Int div paymnt:	n/a	No of shares after	
Fin div paymnt:	n/a	dilution:	n/a
Int net div per share:	nil	P/E ratio:	n/a
Fin net div per share:	nil	Probable CGT?	Yes

Comments:

The plastic supermarket trolleys maker joined AIM via a £4m placing at 50p in February. The funds will help finance new trolley moulds for launch in North America and Europe in early 2005, as well as bolster its marketing efforts. All-plastic trolleys are more durable, easier to move around and do less damage to parked cars than traditional 'wire' competitors. Supercart should make £40,000 profits on £6m sales this calendar year, and £800,000 on £10.75m for 2005.

LATEST REPORTED RESULTS: 2002		PREVIOUS REPORTED RESULTS: 2001	
Turnover:	£1.68m	Turnover:	£2.77m
PTP:	£(425,000)	PTP:	£(207,000)
EPS:	n/a	EPS:	n/a

Supporta (formerly Staffing Ventures) (STF)

Outsourced payroll services provider

10 Bakers Yard, Bakers Row, Farringdon, London, EC1R 3DD Tel: 020-7713 0330; Fax: 020-7814 4700

		holding %
Chairman	Robert Holt	0.7
Chief Executive	Gavin Kaye	0.0
Finance Director	Philip Ellis	0.5
Non-Exec Director	John Williams	0.0

Main Shareholders:

Parys Snowdon	21.6
Unicorn Asset Management	15.5
Rathbone Investment Management	11.4
Ruffer Investment Management	9.1
JO Hambro	8.0

Percentage of free market capital: 14%

Nominated Adviser:	Arbuthnot, Birmingham
AIM Broker:	Arbuthnot, Birmingham
Solicitors:	BPE, Cheltenham
Market Makers:	MLSB; SCAP; WINS
Auditors:	Grant Thornton, Cheltenham
Registrars:	Capita Registrars

Entry on AIM:	14/2/2001	Recent price:	50.0p
Interim results:	Dec	Market cap:	£11.67m
Final results:	Sep	Issue price:	38.0p
Year end:	Mar	Current no of shares:	
Accounts due:	Jul		23,345,675
Int div paymnt:	n/a	No of shares after	
Fin div paymnt:	n/a	dilution:	n/a
Int net div per share:	nil	P/E ratio:	n/a
Fin net div per share:	nil	Probable CGT?	Yes

Comments:

Loss-making Staffing Ventures changed its name to Supporta after Parys Snowdon Payroll reversed into it with an accompanying £4m placing. Acquiring Parys Snowdon Payroll, which provides outsourced payroll, pension and accounts payable services to NHS organisations, was viewed as the best way to grow the group's back office and payroll outsourcing division. Hopefully the deal has boosted revenues and the placing has strengthened the group's balance sheet.

LATEST REPORTED RESULTS: 2003		PREVIOUS REPORTED RESULTS: 2002	
Turnover:	£9.43m	Turnover:	£1.77m
PTP:	£(340,000)	PTP:	£(363,000)
EPS:	(7.0)p	EPS:	(16.6)p

Surface Technology Systems (SRTS)

Supplier of equipment for the manufacture of semiconductors

Imperial Park, Newport, NP10 8UJ Tel: 01633-652400; Fax: 01633-652405; e-mail: enquiries@stsystems.co.uk; web site: www.stsystems.com

		holding %
Chairman	Nigel Randall	0.1
Chief Executive	Ian Smith	0.0
Finance Director	Paul Webb	0.0
Non-Exec Director	Michael Love	0.03

Main Shareholders:

Sumitomo Precision Products	63.8
Amvescap	7.1
Gartmore Investment	5.2
Schroder Investments	4.7
William Partridge	3.2

Percentage of free market capital: 12.2%

Comments:

Surface Technology Systems' markets for specialist capital equipment within areas such as Micro Electro-Mechanical, Photonics, and Wafer Packaging remain tough. And the weakening dollar has reduced margins, forcing the company to restructure. On the upside, orders ticked up strongly in the second half and the year-end forward order book was higher than at the end of 2002. Furthermore, STS has consistently improved its debt position throughout the year.

Nominated Adviser:	Rowan Dartington, Bristol
AIM Broker:	Rowan Dartington, Bristol
Solicitors:	Burges Salmon, Bristol
Market Makers:	ALTI; WINS
Auditors:	Deloitte & Touche, Cardiff
Registrars:	Capita Registrars

ENTRY ON AIM:	8/12/2000	Recent price:	27.5p
Interim results:	Sep	Market cap:	£8.7m
Final results:	Mar	Issue price:	138.0p
Year end:	Dec	Current no of shares:	
Accounts due:	Apr		31,646,015
Int div paymnt:	n/a	No of shares after	
Fin div paymnt:	n/a	dilution:	32,911,392
Int net div per share:	nil	P/E ratio:	n/a
Fin net div per share:	nil	Probable CGT?	Yes

LATEST REPORTED RESULTS:	2002	PREVIOUS REPORTED RESULTS:	2001
Turnover:	£33.82m	Turnover:	£56.67m
PTP:	£(9.88m)	PTP:	£5.33m
EPS:	(23.6)p	EPS:	11.2p

Surface Transforms (SCE)

Designer & maker of carbon fibre reinforced ceramic products

April House, Tarvin Road, Frodsham, WA6 6XN Tel: 01928-735498; Fax: 01928-735352; e-mail: jjf@surface-transforms.com; web site: www.surface-transforms.com

		holding %
Chairman	Derek Whitney	1.7
Managing Director	Julio Faria	25.0
Finance Director	Johannah Stretton	0.0
Non-Exec Director	Kevin D'Silva	1.7

Main Shareholders:

David Levis	5.8
David Clark	10.5

Percentage of free market capital: 53.9%

Comments:

Great progress has been made in the past six months as turnover for the interim period to November increased 66% to £175,000 and pre-tax losses fell 80% to £159,000 thanks to a new business model that focuses on maximising commercial exploitation of its proprietary CFRC technology. It has also won two new contracts with the United States Air Force research laboratory and Dunlop Aerospace.

Nominated Adviser:	John East, London
AIM Broker:	John East, London
Solicitors:	Hammonds, Manchester
Market Makers:	KBCS; WINS
Auditors:	KPMG St James' Square, Manchester M2 2JF
Registrars:	Capita Registrars

Entry on AIM:	24/9/2002	Recent price:	76.5p
Interim results:	Jan	Market cap:	£7.24m
Final results:	Sep	Issue price:	90.0p
Year end:	May	Current no of shares:	
Accounts due:	Oct		9,466,113
Int div paymnt:	n/a	No of shares after	
Fin div paymnt:	n/a	dilution:	n/a
Int net div per share:	nil	P/E ratio:	n/a
Fin net div per share:	nil	Probable CGT?	Yes

LATEST REPORTED RESULTS:	2003	PREVIOUS REPORTED RESULTS:	2002
Turnover:	£240,000	Turnover:	£104,000
PTP:	£(1.12m)	PTP:	£(561,000)
EPS:	(10.9)p	EPS:	(7.5)p

335

Surgical Innovations (SUN)

Surgical equipment distributor

Clayton Park, Clayton Wood Rise, Leeds, LS16 6RF Tel: 0113-230 7597; Fax: 0113-230 7598; e-mail: si@surginno.co.uk; web site: www.surginno.com

		holding %
Chairman	Douglas Liversidge	1.1
Managing Director		
Finance Director	Graham Bowland	0.0
Technical Director	Stuart Moran	1.2

Main Shareholders:

Getz Bros	19.4

Percentage of free market capital: 77.4%

Nominated Adviser:	Westhouse Securities, London
AIM Broker:	Westhouse Securities, London
Solicitors:	Walker Morris, Leeds
Market Makers:	MLSB; SCAP; WINS
Auditors:	Grant Thornton, Leeds
Registrars:	Capita Registrars

ENTRY ON AIM:	7/7/1998	Recent price:	2.75p
Interim results:	Sep	Market cap:	£7.04m
Final results:	Mar	Issue price:	3.0p
Year end:	Dec	Current no of shares:	
Accounts due:	Apr		255,892,311
Int div paymnt:	n/a	No of shares after	
Fin div paymnt:	n/a	dilution:	n/a
Int net div per share:	nil	P/E ratio:	n/a
Fin net div per share:	nil	Probable CGT?	Yes

LATEST REPORTED RESULTS: 2002		PREVIOUS REPORTED RESULTS: 2001	
Turnover:	£2.22m	Turnover:	£1.85m
PTP:	£60,000	PTP:	£36,000
EPS:	0.0p	EPS:	0.0p

Comments:

The tiny surgical products manufacturer's four key areas are licensing, minimally invasive products, blood transfusion products, and Ion Products Solutions. Interim profits stayed flat at £23,000 but sales rose 20% to £1.16m. Sales in the US have picked up, particularly of YelloPort. The group has high hopes for a disposable scissors product and other disposable items. SI remains a minute business in an industry dominated by giants though.

Sutton Harbour (SUH)

Harbour authority operator, property & marine leisure manager

North Quay House, Sutton Harbour, Plymouth, PL4 0RA Tel: 01752-204286; Fax: 01752-205403; web site: www.sutton-harbour.co.uk

		holding %
Chairman	Ellen Winser	5.2
Managing Director	Duncan Godefroy	0.9
Finance Director	Nigel Godefroy	0.2
Non-Exec Director	Malcolm Pearce	1.0

Main Shareholders:

Rotolok/M McCauley	28.7
Vidacos Nominees	8.1
R C Greig Nominees	4.7
Darlington Portfolio Nominees	4.4
Bank of New York Nominees	3.4

Percentage of free market capital: 43%

Nominated Adviser:	Rowan Dartington, Bristol
AIM Broker:	Rowan Dartington, Bristol
Solicitors:	Wolferstans, Plymouth
Market Makers:	KBCS; WINS
Auditors:	KPMG, Plym House, 3 Longbridge Road, Marsh Mills, Plymouth PL6 8LT
Registrars:	Computershare Investor Services

Entry on AIM:	23/12/1996	Recent price:	190.0p
Interim results:	Nov	Market cap:	£23.08m
Final results:	May	Issue price:	12.5p
Year end:	Mar	Current no of shares:	
Accounts due:	Aug		12,146,515
Int div paymnt:	Jan	No of shares after	
Fin div paymnt:	Jul	dilution:	n/a
Int net div per share:	1.8p	P/E ratio:	21.3
Fin net div per share:	3.2p	Probable CGT?	Yes

LATEST REPORTED RESULTS: 2003		PREVIOUS REPORTED RESULTS: 2002	
Turnover:	£9.57m	Turnover:	£8.2m
PTP:	£1.54m	PTP:	£1.59m
EPS:	8.9p	EPS:	9.2p

Comments:

Interims to September from Sutton Harbour were 'satisfactory' and pointed the way to growth. This was an eventful half in which regeneration business moved ahead strongly and the company created its own regional low-cost airline, Air Southwest. Plymouth City Airport enjoyed a stable first half. On the financials, profits came in lower at £628,000 (£722,000), although operating profits were up 6.3% (excluding airline start-up costs) on sales of £3.6m (£4.3m).

SWP   (SWP)

Construction products maker

4th Floor, 3 Bedford Street, London, WC2E 9HD   Tel: 020-7379 7181;   Fax: 020-7379 7090

		holding %
Chairman	Robert Muddimer	0.8
Chief Executive		
Finance Director	Alan Walker	3.2
Exec Director	Alan Smith	5.5

Main Shareholders:

Frances Bell	18.7
HSBC Equity	4.7
Robert Stickings	3.0

Percentage of free market capital: 64.1%

Nominated Adviser:	KBC Peel Hunt, London
AIM Broker:	KBC Peel Hunt, London
Solicitors:	Addleshaw Goddard, London
Market Makers:	KBCS; MLSB
Auditors:	KPMG Audit, 8 Salisbury Square, London, EC4Y 8BB
Registrars:	Capita Registrars

ENTRY ON AIM:	17/6/2002	**Recent price:**	1.1p
Interim results:	Feb	**Market cap:**	£3.75m
Final results:	Nov	**Issue price:**	2.25p
Year end:	Jun	**Current no of shares:**	
Accounts due:	Nov		341,319,028
Int div paymnt:	n/a	**No of shares after**	
Fin div paymnt:	n/a	**dilution:**	n/a
Int net div per share:	nil	**P/E ratio:**	n/a
Fin net div per share:	nil	**Probable CGT?**	**Yes**

LATEST REPORTED RESULTS: 2003		PREVIOUS REPORTED RESULTS: 2002	
Turnover:	£18.36m	**Turnover:**	£16.35m
PTP:	£(714,000)	**PTP:**	£(640,000)
EPS:	(0.2)p	**EPS:**	(0.2)p

Comments:

Profits seem to have taken a perpetual raincheck for construction products maker SWP. Chairman Robert Muddimer described 2003 as a 'particularly frustrating year'. Of the three companies run by SWP, only drainage division Fullflow has shown any signs of progress. Fullflow aims to be the leading 'syphonic' rainwater drainage system supplier in Europe. Sales in France increased 34% to £2.4m. However, operating profits still fell 50%.

Symphony Plastic Technologies   (SYM)

Provider of degradable polythene and related products

Elstree House, Elstree Way, Borehamwood, Hertfordshire WD6 1LE   Tel: 020-8207 5900;   Fax: 020-8207 5960;
e-mail: info@symphonyplastics.co.uk ;   web site: www.symphonyplastics.com

		holding %
Chairman	Christopher Littmoden	0.5
Chief Executive	Michael Laurier	28.4
Finance Director	Ian Bristow	2.3
Operations Director	Keith Frener	3.4

Main Shareholders:

EPI	8.1
R Laurier	4.7
Singer & Friedlander Aim 3	4.3
Crosshill International	4.3

Percentage of free market capital: 41.6%

Nominated Adviser:	Collins Stewart, London
AIM Broker:	Collins Stewart, London
Solicitors:	Kendall Freeman, London
Market Makers:	KBCS; SCAP; WINS
Auditors:	Grant Thornton, Aylesbury, Buckinghamshire
Registrars:	Capita Registrars

Entry on AIM:	30/11/2001	**Recent price:**	21.25p
Interim results:	Sep	**Market cap:**	£9.63m
Final results:	Mar	**Issue price:**	30.0p
Year end:	Dec	**Current no of shares:**	
Accounts due:	Apr		45,332,880
Int div paymnt:	n/a	**No of shares after**	
Fin div paymnt:	n/a	**dilution:**	n/a
Int net div per share:	nil	**P/E ratio:**	n/a
Fin net div per share:	nil	**Probable CGT?**	**Yes**

LATEST REPORTED RESULTS: 2002		PREVIOUS REPORTED RESULTS: 2001	
Turnover:	£4.04m	**Turnover:**	£3.85m
PTP:	£(1.68m)	**PTP:**	£(1.54m)
EPS:	(5.3)p	**EPS:**	(6.6)p

Comments:

The degradable plastics producer's sales powered up 89% last year with operating losses before exceptionals culled by 25%. Encouragingly Symphony is now at cashflow breakeven. The company has evolved from a licensee seller of a limited range, to an owner of its own technology marketing products worldwide. Although UK sales progress has been slower than expected, new markets have been established in Brazil, New Zealand and South Africa.

Synergy Healthcare (SYR)

Outsourced medical support services provider

New Market Drive, Derby, DE24 8SW Tel: 01332-387 100; Fax: 01332-758 817; web site: www.synergyhealthcareplc.uk

		holding %
Chairman	Stephen Wilson	0.2
Chief Executive	Richard Steeves	10.2
Finance Director	Ivan Jacques	0.0
Non-Exec Director	Duncan Nichol	0.0

Main Shareholders:

Framlington Investment Management	10.2
Gartmore	9.9
Merill Lynch	9.3
Credit Suisse Asset Management	8.7
Andrew Fitton	7.9
Percentage of free market capital: 43.6%	

Comments:

Synergy hopes to capitalise on the trend for outsourcing in the NHS, offering cleaning and other services to hospitals via long term contracts of over seven years. Interim pre-tax profits rose 81% to £1.7m on turnover up 25% to £15.3m. Much growth came after acquiring a division of Hays for £11.3m, funded by a placing at 210p. The group is bidding for major contracts with new PFI-backed hospitals. Overall, the 'forward order book' stands at £350m. A full-year profit of £3.8m is predicted.

Nominated Adviser:	Brewin Dolphin, Manchester		
AIM Broker:	Brewin Dolphin, Manchester		
Solicitors:	Taylor Wessing, London		
Market Makers:	KBCS; WINS		
Auditors:	Grant Thornton, Kettering		
Registrars:	Computershare Investor Services		

ENTRY ON AIM:	20/8/2001	**Recent price:**	270.0p
Interim results:	Nov	**Market cap:**	£59.69m
Final results:	Jun	**Issue price:**	128.0p
Year end:	Mar	**Current no of shares:**	
Accounts due:	Jul		22,106,313
Int div paymnt:	Dec	**No of shares after**	
Fin div paymnt:	Aug	**dilution:**	22,578,327
Int net div per share:	1.1p	**P/E ratio:**	36.5
Fin net div per share:	1.6p	**Probable CGT?**	YES

LATEST REPORTED RESULTS: 2003		PREVIOUS REPORTED RESULTS: 2002	
Turnover:	£27.11m	**Turnover:**	£12.65m
PTP:	£2.34m	**PTP:**	£1.46m
EPS:	7.4p	**EPS:**	7.4p

Synigence (suspended 26 Jun 2003) (SYE)

Supplier of health-related information

Portland House, Aldermaston Park, Aldermaston, Reading, Berkshire RG7 4HR Tel: 0118-981 6666; Fax: 0118-981 9801; e-mail: tthompson@synigence.net; web site: www.synigence.co.uk

		holding %
Chairman	Tony Thompson	1.0
Chief Executive	Keith Bushnell	0.9
Finance Director		
Director	Laurence Greetham	6.3

Main Shareholders:

Amvescap	18.1
Grahame Sewell	9.1
NY Nominees	8.6
Nortrust Nominees	5.2
Pharmabio Development	4.8
Percentage of free market capital: 6.9%	

Comments:

Health information business Synigence remains both suspended and in the hands of the administrators, due to doubts over its financial position. Having released no new information to the market since the administrators arrived in August there is little more to report, leaving investors with no option but to watch and wait.

Nominated Adviser:	Collins Stewart, London		
AIM Broker:	Collins Stewart, London		
Solicitors:	Barlow Clyde & Gilbert, London		
Market Makers:	KBCS; SCAP; WINS		
Auditors:	Ernst & Young, Apex Plaza, Reading, Berkshire, RG1 1YE		
Registrars:	Capita Registrars		

Entry on AIM:	6/10/2000	**Recent price:**	6.6p
Interim results:	Sep	**Market cap:**	£5.84m
Final results:	Jun	**Issue price:**	52.0p
Year end:	Dec	**Current no of shares:**	
Accounts due:	Apr		88,543,591
Int div paymnt:	n/a	**No of shares after**	
Fin div paymnt:	n/a	**dilution:**	n/a
Int net div per share:	nil	**P/E ratio:**	n/a
Fin net div per share:	nil	**Probable CGT?**	YES

LATEST REPORTED RESULTS: 2001		PREVIOUS REPORTED RESULTS: 2000	
Turnover:	£413,000	**Turnover:**	£1.98m
PTP:	£(5.96m)	**PTP:**	£(750,000)
EPS:	(13.7)p	**EPS:**	(2.8)p

Systems Union (SUG)

Business software

Systems Union House, 1 Lakeside Road, Farnborough, Hampshire GU14 6XP Tel: 01252-556000; Fax: 01252-556001;
e-mail: marketing_desk@systemsunion.com; web site: www.systemsunion.com

		holding %
Chairman	Bob Morton	10.5
Chief Executive	Paul Coleman	0.1
Finance Director	Antony Sweet	0.01
Non-Exec Director	John Pemberton	4.7

Main Shareholders:

Prudential	10.0
Henderson Invest. Mngmt. Fund	7.6
Schroders Investment Management	6.6
Gartmore Investment Management	5.4
Robert Fleming Holdings	5.1
Percentage of free market capital: 31.8%	

Nominated Adviser:	Panmure Gordon, London
AIM Broker:	KBC Peel Hunt, London;
	Panmure Gordon, London
Solicitors:	Burges Salmon, Bristol
Market Makers:	KBCS; MLSB; WINS
Auditors:	KPMG Audit, Reading
Registrars:	Capita Registrars

ENTRY ON AIM:	1/12/1999	Recent price:	119.0p
Interim results:	Aug	Market cap:	£125.74m
Final results:	Mar	Issue price:	130.0p
Year end:	Dec	Current no of shares:	
Accounts due:	May		105,660,315
Int div paymnt:	n/a	No of shares after	
Fin div paymnt:	n/a	dilution:	106,357,890
Int net div per share:	nil	P/E ratio:	22
Fin net div per share:	nil	Probable CGT?	Yes

LATEST REPORTED RESULTS:	2003	PREVIOUS REPORTED RESULTS:	2002
Turnover:	£78.43m	Turnover:	£74.63m
PTP:	£6.12m	PTP:	£4.32m
EPS:	5.4p	EPS:	3.8p

Comments:

The global software supplier is going from strength to strength. The full year results were better than expected and the company ended the year with £19.6m of cash. It is due to pay an inaugural dividend of 1p. Moreover, due to the acquisition of MIS, annualised revenues were running at £108.4m. Chief executive Paul Coleman claims the current year has started well and reckons the group has a good platform on which to build an even more substantial software company.

Talent (TTV)

Designer and developer of internet applications

9/10 Oasis Park, Eynsham, Oxfordshire OX29 4AL Tel: 01865-887470; Fax: 01865-887450;
e-mail: info@rmrplc.com

		holding %
Chairman	Robert Benton	17.4
Chief Executive	Anthony Humphreys	15.6
Finance Director	Colin Nicholl	3.0
Deputy Chairman	John Cooper	23.5

Main Shareholders:

Duncan Duckett Pension Fund	6.8
Percentage of free market capital: 33.7%	

Nominated Adviser:	John East, London
AIM Broker:	Marshall Securities, London
Solicitors:	Travers Smith Braithwaite,
	London
Market Makers:	ARBT; WINS
Auditors:	Grant Thornton, 1 Westminster
	Way, Oxford OX2 0PZ
Registrars:	Capita Registrars

Entry on AIM:	12/4/2000	Recent price:	19.0p
Interim results:	Jun	Market cap:	£3.08m
Final results:	Mar	Issue price:	120.0p
Year end:	Sep	Current no of shares:	
Accounts due:	Jun		16,210,284
Int div paymnt:	n/a	No of shares after	
Fin div paymnt:	n/a	dilution:	n/a
Int net div per share:	nil	P/E ratio:	n/a
Fin net div per share:	nil	Probable CGT?	Yes

LATEST REPORTED RESULTS:	2003	PREVIOUS REPORTED RESULTS: 7 MONTHS TO 30 SEPT 2002	
Turnover:	£2.92m	Turnover:	£148,000
PTP:	£(480,000)	PTP:	£(938,000)
EPS:	(3.1)p	EPS:	(10.1)p

Comments:

This TV production business continues to progress, thanks in the main to the success of its Test the Nation shows for the BBC. A further four shows of this ilk have already been commissioned as have further projects of CBBC and Disney UK. Talent's latest project is Zeroman, a cartoon about a hapless superhero voiced by Naked Gun star Leslie Nielsen. The company will distribute the 13-episode series in the UK.

Tandem (TND)

Manufacture and distribution of sports and leisure equipment

9a South Street, Crowland, Peterborough PE6 0AH Tel: 01733-211399; Fax: 01733-211933;
e-mail: Paulvicary@apvicary@aol.com; web site: www.falconcycles.co.uk

		holding %
Chairman	Graham Waldron	1.0
Chief Executive		
Finance Director	Mervyn Keene	1.2
Commercial	Paul Vicary	1.1
Director		

Main Shareholders:

Jupiter Asset Mangement	10.1
Venaglass	8.4
Close Investments	7.0

Percentage of free market capital: 68.5%

Nominated Adviser:	KBC Peel Hunt, London
AIM Broker:	KBC Peel Hunt, London
Solicitors:	Eversheds, Nottingham
Market Makers:	KBCS; SCAP; WINS
Auditors:	Deloitte & Touche, Nottingham
Registrars:	Capita Registrars

ENTRY ON AIM:	27/9/2000	**Recent price:**	14.25p
Interim results:	Oct	**Market cap:**	£5.36m
Final results:	Apr	**Issue price:**	5.0p
Year end:	Jan	**Current no of shares:**	
Accounts due:	May		37,585,396
Int div paymnt:	n/a	**No of shares after**	
Fin div paymnt:	n/a	**dilution:**	n/a
Int net div per share:	nil	**P/E ratio:**	71.3
Fin net div per share:	nil	**Probable CGT?**	**YES**

LATEST REPORTED RESULTS:	2003	PREVIOUS REPORTED RESULTS:	2002
Turnover:	£37.32m	**Turnover:**	£35.32m
PTP:	£234,000	**PTP:**	£568,000
EPS:	0.2p	**EPS:**	0.3p

Comments:
Sport and leisure equipment business Tandem has disposed of office water cooler supplier Water Waiter (acquired as a subsidiary of MV Sports in April 2003), for around £2m. Though profitable, management concluded that the business was not compatible with the rest of the Tandem group and thus decided to take the cash and use it to pay down debt. First half figures showed a reduced pre-tax profit of £45,000 from £19m of sales.

Tanfield (formerly Comeleon) (TAN)

Provider of specialist manufacturing processes

Comeleon House, Tanfield Lea Industrial Estate North, Tanfield Lea, Stanley, County Durham DH9 9NX
Tel: 01207-523333; Fax: 01207-523344; e-mail: investors@e-comeleon.com; web site: www.e-comeleon.com

		holding %
Chairman	Jon Pither	0.2
Chief Executive	Roy Stanley	81.6
Finance Director	Timothy Robinson	0.01
Non-Exec Director	Douglas Smith	0.1

Main Shareholders:

BNY Nominees	3.2

Percentage of free market capital: 14.9%

Nominated Adviser:	Brewin Dolphin, Manchester
AIM Broker:	Brewin Dolphin, Manchester
Solicitors:	Ward Hadaway, Newcastle upon Tyne
Market Makers:	KBCS; WINS
Auditors:	Deloitte & Touche, Newcastle upon Tyne
Registrars:	Capita Registrars

Entry on AIM:	14/12/2000	**Recent price:**	7.75p
Interim results:	May	**Market cap:**	£4.78m
Final results:	Dec	**Issue price:**	165.0p
Year end:	Sep	**Current no of shares:**	
Accounts due:	Jan		61,734,716
Int div paymnt:	n/a	**No of shares after**	
Fin div paymnt:	n/a	**dilution:**	n/a
Int net div per share:	nil	**P/E ratio:**	n/a
Fin net div per share:	nil	**Probable CGT?**	**YES**

LATEST REPORTED RESULTS:	2002	PREVIOUS REPORTED RESULTS:	18 MONTHS TO 30 SEP 01
Turnover:	£4.50m	**Turnover:**	£417,000
PTP:	£(3.27m)	**PTP:**	£(4.70m)
EPS:	(24.3)p	**EPS:**	(63.7)p

Comments:
Struggling consumer goods customiser Comeleon moved into the manufacturing sector via the £4.7m reverse takeover of former parent company Tanfield. Headed by Comeleon CEO Roy Stanley, Tanfield operates three core businesses. The first focuses on precision engineering for the automotive industry, the second on systems integration and the third on specialist finishing and coating services. In the year to last March these businesses enabled Tanfield to generate a £4,000 operating profit from £9.5m of sales.

340

Taskcatch (TASK)

5-a-side football pitch developer & operator
6 Ralli Courts, West Riverside, Manchester, M3 5FT Tel: 01942-322256

		holding %
Chairman	Norman Molyneux	0.3
Chief Executive	Jason Lynn	9.9
Finance Director		
Non-Exec Director	John King	0.0

Main Shareholders:

Brendan Larkin	39.5
Ian Currie	4.1
Richard Hughes	3.9

Percentage of free market capital: 42.3%

Nominated Adviser:	WH Ireland, London
AIM Broker:	WH Ireland, London
Solicitors:	Wacks Caller, London
Market Makers:	WINS
Auditors:	PKF, Sovereign House, Queen Street, Manchester M2 5HR
Registrars:	Capita Registrars

ENTRY ON AIM:	31/3/2003	**Recent price:**	40.0p
Interim results:	Sep	Market cap:	£12.68m
Final results:	Mar	Issue price:	28.0p
Year end:	Dec	Current no of shares:	
Accounts due:	May		31,696,750
Int div paymnt:	n/a	No of shares after	
Fin div paymnt:	n/a	dilution:	n/a
Int net div per share:	nil	P/E ratio:	n/a
Fin net div per share:	nil	Probable CGT?	YES

LATEST REPORTED RESULTS: FOR PERIOD TO 31 JAN 2003		PREVIOUS REPORTED RESULTS:	N/A
Turnover:	£138,000	Turnover:	n/a
PTP:	£(54,000)	PTP:	n/a
EPS:	n/a	EPS:	n/a

Comments:

Taskcatch's first acquisition Skylark Thornton took the company into the development and operation of 5-a-side football pitches. More recently, it bought Soccercity for £730,000 – this business operates a two court indoor 5-a-side football centre in Hampshire, and has a track record of profitable trading in this young industry sector. Taskcatch directors insist the demand for high quality football facilities is there – interims to 31 July revealed a £225,070 loss on £274,000 turnover.

---

tecc-IS (TIS)

Investment company
Third Floor, 345 Stockport Road, Manchester, M13 0LF Tel: 0161-273 6050; Fax: 0161-273 6172;
web site: www.tecc-IS.com

		holding %
Chairman	Larry Lipman	0.0
Chief Executive		
Finance Director		
Director	Daniel Kay	0.0

Main Shareholders:

DCM	10.4
Pershing Keen Nominees	6.9
Chase Nominees	4.4
Vidacos Nominees	3.7
Paul Curtis	3.6

Percentage of free market capital: 59.2%

Nominated Adviser:	John East, London
AIM Broker:	John East, London
Solicitors:	Berwin Leighton Paisner, London
Market Makers:	SCAP; WINS
Auditors:	Horwath Clark, Manchester
Registrars:	Capita Registrars

Entry on AIM:	20/9/2000	**Recent price:**	7.0p
Interim results:	Sep	Market cap:	£3.05m
Final results:	Mar	Issue price:	25.0p
Year end:	Dec	Current no of shares:	
Accounts due:	Apr		43,573,000
Int div paymnt:	n/a	No of shares after	
Fin div paymnt:	n/a	dilution:	55,373,000
Int net div per share:	nil	P/E ratio:	n/a
Fin net div per share:	nil	Probable CGT?	No

LATEST REPORTED RESULTS:	2002	PREVIOUS REPORTED RESULTS: 6 JUL 00 TO 31 DEC 01	
Turnover:	n/a	Turnover:	n/a
PTP:	£(635,000)	PTP:	(705,000)
EPS:	(1.5)p	EPS:	(1.8)

Comments:

Experienced chairman Larry Lipman has had problems changing the strategy of this tech-focused investment vehicle. Lipman, who is behind property plays Bizspace and Safeland, wanted to use the group's £2.8m cash pile to buy a majority stake in European self storage concern Espazio. However, tecc-IS' original directors would not approve this and had their contracts terminated and nomad Durlacher resigned. Lipman plans to complete the transaction soon.

Tecteon (TEO)

Echo cancellation software

77 South Audley Street, London, W1K 1JG Tel: 020-7408 1181; Fax: 020-7408 1711;
e-mail: m.hirschowitz@tecteon.com; web site: www.tecteon.com

		holding %
Acting Chairman	Masoud Alikhani	1.1
Chief Executive		
Finance Director		
Non-Exec Director	Ziv Navoth	1.4

Main Shareholders:

New Opportunities Investment Trust	23.8
London Wall Nominees	21.1
I-Fin Services	15.7
HSBC Global Custody Nominee	7.8
Startup Holdings	6.9

Percentage of free market capital: 15.8%

Nominated Adviser:	Seymour Pierce, London
AIM Broker:	Hichens Harrison, London
Solicitors:	Finers Stephens Innocent, London
Market Makers:	MLSB; WINS
Auditors:	Henderson & Co, London
Registrars:	Capita Registrars

ENTRY ON AIM:	28/4/2000	Recent price:	4.5p
Interim results:	Mar	Market cap:	£8.03m
Final results:	Dec	Issue price:	6.5p
Year end:	Jun	Current no of shares:	
Accounts due:	Oct		178,499,673
Int div paymnt:	n/a	No of shares after	
Fin div paymnt:	n/a	dilution:	n/a
Int net div per share:	nil	P/E ratio:	n/a
Fin net div per share:	nil	Probable CGT?	Yes

Comments:

Having cut costs and put a marketing network and sales team in place, Tecteon is hoping to hit breakeven towards the end of 2004 and profits in 2005. Its products save telecoms companies money by improving voice quality and preventing people hanging up. It recently signed two significant contracts but cash is an issue as it recently had to raise £700,000 in a placing for working capital. £1.94m is also due to be paid to creditors within a year.

LATEST REPORTED RESULTS:	2003	PREVIOUS REPORTED RESULTS:	2002
Turnover:	£208,000	Turnover:	£184,000
PTP:	£(1.46m)	PTP:	£(431,000)
EPS:	(1.2)p	EPS:	(0.5)p

Telford Homes (TEF)

Housebuilder

3 Buckingham Court, Rectory Lane, Loughton, Essex IG10 2QZ Tel: 020-8498 6789; Fax: 020-8498 6777;
e-mail: newhomes@telfordhomes.plc.uk; web site: www.telfordhomes.plc.uk

		holding %
Chairman	David Holland	4.0
Chief Executive	Andrew Wiseman	9.3
Finance Director	Jon Di-Stefano	0.4
Managing Director	David Durant	4.0

Main Shareholders:

ISIS Asset Management	15.4
The Puma II Fund	11.0
K P Furlong	8.7
Fielding Nominees	6.4
D G Furlong	5.6

Percentage of free market capital: 23.5%

Nominated Adviser:	Shore Capital, London
AIM Broker:	Shore Capital, London
Solicitors:	SJ Berwin, London
Market Makers:	SCAP; WINS
Auditors:	Moore Stephens, Warwick Lane, London EC4P 4BN
Registrars:	Capita Registrars

Entry on AIM:	14/12/2001	Recent price:	143.5p
Interim results:	Nov	Market cap:	£41.79m
Final results:	May	Issue price:	50.0p
Year end:	Mar	Current no of shares:	
Accounts due:	Jun		29,120,740
Int div paymnt:	Jan	No of shares after	
Fin div paymnt:	Jul	dilution:	n/a
Int net div per share:	1.0p	P/E ratio:	11.3
Fin net div per share:	2.0p	Probable CGT?	Yes

Comments:

Telford specialises in developing blocks of one and two bedroom apartments in the north and east of London. Interim results showed pre-tax profits up 48% to £2.1m and turnover increasing 74% to £15.2m. During the period it lauched four developments, including Abbott's Wharf, which has reservations of 75%. Since interims, it has sold another 22 properties with a sales value of £4.6m. It was also nominated for AIM company of the year in 2003.

LATEST REPORTED RESULTS:	2003	PREVIOUS REPORTED RESULTS:	16 MONTHS TO 31 MAR 02
Turnover:	£25.33m	Turnover:	£8.81m
PTP:	£4.27m	PTP:	£1.33m
EPS:	12.7p	EPS:	10.1p

Tellings Golden Miller (TGM)

Bus services & luxury coach hire provider

The Old Tram Garage, Stanley Road, Twickenham, Middlesex TW2 5NP Tel: 020-8755 7050; Fax: 020-8977 1926;
e-mail: sales@tellings.co.uk; web site: www.tellingsgoldenmiller.co.uk

		holding %
Chairman	Stephen Telling	52.1
Chief Executive	as above	
Finance Director	Robert Hodgetts	0.0
Operations Director	Richard Telling	0.0

Main Shareholders:

Unicorn AIM VCT	6.5

Percentage of free market capital: 21%

Nominated Adviser:	City Financial Associates, London
AIM Broker:	Oriel Securities, London
Solicitors:	Field Fisher Waterhouse, London
Market Makers:	KBCS; SCAP; WINS
Auditors:	Rothman Pantall & Co, London
Registrars:	Computershare Investor Services

ENTRY ON AIM:	1/8/2003	**Recent price:**	132.0p
Interim results:	Sep	**Market cap:**	£29.32m
Final results:	Mar	**Issue price:**	70.0p
Year end:	Dec	**Current no of shares:**	
Accounts due:	Jun		22,209,223
Int div paymnt:	n/a	**No of shares after**	
Fin div paymnt:	n/a	**dilution:**	n/a
Int net div per share:	nil	**P/E ratio:**	146.3
Fin net div per share:	nil	**Probable CGT?**	**YES**

LATEST REPORTED RESULTS:	2002	**PREVIOUS REPORTED RESULTS:**	2001
Turnover:	£21.31m	**Turnover:**	£15.79m
PTP:	£1.51m	**PTP:**	£562,000
EPS:	n/a	**EPS:**	n/a

Comments:

Since publishing maiden interims to June, the bus service provider and luxury coach operator has been awarded another new bus contract by Transport for London. It has also gobbled up the remaining 62.7% of bus and coach fleet operator Burtons. Tellings Golden Miller will use the deal to expand its bus operations in East Anglia. Those first half figures were excellent, with pre-tax profits accelerating ahead by 169% to £1.47m, as turnover drove 32% higher to £12.7m.

Ten Alps Communications (TAL)

Media company & programme producer

10 Blue Lion Place, Bermondsey, London, SE1 4PU Tel: 020-7089 3686; Fax: 020-7089 3696;
e-mail: Nitil@tenalpsevents.com; web site: www.tenalps.com

		holding %
Chairman	Brian Walden	0.2
Chief Executive	Alex Connock	9.4
Finance Director	Nitil Patel	0.3
Non-Exec Director	Bob Geldof	9.3

Main Shareholders:

Gartmore	7.1
Jack Rubins	6.1
T C N Spencer	6.1
D A Shaw	4.1
N J F O'Hagan	3.7

Percentage of free market capital: 30.4%

Nominated Adviser:	Canaccord Capital, London
AIM Broker:	Canaccord Capital, London
Solicitors:	Reynolds Park Chamberlain, London
Market Makers:	KBCS; MLSB; SCAP; WINS
Auditors:	Bright Grahame Murray, London
Registrars:	Capita Registrars

Entry on AIM:	11/1/2001	**Recent price:**	29.25p
Interim results:	Nov	**Market cap:**	£12.92m
Final results:	Jun	**Issue price:**	1.0p
Year end:	Mar	**Current no of shares:**	
Accounts due:	Jul		44,172,080
Int div paymnt:	n/a	**No of shares after**	
Fin div paymnt:	n/a	**dilution:**	45,218,330
Int net div per share:	nil	**P/E ratio:**	n/a
Fin net div per share:	nil	**Probable CGT?**	**YES**

LATEST REPORTED RESULTS:	2003	**PREVIOUS REPORTED RESULTS:**	2002
Turnover:	£13.06m	**Turnover:**	£10.45m
PTP:	£79,000	**PTP:**	£477,000
EPS:	0.2p	**EPS:**	1.4p

Comments:

Ten Alps has been busy continuing its strategy of 'thinking big'. The Brook Lapping division won a number of contracts including a 70% stake in producing a digital TV channel 'Teachers TV' for the government. 'The brightening up London' event, devised by Bob Geldof, which had artists' images projected onto London's landmarks was also a great success. The company recently acquired profitable factual TV production company 3BM television for a maximum £1.1m.

Tenon (TNO)

Accountancy-based services provider

66 Chiltern St, London, W1V 4JT Tel: 020-7535 1401; Fax: 020-7535 5598;
e-mail: info@tenongroup.com; web site: www.tenongroup.com

		holding %
Chairman	Neil Johnson	0.1
Chief Executive	Andy Raynor	1.2
Finance Director	Matthew Brabin	0.0
Deputy Chairman	Alan McFetrich	0.1

Main Shareholders:

Southwind	9.02
Artemis	8.5
Henderson Investors	6.8
Jupiter Asset Management	6.6
Edinburgh Fund Managers	3.9

Percentage of free market capital: 52.2%

Nominated Adviser:	KBC Peel Hunt, London
AIM Broker:	KBC Peel Hunt, London
Solicitors:	Kendall Freeman, London
Market Makers:	NUMS; WINS
Auditors:	PricewaterhouseCoopers, London
Registrars:	Capita Registrars

Entry on AIM:	30/3/2000	**Recent price:**	36.75p
Interim results:	Sep	**Market cap:**	£57.03m
Final results:	Sep	**Issue price:**	100p
Year end:	Jun	**Current no of shares:**	
Accounts due:	Oct		155,189,184
Int div paymnt:	n/a	**No of shares after**	
Fin div paymnt:	n/a	**dilution:**	n/a
Int net div per share:	nil	**P/E ratio:**	n/a
Fin net div per share:	nil	**Probable CGT?**	Yes

LATEST REPORTED RESULTS:	2002	PREVIOUS REPORTED RESULTS:	2001
Turnover:	£91.95m	**Turnover:**	£55.35m
PTP:	£(114,000)	**PTP:**	£(4.7m)
EPS:	(74.4)p	**EPS:**	(4.6)p

Comments:

The troubled accountancy group is recovering after last year's series of profit warnings, the departure of founder Ian Buckley and a £106m write-off. Buckley had bought 17 small practices advising SMEs with the £40.7m raised on admission. Successful investor Bob Morton, who picked up his stake below 10p, instituted cuts in order to pull the group into profit. This is working, with latest interims showing a £2.1m operating profit with continuing revenues up 20% to £38.7m.

TEP Exchange (TEX)

Operator of electronic trading platform

77 Muswell Hill, London , N10 3PJ Tel: 020-8365 4666; Fax: 020-8365 3666;
e-mail: support@tepexchange.com; web site: www.tepexchange.com

		holding %
Chairman	George Kynoch	0.2
Chief Executive		
Finance Director		
Non-Exec Director	Moses Kraus	19.1

Main Shareholders:

Transcontex	16.1
Surrenda-Link (IOM)	6.5
Wrengate	5.5
Logic Express	5.0
N & A Musry	4.5

Percentage of free market capital: 37.7%

Nominated Adviser:	John East, London
AIM Broker:	Insinger Townsley, London
Solicitors:	Fladgate Fielder, London
Market Makers:	SCAP; WINS
Auditors:	BDO Stoy Hayward, 8 Baker Street, London W1M 1DA
Registrars:	Capita Registrars

Entry on AIM:	10/9/2001	**Recent price:**	0.75p
Interim results:	Jul	**Market cap:**	£1.24m
Final results:	Jun	**Issue price:**	8.0p
Year end:	Dec	**Current no of shares:**	
Accounts due:	Apr		165,303,776
Int div paymnt:	n/a	**No of shares after**	
Fin div paymnt:	n/a	**dilution:**	n/a
Int net div per share:	nil	**P/E ratio:**	n/a
Fin net div per share:	nil	**Probable CGT?**	Yes

LATEST REPORTED RESULTS:	2002	PREVIOUS REPORTED RESULTS:	2001
Turnover:	£909,000	**Turnover:**	£210,000
PTP:	£(699,000)	**PTP:**	£(1.50m)
EPS:	(0.5)p	**EPS:**	(1.8)p

Comments:

TEP's original plan to operate an electronic trading platform allowing financial advisers to deal in their clients' unwanted endowment policies has foundered. A £334,000 interim loss was made as turnover collapsed to just £23,000. Net current liabilities stand at a worrying £453,000. A complicated £275,000 placing saw business partner Surrenda-link take effective control of the group. Surrenda hopes to develop new products for TEP's clients but this may become irrelevant. No news has been issued lately.

Tepnel Life Sciences (TED)

Provider of nucleic acid purification solutions

Heron House, Oaks Business Park, Crewe Road, Wythenshawe, Manchester, M23 9HZ Tel: 0161-946 2200;
Fax: 0161-946 2211; Email: info@tepnel.co.uk; web site: www.tepnel.com

		holding %
Chairman	Alec Craig	0.02
Chief Executive	Benjamin Matzilevich	0.7
Finance Director	Gron Ffoulkes-Davies	0.5
Non-Exec Director	Don Marvin	0.03

Main Shareholders:

Close Asset Management	10.5
Framlington Investment Management	5.5
Barclays Private Bank New York	5.4
Barclays Nominees	4.8
LeggMason Investors Asset Managers	3.2

Percentage of free market capital: 69.3%

Nominated Adviser:	Seymour Pierce, London
AIM Broker:	Seymour Pierce, London
Solicitors:	Halliwell Landau, Manchester
Market Makers:	ARBT; KLWT; MLSB; SCAP; WINS
Auditors:	BDO Stoy Hayward, Manchester
Registrars:	Capita Registrars

ENTRY ON AIM:	16/7/2001	**Recent price:**	10.75p
Interim results:	Sep	Market cap:	£15.02m
Final results:	Mar	Issue price:	20.0p
Year end:	Dec	Current no of shares:	
Accounts due:	May		139,685,245
Int div paymnt:	n/a	No of shares after	
Fin div paymnt:	n/a	dilution:	n/a
Int net div per share:	nil	P/E ratio:	n/a
Fin net div per share:	nil	Probable CGT?	YES

LATEST REPORTED RESULTS: 2002		PREVIOUS REPORTED RESULTS: 2001	
Turnover:	£3.31m	Turnover:	£1.76m
PTP:	£(3.44m)	PTP:	£(2.69m)
EPS:	(3.0)p	EPS:	(5.2)p

Comments:
Tepnel has developed an automated plasmid purifica-tion system, for use in genetic analysis and drug research. Sales are starting to come through for this arm. The group also provides scientific services and has a BioSystems arm serving the food industry. Both these divisions are almost profitable. In the 12 months to last September sales rose 13% to £3.74m as losses were reduced by a third to £2.43m. £4.3m has since been raised in part to pay for Orchid Diagnostics.

Terrace Hill (THG)

Property owner, developer & manager

James Sellars House, 144 West George Street, Glasgow, G2 2HG Tel: 0141-332 2014; Fax: 0141-332 2015;
web site: www.capitaltech.com

		holding %
Chairman	Robert Adair	83.4
Joint CEO	D Ross Macdonald	0.4
Finance Director	Thomas Walsh	0.01
Joint CEO	Nigel Turnbull	0.1

Main Shareholders:

n/a

Percentage of free market capital: 16.1%

Nominated Adviser:	Noble, Edinburgh
AIM Broker:	Seymour Pierce, London
Solicitors:	McGrigor Donald, London
Market Makers:	DURM; WINS
Auditors:	BDO Stoy Hayward, Glasgow
Registrars:	Park Circus Registrars

Entry on AIM:	11/7/1995	**Recent price:**	26.5p
Interim results:	Apr	Market cap:	£41.7m
Final results:	Oct	Issue price:	200.0p
Year end:	Apr	Current no of shares:	
Accounts due:	Oct		157,374,135
Int div paymnt:	Aug	No of shares after	
Fin div paymnt:	Mar	dilution:	n/a
Int net div per share:	0.15p	P/E ratio:	8.8
Fin net div per share:	0.15p	Probable CGT?	No

LATEST REPORTED RESULTS: 18 MONTHS TO 31 OCT '03		PREVIOUS REPORTED RESULTS: 2002	
Turnover:	£39.65m	Turnover:	£4.84m
PTP:	£5.09m	PTP:	£53,000
EPS:	3.0p	EPS:	0.0p

Comments:
Terrace Hill has been snapping up companies of late having acquired property manager Grosvenor Land for £6.22m and commercial property developer Serah Properties for £1.1m. The latter has net assets of £3.4m. The company has admitted tenant demand has been subdued but nonetheless provided excellent year-end results having sold a number of properties including a factory outlet in Rowsley, which made a £2.1m profit. NAV was £46.6m in October.

Tertiary Minerals (TYM)
Tantalum & other metals explorer & developer

Sunrise House, Hulley Road, Hurdsfield Industrial Estate, Macclesfield, Cheshire SK10 2LP Tel: 01625-626203; Fax: 01625-626204; e-mail: info@tertiaryminerals.com; web site: www.tertiaryminerals.com

		holding %
Chairman	Patrick L Cheetham	14.3
Managing Director		
Finance Director		
Non-Exec Director	Donald A McAlister	0.0

Main Shareholders:

Morstan Nominees	10.0
Carole Rowan	8.1
Pershing Keen	7.4
City of London PR	5.3
Tiger Resource Finance	3.7
Percentage of free market capital: 48.2%	

Comments:

Tertiary's shifting of its focus from depressed tantalum onto nickel, copper and gold in Scandinavia has helped the shares rally. The company, which lost an increased £397,000 last year, raised £200,000 at a lowly 8p for the Nottrack nickel prospect in Sweden and has 'key claims' over a potentially high-grade gold, copper and nickel deposit at Kaarasselka in Finland, where it also has a diamond project in the 'Karelian craton'.

Nominated Adviser:	Seymour Pierce, London
AIM Broker:	WH Ireland, Manchester
Solicitors:	Fox Brooks Marshall, Manchester
Market Makers:	SCAP; WINS
Auditors:	PKF, Sovereign House, Queen Street, Manchester M2 5HR
Registrars:	Capita Registrars

ENTRY ON AIM: 18/11/1999	Recent price:	16.75p
Interim results: May	Market cap:	£6.67m
Final results: Dec	Issue price:	n/a
Year end: Sep	Current no of shares:	
Accounts due: Dec		39,793,093
Int div paymnt: n/a	No of shares after	
Fin div paymnt: n/a	dilution:	n/a
Int net div per share: nil	P/E ratio:	n/a
Fin net div per share: nil	Probable CGT?	No

LATEST REPORTED RESULTS: 2003		PREVIOUS REPORTED RESULTS: 2002	
Turnover:	n/a	Turnover:	n/a
PTP:	£(397,000)	PTP:	£(273,000)
EPS:	(1.3)p	EPS:	(1.1)p

Texas Oil & Gas (TXO)
Oil & gas producer

The City Business Centre, 2 London Wall Buildngs, London Wall, London, EC2M 5UU

		holding %
Chairman	Robin Baum	0.0
Chief Executive		
Finance Director	Andrew Glendinning	0.0
Chief Operating Officer	David Chandler	0.0

Main Shareholders:

MC Production & Drilling	23.7
CNT	15.8
Salisbury Merchant Nominees	13.8
Sunvest	13.6
Edinburgh Holdings	11.3
Percentage of free market capital: 8.1%	

Comments:

Texas has been scouting for more oil and gas projects as well as companies to buy or invest in, under oilman Mike Chandler, a near-30% holder after injecting his eastern Texas oil and gas wells into the company. Texas, which lost an interim £140,000, raised £460,000 at 12p to buy half shares in 10 wells in the nearby BC Christian lease and has completed two, tripling production to 100 barrels a day. A punt.

Nominated Adviser:	Nabarro Wells, London
AIM Broker:	CFA Securities, Manchester & Hichens, Harrison & Co, London
Solicitors:	Beveridge Milton, London
Market Makers:	KBCS; SCAP; WINS
Auditors:	BDO Stoy Hayward, Hatfield, Hertfordshire
Registrars:	Capita Registrars

Entry on AIM: 23/9/2002	Recent price:	20.0p
Interim results: Dec	Market cap:	£9.41m
Final results: Sep	Issue price:	5.0p
Year end: Mar	Current no of shares:	
Accounts due: Oct		47,029,333
Int div paymnt: n/a	No of shares after	
Fin div paymnt: n/a	dilution:	n/a
Int net div per share: nil	P/E ratio:	n/a
Fin net div per share: nil	Probable CGT?	No

LATEST REPORTED RESULTS: 2003		PREVIOUS REPORTED RESULTS: 2002	
Turnover:	£287,000	Turnover:	£29,000
PTP:	£(381,000)	PTP:	£(178,000)
EPS:	(1.0)p	EPS:	(1.3)p

THB   (T...)

Insurance broker

Murray House, Murray Road, Orpington, Kent BR5 3QY Tel: 01689-827044; Fax: 01689-883508;
e-mail: personal.lines@thbgroup.co.uk; web site: www.thbgroup.co.uk

		holding %
Chairman	Victor Thompson	27.8
Chief Executive		
Finance Director	Robert Wilkinson	0.8
Exec Director	David Ulph	16.3
Main Shareholders:		
Frank Murphy		4.1

Percentage of free market capital: 47.9%

Nominated Adviser:	Numis, London
AIM Broker:	Numis, London
Solicitors:	Kendall Freeman, London
Market Makers:	NUMS; WINS
Auditors:	Grant Thornton, The Explorer Building, Fleming Way, Manor Royal, Crawley, West Sussex RH10 9GT
Registrars:	Capita Registrars

ENTRY ON AIM:	1/10/2002	Recent price:	104.5p
Interim results:	Dec	Market cap:	£27.69m
Final results:	Sep	Issue price:	n/a
Year end:	Apr	Current no of shares:	
Accounts due:	Oct		26,500,000
Int div paymnt:	Jan	No of shares after	
Fin div paymnt:	Aug	dilution:	n/a
Int net div per share:	2.5p	P/E ratio:	10.5
Fin net div per share:	1.5p	Probable CGT?	No

LATEST REPORTED RESULTS:	2003	PREVIOUS REPORTED RESULTS:	2002
Turnover:	£22.91m	Turnover:	£15.35m
PTP:	£3.83m	PTP:	£3.33m
EPS:	10.0p	EPS:	13.3p

Comments:

A weak US dollar and the loss of US open market terrorism cover sent acquisitive Lloyds' broker THB's interim pre-tax profits down a third to £1m, despite a 33% revenue gain to £13.8m. A higher proportion of binding authorities means the second half will contribute more. Costlier Errors & Omissions cover and competition in the motor fleet market saw disappointing first results from £11.8m acquisition Rarrigini & Rosso.

The Claims People   (CLM)

Insurance claims handler

49 Southwark St, London, SE1 1RU Tel: 020-7357 6636; Fax: 020-7357 6656;
e-mail: peter.morgan@theclaimspeople.com; web site: www.theclaimspeople.com

		holding %
Chairman	John French	0.1
Chief Executive	Barry Whyte	4.1
Finance Director	Peter Morgan	2.8
Operations Director	David Croston	3.3
Main Shareholders:		
ISIS Equity Partners		16.7
Firgrove Investments		7.5
Hargreaves Hale		3.3

Percentage of free market capital: 61.9%

Nominated Adviser:	Grant Thornton, London
AIM Broker:	Durlacher, London
Solicitors:	Eversheds, Manchester
Market Makers:	HOOD; KBCS; WINS
Auditors:	Saffery Champness, London
Registrars:	Melton Registers

Entry on AIM:	24/10/2000	Recent price:	3.0p
Interim results:	Sep	Market cap:	£3m
Final results:	Mar	Issue price:	8.0p
Year end:	Dec	Current no of shares:	
Accounts due:	Apr		100,000,000
Int div paymnt:	n/a	No of shares after	
Fin div paymnt:	n/a	dilution:	n/a
Int net div per share:	nil	P/E ratio:	n/a
Fin net div per share:	nil	Probable CGT?	Yes

LATEST REPORTED RESULTS:	2002	PREVIOUS REPORTED RESULTS:	2001
Turnover:	£1.04m	Turnover:	£303,000
PTP:	£(304,000)	PTP:	£(934,000)
EPS:	(0.5)p	EPS:	(1.8)p

Comments:

Loss adjuster and insurance claims manager The Claims People is on the acquisition trail after turning a full-year loss of £304,000 into a pre-tax profit of £51,000 (swollen by a tax credit to £135,000) on doubled turnover of almost £2m. Moving into motor claims via its 'Verify' inspection service, the company, with a string of blue chip clients, aims to buy companies on an earn-out basis with a mix of shares and cash.

...pham House Group (CPH)

...acquirer and developer

...mes Street, London, WC1N 3DR; web site: www.claphamhousegroup.com

		holding %
Chairman	David Page	7.6
Chief Executive	Paul Campbell	1.7
Finance Director		
Non-Exec Director	Nicholas Donaldson	0.7

Main Shareholders:

JP Morgan	24.5
Chase Nominees	5.2
Shell Petroleum	4.9
HSBC Global	4.9
Rathbone Nominees	4.3

Percentage of free market capital: 46.3%

Nominated Adviser:	Noble & Co, Edinburgh
AIM Broker:	Noble & Co, London
Solicitors:	Marriott Harrison, London
Market Makers:	KBCS; WINS
Auditors:	Baker Tilly, London
Registrars:	Capita Registrars

ENTRY ON AIM: 10/11/2003		Recent price:	125.5p
Interim results:	n/a	Market cap:	£18.89m
Final results:	n/a	Issue price:	100.0p
Year end:	n/a	Current no of shares:	
Accounts due:	n/a		15,050,020
Int div paymnt:	n/a	No of shares after	
Fin div paymnt:	n/a	dilution:	n/a
Int net div per share:	nil	P/E ratio:	n/a
Fin net div per share:	nil	Probable CGT?	YES

LATEST REPORTED RESULTS: N/A		PREVIOUS REPORTED RESULTS: N/A	
Turnover:	n/a	Turnover:	n/a
PTP:	n/a	PTP:	n/a
EPS:	n/a	EPS:	n/a

Comments:

Having raised £14.75m after listing on AIM in November, the restaurant aquisitor and developer has completed its first acquisition. It bought The Real Greek Food Company, which runs three restaurants, for £363,000, plus an earn-out element to be capped at £8.8m. Clapham House's management comprise ex-Pizza Express directors David Page and Paul Campbell. Further acquisitions will be non-pizza-based and predominantly in and around the M25 area.

The Creative Education Corporation (CEC)

Pre-school nurseries developer and operator

25 Harley Street, London, W1G 9BR Tel: 020-7299 1400; Fax: 020-7631 0917

		holding %
Chairman	Christopher Phillips	0.0
Chief Executive	David Alexander	12.0
Finance Director	Rakesh Patel	0.4
Non-Exec Director	John Baker	22.9

Main Shareholders:

n/a

Percentage of free market capital: 35.9%

Nominated Adviser:	Grant Thornton, London
AIM Broker:	Hoodless Brennan, London
Solicitors:	Fladgate Fielder, London
Market Makers:	EVO; HOOD; SCAP; WINS
Auditors:	Fisher Corporate, 11-15 William Rd, London NW1 3ER
Registrars:	Capita Registrars

Entry on AIM:	8/4/2003	Recent price:	5.63p
Interim results:	May	Market cap:	£9.1m
Final results:	Mar	Issue price:	5.0p
Year end:	Dec	Current no of shares:	
Accounts due:	May		161,620,410
Int div paymnt:	n/a	No of shares after	
Fin div paymnt:	n/a	dilution:	n/a
Int net div per share:	nil	P/E ratio:	n/a
Fin net div per share:	nil	Probable CGT?	YES

LATEST REPORTED RESULTS: 2003		PREVIOUS REPORTED RESULTS: 2002	
Turnover:	£318,000	Turnover:	n/a
PTP:	£(577,000)	PTP:	£(35,000)
EPS:	(0.5)p	EPS:	(0.2)p

Comments:

Nursery school provider Creative Education Corporation (CEC) turned in a creditable first full year's trading – marked by its AIM listing in April 2003 and the acquisition of Primary Steps. Since year-end, CEC has expanded its nursery numbers and taken an 18.5% stake in Academy Childcare. These days it operates 11 nurseries and one pre-prep school, and occupancy levels are rising steadily. It hopes to thrive in the highly fragmented UK pre-school childcare market.

The Market Age (TMA)

Financial application service provider

22 Shand Street, London, SE1 2ES Tel: 020-7463 5509; Fax: 020-7463 5550;
e-mail: info@themarketage.com; web site: www.themarketage.com

		holding %
Chairman	Shane Smith*	3.6
Chief Executive	as above	
Finance Director	Richard Hutchinson	8.8
Director	Karren Griffith	6.4

Main Shareholders:

The Smith Trust*	53.9
The MATT	11.2

Percentage of free market capital: 5.9%

*Shane Smith and Karen Griffith have a beneficial and non-beneficial
interests in The Smith Trust respectively

Comments:

Shares in the financial information software provider
have trebled this year after the group, which has
endured heavy losses, unveiled a major contract that
will double revenues and enable it to break even.
Interested punters will shortly be able to find the
company under its new name – Independent
Investment Research. Further contracts have since
been signed. At one point the company had considered
throwing in the towel and becoming a shell.

Nominated Adviser:	Insinger de Beaufort, London	
AIM Broker:	Hoodless Brennan, London	
Solicitors:	Taylor Wessing, London	
Market Makers:	KBCS; WINS	
Auditors:	Ernst & Young, Rolls House, 7 Rolls Buildings, Fetter Lane, London, EC4A 1NH	
Registrars:	Capita Registrars	

ENTRY ON AIM:	2/8/2000	Recent price:	10.0p
Interim results:	Nov	Market cap:	£1.74m
Final results:	Jun	Issue price:	106.0p
Year end:	Feb	Current no of shares:	
Accounts due:	Jun		17,360,063
Int div paymnt:	n/a	No of shares after	
Fin div paymnt:	n/a	dilution:	18,234,960
Int net div per share:	nil	P/E ratio:	n/a
Fin net div per share:	nil	Probable CGT?	Yes

LATEST REPORTED RESULTS: 2002		PREVIOUS REPORTED RESULTS: 15 MONTHS TO FEB 01	
Turnover:	£255,000	Turnover:	£565,000
PTP:	£(2.16m)	PTP:	£(2.39m)
EPS:	(13.0)p	EPS:	(19.1)p

The Medical House (MLH)

Medical information services and products

Unit 8 Riverside Court, Don Road, Attercliffe, Sheffield S9 2TJ Tel: 0114-261 9011; Fax: 0114-243 1597;
e-mail: info@themedicalhouse.com; web site: www.themedicalhouse.com

		holding %
Chairman	Bryan Bodek	0.2
Chief Executive	Ian Townsend	38.1
Finance Director	Stephen Westwood	0.03
Operations Director	Gerard Kemp	36.6

Main Shareholders:

n/a

Percentage of free market capital: 21.7%

Comments:

The developer of needle-free drug delivery systems is
principally focused on the mhi-500, a needle-less injection
system for diabetics, approved by the NHS for prescription use. The group has agreed distribution agreements in
10 territories including South Africa and China. Interim
losses jumped 78% to £0.27m as sales fell 18% to £2.2m.
A recent £1.5m placing at 41p should tide the group
over. Orthopaedics instruments division Eurocut has a
record £3m order book and second half trading is
strong.

Nominated Adviser:	Piper Jaffray, London	
AIM Broker:	Canaccord Capital, Leeds	
Solicitors:	DLA, Leeds	
Market Makers:	GRAB; KBCS; WINS	
Auditors:	KPMG, 1 The Embankment, Neville Street, Leeds, LS1 4DW	
Registrars:	Capita Registrars	

Entry on AIM:	4/9/2000	Recent price:	54.5p
Interim results:	Mar	Market cap:	£32.5m
Final results:	Sep	Issue price:	50.0p
Year end:	Jun	Current no of shares:	
Accounts due:	Oct		59,626,091
Int div paymnt:	n/a	No of shares after	
Fin div paymnt:	n/a	dilution:	n/a
Int net div per share:	nil	P/E ratio:	n/a
Fin net div per share:	nil	Probable CGT?	Yes

LATEST REPORTED RESULTS: 2003		PREVIOUS REPORTED RESULTS: 2002	
Turnover:	£5.19m	Turnover:	£5.32m
PTP:	£(590,000)	PTP:	£(294,000)
EPS:	(0.7)p	EPS:	(0.7)

The Real Good Food Company   (RGD)
Food supplier
Hopton Industrial Estate, London Road, Devizes, Wiltshire SN10 2EU

		holding %
Chairman	Peter Totte	13.8
Chief Executive	John Gibson	4.9
Finance Director		
Non-Exec Director	James Mitchell	3.0

Main Shareholders:

ISIS Investment Management	11.6
Singer & Friedlander	10.9
J M Finn Nominees	6.6

Percentage of free market capital: 49.2%

Comments:
The Real Good Food Company joined AIM in September as a vehicle for the acquisition of food manufacturing companies. Since then it has acquired cake maker Eurofoods/Cool Fresh, pre-packed sandwich specialist Haydens Bakeries and cakes.co.uk. Customers include M&S, Waitrose and Caffe Nero. Interim pre-tax losses were £541,000 but it is achieving cost savings already. Further acquisitions may be made having raised £10m in a December placing.

Nominated Adviser:	John East, London
AIM Broker:	JM Finn, London
Solicitors:	Joelson Wilson, London
Market Makers:	SCAP; WINS
Auditors:	Horwath Clark Maidstone, Kent
Registrars:	Capita Registrars

Entry on AIM: 29/9/2003	**Recent price:**	148.5p
Interim results: Jan	**Market cap:**	£18.8m
Final results: Aug	**Issue price:**	110.0p
Year end: May	**Current no of shares:**	
Accounts due: Sep		12,657,316
Int div paymnt: n/a	**No of shares after**	
Fin div paymnt: n/a	**dilution:**	n/a
Int net div per share: nil	**P/E ratio:**	n/a
Fin net div per share: nil	**Probable CGT?**	**Yes**

LATEST REPORTED RESULTS: 53 WEEKS TO 3 MAY '03	PREVIOUS REPORTED RESULTS: 2002
Turnover: £10.49m	Turnover: £11.38m
PTP: £(726,000)	PTP: £(2.4m)
EPS: n/a	EPS: n/a

The Telecommunications Group (formerly Roxspur) (TTL)
Holding company for a telecommunications services group
The Lodge, Worting Park, Worting, Basingstoke RG23 8PA

		holding %
Chairman	Peter Ryan	0.0
Chief Executive	Michael Hanna	0.0
Finance Director	Julian Synett	0.0
Commercial Director	Graham Pollard	0.0

Main Shareholders:

Alan Dugard	72.4
British Meditrean	14.1
Aberdeen Asset Management	4.2
UBS Asset Management	4.2

Percentage of free market capital: 5.1%

Comments:
The Telecommunciations Group comprises three businesses which merged while reversing into what used to be Roxspur. The group consists of Phone Direct, a wholesaler and distributor of mobile phones; Anglia Telecom, a UK-based mobile phone distributor and fixed line reseller; and Ventelo, a Benelux-based fixed line and mobile phone carrier. A total of 327m shares were issued by Roxspur to satisfy the reverse acquisition, which now respresents 86.5% of the issued shares.

Nominated Adviser:	KBC Peel Hunt, London
AIM Broker:	KBC Peel Hunt, London
Solicitors:	Nabarro Nathanson, London
Market Makers:	KBCS; MLSB; SCAP; WINS
Auditors:	PricewaterhouseCooper, 1 East Parade, Sheffield S1 2ET
Registrars:	Capita Registrars

Entry on AIM: 29/10/2003	**Recent price:**	9.0p
Interim results: Mar	**Market cap:**	£34.04m
Final results: Sep	**Issue price:**	n/a
Year end: Jun	**Current no of shares:**	
Accounts due: Oct		378,262,622
Int div paymnt: n/a	**No of shares after**	
Fin div paymnt: n/a	**dilution:**	n/a
Int net div per share: nil	**P/E ratio:**	0
Fin net div per share: nil	**Probable CGT?**	**Yes**

LATEST REPORTED RESULTS: PERIOD TO 31 MAR '03	PREVIOUS REPORTED RESULTS: N/A
Turnover: n/a	Turnover: n/a
PTP: £(63,000)	PTP: n/a
EPS: n/a	EPS: n/a

themutual.net (TMN)

Internet-based information provider
6/7 St Cross Street, Hatton Garden, London, EC1N 8UB Tel: 020-7440 9310 ; Fax: 020-7831 2727;
e-mail: info@themutual.net; web site: www.themutual.net

		holding %
Chairman	Warren Tayler	0.0
Managing Director	Ben Heaton	11.1
Finance Director	Peter Coveney	3.4
Technical Director	Anna Soobrattee	0.0

Main Shareholders:

Foresight Technology VCT	9.3
Schweco Nominees Limited	7.8
Simon Wajcenberg	7.5
Cairnsford Associates	7.5
Capita IRG Trustees	6.7

Percentage of free market capital: 35.4%

Comments:

Themutual.net continues to build upon the momentum gathered during the last financial year with latest interims showing a 15% increase in sales to £789,000 and cash reserves boosted to £511,000. Pre-tax profits slipped slightly to £219,000, however, due to an accelerated acquisition-related amortisation scheme. On an operational level September's purchase of fellow e-marketing business MyPoints has been the major development, doubling the size of the company's subscriber database to 850,000.

Nominated Adviser:	Durlacher, London		
AIM Broker:	Durlacher, London		
Solicitors:	Field Fisher Waterhouse,		
	London		
Market Makers:	SCAP; WINS		
Auditors:	Menzies, Ashby House, Walton		
	on Thames, Surrey		
Registrars:	Capita Registrars		

ENTRY ON AIM:	30/6/2000	Recent price:	0.2p
Interim results:	Nov	Market cap:	£8.08m
Final results:	Jun	Issue price:	1.0p
Year end:	Apr	Current no of shares:	
Accounts due:	Aug		4,041,716,353
Int div paymnt:	n/a	No of shares after	
Fin div paymnt:	n/a	dilution:	n/a
Int net div per share:	nil	P/E ratio:	n/a
Fin net div per share:	nil	Probable CGT?	YES

LATEST REPORTED RESULTS: 2003		PREVIOUS REPORTED RESULTS: 2002	
Turnover:	£1.37m	Turnover:	£821,000
PTP:	£558,000	PTP:	£(28,000)
EPS:	(0.0)p	EPS:	(0.0)p

Theo Fennell (TFL)

Luxury jewellery designer, manufacturer & retailer
2b Pond Place, 169 Fulham Road, London, SW3 6SP Tel: 020-7591 5000; Fax: 020-7591 5001;
e-mail: neil.goulder@theofennell.com; web site: www.theofennell.com

		holding %
Chairman	Richard Northcott	28.9
Managing Director	Theo Fennell	18.5
Finance Director	Gavin Saunders	0.0
Joint Managing Director	Barbara Anne Snoad	1.9

Main Shareholders:

Centric Investments	21.1

Percentage of free market capital: 26.3%

Comments:

The bijoux jewellery designer is beginning to regain its sparkle as half-year turnover increased by 26% to £7.5m. Since recruiting managing director Barbara Snoad, Cartier's ex-retail director, the company has incorporated better marketing and advertising, enabling operating losses to drop from £300,000 to £90,000 within a year. Controlled expansion by use of concessions and licensing agreements continues with 'Tomfoolery for designers at Debenhams' launching in June.

Nominated Adviser:	Seymour Pierce, London		
AIM Broker:	Seymour Pierce, London		
Solicitors:	Osborne Clarke, London		
Market Makers:	SCAP; WINS		
Auditors:	Grant Thornton, Euston		
	Square, London		
Registrars:	Capita Registrars		

Entry on AIM:	14/6/1996	Recent price:	22.75p
Interim results:	Nov	Market cap:	£3.68m
Final results:	Jun	Issue price:	118.0p
Year end:	Mar	Current no of shares:	
Accounts due:	Sep		16,177,831
Int div paymnt:	n/a	No of shares after	
Fin div paymnt:	n/a	dilution:	21,174,165
Int net div per share:	nil	P/E ratio:	32.5
Fin net div per share:	nil	Probable CGT?	YES

LATEST REPORTED RESULTS: 2003		PREVIOUS REPORTED RESULTS: 2002	
Turnover:	£13.82m	Turnover:	£11.77m
PTP:	£96,000	PTP:	£31,000
EPS:	0.7p	EPS:	0.2p

ThirdForce (formerly Rapid Technology) (THF)

e-learning developer

32B Westland Square, Dublin 2, Ireland, Tel: 00-353 1 235 0279; Fax: 00-353 1 235 0361

		holding %
Chairman	Patrick McDonagh	28.6
Chief Executive	as above	
Finance Director	Eimer McGovern	0.0
Dvlpmt Director	James Barry	11.2

Main Shareholders:

Kirkconnell	13.5
Roger Bannon	10.5
Uta Dickinson	5.0
Diplomat Trust Company	4.6
Churchstanton	3.7

Percentage of free market capital: 9.6%

Comments:

Also quoted on the Developing Companies Market in Dublin, ThirdForce, the former computer technology developer, is now making inroads into the potentially huge e-learning market. Its first acquisition was Electric Paper, a developer and supplier of educational products focused on the computer literacy market. This February, ThirdForce announced the acquisition of AV Edge, a specialist in the production of educational content for TV and DVD.

Nominated Adviser:	English Trust, London		
AIM Broker:	KBC Peel Hunt, London		
Solicitors:	Binchys, Dublin		
Market Makers:	GBMM; KBCS; WINS		
Auditors:	Coopers & Lybrand, George's Quay, Dublin 4		
Registrars:	AIB Bank		

ENTRY ON AIM:	5/12/1997	**Recent price:**	20.5p
Interim results:	Mar	**Market cap:**	£26.77m
Final results:	Nov	**Issue price:**	95.0p
Year end:	Jun	**Current no of shares:**	
Accounts due:	Feb		130,562,354
Int div paymnt:	n/a	**No of shares after**	
Fin div paymnt:	n/a	**dilution:**	n/a
Int net div per share:	nil	**P/E ratio:**	n/a
Fin net div per share:	nil	**Probable CGT?**	YES

LATEST REPORTED RESULTS: 2003		PREVIOUS REPORTED RESULTS: 2002	
Turnover:	n/a	**Turnover:**	n/a
PTP:	£(907,000)	**PTP:**	n/a
EPS:	(3.1)c	**EPS:**	(7.6)c

Thistle Mining (TMG)

Gold miner

10 Dundas Street, Edinburgh, EH3 6HZ Tel: 0131-557-6222; Fax: 0131-557-6333; e-mail: info@thistlemining.com; web site: www.thistlemining.com

		holding %
Chairman	Ian Lang	0.1
Chief Executive	William McLucas	0.8
Finance Director	John Brown	0.0
Non-Exec Director	David Beatty	0.2

Main Shareholders:

Royal Bank Roytor	27.4
International Civil Company	19.7
Resources Investment Trust	10.7
KFAED	9.6
Capital Research & Management company	5.2

Percentage of free market capital: 18.5%

Comments:

A strong rand has hampered Thistle's project to revitalise South Africa's President Steyn gold complex and saw nine-month losses soar to £7.9m. Cash-hungry Thistle, whose latest funding was £18.7m at 12.5p (plus warrants), says it has found a potential new 730,000-oz gold block in Steyn's Eldorado Reef, taking it to 1.2m oz. A £15m loan note funds a feasibility study at Masbate in the Philippines. A punt on a weak rand.

Nominated Adviser:	Grant Thornton, London
AIM Broker:	Canaccord Capital, London
Solicitors:	Dickson Minto W S, Edinburgh
Market Makers:	KBCS; SCAP; WINS
Auditors:	KPMG, 8 Salisbury Square, London EC4Y 8BB
Registrars:	CIBC Mellon Trust

Entry on AIM:	14/8/2002	**Recent price:**	13.5p
Interim results:	Nov	**Market cap:**	£52.83m
Final results:	Mar	**Issue price:**	20.0p
Year end:	Dec	**Current no of shares:**	
Accounts due:	May		391,351,606
Int div paymnt:	n/a	**No of shares after**	
Fin div paymnt:	n/a	**dilution:**	n/a
Int net div per share:	nil	**P/E ratio:**	n/a
Fin net div per share:	nil	**Probable CGT?**	**No**

LATEST REPORTED RESULTS: 2002		PREVIOUS REPORTED RESULTS: 2001	
Turnover:	£63.53m	Turnover:	£10.68m
PTP:	£4.86m	PTP:	£(5.49m)
EPS:	(0.1)p	EPS:	(0.1)p

Thomas Walker (WKT)

Supplier of clothing fasteners

39 St Paul's Square, Birmingham, B3 1QY Tel: 0121-236 5565; Fax: 0121-236 6725

		holding %
Chairman	Bryan Knight	0.0
Chief Executive	Edward Cook	0.0
Finance Director	John Halstead	0.0
Sales & Mktg Director	David Jackson	0.0

Main Shareholders:

T W F Walker	17.5
M H Elliott	12.7
P R Cartwright and others	5.5
J G W Walker	5.4
Thomas Walker Pension Trusts	4.6

Percentage of free market capital: 31.9%

Comments:

This Full List refugee supplies buckles, fasteners and zips to the clothing market, and suffered a 6.7% fall in profits to £57,415 in the first half on a 2.2% sales wane to £1.88m – encouragingly the dividend was maintained. After a confident start to the half, poor performances from garment retailers in the weeks leading up to Christmas spread down to the component supplier. Early indications for 2004 suggest weakness in the clothing market has extended into the New Year.

Nominated Adviser:	Ernst & Young, Birmingham
AIM Broker:	Arbuthnot, Birmingham
Solicitors:	Eversheds, Birmingham
Market Makers:	ARBT; WINS
Auditors:	Ernst & Young, One Colmore Row, Birmingham B3 2DB
Registrars:	Capita Registrars

Entry on AIM:	14/10/2002	**Recent price:**	39.5p
Interim results:	Feb	**Market cap:**	£2.43m
Final results:	Aug	**Issue price:**	39.5p
Year end:	Jun	**Current no of shares:**	
Accounts due:	Oct		6,160,000
Int div paymnt:	Mar	**No of shares after**	
Fin div paymnt:	Nov	**dilution:**	n/a
Int net div per share:	0.15p	**P/E ratio:**	18.8
Fin net div per share:	0.58p	**Probable CGT?**	**Yes**

LATEST REPORTED RESULTS: 2003		PREVIOUS REPORTED RESULTS: 2002	
Turnover:	£3.75m	Turnover:	£3.88m
PTP:	£198,000	PTP:	£170,000
EPS:	2.1p	EPS:	1.8p

Thomson Intermedia (THN)

Media monitoring service provider

58 Farringdon Road, London, EC1R 3BP Tel: 020 7549 4343; Fax: 020-7549 4333;
e-mail: help@thomson-intermedia.com; web site: www.thomson-intermedia.com

		holding %
Chairman	John Napier	0.8
Joint Chief Executive	Sarah Thomson*	28.0
Finance Director	David Trendle	0.1
Joint Chief Executive	Stephen Thomson*	28.0

Main Shareholders:

Herald Investment Trust	12.5
Eaglet Investment Trust	10.7
Strata Investment	3.5

Percentage of free market capital: 13.3%

*Sarah Thomson and Stephen Thomson are married

Comments:

This group provides media monitoring and market research services to corporations. It raised £8m at flotation back in 2000 and has reported a loss in every reporting period since. The year to this January showed an improvement of sorts, with losses down, sales up and operational net cash inflow of £422,000 against a loss of £240,000 last time. The current year has apparently started well with demand for its products growing. Net cash stands at £1.23m.

Nominated Adviser:	Williams de Broe, London
AIM Broker:	Williams de Broe, London
Solicitors:	Jones Day Gouldens, London
Market Makers:	WDBM; WINS
Auditors:	BDO Stoy Hayward, 8 Baker Street, London, W1M 1DA
Registrars:	Computershare Investor Services

ENTRY ON AIM:	5/5/2000	Recent price:	35.0p
Interim results:	Sep	Market cap:	£10.06m
Final results:	Apr	Issue price:	105.0p
Year end:	Jan	Current no of shares:	
Accounts due:	May		28,744,247
Int div paymnt:	n/a	No of shares after	
Fin div paymnt:	n/a	dilution:	30,949,010
Int net div per share:	nil	P/E ratio:	n/a
Fin net div per share:	nil	Probable CGT?	YES

LATEST REPORTED RESULTS: 2003		PREVIOUS REPORTED RESULTS: 2002	
Turnover:	£3.07m	Turnover:	£2.25m
PTP:	£(1.22m)	PTP:	£(3.16m)
EPS:	(4.2)p	EPS:	(11.0)p

Tiger Resource Finance (TIR)

Mining investor

7-8 Kenrick Mews, South Kennsington, London, SW7 3HG Tel: 020-7590 8806; Fax: 020-7589-7806;
e-mail: tiger@tiger-of.com; web site: www.tiger-of.com

		holding %
Chairman	Bruce Rowan	19.0
Chief Executive		
Finance Director		
Director	Michael Nolan	0.3

Main Shareholders:

n/a

Percentage of free market capital: 80%

Comments:

Tiger, one of Aussie investor Bruce Rowan's vehicles, has found favour with last year's doubling of investments to £4.5m and lifting shareholders' funds 65% to £7.1m. Stakes in Alamos Gold, Franconia Minerals, Pacific North West and others thrived, with Cluff Mining the only dog. Rowan now sees limited potential in gold and Tiger is keener on platinum group metal, copper, nickel, zinc and speciality metal companies near production.

Nominated Adviser:	J&E Davy, Dublin
AIM Broker:	WH Ireland, London
Solicitors:	Matheson Ormsby Prentice, Dublin
Market Makers:	KBCS; MLSB; SCAP; WINS
Auditors:	Deloitte & Touche, Earlsfort Terrace, Dublin 2, Ireland
Registrars:	Computershare Investor Services

Entry on AIM:	22/1/2001	Recent price:	2.1p
Interim results:	Aug	Market cap:	£4.95m
Final results:	Mar	Issue price:	2.0p
Year end:	Dec	Current no of shares:	
Accounts due:	Jan		235,680,689
Int div paymnt:	n/a	No of shares after	
Fin div paymnt:	n/a	dilution:	n/a
Int net div per share:	nil	P/E ratio:	21
Fin net div per share:	nil	Probable CGT?	No

LATEST REPORTED RESULTS: 2003		PREVIOUS REPORTED RESULTS: 2002	
Turnover:	n/a	Turnover:	n/a
PTP:	£407,000	PTP:	£423,000
EPS:	0.1p	EPS:	0.2p

Tikit (TIK)

Provider of consultancy services and software solutions

Africa House, 64-78 Kingsway, London, WC2B 6AH Tel: 020-7400 3737; Fax: 020-7400 3738;
e-mail: info@tikit.com; web site: www.tikit.com

		holding %
Chairman	Mike McGoun	11.6
Managing Director	David Lumsden	2.5
Finance Director	Anthony Pearson	0.3
Non-Exec Director	Richard Price	0.1

Main Shareholders:

William Flanagan	16.0
P O' Connor	7.7
Gordon Simpson	7.4
BNYNominees	4.2
Alan Glass	3.7

Percentage of free market capital: 35.6%

Comments:

Legal-sector-focused IT business Tikit's burgeoning reputation received yet another boost in mid-March, as it unveiled a striking set of full year numbers. Perhaps even more impressively, however, the company's sales pipeline and orderbook are said to stand at record levels and the growing regard in which it is held within the legal sector has enabled it to secure a raft of contracts in Europe and the US. A £1.4m pre-goodwill profit is forecast for 2004.

Nominated Adviser:	Charles Stanley, London
AIM Broker:	Charles Stanley, London
Solicitors:	Lawrence Jones, London
Market Makers:	WDBM; WINS
Auditors:	BDO Stoy Hayward, 8 Baker Street, London, W1U 3LL
Registrars:	Capita Registrars

ENTRY ON AIM:	7/6/2001	**Recent price:**	137.5p
Interim results:	Sep	**Market cap:**	£16.89m
Final results:	Mar	**Issue price:**	115.0p
Year end:	Dec	**Current no of shares:**	
Accounts due:	Apr		12,283,866
Int div paymnt:	Oct	**No of shares after**	
Fin div paymnt:	May	**dilution:**	12,537,617
Int net div per share:	0.45p	**P/E ratio:**	45.8
Fin net div per share:	1.05p	**Probable CGT?**	Yes

LATEST REPORTED RESULTS: 2003		**PREVIOUS REPORTED RESULTS:** 2002	
Turnover:	£9.56m	Turnover:	£8.23m
PTP:	£713,000	PTP:	£305,000
EPS:	3.0p	EPS:	1.4p

Tissue Science Laboratories (TSL)

Developer of medical devices

Victoria House, Victoria Road, Aldershot, Hampshire GU11 1EJ Tel: 01252-333002; Fax: 01252-333010;
e-mail: enquiries@tissuescience.com; web site: www.tissuescience.com

		holding %
Chairman	Patrick Paul	21.5
Chief Executive	Martin Hunt	0.0
Finance Director	David Jennings	0.0
Non-Exec Director	Andrew Sealey	0.9

Main Shareholders:

Highland and Universal Securities	7.9
Vertical Fund Associates	6.2
CGNU	4.3
Invesco	3.6
The Paul Foundation	3.0

Percentage of free market capital: 49.6%

Comments:

The maker of Permacol, a soft tissue replacement and repair product, made out of collagen reclaimed from pig skin continues to see sales advance rapidly, thanks to licensing deals with Bard and Zimmer as well as its own efforts. Its product is used in gynaecology, urology, and hernia operations. And a deal has just been signed which may see the material used in head and neck treatments. A £2.6m placing at 120p per share accompanied prelims affected by production problems.

Nominated Adviser:	Panmure Gordon, London
AIM Broker:	Panmure Gordon, London
Solicitors:	Jones Day Gouldens, London
Market Makers:	WEST; WINS
Auditors:	RSM Robson Rhodes, 186 City Road, London EC1V 4DD
Registrars:	Capita Registrars

Entry on AIM:	5/12/2001	**Recent price:**	144.0p
Interim results:	Sep	**Market cap:**	£34.95m
Final results:	Mar	**Issue price:**	146.0p
Year end:	Dec	**Current no of shares:**	
Accounts due:	Apr		24,269,338
Int div paymnt:	n/a	**No of shares after**	
Fin div paymnt:	n/a	**dilution:**	n/a
Int net div per share:	nil	**P/E ratio:**	n/a
Fin net div per share:	nil	**Probable CGT?**	Yes

LATEST REPORTED RESULTS: 2003		**PREVIOUS REPORTED RESULTS:** 2002	
Turnover:	£4.95m	Turnover:	£3.17m
PTP:	£(2.85m)	PTP:	£(2.62m)
EPS:	(11.8)p	EPS:	(10.5)p

Tolent

(TLT)

Building, civil engineering and fit-out work

25 Moorgate Road, Rotherham, South Yorkshire S60 2AD Tel: 01709-828218; Fax: 01709-828499;
e-mail: info@tolent.plc.uk; web site: www.tolent.co.uk

		holding %
Chairman	Stuart Gordon	0.8
Managing Director	John Wood	0.0
Finance Director	Ian Swire	0.1
Non-Exec Director	M R Speakman	0.02

Main Shareholders:

Exeter Asset Management	4.6
Exeter Smaller Companies Income Fund	3.1

Percentage of free market capital: 91.3%

Comments:
Tolent managed to increase profits on lower turnover last year and also benefited from a £320,000 property valuation surplus. With a 'substantial construction workload' for 2004, Tolent is currently working on accountancy software giant Sage's new £58m head-quarters in Newcastle Great Park and a 166,000 sq ft ofice park in south east Leeds. All its investment properties are fully let. NAV was £4.5m in December.

Nominated Adviser:	Brewin Dolphin, Leeds		
AIM Broker:	Brewin Dolphin, Leeds		
Solicitors:	Eversheds, Birmingham		
Market Makers:	CSCS; WINS		
Auditors:	Grant Thornton, 8 West Walk, Leicester LE1 7NH		
Registrars:	Capita Registrars		

ENTRY ON AIM:	1/9/1999	**Recent price:**	123.5p
Interim results:	Sep	**Market cap:**	£15.85m
Final results:	Mar	**Issue price:**	28.0p
Year end:	Dec	**Current no of shares:**	
Accounts due:	Apr		12,832,626
Int div paymnt:	Sep	**No of shares after**	
Fin div paymnt:	Jul	**dilution:**	n/a
Int net div per share:	2.25p	**P/E ratio:**	8.0
Fin net div per share:	2.5p	**Probable CGT?**	Yes

LATEST REPORTED RESULTS: 2003		**PREVIOUS REPORTED RESULTS:** 2002	
Turnover:	£117.1m	Turnover:	£125.83m
PTP:	£2.87m	PTP:	£2.58m
EPS:	15.5p	EPS:	13.6p

Tom Hoskins

(TMH)

Cash shell

131 Waterloo Road, London SE1 8UR Tel: 020-7401 9876; Fax: 020-7928 1880; web site: www.tomhoskins.co.uk

		holding %
Chairman	Geoffrey Hoodless	0.0
Chairman		
Managing Director		
Finance Director		

Main Shareholders:

Fairacres	11.6
David Clarke	11.6
Weighbridge	6.6

Percentage of free market capital: 70.2%

Comments:
The failed country pub operator currently has no cash to speak of but continues to look for suitable acquisition targets via a reverse takeover. In the interim, it incurred administrative charges of £24,575, but its largest shareholder HBBC has guaranteed ongoing funding. The new chairman is Geoffrey Hoodless, connected with corporate brokers Hoodless Brennan.

Nominated Adviser:	Corporate Synergy, London		
AIM Broker:	KBC Peel Hunt, London		
Solicitors:	Eversheds, London		
Market Makers:	KBCS; WINS		
Auditors:	BDO Stoy Hayward, 69 Tweedy Rd, Bromley, Kent BR1 3WA		
Registrars:	Capita Registrars		

Entry on AIM:	9/5/1996	**Recent price:**	1.75p
Interim results:	Nov	**Market cap:**	£0.47m
Final results:	Aug	**Issue price:**	40.0p
Year end:	Feb	**Current no of shares:**	
Accounts due:	May		26,751,430
Int div paymnt:	n/a	**No of shares after**	
Fin div paymnt:	n/a	**dilution:**	n/a
Int net div per share:	nil	**P/E ratio:**	n/a
Fin net div per share:	nil	**Probable CGT?**	Yes

LATEST REPORTED RESULTS: 2003		**PREVIOUS REPORTED RESULTS:** 2002	
Turnover:	n/a	Turnover:	£66,000
PTP:	£(40,000)	PTP:	£707
EPS:	(0.2)p	EPS:	0.0p

Top Ten (TTH)

Bingo clubs operator

Unit 8 ,Verulam Industrial Estate, 224 London Road, St Albans, Hertfordshire AL1 9JF Tel: 01727-850793;
Fax: 01727-837804; e-mail: headoffice@toptenbingo.co.uk

		holding %
Chairman	Aubrey Brocklebank	0.1
Deputy Chairman	Samuel Weston	0.0
Finance Director	Alan Weston	0.0
Non-Exec Director	Richard Simons	0.0

Main Shareholders:
Anstruther Properties   47.7

Percentage of free market capital: 28.4%

Comments:

The bingo and social club operator increased interim pre-tax profits by 98% to £530,208. Turnover jumped 43% to £5.3m. Since September, it has also acquired a further eight licensed bingo clubs and four amusement arcades for £5.8m. This was partly funded by a placing and open offer in November raising £4.65m. Seven of the clubs are freehold and Top Ten intends to refurbish all the sites and looks set to benefit from forthcoming gambling deregulation.

Nominated Adviser:	Nabarro Wells, London
AIM Broker:	Charles Stanley, London
Solicitors:	Finers Stephens Innocent, London
Market Makers:	SCAP; WINS
Auditors:	Jeffreys Henry, Finsgate, 5-7 Cranwood Street EC1V 9EE
Registrars:	Capita Registrars

ENTRY ON AIM:	12/7/1999	Recent price:	7.0p
Interim results:	Mar	Market cap:	£26.69m
Final results:	Jun	Issue price:	65.0p
Year end:	Jun	Current no of shares:	
Accounts due:	Nov		381,301,280
Int div paymnt:	n/a	No of shares after	
Fin div paymnt:	n/a	dilution:	n/a
Int net div per share:	nil	P/E ratio:	n/a
Fin net div per share:	nil	Probable CGT?	Yes

LATEST REPORTED RESULTS: 52 WEEKS TO 30 MAR 03		PREVIOUS REPORTED RESULTS: 1 JUL 01 TO 31 MAR 02	
Turnover:	£8.23m	Turnover:	£82,000
PTP:	£579,000	PTP:	£(89,000)
EPS:	0.2p	EPS:	(0.4)p

Torday & Carlisle (TDC)

Investor in undervalued businesses

Standard Way, Northallerton, North Yorkshire, DL6 2XA Tel: 01609-788716; Fax: 01609-761040

		holding %
Chairman	James Leek	10.3
Chief Executive		
Finance Director	Tony Morley	0.2
Non-Exec Director	Magnus Mowat	0.8

Main Shareholders:

V & P Midlands   27.4
R Adair   6.3

Percentage of free market capital: 44.7%

Comments:

2003 was a good year for Torday & Carlisle, a company whose directors have significant stakes – aligning their interests with shareholders – and which continues to return cash to shareholders through buy-backs. Underlying profits at its two core subsidiaries E Wood and Solvitol, and 50% associate LD, powered up by 34%. Specialist surface coatings arm E Wood scored record results, although formulated chemicals business Solvitol had a disappointing year.

Nominated Adviser:	Altium Capital, London
AIM Broker:	Brewin Dolphin, Glasgow
Solicitors:	Hammonds, London
Market Makers:	KBCS; MLSB; SCAP; WINS
Auditors:	KPMG, Newcastle upon Tyne
Registrars:	Capita Registrars

Entry on AIM:	17/12/2001	Recent price:	78.5p
Interim results:	Sep	Market cap:	£13.38m
Final results:	Mar	Issue price:	20.0p
Year end:	Dec	Current no of shares:	
Accounts due:	Apr		17,038,524
Int div paymnt:	n/a	No of shares after	
Fin div paymnt:	Jun	dilution:	n/a
Int net div per share:	nil	P/E ratio:	10.3
Fin net div per share:	0.6p	Probable CGT?	Yes

LATEST REPORTED RESULTS: 2003		PREVIOUS REPORTED RESULTS: 2002	
Turnover:	£32.61m	Turnover:	£35.78m
PTP:	£1.55m	PTP:	£2.47m
EPS:	7.6p	EPS:	5.6p

Torex Retail (TRX)

Software company
Telfer House, Range Road, Witney, Oxfordshire OX29 0YN Tel: 0870-050 9900; Fax: 0870-050 9901

		holding %
Acting Chairman	Robert Loosemore	18.7
Chief Executive	as above	
Finance Director		
Non-Exec Director	Colin Wall	0.0

Main Shareholders:

Schroder	9.8
ISIS	8.7
New Star Asset	6.9
Artemis	6.5
JP Morgan	6.5

Percentage of free market capital: 26.4%

Comments:

Having been deemed surplus to requirements by parent company Torex following its merger with health-sector focused IT business iSoft in late 2003, Torex Retail floated on AIM in its own right. Former director Robert Loosemore returned to lead the £64.5m buyout, with the aid of a powerful pod of VC backers. With annual profits pushing £10m and a roster of customers including Diesel, Hamleys and Everton Football Club, it is easy to see why so many were eager to lend their support.

Nominated Adviser:	Evolution Beeson Gregory, London
AIM Broker:	Evolution Beeson Gregory, London
Solicitors:	Clark Holt, Swindon
Market Makers:	WINS
Auditors:	Hurst Morrison THomson, Henley-on-Thames, Oxfordshire
Registrars:	Capita Registrars

ENTRY ON AIM:	2/3/2004	**Recent price:**	57.5p
Interim results:	Sep	**Market cap:**	£88.29m
Final results:	Mar	**Issue price:**	65.5p
Year end:	Dec	**Current no of shares:**	
Accounts due:	Apr		153,541,523
Int div paymnt:	n/a	**No of shares after**	
Fin div paymnt:	n/a	**dilution:**	n/a
Int net div per share:	nil	**P/E ratio:**	n/a
Fin net div per share:	nil	**Probable CGT?**	Yes

LATEST REPORTED RESULTS: 2003		PREVIOUS REPORTED RESULTS: 2002	
Turnover:	£67.56m	Turnover:	£62.59m
PTP:	£9.92m	PTP:	£5.95m
EPS:	n/a	EPS:	n/a

Totally (TLY)

Producer of specialist web sites and portals
610-611 Highgate Studios, 53-79 Highgate Road, Kentish Town, London, NW5 1TL Tel: 020-7692 6929;
Fax: 020-7692 6689; e-mail: richardb@totallyplc.com; web site: www.totallyplc.com

		holding %
Chairman	Michael Sinclair	17.6
Managing Director	Steven Burns	11.5
Finance Director	Adam Becker	1.4
Director	David Levitt	3.9

Main Shareholders:

Schweco Nominees	9.9
A Margolis	8.4
Adam Crow	4.9
Daniel Whiteman	3.2

Percentage of free market capital: 1.3%

Comments:

Jewish-community focused media and communications business Totally has enhanced its US presence further through the all-share acquisition of the New England-based Jewish Advocate Publishing Corporation for £900,000. To Totally chief executive Steve Burns the move marks an important step in the company's international expansion – a joint venture with another US firm Ha'aretz is now well established. Interim losses were reduced from £139,175 to £100,000.

Nominated Adviser:	John East, London
AIM Broker:	Insinger Townsley, London
Solicitors:	SJ Berwin, London
Market Makers:	SCAP; WINS
Auditors:	KPMG Audit, 8 Salisbury Square, London EC4Y 8BB
Registrars:	Capita Registrars

Entry on AIM:	31/1/2000	**Recent price:**	4.75p
Interim results:	Aug	**Market cap:**	£3.74m
Final results:	Jun	**Issue price:**	40.0p
Year end:	Dec	**Current no of shares:**	
Accounts due:	May		78,689,709
Int div paymnt:	n/a	**No of shares after**	
Fin div paymnt:	n/a	**dilution:**	n/a
Int net div per share:	nil	**P/E ratio:**	n/a
Fin net div per share:	nil	**Probable CGT?**	Yes

LATEST REPORTED RESULTS: 2002		PREVIOUS REPORTED RESULTS: 2001	
Turnover:	£1.69m	Turnover:	£1.46m
PTP:	£(415,000)	PTP:	£(3.05m)
EPS:	(0.9)p	EPS:	(9.8)p

Tottenham Hotspur (TTNM)

Football club operator

Bill Nicholson Way, 748 High Road, Tottenham, London, N17 0AP Tel: 020-8365 5000; Fax: 020-8365 5175

		holding %
Chairman	Daniel Levy	0.0
Chief Executive		
Finance Director	Matthew Collecott	0.0
Vice Chairman	David Buchler	0.0

Main Shareholders:

ENIC	29.8
Armshold	13.0
Hodram	9.0

Percentage of free market capital: 48.2%

Nominated Adviser:	Seymour Pierce, London	
AIM Broker:	Seymour Pierce, London	
Solicitors:	Olswang, London	
Market Makers:	KBCS; MLSB; WINS	
Auditors:	Deloitte & Touche, London	
Registrars:	Capita Registrars	

ENTRY ON AIM:	23/1/2004	**Recent price:**	21.5p
Interim results:	Mar	**Market cap:**	£21.94m
Final results:	Sep	**Issue price:**	25.0p
Year end:	Jun	**Current no of shares:**	
Accounts due:	Oct		102,041,520
Int div paymnt:	n/a	**No of shares after**	
Fin div paymnt:	n/a	**dilution:**	n/a
Int net div per share:	nil	**P/E ratio:**	n/a
Fin net div per share:	nil	**Probable CGT?**	**YES**

LATEST REPORTED RESULTS: 2003		PREVIOUS REPORTED RESULTS: 2002	
Turnover:	£10.91m	Turnover:	£26.71m
PTP:	£(12.65)	PTP:	£(8.16m)
EPS:	n/a	EPS:	n/a

Comments:
Tottenham's interims to December saw turnover rise a meagre 1.2% to £33.2m and narrower losses of £3m (£8.6m). Turnover was aided by better gate receipts, despite the fact actual Premier League attendances were down. The once glamorous North London football giant and Full List refugee marches on with secured funding after a successful share issue in January. Spurs invested heavily in the squad during the summer and winter transfer windows.

Touchstone (TSE)

IT services

5-6 Beauchamp Court, Victors Way, High Barnet, Herts EN5 5TZ Tel: 020-8275 3400; Fax: 020) 8441 5442;
e-mail: moreinfo@touchstone.co.uk

		holding %
Chairman	David Thompson	0.1
Chief Executive	Keith Birch	29.2
Finance Director	Christian Butler	0.8
Commercial	David Birch	15.7
Director		

Main Shareholders:

Phillip Birch	19.6
ISIS Asset Management	9.6
Chase Nominees	4.0
N.V.PensioenVerzekeringsMaatschappij	3.1

Percentage of free market capital: 15.7%

Nominated Adviser:	Teather & Greenwood, London	
AIM Broker:	Teather & Greenwood, London	
Solicitors:	Taylor Wessing, London	
Market Makers:	TEAM; WINS	
Auditors:	KPMG, 8 Salisbury Square, London EC4Y 8BB	
Registrars:	Capita Registrars	

Entry on AIM:	22/8/2003	**Recent price:**	112.5p
Interim results:	Nov	**Market cap:**	£11.68m
Final results:	Jun	**Issue price:**	n/a
Year end:	Mar	**Current no of shares:**	
Accounts due:	Sep		10,380,045
Int div paymnt:	May	**No of shares after**	
Fin div paymnt:	Nov	**dilution:**	n/a
Int net div per share:	1.0p	**P/E ratio:**	12.2
Fin net div per share:	2.0p	**Probable CGT?**	**YES**

LATEST REPORTED RESULTS: 2003		PREVIOUS REPORTED RESULTS: 2002	
Turnover:	£14.25m	Turnover:	£14.19m
PTP:	£1.53m	PTP:	£1.77m
EPS:	9.2p	EPS:	11.4p

Comments:
It's been a busy six months for this Full List refugee engaged in the supply of software and related services in the SunSystems, MS Great Plains and CRM space. Its most recent interims were lacklustre, showing a slight rise in turnover to £6.95m and a meagre profit before tax. Since then it has been on the acquisition trail, buying the Sage CRM business of Brown & Co from the liquidators and two other IT services groups for a maximum of £725,000. These last two outfits were loss making.

Toye & Company
Military regalia manufacturer and retailer

(TOYE)

Regalia House, 19-21 Great Queen Street, London, WC2B 5BE Tel: 020-7242 0471; Fax: 020-7831 8692;
web site: www.toye.com

		holding %
Chairman	Bryan Toye*	38.7
Chief Executive	as above	
Finance Director		
Non-Exec Director	Nicolas Wills	12.0
Main Shareholders:		
Stephen Elias		7.3
Ruth Green		4.0

Percentage of free market capital: 26.8%

*37.55% of these share are held as a Trustee

Nominated Adviser:	WH Ireland, London
AIM Broker:	WH Ireland, London
Solicitors:	Ashursts, London
Market Makers:	WINS
Auditors:	PKF, New Garden House, 78 Hatton Garden, London EC1N 8JA
Registrars:	Capita Registrars

Entry on AIM:	15/5/2003	Recent price:	48.0p
Interim results:	Nov	Market cap:	£1.08m
Final results:	Apr	Issue price:	43.0p
Year end:	Dec	Current no of shares:	
Accounts due:	Jun		2,248,000
Int div paymnt:	n/a	No of shares after	
Fin div paymnt:	n/a	dilution:	n/a
Int net div per share:	nil	P/E ratio:	96.0
Fin net div per share:	nil	Probable CGT?	Yes

LATEST REPORTED RESULTS: 2002		PREVIOUS REPORTED RESULTS: 2001	
Turnover:	£7.87m	Turnover:	£8.19m
PTP:	£12,000	PTP:	£53,000
EPS:	0.5p	EPS:	2.3p

Comments:
Toye markets, sells and makes military and other regalia, such as medals, enamel gifts, honours caps and badges. With the surge in demand precipitated by 2002's Golden Jubilee now a distant memory, however, times are tough for the company, first half profits almost halving from £24,000 to £12,400. The regalia market is showing few signs of growth at home and overseas customers frequently don't have sufficient funds to make purchases.

TradingSports Exchange Systems
Person-to-person betting exchange system provider

(TES)

13 Princeton Court, 55 Felsham Road, London, SW15 1AZ Tel: 020-8780 6000; Fax: 020-8780 6060;
e-mail: info@tradingsports.com; web site: www.tradingsports.com

		holding %
Chairman	Joseph Tighe	14.9
Chief Executive	as above	
Finance Director		
Chief Technical Officer	Graham Twaddle	5.6
Main Shareholders:		
Benjamin Arbib		8.0
Nicholas Jones		4.8
Jake Ulrich		3.7

Percentage of free market capital: 52.4%

Nominated Adviser:	Evolution Beeson Gregory, London
AIM Broker:	Evolution Beeson Gregory, London
Solicitors:	Mayer, Brown, Rowe & Maw, London
Market Makers:	EVO; SCAP; WINS
Auditors:	Nexia Audit, London
Registrars:	Capita Registrars

Entry on AIM:	29/5/2003	Recent price:	37.5p
Interim results:	Sep	Market cap:	£3.94m
Final results:	Mar	Issue price:	115.0p
Year end:	Dec	Current no of shares:	
Accounts due:	May		10,494,261
Int div paymnt:	n/a	No of shares after	
Fin div paymnt:	n/a	dilution:	n/a
Int net div per share:	nil	P/E ratio:	n/a
Fin net div per share:	nil	Probable CGT?	Yes

LATEST REPORTED RESULTS: 1 Jan 2002 to 31 Dec 2002		PREVIOUS REPORTED RESULTS: 15 Aug 2000 to 31 Dec 2001	
Turnover:	£33,000	Turnover:	n/a
PTP:	£(2.22m)	PTP:	£(670,000)
EPS:	(83.2)p	EPS:	(32.8)p

Comments:
The provider of person-to-person betting exchange systems recently announced a massive milestone, the launch of Binexx.com. This is the financial betting exchange of City Index, and the company's first deal with a major FSA-regulated City firm. This news followed expansion into the European market through a deal with Golanta Sports. Maiden interims to June revealed pre-tax losses of £846,000 on £25,000 of sales – on a pro forma basis, turnover was £91,000.

Trans-Siberian Gold (TSG)

Gold mining

Unit B1, Church Barn, Old Farm Business Centre, Church Road, Toft, Cambridge CB3 7RF Tel: 01223-262258;
Fax: 01223-264995; e-mail: info@trans-siberiangold.com

		holding %
Chairman	Jeremy Marshall	0.4
Managing Director	Jocelyn Waller	3.2
Finance Director	Simon Olsen	0.0
Non-Exec Director	Philip Bowring	1.7

Main Shareholders:

Firebird Funds	7.4
L-R Global Partners	5.9
The Throgmorton Trust	4.7

Percentage of free market capital: 72.3%

Comments:

Trans-Siberian's price has so far been unable to recover from profit-taking by favoured pre-float discount punters. Headed by ex-Avocet boss Jocelyn Waller, the company claims a 2.3m-oz gold resource of Veduga in western Siberia and 648,000 oz of gold and 1.4m oz of silver at Asacha-Rodnikova in far eastern Russia. Veduga could start open-pit before going underground. Speculative.

Nominated Adviser:	Collins Stewart, London
AIM Broker:	Collins Stewart, London
Solicitors:	Freshfields Bruckhaus Deringer, London
Market Makers:	CSCS; EVO; WINS
Auditors:	PricewaterhouseCoopers, London
Registrars:	Capita Registrars

ENTRY ON AIM: 25/11/2003		**Recent price:**	121.0p
Interim results:	Jan	**Market cap:**	£34.55m
Final results:	Jul	**Issue price:**	150.0p
Year end:	Mar	**Current no of shares:**	
Accounts due:	Aug		28,550,779
Int div paymnt:	n/a	**No of shares after**	
Fin div paymnt:	n/a	**dilution:**	n/a
Int net div per share:	nil	**P/E ratio:**	n/a
Fin net div per share:	nil	**Probable CGT?**	**No**

LATEST REPORTED RESULTS: 2002		PREVIOUS REPORTED RESULTS: 2001	
Turnover:	n/a	Turnover:	n/a
PTP:	$(589,826)	PTP:	$(183,154)
EPS:	(0.1)c	EPS:	(0.2)c

Transcomm (TRC)

Mobile data communications systems provider

Heathrow Boulevard, 280 Bath Road, West Drayton, Middlesex UB7 0DQ Tel: 020-8990 9090; Fax: 020-8990 9110;
e-mail: info@transcomm.uk.com; web site: www.transcomm.uk.com

		holding %
Chairman	Rod Matthews	0.03
Chief Executive	Andrew Carver	0.0
Finance Director	Russell Backhouse	0.01
Non-Exec Director	Aubrey Brocklebank	0.2

Main Shareholders:

Andrew Fitton	7.0
Clydesdale Bank Noms Ltd MGC	5.9
AIM Trust	5.1
Clydesdale Bank Noms Ltd MGIN	4.9
M & G Fund	4.7

Percentage of free market capital: 48.4%

Comments:

Mobile data specialist Transcomm has received an offer 'which may or may not lead' to a bid being made for the company. Aside from revealing that any such offer is unlikely to exceed 15.5p a share further details have yet to emerge. The news came on the back of a mixed set of interim numbers to June, revealing an 11% fall in revenues to £6.4m but an improvement in profits from £33,300 to £169,500.

Nominated Adviser:	Nabarro Wells, London
AIM Broker:	Panmure Gordon, London
Solicitors:	Dickinson Dees, Newcastle
Market Makers:	ALTI; MLSB; SCAP; WEST; WINS
Auditors:	KPMG Audit, Cricklade Ct, Swindon, SN1 3EY
Registrars:	Connaught St Michaels

Entry on AIM:	1/3/1999	**Recent price:**	15.25p
Interim results:	Aug	**Market cap:**	£15.68m
Final results:	Mar	**Issue price:**	17.5p
Year end:	Dec	**Current no of shares:**	
Accounts due:	Apr		102,820,084
Int div paymnt:	n/a	**No of shares after**	
Fin div paymnt:	n/a	**dilution:**	112,344,319
Int net div per share:	nil	**P/E ratio:**	n/a
Fin net div per share:	nil	**Probable CGT?**	**Yes**

LATEST REPORTED RESULTS: 2002		PREVIOUS REPORTED RESULTS: 2001	
Turnover:	£13.83m	Turnover:	£15.67m
PTP:	£33,000	PTP:	£(11.09m)
EPS:	0.0p	EPS:	0.0p

Transense Technologies (TRT)

Technology developer for automotive industry

66 Heyford Park, Upper Heyford, Bicester, Oxon OX25 5HD Tel: 01869-238380; Fax: 01869-238381;
e-mail: mailbox@transense.co.uk; web site: www.transense.co.uk

		holding %
Chairman	Peter Woods	0.4
Chief executive	James Perry	4.5
Finance Director	Howard Pearl	0.5
Research Director	Anthony Lonsdale	5.4

Main Shareholders:

Friends Ivory & Sime	15.1
B Lonsdale	4.8
LeggMason Investors Asset Managers	4.8
Equitable Life Assurance	3.9
A J Ingham	3.4
Percentage of free market capital: 56.1%	

Comments:

Transense has still to see its patents and technology put into commercial production. Although it has announced another licensing agreement, turnover is still pretty small (£180,000 at the interims) and losses continue unabated. It has also extended its agreement with 3DM, which netted it only a further £50,000. There is some hope, however, as all passenger vehicles under 10,000 lbs in the US now have to attach tyre sensors, but competition abounds.

Nominated Adviser:	Bridgewell, London		
AIM Broker:	Bridgewell, London		
Solicitors:	Travers Smith Braithwaite, London		
Market Makers:	BGWL; SCAP; KBCS; WINS		
Auditors:	BDO Stoy Hayward, 69 Tweedy Road, Bromley, Kent BR1 3WA		
Registrars:	Capita Registrars		

ENTRY ON AIM: 15/12/1999		**Recent price:**	50.75p
Interim results:	Sep	**Market cap:**	£27.03m
Final results:	Mar	**Issue price:**	25.0p
Year end:	Dec	**Current no of shares:**	
Accounts due:	Apr		53,266,474
Int div paymnt:	n/a	**No of shares after**	
Fin div paymnt:	n/a	**dilution:**	n/a
Int net div per share:	nil	**P/E ratio:**	n/a
Fin net div per share:	nil	**Probable CGT?**	Yes

LATEST REPORTED RESULTS: 2002		PREVIOUS REPORTED RESULTS: 2001	
Turnover:	£112,000	Turnover:	£191,000
PTP:	£(1.26m)	PTP:	£(918,000)
EPS:	(2.4)p	EPS:	(1.8)p

Transport Systems (TSY)

Traffic management services supplier

c/o Forest Traffic Systems, Albany Street, Newport, Gwent NP20 5NJ Tel: 01633-850222; Fax: 01633-822000;
e-mail: rosswilliams@foresttraffic.co.uk

		holding %
Chairman	Christopher Powell	6.4
Chief Executive	Ian Martin	3.3
Finance Director	Kevin Allen	2.3
Director of Ops	Ross Williams	1.8

Main Shareholders:

Capita Trust Company	10.4
Talisman First VCT	10.4
Rathbone Nominees	8.2
Bank of New York	6.7
HSBC Global Custody Nominees	6.1
Percentage of free market capital: 19.4%	

Comments:

Transport Systems is in a turnaround phase under its strengthened management team. Interims to September revealed a move from losses to a £101,507 pre-tax profit – before amortisation – on revenues lifted 13.4% to £1.47m. Trading at Forest Traffic Signals is buoyant, there's plenty of demand for its traffic management services and the traffic light fleet has been expanded. Meanwhile, Forest Highways has a strong order book and expects a 'high workload' for the rest of the year.

Nominated Adviser:	Teather & Greenwood, London		
AIM Broker:	Teather & Greenwood, London		
Solicitors:	Edwards Geldard, Cardiff		
Market Makers:	KBCS; WINS		
Auditors:	Baker Tilly, 2 Bloomsbury Street, London WC1B 3ST		
Registrars:	Capita Registrars		

Entry on AIM: 31/1/2001		**Recent price:**	16.0p
Interim results:	Dec	**Market cap:**	£2.97m
Final results:	Jun	**Issue price:**	10.0p
Year end:	Mar	**Current no of shares:**	
Accounts due:	Nov		18,581,961
Int div paymnt:	n/a	**No of shares after**	
Fin div paymnt:	n/a	**dilution:**	n/a
Int net div per share:	nil	**P/E ratio:**	n/a
Fin net div per share:	nil	**Probable CGT?**	Yes

LATEST REPORTED RESULTS: 2003		PREVIOUS REPORTED RESULTS: 2002	
Turnover:	£2.65m	Turnover:	£2.48m
PTP:	£(344,000)	PTP:	£(380,000)
EPS:	(3.0)p	EPS:	(4.5)p

TranXenoGen (TXN)

Protein drug manufacturer

800 Boston Turnpike, Shewsbury, Massachusetts 01545 USA, Tel: 00-1 508 9364200; Fax: 00-1 508 8422786; web site: www.tranxenogen.com

		holding %
Chairman	Dr Kim Sze Tan	5.7
Chief Executive	George Uveges	3.0
Finance Director	Pat Muggy	0.0
Vice President	Paul DiTullio*	23.6

Main Shareholders:

CTD Riflemen's Partnership	12.8
Steven Parkinson	10.7
Karl Ebert	10.7
Nigel Wray	10.0
Pershing Keen Nominees	7.0

Percentage of free market capital: 23.6%

*Includes 3,850,000 shares held by the CDT Riflemen's Partnership, of which Mr DiTullio is a limited partner

Comments:

This US company's chickens lay eggs containing specific therapeutic human proteins. These will produce insulin, human serum albumin and human growth hormone. It has deals with Abbot Labs, Amgen and an agreement to produce two vaccines. The group has also patented its Gene-Testes 'transfection' technology to produce trangenic animals. At the end of 2003 only $2.2m cash remained. Cost cutting measures have been introduced but a fundraising is really needed.

Nominated Adviser:	Insinger de Beaufort, London		
AIM Broker:	Insinger Townsley, London		
Solicitors:	CMS Cameron McKenna,		
	London; Palmer & Dodge,		
	Boston, US		
Market Makers:	NUMS; WEST; WINS		
Auditors:	Deloitte & Touche, Abbey		
	Street, Reading, RG1 3BD		
Registrars:	Capita Registrars		

ENTRY ON AIM:	18/7/2000	Recent price:	7.75p
Interim results:	Sep	Market cap:	£2.5m
Final results:	Mar	Issue price:	200.0p
Year end:	Dec	Current no of shares:	
Accounts due:	Apr		32,195,000
Int div paymnt:	n/a	No of shares after	
Fin div paymnt:	n/a	dilution:	37,550,000
Int net div per share:	nil	P/E ratio:	n/a
Fin net div per share:	nil	Probable CGT?	Yes

LATEST REPORTED RESULTS: 2003		PREVIOUS REPORTED RESULTS: 2002	
Turnover:	n/a	Turnover:	$33,000
PTP:	$(4.35m)	PTP:	$(4.42m)
EPS:	(0.1)c	EPS:	(0.1)c

Tricorn (TCN)

Environmental engineer

P O Box 179, Spring Lane, Malvern, Worcestershire WR14 1ZY Tel: 01684-569956 ; Fax: 01684-572540; e-mail: ra@tricorn.uk.com

		holding %
Chairman	Nicholas Paul	0.4
Chief Executive	Steven Cooper	0.0
Finance Director		
Director	Roger Allsop	43.6

Main Shareholders:

Gartmore	15.0
Forest Nominees	5.4
Rock Nominees	5.3

Percentage of free market capital: 24.6%

Comments:

Tricorn enjoyed a strong half to September, with cost cutting showing through and revenues rising across the board. Losses were pared back from £452,000 to £95,000 on improved turnover of £2.9m (£2.1m). Tube manipulation specialist Malvern Tubular Components continued its drive for lean manufacturing, Redman Fittings made steady progress and Isssquared successfully completed its pipeline inspection system project for a water company consortium.

Nominated Adviser:	Collins Stewart, London
AIM Broker:	Collins Stewart, London
Solicitors:	Halliwell Landau, Manchester
Market Makers:	CSCS; WINS
Auditors:	Grant Thornton, 111 Edmund
	Street, Birmingham B3 2HJ
Registrars:	Neville Registrars

Entry on AIM:	5/12/2001	Recent price:	10.25p
Interim results:	Dec	Market cap:	£2.98m
Final results:	Aug	Issue price:	30.0p
Year end:	Mar	Current no of shares:	
Accounts due:	Apr		29,110,000
Int div paymnt:	n/a	No of shares after	
Fin div paymnt:	n/a	dilution:	n/a
Int net div per share:	nil	P/E ratio:	n/a
Fin net div per share:	nil	Probable CGT?	Yes

LATEST REPORTED RESULTS: 2003		PREVIOUS REPORTED RESULTS: 2002	
Turnover:	£4.32m	Turnover:	£4.92m
PTP:	£(1.61m)	PTP:	£(638,000)
EPS:	(5.5)p	EPS:	(2.7)p

Triple Plate Junction (formerly Names.co Internet) (TPJ)
Exploration of Vietnamese mineral assets
105 Piccadilly, London, W1J 7NJ Tel: 020-7499 1400; Fax: 020-7499 1455; e-mail: info@names.co.uk

		holding %
Chairman	Ian Gowrie-Smith	0.0
Chief Executive	Geoffrey Walsh	0.0
Finance Director	David Lees	4.0
Exploration Director	William Howell	0.0

Main Shareholders:

Candice	27.2
Thornaby	23.6
Merlin Group	15.3
The Beausoleil Settlement	8.6
Pershing Keen	4.6

Percentage of free market capital: 7.43%

Comments:

Aussie entrepreneur Ian Gowrie Smith (of Medeva fame) floated former web-linked flop Names.co as Triple Plate to probe gold prospects in Vietnam. Run by ex-Lonrho stalwart Geoff Walsh, Triple Plate has a joint venture with US giant Newmont to develop a mine at Pu Sam Cap and joint ventures with the Tiberon group at Xi Pa, A Bang and Lang Vai. Distinctly speculative, though Gowrie Smith has a money-making record.

Nominated Adviser:	John East, London
AIM Broker:	Insinger Townsley, London
Solicitors:	Stringer Saul, London
Market Makers:	SCAP; WINS
Auditors:	Grant Thornton, London Thames Valley Office, Churchill House, Chalvey Road East, Slough, Berks SL1 2LS
Registrars:	Capita Registrars

ENTRY ON AIM:	27/6/2000	**Recent price:**	42.5p
Interim results:	Dec	**Market cap:**	£15.35m
Final results:	Sep	**Issue price:**	n/a
Year end:	Mar	**Current no of shares:**	
Accounts due:	Aug		36,115,278
Int div paymnt:	n/a	**No of shares after**	
Fin div paymnt:	n/a	**dilution:**	n/a
Int net div per share:	nil	**P/E ratio:**	n/a
Fin net div per share:	nil	**Probable CGT?**	Yes

LATEST REPORTED RESULTS: 2003		PREVIOUS REPORTED RESULTS: 2002	
Turnover:	£1.10m	**Turnover:**	£1.08m
PTP:	£(134,000)	**PTP:**	£34,000
EPS:	(0.1)p	**EPS:**	0.0p

TripleArc (TPA)
Provider of integrated procurement solutions for the printing industry
Linhope House, 36a Linhope Street, London, NW1 6HU Tel: 020-7258 6290; Fax: 020-7258 6271; e-mail: info@triplearc.com; web site: www.triplearc.com

		holding %
Chairman	Tim Brettel	6.7
Chief Executive	Jason Cromack	2.3
Finance Director	Peter Houston	0.2
Non-Exec Director	David Wong	10.4

Main Shareholders:

Nigel Edgely	4.2

Percentage of free market capital: 71.3%

Comments:

2003 was a huge year for the print procurement solutions venture, with the highlight being the November acquisition of Access Plus. This deal turned the group into one of the UK's major print management companies – this is one of the most exciting and the fastest growing sector of the print industry, growing at about 15% a year. Turnover and operating profits powered ahead dramatically buoyed by continued growth at g12 and a 6-week contribution from Access Plus.

Nominated Adviser:	Canaccord Capital, London
AIM Broker:	Canaccord Capital, London
Solicitors:	Berwin Leighton Paisner, London
Market Makers:	KBCS; SCAP; WINS
Auditors:	KPMG, 1 Stokes Place, St Stephen's Green, Dublin 2
Registrars:	Computershare Investor Services

Entry on AIM:	10/12/2001	**Recent price:**	15.75p
Interim results:	Sep	**Market cap:**	£31.66m
Final results:	Jun	**Issue price:**	30.0p
Year end:	Dec	**Current no of shares:**	
Accounts due:	Apr		201,021,350
Int div paymnt:	n/a	**No of shares after**	
Fin div paymnt:	n/a	**dilution:**	n/a
Int net div per share:	nil	**P/E ratio:**	n/a
Fin net div per share:	nil	**Probable CGT?**	Yes

LATEST REPORTED RESULTS: 2003		PREVIOUS REPORTED RESULTS: 2002	
Turnover:	£20.86m	**Turnover:**	£7.01m
PTP:	£(35,000)	**PTP:**	£(2.98m)
EPS:	(0.3)p	**EPS:**	(4.6)p

UA   (UAS)

Livestock marketing services and property investment

Perth Agricultural Centre, East Huntingtower, Perth, PH1 3JJ Tel: 01738-626183; Fax: 01738-474160;
e-mail: enquiries@uagroup.co.uk; web site: www.uagroup.co.uk

		holding %
Chairman	Peregrine Moncreiffe	11.1
Chief Executive	David Danson	1.9
Finance Director	Suzanne Grahame	1.1
Marketing Director	David Leggat	1.0

Main Shareholders:

UA Trustees	6.6
John Izat	4.7
David Barry	3.9

Percentage of free market capital: 64.3%

Comments:

The property service and livestock marketing company continues to capitalise on its property assets. It recently sold a farm in Polnaise, Stirling for £700,000, which was £580,000 above book value. The company is developing properties and has acquired a 23-acre estate in Pirnhall, also in Stirling, part of which will be devploed into a livestock market. On the trading side, it has 25% market share of the livestock marketing business in Scotland.

Nominated Adviser:	Charles Stanley, London		
AIM Broker:	Charles Stanley, London		
Solicitors:	Burness, Edinburgh		
Market Makers:	MLSB; WINS		
Auditors:	Grant Thornton, 1/4 Atholl Crescent, Edinburgh EH3 8LQ		
Registrars:	Lloyds TSB Registrars		

ENTRY ON AIM:	15/9/1995	**Recent price:**	745.0p
Interim results:	Nov	**Market cap:**	£26.3m
Final results:	Apr	**Issue price:**	107.5p
Year end:	Jan	**Current no of shares:**	
Accounts due:	May		3,530,290
Int div paymnt:	Nov	**No of shares after**	
Fin div paymnt:	Jun	**dilution:**	n/a
Int net div per share:	2.0p	**P/E ratio:**	74.5
Fin net div per share:	3.0p	**Probable CGT?**	Yes

LATEST REPORTED RESULTS: 2003		PREVIOUS REPORTED RESULTS: 2002	
Turnover:	£15.76m	Turnover:	£10.18m
PTP:	£421,000	PTP:	£(993,000)
EPS:	10.0p	EPS:	(26.4)p

UBC Media   (UBC)

Audio and new media content producer

50 Lisson Street, London, NW1 5DF Tel: 020-7453 1600; Fax: 020-7723 6132; e-mail: info@ubcmedia.com;
web site: www.ubcmedia.com

		holding %
Chairman	Michael Peacock	6.1
CEO	Simon Cole	17.2
Finance Director	Jennifer Donald	0.1
Programme Director	Timothy Blackmore	13.0

Main Shareholders:

Noel Edmonds (Non-Exec Director)	9.0
Herald Investment Trust	4.0
Stanlife Nominees	3.9
Universities Superannuation	3.4
GWR	3.3

Percentage of free market capital: 33.1%

Comments:

UBC is one of the biggest suppliers of entertainment and news services to the radio sector, and one of the largest suppliers of programming to the BBC. It also owns the Classic Gold Digital Network, is part of the MRX digital radio consortium and owns all of OneWorld Radio, the national commercial digital radio station. The past six months have seen deals with the BBC, EMAP, CNN Group and the Guardian Media Group amongst others. But profits aren't expected this year or next.

Nominated Adviser:	Hoare Govett, London		
AIM Broker:	Hoare Govett, London; Seymour Pierce, London		
Solicitors:	Wragge & Co, Birmingham		
Market Makers:	MLSB; SCAP; WINS		
Auditors:	PricewaterhouseCoopers, 1 Embankment Place, London WC2N 6NN		
Registrars:	Capita Registrars		

Entry on AIM:	3/7/2000	**Recent price:**	35.5p
Interim results:	Nov	**Market cap:**	£56.17m
Final results:	Jul	**Issue price:**	25.0p
Year end:	Mar	**Current no of shares:**	
Accounts due:	Jul		158,237,228
Int div paymnt:	n/a	**No of shares after**	
Fin div paymnt:	n/a	**dilution:**	n/a
Int net div per share:	nil	**P/E ratio:**	n/a
Fin net div per share:	nil	**Probable CGT?**	Yes

LATEST REPORTED RESULTS: 2003		PREVIOUS REPORTED RESULTS: 2002	
Turnover:	£10.32m	Turnover:	£9.19m
PTP:	£(2.10m)	PTP:	£(3.03m)
EPS:	(1.4)p	EPS:	(2.2)p

ukbetting

(UKB)

Gambling website operator

3rd Floor, 14 Waterloo Place, London, SW1Y 4AR Tel: 020-7004 2805; Fax: 020-7004 2802;
e-mail: siobhan@ukbetting.com; web site: www.plc.ukbetting.com

		holding %
Chairman	David Sieff	0.3
Chief Executive	Eric Semel	3.0
Finance Director	Andrew Galvin	0.0
Vice Chairman	Peter Dubens	3.2

Main Shareholders:

UBS Investment Bank	19.0
Fidelity International	5.6
Herald Investment Trust	5.3
Canada Life Marketing Group	3.6

Percentage of free market capital: 55.6%

Comments:

The online betting and sports content company has been on the acquisition trail buying Rivals Digital Media, an online sports content business for £2m and Oddschecker, a UK odds comparison service for £4.75m. It has also confirmed it is in talks regarding a further acquisition presently. TEAMtalk, its in-store media operation, has also gained new business by providing radio services to tile retailer Topps Tiles and Littlewood's Index stores.

Nominated Adviser:	Collins Stewart, London		
AIM Broker:	Collins Stewart, London		
Solicitors:	Stringer Saul, London		
Market Makers:	BGMM; SCAP; WINS		
Auditors:	Grant Thornton, 31 Carlton Crescent. Southampton SO15 2EW		
Registrars:	Melton Registrars		

Entry on AIM:	7/8/2001	**Recent price:**	72.0p
Interim results:	Jan	**Market cap:**	£65.04m
Final results:	Sep	**Issue price:**	25.0p
Year end:	Jun	**Current no of shares:**	
Accounts due:	Oct		90,331,735
Int div paymnt:	n/a	**No of shares after**	
Fin div paymnt:	n/a	**dilution:**	n/a
Int net div per share:	nil	**P/E ratio:**	n/a
Fin net div per share:	nil	**Probable CGT?**	YES

LATEST REPORTED RESULTS:	2002	PREVIOUS REPORTED RESULTS:	2001
Turnover:	£39.08m	Turnover:	£5.16m
PTP:	£(8.83m)	PTP:	£(2.60m)
EPS:	(19.3)p	EPS:	(18.3)p

Ultimate Finance (UFG)

Cash flow finance provider

11 St James's Square, Manchester, M2 6WH Tel: 0161-832 2174; Fax: 0161-833 0935

		holding %
Chairman	Clive Garston	1.3
Chief Executive	Brian Sumner	10.7
Finance Director		
Managing Director	Richard Pepler	0.2

Main Shareholders:

WH Ireland	27.5
Glenmore Investments	13.0

Percentage of free market capital: 40.5%

Nominated Adviser:	Dawnay Day, London
AIM Broker:	WH Ireland, Manchester
Solicitors:	Halliwell Landau, Manchester
Market Makers:	KBCS; SCAP; WINS
Auditors:	KPMG Audit, 1 The Embankment, Neville Street, Leeds LS1 4DW
Registrars:	Neville Registrars

Entry on AIM:	12/6/2002	Recent price:	18.5p
Interim results:	Jan	Market cap:	£2.08m
Final results:	Sep	Issue price:	24.0p
Year end:	Apr	Current no of shares:	
Accounts due:	Oct		11,223,372
Int div paymnt:	n/a	No of shares after	
Fin div paymnt:	n/a	dilution:	13,863,372
Int net div per share:	nil	P/E ratio:	n/a
Fin net div per share:	nil	Probable CGT?	Yes

LATEST REPORTED RESULTS: 10 Jan '02 to 30 Jun '03		PREVIOUS REPORTED RESULTS: N/A	
Turnover:	£485,000	Turnover:	n/a
PTP:	£(663,000)	PTP:	n/a
EPS:	(5.9)p	EPS:	n/a

Comments:

Ultimate provides invoice discounting, factoring and trade financing services. Last year's float brought in £1.82m, although this was heavily underwritten by broker WH Ireland who retains a hefty holding. The group also has a £4.5m facility to draw on from the Bank of Scotland. Latest interims saw client turnover rise by £12.9m to £17.5m. This helped losses reduce by 62% to £0.17m. So far £3.4m has been advanced to 81 clients. The group has a tough bad debts policy as well.

Ultimate Leisure (ULG)

Bar operator

26 Mosley Street, Newcastle upon Tyne, NE1 1DF Tel: 0191-261 8800; Fax: 0191-221 2282;
e-mail: ultimate.leisure@virgin.net; web site: www.ultimateleisure.com

		holding %
Chairman	Jon Pither	0.6
Chief Executive	Allan Rankin	18.4
Finance Director	Craig Bell	0.03
Managing Director	Robert Senior	0.3

Main Shareholders:

S Rankin	16.5
J R Rankin	16.5
Vanot	12.7
Pacific 2000 Trust	6.6
M & G	6.1

Percentage of free market capital: 13.4%

Nominated Adviser:	Brewin Dolphin, Newcastle
AIM Broker:	Brewin Dolphin, Newcastle
Solicitors:	Mincoffs, Newcastle upon Tyne
Market Makers:	BGMM; WINS
Auditors:	KPMG, Quayside House, 110 Quayside, Newcastle upon Tyne
Registrars:	Capita Registrars

Entry on AIM:	29/7/1999	Recent price:	332.0p
Interim results:	Feb	Market cap:	£80.91m
Final results:	Sep	Issue price:	145.0p
Year end:	Jun	Current no of shares:	
Accounts due:	Oct		24,369,826
Int div paymnt:	Apr	No of shares after	
Fin div paymnt:	Nov	dilution:	n/a
Int net div per share:	1.66p	P/E ratio:	12.4
Fin net div per share:	4.34p	Probable CGT?	Yes

LATEST REPORTED RESULTS: 2003		PREVIOUS REPORTED RESULTS: 2002	
Turnover:	£26.50m	Turnover:	£20.57m
PTP:	£6.77m	PTP:	£5.18m
EPS:	26.7p	EPS:	20.8p

Comments:

Ultimate, with its 'Beach' and 'Coyote Wild' bar concepts, continues to produce excellent results. The group recently acquired a large freehold site in Belfast comprising two bars and a nightclub with capacity for over 1,000 people. Having raised £20m in October, its gearing has dropped from 86% in June to 15%. Maintaining a strategy of purchasing freehold sites, it also has the 'financial firepower' to continue further expansion activities.

Univent (UVT)

Nursing & rest homes operator

Dunraven House, Weighton Road, Penge, London, SE20 8SX Tel: 020-8659 2340; Fax: 020-8778 8711;
e-mail: univentplc@freeuk.com

		holding %
Chairman	Timothy SK Yeo	1.4
Managing Director	Alain J Leong-Son	32.7
Finance Director	Guillame M Leong-Son	12.6
Director	Paul D Boylan	23.8

Main Shareholders:

Kingston Nominees	7.7
Excellon Investments	4.6
Asset Nominees	4.5
Malen Pillay	3.7
Regional Nominees	3.1

Percentage of free market capital: 5.9%

Nominated Adviser:	Teather & Greenwood, London
AIM Broker:	Hichens Harrison, London
Solicitors:	Finers Stephens Innocent, London
Market Makers:	KBCS; WINS
Auditors:	PKF, Park St, Guildford, GU1 4HN
Registrars:	Assets International Management

ENTRY ON AIM:	28/9/1995	**Recent price:**	41.5p
Interim results:	Jun	**Market cap:**	£3.79m
Final results:	Mar	**Issue price:**	40.0p
Year end:	Sep	**Current no of shares:**	
Accounts due:	Mar		9,125,000
Int div paymnt:	n/a	**No of shares after**	
Fin div paymnt:	n/a	**dilution:**	n/a
Int net div per share:	nil	**P/E ratio:**	46.1
Fin net div per share:	nil	**Probable CGT?**	Yes

LATEST REPORTED RESULTS:	2002	PREVIOUS REPORTED RESULTS:	2001
Turnover:	£3.31m	**Turnover:**	£2.86m
PTP:	£129,000	**PTP:**	£161,000
EPS:	0.9p	**EPS:**	1.1p

Comments:

The nursing homes operator, chaired by shadow trade minister Tim Yeo, recorded a 52% recovery in profits during 2003 after a depressed previous year. Operating margins have been improved as the group's care staff agency extended its geographical reach. One weak spot is the nursery next to the Halifax home, which is struggling. Gearing stands at its lowest level for seven years, helped by a revaluation of assets. NAV stands at £3.33m. A final dividend of 0.5p has been declared.

Universal Direct (UDI)

Re-seller of discounted electronic goods

11-13 The Vineyard, Abingdon, OX14 3PX Oxfordshire, Tel: 020-7706 3000; Fax: 020-7723 0386

		holding %
Chairman	Edward Adams	12.9
Chief Executive		
Finance Director	Andrew Flatt	7.9
Non-Exec Director	Gary Shoefield	0.0

Main Shareholders:

Robin Jones	8.6
TD Waterhouse	4.7
David Holyoak	4.3
Pershing Keen	4.0
Bybrook	3.6

Percentage of free market capital: 47.4%

Nominated Adviser:	Beaumont Cornish, London
AIM Broker:	Insinger Townsley, London
Solicitors:	Moore & Blatch, London
Market Makers:	KBCS; MLSB; SCAP; WINS
Auditors:	BDO Stoy Hayward, 8 Baker Street, London W1M 1DA
Registrars:	Capita Registrars

Entry on AIM:	20/1/2000	**Recent price:**	26.0p
Interim results:	Sep	**Market cap:**	£1.18m
Final results:	Jul	**Issue price:**	n/a
Year end:	Mar	**Current no of shares:**	
Accounts due:	Jul		4,544,913
Int div paymnt:	n/a	**No of shares after**	
Fin div paymnt:	n/a	**dilution:**	n/a
Int net div per share:	nil	**P/E ratio:**	n/a
Fin net div per share:	nil	**Probable CGT?**	Yes

LATEST REPORTED RESULTS:	2003	PREVIOUS REPORTED RESULTS:	2002
Turnover:	£4.78m	**Turnover:**	£4.47m
PTP:	£(985,000)	**PTP:**	£(9.07m)
EPS:	(0.2)p	**EPS:**	(2.1)p

Comments:

This company's sole operating business these days is Universal Consumer Products, or 'UCP', a business acquired for £2.5m cash in a reverse deal last April. UCP buys and resells consumer electronics and other hardware items from manufacturers and retailers. These could be obsolete goods, or customer returns, which are then sold to independent discount retailers. For the half to September, the loss before tax was £149,000 on continuing sales of £2.54m.

Universe (UNG)

Payment systems developer

55 Queen Anne Street, London, W1G 9JR Tel: 02380-689 200; Fax: 02380-689 201;
e-mail: webmaster@universe-group.co.uk; web site: www.universe-group.co.uk

		holding %
Chairman	George Welham	0.03
Chief Executive	Ray Mackie	15.2
Finance Director	Eddie Paul	0.02
Non-Exec Director	Barrie Brinkman	1.6

Main Shareholders:

Pershing Nominees	4.0
Sharelink Nominees	3.8
Robert Sutton	3.1

Percentage of free market capital: 72.2%

Nominated Adviser:	Charles Stanley, London
AIM Broker:	Charles Stanley, London
Solicitors:	Travers Smith Braithwaite, London
Market Makers:	MLSB; TEAM; WINS
Auditors:	KPMG Audit, 8 Salisbury Square, London EC4Y 8BB
Registrars:	Capita Registrars

ENTRY ON AIM:	20/2/1998	**Recent price:**	25.5p
Interim results:	Sep	**Market cap:**	£14.74m
Final results:	Mar	**Issue price:**	44.0p
Year end:	Dec	**Current no of shares:**	
Accounts due:	Mar		57,806,023
Int div paymnt:	Oct	**No of shares after**	
Fin div paymnt:	May	**dilution:**	n/a
Int net div per share: 0.54p		**P/E ratio:**	10.2
Fin net div per share: 1.17p		**Probable CGT?**	**YES**

LATEST REPORTED RESULTS: 2002		PREVIOUS REPORTED RESULTS: 2001	
Turnover:	£34.49m	Turnover:	£58.99m
PTP:	£889,000	PTP:	£858,000
EPS:	2.5p	EPS:	0.4p

Comments:

2003 was a year of major transition for the retail and information systems company. Retail technology arm HTEC 'manfully' played the role of sole profit provider as the bureaux de change operations struggled and money transfer arm First Remit went through its gestation period. In a tricky year Universe managed to lift turnover, but it swung to losses after restructuring and the write-off of development costs at First Remit. Operating profits were modestly higher.

Urbium (URM)

Bar nightclub operator

Vernon House, 40 Shaftesbury Avenue, London, W1D 7ER Tel: 020-7434 0030; Fax: 020-7434 1413;
web site: www.urbium.com

		holding %
Chairman	John Conlan	0.2
Managing Director	Robert Cohan	0.0
Finance Director	Steven Palmer	0.01
Non-Exec Director	The Viscount Astor	0.8

Main Shareholders:

Schroder Investment Managment	6.8
The Clark Group Pension Scheme	5.0
Fidelity Investments	4.1
Standard Lfe Investments	3.3

Percentage of free market capital: 52%

Nominated Adviser:	Numis, London
AIM Broker:	Numis, London
Solicitors:	Norton Rose & Berwin Leighton Paisner, London
Market Makers:	ARBT; CSFB; KBCS; MLSB; SCAP; WEST; WINS
Auditors:	KPMG Audit, 8 Salisbury Square, London EC4Y 8BB
Registrars:	Capita Registrars

Entry on AIM:	17/5/2002	**Recent price:**	583.0p
Interim results:	Sep	**Market cap:**	£60.37m
Final results:	Feb	**Issue price:**	14.25p
Year end:	Dec	**Current no of shares:**	
Accounts due:	Apr		10,354,593
Int div paymnt:	n/a	**No of shares after**	
Fin div paymnt:	n/a	**dilution:**	n/a
Int net div per share:	nil	**P/E ratio:**	23.9
Fin net div per share:	nil	**Probable CGT?**	**YES**

LATEST REPORTED RESULTS: 2003		PREVIOUS REPORTED RESULTS: 2002	
Turnover:	£67.56m	Turnover:	£62.74m
PTP:	£3.47m	PTP:	£4.26m
EPS:	24.4p	EPS:	11.3p

Comments:

Unlike rival high street bar operators, Urbium is going from stength to strength with good year-end figures despite difficult trading conditions. The owners of the seven-strong Tiger Tiger chain now operates 16 bars in the West End of London and has acquired a further two bars, aiming to be the market leader in the City of London. It also plans to open smaller formats of Tiger Tiger throughout the UK, with the first in Aberdeen this summer.

Vantis (VTS)

Professional services business

82 St John Street, London, EC1M 4JN Tel: 020-7417 0417; web site: www.vantisplc.com

		holding %
Chairman	Paul Gourmand	0.0
Chief Executive	Paul Jackson	20.1
Finance Director	Trevor Applin	11.3
Exec Director	Nigel Hamilton-Smith	5.2

Main Shareholders:

Barrie Dunning	11.7
Andrew Scott	6.9

Percentage of free market capital: 25.0%

Nominated Adviser:	Charles Stanley, London
AIM Broker:	Charles Stanley, London
Solicitors:	Mayer, Brown, Rowe & Maw, London
Market Makers:	NUMS; WINS
Auditors:	BDO Stoy Hayward, Epsom, Surrey
Registrars:	Capita Registrars

ENTRY ON AIM:	1/5/2002	Recent price:	124.5p
Interim results:	Dec	Market cap:	£51.49m
Final results:	Sep	Issue price:	90.0p
Year end:	Mar	Current no of shares:	
Accounts due:	Aug		41,361,298
Int div paymnt:	Feb	No of shares after	
Fin div paymnt:	Sep	dilution:	n/a
Int net div per share: 0.94p		P/E ratio:	18
Fin net div per share: 2.065p		Probable CGT?	Yes

LATEST REPORTED RESULTS: YEAR TO 30 APR 2003		PREVIOUS REPORTED RESULTS: N/A	
Turnover:	£18.65m	Turnover:	n/a
PTP:	£3.07m	PTP:	n/a
EPS:	6.9p	EPS:	n/a

Comments:

Vantis, like Tenon and Numerica, joined AIM to build an accountancy business. But unlike its start-up rivals it already had a 16-year history of acquisitive growth. Since admission the group has made several acquisitions – the latest was insolvency specialist Redhead French for £7.8m. More can be expected following a number of placings, pulling in nearly £6m. Interim revenues rose 30% to £10.2m, producing a profit before tax, interest and goodwill of £1.8m, up 29%. Gearing was reduced to 53%.

Vebnet (formerly Stockbourne) (VBT)

Software applications for employee benefits

The Courtyard, New Lodge, Drift Road, Winkfield, Windsor, Berkshire SL4 4RR Tel: 01344-884 662; Fax: 01344-884 878

		holding %
Chairman	Derek Scott	1.1
Chief Executive	Gerard O'Neill	13.1
Finance Director	Stephen Thurlow	3.1
Deputy Chairman	Dr Nairn	11.2

Main Shareholders:

Cross Atlantic Capital	28.9
Liontrust	5.6
Shaun Clarkin	3.2

Percentage of free market capital: 32.1%

Nominated Adviser:	Brewin Dolphin, Edinburgh
AIM Broker:	Brewin Dolphin, Edinburgh
Solicitors:	Dundas & Wilson, Edinburgh
Market Makers:	KBCS; WINS
Auditors:	LWC Audit Limited, Edinburgh
Registrars:	Capita Registrars

Entry on AIM:	15/1/2003	Recent price:	147.5p
Interim results:	Mar	Market cap:	£12.44m
Final results:	Sep	Issue price:	56.0p
Year end:	Jun	Current no of shares:	
Accounts due:	Mar		8,435,193
Int div paymnt:	n/a	No of shares after	
Fin div paymnt:	n/a	dilution:	n/a
Int net div per share:	nil	P/E ratio:	n/a
Fin net div per share:	nil	Probable CGT?	Yes

LATEST REPORTED RESULTS: 2003		PREVIOUS REPORTED RESULTS: 2002	
Turnover:	£668,000	Turnover:	£25,000
PTP:	£(1.26m)	PTP:	£(1.51m)
EPS:	(20.0)p	EPS:	(31.0)p

Comments:

The provider of technology for employee benefit solutions more than doubled its turnover to £380,000 in the half to December, although losses came in wider at £610,000 (£516,000). Encouragingly, the number of employees using its core FIX&FLEX product rose 60% to 14,187 and new clients reported included British American Tobacco and Parsons Brinkerhoff. Vebnet is on course to reach cash breakeven at the operating level in 2004.

Venturia

Cash shell

Parklands Lodge, Charcoal Road, Altrincham, Cheshire WA14 4RT Tel: 0161-929 1129; Fax: 0161-929 6855;
web site: www.buyersguide.co.uk

		holding %
Chairman	Martin Robinson	0.0
Chief Executive	Robert Cory	0.0
Finance Director		
Non-Exec Director	Alan Clarke	0.0

Main Shareholders:

Armstrong Brooks	95.3

Percentage of free market capital: n/a

Comments:

Cash shell Venturia ditched its online advertising operations way back in 2002 and has yet to find a suitable acquisition. Directors claim Venturia remains on the hunt for businesses which are peripheral to industrial and commercial property, or technology businesses. For 2003, the company reported a disappointing £129,527 loss, although it traded profitably during the second half. At the December year-end, Venturia had £2.9m in cash resources.

Nominated Adviser:	Corporate Synergy, London
AIM Broker:	Daniel Stewart, London
Solicitors:	Halliwell Landau, London;
	McFadden, Pilkington & Ward, London
Market Makers:	CSCS; KBCS; WINS
Auditors:	PKF, Manchester
Registrars:	Lloyds TSB Registrars

ENTRY ON AIM:	7/8/2000	**Recent price:**	3.0p
Interim results:	Sep	**Market cap:**	£2.62m
Final results:	Mar	**Issue price:**	29.0p
Year end:	Dec	**Current no of shares:**	
Accounts due:	Apr		87,250,000
Int div paymnt:	n/a	**No of shares after**	
Fin div paymnt:	n/a	**dilution:**	n/a
Int net div per share:	nil	**P/E ratio:**	n/a
Fin net div per share:	nil	**Probable CGT?**	No

LATEST REPORTED RESULTS: 2002		PREVIOUS REPORTED RESULTS: 2001	
Turnover:	£228,000	Turnover:	£1.23m
PTP:	£(880,000)	PTP:	£(882,000)
EPS:	(1.0)p	EPS:	(1.0)p

VI

(VIG)

Design, manufacture and distribution of CAD software

The Mill, Brimscombe, Stroud, Glos. GL5 2QG Tel: 01453-732900; Fax: 01453-887444; e-mail: vero@vero.co.uk;
web site: www.vero-software.com

		holding %
Chairman	Stephen Palframan	0.0
Chief Executive	Donald Babbs	23.0
Finance Director		
Dvlptmt Director	Gerard O'Driscoll	2.6

Main Shareholders:

Ezio Galardo	17.2
Chase Nominees	14.8
Rathbones Nominees	10.4
Artemis AIM VCT	6.5
Marino Cignetti	5.9

Percentage of free market capital: .7%

Comments:

The computer-aided design software developer is recovering from a dismal 2002 performance. First half losses reduced by £130,000 to £227,000 as sales surged 36% to £4.4m. In a bid to hasten the turnaround, new sales offices have been opened in Canada, France and Japan, while a series of product upgrades have been released. Cash reserves remain strong so VI has plenty of time on its side. Consolidation in the highly fragmented CAD software market, however, should be expected.

Nominated Adviser:	Grant Thornton, London
AIM Broker:	Durlacher, London
Solicitors:	Addleshaw Goddard, London
Market Makers:	DURM; WINS
Auditors:	Moore Stephens, Warwick Lane, London EC4P 4BN
Registrars:	Capita Registrars

Entry on AIM:	3/4/1998	**Recent price:**	16.75p
Interim results:	Sep	**Market cap:**	£6.24m
Final results:	Apr	**Issue price:**	50.0p
Year end:	Dec	**Current no of shares:**	
Accounts due:	Apr		37,261,166
Int div paymnt:	n/a	**No of shares after**	
Fin div paymnt:	n/a	**dilution:**	37,443,023
Int net div per share:	nil	**P/E ratio:**	n/a
Fin net div per share:	nil	**Probable CGT?**	Yes

LATEST REPORTED RESULTS: 2002		PREVIOUS REPORTED RESULTS: 2001	
Turnover:	£7.54m	Turnover:	£6.46m
PTP:	£70,000	PTP:	£726,000
EPS:	(0.7)p	EPS:	2.1p

(VRA)

...gement service provider

Campus South, Queensferry Road, Dunfermaline, KY11 8PL Tel: 01383-748 000;
...ail: info@vianet.co.uk; web site: www.vianet.co.uk

		holding %
	John May	0.5
	Ian Orrock	2.2
Finance Director	Alastair Kerr	0.3
Non-Exec Director	Brian McGhee	0.2

Main Shareholders:

Willbro Nominees	22.5
Canada Trust	12.1
Adam & Company Nominees	11.3
Singer & Friedlander AIM 3 VCT	10.7
Vidacos	5.1

Percentage of free market capital: 19.7%

Comments:

The vending machine technology developer has agreed a licensing deal with telecoms group Alcatel. The two companies will work together to allow vending machine operators to check their property remotely using mobile phone technology. In return, Vianet will receive a £265,000 fee up front, followed by a similar sum later. Following this the company raised £3.3m in an oversubscribed 6p offer. The group now has 600 units operating or ordered – 150 are run by Red Bull.

Nominated Adviser:	Brewin Dolphin, Edinburgh
AIM Broker:	Brewin Dolphin, Glasgow
Solicitors:	Shepherd & Wedderburn WS, Edinburgh
Market Makers:	BGMM; WINS
Auditors:	Grant Thornton, 1-4 Atholl Crescent, Edinburgh EG3 8LQ
Registrars:	Capita Registrars

Entry on AIM:	29/3/2000	**Recent price:**	9.75p
Interim results:	Jun	**Market cap:**	£12.55m
Final results:	Dec	**Issue price:**	130.0p
Year end:	Sep	**Current no of shares:**	
Accounts due:	Jan		128,685,221
Int div paymnt:	n/a	**No of shares after**	
Fin div paymnt:	n/a	**dilution:**	n/a
Int net div per share:	nil	**P/E ratio:**	n/a
Fin net div per share:	nil	**Probable CGT?**	Yes

LATEST REPORTED RESULTS: 2003		PREVIOUS REPORTED RESULTS: 2002	
Turnover:	£34,000	Turnover:	£13,000
PTP:	£(2.06m)	PTP:	£(1.96m)
EPS:	(3.1)p	EPS:	(6.3)p

Victory Corporation (VRY)

Retailer

Salisbury House, City Fields, Tangmere, Chichester, West Sussex PO20 2FP Tel: 01243-622226; Fax: 01243-622339

		holding %
Chairman	John Jackson	0.0
Chief Executive		
Finance Director	Clive Bruce	0.0
Marketing Director	Ros Simmons	0.0

Main Shareholders:

Virgin Retail Investment Holdings	89.0

Percentage of free market capital: 10.9%

Comments:

Victory Corporation's focus on Virgin Cosmetics, having ditched retail clothing arm Capo, helped it report a strong first half. Turnover rose 42% to £26m with losses pared back 57% to £1.5m. Virgin Cosmetics Direct, accounting for 83% of cosmetics sales, saw a 41% sales rise and independent sales consultants grew in number by 17% to 9,153. Directors are cautious on the full year, as high consumer credit and rising mortgage rates have hit consumer spending.

Nominated Adviser:	Seymour Pierce, London
AIM Broker:	Seymour Pierce, London
Solicitors:	Harbottle & Lewis, London
Market Makers:	SGSL; UBSW; WINS
Auditors:	KPMG Audit, 8 Salisbury Square, London EC4Y 8BB
Registrars:	Capita Registrars

Entry on AIM:	17/10/1996	**Recent price:**	207.5p
Interim results:	Dec	**Market cap:**	£23.43m
Final results:	Jun	**Issue price:**	58.0p
Year end:	Mar	**Current no of shares:**	
Accounts due:	Aug		11,292,287
Int div paymnt:	n/a	**No of shares after**	
Fin div paymnt:	n/a	**dilution:**	n/a
Int net div per share:	nil	**P/E ratio:**	n/a
Fin net div per share:	nil	**Probable CGT?**	Yes

LATEST REPORTED RESULTS: 2003		PREVIOUS REPORTED RESULTS: 2002	
Turnover:	£57.62m	Turnover:	£47.5m
PTP:	£(7.94m)	PTP:	£(3.99m)
EPS:	(1.5)p	EPS:	(0.8)p

Vietnam Opportunity Fund (VOF)
Investment company
PO Box 309GT, Ugland House, South Church Street, George Town, Grand Cayman, Cayman Islands,

		holding %
Chairman	Koon Choi	0.0
Chief Executive	Horst Geicke	7.4
Finance Director		
Director	Robert Knapp	0.0

Main Shareholders:

Millennium Partners	26.3
Ideal Trade Investments	15.8
Deutsche Bank	13.2
The Value Catalyst Fund	10.5
Omni Worldwide	5.3
Percentage of free market capital:	17.9%

Comments:
Investment manager Vina Capital has invested nearly a third of the $9.5m raised prior to admission in three investments in Vietnam. Two are unlisted concerns and one is the privatised Vietnamese milk producer. The country has moved from a centrally controlled economy to a more market-based system in recent years and Vina hopes to make the most of these liberal reforms. Despite the dong to dollar exchange rate remaining stable, any investment in this area still comes with large risks. Returns will be paid in dividends.

Nominated Adviser:	Grant Thornton, London
AIM Broker:	Collins Stewart, London
Solicitors:	Lawrence Graham, London
Market Makers:	CSCS; WINS
Auditors:	Grant Thornton, 15th Floor, Bitexco Building, 19-25 Nguyen Hue, District 1, Ho Chi Minh City, Vietnam
Registrars:	HSBC

ENTRY ON AIM:	30/9/2003	**Recent price:**	1.2p
Interim results:	n/a	**Market cap:**	£0.11m
Final results:	n/a	**Issue price:**	n/a
Year end:	n/a	**Current no of shares:**	
Accounts due:	n/a		9,500,000
Int div paymnt:	n/a	**No of shares after**	
Fin div paymnt:	n/a	**dilution:**	n/a
Int net div per share:	nil	**P/E ratio:**	n/a
Fin net div per share:	nil	**Probable CGT?**	No

LATEST REPORTED RESULTS:		PREVIOUS REPORTED RESULTS:	
	N/A		N/A
Turnover:	n/a	**Turnover:**	n/a
PTP:	n/a	**PTP:**	n/a
EPS:	n/a	**EPS:**	n/a

Virotec International (VTI)
Removal of toxic metals from waste water
PO Box 188, Hope Island, 4212, Queensland Australia, Tel: 00-1 61 7 5530 8014; Fax: 00-1 61 7 5530 8052;
e-mail: mail@virotec.com; web site: www.virotec.com

		holding %
Chairman	Brian Sheeran	1.6
Chief Executive		
Finance Director	Bruno Bamonte	0.7
Non-Exec Director	Michael Nissen	3.9

Main Shareholders:

Odd Lot Nominees	10.9
Fidelity Investments	10.0
Mr N. Wray	7.6
Prestbury Investments	4.1
Mr N. Leslau	4.1
Percentage of free market capital:	53.7%

Comments:
Virotec focuses on environmental services and mining. Its Basecon treatment turns toxic 'red mud' produced from alumina manufacture into transportable waste product and Bauxsol uses the same waste to clean up contaminated water supplies. It has recently been part of a successful tender for an arsenic-contaminated site in Albania worth £760,000, of which it will receive 30% of the proceeds. Revenues are small and losses are still substantial.

Nominated Adviser:	Numis, London
AIM Broker:	Numis, London
Solicitors:	Fox Brooks Marshall, Manchester
Market Makers:	ALTI; SCAP; SGSL; WDBM; WINS
Auditors:	KPMG, Queensland 4217, Australia
Registrars:	Computershare Investor Services

Entry on AIM:	18/7/2001	**Recent price:**	21.25p
Interim results:	Mar	**Market cap:**	£41.12m
Final results:	Sep	**Issue price:**	14.0p
Year end:	Jun	**Current no of shares:**	
Accounts due:	Oct		193,493,841
Int div paymnt:	n/a	**No of shares after**	
Fin div paymnt:	n/a	**dilution:**	n/a
Int net div per share:	nil	**P/E ratio:**	n/a
Fin net div per share:	nil	**Probable CGT?**	Yes

LATEST REPORTED RESULTS:		PREVIOUS REPORTED RESULTS:	
	2003		2002
Turnover:	A$1.66m	**Turnover:**	A$1.54m
PTP:	A$(5.62m)	**PTP:**	A$(5.12m)
EPS:	Ac(0.0)	**EPS:**	Ac(0.0)

Virtue Broadcasting (VTB)
Distributor of digital media
Tornado House, Pound Lane, Marlow, Buckinghamshire SL7 2AF Tel: 01628-498 600; Fax: 01628-498610;
e-mail: ir@tornadogroup.com; web site: www.tornadogroup.com

		holding %
Chairman	Michael Neville	0.3
Chief Executive	Klaus Ackerstaft	0.2
Finance Director	James Ormondroyd	0.0
Non-Exec Director	Giles English	8.6

Main Shareholders:

Interoute Finance	13.4
John Kinnear	6.4
S Campbell	4.7
MVI Group	4.5
Zodiak Venture Capital	4.5

Percentage of free market capital: 46%

Comments:
Virtue Broadcasting has been on the acquisition trail of late and there is no sign of this abating. In 2003, it purchased communications solutions provider Unit.net and Swedish webcasting and content distribution company Kamera Holdings, the latter for £2.4m. To assist in paying for the acquisitions, it raised £1.8m through two placings at a 30% discount. The company is now looking to raise further funds to finance new acquisitions in its pipeline.

Nominated Adviser:	Brewin Dolphin, Leeds
AIM Broker:	Brewin Dolphin, Newcastle
Solicitors:	Taylor Wessing, London
Market Makers:	KBCS; MLSB; SCAP; WINS
Auditors:	PricewaterhouseCoopers, London
Registrars:	Capita Registrars

Entry on AIM:	7/3/2000	**Recent price:**	4.25p
Interim results:	Sep	**Market cap:**	£9.23m
Final results:	Jun	**Issue price:**	86.5p
Year end:	Dec	**Current no of shares:**	
Accounts due:	May		217,076,596
Int div paymnt:	n/a	**No of shares after**	
Fin div paymnt:	n/a	**dilution:**	n/a
Int net div per share:	nil	**P/E ratio:**	n/a
Fin net div per share:	nil	**Probable CGT?**	**Yes**

LATEST REPORTED RESULTS:		PREVIOUS REPORTED RESULTS:	
	2002		**2001**
Turnover:	£2.21m	**Turnover:**	£1.72m
PTP:	£(9.86m)	**PTP:**	£(9.48m)
EPS:	(9.1)p	**EPS:**	(9.9)p

Vista Group (VST)
PVC door manufacturer
Unit 1, Prenton Way, North Cheshire Trading Estate, Wirral, Merseyside CH43 3DU

		holding %
Chairman	Gavin Johnson	10.0
Chief Executive	Georg Sadler	25.0
Finance Director		
Non-Exec Director	Keith Salisbury	6.6

Main Shareholders:

Ian Currie	8.7
Richard Hughes	8.7
Michael Halsall	6.4
Amanda Johnson	5.0
Paul Stanton	4.0

Percentage of free market capital: 22.7%

Comments:
Vista is a maker of door panels and composite doors from PVC, glass reinforced polymer and foam. Customers include local authorities and house builders, with demand being driven by new building. But the most significant growth is coming from the home improvement and social housing markets, where its products suit because of their durability, higher security and low maintenance. Vista made pre-tax profits of £818,000 last year, on a turnover of £6.4m.

Nominated Adviser:	WH Ireland, Manchester
AIM Broker:	WH Ireland, Manchester
Solicitors:	Wacks Caller, Manchester
Market Makers:	WINS
Auditors:	Chadwick, Tevevision House, 10/12 Mount Street, Manchester M2 4JU
Registrars:	Neville Registrars

Entry on AIM:	19/12/2003	**Recent price:**	100.5p
Interim results:	Sep	**Market cap:**	£15.46m
Final results:	Mar	**Issue price:**	95.0p
Year end:	Dec	**Current no of shares:**	
Accounts due:	Jun		15,382,116
Int div paymnt:	n/a	**No of shares after**	
Fin div paymnt:	n/a	**dilution:**	n/a
Int net div per share:	nil	**P/E ratio:**	n/a
Fin net div per share:	nil	**Probable CGT?**	**Yes**

LATEST REPORTED RESULTS:		PREVIOUS REPORTED RESULTS:	
	2002		**2001**
Turnover:	£6.39m	**Turnover:**	£5.40m
PTP:	£818,000	**PTP:**	£1.01m
EPS:	n/a	**EPS:**	n/a

Vitesse Media (VIS)

Print and on-line publishing

95 Aldwych, London, WC2B 4JF Tel: 020-7430 9777; Fax: 020-7430 9888;
e-mail: info@vitessemedia.com; web site: www.vitessemedia.com

		holding %
Chairman	Sara Williams	49.0
Chief Executive	as above	
Finance Director	Nicola Brookes	0.1
Editorial Director	Leslie Copeland	0.0

Main Shareholders:

Bob Morton	14.4
Artemis AIM VCT	12.8
Peter Williams (non-exec director)	7.0

Percentage of free market capital: 16.6%

Comments:

Vitesse, a leading print and online publisher in the enterprise sector, turned a £51,000 loss into a pre-tax profit of £30,000 at the interim stage. The group, whose products include Growth Company Investor, Business XL, The AIM Guide, and the Lloyds TSB Small Business Guide, increased revenues nearly 6% to £0.95m. Since these results, the group has completed two small acquistions, buying investment website thewrongprice.com and the Investor All-Star Awards, a prestigious annual event for the investment and venture capital community.

Nominated Adviser:	KBC Peel Hunt, London
AIM Broker:	KBC Peel Hunt, London
Solicitors:	Mayer, Brown, Rowe & Maw, London
Market Makers:	KBCS; WINS
Auditors:	Baker Tilly, 2 Bloomsbury Street, London WC1B 3ST
Registrars:	Computershare Investor Services

Entry on AIM:	3/10/2001	**Recent price:**	32.0p
Interim results:	Sep	**Market cap:**	£4.18m
Final results:	Apr	**Issue price:**	24.5p
Year end:	Jan	**Current no of shares:**	
Accounts due:	May		13,047,844
Int div paymnt:	n/a	**No of shares after**	
Fin div paymnt:	n/a	**dilution:**	14,051,685
Int net div per share:	nil	**P/E ratio:**	n/a
Fin net div per share:	nil	**Probable CGT?**	Yes

LATEST REPORTED RESULTS:	2003	PREVIOUS REPORTED RESULTS:	2002
Turnover:	£1.50m	Turnover:	£1.37m
PTP:	£(363,000)	PTP:	£(45,000)
EPS:	(2.8)p	EPS:	(0.4)p

Vitesse Media plc

Providing essential insights for entrepreneurs & investors

Founded in 1997, **Vitesse Media** is a growing publishing and media business, specialising in business, investment and tax. Its titles include:

Business

Business XL, www.smallbusiness.co.uk, Lloyds TSB Small Business Guide, www.growthbusiness.co.uk, The AIM Guide

Tax

Tax-Effective Investor, Lloyds TSB Tax Guide, www.taxguide.co.uk

Investment

Growth Company Investor, www.growthcompany.co.uk, www.smallcompanies.co.uk, www.thewrongprice.com

Events

Growth Company Awards, Quoted Company Awards, Investor Allstars

The company's focus is on its high-quality content, its customer care and its profitability. Visit www.vitessemedia.com for more details.

95 Aldwych, London WC2B 4JF
Tel:020-7430 9777 Fax:020-7430 9888
info@growthcompany.co.uk

Vitesse Media plc

Volvere (VLE)

Investment vehicle
9-11 Grosvenor Gardens, London, SW1W 0BD

		holding %
Chairman	Sir Stanley Kalms	6.9
Chief Executive	Jonathan Lander*	9.7
Finance Director	Nicholas Lander	0.7
Non-Exec Director	Neil Ashley**	13.9

Main Shareholders:

Dawnay Day International	13.9
Friedman Billings Ramsey	13.9
JP Morgan Fleming Asset Management	9.7
United Gulf Bank	7.8
Dawnay Day Lander*	6.9

Percentage of free market capital: 11.1%

* Jonathan Lander's holding includes that of Dawnay Day Lander
** Neil Ashley's holding includes that of Jasmine Trustees (6.9%)

Comments:

Last May this turnaround specialist bought Vectra, a loss-making division of support services giant Amey for £2m cash. Vectra has clients in the oil, gas, nuclear, transport, defence and other sectors. Backers include Dixons legend Sir Stanley Kalms and Amey's founder Neil Ashley. The team is led by Jonathan Lander of bank Dawnay Day Lander and assisted by Kalms' son Richard. At the end of the year net assets stood at £4m, of which cash was £3.3m. Vectra made a £0.5m profit on £7.1m turnover.

Nominated Adviser:	Dawnay Day, London
AIM Broker:	Teather & Greenwood, London
Solicitors:	Hammonds, London
Market Makers:	TEAM; WINS
Auditors:	Deloitte & Touche, Reading, Berkshire
Registrars:	Capita Registrars

ENTRY ON AIM: 24/12/2002	**Recent price:**	175.0p
Interim results:	Aug	**Market cap:**	£6.32m
Final results:	Mar	**Issue price:**	100.0p
Year end:	Dec	**Current no of shares:**	
Accounts due:	Aug		3,609,720
Int div paymnt:	n/a	**No of shares after**	
Fin div paymnt:	n/a	**dilution:**	n/a
Int net div per share:	nil	**P/E ratio:**	n/a
Fin net div per share:	nil	**Probable CGT?**	**No**

LATEST REPORTED RESULTS: INTERIM RESULTS TO 30 JUNE '03	PREVIOUS REPORTED RESULTS: N/A
Turnover: £1.31m	**Turnover:** n/a
PTP: £(186,000)	**PTP:** n/a
EPS: (6.1)p	**EPS:** n/a

Voss Net (VOS)

Learning services supplier
42-46 High Street, Esher, Surrey, KT10 9QY Tel: 01753-737800; Fax: 01753-737850;
e-mail: enquiries@vossnet.co.uk; web site: www.vossnet.co.uk

		holding %
Chairman	Leo Knifton	0.0
Managing Director	Jeremy Gilbert	10.6
Finance Director	Robert Burns*	0.3
Director	Nigel Weller	0.0

Main Shareholders:

Zaika Limited	29.9
Westcombe Investments	15.6
International Advance	6.9
Thibault Capital Markets	6.6
Westcombe Investments	5.3

Percentage of free market capital: 24.8%

*Robert Burns holds a 25% indirect interest in 55,555 shares

Comments:

Having recently disposed of freight software systems subsidiary Sigma to management (generating a £21,000 profit), Voss Net now focuses exclusively on its training operations. The problem is that, following a dispute with a London college with regard to unpaid invoices, this division endured a difficult first half of 2003 and so last year's £175,000 interim profit turned into a £338,423 loss. Fortunately much of the cash owed has since been recouped.

Nominated Adviser:	City Financial Associates, London
AIM Broker:	City Financial Associates, London
Solicitors:	Watson, Farley & Williams, London
Market Makers:	SCAP; WINS
Auditors:	Hugill, 18 Bedford Row, London WC1R 4EB
Registrars:	Capita Registrars

Entry on AIM: 14/8/1995	**Recent price:**	1.25p
Interim results:	Jan	**Market cap:**	£2.04m
Final results:	Sep	**Issue price:**	143.0p
Year end:	Nov	**Current no of shares:**	
Accounts due:	Nov		163,036,902
Int div paymnt:	n/a	**No of shares after**	
Fin div paymnt:	n/a	**dilution:**	n/a
Int net div per share:	nil	**P/E ratio:**	n/a
Fin net div per share:	nil	**Probable CGT?**	**YES**

LATEST REPORTED RESULTS: 2002	PREVIOUS REPORTED RESULTS: 2001
Turnover: £1.13m	**Turnover:** £921,000
PTP: £(321,000)	**PTP:** £(1.06m)
EPS: (0.9)p	**EPS:** (13.3)p

Walker Greenbank (WGB)

Wall coverings & fabrics designer & distributor

Bradbourne Drive, Tilbrook, Milton Keynes, Buckinghamshire MK7 8BE Tel: 08708-300365; Fax: 08708-300364;
web site: www.walkergreenbank.com

		holding %
Chairman	Ian Kirkham	0.2
Chief Executive		
Finance Director	John Sach	0.1
Non-Exec Director	Peter Harkness	0.2

Main Shareholders:

Union Discount Company	30.0
Merrill Lynch	6.1
Walker Greenbank EBT	4.3
British Airways Pension Trustees	4.2
Framlington	3.4

Percentage of free market capital: 51.6%

Comments:

Wall coverings and furnishing fabrics business Walker Greenbank is slowly emerging from the gloom. The first half saw sales drop by £4m to £21m but losses, on an operating level at least, were reduced slightly, while debts were cut by £2.5m to a three-year low of £4.8m. Moreover a second-half trading update has confirmed that losses continue to fall. A £4.7m sale and lease-back of the company's Milton Keynes base should ensure further debt reduction.

Nominated Adviser:	Brewin Dolphin, London		
AIM Broker:	Brewin Dolphin, London		
Solicitors:	CMS Cameron McKenna, London		
Market Makers:	WINS		
Auditors:	PricewaterhouseCoopers, London		
Registrars:	Capita Registrars		

ENTRY ON AIM:	15/4/2003	**Recent price:**	14.75p
Interim results:	Oct	**Market cap:**	£8.7m
Final results:	Apr	**Issue price:**	1.1p
Year end:	Jan	**Current no of shares:**	
Accounts due:	May		59,006,162
Int div paymnt:	n/a	**No of shares after**	
Fin div paymnt:	n/a	**dilution:**	n/a
Int net div per share:	nil	**P/E ratio:**	n/a
Fin net div per share:	nil	**Probable CGT?**	Yes

LATEST REPORTED RESULTS: 2003		PREVIOUS REPORTED RESULTS: 2002	
Turnover:	£58.26m	**Turnover:**	£61.12m
PTP:	£(7.98m)	**PTP:**	£(6.63m)
EPS:	(13.0)p	**EPS:**	(11.7)p

Warthog (WHOG)

Entertainment software developer

10 Eden Place, Cheadle, Cheshire SK8 1AT Tel: 0161-491 5131; Fax: 0161-610 3033;
e-mail: investors@warthog.co.uk; web site: www.warthog.co.uk

		holding %
Chairman	Ian Templeton	0.0
Chief Executive	Ashley Hall	12.4
Finance Director	Simon Elms	2.6
Operations Director	Steven Law	0.5

Main Shareholders:

Close Brothers	10.0
Eric Elms	5.0
Philip Meller	4.8
Nicholas Elms	4.8
Derek Senior	4.1

Percentage of free market capital: 52.9%

Comments:

Embattled games developer Warthog has shifted strategy. It now looks to partner with owners of lucrative intellectual property. This follows a shift in the industry where developers are forced to spend their own cash bidding for projects they might never get. The half to September was dire for Warthog indeed, with profits of £134,000 slipping to a £2.6m loss after provisions against publishers gone bust, and against cancelled and delayed games. Sales softened to £4.95m (£5.4m).

Nominated Adviser:	Evolution Beeson Gregory, London		
AIM Broker:	Evolution Beeson Gregory, London		
Solicitors:	Halliwell Landau, Manchester		
Market Makers:	BGMM; SCAP; WINS		
Auditors:	Baker Tilly, Manchester		
Registrars:	Capita Registrars		

Entry on AIM:	1/2/2003	**Recent price:**	2.5p
Interim results:	Dec	**Market cap:**	£3.07m
Final results:	Jun	**Issue price:**	43.0p
Year end:	Mar	**Current no of shares:**	
Accounts due:	Jul		122,603,610
Int div paymnt:	n/a	**No of shares after**	
Fin div paymnt:	n/a	**dilution:**	n/a
Int net div per share:	nil	**P/E ratio:**	3.6
Fin net div per share:	nil	**Probable CGT?**	Yes

LATEST REPORTED RESULTS: 2003		PREVIOUS REPORTED RESULTS: 2002	
Turnover:	£11.42m	**Turnover:**	£8.86m
PTP:	£(791,000)	**PTP:**	£488,000
EPS:	0.7p	**EPS:**	(0.9)p

Water Hall (WTH)

Landfill and quarrying group

8-10 Leapale Rd, Guildford, Surrey GU1 4JX Tel: 01483-452333; Fax: 01483-452322

		holding %
Chairman	John Leach	0.0
Chief Executive		
Finance Director		
Director	Raschid Abdullah	6.8

Main Shareholders:

Charwell Investments	26.4
Fontwell Investements	20.4
El-Khereiji Trading & Electronics	4.8
Selva	4.8
Intrinsic Value	3.6
Percentage of free market capital: 33.2%	

Comments:

Water Hall has implemented a programme to convert its depleted mineral and landfill reserves to cash while at the same time keeping a tight rein on costs. It is now focusing on its recycling activities and will invest where appropriate. This is after the company failed to receive planning permission for further gravel extraction and landfill operations at the Water Hall Complex where its existing operations are based. The company is in profit. NAV was £2.7m.

Nominated Adviser:	Rowan Dartington, Bristol		
AIM Broker:	Rowan Dartington, Bristol		
Solicitors:	Norton Rose, London		
Market Makers:	KBCS; WINS		
Auditors:	Deloitte & Touche, Reading		
Registrars:	Capita Registrars		
ENTRY ON AIM:	5/7/2001	**Recent price:**	4.0p
Interim results:	Sep	**Market cap:**	£2.25m
Final results:	Apr	**Issue price:**	n/a
Year end:	Dec	**Current no of shares:**	
Accounts due:	May		56,291,102
Int div paymnt:	n/a	**No of shares after**	
Fin div paymnt:	n/a	**dilution:**	n/a
Int net div per share:	nil	**P/E ratio:**	n/a
Fin net div per share:	nil	**Probable CGT?**	Yes

LATEST REPORTED RESULTS: 2002		PREVIOUS REPORTED RESULTS: 2001	
Turnover:	£7.09m	**Turnover:**	£7.13m
PTP:	£(2.80m)	**PTP:**	£(173,000)
EPS:	(5.6)p	**EPS:**	(0.5)p

Watford Leisure (WFC)

Football club operator

Vicarage Road Stadium, Watford, Hertfordshire WD18 0ER Tel: 01923-496000; Fax: 01923-496001;
e-mail: yourvoice@watfordfc.com; web site: www.watfordfc.com

		holding %
Chairman	Graham Simpson	23.0
Chief Executive	as above	
Finance Director		
Non-Exec Director	Andrew Wilson	0.0

Main Shareholders:

Haig Oundjian	15.3
Elton John	8.4
David Lester	7.6
Fordwat	5.2
Strand Associates	4.8
Percentage of free market capital: 27.5%	

Comments:

Watford's losses have continued, affected by the end of Premiership parachute payments and the demise of ITV Digital. The club reached the FA Cup semi-final in 2003 but only came 13th in the 1st Division. Its chief executive has stepped down and its shares consolidated with one share for every 1,000. Recently, it raised £5.25m through a placing for its 'Let's buy back the Vic' campaign in its attempt to buy back the freehold of its Vicarage Road Stadium.

Nominated Adviser:	Strand Partners, London		
AIM Broker:	Seymour Pierce Ellis, Crawley		
Solicitors:	Teacher Stern Selby, London		
Market Makers:	SCAP; WINS		
Auditors:	Chantrey Vellacott DFK, Watford		
Registrars:	Capita Registrars		
Entry on AIM:	2/8/2001	**Recent price:**	82.5p
Interim results:	Mar	**Market cap:**	£8.67m
Final results:	Oct	**Issue price:**	1.0p
Year end:	Jun	**Current no of shares:**	
Accounts due:	Oct		10,511,750
Int div paymnt:	n/a	**No of shares after**	
Fin div paymnt:	n/a	**dilution:**	n/a
Int net div per share:	nil	**P/E ratio:**	n/a
Fin net div per share:	nil	**Probable CGT?**	Yes

LATEST REPORTED RESULTS: 2003		PREVIOUS REPORTED RESULTS: 2002	
Turnover:	£8.67m	**Turnover:**	£16.82m
PTP:	£(10.28m)	**PTP:**	£(7.17m)
EPS:	(0.3)p	**EPS:**	(0.3)p

Wealth Management Software   (WMS)

Financial services software developer and supplier
Fountain House, Great Cornbow, Halesowen, West Midlands B63 3BL Tel: 0121-550 9222; Fax: 0121-550 0722;
e-mail: info@wms-plc.com; web site: www.wms-plc.com

		holding %
Chairman	Paul Newton	7.8
Chief Executive	as above	
Chief Financial	Giles Trigg	0.0
Officer	Paul Foll	4.5
Sales Director		
Main Shareholders:		
Eaglet Investment Trust		23.0
M&G Investment		10.8
Michael Whale		8.1
3i		4.8
Active Capital Trust		3.0
Percentage of free market capital: 26%		

Nominated Adviser:	Evolution Beeson Gregory, London
AIM Broker:	Evolution Beeson Gregory, London
Solicitors:	Pinsents, Birmingham
Market Makers:	BGMM; WINS
Auditors:	Deloitte & Touche, 4 Brindley Place, Birmingham B1 7HZ
Registrars:	Capita Registrars

Entry on AIM:	1/6/2000	Recent price:	14.75p
Interim results:	Sep	Market cap:	£6.19m
Final results:	Mar	Issue price:	130.0p
Year end:	Dec	Current no of shares:	
Accounts due:	Apr		41,967,049
Int div paymnt:	n/a	No of shares after	
Fin div paymnt:	n/a	dilution:	47,884,192
Int net div per share:	nil	P/E ratio:	n/a
Fin net div per share:	nil	Probable CGT?	Yes

LATEST REPORTED RESULTS: 2002		PREVIOUS REPORTED RESULTS: 2001	
Turnover:	£11.0m	Turnover:	£12.01m
PTP:	£(1.06m)	PTP:	£(6.35m)
EPS:	(2.7)p	EPS:	(14.7)p

Comments:

WMS' hitherto impressive turnaround has been rocked by the unexpected news that major client PPML plans to terminate both its licence and support agreements with the company. The management of WMS believe there are no grounds for this termination and thus fees relating to as yet uninvoiced work are being sought. Should these remain unpaid, however, the company's profits will fail to match expectations. First half profits have increased from £15,000 to £208,000.

Weatherly   (WTI)

Cash shell
Carmelite, 50 Victoria Embankment, Blackfriars, London, EC4Y 0DX;
e-mail: info@weatherlysecurities.com; web site: www.weatherlysecurities.com

		holding %
Chairman	Peter Redmond	0.0
Chief Executive		
Finance Director	Fred J Buglion	0.0
Director	Richard Armstrong	5.7
Main Shareholders:		
SJB Ventures		8.9
Merchant House		7.6
Chase Nominees		5.7
Raj de Mendonca		5.7
Foliacura		3.8
Percentage of free market capital: 59%		

Nominated Adviser:	Nabarro Wells, London
AIM Broker:	n/a
Solicitors:	Eversheds, London
Market Makers:	MLSB; SCAP; WINS
Auditors:	BDO Seidman, New York
Registrars:	Capita Registrars

Entry on AIM:	30/5/2000	Recent price:	6.5p
Interim results:	Mar	Market cap:	£2.96m
Final results:	Mar	Issue price:	8.0p
Year end:	Dec	Current no of shares:	
Accounts due:	Apr		45,531,468
Int div paymnt:	n/a	No of shares after	
Fin div paymnt:	n/a	dilution:	n/a
Int net div per share:	nil	P/E ratio:	n/a
Fin net div per share:	nil	Probable CGT?	No

LATEST REPORTED RESULTS: 2002		PREVIOUS REPORTED RESULTS: 2001	
Turnover:	n/a	Turnover:	£12.57m
PTP:	£(1.58m)	PTP:	£(3.34m)
EPS:	(0.8)p	EPS:	(1.8)p

Comments:

Weatherly was due to de-list last year in the wake of potential complaints from clients of the US broker which used to trade under this name until its premises succumbed on 11 September 2001. Now the company has been resurrected as a cash shell seeking a new direction, after being cleaned up by Richard Armstrong and Peter Redmond, the duo behind several other AIM shells. They have managed to inject £250,000 of fresh capital into the business as well at 3p a share.

Web Shareshop (WSS)

Small cap resources investor

123 Goldsworth Road, Woking, Surrey GU21 1LR   Tel: 01483-771992;   Fax: 01483-772087;
e-mail: info@webshareshop.com;   web site: www.webshareshop.co.uk

		holding %
Chairman	Bruce Rowan	27.3
Chief Executive	as above	
Finance Director	John Watkins	2.4
Non-Exec Director	Tony Scutt	0.0

Main Shareholders:

Andrew Neubauer	13.0
John McNair	4.8

Percentage of free market capital: 52.5%

Comments:
Bruce Rowan, 29.9% holder of Web Shareshop, bemoans its 50% discount to assets. Two-thirds are represented by surging Southern African Resources. Mining holdings include Brazilian Diamonds, Gippsland and Beowulf. Among others are My Home and controversial Matisse (formerly Prestige Publishing). Rowan, aiming to add more non-miners, came into Web Shareshop at 2.5p in 2001 and states a target price of 30p.

Nominated Adviser:	Grant Thornton, Portsmouth		
AIM Broker:	Keith Bayley Rogers, London		
Solicitors:	Ronaldsons, London		
Market Makers:	KBCS; WINS		
Auditors:	Grant Thornton, Slough, Bucks SL1 2LS		
Registrars:	Capita Registrars		

ENTRY ON AIM:	5/9/2000	Recent price:	13.5p
Interim results:	Feb	Market cap:	£4.24m
Final results:	Sep	Issue price:	30.0p
Year end:	Jul	Current no of shares:	
Accounts due:	Nov		31,390,430
Int div paymnt:	n/a	No of shares after	
Fin div paymnt:	n/a	dilution:	n/a
Int net div per share:	nil	P/E ratio:	67.5
Fin net div per share:	nil	Probable CGT?	No

LATEST REPORTED RESULTS: 2003		PREVIOUS REPORTED RESULTS: 2002	
Turnover:	£160,000	Turnover:	£429
PTP:	£41,000	PTP:	£(349,000)
EPS:	0.2p	EPS:	(1.5)p

West 175 Media (suspended 12 Aug 2003) (WEP)

Television programme producer and broadcaster

19 High Street, Thames Ditton, Surrey KT7 0EY   Tel: 020-8398 7175;   Fax: 020-8398 7733;
e-mail: pa@west175media.com;   web site: www.west175media.com

		holding %
Chairman	David Montgomery	0.0
Chief Executive	as above	
Finance Director		
Deputy Chairman	C. Sebag-Montefiore	0.7

Main Shareholders:

John Gunn (Non-Exec Director)	10.9
SP Angel	10.8
Invesco Perpetual	8.3
NCL Investment Management	6.9
Goldman Sachs International	4.8

Percentage of free market capital: 46.4%

Comments:
Despite appointing former Mirror Group chief executive David Montgomery as chairman, this group remains troubled. The shares were suspended last August at 1.6p although now the company says 'a third party has been identified' to invest sufficient funds to cover a cash dividend to creditors and, importantly, to settle creditors voluntary arrangement (CVA) fees. When the CVA is arranged, the company says 'further funds will be raised' to enable it to become a shell and 'acquire a suitable business'. Here's hoping.

Nominated Adviser:	Numis, London		
AIM Broker:	Numis, London		
Solicitors:	City Law Partnership, London		
Market Makers:	ALTI; BGMM; MLSB; TEAM; WINS		
Auditors:	Baker Tilly, 2 Bloomsbury Street, London WC1B 3ST		
Registrars:	Capita Registrars		

Entry on AIM:	30/7/1996	Recent price:	1.5p
Interim results:	Dec	Market cap:	£0.34m
Final results:	Sep	Issue price:	125.0p
Year end:	Mar	Current no of shares:	
Accounts due:	Sep		22,558,229
Int div paymnt:	n/a	No of shares after	
Fin div paymnt:	n/a	dilution:	24,853,465
Int net div per share:	nil	P/E ratio:	n/a
Fin net div per share:	nil	Probable CGT?	Yes

LATEST REPORTED RESULTS: 2002		PREVIOUS REPORTED RESULTS: 2001	
Turnover:	$11.91m	Turnover:	$8.70m
PTP:	$(16.87m)	PTP:	$(7.56m)
EPS:	(0.8)c	EPS:	(0.4)c

West Bromwich Albion (WBA)

Professional football club operator

The Tom Silk Building, Halfords Lane, West Bromwich, B71 4BR   Tel: 0121-525 8888;   Fax: 0121-524 3462;
e-mail: baggies@wba.co.uk;   web site: www.wba.co.uk

		holding %
Chairman	Jeremy Peace	31.1
Chief Executive		
Finance Director	Mark Jenkins	0.0
Director	Joseph Brandrick	1.5

Main Shareholders:

Kappa	29.3
Paul Thompson	25.3
A Hale	3.4
John Hale	3.2

Percentage of free market capital: 6.3%

Comments:

Despite relegation from the elite division, the first division outfit is flourishing both on and off the pitch as it attempts to bounce back at the first attempt. Interims to December showed a move from a £300,000 loss to a £700,000 profit, on a lower turnover of £11m (£14.8m) – net funds improved to £1.5m (£600,000). Despite falling average attendances, the figures benefited from high season ticket renewals, as well as strong retail, conference and banqueting revenues.

Nominated Adviser:	Arbuthnot, Birmingham	
AIM Broker:	Arbuthnot, Birmingham	
Solicitors:	DLA, Birmingham	
Market Makers:	ARBT; KBCS; WINS	
Auditors:	Clement Keys, 4/5 Calthorpe Rd, Birmingham B15 1RL	
Registrars:	Neville Registrars	

ENTRY ON AIM:	3/1/1997	**Recent price:**	6500.0p
Interim results:	Mar	**Market cap:**	£5.66m
Final results:	Sep	**Issue price:**	280.0p
Year end:	Jun	**Current no of shares:**	
Accounts due:	Oct		87,107
Int div paymnt:	Jun	**No of shares after**	
Fin div paymnt:	Jun	**dilution:**	139,915
Int net div per share:	nil	**P/E ratio:**	n/a
Fin net div per share:	170.0p	**Probable CGT?**	YES

LATEST REPORTED RESULTS: 2003		PREVIOUS REPORTED RESULTS: 2002	
Turnover:	£28.4m	**Turnover:**	£14.28m
PTP:	£(639,000)	**PTP:**	£2.57m
EPS:	(363.0)p	**EPS:**	118.0p

Western Selection (WSE)

Investment company

25 City Road, London, EC1Y 1BQ   Tel: 020-7448 8950;   Fax: 020-7638 9426;
e-mail: info@westernselection.co.uk;   web site: www.westernselection.co.uk

		holding %
Chairman	DC Marshall	0.1
Managing Director	ARC Barclay	0.1
Finance Director		
Non-Exec Director	JM Robotham	0.2

Main Shareholders:

London Finance & Investment Group	40.5
W T Lamb	11.5
Fidelity Investment Services	6.9
Thomas Charlton	3.5
J A Whybrow & S R M Wilson	3.2

Percentage of free market capital: 33.6%

Comments:

Net assets per share at the idiosyncratic investment concern improved 21% during the second half of 2003 to 24.4p, helped by the markets and a strong performance at marketing services business Creston. Funds are split between a general portfolio and strategic stakes in certain companies. All are cash generative except OFEX-listed Doctors Direct. Another major investment is toiletries producer Swallowfield, where trading has been tough lately. A previous success is rock manager Sanctuary.

Nominated Adviser:	Deloitte & Touche, London	
AIM Broker:	JM Finn, London	
Solicitors:	n/a	
Market Makers:	MLSB; SCAP; WINS	
Auditors:	BDO Stoy Hayward, 69 Tweedy Road, Bromley, Kent BR1 3WA	
Registrars:	Capita Registrars	

Entry on AIM:	17/1/1996	**Recent price:**	15.0p
Interim results:	Feb	**Market cap:**	£6.53m
Final results:	Aug	**Issue price:**	14.0p
Year end:	Jun	**Current no of shares:**	
Accounts due:	Aug		43,511,903
Int div paymnt:	n/a	**No of shares after**	
Fin div paymnt:	Oct	**dilution:**	n/a
Int net div per share:	nil	**P/E ratio:**	25.0
Fin net div per share:	0.52p	**Probable CGT?**	No

LATEST REPORTED RESULTS: 2003		PREVIOUS REPORTED RESULTS: 2002	
Turnover:	n/a	**Turnover:**	n/a
PTP:	£266,000	**PTP:**	£277,000
EPS:	0.6p	**EPS:**	0.6p

Westmount Energy

(WTE)

Energy investor & financier

PO Box 298, 23-25 Broad Street, St Helier, Jersey JE4 8TL Tel: 01534-282591; Fax: 01534-282579;
e-mail: dgwwestmount@aol.com

		holding %
Chairman	Derek G Williams	13.5
Managing Director	as above	
Finance Director		
Director	Marc Yates	1.9

Main Shareholders:

John Saville 7.0

Percentage of free market capital: 75.7%

Nominated Adviser:	Oriel Securities, London
AIM Broker:	Oriel Securities, London
Solicitors:	Clyde & Co, London
Market Makers:	IHCS; KBCS; MLSB; SCAP; WINS
Auditors:	Moore Stephens, St. Helier, Jersey
Registrars:	Capita Registrars

Entry on AIM:	2/10/1995	**Recent price:**	65.0p
Interim results:	Mar	**Market cap:**	£9.68m
Final results:	Nov	**Issue price:**	15.0p
Year end:	Jun	**Current no of shares:**	
Accounts due:	Oct		14,888,361
Int div paymnt:	n/a	**No of shares after**	
Fin div paymnt:	n/a	**dilution:**	n/a
Int net div per share:	nil	**P/E ratio:**	n/a
Fin net div per share:	nil	**Probable CGT?**	No

LATEST REPORTED RESULTS: 2003		PREVIOUS REPORTED RESULTS: 2002	
Turnover:	£101,000	Turnover:	£165,000
PTP:	£(196,000)	PTP:	£(69,000)
EPS:	(1.6)p	EPS:	(0.7)p

Comments:
Westmount changed its passive investment stance by selling its 22% stake in Fusion Oil & Gas to Sterling Energy, another holding, which successfuly bid for Fusion. As a result, Westmount has 17% of Sterling, alone worth 48p a share, and stakes in Desire Petroleum and Eclipse Energy. Westmount, which lost £213,000 last year, also derives royalties on 0.5% of output from the North Sea's P241 licence (the Buchan Field).

Westside Acquisitions

(WST)

Investment business

Regent House, 5-7 Broadhurst Gardens, London, NW6 3RZ Tel: 020-7935 0823

		holding %
Chairman	Richard Owen	11.9
Managing Director	Geoffrey Simmonds	11.9
Finance Director	David Meddings	0.6
Non-Exec Director	John Zucker	3.6

Main Shareholders:

W J Weston	10.6
Galleon Nominees	4.9
Lafferty	3.9
W Roiter	3.6

Percentage of free market capital: 48.1%

Nominated Adviser:	Seymour Pierce, London
AIM Broker:	Seymour Pierce Ellis, Crawley
Solicitors:	Finers Stephens Innocent, London; Roiter Zucker, London
Market Makers:	SCAP; WINS
Auditors:	n/a
Registrars:	Capita Registrars

Entry on AIM:	8/12/1999	**Recent price:**	2.5p
Interim results:	Sep	**Market cap:**	£2.67m
Final results:	Mar	**Issue price:**	2.5p
Year end:	Dec	**Current no of shares:**	
Accounts due:	Jun		106,989,410
Int div paymnt:	n/a	**No of shares after**	
Fin div paymnt:	n/a	**dilution:**	n/a
Int net div per share:	nil	**P/E ratio:**	n/a
Fin net div per share:	nil	**Probable CGT?**	No

LATEST REPORTED RESULTS: 2002		PREVIOUS REPORTED RESULTS: 2001	
Turnover:	£714,000	Turnover:	£579,000
PTP:	£(1.0m)	PTP:	£(421,000)
EPS:	(1.3)p	EPS:	(0.6)p

Comments:
Westside has interests in early-stage companies and advisers to them. So far it has backed a five-a-side football league business and a struggling telecoms training firm amongst others. The directors have successfully rebutted attempts by some shareholders to replace some of the board. A share buyback programme continues and the group recently bought Reverse Takeover Investments, leaving it with £3m in cash at the end of June. Nothing has been reported since.

WH Ireland
Stockbroker

(WHI)

11 St. James's Square, Manchester, M2 6WH Tel: 0161-832 6644; Fax: 0161-833 0935; web site: www.wh-ireland.co.uk

		holding %
Chairman	Sir David Trippier	3.2
Chief Executive	Laurie Beevers	14.7
Finance Director	Derek Ashford	1.2
Managing Director	David Youngman	13.8

Main Shareholders:

Mohammed Marafie	21.4
T Davies*	4.7
John Eastgate	3.9
Nick Alexander	3.7
N Lawrence*	3.3

Percentage of free market capital: 23.1%

*Includes family trusts.

Comments:

The Mancunian small cap stockbroker has benefited from the stock market recovery, managing to turn the previous year's loss into a profit. Acquisitions, particularly of Cardiff brokers, have also helped. Funds under management grew 37% to £209m. WH Ireland's corporate finance team also advised on the highly successful £210 million float of Russian prospector Highland Gold Mining as well as nine others during the year. The first quarter of 2004 has proved bouyant as well.

Nominated Adviser:	Altium Capital, Manchester
AIM Broker:	WH Ireland, Manchester
Solicitors:	Halliwell Landau, Manchester
Market Makers:	ALTI; KBCS; SCAP; WINS
Auditors:	KPMG, 1 The Embankment, Neville Street, Leeds, LS1 4DW
Registrars:	Neville Registrars

Entry on AIM:	27/7/2000	**Recent price:**	80.5p
Interim results:	Aug	**Market cap:**	£16.27m
Final results:	Mar	**Issue price:**	115.0p
Year end:	Nov	**Current no of shares:**	
Accounts due:	Mar		20,215,746
Int div paymnt:	Oct	**No of shares after**	
Fin div paymnt:	Apr	**dilution:**	n/a
Int net div per share:	0.5p	**P/E ratio:**	n/a
Fin net div per share:	0.5p	**Probable CGT?**	No

LATEST REPORTED RESULTS: 2003		PREVIOUS REPORTED RESULTS: 2002	
Turnover:	£9.06m	Turnover:	£6.44m
PTP:	£188,000	PTP:	£(1.54m)
EPS:	0.4p	EPS:	(10.8)p

White Knight Investments
Investment company

(WKI)

138 Park Lane, London, W1K 7AS Tel: 020-7409 3500; Fax: 020-7409 3507

		holding %
Chairman	Malcolm Burne	1.5
Managing Director		
Finance Director	Nathan Steinberg	0.9
Non-Exec Director	Bruce Rowan*	0.0

Main Shareholders:

Sunvest Corporation*	25.5
Momichi	4.6
HSBC	3.8
Paul & Philippa Curtis	3.6
Ivybeam	3.4

Percentage of free market capital: 47.1%

*Bruce Rowan is a controlling shareholder in Sunvest

Comments:

Mining market heavyweights Bobby Danchin, ex-Anglo American director, and South African entrepreneur Rob Still agreed to join White Knight's board after it acquired Mistral Resources, with options on gold prospects in Ghana and Mozambique. Backed by Aussie investor Bruce Rowan, White Knight, which lost a halved £33,000 last year, raised £100,000 in March by selling shares at 4p to Eloro & Exploration.

Nominated Adviser:	Grant Thornton, London
AIM Broker:	Hoodless Brennan, London
Solicitors:	Field Fisher Waterhouse, London
Market Makers:	HOOD; MLSB; WINS
Auditors:	Grant Thornton, Southampton
Registrars:	Melton Registrars

Entry on AIM:	19/5/2000	**Recent price:**	3.5p
Interim results:	Oct	**Market cap:**	£6.67m
Final results:	Sep	**Issue price:**	4.0p
Year end:	Mar	**Current no of shares:**	
Accounts due:	Jul		190,500,000
Int div paymnt:	n/a	**No of shares after**	
Fin div paymnt:	n/a	**dilution:**	n/a
Int net div per share:	nil	**P/E ratio:**	n/a
Fin net div per share:	nil	**Probable CGT?**	No

LATEST REPORTED RESULTS: 2003		PREVIOUS REPORTED RESULTS: 2002	
Turnover:	n/a	Turnover:	n/a
PTP:	£(62,000)	PTP:	£(64,000)
EPS:	(0.1)p	EPS:	(0.1)p

Widney

(WDNY)

Telescopic slides and vehicle window systems manufacturer

Plume Street, Aston, Birmingham, B6 7SA Tel: 0121-327 5500; Fax: 0121-328 4934

		holding %
Chairman	Joe Grimmond	14.5
Chief Executive		
Finance Director	Graham Errington	11.3
Non-Exec Director	Michael Frye	16.8

Main Shareholders:

Gerry Cotterill	11.3
ISIS Asset Management	4.7

Percentage of free market capital: 41.2%

Nominated Adviser:	Williams de Broe, London
AIM Broker:	Williams de Broe, London
Solicitors:	Maclay Murray & Spens, London
Market Makers:	KBCS; WEST; WINS
Auditors:	KMPG, Milton Keynes, Buckinghamshire
Registrars:	Capita Registrars

ENTRY ON AIM:	2/7/2002	**Recent price:**	36.0p
Interim results:	May	**Market cap:**	£7.01m
Final results:	Dec	**Issue price:**	11.0p
Year end:	Sep	**Current no of shares:**	
Accounts due:	Jan		19,476,647
Int div paymnt:	Jun	**No of shares after**	
Fin div paymnt:	Feb	**dilution:**	n/a
Int net div per share: 0.25p		**P/E ratio:**	4.9
Fin net div per share: 0.5p		**Probable CGT?**	Yes

Comments:

Widney makes window systems for specialist vehicles and telescopic slides through its UK arm, along with metal press tools for the car industry through Belcot. Financials improved drastically last year. The group moved from losses to profit before tax on a £5m sales improvement, with strong cash generation bringing down gearing. This was despite tough trading across its various markets with Widney UK seeing weak demand and Belcot up against strong international competition.

LATEST REPORTED RESULTS: 2003		PREVIOUS REPORTED RESULTS: 2002	
Turnover:	£16.87m	Turnover:	£11.9m
PTP:	£(1.18m)	PTP:	£(18.000)
EPS:	7.4p	EPS:	(1.5)p

Wigmore

(WGT)

Provider of maintenance for UK buildings and parks

19 Cavendish Square, London, W1A 2AW Tel: 0845-070 1200; Fax: 0845-070 2300; e-mail: info@fpnm.co.uk

		holding %
Chairman	Peter Hewitt	1.2
Chief Executive		
Finance Director	Peter Grisman	0.2
Non-Exec Director	Keith Lassman	0.3

Main Shareholders:

n/a

Percentage of free market capital: 97.1%

Nominated Adviser:	Seymour Pierce, London
AIM Broker:	Seymour Pierce Ellis, Crawley
Solicitors:	Howard Kennedy, London
Market Makers:	SCAP; WINS
Auditors:	Baker Tilly, 2 Bloomsbury Street, London WC1B 3ST
Registrars:	SLC Registrars

Entry on AIM:	2/1/2002	**Recent price:**	2.75p
Interim results:	Sep	**Market cap:**	£5.77m
Final results:	Jun	**Issue price:**	3.0p
Year end:	Dec	**Current no of shares:**	
Accounts due:	Apr		209,711,111
Int div paymnt:	n/a	**No of shares after**	
Fin div paymnt:	n/a	**dilution:**	n/a
Int net div per share:	nil	**P/E ratio:**	n/a
Fin net div per share:	nil	**Probable CGT?**	Yes

Comments:

Through Speymill, FNPM, and DF Blanchard, Wigmore provides commercial building, construction and property refurbishment services. In the first half, operating losses waxed from £201,000 to £384,000 despite turnover rising 9% to £6.53m, but Wigmore traded profitably in May and June before amortisation. For 2003, the market expects a small pre-tax loss of £5,000, before Wigmore hopefully turns in underlying pre-tax profit of £650,000 for 2004.

LATEST REPORTED RESULTS: 2002		PREVIOUS REPORTED RESULTS: 2001	
Turnover:	£13.61m	Turnover:	£939,000
PTP:	£(763,000)	PTP:	£(584,000)
EPS:	(1.0)p	EPS:	(2.5)p

WILink

Financial information provider

11-12 Wigmore Place, London, W1U 2LU Tel: 020-7436 2223; Fax: 020-7307 1760;
e-mail: communications@wilink.com; web site: www.wilink.com

		holding %
Chairman	Nigel Wray	19.2
Chief Executive	Peter Wakeham	19.4
Finance Director	Nigel Burton	2.1
Non-Exec Director	Graham Morse	12.3

Main Shareholders:

General Employee Benefit Trust	9.7
Herald Investment Trust	5.5

Percentage of free market capital: 30%

Nominated Adviser:	Strand Partners, London
AIM Broker:	Numis, London
Solicitors:	Manches, London
Market Makers:	MLSB; SCAP; WINS
Auditors:	Ernst & Young, London
Registrars:	Capita Registrars

ENTRY ON AIM:	29/11/1999	**Recent price:**	1002.5p
Interim results:	Jun	**Market cap:**	£27.41m
Final results:	Mar	**Issue price:**	n/a
Year end:	Dec	**Current no of shares:**	
Accounts due:	Apr		2,734,145
Int div paymnt:	n/a	**No of shares after**	
Fin div paymnt:	n/a	**dilution:**	3,010,170
Int net div per share:	nil	**P/E ratio:**	n/a
Fin net div per share:	nil	**Probable CGT?**	Yes

LATEST REPORTED RESULTS: 2003		PREVIOUS REPORTED RESULTS: 2002	
Turnover:	£17.68m	**Turnover:**	£20.28m
PTP:	£(61,000)	**PTP:**	£484,000
EPS:	(12.6)p	**EPS:**	17.7p

Comments:

WILink is a provider of investor relations and investment information services in 17 countries in Europe, North America and now Australia. Last year revenue fell 12.8% as the stock markets struggled but operating profits rose 8.7% to £2.6m and earnings per share improved 20.1% to 102.4p, before accounting for goodwill. This happened as a series of share buybacks were made. Net cash stands at £3.6m, or 157p per share.

William Jacks

(JCKS)

Motor car distributor & service provider

Scotch Corner, London Road, Sunningdale, Berkshire SL5 0ER Tel: 01344-625007;
e-mail: info@williamjacks.plc.uk

		holding %
Chairman	Dato Hock	0.0
Chief Executive	John Adair	0.0
Finance Director		
Non-Exec Director	Peter Gadsden	0.0

Main Shareholders:

Jacks International	56.0
Johan Investment	9.8

Percentage of free market capital: 34.2%

Nominated Adviser:	Charles Stanley, London
AIM Broker:	Charles Stanley, London
Solicitors:	Allen & Overy, London
Market Makers:	WINS
Auditors:	Ernst & Young, 7 Rolls Buildings, London EC4A 1NH
Registrars:	Capita Registrars

Entry on AIM:	26/9/2003	**Recent price:**	85.0p
Interim results:	Sep	**Market cap:**	£9.38m
Final results:	May	**Issue price:**	75.5p
Year end:	Jan	**Current no of shares:**	
Accounts due:	Apr		11,037,110
Int div paymnt:	n/a	**No of shares after**	
Fin div paymnt:	n/a	**dilution:**	n/a
Int net div per share:	nil	**P/E ratio:**	23.0
Fin net div per share:	nil	**Probable CGT?**	Yes

LATEST REPORTED RESULTS: 2003		PREVIOUS REPORTED RESULTS: 2002	
Turnover:	£178.28m	**Turnover:**	£181.78m
PTP:	£825,000	**PTP:**	£5.0m
EPS:	3.7p	**EPS:**	35.9p

Comments:

Car dealership William Jacks has had a mixed year following problems with its BMW and Mini dealerships. It disposed of the Cobham and Wimbledon dealerships at a profit and also acquired Dutton-Forshaw Motor's Landrover and Jaguar dealership in Maidstone for £2.3m. Two Volvo businesses were relocated and it acquired a freehold in Brighton. The group came down to AIM against a background of very low margins and precious little support from investors.

ansom & Son (RNSM)

...anufacturer
...fordshire SG5 1LY Tel: 01462-437615; Fax: 01462-420528;
...nsom.com; web site: www.williamransom.com

		holding %
Chai...	Timothy Dye	3.2
Chief Execu...	as above	
Finance Director	Robert Howard	0.1
Non-Exec Director	Christopher Clark	2.6

Main Shareholders:

Jupiter Asset Management	13.1
Liontrust Investment	12.5
Britannic Assurance	6.4
Throgmorton	4.9
Ennismore	4.1
Percentage of free market capital: 49.5%	

Nominated Adviser:	Numis, London		
AIM Broker:	Numis, London		
Solicitors:	Travers Smith Braithwaite, London		
Market Makers:	CLS, MLSB, SCAP,WINS		
Auditors:	RSM Robson Rhodes, Cambridge		
Registrars:	Capita Registrars		

ENTRY ON AIM:	21/7/2003	Recent price:	42.5p
Interim results:	Oct	Market cap:	£11.44m
Final results:	Jun	Issue price:	42.5p
Year end:	Mar	Current no of shares:	
Accounts due:	Aug		26,915,930
Int div paymnt:	Nov	No of shares after	
Fin div paymnt:	Jul	dilution:	n/a
Int net div per share:	0.50p	P/E ratio:	70.8
Fin net div per share:	1.00p	Probable CGT?	YES

LATEST REPORTED RESULTS: 2003		PREVIOUS REPORTED RESULTS: 2002	
Turnover:	£14.73m	Turnover:	£10.65m
PTP:	£269,000	PTP:	£(960,000)
EPS:	0.6p	EPS:	(4.2)p

Comments:

This long-established maker of natural remedies and other drugs moved from the Full List to pursue its acquisition policy. In 2001 Ransom paid £6.75m, funded by debt and a £4.4m placing at 50p, to snap up four consumer products from Roche. These included creams to treat acne, nappy rash and athlete's foot. After selling its Hitchin site for £8.75m, the group plans to acquire other niche products, recently paying £0.58m for certain brands of J.Pickles. One concern is the low margins of these items.

Willington (WLL)

Cold storage and speciality chemicals distributor
Acornfield Road, Knowsley Industrial Park, Liverpool, L33 7YX Tel: 0151-549 1082; Fax: 0151-546 9641;
e-mail: malcolm@intbl.co.uk

		holding %
Chairman	Richard Robinow	8.2
Managing Director	Vincent Troy	0.2
Finance Director	Malcolm Baskerville	0.1
Operations Director	Barrington Bolland	0.1

Main Shareholders:

H M Robinow	60.7
J J Robinow	9.0
J Keatley	4.1
Percentage of free market capital: 15.3%	

Nominated Adviser:	Deloitte & Touche, London
AIM Broker:	Teather & Greenwood, London
Solicitors:	Ashursts, London
Market Makers:	TEAM; WINS
Auditors:	Deloitte & Touche, 9 Charlotte St, Manchester M1 4EU
Registrars:	Capita Registrars

Entry on AIM:	18/12/1998	Recent price:	64.5p
Interim results:	Sep	Market cap:	£5.49m
Final results:	Jun	Issue price:	n/a
Year end:	Dec	Current no of shares:	
Accounts due:	May		8,504,167
Int div paymnt:	n/a	No of shares after	
Fin div paymnt:	n/a	dilution:	n/a
Int net div per share:	nil	P/E ratio:	n/a
Fin net div per share:	nil	Probable CGT?	YES

LATEST REPORTED RESULTS: 2003		PREVIOUS REPORTED RESULTS: 2002	
Turnover:	£26.09m	Turnover:	£32.77m
PTP:	£(297,000)	PTP:	£(575,000)
EPS:	(3.2)p	EPS:	(8.2)p

Comments:

The cold storage and speciality chemical distributor plans to convert shareholdings outside the controlling Robinow family into preference shares and remove the company's AIM listing. Willington's deficit for 2003 was cut from the previous year's £575,000, but that reflected disposals as well as tough trading conditions for the company, which saw sales fall by £7m to £256m. Improved cash flow helped reduce net debt to £4.6m to £1.7m.

Wilshaw (WSW)

Magnet and magnetic components designer and manufacturer

12-14 Hill Street, Richmond, Surrey TW9 1TN Tel: 020-8332 0690; Fax: 020-8332 0669

		holding %
Chairman	Hugh Reynolds	5.7
Chief Executive	as above	
Finance Director	Lesley Innes	0.0
Exec Director	James Laing	0.0

Main Shareholders:

Eaglet Investment Trust	29.9
AXA	4.4
Building & Civil Engineering	3.8
CJ Lea	3.3
Sun Life Int	3.2

Percentage of free market capital: 49.8%

Nominated Adviser:	Collins Stewart, London
AIM Broker:	Collins Stewart, London
Solicitors:	Travers Smith Braithwaite , London
Market Makers:	WINS
Auditors:	KPMG, Arlington Business Park Theale, Reading RG7 4SD
Registrars:	Capita Registrars

ENTRY ON AIM: 19/12/2003		**Recent price:**	12.5p
Interim results:	Nov	Market cap:	£4.9m
Final results:	Jun	Issue price:	n/a
Year end:	Mar	Current no of shares:	
Accounts due:	Aug		39,204,556
Int div paymnt:	Mar	No of shares after	
Fin div paymnt:	Oct	dilution:	n/a
Int net div per share:	5.0p	P/E ratio:	13.9
Fin net div per share:	0.9p	Probable CGT?	Yes

LATEST REPORTED RESULTS: 2003		PREVIOUS REPORTED RESULTS: 2002	
Turnover:	£9.87m	Turnover:	£11.86m
PTP:	£504,000	PTP:	£749,000
EPS:	0.9p	EPS:	1.1p

Comments:

Struggling Wilshaw migrated down from the Full List as part of its ongoing cost cutting programme. The AIM move followed a worrying slide into losses for the half to September. A £414,000 profit made way for losses of £512,000 on a 24% drop in sales to £4m, as demand for its traditional Alnico magnets from the car industry faltered. Thankfully, sales of plastic bonded and soft magnets rose impressively – directors believe there's a future in soft magnetic components.

Winchester Entertainment (Renamed Contentfilm) (WIE)

Film production, sales & UK distribution

19 Heddon Street, London, W1B 4BG Tel: 020-7851 6500; Fax: 020-7851 6505; e-mail: mail@winchesterent.co.uk; web site: www.winchesterent.com

		holding %
Chairman	Huw H Davies	1.1
Chief Executive	Shawn Taylor	0.1
Finance Director		
Non-Exec Director	David Jenkins	0.1

Main Shareholders:

Gary Smith	11.0
Friends Ivory and Sime	9.9
Gartmore	9.8
John Muse	6.0
Alton Irby	6.0

Percentage of free market capital: 52.2%

Nominated Adviser:	Evolution Beeson Gregory, London
AIM Broker:	Evolution Beeson Gregory, London
Solicitors:	Pinsents, Birmingham
Market Makers:	IHCS; MLSB; SCAP; WINS
Auditors:	KPMG Audit, London
Registrars:	Capita Registrars

Entry on AIM:	27/6/1995	Recent price:	26.75p
Interim results:	Dec	Market cap:	£16.9m
Final results:	Jul	Issue price:	100.0p
Year end:	Mar	Current no of shares:	
Accounts due:	Aug		63,177,502
Int div paymnt:	n/a	No of shares after	
Fin div paymnt:	n/a	dilution:	n/a
Int net div per share:	nil	P/E ratio:	n/a
Fin net div per share:	nil	Probable CGT?	Yes

LATEST REPORTED RESULTS: 2003		PREVIOUS REPORTED RESULTS: 2002	
Turnover:	£5.15m	Turnover:	£6.47m
PTP:	£(11.18m)	PTP:	£(8.29m)
EPS:	(40.2)p	EPS:	(27.4)p

Comments:

Winchester's interims showed losses before tax of £2.3m. These didn't include a slug of income from the film The Man Who Sued God, which took £1.1m in the UK alone. However, this pales into insignificance compared to its £9.1m takeover of Content Film, funded by an issue of convertible preference shares. The group also placed shares equivalent to 33.1% of the enlarged company to raise £8.5m and has a new finance facility worth £10.8m from JP Morgan Chase. An exciting future beckons.

World Careers Network

(WOR)

Internet graduate recruitment business

Woodman Works, The Crescent, London, SW19 8DR Tel: 020-8946 9876; Fax: 020-8946 9855;
e-mail: webmaster@wcn.co.uk; web site: www.wcn.co.uk

		holding %
Chairman	Ian Moore	0.4
Managing Director	Charles Hipps	67.0
Finance Director		
Operations Director	David Moore	0.0

Main Shareholders:

Dr Deborah Hipps	5.9
Ms Victoria Hipps	5.9
Generali Portfolio Management	3.8

Percentage of free market capital: 17.1%

Nominated Adviser:	Charles Stanley, London
AIM Broker:	Charles Stanley, London
Solicitors:	Nabarro Nathanson, Reading
Market Makers:	SCAP; WINS
Auditors:	BDO Stoy Hayward, Epsom, Surrey
Registrars:	Capita Registrars

ENTRY ON AIM:	20/3/2000	Recent price:	67.5p
Interim results:	Apr	Market cap:	£5.45m
Final results:	Oct	Issue price:	110.0p
Year end:	Jul	Current no of shares:	
Accounts due:	Nov		8,070,000
Int div paymnt:	n/a	No of shares after	
Fin div paymnt:	n/a	dilution:	8,221,970
Int net div per share:	nil	P/E ratio:	n/a
Fin net div per share:	nil	Probable CGT?	Yes

Comments:

As foreshadowed at half time, WCN moved into profit last year on a 12.5% revenue rise, and those profits exceeded expectations. There was steady growth in the UK despite tough trading conditions and losses were cut at its French operation. The company has completed its transformation into a software business, with software accounting for over 80% of revenues. Its first software client, Corus, has been using its applicant tracking software for four years now.

LATEST REPORTED RESULTS: 2003		PREVIOUS REPORTED RESULTS: 2002	
Turnover:	£1.71m	Turnover:	£1.52m
PTP:	£144,000	PTP:	£(185,000)
EPS:	1.7p	EPS:	(2.3)p

World Travel (suspended 31 October 2003)

(WTL)

Internet-based provider of travel products and information

53 The London Fruit & Wool Exchange, Brushfield Street, London, E1 6EX Tel: 020-7456 1352; Fax: 020-7456 1310;
e-mail: shareholders@wtd.com; web site: www.worldtravelholdings.com

		holding %
Chairman	John Biles	7.0
Chief Executive		
Finance Director	as above	
Technical Director	Henry Ting	15.3

Main Shareholders:

Penlee	9.1
BC Patel	8.4
Aralon	7.3
Clients of Laing & Cruickshank	5.5
REC Holdings	5.5

Percentage of free market capital: 34.1%

Nominated Adviser:	Credit Lyonnais, London
AIM Broker:	Credit Lyonnais, London
Solicitors:	Addleshaw Goddard, London
Market Makers:	CLS.; KBCS; SCAP; WINS
Auditors:	Deloitte & Touche, 1 Surrey Street, London, EC1A 4EJ
Registrars:	Computershare Investor Services

Entry on AIM:	20/9/2000	Recent price:	0.4p
Interim results:	Feb	Market cap:	£0.33m
Final results:	Aug	Issue price:	110.0p
Year end:	Dec	Current no of shares:	
Accounts due:	Apr		81,969,102
Int div paymnt:	n/a	No of shares after	
Fin div paymnt:	n/a	dilution:	n/a
Int net div per share:	nil	P/E ratio:	n/a
Fin net div per share:	nil	Probable CGT?	Yes

Comments:

Last October the shell venture, on the hunt for some kind of reinvention, requested a suspension pending clarification of its financial position. It said that unless it could reach agreement with creditors involving an equity for debt swap or a reduction in creditor claims, the company would fail. There's been no update since. World Travel is a former travel service distribution setup that withdrew from the travel industry. Its most recent accounts were for the half to June 2003.

LATEST REPORTED RESULTS: 2002		PREVIOUS REPORTED RESULTS: 2001	
Turnover:	£21.62m	Turnover:	£23.67m
PTP:	£(1.36m)	PTP:	£(12.62m)
EPS:	(2.1)p	EPS:	(19.2)p

Wyatt (WYT)

Risk consultancy services

The Leaze, Salter Street, Berkeley, Gloucestershire GL13 9DB Tel: 01453-511911; Fax: 01453-511914;
e-mail: mail@wyattgroup.co.uk; web site: www.wyattgroup.co.uk

		holding %
Chairman	Robert Holt	13.1
Chief Executive	as above	
Finance Director		
Non-Exec Director	Reginald Pomphrett	2.6

Main Shareholders:

Ruffer Investment Management	45.2
J Currie	5.6
C Hughes	5.6
RBSTB Nominees	3.9

Percentage of free market capital: 24%

Nominated Adviser:	Rowan Dartington, Bristol
AIM Broker:	Rowan Dartington, Bristol
Solicitors:	BPE, Cheltenham
Market Makers:	SCAP; WINS
Auditors:	Grant Thornton, Cheltenham, Gloucestershire
Registrars:	Capita Registrars

Entry on AIM:	29/3/2001	**Recent price:**	24.5p
Interim results:	Dec	**Market cap:**	£1.63m
Final results:	Sep	**Issue price:**	25.0p
Year end:	Mar	**Current no of shares:**	
Accounts due:	Aug		6,640,000
Int div paymnt:	n/a	**No of shares after**	
Fin div paymnt:	n/a	**dilution:**	n/a
Int net div per share:	nil	**P/E ratio:**	n/a
Fin net div per share:	nil	**Probable CGT?**	Yes

Comments:
Bob Holt, successful chief executive of Mears, wants to build up a series of risk consultancy businesses through Wyatt. Not everything has gone to plan. This year turnover will be half that originally anticipated, 'due to the ill health of a key executive in the main operating unit'. The person involved has now made a full recovery and current trading is encouraging. A £202,000 interim loss was made on £172,000 of turnover. More acquisitions are planned.

LATEST REPORTED RESULTS: 2003		PREVIOUS REPORTED RESULTS: 2002	
Turnover:	£646,000	Turnover:	£175,000
PTP:	£(279,000)	PTP:	£(225,000)
EPS:	(4.0)p	EPS:	(6.4)p

Wynnstay Properties (WSP)

Property owner, developer & manager

Cleary Court, 21 St Swithins Lane, London, EC4N 8AD Tel: 020-7626 3057; Fax: 020-7623 8374;
e-mail: wynnstay@lineone.net

		holding %
Chairman	Philip Collins	27.1
Managing Director	Michael Cheesmer	0.6
Finance Director	Peter Kirkland	0.3
Non-Exec Director	Ian Lockhart	2.2

Main Shareholders:

York & District Inv Co Ltd	11.9
Mr HJA Bird	5.7

Percentage of free market capital: 51.8%

Nominated Adviser:	Charles Stanley, London
AIM Broker:	Charles Stanley, London
Solicitors:	Field Fisher Waterhouse, London
Market Makers:	KBCS; TEAM; WINS
Auditors:	Moore Stephens, Warwick Lane, London EC4P 4BN
Registrars:	Capita Registrars

Entry on AIM:	21/9/1995	**Recent price:**	252.5p
Interim results:	Nov	**Market cap:**	£7.97m
Final results:	Jun	**Issue price:**	n/a
Year end:	Mar	**Current no of shares:**	
Accounts due:	Jun		3,155,267
Int div paymnt:	Dec	**No of shares after**	
Fin div paymnt:	Jul	**dilution:**	n/a
Int net div per share:	2.1p	**P/E ratio:**	13.6
Fin net div per share:	5.1p	**Probable CGT?**	No

Comments:
Wynnstay's interims highlighted the continued malaise in southern England's property market but the company still remains profitable. Turnover fell 1.8% to £748,000 and pre-tax profits dropped 22.8% to £322,000. However, NAV increased slightly to £9.5m. It has recently acquired the Oakcroft Business Centre in Chessington, Surrey for £1.9m and, as with the rest of its portfolio, the units are fully let. Net debt to March stood at £5.4m.

LATEST REPORTED RESULTS: 2003		PREVIOUS REPORTED RESULTS: 2002	
Turnover:	£1.5m	Turnover:	£1.44m
PTP:	£755,000	PTP:	£666,000
EPS:	18.5p	EPS:	15.5p

XecutiveResearch (XEC)

Executive recruitment

105 Piccadilly, London, W1J 7NJ Tel: 020-7647 9876

		holding %
Chairman	David Lees	14.2
Chief Executive		
Finance Director	as above	
Non-Exec Director	Michael Bull	14.2

Main Shareholders:

Evolution Beeson Gregory	21.7
The XecutiveResearch Employee Benefit Trustee	20.5
James Fowler	19.4
Fleming Asset Management	9.9

Percentage of free market capital: n/a

Comments:

Shell venture XecutiveResearch is buying prestige vehicle replacement specialist Accident Exchange in a reverse deal valuing the business at roughly £13.6m. Profitable at operational level since inception in 2001, Accident Exchange provides car hire on credit to motorists involved in accidents where they are not at fault, catering for clients driving marque cars like Porsche, Jaguar, BMW and Audi. The company recovers its charges from the insurer of the driver at fault.

Nominated Adviser:	Insinger de Beaufort, London
AIM Broker:	Insinger Townsley, London
Solicitors:	Stringer Saul, London
Market Makers:	SCAP; WINS
Auditors:	MRI Moores Rowland, London
Registrars:	Capita Registrars

ENTRY ON AIM:	3/5/2002	Recent price:	0.1p
Interim results:	Apr	Market cap:	£0.7m
Final results:	Sept	Issue price:	1.0p
Year end:	Jul	Current no of shares:	
Accounts due:	Oct		695,250,000
Int div paymnt:	n/a	No of shares after	
Fin div paymnt:	n/a	dilution:	n/a
Int net div per share:	nil	P/E ratio:	n/a
Fin net div per share:	nil	Probable CGT?	YES

LATEST REPORTED RESULTS:	2003	PREVIOUS REPORTED RESULTS: 5 MONTHS TO 31 JUL '02	
Turnover:	£93,000	Turnover:	£200,000
PTP:	£(704,000)	PTP:	£(1.84m)
EPS:	n/a	EPS:	n/a

Xpertise (XPG)

IT technical training services

Pacific Road, Atlantic Office Park, Altrincham, Cheshire WA14 5BJ Tel: 0845-757 3888;
e-mail: enquiries@xpertise-consulting.com; web site: www.xpertise.co.uk

		holding %
Chairman	Richard Last	0.0
Managing Director	Ian Johnson	1.4
Finance Director	as above	
Non-Exec Director	Clive Richards	3.9

Main Shareholders:

Lynx	22.1
ISIS Asset management	13.3
Unicorn AIM VCT	12.7
Sphinx	9.1
Singer & Friedlander AIM VCT	6.8

Percentage of free market capital: 7.4%

Comments:

2003 was a very tough year for the IT training company, with losses widening as recession rumbled on in its market. The impressive top-line leap reflected the acquisition of Power Education, a business that was hungrily integrated. Digesting this deal has brought major cost reductions to the group that investors should see in the current year. And capacity in the market is dropping via consolidation and rival business failures. Orders in latter months have also been more encouraging.

Nominated Adviser:	Brewin Dolphin, Manchester
AIM Broker:	Brewin Dolphin, Manchester
Solicitors:	Taylor Wessing, London
Market Makers:	WINS
Auditors:	BDO Stoy Hayward, Manchester
Registrars:	Computershare Investor Services

Entry on AIM:	5/1/1999	Recent price:	1.0p
Interim results:	Sep	Market cap:	£4.19m
Final results:	Mar	Issue price:	25.0p
Year end:	Dec	Current no of shares:	
Accounts due:	Apr		418,947,240
Int div paymnt:	n/a	No of shares after	
Fin div paymnt:	n/a	dilution:	n/a
Int net div per share:	nil	P/E ratio:	n/a
Fin net div per share:	nil	Probable CGT?	YES

LATEST REPORTED RESULTS:	2003	PREVIOUS REPORTED RESULTS:	2002
Turnover:	£10.77m	Turnover:	£4.6m
PTP:	£(2.14m)	PTP:	£(1.15m)
EPS:	(0.7)p	EPS:	(1.6)p

Yamana Gold (YAU)

Mineral mining

150 York Street, Suite 1902, Toronto, Ontario M5H 3S5 Canada,

		holding %
Chairman	Victor Bradley	0.0
Chief Executive	Peter Marrone	0.0
Finance Director		
Director	James Askew	0.0

Main Shareholders:
CDS & Co	40.2
Santa Elina Mines	38.8
Ontario Teachers Pension Plan	5.2

Percentage of free market capital: 15.8%

Comments:
Headed by Canadian entrepreneur Peter Marrone and 38 per cent-owned by Brazilian notable Paulo de Brito, Toronto-quoted Yamana paid £12.3m in August for Brazil's Fazenda Brasiliro property, producing gold at an annual rate of 100,000 oz at US$ 218 an ounce cash cost (against a $400-plus market price). Yamana, which lost £1m in the six months to August, is pursuing other projects at Fazenda Nova and Chapada and could be volatile.

Nominated Adviser:	Canaccord Capital, London
AIM Broker:	Canaccord Capital, London
Solicitors:	Cassels Brock & Blackwell, Toronto
Market Makers:	JEFF; SCAP; WINS
Auditors:	Deloitte & Touche, Vancouver, Canada
Registrars:	Capita Registrars

Entry on AIM: 28/11/2003	**Recent price:**	172.0p
Interim results: Oct	**Market cap:**	£159.32m
Final results: Jul	**Issue price:**	n/a
Year end: Feb	**Current no of shares:**	
Accounts due: Aug		92,628,495
Int div paymnt: n/a	**No of shares after**	
Fin div paymnt: n/a	**dilution:**	n/a
Int net div per share: nil	**P/E ratio:**	n/a
Fin net div per share: nil	**Probable CGT?**	No

LATEST REPORTED RESULTS: 2003		PREVIOUS REPORTED RESULTS: 2002	
Turnover:	n/a	**Turnover:**	$5.84
PTP:	$(2.37m)	**PTP:**	$(11.32m)
EPS:	(0.1)c	**EPS:**	(0.2)c

Yeoman (YGP)

Mobile navigation & positioning technology developer

The Shipyard, Bath Road, Lymington, SO41 3YL Tel: 01590-679777; Fax: 01590-671717;
e-mail: info@yeomangroup.plc.uk; web site: www.yeomangroup.plc.uk

		holding %
Chairman	Gordon Owen	2.2
Chief Executive	Vincent Geake	0.0
Finance Director	Charles H Marshall	0.8
Director	Andrew Melsom	0.0

Main Shareholders:
Artemis Asset Management	16.5
Morley Fund Management	15.0
Liberty Square	8.0
Johnson Fry Unit Trust Managers	7.4
LeggMason Investors	6.5

Percentage of free market capital: 33.6%

Comments:
Yeoman has developed a range of mobile navigation technologies and boasts a series of impressive commercial relationships with the likes of Orange and Vodafone among others. Nonetheless it continues to lose cash by the bucket load, hence the closure of one business and the sale of another last year. Between them these two operations accounted for £5.6m of a £9.8m full year loss. An approach has since been received that may lead to an offer for the remainder of the business.

Nominated Adviser:	Brewin Dolphin, Glasgow
AIM Broker:	Brewin Dolphin, Glasgow
Solicitors:	Reynolds Porter Chamberlain, London
Market Makers:	ALTI; GRAB; MLSB; WINS
Auditors:	BDO Stoy Hayward, 8 Baker Street, London W1U 3LL
Registrars:	Capita Registrars

Entry on AIM: 13/12/1996	**Recent price:**	8.75p
Interim results: Jun	**Market cap:**	£1.98m
Final results: Dec	**Issue price:**	175.0p
Year end: Sep	**Current no of shares:**	
Accounts due: Dec		22,596,719
Int div paymnt: n/a	**No of shares after**	
Fin div paymnt: n/a	**dilution:**	n/a
Int net div per share: nil	**P/E ratio:**	n/a
Fin net div per share: nil	**Probable CGT?**	Yes

LATEST REPORTED RESULTS: 2003		PREVIOUS REPORTED RESULTS: 2002	
Turnover:	£8.76m	**Turnover:**	£12.92m
PTP:	£(9.77m)	**PTP:**	£(12.35m)
EPS:	(40.3)p	**EPS:**	(79.2)p

YM BioSciences
(YMBA)

Drug developer

5045 Orbitor Drive, Building 11, Suite 4000, Mississauga, Ontario, Canada L4W 4Y4 Tel: 00-1 905 629 4959;
Fax: 00-1 905 629 9761; web site: www.ymbiosciences.com

		holding %
Chairman		
Chief Executive	David Allan	1.7
Finance Director		
Non-Exec Director	Tryon Williams	0.1

Main Shareholders:
equity4life	6.5
Financiere Tuileries	4.3
Covington Capital	3.0

Percentage of free market capital: 84.4%

Comments:
This biotech play was set up in Canada back in 1994, and its drugs portfolio is based on technologies licensed from academic centres of excellence. It has three products in clinical development. These include 'lead' breast cancer drug tesmilifene, and two other cancer therapeutics under going trials. The group has recently raised $17m net, which will help fund imminent phase III trials for tesmilifene. Losses hit $2m in the first half.

Nominated Adviser:	Canaccord Capital, London
AIM Broker:	Canaccord Capital, London
Solicitors:	Charles Russell, London
Market Makers:	SCAP; WINS
Auditors:	KPMG, Ontario
Registrars:	Capita Registrars

ENTRY ON AIM:	12/6/2002	**Recent price:**	97.5p
Interim results:	Nov	**Market cap:**	£27.66m
Final results:	Oct	**Issue price:**	179.0p
Year end:	Jun	**Current no of shares:**	
Accounts due:	Oct		28,367,852
Int div paymnt:	n/a	**No of shares after**	
Fin div paymnt:	n/a	**dilution:**	n/a
Int net div per share:	nil	**P/E ratio:**	n/a
Fin net div per share:	nil	**Probable CGT?**	No

LATEST REPORTED RESULTS:	**2003**	**PREVIOUS REPORTED RESULTS:**	**2002**
Turnover:	$273,000	Turnover:	$154,000
PTP:	$(7.38m)	PTP:	$(6.44m)
EPS:	(0.6)c	EPS:	(0.5)c

YooMedia (formely e-district.net)
(YOO)

Developer of interactive family entertainment channel

Aspect Gate, 166 College Road, Harrow, HA1 1BH Tel: 020-8515 2800 ; Fax: 020-8515 2801;

		holding %
Chairman	Michael Sinclair	20.5
Chief Executive	David Docherty	0.2
Non-Exec Director	Bernard Fairman	0.0
Dvlpmt Director	Edmund Abrams	0.6

Main Shareholders:
Foresight Technology VCT	16.3
Columbia Pictures Corp	10.1
Artemis	9.1
Invesco Asset Management	3.1

Percentage of free market capital: 32.9%

Comments:
Interactive TV content producer Yoomedia is expecting slightly lower sales due to a delay of its Dateline digital offering. While its chat and gaming products on cable and Freeview have performed in line with management expectation, Dateline's belated launch means it won't contribute to this year's revenues. The market is expecting sales for the year to reach £1m and losses of circa £5.2m. If all goes according to plan this year, 2004 sales should hit £12.5m with losses reducing to £1m.

Nominated Adviser:	Durlacher, London
AIM Broker:	Durlacher, London
Solicitors:	Denton Wilde Sapte, London
Market Makers:	WEST; WINS
Auditors:	Ernst & Young, 7 Rolls Buildings, London EC4A 1NH
Registrars:	Capita Registrars

Entry on AIM:	7/3/2000	**Recent price:**	41.0p
Interim results:	Sep	**Market cap:**	£43.27m
Final results:	May	**Issue price:**	195.0p
Year end:	Dec	**Current no of shares:**	
Accounts due:	Apr		105,538,075
Int div paymnt:	n/a	**No of shares after**	
Fin div paymnt:	n/a	**dilution:**	n/a
Int net div per share:	nil	**P/E ratio:**	n/a
Fin net div per share:	nil	**Probable CGT?**	Yes

LATEST REPORTED RESULTS:	**2002**	**PREVIOUS REPORTED RESULTS:**	**2001**
Turnover:	£39,000	Turnover:	£15,000
PTP:	£(7.04m)	PTP:	£(3.98m)
EPS:	(9.2)p	EPS:	(5.2)p

Your Space (YSP)

Flexible office space for growing businesses

The Bridge, 12-16 Clerkenwell, London, EC1M 5PQ Tel: 020-73246000; Fax: 020-73246001;
web site: www.yourspaceplc.com

		holding %
Chairman	Christopher Philips	1.6
Chief Executive		
Finance Director	Christopher Tidball	0.0
Exec Director	Laurence Davis	6.7

Main Shareholders:

Pershing Keen	18.2
Shaun Mealey	8.3
J Lancaster	6.8
Lincoln Trust Company	5.0
Ian Ilsley	3.9

Percentage of free market capital: 41.7

Comments:

Your Space (formerly Technology & Internet Property Services) operates in the serviced office market. Its occupancy at its Clerkenwell, Hammersmith and Manchester sites ranged between 81-90% in September and so halved pre-tax losses to £154,000 at the interim stage. Its freeholding at Frampton St in London is fully let. The company also restructured its management team in the first half with Harvey Soning installed as managing director. NAV was £3.8m in September.

Nominated Adviser:	John East, London
AIM Broker:	Insinger Townsley, London
Solicitors:	Fladgate Fielder, London
Market Makers:	SCAP; WINS
Auditors:	Gerald Edelman, 25 Harley Street, London, W1R 2BR
Registrars:	Capita Registrars

Entry on AIM:	7/11/2000	Recent price:	1.75p
Interim results:	Dec	Market cap:	£3.46m
Final results:	Jul	Issue price:	10.0p
Year end:	Mar	Current no of shares:	
Accounts due:	Aug		197,775,442
Int div paymnt:	n/a	No of shares after	
Fin div paymnt:	n/a	dilution:	232,211,157
Int net div per share:	nil	P/E ratio:	n/a
Fin net div per share:	nil	Probable CGT?	Yes

LATEST REPORTED RESULTS: 2003		PREVIOUS REPORTED RESULTS: 2002	
Turnover:	£2.16m	Turnover:	£769,000
PTP:	£(652,000)	PTP:	£(605,000)
EPS:	(0.4)p	EPS:	(0.4)p

Zi Medical (ZIM)

Medical device developer

Unit 4, St Asaph Business Park, St Asaph, Denbighshire LL17 0LJ Tel: 01745-585770; Fax: 01745-585880;
web site: www.zi-medical.co.uk

		holding %
Chairman	Michael Fort	1.2
Managing Director	George Gallagher	10.7
Finance Director		
Non-Exec Director	Robert Nolan	0.5

Main Shareholders:

Rhys Owen	4.6

Percentage of free market capital: 82.8%

Comments:

The medical devices business, which has a worldwide distribution deal with Baxter Healthcare for RedEye, its intravenous drip-monitoring system, took advantage of a soaring share price to raise £2m. The first generation of products is currently being sold, with further models in development. Zi is also working on syringe driver products and other drug delivery items in association with B Braun. The group was started by a 28-year-old ex-Zeneca engineer and reversed into AIM shell BioLife Ventures.

Nominated Adviser:	Brewin Dolphin, Manchester
AIM Broker:	Brewin Dolphin, Manchester
Solicitors:	Halliwell Landau, Manchester
Market Makers:	EVO; KBCS; SCAP; WINS
Auditors:	KPMG, Preston PR2 2YF
Registrars:	Capita Registrars

Entry on AIM:	3/7/2001	Recent price:	16.5p
Interim results:	Aug	Market cap:	£11.86m
Final results:	Jun	Issue price:	6.0p
Year end:	Dec	Current no of shares:	
Accounts due:	Apr		71,878,425
Int div paymnt:	n/a	No of shares after	
Fin div paymnt:	n/a	dilution:	n/a
Int net div per share:	nil	P/E ratio:	n/a
Fin net div per share:	nil	Probable CGT?	Yes

LATEST REPORTED RESULTS: 2002		PREVIOUS REPORTED RESULTS: 2001	
Turnover:	£43,000	Turnover:	n/a
PTP:	£(609,000)	PTP:	£(56,000)
EPS:	(2.0)p	EPS:	(0.5)p

ZincOx Resources (ZOX)

Zinc mining

7 Tanners Yard, London Road, Bagshot, GU19 5HD Tel: 01276-455700; Fax: 01276-850015;
e-mail: info@zincox.com; web site: www.zincox.com

		holding %
Chairman	Noel Masson	8.3
Managing Director	Andrew Woollett	7.4
Finance Director	Peter Fry	0.3
Exploration Director	Michael Foster	2.1

Main Shareholders:

New Opportunities Investment Trust	13.7
Teck Cominco Metals	12.8
Sloane Rolinson Investment Management	6.1
M & G Investment Management	5.6
Hoegh Capital Partners	5.6
Percentage of free market capital: 28.4%	

Nominated Adviser: Numis, London
AIM Broker: Numis, London

Solicitors: Stringer Saul, London
Market Makers: SCAP; WINS

Auditors: Grant Thornton, Southampton

Registrars: Capita Registrars

Entry on AIM: 10/12/2001		**Recent price:**	79.5p
Interim results:	Sep	**Market cap:**	£18.78m
Final results:	Jun	**Issue price:**	120.0p
Year end:	Dec	**Current no of shares:**	
Accounts due:	May		23,627,772
Int div paymnt:	n/a	**No of shares after**	
Fin div paymnt:	n/a	**dilution:**	26,439,878
Int net div per share:	nil	**P/E ratio:**	n/a
Fin net div per share:	nil	**Probable CGT?**	No

LATEST REPORTED RESULTS: 2002		PREVIOUS REPORTED RESULTS: 2001	
Turnover:	n/a	Turnover:	n/a
PTP:	£(1.08m)	PTP:	£(675,000)
EPS:	(0.1)p	EPS:	(0.1)p

Comments:
With zinc back in vogue, Andrew Woollett's ZincOx, long out of favour with its novel zinc oxide treatment process, regained some support on selling its Shaimerden zinc project in Kazakhstan for £4.2m (plus royalties) to focus on recycling. ZincOx, which lost an interim £461,000, has rights to a Russian technology, Polykiln, to make zinc oxide output cheaper and recyle zinc smelter slags, such as ZincOx's at Tsumeb in Namibia.

Zoo Digital (ZOO)

Computer games publisher and DVD technology distributor

Parkhead House, 26 Carver Street, Sheffield, S1 4FS Tel: 0114-241 3700; Fax: 0114-241 3701;
e-mail: info@zoodigitalgroup.com; web site: www.zoodigitalgroup.com

		holding %
Chairman	John Barnes	0.0
Chief Executive	Ian Stewart	21.3
Finance Director	Robert Deri	0.0
Chief Technical Officer	Dr Stuart Green	6.9

Main Shareholders:

M Dalman	6.9
M Newell	6.9
Herald Investment Management	6.8
Alchemy Capital	6.7
Dr Richard Oliver	5.0
Percentage of free market capital: 25.7%	

Nominated Adviser: Noble & Co, London
AIM Broker: Noble & Co, London

Solicitors: DLA, Sheffield
Market Makers: CHMM; WINS

Auditors: PKF, Knowle House, 4 North Park Road, Sheffield S23 3QE
Registrars: Capita Registrars

Entry on AIM:	30/3/2000	**Recent price:**	10.0p
Interim results:	Aug	**Market cap:**	£27.9m
Final results:	Jun	**Issue price:**	85.0p
Year end:	Dec	**Current no of shares:**	
Accounts due:	Apr		279,030,328
Int div paymnt:	n/a	**No of shares after**	
Fin div paymnt:	n/a	**dilution:**	n/a
Int net div per share:	nil	**P/E ratio:**	n/a
Fin net div per share:	nil	**Probable CGT?**	Yes

LATEST REPORTED RESULTS: 2002		PREVIOUS REPORTED RESULTS: 2001	
Turnover:	£1.88m	Turnover:	£724,000
PTP:	£(2.34m)	PTP:	£(8.96m)
EPS:	(1.5)p	EPS:	(8.2)p

Comments:
Zoo's transformation from 3D software developer to computer games distributor is picking up pace. Interims saw sales surge 370% to £1.3m as losses were reduced from £1.2m to £995,000. The second half has so far seen the company acquire 33 games titles from Atari – including the Actua sports range – and launch its own 'Zoo Classics' label. A deal has also been struck with film studio Universal, granting Zoo the right to produce an interactive football DVD game.

Zytronic (ZYT)

Designer and manufacturer of electronic composites

Patterson Street, Blaydon on Tyne, Tyne & Wear NE21 5SG Tel: 0191-414 5511; Fax: 0191-414 0545;
e-mail: info@zytronic.co.uk; web site: www.zytronic.co.uk

		holding %
Chairman	John Kennair	15.9
Chief Executive	Ian Lawson	0.0
Finance Director	Denis Mullan	0.1
Non-Exec Director	Tudor Davies	1.3

Main Shareholders:

HSBC Global Custody Nominees	23.0
Singer & Friedlander Investment Management	10.1
Vidacos	4.2
Artemis	4.1
Gartmore	3.8

Percentage of free market capital: 34.3%

Comments:

Newcastle-based Zytronic achieved a minor turn-around for 2003, but progress remains slow. This partly stems from a lean spell post-9/11, when caution reigned among original equipment manufacturing clients in the electronics sector. Pre-tax losses were cut for the year and in the second half it achieved a £83,000 pre-tax profit. Zytouch is also being trialled for petrol pump applications and has an agreement with touch technology play Elo TouchSystems.

Nominated Adviser:	Brewin Dolphin, Glasgow		
AIM Broker:	Brewin Dolphin, Glasgow		
Solicitors:	Ward Hadaway, Newcastle upon Tyne		
Market Makers:	EVO; KBCS; WINS		
Auditors:	Ernst & Young, Newcastle upon Tyne		
Registrars:	Computershare Investor Services		

ENTRY ON AIM:	6/7/2000	**Recent price:**	66.5p
Interim results:	May	**Market cap:**	£9.5m
Final results:	Dec	**Issue price:**	110.0p
Year end:	Sep	**Current no of shares:**	
Accounts due:	Jan		14,291,539
Int div paymnt:	n/a	**No of shares after**	
Fin div paymnt:	n/a	**dilution:**	14,626,991
Int net div per share:	nil	**P/E ratio:**	n/a
Fin net div per share:	nil	**Probable CGT?**	Yes

LATEST REPORTED RESULTS: 2003		PREVIOUS REPORTED RESULTS: 2002	
Turnover:	£5.69m	**Turnover:**	£5.07m
PTP:	£(368,000)	**PTP:**	£(406,000)
EPS:	(2.2)p	**EPS:**	(2.2)p

Zyzygy (ZYZ)

Shell

6th Floor, The Swiss Centre, 10 Wardour Street, London, W1D 6QF Tel: 020-7758 3200

		holding %
Chairman	Andrew Moore	5.0
Chief Executive	Joanne Sawicki*	48.5
Finance Director		

Main Shareholders:

Worldwide Securities	14.9
Keith Berry	8.5
Donald Kerr	8.5
Paul Crayford*	3.5

Percentage of free market capital: 29%

*Joanne Sawicki and Paul Crayford are married

Comments:

Yet another AIM shell, Zyzygy is now headed by Andy Moore, former UK Independence Party candidate for Solihull and infamous victim of rather personal bulletin board abuse whilst chairman of fellow AIM struggler 10 Group. However, for all his experience – Moore has been a director of 65 companies to date – he has his work cut out to make Zyzygy a success. Cash stands at just £108,000 and there are many more attractive shells seeking reverse deals.

Nominated Adviser:	John East, London		
AIM Broker:	Seymour Pierce Ellis, Crawley		
Solicitors:	KLegal/McGrigor Donald, London		
Market Makers:	BGMM; KBCS; WINS		
Auditors:	Grant Thornton London		
Registrars:	Capita Registrars		

Entry on AIM:	11/8/2000	**Recent price:**	1.0p
Interim results:	Sep	**Market cap:**	£1.34m
Final results:	Jun	**Issue price:**	57.0p
Year end:	Dec	**Current no of shares:**	
Accounts due:	Jul		134,229,294
Int div paymnt:	n/a	**No of shares after**	
Fin div paymnt:	n/a	**dilution:**	n/a
Int net div per share:	nil	**P/E ratio:**	n/a
Fin net div per share:	nil	**Probable CGT?**	Yes

LATEST REPORTED RESULTS: PERIOD TO 30 JUNE		PREVIOUS REPORTED RESULTS: 2001	
Turnover:	£189,000	**Turnover:**	£1.21m
PTP:	£(914,000)	**PTP:**	£(2.4)m
EPS:	(2.4)p	**EPS:**	(14.3)p

AIM:
THE BAKER TILLY ADVISER DIRECTORY

AIM: THE BAKER TILLY ADVISER DIRECTORY

CONTENTS

PAGE

ABOUT BAKER TILLY

The firm

Baker Tilly is a leading firm of chartered accountants and business advisers in the UK, with over 270 partners, 2,000 staff and national coverage through its network of offices. It is the independent UK member firm of Baker Tilly International, which is the 10th largest accountancy network in the world by turnover, represented by 116 firms in 67 countries, has a global fee income of $1.5 billion and 17,000 staff worldwide.

Baker Tilly's clients include high net-worth individuals and growing entrepreneurial companies, including a substantial number of those on AIM.

We have acted as both auditors and reporting accountants to over 80 AIM flotations, and we have partners who are recognised specialists in legislation on the tax benefits that can apply to AIM companies and investors. We are represented on the AIM advisory group of the London Stock Exchange, have written 'A Guide to AIM tax benefits' in association with the Exchange, and conduct the annual 'Taking AIM' survey.

We have a dedicated corporate finance department that provides specialist support to growing businesses – private and quoted – in all aspects of corporate finance, including: acquisition and due diligence advice, management buy-outs and buy-ins, venture capital finance, flotations, valuations, City Code advisory services and public sector work.

Our partners include recognised specialists in tax-related matters, in particular, EIS and VCT legislation.

Due to our broad range of professional skills and services, we provide an active partner-led service to our clients. Our partners and staff have many years' experience drawn from such diverse areas as stock-broking, banking and merchant banking, venture capital and government agencies, including the Inland Revenue. They provide an invaluable breadth of experience when problem-solving or advising our clients.

For further information on our services for AIM, contact Chilton Taylor or Paul Watts on 020-7413 5100, or e-mail chilton.taylor@bakertilly.co.uk or paul.watts@bakertilly.co.uk.

Baker Tilly Aim Accountant of the Year 2003 (Source: Growth Company Awards 2003).

NOMINATED ADVISERS

AIB Corporate Finance

85 Pembroke Road, Ballsbridge, Dublin 4, Ireland, Tel: 00-353 1 667 0233; Fax: 00-353 1 667 0250; email: corporate.finance@aib.ie; Web site: www.aibcf.ie

Contact:	Alan Doherty	**Number of Directors & Executives engaged in:**	
Also act as Nominated Broker?	No	Corporate Finance: Dir:	4
Companies represented on first admission:	0	Exec:	11
Number involved in new issue to raise funds:	0	AIM Activities: Dir:	1
Industry sector preferences:	None	Exec:	3
Geographical preferences:	None		
In-house industry sector analysts?	No	Act for:	n/a
Sectors covered by analysts:	Any		
Prospective AIM companies considered:			
Startups n/a Early stage n/a Established n/a			
Typical transaction parameters:	None		
Split of broking activities:	n/a		
(institutional: private client)			
Underwriting facilities:		Other Offices:	n/a
Can provide:	Yes		
Can arrange:	n/a		
Other activities:	n/a		

Altium Capital

30 St James's Square, London, SW1Y 4AL Tel: 020-7484 4040; Fax: 020-7484 4144; email: garry.levin@altiumcapital.co.uk; Web site: www.altiumcapital.co.uk

Contact:	Garry Levin	**Number of Directors & Executives engaged in:**	
Also act as Nominated Broker?	Yes	Corporate Finance: Dir:	10
Companies represented on first admission:	14	Exec:	11
Number involved in new issue to raise funds:	42	AIM Activities: Dir:	10
Industry sector preferences:		Exec:	11
See below for analyst coverage			
Geographical preferences:	None	Act for: Bright Futures; Connaught; Empire	
In-house industry sector analysts?	Yes	Interactive; Enneurope; Epic; Hawthorn; Imprint	
Sectors covered by analysts: IT; Leisure; Media;		Search & Selection; Inventive Leisure; ITIS; JAB;	
Software; Speciality Retail; Support Services		Online Travel; Torday & Carlisle	
Prospective AIM companies considered:			
Startups Yes Early stage Yes Established Yes			
Typical transaction parameters: Minimum market			
capital - £20m. Minimum funds to be raised - £5m		Other Offices:	
Split of broking activities:	n/a	UK offices	
(institutional: private client)		Manchester Tel: 0161-831 9133 Phillip Adams	
Underwriting facilities:			
Can provide:	Yes		
Can arrange:	Yes		
Other activities: Corporate Finance Advice; Market			
Making; Research; Sales; Sales Trading			

Arbuthnot Securities

2 Lambeth Hill, London, EC4V 4GG Tel: 020-7002 4600;   Fax: 020-7002 4619;
email: FirstnameLastname@arbuthnot.co.uk;   Web site: www.arbuthnot.co.uk

Contact:	Guy Peters	**Number of Directors & Executives engaged in:**	
Also act as Nominated Broker?	Yes	**Corporate Finance:** **Dir:**	8
Companies represented on first admission:	Over 25	**Exec:**	16
Number involved in new issue to raise funds:	Over 15	**AIM Activities:** **Dir:**	4
Industry sector preferences:	None	**Exec:**	9
Geographical preferences:	None		
In-house industry sector analysts?	Yes	**Act for:** AdVal; AIT; Amberley; Chelford; Cradley;	
Sectors covered by analysts:	All	Fayrewood; Highland Timber; International Greetings;	
Prospective AIM companies considered:		INVU; Jennings Brothers; Loades; Mears; Pilkington's	
Startups Yes **Early stage** Yes **Established** Yes		Tiles; SpringHealth Leisure; Staffing Ventures; Thomas	
Typical transaction parameters:	n/a	Walker; West Bromwich Albion	
Split of broking activities:	n/a		
(institutional: private client)			
Underwriting facilities:		**Other Offices:**	
Can provide:	Yes	Birmingham Tel: 0121-632 2100	
Can arrange:	Yes	Edinburgh	
		Glasgow	

Other activities: Corporate Broking; Corporate Finance
Advice; Institutional Research & Sales; Market Making

ARC Associates

3 Finsbury Square, London, EC2A 1LN Tel: 020-7614 4000;   Fax: 020-7614 4001;
email: enquiries@ARCassociates.com;   Web site: www.arcassociates.com

Contact:	Peter Tahany	**Number of Directors & Executives engaged in:**	
Also act as Nominated Broker?	No	**Corporate Finance:** **Dir:**	3
Companies represented on first admission:	n/a	**Exec:**	12
Number involved in new issue to raise funds:	n/a	**AIM Activities:** **Dir:**	3
Industry sector preferences:	Financial Services;	**Exec:**	8
Media; Property; Technology; Telecoms			
Geographical preferences:	UK & Europe	**Act for:**	n/a
In-house industry sector analysts?	Yes		
Sectors covered by analysts: Financial Services; Media;			
Property; Technology; Telecoms			
Prospective AIM companies considered:			
Startups Yes **Early stage** Yes **Established** Yes			
Typical transaction parameters:	£2m-£50m		
Split of broking activities:	n/a	**Other Offices:**	n/a
(institutional: private client)			
Underwriting facilities:			
Can provide:	No		
Can arrange:	Yes		

Other activities: Consultancy Advisory; Corporate
Finance; M&A

ARM Corporate Finance

12 Pepper Street, London, E14 9RP Tel: 020-7512 0191;   Fax: 020-7512 0747;
email: jim.mcgeever.armcf.com;   Web site: www.armcf.com

Contact:	Ian Fenn / Jim McGeever	**Number of Directors & Executives engaged in:**		
Also act as Nominated Broker?	No	**Corporate Finance:**	**Dir:**	4
Companies represented on first admission:	8		**Exec:**	4
Number involved in new issue to raise funds:	8	**AIM Activities:**	**Dir:**	4
Industry sector preferences:	TMT		**Exec:**	4
Geographical preferences:	None			
In-house industry sector analysts?	Yes	**Act for:** Clipper Ventures; Leisureplay; Maisha;		
Sectors covered by analysts:	TMT	Motion Media; Scott Tod; Sirvis IT		

Prospective AIM companies considered:
Startups Yes **Early stage** Yes **Established** Yes
Typical transaction parameters: £1m upwards
Split of broking activities: n/a
(institutional: private client)
Underwriting facilities:
                              Can provide: Yes
                              Can arrange: Yes

Other Offices: n/a

Other activities: Mergers & Acquisitions; Private Equity
Fundraising

Baird

Mint House, 77 Mansell Street, London, E1 8AF Tel: 020-7488 1212;   Fax: 020-7702 3134;
email: nnaylor@rwbaird.com;   Web site: www.baird.com/europe

Contact:	Nicholas Naylor	**Number of Directors & Executives engaged in:**		
Also act as Nominated Broker?	Yes	**Corporate Finance:**	**Dir:**	5
Companies represented on first admission:	4		**Exec:**	10
Number involved in new issue to raise funds:	8	**AIM Activities:**	**Dir:**	5
Industry sector preferences:	Industrial; Healthcare;		**Exec:**	10

Media; Sports & Leisure; Support Services; Retail;
Technology
Geographical preferences: None
In-house industry sector analysts?   Yes
Sectors covered by analysts: Healthcare; Media; Leisure;
Support Services; Retail; Technology
Prospective AIM companies considered:
Startups No **Early stage** Yes **Established** Yes
Typical transaction parameters: None particularly
Split of broking activities: 100:0
(institutional: private client)
Underwriting facilities:
                              Can provide: Yes
                              Can arrange: Yes

Act for: Advanced Medical Solutions; First Property;
Forever Broadcasting; Sinclair Pharma

Other Offices:
Germany; USA

Other activities: Equity Research and Distribution;
Investment Banking; Market Making; Private Equity

Beaumont Cornish

Georgian House, 63 Coleman Street, London, EC2R 5BB Tel: 020-7628 3396;   Fax: 020-7628 3393;
email: corpfin@b-cornish.co.uk;   Web site: www.b-cornish.co.uk

		Number of Directors & Executives engaged in:		
Contact:	Roland Cornish			
Also act as Nominated Broker?	No	Corporate Finance:	Dir:	4
Companies represented on first admission:	8		Exec:	5
Number involved in new issue to raise funds:	7	AIM Activities:	Dir:	4
Industry sector preferences:	All		Exec:	5
Geographical preferences:	All			
In-house industry sector analysts?	n/a	Act for: A Cohen & Co; Brainspark; Bella Media;		
Sectors covered by analysts:	n/a	BWA; Cater Barnard; DawMed Systems; easier;		
Prospective AIM companies considered:		Earthport; Elektron; ESV; Griffin; Huveaux; Incite;		
Startups No Early stage Yes Established Yes		Magnum Power; Medical Marketing International; PC		
Typical transaction parameters:	Flexible	Medics; Oakgate; RII; Universal Direct		
Split of broking activities:	n/a			
(institutional: private client)				
Underwriting facilities:		Other Offices:		n/a
Can provide:	No			
Can arrange:	Yes			

Other activities: General financial advice; Ofex corporate
adviser; Sponsor - Full List

Brewin Dolphin Securities

7 Drumsheugh Gardens, Edinburgh, EH3 7QH Tel: 0131-225 2566;   Fax: 0131-529 0246;
Web site: www.blw.co.uk

		Number of Directors & Executives engaged in:		
Contact:	Vikram Lall			
Also act as Nominated Broker?	Yes	Corporate Finance:	Dir:	12
Companies represented on first admission:	45		Exec:	6
Number involved in new issue to raise funds:	14	AIM Activities:	Dir:	12
Industry sector preferences:	None		Exec:	6
Geographical preferences:	UK generally			
In-house industry sector analysts?	n/a	Act for: 7 Group; Alkane Energy; AMCO; Angus & Ross;		

Sectors covered by analysts: Breweries Pubs Restaurants;
Construction; Chemicals; Electronic & Electrical Equipment;
Engineering; Food Producers & Processors; Health; Household
Goods & Textiles; Leisure and Hotels; Media & Photography;
Mining; Oil & Gas; Other Financial; Paper; Packaging &
Printing; Retail; Software & Computer Services; Support
Services; Telecommunication Services; Transport

Prospective AIM companies considered:

Startups Yes Early stage Yes Established Yes

Typical transaction parameters:	None
Split of broking activities:	n/a
(institutional: private client)	
Underwriting facilities:	
Can provide:	Yes
Can arrange:	Yes

Act for: 7 Group; Alkane Energy; AMCO; Angus & Ross;
AorTech; Beauford; Biolife Ventures; Blavod Black Vodka;
Booth Industries; Capital Management & Investment;
Cavanagh; Clan Homes; Comeleon; Concurrent
Technologies; County Contact Centres; Dobbies Garden
Centres; Firestone Diamonds; Forbidden Technologies;
Gladstone; Henderson Morley; Huveaux; IndigoVision;
Inter Link Foods; James R Knowles; John Swan; Just Car
Clinics; Medical Marketing International; Metnor; Micap;
Netbenefit; Norman Hay; Premier Management;
Quadnetics; Romag; Selector; Stadium; Synergy
Healthcare; tecc-IS; Tolent; Ultimate Leisure; Vebnet;
Vianet; Virtue Broadcasting; Walker Greenbank; Xpertise;
Yeoman; Zytronic

Other activities: Corporate Broking Services; Corporate
Finance Advice; Institutional Research; Private Client
Stockbroking & Fund Management; Takeover & Rule 3 Advice

Other Offices:	
Glasgow	Tel: 0141-221 7733 Elizabeth Kennedy
Manchester	Tel: 0161-839 4222 Mark Brady
Leeds	Tel: 0113-241 0130 Neil Baldwin

Bridgewell

Old Change House, 128 Queen Victoria Street, London, EC4V 4BJ Tel: 020-7003 3000;
Fax: 020-7003 3199; email: john.craven@bridgewell.co.uk; Web site: www.bridgewell.co.uk

Contact: John Craven/Greg Aldridge	**Number of Directors & Executives engaged in:**		
Also act as Nominated Broker? Yes	**Corporate Finance:**	**Dir:**	7
Companies represented on first admission: 16		**Exec:**	11
Number involved in new issue to raise funds: 6	**AIM Activities:**	**Dir:**	7
Industry sector preferences: Construction; Financial Services; General Industrials; Housebuilding; IT; Leisure; Media; Property; Retail; Support Services; Technology		**Exec:**	11
Geographical preferences: None	**Act for:** AFA Systems; Avingtrans; Conygar Investment; Corpora; DDD; Genus; Intelligent Environments; Interior Services; LPA; Premier Direct; SBS; Stonemartin; Transense Technologies		
In-house industry sector analysts? Yes			
Sectors covered by analysts: Construction; Financial Services; General Industrials; Housebuilding; IT; Leisure; Media; Property; Retail; Support Services; Technology			
Prospective AIM companies considered:			
Startups No **Early stage** Yes **Established** Yes	**Other Offices:**		n/a
Typical transaction parameters: Minimum market capital - £10m (other than in exceptional circumstances)			
Split of broking activities: n/a (institutional: private client)			
Underwriting facilities:			
Can provide: Yes			
Can arrange: Yes			
Other activities: Corporate Broking			

British Linen Advisers

12 Melville Street, Edinburgh, EH3 7NS, Tel: 0131-243 8325; Fax: 0131-243 8534;
email info@britishlinen.co.uk; Web site: www.britishlinen.co.uk

Contact: Edward Murray	**Number of Directors & Executives engaged in:**		
Also act as Nominated Broker? No	**Corporate Finance:**	**Dir:**	6
Companies represented on first admission: 2		**Exec:**	6
Number involved in new issue to raise funds: 1	**AIM Activities:**	**Dir:**	6
Industry sector preferences: None		**Exec:**	6
Geographical preferences: UK			
In-house industry sector analysts? No	**Act for:**		n/a
Sectors covered by analysts: n/a			
Prospective AIM companies considered:			
Startups No **Early stage** No **Established** Yes			
Typical transaction parameters: Minimum market capital - £10m. Minimum fundraising - £3m			
Split of broking activities: n/a (institutional: private client)			
Underwriting facilities:	**Other Offices:**		
Can provide: No	London Tel: 020-7710 8800 Richard Davies		
Can arrange: Yes			
Other activities: Corporate Finance Advisory; Debt Advisory			

Canaccord Capital

1st Floor, Brook House, 27 Upper Brook Street, London, W1K 7QF Tel: 020-7518 2777;
Fax: 020-7518 2778/9; email: neil_johnson@canaccordeurope.com; Web site: www.canaccord.com

Contact:	Neil Johnson	**Number of Directors & Executives engaged in:**		
Also act as Nominated Broker?	Yes	**Corporate Finance:**	**Dir:**	4
Companies represented on first admission:	17		**Exec:**	6
Number involved in new issue to raise funds:	43	**AIM Activities:**	**Dir:**	4
Industry sector preferences:	See sector analysts		**Exec:**	6
Geographical preferences:	UK, North America			
and Europe		**Act for:** ADVFN.com; America Mineral Fields; Antrim		
In-house industry sector analysts?	Yes	Energy; Aricom; Bema Gold; Canisp; CES Software; Cluff		
Sectors covered by analysts: Gaming; Life Sciences;		Mining; Corvus Capital; First Calgary Petroleum; First		
Media; Mining; Oil & Gas; Software		Quantum Minerals; Global Energy Development; GMA		
Prospective AIM companies considered:		Resources; Mediwatch; Oilexco; Oriel Resources; Peter		
Startups No **Early stage** Yes **Established** Yes		Hambro Mining; Pixology; Portman; Ramco Energy; Sibir		
Typical transaction parameters:	n/a	Energy; Skiddaw Capital; Symphony Plastic Technologies;		
Split of broking activities:	n/a	Ten Alps Communications; The Medical House; Thistle		
(institutional: private client)		Mining; TripleArc; Yamana Gold; YM BioSciences		
Underwriting facilities:				
	Can provide:	Yes	**Other Offices:**	
	Can arrange:	Yes	1 office in Europe and 25 offices in North America	
Other activities:	n/a			

Cazenove

12 Tokenhouse Yard, London, EC2R 7AN, Tel: 020-7588 2828; Fax: 020-7606 9205;
email mwentworthstanley@cazenove.com; Web site: www.cazenove.com

Contact:	Michael Wentworth-Stanley	**Number of Directors & Executives engaged in:**		
Also act as Nominated Broker?	Yes	**Corporate Finance:**	**Dir:**	n/a
Companies represented on first admission:	n/a		**Exec:**	n/a
Number involved in new issue to raise funds:	n/a	**AIM Activities:**	**Dir:**	n/a
Industry sector preferences:	n/a		**Exec:**	n/a
Geographical preferences:	n/a			
In-house industry sector analysts?	n/a	**Act for:** Inflexion; Radamec		
Sectors covered by analysts:	n/a			
Prospective AIM companies considered:				
Startups n/a **Early stage** n/a **Established** n/a				
Typical transaction parameters:	n/a			
Split of broking activities:	n/a			
(institutional: private client)				
Underwriting facilities:		**Other Offices:**		n/a
	Can provide:	n/a		
	Can arrange:	n/a		
Other activities:	n/a			

Charles Stanley

25 Luke Street, London, EC2A 4AR Tel: 020-7739 8200;   Fax: 020-7739 4307;
Web site: www.charles-stanley.co.uk

Contact:	Richard Thompson/Russell Cook	**Number of Directors & Executives engaged in:**	
Also act as Nominated Broker?	Yes	**Corporate Finance:** Dir:	5
Companies represented on first admission:	n/a	Exec:	4
Number involved in new issue to raise funds:	n/a	**AIM Activities:** Dir:	5
Industry sector preferences:	None	Exec:	4
Geographical preferences:	UK		
In-house industry sector analysts?	Yes	**Act for:** Cassidy Brothers; Celltalk; Centurion	

Sectors covered by analysts: Consumer Goods; Healthcare; Insurance; Leisure; Media & Entertainment; Real Estate; Retailers; Support Services; Technology

Prospective AIM companies considered:

Startups No **Early stage** Yes **Established** Yes

Typical transaction parameters: None particularly

Split of broking activities: n/a
(institutional: private client)

Underwriting facilities:

	Can provide:	No
	Can arrange:	Yes

Other activities: Corporate Broking Services; Corporate Finance Advice; Equity Research; Private Client Stockbroking

Act for: Cassidy Brothers; Celltalk; Centurion Electronics; Computerland UK; Deltex Medical; Feedback; Glisten; Griffin Mining; Highams Systems Services; Honeycombe Leisure; Jourdan; Lawrence; NWF; Parkdean Holidays; Potential Finance; Proactive Sports; samedaybooks.co.uk; Solid State Supplies; Stilo; Supercart; Tikit; UA; Unverse;Vantis; William Jacks; World Careers Network

Other Offices: n/a

City Financial Associates

Pountney Hill House, 6 Laurence Pountney Hill, London, EC4R 0BL Tel: 020-7090 7800;
Fax: 020-7283 6300;   email: enquiry@cityfin.co.uk;

Contact:	Tony Rawlinson	**Number of Directors & Executives engaged in:**	
Also act as Nominated Broker?	Yes	**Corporate Finance:** Dir:	3
Companies represented on first admission:	6	Exec:	3
Number involved in new issue to raise funds:	12	**AIM Activities:** Dir:	3
Industry sector preferences:	UK	Exec:	3
Geographical preferences:	None		
In-house industry sector analysts?	No	**Act for:** 10 Group; 2 Travel; Beaufort; Designer	
Sectors covered by analysts:	n/a		

Prospective AIM companies considered:

Startups Yes **Early stage** Yes **Established** Yes

Typical transaction parameters: Raising £250,000-
£10m for smaller companies. Market cap £1m–£50m

Split of broking activities:
(institutional: private client)

Underwriting facilities:

	Can provide:	No
	Can arrange:	Yes

Other activities: n/a

Act for: 10 Group; 2 Travel; Beaufort; Designer Vision; Dinkie Heel; Documedia Solutions; Fundamental-E Investments; Interactive Digital Solutions; Mosaique; Oak Holdings; Overnet Data; Parallel Media; SBS; Setstone; Tellings Golden Miller; Voss Net

Other Offices: n/a

Close Brothers Corporate Finance

10 Crown Place, Clifton Street, London, EC2A 4FT Tel: 020-7655 3100; Fax: 020-7655 8906;
Web site: www.cbcf.com

Contact:	Mark Napier	**Number of Directors & Executives engaged in:**	
Also act as Nominated Broker?	No	**Corporate Finance:** Dir:	24
Companies represented on first admission:	3	Exec:	40
Number involved in new issue to raise funds:	3	**AIM Activities:** Dir:	6
Industry sector preferences:	Media; Technology;	Exec:	10
Telecoms; Life Sciences			
Geographical preferences:	None	**Act for:** DCS; Enterprise; Orbis	
In-house industry sector analysts?	Yes		

Sectors covered by analysts: Media; Technology;
Telecoms; Life Sciences
Prospective AIM companies considered:
Startups No **Early stage** Yes, if profitability established
Established Yes

Typical transaction parameters:	Minimum market	**Other Offices:**	n/a
capital - £15m. Minimum funds to be raised - £5m			
Split of broking activities:	n/a		
(institutional: private client)			
Underwriting facilities:			
Can provide:	Yes		
Can arrange:	No		
Other activities:	n/a		

Collins Stewart

9th Floor, 88 Wood Street, London, EC2V 7QR Tel: 020-7523 8350; Fax: 020-7523 8134;
email enquiries@collins-stewart.com; Web site: www.collins-stewart.com

Contact:	Kripa Radhakrishnan	**Number of Directors & Executives engaged in:**	
Also act as Nominated Broker?	Yes	**Corporate Finance:** Dir:	1
Companies represented on first admission:	18	Exec:	7
Number involved in new issue to raise funds:	20	**AIM Activities:** Dir:	1
Industry sector preferences:	None	Exec:	7
Geographical preferences:	None		
In-house industry sector analysts?	Yes		

Sectors covered by analysts: Engineering; Football Clubs;
Healthcare; Information Technology and Internet; Leisure;
Media; Retail; Support Services; Water Companies
Prospective AIM companies considered:
Startups Yes **Early stage** Yes **Established** Yes

Act for: Avanti Capital; BioProgress; Bits Corp; Center Parcs (UK); Chicago Environmental; CI Traders; City Lofts; Cobra Bio-Manufacturing; ComProp; CustomVis; DataCash; Digital Sport; Documedia; Epic Brand Investments; Erinaceous; Flintstone Technologies; Fountains; Halladale; Hartstone; Honeysuckle; Inditherm; Ingenta; International Brand Licensing; Mayborn; Media Square; Milestone; Monterrico Metals; New Media Industries; NewMedia SPARK; PIPEX Communications; Oystertec; Resurge; RWS; Screen; Sirius Financial Solutions; Southampton Leisure; Synigence; Trans-Siberian Gold; Tricorn; Wilshaw

Typical transaction parameters: £20m market cap.	
Miniumum funds to be raised £5m	
Split of broking activities: All Institutional	
(institutional: private client)	
Underwriting facilities:	
Can provide:	Yes
Can arrange:	Yes

Other activities: Investment Trusts; Large and small company broking

Other Offices:
Channel Islands
New York

Corporate Synergy

12 Nicholas Lane, London, EC4N 7BN Tel: 020-7626 2244; Fax: 020-7626 2255;
email info@corporatesynergy.co.uk; Web site: www.corporatesynergy.co.uk

Contact:	Lindsay Mair	**Number of Directors & Executives engaged in:**	
Also act as Nominated Broker?	Yes	**Corporate Finance:** Dir:	4
Companies represented on first admission:	17	Exec:	5
Number involved in new issue to raise funds:	16	**AIM Activities:** Dir:	6
Industry sector preferences:	None	Exec:	10
Geographical preferences:	None		

In-house industry sector analysts? Yes
Sectors covered by analysts: IT; Leisure & Hotels; Media & Entertainment; Mining; Support Services
Prospective AIM companies considered:
Startups No **Early stage** Yes **Established** Yes
Typical transaction parameters: None particularly
Split of broking activities: n/a
(institutional: private client)
Underwriting facilities:

Can provide: No
Can arrange: Yes

Other activities: n/a

Act for: 1st Dental Laboratories; Black Rock Oil & Gas; CMS Webview; Cytomyx; Elite Strategies; Envesta Telecom; Farley; First Derivatives; Hartest; iTrain; Lo-Q; Multi; Sports & Leisure; Tom Hoskins; Venturia

Other Offices:
Newbury 01488-608188

Credit Lyonnais Securities

Broadwalk House, 5 Appold Street, London, EC2A 2DA, Tel: 020-7588 4000; Fax: 020-7588 0278;
Web site: www.creditlyonnais.com

Contact:	Simon Bennett	**Number of Directors & Executives engaged in:**	
Also act as Nominated Broker?	Yes	**Corporate Finance:** Dir:	5
Companies represented on first admission:	5	Exec:	12
Number involved in new issue to raise funds:	2	**AIM Activities:** Dir:	5
Industry sector preferences:	Chemicals;	Exec:	12

Construction; Financial Services; Food; Leisure; Oil; Paper & Packaging; Property; Retail; Support Services; Technology; TMT; Utilities
Geographical preferences: UK/Europe
In-house industry sector analysts? Yes
Sectors covered by analysts: As above
Prospective AIM companies considered:
Startups No **Early stage** Possibly **Established** Yes
Typical transaction parameters: n/a
Split of broking activities: n/a
(institutional: private client)
Underwriting facilities:

Can provide: Yes
Can arrange: Yes

Other activities: Acquisition finance; Market Making; Mergers and Acquisitions

Act for: Bradstock; Heavitree Brewery; Inter-Alliance; Linton Park; Peel Holdings; StatPro; William Ransom & Son

Other Offices:
Frankfurt; Hong Kong; Lyon; New York; Paris

Credit Suisse First Boston

One Cabot Square, London, E14 4QR Tel: 020-7888 8888; Fax: 020-7888 0901;
Web site: www.csfb.com

Contact:	Mark Seligman	**Number of Directors & Executives engaged in:**		
Also act as Nominated Broker?	Yes	**Corporate Finance:**	**Dir:**	430
Companies represented on first admission:	None		**Exec:**	dir & exec
Number involved in new issue to raise funds:	None	**AIM Activities:**	**Dir:**	None
Industry sector preferences:	None		**Exec:**	None
Geographical preferences:	None			
In-house industry sector analysts?	Yes	**Act for:**		n/a
Sectors covered by analysts:	All			

Prospective AIM companies considered:
Startups No **Early stage** No **Established** Yes
Typical transaction parameters: Over £100 million
Split of broking activities:
(institutional: private client)   n/a
Underwriting facilities:

	Can provide:	Yes	**Other Offices:**	n/a
	Can arrange:	Yes		

Other activities: 'Bulge bracket' investment bank

Daniel Stewart

48 Bishopsgate, London, EC2N 4AJ Tel: 020-7374 6789; Fax: 020-7374 6742;
email info@danielstewart.co.uk; Web site: www.danielstewart.co.uk

Contact:	Peter Shea, Alistair Cade	**Number of Directors & Executives engaged in:**		
Also act as Nominated Broker?	Yes	**Corporate Finance:**	**Dir:**	2
Companies represented on first admission:	2		**Exec:**	4
Number involved in new issue to raise funds:	2	**AIM Activities:**	**Dir:**	2
Industry sector preferences:	None		**Exec:**	4
Geographical preferences:	None			
In-house industry sector analysts?	Yes	**Act for:** Matrix Communications		

Sectors covered by analysts: Leisure; Technology
Prospective AIM companies considered:
Startups Yes **Early stage** Yes **Established** Yes
Typical transaction parameters: £2.5–10 million
Split of broking activities: 85:15
(institutional: private client)
Underwriting facilities:

	Can provide:	No	**Other Offices:**	n/a
	Can arrange:	Yes		

Other activities: Corporate Finance; Fund Management;
Mergers & Acquisitions

Dawnay Day Corporate Finance

8-10 Grosvenor Gardens, London, SW1W 0DH Tel: 020-7509 4570; Fax: 020-7509 4575;
email gerald.raingold@dawnay-day.co.uk; Web site: www.dawnayday.co.uk

Contact:	Gerald Raingold	**Number of Directors & Executives engaged in:**	
Also act as Nominated Broker?	No	Corporate Finance: **Dir:**	6
Companies represented on first admission:	3	**Exec:**	4
Number involved in new issue to raise funds:	3	AIM Activities: **Dir:**	4
Industry sector preferences:	n/a	**Exec:**	4
Geographical preferences:	None		
In-house industry sector analysts?	n/a	**Act for:** Falkland Islands; Stylo; Ultimate Finance;	
Sectors covered by analysts: Knowledge of Engineering;		Volvere	
Financial Services; Healthcare; IT; Leisure; Property;			
Retail; Support Services; Textiles			
Prospective AIM companies considered:			
Startups No **Early stage** Possible **Established** Yes			
Typical transaction parameters:	n/a		
Split of broking activities:	n/a	**Other Offices:**	n/a
(institutional: private client)			
Underwriting facilities:			
Can provide:	Yes		
Can arrange:	Yes		
Other activities: Corporate Advisory Services			
Main Market Sponsor			

Deloitte & Touche Corporate Finance

180 Strand, London, WC2R 1BL Tel: 020-7936 3000; Fax: 020-7546 9512;
email rbinks@deloitte.co.uk; Web site: www.deloitte.co.uk

Contact:	Robin Binks/Jonathan Hinton	**Number of Directors & Executives engaged in:**	
Also act as Nominated Broker?	No	Corporate Finance: **Dir:**	30
Companies represented on first admission:	19	**Exec:**	200
Number involved in new issue to raise funds:	26	AIM Activities: **Dir:**	8 Partners
Industry sector preferences:	Covering all sectors	**Exec:**	22 Assistants
Geographical preferences:	None		
In-house industry sector analysts?	No	**Act for:** ASITE; Carbo; COE; Comland Commercial;	
Sectors covered by analysts:	n/a	Conygar Investment; Digital Animations; Western	
Prospective AIM companies considered:		Selection; Willington	
Startups Yes **Early stage** Yes **Established** Yes			
Typical transaction parameters: Minimum market			
capitalisation for new funds - £10m. Minimum funds			
raised - £3m			
Split of broking activities:	n/a	**Other Offices:**	n/a
(institutional: private client)			
Underwriting facilities:			
Can provide:	No		
Can arrange:	Yes		
Other activities: Audit & Business Advisory; Business			
Consulting Services; Corporate Finance Advice; Corporate			
Recovery; General, Modelling & Valuation; Tax Advisory			

Deutsche Bank

6th Floor, Winchester House, Great Winchester Street, London, EC2N 2DB Tel: 020-7545 8000;
Fax: 020-7545 4577; Web site: www.db.com

Contact:	Philip Cowdy	Number of Directors & Executives engaged in:	
Also act as Nominated Broker?	Yes	Corporate Finance: Dir:	n/a
Companies represented on first admission:	n/a	Exec:	n/a
Number involved in new issue to raise funds:	n/a	AIM Activities: Dir:	n/a
Industry sector preferences:	n/a	Exec:	n/a
Geographical preferences:	n/a		
In-house industry sector analysts?	n/a	Act for: Retail Stores	
Sectors covered by analysts:	n/a		
Prospective AIM companies considered:			
Startups n/a Early stage n/a Established n/a			
Typical transaction parameters:	n/a		
Split of broking activities:	n/a		
(institutional: private client)			
Underwriting facilities:		Other Offices:	n/a
Can provide:	n/a		
Can arrange:	n/a		
Other activities:	n/a		

Dolmen Securities

Dolmen House, 4 Earlsfort Terrace, Dublin 2, Ireland, Tel: 00-353 1 633 3800; Fax: 00-353 1 662 3737;
email: info@dbb.ie; Web site: www.dbb.ie

Contact:	Ronan Reid	Number of Directors & Executives engaged in:	
Also act as Nominated Broker?	n/a	Corporate Finance: Dir:	n/a
Companies represented on first admission:	n/a	Exec:	n/a
Number involved in new issue to raise funds:	n/a	AIM Activities: Dir:	n/a
Industry sector preferences:	n/a	Exec:	n/a
Geographical preferences:	n/a		
In-house industry sector analysts?	n/a	Act for:	n/a
Sectors covered by analysts:	n/a		
Prospective AIM companies considered:	n/a		
Startups Early stage Established	n/a		
Typical transaction parameters:	n/a		
Split of broking activities:	n/a		
institutional: private client)	n/a		
Underwriting facilities:		Other Offices:	n/a
Can provide:	n/a		
Can arrange:	n/a		
Other activities:	n/a		

Dresdner Kleinwort Wasserstein

PO Box 560, 20 Fenchurch Street, London, EC3P 3DB Tel: 020-7623 8000; Fax: 020-7283 4667;
email Ishbel.Macpherson@drkw.com; Web site: www.drkw.com

Contact:	Ishbel Macpherson	**Number of Directors & Executives engaged in:**	
Also act as Nominated Broker?	Yes	**Corporate Finance:**	**Dir:**	6
Companies represented on first admission:	1		**Exec:**	15
Number involved in new issue to raise funds:	2	**AIM Activities:**	**Dir:**	Integrated
Industry sector preferences:	Growth		**Exec:**	Integrated
Geographical preferences:	UK		
In-house industry sector analysts?	Yes	**Act for:** InTechnology; Sportingbet.com	
Sectors covered by analysts:	Growth		

Prospective AIM companies considered:

Startups No **Early stage** No **Established** Yes

Typical transaction parameters: Market capitalisation over £100m

Split of broking activities: Integrated approach
(institutional: private client)

Underwriting facilities:

Can provide:	Yes
Can arrange:	n/a

Other Offices:
Operates globally

Other activities: Full service global investment bank

Durlacher

4 Chiswell Street, London, EC1Y 4UP Tel: 020-7459 3600; Fax: 020-7628 3225;
Web site: www.durlacher.com

Contact:	Simon Hirst	**Number of Directors & Executives engaged in:**		
Also act as Nominated Broker?	Yes	**Corporate Finance:**	**Dir:**	5
Companies represented on first admission:	Numerous		**Exec:**	8
Number involved in new issue to raise funds: Numerous		**AIM Activities:**	**Dir:**	5
Industry sector preferences:	Growth, Industrial and		**Exec:**	8

Technology Companies

Geographical preferences: Primarily UK/Europe
In-house industry sector analysts? Yes
Sectors covered by analysts: Various. Emphasis on technology, media, new media, telecoms, life sciences, industrial services and high-growth smaller companies generally.

Act for: Avesco; Cyprotex; Expomedia; Finsbury Food; GTL Resources; Host Europe; ID Data; Image Scan; IMS Maxims; Lighthouse; Matrix Healthcare; Medal Entertainment & Media; Newsplayer; Pursuit Dynamics; Personal; Prestbury; RingProp; Springboard; Straight; themutual.net; YooMedia

Prospective AIM companies considered:

Startups Yes **Early stage** Yes **Established** Yes

Typical transaction parameters: No special parameters
Split of broking activities: n/a
(institutional: private client)

Other Offices:
Regional UK offices

Underwriting facilities:

Can provide:	Yes
Can arrange:	n/a

Other activities: Stategic consultancy research, M&A, fund management, broking, on-line broking and news reporting, private equity and investment. Publisher of the AIM Bulletin

Ernst & Young

Becket House, 1 Lambeth Palace Road, London, SE1 7EU Tel: 020-7951 2000;   Fax: 020-7951 3823;
Web site: www.ey.com/uk

Contact:	Oliver Baker	**Number of Directors & Executives engaged in:**	
Also act as Nominated Broker?	No	**Corporate Finance:** Dir:	15
Companies represented on first admission:	n/a	Exec:	80
Number involved in new issue to raise funds:	n/a	**AIM Activities:** Dir:	1
Industry sector preferences:	n/a	Exec:	7
Geographical preferences:	n/a		
In-house industry sector analysts?	Yes	**Act for:** Black Arrow; London Security; Thomas	
Sectors covered by analysts:	n/a	Walker; web-angel	
Prospective AIM companies considered:			
Startups Yes **Early stage** Yes **Established** Yes			
Typical transaction parameters:	n/a		
Split of broking activities:	n/a		
(institutional: private client)			
Underwriting facilities:		**Other Offices:**	
Can provide:	No	Birmingham: Andrew Raca 0121-535 2604	
Can arrange:	n/a	Leeds: Andrew Kitchingman 0113-298 2505	
		London: John Stephen 020-7951 4462	
Other activities:	n/a		

Evolution Beeson Gregory

100 Wood Street, London, EC2V 7AN Tel: 020-7071 4300;   Fax: 020-7071 4450;
email enquiries@evbg.com;   Web site: www.evbg.com

Contact:	Tom Price/Chris	**Number of Directors & Executives engaged in:**	
Callaway /Tim Worledge/Mike Brennan/ Rob Collins		**Corporate Finance:** Dir:	6
Also act as Nominated Broker?	Yes	Exec:	8
Companies represented on first admission:	42	**AIM Activities:** Dir:	6
Number involved in new issue to raise funds:	68	Exec:	8
Industry sector preferences:	See below		
Geographical preferences:	European	**Act for:** Advance Capital Invest; Advanced Power	
In-house industry sector analysts?	Yes	Components; Aero Inventory; Arlington; ASK Central;	
Sectors covered by analysts: Evolution Beeson Gregory has		Avesco; Bank Restaurant; Blavod Black Vodka; Cape;	
generalist smaller company analysts, plus specialists in		Cardpoint; Chorion; Eckoh Technologies; Faupel Trading;	
Electronics; Games & Gaming; Industrials; Leisure; Life		Focus Solutions; Gaming Corporation; GR; Hat Pin;	
Sciences; Resources; Retail; Services; Software		ImageState; IQE; Landround; Murchison United; Netcall;	
Prospective AIM companies considered:		Ocean Power Technologies; OMG; Osmetech; Paramount;	
Startups No **Early stage** Yes **Established** Yes		Planit; Prezzo; Proteome Sciences; Regal Petroleum;	
Typical transaction parameters: A good management		Reversus; St Barbara Mines; Stagecoach Theatre Arts;	
team with a clear strategy and defensible growth prospects		Sterling Energy; Torex Retail; TradingSports Exchange	
Split of broking activities:	90 :10	Systems; Triple Plate Junction; Warthog; Wealth	
(institutional: private client)		Management Software; Winchester Entertainment	
Underwriting facilities:			
Can provide:	Yes	**Other Offices:**	n/a
Can arrange:	n/a		
Other activities: Corporate Broking Services; Corporate			
Finance Advice; Funding Advice; Mergers and Acquisitions;			
Research; Strategic Financial Advice			

Goodbody Corporate Finance

122 Pembroke Road, Dublin 4, Ireland, Tel: 00-353 1 667 0400; Fax: 00-353 1 667 0280;
Web site: www.goodbody.ie

Contact:	Kathy Morgan	**Number of Directors & Executives engaged in:**		
Also act as Nominated Broker?	Yes	**Corporate Finance:**	**Dir:**	n/a
Companies represented on first admission:	1		**Exec:**	n/a
Number involved in new issue to raise funds:	1	**AIM Activities:**	**Dir:**	n/a
Industry sector preferences:	n/a		**Exec:**	n/a
Geographical preferences:	n/a			
In-house industry sector analysts?	n/a	**Act for:**		n/a
Sectors covered by analysts:	n/a			
Prospective AIM companies considered:				
Startups n/a **Early stage** n/a **Established** n/a				
Typical transaction parameters:	n/a			
Split of broking activities:	n/a			
(institutional: private client)				
Underwriting facilities:		**Other Offices:**		
Can provide:	n/a	Cork		
Can arrange:	n/a			
Other activities:	n/a			

Grant Thornton Corporate Finance

Grant Thornton House, Melton Street, London, NW1 2EP Tel: 020-7383 5100; Fax: 020-7387 5371;
email: corporatefinance@gtuk.com; Web site: www.grant-thornton.co.uk

Contact:	Gerald Beaney/Philip Secrett	**Number of Directors & Executives engaged in:**		
Also act as Nominated Broker?	No	**Corporate Finance:**	**Dir:**	35
Companies represented on first admission:	92		**Exec:**	250
Number involved in new issue to raise funds:	92	**AIM Activities:**	**Dir:**	10
Industry sector preferences:	None		**Exec:**	6
Geographical preferences:	None			
In-house industry sector analysts?	None	**Act for:** 3DM Worldwide; Akaei; Alibi Communications;		
Sectors covered by analysts:	n/a	Avocet Mining; Bond International Software; Bullion		
Prospective AIM companies considered:		Resources; Cabouchon; Cambrian Mining; Capricorn		
Startups Yes **Early stage** Yes **Established** Yes		Resources; Carrwood; Coburg; Digital Classics; Dimension		
Typical transaction parameters:	n/a	Resources; Einstein; EiRx Therapeutics; Eurasia Mining;		
Split of broking activities:	n/a	First Derivatives; Fiske; Gippsland; Glow		
(institutional: private client)		Communications; Golden Prospect; Greenchip Investments;		
Underwriting facilities:		Inflexion; iTrain; KeyWorld Investments; London Asia		
Can provide:	No	Capital; Mean Fiddler Music; Network; On-Line;		
Can arrange:	Yes	Pipehawk; Reefton Mining; SIRA Business Services; Sky		
		Capital; Southern African Resources; Springwood; SRS		
Other activities: Audit & Business Advisory; Corporate		Technologies; The Claims People; The Creative Education		
Finance Advice; Corporate Recovery; Forensic Services;		Corporation; Thistle Mining; VI; Vietnam Opportunity		
General Business Advisory; Company Secretarial Services and		Fund; Web Shareshop; White Knight Investments		
Due Diligence; Project Finance; Taxation; Transaction				
Services		**Other Offices:**		
		39 offices nationwide.		
		For further information please contact National		
		Communications on 020-7383 5100		

Hawkpoint Partners

4 Great St Helens, London, EC3A 6HA Tel: 020-7665 4500;   Fax: 020-7665 4502;
email info@hawkpoint.com;   Web site: www.hawkpoint.com

Contact:	Graham Paton	
Also act as Nominated Broker?	No	
Companies represented on first admission:	4	
Number involved in new issue to raise funds:	3	
Industry sector preferences:	None	
Geographical preferences:	None	
In-house industry sector analysts?	None	
Sectors covered by analysts:	None	

Prospective AIM companies considered:
Startups No Early stage Yes Established Yes
Typical transaction parameters: Minimum market capital £30m

Split of broking activities:	n/a
(institutional: private client)	
Underwriting facilities:	
Can provide:	No
Can arrange:	Yes

Other activities: Our services include Mergers &
Acquisitions, Capital Markets, Restructuring and Strategic
Advice

Number of Directors & Executives engaged in:

Corporate Finance:	**Dir:**	23
	Exec:	42
AIM Activities:	**Dir:**	3
	Exec:	8

Act for: Deep-Sea Leisure; OneClickHR

Other Offices:
Paris
50 Avenue des Champs Elysees
75008 Paris

Hoare Govett

250 Bishopsgate, London, EC2M 4AA Tel: 020-7678 8000;   Web site: www.abnamro.com

Contact:	Philip Davies/Chris Fielding/Justin Jones	
Also act as Nominated Broker?	Yes	
Companies represented on first admission:	n/a	
Number involved in new issue to raise funds:	n/a	
Industry sector preferences:	All sectors considered	
Geographical preferences:	None	
In-house industry sector analysts?	Yes	
Sectors covered by analysts:	Most sectors covered	

Prospective AIM companies considered:
Startups No Early stage Yes Established Yes

Typical transaction parameters:	n/a
Split of broking activities:	n/a
(institutional: private client)	
Underwriting facilities:	
Can provide:	Yes
Can arrange:	n/a

Other activities: Financial adviser and stockbroker

Number of Directors & Executives engaged in:

Corporate Finance:	**Dir:**	3
	Exec:	4
AIM Activities:	**Dir:**	3
	Exec:	4

Act for: GW Pharmaceuticals; NeuTec Pharma; UBC
Media

Other Offices:	n/a

HSBC Bank

Vintners Place, 68 Upper Thames Street, London, EC4V 3BJ Tel: 020-7336 9000;   Fax: 020-7702 3997;

Contact:	John Mellett	**Number of Directors & Executives engaged in:**		
Also act as Nominated Broker?	Yes	**Corporate Finance:**	**Dir:**	50
Companies represented on first admission:	2		**Exec:**	n/a
Number involved in new issue to raise funds:	12	**AIM Activities:**	**Dir:**	4
Industry sector preferences:	None		**Exec:**	12
Geographical preferences:	None			
In-house industry sector analysts?	Yes	**Act for:** Lonrho Africa		
Sectors covered by analysts:	Most sectors			

Prospective AIM companies considered:

Startups No **Early stage** Yes **Established** Yes

Typical transaction parameters:	None particularly	
Split of broking activities:	All institutional	
(institutional: private client)		
Underwriting facilities:		**Other Offices:** n/a
Can provide:	Yes	
Can arrange:	Yes	

Other activities: Corporate Broking; Corporate Finance
Advice; Mergers and Acquisitions; Research

IBI Corporate Finance

26 Fitzwilliam Place, Dublin 2, Ireland, Tel: 00-353 1 661 6633; Fax: 00-353 1 661 6821;
Web site: www.ibicf.ie

Contact:	Leo Casey	**Number of Directors & Executives engaged in:**		
Also act as Nominated Broker?	No	**Corporate Finance:**	**Dir:**	5
Companies represented on first admission:	n/a		**Exec:**	11
Number involved in new issue to raise funds:	n/a	**AIM Activities:**	**Dir:**	n/a
Industry sector preferences:	All		**Exec:**	n/a
Geographical preferences:	n/a			
In-house industry sector analysts?	n/a	**Act for:**		n/a
Sectors covered by analysts:	n/a			

Prospective AIM companies considered:

Startups Yes **Early stage** Yes **Established** Yes

Typical transaction parameters:	Variable	
Split of broking activities:	n/a	
(institutional: private client)		
Underwriting facilities:		**Other Offices:**
Can provide:	Yes	Belfast, Northern Ireland
Can arrange:	No	

Other activities: n/a

ING Bank

60 London Wall, London, EC2 Tel: 020-7767 1000; Fax: 020-7767 7222;

Contact:	Andy Muncer	Number of Directors & Executives engaged in:		
Also act as Nominated Broker?	Yes	Corporate Finance:	Dir:	n/a
Companies represented on first admission:	4		Exec:	n/a
Number involved in new issue to raise funds:	3	AIM Activities:	Dir:	n/a
Industry sector preferences:	n/a		Exec:	n/a
Geographical preferences:	n/a			
In-house industry sector analysts?	n/a	Act for: Andrews Sykes; Seymour Pierce		
Sectors covered by analysts:	n/a			
Prospective AIM companies considered:				
Startups n/a Early stage n/a Established n/a				
Typical transaction parameters:	n/a			
Split of broking activities:	n/a			
(institutional: private client)				
Underwriting facilities:		Other Offices:		
Can provide:	Yes	Lismore House		
Can arrange:	Yes	127 George Street		
		Edinburgh		
Other activities:	n/a	EH2 4JX		

Insinger de Beaufort

44 Worship Street, London, EC2A 2JT Tel: 020-7377 6161; Fax: 020-7655 6897;
email infocorpfin@insinger.com; Web site: www.insinger.com

Contact:	Jasper Allen/Stephen Goschalk	Number of Directors & Executives engaged in:		
Also act as Nominated Broker? Yes, through Insinger Townsley		Corporate Finance:	Dir:	5
			Exec:	1
Companies represented on first admission:	39	AIM Activities:	Dir:	5
Number involved in new issue to raise funds:	41		Exec:	1
Industry sector preferences:	None			
Geographical preferences:	UK and Ireland	Act for: Community Broking; enterpriseAsia;		
In-house industry sector analysts?	Yes	Europasia Education; Fortfield Investments; Future		
Sectors covered by analysts:	Generalist and Mining	Integrated Technologies; Integrated Asset Management;		
Prospective AIM companies considered:		Interactive Gaming; Maelor; Market Age; Noble		
Startups Yes Early stage Yes Established Yes		Investments; Ocean Resources Capital; Penmc;		
Typical transaction parameters: Minimum market capital - £5m		Thirdforce; TranXenoGen; XecutiveResearch		
Split of broking activities:	n/a			
(institutional: private client)		Other Offices:		n/a
Underwriting facilities:				
Can provide:	No			
Can arrange:	Yes			
Other activities: Sponsor to companies on the Official List; Financial adviser on OFEX				

Investec Investment Banking

2 Gresham Street, London, EC2V 7QP Tel: 020-7597 5970; Fax: 020-7597 5120;
Web site: www.investec.com/uk

Contact:		James Grace
Also act as Nominated Broker?		Yes
Companies represented on first admission:		20
Number involved in new issue to raise funds:		11
Industry sector preferences:		Food & General; Food
Manufacturing; Growth Industrial; Healthcare; Leisure; Media;		
Mining; Oil & Gas; Retail; Support Services; Technology;		
Telecoms		
Geographical preferences:		None
In-house industry sector analysts?		Yes
Sectors covered by analysts: Food & General; Food		
Manufacturing; Growth Industrial; Healthcare; Leisure; Media;		
Mining; Oil & Gas; Retail; Support Services; Technology;		
Telecoms; Transport		
Prospective AIM companies considered:		
Startups No **Early stage** Yes, if profitability established		
Established Yes		
Typical transaction parameters:		Market capitalisation
£25m plus preferred		
Split of broking activities:		n/a
(institutional: private client)		
Underwriting facilities:		
	Can provide:	Yes
	Can arrange:	Yes

Other activities: Corporate Broking Services; Corporate
Finance Advice; Research

Number of Directors & Executives engaged in:

Corporate Finance:	**Dir:**	10
	Exec:	15
AIM Activities:	**Dir:**	10
	Exec:	15

Act for: Cluff Mining; Georgica; Hartford; MacLellan;
Melrose; Westmount Energy

Other Offices: n/a

J&E Davy

Davy House, 49 Dawson Street, Dublin 2, Ireland, Tel: 00-353 1 679 6363; Fax: 00-353 1 679 6366;
email: dcf@davy.ie; Web site: www.davy.ie

Contact:		Ivan Murphy
Also act as Nominated Broker?		Yes
Companies represented on first admission:		4
Number involved in new issue to raise funds:		2
Industry sector preferences:		None
Geographical preferences:		Ireland
In-house industry sector analysts?		Yes
Sectors covered by analysts: All major sectors covered		
Prospective AIM companies considered:		
Startups No **Early stage** Yes **Established** Yes		
Typical transaction parameters:		None particularly
Split of broking activities:		n/a
(institutional: private client)		
Underwriting facilities:		
	Can provide:	Yes
	Can arrange:	Yes

Other activities: Corporate Broking Services; Corporate
Finance Advice; Research

Number of Directors & Executives engaged in:

Corporate Finance:	**Dir:**	5
	Exec:	5
AIM Activities:	**Dir:**	2
	Exec:	3

Act for: Alltracel Pharmaceuticals; CPL Resources;
Petroceltic International; Reflex; Tiger Resource
Finance

Other Offices: n/a

John East & Partners

Crystal Gate, 28-30 Worship Street, London, EC2A 2AH Tel: 020-7628 2200; Fax: 020-7628 4473; email: info@johneastpartners.com; Web site: www.johneastpartners.com

Contact:	John East	**Number of Directors & Executives engaged in:**	
Also act as Nominated Broker?	No	Corporate Finance: Dir:	5
Companies represented on first admission:	28	Exec:	1
Number involved in new issue to raise funds:	48	AIM Activities: Dir:	5
Industry sector preferences:	None	Exec:	1
Geographical preferences:	None		

In-house industry sector analysts? No
Sectors covered by analysts: n/a
Prospective AIM companies considered:
Startups No **Early stage** Yes **Established** Yes
Typical transaction parameters: None particularly
Split of broking activities: n/a
(institutional: private client)
Underwriting facilities:
　　　　Can provide: No
　　　　Can arrange: Yes

Other activities: Corporate Finance Advice on all matters including agreed and hostile takeovers

Act for: Bidtimes; Constellation; Equator; Eurolink Managed Services; Eurovestech; Internet Music & Media; Mondas; Napier Brown Foods; Northern Petroleum; Prestige Publishing; Room Service; Silentpoint; Surface Transforms; Talent; tecc-IS; TEP Exchange; The Real Good Food Company; Totally; Triple Plate Junction; Your Space

Other Offices: n/a

KBC Peel Hunt

4th Floor, 111 Old Broad Street, London, EC2N 1PH Tel: 020-7418 8900; Fax: 020-7972 0112; email adam.hart@kbcpeelhunt.com; Web site: www.kbcpeelhunt.com

Contact:	Adam Hart	**Number of Directors & Executives engaged in:**	
Also act as Nominated Broker?	Yes	Corporate Finance: Dir:	2
Companies represented on first admission:	Many	Exec:	12
Number involved in new issue to raise funds:	80+	AIM Activities: Dir:	2
Industry sector preferences:	Most sectors covered,	Exec:	10

other than natural resources
Geographical preferences: None
In-house industry sector analysts? Yes
Sectors covered by analysts: Construction & Building Materials; Engineering; Insurance; IT Hardware; Leisure & Hotels; Pharmaceuticals & Biotechnology; Real Estate; Retail; Software & Computer Services; Support Services
Prospective AIM companies considered:
Startups Yes **Early stage** Yes **Established** Yes
Typical transaction parameters: Subject to the merits of each case
Split of broking activities: 95 :5
(institutional: private client)
Underwriting facilities:
　　　　Can provide: Yes
　　　　Can arrange: Yes

Other activities: Corporate Broking Services; Corporate Finance Advice; Market Making; Mergers & Acquisitions; Research; Private Equity (all on a pan-European basis)

Act for: Abingdon Capital; Acquisitor; Acquisitor (Bermuda); Advanced Technology; Akers Biosciences; Armour Group; Billam; Charteris; Civilian Content; Clover Corporation; Clubhaus; Conister Trust; Contemporary Enterprises; Cybit; Deal Group Media; Dream Direct; Enterprise; eq; FFastFill; General Industries; Harrier; hemscott; I2S; Ideal Shopping Direct; Innovision Research and Technology; Intercede; iomart; IP2IPO; IQ-Ludorum; Knowledge Technology Solutions; Marshall Edwards; Martin Shelton; Meon Capital; Metrodome; Northacre; Offshore Hydrocarbon Mapping; Peel Hotels; RAB Capital; Razorback Vehicles; Sheffield United; Stream; Sunbeach Communications; SWP; Systems Union; Tandem; Tenon; Tom Hoskins; Vitesse Media

Other Offices:
Throughout Europe

KPMG Corporate Finance

8 Salisbury Square, London, EC4Y 8BB Tel: 020-7311 1000; Fax: 020-7311 8252;
Web site: www.kpmg.co.uk/services/cf

Contact: Neil Austin/Richard Barlow/Richard Brown		
Also act as Nominated Broker? No	**Number of Directors & Executives engaged in:**	
Companies represented on first admission: 5	**Corporate Finance:** Dir:	52
Number involved in new issue to raise funds: 3	Exec:	313
Industry sector preferences: None, all sectors covered	**AIM Activities:** Dir:	12
Geographical preferences: None	Exec:	30
In-house industry sector analysts? Yes	**Act for:** Belgravium; Headway; Leeds	
Sectors covered by analysts: All major and many minor sectors		
Prospective AIM companies considered:		
Startups No **Early stage** Yes **Established** Yes		
Typical transaction parameters: None particularly		
Split of broking activities: n/a		
(institutional: private client)	**Other Offices:**	
Underwriting facilities:	Birmingham Tel: 0121-232 3000	Stephen Halbert/
Can provide: No		Charles Cattaneo
Can arrange: Yes	Leeds Tel: 0113-231 3000	Bob Bigley
Other activities: Corporate Finance Advice, including takeovers, mergers & acquisitions, debt advisory services, valuations, private equity and strategic advice		

Macquarie Bank

Level 30, CityPoint, One Ropemaker Street, London, EC2Y 4UP Tel: 020-7065 2000;
Fax: 020-7065 2061

Contact: Nick Peterson		
Also act as Nominated Broker? n/a	**Number of Directors & Executives engaged in:**	
Companies represented on first admission: n/a	**Corporate Finance:** Dir:	n/a
Number involved in new issue to raise funds: n/a	Exec:	n/a
Industry sector preferences: n/a	**AIM Activities:** Dir:	n/a
Geographical preferences: n/a	Exec:	n/a
In-house industry sector analysts? n/a	**Act for:** n/a	
Sectors covered by analysts: n/a		
Prospective AIM companies considered: n/a		
Startups Early stage Established n/a		
Typical transaction parameters: n/a		
Split of broking activities: n/a		
institutional: private client)		
Underwriting facilities:	**Other Offices:** n/a	
Can provide: n/a		
Can arrange: n/a		
Other activities: n/a		

Marshall Securities

Crusader House, 145-157 St John Street, London, EC1V 4RE Tel: 020-7490 3788; Fax: 020-7490 3787

Contact:	John Webb	**Number of Directors & Executives engaged in:**	
Also act as Nominated Broker?	Yes	**Corporate Finance:** Dir:	3
Companies represented on first admission:	2	Exec:	1
Number involved in new issue to raise funds:	6	**AIM Activities:** Dir:	3
Industry sector preferences:	None	Exec:	1
Geographical preferences:	UK generally		
In-house industry sector analysts?	No	**Act for:** Impax	
Sectors covered by analysts:	n/a		

Prospective AIM companies considered:
Startups No **Early stage** Yes **Established** Yes
Typical transaction parameters: None particularly
Split of broking activities: All Institutional investors
institutional: private client)
Underwriting facilities:
　　　　　　Can provide: Yes
　　　　　　Can arrange: Yes

Other Offices: n/a

Other activities: Corporate Finance Advice

Matrix Corporate Finance

Gossard House, 7-8 Savile Row, London, W1S 3PG Tel: 020-7439 6050; Fax: 020-7287 1338;
Web site: www.matrixgroup.co.uk

Contact:	Stephen Mischler	**Number of Directors & Executives engaged in:**	
Also act as Nominated Broker?	No	**Corporate Finance:** Dir:	5
Companies represented on first admission:	1	Exec:	3
Number involved in new issue to raise funds:	nil	**AIM Activities:** Dir:	5
Industry sector preferences:	n/a	Exec:	3
Geographical preferences:	n/a		
In-house industry sector analysts?	n/a	**Act for:** London & Boston Investments	
Sectors covered by analysts:	n/a		

Prospective AIM companies considered:
Startups Yes **Early stage** Yes **Established** Yes
Typical transaction parameters: n/a
Split of broking activities: n/a
(institutional: private client)
Underwriting facilities:
　　　　　　Can provide: n/a
　　　　　　Can arrange: n/a

Other Offices: n/a

Other activities: n/a

Nabarro Wells

Saddlers House, Gutter Lane, Cheapside, London, EC2V 6HS Tel: 020-7710 7400; Fax: 020-7710 7401; email: corpfin@nabarro-wells.co.uk; Web site: www.nabarro-wells.co.uk

Contact: Nigel Atkinson/Hugh Oram/Keith Smith		**Number of Directors & Executives engaged in:**	
Also act as Nominated Broker? No	**Corporate Finance:**	**Dir:**	9
Companies represented on first admission: 42		**Exec:**	0
Number involved in new issue to raise funds: 29	**AIM Activities:**	**Dir:**	7
Industry sector preferences: All sectors covered, but		**Exec:**	0
particular experience in finance, leisure, natural resources			
and technology	**Act for:** African Eagle Resources; Arko; Clean Diesel		
Geographical preferences: None	Technologies; Corpora; Crown Corporation; Cyberes;		
In-house industry sector analysts? No	EmdexTrade; First Calgary Petroleum; Galleon;		
Sectors covered by analysts: All	Gympie Gold; Hardman Resources; Harrogate;		
Prospective AIM companies considered:	Hemisphere Properties; Lloyds British Testing; MG		
Startups No **Early stage** Yes **Established** Yes	Capital; Pathfinder Properties; Portman; Profile Media;		
Typical transaction parameters: None particularly	QuikTraks Network; ReGen Therapeutics; Savoy Asset		
Split of broking activities: n/a	Management; Texas Oil & Gas; Top Ten; Transcomm		
(institutional: private client)			
Underwriting facilities:	**Other Offices: n/a**		
Can provide: No			
Can arrange: Yes			
Other activities: Corporate Finance Advice; Private			
Equity; Venture Capital			

NCB Stockbrokers

3 George's Dock, International Financial Services Centre, Dublin 1, Ireland, Tel: 00-353 1 611 5611; Fax: 00-353 1 611 5987; email: finance-corporate@ncb.ie; Web site: www.ncb.ie

Contact: Helen O' Grady	**Number of Directors & Executives engaged in:**		
Also act as Nominated Broker? No	**Corporate Finance:**	**Dir:**	3
Companies represented on first admission: n/a		**Exec:**	8
Number involved in new issue to raise funds: n/a	**AIM Activities:**	**Dir:**	3
Industry sector preferences: n/a		**Exec:**	8
Geographical preferences: n/a			
In-house industry sector analysts? n/a	**Act for:**		n/a
Sectors covered by analysts: n/a			
Prospective AIM companies considered:			
Startups Yes **Early stage** Yes **Established** Yes			
Typical transaction parameters: n/a			
Split of broking activities: n/a			
(institutional: private client)			
Underwriting facilities:	**Other Offices:**		n/a
Can provide: n/a			
Can arrange: n/a			
Other activities: n/a			

NM Rothschild

82 King Street, Manchester, M2 4WQ Tel: 0161-827 3800; Fax: 0161-832 2554;
Web site: www.nmrothschild.com

Contact:	Greg Cant	**Number of Directors & Executives engaged in:**	
Also act as Nominated Broker?	No	**Corporate Finance:** Dir:	2
Companies represented on first admission:	n/a	Exec:	8
Number involved in new issue to raise funds:	n/a	**AIM Activities:** Dir:	2
Industry sector preferences:	None	Exec:	8
Geographical preferences:	None		
In-house industry sector analysts?	No	**Act for:** Chepstow Racecourse; GW Pharmaceuticals;	
Sectors covered by analysts:	n/a	Peel Holdings	
Prospective AIM companies considered:			
Startups No **Early stage** No **Established** Yes			
Typical transaction parameters:	n/a		
Split of broking activities:	n/a		
(institutional: private client)			
Underwriting facilities:		**Other Offices:**	
Can provide:	Yes	Birmingham, Leeds, London and 50 offices worldwide	
Can arrange:	Yes		
Other activities:	n/a		

Noble & Company

1 Frederick's Place, London, EC2R 8AB Tel: 020-7367 5600; Fax: 020-7796 0020;
email alasdair.robinson@noblegp.com; Web site: www.noblegp.com

Contact:	Alasdair Robinson	**Number of Directors & Executives engaged in:**	
Also act as Nominated Broker?	Yes	**Corporate Finance:** Dir:	9
Companies represented on first admission:	45	Exec:	10
Number involved in new issue to raise funds:	60	**AIM Activities:** Dir:	5
Industry sector preferences: All sectors covered but		Exec:	7
significant experience in Finance; Leisure & Healthcare;			
Media; Oil & Gas; Property & Technology; Retail		**Act for:** Athelney Trust; Avionic Services; Caledonian	
Geographical preferences:	None	Trust; i-documentsystems; Kuju; Longbridge	
In-house industry sector analysts?	Yes	International; Murgitroyd; Numis; Online Travel Corp;	
Sectors covered by analysts: Construction; Engineering;		Optimisa; Palmaris Capital; Terrace Hill; The Clapham	
Finance Sector; Leisure & Healthcare; Media; Oil & Gas;		House Group; Zoo Digital	
Property; Retail; Technology			
Prospective AIM companies considered:			
Startups Yes **Early stage** Yes **Established** Yes		**Other Offices:**	
Typical transaction parameters:	n/a	Edinburgh Tel: 0131-225 9677 Alasdair Robinson	
Split of broking activities:	n/a		
(institutional: private client)			
Underwriting facilities:			
Can provide:	No		
Can arrange:	Yes		
Other activities: Corporate Restructuring; General			
Corporate Finance; Limited partnerships; Mergers and			
acquisitions; Official List Sponsors; Property related Unit			
Trusts; Tax efficient investment vehicles – EIS, VCT, EZT			

NOMINATED ADVISERS

Nomura International

Nomura House, 1 St Martin's-Le-Grand, London, EC1A 4NP Tel: 020-7521 2000;
Fax: 020-7521 3655/6; Web site: www.nomura.co.uk

Contact:	Robert Davies/Charles Spicer	
Also act as Nominated Broker?	n/a	
Companies represented on first admission:	n/a	
Number involved in new issue to raise funds:	n/a	
Industry sector preferences:	n/a	
Geographical preferences:	Europe	
In-house industry sector analysts?	n/a	
Sectors covered by analysts: Healthcare; Technology		
Prospective AIM companies considered:		
Startups Yes **Early stage** Yes **Established** Yes		
Typical transaction parameters:	n/a	
Split of broking activities:	n/a	
(institutional: private client)		
Underwriting facilities:		
Can provide:	Yes	
Can arrange:	Yes	

Number of Directors & Executives engaged in:

Corporate Finance:	**Dir:**	7
	Exec:	20
AIM Activities:	**Dir:**	3
	Exec:	7

Act for: BioFocus; Gaming Insight; LiDCO

Other Offices: n/a

Other activities: M & A Advisory

Numerica

66 Wigmore Street, London, W1U 2HQ Tel: 020-7467 4000; Fax: 020-7467 4040;
email shirin.gandhi@numerica.biz; Web site: www.numerica.biz

Contact:	Shirin Gandhi/Jeff Ward	
Also act as Nominated Broker?	n/a	
Companies represented on first admission:	20	
Number involved in new issue to raise funds:	30	
Industry sector preferences: Charity & Not-for-profit; Hotels, Bars & Restaurants; Italian Businesses; Media; Motor Trade; North American Businesses; Printing; Real Estate & Construction; Recruitment; Retail; Sport; Travel		
Geographical preferences:	None	
In-house industry sector analysts?	None	
Sectors covered by analysts:	n/a	
Prospective AIM companies considered:		
Startups No **Early stage** Yes **Established** Yes		
Typical transaction parameters:	n/a	
Split of broking activities:	n/a	
(institutional: private client)		
Underwriting facilities:		
Can provide:	n/a	
Can arrange:	Yes	

Number of Directors & Executives engaged in:

Corporate Finance:	**Dir:**	8
	Exec:	11
AIM Activities:	**Dir:**	4
	Exec:	3

Act for: n/a

Other Offices:
Birmingham, Bristol, Leicester, Manchester, Marlow, Southampton, Whiteley, Worthing

Other activities: n/a

Numis

Cheapside House, 138 Cheapside, London, EC2V 6LH Tel: 020-7776 1500; Fax: 020-7776 1555;
email mail@numiscorp.com; Web site: www.numiscorp.com

Contact:	Charles Crick/Jag Mundi	**Number of Directors & Executives engaged in:**	
Also act as Nominated Broker?	Yes	**Corporate Finance:** Dir:	8
Companies represented on first admission:	16	Exec:	5
Number involved in new issue to raise funds:	28	**AIM Activities:** Dir:	8
Industry sector preferences:	Aerospace & Defence;	Exec:	5

Industry sector preferences: Aerospace & Defence;
Building & Construction; Consumer; Financial Services; Food
Producers; Food Retail; General Retail; Insurance; Leisure;
Life Sciences; Media; Mining; Support Services; Technology
Geographical preferences: UK
In-house industry sector analysts? Yes
Sectors covered by analysts: Aerospace & Defence; Building
& Construction; Consumer; Financial Services; Food
Producers; Food Retail; General Retail; Insurance; Leisure;
Life Sciences; Media; Mining; Support Services; Technology
Prospective AIM companies considered:
Startups No **Early stage** Yes **Established** Yes
Typical transaction parameters: Minimum market capital
- £15m. Minimum funds to be raised - None
Split of broking activities: All industrial
(institutional: private client)
Underwriting facilities:

	Can provide:	Yes
	Can arrange:	Yes

Other activities: Corporate Finance Advice; Market Making;
Research

Act for: 2 ergo; Alliance Pharma; Ambient; Centaur;
Corac; Domino's Pizza UK & Ireland; Epic Reconstruction;
European Diamonds; FTV; Healthcare Enterprises; Invox;
Jubilee Platinum; Moneybox; Monsoon; Numerica;
Stockcube; THB; Urbium; Virotec; West 175 Media;
WILink; Zincox Resources

Other Offices:
Castle Chambers,
43 Castle Street,
Liverpool L2 9ST
Tel: 0151-225 0800
Fax: 0151-227 9435

Oriel Securities

4 Wood Street, London, EC2V 7JB Tel: 020-7710 7600; Fax: 020-7710 7611;
email info@orielsecurities.com; Web site: www.orielsecurities.com

Contact:	Andrew Edwards	**Number of Directors & Executives engaged in:**	
Also act as Nominated Broker?	Yes	**Corporate Finance:** Dir:	3
Companies represented on first admission:	n/a	Exec:	4
Number involved in new issue to raise funds:	n/a	**AIM Activities:** Dir:	3
Industry sector preferences:	None	Exec:	4

Geographical preferences: n/a
In-house industry sector analysts? Yes
Sectors covered by analysts: Consumer; Food Producers;
Healthcare; Media & Leisure; Oil & Gas; Real Estate;
Retail; Smallcaps; Support Services; Transport
Prospective AIM companies considered:
Startups Yes **Early stage** Yes **Established** Yes
Typical transaction parameters: None
Split of broking activities:
institutional: private client)
Underwriting facilities:

	Can provide:	Yes
	Can arrange:	Yes

Other activities: n/a

Act for: Oasis Healthcare; Sigma Technology;
Westmount Energy

Other Offices: n/a

Panmure Gordon

50 Stratton Street, London, W1J 8LL Tel: 020-7187 2000; Fax: 020-7072 6383;
Web site: www.panmure.com

Contact:	Richard Potts	**Number of Directors & Executives engaged in:**		
Also act as Nominated Broker?	Yes	**Corporate Finance:**	**Dir:**	n/a
Companies represented on first admission:	n/a		**Exec:**	n/a
Number involved in new issue to raise funds:	n/a	**AIM Activities:**	**Dir:**	n/a
Industry sector preferences:	n/a		**Exec:**	n/a
Geographical preferences:	None			
In-house industry sector analysts?	Yes	**Act for:** Coliseum; Genus; Keryx Biopharmaceuticals; Lok 'n Store; NMT; Transcomm; Tissue Science Laboratories		

Sectors covered by analysts: Building & Construction; Engineering; Financials; Food & Beverages; Leisure; Media; Support Services; Technology
Prospective AIM companies considered:
Startups Yes **Early stage** Yes **Established** Yes
Typical transaction parameters: Market capitalisation and size of issue need to be of a size, although there is no specific threshold

Other Offices:
Panmure Gordon is a division of Lazard & Co

Split of broking activities: n/a
(institutional: private client)
Underwriting facilities:
    Can provide: Yes
    Can arrange: Yes

Other activities: n/a

Piper Jaffray

1st Floor, Phoenix House, 18 King William Street, London, EC4N 7US Tel: 020-7743 8700;
Fax: 020-7743 8735; email: david.i.wilson@pjc.com; Web site: www.pjc.com

Contact:	David Wilson	**Number of Directors & Executives engaged in:**		
Also act as Nominated Broker?	No	**Corporate Finance:**	**Dir:**	34
Companies represented on first admission:	n/a		**Exec:**	86
Number involved in new issue to raise funds:	n/a	**AIM Activities:**	**Dir:**	2
Industry sector preferences:	See Sectors covered		**Exec:**	3
Geographical preferences:	UK/US			
In-house industry sector analysts?	65 senior analysts	**Act for:** CeNeSPharmaceuticals; The Medical House		

Sectors covered by analysts: Consumer; Financial Institutions; Healthcare; Manufacturing & Services; Technology
Prospective AIM companies considered:
Startups Yes **Early stage** Yes **Established** Yes
Typical transaction parameters: £10m upwards
Split of broking activities: n/a
(institutional: private client)
Underwriting facilities:

Other Offices:
Chicago; Menlo Park; Minneapolis; New York; San Francisco; Tel Aviv

    Can provide: No
    Can arrange: Yes

Other activities: Banking, Fixed income products, Private Equity, Private Placements

PricewaterhouseCoopers Corporate Finance

1 Embankment Place, London, WC2N 6NN Tel: 020-7583 5000; Fax: 020-7804 4993

Contact:	Peter Clokey	
Also act as Nominated Broker?	No	
Companies represented on first admission:	8	
Number involved in new issue to raise funds:	6	
Industry sector preferences:	None	
Geographical preferences:	None	
In-house industry sector analysts?	Yes	
Sectors covered by analysts:	All major sectors	
Prospective AIM companies considered:		
Startups No Early stage Yes Established Yes		
Typical transaction parameters:	None particularly	
Split of broking activities:	n/a	
(institutional: private client)		
Underwriting facilities:		
Can provide:	No	
Can arrange:	Yes	

Other activities: Corporate Finance Advice

Number of Directors & Executives engaged in:

Corporate Finance:	Dir:	43
	Exec:	230
AIM Activities:	Dir:	6
	Exec:	12

Act for: Numis

Other Offices:

Birmingham	Tel: 0121-265 5000	David Armfield
Manchester	Tel: 0161-236 9191	Colin Gillespie
Southampton	Tel: 023- 8033 0077	J Freeman

RFC Corporate Finance

8th Floor, QV1 Building, 250 St George's Terrace, Perth, Australia, WA 6000 Tel: 00-61 089480 2500;
Fax: 00 61 089480 2511;   email: rfcperth@rfc.com.au; Web site: www.rfc.com.au

Contact:	Stephen Allen
Also act as Nominated Broker?	n/a
Companies represented on first admission:	n/a
Number involved in new issue to raise funds:	n/a
Industry sector preferences:	n/a
Geographical preferences:	n/a
In-house industry sector analysts?	n/a
Sectors covered by analysts:	n/a
Prospective AIM companies considered:	n/a
Startups Early stage Established Typical transaction parameters:	
Split of broking activities:	n/a
(institutional: private client)	
Underwriting facilities:	n/a
Can provide:	n/a
Can arrange:	n/a
Other activities:	n/a

Number of Directors & Executives engaged in:

Corporate Finance:	Dir:	n/a
	Exec:	n/a
AIM Activities:	Dir:	n/a
	Exec:	n/a

Act for: Consolidated Minerals

Other Offices:	n/a

Rowan Dartington Corporate Finance

Colston Tower, Colston Street, Bristol, BS1 4RD Tel: 0117-933 0020; Fax: 0117-933 0024;
email john.wakefield@rowan-dartington.co.uk; Web site: www.rowan-dartington.co.uk

Contact:	John Wakefield	**Number of Directors & Executives engaged in:**	
Also act as Nominated Broker?	Yes	**Corporate Finance:** Dir:	3
Companies represented on first admission:	23	Exec:	2
Number involved in new issue to raise funds:		**AIM Activities:** Dir:	3
50+Industry sector preferences:	None	Exec:	2
Geographical preferences:	None		
In-house industry sector analysts?	Yes	**Act for:** African Diamonds; African Gold; Airsprung Furniture; Bristol & London; Bristol & West Investments; CODASciSys; Compact Power; Creative Recruitment Solutions; CYC; Densitron Technologies; Dickinson Legg; Dipford; Farsight; Gooch & Housego; Holders Technology; Jobs.co.uk; K3 Business Technology; Mercury Recycling; Minco; Montpellier; Pan Andean Resources; Pennant International; Petrel Resources; Photo-Scan; Pubs 'n' Bars; Surface Technology Systems; Sutton Harbour; Water Hall; Wyatt	
Sectors covered by analysts:	Small companies		
Prospective AIM companies considered:			
Startups Yes **Early stage** Yes **Established** Yes			
Typical transaction parameters:	None particularly		
Split of broking activities:	70:30		
(institutional: private client)			
Underwriting facilities:			
Can provide:	No		
Can arrange:	Yes		
		Other Offices:	
		Bath	Tel: 01225-424666
Other activities: Corporate Broking Services; Corporate Finance Advice; Research		Chichester	Tel: 01243-771886
		Exeter	Tel: 01292-410599
		Hereford	Tel: 01432-277003
		Redruth	Tel: 01209-214488
		Taunton	Tel: 01823-257752
		Weston-Super-Mare	Tel: 01934-413355

RP & C International

56 Green Street, London, W1K 6RY Tel: 020-7491 2434; Fax: 020-7499 2893;
email rborg@rpcint.co.uk; Web site: www.rpcint.co.uk

Contact:	Richard Borg	**Number of Directors & Executives engaged in:**	
Also act as Nominated Broker?	No	**Corporate Finance:** Dir:	5
Companies represented on first admission:	1	Exec:	2
Number involved in new issue to raise funds:	Several	**AIM Activities:** Dir:	5
Industry sector preferences:	None, but with experts in Healthcare and Oil & Gas	Exec:	2
Geographical preferences:	None	**Act for:** Global Energy Development, GTL Resources	
In-house industry sector analysts?	No		
Sectors covered by analysts:	n/a		
Prospective AIM companies considered:			
Startups No **Early stage** No **Established** Yes			
Typical transaction parameters: IPO – over £10 miillion Further fundraisings – over £5 million			
Split of broking activities:	n/a	**Other Offices:**	
(institutional: private client)		New York	
Underwriting facilities:			
Can provide:	No		
Can arrange:	Yes		
Other activities:	n/a		

Seymour Pierce

Bucklersbury House, 3 Queen Victoria Street, London, EC4N 8EL Tel: 020-7107 8000; Fax: 020-7107 8100; email: enquiries@seymourpierce.com; Web site: www.seymourpierce.co.uk

Contact:	Richard Feigen	**Number of Directors & Executives engaged in:**		
Also act as Nominated Broker?	Yes	**Corporate Finance:**	**Dir:**	3
Companies represented on first admission:	36		**Exec:**	8
Number involved in new issue to raise funds:	36	**AIM Activities:**	**Dir:**	3
Industry sector preferences:	None		**Exec:**	8
Geographical preferences:	None			

In-house industry sector analysts? Yes

Sectors covered by analysts: Specialised areas: Building and Construction; Biotechnology; IT; Retail; Security; Food Retailing; Media; Leisure; Sport

Prospective AIM companies considered:

Startups No **Early stage** Yes **Established** Yes

Typical transaction parameters:	n/a
Split of broking activities:	n/a
(institutional: private client)	
Underwriting facilities:	
Can provide:	Yes
Can arrange:	Yes
Other activities:	n/a

Act for: Abraxus Investments; actif; Aerobox; Air Music & Media; ARC Risk Management; Artisan(UK); Asfare; ASOS; BioProjects; Buckland Investments; Camelot Capital; Campus Media; Central African Mining & Exploration; Cheerful Scout; Civica; coffeeheaven; Computer Software; Conroy Diamonds & Gold; Croma; Desire Petroleum; Electric Word; Enition; e-Primefinancial; Felix; Flightstore; First Artist; Fulcrum Pharma; Galahad Capital; Gaming Insight; Grosvenor Land; Hansard; Honeygrove Homes; IDN Telecom; Interregnum; Jacques Vert; Legendary Investments; Mano River Resources; Maverick Entertainment; Meriden; Millwall; MOS International; Nature Technology Solutions; Newmark Security; New Millennium Resources; OFEX; patsystems; Pentagon Protection; Raft International; Real Affinity; Reefton Mining; Reflec; Screen FX; SectorGuard; Sefton Resources; Sopheon; SP; Stanley Gibbons; Tecteon; Tepnel Life Sciences; Terrace Hill; Tertiary Minerals; Theo Fennell; Tottenham Hotspur; UBC Media; Victory; Westside Acquisitions; Wigmore

Other Offices: n/a

SG Securities

Exchange House, Primrose Street, London, EC2A 2DD Tel: 020-7638 9000; Fax: 020-7762 5216; Web site: www.socgen.com

Contact:	Andrew Fullerton	**Number of Directors & Executives engaged in:**		
Also act as Nominated Broker?	Yes	**Corporate Finance:**	**Dir:**	5
Companies represented on first admission:	4		**Exec:**	8
Number involved in new issue to raise funds:	3	**AIM Activities:**	**Dir:**	4
Industry sector preferences:	None		**Exec:**	8
Geographical preferences:	UK			

In-house industry sector analysts? Yes - 50 | **Act for:** | n/a

Sectors covered by analysts: All sectors except Property

Prospective AIM companies considered:

Startups No **Early stage** No **Established** Yes

Typical transaction parameters: Resultant market capitalisation usually greater than £30m

Split of broking activities:	95:5
institutional: private client)	
Underwriting facilities:	
Can provide:	Yes
Can arrange:	No

Other Offices:
Leeds Tel: 0113-242 3300

Other activities: Corporate Finance Advice; Derivatives; Market Making; Research

Shore Capital & Corporate

Bond Street House, 14 Clifford Street, London, W1S 4JU Tel: 020-7408 4090; Fax: 020-7408 4091; email: info@shorecap.co.uk; Web site: www.shorecap.co.uk

Contact:	Alex Borrelli/Jonathan Nelson	
Also act as Nominated Broker?		Yes
Companies represented on first admission:		14
Number involved in new issue to raise funds:		16
Industry sector preferences:	Business Services;	
Financials; Food; Leisure; Media; Property; Retail;		
Software; Telecommunications		
Geographical preferences:		None
In-house industry sector analysts?		Yes
Sectors covered by analysts: See industry sector preferences		
Prospective AIM companies considered:		
Startups No **Early stage** Yes **Established** Yes		
Typical transaction parameters:	None particularly	
Split of broking activities:		n/a
(institutional: private client)		
Underwriting facilities:		
	Can provide:	No
	Can arrange:	Yes

Other activities: Corporate Broking Services; Market Making; Private Equity Investment; Stockbroking Services

Number of Directors & Executives engaged in:

Corporate Finance:	**Dir:**	3
	Exec:	3
AIM Activities:	**Dir:**	2
	Exec:	3

Act for: Advance Visual Communications; Birmingham City; BNB Resources; CamAxys; CFA Capital; Fitzhardinge; Formscan; Illuminator; Judges Capital; Merchant House; Orad Hi-Tec; Pilat Media Global; Spring Grove Property Maintenance; Telford Homes

Other Offices:
Liverpool Office

The Atlantic Suite
The Corn Exchange
Fenwick Street
Liverpool L2 7TP
Tel: 0151-600 3700

Smith & Williamson Corporate Finance

No. 1 Riding House Street, London, W1A 3AS Tel: 020-7637 5377; Fax: 020-7323 2714; email corpfinance@smith.williamson.co.uk; Web site: www.smith.williamson.co.uk

Contact:	Dr Azhic Basirov	
Also act as Nominated Broker?		No
Companies represented on first admission:		23
Number involved in new issue to raise funds:		21
Industry sector preferences:		None
Geographical preferences:		None
In-house industry sector analysts?		No
Sectors covered by analysts:		n/a
Prospective AIM companies considered:		
Startups No **Early stage** Yes **Established** Yes		
Typical transaction parameters:	None particularly	
Split of broking activities:		n/a
(institutional: private client)		
Underwriting facilities:		
	Can provide:	No
	Can arrange:	No

Other activities: Corporate Finance
Smith & Williamson combines a firm of Chartered Accountants with an investment management and private banking house

Number of Directors & Executives engaged in:

Corporate Finance:	**Dir:**	7
	Exec:	6
AIM Activities:	**Dir:**	6
	Exec:	5

Act for: Bakery Services; Basepoint; CMS Webview; Gamingking; John Lewis of Hungerford; Longmead; Netb2b2; NWD; OMG; Southern Vectis

Other Offices: n/a

Solomon Hare Corporate Finance

Oakfield House, Oakfield Grove, Clifton, Bristol, BS8 2BN Tel: 0117-933 3344; Fax: 0117-933 3345;
email: Stephen_Toole@solomonhare.co.uk; Web site: www.solomonhare.co.uk

Contact:	Stephen Toole	**Number of Directors & Executives engaged in:**		
Also act as Nominated Broker?	No	Corporate Finance:	Dir:	10
Companies represented on first admission:	4		Exec:	10
Number involved in new issue to raise funds:	4	AIM Activities:	Dir:	7
Industry sector preferences:	None		Exec:	0
Geographical preferences:	South-West			
In-house industry sector analysts?	No	**Act for:** Albemarle & Bond		
Sectors covered by analysts:	n/a			

Prospective AIM companies considered:
Startups No Early stage Yes Established Yes

Typical transaction parameters: None
Split of broking activities: n/a
(institutional: private client)
Underwriting facilities:

Can provide: No — **Other Offices:** 2nd Floor North
Can arrange: Yes — 32 Ludgate Hill, London EC4M 7DR

Other activities: Audit; Insolvency; IT and Management Consultancy; Personal Finance; Taxation

---

Strand Partners

110 Park Street, London, W1K 6NX Tel: 020-7409 3494; Fax: 020-7409 1761;
email mail@strandpartners.co.uk; Web site: www.strandpartners.co.uk

Contact:	Simon Raggett	**Number of Directors & Executives engaged in:**		
Also act as Nominated Broker?	No	Corporate Finance:	Dir:	4
Companies represented on first admission:	10+		Exec:	5
Number involved in new issue to raise funds:	Several	AIM Activities:	Dir:	4
Industry sector preferences:	n/a		Exec:	5
Geographical preferences:	UK			
In-house industry sector analysts?	General analysts			
Sectors covered by analysts:	n/a			

Act for: Hot; Jarvis Porter; London Town; Lonrho Africa; Manpower Software; Sibir Energy; Smart Approach; Streetnames; Watford Leisure; WILink.com

Prospective AIM companies considered:
Startups No Early stage Yes Established Yes

Typical transaction parameters: Up to £500 million
Split of broking activities: n/a
(institutional: private client)
Underwriting facilities:

Can provide: Yes — **Other Offices:** n/a
Can arrange: Yes

Other activities: Investment capability

Teather & Greenwood

Beaufort House, 15 St Botolph Street, London, EC3A 7QR Tel: 020-7426 9000; Fax: 020-7247 0075; email: tg@teathers.com; Web site: www.teathers.com

Contact:	Christopher Hardie/Jeff Keating/	
	Nick Bankes/Mike Sawbridge	
Also act as Nominated Broker?		Yes
Companies represented on first admission:		
30+ in last 5 years		
Number involved in new issue to raise funds:		50+
Industry sector preferences:		None
Geographical preferences:		UK
In-house industry sector analysts?		Yes

Sectors covered by analysts: Banks & Other Financials; Construction & Building Materials; Investment Trusts; Media; Oil & Gas; Pharmaceuticals & Health; Restaurants, Pubs & Breweries/Leisure; Retailers; Small Companies; Software & Computer Services; Support Services

Prospective AIM companies considered:

Startups No **Early stage** No **Established** Yes

Typical transaction parameters: Minimum market capital £10m. Pre-tax over £1m

Split of broking activities: n/a
(institutional: private client)

Underwriting facilities:

	Can provide:	Yes
	Can arrange:	Yes

Other activities: Corporate Broking Services; Corporate Finance Advice; Institutional sales; Market Making; Research; Tax-Efficient Investment

Number of Directors & Executives engaged in:

Corporate Finance:	**Dir:**	5
	Exec:	8
AIM Activities:	**Dir:**	5
	Exec:	8

Act for: Auto Indemnity; Bizspace; BKN International; Blooms of Bressingham; Business Serve; Canterbury Foods; Charlton Athletic; Charterhouse Communications; Coffee Republic; Conder Environmental; CW Residential; Cytomyx; Flomerics; Home Entertainment; Hurlingham Properties; Immedia Broadcasting; Intellexis; Madisons Coffee; Majestic Wine; Mark Kingsley; Monstermob; Mulberry; Myratech.net; Netcentric; Protec; Redbus Interhouse; Touchstone; Transport Systems; Univent; Universe; Volvere; Wynnstay Properties

Other Offices:
Liverpool
8th Floor, India Buildings
Water Street, Liverpool L2 0XR
Tel: 0151-242 0610

Thenberg & Kinde Fondkommission

Stråndvagen 7B, SE-11456 Stockholm, Sweden Tel: 00-46 854 581 574; Fax: 00-46 854 581 565; Web site: www.thenberg.se

Contact:	Fredrik Ljung/Esa Sulkakoski	
Also act as Nominated Broker?		No
Companies represented on first admission:		None
Number involved in new issue to raise funds:		None
Industry sector preferences:		No preferences
Geographical preferences:		Nordic
In-house industry sector analysts?		No
Sectors covered by analysts:		n/a

Prospective AIM companies considered:

Startups Yes **Early stage** Yes **Established** Yes

Typical transaction parameters: n/a

Split of broking activities: n/a
(institutional: private client)

Underwriting facilities:

	Can provide:	No
	Can arrange:	Yes

Other activities: Asset management; Equity brokerage

Number of Directors & Executives engaged in:

Corporate Finance:	**Dir:**	8
	Exec:	n/a
AIM Activities:	**Dir:**	5
	Exec:	n/a
Act for:		n/a

Other Offices:
Våstra Hamngatan 19-21
SE-411 17 Göteborg
Sweden

UBS Warburg

1 Finsbury Avenue, London, EC2M 2PP Tel: 020-7567 8000; Fax: 020-7568 4353;
Web site: www.wdr.com

Contact:	Michael Lacey-Solymar	**Number of Directors & Executives engaged in:**		
Also act as Nominated Broker?	n/a	**Corporate Finance:**	**Dir:**	n/a
Companies represented on first admission:	n/a		**Exec:**	n/a
Number involved in new issue to raise funds:	n/a	**AIM Activities:**	**Dir:**	n/a
Industry sector preferences:	n/a		**Exec:**	n/a
Geographical preferences:	n/a			
In-house industry sector analysts?	n/a	**Act for:**		n/a
Sectors covered by analysts:	n/a			
Prospective AIM companies considered:	n/a			
Startups Early stage Established				
Typical transaction parameters:	n/a			
Split of broking activities:	n/a			
institutional: private client)				
Underwriting facilities:		**Other Offices:**		n/a
Can provide:	n/a			
Can arrange:	n/a			
Other activities:	n/a			

Westhouse Securities

Clements House, 14-18 Gresham Street, London, EC2V 7NN Tel: 020-7601 6100; Fax: 020-7796 2713;
email andrew.smith@westhousesecurities.com; Web site: www.westhousesecurities.com

Contact:	Andrew Smith	**Number of Directors & Executives engaged in:**		
Also act as Nominated Broker?	Yes	**Corporate Finance:**	**Dir:**	4
Companies represented on first admission:	20		**Exec:**	7
Number involved in new issue to raise funds:	24	**AIM Activities:**	**Dir:**	4
Industry sector preferences:	None		**Exec:**	7
Geographical preferences:	None			
In-house industry sector analysts?	Yes	**Act for:** Airbath; Bertam; Brazilian Diamonds;		

Sectors covered by analysts: Mining & Natural
Resources; Small/medium companies, growth companies;
Telecoms, Media, Technology

Act for: Airbath; Bertam; Brazilian Diamonds; Cambridge Mineral Resources; Collins and Hayes; Ensor; Hereward Ventures; Hidefield; Innobox; James Halstead; Lendu; Pilat Technologies; Private & Commercial Finance; Probus Estates; Rowe Evans Investments; Surgical Innovations

Prospective AIM companies considered:
Startups Yes **Early stage** Yes **Established** Yes
Typical transaction parameters: None particularly
Split of broking activities: n/a
(institutional: private client)
Underwriting facilities:
    Can provide: Yes
    Can arrange: n/a

Other activities: Corporate Finance Advice

Other Offices:
Manchester
Contact: Philip Johnson
One King Street,
Manchester M2 6AW
Tel: 0161-838 9140
Fax: 0161-838 9141

WH Ireland

11 St James's Square, Manchester, M2 6WH Tel: 0161-832 6644; Fax: 0161-661 9098;
Web site: www.wh-ireland.co.uk

Contact: David Youngman	**Number of Directors & Executives engaged in:**
Also act as Nominated Broker? Yes	**Corporate Finance:** **Dir:** 6
Companies represented on first admission: 21	**Exec:** 2
Number involved in new issue to raise funds: 14	**AIM Activities:** **Dir:** 6
Industry sector preferences: n/a	**Exec:** 2
Geographical preferences: n/a	
In-house industry sector analysts? n/a	**Act for:** Access Intelligence; Bionex Investments;
Sectors covered by analysts: UK Smaller Companies –	Cityblock; Debt Free Direct; Highland Gold Mining;
Chemicals; Electronics & Electricals; Healthcare;	Leisure Ventures; Palladex; Preston North End;
Household Goods; Leisure; Personal Care; Support	Reflexion Cosmetics; Roshni Investments; Stepquick;
Services	Strategic Retail; Taskcatch; Toye & Company; Vista
Prospective AIM companies considered:	
Startups Yes **Early stage** Yes **Established** Yes	
Typical transaction parameters: n/a	**Other Offices:**
Split of broking activities: n/a	Blackburn, Burnley, Cardiff, Colwyn Bay, Fareham,
(institutional: private client)	Lancaster, London, Malvern, Sydney (Australia),
Underwriting facilities:	Thorpe Bay
Can provide: Yes	
Can arrange: Yes	
Other activities: n/a	

Williams de Broe

6 Broadgate, London, EC2M 2RP Tel: 020-7588 7511; Fax: 020-7588 8860;
Web site: www.wdebroe.com

Contact: Jonathan Gray (London), Ifor Williams	**Number of Directors & Executives engaged in:**
(Birmingham)	**Corporate Finance:** **Dir:** 7
Also act as Nominated Broker? Yes	**Exec:** 12
Companies represented on first admission: 17	**AIM Activities:** **Dir:** 8
Number involved in new issue to raise funds: 20	**Exec:** 12
Industry sector preferences: None	
Geographical preferences: None	**Act for:** ATA; Betinternet.com; CA Coutts; Caledon
In-house industry sector analysts? Yes	Resources; Capcon; Celtic Resources; Centamin Egypt;
Sectors covered by analysts: Most	Centurion Energy; Chepstow Racecourse; Churchill
Prospective AIM companies considered:	China; Clarity Commerce Solutions; CRC; Delcam;
Startups No **Early stage** Yes **Established** Yes	Dwyka Diamonds; Dynamic Commercial Finance;
Typical transaction parameters: Companies with a typi-	Education Development International; Eureka Mining;
cal market capitalisation of £10m or more	Fairplace Consulting; Faroe Petroleum; Futura Medical;
Split of broking activities: 70:30	Gold Mines of Sardinia; MacLellan; Marakand
(institutional: private client)	Minerals; Medoro Resources; Newmarket Investments;
Underwriting facilities:	Oxus Gold; Petra Diamonds; PM; Samuel Heath &
Can provide: Yes	Sons; Solitaire; SouthernEra Resources; Thomson
Can arrange: Yes	Intermedia; Widney
Other activities: Corporate Finance Advice; Fixed Income	**Other Offices:**
Broking; Fund Management; Institutional Broking;	Birmingham Tel: 0121-609 0056 Ifor Williams
Research	Edinburgh Tel: 0131-220 3686 Sid Noble
	Leeds Tel: 0113-243 1619 Joanne Lake

AIM BROKERS

Altium Capital

30 St James's Square, London, SW1 4AL   Tel: 020-7484 4040;   Fax: 020-7484 4010;
email: garry.levin@altiumcapital.co.uk;   Web site: www.altiumcapital.co.uk

Contact: Garry Levin/Tim Richardson	**Number of Directors & Executives engaged in:**
Also act as Nominated Adviser? Yes	**Corporate Finance:** **Dir:** 9
Companies represented on first admission: 21 since 1998	**Exec:** 10
Number involved in new issue to raise funds: 18 since 1998	**AIM Activities:** **Dir:** 4
	Exec: 10
Industry sector preferences: See below	
Geographical preferences: None	**Act for:** Empire Interactive; Epic; Imprint Search &
In-house industry sector analysts? Yes	Selection; ITIS; JAB; Online Travel
Sectors covered by analysts: IT Software & Services; Leisure; Smaller Companies; Speciality Retail; Support Services	
Prospective AIM companies considered:	
Startups No **Early stage** Yes **Established** Yes	
Typical transaction parameters: Minimum market capital - £20m. Minimum funds to be raised - £5m	**Other Offices:**
Split of broking activities: All institutional	Manchester Tel: 0161-831 9133 Phil Adams/Joe Smith
(institutional: private client)	
Underwriting facilities:	
Can provide: Yes	
Can arrange: Yes	
Other activities: Corporate Finance Advice; Market Making; Research; Sales Trading	

Arbuthnot Securities

2 Lambeth Hill, London, EC4V 4GG Tel: 020-7002 4600;   Fax: 020-7002 4619;
email: FirstnameLastname@arbuthnot.co.uk;   Web site: www.arbuthnot.co.uk/securities

Contact: Guy Peters	**Number of Directors & Executives engaged in:**
Also act as Nominated Adviser? Yes	**Corporate Finance:** **Dir:** 8
Companies represented on first admission: Over 20	**Exec:** 16
Number involved in new issue to raise funds: Over 25	**AIM Activities:** **Dir:** 4
Industry sector preferences: None	**Exec:** 9
Geographical preferences: None	
In-house industry sector analysts? Yes	**Act for:** AdVal; Amberley; AIT; Chelford; Cradley;
Sectors covered by analysts: All	Fayrewood; Highland Timber; International Greetings;
Prospective AIM companies considered:	INVU; Jennings Brothers; Loades; Mears; Overnet
Startups Yes **Early stage** Yes **Established** Yes	Data; Pilkington's Tiles; SpringHealth Leisure; Staffing
Typical transaction parameters: n/a	Ventures;Thomas Walker; West Bromwich Albion
Split of broking activities: n/a	
(institutional: private client)	
Underwriting facilities:	**Other Offices:**
Can provide: Yes	Birmingham Tel: 0121-632 2100
Can arrange: Yes	Edinburgh
	Glasgow
Other activities: Corporate Broking; Corporate Finance Advice; Institutional Research & Sales; Market Making	

Astaire & Partners

40 Queen Street, London, EC4R 1HN Tel: 020-7332 2600; Fax: 020-7332 2650;
email: shares@astaire.co.uk; Web site: www.astaire.co.uk

Contact:	Desmond Chapman	**Number of Directors & Executives engaged in:**		
Also act as Nominated Adviser?	No	Corporate Finance:	Dir:	1
Companies represented on first admission:	6		Exec:	1
Number involved in new issue to raise funds:	4	AIM Activities:	Dir:	1
Industry sector preferences:	All except Biotech,		Exec:	1
Natural Resources and Software				
Geographical preferences:	None	Act for:		n/a
In-house industry sector analysts?	No			
Sectors covered by analysts:	n/a			
Prospective AIM companies considered:				
Startups No Early stage Yes Established Yes				
Typical transaction parameters:	None particularly			
Split of broking activities:	90:10			
(institutional: private client)		Other Offices:		n/a
Underwriting facilities:				
Can provide:	No			
Can arrange:	Yes			

Other activities: Corporate Broking Services; Corporate Finance Advice

Baird

Mint House, 77 Mansell Street, London, E1 8AF Tel: 020-7488 1212; Fax: 020-7702 3134;
email: nnaylor@rwbaird.com; Web site: www.rwbaird.com

Contact:	Nicholas Naylor	**Number of Directors & Executives engaged in:**		
Also act as Nominated Adviser?	Yes	Corporate Finance:	Dir:	6
Companies represented on first admission:	4		Exec:	13
Number involved in new issue to raise funds:	8	AIM Activities:	Dir:	4
Industry sector preferences:	Healthcare; Media;		Exec:	13
Retail; Sports & Leisure; Support Services; Technology				
Geographical preferences:	None	Act for: Advanced Medical Solutions; Dickinson Legg;		
In-house industry sector analysts?	Yes	First Property; Forever Broadcasting; Sinclair Pharma		
Sectors covered by analysts: Healthcare; Media; Retail;				
Leisure; Support Services; Technology				
Prospective AIM companies considered:				
Startups No Early stage Yes, if profitability established				
Established Yes				
Typical transaction parameters:	None particularly	Other Offices:		
Split of broking activities:	All Institutional	France, Germany, USA		
(institutional: private client)				
Underwriting facilities:				
Can provide:	Yes			
Can arrange:	Yes			

Other activities: Equity Research and Distribution;
Investment Banking; Market Making; Private Equity

Brewin Dolphin Securities

7 Drumsheugh Gardens, Edinburgh, EH3 7QH Tel: 0131-225 2566; Fax: 0131-529 0246;
Web site: www.blw.co.uk

Contact:	Vikram Lall
Also act as Nominated Adviser?	Yes
Companies represented on first admission:	45
Number involved in new issue to raise funds:	14
Industry sector preferences:	None
Geographical preferences:	UK generally

In-house industry sector analysts? n/a
Sectors covered by analysts: Business Services; Colour Imaging Technology; Construction & Buidling Materials; Electronic & Electrical Equipment; Engineering; Food Producers; General Retailers; Healthcare; Household Goods & Textiles; Internet; Leisure and Hotels; Manufacturing; Media & Photography; Mining; Oil Exploration & Production; Other Financial; Publishing & Printing; Software & Computer Services; Support Services
Prospective AIM companies considered:
Startups Yes Early stage Yes Established Yes

Typical transaction parameters:	None
Split of broking activities:	n/a
(institutional: private client)	
Underwriting facilities:	
Can provide:	Yes
Can arrange:	Yes

Other activities: Corporate Broking Services; Corporate Finance Advice; Institutional Research; Private Client Stockbroking & Fund Management; Takeover & Rule 3 Advice

Number of Directors & Executives engaged in:

Corporate Finance:	Dir:	12
	Exec:	6
AIM Activities:	Dir:	12
	Exec:	6

Act for: Alkane Energy; AMCO; Angus & Ross; AorTech; Beauford; Biolife Ventures; Blavod Black Vodka; Booth Industries; Capital Management & Investment; Cavanagh; Clan Homes; Comeleon; Concurrent Technologies; County Contract Centres; Deep-Sea Leisure; Dobbies Garden Centres; Firestone Diamonds; Forbidden Technologies; Gladstone; Huveaux; IndigoVision; Inter Link Foods; James R Knowles; John Swan & Sons; Just Car Clinics; Medical Marketing International; Metnor; Micap; Netbenefit; Norman Hay; Premier Management; Quadnetics; Romag; Selector; Stadium; Stylo; Synergy Healthcare; tecc-IS; Tolent; Ultimate Leisure; Vebnet; Vianet; Virtue Broadcasting; Walker Greenbank; Xpertise; Yeoman; Zytronic

Other Offices:

Glasgow	Tel: 0141-221 7733	Elizabeth Kennedy
Leeds	Tel: 0113-241 0130	Neil Baldwin
Manchester	Tel: 0161-839 4222	Mark Brady
Newcastle	Tel: 0191-201 3871	Steve Wilson

Bridgewell

Old Change House, 128 Queen Victoria Street, London, EC4V 4BJ Tel: 020-7003 3000;
Fax: 020-7003 3199; Web site: www.bridgewell.co.uk

Contact:	John Craven/Ben Money-Coutts
Also act as Nominated Adviser?	Yes
Companies represented on first admission:	1
Number involved in new issue to raise funds:	2

Industry sector preferences: Construction; Financial Services; General Industrials; Housebuilding; IT; Media ; Property; Support Services

Geographical preferences:	UK
In-house industry sector analysts?	Yes

Sectors covered by analysts: Construction; Engineering; Financial Services; General Industrials; Housebuilding; IT; Leisure; Media; Property; Retail/Consumer; Support Services; Technology
Prospective AIM companies considered:
Startups No Early stage Yes Established Yes
Typical transaction parameters: Minimum market cap £10m (other than in exceptional circumstances)

Split of broking activities:	100%:0%
(institutional: private client)	
Underwriting facilities:	
Can provide:	Yes
Can arrange:	Yes

Other activities: Corporate Advisory

Number of Directors & Executives engaged in:

Corporate Finance:	Dir:	6
	Exec:	11
AIM Activities:	Dir:	6
	Exec:	11

Act for: AFA Systems; Avingtrans; CSS Stellar; DDD; Genus; Intelligent Environments; Interior Services; Premier Direct; SBS; Stonemartin; Transense Technologies

Other Offices:	n/a

Canaccord Capital

1st Floor Brook, 27 Upper Brook Street, London, W1Y 1PD, Tel: 020-7518 2777; Fax: 020-7518 2778; email: neil_johnson@canaccordeurope.com; Web site: www.canaccord.com

Contact:	Neil Johnson	Number of Directors & Executives engaged in:		
Also act as Nominated Adviser?	Yes	Corporate Finance:	Dir:	4
Companies represented on first admission:	14		Exec:	6
Number involved in new issue to raise funds:	20	AIM Activities:	Dir:	4
Industry sector preferences:	See analyst coverage		Exec:	6
Geographical preferences:	Global			
In-house industry sector analysts?	Yes	Act for: ADVFN.com; America Mineral Fields; Antrim Energy; Aricom; Bema Gold; Canisp; CES Software; Cluff Mining; Corvus Capital; First Quantum Minerals; GMA Resources; Mediwatch; Oilexco; Oriel Resources; Peter Hambro Mining; Pixology; Ramco Energy; Skiddaw Capital; Ten Alps Communication; TripleArc; Yamana Gold; YM BioSciences		
Sectors covered by analysts: Gaming; Life Sciences; Media; Mining: Oil & Gas; Software				
Prospective AIM companies considered:				
Startups No Early stage Yes Established Yes				
Typical transaction parameters:	n/a			
Split of broking activities:	All Institutional			
(institutional: private client)				
Underwriting facilities:		Other Offices:		
Can provide:	Yes	2 offices in Europe and 25 offices in North America		
Can arrange:	Yes			
Other activities:	n/a			

Capital International

PO Box 15, Mill Court, Hope Street, Castletown, Isle of Man, IM99 5XH Tel: 01624-828200; Fax: 01624-828201; email: info@capital-iom.com; Web site: www.capital-iom.com

Contact:	Peter Long/Graham Bolton	Number of Directors & Executives engaged in:		
Also act as Nominated Adviser?	No	Corporate Finance:	Dir:	2
Companies represented on first admission:	n/a		Exec:	n/a
Number involved in new issue to raise funds:	n/a	AIM Activities:	Dir:	2
Industry sector preferences:	n/a		Exec:	n/a
Geographical preferences:	n/a			
In-house industry sector analysts?	n/a	Act for: betinternet.com		
Sectors covered by analysts:	n/a			
Prospective AIM companies considered:				
Startups *Early stage *Established *Typical transaction parameters:	n/a			
Split of broking activities:	n/a			
(institutional: private client)				
Underwriting facilities:		Other Offices:		n/a
Can provide:	n/a			
Can arrange:	n/a			
Other activities: Investment management, fund administration, stock broking				

*Capital International provides corporate finance advice and broking services to small- and medium-sized companies based on the Isle of Man

Cazenove

12 Tokenhouse Yard, London, EC2R 7AN, Tel: 020-7588 2828; Fax: 020-7606 9205;
email: mwentworthstanley@cazenove.com; Web site: www.cazenove.com

			Number of Directors & Executives engaged in:		
Contact:	Michael Wentworth-Stanley				
Also act as Nominated Adviser?		Yes	Corporate Finance:	Dir:	n/a
Companies represented on first admission:		n/a		Exec:	n/a
Number involved in new issue to raise funds:		n/a	AIM Activities:	Dir:	n/a
Industry sector preferences:		n/a		Exec:	n/a
Geographical preferences:		n/a			
In-house industry sector analysts?		n/a	Act for: Inflexion; Radamec		
Sectors covered by analysts:		n/a			
Prospective AIM companies considered:					
Startups n/a Early stage n/a Established n/a					
Typical transaction parameters:		n/a			
Split of broking activities:		n/a			
(institutional: private client)					
Underwriting facilities:			Other Offices:		n/a
	Can provide:	n/a			
	Can arrange:	n/a			
Other activities:		n/a			

Charles Stanley

25 Luke Street, London, EC2A 4AR Tel: 020-7739 8200; Fax: 020-7739 4307;
Web site: www.charles-stanley.co.uk

			Number of Directors & Executives engaged in:		
Contact:	Richard Thompson/Russell Cook				
Also act as Nominated Adviser?		Yes	Corporate Finance:	Dir:	5
Companies represented on first admission:		n/a		Exec:	4
Number involved in new issue to raise funds:		n/a	AIM Activities:	Dir:	5
Industry sector preferences:		None		Exec:	4
Geographical preferences:		UK			
In-house industry sector analysts?		Yes	Act for: Cassidy Brothers; Celltalk; Centurion Electronics; Computerland UK; Deltex Medical; Expomedia; Feedback; Glisten; Griffin Mining; Highams Systems Services; Honeycombe Leisure; Jarvis Porter; Jourdan; Lawrence; Motion Media; NWF; Parkdean Holidays; Potential Finance; Proactive Sports; Profile Media; samedaybooks.co.uk; Savoy Asset Management; Solid State Supplies; Stilo; Supercart; Tikit; Top Ten; UA; Vantis; William Jacks; World Careers Network		
Sectors covered by analysts: Consumer Goods; Healthcare; Insurance; Leisure; Media & Entertainment; Real Estate; Retailers; Smaller Companies; Support Services; Technology					
Prospective AIM companies considered:					
Startups No Early stage Yes Established Yes					
Typical transaction parameters:		None particularly			
Split of broking activities:		Principally institutional			
(institutional: private client)					
Underwriting facilities:			Other Offices:		n/a
	Can provide:	No			
	Can arrange:	Yes			
Other activities: Corporate Broking Services; Corporate Finance Advice; Equity Research; Private Client Stockbroking					

Christows

29-30 Cornhill, London, EC3V 3ND Tel: 020-7444 1741; Fax: 020-7444 1749;
email: corp.fin@christows.co.uk; Web site: www.christows.co.uk

Contact:	Len Russell	**Number of Directors & Executives engaged in:**		
Also act as Nominated Adviser?	No	Corporate Finance:	Dir:	1
Companies represented on first admission:	n/a		Exec:	n/a
Number involved in new issue to raise funds:	n/a	AIM Activities:	Dir:	n/a
Industry sector preferences:	n/a		Exec:	n/a
Geographical preferences:	n/a			
In-house industry sector analysts?	n/a	**Act for:** Cabouchon; Cambrian Mining; Hemisphere		
Sectors covered by analysts:	n/a	Properties; Incite; Prestbury; White Knight Investments		
Prospective AIM companies considered:				
Startups No Early stage Yes Established Yes				
Typical transaction parameters:	n/a			
Split of broking activities:	n/a			
(institutional: private client)				
Underwriting facilities:		**Other Offices:**		n/a
Can provide:	n/a			
Can arrange:	n/a			
Other activities:	n/a			

City Financial Associates

Pountney Hill House, 6 Laurence Pountney Hill, London, EC4R 0BL Tel: 020-7090 7800;
Fax: 020-7283 6300; email: enquiry@cityfin.co.uk;

Contact:	Stephen Barclay	**Number of Directors & Executives engaged in:**		
Also act as Nominated Adviser?	Yes	Corporate Finance:	Dir:	3
Companies represented on first admission:	6		Exec:	3
Number involved in new issue to raise funds:	12	AIM Activities:	Dir:	3
Industry sector preferences:	None		Exec:	3
Geographical preferences:	UK			
In-house industry sector analysts?	No	**Act for:** 2 Travel; 10 Group; Designer Vision; Dinkie		
Sectors covered by analysts:	n/a	Heel; Fundamental E-Investments; Interactive Digital		
Prospective AIM companies considered:		Solutions; London Town; Mosaique; Parallel Media;		
Startups Yes Early stage Yes Established Yes		Setstone; Voss Net		
Typical transaction parameters:	Under £10m			
Split of broking activities:	50:50			
(institutional: private client)				
Underwriting facilities:		**Other Offices:**		n/a
Can provide:	No			
Can arrange:	Yes			
Other activities:	n/a			

Collins Stewart

9th Floor, 88 Wood Street, London, EC2V 7QR, Tel: 020-7523 8350; Fax: 020-7523 8134; email: enquiries@collins-stewart.com; Web site: www.collins-stewart.com

Contact:	Kripa Radhakrishnan	**Number of Directors & Executives engaged in:**	
Also act as Nominated Adviser?	Yes	**Corporate Finance:** Dir:	2
Companies represented on first admission:	18	Exec:	8
Number involved in new issue to raise funds:	70	**AIM Activities:** Dir:	2
Industry sector preferences:	None	Exec:	8
Geographical preferences:	None		

In-house industry sector analysts? Yes

Sectors covered by analysts: Engineering; Football Clubs; Healthcare; Information Technology & Internet; Leisure; Media; Retail; Support Services; Water Companies

Prospective AIM companies considered:

Startups No **Early stage** No **Established** Yes

Typical transaction parameters: £20m Market cap; Minimum funds to be raised £5m

Split of broking activities: n/a
(institutional: private client)

Underwriting facilities:

Can provide: Yes

Can arrange: Yes

Other activities: Investment Trusts; Large & small company broking

Act for: Albemarle & Bond; Atlantic Global; Avanti Capital; Base; BioProgress; Bits; Center Parcs (UK); Chicago Environmental; CI Traders; City Lofts; Cobra Bio-Manufacturing; ComProp; CustomVis; DataCash; Documedia Solutions; Erinaceous; Flintstone Technologies; Fountains; Halladale; Hardman Resources; Hartstone; Honeysuckle; Inditherm; Ingenta; International Brand Licensing; Media Square; Milestone; Millfield; Monterrico Metals; New Media Industries; NewMedia SPARK; OneClickHR; Orbis; Oystertec; PIPEX Communications; Resurge; RWS; Screen; Sirius Financial Solutions; Southampton Leisure; Sports and Leisure; Symphony Plastics; Trans-Siberian Gold; Tricorn; ukbetting; Vietnam Opportunity Fund; Wilshaw

Other Offices:
Channel Islands, New York

Collins Stewart (CI)

PO Box 8, 2nd Floor, TSB House, Le Truchot, St Peter Port, Guernsey, GY1 4AE Tel: 01481-731987; Fax: 01481-720018; email: aduquemin@ci.collins-stewart.com; Web site: www.ci.collins-stewart.com

Contact:	Andrew Duquemin	**Number of Directors & Executives engaged in:**	
Also act as Nominated Adviser?	No	**Corporate Finance:** Dir:	3
Companies represented on first admission:	3	Exec:	5
Number involved in new issue to raise funds:	0	**AIM Activities:** Dir:	3
Industry sector preferences:	None	Exec:	5

Geographical preferences: Channel Islands and the Isle of Man

In-house industry sector analysts? Yes

Sectors covered by analysts: n/a

Act for: ComProp

Prospective AIM companies considered:

Startups No **Early stage** Yes **Established** Yes

Typical transaction parameters: None particularly

Split of broking activities: 40:60
(institutional: private client)

Underwriting facilities:

Can provide: Yes

Can arrange: No

Other activities: Asset Management; Corporate Finance Advice (limited to Channel Islands and Isle of Man companies); Fund Management

Other Offices:

Collins Stewart (CI) Limited, PO Box 328, Landes du Marche Vale, Guernsey GY1 3 TY
Collins Stewart (CI) Limited, PO Box 3, 44 Esplanade, St Helier, Jersey JE4 OXQ
Collins Stewart Isle of Man, 7 Auckland Terrace, Parliament Street, Ramsey, Isle of Man IM8 1AF

Corporate Synergy

12 Nicholas Lane, London, EC4N 7BN Tel: 020-7626 2244;   Fax: 020-7626 2255;
email: info@corporatesynergy.co.uk;   Web site: www.corporatesynergy.co.uk

		Number of Directors & Executives engaged in:		
Contact:	Lindsay Mair			
Also act as Nominated Adviser?	Yes	Corporate Finance:	Dir:	4
Companies represented on first admission:	n/a		Exec:	5
Number involved in new issue to raise funds:	n/a	AIM Activities:	Dir:	4
Industry sector preferences:	None		Exec:	4
Geographical preferences:	None			
In-house industry sector analysts?	Yes	Act for: 1st Dental Laboratories; Black Rock Oil & Gas; Farley; First Derivatives; Multi		
Sectors covered by analysts: IT; Leisure & Hotels; Media & Entertainment; Mining; Support Services				
Prospective AIM companies considered:				
Startups No Early stage Yes Established Yes				
Typical transaction parameters:	None particularly			
Split of broking activities:	n/a			
(institutional: private client)		Other Offices:		
Underwriting facilities:		Newbury 01488-608188		
Can provide:	No			
Can arrange:	Yes			
Other activities:	n/a			

Credit Lyonnais Securities

Broadwalk House, 5 Appold Street, London, EC2A 2DA Tel: 020-7588 4000;   Fax: 020-7588 0278;
Web site: www.creditlyonnais.com

		Number of Directors & Executives engaged in:		
Contact:	Simon Bennett			
Also act as Nominated Adviser?	Yes	Corporate Finance:	Dir:	5
Companies represented on first admission:	5		Exec:	12
Number involved in new issue to raise funds:	2	AIM Activities:	Dir:	5
Industry sector preferences:	Chemicals;		Exec:	12
Construction; Food; Leisure; Oil; Paper; Property; Retail; Technology; TMT				
Geographical preferences:	UK/Europe	Act for: Heavitree Brewery; Inter-Alliance; Linton Park; Peel Holdings; StatPro; William Ransom & Son		
In-house industry sector analysts?	Yes			
Sectors covered by analysts:	as above			
Prospective AIM companies considered:				
Startups No Early stage Possibly Established Yes				
Typical transaction parameters:	n/a			
Split of broking activities:	n/a	Other Offices:		
(institutional: private client)		Hong Kong; Lyon; New York; Paris		
Underwriting facilities:				
Can provide:	Yes			
Can arrange:	Yes			
Other activities: Acquisition Finance; Market Making; Mergers and Acquisitions				

Daniel Stewart

48 Bishopsgate, London, EC2N 4AJ Tel: 020-7374 6789; Fax: 020-7374 6742;
email: info@danielstewart.co.uk; Web site: www.danielstewart.co.uk

Contact:	Peter Shea/Alastair Cade	**Number of Directors & Executives engaged in:**	
Also act as Nominated Adviser?	Yes	**Corporate Finance:** **Dir:**	2
Companies represented on first admission:	2	**Exec:**	4
Number involved in new issue to raise funds:	2	**AIM Activities:** **Dir:**	2
Industry sector preferences:	None	**Exec:**	4
Geographical preferences:	None		
In-house industry sector analysts?	Yes	**Act for:** Einstein; Envesta Telecom; Lo-Q; Mean	
Sectors covered by analysts:	Leisure; Technology	Fiddler Muisc; Offshore Telecom; Venturia	
Prospective AIM companies considered:			
Startups Yes **Early stage** Yes **Established** Yes			
Typical transaction parameters:	£2.5-10 million		
Split of broking activities:	85:15		
(institutional: private client)			
Underwriting facilities:		**Other Offices:**	n/a
Can provide:	No		
Can arrange:	Yes		
Other activities: Corporate Finance; Fund Management; Mergers & Acquisitions			

Deutsche Bank

6th Floor, Winchester House, Great Winchester Street, London, EC2N 2DB Tel: 020-7545 8000;
Fax: 020-7545 4577; Web site: www.db.com

Contact:	Philip Cowdy	**Number of Directors & Executives engaged in:**	
Also act as Nominated Adviser?		**Corporate Finance:** **Dir:**	n/a
Companies represented on first admission:	n/a	**Exec:**	n/a
Number involved in new issue to raise funds:	n/a	**AIM Activities:** **Dir:**	n/a
Industry sector preferences:	n/a	**Exec:**	n/a
Geographical preferences:	n/a		
In-house industry sector analysts?	n/a	**Act for:** Retail Stores	
Sectors covered by analysts: n/a			
Prospective AIM companies considered:			
Startups n/a **Early stage** n/a **Established**	n/a		
Typical transaction parameters:	n/a		
Split of broking activities:	n/a		
(institutional: private client)			
Underwriting facilities:		**Other Offices:**	n/a
Can provide:	n/a		
Can arrange:	n/a		
Other activities:	n/a		

Dresdner Kleinwort Wasserstein

PO Box 560, 20 Fenchurch Street, London, EC3P 3DB Tel: 020-7623 8000;   Fax: 020-7283 4667;
email: Ishbel.Macpherson@drkw.com;   Web site: www.drkw.com

		Number of Directors & Executives engaged in:		
Contact:	Ishbel Macpherson			
Also act as Nominated Adviser?	Yes	Corporate Finance:	Dir:	6
Companies represented on first admission:	1		Exec:	15
Number involved in new issue to raise funds:	2	AIM Activities:	Dir:	(Emerging co. team only)
Industry sector preferences:	Growth		Exec:	n/a
Geographical preferences:	UK			
In-house industry sector analysts?	Yes	Act for: InTechnology; Sportingbet.com		
Sectors covered by analysts:	Growth			

Prospective AIM companies considered:
Startups No Early stage No Established Yes
Typical transaction parameters: Mkt cap over £100m
Split of broking activities: Integrated approach
(institutional: private client)
Underwriting facilities:

	Can provide:	Yes
	Can arrange:	n/a

Other Offices:
Operates globally

Other activities: Full service global investment bank

Durlacher

4 Chiswell Street, London, EC1Y 4UP Tel: 020-7459 3600;   Fax: 020-7638 8848;
Web site: www.durlacher.com

		Number of Directors & Executives engaged in:		
Contact:	Simon Hirst			
Also act as Nominated Adviser?	Yes	Corporate Finance:	Dir:	5
Companies represented on first admission:	14		Exec:	4
Number involved in new issue to raise funds:	11	AIM Activities:	Dir:	4
Industry sector preferences: Engineering; Financial;			Exec:	3

Leisure; Internet; IT; Media; Support Services; Technology
Geographical preferences: None
In-house industry sector analysts? Yes
Sectors covered by analysts: Engineering; Financial;
Leisure; Internet; IT; Media; Support Services; Technology
Prospective AIM companies considered:
Startups Yes Early stage Yes Established Yes
Typical transaction parameters: None particularly
Split of broking activities: 50:50
institutional: private client)
Underwriting facilities:

	Can provide:	Yes
	Can arrange:	Yes

Other activities: Consultancy; Corporate Finance Advice;
Institutional and Private Client Broking; Market Making;
Portfolio Management; Research; Traded Options; Venture
Capital

Act for: African Eagle Resources; Archipelago
Resources; Avesco; Clean Diesel Technologies; COE;
Cyberes; Cyprotex; Digital Animations;Digital
Classics; Eurolink Managed Services; Finsbury Foods;
Glow Communications; GTL Resources; Host Europe;
ID Data; Image Scan; IMS Maxims; Lighthouse;
Matrix Healthcare; Medal Entertainment & Media;
Newsplayer; Pursuit Dynamics; Personal; Prestbury;
RingProp; Springboard; Straight; The Claims People;
themutual.net; VI; Yoomedia

Other Offices: n/a

Evolution Beeson Gregory

100 Wood Street, London, EC2V 7AN Tel: 020-7071 4300;   Fax: 020-7071 4450;
email: enquiries@evbg.com;   Web site: www.evbg.com

Contact: Tom Price/Chris Callaway /Tim Worledge/ Mike Brennan/ Rob Collins	**Number of Directors & Executives engaged in:**		
	Corporate Finance:	**Dir:**	6
Also act as Nominated Adviser? Yes		**Exec:**	8
Companies represented on first admission: 44	**AIM Activities:**	**Dir:**	6
Number involved in new issue to raise funds: 63		**Exec:**	8
Industry sector preferences: See below			
Geographical preferences: European	**Act for:** Advance Capital Invest; Advanced Power Components; Aero Inventory; Arlington; ASK Central; Avesco; Avocet Mining; Bank Restaurant; Blavod Black Vodka; Cape; Cardpoint; Chorion; Eckoh Technologies; Faupel Trading; Focus Solutions; Gaming Corporation; GR; Hat Pin; ImageState; IQE; Landround; Murchison United; Netcall; Northern Petroleum; Ocean Power Technologies; OMG; Osmetech; Paramount; Planit; Prezzo; Proteome Sciences; Regal Petroleum; Reversus; St Barbara Mines; Stagecoach Theatre Arts; Sterling Energy; Torex Retail; TradingSports Exchange Systems; Triple Plate Junction; Warthog; Wealth Management Software; Winchester Entertainment		
In-house industry sector analysts? Yes			
Sectors covered by analysts: Evolution Beeson Gregory has generalist smaller company analysts, plus specialists in Electronics; Games & Gaming; Industrials; Leisure; Life Sciences; Resources; Retail;Services;Software			
Prospective AIM companies considered:			
Startups No **Early stage** Yes **Established** Yes			
Typical transaction parameters: Good management team; clear strategy; defensible growth prospects			
Split of broking activities: 90:10			
(institutional: private client)			
Underwriting facilities:			
Can provide: Yes			
Can arrange: n/a	**Other Offices:**		n/a
Other activities: Advice on Funding; Corporate Finance Advice; Fund Management; Mergers and Acquisitions; Research; Strategic Financial Advice			

Fiske

Salisbury House, London Wall, London, EC2M 5QS Tel: 020-7448 4700;   Fax: 020-7256 5365;
email: info@fiskeplc.com;

Contact: Clive Harrison / James Harrison	**Number of Directors & Executives engaged in:**		
Also act as Nominated Adviser? No	**Corporate Finance:**	**Dir:**	1
Companies represented on first admission: 10		**Exec:**	1
Number involved in new issue to raise funds: 9	**AIM Activities:**	**Dir:**	1
Industry sector preferences: None		**Exec:**	3
Geographical preferences: None			
In-house industry sector analysts? No	**Act for:** Bella Media; Bright Futures; BWA; Coburg; enterpriseAsia; Fiske; Future Internet Technologies; Golden Prospect; Greenchip Investments; Harrogate; Oak Holdings		
Sectors covered by analysts: n/a			
Prospective AIM companies considered:			
Startups No **Early stage** No **Established** Yes			
Typical transaction parameters: None particularly			
Split of broking activities: 15:85			
(institutional: private client)			
Underwriting facilities:	**Other Offices:**		n/a
Can provide: Yes			
Can arrange: Yes			
Other activities: Corporate Finance Advice; Research			

Fyshe Horton Finney

Charles House, 148/149 Great Charles Street, Birmingham, B3 3HT Tel: 0121-236 3111;
Fax: 0121-236 4875; email: clive@fyshe.co.uk; Web site: www.fyshe.co.uk

Contact:	Clive Duckitt/Peter Knowles	**Number of Directors & Executives engaged in:**		
Also act as Nominated Adviser?	No	**Corporate Finance:**	**Dir:**	2
Companies represented on first admission:	1		**Exec:**	n/a
Number involved in new issue to raise funds:	n/a	**AIM Activities:**	**Dir:**	1
Industry sector preferences:	n/a		**Exec:**	n/a
Geographical preferences:	n/a			
In-house industry sector analysts?	n/a	**Act for:** Carlisle		
Sectors covered by analysts:	n/a			
Prospective AIM companies considered:				
Startups Yes **Early stage** Yes **Established** Yes				
Typical transaction parameters:	n/a			
Split of broking activities:	90:10			
(institutional: private client)				
Underwriting facilities:		**Other Offices:**		
Can provide:	n/a	Ilkley, Leeds,London, Northampton		
Can arrange:	n/a			
Other activities:	n/a			

Goodbody Corporate Finance

Ballsbridge Park, Ballsbridge, Dublin 4, Ireland, Tel: 00-353 1 667 0400; Fax: 00-353 1 667 0410;
Web site: www.goodbody.ie

Contact:	Carole Corby	**Number of Directors & Executives engaged in:**		
Also act as Nominated Adviser?	Yes	**Corporate Finance:**	**Dir:**	7
Companies represented on first admission:	3		**Exec:**	8
Number involved in new issue to raise funds:	3	**AIM Activities:**	**Dir:**	n/a
Industry sector preferences:	n/a		**Exec:**	n/a
Geographical preferences:	Ireland			
In-house industry sector analysts?	Yes	**Act for:**		n/a
Sectors covered by analysts: Construction & Building Materials; Financial Services; Food; Pharmaceuticals; Technology				
Prospective AIM companies considered:				
Startups n/a **Early stage** n/a **Established** n/a				
Typical transaction parameters:	n/a			
Split of broking activities:	n/a	**Other Offices:**		
(institutional: private client)		Cork, Galway		
Underwriting facilities:				
Can provide:	Yes			
Can arrange:	Yes			
Other activities:	n/a			

Hichens Harrison

Bell Court House, 11 Blomfield, London, EC2M 1LD Tel: 020-7588 5171; Fax: 020-7628 9481;
email: dennis.bailey@hichens.co.uk; Web site: www.hichens.co.uk

Contact:	Dennis Bailey	Number of Directors & Executives engaged in:		
Also act as Nominated Adviser?	No	Corporate Finance:	Dir:	n/a
Companies represented on first admission:	n/a		Exec:	n/a
Number involved in new issue to raise funds:	n/a	AIM Activities:	Dir:	n/a
Industry sector preferences:	n/a		Exec:	n/a
Geographical preferences:	n/a			
In-house industry sector analysts?	n/a	Act for: Capricorn Resources; DawMed Systems; ESV;		
Sectors covered by analysts:	n/a	Knowledge Technology Solutions; RII; Tecteon; Texas		
Prospective AIM companies considered:		Oil & Gas; Univent		
Startups n/a Early stage n/a Established n/a				
Typical transaction parameters:	n/a			
Split of broking activities:	n/a			
(institutional: private client)				
Underwriting facilities:		Other Offices:		n/a
Can provide:	n/a			
Can arrange:	n/a			
Other activities:	n/a			

Hoare Govett

250 Bishopsgate, London, EC2M 4AA Tel: 020-7678 8000; Web site: www.abnamro.com

Contact:	Carol Raymond	Number of Directors & Executives engaged in:		
Also act as Nominated Adviser?	n/a	Corporate Finance:	Dir:	n/a
Companies represented on first admission:	n/a		Exec:	n/a
Number involved in new issue to raise funds:	n/a	AIM Activities:	Dir:	n/a
Industry sector preferences:	n/a		Exec:	n/a
Geographical preferences:	n/a			
In-house industry sector analysts?	n/a	Act for: NeuTec Pharma		
Sectors covered by analysts:	n/a			
Prospective AIM companies considered:	n/a			
Startups Early stage Established				
Typical transaction parameters:	n/a			
Split of broking activities:	n/a			
(institutional: private client)				
Underwriting facilities:	n/a	Other Offices:		n/a
Can provide:	n/a			
Can arrange:	n/a			
Other activities:	n/a			

Hoodless Brennan & Partners

40 Marsh Wall, Docklands, London E14 9TP Tel: 020-7538 1166; Fax: 020-7538 1280;
email: hbp@hoodlessbrennan.com; Web site: www.hoodlessbrennan.com

Contact: Stephen Greenwood (Corporate Finance) Luke Cairns (Corporate Finance Executive)	
Also act as Nominated Adviser?	
Companies represented on first admission: 24	
Number involved in new issue to raise funds: 30	
Industry sector preferences: No preferences - all sectors	
Geographical preferences: No preferences	
In-house industry sector analysts? Yes	
Sectors covered by analysts: Generalist Small Cap Market; Healthcare; Natural Resources; Oil & Gas; Pharmaceurticals; Real Estate; Technologies	
Prospective AIM companies considered:	
Startups Yes **Early stage** Yes **Established** Yes	
Typical transaction parameters: None in particular	
Split of broking activities: 65:35	
(institutional: private client)	
Underwriting facilities:	
Can provide: Yes	
Can arrange: Yes	

Number of Directors & Executives engaged in:

Corporate Finance:	**Dir:**	3
	Exec:	3
AIM Activities:	**Dir:**	3
	Exec:	3

Act for: Akaei; Clipper Ventures; Dimension Resources; DawMed Systems; EiRx Therapeutics; Europasia Education; Gippsland; Henderson Morley; Keyworld Investments; Meriden; On-Line; Reefton Mining; ReGen Therapeutics; The Creative Education Corporation; The Market Age

Other Offices:
1st Floor
43 Temple Row
Birmingham
B2 5LS
Contact: Tim Cofman
Tel: 0121-237 6374
E-mail: tim.cofman@hoodlessbrennan.com

Other activities: Corporate Finance; Institutional Sales; Market Making; Private Equity

HSBC Bank

8 Canada Square, Canary Wharf, London, E14 5HQ Tel: 020-7991 8888; Fax: 020-7991 4454;

Contact: John Mellett	
Also act as Nominated Adviser? Yes	
Companies represented on first admission: 12	
Number involved in new issue to raise funds: 12	
Industry sector preferences: None	
Geographical preferences: None	
In-house industry sector analysts? Yes	
Sectors covered by analysts: Most sectors	
Prospective AIM companies considered:	
Startups No **Early stage** No **Established** Yes	
Typical transaction parameters: Liquidity for institutional shareholders dictates size of deal	
Split of broking activities: All Institutional	
(institutional: private client)	
Underwriting facilities:	
Can provide: Yes	
Can arrange: Yes	

Number of Directors & Executives engaged in:

Corporate Finance:	**Dir:**	35
	Exec:	n/a
AIM Activities:	**Dir:**	2
	Exec:	5

Act for: n/a

Other Offices: n/a

Other activities: Corporate Broking; Corporate Finance Advice; Mergers and Acquisitions; Research

ING Barings

60 London Wall, London, EC2M 5TQ Tel: 020-7767 1000; Fax: 020-7767 7222

Contact:	Andy Muncer	**Number of Directors & Executives engaged in:**		
Also act as Nominated Adviser?	Yes	**Corporate Finance:**	**Dir:**	n/a
Companies represented on first admission:	9		**Exec:**	n/a
Number involved in new issue to raise funds:	8	**AIM Activities:**	**Dir:**	n/a
Industry sector preferences:	n/a		**Exec:**	n/a
Geographical preferences:	n/a			
In-house industry sector analysts?	n/a	**Act for:** Seymour Pierce		
Sectors covered by analysts:	n/a			
Prospective AIM companies considered:				
Startups n/a **Early stage** n/a **Established** n/a				
Typical transaction parameters:	n/a			
Split of broking activities:	n/a			
(institutional: private client)				
Underwriting facilities:		**Other Offices:**		
Can provide:	Yes	Lismore House		
Can arrange:	Yes	127 George Street		
		Edinburgh		
Other activities:	n/a	EH2 4JX		

Insinger Townsley

44 Worship Street, London, EC2A 2JT Tel: 020-7377 6161; Fax: 020-7655 6897;
email: infocorpfin@insinger.com; Web site: www.insinger.com

Contact:	Simon Fox/Nandita Sahgal	**Number of Directors & Executives engaged in:**		
Also act as Nominated Adviser?	Yes, through Insinger	**Corporate Finance:**	**Dir:**	1
de Beaufort			**Exec:**	1
Companies represented on first admission:	26	**AIM Activities:**	**Dir:**	1
Number involved in new issue to raise funds:	49		**Exec:**	1
Industry sector preferences:	None			
Geographical preferences:	None	**Act for:** ASITE; Bullion Resources; Community		
In-house industry sector analysts?	Yes	Broking; Constellation Corporation; Crown		
Sectors covered by analysts: Generalist and Mining		Corporation; Equator; Eurovestech; Fortfield		
Prospective AIM companies considered:		Investments; Interactive Gaming; Internet Music &		
Startups Yes **Early stage** Yes **Established** Yes		Media; London Asia Capital; Penmc; TEP Exchange;		
Typical transaction parameters:	None particularly	Totally; TranXenoGen; Universal Direct;		
Split of broking activities:	n/a	XecutiveResearch; Your Space		
(institutional: private client)				
Underwriting facilities:				
Can provide:	Yes	**Other Offices:**		
Can arrange:	Yes	Geneva (representative office)		

Other activities: Corporate Advisory including Financial
and Group Restructuring; Corporate Broking Services;
Corporate Finance Advice; Corporate International Tax
Planning; MBO's and MBI's; Mergers and Acquisitions;
Research; Stockbroking

Investec Investment Banking

2 Gresham Street, London, EC2V 7QP Tel: 020-7597 5000;   Fax: 020-7597 5097

Contact: Keith Anderson/Erik Anderson/ Nick Thorniley		**Number of Directors & Executives engaged in:**		
Also act as Nominated Adviser?	Yes	**Corporate Finance:**	**Dir:**	10
Companies represented on first admission:	13		**Exec:**	14
Number involved in new issue to raise funds:	13	**AIM Activities:**	**Dir:**	10
Industry sector preferences:	See below		**Exec:**	14
Geographical preferences:	UK bias			
In-house industry sector analysts?	Yes	**Act for:** Cluff Mining; Georgica; Hartford; Melrose		

Sectors covered by analysts: Food Producers &
Processors; Growth Industrials; Healthcare; Leisure;
Media; Mining; Oil & Gas; Retailing - Food & General;
Support Services; Technology; Telecommunications
Prospective AIM companies considered:
Startups Yes **Early stage** Yes **Established** Yes

Typical transaction parameters: Market capitalisation:
£50m-plus preferred
Split of broking activities: All Institutional
(institutional: private client)
Underwriting facilities:

Can provide:	Yes
Can arrange:	Yes

Other Offices: n/a

Other activities: Corporate Finance Advice; Research and
Corporate Broking

J&E Davy

Davy House, 49 Dawson Street, Dublin 2, Ireland Tel: 00-353 1 679 6363;   Fax: 00-353 1 679 6366;
email: dcf@davy.ie;   Web site: www.davy.ie

Contact:	Ivan Murphy	**Number of Directors & Executives engaged in:**		
Also act as Nominated Adviser?	Yes	**Corporate Finance:**	**Dir:**	4
Companies represented on first admission:	1		**Exec:**	6
Number involved in new issue to raise funds:	1	**AIM Activities:**	**Dir:**	2
Industry sector preferences:	None		**Exec:**	3
Geographical preferences:	Ireland			
In-house industry sector analysts?	Yes	**Act for:** CPL Resources; Petroceltic International;		
Sectors covered by analysts: All major sectors covered		Reflex		

Prospective AIM companies considered:
Startups No **Early stage** Yes **Established** Yes
Typical transaction parameters: None particularly
Split of broking activities: n/a
(institutional: private client)
Underwriting facilities:

Can provide:	Yes
Can arrange:	Yes

Other Offices: n/a

Other activities: Corporate Broking Services; Corporate
Finance Advice; Research

JM Finn

Salisbury House, London Wall, London, EC2M 5TA Tel: 020-7628 9688; Fax: 020-7628 7314;
Web site: www.jmfinn.co.uk

		Number of Directors & Executives engaged in:		
Contact:	John Finn			
Also act as Nominated Adviser?	No	**Corporate Finance:**	**Dir:**	n/a
Companies represented on first admission:	3		**Exec:**	n/a
Number involved in new issue to raise funds:	3	**AIM Activities:**	**Dir:**	n/a
Industry sector preferences:	None		**Exec:**	n/a
Geographical preferences:	None			
In-house industry sector analysts?	Yes	**Act for:** 3DM Worldwide; Napier Brown Foods;		
Sectors covered by analysts: Smaller Companies;		Network; Pipehawk; Sky Capital; The Real Good Food		
Technology		Company; Western Selection		
Prospective AIM companies considered:				
Startups Yes **Early stage** Yes, if profitability established				
Established Yes				
Typical transaction parameters: None particularly				
Split of broking activities:	n/a	**Other Offices:**		
(institutional: private client)		St Brandons House		
Underwriting facilities:		29 Great George Street		
		Bristol BS1 5QT		
Can provide:	n/a	Tel: 0117-921 0550		
Can arrange:	n/a			

Other activities: Corporate Finance Advice; Research;
Venture Capital

John East & Partners

Crystal Gate, 28-30 Worship Street, London, EC2A 2AH Tel: 020-7628 2200; Fax: 020-7628 4473;
email: info@johneastpartners.com; Web site: www.johneastpartners.com

		Number of Directors & Executives engaged in:		
Contact:	John East			
Also act as Nominated Adviser?	Yes	**Corporate Finance:**	**Dir:**	5
Companies represented on first admission:	n/a		**Exec:**	1
Number involved in new issue to raise funds:	n/a	**AIM Activities:**	**Dir:**	5
Industry sector preferences:	None		**Exec:**	1
Geographical preferences:	None			
In-house industry sector analysts?	No	**Act for:** Azure; Prestige Publishing; Surface		
Sectors covered by analysts:	n/a	Transforms; tecc-IS		
Prospective AIM companies considered:				
Startups No **Early stage** Yes **Established** Yes				
Typical transaction parameters: None particularly				
Split of broking activities:	n/a			
(institutional: private client)				
Underwriting facilities:		**Other Offices:**	n/a	
Can provide:	No			
Can arrange:	Yes			

Other activities: Corporate Finance Advice on all matters
including agreed and hostile takeovers

KBC Peel Hunt

4th Floor, 111 Old Broad Street, London, EC2N 1PH Tel: 020-7418 8900; Fax: 020-7972 0112;
email: adam.hart@kbcpeelhunt.com; Web site: www.kbcpeelhunt.com

Contact:	Adam Hart	**Number of Directors & Executives engaged in:**	
Also act as Nominated Adviser?	Yes	**Corporate Finance:** **Dir:**	2
Companies represented on first admission:	Many	**Exec:**	12
Number involved in new issue to raise funds:	100+	**AIM Activities:** **Dir:**	2
Industry sector preferences:	Will consider most sec-	**Exec:**	10

tors, other than natural resources

Geographical preferences:	None	**Act for:** Abingdon Capital; Acquisitor; Acquisitor
In-house industry sector analysts?	Yes	(Bermuda); Advanced Technology; Akers Biosciences;
Sectors covered by analysts: Construction & Building		Armour Group; Billam; Charteris; Civilian Content;

Sectors covered by analysts: Construction & Building
Materials; Engineering; Insurance; IT Hardware; Leisure &
Hotels; Pharmaceuticals & Biotechnology; Real Estate;
Retail; Software & Computer Services; Support Services
Prospective AIM companies considered:
Startups Yes **Early stage** Yes **Established** Yes
Typical transaction parameters:
Subject to the merits of each case
Split of broking activities: 95:5
institutional: private client)
Underwriting facilities:
      Can provide: Yes
      Can arrange: Yes
Other activities: Corporate Finance Advice; Market
Making; Mergers and Acquisitions; Other Research; Sales
Distribution; Private Equity (all on a pan-European basis)

Clover Corporation; Clubhaus; Conister Trust;
Connaught; Contemporary Enterprises; Cybit; Deal Group
Media; Dream Direct; Enneurope; Enterprise; eq;
FFastFill; General Industries; Harrier; hemscott; I2S; Ideal
Shopping Direct; Innovision Research and Technology;
Intercede; iomart; IP2IPO; IQ-Ludorum; Knowledge
Technology Solutions; Marshall Edwards; Martin Shelton;
Meon Capital; Metrodome; Murray Financial;
Northacre;Offshore Hydrocarbon Mapping; Peel Hotels;
RAB Capital; Razorback Vehicles; Sheffield United;
Stream; Sunbeach Communications; SWP; Systems
Union; Tandem; Tenon; Thirdforce; Tom Hoskins; Vitesse
Media

Other Offices: Throughout Europe

Keith Bayley Rogers & Co

Sophia House, 76-80 City Road, London, EC1Y 2EQ Tel: 020-7871 2232; Fax: 020-7553 9695;
email: corpfin@wcwb.co.uk

Contact:	Howard Drummon	**Number of Directors & Executives engaged in:**	
Also act as Nominated Adviser?	No	**Corporate Finance:** **Dir:**	1
Companies represented on first admission:	n/a	**Exec:**	4
Number involved in new issue to raise funds:	n/a	**AIM Activities:** **Dir:**	1
Industry sector preferences:	n/a	**Exec:**	4
Geographical preferences:	n/a		
In-house industry sector analysts?	n/a	**Act for:** Arko; Cater Barnard (USA); EmdexTrade;	
Sectors covered by analysts:	n/a	London & Boston Investments; Maisha; MG Capital;	

Prospective AIM companies considered:
Startups No **Early stage** Yes **Established** Yes
Typical transaction parameters: n/a
Split of broking activities: n/a
(institutional: private client)
Underwriting facilities:
      Can provide: n/a
      Can arrange: n/a

Other activities: n/a

Ocean Resources Capital; Petrel Resources; Web
Shareshop

Other Offices: n/a

Marshall Securities

Crusader House, 145-157 St John Street, London, EC1V 4RE Tel: 020-7490 3788;   Fax: 020-7490 3787;

Contact:	John Webb	**Number of Directors & Executives engaged in:**	
Also act as Nominated Adviser?	Yes	**Corporate Finance:** **Dir:**	3
Companies represented on first admission:	3	**Exec:**	1
Number involved in new issue to raise funds:	5	**AIM Activities:** **Dir:**	3
Industry sector preferences:	None	**Exec:**	1
Geographical preferences:	UK generally		
In-house industry sector analysts?	No	**Act for:** Impax; Talent	
Sectors covered by analysts:	n/a		
Prospective AIM companies considered:			
Startups No **Early stage** Yes **Established** Yes			
Typical transaction parameters:	n/a		
Split of broking activities:	All Institutional		
(institutional: private client)			
Underwriting facilities:		**Other Offices:**	n/a
Can provide:	Yes		
Can arrange:	Yes		

Other activities: Corporate Finance Advice

Noble & Company

1 Frederick's Place, London, EC2R 8AB Tel: 020-7367 5600;   Fax: 020-7796 0020;
Web site: www.noblegp.com

Contact:	Jeremy Stephenson	**Number of Directors & Executives engaged in:**	
Also act as Nominated Adviser?	Yes	**Corporate Finance:** **Dir:**	8
Companies represented on first admission:	5	**Exec:**	10
Number involved in new issue to raise funds:	12	**AIM Activities:** **Dir:**	8
Industry sector preferences:	Business Support	**Exec:**	14
Services; Financial Services; Oil & Gas; Property; Retail,			
Leisure & Media; Technology		**Act for:** Avionic Services; i-documentsystems; Kuju;	
Geographical preferences:	None	Longbridge International; Murgitroyd; Optimisa;	
In-house industry sector analysts?	No	Palmaris Capital; The Clapham House Group; Zoo	
Sectors covered by analysts:	n/a	Digital	
Prospective AIM companies considered:			
Startups No **Early stage** No **Established** Yes			
Typical transaction parameters:	n/a		
Split of broking activities:	n/a	**Other Offices:**	
(institutional: private client)		Edinburgh Tel: 0131-225 9766 Alasdair Robinson	
Underwriting facilities:			
Can provide:	No		
Can arrange:	Yes		

Other activities: Corporate Broking; Corporate
Restructuring; General Corporate Finance; Limited partnerships; Mergers and acquisitions; Official List Sponsors;
Property Funds; Property-related Unit Trusts; Tax efficient
investment vehicles – EISs, VCTs, EZTs

Nomura International

Nomura House, 1 St Martin's-Le-Grand, London, EC1A 4NP Tel: 020-7521 2000;
Fax: 020-7521 3655/56; Web site: www.nomura.co.uk

		Number of Directors & Executives engaged in:		
Contact:	Robert Davies/Charles Spicer			
Also act as Nominated Adviser?	No	Corporate Finance:	Dir:	7
Companies represented on first admission:	n/a		Exec:	20
Number involved in new issue to raise funds:	n/a	AIM Activities:	Dir:	3
Industry sector preferences:	n/a		Exec:	7
Geographical preferences:	Europe			
In-house industry sector analysts?	n/a	Act for: LiDCO		
Sectors covered by analysts:	Healthcare; Technology			
Prospective AIM companies considered:				
Startups Yes Early stage Yes Established Yes				
Typical transaction parameters:	n/a			
Split of broking activities:	n/a			
(institutional: private client)				
Underwriting facilities:		Other Offices:		n/a
Can provide:	Yes			
Can arrange:	Yes			

Other activities: M & A Advisory

Numis

Cheapside House, 138 Cheapside, London, EC2V 6LH Tel: 020-7776 1500; Fax: 020-7776 1555;
email: mail@numiscorp.com ; Web site: www.numiscorp.com

		Number of Directors & Executives engaged in:		
Contact:	Charles Crick/Jag Mundi			
Also act as Nominated Adviser?	Yes	Corporate Finance:	Dir:	8
Companies represented on first admission:	16		Exec:	5
Number involved in new issue to raise funds:	28	AIM Activities:	Dir:	8
Industry sector preferences: Aerospace & Defence; Building &			Exec:	5
Construction; Consumer; Financial Services; Food Producers;				
Food Retail; General Retail; Insurance; Leisure; Life Sciences;		Act for: 2 ergo; Alliance Pharma; Ambient; Caledonian		
Media; Mining; Support Services; Technology		Trust; Centaur; Consolidated Minerals; Corac; Domino's		
Geographical preferences:	UK	Pizza UK & Ireland; Epic Reconstruction; European		
In-house industry sector analysts?	Yes	Diamonds; FTV; Gympie Gold; Headway; Healthcare		
Sectors covered by analysts: Aerospace & Defence; Building		Enterprises; Hot; Inter Link Foods; Jubilee Platinum;		
& Construction; Consumer; Financial Services; Food		Leeds; Maelor; Moneybox; Monsoon; Numerica; Pursuit		
Producers; Food Retail; General Retail; Insurance; Leisure;		Dynamics; Stockcube; THB; Urbium; Virotec; West 175		
Life Sciences; Media; Mining; Support Services; Technology		Media; WILink.com; Zincox Resources		
Prospective AIM companies considered:				
Startups Yes Early stage Yes Established Yes				
Typical transaction parameters: Minimum market capital		Other Offices:		
- £15m. Minimum funds to be raised: None		Castle Chambers		
Split of broking activities: All Institutional		43 Castle Street		
institutional: private client)		Liverpool		
Underwriting facilities:		L2 9ST		
Can provide:	Yes	Tel: 0151-225 0800		
Can arrange:	Yes	Fax: 0151-227 9435		
Other activities: Corporate Finance Advice; Institutional				
Sales; Market Making; Research				

Oriel Securities

4 Wood Street, London, EC2V 7JB Tel: 020-7710 7600;   Fax: 020-7710 7609;
email: info@orielsecurities.com;   Web site: www.orielsecurities.com

Contact:	Andrew Edwards	Number of Directors & Executives engaged in:		
Also act as Nominated Adviser?	Yes	**Corporate Finance:**	**Dir:**	3
Companies represented on first admission:	n/a		**Exec:**	4
Number involved in new issue to raise funds:	n/a	**AIM Activities:**	**Dir:**	3
Industry sector preferences:	None		**Exec:**	4
Geographical preferences:	n/a			
In-house industry sector analysts?	Yes	**Act for:** Hardman Resources; Oasis Healthcare; Sigma		

Sectors covered by analysts: Consumer; Food Producers; Healthcare; Media & Leisure; Oil & Gas; Real Estate; Retail; Smallcaps; Support Services; Transport
Technology; Tellings Golden Miller; Westmount Energy

Prospective AIM companies considered:
Startups Yes **Early stage** Yes **Established** Yes
Typical transaction parameters:

Split of broking activities:	n/a	**Other Offices:**	n/a

(institutional: private client)
Underwriting facilities:

	Can provide:	Yes
	Can arrange:	Yes

Other activities: n/a

Panmure Gordon

50 Stratton Street, London, W1J 8LL Tel: 020-7187 2000;   Fax: 020-7072 6383;
Web site: www.panmure.com

Contact:	Richard Potts	Number of Directors & Executives engaged in:		
Also act as Nominated Adviser?	Yes	**Corporate Finance:**	**Dir:**	n/a
Companies represented on first admission:	n/a		**Exec:**	n/a
Number involved in new issue to raise funds:	n/a	**AIM Activities:**	**Dir:**	n/a
Industry sector preferences:	n/a		**Exec:**	n/a
Geographical preferences:	None			
In-house industry sector analysts?	Yes	**Act for:** Coliseum; InTechnology; Interior Services;		

Sectors covered by analysts: As above plus others
Inventive Leisure; Keryx Biopharmaceuticals; Lok 'n
Prospective AIM companies considered:
Store; NMT; Tissue Science Laboratories; Transcomm;
Startups Yes **Early stage** Yes **Established** Yes
Systems Union
Typical transaction parameters: Market capitalisation and size of issue need to be of a size, although there is no specific threshold

Split of broking activities:	n/a	**Other Offices:**
(institutional: private client)		Panmure Gordon is a division of Lazard & Co

Underwriting facilities:

	Can provide:	Yes
	Can arrange:	Yes

Other activities: Convertibles; Corporate Broking Services; Corporate Finance Advice; Equity Capital Markets; High Yield Derivatives; Mergers & Acquisitions; Research

Phillip Securities (UK)

83-85 Mansell Street, London, E1 8AN Tel: 020-7553 8821; Fax: 020-7369 9889;
email: corpbroker@phillip-uk.com; Web site: www.phillip-uk.com

Contact:	Nicholas Bealer/Linus Lim	Number of Directors & Executives engaged in:		
Also act as Nominated Adviser?	No	Corporate Finance:	Dir:	n/a
Companies represented on first admission:	1		Exec:	n/a
Number involved in new issue to raise funds:	2	AIM Activities:	Dir:	n/a
Industry sector preferences:	Technology		Exec:	n/a
Geographical preferences:	UK, Far East			
In-house industry sector analysts?	No	Act for: Quiktrak Networks		
Sectors covered by analysts:	n/a			
Prospective AIM companies considered:				
Startups Yes Early stage Yes Established Yes				
Typical transaction parameters:				
Split of broking activities:				
(institutional: private client)				
Underwriting facilities:		Other Offices:		
Can provide:	n/a	Branch network across Asia		
Can arrange:	n/a			

Other activities: Ethical investments; UK and Far East equity

---

Rowan Dartington Corporate Finance

Colston Tower, Colston Street, Bristol, BS1 4RD Tel: 0117-933 0020; Fax: 0117-933 0024

Contact:	John Wakefield	Number of Directors & Executives engaged in:	
Also act as Nominated Adviser?	Yes	Corporate Finance: Dir:	3
Companies represented on first admission:	Approx 40	Exec:	2
Number involved in new issue to raise funds:	50+	AIM Activities: Dir:	3
Industry sector preferences:	None	Exec:	2
Geographical preferences:	None		
In-house industry sector analysts?	Yes	Act for: African Diamonds; African Gold; Airsprung	
Sectors covered by analysts:	Smaller companies	Furniture; Bristol & London; Bristol & West Investments;	
Prospective AIM companies considered:		CODASciSys; Compact Power; Creative Recruitment	
Startups No Early stage Yes Established Yes		Solutions; CYC; Densitron Technologies; Dickinson	
Typical transaction parameters:	None particularly	Legg; Dipford; Farsight; Gooch & Housego; Hawthorn;	
Split of broking activities:	70:30	Holders Technology; K3 Business Technology; Mercury	
institutional: private client)		Recycling; Minco; Montpellier; Pan Andean Resources;	
Underwriting facilities:		Pennant International; Petrel Resources; Photo-Scan;	
Can provide:	No	Pubs 'n' Bars; Surface Technology Systems; Sutton	
Can arrange:	Yes	Harbour; Water Hall; Wyatt	

Other activities: Corporate Finance Advice; Private Client Fund Management; Research; Stockbroking	Other Offices:	Redruth
	Bath	Tel: 01209-214488
	Tel: 01225-424666	Taunton
	Chichester	Tel: 01823-257752
	Tel: 01243-771886	Weston-Super-Mare
	Hereford	Tel: 01934-413355
	Tel: 01432-277003	

Schroder Salomon Smith Barney (Salomon Brothers UK Equity)

Citigroup Centre, 33 Canada Square, Canary Wharf, London, E14 5LB Tel: 020-7986 4000;
Fax: 020-7986 2266;

Contact: Kamal Tabet	**Number of Directors & Executives engaged in:**
Also act as Nominated Adviser? Yes	**Corporate Finance:** **Dir:** n/a
Companies represented on first admission: 2	**Exec:** n/a
Number involved in new issue to raise funds: 2	**AIM Activities:** **Dir:** n/a
Industry sector preferences: n/a	**Exec:** n/a
Geographical preferences: n/a	
In-house industry sector analysts? n/a	**Act for:** n/a
Sectors covered by analysts: All major sectors	
Prospective AIM companies considered:	
Startups n/a **Early stage** Yes **Established** Yes	
Typical transaction parameters: $50m and above capital raising	
Split of broking activities: n/a	
(institutional: private client)	**Other Offices:**
Underwriting facilities:	SSSB has offices in all major global financial centres
Can provide: Yes	
Can arrange: Yes	
Other activities: n/a	

Seymour Pierce

Bucklersbury House, 3 Queen Victoria Street, London, EC4N 8EL Tel: 020-7107 8000;
Fax: 020-7107 8102;   email: enquiries@seymourpierce.com;   Web site: www.seymourpierce.co.uk

Contact: Richard Feigen	**Number of Directors & Executives engaged in:**
Also act as Nominated Adviser? Yes	**Corporate Finance:** **Dir:** 3
Companies represented on first admission: 55	**Exec:** 8
Number involved in new issue to raise funds: 201	**AIM Activities:** **Dir:** 3
Industry sector preferences: None	**Exec:** 8
Geographical preferences: None	
In-house industry sector analysts? Yes	**Act for:** 10 Group; Abraxus Investments; actif; Aerobox;
Sectors covered by analysts: Specialised areas:	Air Music & Media; Alibi Communications; Artisan
Biotechnology; Building & Construction; Food Retailing;	(UK); Asfare; Bidtimes; BioProjects; Bond International
IT; Leisure; Media; Retail; Security; Sport; Textiles; Split	Software; Buckland; Camelot Capital; Campus Media;
Investment Trusts	Civica; Computer Software; Croma; Desire Petroleum;
Prospective AIM companies considered:	Earthport; Electric Word; Elite Strategies; Enition;
Startups No **Early stage** Yes **Established** Yes	e-primefinancial; Felix; First Artist; Flightstore; Fulcrum
Typical transaction parameters: None particularly	Pharma; Gaming Insight; Hansard; Hartest; IDN Telecom;
Split of broking activities: n/a	Integrated Asset Management; Interregnum; Jacques Vert;
(institutional: private client)	Legendary Investments; MOS International; NWD;
Underwriting facilities:	OFEX; Patsystems; Private & Commercial Finance; Raft
Can provide: Yes	International; Real Affinity; Reflec; Screen FX;
Can arrange: Yes	Silentpoint; Sopheon; SP; Stanley Gibbons; Streetnames;
Other activities: n/a	Tepnel Life Sciences; Terrace Hill; Theo Fennell;
	Tottenham Hotspur; UBC Media; Victory
	Other Offices: n/a

Seymour Pierce Ellis

Jubilee Walk, Three Bridges, Crawley, West Sussex, RH10 1LQ Tel: 01293-517744; Fax: 01293-521093;
email: ellis@seymourpierce.com; Web site: www.seymourpierce.com

Contact:	Neil Badger	**Number of Directors & Executives engaged in:**	
Also act as Nominated Adviser?	No	**Corporate Finance:** **Dir:**	4 (Broking)
Companies represented on first admission:	n/a	**Exec:**	1 (Broking)
Number involved in new issue to raise funds:	n/a	**AIM Activities:** **Dir:**	4
Industry sector preferences:	None	**Exec:**	1
Geographical preferences:	None		
In-house industry sector analysts?	Yes	**Act for:** ARC Risk Management; ASOS; Bakery	
Sectors covered by analysts:	All	Services; Beaufort International; Billam; Camelot	
Prospective AIM companies considered:		Capital; Cater Barnard; Central African Mining &	
Startups No **Early stage** No **Established** Yes		Exploration; CFA Capital; Cheerful Scout; coffeeheaven;	
Typical transaction parameters: None particularly		Coffee Republic; Conroy Diamonds & Gold; CybIT;	
Split of broking activities:	10:90	Envesta; Flintstone Technologies; Galahad Gold;	
(institutional: private client)		Gamingking; Griffin Mining; Grosvenor Land;	
Underwriting facilities:		Honeygrove Homes; John Lewis of Hungerford; Mano	
Can provide:	Yes	River Resources; Maverick Entertainment; Millwall;	
Can arrange:	Yes	Nature Technology Solutions; Netb2b2; New Millennium	
		Resources; Newmark Security; Pentagon Protection;	
Other activities: Corporate Broking; Private Client		SectorGuard; Sefton Resources; Sira Business Services;	
Stockbroking; Research; US Trading		Southern African Resources; Watford Leisure; Westside	
		Acquisitions; Wigmore; Zyzygy	
		Other Offices:	n/a

SG Securities (London)

Exchange House, Primrose Street, Broadgate, London, EC2A 2DD Tel: 020-7638 9000;
Fax: 020-7762 5216; Web site: www.socgen.com

Contact:	Andrew Fullerton	**Number of Directors & Executives engaged in:**	
Also act as Nominated Adviser?	Yes	**Corporate Finance:** **Dir:**	5
Companies represented on first admission:	3	**Exec:**	8
Number involved in new issue to raise funds:	4	**AIM Activities:** **Dir:**	2
Industry sector preferences:	None	**Exec:**	2
Geographical preferences:	UK		
In-house industry sector analysts?	Yes - 50	**Act for:**	n/a
Sectors covered by analysts: All sectors except Property			
Prospective AIM companies considered:			
Startups No **Early stage** No **Established** Yes			
Typical transaction parameters: Resultant market capi-			
talisation usually greater than £30m			
Split of broking activities:	95:5		
institutional: private client)		**Other Offices:**	n/a
Underwriting facilities:			
Can provide:	Yes		
Can arrange:	No		
Other activities: Corporate Finance Advice; Research			

Shore Capital Stockbrokers

Bond Street House, 14 Clifford Street, London, W1S 4JU Tel: 020-7408 4080; Fax: 020-7408 4081;
email: info@shorecap.co.uk; Web site: www.shorecap.co.uk

Contact: Alex Borrelli/Jonathan Nelson	**Number of Directors & Executives engaged in:**		
Also act as Nominated Adviser? Yes	**Corporate Finance:**	**Dir:**	3
Companies represented on first admission: 14		**Exec:**	3
Number involved in new issue to raise funds: 16	**AIM Activities:**	**Dir:**	2
Industry sector preferences: Business Services;		**Exec:**	3
Financials; Food; Leisure; Media; Property; Retail;			
Software; Technology; Telecommunications	**Act for:** Advance Visual Communications;		
Geographical preferences: None	Birmingham City; BNB Resources; CamAxys;		
In-house industry sector analysts? Yes	Fitzhardinge; Formscan; Illuminator; Judges Capital;		
Sectors covered by analysts: See industry sector	Manpower Software; Merchant House; Orad Hi-Tec		
preferences	Systems; Pilat Media Global; Raven Mount; Spring		
Prospective AIM companies considered:	Grove Property Maintenance; Telford Homes		
Startups No **Early stage** Yes **Established** Yes			
Typical transaction parameters: None particularly	**Other Offices:**		
Split of broking activities: n/a	Liverpool Office		
(institutional: private client)	The Atlantic Suite		
Underwriting facilities:	The Corn Exchange		
Can provide: No	Fenwick Street		
Can arrange: Yes	Liverpool L2 7TP		
	Tel: 0151-600 3700		
Other activities: Corporate Broking; Corporate Finance			
Advice; Market Making; Private Equity Investment			

Teather & Greenwood

Beaufort House, 15 St. Botolph Street, London, EC3A 7QR Tel: 020-7426 9000; Fax: 020-7247 0075;
email: tg@teathers.com; Web site: www.teathers.com

Contact: Christopher Hardie/Jeff Keating/	**Number of Directors & Executives engaged in:**		
Nick Bankes/Mike Sawbridge	**Corporate Finance:**	**Dir:**	4
Also act as Nominated Adviser? Yes		**Exec:**	3
Companies represented on first admission: 30+ in last 5	**AIM Activities:**	**Dir:**	4
years		**Exec:**	3
Number involved in new issue to raise funds: 50+			
Industry sector preferences: None	**Act for:** Auto Indemnity; Basepoint; Belgravium; Biofocus;		
Geographical preferences: UK	Bizspace; Blooms of Bressingham; Business Serve; Canterbury		
In-house industry sector analysts? Yes	Foods; Charlton Athletic; Charterhouse Communications;		
Sectors covered by analysts: Banks & Other Financials;	Chepstow Racecourse; Coffee Republic; Comland		
Construction & Building Materials; Investment Trusts; Media;	Commercial; Conder Environmental; CW Residential;		
Oil & Gas; Pharmaceuticals & Health; Restaurants, Pubs &	Cytomyx; Flomerics; Genus; Home Entertainment;		
Breweries/Leisure; Retailers; Small Companies; Software &	Hurlingham Properties; Immedia Broadcasting; Intellexis;		
Computer Services; Support Services	Lloyds British Testing; London Security; Longmead; LPA;		
Prospective AIM companies considered:	Madisons Coffee; Majestic Wine; Mark Kingsley; Mondas;		
Startups Yes **Early stage** Yes **Established** Yes	Monstermob; Mulberry; Myratech.net; Netcentric; Pathfinder		
Typical transaction parameters: Minimum market capital	Properties; Protec; Redbus Interhouse; Smart Approach;		
- £10m. PBT £1m+	Southern Vectis; Stonemartin; Transport Systems; Touchstone;		
Split of broking activities: n/a	Universe; Univent; Volvere; Willington; Wynnstay Properties		
institutional: private client)			
Underwriting facilities:	**Other Offices:**		
Can provide: Yes	Liverpool		
Can arrange: Yes	8th Floor		
Other activities: Corporate Broking Services; Corporate	India Buildings		
Finance Advice; Institutional sales; M&A; Market making;	Water Street		
Research; Tax efficient investment	Liverpool L2 0XR		
	Tel: 0151-242 0610		

The Share Centre

Oxford House, Oxford Road, Aylesbury, Buckinghamshire, HP21 8SZ Tel: 0800-800008;
Fax: 01296-414140; email: info@share.co.uk; Web site: www.share.com

Contact:	Iain Wallace	**Number of Directors & Executives engaged in:**		
Also act as Nominated Adviser?	No	Corporate Finance:	Dir:	2
Companies represented on first admission:	0		Exec:	1
Number involved in new issue to raise funds:	0	AIM Activities:	Dir:	2
Industry sector preferences:	n/a		Exec:	2
Geographical preferences:	n/a			
In-house industry sector analysts?	Yes	Act for: Elektron		
Sectors covered by analysts:	All			

Prospective AIM companies considered:
Startups Yes **Early stage** Yes **Established** Yes
Typical transaction parameters: n/a
Split of broking activities: All private investors
(institutional: private client)
Underwriting facilities: **Other Offices:** n/a
      Can provide: No
      Can arrange: No

Other activities: Employee Share Schemes; Fundraising;
ShareMark trading platform

Westhouse Securities

Clements House, 14-18 Gresham Street, London, EC2R 7HE Tel: 020-7601 6100; Fax: 020-7796 2476;
email: suzanne.johnson-walsh@westhousesecurities.com; Web site: www.westhousesecurities.com

Contact:	Suzanne Johnson-Walsh	**Number of Directors & Executives engaged in:**		
Also act as Nominated Adviser?	Yes	Corporate Finance:	Dir:	4
Companies represented on first admission:	18		Exec:	9
Number involved in new issue to raise funds:	24	AIM Activities:	Dir:	4
Industry sector preferences:	None		Exec:	9
Geographical preferences:	None			
In-house industry sector analysts?	Yes			

Sectors covered by analysts: Electronics; Housebuilding; Household Goods; IT Hardware; Mining; Packaging; Software; Support Services; Textiles

Act for: Airbath; Bertam; BKN International; Brazilian Diamonds; Cambridge Mineral Resources; Collins and Hayes; Ensor; Hereward Ventures; Hidefield; Innobox; James Halstead; Lendu; Pilat Technologies; Probus Estates; Rowe Evans Investments; Surgical Innovations

Prospective AIM companies considered:
Startups Yes **Early stage** Yes **Established** Yes
Typical transaction parameters: None particularly
Split of broking activities: Mainly Institutional
(institutional: private client)
Underwriting facilities:
      Can provide: Yes
      Can arrange: Yes

Other Offices:
Manchester
Contact: Philip Johnson
One King Street,
Manchester M2 6AW
Tel: 0161-838 9140
Fax: 0161-838 9141

Other activities: Finance; Research

WH Ireland

11 St James's Square, Manchester, M2 6WH Tel: 0161-832 6644; Fax: 0161-661 9098;
Web site: www.wh-ireland.co.uk

Contact:	David Youngman	**Number of Directors & Executives engaged in:**		
Also act as Nominated Adviser?	Yes	**Corporate Finance:**	**Dir:**	6
Companies represented on first admission:	18		**Exec:**	2
Number involved in new issue to raise funds:	14	**AIM Activities:**	**Dir:**	6
Industry sector preferences:	None		**Exec:**	2
Geographical preferences:	None			
In-house industry sector analysts?	Yes	**Act for:** Access Intelligence; Bionex Investments;		

Sectors covered by analysts: UK Smaller Companies - Chemicals; Electronics & Electricals; Healthcare; Household Goods; Leisure; Personal Care; Support Services,

Prospective AIM companies considered:
Startups Yes **Early stage** Yes **Established** Yes

Typical transaction parameters:	n/a
Split of broking activities:	n/a
(institutional: private client)	
Underwriting facilities:	
Can provide:	Yes
Can arrange:	Yes
Other activities:	n/a

Act for: Access Intelligence; Bionex Investments; Black Arrow; Carrwood; Cityblock; Compass Financial; Debt Free Direct; Eurasia Mining; Highland Gold Mining; Leisure Ventures; Palladex; Preston North End; Reflexion Cosmetics; Roshni Investments; Stepquick; Strategic Retail; Taskcatch; Tertiary Minerals; Tiger Resource Finance; Toye & Company; Ultimate Finance; Vista; WH Ireland

Other Offices:
Blackburn; Burnley; Cardiff; Colwyn Bay; Fareham; Lancaster; London; Malvern; Thorpe Bay; Sydney (Australia);

Williams de Broe

6 Broadgate, London, EC2M 2RP Tel: 020-7588 7511; Fax: 020-7588 8860;
Web site: www.wdebroe.com

Contact:	Jonathan Gray (London),	**Number of Directors & Executives engaged in:**		
	Ifor Williams (Birmingham)	**Corporate Finance:**	**Dir:**	7
Also act as Nominated Adviser?			**Exec:**	12
Companies represented on first admission:	14	**AIM Activities:**	**Dir:**	8
Number involved in new issue to raise funds:	14		**Exec:**	12
Industry sector preferences:	None			
Geographical preferences:	None	**Act for:** ATA; betinternet.com; CA Coutts; Caledon		
In-house industry sector analysts?	Yes			
Sectors covered by analysts:	Most			

Prospective AIM companies considered:
Startups No **Early stage** Yes **Established** Yes

Typical transaction parameters: Companies with a market capitalisation typically of £10m

Split of broking activities:	70:30
(institutional: private client)	
Underwriting facilities:	
Can provide:	Yes
Can arrange:	Yes

Other activities: Corporate Finance Advice; Fixed Income Broking; Fund Management; Institutional Broking; Research

Act for: ATA; betinternet.com; CA Coutts; Caledon Resources; Capcon; Celtic Resources; Centamin Egypt; Centurion Energy; Chepstow Racecourse; Churchill China; Clarity Commerce Solutions; CRC; Delcam; Dwyka Diamonds; Dynamic Commercial Finance; Education Development International; Eureka Mining; Fairplace Consulting; Faroe Petroleum; Futura Medical; Gold Mines of Sardinia; MacLellan; Marakand Minerals; Medoro resources; Newmarket Investments; Oxus Gold; Petra Diamonds; PM; Samuel Heath; Solitaire; Southern Era Resources; Thomson Intermedia; Widney

Other Offices:

Birmingham	Tel: 0121-609 0050	Ifor Williams
Edinburgh	Tel: 0131-220 3686	Sid Noble
Leeds	Tel: 0113-243 1619	Joanne Lake

ACCOUNTANTS

Baker Tilly

2 Bloomsbury Street, London, WC1 3ST Tel: 020-7413 5100; Fax: 020-7413 5101;
email: chilton.taylor@bakertilly.co.uk paul.watts@bakertilly.co.uk; Web site: www.bakertilly.co.uk

Contact: Chilton Taylor / Paul Watts	**Number of Partners & Assistants engaged in advising companies in relation to AIM:**
Number of AIM new issues worked on as:	**Partners:** 20 **Assistants:** 50
Reporting Accountants: 100	Act for: 1st Dental Laboratories; Advanced Medical Solutions; ASITE;
Auditors to AIM Company: 66	ARC Risk Management; Azure Holdings; Biofocus; Bond International
Corporate Finance Adviser: Yes	Software; Business Serve; Capricorn Resources; Cavanagh; Central African
In Another Role: EIS/VCT Advisers	Mining & Exploration; Charteris; Chorion; City Lofts; Clubhaus; Concurrent
Industry sector preferences: None	Technologies; Crown Corporation; DataCash; DawMed Systems; Electric
In-house industry sector analysts: Yes	Word; Elektron; Epic; Eurolink Managed Services; Ffastfill; First Artist;
Sectors covered by analysts: All sectors	Fitzhardinge; Hemisphere Properties; Honeycombe Leisure; Honeygrove;
Typical transaction parameters: All sizes	hot group; Hunters Leisure; Innovision Research & Technology; Intelligent
Member of professional or regulatory association or	Environments; Internet Business; Landround; Legendary Investments;
authority: Baker Tilly - Institute of Chartered Accountants	Loades; Lok'n'store; Maelor; MOS International; Myratech.net; Netcentric;
in England & Wales, Baker Tilly & Co Limited and Baker	NWD; Online Travel; Pathfinder Properties; Pilat Media Global; Potential
Tilly Financial Services - Financial Services Authority	Finance; Profile Media; Raft International; Real Affinity; Resurge;
Other activities: Via Baker Tilly and controlled compa-	Silentpoint; Sky Capital Holdings; Southern African Resources; Stilo
nies: Accountancy; Audit; Business Recovery; Financial	International; The Clapham House Group; ThreeW.net; Transport Systems;
Services; Financial Strategic Planning; Forensic	Universe; Vitesse Media; Warthog; West 175 Media; Wigmore
Accounting; Insurance; IT Consultancy; Litigation	
Support; Pensions; Personal & Corporate Tax; Taxation;	**Other Offices:** Basingstoke, Birmingham, Brighton; Bristol,
VAT	Bromley, Bury St Edmunds, Chelmsford, Chester, Coventry,
	Edinburgh, Gatwick-Crawley, Glasgow, Grimsby, Guildford,
	Hereford, Hull, Ipswich, Leeds, Lerwick, Liverpool, London,
	Manchester, Milton Keynes, Newcastle, Newmarket, Norwich,
Independent member of Baker Tilly International, over 116	Peterborough, Spalding, Stoke on Trent, Tunbridge Wells,
firms in 67 countries	Warrington, Watford, Yeovil

BDO Stoy Hayward

8 Baker Street, London, W1U 3LL Tel: 020-7486 5888; Fax: 020-7487 3686;
email: firstname.lastname@bdo.co.uk; Web site: www.bdo.co.uk

Contact: Stephen Bourne	**Number of Partners & Assistants engaged in advising companies in relation to AIM:**
Number of AIM new issues worked on as:	**Partners:** 15
Reporting Accountants: 55	**Assistants:** 100
Auditors to AIM Company: 77	
Corporate Finance Adviser: n/a	Act for: actif; Armour; Artisan (UK); ASK Central; Bella
In Another Role: n/a	Media; BioProjects; Bits Corp; Blazepoint; Capital
Industry sector preferences: Business Services;	Management & Investment; Cassidy Brothers; Centurion
Hospitality; Marketing; Media; Property; Retail	Electronics; COE; Coffee Republic; Contemporary Enterprises;
In-house industry sector analysts: n/a	Corvus Capital; CW Residential; DataCash; Equator; Eurolink
Sectors covered by analysts: n/a	Managed Services; Excel Airways; Feedback; Flomerics; FTV;
Typical transaction parameters: None particularly	Futura Medical; Gaming Insight; Grosvenor Land; Harrogate;
Member of professional or regulatory association or	Hartford; Hat Pin; Highams; Host Europe; Illuminator; Incite;
authority: ICAEW	IQ-Ludorum; London Town; Longbridge International; Lo-Q;
Other activities: Audit; Corporate Finance; Corporate	Marakand Minerals; Mark Kingsley; Milestone; Millwall;
Recovery; Management Consultancy; Tax Consultancy	Multi; Netbenefit; Newmark; New Media Industries; Norman
	Hay; Osmetech; Paramount; Parallel Media; Pentagon
	Protection; Prezzo; Reflec; Regal Petroleum; ReGen
	Therapeutics; Ringprop; RWS; Silentpoint; Solid State Supplies;
	Sportingbet.com; SpringHealth Leisure; Streetnames; TEP
	Exchange; Tepnel Life Sciences; Terrace Hill; Thomson
	Intermedia; Tikit; Tom Hoskins; Topnotch Health Clubs;
	Transense Technologies; Vantis; Vebnet; Weatherly; Western
	Selecton; World Careers Network; Xpertise; Yeoman
	Other Offices:
	20 throughout the UK and Ireland

Bright Grahame Murray

124/130 Seymour Place, London, W1H 1BG, Tel: 020-7402 5201; Fax: 020-7402 6659;
email: post@bgm.co.uk; Web site: www.bgm.co.uk

Contact:	Robert Feld/Robert Moore	
Number of AIM new issues worked on as:		
Reporting Accountants:	None	
Auditors to AIM Company:	3	
Corporate Finance Adviser:	None	
In Another Role:	3	
Industry sector preferences:	n/a	
In-house industry sector analysts:	No	
Sectors covered by analysts:	n/a	
Typical transaction parameters:	n/a	
Member of professional or regulatory association or authority: ICAEW		
Other activities: Audit; Payroll services; Taxation; Transaction services		

Number of Partners & Assistants engaged in advising companies in relation to AIM:

Partners: 3
Assistants: 3

Act for: Elektron; Hartest; Ten Alps Communications

Other Offices: n/a

Chadwick

Television House, 10-12 Mount St, Manchester, M2 5NT Tel: 0161-832 6088; Fax: 0161-834 9053;
email: pjones@chadwk.co.uk; Web site: www.chadwick.ac

Contact:	Peter Jones	
Number of AIM new issues worked on as:		
Reporting Accountants:	5	
Auditors to AIM Company:	5	
Corporate Finance Adviser:	n/a	
In Another Role:	n/a	
Industry sector preferences:	n/a	
In-house industry sector analysts:	n/a	
Sectors covered by analysts:	n/a	
Typical transaction parameters:	n/a	
Member of professional or regulatory association or authority:	ICAEW	
Other activities:	n/a	

Number of Partners & Assistants engaged in advising companies in relation to AIM:

Partners: 4
Assistants: 6

Act for: Access Intelligence; Community Broking; Ensor; Readybuy; Vista

Other Offices:
Tower Building, Water St, Liverpool L3 1PQ

Chantrey Vellacott DFK

Gresham House, 53 Clarendon Road, Watford, Herts, WD17 1LR   Tel: 01923-255111;
Fax: 01923-241300;   Web site: www.cvdfk.com

Contact: Laurie Batten	**Number of Partners & Assistants engaged in advising companies in relation to AIM:**
Number of AIM new issues worked on as:	
Reporting Accountants: n/a	**Partners:** n/a
Auditors to AIM Company: n/a	**Assistants:** n/a
Corporate Finance Adviser: n/a	**Act for:** Bionex Investments; Farley; Ocean Resources
In Another Role: n/a	Capital; Watford Leisure
Industry sector preferences: n/a	
In-house industry sector analysts: n/a	
Sectors covered by analysts: n/a	
Typical transaction parameters: n/a	
Member of professional or regulatory association or authority: n/a	
Other activities: n/a	
	Other Offices: n/a

CLB Corporate Finance

Aldwych House, 81 Aldwych, London, WC2B 4HP Tel: 020-7242 2444;   Fax: 020-7242 1117;
Web site: www.clb.co.uk

Contact: Ken Clarke	**Number of Partners & Assistants engaged in advising companies in relation to AIM:**
Number of AIM new issues worked on as:	
Reporting Accountants: n/a	**Partners:** 7
Auditors to AIM Company: n/a	**Assistants:** 8
Corporate Finance Adviser: n/a	**Act for:** Arko; CFA Capital; Designer Vision; MG Group;
In Another Role: n/a	Symphony Plastic Technologies
Industry sector preferences: n/a	
In-house industry sector analysts: n/a	
Sectors covered by analysts: n/a	
Typical transaction parameters: n/a	
Member of professional or regulatory association or authority: ICAEW, FSA	
Other activities: n/a	
	Other Offices: Manchester

Deloitte & Touche

Stonecutter Court, 1 Stonecutter Street, London, EC4A 4TR Tel: 020-7936 3000; Fax: 020-7546 9512;
Web site: www.deloitte.co.uk

Contact:	Richard Collins
Number of AIM new issues worked on as:	
Reporting Accountants:	n/a
Auditors to AIM Company:	n/a
Corporate Finance Adviser:	n/a
In Another Role:	n/a
Industry sector preferences:	n/a
In-house industry sector analysts:	n/a
Sectors covered by analysts:	n/a

Typical transaction parameters: Minimum market capitalisation for new funds - £10m. Minimum funds raised - £3m

Member of professional or regulatory association or authority: ICAEW

Other activities: Corporate Finance Advice, Due Diligence

Number of Partners & Assistants engaged in advising companies in relation to AIM:

Partners:	n/a
Assistants:	n/a

Act for: Abraxus Investments; African Diamonds; Ambient; Arko; Bertam; betinternet.com; Bizspace; Bradstock; Celtic Resources; CI Traders; Clubhaus; Comeleon; Constellation; Cradley; Delcam; Densitron Technologies; Dobbies Garden Centres; easier; Enterprise; Envesta; ESV; Fiske; Focus Solutions; Fortfield Investments; Georgica; GW Pharmaceuticals; Halladale; Hemscott; Inter-Alliance; Intercede; Interior Services; iomart; IQE; ITIS; Jarvis Porter; K3 Business Technology; Lendu; LiDCO; Longmead; Mano River Resources; Matrix Healthcare; Medal Entertainment & Media; Medical Marketing International; Melrose; Millfield; Minco; Motion Media; Mulberry; NewMedia SPARK; Newsplayer; Ocean Power Technologies; OFEX; Oilexco; Pacific Media; Pan Andean Resources; Paradigm Media Investments; Peel Hotels; Penmc; Petrel Resources; Pixology; Proactive Sports; Proteome Sciences; Redbus Interhouse; Rowe Evans Investments; Screen; Sigma Technology; Sirius Financial Solutions; Southampton Leisure; Springboard; Sterling Energy; Stonemartin; Tiger Resource Finance; Tissue Science Laboratories; TranXenoGen; Volvere; Wealth Management Software; Willington; World Travel; Yamana Gold; Zoo Digital

Other Offices:
Aberdeen; Bath; Belfast; Birmingham; Bracknell; Bristol; Cambridge; Cardiff; Crawley; Edinburgh; Epsom; Glasgow; Isle of Man; Leeds; Liverpool; Manchester; Newcastle-upon-Tyne; Nottingham; Reading; Southampton; St Albans

Dow Schofield Watts LLP

The White House, Greenalls Avenue, Warrington, Cheshire, WA4 6HL Tel: 01925-438048;
Fax: 01925-438049; email: mark@thebiggestname.com; Web site: www.thebiggestname.com

Contact:	James Dow/Mark Watts
Number of AIM new issues worked on as:	
Reporting Accountants:	n/a
Auditors to AIM Company:	n/a
Corporate Finance Adviser:	n/a
In Another Role:	n/a
Industry sector preferences:	Most sectors covered
In-house industry sector analysts:	n/a
Sectors covered by analysts:	n/a
Typical transaction parameters:	n/a

Member of professional or regulatory association or authority: ICAEW

Other activities: Acquisitons & disposals; Private equity; Strategic advice

Number of Partners & Assistants engaged in advising companies in relation to AIM:

Partners:	3
Assistants:	n/a

Act for: n/a

Other Offices: n/a

Ernst & Young

One Colmore Row, Birmingham, B3 2DB Tel: 0121-535 2245; Fax: 0121-535 2447;
email: Obaker@uk.ey.com; Web site: www.ey.com/uk

Contact:	Oliver Baker
Number of AIM new issues worked on as:	
Reporting Accountants:	n/a
Auditors to AIM Company:	n/a
Corporate Finance Adviser:	n/a
In Another Role:	n/a
Industry sector preferences:	n/a
In-house industry sector analysts:	n/a
Sectors covered by analysts:	n/a
Typical transaction parameters:	n/a
Member of professional or regulatory association or authority:	n/a
Other activities:	n/a

Number of Partners & Assistants engaged in advising companies in relation to AIM:
Partners: n/a Assistants: n/a

Act for: Alkane Energy; Alltracel Pharmaceuticals; Antonov; Archipelago Resources; Bank Restaurant; Black Arrow; Booth Industries; Buyers Guide; CA Coutts; Campus Media; Centamin Egypt; Clan Homes; Clean Diesel Technologies; Cobra Bio-Manufacturing; Consolidated Minerals; Cyprotex; Digital Animations; Documedia; Domino's Pizza UK & Ireland; Earthport; Fayrewood; Flintstone Technologies; Fulcrum Pharma; Genus; Global Energy Development; Gold Mines of Sardinia; Gympie Gold; Heavitree Brewery (The); Highland Gold Mining; Home Entertainment; Honeysuckle; ImageState; Imprint Search & Selection; IMS Maxims; International Brand Licensing; Leisure Ventures; LTG Technologies; Majestic Wine; Marshall Edwards; Monstermob; Netcentric; Newmarket Investments; Northern Petroleum; Orbis; Oystertec; Parkdean Holidays; Petroceltic International; Pilat Media Global; Pilkington's Tiles; PrimeEnt; Private & Commercial Finance; Quayle Munro; Romag; Sibir Energy; Sinclair Pharma; Smart Approach; Sopheon; Stockcube; Synigence; The Market Age; Thomas Walker; Tricorn; Water Hall; WILink.com; William Jacks; Zytronic

Other Offices: Aberdeen, Belfast, Birmingham, Bristol, Cambridge, Cardiff, Edinburgh, Exeter, Glasgow, Hull, Inverness, Leeds, Liverpool, Luton, Manchester, Newcastle upon Tyne, Nottingham, Reading, Southampton, Swindon

Ford Campbell

City Wharf, New Bailey Street, Manchester, M3 5ER Tel: 0161-819 2500; Fax: 0161-839 9990;
email: gtravis@ford-campbell.co.uk; Web site: www.ford-campbell.com

Contact:	Graham Travis
Number of AIM new issues worked on as:	
Reporting Accountants:	n/a
Auditors to AIM Company:	n/a
Corporate Finance Adviser:	n/a
In Another Role:	n/a
Industry sector preferences:	n/a
In-house industry sector analysts:	n/a
Sectors covered by analysts:	n/a
Typical transaction parameters:	n/a
Member of professional or regulatory association or authority:	n/a
Other activities:	n/a

Number of Partners & Assistants engaged in advising companies in relation to AIM:
Partners: n/a
Assistants: n/a

Act for: Prestbury

Other Offices: n/a

Gerald Edelman

25 Harley Street, London, W1G 9BR Tel: 020-7299 1400;   Fax: 020-7299 1401;
email: rpatel@geraldedelman.com;   Web site: www.geraldedelman.com

Contact:	RR Patel
Number of AIM new issues worked on as:	
Reporting Accountants:	14
Auditors to AIM Company:	10
Corporate Finance Adviser:	3
In Another Role:	3
Industry sector preferences:	Internet; Investment; Media; Property; Publishing; Sports
In-house industry sector analysts:	No
Sectors covered by analysts:	n/a
Typical transaction parameters:	£5m - £50m
Member of professional or regulatory association or authority: ICAEW	
Other activities: Audit; Business Development Services; Corporate Finance; Financial Services; Forensic Accounting; Insolvency; Litigation Support; Taxation	

Number of Partners & Assistants engaged in advising companies in relation to AIM:

Partners:	3
Assistants:	5

Act for: Hansard; Internet Music & Media; London Asia Capital; Mean Fiddler Music; Microcap Equities; Premier Management; Prestige Publishing; Sports & Leisure; Your Space

Other Offices:
Edelman House, 1238 High Road, Whetstone, London N20 0LH;
Suite 2, Kent House, Station Road, Ashford, Kent TN23 1PP

Gerald Kreditor & Co

Tudor House, Llanvanor Road, London, NW2 2AQ Tel: 020-8209 1535;   Fax: 020-8209 1923;

Contact:	M Rosen
Number of AIM new issues worked on as:	
Reporting Accountants:	None
Auditors to AIM Company:	None
Corporate Finance Adviser:	n/a
In Another Role:	n/a
Industry sector preferences:	None
In-house industry sector analysts:	No
Sectors covered by analysts:	n/a
Typical transaction parameters:	None
Member of professional or regulatory association or authority: ICAEW	
Other activities: Audit; Corporate Finance Advice; Taxation and Other	

Number of Partners & Assistants engaged in advising companies in relation to AIM:

Partners:	2 Partners
Assistants:	3 Others

Act for: GR

Other Offices:	n/a

471

Grant Thornton

Grant Thornton House, 22 Melton Street, London, NW1 2EP Tel: 020-7383 5100; Fax: 020-7387 5371; email: corporatefinace@gtuk.com; Web site: www.grant-thornton.co.uk

Contact: Martin Goddard	**Number of Partners & Assistants engaged in advising companies in relation to AIM:**
Number of AIM new issues worked on as:	**Partners:** 21 **Assistants:** 50
Reporting Accountants: 134	
Auditors to AIM Company: 87	**Act for:** AdVal; ADVFN.com; African Eagle Resources; Akaei;
Corporate Finance Adviser: 92	Alliance Pharma; Amco; Asfare; Auto Indemnity; Avocet Mining;
In Another Role: n/a	Bidtimes; Billam; BioProgress; Blooms of Bressingham; Buckland
Industry sector preferences: None	Investments; Bullion Resources; Cabouchon; Cambridge Mineral
In-house industry sector analysts: No	Resources; Canisp; Cardpoint; Charterhouse Communications; coffee-
Sectors covered by analysts: n/a	heaven; Corac; County Contact Centres; CRC; CSS Steller; CybIT;
Typical transaction parameters: None	Cyprotex; DDD; Deal Group Media; Dream Direct; EiRx Therapeutics;
Member of professional or regulatory association or	Empire Interactive; Erinaceous; Eurovestech; Future Internet
authority: ICAEW; Authorised by the FSA	Technologies; Galleon; Gaming Corporation; Gamingking; Glow
Other activities: Audit and Business Advisory; Corporate	Communications; GMA Resources; Gold Mines of Sardinia; Golden
Finance Advice; Corporate Recovery; Forensic Services;	Prospect; Griffin Mining; Hartford; Hereward Ventures; Highland
Company Secretarial Services; Due Diligence; Project	Timber; Ideal Shopping Direct; i-documentsystems; Ingenta; Interactive
Finance; Taxation; Transaction Services	Digital Solutions; Inter Link Foods; iTrain; Jourdan; Jubilee Platinum;
	Judges Capital; Keyword Investments; Lloyds British Testing;
	Manpower Software; Mears; Media Square; Meriden; Monterrico
	Metals; OMG; On-Line; Optimiser; Peerless Technology Systems;
	Personal; Sports Reasource; Spring Grove Property Maintenance;
	Springwood; Staffing Ventures; Straight; Surgical Innovations;
	Symphony Plastic Technologies; Synergy Healthcare; THB; Theo
	Fennell; Tolent; Tricorn; Triple Plate Junction; UA; Vianet; Web
	Shareshop; White Knight Investments; World Life Sciences; Wyatt;
	Zincox Resources
	Other Offices: 36 offices nationwide. For further information contact National Communications on 020-7383 5100

Hacker Young

St Alphage House, 2 Fore Street, London, EC2Y 5DH Tel: 020-7216 4600; Fax: 020-7628 3069; email: m.egan@hackeryoung.com / m.savage@hackeryoung.com; Web site: www.hackeryoung.co.uk

Contact: Michael P W Egan/Martin Savage	**Number of Partners & Assistants engaged in advising companies in relation to AIM:**
Number of AIM new issues worked on as: ·	**Partners:** 9 Partners
Reporting Accountants: 6	**Assistants:** 8 Managers
Auditors to AIM Company: 6	
Corporate Finance Adviser: No	**Act for:** Black Rock Oil & Gas; Desire Petroleum;
In Another Role: Yes	Gladstone; Mercury Recycling; SIRA Business Services
Industry sector preferences: Open	
In-house industry sector analysts: n/a	
Sectors covered by analysts: Open	
Typical transaction parameters: Open	
Member of professional or regulatory association or	
authority: ICAEW; Financial Services Authority	
Other activities: Arbitration and Management	
Consultancy; Audit; Business Advisory & Accounting;	
Company Secretarial; Corporate Finance; Forensic	
Accountancy; Payroll Services; Taxation; Turnaround and	
Recovery	
	Other Offices: Birmingham (Winross Hacker Young); Brighton, Cambridge (George Hay); Chester; Manchester; Nottingham; Sunderland (Torgersens); Wrexham, York (Calvert Smith & Co)

Hill Wooldridge

107 Hindes Road, Harrow, Middlesex, HA1 1RU Tel: 020-8427 1944; Fax: 020-8863 2081;
email: hillwool@msn.com

Contact: John Soughton	**Number of Partners & Assistants engaged in advising companies in relation to AIM:**
Number of AIM new issues worked on as:	**Partners:** 2
Reporting Accountants: 0	**Assistants:** 2
Auditors to AIM Company: 3	
Corporate Finance Adviser: 0	**Act for:** Bakery Services; coffeeheaven; John Lewis of
In Another Role: n/a	Hungerford
Industry sector preferences: None	
In-house industry sector analysts: No	
Sectors covered by analysts: n/a	
Typical transaction parameters: None	
Member of professional or regulatory association or authority: ICAEW	
Other activities: Audit and Business Advisory; Corporate Finance Advice; Tax Advisory	

Other Offices:
Brentwood - Contact: T J Horner
55 Crown Street, Brentwood, Essex CM14 4BD; Tel:
01277-215402; Fax: 01277-262833

HLB AV AUDIT

66 Wigmore Street, London, W1H 2HQ Tel: 020-7467 4000; Fax: 020-7467 4040;
Web site: www.avaudit.com

Contact: Shirin Gandhi	**Number of Partners & Assistants engaged in advising companies in relation to AIM:**
Number of AIM new issues worked on as:	**Partners:** 3
Reporting Accountants: 3	**Assistants:** 4
Auditors to AIM Company: 6	
Corporate Finance Adviser: 2	**Act for:** Cheerful Scout; ComProp; Healthcare Enterprise
In Another Role: Shareholder and Board members of Kennedy Gee Corporate Finance - a nominated adviser	
Industry sector preferences: Consumer Products; Electronics; Engineering; Food and Beverage; Healthcare; Leisure; Software, Internet and IT	
In-house industry sector analysts: Yes	
Sectors covered by analysts: Retail; Industrial Products; Utilities and IT	
Typical transaction parameters: None particularly	
Member of professional or regulatory association or authority: ICAEW	
Other activities: Audit; Corporate Finance Advice; Financial Services Authority; Taxation	

Other Offices:
Birmingham; Bristol; Leicester; Manchester;
Southampton

Horwath Corporate Finance

25 New Street Square, London, EC4A 3LN Tel: 020-7353 1577;   Fax: 020-7353 2803;
email: george.cranston@horwath.co.uk;   Web site: www.horwathcw.com

Contact:	George Cranston/Peter Varley	**Number of Partners & Assistants engaged in advising companies in relation to AIM:**	
Number of AIM new issues worked on as:		**Partners:**	3
Reporting Accountants:	42	**Assistants:**	6
Auditors to AIM Company:	11	**Act for:** Aerobox; Aero Inventory; ASOS; Bright Futures; CYC; Debt Free Direct; Finsbury Food; Hawthorn; Napier Brown Foods; SP; tecc-IS; The Real Good Food Company; Westside Acquisitions	
Corporate Finance Adviser:	n/a		
In Another Role:	n/a		
Industry sector preferences:	None		
In-house industry sector analysts:	No		
Sectors covered by analysts:	n/a		
Typical transaction parameters:	£2 - £25m		
Member of professional or regulatory association or authority: ICAEW; Financial Services Authority			
Other activities: Acquisition and Disposals; Audit; Capital Raising and Refinancing; Corporate Finance Advice; Taxation			
		Other Offices:	n/a

Kingston Smith

Devonshire House, 60 Goswell Road, London, EC1M 7AD Tel: 020-7566 4000;   Fax: 020-7566 4010;
email: cf@kingstonsmith.co.uk;   Web site: www.kingstonsmith.co.uk

Contact:	Steven Neal	**Number of Partners & Assistants engaged in advising companies in relation to AIM:**	
Number of AIM new issues worked on as:			
Reporting Accountants:	20	**Partners:**	14
Auditors to AIM Company:	7	**Assistants:**	15
Corporate Finance Adviser:	10	**Act for:** Air Music & Media; Hidefield; Northacre; Pubs 'n' Bars	
In Another Role:	n/a		
Industry sector preferences: Construction; Entertainment; Financial Services; Leisure & Tourism; Manufacturing; Marketing; Mining; Property; Retail			
In-house industry sector analysts:	n/a		
Sectors covered by analysts:	n/a		
Typical transaction parameters:	£0.5m - £100m		
Member of professional or regulatory association or authority:	ICAEW		
Other activities:	n/a		
		Other Offices: Surrey House, Surrey Sreet, Redhill, Surrey RH1 1RH; 800 Uxbridge Road, Hayes, Middlesex UB4 0RS; Orbital House, 20 Eastern Road, Romford, Essex RM1 3DP; 105 St Peter Street, St Albans, Hertfordshire AL1 3EJ; Quadrant House, 80-82Regent Street, London W1B 5RP	

KPMG

8 Salisbury Square, London, EC4Y 8BB Tel: 020-7311 1000; Fax: 020-7311 1641;
email: tony.fry@kpmg.co.uk; Web site: www.kpmg.com

Contact:	Katrina Pringle/Tony Fry
Number of AIM new issues worked on as:	
Reporting Accountants:	62
Auditors to AIM Company:	62
Corporate Finance Adviser:	6
In Another Role:	n/a
Industry sector preferences:	None
In-house industry sector analysts:	n/a
Sectors covered by analysts:	All
Typical transaction parameters:	n/a
Member of professional or regulatory association or authority:	ICAEW
Other activities:	n/a

Number of Partners & Assistants engaged in advising companies in relation to AIM:
Partners: 50   Assistants: 350

Act for: 10 Group; Acquisitor; Acquisitor (Bermuda); Advanced Technology; AFA Systems; America Mineral Fields; Atlantic Global; Avesco; Bristol & London; Caledonian Trust; Celltalk; CES Software; Chelford; Chepstow Racecourse; Chicago Environmental; Chorion; Cluff Mining; CODASciSys; Coliseum; Computerland UK; Conder Environmental; Conister Trust; Connaught; Cyberes; DCS; Deep-Sea Leisure; Dynamic Commercial Finance; Enneurope; Epic; Epic Reconstruction; Epic Brand Investments; Eurasia Mining; Expomedia; Falkland Islands; Faroe Petroleum; Faupel Trading; Finsbury Food; First Calgary Petroleums; First Derivatives; Flightstore; Flomerics; Forbidden Technologies; General Industries; GTL Resources; Headway; HPD Exploration; Huveaux; Immedia Broadcasting; IndigoVision; International Greetings; Internet Business Group; Inveresk;Invox; James R Knowles; Jennings Brothers; Keryx Biopharamaceuticals; Leeds; London Security; Madisons Coffee; Maelor; Metnor; Murchison United NL; Murgitroyd; NeuTec Pharma; New Millennium Resources; OverNet Data; Photoscan; PIPEX Communications; PM; Premier Direct; Preston North End; Probus Estates; Raven Mount; Razorback Vehicles; Retail Stores; Sibir Energy; Southern Vectis; Stream; Surface Transforms; Systems Union; Touchstone; Thistle Mining; Totally; Transcomm; TripleArc; Ultimate Finance; Ultimate Leisure; United Industries; Urbium; Victory Corporation; Virotec; Wealth Management Software; web-angel; WH Ireland; Widney; Wilshaw; Winchester Entertainment; YM BioSciences

Other Offices:
UK regional offices

MacIntyre Hudson

Greenwood House, 4/7 Salisbury Court, London, EC4Y 8BT Tel: 020-7583 7575; Fax: 020-7583 2081;
email: londoncity@macintyrehudson.co.uk; Web site: www.macintyrehudson.co.uk

Contact:	Chris Sutton/Mike Kay
Number of AIM new issues worked on as:	
Reporting Accountants:	3
Auditors to AIM Company:	4
Corporate Finance Adviser:	n/a
In Another Role:	n/a
Industry sector preferences:	n/a
In-house industry sector analysts:	n/a
Sectors covered by analysts:	n/a
Typical transaction parameters:	£2m - £30m
Member of professional or regulatory association or authority: Institute of Chartered Accountants in England & Wales	
Other activities:	n/a

Number of Partners & Assistants engaged in advising companies in relation to AIM:
Partners:	6
Assistants:	5

Act for: Avionic Services; Matrix Communications; Solitaire

Other Offices:
Bedford; Chelmsford; High Wycombe; Leicester; Milton Keynes; Northampton; Peterborough

ACCOUNTANTS

Moore Stephens

1 Snow Hill, London, EC1A 2EN Tel: 020-7334 9191; Fax: 020-7334 7978;
email: arthur.davey@moorestephens.com; Web site: www.moorestephens.co.uk

Contact:	Arthur Davey	
Number of AIM new issues worked on as:		
Reporting Accountants:	18	
Auditors to AIM Company:	n/a	
Corporate Finance Adviser:	n/a	
In Another Role:	n/a	
Industry sector preferences:	Financial Services;	
Insurance; Property; Shipping		
In-house industry sector analysts:	No	
Sectors covered by analysts:	n/a	
Typical transaction parameters:	n/a	

Member of professional or regulatory association or authority: ICAEW; FSA

Other activities: Audit accounting and assurance; Capital raising; Company disposals and business grooming; Due diligence; M & A; Reconstruction; Taxation

Number of Partners & Assistants engaged in advising companies in relation to AIM:

Partners:	2
Assistants:	8

Act for: 7 Group; 10 Group; Aricom; Formscan; Henderson; Integrated Asset Management; JAB; Online Technologies; Peter Hambro Mining; Samuel Heath & Sons; Telford Homes; VI; Westmount Energy; Wynnstay Properties

Other Offices:	24
Offices in the UK	

MRI Moores Rowland

3 Sheldon Square, Paddington, London , W2 6PS Tel: 020-7470 0000; Fax: 020-7339 9019;
email: mrilondon@mrimr.com; Web site: www.mrimr.com

Contact:	Robin Stevens/Stephen Bullock	
Number of AIM new issues worked on as:		
Reporting Accountants:	12	
Auditors to AIM Company:	10	
Corporate Finance Adviser:	0	
In Another Role:	n/a	
Industry sector preferences:	n/a	
In-house industry sector analysts:	n/a	
Sectors covered by analysts:	n/a	
Typical transaction parameters:	n/a	

Member of professional or regulatory association or authority: ICAEW

Other activities: Corporate finance advisory; Share incentive consulting; Tax consultancy & compliance; Wealth management services

Number of Partners & Assistants engaged in advising companies in relation to AIM:

Partners:	6
Assistants:	n/a

Act for: Impax; Honeygrove Homes; ReGen Therapeutics; Xecutive Research

Other Offices:	
24 offices in the UK	

Nunn Hayward

66/70 Coombe Road, New Malden, Surrey, KT3 4QW Tel: 020-8336 2166; Fax: 020-8336 2038

Contact:	Peter Hayward
Number of AIM new issues worked on as:	
Reporting Accountants:	0
Auditors to AIM Company:	2
Corporate Finance Adviser:	0
In Another Role:	0
Industry sector preferences:	None
In-house industry sector analysts:	No
Sectors covered by analysts:	n/a
Typical transaction parameters:	None
Member of professional or regulatory association or authority:	ICAEW
Other activities:	Audit; Taxation;
Corporate Recovery	

Number of Partners & Assistants engaged in advising companies in relation to AIM:

Partners: 2
Assistants: 1

Act for: Charlton Athletic; NBA Quantum

Other Offices:
Gerrards Cross   Tel: 01753-88211 - Ian Nunn

PKF

Farringdon Place, 20 Farringdon Road, London, EC1M 3AP Tel: 020-7065 0000; Fax: 020-7065 0650;
email: jeff.harris@uk.pkf.com; Web site: www.pkf.co.uk

Contact:	Jeff Harris
Number of AIM new issues worked on as:	
Reporting Accountants:	42
Auditors to AIM Company:	25
Corporate Finance Adviser:	n/a
In Another Role:	n/a

Industry sector preferences: All sectors considered. Particular experience of Biotechnology and Pharmaceuticals; Food; Hotels and Leisure; Financial Services; Mining and Mineral Extraction; Recruitment; Telecommunications; Multimedia; IT; Internet; Software; Technology; Transportation and Manufacturing
In-house industry sector analysts: Yes
Sectors covered by analysts: Hotel and Leisure
Typical transaction parameters: n/a
Member of professional or regulatory association or authority: Institute of Chartered Accountants in England and Wales. Regulated by the FSA for mainstream corporate finance work.
Other activities: Within corporate finance: acquisitions and disposals; fundraising; MBO/MBIs; privatisations; Stock Exchange transactions; valuations. Other services: audit and accountancy; business advisory services; company secretarial; corporate recovery; financial services; management consultancy; taxation

Number of Partners & Assistants engaged in advising companies in relation to AIM:

Partners: 26
Assistants: 40

Act for: Arko; ATA; CamAxys; Canterbury Foods; Cityblock; Computer Software; CustomVis; European Diamonds; Firestone Diamonds; Flintstone Technologies; Glisten; I2S; ID Data; Innobox; Meriden; Network; Numis; Protec; Quadnetics; Stagecoach Stepquick; Strategic Retail; Theatre Arts; Taskcatch; Tertiary Minerals; Toye & Company; Univent; Venturia; Zoo Digital

Other Offices:
30 offices throughout the UK

PricewaterhouseCoopers

1 Embankment Place, London, WC2N 6RH Tel: 020-7583 5000; Fax: 020-7822 4652;

Contact:	Brad Douglas
Number of AIM new issues worked on as:	
Reporting Accountants:	75
Auditors to AIM Company:	78
Corporate Finance Adviser:	6
In Another Role:	n/a
Industry sector preferences:	None
In-house industry sector analysts:	n/a
Sectors covered by analysts:	n/a
Typical transaction parameters:	All ranges

Member of professional or regulatory association or authority: ICAEW

Other activities: Lines of Service: Assurance and Business Advisory Services; Business Process Outsourcing; Business Recovery Services; Financial Advisory Services; Global Human Resource Solution; Management Consulting Services; Tax and Legal Services

Number of Partners & Assistants engaged in advising companies in relation to AIM:

Partners:	20
Assistants:	100

Act for: Advanced Power Components; Airsprung Furniture; Antrim Energy; AorTech; Avanti Capital; Avingtrans; Belgravium; Bema Gold; Brazilian Diamonds; Bullough; Caledon Resources; Cape; Carbo; Carlisle; Carrwood; CeNeS; Center Parcs (UK); Centurion Energy; Churchill China; Convergent Communications; Deltex Medical; Dickinson Legg; Dinkie Heel; Dwyka Diamonds; Eckoh Technologies; eq; Farsight; First Property; First Quantum Minerals; Forever Broadcasting; Fountains; Gooch & Housego; Gympie Gold; Inflexion; Ingenta; Intelligent Environments; Inventive Leisure; IP2IPO; Jacques Vert; James Halstead; Just Car Clinics; Lamont; Lighthouse Group; Linton Park; Lombard Medical; London Security; MacLellan; Magnum Power; Monsoon; Montpellier; Murray Financial; NMT; Noble Investments; NWF; Oasis Healthcare; OneClickHR; Oxus Mining; patsystems; Pursuit Dynamics; Ramco Energy; Scipher; SouthernEra Resources; St Barbara Mines; Stadium; Stylo; Tenon; The Telecommunications Group; Thirdforce; Torday & Carlisle; Trans-Siberian Gold; UBC Media; Virtue Broadcasting; Walker Greenbank; YooMedia

Other Offices:
UK offices outside of London: 36

Rees Pollock

7 Pilgrim Street, London, EC4V 6DR Tel: 020-7329 6404; Fax: 020-7329 6408; email: catherine@reespollock.co.uk; Web site: www.reespollock.co.uk

Contact:	Catherine Kimberlin
Number of AIM new issues worked on as:	
Reporting Accountants:	5
Auditors to AIM Company:	5
Corporate Finance Adviser:	n/a
In Another Role:	n/a
Industry sector preferences:	None
In-house industry sector analysts:	No
Sectors covered by analysts:	n/a
Typical transaction parameters:	None

Member of professional or regulatory association or authority: ICAEW

Other activities: Audit; Corporate Finance Advice; Litigation Support; Taxation

Number of Partners & Assistants engaged in advising companies in relation to AIM:

Partners:	5
Assistants:	6

Act for: A Cohen & Co; Conygar Investment; Fairplace Consulting; Galahad Gold

Other Offices: n/a

RSM Robson Rhodes LLP

186 City Road, London, EC1V 2NU Tel: 020-7251 1644; Fax: 020-7253 3498;
email: marketing@rsmi.co.uk; Web site: www.rsmi.co.uk

Contact:	Natasha Newman
Number of AIM new issues worked on as:	
Reporting Accountants:	Yes
Auditors to AIM Company:	Yes
Corporate Finance Adviser:	Yes
In Another Role:	n/a
Industry sector preferences:	Construction;

Engineering & manufacturing; Leisure & lifestyle;
Property

In-house industry sector analysts:	n/a
Sectors covered by analysts:	n/a
Typical transaction parameters:	None

**Member of professional or regulatory association or
authority:** ICAEW; Regulated by the Financial Services
Authority

Other activities:	n/a

**Number of Partners & Assistants engaged in advising
companies in relation to AIM:**

Partners:	8
Assistants:	n/a

Act for: Auto Indemnity; Birmingham City; BNB
Resources; EmdexTrade; Hartstone; Holders Technology;
LPA; Mondas; Pipehawk; PNC Telecom; Radamec; Veos;
William Ransom & Son

Other Offices:
Birmingham, Bristol, Cambridge, Dublin, Edinburgh,
Hemel, Leeds, London, Manchester

Saffery Champness

Lion House, Red Lion Street, London, WC1R 4GB Tel: 020-7841 4000; Fax: 020-7841 4100;
email: corporate.finance@saffery.com; Web site: www.saffery.com

Contact: Nick Gaskell / Lorenzo Mosca / Stewart Garrard	
Number of AIM new issues worked on as:	
Reporting Accountants:	15
Auditors to AIM Company:	7
Corporate Finance Adviser:	0
In Another Role:	6
Industry sector preferences:	None
In-house industry sector analysts:	Yes
Sectors covered by analysts:	High-tech products and

communications; Leisure; Media and Entertainment;
Property; Financial Services; Healthcare; Food Industry;
Sport, TV and Film Industry

Typical transaction parameters:	None

**Member of professional or regulatory association or
authority:** Institute of Chartered Accountants in England
and Wales
Other activities: Audit; Business Advisory; Consultancy;
Corporate Finance Advice; Human Resource Support;
Litigation Support; Research; Taxation

**Number of Partners & Assistants engaged in advising
companies in relation to AIM:**

Partners:	6
Assistants:	8

Act for: Claims People; Croma; Harrier; Intellexis; PC
Medics; Savoy Asset Management; Talent; Ten Alps
Communications

Other Offices:
Bournemouth, Bristol, Edinburgh, Guernsey, Harrogate,
High Wycombe, Inverness, Manchester, Peterborough

Smith & Williamson

No 1 Riding House Street, London, W1A 3AS Tel: 020-7637 5377; Fax: 020-7436 5438;
email: <recipient>@smith.williamson.co.uk; Web site: www.smith.williamson.co.uk

Contact:	Ian Burns/Philip Quigley	**Number of Partners & Assistants engaged in advising companies in relation to AIM:**	
Number of AIM new issues worked on as:		**Partners:**	8
Reporting Accountants:	2	**Assistants:**	10
Auditors to AIM Company:	6	**Act for:** Beaufort; Blavod Black Vodka; Ffastfill; Metrodome; SectorGuard; Web Shareshop	
Corporate Finance Adviser:	13		
In Another Role:	n/a		
Industry sector preferences:	None		
In-house industry sector analysts:	No		
Sectors covered by analysts:	n/a		
Typical transaction parameters:	None particularly		

Member of professional or regulatory association or authority: Institute of Chartered Accountants in England & Wales

Other activities: Audit; Corporate Finance; IT and Management Consulting; Taxation (corporate and personal) and pensions (corporate and personal).

Other Offices:		
Guildford	Tel: 01483-407100	Michael Bishop
Salisbury	Tel: 01722-411881	Chris Appleton
Tunbridge Wells	Tel: 01892-529922	Neale Jackson
Whetstone	Tel: 020-8446 4371	Doug Hall
Worcester	Tel: 01905-730100	Neil Hickling

Solomon Hare

Oakfield House, Oakfield Grove, Clifton, Bristol, BS8 2BN Tel: 0117-933 3344; Fax: 0117-933 3345;
email: stephen_toole@solomonhare.co.uk; Web site: www.solomonhare.co.uk

Contact:	Stephen Toole	**Number of Partners & Assistants engaged in advising companies in relation to AIM:**	
Number of AIM new issues worked on as:			
Reporting Accountants:	9	**Partners:**	10
Auditors to AIM Company:	9	**Assistants:**	10
Corporate Finance Adviser:	5	**Act for:** 2 Travel; 3DM Worldwide; Albemarle & Bond; Arlington; Clarity Commerce Solutions; Compact Power; Stanley Gibbons	
In Another Role:	n/a		
Industry sector preferences:	None		
In-house industry sector analysts:	No		
Sectors covered by analysts:	n/a		
Typical transaction parameters:	None		

Member of professional or regulatory association or authority: ICAEW and the SFA

Other activities: Audit; Corporate Finance Advice; Insolvency; IT and Management Consultancy; Personal Finance; Taxation

Other Offices:
Solomon Hare,
2nd Floor North,
32 Ludgate Hill,
London EC4M 7DR

Tenon Corporate Finance

Charnwood House, Gregory Boulevard, Nottingham, NG7 6NX Tel: 0115-955 2000; Fax: 0115-918 4301;
email: ian.beswick@tenongroup.com; Web site: www.tenongroup.com

Contact:	Ian Beswick/Julian Clough	

Number of AIM new issues worked on as:

Reporting Accountants:	8
Auditors to AIM Company:	4
Corporate Finance Adviser:	n/a
In Another Role:	n/a

Industry sector preferences: Small to mid-market companies in any sector

In-house industry sector analysts:	No
Sectors covered by analysts:	n/a
Typical transaction parameters:	£0.5m - £100m

Member of professional or regulatory association or authority: FSA

Other activities: Audit; Business Services; Corporate Finance; Corporate Recovery; Financial Services; Forensic; Outsourcing; Tax

Number of Partners & Assistants engaged in advising companies in relation to AIM:

Partners:	3
Assistants:	3

Act for: Basepoint; Inditherm

Other Offices:
Nationwide

MARKET MAKERS

MARKET MAKERS

ABN AMRO EQUITIES (ABN)
250 Bishopgate, London EC2M 4AA Tel: 020-7678 8000; Fax: 020-7256 9000; Web site: www.abnamro.com

AITKEN CAMPBELL (AITK)
Ground Floor, 2 Central Quay, 89 Hidepark Street, Glasgow G3 8BW Tel: 0141-248 6966; Fax: 0141-221 5797

ALTIUM CAPITAL (ALTI)
30 St James's Square, London SW1 4AL Tel: 020-7484 4040; Fax: 020-7484 4010;
E-mail: sonia.hough@altiumcapital.co.uk Web site: www.altiumcapital.com

ARBUTHNOT (ARBT)
Arbuthnot House, 20 Ropemaker Street, London EC2Y 9AR Tel: 020-7012 2000; Fax: 020-7002 4619;
Web site: www.arbuthnot.co.uk

BRIDGEWELL SECURITIES (BGWL)
Old Change House, 128 Queen Victoria Street, London EC4V 4BJ Tel: 020-7003 3000; Fax: 020-7003 3299;
E-mail: general@gilbert-elliott.co.uk Web site: www.bridgewell.com

CAZENOVE SECURITIES (CAZN)
20 Moorgate, London EC2R 6DA Tel: 020-7588 2828; Fax: 020-7606 9205;
E-mail:firstname.lastname@cazenove.com Web site: www.cazenove.com

CITIGROUP (CITI)
33 Canada Square, Canary Wharf, London E14 5LB Tel: 020-7986 4000; Fax: 020-7986 2266
Web site: www.citigroup.com

COLLINS STEWART (CSCS)
9th Floor, 88 Wood Street, London EC2V 7QR Tel: 020-7523 8000; Fax: 020-7523 8131;
E-mail: enquiries@collins-stewart.com Web site: www.collins-stewart.com

CREDIT LYONNAIS SECURITIES (CLS.)
Broadwalk House, 5 Appold Street, London EC2A 2DA Tel: 020-7588 4000; Fax: 020-7214 5002;
Web site: www.creditlyonnais.com

CREDIT SUISSE FIRST BOSTON EQUITIES (CSFB)
One Cabot Square, London E14 4QJ Tel: 020-7888 8888; Fax: 020-7888 1600;
E-mail: firstname.lastname@csfb.com Web site: www.csfb.com

DEUTSCHE ASSET MANAGEMENT (DMG.)
1 Appold Street, London EC2A 2UU Tel: 020-7545 6000; Fax: 020-7545 0321;
Web site: www.deam.co.uk

DURLACHER (DURM)
4 Chiswell St, London EC1Y 4UP Tel: 020-7459 3600 Fax: 020-7638 8848; Web site: www.durlacher.com

EVOLUTION BEESON GREGORY (EVO)
100 Wood Street, London EC2V 7AN Tel: 020-7488 4040; Fax: 020-7702 4288;
Web site: www.evolution-group.com

GOODBODY STOCKBROKERS (GOOD)
Ballsbridge Park, Ballsbridge, Dublin 4 Ireland Tel: 00-353 1 641 0434; Fax: 00-353 1 667 2111;
E-mail: goodbody@goodbody.ie Website: www.goodbody.ie

HOODLESS BRENNAN AND PARTNERS (HOOD)
40 Marsh Wall, Docklands, London E14 9TP Tel: 020-7538 1166; Fax: 020-7538 1280;
E-mail: hbp@hoodlessbrennan.com Web site: www.hoodlessbrennan.com

HSBC SECURITIES (HSBC)
8 Canada Square, London E14 5HQ Tel: 020-7991 8888; Fax: 020-7336 9500; Web site: www.hsbc.com

INVESTEC BANK (INV)
2 Gresham Street, London EC2V 7QP Tel: 020-7597 5000; Fax: 020-7597 5120;
Web site: www.investec.com/uk

MARKET MAKERS

J & E DAVY (DAVY)
Davy House, 49 Dawson Street, Dublin 2, Republic of Ireland Tel: 00-353 1 679 788

JEFFERIES (JEFF)
Bracken House, One Friday Street, London EC4M 9JA Tel: 020-7618 3500; Fax: 020-7618 3760;
Web site: www.jefco.com

JP MORGAN SECURITIES (JPMS)
60 Victoria Embankment, London EC4Y 0JP Tel: 020-7600 2300; Fax: 020-7325 8267;
Web site: www.jpmorgan.com

KBC PEEL HUNT (KBCS)
111 Old Broad Street, London EC2N 1PH Tel: 020-7418 8900; Fax: 020-7417 4686;
E-mail: firstname.lastname@kbcpeelhunt.com Web site: www.kbcpeelhunt.com

KLEINWORT BENSON SECURITIES (KLWT)
20 Fenchurch Street, London EC3P 3DB Tel: 020-7623 4069; Fax: 020-7623 4069;
E-mail: firstname.lastname@drkw.com Web site: www.drkw.com

LEHMAN BROTHERS (LEHM)
25 Bank Street, London E145LE Tel: 020-7102 1000; Web site: www.lehman.com

MERRILL LYNCH INTERNATIONAL (MLSB)
2 King Edward Street, London EC1A 1HQ Tel: 020-7628 1000; Fax: 020-7772 1902;
E-mail: carina_brahmania@ml.com Web site: www.ml.com

NOMURA INTERNATIONAL (NMRA)
Nomura House, 1 St Martin's-Le-Grand, London EC1A 4NP Tel: 020-7521 2000; Fax: 020-7521 2121;
E-mail: firstname.lastname@nomura.co.uk Web site: www.nomura.co.uk

NUMIS (NUMS)
Cheapside House, 138 Cheapside, London EC2V 6LH Tel: 020-7776 1500; Fax: 020-7776 1555;
E-mail: mail@numiscorp.com Web site: www.numiscorp.com

ROBERT W BAIRD (BARD)
Mint House, 77 Mansell Street, London E1 8AF Tel: 020-7488 1212; Fax: 020-7702 3134;
Web site: www.rwbaird.com

SG SECURITIES (LONDON) (SGSL)
Exchange House, Primrose Street, Broadgate, London EC2A 2DD Tel: 020-7762 4444;
Fax: 020-7762 4555; E-mail: firstname.lastname@socgen.co.uk Web site: www.socgen.com

SHORE CAPITAL STOCKBROKERS (SCAP)
Bond Street House, 14 Clifford Street, London W1S 4JU Tel: 020-7408 4080; Fax: 020-7408 4081;
E-mail: info@shorecap.co.uk Web site: www.shorecap.co.uk

TEATHER & GREENWOOD (TEAM)
Beaufort House, 15 St. Botolph Street, London EC3A 7QR Tel: 020-7426 9000; Fax: 020-7426 9595;
E-mail: firstname.lastname@teathers.com Web site: www.teathers.com

UBS INVESTMENT BANK (UBS.)
100 Liverpool Street, London EC2M 2RH Tel: 020-7567 8000; Fax: 020-7568 4800;
Web site: www.ubsw.com

PANMURE GORDON (PMUR)
Woolgate Exchange, 25 Basinghall Street, London EC2V 5HA Tel: 020-7187 2000;
Web site: www.panmure.com

WILLIAMS DE BROE (WDBM)
6 Broadgate, London EC2M 2RP Tel: 020-7588 7511; Fax: 020-7588 1702;
Web site: www.wdebroe.com

WINTERFLOOD SECURITIES (WINS)
Atrium Building, Cannon Bridge, 25 Dowgate Hill, London EC4R 2GA Tel: 020-7621 0004;
Fax: 020-7623 9482; E-mail: enquiries@wins.co.uk Web site: www.wins.co.uk

REGISTRARS

Assets International Management

Beech Hurst, Waterhouse Lane, PO Box 82, Tadworth, Surrey, KT29 6LE Tel: 01737-830010;
Fax: 01737-832393

Contact:	Bill Leong	**Engaged by:**	Univent
Other offices:	n/a		
Companies acted for on first admission:	2		
Number currently engaged by:	1		
Geographical preferences:	None		
Typical transaction parameters:	None particularly		
Tied relationships:	n/a		

Capita Registrars

7th Floor, Phoenix House, 18 King William Street, London, EC4N 7HE, Tel: 020-7800 4120;
Fax: 020-7800 4194; email: development@capitaregistrars.com; Web site: www.capitaregistrars.com

Contact: Paul Etheridge	International Software; Brainspark; Bright Futures;
Other offices: Beckenham, Bristol, City, Dublin,	Booth Industries; Brazilian Diamonds; Bright Futures;
Edinburgh, Huddersfield, Jersey	Buckland; Bullion Resources; BWA; CA Coutts;
Companies acted for on first admission: 132	Cabouchon; Cape; Capital Management & Investment;
Number currently engaged by: Approx 75%	Capricorn Resources; CamAxys; Cambrian Mining;
Geographical preferences: All of the UK and int'l	Cambridge Mineral Resources; Canisp; Canterbury
Typical transaction parameters: n/a	Foods; Capcon; Carbo; Cardpoint; Carlisle; Cater
Tied relationships: n/a	Barnard; Cater Barnard (USA); Cavanagh; Celltalk;

Engaged by: 1st Dental Laboratories; 2 Travel; 3DM Worldwide; Abingdon Capital; Abraxus Investments; Acquisitor; Acquisitor (Bermuda); actif; ADVFN.com; AdVal; Advance Visual Communications; Advanced Medical Solutions; Advanced Technology; Aerobox; Aero Inventory; African Eagle Resources; Airbath; Airsprung Furniture; AIT; Akaei; Albemarle & Bond; Alibi Communications; Alliance Pharma; Amberley; Ambient; Amco; Angus & Ross; Antonov; Antrim Energy; ARC Risk Management; Aricom; Arko; Arlington; Armour Trust; Artisan UK; ASITE; ASOS; Atlantic Global; Avanti Capital; Avesco; Avingtrans; Avionic Services; Bakery Services; Base; Basepoint; Beauford; Beaufort; Belgravium; Bella Media; betinternet.com; BioFocus; Bionex Investments; BioProgress; BioProjects; Birmingham City; Bits Corp; Bizspace; Blavod Extreme Spirits; Blooms of Bressingham; BNB Resources; Bond

Center Parcs (UK); Central African Mining & Exploration; Centurion Electronics; Centurion Energy; CES Software; CFA Capital; Charlton Athletic; Charterhouse Communications; Charteris; Cheerful Scout; Chelford; Chorion; Cityblock; City Lofts; Civilian Content; Clarity Commerce Solutions; Clean Diesel Technologies; Clipper Ventures; Clubhaus; Cluff Mining; CMS Webview; Cobra Bio-Manufacturing; Coburg; coffeeheaven; Coffee Republic; Coliseum; Collins & Hayes; Comeleon; Comland Commercial; Community Broking; Computerland UK; Computer Software; Concurrent Technology; Conder Environmental; Connaught; Constellation; Contemporary Enterprises; Corac; Cradley; Crown Corporation; CRC; CSS Stellar; CustomVis; CW Residential; CyberChina; Cyberes; CybIT; Cyprotex; Cytomyx; DataCash; DCS; Deal Group Media; Debt Free Direct; Deltex Medical; Densitron Technologies;

Designer Vision; Desire Petroleum; Digital Animations; Digital Classics; Dimension Resources; Dinkie Heel; Documedia; Domino's Pizza; Dream Direct; Dynamic Commercial Finance; Eagle Eye Telematics; Earthport; easier; Eckoh Technologies; Education Development International; Einstein Channel; EiRx Therapeutics; Elektron; Elite Strategies; EmdexTrade; Empire Interactive; Enneurope; Ensor; Envesta Telecom; Enterprise; enterpriseAsia; E-Primefinancial; Equator; eq; Erinaceous; Eurasia Mining; Eurolink Managed Services; Europasia Education; Eurovestech; Expomedia; Fairplace Consulting; Falkland Islands; Farley; Faroe Petroleum; Farsight; Fayrewood; Feedback; Ffastfill; Finsbury Food; Firestone Diamonds; First Artist; First Derivatives; First Property; Fiske; Fitzhardinge; Flintstone Technologies; Flomerics; Focus Solutions; Forbidden Technologies; Forever Broadcasting; Fountains; FTV; Fulcrum Pharma; Fundamental-E Investments; Futura Medical; Future Integrated Technology; Gaming Corporation; Gaming Internet; Gamingking; Gaming Investments; Georgica; Gladstone; Glisten; Glow Communications; Global Energy Development; GMA Resources; Golden Prospect; Gold Mines of Sardinia; Gooch & Housego; Greenchip Investments; Griffin Mining; Grosvenor Land; GW Pharmaceuticals; Halladale; Hansom; Harrogate; Harrier; Hartest; Hartford; Hartstone; Hat Pin; Hawthorn; Headway; Healthcare Enterprise; Health Media; hemscott; Hereward Ventures; Hidefield; Highams Systems Services; Highland Gold Mining; Holders Technology; Honeycombe Leisure; Honeysuckle; Host Europe; Hot Group; HPD Exploration; Hurlingham; ID Data; Ideal Shopping Direct; IDN Telecom; Illuminator; Image Scan; ImageState; Impax; Imprint Search & Selection; IMS Maxims; Incite; Inditherm; Ingenta; InTechnology; Integrated Asset Management; Intellexis; Interactive Digital Solutions; Inter Link Foods; Inter-Alliance; Interior Services; International Brand Licensing; International Greetings; Internet Business Group; Internet Music & Media; Interregnum; Inventive Leisure; INVU; Iomart; IP2IPO; IQE; IQ-Ludorum; ITIS; iTrain; JAB; James R Knowles; Jarvis Porter; John Lewis of Hungerford; Jubilee Platinum; Judges Capital; Just Car Clinics; K3 Business Technology; KeyWorld Investments; Knowledge Technology Solutions; Kuju; Landround; Lawrence; Leeds; Legendary Investments; Leisure Ventures; Lendu; LiDCO; Lighthouse; Linton Park; Lloyds British Testing; Lok 'n Store; London & Boston Investments; London Asia Capital; London Security; Longbridge; Longmead; Lo-Q; LTG Technologies; Maclellan; Madisons Coffee; Maelor; Magnum Power; Maisha; Majestic Wine; Mano River Resources; Manpower Software; Marakand Minerals; Mark Kingsley; Marshall Edwards; Martin Shelton; Matrix Communications; Matrix Healthcare; Mayborn; Mean Fiddler Music; Mears; Medal Entertainment & Media; Medi-Watch; Medical Marketing International; Merchant House; Mercury Recycling; Metnor; Metrodome; MG Capital; Microcap Equities; Milestone; Mondas; Monsoon; Monterrico Metals; Montpellier; MOS International; Mosaique; Motion Media; Multi; Murgitroyd; Myratech.net; Napier Brown Foods; NBA Quantum; NetB2B2; Netbenefit; Newmarket Investments; Newmark Security; NewMedia SPARK; New Media Industries; Newsplayer; Noble Investments; Northacre;

NWD; NWF; Oasis Healthcare; Ocean Resources Capital; OFEX; OMG; OneClickHR; On-Line; Optimisa; Orbis; Osmetech; OverNet Data; Oxus Mining; Palmaris Capital; Paramount; Parkdean Holidays; Pathfinder Properties; Peel Holdings; Pennant; Pentagon Protection; Personal Group; Peter Hambro Mining; Petra Diamonds; Pilat Media Global; Pilat Technologies; PipeHawk; PIPEX Communications; Pixology; PM; PNC Telecom; Potential Finance; Premier Direct; Premier Management; Premisys; Prestbury; Prestige Publishing; PrimeEnt; Proactive Sports; Probus Estates; Profile Media; Protagona; Proteome Sciences; Pubs 'n' Bars; Quadnetics; Quayle Munro; Quiktrak Networks; Raft International; Ramco Energy; Raven Mount; Razorback Vehicles; Real Affinity; Redbus Interhouse; ReGen Therapeutics; Resurge; Retail Stores; Reversus; RII; Robotic Technology Systems; Room Service; RWS; samedaybooks.co.uk; Samuel Heath & Sons; Savoy Asset Management; SBS; Scipher; Screen; SectorGuard; Selector; Setstone; Sheffield United; Sibir Energy; Sigma Technology; Sinclair Pharma; SIRA Business Services; Sirius Financial Solutions; Silentpoint; Sky Capital; Smart Approach; Solid State Supplies; Solitaire; Sopheon; Southern African Resources; Southern Vectis; SP; Sports and Leisure; Sportingbet.com; Sports Internet; Springboard; Springwood; Spring Grove Property Maintenance; Stadium; Staffing Ventures; Stagecoach Theatre Arts; Stanley Gibbons; StatPro; Stenoak Associated Services; Stepquick; Sterling Energy; Stilo; Stockcube; Stonemartin; Straight; Stream; Streetnames; Sunbeach Communications; Surface Technology Systems; Surface Transforms; Surgical Innovations; SWP; Symphony Plastic Technologies; Synigence; Systems Union; Talent; Tandem; Taskcatch; tecc-IS; Tecteon; Telford Homes; Ten Alps Communications; Tenon; TEP Exchange; Tepnel Life Sciences; Tertiary Minerals; Texas Oil & Gas; THB; The Claims People; The Clapham House Group; The Creative Education Corporation; The Market Age; The Medical House; themutual.net; Theo Fennell; The Real Good Food Company; The Telecommunications Group; Thomas Walker; Tikit; Tissue Science Laboratories; Tolent; Tom Hoskins; Topnotch Health Clubs; Top Ten; Torday & Carlisle; Tornado; Totally; Touchstone; Toye & Company; TradingSports Exchange Systems; Transcomm; Transense Technologies; Transport Systems; Trans-Siberian Gold; TranXenoGen; Triple Plate Junction; UBC Media; Ultimate Leisure; United Industries; Universe; Urbium; Vantis; Vebnet; Veos; VI; Vianet; Victory Corporation; Volvere; Voss Net; Walker Greenbank; Warthog; Water Hall; Watford Leisure; Wealth Management Software; Weatherly; Web–angel; Web Shareshop; Western Selecton; Westmount Energy; Westside Acquisitions; White Knight Investments; Widney; WILink.com; William Jacks; William Ransom & Son; Willington; Wilshaw; Winchester Entertainment; World Careers Network; World Sport; Wyatt; Wynnstay Properties; XecutiveResearch; Yamana Gold; Yeoman; YM BioSciences; YooMedia; Your Space; Zi Medical; Zincox Resources; Zoo Digital; Zyzygy

Computershare Investor Services

PO Box 82, The Pavilions, Bridgwater Road, Bristol, BS99 7NH Tel: 0870-702 0000;
Fax: 0870-703 6101; email: bd@compuershare.co.uk; Web site: www.computershare.com

Contact:	Chris Guy, business development manager	**Engaged by:** 7 Group; 10 Group; A Cohen & Co; Advance
	0870-703 6025	Capital Invest; Affinity Internet; African Gold; Alkane Energy;
		Alltracel Pharmaceuticals; America Mineral Fields; Asfare; ASK
Other offices:		Central; Auto Indemnity; Bema Gold; Billam; Black Arrow; Black
Channel Islands: Tel: 01534-825200		Rock Oil & Gas; Bristol and West Investments; Campus Media;
Dublin: Tel: 00-353 1 21633100		Celtic Resources; Centamin Egypt; Chepstow Racecourse;
Edinburgh: Tel: 0870-702 0010		Chicago Environmental; CI Traders; Clover; CODASciSys; COE;
London: Tel: 020-7920 0010		Compact Power; Consolidated Minerals; CPL Resources; DDD;
		Deep Sea Leisure; Dickinson Legg; Dipford; Dwyka Diamonds;
		Electric Word; Ennex; Epic Brand Investments; Eureka Mining;
Companies acted for on first admission:	61	European Diamonds; First Calgary Petroleums; General
		Industries; GTL Resources; Gympie Gold; Hansard; Hardman
Number currently engaged by:	Approx 50%	Resources; Heavitree Brewery; Highland Timber; I2S; IES;
		Immedia Broadcasting; IndigoVision; Innovision Research and
Geographical preferences:	None	Technology; Intelligent Environments; Intercede; Inveresk;
		Jacques Vert; James Halstead; Jennings Brothers; Melrose;
Typical transaction parameters:	n/a	Mezzanine; Micap; Monstermob; Mulberry; Murchison United
		NL; Nature Technology Solutions; Netcentric; Network; New
Tied relationships:	n/a	Millennium Resources; Micap; Millwall; NMT; Numis; Oak
		Holdings; Ocean Power Technologies; Oilexco; Pan Andean
		Resources; Paradigm Media; patsystems; Peel Hotels; Petroceltic
		International; Pilkington's Tiles; Portman; Prezzo; Private and
		Commercial Finance; Pursuit Dynamics; Radamec; Reefton
		Mining; Reflec; Reflex; Regal Petroleum; Romag; Sefton
		Resources; SRS Technology; St Barbara Mines; Sutton Harbour;
		Synergy Healthcare; Teather & Greenwood; Tellings Golden
		Miller; Thomson Intermedia; TripleArc; Virotec; Vitesse Media;
		Xpertise; Zytronic

Lloyds TSB Registrars

The Causeway, Worthing, West Sussex, BN99 6DA Tel: 0870-600 3964; Fax: 01903-833452;
Web site: www.lloydstsb-registrars.co.uk / www.shareview.co.uk

Contact:	Justin Cooper	**Engaged by:** Andrews Sykes; AorTech; Avocet
		Mining; Bradstock; Caledonian Trust; CeNeS
Other offices:	Birmingham, Edinburgh	Pharmaceuticals; Churchill China; County Contact
		Centres; Dobbies Garden Centres; Epic; Genus; Home
Companies acted for on first admission:	n/a	Entertainment; Huveaux; Inflexion; Jourdan; Lonrho
		Africa; NeuTec Pharma; Norman Hay; Online Travel
Number currently engaged by:	n/a	Corp; Oystertec; Photo-Scan; Preston North End;
		RingProp; Southampton Leisure; Stylo; UA; Venturia
Geographical preferences:	n/a	
Typical transaction parameters:	n/a	
Tied relationships:	n/a	

Neville Registrars

18 Laurel Lane, Halesowen, West Midlands, B63 3DA Tel: 0121-585 1131; Fax: 0121-585 1132;
email: nevilles@waverider.co.uk

Contact:	Brian Cox	**Engaged by:** Access Intelligence; Air Music & Media; Bidtimes; Bristol & London; Camelot Capital;
Other offices:	n/a	Carrwood; Corpora; Croma; DawMed Systems; Delcam; Flightstore; Formscan; Galahad Gold;
Companies acted for on first admission:	31	Galleon; Henderson Morley; Innobox; Invox; Loades; Maverick Entertainment; Media Square; Meriden;
Number currently engaged by:	6	Netcall; Northern Petroleum; PC Medics; Scott Tod; Strategic Retail; Tricorn; Ultimate Finance; Vista; West
Geographical preferences:	None	Bromwich Albion; WH Ireland
Typical transaction parameters:	None particularly	
Tied relationships:	n/a	

Park Circus Registrars

James Sellars House, 144 West George Street, Glasgow, G2 2HG Tel: 0141-353 2620;
Fax: 0141-353 2296; Web site: www.pcregistrars.co.uk

Contact:	June McDowall	**Engaged by:**
Other offices:	None	Athelney Trust; Clan Homes; i-documentsystems
Companies acted for on first admission:	8	
Number currently engaged by:	3	
Geographical preferences:	None	
Typical transaction parameters:	None particularly	
Tied relationships:	n/a	

REGISTRARS

Share Registrars

Craven House, West Street, Farnham, Surrey, GU9 7EN Tel: 01252-733683 Fax: 01252-717233
email: johns@mspsecretaries.co.uk Web site: www.shareregistrars.uk.com

Contact:	John Stuttaford	**Engaged by:**
Other offices:	n/a	Archipelago Resources; Centaur; CFA Capital; Conygar Investment; Hemisphere Properties; Mosaique;
Companies acted for on first admission:	4	Namibian Resources; Quintessentially English; ukbetting; Web Shareshop
Number currently engaged by:	n/a	
Geographical preferences:	n/a	
Typical transaction parameters:	n/a	
Tied relationships:	n/a	

SLC Registrars

42-46 High Street, Esher, Surrey, KT10 9QY Tel: 01372-467308;   Fax: 01372-463620;
email: slc@davidvenus.com;   Web site: www.davidvenus.com/slc

Contact:	DW Armour	**Engaged by:**
Other offices:	n/a	Honeygrove Homes; London Town; Wigmore
Companies acted for on first admission:	4	
Number currently engaged by:	3	
Geographical preferences:	None	
Typical transaction parameters:	None particularly	
Tied relationships: SLC Registrars are wholly owned by David Venus & Company		

Stanley Wilkinson

288/290 Church Street, Blackpool, FY1 3QA Tel: 01253-622324

Contact:	Carol Wilkinson	**Engaged by:**	Cassidy Brothers
Other offices:	n/a		
Companies acted for on first admission:	1		
Number currently engaged by:	0		
Geographical preferences:	None		
Typical transaction parameters:	5,000 shareholders		
Tied relationships:	n/a		

FINANCIAL PUBLIC RELATIONS CONSULTANTS

4C Communications

45 Russell Square, London, WC1B 4JP Tel: 020-7907 4761; email: ccorbett@4ccomms.co.uk;
Web site: www.4ccomms.co.uk

Contact:	Carina Corbett	Number of Directors & Executives engaged in: Financial PR Activities:	
Other Offices:	n/a	Dir:	1
		Exec:	1
Number of AIM Companies acting for:	3		
Engaged by: Avocet Mining; First Calgary Petroleum; First Quantum Minerals			
Member of Professional Body: Investor Relations Society			
		Additional Information:	n/a

Bankside Consultants

St Mary Abchurch House, 123 Cannon Street, London, EC4N 5AU Tel: 020-7444 4140;
Fax: 020-7444 4184; email: mail@bankside.com; Web site: www.bankside.com

Contact:	Libby Moss	Number of Directors & Executives engaged in: Financial PR Activities:	
Other Offices: Brussels; Dubai; Frankfurt; Hong Kong; Johannesburg; New York; Paris; Sydney; Zurich		Dir:	7
		Exec:	14
Number of AIM Companies acting for:	17		
Engaged by: 3DM Worldwide; Asfare; BNB Resources; Cardpoint; City Lofts; Cyprotex; First Quantum Minerals; Home Entertainment; ID Data; Jarvis Porter; Jennings Brothers; LIDCO; Monterrico Metals; Quadnetics; Radamec; Stilo International			
Member of Professional Body: Institute of Public Relations		Additional Information: Bankside advises UK and international companies listed on OFEX; Nasdaq; Nasdaq OTC Bulletin Board
		Services offered: Media & investor relations strategy and implementation; transaction support (particularly in connection with IPOs, other capital raisings, takeovers, mergers, acquisitions and disposals); corporate and business-to-business communications; advocacy and issues management.

Beattie Financial

4th Floor, 37/39 Lime Street, London, EC3M 7AY Tel: 020-7398 3300; Fax: 020-7398 0003;
email: james.chandler@beattiefinancial,com; Web site: www.beattiemedia.co.uk

Contact:	James Chandler	**Number of Directors & Executives engaged in:**	
		Financial PR Activities:	
Other Offices: Aberdeen; Leeds; London; Dublin;		**Dir:**	4
Dundee; Falkirk; Glasgow		**Exec:**	5
Number of AIM Companies acting for:	11		
Engaged by: Epic; Glisten; James R Knowles; Inter Link Foods; Maelor; Magnum Power; Napier Brown Foods; Reversus; Scott Tod; Tikit; Topnotch Health Clubs; Xpertise			
Member of Professional Body:	n/a		
		Additional Information:	n/a

Bell Pottinger Financial

6th Floor, Holborn Gate, 330 High Holborn, London, WC1V 7QD Tel: 020-7861 3232;
Fax: 020-7861 3233; email: financial@bell-pottinger.co.uk; Web site: www.bell-pottinger-financial.com

Contact:	Jonathan Brill/Billy Clegg	**Number of Directors & Executives engaged in:**	
		Financial PR Activities:	
Other Offices: Holding company: Chime Communications		**Dir:**	6
		Exec:	22
Number of AIM Companies acting for:	12		
Engaged by: Cyberes; CybIT; Dobbies Garden Centres; Georgica; Halladale; Huveaux; Monstermob; Osmetech; Sibir Energy; Stonemartin			
Member of Professional Body:	n/a		
		Additional Information:	n/a

Biddicks

Mercury House, Triton Court, 14-18 Finsbury Square, London, EC2A 1BR Tel: 020-7448 1000; Fax: 020-7448 1010;   email: info@biddicks.co.uk;   Web site: www.biddicks.co.uk

Contact: Zoe Biddick / Katie Tzouliadis	Number of Directors & Executives engaged in: Financial PR Activities:	
Other Offices: n/a	Dir:	3
	Exec:	3
Number of AIM Companies acting for: 15		
Engaged by: Arko; Charteris; Computerland; Connaught; Gold Mines of Sardinia; K3 Business Technology; Leisure Ventures; Premier Direct; Protec; Raft International; Stream; Ultimate Finance; W H Ireland; Zi Medical		
Member of Professional Body: n/a		
	Additional Information:	n/a

Binns & Co Public Relations

9th Floor, Citypoint, 1 Ropemaker St, London EC2Y 9HT Tel: 020-7786 9600;   Fax: 020-7786 9606; email: peter.binns@binnspr.co.uk;   Web site: www.binnspr.co.uk

Contact: Peter Binns/Paul McManus/Paul Vann	Number of Directors & Executives engaged in:	
Other Offices: Binns Winningtons 11 Whiteladies Road Clifton, Bristol BS8 1PB	Financial PR Activities:	
	Dir:	5
	Exec:	6
Number of AIM Companies acting for: 15		
Engaged by: African Diamonds; African Gold; Airbath; Atlantic Global; Base; Bizspace; Bristol & West Investments; Campus Media; Clarity Commerce Solutions; CodaSciSys; Cyberchina; Dinkie Heel; Dipford; eq; Galleon; GMA Resources; Hardman Resources; Mediwatch; Mercury Recycling; Minco; Pan Andean Resources; Pennant; Pentagon Protection; Petrel; PM; RingProp; Screen; Stadium; Surface Technology Systems; Sutton Harbour; Zoo Digital		
	Additional Information:	n/a
Member of Professional Body: PRCA (Public Relations Consultants Association); Worldcom		

Bishopsgate Communications

4/5 North Mews, London, WC1N 2JP Tel: 020-7430 1600;   Fax: 020-7430 2226;
email: info@bishopsgatecommunications.com;   Web site: www.bishopsgatecommunications.com

Contact:	Maxine Barnes	Number of Directors & Executives engaged in: Financial PR Activities:	
Other Offices:	n/a	Dir:	1
		Exec:	2
Number of AIM Companies acting for:	8		

Engaged by: Acquisitor; Acquisitor (Bermuda); ARC Risk Management; Billam; Dimension Resources; Europasia; Henderson Morley; Sunbeach Communications

Member of Professional Body:	n/a

Additional Information: n/a

Britton Financial PR

62 Britton Street, London, EC1M 5UY Tel: 020-7689 6095;   Fax: 020-7251 2545;
email: tim@blackstonecomms.demon.co.uk;

Contact	Tim Blackstone /Gary Middleton	Number of Directors & Executives engaged in: Financial PR Activities:	
Other Offices:	n/a	Dir:	n/a
		Exec:	n/a
Number of AIM Companies acting for:	8		

Engaged by: e-primefinancial; Eurasia Mining; European Diamonds; Galahad Gold; Murchison United NL; Pipehawk; Pubs 'n' Bars

Member of Professional Body:	n/a

Additional Information: n/a

Brown Lloyd James Financial

25 Lower Belgrave Street, London, SW1W ONR Tel: 020-7491 7776; Fax: 020-7591 9611;
email: pr@blj.co.uk; Web site: www.brownlloydjames.com

Contact:	Christopher Joll	**Number of Directors & Executives engaged in:**		
		Financial PR Activities:		
Other Offices:	n/a		**Dir:**	n/a
			Exec:	n/a
Number of AIM Companies acting for:	n/a			
Engaged by:	Center Parcs			
Member of Professional Body:	n/a			
		Additional Information:		n/a

Brunswick

16 Lincoln's Inn Fields, London, WC2A 3ED Tel: 020-7404 5959; Fax: 020-7831 2823;

Contact:	Katya Reynier	**Number of Directors & Executives engaged in:**		
		Financial PR Activities:		
Other Offices:	n/a		**Dir:**	n/a
			Exec:	n/a
Number of AIM Companies acting for:	n/a			
Engaged by:	Blavod Extreme Spirits			
Member of Professional Body:	n/a			
		Additional Information:		n/a

Buchanan Communications

107 Cheapside, London, EC2V 6DN Tel: 020-7466 5000; Fax: 020-7466 5001;
email: marke@buchanan.uk.com; Web site: www.buchanan.uk.com

		Number of Directors & Executives engaged in: Financial PR Activities:	
Contact:	Mark Edwards		
Other Offices:	Leeds	**Dir:**	11
		Exec:	15
Number of AIM Companies acting for:	47		

Engaged by: Advanced Medical Solutions; ADVFN.com; Aero Inventory; Alizyme; Antonov; Bond International Software; Biofocus; Churchill China; Cobra Bio-manufacturing; Coffee Republic; Coliseum; Comeleon; Corac; Dickinson Legg; Digital Animation; Domino's Pizza; Eckoh Technologies; Excel Airways; Faupel Trading; Fayrewood; Flomerics; Fountains; Fulcrum Pharmaceuticals; Genus; Global Energy Development; Gooch & Housego; GTL; Image Scan; Immedia Broadcasting; Imprint Search & Selection; Kuju; Majestic Wine; Medical Marketing International; Milestone; Numerica; Oasis Healthcare; OneClickHR; Orad Hi Tech; Oystertec; Profile Media; Regal Petroleum; Resurge; SRS Technology; Symphony Plastic Technologies; Trading Sports; Universe; Vantis; Wealth Management Software

Additional Information: n/a

Member of Professional Body: n/a

Capital PR

78 Cannon Street, London, EC4N 6NQ Tel: 020-7618 6560; Fax: 020-7618 8099;
email: jbd@capitalww.com; Web site: www.capital.com.au

		Number of Directors & Executives engaged in: Financial PR Activities:	
Contact:	Jackie Brock-Doyle		
Other Offices:	Perth, Sydney	**Dir:**	4
		Exec:	5
Number of AIM Companies acting for:	0		
Engaged by:	n/a		
Member of Professional Body:	Yes		

Additional Information: n/a

Cardew Chancery

12 Suffolk Street, London, SW1Y 4HG Tel: 020-7930 0777; Fax: 020-7925 0646;
email: richard.fallowfield@cardewchancery.com; Web site: www.cardewchancery.com

Contact:	Richard Fallowfield	Number of Directors & Executives engaged in: Financial PR Activities:	
Other Offices:	n/a	Dir:	7
		Exec:	13
Number of AIM Companies acting for:	5		
Engaged by: i-documentsystems; Judges Capital; Murgitroyd; Online Travel Corporation; Theo Fennell			
Member of Professional Body:	n/a		
		Additional Information:	n/a

Citigate Dewe Rogerson

3 London Wall, London, EC2M 5SY Tel: 020-7638 9571; Fax: 020-7628 3444;
email: patrick.donovan@citigatedr.co.uk; Web site: www.citigatedr.co.uk

Contact:	Patrick Donovan	Number of Directors & Executives engaged in: Financial PR Activities:	
Other Offices:	Birmingham; Leeds	Dir:	45
		Exec:	49
Number of AIM Companies acting for:	14		
Engaged by: BioFocus; Carrwood; Collins & Hayes; Delcam; Education Development International; Focus Solutions; Inflexion; ITIS; Leeds; Media Square			
Member of Professional Body:	n/a		
		Additional Information:	n/a

City of London

Mercury House, Triton Court, Finsbury Square, London, EC2A 1BR Tel: 020-7628 5518;
Fax: 020-7628 8555; email: office@cityoflondonpr.co.uk; Web site: www.cityoflondonpr.co.uk

Contact:	John Greenhalgh	**Number of Directors & Executives engaged in: Financial PR Activities:**	
Other Offices:	n/a	**Dir:**	2
		Exec:	2
Number of AIM Companies acting for:	2		
Engaged by: Conroy Diamonds & Gold; Tertiary Minerals			
Member of Professional Body:	n/a		
		Additional Information:	n/a

City Profile

7-9 Copthall Avenue, London, EC2R 7NJ Tel: 020-7448 3244; Fax: 020-7448 3245;
email: simon.courtenay@city-profile.com; Web site: www.city-profile.com

Contact:	Simon Courtenay	**Number of Directors & Executives engaged in: Financial PR Activities:**	
Other Offices:	n/a	**Dir:**	3
		Exec:	4
Number of AIM Companies acting for:	2		
Engaged by: Deal Group Media; Interior Sevices			
Member of Professional Body:	n/a		
		Additional Information:	n/a

CityRoad Communications

7th Floor Roman House, Wood Street, London, EC2Y 5BA Tel: 020-7334 0243; Fax: 020-7334 0244;
Web site: www.cityroad.uk.com

Contact:	Paul Quade	Number of Directors & Executives engaged in: Financial PR Activities:	
Other Offices:	n/a	Dir:	4
		Exec:	3
Number of AIM Companies acting for:	2		
Engaged by: Athelney Trust; Landround			
Member of Professional Body:	n/a		
		Additional Information: Act for three OFEX companies: Appian Technology, Branded Leisure and Croma	

College Hill Associates

78 Cannon Street, London, EC4N 6HH Tel: 020-7457 2020; Fax: 020-7248 3295;
email: pr@collegehill.com; Web site: www.collegehill.com

Contact:	Tony Friend	Number of Directors & Executives engaged in: Financial PR Activities:	
Other Offices:	Johannesburg	Dir:	19
		Exec:	30
Number of AIM Companies acting for:	32		
Engaged by: Advanced Technology; Ask Central; Avanti Capital; Cape; Cluff Mining; ComputerLand (UK); Concurrent Technologies; Contemporary Enterprises; Falkland Islands; Faroe Petroleum; First Calgary Petroleums; Fitzhardinge; Forbidden Technologies; Healthcare Enterprise; Hartford; Hemscott; Innovision; Inventive Leisure; Lok n Store; Mondas; Montpellier; Netcall; Northacre; Parkdean Holidays; Ramco; Synergy Healthcare; Tellings Golden Miller; Tenon; Thomson Intermedia; TranXenoGen; Vianet; Widney			
		Additional Information:	n/a
Member of Professional Body:	n/a		

504

Conduit PR

107-111 Fleet Street, London, EC4A 2AB Tel: 020-7936 9095; Fax: 020-7936 9100;
email: leesa@conduitpr.com; Web site: www.conduitpr.com

Contact:	Leesa Peters	**Number of Directors & Executives engaged in: Financial PR Activities:**	
Other Offices: Edinburgh, Johannesburg, Perth, Sydney, Montreal		**Dir:**	3
		Exec:	6
Number of AIM Companies acting for:	20		
Engaged by: African Eagle; Aztec Resources; Cambridge Minerals; Celtic Resources; Clipper Ventures; Dwyka Diamonds; Eureka Mining; Firestone Diamonds; Gippsland; Golden Prospect; Goldstone Resources; Hereward Ventures; HPD Exploration; Minco; Murchison United; Palladex; Parallel Media; Patagonia Gold; Thistle Mining; ZincOx Resources		**Additional Information:**	n/a
Member of Professional Body:	n/a		

De Facto Communications

No 1 London Wall Buildings, London Wall, London, EC2M 5PG Tel: 020-7496 3300;
Fax: 020-7496 3355; email: info@defacto.com; Web site: www.defacto.com

Contact:	Louise Sarup	**Number of Directors & Executives engaged in: Financial PR Activities:**	
Other Offices:	Munich	**Dir:**	2
		Exec:	4
Number of AIM Companies acting for:	1		
Engaged by:	Tepnel Life Sciences		
Member of Professional Body: Investor Relations Society		**Additional Information:**	n/a

Financial Dynamics

Holborn Gate, 26 Southampton Buildings, London, WC2A 1PB Tel: 020-7831 3113; Fax: 020-7405 8007; Web site: www.fd.com

		Number of Directors & Executives engaged in: Financial PR Activities:	
Contact:	Tim Spratt		
Other Offices:	n/a	**Dir:**	n/a
		Exec:	n/a
Number of AIM Companies acting for:	7		
Engaged by: BioProjects; CES Software; Clubhuas; Deltex Medical; Earthport; InTechnology; Inter-Alliance; INVU; Maelor; NeuTec Pharma; NMT; PIPEX Communications; Scipher; UKbetting;			
Member of Professional Body:	n/a		
		Additional Information:	n/a

Finsbury

52-58 Tabernacle Street, London, EC2A 4NJ Tel: 020-7251 3801; Fax: 020-7251 4112; email: info@finsbury.com; Web site: www.finsbury.com

		Number of Directors & Executives engaged in: Financial PR Activities:	
Contact:	Anthony Silverman		
Other Offices:	n/a	**Dir:**	n/a
		Exec:	n/a
Number of AIM Companies acting for:	n/a		
Engaged by:	Conygar Investment		
Member of Professional Body:	n/a		
		Additional Information:	n/a

Gavin Anderson & Company

85 Strand, London, WC2R 0DW Tel: 020-7554 1400; Fax: 020 7554 1488;
email: gavinfo@gavinanderson.co.uk; Web site: www.gavinanderson.com

Contact:	Richard Constant	Number of Directors & Executives engaged in: Financial PR Activities:	
Other Offices:	n/a	Dir:	12
		Exec:	30
Number of AIM Companies acting for:	n/a		
Engaged by:	Romag; Micap; Numis; Yeoman		
Member of Professional Body:	n/a		
		Additional Information:	n/a

Gresham

Bloomsbury House, 4 Bloomsbury Square, London, WC1A 2RP Tel: 020-7404 9000;
Fax: 020-7404 9001; email: info@greshampr.com; Web site: www.greshampr.com

Contact:	Neil Boom	Number of Directors & Executives engaged in: Financial PR Activities:	
Other Offices:	n/a	Dir:	1
		Exec:	4
Number of AIM Companies acting for:	4		
Engaged by: Angus & Ross; CA Coutts; KnowledgeTechnology Solutions; Surface Transforms			
Member of Professional Body:	n/a		
		Additional Information:	n/a

Haggie Financial

Roman House, Wood Street, London, EC2Y 5BM Tel: 020-7417 8989; Fax: 020-7417 8247;
email: david@haggie.co.uk; Web site: www.haggie.co.uk

Contact: David Haggie	Number of Directors & Executives engaged in: Financial PR Activities:
Other Offices: n/a	Dir: 4
	Exec: 4
Number of AIM Companies acting for: 4	
Engaged by: Epic Brand Investments; Highams; THB; Thirdforce	
Member of Professional Body: n/a	
	Additional Information: n/a

Hansard Communications

14 Kinnerton Place South, London, SW1X 8EA Tel: 020-7245 1100; Fax: 020-7245 0909;
email: mail@hansardcommunications.com; Web site: www.hansardcommunications.com

Contact: Paul Foulger	Number of Directors & Executives engaged in: Financial PR Activities:
Other Offices: n/a	Dir: 2
	Exec: 4
Number of AIM Companies acting for: 21	
Engaged by: Artisan (UK); Croma; Densitron; Dynamic Commercial Finance; Flintstone Technologies; Hansard; Hartest; Hay & Robertson; Hemisphere Properties; Incite; International Brand Licensing; Matrix Communications; Mean Fiddler Music; Microcap Equities; Nature Technology Solutions; Northern Petroleum; NWD; PNC Telecom; Room Service; Sky Capital; Sopheon; Sports & Leisure; The Creative Education Corporation; Wigmore	
	Additional Information: n/a
Member of Professional Body: FCCA	

Hill & Knowlton Financial

35 Red Lion Square, London, WC1R 4SG Tel: 020-7413 3000; Fax: 020-7973 4466;
email: apayne@hillandknowlton.com; Web site: www.hillandknowlton.com

Contact:	Anthony Payne	Number of Directors & Executives engaged in: Financial PR Activities:	
Other Offices:	68 offices in 34 countries	Dir:	2
		Exec:	4
Number of AIM Companies acting for:	1		
Engaged by:	betinternet		
Member of Professional Body: IPR, PRCA			
		Additional Information:	n/a

Holborn

12 Nicholas Lane, London, EC4N 7BN Tel: 020-7929 5599;   Fax: 020-7929 3999;
email: info@holbornpr.co.uk; Web site: www.holbornpr.co.uk

Contact:	David Bick	Number of Directors & Executives engaged in: Financial PR Activities:	
Other Offices:	n/a	Dir:	10
		Exec:	4
Number of AIM Companies acting for:	16		
Engaged by: Bidtimes; Cabouchon; Corvus Capital; Honeycombe Leisure; Innobox; Internet Music & Media; Madisons Coffee; Meriden; Personal; Petroceltic International; Seymour Pierce; Silentpoint; Solitaire; Springhealth Leisure; Touchstone			
Member of Professional Body:	n/a		
		Additional Information:	n/a

Hudson Sandler

29 Cloth Fair, London, EC1A 7NN Tel: 020-7796 4133; Fax: 020-7796 3480;
email: piers.hooper@hspr.co.uk; Web site: www.hudsonsandler.co.uk

Contact:	Piers Hooper	Number of Directors & Executives engaged in: Financial PR Activities:	
Other Offices:	n/a	Dir:	8
		Exec:	20
Number of AIM Companies acting for:	7		
Engaged by: Actif; Advance Capital Invest; Ingenta; Jacques Vert; James Halstead; Patsystems; SP Holdings			
Member of Professional Body:	n/a		
		Additional Information:	n/a

IKON Associates

6 Quarry Street, Guildford, Surrey, GU1 3UR Tel: 01483-535102; Fax: 01483-535103;
email: adrian@ikonassociates.com; Web site: www.ikonassociates.com

Contact:	Adrian Shaw	Number of Directors & Executives engaged in: Financial PR Activities:	
Other Offices:	n/a	Dir:	2
		Exec:	2
Number of AIM Companies acting for:	3		
Engaged by: Dream Direct; Ideal Shopping Direct; Proteome Sciences			
Member of Professional Body:	n/a		
		Additional Information: Specialises in advising entrepreneurial and enterprising businesses. It provides financial PR, corporate PR, marketing and corporate branding.	

ing media

31 Earl St, London, EC2A 2AL Tel: 020-7247 8334; Fax: 020-7247 9568;
email: leanne@ing-media.com; Web site: www.ing-media.com

Contact:	Leanne Tritton	**Number of Directors & Executives engaged in: Financial PR Activities:**	
Other Offices:	n/a	**Dir:**	n/a
		Exec:	n/a
Number of AIM Companies acting for:	1		
Engaged by:	OFEX		
Member of Professional Body:	n/a		
		Additional Information:	n/a

M: Communications

1 Ropemaker Street, 9th Floor, London, EC2Y 9HT Tel: 020-7153 1530;
email: info@mcomgroup.com; Web site: www.mcomgroup.com

Contact:	Nick Miles	**Number of Directors & Executives engaged in: Financial PR Activities:**	
Other Offices:	n/a	**Dir:**	n/a
		Exec:	n/a
Number of AIM Companies acting for:	n/a		
Engaged by: Melrose			
Member of Professional Body:	n/a		
		Additional Information:	n/a

511

Marshall Robinson Roe

10 Greycoat Place, London, SW1P 1SB Tel: 020-7960 6007; Fax: 020-7117 1401;
email: mail@marshallrobinsonroe.com; Web site: www.marshallrobinsonroe.com

		Number of Directors & Executives engaged in: Financial PR Activities:	
Contact:	Andrew Marshall / Richard Robinson		
Other Offices:	n/a	**Dir:**	2
		Exec:	2
Number of AIM Companies acting for:	13		
Engaged by: Cytomyx; Digital Classics; KeyWorld Investments; Lloyds British Testing; ReGen Therapeutics; Sefton Resources; The Claims People; Top Ten; Transcomm			
Member of Professional Body: Investor Relations Society; Institute of Directors			
		Additional Information:	n/a

Merlin Financial Communications

Old Change House, 128 Queen Victoria Street, London, EC4V 4BJ Tel: 020-7653 6620;
Fax: 020-7653 6621 email:contact@merlinpr.com

		Number of Directors & Executives engaged in: Financial PR Activities:	
Contact:	David Simonson		
Other Offices: n/a		**Dir:**	6
		Exec:	6
Number of AIM Companies acting for:	7		
Engaged by: Ambient; Aricom; Interregnum; Newsplayer; Peter Hambro Mining; VI; Warthog; Westmount Energy			
Member of Professional Body:	n/a		
		Additional Information:	n/a

Parkgreen Communications

1st Floor, Ireland House, 150 New Bond Street, London, W1S 2AQ email: info@parkgreenmedia.com;
Web site: www.parkgreencommunications.com

Contact:	Justine Howarth	**Number of Directors & Executives engaged in:** **Financial PR Activities:**	
Other Offices:	n/a	**Dir:**	3
		Exec:	9
Number of AIM Companies acting for:	7		
Engaged by: Bullion Resources; Cambrian Mining; Intellexis; Jubilee Platinum; Petra Diamonds; Texas Oil & Gas; Tiger Resource Finance			
Member of Professional Body:	n/a		
		Additional Information:	n/a

Penrose

2nd Floor, 30-34 Moorgate, London, EC2R 6PJ Tel: 020-7786 4888; Fax: 020-7786 4889;
email: gillianm@penrose.co.uk; Web site: www.penrose.co.uk

Contact:	Gillian McKinlay	**Number of Directors & Executives engaged in:** **Financial PR Activities:**	
Other Offices:	n/a	**Dir:**	3
		Exec:	14
Number of AIM Companies acting for:	1		
Engaged by:	Telford Homes		
Member of Professional Body:	n/a		
		Additional Information:	n/a

Polhill Communications

Dome House, 48 Artillery Lane, London, E1 7LS Tel: 0207-655 0500; Fax: 0207-655 0501;
Web site: www.polhill.com

Contact:	Chris Harvey	Number of Directors & Executives engaged in: Financial PR Activities:	
Other Offices:	n/a	Dir:	4
		Exec:	22
Number of AIM Companies acting for:	1		
Engaged by: Inter-Alliance			
Member of Professional Body:	n/a		
		Additional Information:	n/a

Pollen Associates

Three Firs House, Bramshott Chase, Hindhead, GU26 6DG Tel: 01428-608860; Fax: 01428-608890;
email: richard.pollen@pollenassociates.com; Web site: www.pollenassociates.com

Contact:	Richard Pollen	Number of Directors & Executives engaged in: Financial PR Activities:	
Other Offices:	n/a	Dir:	1
		Exec:	1
Number of AIM Companies acting for:	1		
Engaged by: Chelford			
Member of Professional Body: Institute of Public Relations, Institute of Directors; Corporate & Financial Group (Chairman)			
		Additional Information: Corporate communications counselling to senior management	

Positive Profile

Hamilton House, 1 Temple Avenue, London, EC4Y 0HA Tel: 020-7489 2028; Fax: 020-7427 0777;
email: HenryG@PositiveProfile.com; Web site: www.PositiveProfile.com

Contact:	Henry L Gewanter	**Number of Directors & Executives engaged in:** **Financial PR Activities:**	
Other Offices:	n/a	**Dir:**	4
		Exec:	2
Number of AIM Companies acting for:	1		
Engaged by: Terrace Hill			
Member of Professional Body: Chartered Institute of Bankers; Institute of Public Relations; Chartered Institute of Marketing; Institute of Direct Marketing; Royal Society of Arts; Association of Banking Teachers; Consumers' Association; Institute of Direct Marketing; Institute of Civil Engineers		**Additional Information:**	n/a

Redleaf Communications

9-13 Andrew Street, London, EC4A 3AF Tel: 020-7955 1410; Fax: 020-7955 1429;
email: ek@redleafpr.com; Web site: www.redleafpr.com

Contact:	Emma Kane/Nick Lambert	**Number of Directors & Executives engaged in:** **Financial PR Activities:**	
Other Offices: n/a		**Dir:**	2
		Exec:	13
Number of AIM Companies acting for:	9		
Engaged by: African Diamonds; Cluff Mining; Finsbury Foods; Galahad Gold; Millfield; Pan Andean Resources; Petrel Resources; Transense Technologies			
Member of Professional Body: Institute of Public Relations; ProShare		**Additional Information:** Provide specialist retail investor service	

Roman River Communications

The Courtyard, Wetheringsett Hall, Wetheringsett, Stowmarket, Suffolk, IP14 5PW Tel: 01449-768907; Fax: 01449-768877; email: james.bendall@romanriver.fsnet.co.uk;

Contact:	James Bendall	Number of Directors & Executives engaged in: Financial PR Activities:	
Other Offices:	n/a	Dir:	1
		Exec:	1
Number of AIM Companies acting for:	2		
Engaged by: Advanced Power Components; Avionic Services			
Member of Professional Body:	n/a		
		Additional Information:	n/a

Simon Mountford Communications

The Old School, Newton on Ouse, York, YO30 2BN Tel: 01347-844 844; Fax: 01347-848 301; email: pr@simon-mountford.co.uk; Web site: www.simon-mountford.co.uk

Contact:	Simon Mountford	Number of Directors & Executives engaged in: Financial PR Activities:	
Other Offices:	n/a	Dir:	1
		Exec:	1
Number of AIM Companies acting for:	2		
Engaged by:	COE; Straight		
Member of Professional Body: Chartered Institute of Journalists			
		Additional Information:	n/a

Smith Grundon & Partners

9 Carmelite Street, London, EC4Y 0DR Tel: 020-7072 8616; Fax: 020-7072 8625;
email: mail@smithgrundon.co.uk; Web site: www.smithgrundon.co.uk

Contact:	Andrew Smith	**Number of Directors & Executives engaged in:**
		Financial PR Activities:
Other Offices:	n/a	**Dir:** n/a
		Exec: n/a
Number of AIM Companies acting for:	1	
Engaged by: Strategic Retail		
Member of Professional Body:	n/a	
		Additional Information: n/a

Smithfield

78 Cowcross Street, London, EC1M 6HE Tel: 020-7360 4900; Fax: 020-7253 6988;
email: rhoare@smithfieldfinancial.com; Web site: www.smithfieldgroup.com

Contact:	Reg Hoare	**Number of Directors & Executives engaged in:**
		Financial PR Activities:
Other Offices:	n/a	**Dir:** 6
		Exec: 12
Number of AIM Companies acting for:	2	
Engaged by: AFA Systems; Sportingbet		
Member of Professional Body:	n/a	
		Additional Information: n/a

St Brides Media & Finance

46 Bedford Row, London, WC1R 4LR Tel: 020-7242 4477; Fax: 020-7242 4488;
email: info@sbmf.co.uk;

Contact: Ian James, Hugo de Salis, Isabel Crossley	**Number of Directors & Executives engaged in: Financial PR Activities:**	
Other Offices: n/a	**Dir:**	3
	Exec:	n/a
Number of AIM Companies acting for: 19		
Engaged by: 2 Travel; Abraxus Investments; Beaufort; Capricorn Resources; Central African Mining & Exploration; CFA Capital; Cheerful Scout; DataCash; Honeygrove Group; hot group; Interactive Digital Solutions; Mark Kingsley; Oak Holdings; Private & Commercial Finance; Pursuit Dynamics; SectorGuard; Southern African Resources; Terrace Hill; Vitesse Media; Westside Acquisitions	**Additional Information:**	n/a
Member of Professional Body: n/a		

Tavistock Communications

131 Finsbury Pavement, London, EC2A 1NT Tel: 020-7920 3150; Fax: 020-7920 3151;
email: jwest@tavistock.co.uk; Web site: www.tavistock.co.uk

Contact: John West	**Number of Directors & Executives engaged in: Financial PR Activities:**	
Other Offices: Düsseldorf, Frankfurt, Zurich	**Dir:**	6
	Exec:	14
Number of AIM Companies acting for: 15		
Engaged by: Award International; Centurion Electronics; DawMed Systems; Envesta Telecom; Erinaceous; First Property; Flightstore; Giardino; Glow Communications; Maverick Entertainment; Medal Entertainment & Media; NetB2B2; NWF; Pathfinder Properties; Sheffield United		
Member of Professional Body: n/a	**Additional Information:**	n/a

Tulchan Communications

8th Floor, 21 New Fetter Lane, London, EC4A 1AE Tel: 020-7353 4200; Fax: 020-7353 4201;
email: enquiries@tulchangroup.com ; Web site: www.tulchangroup.com

Contact:	Andrew Honnor	Number of Directors & Executives engaged in: Financial PR Activities:	
Other Offices:	n/a	Dir:	1
		Exec:	4
Number of AIM Companies acting for:	17		
Engaged by:	n/a		
Member of Professional Body:	n/a		
		Additional Information:	n/a

Walters Associates

15-16 Pembroke Mews, London, W8 6ER Tel: 020-7938 2441; Fax: 020-7937 6450;
email: alex@waltersassociates.uk.com;

Contact:	Alex Walters	Number of Directors & Executives engaged in: Financial PR Activities:	
Other Offices:	None	Dir:	n/a
		Exec:	n/a
Number of AIM Companies acting for:	2		
Engaged by: Host Europe; PC Medics			
Member of Professional Body:	n/a		
		Additional Information:	n/a

Weber Shandwick/Square Mile

Fox Court, 14 Gray's Inn Road, London, WC1X 8WS Tel: 020-7067 0700; Fax: 0870-990 5481; email: cmlynch@webershandwick.com; Web site: www.webershandwick.com

		Number of Directors & Executives engaged in: Financial PR Activities:	
Contact:	Chris Lynch		
Other Offices: Africa, Asia Pacific, Europe, Latin America, Middle East and North America		**Dir:**	12
		Exec:	20
Number of AIM Companies acting for:	14		
Engaged by: Alterian; CRC; CustomVis; Empire Interactive; Enterprise; GamingKing; GW Pharmaceuticals; Redbus Interhouse; StatPro; TripleArc; Urbium; Volvere;			
Member of Professional Body:	n/a		
		Additional Information:	n/a

WMC Communications

7 Cheval Place, Knightsbridge, London, SW7 1EW Tel: 020-7591 3999; email: alex.glover@wmccommunications.com; Web site: www.wmccommunications.com

		Number of Directors & Executives engaged in: Financial PR Activities:	
Contact:	Alex Glover		
Other Offices:	n/a	**Dir:**	3
		Exec:	3
Number of AIM Companies acting for:	2		
Engaged by: First Artist; Mulberry			
Member of Professional Body:	n/a		
		Additional Information:	n/a

SOLICITORS

Addleshaw Goddard

150 Aldersgate Street, London, EC1A 4EJ Tel: 020-7606 8855;   Fax: 020-7606 4390;
email: info@addleshawgoddard.com;   Web site: www.addleshawgoddard.com

Contact: Simon Griffiths	
Number of AIM new issues worked on as:	
adviser to the Company: Over 70	
adviser to the NOMAD: Over 50	
any other capacity: n/a	
Industry sector preferences: n/a	
In-house industry sector analysts: n/a	
Sectors covered: n/a	
Transaction parameters (typical): n/a	
Member of professional or regulatory body: n/a	

Number of 'fee-earners' engaged in advising companies in relation to AIM:

Partners:	15
Assistants:	30

Act for: Antonov; Axiomlab; Churchill China; Clover; Coliseum; Comland Commercial; Cyprotex; Deal Group Media; Falkland Island; Harrier; Interior Services; Inventive Leisure; Noble Investments; Oystertec; Peel Holdings; Pilkington's Tiles; Preston North End; Pubs 'n' Bars; Raft International; Reflec; SBS; Sportingbet; SWP; THB; Tikit; Transense Technologies; Vebnet; VI

Other Offices:
Brussels; Cannon Street, London; Leeds; Manchester

Ashursts

Broadwalk House, 5 Appold St, London, EC2A 2HA Tel: 020-7638 1111;
Fax: 020-7638 1112;   Web site: www.ashursts.com

Contact: Michael Robins	
Number of AIM new issues worked on as:	
adviser to the Company: 49	
adviser to the NOMAD: n/a	
any other capacity: n/a	
Industry sector preferences: All sectors	
In-house industry sector analysts: Yes	
Sectors covered: We cover many sectors. The firm has a very large and diverse corporate client base	
Transaction parameters (typical): Any size	
Member of professional or regulatory body: Regulated by The Law Society	

Number of 'fee-earners' engaged in advising companies in relation to AIM:

Partners:	43
Assistants:	181

Act for: Alkane Energy; Beaufort; European Diamonds; Inter-Alliance; Innovision Research and Technology; NeuTec Pharma; Orbis; Osmetech; Redbus Interhouse; Rowe Evans Investments; Scipher; Solid State Supplies; Surgical Innovations; Toye & Company; Vebnet

Other Offices:
Brussels; Frankfurt; Madrid; Milan; Munich; New Delhi; New York; Paris; Singapore; Tokyo

Berwin Leighton Paisner

Adelaide House, London Bridge, London, EC4R 9HA Tel: 020-7427 1218;
Fax: 020-7760 1111; email: david.collins@blplaw.com; Web site: www.blplaw.com

Contact: David Collins	**Number of 'fee-earners' engaged in advising companies in relation to AIM:**
Number of AIM new issues worked on as:	**Partners:** 22
adviser to the Company: Over 50	**Assistants:** 40
adviser to the NOMAD: Over 50	
any other capacity: Over 50	
Industry sector preferences: Business Services; Gaming; Healthcare; Hotels; Leisure; Media; Mining; Outsourcing; Real Estate; Retail; Technology	**Act for:** betinternet.com; Bidtimes; Bradstock; Chorion; Corvus Capital; CSS Stellar; Gaming Insight; Innobox; Intercede; Internet Music & Media; ITIS;
In-house industry sector analysts: No	London Asia Capital; Numerica; Microcap Equities;
Sectors covered: n/a	Monsoon; NWD; Orad Hi-Tec Systems; Pilat Technologies; PNC Telecom; Raven Mount;
Transaction parameters (typical): All	Silentpoint; Stagecoach Theatre Arts; Streetnames;
Member of professional or regulatory body: British Retail Consortium, QCA, The Law Society	tecc-IS; Tecteon; themutual.net; TripleArc; Urbium
	Other Offices: Brussels and alliance offices in New York, Paris, Milan and Rome

Binchys

40 Lower Baggot Street, Dublin 2, Ireland Tel: 00-353 1 661 6144; Fax: 00-353 1 676 0189;
email: info@binchys.com; Web site: www.binchys.com

Contact: Jennifer Caldwell	**Number of 'fee-earners' engaged in advising companies in relation to AIM:**
Number of AIM new issues worked on as:	**Partners:** n/a
adviser to the Company: n/a	**Assistants:** n/a
adviser to the NOMAD: n/a	
any other capacity: n/a	
Industry sector preferences: n/a	**Act for:** betinternet; Thirdforce
In-house industry sector analysts: n/a	
Sectors covered: n/a	
Transaction parameters (typical): n/a	
Member of professional or regulatory body: n/a	
	Other Offices: n/a

Bircham Dyson Bell

50 Broadway, London, SW1H 0BL Tel: 020-7227 7000;   Fax: 020-7222 3480;
email: davidgoodman@bdb-law.co.uk;   Web site: www.bdb-law.co.uk

Contact: David Goodman/John Turnbull	**Number of 'fee-earners' engaged in advising**
Number of AIM new issues worked on as:	**companies in relation to AIM:**
adviser to the Company: 11	**Partners:** 3
adviser to the NOMAD: 2	**Assistants:** 3
any other capacity: 1	
Industry sector preferences: n/a	**Act for:** BWA; CW Residential; Eagle Eye Telematics;
In-house industry sector analysts: No	EiRx Therapeutics; Integrated Asset Management;
Sectors covered: n/a	Jarvis Porter; Metrodome; NWD; Paramount; PNC
	Telecom; PrimeEnt
Transaction parameters (typical): £1m-£20m	
Member of professional or regulatory body: The Law Society	
	Other Offices:
	Cardiff; Edinburgh; Brussels

BPE

St James's House, St James's Square, Cheltenham, Gloucestershire, GL50 3PR
Tel: 01242-248211;   Fax: 01242-226712;   email: jwo@bpe.co.uk;   Web site: www.bpe.co.uk

Contact: John Workman	**Number of 'fee-earners' engaged in advising**
Number of AIM new issues worked on as:	**companies in relation to AIM:**
adviser to the Company: 8	**Partners:** 3
adviser to the NOMAD: 1	**Assistants:** 2
any other capacity: n/a	
Industry sector preferences: None	**Act for:** DawMed Systems; Mears; Staffing Ventures;
In-house industry sector analysts: No	Wyatt
Sectors covered: n/a	
Transaction parameters (typical): £2m-£15m	
Member of professional or regulatory body: n/a	
	Other Offices:
	11 Guilford Street
	London WC1N 1DT
	Tel: 020-7404 0456
	Fax: 020-7430 2300
	Somerset House
	37 Temple Street
	Birmingham B2 5DP
	Tel: 0121-631 8400
	Fax: 0121-631 8402

Burges Salmon

Narrow Quay House, Narrow Quay, Bristol, BS1 4AH Tel: 0117-939 2000;
Fax: 0117-902 4400; email: email@burges-salmon.com; Web site: www.burges-salmon.com

Contact:	Christopher Godfrey	**Number of 'fee-earners' engaged in advising companies in relation to AIM:**	
Number of AIM new issues worked on as:			
adviser to the Company:	15+	**Partners:**	8
adviser to the NOMAD:	3	**Assistants:**	20
any other capacity:	n/a		
Industry sector preferences:	None	**Act for:** Airsprung Furniture; Albemarle & Bond; Arlington; Bristol & London; CODASciSys; Connaught; Dinkie Heel; Dipford; Gooch & Housego; Motion Media; Surface Technology Systems; Systems Union	
In-house industry sector analysts:	n/a		
Sectors covered:	n/a		
Transaction parameters (typical):	None		
Member of professional or regulatory body: BVCA; CBI; Quoted Companies Alliance; The Law Society			

Other Offices:
London

Burness

50 Lothian Road, Festival Square, Edinburgh, EH3 9WJ Tel: 0131-473 6000;
Fax: 0131-473 6006; email: edinburgh@burness.co.uk; Web site: www.burness.co.uk

Contact:	Peter Lawson	**Number of 'fee-earners' engaged in advising companies in relation to AIM:**	
Number of AIM new issues worked on as:			
adviser to the Company:	8	**Partners:**	5
adviser to the NOMAD:	5	**Assistants:**	5
any other capacity:	3		
Industry sector preferences:	n/a	**Act for:** Angus & Ross; Beauford; i-documentsystems; Ramco; UA	
In-house industry sector analysts:	No		
Sectors covered:	n/a		
Transaction parameters (typical):	£2m-£50m		
Member of professional or regulatory body: The Law Society of Scotland, Securities Institute			

Other Offices:
Glasgow

Charles Russell

8 - 10 New Fetter Lane, London, EC4A 1RS Tel: 020-7203 5000; Fax: 020-7203 0200;
email: enquiry@cr-law.co.uk; Web site: www.cr-law.com

Contact:	Simon Gilbert	
Number of AIM new issues worked on as:		
adviser to the Company:	9	
adviser to the NOMAD:	7	
any other capacity:	4	
Industry sector preferences: Covers most sectors including Biotech; IT; IP and Natural Resources		
In-house industry sector analysts:	n/a	
Sectors covered:	n/a	
Transaction parameters (typical):	n/a	
Member of professional or regulatory body: Law Society		

Number of 'fee-earners' engaged in advising companies in relation to AIM:

Partners:	8
Assistants:	15

Act for: 3DM Worldwide; Bema Gold; Corac; Immedia Broadcasting; Montpellier; Network; Pennant; Samedaybooks; YM BioSciences

Other Offices:
Cheltenham; Guildford

Clifford Chance

200 Aldersgate Street, London, EC1A 4JJ Tel: 020-7600 1000; Fax: 020-7600 5555;
Web site: www.cliffordchance.com

Contact:	Simon Tinkler	
Number of AIM new issues worked on as:		
adviser to the Company:	n/a	
adviser to the NOMAD:	n/a	
any other capacity:	n/a	
Industry sector preferences:	n/a	
In-house industry sector analysts:	n/a	
Sectors covered:	n/a	
Transaction parameters (typical):	n/a	
Member of professional or regulatory body:	n/a	

Number of 'fee-earners' engaged in advising companies in relation to AIM:

Partners:	n/a
Assistants:	n/a

Act for: CI Traders; Melrose

Other Offices:	n/a

Clyde & Co

51 Eastcheap, London, EC3M 1JP Tel: 020-7623 1244;   Fax: 020-7623 5427;
email: gary.thorpe@clyde.co.uk;   Web site: www.clydeco.com

Contact: Gary Thorpe/Andrew Baker	**Number of 'fee-earners' engaged in advising companies in relation to AIM:**
Number of AIM new issues worked on as:	
adviser to the Company: 5	**Partners:** 5
adviser to the NOMAD: 18	**Assistants:** 17
any other capacity: n/a	
Industry sector preferences: None	**Act for:** Faroe Petroleum; Longmead; Web Shareshop; Westmount Energy
In-house industry sector analysts: No	
Sectors covered: All sectors are/can be covered	
Transaction parameters (typical): No limits	
Member of professional or regulatory body: Quoted Companies Alliance, The Law Society	

Other Offices:
Belgrade; Cardiff; Guildford; Caracas; Dubai; Hong Kong; Paris; Piraeus; Singapore; St Petersburg

CMS Cameron McKenna

Mitre House, 160 Aldersgate Street, London, EC1A 4DD Tel: 020-7367 3000;
Fax: 020-7367 2000; email: info@cmck.com; Web site: www.law-now.com

Contact: Louise Wallace/John Burton	**Number of 'fee-earners' engaged in advising companies in relation to AIM:**
Number of AIM new issues worked on as:	
adviser to the Company: n/a	**Partners:** 25
adviser to the NOMAD: 10	**Assistants:** 41
any other capacity: n/a	
Industry sector preferences: All areas covered	**Act for:** Andaman Resources; DCS; Galleon; Hartford; IQ Ludorum; Interior Services; OneClickHR; Oxus Mining; Photo-Scan; TranXenoGen; Walker Greenbank
In-house industry sector analysts: n/a	
Sectors covered: CMS Cameron McKenna is a full service law firm advising on a wide range of sectors within the UK and overseas.	
Transaction parameters (typical): Market cap of £10m+ at flotation	
Member of professional or regulatory body: The Law Society	

Other Offices:
Aberdeen; Bristol; Amsterdam; Arnhem; Beijing; Belgrade; Berlin; Bratislava; Brussels; Bucharest; Budapest; Buenos Aires; Casablanca; Chemnit; Dresden; Düsseldorf; Frankfurt; Hamburg; Hilversum; Hong Kong; Leipzig; Lyon; Madrid; Milan; Moscow; Munich; New York; Paris; Prague; Rome; Stuttgart; Utrecht; Vienna; Warsaw; Zürich
Associated Offices: Toronto; Washington DC

SOLICITORS

Dechert

2 Serjeants' Inn, London, EC4Y 1LT Tel: 020-7583 5353; Fax: 020-7353 3683;
email: advice@eu.dechert.com; Web site: www.dechert.com

Contact: David Vogel	
Number of AIM new issues worked on as:	
adviser to the Company: Over 20	
adviser to the NOMAD: 9	
any other capacity: n/a	
Industry sector preferences: Corporate Finance; Financial Services; Insurance; Pharmaceuticals & Biotech; Property; Retail	
In-house industry sector analysts: n/a	
Sectors covered: n/a	
Transaction parameters (typical): n/a	
Member of professional or regulatory body: The Law Society	

Number of 'fee-earners' engaged in advising companies in relation to AIM:

Partners:	11
Assistants:	20

Act for: BioProgress; Bizspace; Fiske; Madisons Coffee; Numis; Retail Stores; Savoy Asset Management

Other Offices:
Boston; Brussels; Frankfurt; Harrisburg; Hartford Luxembourg; Newport Beach; New York; Palo Alto; Paris; Philadelphia; Princeton; San Francisco; Washington

---

Denton Wilde Sapte

1 Fleet Place, London, EC4M 7WS Tel: 020-7246 7000; Fax: 020-7246 7777;
email: info@dentonwildesapte.com; Web site: www.dentonwildesapte.com

Contact: Neil Vickers	
Number of AIM new issues worked on as:	
adviser to the Company: 8	
adviser to the NOMAD: 1	
any other capacity: n/a	
Industry sector preferences: Aviation; Banking; Energy; E-commerce; Media and Technology; Rail; Retail; Telecoms	
In-house industry sector analysts: Yes	
Sectors covered: All	
Transaction parameters (typical): None	
Member of professional or regulatory body: International Bar Association	

Number of 'fee-earners' engaged in advising companies in relation to AIM:

Partners:	18
Assistants:	66

Act for: Hot; Parallel Media; YooMedia

Other Offices:
London; Milton Keynes; Abu Dhabi; Almaty; Beijing; Brussels; Cairo; Dubai; Gibraltar; Hong Kong; Istanbul; Moscow; Muscat; Paris; Singapore; Tokyo

Dickinson Dees

St Ann's Wharf, 112 Quayside, Newcastle-upon-Tyne, NE99 1SB Tel: 0191-279 9000;
Fax: 0191-279 9100; email: sean.nicolson@dickinson-dees.com; Web site: www.dickinson-dees.com

Contact:	Sean Nicolson	**Number of 'fee-earners' engaged in advising**	
Number of AIM new issues worked on as:		**companies in relation to AIM:**	
adviser to the Company:	4	**Partners:**	10
adviser to the NOMAD:	n/a	**Assistants:**	18
any other capacity:	5		
Industry sector preferences:	None	**Act for:** Caledonian Trust; Parkdean Holidays;	
In-house industry sector analysts:	n/a	Transcomm	
Sectors covered:	n/a		
Transaction parameters (typical):	No limits		
Member of professional or regulatory body: The Law			
Society			

Other Offices:
Tees Valley; Brussels

Dickson Minto

Royal London House, 22-25 Finsbury Square, London, EC2A 1DX Tel: 020-7628 4455;
Fax: 020-7628 0027; Web site: www.dicksonminto.com

Contact:	Alastair R Dickson	**Number of 'fee-earners' engaged in advising**	
Number of AIM new issues worked on as:		**companies in relation to AIM:**	
adviser to the Company:	n/a	**Partners:**	n/a
adviser to the NOMAD:	n/a	**Assistants:**	n/a
any other capacity:	n/a		
Industry sector preferences:	n/a	**Act for:** Inveresk; Quayle Munro; Thistle Mining	
In-house industry sector analysts:	n/a		
Sectors covered:	n/a		
Transaction parameters (typical):	n/a		
Member of professional or regulatory body:	n/a		

Other Offices: n/a

SOLICITORS

DLA

City Office, 3 Noble Street, London, EC2V 7EE Tel: 08700-111 111; Fax: 020-7796 6666; email: mark.taylor@dla.com, alex.tamlyn@dla.com; Web site: www.dla.com

Contact: Mark Taylor/Alex Tamlyn
Number of AIM new issues worked on as:
   adviser to the Company: 10
   adviser to the NOMAD: 5
   any other capacity: 17
Industry sector preferences: The firm advises on most sectors and has had recent experience in the following: Engineering & Machinery; Health; Leisure, Entertainment & Hotels; Media & Photography; Software & Computer Services; Speciality & Other Finance
In-house industry sector analysts: n/a
Sectors covered: We have the resources and expertise to meet the needs of all major sectors.
Transaction parameters (typical): n/a
Member of professional or regulatory body: QCA, The British Venture Capital Association, The Law Society
	Number of 'fee-earners' engaged in advising companies in relation to AIM:
	Partners: 15
	Assistants: 29
	Act for: Advance Visual Communications; Belgravium Technologies; Carbo; Cavanagh; CMS Webview; COE; Conder Environmental; Cradley; Earthport; Empire Interactive; Enterprise; Envesta Telecom; Excel Airways; Galleon; Genus; Headway; Inter-Alliance; Inventive Leisure; INVU; Jarvis Porter; Just Car Clinics; Lawrence; Leeds; Lighthouse; Lonrho Africa; Matrix Healthcare; Media Square; Merchant House; Norman Hay; Pilkington's Tiles; Pixology; PrimeEnt; Proactive Sports; Sheffield United; Sirius Financial Solutions; Southern Vectis; Springboard; Stylo; The Medical House; West Bromwich Albion; Zoo Digital

	Other Offices: UK Offices: Birmingham; Bradford; Edinburgh; Glasgow; Leeds; Liverpool; Manchester; Sheffield Overseas Offices: Antwerp; Bangkok; Brussels; Hong Kong; Madrid; Sarajevo; Singapore; Shanghai; Vienna; Zagreb DLA Group Offices*: Denmark; France; Germany; Italy; Netherlands; Norway; Sweden *DLA is a member firm of D&P, an international association of law firms

Dundas & Wilson CS

Saltire Court, 20 Castle Terrace, Edinburgh, EH1 2EN Tel: 0131-228 8000; Fax: 0131-228 8888; email: michael.polson@dundas-wilson.com; Web site: www.dundas-wilson.com

Contact: Michael B Polson/Colin Lawrie
Number of AIM new issues worked on as:
   adviser to the Company: 8
   adviser to the NOMAD: 4
   any other capacity: 4
Industry sector preferences: n/a
In-house industry sector analysts: n/a
Sectors covered: Financial; Hi-Tech; Manufacturing
 	
Transaction parameters (typical): £1m-£20m
Member of professional or regulatory body: The Law Society of Scotland
	Number of 'fee-earners' engaged in advising companies in relation to AIM:
	Partners: 8
	Assistants: 19
	Act for: Cavanagh; DA Group; Vebnet

	Other Offices: Glasgow; London

DWF
Havester House, 37 Peter St, Manchester, M2 5GB Tel: 0161-603 5000

Contact: Andrew Needham	**Number of 'fee-earners' engaged in advising companies in relation to AIM:**
Number of AIM new issues worked on as:	
adviser to the Company: 4	**Partners:** 4
adviser to the NOMAD: n/a	**Assistants:** 0
any other capacity: n/a	
Industry sector preferences: n/a	**Act for:** Access Intelligence; Inter Link Foods;
In-house industry sector analysts: n/a	Inventive Leisure; Monstermob; Readybuy; Reflec
Sectors covered: n/a	
Transaction parameters (typical): n/a	
Member of professional or regulatory body: The Law Society	
	Other Offices: Liverpool; Warrington

Eversheds
Senator House, 85 Queen Victoria St, London, EC4V 4JL Tel: 020-7919 4500;
Fax: 020-7919 4919; email: neilmatthews@eversheds.com; Web site: www.eversheds.com

Contact: Neil Matthews	**Number of 'fee-earners' engaged in advising companies in relation to AIM:**
Number of AIM new issues worked on as:	
adviser to the Company: 50+	**Partners:** 30
adviser to the NOMAD: 50+	**Assistants:** 50
any other capacity: n/a	
Industry sector preferences: All sectors covered.	**Act for:** 2 Travel; AFA Systems; Amco; Artisan (UK);
In-house industry sector analysts: Yes	Bakery Services; Bidtimes; CamAxys; Canterbury
Sectors covered: All	Foods; CeNeS; Claims People; coffeeheaven;
	Computerland UK; Debt Free Direct; Eurasia Mining;
Transaction parameters (typical): £1m-£100m	Fieldens; G.R.; Glisten; Huveaux; James Halstead;
Member of professional or regulatory body: British Venture Capital Association; CBI Corporate Law Panel; CISCO; ICAEW (Corporate Finance Faculty); The Law Society	James R Knowles; K3 Business Technology; Landround; LPA; Meriden; NetB2B2; Oasis Healthcare; Peel Holdings; Reversus; Sinclair Pharma; Tandem; Tepnel Life Sciences; The Claims People; Thomas Walker; Tolent; Weatherly
	Other Offices: Birmingham; Cambridge; Cardiff; Copenhagen; Ipswich; Leeds; Manchester; Newcastle; Norwich; Nottingham; Brussels; Paris
	Associated Offices: Hong Kong; Kuala Lumpur; Milan; Rome; Shanghai; Singapore; Sofia

Faegre Benson Hobson Audley

7 Pilgrim Street, London, EC4V 6LB Tel: 020-7450 4500; Fax: 020-7450 4545; email: lawyers@faegre.co.uk; Web site: www.faegre.co.uk

Contact:	Max Audley	
Number of AIM new issues worked on as:		
adviser to the Company:	22	
adviser to the NOMAD:	30	
any other capacity:	n/a	

Industry sector preferences: Biotechnology; E-commerce; Financial Services; Innovation and Technology; Natural Resources
In-house industry sector analysts: No
Sectors covered: n/a

Transaction parameters (typical): No typical parameters
Member of professional or regulatory body: British Venture Capital Association; Quoted Companies Alliance; The Law Society of England & Wales

Number of 'fee-earners' engaged in advising companies in relation to AIM:

Partners:	3
Assistants:	5

Act for: A Cohen & Co; BioProjects; Clean Diesel Technologies; Greenchip Investments; Gympie Gold; Impax; Judges Capital; Lighthouse; Ringprop; SouthernEra Resources; StatPro

Other Offices:
Boulder; Denver; Des Moines; Frankfurt; Minneapolis Shanghai

Field Fisher Waterhouse

35 Vine Street, London, EC3N 2AA Tel: 020-7861 4000; Fax: 020-7488 0084; email: info@ffw.com; Web site: www.ffw.com

Contact:	Anthony Brockbank	
Number of AIM new issues worked on as:		
adviser to the Company:	More than 53	
adviser to the NOMAD:	50	
any other capacity:	n/a	

Industry sector preferences: n/a
In-house industry sector analysts: Yes
Sectors covered: Franchising; Information Technology; Internet; Investment Funds; Leisure; Media; Natural Resources; Rail; Sport; Telecoms; Travel

Transaction parameters (typical): £0.5m-£150m
Member of professional or regulatory body: AUTIF; City of London Law Society; Institute of Tourism; International Bar Association; Rail Study Association; The Law Society

Number of 'fee-earners' engaged in advising companies in relation to AIM:

Partners:	5
Assistants:	8

Act for: 10 Group; ADVFN; Akaei; Avocet Mining; Brazilian Diamonds; Bullion Resources; Cabouchon; CFA Capital; Designer Vision; Digital Classics; Dimension Resources; Dinkie Heel; Einstein; EmdexTrade; Equator; FFastFill; GMA Resources; Hemisphere Properties; Hidefield; Jacques Vert; Mediwatch; Mosaique; NBA Quantum; Newmark Security; Oak Holdings; OFEX; On-Line; Tellings Golden Miller; themutual.net; Wynnstay Properties; Zyzygy

Other Offices: n/a

Finers Stephens Innocent

179 Great Portland Street, London, W1W 5LS Tel: 020-7323 4000; Fax: 020-7580 7069;
email: areeback@fsilaw.co.uk; Web site: www.fsilaw.com

Contact:	Ashley Reeback	**Number of 'fee-earners' engaged in advising companies in relation to AIM:**
Number of AIM new issues worked on as:		
adviser to the Company:	10	**Partners:** 4
adviser to the NOMAD:	2	**Assistants:** 4
any other capacity:	n/a	
Industry sector preferences:	Gaming and leisure	**Act for:** Centurion Electronics; Cheerful Scout; Mean Fiddler Music; Sportingbet; Tecteon; Top Ten; Totally; Univent; Westside Acquisitions; YooMedia
companies; Technology		
In-house industry sector analysts:	No	
Sectors covered:	n/a	
Transaction parameters (typical):	£1m-£20m	
Member of professional or regulatory body: No		

Other Offices:
None

Fladgate Fielder

25 North Row, London, W1K 6DJ Tel: 020-7323 4747; Fax: 020-7629 4414;
Web site: www.fladgate.com

Contact:	Nicolas Greenstone	**Number of 'fee-earners' engaged in advising companies in relation to AIM:**
Number of AIM new issues worked on as:		
adviser to the Company:	5	**Partners:** 6
adviser to the NOMAD:	n/a	**Assistants:** 4
any other capacity:	4	
Industry sector preferences:	None	**Act for:** Air Music & Media; Canisp; PC Medics; Prestige Publishing; Spring Grove Property Maintenance; TEP Exchange; The Creative Education Corporation; Your Space
In-house industry sector analysts:	No	
Sectors covered:	n/a	
Transaction parameters (typical):	£10m-£55m	
Member of professional or regulatory body: The Law Society		

Other Offices: n/a

SOLICITORS

Fox Brooks Marshall

Century House, St Peters Square, Manchester, Tel: 0161-236 7766; Fax: 0161-236 7794;
email: fbm@foxbrooks.co.uk

Contact: Andrew Wright/Simon Ledbrooke	**Number of 'fee-earners' engaged in advising**
Number of AIM new issues worked on as:	**companies in relation to AIM:**
adviser to the Company: 12	**Partners:** 5
adviser to the NOMAD: 9	**Assistants:** 5
any other capacity: n/a	
Industry sector preferences: Exploration; Mining; Technology	**Act for:** African Eagle Resources; Gold Mines of Sardinia; Highland Gold Mining; St Barbara Mines; Tertiary Minerals; Virotec
In-house industry sector analysts: n/a	
Sectors covered: n/a	
Transaction parameters (typical): n/a	
Member of professional or regulatory body: The Law Society	
	Other Offices: n/a

Freshfields Bruckhaus Deringer

65 Fleet Street, London, EC4Y 1HS Tel: +44 20 7936 4000 Fax: +44 20 7832 7001
Tel: 020-7936 4000; Fax: 020-7832 7001; Web site: www.freshfields.com

Contact: Peter Jeffcote	**Number of 'fee-earners' engaged in advising**
Number of AIM new issues worked on as:	**companies in relation to AIM:**
adviser to the Company: n/a	**Partners:** n/a
adviser to the NOMAD: n/a	**Assistants:** n/a
any other capacity: n/a	
Industry sector preferences: n/a	**Act for:** Eckoh Technologies; Trans-Siberian Gold
In-house industry sector analysts: n/a	
Sectors covered: Transaction parameters (typical): n/a	
Member of professional or regulatory body: n/a	
	Other Offices: n/a

Gately Wareing

Windsor House, 3 Temple Row, Birmingham, B2 5JR Tel: 0121-234 0000;
Fax: 0121-234 0003; email: Pcliff@gateleywareing.com; Web site: www.gateleywareing.com

Contact:		Paul Cliff
Number of AIM new issues worked on as:		
adviser to the Company:		5
adviser to the NOMAD:		5
any other capacity:		n/a
Industry sector preferences:		n/a
In-house industry sector analysts:		n/a
Sectors covered:		n/a
Transaction parameters (typical):		Any
Member of professional or regulatory body: The Law Society		

Number of 'fee-earners' engaged in advising companies in relation to AIM:

Partners:	3
Assistants:	3

Act for: Cobra Biomanufacturing; Lloyds British Testing; ML Laboratories

Other Offices:
Leicester; Nottingham

Gold Mann & Co

4 Chiswell Street, 5th Floor, London, EC1Y 4UP Tel: 020-7786 2100; Fax: 020-7786 2101

Contact:		Mark Hartley
Number of AIM new issues worked on as:		
adviser to the Company:		n/a
adviser to the NOMAD:		n/a
any other capacity:		n/a
Industry sector preferences:		n/a
In-house industry sector analysts:		n/a
Sectors covered: Transaction parameters (typical):		n/a
Member of professional or regulatory body:		n/a

Number of 'fee-earners' engaged in advising companies in relation to AIM:

Partners:	n/a
Assistants:	n/a

Act for: AFA Systems; Capcon; Maverick Entertainment

Other Offices:	n/a

SOLICITORS

Hale and Dorr

Alder Castle, 10 Noble Street, London, EC2V 7QJ Tel: 020-7645 2400;   Fax: 020-7645 2424; email: naujoks@bhd.com; Web site: www.haledorr.com

Contact: Joe Pillman/Kate Eavis	**Number of 'fee-earners' engaged in advising**
Number of AIM new issues worked on as:	**companies in relation to AIM:**
adviser to the Company: 4	**Partners:** 3
adviser to the NOMAD: n/a	**Assistants:** 7
any other capacity: n/a	
Industry sector preferences: Biotechnology; Life Sciences; Technology	**Act for:** Akers Biosciences; CRC; Ocean Power Technologies; ReGen Therapeutics; Screen
In-house industry sector analysts: No	
Sectors covered: n/a	
Transaction parameters (typical): n/a	
Member of professional or regulatory body: The Law Society of England & Wales	**Other Offices:**
	Park Gate
	25 Milton Park
	Oxford OX14 4SH
	Tel: 01235-823 000
	Fax: 01235-823 030
	Maximilianstrasse 31
	D-80539 München
	Germany
	Tel: 00-49 89 24 213 0
	Fax: 00-49 89 24 213 213

Halliwell Landau
75 King William Street, London, EC4N 7BE   Tel: 020-7929 1900, Fax: 020-7929 4800, St James's Court, Brown Street, Manchester, M2 2JF Tel: 0161-835 3003; Fax: 0161-835 2994; email: crg@halliwells.co.uk acraig@halliwells.co.uk;   Web site: www.halliwells.co.uk

Contact: Clive Garston (London)/Alec Craig (Manchester)	**Number of 'fee-earners' engaged in advising**
Number of AIM new issues worked on as:	**companies in relation to AIM:**
adviser to the Company: 9 in the last 12 months	**Partners:** 14
adviser to the NOMAD: 4 in the last 12 months	**Assistants:** 25
any other capacity: n/a	
Industry sector preferences: Biotechnology; Healthcare; Leisure; Technology	**Act for:** 1st Dental Laboratories; Cardpoint; Carrwood; Celltalk; Eagle Eye Telematics; Hansard; Leisure
In-house industry sector analysts: n/a	Ventures; MacLellan; Netcall; Resurge; Sports &
Sectors covered: n/a	Leisure; Tepnel Life Sciences; Tricorn; Ultimate Finance; Warthog; WH Ireland; Zi Medical
Transaction parameters (typical): >£1m	
Member of professional or regulatory body: CBI; The Law Society	
	Other Offices:
As individuals:	Sheffield
American Bar Association; Institute of Directors; Securities Institute	

Hammonds

7 Devonshire Square, Cutlers Garden, London, EC2M 4YH Tel: 0870-839 0000;
Fax: 0870-839 1001; email: enquiries@hammonds.com; Web site: www.hammonds.com

Contact: Martin Thomas / Tim Jackson-Smith	**Number of 'fee-earners' engaged in advising companies in relation to AIM:**
Number of AIM new issues worked on as:	
adviser to the Company: 15	**Partners:** 24
adviser to the NOMAD: 23	**Assistants:** 60
any other capacity: n/a	
Industry sector preferences: n/a	**Act for:** CustomVis; Cyberes; Dream Direct; Dynamic
In-house industry sector analysts: Yes	Commercial Finance; Eurolink Managed Services;
Sectors covered: Chemical; Utilities; Engineering;	Focus Solutions; FTV; Honeycombe Leisure; Host
Pharmaceuticals	Europe; Ideal Shopping Direct; Intellexis; Inter Link
	Foods; John Lewis of Hungerford; Penmc; PIPEX
Transaction parameters (typical): £1m	Communications; PM; Proactive Sports; Reefton
Member of professional or regulatory body: BVCA;	Mining; SP; Stockcube; Surface Transforms; Volvere
CBI; Energy Industries Council; IoD; The Law Society	

Other Offices:
Birmingham; Leeds; Manchester; Berlin; Brussels; Hong Kong; Madrid; Milan; Munich; Paris; Rome, Turin

Harbottle & Lewis

Hanover House, 14 Hanover Square, London, W1S 1HP Tel: 020-7667 5000;
Fax: 020-7667 5100; email: collin.howes@harbottle.com; Web site: www.harbottle.com

Contact: Mark Bertram/Tim Parker	**Number of 'fee-earners' engaged in advising companies in relation to AIM:**
Number of AIM new issues worked on as:	
adviser to the Company: 5	**Partners:** 4
adviser to the NOMAD: 1	**Assistants:** 0
any other capacity: n/a	
Industry sector preferences: Advertising, Travel;	**Act for:** First Property; Mean Fiddler Music; Victory
Communications; e-commerce; Entertainment; Leisure;	
Media; Sport and Technology	
In-house industry sector analysts: No	
Sectors covered: n/a	
Transaction parameters (typical): £1m-£150m	
Member of professional or regulatory body: American	
Bar Association; Association of Entertainment Lawyers;	**Other Offices:** n/a
Computer Law Association; Employment Lawyers	
Association; European Air Law Association; International	
Bar Association; News Producers Alliance; Radio	
Academy; Royal Aeronautical Society; Royal Television	
Society; Society for Computers and Law	

Herbert Smith

Exchange House, Primrose Street, London, EC2A 2HS Tel: 020-7374 8000;
Fax: 020-7374 0888; email: contact@herbertsmith.com; Web site: www.herbertsmith.com

Contact: Henry Raine	Number of 'fee-earners' engaged in advising companies in relation to AIM:
Number of AIM new issues worked on as:	
adviser to the Company: 4	Partners: 5
adviser to the NOMAD: n/a	Assistants: 20
any other capacity: n/a	
Industry sector preferences: None	Act for: Cape; Georgica; LiDCO; Razorback Vehicles
In-house industry sector analysts: Yes	
Sectors covered: Leisure and Sport; Pharmaceuticals and Healthcare (not necessarily just AIM)	
Transaction parameters (typical): over £10m (market cap)	
Member of professional or regulatory body: CISCO; UK Bio-industry Association	**Other Offices:**
	Bangkok; Beijing; Brussels; Hong Kong; Moscow; Paris; Shanghai; Singapore; Tokyo

Howard Kennedy

19 Cavendish Square, London, W1A 2AW Tel: 020-7636 1616; Fax: 020-7491 2899;
email: enquiries@howardkennedy.com; Web site: www.howardkennedy.com

Contact: Keith Lassman	Number of 'fee-earners' engaged in advising companies in relation to AIM:
Number of AIM new issues worked on as:	
adviser to the Company: n/a	Partners: 10
adviser to the NOMAD: n/a	Assistants: 8
any other capacity: n/a	
Industry sector preferences: n/a	Act for: 7 Group; ASK Central; Contemporary Enterprises; Hurlingham; Longbridge International; Prezzo; Stilo; Wigmore
In-house industry sector analysts: n/a	
Sectors covered: Aviation; Information Technology; Leisure, Entertainment & Hotels; Other Finance; Property; Retail	
Transaction parameters (typical): n/a	
Member of professional or regulatory body: FSA; The Law Society	**Other Offices:** n/a

Irwin Mitchell

21 Queen Street, Leeds, LS1 2TW Tel: 0870-150 0100;   Fax: 0113-234 3322;
Web site: www.imonline.co.uk

Contact:	Kevin Cunningham	
Number of AIM new issues worked on as:		
adviser to the Company:	n/a	
adviser to the NOMAD:	n/a	
any other capacity:	n/a	
Industry sector preferences:	n/a	
In-house industry sector analysts:	n/a	
Sectors covered:	n/a	
Transaction parameters (typical):	n/a	
Member of professional or regulatory body:	n/a	

Number of 'fee-earners' engaged in advising companies in relation to AIM:

Partners:	n/a
Assistants:	n/a

Act for: MOS International; Sunbeach Communications

Other Offices: n/a

Joelson Wilson

70 New Cavendish Street, London, W1G 8AT Tel: 020-7580 5721;   Fax: 020-7580 2251;
email: sac@joelson-wilson.co.uk;   Web site: www.joelson-wilson.co.uk

Contact:	Sheldon Cordell	
Number of AIM new issues worked on as:		
adviser to the Company:	n/a	
adviser to the NOMAD:	n/a	
any other capacity:	n/a	
Industry sector preferences:	n/a	
In-house industry sector analysts:	n/a	
Sectors covered: Transaction parameters (typical):	n/a	
Member of professional or regulatory body:	n/a	

Number of 'fee-earners' engaged in advising companies in relation to AIM:

Partners:	n/a
Assistants:	n/a

Act for: actif; Napier Brown Foods; The Real Good Food Company

Other Offices: n/a

Jones Day Gouldens

10 Old Bailey, London, EC4M 7NG   Tel: 020-7583 7777;   Fax: 020-7583 6777;
email: info@gouldens.com;   Web site: www.gouldens.com

Contact:		Hilary Winter/Jane Wandby
Number of AIM new issues worked on as:		
adviser to the Company:		n/a
adviser to the NOMAD:		n/a
any other capacity:		n/a
Industry sector preferences:		n/a
In-house industry sector analysts:		n/a
Sectors covered:		n/a
Transaction parameters (typical):		n/a
Member of professional or regulatory body:		n/a

Number of 'fee-earners' engaged in advising companies in relation to AIM:

Partners:	19
Assistants:	25

Act for: Bits Corp; Brainspark; easier; Enneurope; Internet Business Group; Inveresk; Jourdan; Manpower Software; Oak Holdings; Sibir Energy; Smart Approach; Southampton Leisure; Thomson Intermedia; Tissue Science Laboratories

Other Offices: n/a

Kendall Freeman

43 Fetter Lane, London, EC4A 1JU Tel: 020-7583 4055;   Fax: 020-7353 7377;
email: richardspiller@kendallfreeman.com;   Web site: www.kendallfreeman.com

Contact:		Richard Spiller/Ashwani Kochhar
Number of AIM new issues worked on as:		
adviser to the Company:		12
adviser to the NOMAD:		6
any other capacity:		None
Industry sector preferences:		Insurance
In-house industry sector analysts:		n/a
Sectors covered:		n/a
Transaction parameters (typical):		No limits
Member of professional or regulatory body:		The Law Society

Number of 'fee-earners' engaged in advising companies in relation to AIM:

Partners:	2
Assistants:	8

Act for: Numis; Tenon; THB

Other Offices: n/a

Kerman & Co

7 Savoy Court, The Strand, London, WC2R 0ER Tel: 020-7539 7272; Fax: 020-7240 5780;
Web site: www.kermanco.com

Contact: Richard Stanton-Reid		**Number of 'fee-earners' engaged in advising**	
Number of AIM new issues worked on as:		**companies in relation to AIM:**	
adviser to the Company:	1	**Partners:**	2
adviser to the NOMAD:	0	**Assistants:**	2
any other capacity:	0		
Industry sector preferences:	n/a	**Act for:** Celtic Resources, Eureka Mining; Oxus Gold	
In-house industry sector analysts:	n/a		
Sectors covered:	n/a		
Transaction parameters (typical):	n/a		
Member of professional or regulatory body: The Law Society			
		Other Offices: Almety, Kazakhstan	

KLegal

1-2 Dorset Rise, London, EC4Y 8AE, Tel: 020-7694 2500; Fax: 020-7694 2501;
email: Emma.steward@klegal.co.uk; Web site: www.klegal.co.uk

Contact: Ian Binnie/David Mandell		**Number of 'fee-earners' engaged in advising**	
Number of AIM new issues worked on as:		**companies in relation to AIM:**	
adviser to the Company:	n/a	**Partners:**	9
adviser to the NOMAD:	n/a	**Assistants:**	4
any other capacity:	3		
Industry sector preferences: Brands; Life Sciences; Retail; Technology		**Act for:** Advance Capital Invest; Halladale; iomart; Legendary Investments; Preston North End; Seyour Pierce; Stagecoach Theatre Arts	
In-house industry sector analysts:	n/a		
Sectors covered:	n/a		
Transaction parameters (typical):	£5m plus		
Member of professional or regulatory body: The Law Society of England & Wales; The Law Society of Scotland		**Other Offices:** Belfast; Edinburgh	
		KLegal is a member of KLegal International Network of firms.	

541

Kuit Steinart Levy

3 St Mary's Parsonage, Manchester, M3 2RD Tel: 0161-832 3434;   Fax: 0161-832 6650;
Web site: www.kuits.com

Contact:	Rob Buckley, Kirsti Pinnell	Number of 'fee-earners' engaged in advising companies in relation to AIM:	
Number of AIM new issues worked on as:			
adviser to the Company:	n/a	Partners:	2
adviser to the NOMAD:	n/a	Assistants:	3
any other capacity:	n/a		
Industry sector preferences:	n/a	Act for: Aerobox; Bright Futures; Mercury Recycling; ASOS	
In-house industry sector analysts:	n/a		
Sectors covered:	n/a		
Transaction parameters (typical):	£20m		
Member of professional or regulatory body: The Law Society			
		Other Offices:	n/a

Latham & Watkins

99 Bishopsgate, 11th Floor, London, EC2M 3XF Tel: 020-7710 1000;   Fax: 020-7374 4460;
Web site: www.lw.com

Contact:	Nigel Campion-Smith	Number of 'fee-earners' engaged in advising companies in relation to AIM:	
Number of AIM new issues worked on as:			
adviser to the Company:	4	Partners:	4
adviser to the NOMAD:	n/a	Assistants:	8
any other capacity:	n/a		
Industry sector preferences:	No	Act for: CI Traders; Comprop; Epic Brand Investments; Epic Reconstruction	
In-house industry sector analysts:	No		
Sectors covered:	n/a		
Transaction parameters (typical):	n/a		
Member of professional or regulatory body: Solicitors (Law Society)			
		Other Offices: Boston; Brussels; Chicago; Frankfurt; Hamburg; Hong Kong; Los Angeles; Milan; Moscow; New Jersey; New York; Northern Virginia; Orange County; Paris; San Diego; San Francisco; Silicon Valley; Singapore; Tokyo; Washington D C	

Lawrence Graham

190 Strand, London, WC2R 1JN Tel: 020-7379 0000; Fax: 020-7379 6854;
email: info@lawgram.com; Web site: www.lawgram.com

Contact: Hugh Maule	**Number of 'fee-earners' engaged in advising companies in relation to AIM:**
Number of AIM new issues worked on as:	
adviser to the Company: IPO: 22, Secondary issues: 23	**Partners:** 7
adviser to the NOMAD: IPO: 32; Secondary issues: 14	**Assistants:** 10
any other capacity: Number of joint AIM/DCM issues: 4;	
Uplift to Full List from AIM: 7	**Act for:** Archipelago Resources; ATA; Cater Barnard;
Industry sector preferences: All	City Lofts; Coffee Republic; Crown Corporation; HPD
In-house industry sector analysts: No	Exploration; Milestone; Millfield; Pipehawk; Protec;
Sectors covered: All sectors can be covered, including:	Stream; Vietnam Opportunity Fund
Corporate Services;Financial Intermediaries; Leisure &	
Entertainment; IT; Mining; Outsourcing; Property;	
Publishing & Media; Recruitment; Retail; Security;	
Telecoms	
	Other Offices: n/a
Transaction parameters (typical): £5m-£200m	
Member of professional or regulatory body: The Law	
Society	

Lewis Silkin

12 Gough Square, London, EC4A 3DW Tel: 020-7074 8004; Fax: 020-7832 1758;
email: clare.grayston@lewissilkin.com; Web site: www.lewissilkin.com

Contact: Clare Grayston	**Number of 'fee-earners' engaged in advising companies in relation to AIM:**
Number of AIM new issues worked on as:	
adviser to the Company: 7	**Partners:** 5
adviser to the NOMAD: 53	**Assistants:** 7
any other capacity: n/a	
Industry sector preferences: None	**Act for:** Hat Pin; Newsplayer; Staffing Ventures; TEP
In-house industry sector analysts: No	Exchange
Sectors covered: Construction; Corporate Services;	
Employment; Litigation and Dispute Resolution;	
Marketing Services; Project Finance; Property; Sport;	
Technology and Communications	
Transaction parameters (typical): £2m-£100m	
Member of professional or regulatory body:	**Other Offices:**
Employment Lawyers Association; European Advertising	Oxford
Lawyers Association; Investor Relations Society; The Law	
Society; Society for Computers in Law; Society of	
Construction Lawyers; Society of Share Scheme	
Practitioners	

SOLICITORS

Lovells

Atlantic House, 50 Holborn Viaduct, London, EC1A 2FG Tel: 020-7296 2000;
Fax: 020-7296 2001; email: information@lovells.com; Web site: www.lovells.com

Contact: Andrew Carey, Richard Ufland	Number of 'fee-earners' engaged in advising companies in relation to AIM:
Number of AIM new issues worked on as:	
adviser to the Company: Numerous	**Partners:** as required
adviser to the NOMAD: Numerous	**Assistants:** as required
any other capacity: Numerous	
Industry sector preferences: None	**Act for:** Bertam; Proteome Sciences; Radamec
In-house industry sector analysts: No	
Sectors covered: n/a	
Transaction parameters (typical): n/a	
Member of professional or regulatory body: The Law Society	

Other Offices:
Alicante; Amsterdam; Beijing; Berlin; Brussels; Budapest; Chicago; Dusseldorf; Frankfurt; Hamburg; Ho Chi Minh City; Hong Kong; Milan; Moscow; Munich; New York; Paris; Prague; Rome; Singapore; Tokyo; Vienna; Warsaw; Washington DC; Zagreb

MacFarlanes

10 Norwich Street, London, EC4A 1BD Tel: 020-7831 9222; Fax: 020-7831 9607;
Web site: www.macfarlanes.com

Contact: Simon Martin	Number of 'fee-earners' engaged in advising companies in relation to AIM:
Number of AIM new issues worked on as:	
adviser to the Company: Numerous	**Partners:** as required
adviser to the NOMAD: Numerous	**Assistants:** as required
any other capacity: n/a	
Industry sector preferences: None	**Act for:** Conygar Investment; I2S; Quadnetics; Reflex; Tenon
In-house industry sector analysts: None	
Sectors covered: n/a	
Transaction parameters (typical): n/a	
Member of professional or regulatory body: The Law Society	

Other Offices: n/a

Maclay Murray & Spens

10 Foster Lane, London, EC2V 6HR Tel: 020-7606 6130;   Fax: 020-7600 0992;
email: jonathan.brooks@mms.co.uk;   Web site: www.mms.co.uk

Contact: Jonathan Brooks	**Number of 'fee-earners' engaged in advising**
Number of AIM new issues worked on as:	**companies in relation to AIM:**
adviser to the Company: 8	**Partners:** 14
adviser to the NOMAD: 6	**Assistants:** 28
any other capacity: n/a	
Industry sector preferences: Beverages; Engineering;	**Act for:** Bella Media; BKN International; Blavod
Healthcare; Life Sciences; Media; Natural Resources;	Extreme Spirits; LTG Technologies; Manpower
Technology	Software; New Media Industries; Private &
In-house industry sector analysts: n/a	Commercial Finance; Widney
Sectors covered: n/a	
Transaction parameters (typical): Up to 100 million	
Member of professional or regulatory body: BUCA; Lex	
Mundi; The Law Society	**Other Offices:**
	Aberdeen; Brussels; Edinburgh; Glasgow

Manches

Aldwych House, 81 Aldwych, London, WC2B 4RP Tel: 020-7404 4433;   Fax: 020-7430 1133

Contact: Christopher Owen/Matthew Martin	**Number of 'fee-earners' engaged in advising**
Number of AIM new issues worked on as:	**companies in relation to AIM:**
adviser to the Company: 4	**Partners:** 8
adviser to the NOMAD: n/a	**Assistants:** 8
any other capacity: n/a	
Industry sector preferences: Growing business, particu-	**Act for:** Comland Commercial; Pan Andean Resources;
larly in area of hi-tech media and publishing	WILink.com
In-house industry sector analysts: Yes	
Sectors covered: Biotechnology; Insurance; IT; Media;	
Publishing; Telecoms	
Transaction parameters (typical): n/a	
Member of professional or regulatory body: n/a	**Other Offices:**
	Oxford

Marriott Harrison

12 Great James Street, London, WC1N 3DR   Tel: 020-7209 2000;   Fax: 020-7209 2001;
email: Duncan.innes@marriottharrison.co.uk;   Web site: www.marriottharrison.com

Contact:		Duncan Innes
Number of AIM new issues worked on as:		
adviser to the Company:		6
adviser to the NOMAD:		10
any other capacity:		4
Industry sector preferences:	Media & Technology; Travel	
In-house industry sector analysts:		No
Sectors covered:		n/a
Transaction parameters (typical):		n/a
Member of professional or regulatory body: The Law Society, Securities Institute		

Number of 'fee-earners' engaged in advising companies in relation to AIM:

Partners:	4
Assistants:	4

Act for: Beaufort; Clapham House; Online Travel

Other Offices:　　　　　　　　　　　　　　n/a

Martineau Johnson

St Philips House, St Philips Place, Birmingham, B3 2PP Tel: 0121-200 3300;
Fax: 0121-200 3330;   email: lawyers@marjohn.com;   Web site: www.martineau-johnson.co.uk

Contact:	Roger Blears
Number of AIM new issues worked on as:	
adviser to the Company:	n/a
adviser to the NOMAD:	n/a
any other capacity:	n/a
Industry sector preferences:	n/a
In-house industry sector analysts:	n/a
Sectors covered:	n/a
Transaction parameters (typical):	n/a
Member of professional or regulatory body:	n/a

Number of 'fee-earners' engaged in advising companies in relation to AIM:

Partners:	n/a
Assistants:	n/a

Act for: Booth Industries; Loades

Other Offices:　　　　　　　　　　　　　　n/a

Masons

30 Aylesbury Street, London, EC1R 0ER Tel: 020-7490 4000; Fax: 020-7490 2545;
email: victor.hawrych@masons.com; Web site: www.masons.com

Contact:	Victor Hawrych	**Number of 'fee-earners' engaged in advising**		
Number of AIM new issues worked on as:		**companies in relation to AIM:**		
adviser to the Company:	n/a	**Partners:**		3
adviser to the NOMAD:	n/a	**Assistants:**		6
any other capacity:	12			
Industry sector preferences:	All	**Act for:** Charteris; IP2IPO; Nature Technology		
In-house industry sector analysts:	Yes	Solutions; Pathfinder Properties; Sefton Resources		
Sectors covered: Construction; Energy; Engineering;				
Information & Technology; Property				
Transaction parameters (typical):	All			
Member of professional or regulatory body:	n/a			
		Other Offices:		
		Bristol; Glasgow; Leeds; Manchester; Brussels;		
		Dublin; Guangzhou; Hong Kong; Singapore		

Matheson Ormsby Prentice

30 Herbert Street, Dublin 2, Ireland   Tel: 00-353 1 619 9000;   Fax: 00-353 1 619 9010;
email: mop@mop.ie; Web site: www.mop.ie

Contact:	Edward Miller	**Number of 'fee-earners' engaged in advising**		
Number of AIM new issues worked on as:		**companies in relation to AIM:**		
adviser to the Company:	n/a	**Partners:**		n/a
adviser to the NOMAD:	n/a	**Assistants:**		n/a
any other capacity:	n/a			
Industry sector preferences:	n/a	**Act for:** Fayrewood; Tiger Resource Finance		
In-house industry sector analysts:	n/a			
Sectors covered:	n/a			
Transaction parameters (typical):	n/a			
Member of professional or regulatory body:	n/a			
		Other Offices:		n/a

Mayer Brown Rowe & Maw

11 Pilgrim Street, London, EC4V 6RW Tel: 020-7248 4282;   Fax: 020-7248 2009;
email: london@eu.mayerbrownrowe.com;   Web site: www.mayerbrownrowe.com/london

Contact:	Stephanie Bates/Fiona Holland/	
	Stephen Bottomley	
Number of AIM new issues worked on as:		
adviser to the Company:	7	
adviser to the NOMAD:	4	
any other capacity:	n/a	
Industry sector preferences:	All sectors covered;	
most notable specialist industry groups: Pharmaceuticals		
and biotech; Communications (including telecoms, cable		
TV, broadcasting and satellite); Media; Professions;		
Publishing		
In-house industry sector analysts:	n/a	
Sectors covered:	n/a	
Transaction parameters (typical):	n/a	
Member of professional or regulatory body: Regulated		
by The Law Society		

Number of 'fee-earners' engaged in advising companies in relation to AIM:

Partners:	18
Assistants:	24

Act for: Gamingking; GW Pharmaceuticals; Inter-Alliance; PIPEX Communications; TradingSports Exchange Systems; Vantis; Vitesse Media

Other Offices:
Manchester; Brussels; Charlotte; Chicago; Cologne; Frankfurt; Houston; Los Angeles; New York; Palo Alto; Paris; Washington DC

McClure Naismith

292 St Vincent Street, Glasgow, G2 5TQ Tel: 0141-204 2700;   Fax: 0141-248 3998;
email: glasgow@mcclurenaismith.com;   Web site: www.mcclurenaismith.com

Contact:	Kenneth Chrystie
Number of AIM new issues worked on as:	
adviser to the Company:	n/a
adviser to the NOMAD:	n/a
any other capacity:	n/a
Industry sector preferences:	n/a
In-house industry sector analysts:	n/a
Sectors covered:	n/a
Transaction parameters (typical):	n/a
Member of professional or regulatory body:	n/a

Number of 'fee-earners' engaged in advising companies in relation to AIM:

Partners:	n/a
Assistants:	n/a

Act for: Clan Homes; Murgitroyd

Other Offices: n/a

McFadden Pilkington & Ward
City Tower, Level 4, 40 Basinghall Street, London, EC2V 5DE Tel: 020-7638 8788;
Fax: 020-7638 8799; Web site: www.mpw-lawyers.com

Contact: John McFadden	**Number of 'fee-earners' engaged in advising**
Number of AIM new issues worked on as:	**companies in relation to AIM:**
adviser to the Company: n/a	**Partners:** n/a
adviser to the NOMAD: n/a	**Assistants:** n/a
any other capacity: n/a	
Industry sector preferences: n/a	**Act for:** Arko; Buckland; Venturia
In-house industry sector analysts: n/a	
Sectors covered: n/a	
Transaction parameters (typical): n/a	
Member of professional or regulatory body: n/a	
	Other Offices: n/a

McGrigors
Pacific House, 70 Wellington Street, Glasgow, G2 6SB Tel: 0141-248 6677;
Fax: 0141-221 1390; email: marketing@mcgrigors.com; Web site: www.mcgrigors.com

Contact: Colin Gray	**Number of 'fee-earners' engaged in advising**
Number of AIM new issues worked on as:	**companies in relation to AIM:**
adviser to the Company: n/a	**Partners:** 11
adviser to the NOMAD: 12	**Assistants:** 16
any other capacity: n/a	
Industry sector preferences: None	**Act for:** Advance Capital Invest; Antrim Energy;
In-house industry sector analysts: Yes	Halladale; iomart; Legendary Investments; Preston
Sectors covered: All sectors covered with particular	North End; Seymour Pierce; Stagecoach Theatre Arts;
expertise in retail, technology, sport and biomedical	Zyzygy
Transaction parameters (typical): £5m-£100m	
Member of professional or regulatory body: The Law	
Society of Scotland; The Law Society of England & Wales	**Other Offices:**
	Belfast; Edinburgh; London

SOLICITORS

Memery Crystal

44 Southampton Buildings, London, WC2A 1AP Tel: 020-7242 5905; Fax: 020-7242 2058;
email: info@memerycrystal.com; Web site: www.memerycrystal.com

Contact: Lesley Gregory	**Number of 'fee-earners' engaged in advising companies in relation to AIM:**
Number of AIM new issues worked on as:	
adviser to the Company: 43	**Partners:** 8
adviser to the NOMAD: 88	**Assistants:** 5
any other capacity: 0	
Industry sector preferences: No preference	**Act for:** AdVal; Avionic Services; Centurion Energy; CFA Capital; Cheerful Scout; Clipper Ventures; Cobra Bio-Manufacturing; Cytomyx; Electric Word; e-Primefinancial; Erinaceous; Futura Medical; Glow Communications; Honeygrove Homes; i-documentsystems; Intellexis; International Brand Licensing; Invox; Multi; New Millennium Resources; Petra Diamonds; Seymour Pierce
In-house industry sector analysts: No	
Sectors covered: n/a	
Transaction parameters (typical): £2m-£50m	
Member of professional or regulatory body: The Law Society, Women In Management	
	Other Offices: n/a

Morgan Cole

Bradley Court, Park Place, Cardiff, CF10 3DP Tel: 02920-385 385; Fax: 02920-385 300;
email: robert.cherry@morgan-cole.com; Web site: www.morgan-cole.com

Contact: Robert Cherry	**Number of 'fee-earners' engaged in advising companies in relation to AIM:**
Number of AIM new issues worked on as:	
adviser to the Company: 7	**Partners:** 4
adviser to the NOMAD: n/a	**Assistants:** 6
any other capacity: n/a	
Industry sector preferences: None	**Act for:** Celltalk; CRC; General Industries; Screen; SpringHealth Leisure
In-house industry sector analysts: Yes	
Sectors covered: Energy; Leisure; Technology; Telecoms	
Transaction parameters (typical): £1m-£50m	
Member of professional or regulatory body: n/a	
	Other Offices: Cardiff; London; Oxford; Reading; Swansea

Nabarro Nathanson

Lacon House, Theobald's Road, London, WC1X 8RW Tel: 020-7524 6000; Fax: 020-7524 6524; email: g.taylor@nabarro.com, w.taylor@nabarro.com; Web site: www.nabarro.com

Contact:	Glyn Taylor/Warren Taylor	**Number of 'fee-earners' engaged in advising companies in relation to AIM:**	
Number of AIM new issues worked on as:			
adviser to the Company:	More than 75	**Partners:**	5
adviser to the NOMAD:	More than 75	**Assistants:**	15
any other capacity:	More than 75		
Industry sector preferences:	None	**Act for:** Avingtrans; CA Coutts; Chelford; Dwyka Diamonds; Expomedia; Flomerics; Formscan; Medal Entertainment; Netbenefit; NewMedia SPARK; Premier Management; SectorGuard; SIRA Business Services; Stanley Gibbons; Stonemartin; The Telecommunications Group; Vebnet; World Careers Network; World Telecom	
In-house industry sector analysts:	No		
Sectors covered:	n/a		
Transaction parameters (typical):	n/a		
Member of professional or regulatory body: The Law Society			
		Other Offices: Reading; Sheffield; Brussels	

Nicholson Graham & Jones

110 Cannon Street, London, EC4N 6AR Tel: 020-7648 9000; Fax: 020-7648 9001; email: info@ngj.co.uk; Web site: www.ngj.co.uk

Contact:	Kevin McGuinness	**Number of 'fee-earners' engaged in advising companies in relation to AIM:**	
Number of AIM new issues worked on as:			
adviser to the Company:	(in past 12 months) 4	**Partners:**	5
adviser to the NOMAD:	(in past 12 months) 2	**Assistants:**	10
any other capacity:	(in past 12 months) 0		
Industry sector preferences: Distribution; Finance; Leisure & Travel; Manufacturing; Media & Sport; PFI; Property; Real Estate; Retail; Technology		**Act for:** Caledon Resources; Expomedia; Home Entertainment; Knowledge Technology Solutions; Peel Hotels; Sky Capital; WH Ireland	
In-house industry sector analysts:	No		
Sectors covered:	n/a		
Transaction parameters (typical):	n/a		
Member of professional or regulatory body: BVCA; The Law Society of England & Wales		**Other Offices:** Brussels	

Norton Rose

Kempson House, Camomile Street, London, EC3A 7AN Tel: 020-7283 6000;
Fax: 020-7283 6500; email: corpfin@nortonrose.com; Web site: www.nortonrose.com

Contact: Simon FT Cox	**Number of 'fee-earners' engaged in advising companies in relation to AIM:**
Number of AIM new issues worked on as:	
adviser to the Company: 23	**Partners:** 33
adviser to the NOMAD: 30	**Assistants:** 80
any other capacity: n/a	
Industry sector preferences: None, but a significant proportion of deals are in the Technology & Media and Energy & Mining sectors.	**Act for:** Alliance Pharma; Aricom; Avesco; Coliseum; DDD; Global Energy Development; Healthcare Enterprise; InTechnology; Peter Hambro Mining; Potential Finance; Profile Media
In-house industry sector analysts: Yes	
Sectors covered: All	
Transaction parameters (typical): No limit	
Member of professional or regulatory body: The Law Society	**Other Offices:**
	London; Amsterdam; Athens; Bahrain; Bangkok; Beijing; Brussels; Cologne; Frankfurt; Hong Kong; Milan; Moscow; Munich; Paris; Piraeus; Singapore; Warsaw
	Associate Offices: Jakarta; Prague

O'Donnell Sweeney

Earlsfort Centre, Earlsfort Terrace, Dublin 2, Tel: 00-353-1-664 4200;
Fax: 00-353-1-664 4300; email: r@odonnellsweeney.ie; Web site: www.odonnellsweeney.ie

Contact: Tony McGovern	**Number of 'fee-earners' engaged in advising companies in relation to AIM:**
Number of AIM new issues worked on as:	
adviser to the Company: n/a	**Partners:** 4
adviser to the NOMAD: n/a	**Assistants:** 6
any other capacity: n/a	
Industry sector preferences: n/a	**Act for:** Alltracel Pharmaceuticals; Fortfield Investments
In-house industry sector analysts: n/a	
Sectors covered: n/a	
Transaction parameters (typical): n/a	
Member of professional or regulatory body: The Law Society of Ireland	
	Other Offices: n/a

Olswang

90 High Holborn, London, WC1V 6XX Tel: 020-7067 3000; Fax: 020-7208 8800;
email: pxb@olswang.com; Web site: www.olswang.com

Contact: Paul Blackmore	**Number of 'fee-earners' engaged in advising companies in relation to AIM:**		
Number of AIM new issues worked on as:			
adviser to the Company: 26	**Partners:**	16	
adviser to the NOMAD: 6	**Assistants:**	32	
any other capacity: n/a			
Industry sector preferences: None, but have specialists in all media, communications and technology sectors, as specified below	**Act for:** Ambient; Asfare; Basepoint; Conroy Diamonds & Gold; Harrier; Lo-Q; Paradigm Media Investments; Protec; Stenoak Associated Services; Topnotch Health Clubs; West 175 Media		
In-house industry sector analysts: Yes			
Sectors covered: Advertising; Computing Technologies; E-commerce and Internet; IT/IP; Media - Film, TV, Radio, Digital, Cable, Retail; Satellite; Telecommunications			
Transaction parameters (typical): All	**Other Offices:** Brussels; Reading		
Member of professional or regulatory body: BVCA; Easdaq; The Law Society			

Osborne Clarke

Hillgate House, 26 Old Bailey, London, EC4M 7HW Tel: 020-7809 1020; Fax: 020-7809 1021;
email: simon.fielder@osborneclarke.com; Web site: www.osborneclarke.com

Contact: Simon Fielder	**Number of 'fee-earners' engaged in advising companies in relation to AIM:**		
Number of AIM new issues worked on as:			
adviser to the Company: 20	**Partners:**	11	
adviser to the NOMAD: 10	**Assistants:**	40	
any other capacity: As solicitors to the company or issue - 30			
Industry sector preferences: n/a	**Act for:** Bristol & West Investments; Cambridge Mineral Resources; CES Software; Compact Power; Desire Petroleum; Dickinson Legg; easier; Hereward Ventures; Holders Technology; Kuju; Majestic Wine; Mosaique; Mulberry; Regal Petroleum; Solitaire; Theo Fennell; Tribal Group		
In-house industry sector analysts: Yes			
Sectors covered: Advertising and Marketing; Employment; Financial; IT and Telecoms; Property; Retail Sectors			
Transaction parameters (typical): £20m upward	**Other Offices:** Bristol; Thames Valley; Barcelona; Brussels; Cologne; Copenhagen; Milan; Paris; Rotterdam; Silicon Valley		
Member of professional or regulatory body: BVCA; Finance Leasing Association; Securities Association Institute of Directors; The Law Society			

Pinsents

Dashwood House, 69 Old Broad Street, London, EC2M 1NR Tel: 020-7418 7000;
Fax: 020-7418 7050; email: gareth.edwards@pinsents.com; Web site: www.pinsents.com

Contact: Gareth Edwards	**Number of 'fee-earners' engaged in advising companies in relation to AIM:**
Number of AIM new issues worked on as:	
adviser to the Company: 22	**Partners:** 19
adviser to the NOMAD: 14	**Assistants:** 35
any other capacity: 2	
Industry sector preferences: None	**Act for:** Acquistor; Acquisitor (Bermuda); Bank
In-house industry sector analysts: Yes	Restaurant; Billam; BNB Resources; Capital
Sectors covered: Automotive; Biotechnology; B2B;	Management & Investment; CybIT; Education
Computer Software; Education; Forestry; Hi-Tec; Internet;	Development International; Fairplace Consulting; First
New Media; Property; Restaurants; Retail; Support	Property; Fountains; Fulcrum Pharma; Honeycombe
Services; Telecoms	Leisure; Matrix Communications; Mayborn; Oystertec;
	Quadnetics; Stadium; Wealth Management Software;
Transaction parameters (typical): £3.5m-£130m	Winchester Entertainment
Member of professional or regulatory body: The Law	
Society	**Other Offices:**
	Birmingham; Leeds; Manchester; Brussels

Reynolds Porter Chamberlain

Chichester House, 278/282 High Holborn, London, WC1V 7HA Tel: 020-7242 2877;
Fax: 020-7242 1431; Web site: www.rpc.co.uk

Contact: Christopher Newsholme	**Number of 'fee-earners' engaged in advising companies in relation to AIM:**
Number of AIM new issues worked on as:	
adviser to the Company: 10	**Partners:** 4
adviser to the NOMAD: 1	**Assistants:** 7
any other capacity: n/a	
Industry sector preferences: n/a	**Act for:** Firestone Diamonds; Lombard Medical;
In-house industry sector analysts: n/a	Stockcube; Ten Alps Communications; Yeoman
Sectors covered: n/a	
Transaction parameters (typical): £5-100 million	
Member of professional or regulatory body: n/a	
	Other Offices:
	London

Richards Butler

Beaufort House, 15 St Botolph Street, London, EC3A 7EE Tel: 020-7247 6555;
Fax: 020-7247 5091; email: jfw@richardsbutler.com; Web site: www.richardsbutler.com

Contact: James Wilkinson	**Number of 'fee-earners' engaged in advising**
Number of AIM new issues worked on as:	**companies in relation to AIM:**
adviser to the Company: n/a	**Partners:** 11
adviser to the NOMAD: n/a	**Assistants:** 15
any other capacity: n/a	
Industry sector preferences: Bio-technology; Insurance; Leisure/Media; Property & Construction; TMT; Transport	**Act for:** Blooms of Bressingham; Hemscott; MG Capital; Millwall; Mondas; Numis; Stilo
In-house industry sector analysts: No	
Sectors covered: n/a	
Transaction parameters (typical): No limits	
Member of professional or regulatory body: Law Society; Quoted Companies Alliance	**Other Offices:** Abu Dhabi; Athens; Beijing; Hong Kong; Paris; Piraeus
	Associated Ofiices: Doha; Muscat; Sao Paulo

Salans

Clements House, 14-18 Gresham Street, London , EC2V 7NN Tel: 020-7509 6000;
Fax: 020-7726 6191; Web site: www.salans.com

Contact: Philip Enoch	**Number of 'fee-earners' engaged in advising**
Number of AIM new issues worked on as:	**companies in relation to AIM:**
adviser to the Company: 4 in 2002	**Partners:** 6
adviser to the NOMAD: n/a	**Assistants:** 8
any other capacity: n/a	
Industry sector preferences: Betting & gaming; Minerals & natural resources; Motor trade	**Act for:** Abraxus Investments; Andrews Sykes; Capricorn Resources; Central African Mining & Exploration; Grosvenor Land; Health Media; London Security; Raft; RWS; Southern African Resources; Sterling Energy
In-house industry sector analysts: n/a	
Sectors covered: n/a	
Transaction parameters (typical): £1 - £500m	
Member of professional or regulatory body: The Law Society	**Other Offices:** Almaty; Baku; Moscow; New York; Paris; St Petersburg; Ukraine; Warsaw

Shakespeares

Somerset House, Temple Street, Birmingham, B2 5DJ Tel: 0121-632 4199;
Fax: 0121-643 2257; email: info@shakespeares.co.uk; Web site: www.shakespeares.co.uk

Contact:	Richard Baizley	**Number of 'fee-earners' engaged in advising**	
Number of AIM new issues worked on as:		**companies in relation to AIM:**	
adviser to the Company:	n/a	**Partners:**	
adviser to the NOMAD:	n/a	**Assistants:**	n/a
any other capacity:	n/a		
Industry sector preferences:	n/a	**Act for:** Creative Recruitment Solutions; Samuel Heath	
In-house industry sector analysts:	n/a	& Sons	
Sectors covered:	n/a		
Transaction parameters (typical):	n/a		
Member of professional or regulatory body:	n/a		
		Other Offices:	n/a

Shepherd+ Wedderburn

Saltire Court, 20 Castle Terrace, Edinburgh, EH1 2ET Tel: 0131-228 9900; Fax: 0131-228
1222; email: james.will@shepwedd.co.uk; Web site: www.shepwedd.co.uk

Contact:	James Will	**Number of 'fee-earners' engaged in advising**	
Number of AIM new issues worked on as:		**companies in relation to AIM:**	
adviser to the Company:	Over 20	**Partners:**	6
adviser to the NOMAD:	Over 15	**Assistants:**	12
any other capacity:	n/a		
Industry sector preferences:	All sectors covered	**Act for:** Deep-Sea Leisure; FTV; IndigoVision; John	
In-house industry sector analysts:	n/a	Swan & Sons; Magnum Power; Micap; NMT; Palmaris	
Sectors covered:	n/a	Capital; Sigma Technology; Vianet	
Transaction parameters (typical):	n/a		
Member of professional or regulatory body: The Law			
Society of Scotland			

Other Offices:

155 St Vincent Street
Glasgow
G2 5NR   Tel: 0141-566 9900   Fax: 0141-565 1222

6th Floor
Bucklersbury House Fax:
83 Cannon Street
London
EC4N 8SW   Tel: 020-7763 3200   020-7763 3250

Simmons & Simmons

CityPoint, One Ropemaker Street, London, EC2Y 9SS Tel: 020-7628 2020; Fax: 020-7628 2070;
email: enquiries@simmons-simmons.com; Web site: www.simmons-simmons.com

Contact: Stuart Evans/Ed Lukins/Charles Mayo		**Number of 'fee-earners' engaged in advising**	
Number of AIM new issues worked on as:		**companies in relation to AIM:**	
adviser to the Company:	2	**Partners:**	9
adviser to the NOMAD:	n/a	**Assistants:**	12
any other capacity:	0		
Industry sector preferences: No preferences, but have seen a lot of activity in Biotechnology and High Technology		**Act for:** Center Parcs (UK); ID Data; Optimisa	
In-house industry sector analysts: Yes			
Sectors covered: Banking; Biotech; Chemicals; Computer; Construction; Corporate Finance; Employee Benefits; Energy; Environmental Litigation; Hotels & Leisure; Insurance; International Arbitration; Media & Technology; Pension and Trusts; Pharmaceuticals; Professional Liability; Property; Safety Management; Shipping; Sport;Telecoms		**Other Offices:** Abu Dhabi; Brussels; Düsseldorf; Frankfurt; Hong Kong; Lisbon; Madrid; Milan; Netherlands; New York; Padua; Paris; Rome; Shanghai; Tokyo	
Transaction parameters (typical): n/a			
Member of professional or regulatory body: CISCO; City of London Law Soc; City of London Solicitor's Company; Institute of Directors; International Securities Market Assoc; Investors' Compensation Scheme; The Law Soc; London Invest Banking Assoc; London Chamber of Comm and Ind; London Invest Banking Assoc; Securities Trust			

SJ Berwin

222 Grays Inn Road, London, WC1X 8XF Tel: 020-7533 2222; Fax: 020-7533 2000;
email: info@sjberwin.com; Web site: www.sjberwin.com

Contact: Delphine Currie		**Number of 'fee-earners' engaged in advising**	
Number of AIM new issues worked on as:		**companies in relation to AIM:**	
adviser to the Company: (past 12 months) 1		**Partners:**	23
adviser to the NOMAD:	5	**Assistants:**	47
any other capacity:	1		
Industry sector preferences: E-commerce; Finance; IT & Telecommunications; Leisure; Media; Natural Resources; Pharmaceuticals & Healthcare; Real Estate; Retail; Sport; Technology		**Act for:** AIT; Alibi; Axiomlab; Birmingham City; Bristol & West Investments; Eurovestech; Finsbury Food; First Artist; First Calgary Petroleum; First Quantum Minerals; Fitzhardinge; Heavitree Brewery; Interregnum; PIPEX Communications; Safestore; Seymour Pierce; Sportingbet; Telford Homes; ukbetting	
In-house industry sector analysts: No			
Sectors covered: n/a			
Transaction parameters (typical): £2m-£50m		**Other Offices:** Berlin; Brussels; Frankfurt; Madrid; Munich; Paris	
Member of professional or regulatory body: The Law Society			

Slaughter & May

One Bunhill Row, London, EC1Y 8YY Tel: 020-7600 1200; Fax: 020-7090 5000;
Web site: www.slaughterandmay.com

Contact:	Christopher Saul	
Number of AIM new issues worked on as:		
adviser to the Company:	n/a	
adviser to the NOMAD:	n/a	
any other capacity:	n/a	
Industry sector preferences:	n/a	
In-house industry sector analysts:	n/a	
Sectors covered:	n/a	
Transaction parameters (typical):	n/a	
Member of professional or regulatory body:	n/a	

Number of 'fee-earners' engaged in advising companies in relation to AIM:

Partners:	n/a
Assistants:	n/a

Act for: CamAxys; Cluff Mining

Other Offices: n/a

Stallard

Centurion House, 37 Jewry Street, London, EC3N 2ER, Tel: 020-7423 1000; Fax: 020-7481 3002;
email: keith.robinson@stallardlaw.co.uk; Web site: www.stallardlaw.co.uk

Contact:	Keith Robinson	
Number of AIM new issues worked on as:		
adviser to the Company:	Over 6 (2 Last year)	
adviser to the NOMAD:	3	
any other capacity:	2	
Industry sector preferences:	n/a	
In-house industry sector analysts:	n/a	
Sectors covered:	n/a	
Transaction parameters (typical):	n/a	
Member of professional or regulatory body: FSA; The Law Society		

Number of 'fee-earners' engaged in advising companies in relation to AIM:

Partners:	3
Assistants:	2

Act for: Image Scan; Maisha; Ocean Resources Capital; Ofex; Scott Tod

Other Offices: n/a

Stephenson Harwood

One St Paul's Churchyard, London, EC4M 8SH Tel: 020-7329 4422; Fax: 020-7606 0822;

Contact:	William Saunders
Number of AIM new issues worked on as:	
adviser to the Company:	n/a
adviser to the NOMAD:	n/a
any other capacity:	n/a
Industry sector preferences:	n/a
In-house industry sector analysts:	n/a
Sectors covered:	n/a
Transaction parameters (typical):	n/a
Member of professional or regulatory body:	n/a

Number of 'fee-earners' engaged in advising companies in relation to AIM:

Partners:	n/a
Assistants:	n/a

Act for: BNB Resources; Constellation

Other Offices: n/a

Stringer Saul

17 Hanover Square, London, W1S 1HU Tel: 020-7917 8500; Fax: 020-7917 8555;
email: law@stringersaul.co.uk; Web site: www.stringersaul.co.uk

Contact:	Nigel Gordon
Number of AIM new issues worked on as:	
adviser to the Company:	30
adviser to the NOMAD:	n/a
any other capacity:	n/a
Industry sector preferences:	Financial Services

companies; Investment companies and High Technology companies – particularly in the Pharmaceutical sector; Natural Resources companies

In-house industry sector analysts:	None
Sectors covered:	n/a
Transaction parameters (typical):	£1m-£30m

Member of professional or regulatory body:
The Bio-industry Association; The Law Society

Number of 'fee-earners' engaged in advising companies in relation to AIM:

Partners:	4
Assistants:	2

Act for: Abingdon Capital; Avanti Capital; Bionex Investments; County Contact Centres; Einstein; Farley; Golden Prospect; Greenchip Investments; Jubilee Platinum; Mano River Resources; Marakand Minerals; PrimeEnt; Probus Estates; Triple Plate Junction; White Knight Investments; XecutiveResearch; Zincox Resources

Other Offices:
None

SOLICITORS

Taylor Wessing

Carmelite, 50 Victoria Embankment, Blackfriars, London, EC4Y 0DX Tel: 020-7300 7000;
Fax: 020-7300 7100; email: london@taylorwessing.com; Web site: www.taylorwessing.com

Contact: Gary Moss	
Number of AIM new issues worked on as:	
adviser to the Company: Over 25	
adviser to the NOMAD: Over 10	
any other capacity: 1	
Industry sector preferences: n/a	
In-house industry sector analysts: n/a	
Sectors covered: n/a	
Transaction parameters (typical): Flexible	
Member of professional or regulatory body: The Law Society	

Number of 'fee-earners' engaged in advising companies in relation to AIM:

Partners:	3
Assistants:	8

Act for: Aero Inventory; AIT; African Gold; Artisan UK; Bella Media; Chicago Environmental; Documedia Solutions; EnterpriseAsia.com; Epic Brands Investment; Faupel Trading; Imagestate; Intelligent Environments; Local Inns; Montpellier; OMG; Quadnetics; Synergy Healthcare; The Market Age; Xpertise

Other Offices:
Alicante; Berlin; Brussels; Cambridge; Dubai; Dusseldorf; Frankfurt; Hamburg; Munich; Shanghai

Thomas Eggar

The Corn Exchange, Baffins Lane, Chichester, PO19 1GE Tel: 01243-786111;
Fax: 01243-775640; email: nick.rutter@thomaseggar.com; Web site: www.thomaseggar.com

Contact: Nick Rutter	
Number of AIM new issues worked on as:	
adviser to the Company: 3	
adviser to the NOMAD: n/a	
any other capacity: n/a	
Industry sector preferences: n/a	
In-house industry sector analysts: n/a	
Sectors covered: n/a	
Transaction parameters (typical): n/a	
Member of professional or regulatory body: The Law Society	

Number of 'fee-earners' engaged in advising companies in relation to AIM:

Partners:	3
Assistants:	2

Act for: iTrain; RingProp

Other Offices:
Harsham; London; Reigate; Warthing

Travers Smith Braithwaite

10 Snow Hill, London, EC1A 2AL Tel: 020-7295 3000; Fax: 020-7295 3500;
email: David.Adams@TraversSmith.com; Web site: www.traverssmith.com

Contact: David Adams	**Number of 'fee-earners' engaged in advising**
Number of AIM new issues worked on as:	**companies in relation to AIM:**
adviser to the Company: 1	**Partners:** 8
adviser to the NOMAD: 1	**Assistants:** 13
any other capacity: 8	
Industry sector preferences: n/a	**Act for:** Cape; Ingenta; Interior Service; Newmark
In-house industry sector analysts: No	Security; Peel Holdings; Planit Holdings; Stonemartin;
Sectors covered: Breweries; Construction; Engineering;	Transense Technologies Group; Universe; William
Leisure; Property; Retail; Services; TMT	Ransom & Son
Transaction parameters (typical): £10m-£1bn	
Member of professional or regulatory body: The Law	
Society	**Other Offices:**
	Berlin; Paris

Wacks Caller

Steam Packet House, 76 Cross Street, Manchester, M2 4JU Tel: 0161-957 8888;
Fax: 0161-957 8899; email: law@wackscaller.com; Web site: www.wackscaller.com

Contact: Stephen Chadwick	**Number of 'fee-earners' engaged in advising**
Number of AIM new issues worked on as:	**companies in relation to AIM:**
adviser to the Company: None	**Partners:** 7
adviser to the NOMAD: n/a	**Assistants:** 6
any other capacity: 30	
Industry sector preferences: n/a	**Act for:** Axiomlab; Cityblock; Eagle Eye Telematics;
In-house industry sector analysts: n/a	Fundamental-E Investments; Harrogate; Hot;
Sectors covered: n/a	Stepquick; Strategic Retail; Taskcatch; Vista; Wyatt
Transaction parameters (typical): n/a	
Member of professional or regulatory body: The Law	
Society	**Other Offices:** n/a

SOLICITORS

Walker Morris

Kings Court, 12 King Street, Leeds, LS1 2HL Tel: 0113-283 2500; Fax: 0113-245 9412;
email: reach@walkermorris.co.uk; Web site: www.walkermorris.co.uk

Contact:	Peter Smart	**Number of 'fee-earners' engaged in advising**		
Number of AIM new issues worked on as:		**companies in relation to AIM:**		
adviser to the Company:	n/a		**Partners:**	n/a
adviser to the NOMAD:	n/a		**Assistants:**	n/a
any other capacity:	n/a			
Industry sector preferences:	n/a	**Act for:** Airbath; Collins & Hayes; Leeds; London		
In-house industry sector analysts:	n/a	Security; Straight; Stylo; Surgical Innovations		
Sectors covered:	n/a			
Transaction parameters (typical):	n/a			
Member of professional or regulatory body:	n/a			
		Other Offices:		n/a

Ward Hadaway

Sandgate House, 102 Quayside, Newcastle Upon Tyne, NE1 3DX Tel: 0191-204 4000;
Fax: 0191-204 4001; email: enquiries@wardhadaway.com; Web site: www.wardhadaway.com

Contact:	David Crone	**Number of 'fee-earners' engaged in advising**		
Number of AIM new issues worked on as:		**companies in relation to AIM:**		
adviser to the Company:	n/a		**Partners:**	n/a
adviser to the NOMAD:	n/a		**Assistants:**	n/a
any other capacity:	n/a			
Industry sector preferences:	n/a	**Act for:** Romag; Tanfield; Zytronic		
In-house industry sector analysts:	n/a			
Sectors covered:	n/a			
Transaction parameters (typical):	n/a			
Member of professional or regulatory body:	n/a			
		Other Offices:		n/a

Watson Farley & Williams

15 Appold St, London, EC2A 2HB Tel: 020-7814 8000; Fax: 020-7814 8141/2;
email: jmellmann@wfw.com; Web site: www.wfw.com

Contact:	Jan Mellmann	**Number of 'fee-earners' engaged in advising**	
Number of AIM new issues worked on as:		**companies in relation to AIM:**	
adviser to the Company:	26	**Partners:**	4
adviser to the NOMAD:	10	**Assistants:**	8
any other capacity:	n/a		
Industry sector preferences: All sectors covered, but particular expertise in banks, investment companies, IT, mining, oil & gas, telecommunications services and transport		**Act for:** Black Rock Oil & Gas; Consolidated Minerals; Hardman Resources; RII; Voss Net	
In-house industry sector analysts:	n/a		
Sectors covered:	n/a		
Transaction parameters (typical):	n/a		
Member of professional or regulatory body: The Law Society		**Other Offices:** Bangkok; New York; Paris; Piraeus; Rome;Singapore	

Wedlake Bell

16 Bedford Street, Covent Garden, London, WC2E 9HF Tel: 020-7395 3000;
Fax: 020-7836 9966; email: info@wedlakebell.com; Web site: www.wedlakebell.com

Contact:	Adam Walker/Stuart Robertson	**Number of 'fee-earners' engaged in advising**	
Number of AIM new issues worked on as:		**companies in relation to AIM:**	
adviser to the Company:	10	**Partners:**	5
adviser to the NOMAD:	6	**Assistants:**	8
any other capacity: (Adviser to the broker) 28+			
Industry sector preferences:	No	**Act for:** ARC Risk Management; Auto Indemnity;	
In-house industry sector analysts:	No	Blooms of Bressingham; Hartest; Martin Shelton	
Sectors covered:	n/a		
Transaction parameters (typical):	All		
Member of professional or regulatory body: Quoted Companies Alliance; The Law Society		**Other Offices:** Guernsey Member of TELFA (Trans-European Law Firms Alliance) with offices throughout Europe Alliance with US law firm Fredrikson & Byron	

SOLICITORS

William Fry

Fitzwilton House, Wilton Place, Dublin 2, Ireland, Tel: 00 353 1 639 5000;
Fax: 00 353 1 639 5333; email: central.mail@williamfry.ie; Web site: www.williamfry.ie

Contact:		Carol McNellis
Number of AIM new issues worked on as:		
adviser to the Company:		n/a
adviser to the NOMAD:		n/a
any other capacity:		n/a
Industry sector preferences:		n/a
In-house industry sector analysts:		n/a
Sectors covered:		n/a
Transaction parameters (typical):		n/a
Member of professional or regulatory body:		n/a

Number of 'fee-earners' engaged in advising companies in relation to AIM:

Partners:	n/a
Assistants:	n/a

Act for: Conroy Diamonds & Gold; CPL Resources

Other Offices: n/a

Withers

16 Old Bailey, London, EC4M 7EG Tel: 020-7597 6000; Fax: 020-7597 6543;
email: hugh.devlin@withersworldwide.com; Web site: www.withersworldwide.com

Contact:	Hugh Devlin
Number of AIM new issues worked on as:	
adviser to the Company:	14
adviser to the NOMAD:	n/a
any other capacity:	40 (Solicitors to the placing)
Industry sector preferences:	Biotech; Financial Services; HR
In-house industry sector analysts:	No
Sectors covered:	n/a
Transaction parameters (typical):	£2.5m-£150m
Member of professional or regulatory body: The Law Society	

Number of 'fee-earners' engaged in advising companies in relation to AIM:

Partners:	7
Assistants:	12

Act for: Highams Systems Services; Newmarket Investments

Other Offices:
Milan; New Haven; New York

Wragge & Co

55 Colmore Row, Birmingham, B3 2AS Tel: 0121-233 1000; Fax: 0121-214 1099;
email: mail@wragge.com; Web site: www.wragge.com

Contact:	Julian Henwood	**Number of 'fee-earners' engaged in advising**	
Number of AIM new issues worked on as:		**companies in relation to AIM:**	
adviser to the Company:	20	**Partners:**	5
adviser to the NOMAD:	3	**Assistants:**	15
any other capacity:	n/a		
Industry sector preferences:	None	**Act for:** Advanced Medical Solutions; Campus Media;
In-house industry sector analysts:	n/a	Delcam; Focus Solutions; Henderson Morley; IDN

Sectors covered: Act for AIM clients in Engineering; Financial Services; Internet; Media; Software; Technology and Telecom sectors. Client-base generally covers all industry sectors

Telecom; Inter-Alliance; SRS Technology; UBC Media

Transaction parameters (typical): £10m-£250m
Member of professional or regulatory body: American Intellectual Property Law Association; Association of Counsel's Secretaries and Solicitors; British Computer Society; Chartered Institute of Arbitrators; Chartered Institute of Patent Agents; Insolvency Practitioners Association; The Consequential Loss Society; The Institute of Directors; The Law Society; The Liabilities Society; The Quoted Companies Alliance

Other Offices:
Brussels; London

USEFUL INFORMATION

AIM TEAM CONTACT DETAILS

London Stock Exchange
Old Broad Street
London
EC2N 1HP

Tel: 020-7797 1000
Fax: 020-7797 2099

Internet: http://www.londonstockexchange.com/aim

Head of AIM: Martin Graham

Deputy Head of Aim   Mathew Wootton

AIM Policy: Gillian Watson

AIM Admissions: Gemma Bragoli

AIM Regulation: Ray Knowles
                           Catherine Saunders
                           Claire Brown
                           Philip Howard
                           Chris Allison

London Stock Exchange regional offices

London & South:
Nick Langford   020-7797 4403
Satty Bains   020-7797 3252
Claire Dorrian   020-7797 2074

Midlands & the East
Nemone Wynn Evans   0121-236 9181

Midlands & the West
Mark Russon   0121-236 9181

Yorkshire & North
John Holland   0113-243 0738

Scotland & Ireland:
David Robertson   0141-221 7060

Overseas
Shelley England   020-7797 4363